Part 2

chs 13

14

15

16

17

19

21

Auditing

KENT Series in Accounting

THIRD EDITION

Auditing: Theory and Practice

C. William Thomas
Baylor University

Bart H. Ward
University of Oklahoma

Emerson O. Henke
Baylor University

PWS-KENT Publishing Company
Boston

PWS–KENT
Publishing Company

*To our wives, Mary Ann, Mickey, and Be,
for their loving support in writing this book*

PWS-KENT Publishing Company is a division of Wadsworth, Inc.

Material from the Uniform CPA Examinations for the years 1951 through November 1989, copyrighted by the American Institute of Certified Public Accountants, Inc., is reprinted or adapted with permission.

This book contains various questions from the Certified Internal Auditor Examinations, by The Institute of Internal Auditors, Inc. Copyright various years by The Institute of Internal Auditors, Inc., 249 Maitland Avenue, Altamonte Springs, Florida 32701. Reprinted with permission.

This book contains a question from the December 1982 CMA Examination. Copyright 1982, Institute of Certified Management Accountants, 10 Paragon Drive, Montvale, New Jersey 07645-1759. Reprinted with permission.

Library of Congress Cataloging-in-Publication Data

Thomas, C. William.
    Auditing : theory and practice / C. William Thomas, Bart H. Ward, Emerson O. Henke.—3rd ed.

        p.   cm.
    Includes index.
    ISBN 0-534-92074-8
    1. Auditing.   I. Ward, Bart H.   II. Henke, Emerson O.
    III. Title.
    HF5667.T45   1991
        657'.45—dc20   90-38459
                                                                    CIP

Sponsoring Editor: Al Bruckner   *Assistant Editor:* Deirdre Lynch
Production Coordinator: Robine Andrau   *Manufacturing Coordinator:* Peter D. Leatherwood   *Production:* Cece Munson/The Cooper Company
Interior Designer: John Edeen   *Cover Designer:* Robine Andrau   *Cover Photo:* Slide Graphics of New England, Inc.   *Cover Printer:* Henry N. Sawyer Company   *Typesetter:* G&S Typesetters, Inc.   *Printer and Binder:* R. R. Donnelley & Sons Company

Printed in the United States of America

91 92 93 94 95 — 10 9 8 7 6 5 4 3 2 1

Contents

PART **I**

The Audit: Its Nature and Environment   1

CHAPTER **1**
Conceptual Framework Underlying the Audit   3

CHAPTER **2**
AICPA Auditing and Quality Control Standards   25

CHAPTER **3**
Professional Ethics   47

CHAPTER **4**
Accountants' Legal Liability   95

P A R T **II**

The Financial Statement Audit: Process and Principles   141

C H A P T E R **5**
Evidence, Audit Risk, and Materiality   143

C H A P T E R **6**
Audit Objectives and Procedures   187

CHAPTER **7**
Planning the Audit   229

CHAPTER **8**
The Effects of the Control Structure on the Audit   273

P A R T **III**

Auditing Tools and Techniques   377

P A R T **IV**

The Application of Audit Theory in Practice   541

CHAPTER **15**
**The Audit of Selected Accounts in the Acquisitions
and Expenditures System**   645

CHAPTER **16**
The Payroll System and Related Accounts   681

CHAPTER **17**

The Production and Conversion System 715

CHAPTER **18**

The Financing and Investing System 765

C H A P T E R **19**
The Audit of Cash   825

C H A P T E R **20**
Completing the Audit   861

PART **V**

Reports and Other Services   903

CHAPTER **21**
The Audit Report   905

CHAPTER **22**
Other Types of Reports   949

Preface

Auditing: Theory and Practice, Third Edition, is designed for use in a one- or two-course sequence in either an introductory or a graduate level auditing course. It is divided into five logically sequenced parts and covers the subject of auditing, with an optimum blend of theory and application.

Part I, The Audit: Its Nature and Environment, introduces the student to the nature and environment of the audit. The conceptual framework that surrounds audits of every type is first discussed, and different types of auditing—financial, internal, and governmental—are differentiated and contrasted. The generally accepted auditing standards of the American Institute of Certified Public Accountants (AICPA), the ethical foundations of the auditing profession, and the legal liability of accountants are addressed.

In Part II, The Financial Statement Audit: Process and Principles, we begin to develop the process and principles that underlie the financial statement audit. The concepts of audit risk and materiality are introduced as a necessary prerequisite for determining the nature, timing, and extent of evidence that must be gathered to support financial statement balances. The theory of evidence is addressed, along with the financial statement assertions, verification of which is the objective of the financial statement audit. Audit objectives and procedures are then developed as natural extensions of the financial statement assertions. Next, the planning phase of the audit is discussed. We also explain the effects of the internal control structure and the computer environment on the audit.

Part III, Auditing Tools and Techniques, presents the tools that are used by the modern auditor to gather evidence. These include mainframe and microcomputers as well as sampling techniques for tests of controls and substantive tests of details.

In Part IV, The Application of Audit Theory in Practice, we explain how the theoretical concepts of auditing, developed in Chapters 1 through 12, are applied to the various systems of the business that support the financial statements. These systems are revenue and collections, acquisition and expenditures, payroll, production and conversion, and financing and investing. A separate chapter includes a discussion of the special audit procedures related to the cash balance. The final chapter in this part of the text explains the procedures that are involved during the completion phase of the audit.

Part V, Reports and Other Services, discusses the various types of reports that are associated with audited financial statements and other services that are performed by public accountants. Chapter 24 is concerned with the special concepts, standards, objectives, and procedures that are associated with internal, operational, and governmental auditing.

Auditing: Theory and Practice, Third Edition, is organized to deal in a comprehensive manner with the standards that need to be followed in performing independent as well as other types of audits. Each chapter is supplemented with extensive questions, cases, and problems from CPA, CIA, and CMA examinations that can be used to enlarge the student's understanding of the chapter. Appendices, including illustrative working papers from an actual audit, questionnaires, and analytical schedules, are provided for use as reference materials. A brief integrated case study, *T&H, Inc.,* begins in Chapter 7 with the discussion of audit planning; it continues in Chapters 8 and 20, where concepts of internal control and completion of the audit are treated. A student data disk for the case is available.

Specific Features

- The text provides comprehensive coverage of the independent audit with an effective blending of theory and practice. Governmental auditing and internal auditing are discussed and compared with the independent audit.
- Chapter 3 introduces the student to the Code of Professional Conduct of the AICPA and the Code of Professional Ethics for internal auditors. Included in this chapter are revised case study materials to assist the student in developing the ability to make well-reasoned ethical decisions.
- Chapter 4 provides comprehensive coverage of the legal environment facing accountants. Included are a full discussion of the auditor's civil and criminal liability and the measures being taken by the accounting profession to cope with the problem of legal liability. The Expectations Gaps standards are presented, with emphasis on the auditor's increased responsibilities to plan the audit to detect material errors and irregularities. The illegal acts having a direct and material impact on the financial statements and the tort reform movement that is now active at both the federal and state levels are also discussed.
- Chapters 5 through 9, which form the heart of the book, focus on the process involved in conducting the financial statement audit. Diagrams describing the process are included and are highlighted showing the phase of the process that is covered in that particular chapter.
- Chapter 10 introduces the student to the use of the computer in performing an audit and covers the use of both mainframe hardware and microcomputer equipment in various phases of the audit.
- Chapters 11 and 12 cover sampling techniques that are used for tests of controls and substantive tests. Chapter 12 has been updated to include a discussion of regression analysis as a statistical tool that may be used for analytical procedures in the modern audit.

- Part III takes a transaction cycle approach and covers the full audit of the five basic transaction cycles of the business. For each of these cycles, full coverage of the auditor's understanding of the control structure precedes the discussion of related detection risk procedures. EDP controls and the use of the computer are integrated into the explanation of the audit of each of these cycles. This organization ensures a clear, complete presentation of the audit of each cycle.
- A uniform set of audit working papers, adapted from an actual audit, is presented in appendices to Chapters 13 through 20. They make it easier for the instructor to illustrate (and for the student to understand) how the various working papers form an integrated body of evidence that supports the audit report.
- All theoretical and applications chapters have been updated for the "Expectation Gap" auditing standards, issued in 1988 and effective in financial statement audits beginning in 1989.
- Chapter 23 includes a full discussion of the attestation standards, which will serve as extensions of the attest function to nonaudit services in the 1990s and beyond.
- Chapter 24 provides full coverage of the GAO's revised auditing standards (1988) for audits of governmental programs and entities, including audits covered under the Single Audit Act of 1984. Discussions of internal and operational auditing have also been updated and expanded.
- A large number of multiple-choice questions adopted from professional certification examinations are included with the chapters. These questions are particularly useful in assuring comprehensive coverage and in preparing people for CPA, CIA, and CMA examinations. When used with the diagnostic comments included in the Solutions Manual, these questions can be effective for individual study as well as classroom discussion.
- We have also included a significant number of applications problems with the text material in Part IV. These applications problems, some of which have been adapted for use with the microcomputer, provide the student with an opportunity to apply auditing procedures to selected financial statement data.

Acknowledgments

We are indebted to a number of organizations, major accounting firms, and people for their assistance and inspiration in producing this text. Specifically, we acknowledge the American Institute of Certified Public Accountants for permission to quote extensively from Statements on Auditing Standards, the Code of Professional Conduct, Uniform CPA Examinations, and other publications. We are indebted to the Institute of Internal Auditors and the National Association of Accountants for permitting us to use certain of their materials, including problems from past CIA and CMA examinations. The U.S. General Accounting Office has permitted us to quote from Generally Accepted Auditing Standards for that organization. We also wish to acknowledge the significant contributions of KPMG Peat Marwick, Coopers & Lybrand, Deloitte & Touche, Ernst & Young, Arthur Andersen and Co., and Grant Thornton, which allowed us to use certain materials from their publications.

We would like to express our appreciation to Cathy Talbert and Evelyn Hupp for their untiring work in typing and retyping the Solutions Manual and other ancillary material as the book was being produced. Finally, the loving support of our wives, Mary Ann, Be, and Mickey, is gratefully acknowledged.

We are also indebted to the following reviewers for their helpful criticisms and suggestions: Victor E. Antrosiglio, Jersey City State College; Walter G. Austin, University of Texas at El Paso; Stephen Fogg, Temple University; Doris A. Granatowski, Southern Connecticut State University; K. G. Janardan, Eastern Michigan University; Malcolm H. Lathan, Jr., University of Virginia; Philip H. Siegel, University of Houston; and Wally Smieliauskas, University of Toronto.

The Audit:
Its Nature
and Environment

CHAPTER 1

Conceptual Framework Underlying the Audit

Objectives

- ☐ **1.** Define the process, characteristics, and objectives of auditing.
- ☐ **2.** Relate the definition of auditing to the three broad types: independent, internal, and governmental.
- ☐ **3.** Describe how the economic environment contributes to the need for independent audits.
- ☐ **4.** Identify the professional organizations that influence independent auditing.
- ☐ **5.** Describe the attest function and how it relates to the overall audit function.
- ☐ **6.** Identify and describe the parts of the standard audit report that is the final product of the independent audit.

In this chapter we introduce the conceptual framework underlying the audit, with particular emphasis on the independent audit.

Auditing Defined

Auditing is a process in which one person verifies the assertions of another. A committee of the American Accounting Association (AAA) has broadly defined auditing as follows:

☑ **Objective 1**
Define auditing

> . . . a systematic process of objectively obtaining and evaluating evidence regarding assertions about economic actions and events to ascertain the degree of correspondence between those assertions and established criteria and communicating the results to interested users.[1]

This definition encompasses all the different types of auditing—independent audits performed by professional certified public accountants, internal audits performed by employees of business entities, and governmental audits performed by employees of the U.S. General Accounting Office (GAO).

The AAA definition describes an audit as a *systematic process*. Therefore, it must be based on a sound conceptual framework that includes the generally accepted auditing standards that are developed and explained in Chapter 2. The phrase *objectively obtaining and evaluating evidence* describes the basic nature of the audit process. No matter what type of auditing is being performed, the evidence-gathering process should, above all else, be objective—that is, not subject to the biases of the observer. The evidence itself may possess varying degrees of objectivity, but the auditor must retain an objective mental attitude throughout the evidence-gathering and evaluating stages of the audit.

Another phase, *assertions about economic actions and events,* suggests that the audit can involve an examination of any of the following (not an all-inclusive list):

- An entity's historical financial statements.
- An entity's projected financial statements.
- An entity's internal control structure.
- An entity's internal data.

☑ **Objective 2**
Relate definition to the three types of audits

Figure 1–1 contains a brief summary of the comparison between independent, internal, and governmental (GAO) audits on two dimensions: (1) the source of economic assertions that are the basis of the evidence-gathering process and (2) the established criteria against which those assertions are usually judged.

The three types of auditing may differ based on the types of economic assertions that are the subject of the audit. For example, **independent auditors** seek to verify the economic assertions embodied in the systems that support an entity's external financial statements. Those assertions are (1) existence/occurrence, (2) completeness, (3) rights/obligations, (4) valuation, and (5) presentation/disclosure. **Internal auditors**, although sometimes concerned with assertions con-

Figure 1–1 ▰▰▰▱▱▭▭

Comparison of Independent, Internal, and GAO Audits

Dimension	Independent	Internal	GAO
Economic assertions (sources)	External financial statements	Internal reports and controls	Both
Established criteria	GAAP	Internal standards of entity, laws and regulations of governmental bodies	Both

tained in external financial statements, have the primary function of verifying the company's compliance with internal profitability goals and with established policies of management regarding internal controls. **Governmental (GAO) auditors** may be concerned with adherence of the entity to external reporting requirements as well as to whether the entity has operated in compliance with laws and regulations, including those pertaining to controls and those pertaining to efficiency and economy in the use of resources.

The *established criteria* against which economic assertions are evaluated must be, to a large degree, uniform and mutually understandable to both preparer and user groups. For independent audits and external reporting, established criteria are commonly referred to as *generally accepted accounting principles* (GAAP). The conceptual basis underlying these principles is discussed later in this chapter. Well-defined bases of accounting other than GAAP may also serve as acceptable criteria against which assertions can be evaluated. For a governmental audit, established criteria may consist of rules and regulations within which the entity operates as well as GAAP. For an *operational audit* (a particular type of internal audit) the criteria may be budgets or other standards of efficiency and effectiveness established by the managerial policy of the company.

Communicating the results to interested users involves the preparation of an audit report to communicate the results of the auditor's examination to the users of the information. The format and content of audit reports vary with the type of audit performed and the circumstances under which the report is issued. Figure 1–3 (later in this chapter) illustrates the standard unqualified audit report that is issued by independent auditors to accompany external financial statements. Chapter 21 contains a full discussion of the circumstances in which auditors may diverge from the standard wording illustrated in Figure 1–3.

In Chapters 1 through 4 of this text we consider the general nature of the independent audit. Professional standards for independent auditors are discussed, along with ethical and quality control standards of the public accounting profession. The legal environment that has contributed to the formulation of standards for independent audits is also addressed.

Chapter 24 is devoted to discussion of standards for operational and internal audits as well as audits of governmental entities and programs. In that chapter, we also illustrate the various types of reports that may result from internal or governmental audits.

The Economic Environment and the Independent Audit

☑ **Objective 3**
Describe how the economic environment contributes to the need for independent audits

The environment in which modern economic activities are conducted is extremely complex. In the private sector, which is composed of businesses ranging from small, single-owner entities to large corporations, decisions relating to the internal affairs of an enterprise, as well as lending and investment decisions of creditors and investors, must be made daily. In the public sector (government), interested parties must decide whether managers are complying with the controls placed on them and whether the entity is operating efficiently and effectively. In these situations the personal interests of managers may conflict with those of the entity's owners or constituents. Therefore, managers must collect and report financial information about the entity that communicates the results of their activities to those groups. In doing that, user needs must be identified for the purpose of establishing the nature of the data to be communicated. Because of the potential bias of management in identifying and presenting such information, there is a need for independent verification of the data to assure fairness of presentation.

Communicating Economic Data

To assist investors, creditors, and other interested parties (user groups) in making informed decisions, financial managers must provide information about the entity's economic resources and obligations at specified points in time and changes in those resources and obligations over periods of time. These types of economic assertions are called *financial statements*. Economic assertions, however, are not limited to financial statements; they can also include statistical data, charts, tables, and related narrative information. We often use the term *financial data* to describe the financial statements and the comments, charts, etc., relating to those statements. Although we shall give some attention to the communication of internal financial information to internal managers, *we are primarily concerned with communicating the financial data required by external interested parties*.

The Need for Unbiased Data

Preparers of financial data include the financial managers of enterprises and persons at various levels of responsibility within these enterprises. Like the user groups mentioned in the previous paragraph, preparers of financial information have their own operating goals. However, since it may be assumed that each person places primary importance on maximizing her or his own welfare, *the goals of the persons preparing the information will often be different from those of the persons using it*. For example, whereas the external users of financial information seek data that will aid them in making investment or credit decisions, the providers of the information want to maximize the image and remuneration associated with their work. Such motivations can cause the preparers of financial information to incorporate personal biases into those data.

Because of the complex nature of the business and regulatory environment within which financial information is reported, and because of the large number of transactions processed, there is also the possibility that financial information will be recorded erroneously. In isolated cases, financial data may even be intentionally misrepresented by preparers. Since the measured performance of managers—and in some instances their immediate incomes (bonuses, incentives, etc.)—may be directly affected by the reported operating results of the entity, unverified financial information from preparers may be biased to reflect economic events in a light that is most favorable to them.

The Need for Independent Verification of Reported Data

We can summarize our observations to this point by concluding that *there may be a conflict of interests between the providers of financial information and the external interested parties using that information.* Therefore, for external users to have assurance that the financial data they receive is complete, consistent, and fairly presented, the data must be verified (audited). To meet this need, each user might attempt personally to verify the information, but in most cases this would be impracticable because the typical investor or creditor has neither the time nor the required skills. *Therefore, it generally becomes cost-effective and desirable to hire independent and technically competent professionals to verify the credibility of the data.*

Meeting the Need for Independent Verification

The accounting profession has responded to the need for independent verification of financial data by providing independent auditing services. As shown in Figure 1–2 the auditor, operating as an objective, independent party, conducts an evidence-gathering process regarding the economic assertions that are being examined. Evidence that is examined may consist of underlying accounting data, such as general and subsidiary ledgers, accounting manuals, and other data that are the same as those used by preparers to construct the accounting reports. However, the auditor's evidence will also consist of corroborating (documentary) material, such as invoices from vendors supporting the existence and proper valuation of accounts payable or confirmation letters to various outside parties supporting the existence of accounts receivable. In addition, the auditor may make his or her own observations regarding evidence supporting the economic assertions. Such observations may be necessary, for example, to determine whether physical inventories of merchandise or property and equipment, contained in the financial statements, actually exist. The auditor may also find it necessary to recalculate many of the mathematical calculations found in the primary reports and to make pertinent inquiries of persons associated with the primary communication process. Evidence from these and other sources is evaluated by

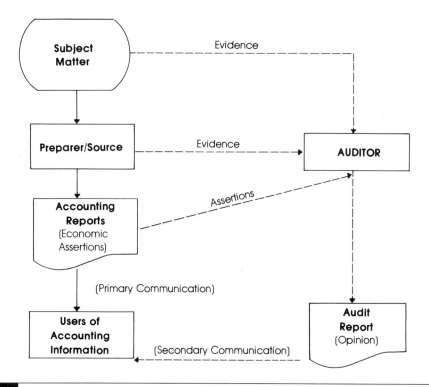

Figure 1–2 ▪▬▬

The Communication Process for Audit Reports

Source: "Report of the Committee to Prepare a Statement of Basic Auditing Concepts," *Accounting Review*, Supplement (1972): 27.

the auditor, who must then, as an accounting expert, compare the economic assertions with established criteria (including GAAP or some other well-defined basis of accounting) and form a judgment as to whether those assertions are presented within reasonable limits of economic reality. Evidence thus obtained provides the auditor with a reasonable basis for expressing an opinion in the audit report or secondary communication. Audit reports by independent professionals that are based on such an evidence-gathering process lend credibility to the economic assertions of various business entities.

It is important to recognize at this point that *no audit can provide complete assurance* that the financial statements are free from material error arising either from honest mistakes made by preparers of the information or from intentional misrepresentations. The reasons for this observation are many. First, accounting concepts reflected in financial statements are often ambiguous and subject to interpretation by the preparers. As an example, consider the disclosure of loss contingencies required by FASB Statement 5. Adequate disclosure is subject to interpretation of both probability and range of loss of a somewhat unpredictable future event. The results—in this case, the financial statements—cannot be more accurate and reliable than the underlying accounting measurement methods permit. In addition, a variety of factors limit the auditing process itself. For example, financial statement balances are most often the result of thousands of transactions, the audit of each of which would not be cost-effective. As a result, some degree of *uncertainty* (risk) always exists as to the appropriateness of the audit report. We will deal with audit risk at length in later chapters.

Professional Organizations That Influence Auditing

☑ **Objective 4**
Identify the professional organizations that influence independent auditing

A number of professional organizations influence the way in which the independent verification of financial statements is carried out. The most prominent of these organizations is the American Institute of Certified Public Accountants (AICPA). One of the most important objectives of the AICPA is to promote and maintain high standards of professional conduct, both technically and ethically. To meet this objective, the AICPA has established four divisions, as follows:

1. Auditing Standards Division.
2. Division for CPA Firms.
3. Quality Control Review Division.
4. Professional Ethics Division.

The last three of these divisions are discussed in later chapters.

Auditing Standards Division of the AICPA

The Auditing Standards Division consists of the **Auditing Standards Board** (formerly the Auditing Standards Executive Committee), plus an advisory council that monitors the board's activities, various task forces, and administrative staff. The primary function of the Auditing Standards Board is to issue authoritative pronouncements, called Statements on Auditing Standards (SAS). These standards provide guidelines for developing and applying audit procedures and for reporting the findings of the audit. We will refer to these statements throughout this text. Statements on Auditing Standards are interpretations of the ten basic generally accepted auditing standards (GAAS), discussed in Chapter 2. Departures from these standards must be justified by the auditor. The penalty for failure to provide justification can include disciplinary action by the AICPA. Periodically, these individual statements are codified into a single volume entitled *Codification of Statements on Auditing Standards*. In addition to Statements on Auditing Standards, the Auditing Standards Division also issues interpretations of SASs (which explain their applicability in certain circumstances); Industry Audit Guides (which contain auditing and reporting requirements for various industries); Statements of Position of the Division, Auditing Research Monographs, and Auditing Procedures Studies.

Financial Accounting Standards Board

The **Financial Accounting Standards Board** (FASB), consisting of seven full-time members chosen from business and academic environments, is an independent body whose primary responsibility is the development of standards for external financial accounting and reporting. The FASB was established in 1973 as the result of a lengthy study by members of the accounting profession concerning improvements needed in the standard-setting process. The FASB superseded the Accounting Principles Board (APB) of the AICPA which, until 1973, was responsible for determining appropriate accounting principles. Authoritative pronouncements issued by the FASB and the APB are discussed later in this chapter.

State Board of Public Accountancy

In addition to national and state organizations and rule-making bodies, each state has its own Board of Public Accountancy. The primary responsibility of these boards usually is to administer the state laws governing the practice of public accountancy within each state. Those laws relate to certification, licensing, professional conduct, and (in some cases) continuing professional education of public accountants. Although state boards are not affiliated directly with the AICPA or state societies of CPAs, they work with these organizations in monitoring the professional conduct of public accountants.

Securities and Exchange Commission

The **Securities and Exchange Commission** (SEC) is a governmental body created by the Securities and Exchange Act of 1934. It has the authority to issue technical standards governing the presentation of financial reports for companies whose securities are offered for public sale or are subsequently traded on the stock exchanges or on over-the-counter markets. We call these companies *public entities*. In effect, the SEC has been granted the authority to establish GAAP for such companies. They have traditionally delegated this authority to the AICPA and, more recently, to the FASB. In some instances, however, SEC disclosure requirements extend beyond those required by GAAP. The SEC requirements are issued in the form of Accounting Series Releases (ASR).

The Attest Function: A Primary Responsibility of the Auditor

☑ **Objective 5**
Describe the attest function

The term **attest** refers to the issuance, by an independent party, of a written statement that expresses a conclusion regarding the assertions of another party. In that statement, the attestor gives some assurance to the users of the information that the economic assertions contained therein are fairly presented in accordance with a given set of criteria. We will discuss the range of attest services that are available to the independent accountant later in this section and in later chapters.

The audit is the highest form of attest service that may be performed. The primary responsibility of the independent auditor is to assure the investing and lending public that assertions contained in external financial statements of an entity are objectively and fairly presented. That assurance is accomplished by issuing an audit report attesting to fairness of presentation of the audited financial statements. In this section we explain the responsibilities of the auditor associated with the attest function by

- Examining the key elements of the standard audit report.
- Relating the historical development of the attest function to the evolution of the independent audit.
- Showing the importance of verifying fairness of presentation.
- Explaining how the principle of materiality and the concept of relative risk enter into the expression of an audit opinion.
- Noting briefly the kinds of decisions that the auditor must make as he or she performs the attest function.

Elements of the Standard Audit Report

☑ **Objective 6**
Identify and describe parts of the standard audit report

The auditor performs the attest function by issuing an audit report (see Figure 1–3), dated as of the day that all audit field-work procedures were completed. The auditor's signature at the bottom of the conventional *unqualified audit report* means that the audit has been completed and that the financial statements are judged to be free from material misstatements (either intentional or unintentional) when measured against the criteria of generally accepted accounting principles (GAAP). It is implied that if the auditor had found material misstatements that the client refused to correct, that fact would have been indicated in the report before it was signed.

A closer look at the standard audit report reveals that it contains six important parts: (1) the title, (2) the introductory paragraph, (3) the scope paragraph, (4) the opinion paragraph, (5) the signature, and (6) the date.

The title, "Independent Auditor's Report," communicates to readers that the person(s) conducting the audit does not have any relationship(s) with the company being audited that would create the impression that a conflict of interests exists. As explained earlier, absence of conflict of interest on the part of the auditor is central to the value of the attest function.

The body of the audit report is composed of three paragraphs. The *introductory* paragraph explains that the financial statements have been audited. Notice that very specific reference is given to the *exact* financial statements audited and the dates of each. Furthermore, a clear statement is given to differentiate the responsibility of management from the responsibility of the auditor. The responsibility of management is to prepare the financial statements; the responsibility of

Figure 1-3

Standard Audit Report

(1)   **Independent Auditor's Report**

(2)   We have audited the accompanying balance sheets of X Company as of
December 31, 19x2 and x1, and the related statements of income, retained
earnings, and cash flows for the years then ended. These financial statements
are the responsibility of the Company's management. Our responsibility is to express an opinion on these financial statements based on our audits.

(3)   We conducted our audits in accordance with generally accepted auditing
standards. Those standards require that we plan and perform the audit to obtain
reasonable assurance about whether the financial statements are free of material misstatement. An audit includes examining, on a test basis, evidence supporting the amounts and disclosures in the financial statements. An audit also includes assessing the accounting principles used and the significant estimates
made by management, as well as evaluating the overall financial statement presentation. We believe that our audits provide a reasonable basis for our opinion.

(4)   In our opinion, the financial statements referred to above present fairly, in all
material respects, the financial position of X Company at December 31, 19x2
and 19x1, and the results of its operations and its cash flows for the years then
ended in conformity with generally accepted accounting principles.

(5)   Best and Company
Certified Public Accountants

(6)   March 21, 19x3

the auditor is to audit them. Management, and not the auditor, is primarily responsible for the assertions contained in the financial statements.

The second paragraph is known as the *scope paragraph* because it states the
nature of the services (audit) that were performed by the accountant. Thus, the
paragraph is intended to aid in the interpretation of the function and limitations
of an audit. The first sentence indicates that the audit was conducted in accordance with generally accepted auditing standards (GAAS). The second sentence
explains the basic objective of the audit, which is to provide reasonable (but not
absolute) assurance that financial statements are free of material misstatement.
Procedures that are included in the audit are then described in general terms.
We are informed that evidence supporting the amounts and disclosures in the
financial statements has been examined on a test basis. In addition, we are assured that the auditor has made an assessment of the accounting principles used
and the significant estimates made by management.

Finally, the *opinion paragraph* expresses the auditor's opinion as to whether the
financial statements are *fairly presented*. The phrase *in all material respects* is a
warning that the auditor does not attest to the absolute accuracy of the financial
statements. We will discuss further the meaning of *fairly presented* and *in all material respects* later in this chapter.

The audit report is usually signed on behalf of the firm by the CPA who has final responsibility for the engagement (usually the engagement partner). The date of the audit report is the last day of audit field work.

Generally Accepted Accounting Principles

Statement 4 of the Accounting Principles Board (APB) defines GAAP as follows:

> **Generally accepted accounting principles** encompass the conventions, rules, and procedures necessary to define accepted accounting practice at a particular time. The standard of generally accepted accounting principles includes not only broad guidelines of general application but also detailed practices and procedures.[2]

These guidelines, practices, and procedures have evolved over the life of the accounting profession and are, therefore, reflected in accounting textbooks and official pronouncements coming from the Committee on Accounting Procedures, the Accounting Principles Board (APB) of the AICPA, and the Financial Accounting Standards Board (FASB). You have studied these principles, practices, and procedures in your financial accounting courses. The FASB is currently the authoritative body charged with resolving questions relating to GAAP.

The Government Accounting Standards Board (GASB) has been designated as the authoritative body to issue accounting principles for state and local governments. Under the AICPA Code of Professional Conduct, the APB opinions and the accounting research bulletins issued by the AICPA, as well as FASB and GASB statements and interpretations, qualify as elements of GAAP. However, accounting interpretations issued by the AICPA *do not qualify* as elements of generally accepted accounting principles.

Statement on Auditing Standards 43, presented in Section 411 of the Codified Auditing Standards (AU411.05),* clarifies the order of authority for sources of established accounting principles that an auditor should follow in determining whether an accounting principle is generally accepted. "The House of GAAP," shown in Figure 1–4 reflects one interpretation of the foundation and building blocks that constitute generally accepted accounting principles and the authoritative literature that contain them. As you can see, the house rests on a basic foundation of assumptions and principles that are generally accepted by accountants.[3] Successive floors of the house contain the hierarchy of established rules that have been written by authoritative bodies, such as the FASB, the AICPA, and others.

An understanding of the phrase *fairly presented* is not complete without some knowledge of the historical evolution of the attest function, which is presented next.

---

*Statements on Auditing Standards are periodically codified into single volumes. The *AU* reference (AU411.05 in this case) refers to the section and paragraphs of the codification in which the SAS is found. This referencing system will be used throughout this text.

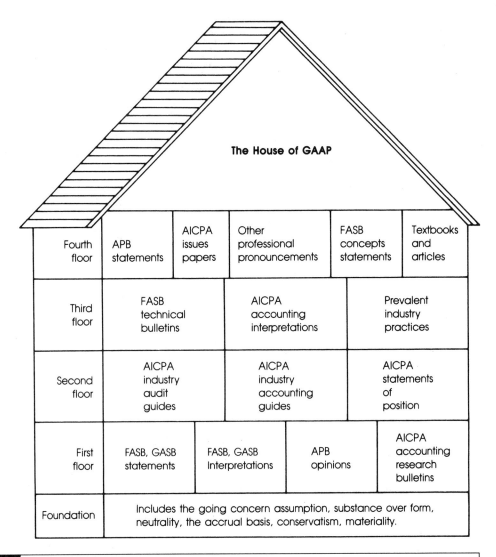

The House of GAAP

Fourth floor	APB statements	AICPA issues papers	Other professional pronouncements	FASB concepts statements	Textbooks and articles
Third floor	FASB technical bulletins		AICPA accounting interpretations		Prevalent industry practices
Second floor	AICPA industry audit guides		AICPA industry accounting guides		AICPA statements of position
First floor	FASB, GASB statements	FASB, GASB Interpretations		APB opinions	AICPA accounting research bulletins
Foundation	Includes the going concern assumption, substance over form, neutrality, the accrual basis, conservatism, materiality.				

Figure 1-4

The House of GAAP

Source: Deloitte & Touche. Used with permission.

Development of the Attest Function

Throughout the early history of the auditing profession there was little need for the attest function as it is performed today. There were no laws requiring an opinion on the financial statements and there was little reliance on public investors for funds. During those times, audits were performed primarily for managers who were also owners. They were, therefore, directed primarily toward discovering bookkeeping irregularities and fraudulent activities on the part of employees. For example, an early auditing text written by Lawrence R. Dicksee indicated that auditing had a threefold objective—the detection of fraud, the detection of technical errors, and the detection of errors of principle.[4]

Audits during that period also centered on the examination of the balance sheet, which was often the only published financial statement. In view of the objective of discovering bookkeeping irregularities and internal fraud, the examination typically included a rather complete verification of transactions against supporting documents. In many instances this was interpreted to require a detailed check of all transactions. These audits relied almost completely on internal evidence, which meant that the *certified* statements were simply proved to be consistent with the account balances on the books. The following audit report, typical of those used during the early years of the profession, can be compared to the standard report presented in Figure 1–3 to show the difference between the type of work done by the auditor prior to 1920 and that done today:

> We have audited the books and accounts of the ABC Company for the year ended December 31, 1915, and we certify that, in our opinion, the above balance sheet sets forth its position as at the termination of that year and that the company profit and loss account is correct.[5]

Perhaps the most authoritative publication on auditing during the period from 1912 to 1957 was the Montgomery auditing text. The changes in auditing objectives are clearly reflected in the various editions of this text. In the earlier editions, Montgomery stated that the detection or prevention of fraud and the detection or prevention of errors were the primary objectives of the audit. He gave less emphasis to the fraud objective in subsequent editions and, finally, in his 1957 edition stated that it was a *responsibility not assumed.* At that time, he emphasized the attest function as the primary responsibility of the auditor.

The changes reflected in the Montgomery text were associated with changes in the business environment. Beginning in the 1920s, firms began to rely more heavily on capital from public investors. This generally took the form of stock being sold to third-party investors not affiliated with the firm in a managerial capacity.

The legal responsibility of the auditor for meeting third-party needs for fairly presented financial information was first emphasized by the courts in the *Ultramares* v. *Touche* case.[6] In this case, a third-party creditor sued the auditors for negligence and fraud in the performance of the audit because of a loss suffered on a loan made to Fred Stern and Company. *This legal case is important because it established a basis for third-party action against an auditor for serious negligence in the proof of account balances.* The case led to a greater emphasis on the development of external support for such things as accounts receivable through confirmation procedures.

Another milestone in the movement toward emphasizing the attest function occurred in 1933. During that year the Securities Act was passed by Congress.

This act further increased the auditor's potential liability to third parties. A year later Congress passed the Securities Exchange Act, which was designed to regulate public security trading. Congress created the Securities and Exchange Commission (SEC) as an agency to regulate those activities.

In the late 1930s, the *McKesson & Robbins* case further emphasized the need for objectively developed financial statements for which selected account balances are verified against external evidence. Largely as a result of this case, the AICPA issued a pronouncement *requiring auditors to gather independent and external evidence regarding the existence of accounts receivable and inventory when those accounts were material. This case led to the establishment of ten generally accepted auditing standards*, which are still the foundation of the present-day auditing process. As a result of this case, the SEC, in addition to recommending the gathering of external evidence, also stated that (1) the stockholders should hire the auditor, (2) the audit report should be addressed to the stockholders, and (3) the auditors should attend stockholders meetings for the purpose of answering questions posed by that group.

Expansion of the Attest Function

During the years from 1940 to 1980, the attest function was generally limited to expressing a positive opinion on historical financial statements, based on an audit in accordance with generally accepted auditing standards. However, during the past decade the changing business environment has again dictated that the CPA expand the scope of services provided to include a variety of *nonaudit services* and to provide *assurances other than the audit opinion* on *either historical or prospective* financial assertions. It is becoming commonplace for clients to request that the CPA (1) *examine* financial assertions that are not intended to be presented in conformity with generally accepted accounting principles; (2) *review*, rather than audit, a set of historical or prospective financial assertions and express an appropriate written communication; or (3) *apply agreed-upon procedures* not constituting a full audit examination to a set of historical or prospective financial assertions.

In response to the changing marketplace for accounting services, the Auditing Standards Board and the Accounting and Review Services Committee have revised the definition of the *attest engagement* as follows:

> An *attest engagement* is one in which a practitioner is engaged to issue or does issue a written communication that expresses a conclusion with respect to the reliability of a written assertion that is the responsibility of another party.[7]

This definition is broad enough to include not only audit engagements but also many types of nonaudit services that require other forms of assurance. In addition, eleven Attestation Standards have been promulgated by the AICPA to serve as overall guidelines for attest services.[8] These standards are general in nature and serve as a framework within which generally accepted auditing standards, accounting and review standards, and standards regarding prospective financial statements may be applied. Nonaudit services that fall under the general authority of the attestation standards are covered in Chapter 23.

Emphasis on Fairness of Presentation

As we examine the standard audit report currently used by independent auditors, we note that the terms *true* and *correct*, historically used by auditors to express their findings relating to the financial statements, have been replaced by the phrase **fairly presented**. This change in terminology has occurred as the profession has recognized that there is no such thing as a completely correct set of financial statements. The meaning of *fairly presented* is partially clarified by Statement on Auditing Standards SAS 5 (AU411). That statement requires that before signing an opinion stating that the statements are fairly presented, the auditor must judge whether each of the following criteria has been met:

- Accounting principles selected and applied have general acceptance.
- Accounting principles are appropriate in the circumstances.
- Financial statements, including related notes, are appropriately informative.
- Information presented in the financial statements is classified and summarized in a reasonable manner.
- Financial statements appropriately reflect the underlying events and transactions within a range of acceptable limits that are reasonable and practical to attain.[9]

This standard emphasizes the importance of the judgments to be made by the auditor as the audit is being performed and the audit report is being written.

Materiality and Relative Risk

Figure 1–4 showed us that materiality is part of the foundation underlying GAAP. In the process of recording, classifying, and summarizing the financial data, many judgments have to be made that could cause the specific data presented in the financial statements to differ. Realistically, little is to be gained by pursuing a goal of precise correctness. Instead, the accounting profession has adopted the *principle of materiality*, which, in effect, says that the accountant, in making decisions relating to the accounting process, should be concerned only with those things that have a significant effect on the judgment processes of users of financial statement data. As a result, the auditor must judge whether or not reported results are within a *range of acceptable limits*.[10]

As a general rule, the accountant considers an item to be material if an error in it, or its omission, *would cause a prudent individual, who can use financial statements intelligently, to change a decision that might be made on the basis of those statements.* Sometimes percentages relating the individual item to the balance in an account, to total assets, or to net income may be established by an auditor or an auditing firm as a basis for judging **materiality**. In the use of such guidelines, however, specific percentage relationships should be evaluated in the light of the way the item being considered affects all other items relating to it. For example, an error in inventory that is insignificant in relationship to total inventory may be significant if net income will be misstated by the amount of the inventory error. Another important factor to consider is the effect that an error may have on trends and on the relative change in an item.

Audit Reports Other Than Unqualified

The findings of the audit may cause the auditor to conclude that the standard audit report illustrated in Figure 1–3 is not appropriate. In these cases, the report must be changed to communicate appropriately facts and circumstances as well as the changed conclusions of the auditor.

In general, departures from the standard report language may fall into two categories: (1) report qualifications and (2) modifications of the unqualified audit report. Because of the circumstances surrounding them, report qualifications are generally considered more critical than report modifications.

Audit reports may be *qualified* for one of two reasons:

1. The *scope* of the audit may have been affected by the auditor's inability to gather sufficient, competent evidential matter to support the assertions in part or all of the financial statements. For example, the auditor may be unable to obtain evidence supporting the existence assertion for inventories by observing them. If the scope limitation materially affects only a part of the financial statements, a *qualified audit report* is appropriate. However, if the limitation is material with respect to the *financial statements taken as a whole* (all parts of the current period's financial statements plus all prior years presented for comparative purposes), then a *disclaimer of opinion* is appropriate. A disclaimer is the auditor's statement that an opinion cannot be expressed.

2. The auditor might have discovered an *error or irregularity* in the financial statements that remains uncorrected by the client. Errors are unintentional mistakes, such as mistakes in application of GAAP or mathematical mistakes. Irregularities are intentional misstatements by management or employees. If an error is material to only an isolated part of the financial statements (such as accounts receivable, for example) then a *qualified audit opinion* is appropriate. On the other hand, if the error is material with respect to the financial statements taken as a whole, or if an irregularity exists, an *adverse opinion* is appropriate. The adverse opinion is the auditor's conclusion that the financial statements do not present fairly, in all material respects, the entity's financial position, results of operations, and cash flows.

Qualified audit reports, as well as modified unqualified reports, are discussed at length in Chapter 21.

Summary

In this chapter we have introduced the conceptual framework underlying the audit, with particular emphasis on the independent audit conducted by the certified public accountant. We defined auditing as a systematic process of objectively obtaining and evaluating evidence regarding assertions about economic actions and events to ascertain the degree of correspondence between those assertions and established criteria, and communicating the results to interested users.

We examined the economic environment that necessitates the independent audit and that gives meaning to the audit function. We then discussed the professional organizations that influence independent auditing, such as the AICPA, the FASB, the SEC, and others. We described the independent auditor's primary function, which is to attest to the fairness of financial statements. That function was explained by examining the elements of the auditor's standard audit report. We also briefly discussed the circumstances in which a qualified audit report would be issued.

Auditing Vocabulary

p. 10 **attest:** The issuance, by an independent party, of a written statement that expresses a conclusion regarding the assertions of another party.

p. 4 **auditing:** A systematic process of objectively obtaining and evaluating evidence regarding assertions about economic actions and events to ascertain the degree of correspondence between those assertions and established criteria and communicating the results to interested users.

p. 9 **Auditing Standards Board:** The unit of the American Institute of Certified Public Accountants (AICPA) that issues authoritative pronouncements, called Statements on Auditing Standards (SASs).

p. 17 **fairness of presentation:** A phrase meaning that generally accepted accounting principles (GAAP) have been followed in the preparation of financial statements and that, in cases in which choices have existed, the selection was the most appropriate GAAP.

p. 10 **Financial Accounting Standards Board:** An independent rule-making body consisting of seven full-time members from the business and academic community whose primary responsibility is the development of standards for external and financial reporting.

p. 13 **generally accepted accounting principles (GAAP):** The conventions, rules, and procedures necessary to define accepted accounting practice at a particular time.

p. 5 **governmental (GAO) auditors:** Auditors who obtain evidence regarding assertions contained in external financial statements of a government program as well as evidence of compliance on the part of the government program with applicable laws and regulations.

p. 4   **independent auditors:**   Auditors who obtain evidence regarding assertions in external financial statements and, using GAAP as the usual criteria, determine and report whether those financial statements are fairly presented.

p. 4   **internal auditors:**   Auditors who obtain evidence regarding the assertions contained in internal reports, and, using internally generated criteria of the company or laws or regulations, determine and report whether those assertions are in accordance with management's stated criteria.

p. 17   **materiality:**   A threshhold of significance to a decision maker. An accountant considers an item to be material if an error in it, or an omission, would cause a prudent user to change a decision.

p. 10   **Securities and Exchange Commission (SEC):**   A governmental body that has the authority to issue technical standards governing the presentation of financial reports for companies whose securities are offered for public sale or are subsequently traded on the stock exchanges or on the over-the-counter markets.

Notes

1. "Report of the Committee to Prepare a Statement of Basic Auditing Concepts," *Accounting Review*, Supplement (1972): 18.
2. American Institute of Certified Public Accountants, *APB Statement 4, Basic Concepts and Accounting Principles Underlying Financial Statement of Business Enterprise* (New York: AICPA, 1970): 54–55.
3. Deloitte Haskins & Sells (predecessor of Deloitte & Touche), *The Week in Review* (New York: July 13, 1984): 4, as interpreted from article in *Journal of Accountancy* by Steven Rubin, Technical Manager of AICPA's Accounting Standards Division. Used with permission.
4. Lawrence R. Dicksee, *Auditing* (New York: Ronald Press, 1905): 54.
5. George Cochrane, "The Auditor's Report: Its Evolution in the U.S.A." *Accountant* (November 1950): 448–60.
6. *Ultramares Corporation* v. *Touche* (255 N.Y. 170, 174 N.E. 441, 1931).
7. *Statement on Standards for Attestation Engagements* (New York: AICPA, 1986): 5.
8. Ibid.
9. Statement on Auditing Standards (SAS) 5 (AU411), paragraph .04 (New York: AICPA, 1975), as amended by SAS 43 (AU1010) (New York: AICPA, 1982).
10. Ibid.

Questions for Class Discussion

Q1-1   What is meant by the term *auditing*?

Q1-2   Why are independent audits required in our present-day economic environment?

Q1-3   What, in general, does the public accountant do in performing an independent audit?

Q1-4   What device does the public accountant use in communicating to the public his or her findings after completing an independent audit of a company's financial statements?

Q1-5 What is the most important professional organization for practicing certified public accountants?

Q1-6 What is the relationship of the American Institute of Certified Public Accountants to the auditing profession?

Q1-7 What is the relationship of the Financial Accounting Standards Board to the accounting profession?

Q1-8 What is the relationship of the Securities and Exchange Commission to published financial statements?

Q1-9 What is meant by the term *generally accepted auditing standards*? How is it used in the standard audit report?

Q1-10 How do the statements on auditing standards relate to generally accepted auditing standards?

Q1-11 What is meant by the term *generally accepted accounting principles*? How is that term used in the standard audit report?

Q1-12 Have auditors always assumed a responsibility for expressing an opinion regarding fairness of statement presentation? Discuss.

Q1-13 Has the federal government shown any interest in the way accountants perform the auditing function? Explain.

Q1-14 Does the fact that an auditor expresses an opinion that the financial statements of a client are fairly presented mean that they are free from error? Explain.

Short Cases

C1-1 Jaime Gomez is president of the Gomez Manufacturing Company, a small corporation manufacturing air-conditioning units. Until recently the company has had no need for credit other than open account obligations associated with the purchases of raw materials. However, the volume of business has grown significantly during the last year, and as a result Mr. Gomez is seeking to establish a line of credit with a local bank. The bank has asked Mr. Gomez for audited financial statements for the company covering its most recent fiscal period. Mr. Gomez states that he sees no reason for such a request because the company has an excellent internal auditing staff that monitors all accounting activities. For that reason, he feels certain that his financial statements are fairly presented.

Required: Explain to Mr. Gomez why the bank insists on independently audited financial statements.

C1-2 Your public accounting firm has just completed an audit of the financial statements of the Swanson Corporation and has delivered an unqualified audit report to the company's board of directors. Julia Burnett, the president of the company, states that she considers the independent audit to be a nonproductive activity because it has produced no significant changes in the financial statements. She, therefore, concludes that the fees paid for the audit constitute a waste of the company's resources.

Required: Respond to the position taken by Ms. Burnett.

C1-3 Your father recently purchased 100 shares of Nelco Corporation stock. As a stockholder, he has just received the company's annual report. He observes that the public accounting firm of Alfred Ciri and Company has audited the financial statements and presented an unqualified opinion regarding the fairness of the financial statements. In discussing the annual report with you, he states that he presumes that the public accounting firm has prepared the financial statements and that, since they have rendered an unqualified opinion on those statements, his investment is a good one.

Required: Respond to your father's observations.

C1-4 Aaron Wluka is a businessman not familiar with the accounting profession; he has just learned that the American Institute of Certified Public Accountants is the principal organization of CPAs. He has also learned that this organization has established the generally accepted auditing standards referred to in the standard audit report that he has just finished reading. In discussing the report with you, Wluka states that he assumes that the AICPA also establishes generally accepted accounting principles, another term included in the report. He says that if that is the case, he questions the desirability of CPAs' establishing their own auditing standards and generally accepted accounting principles without other elements of the business world having input into the establishment of those standards and practices.

Required: Respond to Wluka's concerns.

C1-5 James Ball, a friend of yours, is interested in the stock of Rich Corporation. He has observed the *fairly presented* phrase in the independent auditor's report and states that he interprets this to mean that the assets and liabilities shown in the balance sheet have a current value equal to the amounts shown for them.

Required: Explain to James what the *fairly presented* phrase means in the audit report.

Problems

P1-1 Select the best answer for each of the following questions.

    a. The independent audit is important to readers of financial statements because it

        1. Determines the future stewardship of the management of the company whose financial statements are audited.

        2. Measures and communicates financial business data included in financial statements.

        3. Involves the objective examination of and reporting on management-prepared statements.

        4. Reports on the accuracy of all information in the financial statements.

    b. Which of the following *best* describes why an independent auditor reports on financial statements?

        1. A management fraud may exist, and it is more likely to be detected by independent auditors.

        2. Different interests may exist between the company preparing the statements and the persons using the statements.

        3. A misstatement of account balances may exist and is generally corrected as the result of the independent auditor's work.

        4. A poorly designed internal control system may exist.

   c. An independent audit aids in the communication of economic data because the audit
1. Confirms the accuracy of management's financial representations.
2. Lends credibility to the financial statements.
3. Guarantees that financial data are fairly presented.
4. Assures the readers of financial statements that any fraudulent activity has been corrected.

   d. Auditing interpretations, which are issued by the staff of the AICPA Auditing Standards Division to provide timely guidance on the application of pronouncements of the Auditing Standards Board, are
1. Less authoritative than a pronouncement of the Auditing Standards Board.
2. Equally authoritative as a pronouncement of the Auditing Standards Board.
3. More authoritative than a pronouncement of the Auditing Standards Board.
4. Nonauthoritative opinions that are issued without consulting members of the Auditing Standards Board.

(AICPA adapted)

P1-2 Select the best answer to each of the following items.

   a. Which of the following publications does *not* qualify as a statement of generally accepted accounting principles under the AICPA Code of Professional Conduct?
1. AICPA Accounting Research Bulletins and APB Opinions.
2. Accounting interpretations issued by the AICPA.
3. Statements of Financial Standards issued by the FASB.
4. Accounting interpretations issued by the FASB.

   b. The auditor's judgment concerning the overall fairness of the presentation of financial position, results of operations, and changes in financial position is applied within the framework of
1. Quality control.
2. Generally accepted auditing standards that include the concept of materiality.
3. The auditor's evaluation of the audited company's internal control.
4. Generally accepted accounting principles.

   c. Which one of the following statements is correct concerning the concept of materiality?
1. Materiality is determined by reference to guidelines established by the AICPA.
2. Materiality depends only on the dollar amount of an item relative to other items in the financial statements.
3. Materiality depends on the nature of an item rather than the dollar amount.
4. Materiality is a matter of professional judgment.

   d. The auditor's opinion makes reference to generally accepted accounting principles (GAAP). Which of the following *best* describes GAAP?
1. The interpretations of accounting rules and procedures by certified public accountants on audit engagements.
2. The pronouncements made by the Financial Accounting Standards Board and its predecessor, the Accounting Principles Board.
3. The guidelines set forth by various governmental agencies that derive their authority from Congress.
4. The conventions, rules, and procedures that are necessary to define the accepted accounting practices at a particular time.

    e. A publicly held company that disagrees with the independent auditor on a significant matter affecting its financial statements has several courses of action. Which of the following courses of action would be *inappropriate*?

      1. Appeal to the Financial Accounting Standards Board to review the significant matter.

      2. Modify the financial statements by expressing in the footnotes its viewpoint with regard to the significant matter.

      3. Ask the auditor to refer in the auditor's opinion to a client footnote that discusses the client's point-of-view with regard to the significant matter.

      4. Engage another independent auditor.

    f. When compared to the auditor of fifty years ago, today's auditor places less relative emphasis on

      1. Confirmation.

      2. Examination of documentary support.

      3. Overall tests of ratios and trends.

      4. Physical observation.

(AICPA adapted)

P1-3 The audit has been described as a necessary function to management, investors, creditors, and others. In addition, audits can be beneficial for small as well as large companies.

Required:

    a. Discuss the value of the audit for

      1. A large publicly traded company.

      2. A small closely held private company.

    b. Discuss some of the factors that make an audit necessary.

    c. Define the term *attest* and discuss its evolution.

P1-4 Mueller, the sole owner of a small hardware business, has been told that the business should have financial statements reported on by an independent CPA. Mueller, having some bookkeeping experience, has personally prepared the company's financial statements and does not understand why such statements should be examined by a CPA. Mueller discussed the matter with Mitchell, a CPA, and asked her to explain why an audit is considered important.

Required:

    a. Describe the objectives of an independent audit.

    b. Discuss ways in which an independent audit may be beneficial to Mueller.

(AICPA adapted)

CHAPTER 2

AICPA Auditing and Quality Control Standards

Objectives

- ☐ **1.** Describe the relationship between auditing standards and auditing procedures.
- ☐ **2.** Describe the standard-setting process of the AICPA.
- ☐ **3.** Discuss the ten generally accepted auditing standards of the AICPA.
- ☐ **4.** Discuss the relationship of quality control standards to generally accepted auditing standards and to other standards issued by the AICPA.

Standards are measures of quality against which the performance of individuals or groups can be compared. The primary purpose of this chapter is to discuss the generally accepted auditing standards of the American Institute of Certified Public Accountants (AICPA), which are the professional standards that underlie independent auditing services.

As we mentioned in Chapter 1, audits are but one (the highest) form of attestation services performed by independent accountants. Other such services include reviews and engagements to apply agreed-on procedures to either historical or prospective financial assertions of others. The AICPA has issued a series of *attestation standards* that govern all attest engagements but that apply principally to nonaudit services. Those standards are discussed in Chapter 23.

Professional standards for the practice of internal auditing are established by the Institute of Internal Auditors (IIA). Professional standards for audits of governmental programs, organizations, activities, and functions are maintained by the General Accounting Office of the United States Government (GAO). Since internal and GAO audits have certain similarities, we will reserve discussion of the standards for those types of engagements until Chapter 24.

Relationship between Standards and Procedures

☑ **Objective 1**
Describe the relationship between auditing standards and auditing procedures

The term **auditing standards** refers to rules set by a governing authority to measure quality of performance. Standards are somewhat conceptual in nature and tend to be constant over time. In contrast, **auditing procedures** are acts to be performed that help to assure that certain objectives are achieved. In the practice of independent auditing, standards may be regarded as the broad guidelines established by the AICPA and other authorities as measures of quality of the auditor's performance. Procedures are the means by which the broad qualitative standards are carried out in practice. For example, one of the generally accepted field-work standards of auditing requires that sufficient, competent evidential matter be obtained to provide a reasonable basis of support for the audit opinion. To partially satisfy this standard with respect to the existence assertion for the cash account in the financial statements, the auditor would usually follow the procedure of obtaining letters of confirmation of cash in banks from the appropriate financial institutions.

Standard-Setting Process

☑ **Objective 2**
Describe the standard-setting process of the AICPA

As we discussed in Chapter 1, the Auditing Standards Board of the American Institute of Certified Public Accountants (AICPA) has the principal authority to issue standards governing the practice of independent auditing in the United States. The board consists of twenty-one members chosen from the fields of public accounting, industry, government, and education. Generally, for a standard to be adopted, a two-thirds majority vote must be obtained.

For a pronouncement to be adopted, the following sequence of events must generally be followed:

1. The need for the pronouncement must be identified, usually through response to comments of practitioners, regulatory pressure from groups such as the SEC, or litigation (see Chapter 4).
2. A research process takes place in which issues are analyzed, data are gathered on current practice, existing literature is reviewed, and alternative approaches to problems are proposed. A task force of practitioners and AICPA staff is responsible for this step.
3. The proposed pronouncement is discussed by the board, and alternative courses of action are evaluated. A draft of the proposal is developed and is usually revised after each round of discussions.
4. The board votes on whether to issue the pronouncement for exposure to the profession and other interested parties. At least a two-thirds vote is required for approval. An exposure draft of the pronouncement is distributed for comment to all CPA firms with AICPA members, regulatory bodies such as

the SEC, and other interested parties. Written responses to the exposure draft are elicited from all. At least ninety days are allowed for the exposure draft period.

5. Comments are received, reviewed, and evaluated by the board. If comments reveal issues that have not previously been considered, the board will reconsider its position.

6. The board votes again. If the pronouncement receives at least two-thirds majority vote, it is adopted as a Statement on Auditing Standards and is issued in numerical sequence with previously issued standards.

7. The newly adopted standard is implemented by practitioners. In most cases, several months will elapse between the date of issuance and the date of required implementation. The purpose of this time lag is to give practitioners time to assimilate the new material and to develop internal guidelines for implementation of the pronouncement within their respective firms.

Generally Accepted Auditing Standards

☑ **Objective 3**
Discuss the ten generally accepted auditing standards

The generally accepted auditing standards of the AICPA prescribe the personal and professional qualities that the independent auditor should possess, as well as the judgment that should be exercised in the performance of the audit and in the issuance of the report. There are ten auditing standards, categorized as general standards, standards of field work, and standards of reporting. Figure 2–1 contains a listing of these standards, which are discussed in the sections that follow.

General Standards

The **general standards** pertain to personal qualities of the practitioner, including the ability to make informed judgments about the assertions to which he or she is attesting. General standards include the professional qualifications of the auditor and the quality of the work performed during the field work and reporting stages of the engagement.

Adequate Technical Training and Proficiency

Both formal education and experience are required of the independent auditor to make him or her proficient. The formal educational background of an auditor should include not only financial accounting and reporting, but other business areas as well as the liberal arts. The practitioner should be proficient in analytical, critical, and investigative skills. These skills require a solid formal educa-

Figure 2–1 ▮▬▬▬▬▬▬▬▬▬▬▬▬▬▬▬▬▬▬▬▬▬▬▬▬▬▬▬▬▬▬▬▬▬▬

Generally Accepted Auditing Standards of the AICPA

General Standards

1. The examination is to be performed by a person or persons having adequate technical training and proficiency as an auditor.
2. In all matters relating to the assignment, an independent mental attitude is to be maintained by the auditor or auditors.
3. Due professional care is to be exercised in the performance of the examination and the preparation of the report.

Standards of Field Work

1. The work is to be adequately planned and assistants, if any, are to be properly supervised.
2. A sufficient understanding of the internal control structure is to be obtained to plan the audit and to determine the nature, timing, and extent of tests to be performed.
3. Sufficient competent evidential matter is to be obtained through inspection, observation, inquiries, and confirmation to afford a reasonable basis for an opinion regarding the financial statements under examination.

Standards of Reporting

1. The report shall state whether the financial statements are presented in accordance with generally accepted accounting principles.
2. The report shall identify those circumstances in which such principles have not been consistently observed in the current period in relation to the preceding period.
3. Informative disclosures in the financial statements are to be regarded as reasonably adequate unless otherwise stated in the report.
4. The report shall contain either an expression of opinion regarding the financial statements, taken as a whole, or an assertion to the effect that an opinion cannot be expressed. When an overall opinion cannot be expressed, the reasons therefor should be stated. In all cases in which an auditor's name is associated with financial statements, the report should contain a clear-cut indication of the character of the auditor's examination, if any, and the degree of responsibility he is taking.

Later in the text, we devote whole chapters or sections of chapters to discussion of topics related to these standards. Those chapters are as follows:

Chapter	Topic
3	General standards (included in coverage of the AICPA Code of Professional Conduct)
4	Due professional care (included in legal liability)
5, 6,	Evidence, audit risk, materiality
7	Planning and supervision
8, 9	Understanding the internal control structure
10–20	Applications and tools
21–23	Reports
24	Relationship to Generally Accepted Government Auditing Standards (GAGAS)

tion in both accounting and auditing, as well as related fields of business, logic, mathematics, and communications.

Formal education generally includes not only a college or university degree, but also a certain number of classroom hours of continuing professional education per year (up to forty hours in most states) after obtaining the degree and professional certification. The foundation for the application of all auditing procedures is *seasoned judgment*. No matter how much formal education the auditor possesses, formal education alone is not sufficient to meet this standard. It must be supplemented by extensive experience to enable the practitioner to make the judgments required in a typical audit engagement. Persons at every subordinate level must spend time in on-the-job training and be supervised and reviewed regularly by more experienced persons. These stringent requirements for extensive formal and continuing education and experience are based on the underlying belief that it is the professional obligation of the independent auditor to the public, to the client, and to fellow practitioners to be technically and experientially competent.

Independence in Mental Attitude

Independence is the very cornerstone of the attest function, regardless of whether audit, review, or other types of attest services are being performed. Without it, attest services are meaningless and worthless to users of financial statements and other assertions. For example, the justification for the economic value of the audit report (the primary tangible product of the audit) is that it provides an unbiased opinion of an informed observer as to the propriety of accounting information. The auditor's opinion would be of no social or economic value if the auditor were not independent of the client.

The concept of independence follows logically from the underlying belief that there must be no conflict of interest between the attestor and the client; that is, the persons performing the audit services must have no relationship with the entity that could cause them to gain financially from improprieties in the financial statements, thus sacrificing the necessary attitude of professional skepticism. In addition, if nonattest services (management advisory services, tax services, etc.) are being performed concurrently with audit or other attest services, those services must take a role of secondary importance to the attest responsibility. The attestor must, both in thought and in appearance, be a person who exercises independent judgment in planning the engagement, gathering the evidence, and writing the report.

Independence, from a conceptual standpoint, is a two-pronged issue. The attestor must be independent both in *fact* and in *appearance*. Independence in fact is an intellectually honest state of mind. The attestor may, in some situations, be the only person capable of assessing this facet of independence. Beyond being independent, however, the attestor must *avoid situations* (such as stock ownership or management relationships with the client) that may cause third parties to view the relationship with the client as one entangled with conflict of interests.

We will discuss these issues more specifically in Chapter 3, when we consider the attestor's ethical responsibilities for independence.

Due Professional Care

The third general auditing standard calls for the exercise of **due professional care** in the conduct of the engagement. Because of professional obligations to the general public, the concept of due professional care concerns what the auditor does and how well it is done. Every person who offers services to the general public assumes the responsibility of performing as a professional with the degree of skill commonly possessed by others in the field. The concept of due care imposes a level of performance responsibility that must be met by all persons involved in the engagement, from planning to preparation of the report. For example, the auditor must exercise due care in judging whether the evidence is both sufficient and competent to provide support for the audit report. This judgment requires a critical review of the work done at every level of supervision.

The due-care concept recognizes, however, that persons who perform attest services, like all other human beings, are subject to mistakes in judgment. Such errors occur in every profession, and allowances must be provided for them. The auditor, who undertakes a service in good faith, is not infallible. He or she is liable to the client and, as has been shown in the courts many times, to third parties for negligence, bad faith, or dishonesty, but not for mistakes in judgment.

Standards of Field Work

Standards of audit field work govern the actual process of evidence gathering at the client's place of business. The three broad standards in this area require adequate planning and supervision of the work, proper understanding of the control structure of the client, and the gathering of sufficient, competent evidential matter to support the audit opinion.

Proper Planning and Supervision

Underlying the planning and supervision standard is the concept of due professional care (discussed in the previous section). To exercise proper care on an audit engagement, attention should be given to the timing factors involved in accepting the engagement, to adequate planning of the actual procedures, and to appropriately appointing and supervising assistants on the engagement.

Planning for an audit engagement essentially means developing an overall *strategy* for the nature, timing, and extent of procedures to be performed. Generally, the nature of the detailed procedures required on financial statement bal-

Figure 2–2 ∎

Attestation Risk (*RA*)

$RA = IR \times IC \times DR$

where *RA* = the risk that a practitioner may fail to appropriately modify the attest report on an assertion that is materially misstated

IR = Inherent risk

IC = Control risk (assessed on audits only)

DR = Detection risk

ances during the audit function is more extensive than for other types of attest services. However, the procedures required for planning the engagement are relatively common for all types of attest engagements. Specifically, the practitioner should become thoroughly familiar with the *industry* in which the client operates, as well as the *operating practices of the client*, including the extent to which computers are utilized by the client to process information.

The overriding consideration during the planning stages of the engagement is control of **attestation risk**. As shown in Figure 2–2, attestation risk is essentially the risk that the practitioner may fail to appropriately modify the attest report on an assertion that is materially misstated. The two major components of attestation risk are (1) the risk that the assertion itself contains errors that have been undetected by the client and (2) the risk that the practitioner will not detect such errors. The first of these risks consists of two subparts: **inherent risk** and **control risk**. Inherent risk is the risk that the assertion itself, because of its nature or because of the environmental factors surrounding the industry or company, might be intentionally or unintentionally misstated. Control risk will be discussed in the next section.

Detection risk is the risk that the procedures employed by the attestor will be ineffective to detect misstatements in the assertions to which the attest statement is attached. Ineffective tests, errors in judgment, and insufficient evidence on which to base conclusions are all examples of detection risk. The attestor alone is responsible for detection risk. Although not directly responsible for inherent risk and control risk, *the attestor is responsible for assessing both inherent risk and control risk,* and for using the findings of those assessments in designing the nature, timing, and extent of procedures to be performed on the assertions. Assessments of inherent risk and control risk are made during the planning stages of the engagement.

We will further develop the concept of attestation risk, as applied specifically to the audit engagement, in Chapters 5 through 8.

A large part of controlling detection risk involves proper *supervision* of assistants. The supervision standard requires the more experienced practitioner to direct the work of assistants, to keep them informed on the objectives of the engagement as well as other matters that affect them, to review their work, and to help settle differences of opinion whenever they arise.

Understanding the Control Structure

The second field-work standard of auditing requires the auditor to obtain an understanding of the control structure of every audit client. After reaching an understanding that is sufficient to plan the engagement, the auditor will form an assessment of **control risk** for the engagement. Control risk is the risk that the internal control system that produced the assertion is not sufficiently strong to prevent, detect, or correct intentional or unintentional misstatements. When combined with the assessment of inherent risk, the auditor's assessment of control risk will be the basis for the auditor's decision regarding the nature, timing, and extent of audit procedures to be performed on the financial assertions.

The second standard of audit field work is unique to the audit function and is specifically applicable only to audit engagements. Nonaudit attest services, such as reviews and engagements to perform agreed-on procedures, are less extensive in terms of verification procedures than an audit. Clients who desire lesser services than a full-scope audit often do not need and cannot afford the added expense of a study and evaluation of the control system. In addition, some types of nonaudit attestation services require verification of assertions (such as aspects of information about computer software) that are unrelated to the control system.

The theory that underlies the second standard of audit field work is based on the logical proposition that a strong system of internal control provides more reliable information; thus, when strong internal control exists, there is less risk that financial statements contain material misstatements. An inverse relationship is assumed, therefore, between the quality of the internal control system and the probability of a material error being emitted from the system. The lower the auditor's assessment of control risk, the less necessary it will be to perform extensive and costly tests of the financial statement balances produced by the control system. Chapters 8 through 11 deal with the process by which the auditor conducts the assessment of control risk.

Sufficient Competent Evidence to Support Conclusions

The third audit standard of field work requires that the evidence supporting an audit report be both sufficient and competent to support an opinion, and that it include the specific procedures of *inspection, observation, confirmation, and verbal inquiry*.

Sufficiency refers to the *quantity* of evidence needed to support the audit opinion. Because of the costs associated with the audit process, it is usually impossible to examine 100 percent of the transactions that support a particular account balance or class of transactions. Thus, *sampling* is often necessary. Through the process of sampling, the auditor will select a representative number of transactions or items that comprise an account balance. He or she will then apply an appropriate audit procedure to those items and determine the amount of error in the sample. Then, the sample results will be extrapolated, or projected, to the entire account balance or class of transactions to estimate the error in the entire population. That error is then compared to a predetermined threshhold of maximum tolerable error (materiality), and a decision is reached about the fairness of presentation of the balance.

Because the process of sampling is used, there will always be a risk that the sample did not contain the same characteristics as the auditor would have found had he or she examined the entire population. The decision regarding sufficiency concerns the question "how large a sample should be selected?" The answer to that question inevitably is "large enough to enable a reasonably accurate estimate of the error in the population, while controlling sampling risk at a reasonably low level."

The term **competency** refers to the *quality* of evidence needed to support an audit opinion. Embodied in the issue of competency are the qualities of **validity** and **relevance**. To be valid, evidence must be capable of supporting a particular financial assertion. To be relevant, evidence must pertain directly to the assertion being tested. For example, in auditing inventories, auditors must gather evidence supporting the financial assertion of existence. The most competent evidence that can be gathered (i.e., the most valid and the most relevant evidence) in support of this assertion is the physical observation and test counting of the client's inventories.

Within certain broad guidelines, the auditor is free to exercise *professional judgment* in deciding the nature, timing, and extent of evidential matter to be gathered in support of the assertions that are the subject of the engagement. We will discuss all of these issues more completely when we consider evidence in Chapter 5.

Standards of Reporting

The report is the primary tangible product of the attest engagement. The report must be as informative as possible. It must be clear and concise and must adequately communicate both the nature of the attest service performed and the degree of assurance that is given by the attestor. As we discuss the reporting standards of auditing, it would be helpful to refer again to Figure 1–3 (page 12), which illustrates the independent auditor's report. As we discuss each standard, we will point out how that report complies with it.

Statements in Accordance with GAAP

The underlying theoretical postulate for the reporting standards is that *fair presentation implies the use of generally accepted accounting principles*. Embodied in the phrase "present fairly" in the opinion paragraph in Figure 1–3 are the concepts of accounting propriety, adequate disclosure, and audit obligation. *Accounting propriety* and *adequate disclosure* pertain to the faithfulness with which reported financial data portray the realities of an enterprise's financial resources and obligations at one point in time and changes in those resources and obligations over a period of time. *Audit obligation* pertains to the faithfulness (or due care) with which the auditor discharges his or her responsibility to judge propriety and adequate disclosure of the financial data. As discussed in Chapter 1, the phrase *present fairly* has been interpreted by Section 411 of the auditing standards to mean:

1. Presented in accordance with generally accepted accounting principles.
2. In cases in which the auditor has a choice among several generally accepted accounting principles, the selection of the most appropriate accounting principles.
3. A proper application of the standard of materiality to the disclosures in the financial statements.
4. Within a range of acceptable limits that are reasonable and practicable to attain under the circumstances.

In the first audit reporting standard, the requirements that the report shall state whether the financial statements are presented in accordance with GAAP implies that GAAP is the usual criterion against which fairness of presentation is judged. This is true any time the financial statements *purport* to present *financial position and results of operations*. In some cases financial statements may present other widely accepted and understood information, such as cash flow and assets and liabilities arising from cash transactions. In these circumstances, there may be other acceptable comprehensive bases of accounting than GAAP that may be used for judging fairness of presentation. Those other bases are discussed in Chapter 22. Unless either GAAP or another generally accepted comprehensive basis of accounting are used, the statements will be deemed "not presented fairly"—unless, as is rarely the case, the auditor can show that adherence to one of these bases of accounting would have caused the information to be misleading.

Lack of Consistency in Application of GAAP

The second audit standard of reporting requires the audit report to be modified whenever GAAP have not been consistently applied. Consistency is one of the generally accepted accounting principles. Therefore, the phrase "present fairly . . . in accordance with generally accepted accounting principles" in the standard report (Figure 1–3) implies that GAAP have been consistently observed. However, whenever accounting changes occur that affect consistency, readers who are attempting to interpret comparative changes between accounting periods should be advised that the lack of comparability is due to changes in accounting principles or methods rather than to real economic changes. Auditors' modified reports for lack of consistency are discussed in Chapter 21.

Adequate Informative Disclosures

The third audit reporting standard requires the auditor to disclose in the audit report any financial data considered necessary for fair presentation, if those data are omitted from the body or footnotes of the financial statements by the preparers of the information. Stated in another way, adequate disclosure may be presumed by the reader of the financial statements unless the audit report states that necessary disclosures are lacking. Therefore, when the readers of financial statements see an unqualified audit report such as the one illustrated in Figure 1–3, they may properly infer that the auditor has reached the conclusion that no further disclosures are necessary for fair presentation.

Note that the financial statements, including related footnotes, are the property of the client. Although the auditor can *recommend* that changes be made in those statements, the ultimate decision about what information will or will not be included rests with the client.

Expression of an Opinion or Disclaimer

The fourth standard is the most complicated of all the reporting standards. Its application is also more far-reaching than any of the others. It contains three important statements, and we will analyze and discuss the implications of each.

1. The report shall contain either an expression of opinion regarding the financial statements taken as a whole or an assertion to the effect that an opinion cannot be expressed.

When a CPA is associated with a set of financial statements, he or she must always either express one type of opinion (unqualified, qualified, or adverse) or disclaim an opinion (state that no opinion can be expressed) with regard to the financial statements taken as a whole. The phrase *financial statements, taken as a whole* applies to the financial statements for the current period as well as those of one or more previous periods that are presented for comparative purposes.

2. When an overall opinion cannot be expressed, the reasons therefor should be stated.

When an opinion on financial statements is disclaimed, the accountant has a reporting obligation to explain the reason for the disclaimer. Among the possible reasons are limitations in scope of the audit engagement and lack of auditor independence. These and other reasons to disclaim an audit opinion will be discussed in Chapter 21.

3. In all cases in which an auditor's name is associated with financial statements, the report should contain a clear-cut indication of the character of the auditor's examination, if any, and the degree of responsibility he is taking.

Association is defined by SAS 26 (AU504) as either (1) consent by the accountant to the use of his or her name in a report, document, or written communication containing the financial statements or (2) submission by the accountant to a client of financial statements the accountant has prepared or assisted in preparing, whether or not the accountant's name is appended to the statements.

Quality Control Standards

☑ **Objective 4**
Discuss quality
control standards
and their
relationship to
generally
accepted auditing
standards

Generally accepted auditing standards define the correct conduct of an *audit engagement*. In contrast, **quality control standards** define the correct conduct of the *overall operations of a public accounting firm*. Their purpose is to provide reasonable assurance that CPA firms who provide audit, accounting, and review services conform to professional standards.

Quality control standards are issued by the quality control standards committee, which is a senior technical committee of the AICPA. Firms that are members of the AICPA Division for CPA Firms are required to adhere to quality control standards.

Characteristics of a Quality Control System

A system of quality control for a CPA firm should encompass its organizational structure and the policies and procedures adopted to provide reasonable assurance that the firm is complying with professional standards. Although firm size, nature of practice, organization, and cost-benefit considerations affect the nature of a particular firm's quality control system, the following elements should be considered:

- Independence.
- Assigning personnel to engagements.
- Consultation.
- Supervision.
- Hiring.
- Professional development.
- Advancement.
- Acceptance and continuance of clients.
- Inspection.

Many of these elements are interrelated. For example, a firm's hiring policies might affect its professional development and advancement policies. Furthermore, the specific nature and extent of a firm's quality control policies and procedures depend on such factors as a firm's size and the nature of a firm's practice, its organization, and whether the cost of implementing the policies would outweigh the expected benefits. We now briefly describe the standards established for each of the elements and discuss the AICPA enforcement of them.

Independence.   *Independence* has the same meaning as an operating standard for a firm as it has for the activities of the individual accountant. The significance of independence as a quality control standard is that it *requires the firm to establish policies and procedures for implementation of the independence rule* of the Code of Professional Conduct (Chapter 3). Such procedures might include (1) requiring all personnel to adhere to the independence rules of the AICPA, state CPA society, state board of accountancy, and other bodies, including the SEC, when applicable; (2) communicating the firm's policy with respect to independence to all personnel; (3) monitoring compliance with the firm's policies in the area of independence; (4) confirming the independence of the other auditing firm(s), when acting as principal auditor.

Assignment of Personnel.   Care should be taken to be sure that persons assigned to perform various audit tasks possess the technical training and proficiency required. The firm should adopt policies and procedures to make sure that these criteria are met. They may include (1) timely identification of staff requirements for each specific engagement; (2) designation of persons to be responsible for assignment of personnel to engagements; (3) planning for a firm's total personnel needs for all engagements; and (4) use of time budgets and scheduling practices to establish manpower requirements and to schedule field work.

Consultation.   Consultation services should be used when complex accounting and auditing questions arise on an engagement. Policies and procedures to implement this standard include the referral of complex or specialized technical accounting and auditing questions to designated experienced personnel within the firm. Another recourse is to refer questions to a division or group in the AICPA or state CPA society established to handle technical inquiries. This standard also implies the need for maintaining a technical reference library for staff use.

Supervision.   The work of all aspects of the accounting firm's practice should be adequately supervised at all levels. Policies and procedures to implement this standard require planning for all engagements, including assignment of personnel to engagements, development of background information on clients, and development of an overall engagement strategy. Operating policies should also require a review process for all work papers, audit reports, and financial statements, as well as the use of standard forms, checklists, and questionnaires.

Hiring.   To ensure minimum standards of quality among entry-level personnel, the firm should establish recruiting policies throughout the firm to obtain well-qualified candidates. It should establish an appropriate experience requirement for an applicant to be considered for an advanced starting position. A background investigation should be required for all new personnel. Employees acquired through merger with or the acquisition of another firm should be appropriately indoctrinated into the firm's operating policies.

Professional Development.   The professional development standard requires the firm to establish continuing professional education (CPE) activities in the form of *on-the-job training* and *classroom instruction* to keep employees abreast of the ever-increasing number of technical standards emerging from various authoritative groups. To implement this standard of professional development, a firm should undertake the following procedures: (1) provide instruction as needed to personnel on job assignments; (2) require personnel to attend formal CPE programs conducted by the firm, by a college or university, or by a professional organization; (3) distribute written communications regarding the firm's policy on various technical issues to all personnel; and (4) make copies or summaries of new technical pronouncements (FASB standards, SASs, etc.) available to all personnel.

Advancement.   The CPA firm should establish procedures that prevent employees from advancing to higher positions within the firm before they are capable of handling the responsibilities of those positions. Each employee's moral character, intelligence, judgment, and motivation should be carefully evaluated before he or she is promoted. This requires the firm to establish qualifications deemed necessary for various levels of responsibility within the firm and to make use of evaluations by supervisors and, in some cases, subordinates. In addition, there should be partner committees to review the qualifications of individuals being considered for promotion.

Acceptance and Continuance of Clients.   The CPA firm should adopt policies and procedures to give guidance in the decision of whether to accept an engagement from a prospective client and whether to continue an engagement with an existing client. Policies such as these, when followed, help to minimize the likelihood of the CPA's association with a client whose management lacks integrity. Implementing policies include such things as (1) preengagement inquiry and review, (2) review of financial statements of prospective clients, and (3) evaluation of the firm's ability to service the client.

Inspection.   Finally, there should be a periodic *inspection of a firm's overall quality control program*, to help assure that it is working effectively. This inspection program may be accomplished internally by members of the management group of the firm, but most often it is accomplished by voluntarily submitting to a peer review.

The quality (peer) review process, which is the procedural process by which quality control standards are implemented, is discussed in Chapter 3.

Summary

In this chapter, we have attempted to lay the foundation for the study of the independent audit. That foundation is embodied in the generally accepted auditing standards of the AICPA. We learned that auditing standards are broad guidelines that serve as a measure of performance for independent auditors. In contrast, auditing procedures are acts to be performed that fulfill the objectives embodied in the standards.

We discussed the steps in the standard-setting process. These steps reveal the stages that a proposed pronouncement must pass through before being adopted as a standard by the profession. You should realize that the process is quite involved and deliberate and that much thought and discussion precedes the issuance of new auditing standards.

We then systematically reviewed the three major groups of generally accepted auditing standards: general standards, standards of field work, and standards of reporting. As we did so, we discussed the conceptual background of the standards, pointing out why they are important.

We concluded the chapter with a discussion of the quality control standards of the AICPA. Quality control standards are the means by which the generally accepted auditing standards and other professional standards are implemented in accounting practice.

Auditing Vocabulary

p. 35 **association:**   Either (1) the consent to the use of one's name in a document containing financial statements or (2) the submission of financial statements the accountant has prepared or assisted in preparing.

p. 31 **attestation risk:**   The risk that an attestor may fail to appropriately modify the attest report on an assertion that is materially misstated.

p. 26 **auditing procedures:**   Acts to be performed that help to assure that objectives will be achieved and standards met.

p. 26 **auditing standards:**   Rules set by a governing authority to measure quality of performance.

p. 33 **competency:**   The quality of evidence needed to support the audit opinion. Embodied in the concept of competency are both **validity** and **relevance**.

p. 32 **control risk:**   The risk that the internal control structure that produced the assertion is not sufficiently strong to prevent, detect, or correct intentional or unintentional misstatements.

p. 31 **detection risk:**   The risk that the procedure employed by the attestor will be ineffective to detect misstatements in the assertions to which the attest report is attached.

p. 30 **due professional care:**   The exercise of the same level of care commonly possessed by all others who are adequately technically trained in the field.

p. 27 **general standards:**   Standards that govern personal qualities of the practitioner, including the ability to make informed judgments about assertions to which he or she is attesting, as well as adequate training and proficiency, independence, and due professional care.

p. 29 **independence:**   The freedom from conflict of interests and the absence of relationships with clients that might cause third parties to infer conflict of interests.

p. 31 **inherent risk:**   The risk that a financial assertion itself, because of its nature or the environmental factors surrounding the industry or company, might be intentionally or unintentionally misstated.

p. 36 **quality control standards:**   Standards that govern the conduct of an accounting practice and encompass the organizational structure, policies, and procedures of a firm to provide reasonable assurance that it is complying with professional standards.

p. 32 **sufficiency:**   The quantity of evidence needed to support the audit opinion.

Questions for Class Discussion

Q2-1 Define the term *standard*.

Q2-2 In general, how do auditing standards differ from auditing procedures? Describe the three major categories of AICPA auditing standards. Paraphrase each standard.

Q2-3 What are three of the major sources of new auditing standards?

Q2-4 Why does it generally take from six months to several years to issue an auditing standard?

Q2-5 What groups are represented on the Auditing Standards Board? Why?

Q2-6 What is the justification for having generally accepted auditing standards?

Q2-7 Why can't a student just graduated from college conduct an audit engagement from beginning to end without being supervised?

Q2-8 Describe the term *independence*.

Q2-9 Why is independence a necessary part of every attest engagement?

Q2-10 What does the term *due professional care* mean? What responsibility does the auditor have in this regard?

Q2-11 What is involved in the planning of an audit engagement? How long do you think it should take?

Q2-12 What are the elements of supervision that should be part of the relationship between an audit supervisor and his or her staff?

Q2-13 What risk, if any, is associated with the issuance of an attest engagement report?

Q2-14 What is *inherent risk*? Why can't the auditor control it?

Q2-15 What is *control risk*? What type of attest service requires its assessment? Why?

Q2-16 Describe the term *detection risk*. What must be done for the attestor to control it?

Q2-17 Why do audits generally require more extensive verification procedures for assertions than other types of attest services?

Q2-18 Why must evidence be gathered by the auditor? Describe the general qualities that evidence should possess.

Q2-19 What is the purpose of the first audit standard of reporting?

Q2-20 In Figure 1–3, the standard unqualified audit report states that the financial statements are "fairly presented in all material respects." Explain the meaning of that statement.

Q2-21 What is the purpose of the second standard of audit reporting?

Q2-22 Why may we say that the third audit standard of reporting is an "implied standard"?

Q2-23 What is the purpose of the fourth audit standard of reporting? How is that purpose accomplished?

Q2-24 What relationship exists between quality control standards for public accounting firms and the generally accepted auditing standards of the AICPA?

Q2-25 What is the relationship between a CPA firm's hiring practices and the maintenance of quality control within the firm?

Q2-26 What is the justification behind the quality control standard related to acceptance and continuance of clients? How does a typical CPA firm adhere to this rule?

Q2-27 How is the participation of a firm's employees in continuing professional education programs related to the maintenance of quality control for the CPA firm?

Short Cases

C2-1 Emilio Rodriguez is a local practitioner in the town of Escondido, Texas. For the past twenty years, since he graduated from the State University, his client base has consisted mostly of individual, trust, and corporate tax clients. In April of this year, Huck Manufacturing Company, owned by Rodriguez's brother, Julio, moved its plant and main base of operations to Escondido. Desiring to build the local economy, Julio has asked Emilio to visit with him next week concerning the possibility of performing the annual audit.

Required:
  a. What is the meaning of the term *attest engagement*?
  b. Is there a possibility that Huck might need attest services? What kinds might they need?
  c. What is the risk associated with issuance of an attest report?
  d. List the general auditing standards. Discuss whether Emilio is qualified, on the basis of the facts stated above, to perform an audit for Huck Manufacturing Company.
  e. What advice would you give to Emilio?

C2-2 A local certified public accountant has expressed opposition to the requirement established by his state society that he participate in at least forty hours of continuing professional education each year. He states that he has a college degree and has passed the CPA examination and, therefore, sees no need for additional professional education.

Required: Respond to the local certified public accountant.

C2-3 The Able Corporation has been asked by its bank to present statements audited by a certified public accountant in connection with a loan application. A local CPA, who owns stock in the company, would like to perform the audit. He states that he knows that he can be independent in performing the audit in spite of the fact that he owns stock in the company. Another CPA claims that the first one does not meet the standard of independence and therefore cannot accept the engagement.

Required:
  a. Explain the justification for the position expressed by the second CPA.
  b. Would the first CPA be qualified to perform audit services for the client? Why or why not?

C2-4 Shady Graves, the president of Shady Corporation, is widely suspected of having connections with personalities whose integrity is questionable. He recently asked a local certified public accountant to audit the Shady Corporation. The local CPA refused to accept the engagement. Shady says he does not understand why the CPA has rejected the opportunity to perform the audit.

Required: Discuss the probable justification of the certified public accountant's action in this case.

Problems

P2-1   Select the best answer to each of the following questions relating to auditor independence.
   a. An independent auditor must be without bias with respect to the financial statements of a client in order to
      1. Comply with the laws established by governmental agencies.
      2. Maintain the appearance of separate interests on the part of the auditor and the client.
      3. Protect against criticism and possible litigation from stockholders and creditors.
      4. Ensure the impartiality necessary for an expression of the auditor's opinion.
   b. What is the meaning of the generally accepted auditing standard that requires the auditor to be independent?
      1. The auditor must be without bias with respect to the client under audit.
      2. The auditor must adopt a critical attitude during the audit.
      3. The auditor's sole obligation is to third parties.
      4. The auditor may have a direct ownership interest in his client's business if it is not material.

(AICPA adapted)

P2-2   Select the best answer to each of the following questions relating to the meaning and application of generally accepted auditing standards.
   a. Which of the following best describes what is meant by generally accepted auditing standards?
      1. Pronouncements issued by the Auditing Standards Board.
      2. Procedures to be used to gather evidence to support financial statements.
      3. Rules acknowledged by the accounting profession because of their universal compliance.
      4. Measures of the quality of the auditor's performance.
   b. Which of the following is *not* required by the generally accepted auditing standard that states that due professional care is to be exercised in the performance of the examination?
      1. Observance of the standards of field work and reporting.
      2. Critical review of the audit work performed at every level of supervision.
      3. Degree of skill commonly possessed by others in the profession.
      4. Responsibility for losses because of errors of judgment.
   c. Auditing standards differ from auditing procedures in that procedures relate to
      1. Measures of performance.
      2. Auditing principles.
      3. Acts to be performed.
      4. Audit judgments.
   d. Statements on Auditing Standards issued by the AICPA's Auditing Standards Board are

1. Part of the generally accepted auditing standards under the AICPA Code of Professional Conduct.
2. Interpretations of generally accepted auditing standards under the AICPA Code of Professional Conduct, and departures from such statements must be justified.
3. Interpretations of generally accepted auditing standards under the AICPA Code of Professional Conduct, and such statements must be followed in every engagement.
4. Generally accepted auditing procedures that are not covered by the AICPA Code of Professional Conduct.

e. A CPA is most likely to refer to one or more of the three general auditing standards in determining
1. The nature of the CPA's report qualification.
2. The scope of the CPA's auditing procedures.
3. Requirements for the review of internal control.
4. Whether the CPA should undertake an audit engagement.

f. The first general standard of generally accepted auditing standards, which states in part that the examination is to be performed by a person or persons having adequate technical training, requires that an auditor have
1. Education and experience in the field of auditing.
2. Ability in the planning and supervision of the audit work.
3. Proficiency in business and financial matters.
4. Knowledge in the areas of financial accounting.

g. Which of the following is mandatory if the auditor is to comply with generally accepted auditing standards?
1. Possession by the auditor of adequate technical training.
2. Use of analytical procedures in all phases of audit engagements.
3. Use of statistical sampling whenever feasible on an audit engagement.
4. Confirmation by the auditor of material accounts receivable balances.

h. Due professional care requires
1. A critical review of the work done at every level of supervision.
2. The examination of all corroborating evidence available.
3. The exercise of error-free judgment.
4. A study and review of internal accounting control that includes compliance tests.

i. The objective of the consistency standard is to provide assurance that
1. There are *no* variations in the format and presentation of financial statements.
2. Substantially different transactions and events are *not* accounted for on an identical basis.
3. The auditor is consulted before material changes are made in the application of accounting principles.
4. The comparability of financial statements between periods is *not* materially affected by changes in accounting principles without disclosure.

(AICPA adapted)

P2-3 Select the best answer for each of the following items relating to maintenance of quality controls for an accounting firm.
a. In pursuing its quality control objectives with respect to acceptance of a client, a CPA firm is *not* likely to
1. Make inquiries of the proposed client's legal counsel.

    2. Review financial statements of the proposed client.

    3. Make inquiries of previous auditors.

    4. Review the personnel practices of the proposed client.

  b. In pursuing its quality control objectives with respect to assigning personnel to engagements, a firm of independent auditors may use policies and procedures such as

    1. Designating senior qualified personnel to provide advice on accounting or auditing questions throughout the engagement.

    2. Requiring timely identification of the staffing requirements of specific engagements so that enough qualified personnel can be made available.

    3. Establishing at entry levels a policy for recruiting that includes minimum standards of academic preparation and accomplishment.

    4. Requiring auditing personnel to have current accounting and auditing literature available for research and reference purposes throughout the engagement.

  c. A CPA establishes quality control policies and procedures for deciding whether to accept a new client or continue to perform services for a current client. The primary purpose for establishing such policies and procedures is

    1. To enable the auditor to attest to the integrity or reliability of a client.

    2. To comply with the quality control standards established by regulatory bodies.

    3. To minimize the likelihood of association with clients whose managements lack integrity.

    4. To lessen the exposure to litigation resulting from failure to detect irregularities in client financial statements.

  d. To achieve effective quality control, a firm of independent auditors should establish policies and procedures for

    1. Determining the minimum procedures necessary for unaudited financial statements.

    2. Setting the scope of audit work.

    3. Deciding whether to accept or continue a client.

    4. Setting the scope of internal control study and evaluation.

  e. The *least* important evidence of a CPA firm's evaluation of its system of quality controls concerns the CPA firm's policies and procedures with respect to

    1. Employment (hiring).

    2. Confidentiality of engagements.

    3. Assigning personnel to engagements.

    4. Determination of audit fees.

  f. In connection with the element of professional development, a CPA firm's system of quality control should ordinarily provide that all personnel

    1. Have the knowledge required to enable them to fulfill responsibilities assigned.

    2. Possess judgment, motivation, and adequate experience.

    3. Seek assistance from persons having appropriate levels of knowledge, judgment, and authority.

    4. Demonstrate compliance with peer review directives.

(AICPA adapted)

P2-4 Jennifer Ray, the owner of a small company, asked Thorvald Holm, CPA, to conduct an audit of the company's records. Ray told Holm that an audit had to be completed in time to submit audited financial statements to a bank as part of a loan application. Holm immediately accepted the engagement and agreed to provide an auditor's report within three weeks.

Holm hired two accounting students to conduct the audit and spent several hours telling them exactly what to do. Holm told the students not to spend time reviewing the controls but instead to concentrate on proving the mathematical accuracy of the ledger accounts and summarizing the data in the accounting records that support Ray's financial statements. The students followed Holm's instructions and after two weeks gave Holm the financial statements, which did not include footnotes. Holm reviewed the statements and prepared an unqualified auditor's report. His report, however, did not refer to generally accepted accounting principles nor to the year-to-year application of such principles.

Required: Briefly describe each of the generally accepted auditing standards and indicate how the action(s) of Holm resulted in a failure to comply with *each* standard.

Organize your answer as follows:

Brief Description of Generally Accepted Auditing Standards	Holm's Actions Resulting in Failure to Comply with Generally Accepted Auditing Standards

(AICPA adapted)

P2-5 You have accepted the engagement of examining the financial statements of the Thorne Company, a small manufacturing firm that has been your client for several years. Because you were busy writing the report for another engagement, you sent an assistant accountant to begin the audit with the suggestion that she start with the accounts receivable. Using the prior year's working papers as a guide, the assistant prepared a trial balance of the accounts, aged them, prepared and mailed positive confirmation requests, examined underlying support for charges and credits, and performed such other work as she deemed necessary to obtain reasonable assurance about the validity and collectability of the receivables. At the conclusion of her work, you reviewed the working papers that she prepared and found that she had carefully followed the prior year's working papers.

Required: The opinion rendered by a CPA states: "Our examination was made in accordance with generally accepted auditing standards. . . ."

List the three generally accepted standards of field work. Relate them to the illustration in this case by indicating how they were fulfilled or, if appropriate, how they were not fulfilled.

(AICPA adapted)

CHAPTER 3

Professional Ethics

Objectives

☐ **1.** Have a grasp of the meaning of ethics, as well as how the guiding principles of ethics that govern the accounting profession apply to you.

☐ **2.** Have an appreciation for the historical development of the AICPA Code of Professional Conduct.

☐ **3.** Know the composition of the AICPA Code of Professional Conduct and be able to apply the provisions of the Code to simple fact situations.

☐ **4.** Be able to recognize both internal and external incentives for maintaining high standards of professional conduct among certified public accountants.

One of the distinguishing marks of a profession is that its members impose on themselves codes of professional conduct. Codes of ethical conduct are characteristic of the fields of law, medicine, accounting, and many other professions. In this chapter we consider the general nature of ethics, with particular attention to the nature and content of the AICPA Code of Professional Conduct.

Appendixes A, B, C, and D present selected AICPA Interpretations of the code; Appendix E is the Code of Ethics for the Institute of Internal Auditors.

General Concepts of Ethics

☑ **Objective 1**
Grasp the meaning
of ethics

Ethics may be defined as *a discipline dealing with good and evil and with moral duty*.[1] By implication ethics involves reflective choice in establishing standards of right and wrong. The phrase *standards of right and wrong* suggests that the basic subject of ethics is the establishment of criteria for right behavior and, consequently, the identification of wrong behavior.

We establish parameters for right and wrong behavior because of the need for order in society and because self-serving desires tend to influence the actions of all persons to a greater or lesser degree. Parameters that define right and wrong behavior are established in society through a system of statutory and common law. However, usually within these boundaries, we find that most individuals have established written or unwritten moral codes for themselves that enforce *a higher standard than that imposed by law*. These codes deal with the way we treat others and the way we restrain our selfish desires in deference to the rights and expectations of others; this behavior and its underlying beliefs are the essence of *ethics*.

Although each person may have a unique philosophy of what is right and what is wrong, our individual perspectives on ethics are shaped by our cultural, socioeconomic, and religious backgrounds. Many people, for instance, draw on their religious beliefs as standards for the establishment of personal ethical principles.

A good portion of the Old Testament in the Bible contains laws that form the basis of much of the moral code for the Judeo-Christian world. In addition, the Christian philosophy of life, begun by Jesus of Nazareth and promoted by his followers through the centuries, requires behavior that is opposite to that which would promote our short-term selfish interests. The Christian philosophy goes beyond even the standards of the Old Testament in promoting the spirit versus the letter of moral law. For those who accept the whole biblical philosophy as the ultimate in good behavior, it is ethical to live within those constraints, even though the legal system does not require it. Those who espouse other beliefs may also, because of cultural, religious, or ethnic background, incorporate rules of conduct in their personal lives that require a higher standard of behavior than that imposed by law.

Regardless of the differences that may exist in the way individuals make ethical choices, the public, as well as the government and the business community, have a right to expect *consistent standards of integrity and competence* from members of professions on whom they depend for certain things. Codes of ethics are, therefore, established by professional groups as *self-imposed and self-enforced constraints* on behavior, and these codes provide the basis for outsiders' expectations of the conduct of the group's members.

Professional Responsibilities

☑ **Objective 1**
Grasp the guiding
principles for
conduct in the
accounting
profession

The term **profession** is used to describe a group of people pursuing a learned art as a common calling *in the spirit of public service*[2] and at the same time pursuing a means of livelihood. The practices of accounting by certified public accountants and certified internal auditors have, when measured against the definition cited above, been held to be professions. Generally speaking, people engaged in professional activities, as defined above, are proud of their affiliations and, because they are professionals, regulate themselves by imposing constraints on their conduct. Realistically, the codifications of these standards of behavior serve two purposes. First, the codes set out for the members of the profession the *pattern of behavior expected of them* if they are to continue in the profession. Equally important, however, is the fact that the code of conduct *discloses to the public the self-imposed standards* within which the profession operates; in that way, the code improves the image of the profession, lends credibility to reports rendered by professionals, and helps professionals perform service functions more effectively.

Public Accounting as a Profession

The specific code of conduct within which a professional operates is partly determined by the nature of the group's professional responsibilities. The internal auditor, for example, performs essentially a single function (auditing) and has responsibilities to one group (management of the company). The Code of Ethics of the Institute of Internal Auditors is directed, therefore, toward the professional practice of internal auditing. The certified public accountant, however, logically operates under slightly different interpretations of a single code of behavior in the performance of each of the various types of public accounting services. For example, the code of conduct expected of the certified public accountant in providing tax services or management advisory services is slightly different from the one expected of the same person performing an independent audit. As is the case in any profession, the code of conduct for the work depends ultimately on the self-imposed *ethical standards the public is expecting the professional to adhere to in the task being performed*. In the paragraphs that follow, we examine the broad ethical concepts that define behavior expected of the accountant who *holds himself or herself out* to be a CPA in the *performance of all professional services*: auditing, tax services, management advisory services (MAS), and accounting and review services. We then show how the elements of that behavior pattern provide the basis for the AICPA Code of Professional Conduct.

Because the certified public accountant has responsibilities to both the public and clients, he or she must exhibit behavior that promotes the appearance of integrity, objectivity, and independence. Furthermore, the public accountant must be willing to maintain a *confidential relationship* with each client, as well as to accept responsibility for being *professionally competent* to perform various types of engagements. He or she has additional responsibilities to maintain *appropriate relationships with colleagues* in the profession and to *enhance the image of the profession.* Professional expectations thus require the accountant to accept a code of conduct that will promote such relationships and at the same time present a favorable image to the public.

From the foregoing observations, we can conclude that the development of a code of conduct for the professional is at least partially motivated by an attitude of *intelligent selfishness.* This means that the code is to some extent accepted by the profession because it is judged, over the long run, to be the best course of action for the profession and therefore ultimately beneficial to individuals engaged in the profession. Stated another way, the acceptance of the constraints included in a code of conduct may reduce the short-term material benefits available to the professional, but over the long run the members of the profession will realize greater material and other benefits than they would without the constraints.

Regulatory Bodies Involved

Conceptually, the practicing certified public accountant is subject to a number of agency-imposed codes of behavior. The CPA certificate, for example, is granted by the state in which the accountant practices. As a result, each state has a public agency generally called a State Board of Public Accountancy, which regulates public accounting practice within the state. In the process of accepting and discharging this responsibility, many state boards have issued codes of conduct setting out the behavioral constraints expected of all certified public accountants in their states.

In most states, CPAs have also voluntarily created an organization called the State Society (or Association) of Certified Public Accountants. These organizations have a number of operating objectives, one of which is to enhance the reputation of professional accounting within the state. In working toward that goal, each of these organizations typically carries on continuing professional education activities and generally establishes its own code of conduct for members of the society. We should note, however, that a state society code of conduct is enforceable by the state society only against those accountants who voluntarily join the organization. This may include most but not all the CPAs within a particular state.

The most comprehensive code of conduct for the accounting profession has been established by the American Institute of Certified Public Accountants. The codes imposed by the state boards and state societies generally incorporate the significant elements of the AICPA code. Again, however, because membership in the AICPA is voluntary, some accountants involved in the practice of public accounting are not members of the AICPA. Nevertheless, because the AICPA is a national organization having close ties with state societies and state boards, the *AICPA Code of Professional Conduct* more than any other code reflects the behavior patterns generally expected of professional accountants. It should be noted that when a CPA is licensed to practice accounting in a particular state and is also a member of the AICPA and state society of CPAs, he or she is subject to three codes of professional conduct. If, with regard to a matter of ethics, a provision of one of these codes is more stringent in that provision than the others, *the CPA must always abide by the most restrictive provision*.

AICPA Code of Professional Conduct

The American Institute of Certified Public Accountants (AICPA) is the most important national organization in which practicing public accountants may hold membership. Organized in 1887 as the American Association of Public Accountants (AAPA), it has been the primary professional organization for practicing certified public accountants for more than one hundred years. One of its many services to the profession has been the development of the AICPA Code of Professional Conduct. Because this code of conduct is national in scope and most of the other codes of conduct are derived from it, we now consider the development and present content of that code by

1. Briefly tracing the historical background of the present code.
2. Describing the profession's most recent efforts at restructuring professional standards.
3. Outlining the six principles of ethics that form the enforceable basis for professional conduct for CPAs.
4. Describing the rules portion of the code.
5. Relating the contents of the code to the general ethical responsibilities of public accountants.

Historical Background[3]

☑ **Objective 2**
Appreciate the historical development of AICPA Code of Professional Conduct

In the early 1900s, with the growth of the Industrial Revolution in the United States, members of the American Association of Public Accountants (AAPA) began to recognize that, in their capacity as auditors of growing industries, they were subject to increasing scrutiny by the public. As fledgling industries matured, investors, bankers, and governmental agencies that relied on financial statements of these businesses to make decisions began to express greater expectations of accountants for consistent standards of behavior. The accounting profession, recognizing its need for self-regulation, was coming of age.

In 1916 the name of the association was changed to the Institute of Accountants in the United States of America (AIA). In 1917 the AIA adopted its first code of ethics. The code was a very simple one, having only eight *do not* rules that prohibited the accountant from

1. Describing the firm as *members of the Institute* if it were not in fact a partnership in which all partners are Institute members.
2. Expressing an opinion on financial statements containing an essential misstatement of fact or an omission of anything that would amount to an essential misstatement.

3. Allowing anyone to practice in a member's name who was not his or her partner, his or her employee, or a member of the Institute.
4. Sharing fees with the laity or accepting rebates or *kickbacks* from the laity.
5. Engaging in any activity incompatible or inconsistent with the member's accounting practice.
6. Expressing an opinion on financial statements not examined under the supervision of the member, the member's partner or employee, a member of the Institute, or a member of a similar association abroad.
7. Attempting to influence legislation or governmental regulation affecting the accounting profession without advising the Institute.
8. Soliciting the clients or encroaching upon the business of another member of the Institute.[4]

Although many of the eight provisions included in the first code are either expressly or implicitly part of the present AICPA Code of Professional Conduct, some of the areas of much concern now were not even mentioned originally. For example, we find no mention of the public interest, integrity, objectivity, independence, or other distinguishing marks of the present code. The apparent shift in emphasis in the code is because the nature of the CPA's services (and corresponding responsibilities) are more complete and more complex in contemporary practice than in those days.

The original code has been revised over the years and expanded to meet the needs of the changing environment of auditing practice. As the attest function became more important, the need for independence became more important. As a result, a rule to require *independence in appearance as well as independence in fact* for accountants who perform audits was adopted and subsequently strengthened.

In recent years, public accountants have seen the management advisory services part of their work increase significantly. The combination of this type of service with the auditing responsibility has repeatedly raised a question as to whether one auditing firm could perform both of these services for a particular client and still maintain the appearance of independence. The present position of the AICPA is that there is danger that the accountant's independence may be questioned if management accepts the proposals of the public accountant without subjecting them to critical review. The general conclusion, however, is that *the performance of management advisory services does not negate the consultant's independence.*

Of particular importance in the revision process was the restatement of the code in 1973. At that time, the code restatement committee developed a conceptual foundation for the code by presenting a philosophical essay on the concepts from which the rules of conduct should flow and showing why these concepts are important to the profession. That essay concluded that the conduct toward which CPAs should strive is embodied in five broad ethical goals stated as *affirmative ethical principles,* as follows:

- *Independence, integrity, and objectivity.* This principle requires that a certified public accountant acting in any capacity should maintain his or her integrity and objectivity and, when engaged in the practice of auditing, should be independent of those being served.

- *Competence and technical standards.* The essay states that a certified public accountant should always observe the profession's technical standards and strive continuously to improve his or her competence and quality of services.
- *Responsibilities to clients.* This principle requires the certified public accountant to be fair and candid with clients and serve them with professional concern for their best interests consistent with his or her responsibility to the public.
- *Responsibilities to colleagues.* This principle requires the certified public accountant to adhere to standards of conduct that will promote cooperation and good relations among members of the profession.
- *Other responsibilities and practices.* This principle requires the certified public accountant to adhere to standards of conduct that will enhance the stature of the profession and its ability to serve the public.[5]

A second section, *rules of conduct*, was designed to spell out more specifically the behavior patterns expected of accountants in the process of achieving those goals. Recognizing that rules are subject to interpretation, the committee added a third section, *interpretation of the rules*. That section was intended to explain the application and scope of the rules. The interpretations were subdivided in accordance with the five basic concepts just described. Interpretations are not themselves enforceable, but anyone who departs from the guidelines set therein must be prepared to justify the departure in a disciplinary hearing.

Between 1973 and 1977, a section entitled *Ethics Rulings* was added. This section included ongoing questions and answers relating to specific acts that the accountant might encounter. These rulings, updated to the present time, are included in the present ethics standards.

Another revision of the rules of conduct was also approved in 1978. This publication included two new sections—one setting out the *objectives of the American Institute of Certified Public Accountants* and another describing the *professional practice of certified public accountants*. These two segments of the publication served to further point up the relationship between the environment in which certified public accountants operate and the code of conduct prescribing the behavior expected of them.

The Anderson Committee: Restructuring Professional Standards[6]

In recent years, the accounting profession has come under the increasing scrutiny of Congress, the media, various regulatory agencies of the federal government, and the public. The changing business environment, an increased number of business failures, and negative publicity caused by a few unscrupulous persons within the professional accounting community have caused various members of society to criticize the profession and to question whether we are measuring up to the public's expectations. Some of this criticism has been the result of misinformation as to the role that the audit plays in the financial reporting process, as well as the impact of nonaudit services (in particular, management advisory services) on the independence of the auditor. However, legitimate concerns exist about the behavior of the CPA in a changing business environment that demands an increasing scope of services as well as the commitment of the accounting profession to serve the public interest and to retain public confidence.

In October 1983 the AICPA appointed a special committee to study the relevance and effectiveness of standards of professional conduct for CPAs. More commonly known by the last name of its chairman, George D. Anderson, the committee was given the basic charge to consider the changing economic, social, legal, and regulatory climate; to thoroughly assess the relevance and effectiveness of existing ethical standards; to evaluate the role of the AICPA in establishing standards; and to recommend a course of action for the profession.

After three years of debate, in 1986 the committee issued its report entitled "Restructuring Professional Standards to Achieve Professional Excellence in a Changing Environment." The final report, approved by the membership of the AICPA in January 1988, included recommendations in four broad areas:

- Restructuring the AICPA Code of Professional Conduct into two sections: (1) principles of conduct that are positively stated and goal oriented and (2) revised rules of performance and behavior.
- Guidance to practitioners in making judgments regarding the scope and nature of services that may be performed, as well as adherence to professionalism in the performance of those services.
- Establishing a new program for monitoring accounting practice and for improving its quality and consistency.
- Establishing mandatory continuing professional education for all members of the AICPA and a requirement for a postbaccalaureate education by the year 2000 for those planning to enter the accounting profession.

The Anderson Report was approved by a margin of approximately 80 percent of the membership of the AICPA. This overwhelming display of support expressed the profession's sincere intention to achieve and maintain the highest standards of excellence into the second century of the profession's existence. The sections that follow describe the revised Code of Professional Conduct as well as the other three provisions of the Anderson Report.

Composition, Applicability, and Compliance[7]

Objective 3
Know the composition of AICPA Code of Professional Conduct

One of the valid criticisms leveled against the former code of professional conduct was its composition. Although it had been revised several times, the rules were still stated in the form of *do nots*. In contrast, the revised code is more *positively stated* and *goal oriented*. It defines ethical conduct in terms of what it should be, not just in terms of the boundaries for unethical conduct that should be avoided. The code consists of two sections: (1) broad principles, which provide the framework; and (2) enforceable rules, which govern the performance of professional services by the membership. The Council of the AICPA is authorized to designate bodies to write technical standards that interpret the rules, and the bylaws of the AICPA require adherence to the rules and to technical standards. Interpretations and rulings of the former code will remain in effect until further updating action is required by the Professional Ethics Committee.

In contrast to the former code of professional conduct, the revised code is applicable to *all* members—those in public practice, industry, government, and education. Under the former structure, only a few of the rules were applicable to members who were not in public practice. In this respect, the revision of the code strengthened its influence over the membership.

As in the past, compliance with the code is expected to be primarily on a voluntary basis. However, strong reinforcement is provided by peers with the addition of mandatory quality review (covered later in this chapter), public opinion, and ultimately by disciplinary proceedings against members who fail to comply with the rules.

Principles of Ethical Conduct

Six principles form the framework for the rules of conduct. These principles are intended to express the foundations of ethical behavior for accountants.

Article I. Responsibilities. In carrying out their responsibilities as professionals, members should exercise sensitive professional and moral judgments in all their activities.

As professionals, we are responsible not only to those who use our services but to each other, to improve the art of accounting and to maintain the public's confidence in the profession.

Article II. The Public Interest. Members should accept the obligation to act in a way that will serve the public interest, honor the public trust, and demonstrate commitment to professionalism.

The accounting profession's public consists of **clients**, credit grantors, and the business and financial community, among others. The CPA must pledge to direct his or her efforts toward the collective well-being of the community, regardless of the type of services that are being performed. The CPA must behave at all times with integrity and objectivity, exercising due care in both the scope and the nature of the services that are performed for the public.

Article III. Integrity. To maintain and broaden public confidence, members should perform all professional responsibilities with the highest sense of integrity.

Integrity is the bedrock upon which all professional conduct rests. Among other things, it requires the CPA to be *honest, candid,* and to *respect the client's confidentiality.* Integrity also requires observance of the principles of objectivity, independence, and due care (discussed below). Although the rules of conduct cover many specific circumstances, there will invariably be those times in which deeds or decisions are being contemplated for which no specific rule exists. At those time, the CPA should ask, "Am I doing what a person of integrity would do, in substance as well as form?"

Article IV. Objectivity and Independence. A member should maintain objectivity and be free of conflicts of interest in discharging professional responsibilities. A member in public practice should be independent in fact and appearance when providing auditing and other attestation services.

The principle of objectivity implies a state of mind that should be maintained by the CPA in the **practice of public accounting**, regardless of the type of **professional service** he or she is performing—attest, tax, or management advisory services. The principle also applies to the CPA who is employed in private industry, government, or education. Objectivity implies impartiality, intellectual honesty, and freedom from conflicts of interest on the part of the CPA at all times. The CPA must not subordinate his or her judgment to others, regardless of who the employer is.

Independence, as discussed in Chapter 2, is a concept that applies only when the CPA is performing attest services. To maintain independence, the CPA must be both independent in fact (in the mind) and in appearance. This requires the CPA in public practice to continually assess the relationship with the client and to avoid relationships that would impair independence, such as stock ownership or managerial relationships with the client, while performing attest related services. Many CPA firms go beyond the letter of the law on this rule and maintain attest independence from all clients, including those for whom only nonattest services are performed.

Independence, integrity, and objectivity are included in the rules section as well as in the principles section. We will discuss all of these concepts in more detail later in the chapter.

Article V. Due Care. A member should observe the profession's technical and ethical standards, strive continually to improve competence and the quality of services, and discharge professional responsibility to the best of the member's ability.

The goal in rendering professional services is excellence. To achieve excellence, the CPA is expected to be diligent in discharging professional duties to the best of his or her ability. The CPA first obtains competence for the job from formal education. Continuing professional education, however, must be pursued as a lifelong goal. Competence, once achieved, assures that the CPA can exercise mature judgment in the difficult decisions that he or she will face. If for some reason the CPA is self-judged to be lacking competence for a particular task, it is up to him or her to obtain the level of competence necessary or to refer the engagement to someone who possesses the expertise for the job. All work performed by the CPA should be adequately planned, and assistants, if any, should be adequately supervised.

Article VI. Scope and Nature of Services. A member in public practice should observe the Principles of the Code of Professional Conduct in determining the scope and nature of services to be provided.

In this era of constant change, new businesses emerge and existing ones struggle for survival. More and more demands are going to be placed on the CPA to provide expansion of both the scope and the nature of professional services. This principle, therefore, is intended to be dynamic in its application. Within broad guidelines, the CPA is free to decide the nature and scope of services to clients. However, caution is given that *all* services should be performed in accordance with professional standards. For example, in keeping with the standard regarding integrity, the CPA is reminded that service and the public trust are not to be subordinated to personal gain in the decision as to scope and nature of services. In addition, all such services should be performed with an attitude of objectivity, requiring that the CPA be free from conflict of interest situations with the client at all times. Due care should be exercised by the CPA to assure that sound judgment is behind each decision.

Members are required to practice in firms that have in place internal quality-control procedures to ensure that the highest professional standards will be carried out in all aspects of the practice. We will review the process of quality control later in this chapter.

Rules of Conduct

The Rules of Conduct portion of the AICPA Code of Professional Conduct sets forth enforceable guidelines to govern the conduct of members with regard to (1) independence, integrity, and objectivity; (2) compliance with professional standards including accounting, auditing, and other technical standards; (3) client responsibilities; and (4) other responsibilities. We will discuss these responsibilities in the paragraphs that follow.

Independence, Integrity, and Objectivity

> Rule 101: Independence. A member in public practice shall be independent in the performance of professional services as required by standards promulgated by bodies designated by Council.

As stated in the previous chapter, independence on the part of the CPA is required whenever *attest* services are performed. These include auditing, review, and engagements to apply agreed-on procedures for the client, of which the outcome is a written statement that expresses a conclusion regarding the assertions of another party. The assertions may be in the form of either historical or prospective financial statements, or may consist of statements not constituting financial statements, such as compliance of the company with the provisions of a loan or other agreement.

As stated earlier, independence is conceptually a two-pronged issue. First, the attestor must *be* independent in mental attitude. Independence is a state of mind known only to the attestor and cannot be judged by another. Therefore, to make the rule operational in practice, the accountant is required to maintain the *appearance of independence* to outsiders who might observe the client-accountant relationship. An *interpretation* of the independence rule (see Appendix 3–A) prohibits the CPA from two specific relationships with the client during specified periods of time:

Financial Interests. During the period of the professional engagement or at the time of expressing an opinion, the member or a member's firm had or was committed to acquire *any direct financial interest* or *a material indirect financial interest* in the enterprise. In this respect, any interests that were held by the CPA's spouse, minor children, or other dependents are considered held by him or her and are thus considered a direct financial interest.

☑ **Objective 3**
Apply rules of professional conduct to fact situations

EXAMPLE 1
The firm of Brown, Herman, and Duncan has been engaged to perform the annual audit of CMR, Inc. Last year, the wife of Norman Duncan, partner, acquired a 1 percent interest in the stock of CMR, Inc. The stock interest is considered a direct financial interest in CMR by Norman Duncan. Neither he nor the firm would be considered independent.

EXAMPLE 2
Same facts as Example 1, except that Duncan's wife sold the stock before the engagement was accepted by the firm. Duncan's and the firm's independence is not considered impaired.

EXAMPLE 3
Same facts, except that Duncan was the trustee of an educational trust for the benefit of his children. The trust owned shares in CMR, Inc. Neither Duncan nor the firm is independent.

Managerial Relationships. The CPA is prohibited from being connected with the enterprise as a promoter, underwriter, voting trustee, officer, director, or in any other capacity equivalent to that of a member .of management or an employee. For purposes of this interpretation, an additional prohibited time period is added: the time covered by the financial statements.

EXAMPLE 4
Yolanda Ybarra, CPA, was vice-president and controller of Bass Plastics, Inc. during the 19X1 calendar year. In December of that year, Ybarra decided to resign her position as controller and to go into public practice. Bass has approached her with the proposal that she perform the audit of the 19X1 financial statements. Ybarra would not be considered independent for this purpose.

As you can see, these two interpretations provide for only the most basic understanding of the meaning and application of the independence rule. Additional interpretations, summarized in Appendix 3–A, lend clarity to the effects of the following on the independence of the member and/or the firm:

- Directorships.
- Relationships of retired partners.
- Performance of accounting services.
- Meaning of certain terminology.
- Actual or threatened litigation.
- Certain financial interests of the CPA.

> Rule 102: Integrity and Objectivity. In the performance of any professional service, a member shall maintain objectivity and integrity, and shall be free of conflicts of interest, and shall not knowingly misrepresent facts or subordinate his or her judgment to others.

The requirement for integrity and objectivity applies to all areas of the certified public accountant's practice (attest as well as nonattest services). It also applies to all members of the AICPA who are in nonpublic positions, such as those with industry, government, and education. Although an accountant who is not engaged in attestation services is not required to adhere to the independence standard of Rule 101, he or she *still has the responsibility to maintain an impartial attitude* and to be *free from conflicts of interest* that could impair objectivity.

EXAMPLE 5
Jim Mimms, CPA, engages only in tax preparation and planning work for his client, Relex, Inc. Yesterday, the management of Relex presented Mimms with a schedule of deductions for the yearly tax return. Mimms is convinced by valid evidence that the deductions are overstated. He should not sign the corporate tax return as preparer until all questions are resolved to his satisfaction and errors, if any, are corrected.

EXAMPLE 6
Todd Harper is the engagement partner for a management advisory services engagement for Big, Incorporated. Field work has been completed and recommendations have been made for significant changes in the information system of Big. The chairman of Big's board of directors informs Harper that they will implement all changes, as long as Harper will supervise operations of the company for two years following completion of the installation. Harper may not accept the assignment, since in so doing he would be assuming the role of management, impairing the firm's objectivity, and creating the impression of a conflict of interests.

Compliance with Professional Standards

The 200 series of the Rules (see Appendix 3–B for interpretations) deals with compliance of all CPAs with applicable technical standards for all areas of accounting practice. It also establishes the CPA's responsibility in all circumstances in which reports are required regarding the conformity of assertions with generally accepted accounting principles (GAAP).

> Rule 201. General Standards. A member shall comply with the following standards and with any interpretations thereof by bodies designated by Council.

    A. Professional Competence. Undertake only those professional services that the member or the member's firm can reasonably expect to be completed with professional competence.

    B. Due Professional Care. Exercise due professional care in the performance of professional services.

    C. Planning and Supervision. Adequately plan and supervise the performance of professional services.

    D. Sufficient Relevant Data. Obtain sufficient relevant data to afford a reasonable basis for conclusions or recommendations in relation to any professional services performed.

On first glance, the four parts of this rule so strongly resemble two of the general standards and two of the field work standards of auditing (Chapter 2) as to merely repeat them. However, these rules are much broader than the auditing standards. In fact, they form the ethical basis for those standards. Notice that the phrase *professional services* is used instead of *engagement*. These four rules are therefore applicable to all professional services that CPAs perform in public practice.

> Rule 202. Compliance with Standards. A member who performs auditing, review, compilation, management advisory, tax, or other professional services shall comply with standards promulgated by bodies designated by Council.

Separate standard-setting bodies of the AICPA are charged with promulgating standards relating to all of the following areas of professional practice: (1) auditing, (2) compilation and review, (3) management advisory services, and (4) taxation. The CPA who performs any of these professional services (regardless of whether he or she is in public practice) must adhere to appropriate standards. In the area of auditing, generally accepted standards are incorporated into statements on auditing standards (SASs). Similarly, there are regularly published statements for accounting (compilation) and review services and for management advisory services. In the area of tax practice, the guidelines are less authoritative than for other areas of practice and are incorporated into statements on responsibilities in tax practice. The accountant's responsibilities under non-audit service standards are discussed in Chapter 23.

> Rule 203. Accounting Principles. A member shall not (1) express an opinion or state affirmatively that the financial statements or other financial data of any entity are presented in conformity with generally accepted accounting principles or (2) state that he or she is not aware of any material modifications that should be made to such statements or data in order for them to be in conformity with generally accepted accounting principles, if such statements or data contain any departure from an accounting principle promulgated by bodies designated by Council to establish such principles that has a material effect on the statements or data taken as a whole. If, however, the statements or data contain such a departure and the member can demonstrate that due to unusual circumstances the financial statements or data would otherwise have been misleading, the member can comply with the rule by describing the departure, its approximate effects, if practicable, and the reasons why compliance with the principle would result in a misleading statement.

Whenever a CPA has been engaged to attest (either audit, review, or perform agreed-upon procedures) to assertions in financial statements or other financial data, the criteria that are used as the yardstick for measuring fairness of presentation are usually GAAP. The Financial Accounting Standards Board (FASB) has been designated as the primary body authorized to promulgate GAAP. A glance back to Figure 1–4 will reveal other sources of GAAP. This rule states that the CPA shall not attest to the fairness of financial data that purport to present GAAP, if the data contains a departure from a statement of an authoritative body designated to establish GAAP, unless the CPA can justify the departure and can establish that adherence to GAAP would have caused the data to be misleading. Examples of such departures are new legislation or the evolution of a new form of business transaction not previously addressed by traditional accounting principles.

Responsibilities to Clients

The 300 series of the rules (see Appendix 3–C for interpretations) deals generally with the CPA's responsibilities to clients. Two rules govern this aspect of public accounting practice: (1) Rule 301, which protects confidential client information, and (2) Rule 302, which prohibits acceptance of a contingent fee.

> Rule 301. Confidential Client Information. A member in public practice shall not disclose any confidential client information without the specific consent of the client.
>
> This rule shall not be construed (1) to relieve a member of his or her professional obligations under rules 202 and 203, (2) to affect in any way the member's obligation to comply with a validly issued and enforceable subpoena or summons, (3) to prohibit review of a member's professional practice under AICPA or state CPA society authorization, or (4) to preclude a member from initiating a complaint with or responding to any inquiry made by a recognized investigative or disciplinary body.
>
> Members of a recognized investigative or disciplinary body and professional practice reviewers shall not use to their own advantage or disclose any member's confidential client information that comes to their attention in carrying out their official responsibilities. However, this prohibition shall not restrict the exchange of information with a recognized investigative or disciplinary body or affect, in any way, compliance with a validly issued and enforceable subpoena or summons.

It is vital to the integrity of the professional accountant that information passing between him or her and the client be kept confidential. Such information, if made public, could damage the clients' businesses and injure the reputation of the CPA. For this reason, in most instances, the client must give specific permission for the CPA to divulge information that passed between them. Likewise, it is vital to the integrity of the profession that members who serve on disciplinary boards keep information to themselves.

Privileged communication is common in many professions. Lawyers, doctors, and members of the clergy have the benefits of privileged communication with clients. However, the CPA does not enjoy the same privileged communication with his clients as other professionals do with theirs. The CPA, perhaps more than any other professional, is expected to honor the public's interests above those of all others, including the client. As a striking example of this public duty, the AICPA acknowledges that the confidentiality rule does not prevent the accountant from responding to a validly issued subpoena or summons by a court of law. In other words, a CPA's working papers can be subpoenaed and used against the client or even the CPA in a court of law. In recent years, in fact, the Supreme Court has upheld the ruling that accountants' working papers are not privileged communication even in tax matters, although it is likely that similar working papers of an attorney regarding the same matters would be privileged.[8]

There are several other notable exceptions to the confidentiality rule. The rule does not apply, for example, whenever the issue is the CPA's responsibility for compliance with professional standards (covered in Rule 202) or reporting as to whether the client's financial statements are in accordance with GAAP (covered in Rule 203).

<table>
<tr>
<td>

☑ **Objective 3**
Apply rules of professional conduct to fact situations

</td>
<td>

EXAMPLE 7
Tena Williams, CPA, has been attempting to audit the financial statements of Shop-Right Foods, Inc. The controller of Shop-Right has imposed a restriction on Ms. Williams's audit work by refusing to allow her to observe the taking of physical inventories. Although she has tried to perform alternative procedures to assure herself as to the existence and completeness of inventories, she has been unable to do so. The facts surrounding the conflict must be disclosed in the audit report, and the report must be appropriately qualified. The same would be the case if the client had refused to make a material disclosure in the financial statements or had committed uncorrected material errors or irregularities.

</td>
</tr>
</table>

The confidentiality rule does not protect the CPA's working papers whenever they are being subjected to a quality review by another firm, under the AICPA's standards for quality reviews (covered later in this chapter). Likewise, the rule does not prevent a CPA from initiating a complaint against another CPA with a recognized disciplinary body whenever a violation of professional conduct has been discovered.

Rule 302. Contingent Fees. Professional services shall not be offered or rendered under an arrangement whereby no fee will be charged unless a specified finding or result is attained, or where the fee is otherwise contingent upon the findings or results of such services. However, a member's fees may vary depending, for example, on the complexity of services rendered.

Fees are not regarded as being contingent if fixed by courts or other public authorities, or, in tax matters, if determined based on the results of judicial proceedings or the findings of governmental agencies.

Contingent fees are defined as fees that are based on the outcome of the engagement. *Outcome* is usually defined as the achievement of a specified finding or result. For example, a contingent fee for a consulting engagement might be stated in the engagement letter as follows: "A fee not less than 20 percent of the amount of savings in operating expenses over the previous year will be charged. However, in no case will the fee for the engagement be less than $100,000."

As of the date of this writing, contingent fees are prohibited for certain attest services for CPAs in public practice because such fees create the appearance of a conflict of interests and thus affect the CPA's attestation independence. For example, if CPA firms were allowed to charge audit fees based on 10 percent of net income after taxes on the client's financial statements, the objectivity of the firm would be impaired to the extent that the audit report would be worthless.

Significant changes have occurred recently in the contingent fees rule, as well as the rule prohibiting commissions (Rule 503, discussed later in this chapter). These reflect the changing nature of accounting practice in the United States. For the first ninety years of its existence, the attest function (primarily audit) was the *bread and butter* of the accounting profession. Both contingent fees and commissions have traditionally been prohibited for CPAs because of their effects on the independence of auditors. In the last decade, however, clients have begun to demand expanded and more comprehensive services from accountants, such as investment and tax counseling and a variety of other nonattest services. At the same time, advertising by CPA firms has been greatly increased, causing greater competition among CPA firms for audits. This has made the audit practices of many CPA firms less profitable, forcing them to seek new and more profitable services to clients. Also, the financial services industry has emerged to compete with the public accounting industry for such services as investment counseling and tax planning. Practitioners have found it hard to compete with non-CPA financial planners and attorneys who also perform financial planning services for clients, and whose codes of professional conduct allow contingent fees, unlimited advertising, and commissions.

The Federal Trade Commission, with the support of some CPAs, brought pressure against AICPA to change the Code of Professional Conduct to allow commissions and contingent fees on nonattest engagements. The government contended that both of these prohibitive rules constituted an effort on the part of the profession to unlawfully restrict free trade. Thus, some CPAs are presently engaged in nonattest professional services in which contingent fees and commissions are charged. However, it should be remembered that certain state boards and state societies have more restrictive rules that still prohibit such practices. In those jurisdictions, CPAs must follow the more restrictive rules. In addition, it is generally agreed that, if attest services (audits, reviews, or engagements to apply agreed-upon procedures) are being performed simultaneously with nonattest services for the same client, contingent fees and commissions are inappropriate.

Other Responsibilities and Practices

Members of the AICPA should adhere to four basic rules in meeting their other responsibilities: members (1) should not commit acts discreditable to the profession, (2) should advertise only under the limitations imposed by the Code, (3) should not accept or pay commissions for engagements or referrals, and (4) should practice only in certain business forms. (See Appendix 3–D for interpretations.)

Rule 501. Acts Discreditable to the Profession. A CPA shall not commit an act discreditable to the profession.

An act discreditable to the profession is an act that hinders the CPA's objectivity in performing professional services. Examples of acts discreditable to the profession include refusal to return client records and discrimination in employment practices by CPA firms.

Rule 502. Advertising and Other Forms of Solicitation. A member in public practice shall not seek to obtain clients by advertising or other forms of solicitation in a manner that is false, misleading, or deceptive. Solicitation by the use of coercion, overreaching, or harassing conduct is prohibited.

From the early days of the accounting profession until 1978, advertising in any form was strictly prohibited, because of its potential to impair the CPA's objectivity in rendering services. The term *advertising* included *solicitation*, which is an uninvited proposal to render services to a specified party. Beginning in 1978, however, and continuing over the next decade, the rules restricting advertising for CPAs have been relaxed significantly. As in the case of contingent fees and commissions, the Federal Trade Commission has ruled that the prohibition of advertising was a violation of federal antitrust laws.

Under the present rule, advertising by CPAs may generally be classified into two broad categories: (1) permitted advertising and (2) false, misleading, or deceptive advertising. Limits on permitted advertising are quite flexible, thus allowing all of the following:

- Names, addresses, telephone numbers, number of partners shareholders or employees, office hours, foreign language competence, and date the firm was established.
- Services offered and fees for those services, including hourly rates and fixed fees.
- Educational and professional attainments, including date and place of certifications, schools attended, dates of graduation, degrees received, and memberships in professional associations.
- Published statements of position relating to a subject of public interest and containing the member's name.
- Persuasive advertisements intended to attract new clients, as long as the advertisements do not include information that is clearly false or misleading.
- Solicitation, including a direct uninvited solicitation of business to clients of competitors, as long as the solicitation is not based on coercion, overreaching, or harassing conduct.
- Self-designation as an industry expert, unless such designation is misleading.

There are no restrictions as to the type of advertising media, frequency of placement, size, artwork, or type style.

On the other hand, Rule 502 prohibits false, misleading, or deceptive advertising. As the Code has become more and more liberalized toward permission of most types of advertising and solicitation, the distinction between acceptable and false, misleading, or deceptive advertising has become less and less discernable. In general, misleading or deceptive advertising would include activities that

- Create false or unjustified expectations of favorable results.
- Imply the ability to influence courts, tribunals, or regulatory agencies.
- Imply that a particular service would be performed for a stated fee when it is obvious to the practitioner that the actual fee will be larger.

EXAMPLE 8
Irving Markup, CPA, advertises in the newspaper that his firm employs former field agents of the Internal Revenue Service and thus has greater ability than competing firms to influence the judgment of the IRS in audits. Such advertising is misleading and unethical.

EXAMPLE 9
Florence Sharpness, CPA, solicits business from a prospective tax client by telling them that the fee for their Corporate tax return will be $500. It is clear to Ms. Sharpness at the time that the fee will actually be $1,000 due to complications of which she is aware at the time the engagement is proposed. Such an action is generally considered unethical.

Rule 503. Commissions. The acceptance by a member in public practice of a payment for the referral of products or services of others to a client is prohibited. Such action is considered to create a conflict of interest that results in a loss of objectivity and independence.

A member shall not make a payment to obtain a client. This rule shall not prohibit payments for the purchase of an accounting practice or retirement payments to individuals formerly engaged in the practice of public accounting or payments to their heirs or estates.

As discussed earlier under Rule 302 (contingent fees) the emergence of the financial planning industry in the past decade has produced a dilemma for CPAs who perform these kinds of services for clients. Non-CPAs who have achieved the professional designation of *certified financial planner* (CFP) routinely give financial and tax advice to clients in direct competition with the CPA. However, the services of a CFP may include sale of insurance and securities to clients, both of which involve compensation in the form of a commission. Under the present Code of Conduct, accountants are not allowed to engage in the sale of products or services to clients in exchange for commissions while performing attest services for the same clients.

As mentioned in the discussion under Rule 302, the Federal Trade Commission has opposed the accounting profession with respect to contingent fees and commissions, alleging that prohibition of these forms of compensation constitute unlawful violation of free trade. In response, the AICPA has agreed to permit such fees for nonattest services. However, as mentioned under Rule 302, many state boards and societies' rules still prohibit such fee arrangements.

As the rules that limit not only advertising, but also commissions, contingent fees, and other activities, have gradually been relaxed over time, CPAs should be encouraged to revert to Article III under Principles of Ethical Conduct, discussed earlier. This broad principle of ethics encourages members, in all of their activities, to perform all professional responsibilities with the highest sense of *integrity*. Individual circumstances not specifically prohibited by the rules should be addressed with the following question: "What would a person of integrity do, in substance as well as form?" In such circumstances, practitioners would do well to let conscience be the guide for proper conduct, and to have the moral courage to be true to personal convictions.

> Rule 505. Form of Practice and Name. A member may practice public accounting only in the form of a proprietorship, a partnership, or a professional corporation whose characteristics conform to resolutions of Council.
>
> A member shall not practice public accounting under a firm name that is misleading. Names of one or more past partners or shareholders may be included in the firm name of a successor partnership or corporation. Also, a partner or shareholder surviving the death or withdrawal of all other partners or shareholders may continue to practice under such name which includes the name of past partners or shareholders for up to two years after becoming a sole practitioner.
>
> A firm may not designate itself as "Members of the American Institute of Certified Public Accountants" unless all of its partners or shareholders are members of the Institute.

Before 1969, all public accounting practice was carried out through the medium of proprietorships or partnerships. However, in response to the strong desire on the part of accountants to operate within a corporate framework, the council of the AICPA approved in 1969 a resolution allowing public accountants to render services through a professional corporation as well as the other two forms.

The rule limits to two years the amount of time that a sole practitioner may retain the name of a partnership or corporation after the death or withdrawal of the other members of the firm. In addition, firms are prevented from representing on letterhead or in other forms that they are members of the AICPA unless all partners or shareholders of the firm are members. This portion of the rule prevents the CPA from entering into partnership or other business arrangements with non-CPAs who might unduly or unknowingly abuse the status of the designation *certified public accountant* or cause conflicts of interests for the CPA.

Incentives for Maintaining Ethical Conduct

☑ **Incentive 4**
Recognize incentives for maintaining quality of practice

The major incentive for maintaining ethical conduct should be personal and voluntary by the certified public accountant. Experience has shown that, in the overwhelming majority of cases, CPAs strive to maintain ethical conduct so that the integrity and image of the profession will be protected and public confidence maintained. A recent Gallup poll confirmed that certified public accountants are considered to be among the highest in integrity by the general public.

Joint Ethics Enforcement Program (JEEP)

A joint ethics enforcement program (JEEP) for ethical conduct of CPAs exists between the AICPA and the various state societies of CPAs. Under the program, the Professional Ethics Division of the AICPA cooperates with the ethics committees of the various state societies. On receiving a complaint involving a member, a particular state society has the option to review and deal with the matter themselves or to refer the case to the Professional Ethics Division. Regardless of which body deals with the complaint, the first action to be taken is to initiate an inquiry into the matter to ascertain the validity of the complaint as well as the appropriate response. Depending on the outcome of this inquiry, complaints are disposed of in one of the following ways: (1) if no deficiencies are found, the complaint will be terminated; (2) for minor violations, educational and remedial or corrective actions will be required; (3) for complaints involving compliance with technical or independence standards, the practice-monitoring committee of the state society will be informed for appropriate action; or (4) for serious deficiencies or refusal on the part of a member to cooperate, the matter will be presented to the Joint Trial Board for disciplinary action.

The *Joint Trial Board* consists of thirty-six members from across the nation, selected by the AICPA Nominations Committee on referral, three members from each of twelve geographical regions. Hearings are conducted by subboards consisting of at least five board members appointed to maximize representation from the general area in which the involved member resides. Disciplinary action for the member may range from a reprimand to expulsion from the institute and from the state society. Trial boards are required to publish the names of all members found guilty of ethics violations.

CPAs value memberships in both the AICPA and various state societies because of the enhancement that such memberships provide for one's professional image. Nevertheless, these memberships are voluntary, and in the final analysis, the only organizations through which ethical behavior may be imposed on all CPAs are the state boards of public accountancy. These bodies also have ethics trial boards to receive complaints involving licensees within a particular state. Ultimately, the decisions of various trial boards of both the AICPA and the various state boards of public accountancy may be appealed to the Federal District Court System. Action taken by the AICPA in a particular matter against a member may in turn cause the state board to act, perhaps even to suspend or revoke the member's CPA certificate or license to practice. It is also possible that an accountant's license or permit to practice will be suspended or revoked by governmental authority.

Quality Review Programs

Before 1988, no mandatory program existed to monitor the quality of audit and accounting practice in the United States. The AICPA did, however, have a voluntary program that was administered by its Division for CPA Firms. Established in 1978, the division is composed of two sections: the SEC Practice Section (SECPS) and the Private Companies Practice Section (PCPS). The objectives of the division are to improve the quality of practice by CPA firms, to establish and maintain an effective system of self-regulation, and to provide a forum for making known views on professional matters. Requirements for membership in both of these sections include the following:

1. Adhere to quality control standards established by the AICPA Quality Control Standards Committee.
2. Submit to quality reviews of their accounting and auditing practice every three years or at such additional times as designated.
3. Ensure that all their professionals participate in forty hours of continuing professional education annually.
4. Maintain minimum amounts and types of liability insurance.[9]

In 1988, with the passage of the Anderson Committee Report, the AICPA established a *practice-monitoring requirement* for all its members in public practice. A mandatory quality review program is being implemented under this requirement that will give primary emphasis to assuring quality performance and to reducing or eliminating substandard performance throughout the profession. Disciplinary actions will be taken against members in public practice who fail to cooperate or who exhibit serious deficiencies in their practices that cannot be dealt with by remedial or corrective actions. To enroll in the program, a firm will be required to agree to the following, among other things:

1. To adhere to the applicable quality control standards of the AICPA (covered in Chapter 2).
2. To require AICPA membership of all proprietors, partners, and/or shareholders.
3. To undergo a quality review of its accounting and auditing practice every three years (only firms that offer audit services must have site reviews).
4. To file annual compliance reports with the AICPA.
5. To allow the AICPA to disclose information on the firm's compliance.
6. To comply with established rules and regulations, to cooperate with review personnel, and to accept final decisions on disciplinary matters.
7. To ensure that AICPA members in the firm meet their continuing professional education requirements.

Quality reviews are conducted to ascertain whether quality control standards are being carried out. It is common for one CPA firm to engage another CPA firm to conduct the review for a particular year. Reciprocal reviews are not permitted. It is important to remember that, for the review to be conducted effectively, the reviewing firm must gain access to the working papers of the firm being reviewed. Rule 301 of the Code of Professional Conduct (confidential client information) has been amended to allow such access, as long as the information is kept confidential among the parties associated with the review. Care should be exercised to ensure that members of the reviewing team and their firm maintain independence with respect to reviewed firms and their clients.

The elements of the firm's quality control system are reviewed, as well as policies and procedures to document and communicate them to personnel. In addition, the firm's compliance with membership requirements of the practice section is evaluated. At the completion of the review, the review team provides the reviewed firm with a formal report, along with any necessary suggestions as to needed improvements in the system of quality control.

The Securities and Exchange Commission

The Securities and Exchange Commission (SEC) was established in 1934 with the authority to define the content and form of financial statements and other reports submitted to it. This authority is interpreted to include the methods of accounting used to derive those statements. Over the years the SEC has delegated to the private sector (the AICPA and the FASB) the general responsibility for the establishment of accounting principles, including the ethical constraints under which public accountants are to operate. However, the SEC has seen fit to issue rules and interpretations, through the medium of *Accounting Series Releases*, specifying procedures and ethical interpretations to be applied to situations involving filings with it.

Insofar as auditors' independence is concerned, the positions of the AICPA and SEC are slightly different in regard to two areas. First, with the exception of audit fee arrangements, the SEC interprets any business transaction between an auditor and a client as a *direct financial interest* as defined earlier. Second, the SEC interprets almost any form of recordkeeping for clients (manual or EDP) as an impairment to independence.[10] The SEC feels that the accountant cannot objectively audit books and records that he or she has maintained for the client. Also, renting computer time to a client is considered by the SEC to be a business transaction with the client and, therefore, to adversely affect the independence of the CPA. As a result, the *SEC's interpretations of independence are generally more stringent than those of the AICPA.*

Aside from the presently existing differences of opinion cited above, it is important to recognize that over the years the SEC has, without question, had considerable influence on the general content of the AICPA Code of Professional Conduct. Generally speaking, the AICPA has been inclined to amend its code toward compliance with SEC expectations for the accountant engaged in work with the SEC. As a result, the present AICPA code is probably more stringent than it would have been without the influence of the SEC.

Ethical Responsibilities Related to Legal Liability

As we have indicated in the preceding paragraphs, ethical violations are disciplined by the profession. It is important, however, to observe that *violations of the code of conduct can lead to legal liability.* This can occur when either a client or a third party can demonstrate in the courts that a loss has been suffered because the accountant violated ethical requirements such as those relating to independence, competence, or confidential relationship with the client. Therefore, the accountant may suffer not only embarrassment by the professional discipline described in the preceding paragraphs but may also suffer financially as a result of loss of clients and potential litigation.

We should also observe that the establishment of an accountant's legal liability can lead to discipline for ethics violations. Discipline would occur when the legal action was taken simply because the ethics enforcement organization was unaware of the ethics violation relating to the legal liability until it was disclosed in the courts. Indictment and conviction of a felony crime, including filing or assistance with false tax returns, constitutes an act discreditable to the accounting profession (Rule 501) and can lead to suspension of membership in the AICPA or State Society of CPAs, as well as revocation of the license to practice by the State Board of Public Accountancy.

Enhancing Auditor Independence through Audit Committees

Independence is the cornerstone of the auditing profession. Without it, the audit opinion would be meaningless. Independence has been held to be so vital to the auditor-client relationship that provisions have been made for it in both generally accepted auditing standards (Chapter 2) and the Code of Professional Conduct. Yet, for all its importance in the literature, CPAs have traditionally had difficulty in maintaining the appearance of independence with audit clients.

Public accounting is a service-oriented profession. Concurrent services to clients can include not only auditing but also management advisory services, tax services, and accounting and review services. All of these services require a more client-advocacy-related approach (less independence) than audit services. The profession has been compelled to recognize that the dual roles of client advocate and auditor can conflict, at least in theory, and potentially impair the credibility of the audit opinion by exposing auditors to undue client influences. The establishment of *audit committees* has provided at least a partial solution to the many unresolved conflicts in this arena.

The New York Stock Exchange, in 1978, mandated that domestic companies with listed securities establish *audit committees* made up entirely of *outside directors*—directors who are neither officers nor employees of the client and who are not closely related by family or financial ties to company management. In 1979 the American Stock Exchange strongly recommended similar action for its listed companies. Throughout the years, other groups, such as the SEC and the National Commission on Fraudulent Financial Reporting (Chapter 4), have advocated the use of audit committees. Although not universally required, audit committees may operate effectively in both nonpublic and public companies.

Audit committees serve a vital function in overseeing the accounting and financial reporting policies and practices of the companies. In so doing, they help boards of directors fulfill responsibilities and help maintain liaisons between the boards and both internal and external auditors. Although no specific functions have been prescribed for audit committees, their duties usually include

- Approving the appointment and retention of the independent auditor.
- Reviewing the proposed scope and audit approach.

- Receiving and reviewing the findings of the audit (both internal and external), including the audit report, financial statements, and supplementary reports, such as the report on internal control.
- Exercising vigilant and informed oversight of the financial reporting process, including the company's internal controls.
- Considering the selection of accounting policies.
- Reviewing internal auditor recommendations.

Audit committees should enhance the quality of the independent audit by reinforcing auditor independence while strengthening the probability that audit suggestions and recommended improvements will be implemented by management. In the long run, the audit committee should strengthen the company by giving the board of directors insight into potential problem areas, with greater incentive to improve accounting and operating policies.

Summary

In this chapter we have discussed the ethics underlying the public accounting profession. We observed that a certain level of behavior, more restrictive than that prescribed by law, is expected of persons involved in professional activities. Codes of professional conduct are established to provide guidelines for that behavior and to enhance the image of the profession. In the long run such restrictions are also materially beneficial to the profession.

Although it is true that most ethics violations are defined in terms of the code adopted by the state society or state board, these codes are generally consistent with the provisions of the AICPA Code of Professional Conduct. Therefore, considerable attention was given to the rules included in that code. Interpretations of the rules are included in appendixes at the end of the chapter.

We explained how the quality review process is used to monitor adherence to AICPA standards of quality control. We also dealt briefly with the ethics enforcement process for both individual CPAs and public accounting firms.

In the last part of the chapter, we explained that, although ethics violations are subject to punishment only by the profession, they can also become the basis for actions involving legal liability.

Auditing Vocabulary

p. 55   **client:**   Any person or entity, other than the member's employer, that engages a member or firm to perform professional services.

p. 48   **ethics:**   A discipline dealing with good and evil and with moral duty; involves reflective choice in establishing standards of right and wrong.

p. 49   **holding out:**   Any action, expressed or implied, that informs others of one's status as a CPA.

p. 56   **practice of public accounting:**   Performance of professional services for clients, by a member or a member's firm, while holding out as a CPA.

p. 49   **profession:**   A group of people pursuing a learned art as a common calling in the spirit of public service.

p. 56   **professional services:**   Professional services are those services for which written standards have been promulgated and include all services performed by a member while holding out as a CPA.

Appendix 3–A: Selected AICPA Interpretations* of Rule 101 on Independence

101-1. Independence

Independence shall be considered to be impaired if, for example, a member had any of the following transactions, interests, or relationships:

A. During the period of a professional engagement or at the time of expressing an opinion, a member or a member's firm

1. Had or was committed to acquire any direct or material indirect financial interest in the enterprise.

2. Was a trustee of any trust or executor or administrator of any estate if such trust or estate had or was committed to acquire any direct or material indirect financial interest in the enterprise.

3. Had any joint, closely held business investment with the enterprise or with any officer, director, or principal stockholders thereof that was material in relation to the member's net worth or to the net worth of the member's firm.

4. Had any loan to or from the enterprise or any officer, director, or principal stockholder of the enterprise. This proscription does not apply to the following loans from a financial institution when made under normal lending procedures, terms, and requirements:

    a. Loans obtained by a member or a member's firm that are not material in relation to the net worth of such borrower.

    b. Home mortgages.

    c. Other secured loans, except loans guaranteed by a member's firm which are otherwise unsecured.

B. During the period covered by the financial statements, during the period of the professional engagement, or at the time of expressing an opinion, a member or a member's firm

---

*To be renumbered in future editions of Code.

Appendix 3–A is from *Rules of Conduct* (New York: AICPA, 1990). Copyright © 1990 by the American Institute of Certified Public Accountants, Inc.

1. Was connected with the enterprise as a promoter, underwriter, or voting trustee, as a director or officer, or in any capacity equivalent to that of a member of management or of an employee.
2. Was a trustee for any pension or profit-sharing trust of the enterprise.

The above examples are not intended to be all-inclusive.

101-2. Directorships

Members are often asked to lend the prestige of their name as a director of a charitable, religious, civic, or other similar type of nonprofit organization whose board is large and representative of the community's leadership. An auditor who permits his name to be used in this manner would not be considered lacking in independence under Rule 101 so long as he does not perform or give advice on management functions, and the board itself is sufficiently large that a third party would conclude that his membership was honorary.

101-3. Retired Partners and Independence of the Firm

A retired partner having a relationship of a type specified in Rule 101 with a client of his former firm would not be considered as impairing the firm's independence with respect to the client provided that he is no longer active in the firm, that the fees received from such client do not have a material effect on his retirement benefits, and that he is not held out as being associated with his former partnership.

101-4. Accounting Services

Members in public practice are sometimes asked to provide manual or automated bookkeeping or data processing services to clients who are of insufficient size to employ an adequate internal accounting staff. Computer systems design and programming assistance are also rendered by members either in conjunction with data processing services or as a separate engagement. Members who perform such services and who are engaged in the practice of public accounting are subject to the bylaws and rules of conduct.

On occasion members also rent *block time* on their computers to their clients but are not involved in the processing of transactions or maintaining the client's accounting records. In such cases the sale of block time constitutes a business rather than a professional relationship and must be considered together with all other relationships between the member and his client to determine if their aggregate impact is such as to impair the member's independence.

When a member performs manual or automated bookkeeping services, concern may arise whether the performance of such services would impair his audit independence—that the performance of such basic accounting services would cause his audit to be lacking in a review of mechanical accuracy or that the accounting judgments made by him in recording transactions may somehow be less reliable than if made by him in connection with the subsequent audit.

Members are skilled in, and well accustomed to, applying techniques to control mechanical accuracy, and the performance of the record-keeping function should have no effect on application of such techniques. With regard to accounting judgments, if third parties have confidence in a member's judgment in performing an audit, it is difficult to contend that they would have less confidence where the same judgment is applied in the process of preparing the underlying accounting records.

Nevertheless, a member performing accounting services for an audit client must meet the following requirements to retain the appearance that he is not virtually an employee and therefore lacking in independence in the eyes of a reasonable observer:

- The CPA must not have any relationship or combination of relationships with the client or any conflict of interest that would impair his integrity and objectivity.
- The client must accept the responsibility for the financial statements as his own. A small client may not have anyone in his employ to maintain accounting records and may rely on the CPA for this purpose. Nevertheless, the client must be sufficiently knowledgeable of the enterprise's activities and financial condition and the applicable accounting principles so that he can reasonably accept such responsibility, including, specifically, fairness of valuation and presentation and adequacy of disclosure. When necessary, the CPA must discuss accounting matters with the client to be sure that the client has the required degree of understanding.
- The CPA must not assume the role of employee or of management conducting the operations of an enterprise. For example, the CPA shall not consummate transactions, have custody of assets, or exercise authority on behalf of the client. The client must prepare the source documents on all transactions in sufficient detail to identify clearly the nature and amount of such transactions and maintain an accounting control over data processed by the CPA, such as control totals and document counts. The CPA should not make changes in such basic data without the concurrence of the client.
- The CPA, in making an examination of financial statements prepared from books and records he has maintained completely or in part, must conform to generally accepted auditing standards. The fact that he has processed or maintained certain records does not eliminate the need to make sufficient audit tests.

When a client's securities become subject to regulation by the Securities and Exchange Commission or other federal or state regulatory body, responsibility for maintenance of the accounting records, including accounting classification decisions, must be assumed by accounting personnel employed by the client. The assumption of this responsibility must commence with the first fiscal year after the client's securities qualify for such regulation.

101-5. Meaning of the Phase *Normal Lending Procedures, Terms, and Requirements*

Interpretation 101-1 (A)(4) prohibits loans to a member from his client except for certain specified kinds of loans from a client financial institution when made under *normal lending procedures, terms, and requirements*. The member would meet the criteria prescribed by this rule if the procedures, terms, and requirements relating to his loan are reasonably comparable to those relating to other loans of a similar character committed to other borrowers during the period in which the loan to the member is committed.

101-6. The Effect of Actual or Threatened Litigation on Independence

[Partially omitted.] Rule of Conduct 101 prohibits the expression of an opinion on financial statements of an enterprise unless a member and his firm are independent with respect to the enterprise. In some circumstances, independence may be considered impaired as a result of litigation or the expressed intention to commence litigation.

Litigation between Client and Auditor.   When the present management of a client company commences, or expresses an intention to commence, legal action against the auditor, the auditor and the client management may be placed in adversary positions in which the management's willingness to make complete disclosures and the auditor's objectivity may be affected by self-interest.

. . . Independence may be impaired whenever the auditor and his client company or its management are in threatened or actual positions of material adverse interests by reason of actual or intended litigation. Because of the complexity and diversity of the situations of adverse interests that may arise, however, it is difficult to prescribe precise points at which independence may be impaired. The following criteria are offered as guidelines:

1. The commencement of litigation by the present management alleging deficiencies in audit work for the client would be considered to impair independence.
2. The commencement of litigation by the auditor against the present management alleging management fraud or deceit would be considered to impair independence.
3. An expressed intention by the present management to commence litigation against the auditor alleging deficiencies in audit work for the client is considered to impair independence if the auditor concludes that there is a strong possibility that such a claim will be filed.
4. Litigation not related to audit work for the client (whether threatened or actual) for an amount not material to the member's firm or to the financial statements of the client company would not usually be considered to affect the relationship in such a way as to impair independence.

Litigation by Security Holders. The auditor may also become involved in litigation (*primary litigation*) in which he and the client company or its management are defendants. Such litigation may arise, for example, when one or more stockholders bring a stockholders' derivative action or a so-called class action against the client company or its management, officers, directors, underwriters, or auditors under the securities laws. Such primary litigation in itself would not alter fundamental relationships between the client company or its management and auditor and therefore should not be deemed to have an adverse impact on the auditor's independence. These situations should be examined carefully, however, since the potential for adverse interests may exist if cross-claims are filed against the auditor alleging that he is responsible for any deficiencies or if the auditor alleges fraud or deceit by the present management as a defense.

Effects of Impairment of Independence. If the auditor believes that the circumstances would lead a reasonable person having knowledge of the facts to conclude that the actual or intended litigation poses an unacceptable threat to the auditor's independence, he should either (a) disengage himself to avoid the appearance that his self-interest would affect his objectivity or (b) disclaim an opinion because of lack of independence.

101-7. The effect on Independence of Financial Interests in Nonclients' Investor or Investee Relationships with a Member's Client

This interpretation deals with the effect on the appearance of independence of financial interests in nonclients that are related in various ways to a client. For purposes of the interpretation, the following terms are relevant:

1. *Client*. The enterprise with whose financial statements the member is associated.
2. *Member*. Those individuals identified in the term *he or his firm*, as defined in Interpretation 101-9.
3. *Investor*. (a) A parent corporation or (b) another investor (including a natural person but not a partnership) that holds an interest in another company (*investee*), but only if the interest gives such other investor the ability to exercise significant influence over operating and financial policies of the investee. (In the case of a member holding a direct financial interest in a partnership that invests in his client, that member is deemed to hold a direct financial interest in the client through attribution, and thus is not independent.)
4. *Investee*. (a) A subsidiary corporation or (b) an entity that is subject to significant influence from an investor.
5. *Material investee*. An investee is presumed to be material if
   a. The investor's aggregate carrying amount of investment in and advances to the investee exceeds 5 percent of the investor's consolidated total assets, or
   b. The investor's equity in the investee's income from continuing operations before income taxes exceeds 5 percent of the investor's consolidated income from continuing operations before income taxes.

6. *Material financial interest.* One that exceeds 5 percent of the member's net worth. Financial interests in more than one investee of one investor are aggregated for this purpose.

Where a nonclient investee is material to a client investor, any direct or material indirect financial interest of a member in the nonclient investee would be considered to impair the member's independence with respect to the client. Likewise, where a client investee is material to a nonclient investor, any direct or material indirect financial interest of a member in the nonclient investor would be considered to impair the member's independence with respect to the client.

The remainder of this interpretation discusses whether, in other situations, a member's financial interest in nonclient investors or nonclient investees of an audit client will impair the member's independence. Those situations are (1) nonclient investee is not material to client investor, and (2) client investee is not material to nonclient investor.

101-9. The Meaning of Certain Independence Terminology and the Effect of Family Relationships on Independence*

Member or Member's Firm.   A *member* (as used in rule 101) and *a member or a member's firm* (as used in interpretation 101-1) include

1. The member's firm and its proprietors, partners, or shareholders. A member's firm is defined as a proprietorship, partnership, or professional corporation or association engaged in the practice of public accounting.
2. All individuals[†] participating in the engagement, except those who perform only routine clerical functions, such as typing and photocopying.
3. All individuals[†] with a managerial position located in an office participating in a significant portion of the engagement.
4. Any entity (for example, partnership, corporation, trust, joint venture, or pool) whose operating, financial, or accounting policies can be controlled (see definition of control for consolidation purposes in Financial Accounting Standards Board [FASB] Statement No. 94) by one or more of the persons described in (1) through (3) or by two or more such pesons if they choose to act together.

A member or a member's firm does not include an individual[†] solely because he or she was formerly associated with the client in any capacity described in interpretation 101-1-B, if such individual[†] has disassociated himself or herself from the client and does not participate in the engagement for the client covering any period of his or her association with the client.

---

*From Exposure Draft, *Omnibus Proposal of Professional Ethics Division* (New York: AICPA, May 22, 1990).
†Refers to individuals irrespective of their functional classification (for example, audit, tax, or management advisory services) and includes employees and contractors, except specialists as discussed in AU section 336.

A member or a member's firm includes individuals who provide services to clients and are associated with the client in any capacity described in interpretation 101-1-B, if the individuals are located in an office participating in a significant portion of the engagement.

Managerial Position.   The organizations of firms vary; therefore, whether an individual has a managerial position depends on the responsibilities and how he or she or the position itself is held out to clients and third parties. The following are some, but not necessarily all, of the responsibilities that suggest that an individual has a managerial position:

1. Continuing responsibility for the overall planning and supervision of engagements for specified clients
2. Authority for determining that an engagement is complete subject to final partner approval if required
3. Responsiblity for client relationships (for example, negotiating and collecting fees for enagements, marketing the firm's services)
4. Existence of profit sharing as a significant feature of total compensation
5. Responsibility for overall management of the firm, development or establishment of firm policies on technical matters, and implementation of or compliance with the following nine elements of quality control:
   a. Independence
   b. Assigning personnel to engagements
   c. Consultation
   d. Supervision
   e. Hiring
   f. Professional development of personnel
   g. Advancement of personnel
   h. Acceptance and continuance of clients
   i. Inspection of compliance with policies and procedures

Significant Influence.   A person or entity can exercise significant influence over the operating, financial, or accounting policies of another entity if, for example, the person or entity

1. Is connected with the entity as a promoter, underwriter, voting trustee, general partner, or director (other than an honorary director as defined in the code of conduct).
2. Is connected with the entity in a policy-making position related to the entity's primary operating, financial or accounting policies, such as chief executive officer, chief operating officer, chief financial officer, or chief accounting officer.
3. Meets the criteria established in Accounting Principles Board Opinion No. 18, *The Equity Method of Accounting for Investments in Common Stock*, and its interpretations to determine the ability of an investor to exercise such influence with respect to an entity.

The foregoing examples are not necessarily all-inclusive.

Office Participating in a Significant Portion of the Engagement.   An office would be considered to be participating in a significant portion of an engagement if the office had primary client responsibility for a multioffice engagement. In addition, professional judgment must be exercised in deciding whether any other office participates in a significant portion of a multioffice engagement. For example, an office would be considered to be participating in a significant portion of the engagement if the office's engagement hours or fees are material to total engagement hours or fees or if the office's responsibility for reporting, whether internally or externally, on a portion of the engagement relates to a material amount of assets or income (loss) before income taxes of the client.

The foregoing examples are not necessarily all-inclusive of the situations in which an office may be considered to be participating in a significant portion of the engagement.

Spouses and Dependent Persons.   The term *member* includes spouses (whether or not dependent) and dependent persons (whether or not related) for all purposes of complying with rule 101 subject to the following exception.

The exception is that the independence of the member and the member's firm will not normally be impaired solely because of employment of a spouse or dependent person by a client if the employment is in a position that does not allow "significant influence" over the client's operating, financial, or accounting policies. However, if such employment is in a position in which the person's activities are audit-sensitive (even though not a position of significant influence), the member should not participate in the engagement.

In general, a person's activities would be considered audit-sensitive if such activities are normally an element of or subject to significant internal accounting controls. For example, the following positions, which are not intended to be all inclusive, would normally be considered audit-sensitive (even though not positions of significant influence): cashier, internal auditor, accounting supervisor, purchasing agent, or inventory warehouse supervisor.

Nondependent Close Relative.   The term *member* excludes nondependent close relatives of the persons described in (1) through (3) of that definition. Nevertheless, in circumstances discussed below, the independence of a member or a firm can be impaired because of a nondependent close relative.

Close relatives are nondependent children, stepchildren, brothers, sisters, grandparents, parents, and their respective spouses. Close relatives do not include the brothers and sisters of the member's spouse.

The independence of a member's firm would be considered to be impaired with respect to the enterprise if:

1. During the period of the professional engagement or at the time of expressing an opinion, an individual participating in the engagement has a close relative with a financial interest in the enterprise that was material to the close relative and of which the individual participating in the engagement has knowledge.
2. During the period covered by the financial statements, during the period of the professional engagement, or at the time of expressing an opinion

a. An individual participating in the engagement has a close relative who could exercise significant influence over the operating, financial, or accounting policies of the enterprise or who is otherwise employed in a position where the person's activities are "audit-sensitive" or

b. A proprietor, partner, shareholder, or individual with a managerial position, any of whom are located in an office participating in a significant portion of the engagement, has a close relative who could exercise significant influence over the operating, financial, or accounting policies of the enterprise.

Other Considerations. Members must be aware that it is impossible to enumerate all circumstances wherein the appearance of a member's independence might be questioned by third parties. For example, a member's relationship with a cohabitant may be equivalent to that of a spouse. In addition, in situations involving assessment of the association of any relative or dependent person with a client, members must consider whether the strength of personal and business relationships between the member and the relative or dependent person, considered in conjunction with the specified association with the client, would lead a reasonable person aware of all the facts, and taking into consideration normal strength of character and normal behavior under the circumstances, to conclude that the situation poses an unacceptable threat to the member's objectivity and appearance of independence.

Appendix 3–B: Selected AICPA Interpretations of Rules 201 and 202 Relating to Compliance with Technical Standards

201-1. Competence

A member who accepts a professional engagement implies that he has the necessary competence to complete the engagement according to professional standards, applying his knowledge and skill with reasonable care and diligence, but he does not assume a responsibility for infallibility of knowledge or judgment.

Competence in the practice of public accounting involves both the technical qualifications of the member and his staff and his ability to supervise and evaluate the quality of the work performed. Competence relates both to knowledge of the profession's standards, techniques, and the technical subject matter involved, and to the capability to exercise sound judgment in applying such knowledge to each engagement.

The member may have the knowledge required to complete an engagement professionally before undertaking it. In many cases, however, additional research or consultation with others may be necessary during the course of the

Appendix 3–B is from *Rules of Conduct* (New York: AICPA, 1990). Copyright © 1990 by the American Institute of Certified Public Accountants, Inc.

engagement. The need for research does not ordinarily represent a lack of competence, but rather is a normal part of the professional conduct of an engagement.

However, if a CPA is unable to gain sufficient competence through these means, he should suggest, in fairness to his client and the public, the engagement of someone competent to perform the needed service, either independently or as an associate.

203-1. Departures from Established Accounting Principles

Rule 203 was adopted to require compliance with accounting principles promulgated by the body designed by the council to establish such principles. There is a strong presumption that adherence to officially established accounting principles would in nearly all instances result in financial statements that are not misleading.

However, in the establishment of accounting principles it is difficult to anticipate all of the circumstances to which such principles might be applied. This rule therefore recognizes that on occasion there may be unusual circumstances in which the literal application of pronouncements on accounting principles would have the effect of rendering financial statements misleading. In such cases, the proper accounting treatment is that which will render the financial statements not misleading.

The question of what constitutes unusual circumstances as referred to in Rule 203 is a matter of professional judgment involving the ability to support the position that adherence to a promulgated principle would be regarded generally by reasonable men as producing a misleading result.

Examples of events that may justify departures from a principle are new legislation or the evolution of a new form of business transaction. An unusual degree of materiality or the existence of conflicting industry practices are examples of circumstances that would not ordinarily be regarded as unusual in the context of Rule 203.

203-2. Status of FASB Interpretations

The council is authorized under Rule 203 to designate a body to establish accounting principles and has designated the Financial Accounting Standards Board as such body. The council also has resolved that FASB Statements of Financial Accounting Standards, together with those Accounting Research Bulletins and APB Opinions not superseded by action of the FASB, constitute accounting principles as contemplated in Rule 203.

In determining the existence of a departure from an accounting principle established by a Statement of Financial Accounting Standards, Accounting Research Bulletin, or APB Opinion encompassed by Rule 203, the division of professional ethics will construe such Statement, Bulletin, or Opinion in the light of any interpretation thereof issued by the FASB.

Appendix 3–C: Selected AICPA Interpretations of Rule 301 on Responsibilities to Clients

301-1. Confidential Information and Technical Standards

The prohibition against disclosure of confidential information obtained in the course of a professional engagement does not apply to disclosure of such information when required to properly discharge the member's responsibility according to the profession's standards. The prohibition would not apply, for example, to disclosure, as required by Section 561 of Statement of Auditing Standards 1, of subsequent discovery of facts existing at the date of the auditor's report that would have affected the auditor's report had he been aware of such facts.

Appendix 3–D: Selected AICPA Interpretations of Rules 501, 502, and 505 on Other Responsibilities

501-1. Client's Records and Accountant's Work Papers

[Partially omitted.] Retention of client records after a demand is made for them is an act discreditable to the profession in violation of Rule 501. The fact that the statutes of the state in which a member practices may specifically grant him a lien on all client records in his possession does not change the ethical standard that it would be a violation of the code to retain the records to enforce payment.

A member's working papers are his property and need not be surrendered to the client. However, in some instances a member's working papers will contain data that should properly be reflected in the client's books and records but that for convenience have not been duplicated therein, with the result that the client's records are incomplete. In such instances, the portion of the working papers containing such data constitutes part of the client's records, and copies should be made available to the client on request.

501-2. Discrimination in Employment Practices

Discrimination based on race, color, religion, sex, age, or national origin in hiring, promotion, or salary practices is presumed to constitute an act discreditable to the profession in violation of Rule 501.

501-3. Failure to Follow Standards and/or Procedures or Other Requirements in Governmental Audits

Engagements for audits of government grants, government units, or other recipients of government monies typically require that such audits be in compliance with government audit standards, guides, procedures, statutes, rules, and regulations, in addition to generally accepted auditing standards. If a member has accepted such an engagement and undertakes an obligation to follow specified government audit standards, guides, procedures, statutes, rules, and regulations, in addition to generally accepted auditing standards, he is obligated to follow such requirements. Failure to do so is an act discreditable to the profession in violation of Rule 501, unless the member discloses in his report the fact that such requirements were not followed and the reasons therefor.

501-4. Negligence in Preparation of Financial Statements or Records

A member who, by virtue of his negligence, makes, or permits or directs another to make, false and misleading entries in the financial statements or records of an entity shall be considered to have committed an act discreditable to the profession in violation of rule 501.

502-2. False, Misleading, or Deceptive Acts

Advertising or other forms of solicitation that are false, misleading, or deceptive are not in the public interest and are prohibited. Such activities include those that

1. Create false or unjustified expectations of favorable results.
2. Imply the ability to influence any court, tribunal, regulatory agency, or similar official body.
3. Contain a representation that specific professional services in current or future periods will be performed for a stated fee (or range) when it is likely at the time of the representation that the actual fee will be substantially higher, without notification of the client.
4. Contain any other representation that would be likely to cause a reasonable person to misunderstand or be deceived.

Appendix 3-E: The Institute of Internal Auditors Code of Ethics*

THE INSTITUTE OF INTERNAL AUDITORS

CODE OF ETHICS

PURPOSE: A distinguishing mark of a profession is acceptance by its members of responsibility to the interests of those it serves. Members of The Institute of Internal Auditors (Members) and Certified Internal Auditors (CIAs) must maintain high standards of conduct in order to effectively discharge this responsibility. The Institute of Internal Auditors (Institute) adopts this *Code of Ethics* for Members and CIAs.

APPLICABILITY: This *Code of Ethics* is applicable to all Members and CIAs. Membership in The Institute and acceptance of the "Certified Internal Auditor" designation are voluntary actions. By acceptance, Members and CIAs assume an obligation of self-discipline above and beyond the requirements of laws and regulations.

The standards of conduct set forth in this *Code of Ethics* provide basic principles in the practice of internal auditing. Members and CIAs should realize that their individual judgment is required in the application of these principles.

CIAs shall use the "Certified Internal Auditor" designation with discretion and in a dignified manner, fully aware of what the designation denotes. The designation shall also be used in a manner consistent with all statutory requirements.

Members who are judged by the Board of Directors of The Institute to be in violation of the standards of conduct of the *Code of Ethics* shall be subject to forfeiture of their membership in The Institute. CIAs who are similarly judged also shall be subject to forfeiture of the "Certified Internal Auditor" designation.

STANDARDS OF CONDUCT

    I. Members and CIAs shall exercise honesty, objectivity, and diligence in the performance of their duties and responsibilities.

    II. Members and CIAs shall exhibit loyalty in all matters pertaining to the affairs of their organization or to whomever they may be rendering a service. However, Members and CIAs shall not knowingly be a party to any illegal or improper activity.

    III. Members and CIAs shall not knowingly engage in acts or activities which are discreditable to the profession of internal auditing or to their organization.

    IV. Members and CIAs shall refrain from entering into any activity which may be in conflict with the interest of their organization or which would prejudice their ability to carry out objectively their duties and responsibilities.

    V. Members and CIAs shall not accept anything of value from an employee, client, customer, supplier, or business associate of their organization which would impair or be presumed to impair their professional judgment.

    VI. Members and CIAs shall undertake only those services which they can reasonably expect to complete with professional competence.

    VII. Members and CIAs shall adopt suitable means to comply with the *Standards for the Professional Practice of Internal Auditing*.

    VIII. Members and CIAs shall be prudent in the use of information acquired in the course of their duties. They shall not use confidential information for any personal gain nor in any manner which would be contrary to law or detrimental to the welfare of their organization.

    IX. Members and CIAs, when reporting on the results of their work, shall reveal all material facts known to them which, if not revealed, could either distort reports of operations under review or conceal unlawful practices.

    X. Members and CIAs shall continually strive for improvement in their proficiency, and in the effectiveness and quality of their service.

    XI. Members and CIAs, in the practice of their profession, shall be ever mindful of their obligation to maintain the high standards of competence, morality and dignity promulgated by The Institute. Members shall abide by the *Bylaws* and uphold the objectives of The Institute.

---

*Adopted by Board of Directors July, 1988

Notes

1. *New Merriam-Webster Pocket Dictionary* (New York: Pocket Books, 1964): 168.
2. Floyd W. Windall and Robert N. Corley, *The Accounting Professional* (Englewood Cliffs, N.J.: Prentice-Hall, 1980): 198.
3. Much of the material in this section excerpted from Herman J. Lowe, "Ethics in Our 100-Year History," *Journal of Accountancy* (May 1987): 78–87.
4. Thomas J. Higging, "Professional Ethics: A Time for Reappraisal," *Journal of Accountancy* (March 1962): 29–35.
5. *Restatement of the Code of Professional Ethics* (New York: AICPA, 1972): 7.
6. Much of the material in this section excerpted from George D. Anderson and Robert C. Ellyson, "Restructuring Professional Standards: the Anderson Report," *Journal of Accountancy* (September 1986): 92–104.
7. Material in this section excerpted from *Plan to Restructure Professional Standards* (New York: AICPA, 1987).
8. *U.S. v. Smith* (1974, DC Miss) 373 F Supp. 14.
9. Windall and Corley, p. 137.
10. SEC Accounting Series Releases 126 and 234.

Questions for Class Discussion

Q3-1   What does the term *ethics* mean?

Q3-2   What distinguishes a profession from a vocation?

Q3-3   Why do the members of a profession adopt a code of conduct governing their behavior? Discuss.

Q3-4   What relationship exists between a society's code of law and a code of professional conduct adopted by a segment of that society?

Q3-5   How does a profession's code of professional conduct relate to the services performed by that profession? Discuss.

Q3-6   Is a code of professional conduct selfishly beneficial to a profession? Explain.

Q3-7   Who is responsible for enforcing the provisions of a code of professional conduct? Explain how that process occurs in the AICPA.

Q3-8   A CPA is typically licensed to practice by the board of public accountancy for a particular state. Why, then, does the accounting profession give so much attention to the provisions of the AICPA Code of Professional Conduct?

Q3-9   What are the relationships between the six broad ethical principles underlying the AICPA Code of Professional Conduct and the practice of accountancy?

Q3-10   Is the certified public accountant governed by the same rules of conduct in performing all public accounting services? Discuss.

Q3-11   Explain the responsibility for adherence to the AICPA Code of Professional Conduct for members who are not in public practice. Would it be more or less difficult for these members to comply than for those in public practice? Explain.

Q3-12 The first code of professional conduct adopted by the AICPA contained no reference to the need for independence in the performance of attestation services. Why has that changed in later revisions?

Q3-13 What is the difference between being independent and appearing to be independent? Why is the appearance of independence important to the CPA who performs attest services?

Q3-14 How are competence and technical standards associated with the AICPA Code of Professional Conduct?

Q3-15 What is meant by a *contingent fee*? Give an example. Under what circumstances are contingent fees allowable under the AICPA Code of Professional Conduct? Under what circumstances are contingent fees not allowed? Why?

Q3-16 What is meant by the phrase *acts discreditable to the profession*?

Q3-17 What is meant by the phrase *in the public interest*?

Q3-18 What relationship exists between quality control standards for public accounting firms and the profession's code of professional conduct?

Q3-19 What is meant by the phrase *quality review*? How does it relate to the maintenance of quality control standards?

Q3-20 What influence has the SEC had on the AICPA Code of Professional Conduct?

Q3-21 What is likely to happen in the event that a certified public accountant violates the profession's code of conduct?

Q3-22 What is likely to happen if a public accounting firm is found to be deficient in maintaining appropriate quality control standards?

Q3-23 What is the relationship between ethical responsibilities and potential legal liability for public accountants?

Short Cases

C3-1 Ben Seastrunk, a BBA graduate of a small midwestern university, recently took a job with Sleeper and Sleeper, CPAs, a local firm in his hometown of Midwest City, Nebraska. After he had worked for the firm for six months, a partner of the firm, Loc Tran, invited Seastrunk into his office for his semiannual review.

"Seastrunk, I like you," Tran told the young man. "I believe you have what it takes to succeed in this business. I want to give you a little advice, son. It's a dog-eat-dog world out there, and only the strong survive. We're adopting a more aggressive policy of client service to try to expand our share of the market for clients in this town. We're planning on developing a drastically lower first-year fee structure to attract new clients and undercut the competition. We figure that we can cut a few corners on each engagement to save dollars off the fees, and next year we can increase fees above their former levels to more than make up the difference.

"In addition, I'd like to talk to your father this year about taking him on as an audit client next year. You know, that $45,000 fee he's paying Arthur Crumley would surely do a lot for our P & L. And who knows, we might even be able to work up a little bonus for you of, say, 10 percent off the top. You aren't a CPA yet, so it won't hurt you a bit professionally, and nobody in this town would dare sue me for violating the code of ethics. Besides, no one needs to know anything about this conversation except you and me. Right, son?"

Required:
  a. Evaluate Tran's statements in light of the AICPA Code of Professional Conduct.
  b. Were any of Tran's statements, while not a violation of the AICPA Code of Professional Conduct, personally objectionable?
  c. Are lawsuits generally the recourse sought by other professionals when a CPA violates the Code of Professional Conduct of the AICPA? If not, what other recourse is available against Tran and the firm of Sleeper and Sleeper?

C3-2   Joyce Gilbert and Elissa Bradley formed a corporation called Financial Services, Inc., each woman taking 50 percent of the authorized common stock. Gilbert is a CPA and a member of the American Institute of CPAs. Bradley is a CPCU (Chartered Property Casualty Underwriter). The corporation performs auditing and tax services under Gilbert's direction and insurance services under Bradley's supervision. The opening of the corporation's office was announced by a three-inch, two-column "card" in the local newspaper.

One of the corporation's first audit clients was the Grandtime Company. Grandtime had total assets of $600,000 and total liabilities of $270,000. In the course of her examination, Gilbert found that Grandtime's building with a book value of $240,000 was pledged as security for a ten-year-term note in the amount of $200,000. The client's statement did not mention that the building was pledged as security for the ten-year-term note.

Gilbert realized that the failure to disclose the lien did not affect either the value of the assets or the amount of the liabilities. Because her examination was satisfactory in all other respects, Gilbert rendered an unqualified opinion on Grandtime's financial statements. About two months after the date of her opinion, Gilbert learned that an insurance company was planning to loan Grandtime $150,000 in the form of a first-mortgage note on the building. Realizing that the insurance company was unaware of the existing lien on the building, Gilbert had Bradley notify the insurance company of the fact that Grandtime's building was pledged as security for the term note.

Shortly after the events described above, Gilbert was charged with a violation of professional conduct.

Required: Identify and discuss the ethical implications of those acts by Gilbert that were in violation of the AICPA Code of Professional Conduct.   *(AICPA adapted)*

C3-3   You have been elected treasurer of your local church. The church board recently adopted a policy whereby emergency financial needs of the members could be met through an emergency benevolence fund. The church's policy is that members may designate special church offerings to be used for meeting the needs of church members who are in dire financial straits. These needs are to be screened by a special committee of which you have been appointed chairperson.

Shortly after that policy was approved, you were approached by the chairman of the church board, who has a son in a seminary supported by your denomination about 100 miles away from your city. The chairman (also the wealthiest and most influential member of the church) told you that he had decided to support his son through the church benevolence fund. His plan is to give an extra $500 per month to the church, designated for his son, and he wants you to direct that the money be so disbursed. He plans to deduct the extra $6,000 given by him to the church as part of charitable contributions on his personal tax return.

Required:
  a. Would you accommodate the chairman of the church board?

b. If you decided to accommodate the chairman of the board, which provision of the AICPA's Code of Professional Conduct would you be violating, if any? Does this answer affect your response to question (a)?

C3-4 Alex Blum, a retired partner of your CPA firm, has just been appointed to the board of directors of Palmore Corporation, your firm's client. Blum is also an ex officio member of your firm's MAS advisory committee, which meets monthly to discuss MAS problems of the partnership's clients, some of which are competitors of Palmore Corporation. Your partnership pays Blum $200 for each advisory committee meeting attended plus a monthly retirement benefit, fixed by a retirement plan policy, of $2,000.

Required: Discuss the effect of Blum's appointment to the board of directors of Palmore Corporation on the partnership's independence in expressing an opinion on Palmore Corporation's financial statements. Are there other matters of ethics involved in this situation? *(AICPA adapted)*

C3-5 An auditor's report was appended to the financial statements of Worthmore, Inc. The statements consisted of a balance sheet as of November 30, 19X8, and statements of income, retained earnings, and cash flows for the year then ended. The first two paragraphs of the report contained the wording of the unqualified standard report, and a third paragraph read as follows:

"The wives of two partners of our CPA firm owned a material investment in the outstanding common stock of Worthmore, Inc., during the fiscal year ended November 30, 19X8. These individuals disposed of their holdings on December 3, 19X8, in a transaction that did not result in a profit or a loss. This information is included in our audit report in order to comply with disclosure requirements of the Rules of Conduct of the American Institute of Certified Public Accountants.

Bell & Davis
Certified Public Accountants"

Required:
a. Was the CPA firm of Bell & Davis independent with respect to the fiscal 19X8 audit of Worthmore, Inc.'s financial statements? Explain.
b. Do you find Bell & Davis's audit report satisfactory? Explain.
c. Assume that no members of Bell & Davis or any members of their families held any financial interests in Worthmore, Inc., during 19X8. For each of the following cases, indicate if independence would be lacking for Bell & Davis, assuming that Worthmore, Inc., is a profit-seeking enterprise. In each case, explain why independence would or would not be lacking.
   1. Two directors of Worthmore, Inc., became partners in the CPA firm of Bell & Davis on July 1, 19X8, resigning their directorships on that date.
   2. During 19X8, the former controller of Worthmore, now a Bell & Davis partner, was frequently called on for assistance by Worthmore. He made decisions for Worthmore's management regarding fixed asset acquisitions and the company's product marketing mix. In addition, he conducted a computer feasibility study for Worthmore. *(AICPA adapted)*

C3-6 A client, without consulting its CPA, has changed its accounting so that it is not in accordance with generally accepted accounting principles. During the regular engagement, the CPA discovers that the statements based on the accounts are so grossly misleading that they might be considered fraudulent.

Required:
  a. Discuss the action to be taken by the CPA.
  b. In this situation, what obligation does the CPA have to outsiders if he or she is replaced? Discuss briefly.
  c. In this situation, what obligation does the CPA have to a new auditor if he or she is replaced? Discuss briefly.

C3-7   The Miller Corporation is indebted to Delores Ruiz, CPA, for unpaid fees and has offered to give her unsecured, interest-bearing notes.

Required: Decide whether the CPA's acceptance of these notes would have any bearing on her independence in the engagement with the Miller Corporation. Would your conclusion be the same if Miller Corporation had offered to give Ruiz 200 shares of its common stock (after which 10,200 shares would be outstanding)? Discuss all facets of these two separate situations.   *(AICPA adapted)*

C3-8   Richard Royal recently moved to Center City, Illinois and joined a local church. On learning that Royal was a CPA, the church board elected Royal as church treasurer for the year 19X2. At the same time, the board asked Royal to perform the annual audit of the church for the fiscal year 19X1. Royal has agreed to perform the audit for no fee.

Required:
  a. Discuss the ethical implications of Royal's acceptance of the 19X1 audit.
  b. Does the fact that Royal would perform the audit for no fee have any bearing on your decision in question (a)?
  c. What could Royal do, if anything, that would allow him to accept the church engagement within the rules of the AICPA Code of Conduct?

C3-9   An accounting firm has been told that it should subject itself to quality review. A partner in the firm objects to this practice and observes that other business enterprises are not subject to such reviews. He maintains that the way his firm conducts its activities should not be of interest to anyone else because the competitive market for accountants' services will cause the more efficient firms to prosper and the less efficient ones not to prosper.

Required: Explain to the partner why the operations of his firm should be subject to quality review.

C3-10   Dean Young, CPA, is the managing partner of the Florence, Italy, office of the international accounting firm of Biggest and Best, CPAs. Within the city are two very large advertising agencies, La Donna Ltd. and La Bella Ltd. Both agencies are audit clients of Biggest and Best, and Young is the engagement partner for both audits.
    La Donna is a subsidiary of a United States-based New York Stock Exchange company. The parent company, based in Dallas, Texas, is a client of Biggest and Best in that city. La Bella is also a subsidiary of a New York Stock Exchange company, based in Atlanta, Georgia, who is a client of Biggest and Best in that city. Both the Dallas and Atlanta offices have engaged the Florence office to perform the audit field work on the Italian subsidiaries and to issue the audit reports thereon to them.
    La Bella is a customer of La Donna. The president of La Bella has been instrumental in the relationship that has been established between the two agencies. La Bella regularly places advertising with a television station in Florence, using La Donna as an intermediary, because of the expertise that some personnel with La Donna have in television markets. As part of a volume discount arrangement, the television station regularly pays

rebates to agencies that place large amounts of advertising with the station. The amount of those rebates is based on a contract between the agency and the television station.

In the process of auditing the financial statements of La Donna, the senior CPA on the engagement discovers that, to retain the relationship between the two advertising agencies, the management of La Donna has felt obligated to instruct the television station as follows: (1) to pay the full contracted rebate amount to La Donna; (2) to pay an "additional amount" to "a high level executive" (unnamed) in La Bella. The payment of the additional amount is made in the form of a cashier's check drawn to "bearer." Since Biggest and Best do not audit the financial statements of the television station, they do not have access to the canceled checks of that entity to ascertain the name of the endorsee of the check for the additional amount.

Both the parent of La Donna and the parent of La Bella have strict codes of ethical conduct that prohibit employees from accepting or paying bribes or kickbacks from officials of other companies.

Required:

a. Do you feel that anything unethical has occurred as the result of the above transactions between the television stations, La Donna, and the high level executive in La Bella? Why or why not?

b. Describe the ethical dilemma, if any, faced by Dean Young, the partner in charge of the Florence office? Arrange your discussion points as follows:
1. The parties to the problem.
2. The choices that Young faces.
3. The potential consequences of each choice to the parties involved.

c. If you were Young, which choice would you make? Why?

C3-11   Michael White, CPA, is controller of Birdsong Industries, Inc. Birdsong is the subsidiary of Big Conglomerate, Inc. White reports to Russell Conger, president of Birdsong, as well as to the controller of Big Conglomerate and to its audit committee. Conger is the son-in-law of the Chairman of the Board of Big Conglomerate and the nephew of the Chairman of the audit committee.

To impress his father-in-law, Conger has been pushing the sales staff of Birdsong to pad sales figures so that profits would look better than they are. When White discovered overstated sales figures in the internal reports of the company, he confronted Conger. Conger threatened to use his position to see to it that White is fired if he reports Conger to the audit committee.

Required:

a. Critique the internal organizational structure of Big Conglomerate, Inc. What probability would you set (low, medium, or high) that the audit committee of Big is effective or ineffective? Why?

b. Describe White's choices and the potential consequences of each.

c. Does the AICPA Code of Professional Conduct address this situation? In what way?

d. If you were White, what would you do? Why?

Problems

P3-1   Select the best answer to the following questions.

a. Which of the following statements best describes why the profession of certified public accountants has deemed it essential to promulgate a code of conduct and to establish a mechanism for enforcing observance of the code:

1. A distinguishing mark of a profession is its acceptance of responsibility to the public.
2. A prerequisite to success is the establishment of an ethical code that stresses primarily the professional's responsibility to clients and colleagues.
3. A requirement of most state laws calls for the profession to establish a code of ethics.
4. An essential means of self-protection for the profession is the establishment of a code of conduct.

b. The AICPA Code of Professional Conduct requires compliance with accounting principles promulgated by the body designated by AICPA Council to establish such principles. The pronouncements covered by the code include all of the following *except*
1. Opinions issued by the Accounting Principles Board.
2. AICPA Accounting Research Studies.
3. Interpretations issued by the Financial Accounting Standards Board.
4. AICPA Accounting Research Bulletins.

c. The AICPA Code of Professional Conduct recognizes that the reliance of the public, the government, and the business community on sound financial reporting imposes particular obligations on CPAs. The code derives its authority from
1. Public laws enacted over the years.
2. General acceptance of the code by the business community.
3. Requirements of governmental regulatory agencies, such as the Securities and Exchange Commission.
4. Bylaws of the American Institute of Certified Public Accountants.

d. A CPA's retention of client records as a means of enforcing payment of an overdue audit fee is an action that is
1. Considered acceptable by the AICPA Code of Professional Conduct.
2. Ill-advised, since it would impair the CPA's independence with respect to the client.
3. Considered discreditable to the profession.
4. A violation of generally accepted auditing standards.

P3-2 Select the best answer for each of the following items relating to the maintenance of objectivity and integrity in performing an audit.

a. An auditor strives to achieve independence in appearance in order to
1. Maintain public confidence in the profession.
2. Become independent in fact.
3. Comply with the generally accepted auditing standards of field work.
4. Maintain an unbiased mental attitude.

b. A CPA purchased stock in a client corporation and placed it in a trust as an educational fund for the CPA's minor child. The trust securities were not material to the CPA but were material to the child's personal net worth. Would the independence of the CPA be considered impaired with respect to the client?
1. Yes, because the stock would be considered a direct financial interest and, consequently, materiality is *not* a factor.
2. Yes, because the stock would be considered an indirect financial interest that is material to the CPA's child.
3. No, because the CPA would *not* be considered to have a direct financial interest in the client.
4. No, because the CPA would *not* be considered to have a material indirect financial interest in the client.

   c. A CPA audits the financial statements of a local bank. According to the AICPA Code of Professional Conduct, the appearance of independence ordinarily would *not* be impaired if the CPA
      1. Serves on the bank's committee that approves loans.
      2. Owns several shares of the bank's common stock.
      3. Obtains a short-term loan from the bank.
      4. Uses the bank's time-sharing computer service to solve client-related problems.
   d. During the course of an audit, the client's controller asks your advice on how to revise the purchase journal so as to reduce the amount of time his staff takes in posting. How should you respond?
      1. Explain that under the AICPA Code of Professional Conduct you cannot give advice on management advisory service areas at the same time you are doing an audit.
      2. Explain that under the AICPA Statement on Management Advisory Services informal advice of this type is prohibited.
      3. Respond with definite recommendations based on your audit of these records, but state that you will not assume any responsibility for any changes unless your specific recommendations are followed.
      4. Respond as practicable at the moment and express the basis for your response so it will be accepted for what it is.
   e. Which of the following *best* describes why publicly traded corporations follow the practice of having the outside auditor appointed by the audit committee of the board of directors or elected by the stockholders?
      1. To comply with the regulations of the Financial Accounting Standards Board.
      2. To emphasize auditor independence from the management of the corporation.
      3. To encourage a policy of rotation of the independent auditors.
      4. To provide the corporate owners with an opportunity to voice their opinion concerning the quality of the auditing firm selected by the directors.
   f. An auditor is about to commence a recurring annual auditing engagement. The continuing auditor's independence would ordinarily be considered to be impaired if the prior year's audit fee
      1. Was only partially paid and the balance is being disputed.
      2. Has *not* been paid and will *not* be paid for at least twelve months.
      3. Has *not* been paid and the client has filed a voluntary petition for bankruptcy.
      4. Was settled by litigation.   (AICPA adapted)

P3-3 Select the best answer to each of the following items relating to maintenance of confidence and fees charged for accounting services.
   a. The AICPA Code of Professional Conduct states that a CPA shall not disclose any confidential information obtained in the course of a professional engagement except with the consent of the client. This rule should be understood to preclude a CPA from responding to an inquiry made by
      1. The trial board of the AICPA.
      2. An investigative body of a state CPA society.
      3. A CPA/shareholder of the client corporation.
      4. An AICPA voluntary quality review body.
   b. In which one of the following situations would a CPA be in violation of the AICPA Code of Professional Conduct in determining his fee?
      1. A fee based on whether the CPA's audit report on the client's financial statements results in the approval of a bank loan.
      2. A fee based on the outcome of a bankruptcy proceeding.

3. A fee based on the nature of the service rendered and the CPA's particular expertise instead of the actual time spent on the engagement.

4. A fee based on the fee charged by the prior auditor.

c. The profession's ethical standards would most likely be considered to have been violated when the CPA represents that specific consulting services will be performed for a stated fee and it is apparent at the time of the representation that the

1. CPA would *not* be independent.

2. Fee was a competitive bid.

3. Actual fee would be substantially higher.

4. Actual fee would be substantially lower than the fees charged by other CPAs for comparable services.   *(AICPA adapted)*

P3-4 Which of the following actions, if any, would constitute a violation of the AICPA's Code of Professional Conduct with respect to advertising? Explain your opinion for each case.

a. A CPA moves office locations and advertises the new address and telephone number in the local newspaper.

b. A CPA publishes a monthly newsletter on financial management. The CPA firm's name is featured prominently on the front of the newsletter.

c. A CPA's advertisement contains the words: "Hassled by the Feds? Don't worry. We provide peace of mind."

d. A CPA places his name and address in the yellow pages of the telephone book enclosed in a box, with the firm's logo included, and the name and telephone number in boldface type.

e. A CPA places an advertisement in the local newspaper stating his name, address, telephone number, fees for various services, and expertise in farm and ranch taxation.

f. A CPA, knowing that a prospective client is already the client of another CPA, solicits the tax engagement of the client, promising that the fee will be no more than $1,000 and that, if the client is audited, the CPA will attend the audit at no extra charge.

g. Same as (f), except that the CPA has knowledge that the actual fee is more likely to be $1,500.

P3-5 Commissions and contingent fees are prohibited on certain types of professional accounting engagements. Evaluate each of the following situations in light of the AICPA Code of Professional Conduct. Justify your answers.

a. Janice Peavley, CPA, is approached by a prospective audit client, who promises to pay her "10 percent of the amount you increase net income from my own computations."

b. David Stevens, CPA and tax specialist, has been approached by a prospective client to perform the 19x9 annual audit. Since Stevens does not perform audit services, he refers the engagement to his friend Ben Mattox and accepts a $1,000 referral fee from Mattox.

P3-6 Each of the following cases involves possible violations of the AICPA's Code of Professional Conduct. For each situation, state whether a violation of the code has occurred and why.

a. Rudolph Ross, CPA, provides bookkeeping, tax, and auditing services for one of his firm's clients. Since Ross's firm is small, one person typically performs all of the above services.

    b. Jack Pritchett, CPA, was convicted of possession of marijuana after two marijuana cigarettes were found on his person during a raid of a local discotheque and bar.

    c. Donna Eberhart, CPA, is presently employed by C. P. Smart & Co., CPAs, and seeks employment with Goode & Co., CPAs. Ms. Eberhart informs Goode & Co. that she works for another firm in the same locale but refuses to allow them to contact Smart. Goode & Co. hire Eberhart without notifying Smart & Co.

    d. Margaret Teitelbaum, CPA, belongs to Ridgecrest Country Club, membership in which involves the acquisition of a pro rata share of equity or debt securities. The club asks Teitelbaum to perform its annual audit, and she accepts the engagement.

    e. A brother of John Sealy, CPA, is a stockholder and one of four vice-presidents of a closely held corporation that is located in the same city as Sealy's public accounting practice. The company asks Sealy to perform the annual audit, and Sealy accepts.

    f. Same as (**e**), except that the corporation is in a city 3,000 miles away from Sealy's practice.

    g. Maria Leipold, CPA, has a client, Alpha Corporation, which has been unable to meet its current obligations due to severely depressed economic conditions. The corporation owes Leipold $5,200 in unpaid audit fees from the previous year. They persuade her to perform their current audit, after giving her a promissory note for her unpaid fees.

    h. Arthur Anderby Co., on behalf of a client, engages in "executive search," which involves recruiting and hiring a company controller.

    i. Jack Thorp, a CPA in public practice, wishes to also be a representative of a computer tax service. The computer organization provides services only to tax practitioners. Thorp uses his professional contacts to introduce possible clients to the computer service.

    j. Morgan and Sons, CPAs, designates itself on its letterhead as "Members of the American Institute of Certified Public Accountants." Morgan is a member of the AICPA, but neither of his sons is a member.

P3-7   For many years the financial and accounting community has recognized the importance of the use of audit committees and has endorsed their formation.

    At this time, the use of audit committees has become widespread. Independent auditors have become increasingly involved with audit committees and, consequently, have become familiar with their nature and function.

Required:

    a. Describe what an audit committee is.

    b. Identify the reasons why audit committees have been formed and are currently in operation.

    c. What are the functions of an audit committee?   *(AICPA adapted)*

CHAPTER 4

Accountants' Legal Liability

Objectives

☐ **1.** Understand the litigious nature of the present-day auditing environment.
☐ **2.** How to avoid a civil lawsuit.
☐ **3.** How to avoid a criminal lawsuit.
☐ **4.** How the accounting profession is responding to legal pressures.
☐ **5.** How to search for, detect, and report errors and irregularities.
☐ **6.** How to respond to illegal acts of a client.
☐ **7.** How to search for and report related-party transactions.

In preceding chapters we examined the profession of auditing and the relationships of the independent auditor to the various groups using the results of the audit. We developed and discussed the conceptual framework within which an audit is performed. From those sources it became clear that the independent auditor, even though engaged by the company whose records are being audited, has responsibilities to various third-party users as well as to the client. In performing independent auditing services, *the auditor becomes responsible to both the client and third parties.* A part of the benefits associated with an audit, therefore, springs from the liability the auditor takes for appropriately discharging those responsibilities through the attest function.

In this chapter we describe and analyze the auditor's legal liability, both to the client and to third-party users of audited data. The appendix to this chapter contains summaries of key court cases that illustrate the application of the legal concepts covered in the chapter.

As we move through this chapter, it is important to recognize not only the current legal implications associated with the independent auditor's work, but also *the ways in which legal actions against accountants have influenced the profession.*

The Present-Day Auditing Environment

☑ **Objective 1**
Understand the litigious environment surrounding the public accounting profession

Prior to the 1920s, the auditor had little responsibility to anyone other than the client. Also, the general inclination of the public was to rely less on legal action at that time. Only a minimal number of lawsuits were lodged against auditors during those years. However, with the development of the attest function throughout the past 75 years and the resultant establishment of legal liability to third parties, legal actions against public accounting firms have increased, particularly during the past three decades. The recent increase has been, to some extent, caused by changes in general attitudes: people have come to rely more heavily on legal action in *all* types of controversies.

We begin our coverage of legal liability by analyzing the current environment in which the independent auditor operates. We accomplish this by (1) identifying and defining pertinent legal terminology and (2) examining some of the more important reasons for litigation against public accountants.

Pertinent Legal Terminology

The liability for violating the numerous statutes enacted to protect the investing public may be either civil or criminal. Although it is difficult to draw a precise distinction between these two types of liability, *criminal liability* occurs when an act considered to be a wrong against society is committed. As a result of such violations, the offender can be fined or imprisoned, or both. On the other hand, *civil liability* involves a violation of the rights of some specific party, such as the client or a third party. The penalty for a civil offense will be payment of damages. Some conduct can expose the accountant to both civil and criminal liability. We elaborate on each of these terms later in the chapter.

The term *negligence* describes the failure to exercise the degree of care that a reasonable person would exercise under similar circumstances. The auditor is expected to exercise reasonable care in performing an audit. The *standard of reasonable care* for accountants is measured by the level of quality, accuracy, and completeness expected of the average accountant. Honest inaccuracies and errors of judgment do not give rise to liability for negligence so long as it can be shown that the accountant has exercised reasonable care. Negligence as a cause of liability is subdivided into *ordinary negligence* and *gross negligence*. The first of these is characterized as a *lack of reasonable care* in the performance of professional accounting tasks. Gross negligence, on the other hand, is characterized as the *lack of even minimum care* in performing professional duties, thereby indicating *reckless disregard for duty and responsibility*.[1] This type of negligence can lead to a charge of constructive fraud.

Fraud is defined as an intentional act of deceit, designed to obtain an unjust advantage, that results in injury to the rights or interests of another. *Scienter* ("sigh enter" or "see enter") is a mental state embracing intent to deceive, manipulate, or defraud. In most cases, it has been shown that *knowledge of client fraud* is sufficient to prove scienter. *Constructive fraud*, however, can occur with proof of gross negligence, without a conscious intent to deceive.

Privity of contract defines the contractual relationship between two parties. In auditing contracts, usually made formal by the engagement letter, the parties generally possessing privity of contract are the auditor and the *client* (who, in most cases, is the person to whom the audit report is addressed). It is important under common law, in certain legal jurisdictions, to establish privity, because clients who have privity of contract have certain rights of recovery against auditors that third parties do not have.

The auditor's defense in most lawsuits involves convincing the court of his or her *due diligence*—that is, adherence to generally accepted auditing standards (GAAS) and generally accepted accounting principles (GAAP) in performing the audit. In this phase of the defense, the attorney for the auditor will often seek *expert testimony*—which is generally the testimony of another CPA as to whether, in that witness's opinion, the auditor has adhered to GAAS/GAAP. In such cases three types of questions are likely to arise: *questions of the facts* in the situation, the *question of the law* governing the situation, and *questions involving a mixture of fact and law*.[2] The expert witness can be particularly helpful in interpreting questions of fact—such as whether or not the accounting or auditing criteria have been met. It is also important to observe at this point that the Securities and Exchange Commission and the courts may impose higher standards of performance than those implied by adherence to GAAP and GAAS. Therefore, expert testimony is not necessarily binding in cases involving possible violations of Securities and Exchange Commission regulations.

Civil liability cases generally involve contractual or intentional tort of fraud violations. Violations of contractual arrangements may be either expressed or implied. *Expressed contractual violations* occur when one of the parties to a contract fails to carry out his or her responsibilities as stated in the contract. *Implied contractual violations*, however, can occur when there was a failure on the part of one party to meet the obligations implied by his or her *relationship* to the activities being performed.

Intentional tort of fraud violations involve intentional injury or wrong to another party. As they relate to auditing, they require proof of the following allegations for damages to be assessed:

- It must be shown that the action was committed with *intention to mislead the users* of the data.
- There must be a *false representation* or *concealment*.
- The plaintiff must show that *he or she relied on the false statements*.
- It must be shown that the *plaintiff was injured as a consequence of reliance on the audited statements*.[3]

The burden of proof for various allegations can fall on the plaintiff (client or third party) or the auditor, depending on whether the suit is brought under common law or statutory (SEC) law, as explained later in the chapter.

Another term that has become important in recent legal actions is the *class action lawsuit*: this involves collective actions in which the plaintiff represents a class of persons similarly situated. For example, one stockholder, suing for damages on the basis of false information included in the financial statements, may, under proper conditions, file the suit as a class action suit on behalf of all of the stockholders. The verdict in the case then would apply to all stockholders included in the class action.

Litigious Climate for Auditors[4]

Figure 4–1 presents in summary form the highly litigious environment in which not only accountants but also architects, doctors, and lawyers must practice. The stampede to the courtroom by plaintiffs to recover enormous sums from professionals is thought by some to threaten the future of the judicial system in America by overloading the dockets of state and federal courts with frivolous lawsuits. The American judicial system has produced more lawsuits against accountants alone in the past fifteen years than in the entire previous history of the accounting profession. In the period between 1980 and 1988, the largest accounting firms paid over $250,000,000 in settlements of mostly audit-related cases.

One of the principal factors in this avalanche of litigation is the unethical distortion of the concept of free enterprise and competition to one of unrestrained greed on the part of individuals who would stop at nothing to get rich quickly, no matter what the cost to others in society. Moreover, the attitude is held by many that they are not responsible for their own actions, including their mistakes. Whenever an injury is suffered, someone else must always pay. There is the erroneous notion that if those footing the bill are nameless people with *deep pockets* (insurance companies of CPA firms and other professionals) then no one really pays.

The legal system in the United States has contributed to the problem. It is easier to bring a lawsuit against another person in the United States than in most other countries in the free world. In many states, judges are elected rather than appointed. Thus there is a tendency for courts to be biased toward the plaintiff in civil cases. In addition, there has been a proliferation of litigation-oriented attorneys over the past thirty years (one attorney now exists for every 390 Americans). In civil cases, attorneys often are engaged on a contingent fee basis (as much as one-third of the damages awarded).

Laws at both the state and federal levels have created inequities for defendants in civil lawsuits. The concept of **joint and several liability** at the state level apportions the responsibility for wrongdoing among the various parties of a lawsuit under the concept of *comparative negligence*. If, for example, a plaintiff sued a bankrupt company and its independent auditor, the court might rule that the plaintiff was 10 percent responsible, the bankrupt company 60 percent responsible, and the auditors 30 percent responsible. The plaintiff's judgment would thus be 90 percent of the damages. Under the joint and several liability statutes, however, the CPA firm might ultimately have to pay for all of the damages because the firm is deemed *jointly* as well as *severally* liable. Since the company

Figure 4-1 ■■■

Everybody Pays: The Harsh Trends of Civil Suits

Evidence of the trend toward excessive compensation of plaintiffs is all around us. Both the number of lawsuits and the dollar amounts of awards and out-of-court settlements are climbing:

• The number of lawsuits filed annually in federal courts jumped from 86,000 to 239,000 between 1962 and 1982.

• By 1985, 8 million lawsuits were pending in state and local courts—that's about 1 suit for every 20 adult Americans.

• A 1987 Rand Corporation analysis of civil jury awards shows staggering increases over the last 25 years. The average malpractice jury award in Cook County, Illinois, for example, increased by 2,167 percent between 1960 and 1984.

These trends have been hitting accountants hard. For those who practice in a partnership, their personal assets as well as their investments in the partnership are at risk. And this is no mere theoretical matter:

• More suits have been filed against accountants in the past 15 years than in the entire previous history of the profession.

• The number of lawsuits reported to the special investigations committee of the American Institute of CPAs SEC practice section has increased in each of the last six years.

According to available data, the largest accounting firms collectively have paid more than $250 million in settlements of mostly audit-related lawsuits since 1980.

Inevitably, the ground swell of litigation and the quantum leap in awards to plaintiffs have made it nearly impossible for CPA firms and their insurers to predict the future standards to which the courts will hold the profession, and this uncertainty has destabilized the market for professional liability insurance. Premiums are escalating, coverage is shrinking and many carriers have ceased to offer *any* such insurance. Here are some telling examples:

• Insurance premiums for the largest CPA firms have multiplied by a factor of five since 1984; at the same time, available commercial coverage has been cut in half. And deductibles have increased many times over.

• The AICPA liability insurance plan's 1980 premium for firms with 25 professionals was about $64 a person for $1 million in coverage. By 1986 the premium had risen to about $1,160 a person—and the deductible had doubled.

• One out of five firms responding to a recent Wisconsin Institute of CPAs survey of its members indicated that it had been forced to drop its professional insurance coverage.

But there is fallout for the public, too. Consumers will pay, through increased costs of goods and services and through ever-higher insurance premiums. And let's not forget the transaction costs associated with civil suits. The Rand Corporation has estimated that, of the $29 billion to $36 billion spent on general litigation terminated in 1985, plaintiffs received only half. Legal fees and other litigation-related costs ate up the rest.

Reprinted with permission from *Journal of Accountancy*, September 1987, p. 119. Copyright © 1987 by American Institute of Certified Public Accountants, Inc., and Arthur Andersen & Co.

who was 60 percent responsible for the damages is bankrupt and unable to pay, the CPA firm, who likely carries professional liability insurance, would be forced to bear the entire burden.

During the past thirty years, regulatory and social welfare legislation at the federal level, often purposely drafted by Congress to be vague and ambiguous, has invited recourse to the courtroom as the means to solve every problem. Moreover, loopholes have been created that can cause unintended consequences for accountants. A glaring example is the **Racketeer-Influenced and Corrupt Organization (RICO)**, statutes of the early 1970s. This legislation, aimed at organized crime, defines *racketeering* very loosely as any two instances over a ten-year period of a variety of offenses, including securities fraud and mail fraud, two vaguely defined violations that are commonly alleged against CPAs. One of the many punishments for violations of the RICO statutes is treble damages. Thus, auditors who fail to detect client fraud can be forced to pay three times the amount of monetary damages incurred by plaintiffs.

Not to be ignored, unfortunately, are the actions of corrupt accountants. Although the vast majority of audits are performed by scrupulously honest and upright individuals, a few notable failures have caused great damage to the entire profession. In the acclaimed *ESM Securities* scandal, for example, an audit partner in a national accounting firm accepted a bribe for remaining silent after discovering a $300 million fraudulent scheme that eventually threatened to bankrupt many municipal governments from Ohio to Texas, as well as the savings and loan industry in Ohio.

The Expectations Gap

ESM and other scandals attracted the attention, in 1985, of the *House Subcommittee on Oversight and Investigations.* Chaired by Rep. John D. Dingell (D-Mich.), the subcommittee conducted hearings that lasted for months and involved testimony from the highest officials in public accounting as well as the SEC. Emerging from the hearings were a multitude of ethical questions regarding an **expectations gap** that existed between performance of auditors and expectations of the general public. Among those questions were

- Should auditors accept additional responsibility for uncovering *fraud and illegal acts* of clients?
- Should auditors take on additional responsibility for evaluating and communicating whether a company is a *going concern*?
- Should *communications* from accountants regarding the nature and limitations of the audit function in general be improved?[5]

Largely in response to Congressional pressure and adverse publicity, the **Commission on Fraudulent Financial Reporting** was appointed in October 1985. The six-member commission was composed of representatives of the AICPA, the AAA, the Institute of Internal Auditors (IIA), the Financial Executives Institute (FEI), and the National Association of Accountants (NAA). The final report of the Commission, issued in 1987, contained recommendations for sweeping reforms in the process by which financial information is reported to the public. Those recommendations are included in a later section of this chapter. Before we consider the response of the accounting profession to the perils of the litigious age, however, let us first examine the legal theories that define traditional civil and criminal liability of accountants.

Civil Liability of Auditors

☑ **Objective 2**
Avoid civil liability

Most lawsuits against auditors involve claims for damages to clients or third parties and thus represent what is described as *civil liabilities*. We now explain how they may be claimed *under common law, under the securities acts*, and *in connection with the responsibility for detection of fraud*.

Civil Liability to Clients under Common Law

Common law includes a system of jurisprudence that originated in England and is based on *judicial precedent* rather than legislative enactments. Its principles are determined basically by the social needs of the community and, therefore, can change with changes in such needs. Many contracts, including those between an auditor and a client, are governed by the contents of the contract—as interpreted within the common-law system. Therefore, as observed earlier, an auditor's liability to clients may involve a *breach of contract* or *tort liability*. The latter is based on failure to carry out a duty created by either social policy or social policy in combination with the contract.

As explained earlier, an accountant's contractual responsibilities to the client may either be expressed or implied. For example, the expressed duties are those spelled out by the terms of the contract. On the other hand, the implied duties are those that the courts have previously determined to be a part of every contract, whether or not they are specifically included in the terms of the contract. These implied responsibilities constitute the primary source of *legal liability for negligence*. For example, the accountant has an implied contractual duty not to perform in a negligent or fraudulent manner. The client, on the other hand, has an implied contractual responsibility not to interfere with or prevent the accountant from performing the elements of the audit. *The test for negligence involves determining whether the accountant has exercised reasonable care under the circumstances.* Within this interpretation of the law, the accountant may also be held liable for acts or omissions that amount to actual or constructive fraud. *To constitute actual fraud the acts or omissions must be intentional and have the intent to deceive.* Constructive fraud, on the other hand, involves acts or omissions occurring because of gross negligence without a conscious intent to deceive.

As shown in Figure 4–2 (column 1) clients may generally recover damages from the auditor if they can *allege and prove* the following things:

- The financial statements attested to by the auditor were *misleading*.
- The client *relied* on the financial statements.
- *Damages* (monetary losses) were suffered by the client.

Figure 4–2 ▪▪▪▪▪

The Auditor's Civil Liability

		Statutory law	
		Clients and all third parties (any purchaser)	
Common law			
Clients and third-party beneficiaries	Third parties	Securities Act of 1933	Securities Exchange Act of 1934
Basis for suit if alleged and proven:			
Misleading financial statements	Misleading financial statements	Misleading financial statements*	Misleading financial statements
Reliance	Reliance	Damages (loss)	Reliance
Damages (loss)	Damages (loss)		Damages (loss)
Proximate cause	Proximate cause		Proximate cause
Auditor negligence	Auditor gross negligence (constructive fraud) or actual fraud		
Breach of contract			
Auditor's defense:			
Due diligence	Due diligence	Due diligence	Due diligence
Contributory negligence		Lack of causation	Lack of knowledge of misleading statements
Lack of causation		Others	
Burden of proof for negligence:			
Plaintiff	Plaintiff	Defendant (accountant)	Defendant (accountant)

*Reliance not necessary unless a twelve-month statement of earnings (beginning after effective date of registration statement) is issued.

- The *cause* of the damages was linked to the auditor's breach of duty to perform with due diligence.
- The auditor was *negligent* (that is, that he or she failed to exercise due professional care in the engagement and thus did not follow generally accepted auditing standards).

Additionally, clients may sue the auditor for breach of contract.
    The auditor's main lines of defense are

- *Due diligence.* The audit was conducted with due professional care, and in accordance with generally accepted auditing standards.
- *Contributory negligence.* The client's own negligence was a contributing factor in the client's loss. As stated previously, most states follow the concept of *comparative negligence* by apportioning responsibility between the parties.
- *Lack of causation.* The client's loss was not due to the CPA's actions, even if he or she were negligent.

Civil Liability to Third Parties under Common Law

Third-party lawsuits (such as those brought by creditors or stockholders of the client) generally seek recovery of losses alleged to have been suffered because of reliance on audited financial data. Since the auditor has no contract with these parties, they ordinarily do not obtain the same rights as the client against the auditor in a civil action. However, in special cases they may be named *third-party beneficiaries* and thus obtain the same rights as the client (column 1, Figure 4–2).

Third-party beneficiaries are people whom the contracting parties intended to receive primary benefits of the accountant's services. Beyond that vague definition, however, there are inconsistent interpretations of the term among various jurisdictions. Thus, courts' interpretations of whether third parties may recover from an auditor for ordinary negligence depend on the state in which the suit is brought. A look into the case law history will help to explain.

Ultramares v. *Touche* was the first and most important precedent case in common law involving third-party recovery of damages against auditors, decided by the Supreme Court of New York in 1931. Ultramares was a factoring company that in 1923 loaned money to Fred Stern and Company on the basis of false financial statements audited by Touche, Niven & Co. Ultramares sued Touche for both negligence and fraud because the firm had failed to detect that the records of the company were false. The charge of negligence was ultimately disallowed because Ultramares was not specifically named in the contract as relying on the financial statements. The court, however, refused to disallow the charge of fraud. At that point the case was settled out of court. The court held that Ultramares could not recover on the basis of ordinarily negligence, because, in the words of the judge:

> If liability for negligence exists, a thoughtless slip or blunder, the failure to detect a theft or forgery beneath the cover of deceptive entries, may expose the accountants to a liability in an indeterminate amount for an indeterminate time to an indeterminate class.[6]

The court held that for third parties not specifically named in the contract to recover from the auditor, they would have to prove *gross negligence* (failure to exercise even slight care) on the part of the auditor. The court continued, however, by saying that had Ultramares been specifically named in the contract, it would have been a *third-party beneficiary* and would have enjoyed the same privilege of recovery as the client. The *Ultramares* rule has been upheld in Colorado, Florida, Georgia,[7] and was recently reconfirmed in New York in *Credit Alliance Corporation* v. *Arthur Andersen & Co.* (New York, 1985).

Other Interpretations. Over the years, legal scholars have tended to liberalize the definition of third-party beneficiary in their writings. In *Restatement (Second) of Torts* (a legal treatise that interprets the application of common law) the liability for failing to exercise due care and for supplying false information to third parties is extended to *a limited group of persons for whose benefit and guidance* the information is supplied. Thus liability for ordinary negligence is extended to that limited class of individuals who can be *reasonably foreseen* to be relying on the contract between the auditor and the client.

A leading case to illustrate the *Restatement of Torts* rule is *Rusch Factors, Inc.* v. *Levin* (Rhode Island, 1968). In this case, Rusch Factors was a factoring company who loaned money to a corporation on the basis of its audited financial statements. Levin, the auditor, was aware when engaged by the corporation that the financial statements were to be used for the purpose of obtaining a loan. However, the name of the potential lender was not specified in the contract. The corporation went into receivership and Rusch Factors, able to collect only a portion of the loan, sued Levin for failure to exercise due care in the audit. Levin's attorney argued that, since Rusch Factors did not have privity of contract, they could not recover from Levin by proving his negligence. The court held against the CPA, concluding:

> Why should an innocent reliant party be forced to carry the weighty burden of an accountant's professional malpractice? Isn't the risk of loss more easily distributed and fairly spread by imposing it on the accounting profession, which can pass the cost of insuring risk on to its customers, who can in turn pass the cost on to the entire consuming public?[8]

The *Restatement of Torts* rule has been upheld in Iowa, Texas, Missouri, Minnesota, Kentucky, Ohio, and New Hampshire in various cases over the past twenty years.[9]

In 1983, the New Jersey Supreme Court took the *Restatement of Torts* interpretation of third-party liability one step further than *Rusch Factors*. In *H. Rosenblum, Inc.* v. *Adler* the liability of the auditor for ordinary negligence was extended to cover all parties whom the auditor *should reasonably foresee* as recipients of the audited financial statements. Rosenblum, who owned two corporations engaged in the retail catalog gift business, agreed to merge those businesses into Giant Stores Corporation, a large discount chain. Rosenblum, alleging that he relied on the audited statements of Giant, accepted stock of Giant stores in exchange for his interests in the two corporations. Giant had been audited by Touche Ross & Co., who had attested to the fairness of presentation of Giant's financial statements in its annual reports for the years 1969 through 1972. The financial statements were subsequently found to be fraudulent, and the stock proved to be worthless. Rosenblum sued Touche Ross & Co. for damages suffered because of their negligence. Touche Ross asserted in their defense that they had neither a privity relationship with Rosenblum nor a relationship that would cause them to believe that Rosenblum was a third-party beneficiary. The court held as follows:

> When an independent auditor furnishes an opinion with no limitation in the certificate as to whom the company may disseminate the financial statements, he has the duty to *all those whom the auditor should reasonably foresee as recipients* from the company of the

statements for its proper business purposes, provided that recipients rely on the statements pursuant to those business purposes.[10]

Rosenblum, the most liberal interpretation of accountant's liability to third parties to date, has been used as precedent law in Wisconsin[11] as well as in New Jersey.

Reference to Figure 4–1 and the discussion in the last section will confirm that the liberalized interpretation of the definition of third-party beneficiary has been a major contributing factor in the *stampede to the courtroom* that we have witnessed in the past twenty years. One result is a liability insurance crisis of unprecedented magnitude. Insurance premiums for the largest CPA firms have increased fivefold since 1984, while available coverage has been cut in half. Many insurance carriers have ceased to offer any such insurance.

In summary, we may say that the negligent CPA's liability to third parties in most states generally depends on whether that party can meet the definition of third-party beneficiary. Of great importance is whether under state statute the definition of third-party beneficiary follows the strict definition of *Ultramares* or the more lenient definition of the *Restatement of Torts.* At the extreme, some states may in effect nullify completely the definition of third-party beneficiary by stating that *all parties* who should be foreseen by the auditor to be relying on his or her report should be allowed to recover. The determination of the matter is in the hands of the various states. Thus, the outcome for a particular set of facts may be different depending on the state in which the case is tried.

Civil liability to third parties for *fraud* (deceit) can exist whether the services were intended primarily for the benefit of third parties or for the benefit of the client. In such a situation, however, the third party must show that reasonable reliance was placed on the auditor's work. The common law elements of deceit in general are[12]

- A false representation of material fact made by the defendant.
- Knowledge or belief of falsity, technically described as *scienter.*
- An intent that the plaintiff rely on the false representation.
- Justifiable reliance on the false representation.

Civil Liabilities under the Security Acts

In the preceding paragraphs we have discussed the accountant's civil liability based on common law. The auditor may also be liable for such liability under the federal statutes included in the Securities Act of 1933 and the Securities Exchange Act of 1934. These statutes were enacted to provide certain protections for the investing public—judged to be necessary partly as a result of the stock market crash of 1929.

The *Securities Act of 1933* was designed to provide the investing public with appropriate information to allow evaluation of the merits of new security issues. The act requires companies issuing securities for public sale to file a registration statement with the Securities and Exchange Commission prior to offering such securities for sale. The registration statement (Form S-1) includes facts concerning the securities to be issued along with audited financial statements. Section 11(a) of the act makes the accountant liable for any false statements in the registration statement of the prospectus, which includes essentially the same financial information as that included in the registration statement.

The auditor preparing the registration statement can be held liable to any purchaser of an initial issue of securities covered by the registration statement if it contains false statements or material omissions.[13] The investor is required to prove the existence of the false statement or material omission and that the security purchased was offered through the inaccurate registration statement. It is not necessary for the purchaser to prove reliance on the accountant's error unless a twelve-month earnings statement has been issued for a period after the effective date of the registration statement. However, *recent cases suggest that accountants may not generally be held liable unless their work was fraudulent or performed with reckless disregard for known facts.*[14] Thus, the accountant must prove that he or she has exercised due diligence by showing that after reasonable investigation there was reasonable basis for presenting the data as shown in the registration statement. On failing to prove due diligence, the accountant may try to prove that the plaintiff's loss was caused by something other than the misleading financial statements (lack of *causation*). Other available defenses include

- The financial statements are not misleading.
- Misstatements or omissions are not material.
- The plaintiff knew of the misstatement.
- The statute of limitations has expired.

The *Securities Exchange Act of 1934* is designed to regulate the national securities exchanges, including the securities listed on those exchanges. It requires each listed company to submit to the Securities and Exchange Commission an annual report commonly referred to as *Form 10-K*. This report includes audited financial statements that constitute the chief source of the accountant's liability under this act.

Liability for fraud exists under Section 10(b) of the Securities Exchange Act of 1934. Rule 10b-5, promulgated in 1942, defines liability for fraud under that act as follows:

> It shall be unlawful for any person, directly or indirectly, by the use of any means or instrumentality of interstate commerce, or of the mails, or of any facility of any national securities exchange,
>
> 1. To employ any device, scheme, or artifice to defraud,
> 2. To make any untrue statement of a material fact or to omit a material fact necessary in order to make the statements made, in light of the circumstances under which they were made, not misleading, or
> 3. To engage in any act, practice, or course of business that operates or would operate as a fraud or deceit on any person in connection with the purchase or sale of any security.[15]

The accountant must exercise due diligence in work relating to this act to avoid liability. The *Ernst and Ernst* v. *Hochfelder et al.* case has been especially important in interpreting *the due diligence requirement* especially as it relates to possible fraudulent activity. Specifically, it showed that negligence alone on the part of the auditor is not sufficient evidence to prove the intent to defraud required for establishing liability under the antifraud provision of the Securities Exchange Act of 1934.

For the accountant to be held liable under the 1934 Act, the investor must prove (1) the materiality of the false or misleading statement; (2) the security was purchased or sold at a price that was influenced by the false or misleading statement; (3) reliance on the statement caused the loss; and (4) scienter. The auditor must prove that he or she acted in good faith with no knowledge of a misleading statement.

Figure 4–2 was presented to help you see the circumstances in which the auditors may be held liable to clients and third parties for negligence and to summarize the auditor's legal position under both common law and statutory law. As the figure shows, the main differences between the auditor's civil liability under common and statutory law are these:

1. Under common law, the rights of clients and third-party beneficiaries are more extensive than the rights of third parties. Specifically, *third parties must prove gross negligence to recover from the auditor, whereas clients and third-party beneficiaries must prove only ordinary negligence.* In contrast, under statutory law there is no distinction between the rights of the two groups. Any purchaser of securities may sue the accountant.

2. Under common law, the burden of proof for proving negligence of the auditor rests on the plaintiff (client or third party). *Under statutory law, the auditor has the burden of proving that he or she was not negligent.* In addition, under the Securities Act of 1933, the plaintiff need not show reliance on misleading financial statements or proximate cause unless the security was purchased after the registrant filed an income statement covering a twelve-month period beginning after the effective date of the registration statement.

Auditor's Criminal Liability

☑ **Objective 3**
Avoid criminal
lawsuit.

Most of the lawsuits against accountants have involved the recovery of damages for alleged civil liability. Criminal liability can occur, however, when an act considered to be a *wrong against society* is committed. Certain willful violations of the provisions included in both the Securities Act of 1933 and the Securities Exchange Act of 1934, as well as certain violations of the Internal Revenue Code, can subject the offender to criminal penalties in the form of a fine and/or a possible prison term. In addition, states have enacted laws calling for the recognition of criminal liability for certain other activities often involving accountants.

Willful Violation and Fraud

Generally speaking, a *crime must involve both an act and criminal intent.* The intent, however, may be implied from the facts in the case because the accused party is presumed to intend to achieve the natural and probable consequences of his or her acts. The Securities Act of 1933 states that willful violations of its provision constitute a crime under the following conditions:

> Any person who willfully violates any provisions of this title or the rules and regulations promulgated by the commission under authority thereof; or any person who willfully, in a registration statement filed under this title, makes any untrue statement of a material fact or omits the statement of any material facts required to be stated therein, or are necessary to make the statements therein not misleading, shall upon conviction, be fined not more than $10,000 or imprisoned not more than 5 years, or both.[16]

The key element of this provision of the act is the interpretation of the word *willfully.* The normal expectation is that the accountant will exercise "due diligence" in the performance of all tasks undertaken. Failure to do so can be construed as a willful violation of the act.

The Securities Exchange Act of 1934 calls for criminal action for false and misleading statements. Specifically, the act includes the following provision as part of Section 32:

> Any person who willfully violates any provision of this title or any rule or regulation thereunder . . . or any person who willfully and knowingly makes or causes to be made any statement in any application, report, or document required to be filed under this title or any rule or regulation thereunder . . . which . . . was false or misleading with respect to any material fact shall upon conviction be fined not more than $10,000 or imprisoned not more than 5 years, or both.[17]

The *Continental Vending* case, summarized in the appendix, can help us in interpreting this section of the 1934 Act. In that case, the court required accountants to disclose what they know when they have reason to believe that a corporation is being operated for the primary benefit of related-party shareholders/managers rather than in the interest of all stockholders. It also makes a point of the fact that compliance with generally accepted accounting principles is not an absolute defense in a criminal case.

U.S. v. *Natelli, U.S.* v. *Weiner (Equity Funding),* and *ESM Securities,* all summarized in the appendix to this chapter, are other examples of cases in which criminal penalties have been imposed on accountants for illegal activities.

Liabilities of the Tax Practitioner

The CPA who prepares tax returns for clients should remember that individuals engaged in practice before the Internal Revenue Service (IRS) are subject to both civil and criminal penalties under the Internal Revenue Code for making false statements and for other negligent or fraudulent misconduct. Civil penalties in tax practice were imposed on CPAs for the first time in the Tax Reform Act of 1976 and were increased in the Tax Equity and Fiscal Responsibility Act of 1982. The basis for liability under these acts is an understatement of the federal income tax liability of the taxpayer. A final determination of the tax liability by the IRS or the courts is not a necessary condition for establishing an understatement of that liability. Where the understatement is due to the negligent or intentional disregard of the income tax rules and regulations, the penalty is $250. The penalty is assessed on the *preparer*, and not necessarily on the employing firm. In the event of a trial, the burden of proof is on the preparer to show that he or she was not at fault. Where it is found that understatement is *willful*, the preparer's penalty is $1,000. In addition, the Tax Reform Act imposes the following *civil penalties* on preparers for the following offenses:

- $50 for failure to furnish the client with a copy of the tax return.
- $50 for failure to retain either a copy of all returns prepared or a list of all taxpayers and their taxpayer identification numbers.
- $50 for failure to provide the preparer's tax identification number on the tax return.
- $50 for failure to sign the return.
- $500 for each taxpayer's income tax check endorsed or otherwise negotiated by the preparer.
- $1,000 or, if less, 100 percent of the gross income derived by persons found to be promoting *abusive tax shelters*.
- $1,000 ($10,000 for corporate returns) for persons who aid and abet in the preparation of false documents that understate tax liability.

Criminal penalties are imposed on preparers under Section 7206 of the Internal Revenue Code for aid or assistance in preparation of fraudulent tax returns. Under this section, an accountant found guilty of such acts may be fined not more than $100,000 or imprisoned not more than three years, or both, in addition to costs of prosecution.

The Profession's Response to the Perils of a Litigious Age

☑ **Objective 4**
Understand the accounting profession's response to legal pressures.

Without question, the legal penalties imposed on accountants and the public disclosure of these penalties have moved the profession to reexamine and strengthen its technical standards and to enforce compliance with them. For example, the Code of Professional Conduct (summarized in Chapter 3) has been totally revised, and quality (peer) reviews have been made mandatory for CPA firms.

The Commission on Fraudulent Financial Reporting

Perhaps the most sweeping response to the *expectations gap* mentioned earlier in this chapter has been the work of the Commission on Fraudulent Financial Reporting. As mentioned earlier, the commission was formed in 1985 shortly after the Dingell Committee Hearings in the U.S. House of Representatives. The blue-ribbon panel of six was composed of representatives from industry, government, education, and accountants engaged in public practice. The intent of the commission was to perform a comprehensive study of the causes of fraudulent financial reporting, and to provide in their report a balanced response to the problem. In particular, one of the objectives of the commission was to examine the role of the independent public accountant in detecting fraud, focusing particularly on whether the detection of fraudulent financial reporting had been neglected or insufficiently addressed.

The final report of the Commission was issued in October 1987. Included in the *balanced response* of the commission were recommendations for

1. The public company,
2. The independent public accountant,
3. The SEC and enforcement authorities, and
4. Education.

These recommendations are summarized below:

For the *public company*, management should take steps to assure that the *tone at the top* reflects a serious attitude about fraudulent financial reporting. In addition, all public companies are encouraged to have effective *internal audit* functions (see Chapter 5). *Audit committees* should play a vital role in the public company. In addition, *management should render its own report* to shareholders, acknowledging its responsibility for the financial statements, and giving periodic reports on the effectiveness of internal controls. Finally, the issue of **opinion shopping** is addressed. For this purpose, *opinion shopping* means the process of searching out other auditors if the company's management disagrees with the present auditor regarding a financial reporting issue. The Commission recommended that before opinion shopping were practiced, the audit committee of the company should be informed.

For the *independent public accountant*, it was recommended that an *expanded responsibility* for detection of fraud be assumed and that *capabilities for fraud detection be improved*. In addition, the *assurance of audit quality* was strengthened by (1) requiring additional quality reviews for all new public clients added to the firm; (2) specifying improved guidelines for second-partner review on public clients; and (3) encouraging greater sensitivity within the accounting firm to pressures that may adversely impact audit quality. Recommendations to improve *communications* of public accountants were made. These included changes in the standard audit report (see Chapter 21). Finally, changes were recommended in the process of *setting audit standards* to give more participation to user groups. In the next section, we discuss the *expectation gap* auditing standards issued early in 1988 to respond to these recommendations.

Recommendations for the *SEC and enforcement authorities* include (1) new SEC sanctions and greater criminal prosecution for persons committing acts of fraudulent financial reporting; (2) improved regulation of the accounting profession; (3) adequate resources to fulfill its expanded responsibilities; (4) improved federal regulation of financial institutions; (5) improved oversight by state boards of public accountancy; and (6) tort reform to end some of the abuses cited earlier in the chapter and to head off a liability insurance crisis in America.

For *education*, the Commission recommended (1) expanded curricula to require increased exposure to analytical skills and problem-solving; (2) education on factors that cause fraud and ways to avoid it; (3) stress on the importance of the control environment within companies; (4) stress on the importance of the assessment of control risk in an audit engagement; (5) improvement in students' capabilities to communicate; (6) improvement in students' understanding of the regulatory environment; (7) increased emphasis on business ethics in the curriculum; and (8) changing the content of professional examinations and continuing professional education to include topics on fraudulent financial reporting.

Proposals for Tort Reform

To counter the inequities of the joint and several liability concept, professional organizations in many states have launched campaigns for **tort reform** legislation. In essence, a successful tort reform program would limit the liability of a party to a lawsuit to the proportionate responsibility of that party for the damages suffered. In the example cited earlier for joint and several liability, the auditor's exposure would be limited to 30 percent of the damages sustained by the plaintiff, since only 30 percent of the monetary damages were caused by the negligence of the CPA.

Tort reform is seen as necessary by the AICPA and other professional accounting organizations, as well as governing organizations of other professions, as the only lasting solution to the liability insurance crisis facing the learned professions today. As of the date of this writing, many states have tort reform legislation in force or pending.

The Expectations Gap Auditing Standards

In January 1988, in response to the Commission for Fraudulent Financial Reporting's recommendations for the accounting profession, the Auditing Standards Board issued nine new statements on auditing standards. The purpose of the issuance of these standards was to address and to help eliminate the so-called *gap* between public and financial statement users' expectations and the responsibilities assumed by auditors in the professional standards. Figure 4–3 summarizes the nine standards (SAS) into four categories.[18]

1. Standards to enhance the auditor's responsibility and capability to detect fraud and illegal acts.
2. Standards to provide for more effective audits.
3. Standards requiring improved external communications.
4. Standards requiring improved internal communications.

Figure 4–3 ▬▬▬

The Expectation Gap Statements on Auditing Standards

Detection of fraud and illegal acts
• SAS no. 53, *The Auditor's Responsibility to Detect and Report Errors and Irregularities*
• SAS no. 54, *Illegal Acts by Clients*

More effective audits
• SAS no. 55, *Consideration of the Internal Control Structure in a Financial Statement Audit*
• SAS no. 56, *Analytical Procedures*
• SAS no. 57, *Auditing Accounting Estimates*

Improved external communications
• SAS no. 58, *Reports on Audited Financial Statements*
• SAS no. 59, *The Auditor's Consideration of an Entity's Ability to Continue as a Going Concern*

Improved internal communications
• SAS no. 60, *Communication of Internal Control Structure Related Matters Noted in an Audit*
• SAS no. 61, *Communication with Audit Committees*

Reprinted with permission from *Journal of Accountancy*, "The Expectation Gap Auditing Standards" (April 1988), p. 37. Copyright © 1988 by American Institute of Certified Public Accountants, Inc.

Responsibilities Relating to Errors and Irregularities[19]

We will briefly summarize SAS No. 53, entitled *The Auditor's Responsibility to Detect and Report Errors and Irregularities*, and SAS No. 54, entitled *Illegal Acts by Clients*. In addition, we will review another existing standard entitled *The Effects of Related Party Transactions*. Other standards have application in later chapters and will be discussed at the appropriate time.

☑ **Objective 5**
How to search for, detect, and report errors and irregularities.

The term **errors** refers to *unintentional* misstatements or omissions in financial statements. Errors include inadvertent mistakes in gathering or processing accounting data, incorrect accounting estimates as a result of oversight or misinterpretation of facts, and mistakes in the application of accounting principles that affect the classification or disclosure of a financial statement item.

The term **irregularities** refers to *intentional* misstatements or omissions in financial statements. Irregularities include *fraudulent financial reporting*, the purpose of which is to mislead decision makers (often called management fraud) and misappropriation of assets, sometimes referred to as *defalcations*. Irregularities often involve manipulation or falsification of accounting records or supporting documents, misrepresentation or intentional omission of significant information, or deliberate misapplication of accounting principles that affect the disclosures in financial statements.

The Auditor's Responsibility to Detect Errors and Irregularities

Generally accepted auditing standards require that *an audit examination should be designed to detect material misstatements that result from errors and irregularities.* In fact, that responsibility is the stated purpose of the audit in the audit report (Figure 1–3). Prior to the *expectation gap* standards, the profession assumed only the responsibility of *searching for* errors or irregularities in the typical audit examination. In addition to increasing the auditor's responsibility for detection of errors and irregularities, the new standard sets far more specific guidelines to assist the auditor in detection.

Characteristics of some errors and irregularities may make them harder than others to detect. Such factors as *materiality* of the amount involved, skillfulness of perpetrators in *concealment*, and the quality of the *control structure* of the company affect the auditor's ability to detect errors and irregularities. In addition, *financial statement effects* of some errors or irregularities can make them more difficult to detect than others. For example, an irregularity of *overstatement* of accounts receivable is usually readily detectable through the audit confirmation. On the other hand, if a liability is *understated* or unrecorded, the perpetrator might destroy all evidence related to the liability, making it harder for the auditor to detect. Some irregularities involve such things as forgery of documents and collusion among company employees (two extremely difficult things to detect); the audit examination planned and executed in accordance with generally accepted auditing standards cannot necessarily be expected to detect all such events. Therefore, the discovery of errors and irregularities after the issuance of an unqualified audit report is not necessarily evidence that the auditor should have detected them.

In controlling for the possibility of material errors and irregularities in the financial statements, the auditor should keep two concepts in mind: *due care* and *professional skepticism.* The concept of **due care** has its roots in law, as we discussed earlier, and requires the auditor to exercise the same degree of care that any other prudent and technically trained person would exercise during the *planning, performance,* and *evaluation* stages of the evidence-gathering process. For example, during the planning stages of the audit, the auditor should consider management, operating, industry, and engagement characteristics that might heighten the risk of occurrence of an irregularity. In addition, the control environment of the company should be thoroughly understood, including management's policies and attitudes toward detecting errors and irregularities.

By assuming an attitude of **professional skepticism,** the auditor does not assume that management is necessarily dishonest or honest. Instead, the auditor must strive to maintain an attitude of an impartial referee in an athletic contest. He or she objectively and independently gathers and evaluates the evidence supporting the assertions on the financial statements and concludes on the basis of that evidence whether the financial statements are fairly presented.

The auditor should form a preliminary assessment of the risk of occurrence of certain types of errors and irregularities during the planning stages of the audit, as discussed above. For example, the auditor would perform preliminary analytical procedures on selected financial statement ratios and related data to form an expectation regarding the risk of misstatement of various accounts. After these and other planning procedures are performed, a preliminary audit plan is developed that consists of an audit program containing procedures deemed appropriate for the level of risk of misstatement assumed.

As the audit progresses, results of certain audit procedures may cause the auditor to change his or her expectations with regard to the probability of occurrence of errors and irregularities. For example, analytical procedures such as gross profit analysis may disclose significant differences from the auditor's expectations regarding balances in the sales or inventory accounts. Alternatively, the auditor may find significant differences between the amount of a control account, such as accounts receivable, and the total of the accounts receivable subsidiary ledger. Significant differences between client and customer records for certain accounts receivable may be discovered during the confirmation process. Some of the transactions examined by the auditor may lack sufficient documentation. All of these circumstances might cause the appropriately skeptical auditor to revise his or her expectations regarding the occurrence of errors or irregularities. In such cases, the auditor should reconsider the nature, timing, and extent of audit procedures to accommodate a higher risk of misstatement than that previously planned.

Evaluation of Audit Test Results

As the audit progresses, a record should be kept of all differences between the amounts shown on client's records and those obtained by the auditor from supporting evidential matter. In addition, because irregularities are intentional, implications exist beyond direct monetary effects on the financial statements. Proper note should be made of all irregularities.

At the end of the audit, all audit differences should be accumulated and summarized. Since these differences represent errors, their combined impact on the financial statements of the company should be calculated and evaluated in terms of materiality. The nature and effect of material errors on the financial statements should be communicated to management at least one level above that at which they occurred. Usually, the client's response will be to correct the errors and to make the appropriate disclosures. If the client refuses to make the necessary corrections and disclosures, the item assumes the nature of an irregularity and must be dealt with as discussed below.

The Effect of Irregularities on the Audit Report

The auditor's response to irregularities depends on the materiality of the item. If the irregularity has an immaterial effect on the financial statements, there is no need for revision of the financial statements or the auditor's opinion. However, if the impact of the irregularity on the financial statements is material, the auditor should insist that the statements be revised. If the client refuses to comply with the auditor's request, the auditor should express an *adverse opinion* on the financial statements.

If, for some reason, the auditor is prevented from applying necessary procedures, or if after the application of extended procedures, the auditor remains uncertain about whether irregularities materially affect the financial statements, he or she should issue a *disclaimer of opinion* on the financial statements, indicate the findings of the engagement to the client's board of directors, and in some cases withdraw from the audit engagement.

Other Communications Concerning Errors and Irregularities

The auditor has a responsibility to communicate proposed audit adjustments to the audit committee or board of directors of the company, whether or not the adjustments are actually recorded by the entity. In addition, the auditor has a responsibility to communicate with these groups with respect to any material irregularities that were discovered as a result of the audit. Irregularities that are individually immaterial may be aggregated for purposes of these discussions.

It is not ordinarily a part of the auditor's responsibility to discuss irregularities with parties other than the client's audit committee or board of directors. As we discussed in Chapter 3, it is usually considered a violation of the Code of Professional Conduct (Rule 301) to do so. However, the following circumstances are exceptions: (1) the entity reporting an auditor change to the SEC (to prevent opinion shopping); (2) the auditor reporting to a successor auditor under the general permission of the client (see Chapter 7); (3) response to a subpoena; and (4) response to a funding or other specified governmental agency whenever the audit involves financing of a government program. Since these cases have potential legal and ethical ramifications, the auditor should normally consult his or her attorney before proceeding with discussions involving parties other than the client.

Illegal Acts by Clients[20]

☑ **Objective 6**
How to respond to illegal acts of clients

What should an auditor do when he or she discovers that the client has violated the law? This question first became a vital issue to the auditing standards board in the late 1970s, after Congress passed the Foreign Corrupt Practices Act of 1977. That act required public companies to refrain from making bribes to foreign governments and to maintain systems of internal control sufficient to prevent bribes from occurring. In response, the AICPA issued SAS No. 17, which disclaimed responsibility on the part of the auditor for detecting **illegal acts.** After all, auditors are neither policemen nor attorneys, and in many cases they lack the expertise to determine whether a client act is illegal. No specific procedures were prescribed in the standard to enable the auditor to discern if illegal acts were taking place. However, the auditor was required to report suspected illegal acts to a level of management at least one level above that at which such acts occurred. Appropriate action could be taken by the client both to correct the illegality and to properly disclose the act, along with its financial statement impact, if any.

SAS No. 54, *Illegal Acts by Clients*, also a product of the *expectation gap* project, supersedes SAS 17, expanding and clarifying the auditor's responsibility in this area. Illegal acts are defined as violations of laws or governmental regulations *other than irregularities*, which were discussed in the previous section. Examples include violations of state or federal laws, such as tax laws and regulations, or violations of contract terms with third parties, that affect the nature of disclosures either in the body or the footnotes to the financial statements.

Characteristics of illegal acts that should be considered in defining the auditor's responsibilities with respect to illegal acts include (1) dependence on legal judgment and (2) relationship of the illegal act to the financial statements. With respect to the first characteristic, the profession still disclaims responsibility for making judgments as to legality of an act *per se*. With respect to the second characteristic, the further removed an illegal act is from events or transactions reflected in the financial statements, the less capable is the auditor to recognize and evaluate it. Such laws or regulations as occupational safety and health (OSHA), food and drug administration (FDA), environmental protection (EPA), and antitrust activities of the entity are examples. However, for those illegal acts that have a *direct and material impact on the financial statements*, the auditor's responsibility for detecting and reporting such acts is the same as for errors and irregularities, discussed in the preceding section.

Specific procedures are prescribed (1) in the absence of evidence concerning possible illegal acts and (2) in response to possible illegal acts. Audit procedures should routinely include *inquiries of management* concerning

- The client's compliance with laws and regulations.
- The client's policies relative to the prevention of illegal acts.
- The use of directives and internal policies to enforce conduct within the company that is within the law.

The auditor obtains *confirmation of litigation* in progress or threatened against the company from the company's attorney. In addition, the auditor generally obtains *written representations* from the client regarding compliance with applicable laws and regulations, as well as loss contingencies that should be disclosed in connection with litigation. These representations are included in the *client representation letter*, which is discussed in detail in later chapters.

Normal audit procedures might reveal specific information concerning illegal acts. Examples include unauthorized or improperly recorded transactions, incomplete transactions, or transactions deliberately recorded in the wrong period. Evidence of investigations by governmental agencies, or payment of large amounts for unspecified services to *consultants*, affiliates, or employees might be a telltale sign of illegal activities. Large payments of cash, payments to government officials, or failure to file tax returns should also raise the auditor's level of skepticism regarding the legality of the client's activities. In such cases, additional audit procedures are generally necessary. The auditor should

- Inquire of management at a level above the persons involved to obtain information on the nature of the act.
- Consult with the client's legal counsel or other specialists about applications of law and possible effects of the act on the financial statements.
- Apply additional procedures as necessary to obtain an understanding of the nature of the acts. These might include examination of supporting documents, confirmation of significant information with outside parties, and examining board of directors' minutes regarding authorization of the transaction.

If the auditor concludes, based on the above information, that the act(s) of the client is in fact illegal, he or she should consider the effects of disclosure of the item on the financial statements. In this regard, remember that *contingent* effects of an illegal act can be more material than the immediate effects of the act itself. For example, if a company is engaging in illegal activity, it could result in future loss of revenue, or even litigation that could threaten the survival of the company.

The auditor should consider the implications of a discovered illegal act to the other aspects of the engagement. In particular, if the client appears to ignore or conceal illegal activity, the auditor may have cause to disbelieve other representations that have been made by the client.

The auditor should communicate with the audit committee, or other group having equivalent authority, giving them pertinent details of the illegal activity along with its financial statement ramifications. If senior management is involved, the auditor should communicate directly with the audit committee and appropriate remedial action should be taken by the board of directors of the company.

Illegal activities by clients can have the following impact on the audit report:

- Material undisclosed illegal acts should be accompanied by a qualified or an adverse audit opinion.
- If the auditor is prevented by the client from obtaining sufficient competent evidence regarding the illegal act, he or she should issue a disclaimer of opinion. If the limitation regarding evidence is not imposed by the client, the auditor may issue a qualified opinion due to a limited-scope engagement.
- If the client refuses to accept the report, the CPA should withdraw from the engagement, setting forth the reasons in a letter to the audit committee.

Normally, disclosures to parties outside the client regarding illegal acts are covered by the client confidentiality rule (301) of the Code of Professional Conduct. However, exceptions are provided in the following cases:

- Disclosure to the SEC when the auditor has withdrawn or been discharged.
- Disclosure to a successor auditor when the successor makes inquiries under the client's permission.
- Disclosure to a court in response to a subpoena.
- Disclosure to a funding agency or other specified agency in accordance with governmental audit requirements.

Effect of Related-Party Transactions

☑ **Objective 7**
How to search for and report related-party transactions

The auditing process depends, to some extent, on the assumption that each of the parties to a business transaction will seek to maximize expected economic benefits from the transaction. This can be expected to occur if the parties to the transaction have opposite interests (deal at arm's length). In situations where this arm's length dealing does not occur (**related-party transactions**), improper values can be introduced into the accounting records. The *Continental Vending* case (discussed in the appendix) showed the effects this kind of abuse can have.

SAS 45 (AU334) relates to FASB Statement 57, which defines the related parties of a company to be its affiliates, principal owners, management, and immediate members of their families, entities accounted for by the equity method, or any other party that might significantly influence or be significantly influenced by the company so as to be prevented from pursuing its own separate interests. Although generally accepted auditing standards cannot be expected to provide assurance that all of the related-party transactions will be disclosed, SAS 45 requires that special attention be given to identifying and examining material related-party transactions to ascertain the economic substance of those transactions. Furthermore, the auditor is required to ascertain proper disclosure of those transactions in accordance with FASB Statement 57. That disclosure includes (a) the nature of the material related-party relationship; (b) a description of the related-party transaction, including amounts, if applicable; (c) the effects of any change in terms between the related parties from those used in prior periods; (d) if not apparent in the financial statements, the terms, manner of settlement, and amount due to or from related parties; and (e) if the existence of the control relationship has the potential of producing operating results or financial positions that differ from those that would result from an arm's length relationship, disclosure must be made of the nature of such ownership or management control.

Summary

In this chapter we analyzed and discussed the legal implications of the independent auditor's responsibilities that we first took up in Chapter 1. We began by defining pertinent legal terminology. Then we observed that present-day auditing activities are carried out in a highly litigious environment.

We explained the relationship between the auditor's work and possible legal liability. We saw that, with the development of the attest function, auditors have, to an increasing degree, been held liable to third parties. This in turn has influenced the profession toward the codification of generally accepted auditing standards (GAAS) and the establishment of various interpretations through the medium of Statements on Auditing Standards (SAS). Legal actions against accountants have also influenced the code of ethics and have encouraged the profession to develop quality control (peer review) standards for public accounting firms.

In the last part of the chapter we examined the posture that accountants are assuming in today's litigious world. That posture is probably best defined in selected recommendations of the Commission on Fraudulent Financial Reporting, which resulted in the issuance of nine *expectation gap* auditing standards in 1988, as well as a revised Code of Professional Conduct for CPAs.

Auditing Vocabulary

p. 100 **Commission on Fraudulent Financial Reporting:** This Commission, appointed in 1985, comprised representatives of the AICPA, the AAA, the Institute of Internal Auditors (IIA), the Financial Executives Institute (FEI), and the National Association of Accountants (NAA).

p. 113 **due care:** Requires the auditor to exercise the same degree of care that any other prudent and technically trained person would exercise during the planning, performance, and evaluation stages of the evidence-gathering process.

p. 112 **errors:** Unintentional misstatements or omissions in the financial statements.

p. 100 **expectations gap:** A phrase first cited by the House Subcommittee on Oversight and Investigations, chaired by Representative John D. Dingell of Michigan. This committee asserted that a gap exists between performance of auditors and expectations of the general public.

p. 115 **illegal acts:** Violations of laws or governmental regulations other than irregularities.

p. 112 **irregularities:** Intentional misstatements or omissions in the financial statements.

p. 98 **joint and several liability:** A liability that apportions the responsibility for wrongdoing among the various parties of a lawsuit under the concept of *comparative negligence*. If a party is *jointly* as well as *severally* liable, he or she might be forced to pay the entire amount of damages suffered by another party, regardless of whether he or she was fully responsible. Under this concept, the party that has the ability to pay is the party that will be responsible, if the other parties who are responsible do not have the funds.

p. 110 **opinion shopping:** The practice of searching out another auditor if the company's management disagrees with the present auditor regarding a financial reporting issue.

p. 113 **professional skepticism:** The attitude that must be taken by an auditor when he or she objectively and independently gathers and evaluates the evidence supporting the assertions on the financial statements and concludes, on the basis of that evidence, whether the financial statements are fairly presented.

p. 100 **Racketeer-Influenced Corrupt Organization (RICO) statutes:** This legislation, aimed at organized crime, defines *racketeering* loosely as any two instances over a ten-year period of a variety of offenses, including securities fraud and mail fraud.

p. 118   **related-party transactions:**   Transactions between the reporting entity and persons who have the ability to materially influence that entity, or who can be influenced by the entity. The auditor is required to ascertain proper disclosure of the substance of transactions between the reporting entity and related parties.

p. 111   **tort reform:**   Legislation that would limit the liability of a party to a lawsuit to the proportionate responsibility of that party for the damages suffered.

APPENDIX 4–A: Selected Common-Law Cases

McKesson & Robbins Case (1940)

McKesson & Robbins was a wholesale drug company registered under the Securities Exchange Act. Price Waterhouse and Company served as its auditors. The company was alleged to have owned a Canadian subsidiary through which a significant part of its activities were conducted. Over several years, through massive collusion on the part of the president of the company and other key officers, fictitious documents were used to create fictitious receivables and inventory on the books of the Canadian subsidiary.

In 1940, the Securities and Exchange Commission conducted an investigation and concluded that the auditors were negligent and that the gross discrepancies reflected in the records of the company should have been discovered during the course of the audits. At the same time, however, the SEC conceded that the auditors had followed procedures considered acceptable at the time the audit was performed. Price Waterhouse and Company contended that their examination was not designed to detect fraud, particularly where collusion of the type present in this case existed.

As a direct result of this case, the accounting profession required that accounts receivable and inventory be validated in the future from external and independent sources. This was interpreted to mean confirmation of accounts receivable and observation of the inventory process. Ultimately, this case was a basic, motivating force—causing the accounting profession to adopt presently existing generally accepted accounting standards (GAAS).

The *1136 Tenants Corporation* v. *Max Rothenberg and Company* (1971)

This case involved the preparation of unaudited financial statements by the accountant for the 1136 Tenants Corporation (an apartment cooperative), which was being defrauded by its leasing agent. There was apparently a misunderstanding between the corporation and the accountant as to the nature and extent of the services to be rendered. The accountant orally agreed to write up transactions and to prepare periodic financial statements for the corporation. The fee was set at $50 per month. No letter had been written confirming the terms of the engagement. The owners apparently thought that an audit should be performed, whereas the accountants understood the services to be confined to write-up work. In this particular instance, some auditing procedures were followed, which apparently caused the judge to construe the services to be an audit. There were a number of missing invoices, which the accountant failed to follow up but listed in his working papers. However, no independent verifications of the account balances were made. A statement to this effect was made in the transmittal letter accompanying the financial statements. The financial statements, although they referred to the transmittal letter, were not marked "unaudited."

When it was later discovered that the defalcations had been committed by the leasing agents of the 1136 Tenants Corporation, the accountants were sued by the owners for negligence in failure to discover the fraud. The court decided in favor of the owners and $237,000 in damages were awarded to the plaintiffs.

This case is important because it established liability of the accountant for failure to discover fraud in connection with the preparation of unaudited statements. The case emphasizes the need for a written engagement letter and a clearly worded disclaimer in connection with this type of service.

Appendix 4–B: Statutory Law Cases

Fischer v. Kletz (Yale Express Case) (1967)

This case involved a class action suit against Peat, Marwick, Mitchell & Co. Shareholders in this case sought to establish liability on the auditor's part for failure to call to their attention previous audited financial statements later discovered to contain false data.

The public accountants in this case had audited the financial statements of the Yale Express System for the year ended December 31, 1963. The audit report was dated March 31, 1964. Later, during 1964, Peat, Marwick, Mitchell & Co. was engaged to perform a special study of Yale's past and current operations. During this nonaudit engagement, the accountants discovered that certain figures in the annual report were substantially false and misleading. Although this information was discovered some time late in 1964, the findings were not released until May of 1965. The plaintiffs contended that this delay, in terms of silence and inaction, was a violation of the public accountants' responsibilities relating to the previously audited financial statements.

This case has at least two interesting aspects: First, it points up the problem that can occur when a public accounting firm serves a client in two capacities. In this case, Peat, Marwick, Mitchell & Co. provided independent auditing services with respect to the financial statements for the year ended December 31, 1963. In 1964, they were employed by Yale Express in a management advisory capacity. It was while serving in this capacity that the errors in the audited financial statements were discovered. The court held that the nature of the services being performed at the time previous errors were discovered was irrelevant when related to the CPA's reporting responsibility. The second point of interest involves the determination of the accountant's responsibility for disclosing errors in previously audited financial statements after the audit report has been issued.

Partially as a result of this case, Section 561 ("Subsequent Discovery of Facts Existing at the Date of the Auditor's Report") was incorporated into SAS 1 in 1972. That statement requires that the auditor should, as soon as practicable after such subsequent information becomes known to him or her, discuss the matter with the client at an appropriate level of management. If the auditor concludes that action should be taken to prevent future reliance on the audit report, the client should be advised to make appropriate disclosure of the newly discovered facts and their impact on the financial statements to persons who are known to be currently relying or who are likely to rely on the financial statements and related auditor's report. If the client refuses to make the appropriate disclosures, it is then the responsibility of the CPA to see that the disclosures are made.

Escott et al. v. Bar Chris Construction Corporation et al. (1968)

In this case the holders of certain convertible debentures of Bar Chris Construction Corporation brought an action under Section 11 of the Securities Act of 1933, alleging that the registration statement of the company contained material false statements and material omissions. Among the defendants were the auditors of Bar Chris: Peat, Marwick, Mitchell & Co.

Bar Chris Construction Corporation was engaged in constructing bowling alleys. Its sales increased dramatically in the late 1950s. Its method of operation called for construction with a comparatively small down payment, the balance being paid in notes that Bar Chris subsequently discounted with factors. On at least one occasion, Bar Chris practiced a method of financing that was, in substance, a sale and leaseback arrangement. Construction operations were accounted for on the percentage-of-completion method.

In this case, a judgment was rendered in favor of third-party plaintiffs who brought action under the law covering false statements and misleading omissions in a registration statement. Among the charges and holdings of the court against the statements were these:

- The percentage-of-completion method was erroneous and misleading, and even if use of the method was appropriate, its application in this case caused misleading statements. The court held that use of the method was appropriate but that it had been misapplied.

- There was inappropriate accounting for sale and leaseback arrangements. Bar Chris had sold a bowling alley to a factoring company, which, in turn, had leased it back to a consolidated subsidiary of Bar Chris. This transaction was treated as a sale by Bar Chris in its consolidated financial statements. It is important to note that this sale occurred in 1960, prior to issuance of APB Opinion No. 5 in 1964. Before 1964, GAAP allowed profits to be recognized on such sales, as long as the transaction was fully disclosed. In ruling that this practice was inappropriate, the court in effect decided that GAAP did not necessarily result in fairness of presentation.

- There was understatement of allowance for doubtful accounts and overstatement of receivables by inclusion of sales to a consolidated subsidiary.

- There was understatement of direct and contingent liabilities.

These misstatements resulted in an apparent overstatement of earnings and an overstatement of the current ratio. The court ruled that a 16 percent overstatement of earnings and a 15 percent overstatement of earnings per share was not material. Although the court's reason for this ruling was not explicitly stated, it has been speculated that recognition was given to the company's already rapid growth in spite of the error and the fact that debentures (creditor claims) were being issued. Since prospective creditors normally are more interested in a company's ability to pay than its profitability, perhaps the net income error was construed to be less important than the error in current ratio. Consistent with that thought, the court did rule that the overstatement in the firm's current ratio (2.6:1 vs. 2.9:1) was material.

The defenses given by all defendants, including Peat, Marwick, Mitchell & Co., included due diligence. However, evidence showed that the team conducting the field work had been negligent in their audit, particularly in the S-1 review, which covered subsequent events up to the effective date of the registration statement.

This case showed that the portion of the 1933 Securities Act pertaining to accountants' liability can be used as a basis for third parties' suits against auditing firms.

The judge presiding over the case asserted in his opinion that accountants should not be held to a standard higher than that recognized by their profession, and that he did not hold them to such a standard. On the contrary, the accountants' work did not come up to that standard. Consequently, they were liable to third parties for their negligence. The *Bar Chris* case demonstrates, too, that the courts are willing to choose between alternate accounting principles when they believe that the application of a certain practice does not result in fair presentation of information in financial statements. It also showed that the court is willing to make some rather specific interpretations of the principle of materiality.

United States v. Simon (Continental Vending Case) (1969)

In this case, Carl Simon, a senior partner with Lybrand Ross Brothers and Montgomery, and two other members of that firm were convicted of drawing up and certifying false or misleading financial statements of Continental Vending Machine Corporation. A key element of the trial involved transactions between Continental Vending, its affiliate, Valley Commercial Corporation, and Roth, the president of Continental Vending. Roth also controlled the operations of Valley Commercial Corporation. Over a period of years, Valley Commercial Corporation became deeply indebted to Continental Vending. Further analysis showed that Valley had lent Roth an amount approximately equal to the amount owed to Continental. Roth was unable to pay but offered to secure the indebtedness with his equity in stocks, bonds, and other securities of Continental and another company if this would be acceptable. He also agreed to post as collateral a mortgage on his house and furnishings. Over a short period of time, the market value of the collateral supporting the receivable from Valley declined to the point where it was worth only $395,000. This was collateral pledged to cover receivables of approximately 3.5 million dollars. Other issues involved improperly netting receivables against payables and inadequate footnote disclosure of the substance of the entire transaction between Roth, Valley, and Continental.

In the trial, eight expert witnesses (independent accountants) testified generally that the footnote disclosure of the Valley receivable was not inconsistent with generally accepted accounting principles. The dominating issue, however, centered around the president's diversion of corporate funds to his personal benefit. It was concluded that one of the accountants knew this had been occurring and that Simon, the partner in charge of the engagement, must have had a good reason to suspect what was occurring. The court concluded that the accountants failed to discharge their responsibilities appropriately—both because of an inadequate disclosure of the situation and because of not appropriately describing the situation about the securities pledged as collateral. The accountants were also cited for failure to insist that Roth mortgage his house and furnishings as additional collateral. The government also provided additional evidence of criminal intent in the form of conflicting statements by defendants and contradictions by other witnesses.

Simon and the other two accountants were convicted and fined for their failure to make proper disclosure of the circumstances surrounding the loan to Valley.

This case clearly imposes on auditors a responsibility (with possible criminal penalties) to disclose what they know about the client when there is reason to believe that a corporation is being operated primarily for the benefit of management rather than in the interest of all stockholders. Aspects of the case can clearly be seen in current auditing standards, which require disclosure of all related parties and the substance of transactions between them.

United States v. Weiner (Equity Funding Case) (1973)

This case, like the *McKesson & Robbins* case, involved massive collusion on the part of higher management with the objective of falsifying assets and earnings. Traditionally, auditors assume the integrity of client top-level management. This case clearly demonstrates that such an assumption may be inappropriate.

Equity Funding Corporation of America was engaged in investing mutual funds and money received from sales of capital stock and in selling life insurance to stockholders. During the early 1960s, the earnings of the company grew rapidly. However, as mutual funds lost some of their glamour, the management was apparently unwilling to acknowledge the consequences of that situation. As a result, dummy customers were made up and false information was stored in computer files. A set of computer programs was used to conceal the deception. By doing this, Equity Funding secured advances from other insurance companies on a co-insurance arrangement. However, a sizable number of the policies never existed, and as a result, the insurance companies lost most of what they had advanced to Equity Funding.

Over a period of years several CPA firms worked on the audits of Equity Funding, but none detected the fraud. When the facts finally became known, the case was a serious embarrassment to the accounting profession. It clearly demonstrated that an auditor's assumption regarding the honesty of top-level management had to be reexamined. The most direct effect of this case was to cause the issuance of Statement on Auditing Standards 16 (the predecessor to SAS 53 entitled "The Auditor's Responsibility to Detect and Report Errors and Irregularities"), which includes comments relating to the auditor's responsibility for detection of management fraud.

United States v. Natelli (1975)

This case is better known as the *National Student Marketing Corporation* case, in which two auditors associated with Peat, Marwick, Mitchell & Co. were charged with violation of the criminal fraud statute of the Securities Exchange Act of 1934.

Natelli was in charge of the audit of the company, whose first issue of stock had risen rapidly during the early months of the company's existence, from $6 per share to $80 per share. The company sold marketing programs to companies for promotional campaigns on college campuses. Many of the programs had required material amounts of development costs before they were ready to be marketed, causing the firm to use the percentage-of-completion method to recognize revenues. This resulted in certain *unbilled receivables* existing on the books of the company, representing commitments from customers. Some $1.7 million of commitments in 1968 were not in writing but were included in the financial statements. Approximately $1 million of these were written off in 1969, after it was discovered that they were not valid. The write-off was spread over a two-year period and included knowingly erroneous retroactive adjustments, which materially overstated income for 1968. Also, in a footnote to the financial statements, the accountants improperly netted together two items, each of which had a material effect on the financial statements, to disclose them as having a net immaterial effect. This was done, apparently, to conceal past mistakes in allowing the recognition of unbilled receivables in the first place. The circumstances and actions on the part of accountants were construed by the court to be a willful violation of the Securities Exchange Act of 1934 and resulted in criminal liability.

Ernst and Ernst v. Hochfelder et al. (1977) and Later Developments

This case involved a suit brought against Ernst and Ernst by a group who had invested in a fraudulent security scheme perpetrated by the president of the First Securities Company in Chicago, a long-time client of Ernst and Ernst. The fraud actually came to light in 1968, when the president committed suicide.

The investors then filed a class action suit for damages against Ernst and Ernst. The accounting firm as accused of negligent conduct because of failure to discover the weakness in internal control, which allowed the fraudulent securities scheme to be perpetrated. The investors, by bringing suit under Rule 10b-5 of the Securities Exchange Act of 1934, were implying, as many had in the past, that a public accountant's ordinary negligence constitutes an act of fraud. It is interesting to note that the court never reached the issue of whether Ernst and Ernst had been negligent. Instead it concluded that the main issue was whether the CPA could be sued for fraud (deceit or scienter) when he or she had merely been ordinarily negligent.

The court was unwilling to extend the scope of Rule 10b-5 of the Securities Exchange Act of 1934 to negligent conduct, and therefore it ruled in favor of the accounting firm. This case has been characterized by some as a turning point in the history of court-awarded judgments to third-party groups. It showed that the auditor's knowledge of client fraud must be proved by the plaintiff before damages can be recovered under the antifraud provisions of the 1934 Act.

In at least one other case since 1976 (*Aaron* v. *SEC*, 1980), the Supreme Court required the SEC to establish scienter in seeking injunctions under the 1934 Act. This decision was based on the reasoning followed in the *Hochfelder* case.

Hochfelder, however, recognized the concept of *aiding or abetting* the fraud of another. The court held that a CPA may be liable, under Rule 10b-5, as an aider or abettor of a person who engages in deception. This topic was one of the issues in the decision of the federal district court in the multimillion dollar case of *The Fund of Funds, Ltd.* v. *Arthur Andersen & Co.* (1982). In that case, a federal district court held that a CPA may be held liable as an aider or abettor, under Section 10(b) and Rule 10b-5, only if three factors are present: (a) a *primary fraud*, that is, fraud by the person who was aided and abetted by the CPA; (b) scienter on the part of the CPA; and (c) substantial assistance by the CPA to the party who committed the primary fraud.

The ESM Securities Scandal (1986)

One of the biggest financial scandals of the 1980s involved a Fort Lauderdale, Florida securities firm and a young partner from the Miami office of Grant Thornton. The case had many of the same trappings as other notable cases mentioned above, such as related-party transactions, adequate technical training and proficiency, and the danger of auditing only one company in an affiliated group. However, there are unique lessons that the profession will learn from ESM. First, the necessity of quality control review for all CPA firms was finally made clear. Second, the fact that professional tax practitioners who work for the same firm as auditors and who service the same clients share the audit team's responsibility to the public and the firm.

ESM is listed here because it typifies the many cases that attracted the adverse attention of the Congress in 1985. That attention precipitated the formation of the Commission on Fraudulent Financial Reporting, which in turn resulted in two major developments in 1988: (1) restructuring of the Code of Professional

Conduct for CPAs, and (2) the issuance of the *expectation gap* standards, summarized in Figure 4–3. Both of these developments are expected to set the course for professional standards of accounting into the twenty-first century.

Notes

1. National Institute of Accountants, *CPA Review: Business Law* (Gainesville, Fla.: National Institute of Accountants, 1988): 6.
2. Denzil Y. Causey, Jr., *Duties and Liabilities of the CPA* (Austin, Tex.: Bureau of Business Research, The University of Texas, 1976): 16–18.
3. Ibid., p. 127.
4. Material in this section is summarized from Robert Mednick, "Accountants' Liability: Coping with the Stampede to the Courtroom," *Journal of Accountancy*, (September 1987), 118–122.
5. Robert J. Sack and Robert Tangreti, "ESM: Implications for the Profession," *Journal of Accountancy* (April 1987), 94–100.
6. 255 N. Y. 170 N. E. 441 (1931).
7. In Florida (*Investment Corp.* v. *Buchman*, 1968); in Colorado (*Stephens Indus., Inc.* v. *Haskins & Sells*, 1971); in Georgia (*McNederland* v. *Barnes*, 1973).
8. 284 F. Supp. 85 (D.R.I., 1968).
9. For example: in Iowa (*Ryan* v. *Kanne*, 1969); in Texas (*Shatterproof Glass Corp.* v. *James*, 1971); in Missouri (*Alama Kraft Manufacturing Co.* v. *Elmer Fox & Co.*, 1973); in Minnesota (*Bonhiver* v. *Graff*, 1976); in Kentucky (*Ingram Industries, Inc.* v. *Nowicki*, 1981); in Ohio (*Haddon View Investments Co.* v. *Coopers & Lybrand*, 1982); in New Hampshire (*Spherex, Inc.* v. *Alexander Grant & Company*, 1982).
10. 93 N. J. 324, 461 A. 2d 138 (1983).
11. See *Citizens States Bank* v. *Timm, Schmidt & Company*, 1983.
12. National Institute of Accountants, 7.
13. Ibid.
14. Ibid., 7–8.
15. Section 10(b) of the Securities Exchange Act of 1934.
16. Section 24 of The Securities Act of 1933.
17. Section 32(a) of The Securities Exchange Act of 1934.
18. Dan M. Guy and Jerry D. Sullivan, "The Expectation Gap Auditing Standards," *Journal of Accountancy* (New York: AICPA, 1988), 36–46.
19. SAS No. 53, *The Auditor's Responsibility to Detect and Report Errors and Irregularities* (New York: AICPA, 1988).
20. SAS No. 54, *Illegal Acts of Clients* (New York: AICPA, 1988).

Questions for Class Discussion

Q4-1 What is the relationship between the benefits typically associated with an audit and the liability of the auditor in connection with the attest function?

Q4-2 What is the difference between criminal liability and civil liability? Discuss.

Q4-3 What is the meaning of the term *negligence* as it is used in legal actions against accountants?

Q4-4 What is the difference between *ordinary negligence* and *gross negligence* as those terms are used in legal actions against accountants?

Q4-5 What is the difference between *fraud* and *constructive fraud*?

Q4-6 What is meant by the term *privity of contract*? How does it relate to actions seeking to recover damages from auditors?

Q4-7 What is meant by the term *expert testimony*? How can such testimony be used in connection with legal action against an auditor?

Q4-8 What is a class action suit? Discuss.

Q4-9 What is the difference between an action based on breach of contract and one based on tort action for negligence?

Q4-10 What is the possibility of a public accountant being held liable to third parties for ordinary negligence in the performance of an audit?

Q4-11 What are the general provisions of the Foreign Corrupt Practices Act?

Q4-12 Do the provisions of SAS 54 and SAS 55 allow the auditor to establish a client's compliance with the Foreign Corrupt Practices Act? Explain.

Q4-13 How should the auditor react to a client's illegal acts that have been determined to have occurred during the audit period? Discuss.

Q4-14 How has the accounting profession responded to the growing loss of credibility that has occurred because of judgments rendered against public accounting firms? Discuss.

Q4-15 What are some of the desirable and undesirable results that have come from the extensive litigation against members of the profession during the 1970s and 1980s? Discuss briefly.

Q4-16 What efforts are being made to establish statutory limitations governing an auditor's liability to third parties? Are these limitations desirable? Discuss.

Q4-17 How has each of the following cases affected the auditing process? (1) The *Ultramares* v. *Touche* case; (2) the *McKesson & Robbins* case; (3) the *Bar Chris Construction Corporation* case; (4) the *Continental Vending* case; (5) the *ESM Securities* case.

Q4-18 Can an accountant be held liable for the discovery of fraud in connection with the preparation of unaudited financial statements? Discuss. (Your discussion should include a reference to the case most pertinent to this question.)

Q4-19 How has the *Equity Funding* case affected the activities of the accounting profession?

Q4-20 What is the significance of the *Ernst and Ernst* v. *Hochfelder* case? Discuss.

Q4-21 What is the historical development of the responsibilities accepted by auditors relating to the discovery of errors and irregularities?

Q4-22 How do errors and irregularities relate to fairness of presentation?

Q4-23 What is the independent auditor's responsibility under generally accepted auditing standards for the discovery of fraud?

Q4-24 What is meant by the term *illegal acts by clients*? What is the auditor's responsibility in connection with such acts?

Q4-25 What is a related-party transaction? Why is the auditor concerned with such transactions?

Q4-26   What is the difference between an accountant's expressed and implied contractual responsibilities to a client?

Q4-27   What is the difference between an accountant's civil liability under common law and his or her civil liability under the Securities Acts?

Q4-28   What difference is there between civil liability and criminal liability actions against auditors?

Q4-29   Under what circumstances may a CPA who prepares tax returns be subject to civil penalties? To criminal penalties? Discuss.

Q4-30   What are the recommendations of the Commission on Fraudulent Financial Reporting as they relate to the profession's response to the perils of our litigious age?

Short Cases

C4-1   Briefly discuss the development of the common law regarding the liability of CPAs to third parties.

(AICPA adapted)

C4-2   The CPA firm of Martinson, Brinks & Sutherland, a partnership, was the auditor for Masco Corporation, a medium-sized wholesaler. Masco leased warehouse facilities and sought financing for leasehold improvements to these facilities. Masco assured its bank that the leasehold improvements would result in a more efficient and profitable operation. Based on these assurances, the bank granted Masco a line of credit.

The loan agreement required annual audited financial statements. Masco submitted to the bank its 19X5 audited financial statements, which showed an operating profit of $75,000; leasehold improvements of $250,000; and net worth of $350,000. In reliance thereon, the bank lent Masco $200,000. The audit report that accompanied the financial statements disclaimed an opinion because the cost of the leasehold improvements could not be determined from the company's records. The part of the audit report dealing with leasehold improvements reads as follows:

"Additions to fixed assets in 19X5 were found to include principally warehouse improvements. Practically all of this work was done by company employees, and the cost of materials and overhead were paid by Masco. Unfortunately, fully complete, detailed cost records were not kept of these leasehold improvements, and no exact determination could be made as to the actual cost of said improvements. The total amount capitalized is set forth in note 4 to the financial statements."

In late 1976, Masco went out of business, at which time it was learned that the claimed leasehold improvements were totally fictitious. The labor expenses charged as leasehold improvements proved to be operating expenses. No item of building material cost had been recorded. No independent investigation of the existence of the leasehold improvements had been made by the auditors.

If the $250,000 had not been capitalized, the income statement would have shown a substantial loss from operations and the net worth would have been correspondingly decreased.

The bank has sustained a loss on its loan to Masco of $200,000 and now seeks to recover damages from the CPA firm, alleging that the accountants negligently audited the financial statements.

Required: Answer the following, setting forth reasons for any conclusions stated.
a. Will the disclaimer of opinion absolve the CPA firm from liability?
b. Are the individual partners of Martinson, Brinks & Sutherland, who did not take part in the audit, liable?

(AICPA adapted)

C4-3 A CPA firm has been named as a defendant in a class action by purchasers of the shares of stock of the Newly Corporation. The offering was a public offering of securities within the meaning of the Securities Act of 1933. The plaintiffs alleged that the firm was either negligent or fraudulent in connection with the preparation of the audited financial statements that accompanied the registration statement filed with the SEC. Specifically, they allege that the CPA firm either intentionally disregarded, or failed to exercise reasonable care to discover, material facts that occurred subsequent to January 31, 19X8, the date of the auditor's report. The securities were sold to the public on March 16, 19X8. The plaintiffs have subpoenaed copies of the CPA firm's working papers. The CPA firm is considering refusing to relinquish the papers, asserting that they contain privileged communication between the CPA firm and its client. The CPA firm will, of course, defend on the merits, irrespective of the question regarding the working papers.

Required: Answer the following, setting forth reasons for any conclusions stated.
a. Can the CPA firm rightfully refuse to surrender its working papers? (See Chapter 3).
b. Discuss the liability of the CPA firm with respect to events that occur in the period between the date of the auditor's report and the effective date of the public offering of the securities.

(AICPA adapted)

C4-4 Justin Marcall is a limited partner of Guarcross, a limited partnership, and is suing a CPA firm that was retained by the limited partnership to perform auditing and tax return preparation services. Guarcross was formed for the purpose of investing in a diversified portfolio of risk capital securities. The partnership agreement included the following provisions:

"The initial capital contribution of each limited partner shall not be less than $250,000; no partner may withdraw any part of his interest in the partnership, except at the end of any fiscal year upon giving written notice of such intention not less than 30 days prior to the end of such year; the books and records of the partnership shall be audited as of the end of the fiscal year by a certified public accountant designated by the general partners, and proper and complete books of account shall be kept and shall be open to inspection by any of the partners or his or her accredited representative."

Marcall's claim of malpractice against the CPA firm centers on the firm's alleged failure to comment, in its audit report, on the withdrawal by the general partners of $2 million of their $2.6 million capital investment, based on back-dated notices, and the lumping together of the $2 million withdrawals with $49,000 in withdrawals by limited partners so that a reader of the financial statement would not be likely to realize that the two general partners have withdrawn a major portion of their investments.

The CPA firm's contention is that its contract was made with the limited partnership, not its partners. It further contends that since the CPA firm had no privity of contract with the third-party limited partners, the limited partners have no right of action for negligence.

Required: Answer the following, setting forth reasons for any conclusions stated.
Discuss the various theories Marcall would rely on to prevail in a lawsuit against the CPA firm.

(AICPA adapted)

C4-5   Farr & Madison, CPAs, audited Glamour, Inc. Their audit was deficient in several respects:
a. Farr & Madison failed to verify properly certain receivables that later proved to be fictitious.
b. With respect to other receivables, although they made a cursory check, they did not detect many accounts that were long overdue and obviously uncollectible.
c. No physical inventory was taken of the securities claimed to be in Glamour's possession, which, in fact, had been sold. Both the securities and cash received from the sales were listed on the balance sheet as assets.
There is no indication that Farr & Madison actually believed that the financial statements were false. Subsequent creditors, not known to Farr & Madison, are now suing on the basis of the deficiencies in the audit described above. Farr & Madison moved to dismiss the lawsuit against it on the basis that the firm did not have actual knowledge of falsity and, therefore, did not commit fraud.

Required: Answer the following, setting forth reasons for any conclusions stated.
May the creditors recover without demonstrating Farr & Madison had actual knowledge of falsity?

(AICPA adapted)

C4-6   Congress has enacted legislation that imposes civil liability and penalties on individuals who are guilty of certain misconduct in connection with their preparing income tax returns for a fee.

Required: Answer the following, setting forth reasons for any conclusions stated.
What potential civil liabilities and penalties to the U.S. government should the practitioner be aware of in connection with the improper preparation of a federal income tax return, and what types of conduct would give rise to these liabilities and penalties?

(AICPA adapted)

C4-7   Whitlow & Company is a brokerage firm registered under the Securities Exchange Act of 1934. The Act requires such a brokerage firm to file audited financial statements with the SEC annually. Mitchell & Moss, Whitlow's CPAs, performed the annual audit for the year ended December 31, 19X9, and rendered an unqualified opinion, which was filed with the SEC along with Whitlow's financial statements. During 1979, Charles, the president of Whitlow & Company, engaged in a huge embezzlement scheme that eventually bankrupted the firm. As a result, substantial losses were suffered by customers and shareholders of Whitlow & Company, including Thaxton, who had recently purchased several shares of stock of Whitlow & Company after reviewing the company's 19X9 audit report. Mitchell & Moss's audit was deficient; if they had complied with generally accepted auditing standards, the embezzlement would have been discovered. However, Mitchell & Moss had no knowledge of the embezzlement nor could their conduct be categorized as reckless.

Required: Answer the following, setting forth reasons for any conclusions stated.
a. What liability to Thaxton, if any, does Mitchell & Moss have under the Securities Exchange Act of 1934?
b. What theory or theories of liability, if any, are available to Whitlow & Company's customers and shareholders under the common law?

(AICPA adapted)

C4-8 The Chriswell Corporation decided to raise additional long-term capital by issuing $5 million of 8 percent subordinated debentures to the public. May, Clark & Company, CPAs, the company's auditors, were engaged to examine the June 30, 19X2, financial statements, which were included in the bond registration statement.

May, Clark & Company completed its examination and submitted an unqualified auditor's report dated July 15, 19X2. The registration statement was filed and later became effective on September 1, 19X2. On August 15, one of the partners of May, Clark & Company called on Chriswell Corporation and had lunch with the financial vice-president and the controller. He questioned both officials on the company's operations since June 30 and inquired whether there had been any material changes in the company's financial position since that date. Both officers assured him that everything had proceeded normally and that the financial condition of the company had not changed materially.

Unfortunately the officers' representation was not true. On July 30, a substantial debtor of the company failed to pay the $400,000 due on its account receivable and indicated to Chriswell that it would probably be forced into bankruptcy. This receivable was shown as a collateralized loan on the June 30 financial statements. It was secured by stock of the debtor corporation, which had a value in excess of the loan at the time the financial statements were prepared but was virtually worthless at the effective date of the registration statement. This $400,000 account receivable was material to the financial condition of Chriswell Corporation, and the market price of the subordinated debentures decreased by nearly 50 percent after the foregoing facts were disclosed.

The debenture holders of Chriswell are seeking recovery of their loss against all parties connected with the debenture registration.

Required: Is May, Clark & Company liable to the Chriswell debenture holders under Section 11 of the Securities Act of 1933? Explain.

(AICPA adapted)

C4-9 Meglow Corporation manufactured ladies' dresses and blouses. Because its cash position was deteriorating, Meglow sought a loan from Bernardi Factors. Bernardi had previously extended $25,000 credit to Meglow but refused to lend any additional money without obtaining copies of Meglow's audited financial statements.

Meglow contacted the CPA firm of Watkins, Winslow & Watkins to perform the audit. In arranging for the examination, Meglow clearly indicated that its purpose was to satisfy Bernardi Factors as to the corporation's sound financial condition and thus to obtain an additional loan of $50,000. Watkins, Winslow & Watkins accepted the engagement, performed the examination in a negligent manner, and rendered an unqualified auditor's opinion. If an adequate examination had been performed, the financial statements would have been found to be misleading.

Meglow submitted the audited financial statements to Bernardi Factors and obtained an additional loan of $35,000. Bernardi refused to lend more than that amount. After several other factors also refused, Meglow finally was able to persuade Maxwell Department Stores, one of its customers, to lend the additional $15,000. Maxwell relied on the financial statements examined by Watkins, Winslow & Watkins.

Meglow is now in bankruptcy, and Bernardi seeks to collect from Watkins, Winslow & Watkins the $60,000 it lent to Meglow. Maxwell seeks to recover from Watkins, Winslow & Watkins the $15,000 it lent Meglow.

Required: Under common law
a. Will Bernardi recover? Explain.
b. Will Maxwell recover? Explain.

(AICPA adapted)

C4-10 A certified public accountant has just completed an audit of the Beta Corporation. A short time later, the client discovers that an employee has embezzled funds during the audit period. The company president has asked the CPA to explain how the embezzlement could have escaped discovery during the audit.

Required: Respond to the client's request.

C4-11 Matthew Goulding, a local certified public accountant, is disturbed by the fact that his congressman has initiated a study of the ways in which certified public accountants conduct their audits of financial statements. He contends that such activities are the concern of the auditor and the client, and therefore he sees no reason why the U.S. Congress should be interested in such matters.

Required: Respond to Matthew.

C4-12 The auditors have just finished their annual audit of the Delta Corporation. Your father, who is president of that company, complains to you, a university accounting major, that the auditors in performing their work seemed to be skeptical about everything they examined. He contends that this attitude of skepticism is not consistent with the requirement that the accountant be objective.

Required: Respond to your father's contentions.

Problems

P4-1 Select the best answer for each of the following items.
    a. The most significant aspect of the *Continental Vending* case was that it
        1. Created a more general awareness of the auditor's exposure to criminal prosecution.
        2. Extended the auditor's responsibility for financial statements of subsidiaries.

       3. Extended the auditor's responsibility for events after the end of the audit period.
       4. Defined the auditor's common-law responsibilities to third parties.

  b. In connection with a lawsuit, a third party attempts to gain access to the auditor's working papers. The client's defense of privileged communication will be successful only to the extent it is protect by the

       1. Auditor's acquiescence in use of this defense.
       2. Common law.
       3. AICPA Code of Professional Ethics.
       4. State law.

  c. The *1136 Tenants* case was important chiefly because of its emphasis on the legal liability of the CPA when associated with

       1. A review of interim statements.
       2. Unaudited financial statements.
       3. An audit resulting in a disclaimer of opinion.
       4. Letters for underwriters.

  d. Which of the following best describes a trend in litigation involving CPAs?

       1. A CPA cannot render an opinion on a company unless the CPA has audited all affiliates of that company.
       2. A CPA may not successfully assert as a defense that the CPA had not motive to be part of a fraud.
       3. A CPA may be exposed to criminal as well as civil liability.
       4. A CPA is primarily responsible for a client's footnotes in an annual report filed with the SEC.

  e. Which of the following is an example of a related party transaction?

       1. An action is taken by the directors of company A to provide additional compensation for vice presidents in charge of the principal business functions of company A.
       2. A long-term agreement is made by company A to provide merchandise or services to company B, a long-time, friendly competitor.
       3. A short-term loan is granted to company A by a bank that has a depositor who is a member of the board of directors of company A.
       4. A nonmonetary exchange occurs whereby company A exchanges property for similar property owned by company B, an unconsolidated subsidiary of company A.

  f. After discovering that a related-party transaction exists, the auditor should be aware that the

       1. Substance of the transaction could be significantly different from its form.
       2. Adequacy of disclosure of the transaction is secondary to its legal form.
       3. Transaction is assumed to be outside the ordinary course of business.
       4. Financial statements should recognize the legal form of the transaction rather than its substance.

P4-2 Select the best answer for each of the following questions relating to the auditor's responsibilities for detection of errors and irregularities, illegal acts, and related-party transactions.

  a. Which of the following statements best describes the auditor's responsibility regarding the detection of material errors and irregularities?

       1. The auditor is responsible for the failure to detect material errors and irregularities only when such failure results from the nonapplication of generally accepted accounting principles.

2. Extended auditing procedures are required to detect material errors and irregularities if the auditor's examination indicates that they may exist.
3. The audit examination should be designed to detect material financial statement misstatements that result from errors and irregularities.
4. Extended auditing procedures are required to detect unrecorded transactions even if there is *no* evidence that material errors and irregularities may exist.

b. When the auditor's regular examination leading to an opinion on financial statements discloses specific circumstances that make him or her suspect that fraud may exist and he or she concludes that the results of such fraud, if any, could *not* be so material as to affect his or her opinion, he or she should
1. Make a note in the working papers of the possibility of a fraud of immaterial amount so as to pursue the matter next year.
2. Reach an understanding with the client as to whether the auditor or the client, subject to the auditor's review, is to make the investigation necessary to determine whether fraud has occurred and, if so, the amount thereof.
3. Refer the matter to the appropriate representatives of the client with the recommendation that it be pursued to a conclusion.
4. Immediately extend the auditing procedures to determine if fraud has occurred and, if so, the amount thereof.

c. When conducting an audit, errors that arouse suspicion of fraud should be given greater attention than other errors. This is an example of applying the criterion of
1. Reliability of evidence.
2. Materiality.
3. Relative risk.
4. Dual-purpose testing.

d. When an independent auditor's examination of financial statements discloses special circumstances that make the auditor suspect that fraud may exist, the auditor's *initial* course of action should be to
1. Recommend that the client pursue the suspected fraud to a conclusion that is agreeable to the auditor.
2. Extend normal auditing procedures in an attempt to detect the full extent of the suspected fraud.
3. Reach an understanding with the proper client representative as to whether the auditor or the client is to make the investigation necessary to determine if a fraud has in fact occurred.
4. Decide whether the fraud, if in fact it should exist, might be of such a magnitude as to affect the auditor's report on the financial statements.

Items e and f are based on the following information:

During the annual audit of BCD Corp., a publicly held company, Smith, CPA, a continuing auditor, determined that illegal political contributions had been made during each of the past seven years, including the year under audit. Smith notified the board of directors of BCD Corp. of the illegal contributions, but they refused to take any action because the amounts involved were immaterial to the financial statements.

e. Smith should reconsider the intended degree of reliance to be placed on the
1. Management representation letter.
2. Preliminary judgment about materiality levels.
3. Letter of audit inquiry to the client's attorney.
4. Prior years' audit programs.

f. Since management took *no* action, Smith should
1. Report the illegal contributions to the Securities and Exchange Commission.

2. Issue an *except for* qualified opinion or an adverse opinion.
3. Disregard the political contributions since the board of directors were notified and the amounts involved were immaterial.
4. Consider withdrawing from the engagement or dissociating from any future relationship with BCD Corp.

g. Which of the auditing procedures listed below would be *least* likely to disclose the existence of related-party transactions of a client during a period under audit?
1. Reading *conflict-of-interest* statements obtained by the client from its management.
2. Scanning accounting records for large transactions at or just prior to the end of the period under audit.
3. Inspecting invoices from law firms.
4. Confirming large purchase and sales transactions with the vendors and/or customers involved.

h. An auditor who is determining the scope of work to be performed concerning possible related-party transactions should
1. Assume that transactions with related parties are outside the ordinary course of business.
2. Determine whether transactions with related parties would have taken place if the parties had *not* been related.
3. Obtain an understanding of management responsibilities and the relationship of each of the parties to the total entity.
4. Establish a basis of accounting principles different from that which would have been appropriate had the parties *not* been related.

i. In connection with the examination of financial statements, an independent auditor could be responsible for failure to detect a material fraud if
1. Statistical sampling techniques were *not* used on the engagement.
2. The auditor planned the work in a hasty and inefficient manner.
3. Accountants performing important parts of the work failed to discover a close relationship between the treasurer and the cashier.
4. The fraud was perpetrated by one client employee, who circumvented the existing internal controls.

j. Because an examination in accordance with generally accepted auditing standards is influenced by the possibility of material errors, the auditor should conduct the examination with an attitude of
1. Professional responsiveness.
2. Conservative advocacy.
3. Objective judgment.
4. Professional skepticism.

k. Under Statements on Auditing Standards, which of the following would be classified as an error?
1. Misappropriation of assets for the benefit of management.
2. Misinterpretation by management of facts that existed when the financial statements were prepared.
3. Preparation of records by employees to cover a fraudulent scheme.
4. Intentional omission of the recording of a transaction to benefit a third party.

(AICPA adapted)

P4-3   A CPA firm was engaged to examine the financial statements of Martin Manufacturing Corporation for the year ending December 31, 19X2. The facts revealed that Martin was in need of cash to continue its operations and agreed to sell its common stock investment in a subsidiary through a private placement. The buyers insisted the proceeds be placed in escrow because of the possibility of a major contingent tax liability that might result from a pending government claim. The payment in escrow was completed in late November 19X2. The president of Martin told the audit partner that the proceeds from the sale of the subsidiary's common stock, held in escrow, should be shown on the balance sheet as an unrestricted current account receivable. The president was of the opinion that the government's claim was groundless and that Martin needed an *uncluttered* balance sheet and a *clean* auditor's opinion to obtain additional working capital from lenders. The audit partner agreed with the president and issued an unqualified opinion on the Martin financial statements, which did not refer to the contingent liability and did not properly describe the escrow arrangement.

The government's claim proved to be valid, and pursuant to the agreement with the buyers, the purchase price of the subsidiary was reduced by $450,000. This adverse development forced Martin into bankruptcy. The CPA firm is being sued for deceit (fraud) by several of Martin's unpaid creditors who extended credit in reliance on the CPA firm's unqualified opinion on Martin's financial statements.

Required:
a. On what facts are the creditors of Martin claiming deceit by the CPA firm?
b. Does the fact that the creditors do not have privity of contract with the CPA firm affect their ability to recover damages?
c. List the general elements of common-law deceit.
d. Will the creditors be able to recover from the CPA firm?

(AICPA adapted)

P4-4   Risk Capital Limited, a Delaware corporation, was considering the purchase of a substantial amount of the treasury stock held by Florida Sunshine Corporation, a closely held corporation. Initial discussions with the Florida Sunshine Corporation began late in 19X1.

Wilson and Wyatt, Florida Sunshine's accountants, regularly prepared quarterly and annual unaudited financial statements. The most recently prepared financial statements were for the year ended September 20, 19X2.

On November 15, 19X2, after protracted negotiations, Risk Capital agreed to purchase 100,000 shares of no par, Class A capital stock of Florida Sunshine at $12.50 per share. However, Risk Capital insisted upon audited statements for calendar year 19X2. The contract made available to Wilson & Wyatt specifically provided:

"Risk Capital shall have the right to rescind the purchase of said stock if the audited financial statements of Florida Sunshine for calendar year 19X2 show a material adverse change in the financial condition of the corporation."

The audited financial statements furnished to Florida Sunshine by Wilson and Wyatt showed no such material adverse change. Risk Capital relied on the audited statements and purchased the treasury stock of Florida Sunshine. It was subsequently discovered that as of the balance sheet date, the audited statements were incorrect and that, in fact, there had been a material adverse change in the financial condition of the corporation. Florida Sunshine is insolvent, and Risk Capital will lose virtually its entire investment.

Risk Capital seeks recovery against Wilson and Wyatt.

Required: Assuming that only ordinary negligence is proven, will Risk Capital prevail

a. Under the principles set forth in *Ultramares* v. *Touche*?

b. Under the principles set forth in *Rusch Factors* v. *Levin*?

(AICPA adapted)

P4-5   Lief Erickson, CPA, has completed the examination of the financial statements of Lexington Products, Inc., on which he plans to express an unqualified audit opinion.

Required:

a. What assurances are provided to the public when the auditor states that the financial statements present the data "fairly . . . in conformity with generally accepted accounting principles"?

b. What are Erickson's responsibilities for the detection of (1) errors or irregularities and (2) illegal acts of personnel of Lexington Products, Inc.? What should Erickson have done if the examination had aroused his suspicions of errors or irregularities? Illegal acts?

c. Given that Erickson is expressing an unqualified audit opinion, what are the possible consequences to him should there be discovery in the future of (1) errors or irregularities or (2) illegal acts?

(AICPA adapted)

P4-6   Lane McWhorter, CPA, was engaged to audit the financial statements of Rudder Construction Co., Inc., a closely held corporation engaged in the construction and operation of car wash and self-storage operations. The percentage-of-completion method was used by Rudder to account for all construction projects. Usually, as Rudder completed a construction project, the building and property were sold to an operator who made a 20 percent down payment and gave an installation note for the balance. Rudder then discounted the note with the Central National Bank and received the proceeds minus the bank discount. Rudder remained contingently liable on all the notes discounted. Economic hard times have fallen on the construction business, and 60 percent of the discounted notes are now in default. In addition, Rudder's own business has fallen off to virtually nothing in the past eight months.

When McWhorter arrived to discuss the 19X3–X4 audit, he noticed that activity had slowed somewhat—the company's parking lot, usually a beehive of activity, was only half full. The controller, David McNeese, assured McWhorter that the slowdown was only temporary and that the company was getting more new contracts in every day. In fact, according to McNeese, new crews were being hired to begin five new projects next week.

As the audit progressed, McWhorter noticed a number of things that disturbed him:

a. The company's internal control structure, which had been represented to McWhorter as excellent, showed a number of compliance deviations.

b. The company's property and equipment ledgers and records for depreciation could not be reconciled to the general ledger.

c. Of the 300 requests for confirmations of accounts receivable that were mailed, only 75 were returned after two mailings.

d. A number of transactions appeared in the general ledger but lacked documentary support.

Required:

a. Define the terms *error* and *irregularity* as used in generally accepted auditing standards. Does it appear that errors may exist in the Rudder Construction Company's financial statements? Does it appear that irregularities may exist?

b. Discuss the responsibility McWhorter has with respect to errors and irregularities in conducting an examination in accordance with generally accepted auditing standards.

c. Discuss the effect that the following factors have on the scope of McWhorter's audit examination:

   1. The integrity of Rudder Construction and its management.

   2. The quality of Rudder's internal control structure.

   3. The other circumstances previously noted.

d. What are the inherent limitations of an audit examination with respect to the detection of errors and irregularities?

e. What should McWhorter do if the procedures he performs indicate that errors or irregularities exist?

P4-7 Patterson, CPA, is auditing the financial statements of Dean Lumber Company, a privately held corporation with 150 employees and ten stockholders, all within the same family. Dean Lumber Company has been in business for many years. However, the financial statements of the company have never been audited. Patterson suspects the possibility of some related-party transactions, because he knows the family quite well through his local church.

Required:

a. Define the term *related-party transaction*, as it is used in generally accepted auditing standards.

b. In the case of Dean Lumber Company, what parties could fall within the category of *related parties*?

c. What should Patterson's chief concerns be with respect to related-party transactions?

d. Describe the procedures that Patterson should follow to identify related-party transactions.

e. What special disclosures, if any, should be made in the audited financial statements of Dean Lumber Company, if related-party transactions are found to exist?

PART **II**

The Financial
Statement Audit:
Process and Principles

CHAPTER 5

Evidence, Audit Risk, and Materiality

Objectives

☐ **1.** Know the process by which the financial statement audit is conducted.
☐ **2.** Know the five basic financial statement assertions, verification of which is the objective of the independent audit.
☐ **3.** Be able to discuss the nature of evidence.
☐ **4.** Be able to recognize the types of evidence that exist.
☐ **5.** Know how to assess audit risk.
☐ **6.** Know how to assess materiality on an audit.

In this part of the text we will present the *process* by which the *financial statement audit* takes place, with emphasis on the *principles* applicable at each stage of the process.

The essence of auditing is embodied in the concept of *evidence.* Recall that in Chapter 1 we defined auditing as "the systematic and objective *process* of obtaining and evaluating evidence regarding . . . economic assertions." The assertions on which we focus in this part are those contained in the *financial statements of a for-profit entity.*

In this chapter, we discuss the theory of evidence as well as the general process by which the third standard of field work is met.

Chapters 6 through 9 deal with the details of the evidence-gathering process. In Chapter 6 we will focus more on the process of evidence gathering than on the principles. We will explore how the auditor verifies the financial statement assertions by forming audit objectives and by performing procedures to satisfy each of the objectives. We will also discuss the timing and documentation of the evidence-gathering process.

Chapter 7 covers planning and assessment of inherent risk, and Chapters 8 and 9 cover assessment of control risk.

The Audit Process

The primary objective of the independent audit is to attest to the fairness of pre-sentation of external financial statements. The standard audit report (Figure 1–3) communicates, among other things, (1) that an evidence-gathering process has taken place in accordance with generally accepted auditing standards; and (2) that, based on the results of the process, which revealed no material uncor-rected errors and irregularities, the financial statements are presented fairly in accordance with generally accepted accounting principles.

Figure 5–1 illustrates the financial statements of a typical manufacturing client, JEP Manufacturing Company, as of March 31, 19X1, with comparative fi-nancial statements as of March 31, 19X0. This company will be used for illustra-

Figure 5–1

JEP Manufacturing Company

B A L A N C E   S H E E T

As of March 31, 19X0 and 19X1

Assets	19X1	19X0
Current Assets:		
Cash	$ 37,815	$ 84,520
Marketable securities	343,272	148,948
Accounts receivable	1,015,032	558,043
Notes receivable	909,539	1,111,337
Prepaid expenses	27,902	28,935
Inventories	873,218	727,240
Deposits	6,311	5,761
Total current assets	3,213,089	2,664,784
Long-term Investments:		
Investment in subsidiary	194,324	179,119
Property, Plant, and Equipment:		
Machinery and equipment	583,360	545,593
Other property	1,256,536	1,188,175
Less accumulated depreciation	(773,050)	(687,592)
Total property, plant, and equipment	1,066,846	1,046,176
Other Assets	72,501	53,827
Total assets	4,546,760	3,943,906

tive purposes throughout Chapters 5 through 20 to illustrate the evidence-gathering process. In the interests of space, the statement of cash flows for the company has been omitted. The assertions embodied in the financial statements are the subject of the evidence-gathering process for the independent audit. More information is given about JEP Manufacturing Company in the appendix to this chapter, which illustrates the process of assessing materiality and audit risk.

The diagram in Figure 5–2 presents a simplified model of the process by which a financial statement audit takes place. The first stage of the process involves *planning*, which is the development of an audit evidence-gathering strategy designed to *minimize audit risk*. Discussed in detail in a later section of this chapter, audit risk is an extension of the concept of attestation risk, which was introduced in Chapter 2. Audit risk is defined in SAS 47 (AU312) as the risk that the auditor may unknowingly fail to modify the opinion on financial statements

Figure 5–1

(continued)

JEP Manufacturing Company

B A L A N C E   S H E E T

As of March 31, 19X0 and 19X1

Liabilities and Stockholders' Equity	19X1	19X0
Current Liabilities:		
Accounts payable	$ 499,760	$ 500,410
Notes payable	—	175,000
Current maturities of long-term debt	81,302	—
Accrued expenses	347,804	232,269
Income taxes payable	279,947	128,610
Total current liabilities	1,403,137	1,036,289
Long-term Liabilities:		
Notes payable	499,857	459,650
Stockholders' Equity:		
Common stock	75,995	75,995
Preferred stock	—	60,200
Additional paid-in capital	34,639	34,639
Treasury stock	(10,122)	(10,122)
Retained earnings	2,737,578	2,287,255
Total stockholders' equity	2,838,090	2,447,967
Total liabilities and stockholders' equity	4,546,760	3,943,906

(continues)

Figure 5–1 ▰▰▰▰

(continued)

JEP Manufacturing Company

T R I A L   B A L A N C E

December 31, 19X1

	Debit	Credit
Cash	$ 37,815	
Marketable securities	343,272	
Accounts receivable—trade	1,008,070	
Accounts receivable—other	6,962	
Notes receivable	5,400	
Costs and estimated earnings	904,139	
Deposits	6,311	
Prepaid expenses	27,902	
Inventory—raw materials	647,417	
Inventory—work in process	194,495	
Inventory—in transit	31,306	
Machinery and equipment	583,359	
Other property	1,256,536	
Accumulated depreciation		$ 773,050
Investment in subsidiary	194,324	
Cash surrender value of life insurance	145,300	
Life insurance policy loan		76,500
Deferred debt expense	3,701	
Accounts payable		499,760
Current maturities of long-term debt		81,302
Accrued expenses		347,804
Federal income taxes payable— current		202,729
Federal income taxes payable— deferred		77,218
Notes payable		499,857
Treasury stock	10,122	
Common stock		75,995
Additional paid-in capital		34,639
Retained earnings		2,285,900
Sales		7,839,589
Cost of sales	5,579,933	
Selling and administrative expenses	1,421,260	
Motor control devices	50,922	
Interest and other income		52,166
Equity in earnings of subsidiary		15,205
Interest expense	61,543	
Income tax expense—current	398,323	
Income tax expense—deferred		56,698
	12,918,412	12,918,412

Figure 5–1 ▰▰▰▰ ▭▭▭▭▭▭▭▭▭▭▭▭▭▭▭▭▭▭▭▭▭▭▭▭▭▭▭▭▭▭▭▭▭▭▭▭▭▭▭

(continued)

JEP Manufacturing Company

COMBINED STATEMENT OF INCOME AND
RETAINED EARNINGS

For the Years Ended March 31, 19X0 and 19X1

	19X1	19X0
Sales	$7,839,589	$6,522,896
Cost of sales	(5,579,933)	(4,939,060)
Gross profit	2,259,656	1,583,836
Selling and administrative expenses	(1,472,182)	(1,009,652)
Operating profit	787,474	574,184
Interest and other income	52,166	51,313
Equity in earnings of subsidiary	15,205	34,668
Interest expense	(61,543)	(80,888)
Income before federal income taxes	793,302	579,277
Federal income taxes—current	(398,323)	(180,107)
Federal income taxes—deferred	56,698	(51,071)
Net income	451,677	348,099
Retained earnings at beginning of year	2,287,255	1,940,406
	2,738,932	2,288,505
Dividends	(1,354)	(1,250)
Retained earnings at end of year	$2,737,578	$2,287,255

JEP Manufacturing Company

MANAGEMENT'S REPORT

The management of JEP Manufacturing Co. is responsible for the financial statements and all other information included in this annual report. The financial statements and related information were prepared in accordance with generally accepted accounting principles and include the informed judgments and estimates of management where exact measurement is not feasible.

The company's internal audit program is designed for constant evaluation of the adequacy and effectiveness of the internal controls. Audits measure adherence to established policies and procedures. The company's formally stated and communicated policies demand high ethical standards of employees.

The Audit Committee of the Board of Directors is composed solely of outside directors. The committee meets periodically with management, internal auditors, and independent public accountants to review the work of each and to satisfy itself that the respective parties are properly discharging their responsibilities. To insure complete independence, representatives of Robert Best & Co., Certified Public Accountants retained by the company to examine its financial statements, have full and free access to meet with the audit committee with or without the presence of management representatives.

Andrew R. Mitchell
Executive Vice President

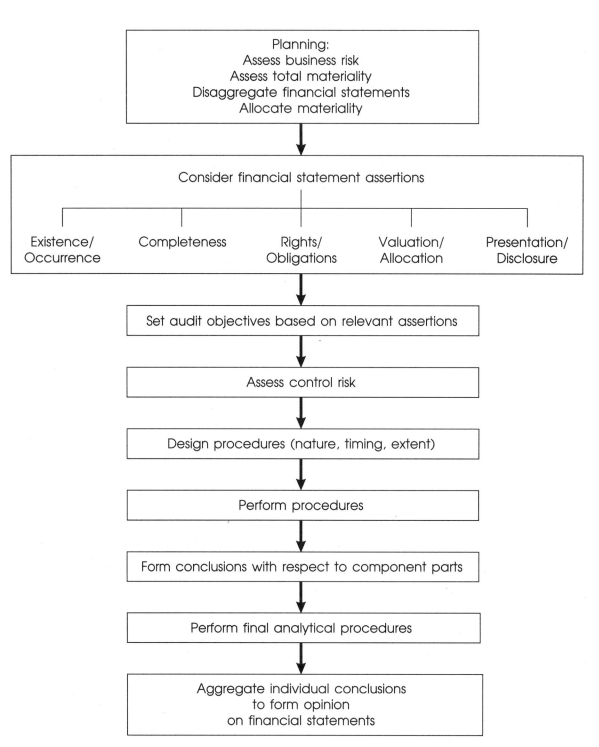

Figure 5–2

Model for the Financial Statement Audit

that are materially misstated. The three component parts of audit risk are (1) inherent risk, (2) control risk, and (3) detection risk.

Inherent risk is assessed by the auditor during the planning stage of the audit. Two levels of inherent risk are generally evaluated: (1) the aggregate level (usually referred to as *business risk*) and (2) the individual account balance level. Inherent risk is the susceptibility to error that is associated with the environment surrounding the industry, company, or accounts. Tools used during the planning stage include discussions with company personnel and others, reading industry literature, and analytical procedures performed on the company's financial and other data. These tools reveal the relative risk of misstatement of various accounts in the financial statements. In addition, the auditor must apply seasoned audit judgment to arrive at a preliminary assessment of *materiality*. Both risk and materiality are covered in detail later.

In conjunction with the planning phase of the process, the auditor must *disaggregate* the financial statements into component parts. Structurally, as shown in Figure 5–1, the financial statements consist of asset, liability, equity, revenue, and expense accounts linked together by accounting systems. For example, revenue and related accounts, accounts receivable, cash receipts, bad debts expense, and related allowance accounts are linked by the *revenue and collections system*. Other systems and related accounts are

- *Acquisition and expenditures system*: Purchases, raw materials inventories, prepaid expenses, property and equipment, operating expenses, accounts payable, and cash disbursements
- *Payroll system*: Payroll expenses and related accruals.
- *Production and conversion system*: Work-in-process, finished goods inventories, cost of goods sold, and related accounts
- *Financing and investing system*: Long-term debt, capital stock and related expense and equity accounts, investments and related revenue and accrual accounts.

Thoughtful and thorough planning helps the auditor to select the accounts in the financial statements that are both material and more susceptible to errors than others and that should therefore be the focus of the financial statement audit.

For *each material component system or account*, the auditor must consider the financial statement assertions embodied in that system or account. Discussed thoroughly in the next section, the universal set of financial assertions that apply to all systems and accounts are (1) existence/occurrence; (2) completeness; (3) rights/obligations; (4) valuation/allocation; and (5) presentation/disclosure. To verify those assertions, the auditor develops a set of audit objectives as the framework of the audit process. Audit objectives are discussed in detail in Chapter 6.

After audit objectives are set for a particular account balance or class of transactions, the auditor must *assess the control risk* associated with the system that produced the account balance. Control risk is the risk that misstatements may be undetected by the client's control system. The auditor must obtain an understanding of the control structure (environment, accounting system, and procedures) that produces the various financial statement assertions. The theory of internal control discussed earlier asserts an inverse relationship between the quality of the system of internal control and the nature, timing, and extent of audit tests that should be performed on the financial statements that are produced by the system. In this sense, a strong internal control system that provides low risk of financial statement misstatement is an excellent source of evidence that the financial statements are fairly presented in accordance with GAAP. Conversely, significant weaknesses in the control structure force the auditor to assess control risk as high, thus preventing reliance on the control structure as evidence for fairness of presentation.

Based on the auditor's assessment of inherent risk and control risk, the auditor is prepared to design an audit program and to perform *detection risk procedures* on the financial statement assertions themselves. Detection risk is defined as the risk that audit procedures performed on the assertions will fail to detect misstatements in the assertions. These procedures, called **substantive tests,** consist largely of inspection of documentary and physical evidence, written confirmations from parties outside the client's business, observation, verbal inquiry, and analytical procedures on financial and other data.

After the evidence-gathering process has taken place for a particular group of accounts, the auditor is prepared to form a conclusion as to whether or not the disclosures in those accounts conform to generally accepted accounting principles. When the process is completed for all important classes of transactions and accounts, the auditor performs final analytical procedures on the financial statements. Analytical procedures are performed at this stage to ascertain whether the conclusions formed by the auditor based on results of detailed procedures corroborate those that one would form based on the relationships that exist among the recorded data in the financial statements. If they do, the auditor is then prepared to form a conclusion (the audit report in Figure 1–3) as to whether the financial statements are, in all material respects, fairly presented in accordance with GAAP.

Financial Statement Assertions

☑ **Objective 2**
Know the five basic financial statement assertions

As stated earlier, auditing is a process of gathering evidence regarding *economic assertions*. In the financial audit, those assertions are the explicit or implicit *representations of management* that are embodied in the various components of the financial statements. As shown in Figure 5–2, **financial statement assertions** can be classified into the following broad categories:[1]

- Existence/occurrence.
- Completeness.
- Rights/obligations.

Fig. 5-2

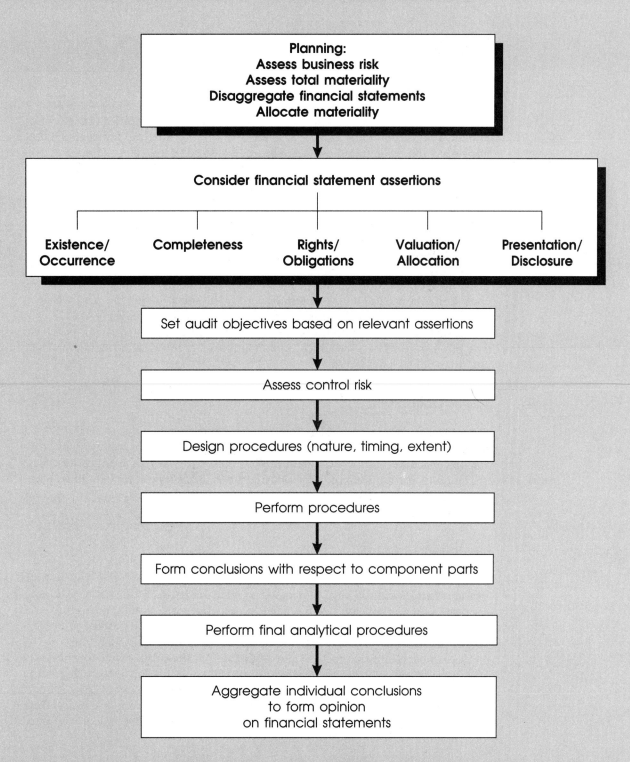

- Valuation/allocation.
- Presentation/disclosure.

Existence/Occurrence

Assertions relating to existence or occurrence deal with whether the assets or liabilities of the company exist at a given date and whether the transactions that generated financial statement accounts actually occurred. For example, if JEP Manufacturing lists the account "Cash" on the balance sheet (Figure 5–1) at $37,815, management is asserting, among other things, that cash exists and that the receipt and disbursement transactions that generated the balance actually occurred.

Completeness

Assertions about completeness deal with whether all transactions and accounts that should be included for presentation in the financial statements are included. If, for example, JEP Manufacturing lists a balance of accounts payable as $499,760, it is asserting that the amount represents a complete accounting of all purchase and other transactions for which unpaid amounts to trade creditors remain as of the financial statement date.

Rights/Obligations

Assertions of rights and obligations pertain to ownership rights of assets and valid obligations for liabilities listed on the balance sheet. For example, by capitalizing machinery and equipment at $583,360, JEP Manufacturing is asserting that it owns the equipment. By disclosing $499,857 as long-term liabilities, management acknowledges the existing obligation for eventual payment of that amount, plus interest.

Valuation/Allocation

Assertions about valuation or allocation relate to whether the appropriate amounts and methods have been used to measure asset, liability, revenue, and expense components of the financial statements, and whether revenue and expense has been properly allocated among financial periods affected. For example, by listing property and equipment as a gross amount of $1,839,896 on the balance sheet, JEP Manufacturing is asserting that the proper valuation method was used to measure the recorded amount (probably historical cost). By listing accumulated depreciation of $773,050 and depreciation expense of $85,458 (part of selling and administrative expenses of $1,472,182), the company is asserting that the proper amount of cost has been allocated against past and current periods' revenue for plant and equipment.

Presentation/Disclosure

Assertions about presentation and disclosure relate to the classifications of the components of the financial statements and the descriptive data included with them. For example, management of JEP Manufacturing has reclassified a portion of long-term notes payable ($81,302) that will mature within one year as a current liability. Thus, management is asserting that this amount will be satisfied with current assets within the next year.

These five basic assertions are common to most financial statement accounts and are the subject of the audit evidence-gathering process. These assertions must be verified successfully by the auditor by obtaining sufficient competent evidential matter. Notice that the last page of Figure 5–1 contains management's report that acknowledges primary responsibility for the financial statements.

The Nature of Audit Evidence

☑ **Objective 3**
Be able to discuss the nature of evidence

The third audit standard of field work requires that sufficient competent evidential matter be obtained through inspection, observation, inquiries, and confirmation to allow the auditor a reasonable basis for expressing an opinion regarding the financial statements under examination. The entire audit process illustrated in Figure 5–2 involves evidence-gathering in some form. Audit **evidence** includes all things that influence the auditor's judgment regarding the conformity of a client's financial presentations to GAAP. The auditor's decision with respect to evidential matter supporting a particular financial statement assertion generally involves three basic considerations: *nature*, or quality of the evidence; *timing*, or period in which the process is performed; and *extent*, or quantity of the evidence. The *extent* of evidence to be gathered relates to the *sufficiency* requirement in the third standard of fieldwork. The *nature* of evidence refers to its *competency*. In the sections that follow, we consider the meanings of these terms more carefully.

Sufficiency of Evidence

In general, **sufficiency** relates to the *amount* or *extent* of evidence necessary to support an informed audit opinion. Since a financial audit is typically based on a *sampling* of the data that underlie the various systems and balances reflected in the financial statements, the pertinent questions to be answered relating to sufficiency of evidence are (1) How much evidence is enough? and (2) How big does a sample have to be to adequately support an audit opinion?

Auditing standards do not provide exact guidelines for judging sufficiency of evidence. On the contrary, the decision of sample size is largely dependent on the auditor's judgment after consideration of the facts associated with the situation. Several factors should be considered by the auditor in making these judgments:

• The nature of the item under examination.
• The materiality threshold for errors and irregularities associated with the item under examination.
• The level of audit risk associated with the item.
• The kinds and competence of evidence that are available.

Although auditing standards do not require the use of statistical sampling methods, statistical literature does give us quantitative determinants of sample size whenever those methods of sampling are used. Even when those methods are not used, the auditor should at least informally take these factors into consideration. They include the variability of the population from which the sample is selected and the size of the population. All of these terms and their effects on sample sizes are discussed at length in Chapters 11 and 12.

The process of drawing and auditing a sample of items is often expensive. It requires a significant amount of time on the part of the auditing firm's personnel and the client's employees who assist on the audit engagement. Therefore, the auditor should always consider *cost-benefit factors* when gathering evidence. To be useful, the cost of audit evidence should not exceed its expected benefits. As we learned in Chapters 1–4, auditors must operate within a very competitive environment. Partly for that reason, the auditor will usually find it necessary to rely on evidence that is *persuasive* rather than totally compelling.[2] Excessive audit-sample sizes can result in inefficient work and excessive fees, which, in turn, may eventually result in the loss of clients. On the other hand, the matter of difficulty and expense involved in testing a particular item is not *in itself* a valid basis for omitting or limiting the test. Conclusions based on inadequate evidence are considered negligent conduct on the part of the auditor and could result in legal exposure, as pointed out in Chapter 4. In summary, we may conclude that sufficiency of evidence means *enough to provide the benefits of adequate support of the audit opinion without being inefficient or negligent.*

Competency of Audit Evidence

Competency refers to the qualities that evidence must possess in order to provide reasonable assurance that the financial statements are presented in accordance with GAAP. Those qualities include (1) validity, (2) relevance, and (3) objectivity.

Validity refers to qualities that will enable the auditor to derive logical conclusions. It may consist of natural or observable objects, which the auditor may see and touch. For example, observing the client's physical inventories or plant and equipment enables the auditor to reach the logical conclusion that these assets exist. Other evidence may be developed logically or mathematically. For example, logically derived evidence includes developing conclusions regarding the truth of verbal evidence presented to the client, or the quality of the client's internal control structure. Recalculation of the client's depreciation expense or accrued liabilities can enable the auditor to reach the conclusion that these computations were made correctly by the client.

Professional standards provide guidelines for judging validity of evidence. The following general guidelines apply:

- Evidence that originates outside the business is generally more reliable than evidence that originates inside the business. We shall explore this later when we discuss the levels of competence of documentary evidence (Figure 5–4).
- Evidence developed under satisfactory conditions of internal control is generally more reliable than evidence developed under poor conditions of internal control.
- Direct personal knowledge obtained by the auditor through inspection, observation, confirmation, and physical examination is generally more persuasive than information obtained through hearsay (i.e., from the client).[3]

Relevance refers to the evidence being related to the financial statement assertion that is being verified. For example, if the auditor is verifying the existence of accounts receivable, evidence that is most relevant is generally considered to be direct confirmation with the customers. On the other hand, if the assertion to be verified is proper disclosure, the auditor would find that analysis of accounts for probable uncollectability and review of client disclosure policies for receivables would provide the most relevant evidence.

Objectivity means that two or more independent parties examining the evidence should draw the same conclusions. For example, if the auditor desires to ascertain that equipment was owned by the client, vendor's invoices and supporting papers showing that the equipment was purchased, received, and paid for should be examined. Such documents have a high degree of objectivity, because, from examining them, two or more auditors would draw the same independent conclusion regarding ownership. If evidence is highly objective, the likelihood of personal bias in judging the results is reduced. In turn, the uncertainty as to the conclusion reached is reduced.

Types of Audit Evidence

☑ **Objective 4**
Be able to recognize the types of evidence

Evidential matter supporting the financial statements can generally be classified into two broad categories: (1) underlying accounting data and (2) all other corroborating evidential matter. Figure 5–3 depicts the *audit evidence tree*, illustrating the two broad types of evidence, along with specific examples of each.

Underlying Accounting Data

Included in **underlying accounting data** are the following client records:

1. The general ledger.
2. Subsidiary ledgers, such as accounts receivable, accounts payable, and fixed assets.

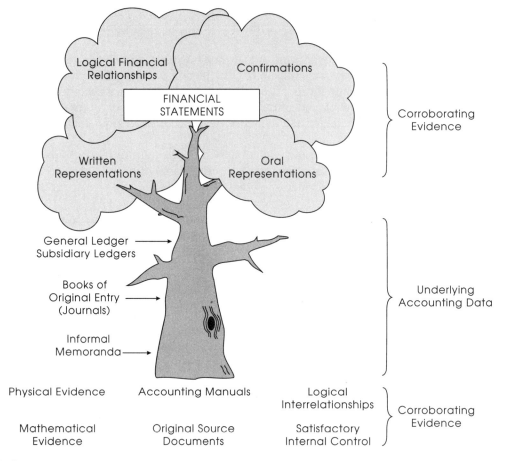

Figure 5–3

The Evidence Tree

3. Books of original entry (journals).
4. Accounting manuals, which document accounting procedures.
5. Informal and memorandum records such as work sheets supporting cost allocations and bank reconciliations.

All of these records directly support the financial statements and make up a valuable part of audit evidence. Tests of underlying accounting information include analytical procedures, retracing the steps followed in the accounting process and in developing the work sheets and allocations involved, recalculation, and reconciliation of related accounting information from different sources. These procedures will be discussed in greater detail in Chapter 6. If the accounting system supporting the underlying accounting information is soundly conceived and carefully maintained, there will be a logical internal consistency about that information which, when discovered by the auditor, gives assurance as to the propriety of the financial statements.

Corroborating Evidential Matter

Underlying accounting data are not considered sufficient evidence to support an opinion regarding the fairness of financial statements. They must be further supported by corroborating evidence. As the term implies, **corroborating evidential matter** lends strength to the auditor's conclusions as to whether the financial statements are fairly presented. Types of corroborating evidence available include (1) physical evidence; (2) statements, both written and oral, by third parties and the client; (3) authoritative documents; (4) mathematical evidence; (5) satisfactory internal control; and (6) interrelationships that exist among the data.[4]

Physical Evidence.   The auditor may examine the physical evidence to verify the client's financial statement assertion of *existence or occurrence*. For example, the physical examination of machinery and equipment in the plant will support the client's assertion of the existence of the equipment. Likewise, physical evidence is generally examined in verifying that marketable securities, inventories, capital stock, notes receivable or payable, and many other types of assets or liabilities exist.

Statements by Third Parties and Clients.   Written statements from outside the client's business, or *confirmations*, are considered excellent evidence. For example, confirmations from banks, customers, and creditors help to verify the financial statement assertions of existence, completeness, and valuation for cash, accounts receivable, and notes payable. Oral evidence is rarely obtained from outside the client's business, but would be considered more competent than similar evidence obtained from inside the client's business. Written representations from the client, usually contained in a *client representation letter*, provide corroborative evidence for the client's verbal responses to auditor inquiries and are considered a weak form of evidence in terms of competency. However, such representations are a necessary part of the evidence that must be obtained on every audit. We will discuss and illustrate the client representation letter in Chapters 6 and 20.

Authoritative Documents.   Documents can provide persuasive evidence with regard to verification of many of the financial statement assertions. For example, a vendor invoice for an item of inventory provides evidence of ownership rights, proper valuation, and existence. A bank statement obtained from the client's bank can provide evidence of existence, valuation, and completeness for the client's cash in bank.

The competency or persuasiveness of *documentary evidence* is largely dependent on (1) where the document originates and (2) whether the document is directly transmitted to the auditor. Documents that originate outside the client's organization generally provide more persuasive evidence than those that originate inside the organization. Also, documents transmitted directly to the auditor from outside parties generally provide more persuasive evidence than documents that first pass through the hands of client employees (thus risking alteration) before reaching the auditor. More specifically, documentary evidence may be classified in descending order of competence as follows:

1. Documents originating outside the client's organization and transmitted directly to the auditor.
2. Documents originating outside the client's organization and held by the client.
3. Documents originating inside the client's organization but circulated outside before being returned directly to the auditor.
4. Documents originating inside the client's organization but circulated outside before being returned to the client.
5. Documents originating inside the client's organization, then transmitted to the auditor.
6. Documents originating inside the client's organization and held by the client.

Examples of documentary evidence falling into each of these six categories are shown in Figure 5–4.

As a general observation, we can conclude that the competence of documentary evidence declines in direct relationship to the opportunity that the client's personnel may have to change the document.

Mathematical Evidence.   The auditor usually obtains mathematical evidence by recalculating the client's computations. Mathematical accuracy of client rec-

Figure 5–4 ■■■

Documentary Evidence Classified by Level of Competence

Level of competence		
Where originated	Where transmitted	Examples
1. Outside	Auditor	Cutoff bank statements
		Audit confirmations
2. Outside	Client	Client's monthly bank statements
		Vendor invoices
3. Inside	Outside, auditor	Canceled checks in cutoff bank statement
4. Inside	Outside, client	Canceled checks in monthly bank statements
5. Inside	Auditor	Client representation letter
6. Inside	Client	Sales invoices
		Sales summaries
		Cost distribution reports
		Shipping documents
		Receiving reports
		Purchase orders

ords is evidence of proper valuation for financial statement accounts. For example, the auditor might *foot* (or re-add) the columns of the cash receipts journal on a test basis to assure that the proper amounts are being obtained before posting to ledger accounts. Depreciation expense, accrued receivables and liabilities, the allowance for doubtful accounts, and bad debts expense, among others, are candidates for mathematical evidence.

Satisfactory Internal Control.   *Strong internal controls* provide excellent evidence that data are being properly captured in the form of transactions valued, summarized, and classified in the financial records. As implied by the second standard of audit field work, an *inverse relationship* is assumed between the quality of the internal control structure and the amount of substantive evidence that must be obtained to verify financial statement assertions. We may infer, then, that the existence of strong controls, functioning as designed, is corroborating evidence that financial statement assertions are proper and that financial statements are presented in accordance with GAAP.

Interrelationships among Recorded Data.   Recorded data that can be shown to be in congruence with evidence from other sources are an excellent source of corroborating evidence. The auditor examines interrelationships among recorded data by performing analytical procedures. The financial statement assertions that are most directly verified by these procedures are valuation and completeness. SAS 56 (AU 329), *Analytical Procedures*, requires analytical procedures during the planning stages of the audit to identify unusual or unexpected relationships for further audit testing, and at the end of the audit to provide corroborative evidence. We will discuss analytical procedures at length in Chapter 7 and later chapters.

On a given engagement, the auditor will examine all of these types of evidence to provide support for financial statement assertions. Selection of evidence to verify a particular assertion should be made on the basis of the qualities of evidence pointed out earlier: relevance, validity, objectivity, and cost-effectiveness. We will discuss the *procedures* used to evaluate evidence in Chapter 6.

We now consider two factors that significantly affect the evidence-gathering process: (1) audit risk and (2) materiality.

Audit Risk

☑ **Objective 5**
Know how to assess audit risk

As long as there have been audited financial statements, those who perform audits have had to deal with the problem of assessing, making allowances for, and eventually accepting some *audit risk*. In Chapter 2, we defined attestation risk as the risk of failing to modify the attest report for a misstated assertion. In the context of the audit, overall **audit risk** is defined as the risk of failing to modify the audit opinion on materially misstated financial statements. It is essential that each audit examination be planned so that the risk of issuing an inappropriate audit opinion is reduced to a sufficiently low level to meet the expectations of users regarding fairness of presentation of the financial statements.

In general, an inappropriate audit opinion can take one of two forms. The auditor may issue an unqualified opinion when, in fact, a qualified opinion or adverse opinion is more appropriate. This situation exists when an undiscovered material error or irregularity has occurred that causes the financial statements to be materially misstated. The cost associated with this kind of risk is potential legal exposure. Conversely, the auditor may decide that he or she must issue a qualified or an adverse opinion when, in fact, an unqualified opinion is more appropriate. In this situation, the typical course of action is almost always to perform additional auditing procedures, which eventually will lead to an appropriate conclusion that the financial statements were not misstated after all. The costs associated with this aspect of overall risk is inefficiency and lost time and fees.

For all practical purposes, auditors are more concerned with the prospect of issuing an inappropriately unqualified opinion than an inappropriately qualified one. For that reason, SAS 47 (AU312) defines total audit risk (RT) as the risk that the auditor may unknowingly fail to modify the opinion on financial statements that are materially misstated. RT is the mathematical complement of the auditor's confidence (C) in the overall fairness of presentation of the financial statements. Thus,

$$RT = 1 - C \tag{1}$$

For example, if the auditor desired to have 95 percent confidence in correctly concluding that the financial statements were fairly stated, the risk of incorrectly making this conclusion (RT) would be

$$1 - .95 = .05$$

RT does not include the following:

- Risk of legal exposure and the related costs involved in defending the auditor when the examination and opinion are appropriate. Such risks are borne jointly by the auditor and the professional liability insurance company. The cost associated with this risk can be minimized over time, since it is a part of the auditor's fee structure.
- Risk that the auditor might mistakenly conclude that financial statements are materially misstated when, in fact, the examination and the unqualified opinion are appropriate. Although costs associated with this type of risk are not negligible, they tend to be associated with audit efficiency and are of less concern to the auditor than the risk of issuing an inappropriately unqualified opinion.

The process of risk assessment involves subjective judgment. No two auditors are likely, therefore, to perform the process in exactly the same way. The subjective assessment of the probability of an unfavorable outcome of an audit is somewhat like the process that meteorologists follow in assessing the likelihood of rain. Current facts must be judgmentally weighed against past experience, and the result, while it may be quantified as a percentage, is still an *educated guess*. Nevertheless, risk assessment during the planning stage is a vital and necessary part of the audit. This risk can usually be assessed with respect to individual accounts; groups of accounts; or classes of transactions, such as accounts receivable, inventories, or sales.

At the individual account balance level, RT can be expressed as the result of the following relational model:

$$RT = IR \times IC \times DR \qquad\qquad (2)$$

where IR is inherent risk, IC is control risk, and DR is detection risk.

Inherent risk (IR) is the susceptibility of the account balance to material error, individually or when aggregated with other balances, assuming there are no related controls to be relied on. IR is a function not only of the relative risk (ease of misappropriation) of the account balance, but also of the *riskiness* of the entity. As with all subjective probability assessments, the success of assessment of inherent risk depends on the seasoned judgment of the auditor. A partial list of factors that might adversely influence IR include

- The liquidity of the account. Highly liquid account balances with high relative risk of misappropriation (cash, marketable securities) have greater IR than nonliquid accounts.
- Accounts highly susceptible to error because of difficulty in calculations have greater IR than those relatively easy to calculate. These accounts might be evidenced by large fluctuations from year to year in the financial statements.
- Accounts characterized by a scarcely visible or nonexistent audit trail are subject to greater IR than those characterized by a highly visible audit trail.
- Company or industry-related environmental factors that affect the account might cause greater IR. These factors include potential insolvency problems, deteriorating economic conditions in the industry, the existence of continued litigation, or other external factors.
- Small, closely held businesses in general have a greater degree of IR than large, widely held businesses, because small, closely held businesses tend to be characterized by small staffs with limited potential for internal control.
- The *tone at the top*—whether management has an appropriately serious attitude toward prevention, detection, or correction of financial statement errors or irregularities.

In general, the more any one or a combination of the above factors influence an account, the greater the inherent risk, thus reducing the auditor's confidence in the appropriateness of the audit opinion, as it relates to that account, without expansion of detection risk procedures.

Sound planning during the early stages of the audit allows for a proper assessment of IR. Specifically, inquiry and preliminary analytical procedure can help to identify accounts with a high level of *IR*, which might demand more of the auditor's attention than other accounts. We will discuss these techniques in greater detail in a later section of this chapter.

Control risk (*IC*) is the risk that material error exists and will not be prevented, detected, or corrected by the client's internal control structure. *IC* is a function of the auditor's judgment of the quality of the internal control structure after an understanding of the structure has been obtained. This factor of the overall risk model will be developed more thoroughly in Chapter 8. Generally, however, it can be said at this point that *IC* affects *RT* in the same manner that *IR* affects *RT*—the greater the risk caused by a poor internal control structure, the greater the *RT*. All other factors remaining equal, less confidence should be placed on the overall audit opinion as it relates to a particular account in such a situation.

Detection risk (*DR*) is the risk that the auditor's substantive tests of balances will lead to the belief that the financial statements do not contain material errors when, in fact, they do, thus causing an inappropriately unqualified audit opinion. This element of the overall audit risk model affects *RT* in the same manner as the other two elements. *Of the three elements in the model, DR is the one that is controllable by the auditor*, because, for planning purposes, there is an inverse relationship between the level of *RT* specified by the auditor and the *nature, timing, and extent* of necessary substantive tests. Assume for a moment that we hold *IR* and *IC* constant. That would mean that specifying a low *RT* (high confidence in the unqualified audit report) would necessitate a low *DR* (high confidence in substantive auditing procedures). Figure 5–5 depicts the relationship between acceptable levels of *DR* and the nature, timing, and extent of necessary substantive tests.

Thus, specifying a low *RT* (high confidence needed in the unqualified audit opinion), with constant *IR* and *IC* risk factors, necessitates one or more of the following actions relating to substantive tests:

1. Use of more effective auditing procedures (thus, their *nature* is affected);
2. Performance of procedures close to the balance sheet date (at final) as opposed to an interim date (thus, their *timing* is affected);
3. Increase in the size of the samples upon which auditing procedures are performed (thus, their *extent* is affected).

Figure 5–5

Effect of Varying Levels of Detection Risk on Nature, Timing, and Extent of Substantive Tests

	High ←—————————— DR ——————————→ Low
Nature	Analytical Procedures ←——————————→ Tests of Details
Timing	Interim ←——————————→ Final
Extent	Small Sample Sizes ←——————————→ Large Sample Sizes

Substantive tests, by *nature*, can be classified into two broad categories: (1) *tests of details*, consisting of inspection of documentary support, confirmation of amounts with outside parties, recalculation of balances, and observation of physical evidence, and (2) analytical procedures, consisting of the study of the relationships (ratios, absolute variations, etc.) between the financial data for material deviations from predicted patterns. Generally speaking, tests of details, because of their nature, are more effective in uncovering the underlying causes of errors in the financial statements than the more general analytical review procedures. Likewise, tests of details are more time-consuming and, thus, are more costly than analytical procedures. The auditor may decide on an optimum mixture of analytical procedures and tests of details, depending on the level of *DR* present.

With respect to *timing*, substantive tests can be performed at any time *after* engagement planning and the preliminary study and evaluation of internal control have been completed.

Generally, if the auditor desires a *low DR* (high confidence in the audit opinion), tests would be concentrated at or near the balance sheet date as opposed to interim dates, which are generally farther from the balance sheet date and involve more risk.

Extent of tests refer to sample size required for a certain level of specified risk. Generally, the lower the desired *DR* specified by the auditor, the larger will be the required sample size.

It is during the planning stages of the audit that the auditor reaches a preliminary conclusion regarding the level of *RT* that is necessary. By performing procedures to allow the preliminary assessment of *IR* and *IC*, the auditor can use the model in Equation (2), along with a predetermined level of *RT*, to calculate the level of *DR* that governs the nature, timing, and extent of substantive audit tests. For example, assume that, as the result of preliminary planning, the client and/or the account being audited is assessed as inherently highly risky. Also assume that the internal control structure is deemed highly risky—that is, the auditor has a low level of confidence that material errors will be prevented or detected by the system. In this case, *DR* must be planned at a low level to maintain the desired level of *RT*. This will require more effective audit tests of financial statement balances, involving rather large sample sizes performed at or near year end. On the other hand, if the auditor is able to reach a conclusion that *IR* and *IC* are acceptably low, given a certain maximum acceptable level of *RT*, a greater level of *DR* is acceptable, allowing for less-extensive detailed tests of the account balance. *Thus, by being able to effectively assess IR and IC during the early stages of the audit, the auditor can actually control the planned level of DR by specifying the nature, timing, and extent of substantive tests necessary to express an unqualified audit opinion.*

Let us illustrate this process with a hypothetical example. Suppose that the auditor wishes to control the maximum acceptable level of *RT* for the accounts receivable account at .05. That is to say, the auditor is willing to accept no more than a 5 percent chance of attesting to the fairness of a materially misstated accounts receivable balance. Suppose, in addition, that the company being audited is small, closely held, and characterized by a multitude of related-party transactions. This may lead the auditor to set *IR* at a very high level. Let us suppose that *IR* is set at 1.0. Because of the company's small size and inability to properly segregate critical functions, *IC* may be set at .80. Using the model specified in Equation (2), the auditor can calculate the level of *DR* that is dictated by this combination of events. Rearranging the elements of Equation (2), we have

$$DR = RT/(IR \times IC) \tag{3}$$

Then,

$$DR = .05/(1.0 \times .80) = .0625$$

Thus, the level of detection risk that is acceptable if the auditor is to keep overall *RT* at the desired maximum level is .0625. *This requires that the auditor plan extensive tests of details on year-end balances.*

Alternatively, suppose that the client is a large, publicly traded corporation, which is traded on the New York Stock Exchange. The company is in an industry that has prospered for years and is expected to continue to do so. Demand for the company's product is very stable, and our experience allows us to conclude that the client's internal control structure is performing effectively. In this case, the auditor may decide to set the level of *IR* at, say, .50 and *IC* at .20. This set of circumstances allows us to calculate *DR* as follows:

$$DR = .05/(.50 \times .20) = .50$$

Thus, to keep the same level of *RT* (.05), the auditor can accept a *DR* as high as .50. This would necessitate far fewer and less detailed tests of the account balance. Instead, the auditor might rely on more analytical (and less costly) tests of the general relationships between the data for his or her assurance of fair presentation. Furthermore, the tests might be performed largely at interim times (during the year) as opposed to the end of the year.

During the planning phase, it is important that the assessment of inherent risk (*IR*) and control risk (*IC*) precede that of *DR*. One reason is that the auditor may decide, on the basis of planning procedures that result in high *IR* and *IC* assessment, not to rely on *IC*. This decision may be reached, for example, when a history of significant errors and/or irregularities in the company's financial records is revealed, or when external factors threaten the solvency or the future of the company. Alternatively, facts learned during the planning stages may lead to the conclusion that the costs associated with further testing of the internal controls may exceed the marginal benefits that could be derived from dependence on the system. The auditor may in these cases feel the need to set either *IR* or *IC* (or both) at 100 percent, making those factors in Equation (3) equal to 1.0. When both *IR* and *IC* are set at 1.0, notice that the full impact of *RT* must be borne by substantive tests. This has the effect of placing a tremendous responsibility on the auditor to design tests of financial statement balances that have a high probability of detecting significant errors and irregularities. During the planning stages of the audit the auditor must begin to gather information that will assist in these important decisions.

We will continue to develop our discussion of the audit risk model in Chapters 8 and 9 as we explore inherent risk and control risk in greater depth. In Chapters 11 and 12 we will break down the detection risk element into its sampling and nonsampling components to show the effects of risk assessment on sample size. In Chapter 11 we will also explain the relationship between SAS 47 (AU312) and SAS 39 (AU350), which explain audit risk, materiality, and sampling.

Materiality

☑ **Objective 6**
Know how to assess materiality on an audit

In Chapter 1, we defined a material financial statement item as a disclosure (or omission) that affects the decision of an informed user of the financial statements. In that sense, materiality relates to financial statement disclosure. The primary responsibility of the client's financial management is to determine whether something is material enough (individually or collectively) to disclose.

Materiality has a slightly different meaning for the auditor. The audit opinion in Figure 1–3 states that the financial statements present fairly, *in all material respects*, the entity's financial position and results of operations. In this sense, the auditor must set in advance a *range of acceptable limits* of error within which it is appropriate to conclude that the client's disclosures meet the standards of GAAP. Then, as the audit progresses, the auditor keeps records of known and likely errors that have not been corrected in specific accounts. At the end of the audit, these errors must be compared with the threshold of error developed as part of planning, to determine whether the financial statements are, in fact, fairly presented.

Steps in Applying the Materiality Standard

There are generally five steps to applying the materiality standard in auditing. They are

During planning stage

1. Setting the preliminary (planning) threshold.
2. Allocation of the preliminary threshold to individual accounts and systems.

During evidence-gathering stage

3. Estimating the total error in specific accounts and systems.
4. Aggregating the errors from specific accounts to form an estimate of total financial statement error.
5. Comparing the total estimate of error with the preliminary threshold.

Planning Materiality

During the planning stages of the audit the need for developing materiality threshold first appears. Although audit risk (discussed in the previous section) and materiality are independently derived factors, they must be considered jointly as decisions are made relating to the planning of the nature, timing, and extent of necessary audit procedures. For example, suppose that the auditor's planning procedures revealed that inherent risk (IR) for a particular account was high. To control the overall risk (RT) of issuing an inappropriately unqualified audit opinion, the auditor might set low materiality thresholds or low detection risk (DR) levels, or a combination of the two. Both of these actions, in turn, would necessitate more effective and more extensive detection risk procedures than would have been the case if inherent risk of misstatement of the account had been assessed at a lower level.

It is essential that the auditor develop a clear perception of what is material during the planning stages of the audit, for at least two reasons. First, early establishment of materiality guidelines provides a threshold for errors and irregularities beyond which the auditor is unwilling to accept misstatements. The guidelines are evidence that the auditor is concerned about material errors from the outset. Furthermore, and perhaps equally important, once those guidelines have been set they also define items and amounts that are *immaterial*. Thus, the auditor is able to focus on the important aspects of the engagement and to perform a more efficient audit—that is, to attain a maximum level of assurance for a minimum cost.

Factors That Affect Planning Materiality

Several factors influence the preliminary materiality decision. Those include

- User groups.
- Financial statement variables that are important to users.
- Quantitative measures
- Qualitative considerations.

With respect to *users*, the auditor should try to identify the intended financial statement user groups during preliminary discussions with the client. The primary purpose for the engagement should be identified as part of audit planning. If the purpose of the audit, for example, is to obtain a bank loan, bank creditors may be logically assumed to be the primary user group. On the other hand, if the purpose of the audit is to satisfy annual reporting requirements under the rules of the SEC for publicly traded companies, the primary user groups may be presumed to be investors and prospective investors.

After primary and other user groups are identified, the auditor should consider those *variables in the financial statements having the most significant impact* on decisions to be made by the identified user group(s). Creditors, for example, might be greatly concerned with the financial statement variables that show the company's ability to repay debts (such as current assets, current liabilities, total assets, total debt, total capital, and the various ratios that are derived from those items). Investors, on the other hand, will be more interested in those financial statement variables that would most directly influence their judgments regarding the company's short-range or long-range profitability (such as sales, net income, net worth, total assets, and the related ratios developed from those items).

To be useful as a decision tool, it is essential that the materiality threshold be *quantified* by the auditor. For example, the auditor may decide that, for a company with $5,000,000 in net income before taxes, the preliminary planning materiality threshold for error will be $250,000 (.05 × $5,000,000). Materiality is usually quantified by expressing it as a percentage of a certain balance sheet or income statement variable. It is important to note, therefore, that materiality is expressed in *relative* rather than absolute terms. Whereas a single or combined error of $250,000 might be material to a company whose net income before taxes was $5,000,000, it would probably not be material to a company whose net income before taxes was $50,000,000.

Although we can cite some general guidelines for materiality thresholds, you must remember that there are *no uniform standards* for judging materiality. Most CPA firms set quantitative materiality guidelines as a matter of *firm policy*. The common standard for aggregate planning materiality, which has evolved through practice, is from 5 to 10 percent of net income before taxes, current assets, or current liabilities. Net income before taxes is used more often than any other variable to judge materiality, because of the perceived impact of that variable on investors' decisions. Since total assets and stockholders' equity generally exceed current assets by a significant amount, the threshold for those variables might be from 3 to 6 percent. If ranges are used (such as 5 to 10 percent) it is clear that errors in excess of the upper bound are material. It is equally clear that errors less than the lower bound are clearly immaterial. For errors that fall inside the range, the auditor would have to weigh the qualitative factors of the decision more carefully.

Qualitative guidelines for aggregate materiality usually involve either inherent risk factors, at the industry or company level, or control risk factors. For example,

1. XYZ Company, a new audit client, is in a highly volatile industry characterized by many business failures. Crane, the auditor, should consider assessing aggregate materiality levels for planning purposes at 5 percent rather than 7 percent of reported net income before taxes, because of the higher-than-normal inherent risk of business failure for the client.
2. The quality of Taurus Company's control structure is extremely low. The company's policies do not provide for cross-checking for accuracy of any transactions, and segregation of duties is inadequate in almost all systems. Because of higher-than-normal control risk, the materiality threshold for transactions produced by the system might be placed at 3 percent of net income before taxes rather than 7 percent.

If the auditor is auditing general-purpose financial statements and is not certain which financial statement variable is most critical to users, he or she might calculate a point estimate of materiality for several critical variables and then select the smaller (more conservative) computation. For example, assume that you are auditing a manufacturing company. Further assume that total assets for the company are $10,000,000, that net income before income taxes is $3,000,000, and that current assets are $5,000,000. You might proceed as follows:

Materiality threshold based on

1. Total assets (.03 × $10,000,000) = $300,000.
2. Net income before tax (.05 × $3,000,000) = $150,000.
3. Current assets (.05 × $5,000,000) = $250,000.

$150,000 would be selected as the materiality threshold because it is the smaller of the three amounts.

Allocation of Preliminary Threshold to Specific Accounts or Systems

As we mentioned in the early part of this chapter and as illustrated in Figure 5–2, to successfully conduct an audit, it is necessary to *disaggregate the financial statements* into component systems or segments. Each of these segments of the financial statements must be audited as a unit. Evidence must then be accumulated that supports the relevant financial assertions in the segment. Errors found in the segment need to be evaluated in terms of whether they materially affect the fair presentation of the segment. Therefore, it is necessary to *allocate planning materiality to each segment* of the financial statements—to set the *range of acceptable limits* or *maximum tolerable error* in advance for fairness of presentation, on an account-by-account basis. Planning materiality will, in turn, help determine the nature, timing, and extent of substantive audit tests that must be performed for each segment.

Most auditors prefer to allocate materiality only to balance sheet accounts, because errors in the balance sheet usually find their offsetting errors in the income statement. Therefore it would not be appropriate to allocate a portion of aggregate materiality to both the related balance sheet account (such as accounts receivable) and income statement account (sales). Since the balance sheet generally has fewer accounts than the income statement, it is generally simpler to confine allocation of materiality to that financial statement.

At least three major factors help determine the allocation of aggregate materiality to a particular segment. They are (1) the relative risk of misstatement of that segment, (2) the relative costs associated with auditing that segment, and (3) the fact that errors of both overstatement and understatement must be considered.

By deciding the relative risk of misstatement of a particular account balance, the auditor is, in effect, assessing *inherent risk* on an account-by-account basis. Factors that may make an account balance riskier than others include

1. Liquidity of the account balance. Generally speaking, the closer the account is to cash, the greater the risk of misstatement, necessitating a lower materiality threshold.
2. Difficulty in estimating the account balance. Some account balances must be

estimated, using certain assumptions. Usually, the more tenuous the assumption, the greater the risk of misstatement, necessitating a lower materiality threshold.
3. The existence of extenuating circumstances, such as related-party transactions, account balances that are in dispute, litigation, or the history of significant errors and irregularities.

The auditor should always be aware of the cost of gathering evidence. The concept of **reasonable assurance** (cost-benefit) should be applied at all times. However, high cost should not be the sole criterion for preventing the auditor from obtaining evidence that is highly necessary to verify critical financial statement assertions. Under ideal conditions, the auditor should balance risk and associated cost to achieve the optimum mixture of evidence for a given account balance.

Because of their nature, certain accounts will be more susceptible to errors of understatement than overstatement, and vice versa. An auditor should keep in mind the business objective of the client. If that objective is to maximize profits, there will be a tendency to overstate assets and understate liabilities. If the auditor learns that certain factors (such as a particular weakness in internal controls) might make a financial statement balance more susceptible to overstatement than understatement, a lower threshold for tolerable error might be specified for the account on the overstatement side than on the understatement side.

Example: The balances in Figure 5–6 comprise the financial statements of Jabo Electronics on December 31, 19X8:
Let's assume that the auditor has decided to use 6 percent of total assets ($60,000) as an aggregate materiality threshold. The auditor learns of a weakness in internal controls that makes it possible that unrecorded purchases in inventory might exist (thus understating both inventories and payables). The plan in Figure 5–7 might be adopted for allocation of the total materiality threshold.

In this case, the auditor might assign a lower-than-normal threshold to cash (only $1,000) because of the higher-than-normal risk of misstatement of the cash account. In addition, the auditor would assign a lower-than normal threshold to inventories and accounts payable (offsetting accounts for purchases) because of

Figure 5–6

Balance Sheet of Jabo Electronics
December 31, 19X8

Assets		Liabilities and Equity	
Cash	100,000	Accounts payable	200,000
Inventories	500,000	Capital stock	100,000
Fixed assets (net)	400,000	Retained earnings	700,000
Total	$1,000,000	Total	$1,000,000

Figure 5–7 ▬▬▬

Allocation of Materiality Threshold for Jabo Electronics

Account Balance	Tolerable Error Overstatement	Tolerable Error Understatement
Cash	$ 1,000	$ 1,000
Inventories/accounts payable	30,000	20,000
Fixed assets	29,000	39,000
	$ 60,000	$ 60,000

the discovered weakness in the internal control structure. A relatively high threshold for tolerable error would be assigned to fixed assets, because of its relatively low risk of misstatement. In addition, a lower threshold would be assigned for overstatement of fixed assets, because the account is more susceptible to errors of overstatement than of understatement.

Materiality during the Evidence-Gathering Stage

Materiality must again be considered as the engagement progresses and the results of audit tests are evaluated. In general, errors that occur on the audit may be divided into two categories: (1) known error and (2) likely error. Known errors are errors that are discovered in specific accounts. For example, the auditor for Jabo might have attempted to audit the cost of a $100,000 item in inventory and found that it was understated by $1,000, thus understating accounts payable by an equal amount.

Likely errors, on the other hand, are *inferred* as the result of the sampling process. Assume, for example, that in addition to the large item mentioned above, the auditor had also tested the values of 100 other inventory items from a total population of 5,000 items and had found them understated by a total of $7,000. In this case, the auditor would be required to extrapolate that error to the total population of 5,000 items as follows:

$7,000/100 = $70 understatement per item.
$70 × 5,000 accounts = $35,000 likely understatement error in the sampled group.

Therefore, the auditor's total estimate of error would be $36,000 ($1,000 known error + $35,000 likely error) in both inventory and accounts payable. This amount should then be compared with the auditor's predetermined (planning) maximum tolerable error for inventory and accounts payable to make the decision as to whether the account balances were fairly stated. In this case, the maximum tolerable error for understatement is $20,000, causing the auditor to infer that both inventory and accounts payable are understated by a material amount.

Materiality at the End of the Audit

Materiality must be considered again at the end of the audit, as the auditor aggregates audit evidence from the various accounting systems and balances and prepares to write the audit report. A record of audit adjustments for errors that have been *passed due to immateriality* should be kept as the audit progresses. Computations should be made as to the aggregate effects of these nonposted adjustments on key financial statement variables (net income, earnings per share, total assets, etc.). If the cumulative effect of these items exceeds the auditor's predetermined materiality threshold for error, appropriate adjustments to the financial statements should be recommended before the audit report is written. We will discuss the audit adjustment process, along with other aspects of completing the engagement, in Chapter 20.

Summary

In this chapter we introduced the process by which evidence is gathered. As the discussion progressed, we focused on key concepts that will be of use throughout the rest of this text: (1) evidence, (2) audit risk, and (3) materiality. We listed the financial statement assertions that are the focus of the evidence-gathering process. We then explored the nature of evidential matter, which included the meanings of the terms *sufficiency* and *competency*. Various types of evidential matter available to the auditor, both underlying accounting data and corroborating evidence, were then discussed. Finally, the two major determinants of the nature, timing, and extent of necessary evidential matter were discussed: audit risk and materiality.

Auditing Vocabulary

p. 159 **audit risk:**   The risk of failing to modify the audit opinion on financial statements that contain a material misstatement. Components of audit risk (RT) are inherent risk (IR), control risk (IC), and detection risk (DR).

p. 154 **competency:**   The qualities that evidence must possess to provide reasonable assurance that the financial statements are presented in accordance with GAAP; those qualities include (1) validity, (2) relevance, and (3) objectivity.

p. 162 **control risk:**   The risk that material error exists and will not be prevented, detected, or corrected by the client's internal control system.

p. 157 **corroborating evidential matter:**   Lends strength to the auditor's conclusions as to whether the financial statements are fairly presented; includes (1) physical evidence, (2) written and oral statements by third parties and the client, (3) authoritative documents, (4) mathematical evidence, (5) satisfactory internal control, and (6) interrelationships that exist among the data.

p. 162   **detection risk:**   The risk that the auditor's substantive tests will lead to the belief that the financial statements do not contain material errors when, in fact, they do, thus causing an inappropriately unqualified audit opinion.

p. 153   **evidence:**   Includes all the things that influence the auditor's judgment regarding the conformity of a client's financial presentations to GAAP. The auditor's decision with respect to evidential matter supporting a particular financial statement assertion generally involves three basic considerations: (1) nature, or quality of evidence; (2) timing, or period of time in which the process is performed; and (3) extent, or quantity of evidence.

p. 150   **financial statement assertions:**   The explicit or implicit representations of management that are embodied in the various components of the financial statements.

p. 161   **inherent risk:**   The susceptibility of an account balance to material error, individually or when aggregated with other balances, assuming there are no related controls to be relied on. Inherent risk (*IR*) is a function not only of the relative risk (ease of misappropriation) of the account balance, but also of the *riskiness* of the entity and the business environment.

p. 165   **materiality:**   The *range of acceptable limits* of error within which it is appropriate to conclude that the client's disclosures meet the standards of GAAP.

p. 155   **objectivity:**   Freedom from bias. To be objective, two or more independent parties examining the evidence should draw the same conclusions. Documentary evidence possesses objectivity because, from examining documents, two or more auditors would draw the same independent conclusion.

p. 169   **reasonable assurance:**   The cost-benefit principle, as applied to auditing, which means that the cost of performing a procedure should not exceed the expected benefits to be derived from that procedure.

p. 155   **relevance:**   Refers to the evidence being related to the financial statement assertion that is being verified.

p. 150   **substantive tests:**   Otherwise known as detection risk procedures, these are tests of the balances in the financial statements. The tests can be performed in one of three ways: (1) as direct tests of the balances, (2) as tests of the transactions that produce the balances, or (3) as analytical procedures. Substantive tests largely involve inspection of documents, written confirmations, observation, and analytical procedures on financial and other data.

p. 153   **sufficiency:**   Relates to the amount or extent of evidence necessary to support an informed audit opinion. Sufficiency answers the question of how much evidence is enough, and how big a sample must be taken to adequately support an audit opinion.

p. 155   **underlying accounting data:**   (See Figure 5–3.) Includes the general ledger, subsidiary ledgers, books of original entry (journals), accounting manuals, and informal and memorandum records such as work sheets supporting cost allocation and bank reconciliations. All of these records directly support the financial statements.

p. 154   **validity:**   Qualities that will enable the auditor to derive logical conclusions.

Appendix 5: Demonstration Problem:
Audit Risk and Planning Materiality
for JEP Manufacturing Company

The primary products produced by JEP are transformers, load-break oil switches, vacuum interruptors, and substations for the electric utility industry, oil industry, and other users of heavy electrical equipment. Transformers and switches comprise the majority of JEP's sales volume and are sold primarily to two customers. JEP specializes in made-to-order products as opposed to standard models.

Figure 5–1 contains the comparative balance sheets and income statements of JEP Manufacturing Company for the years ended March 31, 19X1 and 19X0. It will be helpful to refer to those financial statements as the discussion progresses.

Materiality

As explained earlier in the chapter, a financial statement disclosure is considered material if its inclusion or omission is sufficiently important to influence the decision of an informed user of the financial statements. The auditor considers materiality in terms of errors and irregularities; that is, the auditor must decide, as part of planning, how large an error or irregularity (including omissions) would have to be to cause an informed user to either invest in or lend money to the company by mistake. It is the task of the auditor to apply seasoned judgment to develop (1) an overall materiality threshold and (2) allocated materiality thresholds to the various account balances.

We have stated in the chapter that materiality has qualitative as well as quantitative dimensions. Although this is true, the auditor should reduce his decision regarding materiality for planning purposes to a quantitative measure (dollar amount) and document that conclusion in the working papers.

Overall Limits of Materiality. SAS 47 (AU312) gives little guidance on setting specific materiality thresholds. We have learned from the chapter that the following factors are relevant in reaching a determination:

1. Identification of the primary user group.
2. Determination of the elements of the financial statements having the most significant impact on the primary user group.
3. Application of a quantitative threshold to the relevant financial statement elements.
4. Selection of the smallest threshold of all relevant measures.

Let us assume, for our example, we have learned that the primary user group for JEP Manufacturing Company's financial statements is the stockholders. We may assume that stockholders are interested most in earning the highest possible rates of return on the stock of the company. This implies that net income before taxes would be the most significant variable on the financial statements of JEP Manufacturing Company. Other financial statement variables might also be relevant. For example, total assets or stockholders' equity might be of importance. Materiality thresholds should be applied to each of these variables, and the *smallest* threshold should be used. In our example for JEP,

- Total assets for 19X1 are $4,546,000. The auditor might consider a 3 percent misstatement, or about $136,400, to be material using total assets as the criterion variable.
- Total stockholders' equity is $2,838,000. The auditor might consider a 5 percent misstatement, or $141,900, to be material using stockholders' equity as the criterion variable.
- Net income before taxes for 19X1 is $793,000. The auditor might consider a 5 percent misstatement of net income, or $39,650 (rounded to $40,000), to be material using net income as the criterion variable.

The threshold applied to net income is smallest; therefore that value should be selected. By this choice, the auditors are following the most conservative approach to the audit. The auditors will extend their audit effort, using more effective tests, and taking larger sample sizes than would otherwise be the case, and should achieve even lower levels of risk that total assets or stockholders' equity are not misstated than would have been possible if the thresholds using those variables had been selected.

Allocation of Overall Materiality Threshold. Once the overall threshold for materiality ($40,000) has been determined, the auditor should *allocate* the threshold to the various accounts that would be affected by errors in the financial statements. Balance sheet accounts are generally used for this purpose. But what amount should be allocated to each account? SAS 47 (AU 312) gives no guidance in this respect. The allocation must be done judgmentally. One possibility might be to assign the same percentage of the total materiality threshold to each account as that account bears to the total of all accounts. For example, cash would receive the following allocation for 19X1:

$$38/9,092 \times \$40,000 = \$167$$

Logically, however, other factors may affect the decision and may cause more or less than a proportionate share of the total to be allocated to a particular account. Such factors include the nature of the particular account and its susceptibility to error, or the relative size of the account. For example, inventories for JEP would be both highly susceptible to error and relatively material in size (about 10 percent of the total accounts). Thus, inventories might receive a *less-than proportionate* share of the total $40,000 materiality threshold (say 8 percent). Notice that lowering the proportionate allocation for inventories from $4,000 (10 percent of $40,000) to $3,200 (8 percent of $40,000) causes the auditor to acknowledge the importance of inventories, and to spend more time and effort auditing that account accordingly.

A similar approach would be used to decide the allocation of total materiality to all other accounts on the balance sheet. As explained in the chapter, more or less might be allocated to the overstatement or understatement of an account balance, depending on the relative risks associated with those particular misstatements.

Total Audit Risk

As stated in the chapter, it should be the objective of the typical audit engagement to control total audit risk (*RT*) at a *reasonably low level*. Auditing standards do not require that the level of audit risk be quantified (say at .01 or .05). However, so that we may provide a mathematically tractable illustration, let us assume that it has been decided by the engagement partner to control the total risk of issuance of an inappropriately unqualified audit opinion (*RT*) at .01. Since total confidence in the overall fairness of presentation (*C*) is the mathematical complement of *RT*, the audit partner is implying that he desires 99 percent confidence that the unqualified audit report is, in fact, accompanying financial statements that are free from material misstatement.

If the auditor were to specify an *RT* level of .05, it would imply that the auditor was willing to accept a higher level of risk and thus a lower confidence in the audit opinion. The important thing to remember is that *RT* must be subjectively set by persons who are in supervisory roles on the audit. In addition, there is an *inverse relationship between the level of audit risk specified and the amount of audit effort required to support the opinion*. In specifying an overall *RT* of .01, for example, the auditor would be required to (1) perform more effective audit procedures (2) at or near the end of the fiscal year as opposed to interim dates, and (3) to use larger sample sizes than would be the case of an overall *RT* of .05 had been specified. The auditor must be prepared to support his or her judgment regarding the selection level for *RT*, in light of the circumstances surrounding the engagement. For example, if past extensive audit experience with the client has produced few or no errors or irregularities in the financial statement assertions, the auditor might be satisfied in selecting a higher *RT* than would otherwise have been necessary.

Allocation of *RT* to Individual Account Balances.
The audit risk model is stated as follows:

$$RT = IR \times IC \times DR$$

where *IR* is inherent risk, *IC* is internal control risk, and *DR* is detection risk.

See the chapter for a full explanation of each of these terms.

The audit risk model must be applied at the *individual account balance* level to be operational. In other words, it is not enough merely to set overall *RT* at a level of .01. To operationalize the model, RT must be allocated between the material accounts in the financial statements (cash, marketable securities, accounts receivable, inventories, various liability accounts, etc.). Professional standards give no guidance as to just how this might be done. Once again, the process requires the application of subjective seasoned judgment by the experienced auditor.

One way to allocate RT to individual accounts is to assign the same level to each account balance that is set for the financial statements taken as a whole. Thus, each account balance would have an RT of .01 in our example. On the other hand, it is probably logical for the auditor to base RT for a particular account balance on two factors: materiality of the account and relative risk of misstatement. Accounts that are more material and/or characterized by a higher risk of misstatement (such as cash, inventories, accounts receivable) might receive a .01 level of RT. Accounts that are less material and/or characterized by a lower risk of misstatement (such as prepaid insurance or other assets) might receive a .10 level of RT.

Inherent Risk, Control Risk, and Detection Risk. As explained in the chapter, each account balance must be evaluated in terms of inherent risk (IR) and control risk (IC), so that the proper level of detection risk (DR) may thus be determined. That level of detection risk will then be used in combination with the auditor's planned materiality threshold for the particular account to determine the nature, timing, and extent of the audit evidence that is necessary to reach a conclusion as to the fairness of presentation of the assertions embodied in that balance.

Global factors that influence inherent risk for all accounts include the nature of the industry and business of the client, its past history of errors and irregularities, the integrity of the client, the existence of related-party transactions, and the existence of litigation, to name a few. The auditor learns of these things by *properly planning the audit engagement*. Planning the engagement is the subject of Chapter 7. However, our example for JEP Manufacturing Company gives us a few, if somewhat sketchy, hints as to global factors. The company is a small business engaged in competition with a few very large companies. It has only a few major customers. These factors provide support for setting overall IR at a very high level.

At the individual account balance level, the relative risk of misstatement of a particular account helps to determine its individual IR level. For example, cash, marketable securities and accounts receivable might receive high levels of IR because of their relatively high risk of misstatement. On the other hand, property and equipment or long-term debt might receive relatively low levels of IR because of their relatively low risk of misstatement. For the cash account, which we shall use as an illustration, we may say that, because of the environmental conditions surrounding the company and because of the high inherent risk of misstatement for cash, the inherent risk for that account must be set at its highest level (1.0).

Control risk must also be assessed at the individual account balance level. A sufficient understanding of the control structure of the client must be obtained to perform this assessment. An understanding of the control structure requires the auditor to obtain knowledge of the control environment, the accounting system, and control procedures included in each of these elements of the control structure. That understanding must be obtained on a financial statement assertion-by-assertion basis. For example, the financial statement assertions (discussed in the chapter) for cash would include existence/occurrence, completeness, ownership rights/obligations, valuation, and presentation/disclosure. The control environment and accounting system each might include procedures that are designed to prevent, detect, or correct specific errors or irregularities involving each of these assertions. The auditor must first obtain and document a preliminary understanding of these controls. After that preliminary understanding is reached, the auditor must form a preliminary assessment of control risk for each financial statement assertion. That assessment is made, like all other risk assessments, subjectively, and is based entirely on the seasoned judgment of the auditor. If the auditor concludes that control risk for a particular assertion might be assessed at a still lower level than the preliminary level, further review of the controls and tests of the controls would be necessary. A final assessment is then made for *IC* for those controls. Let us presume that, for purposes of our illustration, we have obtained a preliminary understanding of control risk for all assertions pertaining to cash, and that it is .20.

After an assessment of *IR* and *IC* have been formed for each account balance (and for each financial statement assertion in the case of controls) the auditor is then in a position to determine *DR* and the resultant nature, timing, and extent of tests. For example, in our illustration for the cash account of JEP Manufacturing Company, the determination of the level of *DR* for the cash account is as follows:

$$RT = .01; \quad IR = 1.0; \quad IC = .20$$
$$DR = RT / (IR \times IC) = .01 / (1.0 \times .20) = .05$$

Applying the reasoning of Figure 5–5, an overall *DR* level of .05 for the cash account, plus an allocated $167 materiality threshold from the previous section, implies that detection risk procedures should consist of effective tests of transactions or balances, focused at or near the end of the fiscal year, using sample sizes that are relatively large.

A similar pattern of reasoning should be applied in planning the nature, timing, and extent of the tests for each of the other material accounts in the financial statements.

Notes

1. Statement on Auditing Standards (SAS) 1, Section 326.03 (New York: AICPA, 1980).
2. Ibid., Section 326.20.
3. Ibid., Section 326.19.

4. R. K. Mautz and H. A. Sharaf, *The Philosophy of Auditing* (Sarasota, Fla.: American Accounting Association, 1961), Chapter 5.

Questions for Class Discussion

Q5-1   What is the process by which the financial statement audit takes place?

Q5-2   Why is it necessary to *disaggregate* the financial statements before beginning the audit?

Q5-3   What is audit evidence? What is its relationship to the audit?

Q5-4   What is meant by *sufficiency* as the term pertains to audit evidence?

Q5-5   What is meant by *competency* as the term pertains to audit evidence?

Q5-6   How can the nature of an item influence the auditor's judgment regarding the sufficiency of evidence?

Q5-7   Why is an auditor often willing to accept evidence that is *persuasive* rather than absolutely convincing?

Q5-8   What are the costs of overauditing and underauditing?

Q5-9   What criteria can the auditor apply in determining whether or not sufficient evidence has been gathered during the audit process?

Q5-10   What is meant by *validity* and *relevance* in determining whether evidence is competent?

Q5-11   What does the term *objectivity* mean when applied to audit evidence?

Q5-12   What is the relationship between the *financial statement assertions* and the audit evidence-gathering process?

Q5-13   What are the meanings of these terms: (a) presentation and disclosure; (b) completeness; (c) rights and obligations; (d) existence or occurrence; and (e) valuation or allocation?

Q5-14   What kind of evidence does the auditor examine when the assertion to be verified is *existence*?

Q5-15   What evidence is generally gathered in support of the financial statement assertion of *completeness*?

Q5-16   If you were verifying *ownership rights* for property and equipment, what kind of evidence would you look for?

Q5-17   If you were verifying proper *valuation* for accounts receivable, what kind of evidence would you obtain?

Q5-18   If the financial statement assertion to be verified is *proper disclosure* for long-term debt, what evidence would you obtain?

Q5-19   What is meant by the term *underlying accounting data*? How does it relate to *corroborating evidential matter*?

Q5-20   What are the general criteria for determining the competency of documentary evidence?

Q5-21   What is the relationship between the quality of the system of internal control and evidence? Why must *control risk* be assessed on the audit?

Q5-22   What is the meaning of the term *audit risk*?

Q5-23   What are the component parts of audit risk? Which ones are controllable by the auditor? Which ones are uncontrollable? Why?

Q5-24   What are the factors that influence *inherent risk*?

Q5-25   How does the auditor's assessment of audit risk affect the nature, timing, and extent of substantive tests?

Q5-26   What is the meaning of the term *materiality* as applied to auditing? Why is it important that materiality be estimated as part of planning?

Q5-27   What are the factors that should be considered by the auditor in determining planning materiality?

Q5-28   Why must materiality be considered in the later stages of the audit?

Short Cases

C5-1   During an in-house professional training seminar, a newly employed staff accountant expresses the opinion that the accounting profession should establish specific criteria defining the amount of evidence that should be gathered prior to expressing an opinion as to the fairness of the financial statements. He states that, without such criteria, no two auditing firms would be likely to insist on the same amount of evidence in the same audit engagement.

Required: As discussion leader, respond to the staff accountant's comments.

C5-2   James Manzi, a newly employed staff accountant, is working under your direction on an auditing engagement. He has observed from the audit program that the evidence gathered in examining purchase invoices is looked on as being more competent than the evidence produced by examining sales invoices. He maintains that since each of these documents reflects quantities of goods, prices, and dollar amounts, they should be equally competent.

Required: Explain to your staff accountant why the auditor places greater confidence in the purchase invoice evidence than in the sales invoice evidence.

C5-3   In course of an audit, a valuation error in the amount of $10,000 is discovered during the examination of inventory. Total inventory is valued at approximately $1 million. The staff accountant discovering the error suggests that since the error amounts to only 1 percent of total inventory it can be ignored as being immaterial.

Required: Evaluate the position taken by the staff accountant.

C5-4   Beverly Grillo, a staff accountant working under your supervision, has been charged with the responsibility of reconciling the balance in the cash ledger account with the bank balance. After working with the data for some time, she reports that she is unable to completely reconcile the two balances but that the difference is small and, therefore, in her judgment not material to the audit.

Required: What position would you take in responding to the staff accountant?

C5-5   Russell Green, a staff accountant serving as a member of your audit team, observes that the audit program calls for the internal control structure to be reviewed and for the application of extensive tests of controls to verify that the system is functioning as designed. He observes that the audit program also calls for substantive tests of account balances and transactions. Russell asks you, as the senior accountant in charge, why the audit team has to perform the substantive tests if they are going to place reliance on the system of internal control to be sure that all transactions are valid and properly recorded.

Required: Respond to the staff accountant.

C5-6   In the course of an audit examination, an independent auditor gives serious consideration to the concept of materiality. This concept is inherent in the work of the independent auditor and is important for planning, preparing, and modifying audit programs. The concept of materiality underlies the application of all the generally accepted auditing standards, particularly the standards of field work and reporting.

Required:
a. Briefly describe what is meant by the independent auditor's concept of *materiality*.
b. What are some common relationships and other considerations used by the auditor in judging materiality?
c. Identify how the planning and execution of an audit program might be affected by the independent auditor's concept of materiality.   *(AICPA adapted)*

C5-7   Draco Manufacturing Company is a small, closely held corporation. Allen Mesco, President, is a 90-percent shareholder in the corporation and has obtained sizable loans from the corporation over the past three years. The corporation employs only a single bookkeeper, who, along with Mesco, runs the office and makes daily trips to the bank with deposits. Mesco's policy is that he alone opens the daily mail and then forwards all checks to the bookkeeper for posting and later deposit.

Draco has been the target of several lawsuits by competitors alleging patent infringement. Mesco contends that the lawsuits are completely without merit, after receiving advice from his attorney.

It has become necessary for Draco to obtain a bank loan. The loan officer has insisted that Draco present audited financial statements along with its loan application.

Required: The auditor's substantive tests can be conceived as having three basic properties: nature, timing, and extent. The auditor is required to select a mixture of tests based on his or her assessment of inherent risk and internal controls. By nature, those tests can vary from analytical review to tests of details. The timing of the tests may be at an interim date or at year end. The extent of the tests may vary from small to large sample sizes.
a. On a scale of 0 (least) to 1.0 (greatest), what level of inherent risk would you assign to Draco Corporation? Why?
b. How will your assessment in (a) affect the nature, timing, and extent of your planned substantive auditing procedures?

Problems

P5-1 Select the best answer for each of the following items.

a. The sequence of steps in gathering evidence as the basis of the auditor's opinion is
1. Substantive tests, control risk assessment, and conclusions.
2. Control risk assessment, substantive tests, and conclusions.
3. Control risk assessment, conclusions, and substantive tests.
4. Conclusions, control risk assessment, and substantive tests.

b. In connection with the third generally accepted auditing standard of field work, an auditor examines corroborating evidential matter that includes all of the following *except*
1. Client accounting manuals.
2. Written client representations.
3. Vendor invoices.
4. Minutes of board meetings.

c. Evidential matter supporting the financial statements consists of the underlying accounting data and all corroborating information available to the auditor. Which of the following is an example of corroborating information?
1. Minutes of meetings.
2. General and subsidiary ledgers.
3. Accounting manuals.
4. Work sheets supporting cost allocations.

d. Each of the following might, in itself, form a valid basis for an auditor to decide to omit a test *except* the
1. Relative risk involved.
2. Relationship between the cost of obtaining evidence and its usefulness.
3. Difficulty and expense involved in testing a particular item.
4. Degree of reliance on the relevant internal controls.

e. The risk that an auditor's procedures will lead to the conclusion that a material error does *not* exist in an account balance when, in fact, such error does exist is referred to as
1. Audit risk.
2. Inherent risk.
3. Control risk.
4. Detection risk.   *(AICPA adapted)*

P5-2 Select the best answer for each of the following items.

a. Which of the following types of documentary evidence should the auditor consider the most reliable?
1. A sales invoice issued by the client and supported by a delivery receipt from an outside trucker.
2. Confirmation of an account payable balance mailed by and returned directly to the auditor.
3. A check issued by the company and bearing the payee's endorsement, which is included with the bank statement mailed directly to the auditor.
4. A working paper prepared by the client's controller and reviewed by the client's treasurer.

b. The sufficiency and competency of evidential matter ultimately is based on the
   1. Availability of corroborating data.
   2. Generally accepted auditing standards.
   3. Pertinence of the evidence.
   4. Judgment of the auditor.
c. To be competent, evidence must be both
   1. Timely and substantial.
   2. Reliable and documented.
   3. Valid and relevant.
   4. Useful and objective.
d. Most of the independent auditor's work in formulating an opinion on financial statements consists of
   1. Studying and evaluating internal controls.
   2. Obtaining and examining evidential matter.
   3. Examining cash transactions.
   4. Comparing recorded accountability with assets.
e. Although the validity of evidential matter depends on the circumstances under which it is obtained, three general presumptions have some usefulness. The situations given below indicate the relative reliability a CPA has placed on two types of evidence obtained in different situations. Which of these is an *exception* to one of the general presumptions?
   1. The CPA places more reliance on the balance in the scrap sales account at plant A, where the CPA has made limited tests of transactions because of good internal control, than at point B, where the CPA has made extensive tests of transactions because of poor internal control.
   2. The CPA places more reliance on the CPA's computation of interest payable on outstanding bonds than on the amount confirmed by the trustee.
   3. The CPA places more reliance on the report of an expert on an inventory of precious gems than on the CPA's physical observation of the gems.
   4. The CPA places more reliance on a schedule of insurance coverage obtained from the company's insurance agent than on one prepared by the internal audit staff.
f. Failure to detect material dollar errors in the financial statements is a risk the auditor primarily mitigates by
   1. Performing substantive tests.
   2. Performing compliance tests.
   3. Evaluating internal control.
   4. Obtaining a client representation letter.
g. The following statements were made in a discussion of audit evidence between two CPAs. Which statement concerning evidential matter is not valid?
   1. "I am seldom convinced beyond all doubt with respect to all aspects of the statements being examined."
   2. "I would not undertake that procedure because at best the results would only be persuasive and I'm looking for convincing evidence."
   3. "I evaluate the degree of risk involved in deciding the kind of evidence I will gather."
   4. "I evaluate the usefulness of the evidence I can obtain against the cost of obtaining it." *(AICPA adapted)*

P5-3 Audit risk and materiality should be considered when planning and performing an examination of financial statements in accordance with generally accepted auditing standards. Audit risk and materiality should also be considered together in determining the nature, timing, and extent of auditing procedures and in evaluating the results of those procedures.

Required:

a. 1. Define audit risk.
    2. Describe its components of inherent risk, control risk, and detection risk.
    3. Explain how these components are interrelated.

b. 1. Define materiality.
    2. Discuss the factors affecting its determination.
    3. Describe the relationship between materiality for planning purposes and materiality for evaluation purposes.
                                                        (AICPA adapted)

P5-4 The types of documentary evidence typically obtained by auditors are

a. Bank statements.
b. Confirmation of accounts receivable.
c. Subsidiary accounts receivable ledgers.
d. Minutes of board of directors' and stockholders' meetings.
e. Shipping documents (bills of lading).
f. Cancelled checks.
g. Documents of title for building, land, and other assets.
h. Attorney's letter.
i. Client representation letter.
j. Employment contracts for key executives.
k. Signed W-4 copies from employees.
l. Signed lease agreements.
m. Purchase orders.
n. Payroll time cards.
o. Receiving reports for goods received.
p. Notes payable confirmation.
q. Insurance policies, in force.
r. Remittance advices.
s. Payroll records for gross pay, withholding, etc.

Required:

a. List each of the preceding documents according to
    1. Point of origination.
    2. Where transmitted (to auditor, to client) or held.

b. Classify each of the documents in order of competence. Use the following ordering system:
    1. Very competent (V).
    2. Somewhat competent (SC).
    3. Less competent (L).

c. What criteria should be used for classifying documentary evidence in order of its competence?

P5-5 The third generally accepted auditing standard of field work requires that the auditor obtain sufficient competent evidential matter to afford a reasonable basis for an opinion regarding the financial statements under examination. In considering what constitutes sufficient competent evidential matter, a distinction should be made between underlying accounting data and all other corroborating information available.

Required:
a. Discuss what is generally meant by *underlying accounting data*. Give examples.
b. Discuss what is generally meant by *corroborating information*. Give examples.
c. Discuss procedures the CPA uses to examine (1) underlying accounting data and (2) corroborating information. *(AICPA adapted)*

P5-6 You are the in-charge accountant on the audit of Newco, Inc., a medium-sized manufacturer of electrical equipment. The condensed balance sheet for Newco, Inc., for the year ended May 31, 19X9, is as follows:

Newco, Inc.

BALANCE SHEET

	May 31, 19X9
Assets	
Cash	$ 15,000
Accounts receivable (net)	143,500
Inventory	550,000
Property and equipment (net)	3,541,500
Total assets	$4,250,000

Liabilities and Stockholders' Equity

Liabilities:		
Notes payable		$ 82,000
Trade accounts payable		60,000
Accrued liabilities		75,000
Long-term debt		840,000
Total liabilities		1,057,000
Stockholders' Equity:		
Common Stock		100,000
Retained Earnings:		
Balance, May 31, 19X8	$2,020,000	
Net income for year 19X9	1,573,000	
Dividend, May 31, 19X9	(500,000)	
Balance, May 31, 19X9		3,093,000
Total liabilities and stockholders' equity		$4,250,000

You have determined that the primary users of the financial statements will be the shareholders as well as a large bank from which the company wishes to borrow $1,000,000 to finance a new building.

Required:
a. Determine an aggregate materiality threshold (both overstatement and understatement) for the company's financial statement audit for the year ended May 31, 19X9. Justify your judgment.

b. Allocate the aggregate materiality threshold that you determined in part (a) to the balance sheet accounts of Newco, thus determining maximum tolerable error for each account balance. Include an allocation of both overstatements and understatements to each account. Justify your allocation.

c. [Unrelated to parts (a) and (b)] Assume that maximum tolerable errors for overstatement and understatement were allocated to accounts as stated in the two left-most columns of the table below, and that, after the audit of the financial statements, known and estimated errors were as stated in the two right-most columns. Which accounts would you bring to the attention of management for a recommended adjustment? Why? What additional information would have to be obtained before these accounts could be adjusted?

| | Maximum tolerable error | | Known and likely error | |
	Overstatement	Understatement	Overstatement	Understatement
Cash	$ 1,000	$ 1,000	-0-	-0-
Accounts receivable	2,000	4,000	5,000	2,000
Inventory	5,000	8,000	10,000	15,000
Property and equipment	30,000	42,000	15,000	20,000

CHAPTER 6

Audit Objectives and Procedures

Objectives

☐ **1.** Develop audit objectives as a natural extension of the client's financial statement assertions.
☐ **2.** Describe the details of the evidence-gathering process.
☐ **3.** Write a simple audit program that takes into account the proper nature, timing, and extent of detection risk procedures, given a certain set of audit objectives.
☐ **4.** Document the evidence-gathering process in working papers.

In the last chapter, we introduced the concept of evidence and briefly explained the process of audit evidence gathering. As illustrated by the highlighted sections in the diagram on the following page, in this chapter, we continue that discussion in greater detail by developing a uniform set of audit objectives over various systems and account balances. We then discuss the nature, timing, and extent of the audit procedures that will satisfy those audit objectives.

An appendix to this chapter illustrates the process of evidence-gathering for the cash-in-banks account and includes a simple audit program for the cash account.

Audit Objectives

☑ **Objective 1**
Develop audit objectives

Since the audit examination consists of gathering evidence regarding economic assertions, we may say that the operating objective of the auditor is to *verify* the financial statement assertions of management, which were listed in Chapter 5. This task is accomplished by conducting *auditing procedures* on the underlying accounting data and other corroborating financial data that support those assertions. Auditing procedures are set forth in a document called the *audit program*. But how does the auditor select the appropriate procedures to demonstrate that the audit has been conducted in accordance with generally accepted auditing standards? **Audit objectives** bridge the gap between the client's financial statement assertions and the procedures that are performed to verify those assertions. We typically identify seven audit objectives, some or all of which must be met in verifying each account and related disclosure in the financial statements.

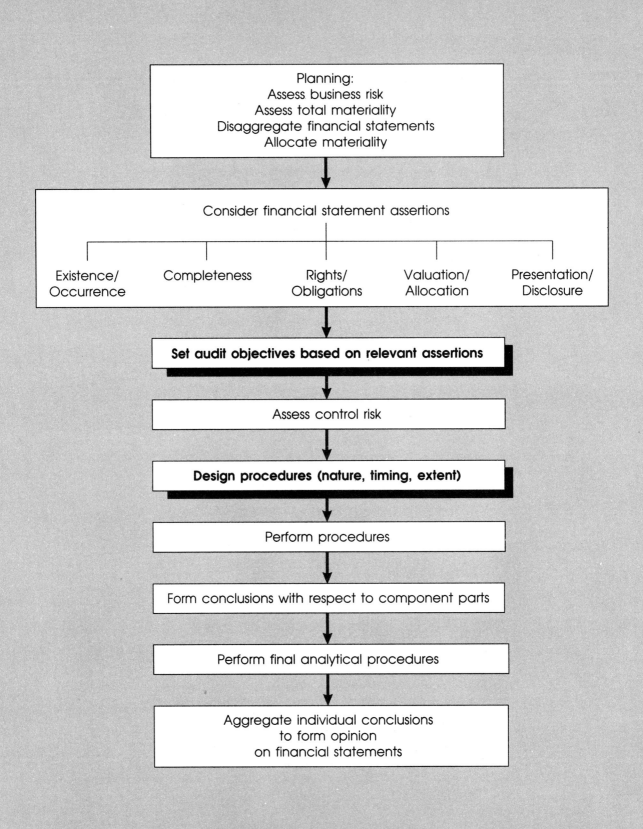

1. Existence.
2. Transaction validity.
3. Ownership/obligation.
4. Valuation.
5. Cutoff.
6. Statement presentation (disclosure).
7. Internal control.

You should notice that, except for one or two significant differences, these audit objectives are almost identical to, and indeed are based mostly on, the financial statement assertions of management. There are two reasons for differences between financial statement assertions and audit objectives. First, management's assertions are not always those of the auditor. The assertions of management regarding existence, completeness, rights and obligations, valuation, allocation, and presentation and disclosure are subject to the verification of the independent auditor. Second, and more important, the auditor's objectives include adherence to the second standard of audit field work, which requires the auditor to take into account, in the selection of auditing procedures, the quality of the client's internal control structure. We consider the effects of the internal control structure on the evidence-gathering process in Chapter 8.

Figure 6–1 shows the relationship between financial statement assertions of management and audit objectives.

Existence

Verification of *existence* is an audit objective for all asset, liability, and owners' equity accounts. The auditor's primary responsibility with respect to asset and equity accounts is to ascertain that the recorded assets and equity capital claims actually exist. Procedures to verify existence depend on the nature of the item and the cost effectiveness of obtaining the evidence.

Figure 6–1

Relationship of Financial Statement Assertions to Audit Objectives

Financial statement assertion	Audit objective*
Existence	Existence
Occurrence	Transaction validity
Rights and obligations	Ownership and obligation
Valuation	Valuation
Allocation; completeness	Cutoff
Presentation (disclosure)	Statement presentation

*In meeting all audit objectives, the auditor takes into account the client's system of internal controls.

Transaction Validity (Occurrence)

The *transaction validity* objective requires the auditor to verify the client's assertion that all transactions recorded during the period *occurred*, and that they are valid reflections of the changes in the company's resources and obligations dur-
The *transaction validity* objective requires the auditor to verify the client's assertion that all transactions recorded during the period *occurred*, and that they are valid reflections of the changes in the company's resources and obligations during the period. Verification of transaction validity requires the auditor to ascertain that *proper documentary support* exists to validate the transactions creating the various account balances. The extent of documentary support required varies with the nature of the client and the transaction, but it is appropriate to observe at this point that some documentary support should exist for all transactions, to enhance their validity. This audit objective applies to all elements of the account balances arising as the result of business transactions.

Ownership

Ownership must be verified for many *assets*. Although possession may be accepted as evidence for ownership of some assets, the auditor must take further steps in ascertaining that many of the recorded assets are in fact owned by the client. The procedure most often used for satisfying this objective is examination of documents evidencing the transfer of title or the current holding of title. For example, deeds can be examined to verify the ownership of real property. Sales contracts, on the other hand, will typically be examined to verify the ownership of inventory. Lease contracts provide the best verification of ownership in the case of assets secured through financing leases. For property belonging to others and leased by the client, the auditor should ascertain that payments for the use of property belonging to others are properly expensed rather than capitalized. For example, payment for the use of noncapitalized (operating) lease property should be properly reflected in the accounts as periodic charges to expense.

With respect to *liabilities*, the ownership objective may be interpreted as establishing that a *bona fide obligation* exists for all recorded liabilities. For example, the auditor should perform tests to ascertain that recorded notes payable represent claims of bona fide creditors. This is normally accomplished by the confirmation with those creditors of all pertinent details of such obligations.

Valuation

Ascertaining appropriate *valuation* is a particularly important audit objective for noncash accounts. Typically, assets are valued at unamortized cost, historical cost, or the lower of historical cost or market value to meet the requirements of GAAP. Recent pronouncements have also mandated the disclosure of price-level—adjusted historical costs, as well as current costs for inventories, property, and equipment of large companies. Historical costs may be verified by examining documentary evidence, such as contracts and vendors' invoices. Market values for marketable securities can be verified by reference to daily prices published in the financial press. Market values of assets such as obsolete inventory, on the other hand, can best be verified be independent appraisals. For the most part, liabilities should be valued at the number of dollars required to liquidate them at the balance sheet date. This audit objective must be met for all non-cash items.

Cutoff

The *cutoff* objective involves verifying the client's assertion that revenues and costs have been completely and properly allocated among the appropriate accounting periods. This requires the auditor to verify that all transactions occurring before the end of an accounting period have been completely recorded as part of that period's activity. Similarly, the auditor must verify that transactions belonging to the next accounting period have not been included in the activity of the period under audit. This objective is often met by examining serially numbered documents around the year end and tracing those documents to the records of the appropriate period. Recalculations of amounts such as depreciation, amortization, and various accruals of income and expenses are also procedures performed in fulfilling the cutoff objective. This audit objective must be met for all elements of the financial statements but is much more important for some items than it is for others.

Statement Presentation (Disclosure)

In meeting the *statement presentation (disclosure) objective*, the auditor is concerned with whether particular components of the financial statements are properly classified, described, and disclosed in accordance with generally accepted accounting principles. For example, in showing accounts receivable on its balance sheet, management is asserting that the accounts are entirely from trade creditors and that a proper allowance has been provided for doubtful accounts. Similarly, management asserts that obligations classified as short-term liabilities in the balance sheet will mature within one year. The auditor must then carry out procedures designed to verify those assertions. Disclosures may be included either in the body of the financial statements or in the footnotes, as appropriate. The *statement presentation objective must be met for all material elements of the financial statements*.

The Process for Detection-Risk Procedures

☑ **Objective 2**
Describe the details of the evidence-gathering process

The audit is a process. In Figure 5–2 we illustrated the various elements of that process, from its planning stages to its completion. We now focus on the detection-risk procedures stage of the audit. At the individual account balance level, the evidence-gathering process consists of the following steps:

1. Identification of the audit objectives that verify relevant financial statement assertions.
2. Establishment of the nature, timing, and extent of auditing procedures to obtain the evidence required to meet the objectives, which requires consideration of
   a. The inherent risk of misstatement of the particular financial statement assertion and
   b. Control risk for the particular financial statement assertion.
3. Gathering the evidence.
4. Performing the auditing procedures.
5. Evaluating the evidence obtained in terms of its sufficiency and competency.
6. Developing a logical conclusion about the audited system or balance, in view of the evidence obtained.

The auditor usually gathers evidence by performing audit tests or sampling. **Sampling** is defined in SAS 39 (AU350) as the application of an auditing procedure to less than 100 percent of the items within an account balance or class for the purpose of evaluating some characteristic of the balance or class.

Sometimes in gathering evidence, sampling is not necessary. For example, when a material account balance (such as property and equipment) consists of only a few transactions (acquisitions and retirements), it may be cost-effective to apply an auditing procedure to 100 percent of the transactions. However, the auditor is more often faced with accounts (such as accounts receivable or sales) that consist of thousands of individual transactions and supporting documents. In such cases the only cost-effective way to gather sufficient competent evidence in support of audit objectives is by sampling.

Notice that sampling is performed to estimate some *characteristic* of the account balance or class. The characteristic to be estimated is, in turn, a function of the particular audit objective. If, for example, the audit objective is related to the internal control structure, the characteristic to be estimated is existence of *specific internal controls*, which is determined by performing tests of controls. We will discuss tests of controls in detail in Chapter 8.

On the other hand, if the audit objective is related to the verification of an account balance or specific financial statement assertion, the test performed will be a *substantive test*. Some audit tests are **dual-purpose tests**, not only of specific internal controls but also of the dollar amount of the account balance. This type of test is often desirable because it is more cost-effective than performing separate tests of controls and dollar amounts.

Figure 6–2 relates audit objectives to auditing procedures, including tests of controls, substantive, and dual-purpose tests, by type of evidence. The specific procedures associated with sampling are covered at length in Chapters 11 and 12.

Types of Substantive Tests

As shown in Figure 6–2, substantive tests can generally be categorized as either *analytical procedures* or *tests of details*. Analytical procedures are designed to test the *reasonableness* of financial disclosures in the light of the surrounding business

Figure 6–2

Relating Audit Objectives to Auditing Procedures by Type of Evidence

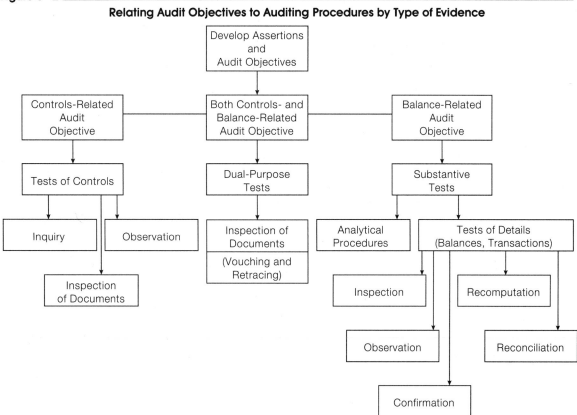

Source: Adapted from Deloitte & Touche. Printed with permission.

environment and other client-specific facts. Analytical procedures range from simple comparisons to the use of complex mathematical models involving the many relationships that might exist among financial and nonfinancial data. The basic premise underlying analytical procedures is that *plausible relationships* may be expected to exist among data. Some of the most obvious interrelationships among recorded data include the following:

- Comparisons of financial information of the current period with comparable information from prior periods.
- Comparisons of achieved results with anticipated results contained in documents such as budgets or forecasts.
- Relationships among elements of financial information within the period (for example, sales and commissions expense).
- Comparisons of company data with those from the industry in which the client operates (for example, gross margins).
- Comparisons of financial information with related nonfinancial information (for example, sales with sales orders).[1]

Because of their cost-effectiveness, analytical procedures are becoming a prominent part of all audits. They are used during the planning stages of the audit to identify areas of high audit risk, so that those areas may be the focus of more concentrated audit effort. Analytical procedures are also used during the audit and at the conclusion of the audit to corroborate the evidence obtained from more detailed tests. We will discuss analytical procedures in greater detail in Chapters 7 and 20.

In contrast to analytical procedures, **tests of details** are designed to detect specific misstatements in account balances that comprise the financial statements. These tests can be further categorized into two subclassifications: (1) **tests of balances** and (2) **tests of transactions**. *Tests of balances* are direct tests of details that make up the ending balances that appear in the financial statements. An example of tests of balances is the confirmation of individual customer accounts that comprise the ending balance of accounts receivable to determine the existence and proper valuation of those accounts. Another example is the observation of raw materials, work in process, and finished goods inventories as of the balance sheet date to determine that they exist.

Tests of transactions consist of an examination of the documents that support the debit and credit entries to various accounts. In the accounts receivable example cited in the previous paragraph, a test of transactions that would corroborate the evidence provided by confirmation would be the examination of a sample of sales invoices and shipping documents that support the debits to individual customers' accounts, as well as the deposit slips that support the credits to the same accounts. In the case of accounts receivable, such tests of transactions often provide support for the audit objectives of existence and proper valuation whenever it is impossible or impracticable to confirm ending customer-account balances.

To verify the financial statement assertions for a specific account balance or class of transactions, the auditor is generally free to select any combination of analytical procedures, tests of balances, and tests of transactions that he or she feels is necessary and sufficient to satisfy the audit objectives.

Direction of Tests

When substantive tests are performed, it is important to define the *direction* toward which tests should be oriented. We may, for example, test financial statement balances for both *overstatement* and *understatement*. Directly testing every balance for both possibilities, however, is inefficient and unnecessary. By deciding in advance the audit objective to be accomplished, we can establish a testing direction of *primary concern*—overstatement or understatement. Because of the self-balancing feature of the financial statements, a direct test of selected entries in one account balance results in an indirect (corollary) test of the offsetting entries in one or more other accounts.

In Figure 6–3 we show how various tests for overstatement and understatement errors in each of four types of accounts (assets, liabilities, revenues, expenses) are related to offsetting tests for errors in one of the other accounts.

Figure 6–3

Audit Test Matrix

Primary (direct) test		Resulting (corollary) test			
(Audit population)		Assets	Liabilities	Revenues	Expenses
Assets	O	U	O	O	U
Liabilities	U	U	O	O	U
Revenues	U	U	O	O	U
Expenses	O	U	O	O	U

Note: O = overstatement; U = understatement.
Source: Deloitte & Touche. Printed with permission.

Primary (direct) tests that are designed primarily to detect errors in audit populations are shown in the left-hand column and should also indirectly discover the related offsetting errors shown in the audit populations in the other four columns. These and other predictable relationships associated with the double-entry system make *the performance of an audit somewhat like putting together a jigsaw puzzle.* In both instances, all the pieces must fit together.

The following example illustrates how the analysis shown in Figure 6–3 can be used. Assume we suspect that accounts receivable may be overstated because of fictitious or erroneous charges. By reference to the analysis, we can conclude that the offsetting credits will cause one of four other errors:

1. Understatement of another asset (such as cash).
2. Overstatement of a liability account (such as customer deposits).
3. Overstatement of a revenue account (such as sales).
4. Understatement of an expense account (such as bad debts expense).

By confirming individual accounts receivable and by **vouching** items from the accounts-receivable accounts to source documents, we should simultaneously discover both the error in the accounts receivable and the offsetting error in the other accounts.

To be overstated, accounts must include either fictitious amounts or overstatement of amounts that actually exist. If, for example, accounts receivable are overstated, some individual customer accounts may include amounts that do not represent valid claims against them. As shown in Figure 6–4, to test for such an overstatement, it is generally best to begin with the recorded balance in the general (and subsidiary) ledger and to obtain evidence in support of the recorded amounts. This can be done by (a) direct confirmation of amounts owed by individual customers; (b) examining collections in the client's cash receipts records of the period following the balance sheet date; or (c) inspecting underlying documents, such as sales invoices and shipping tickets, to ascertain that the original sales were properly recorded. The important thing to note here is that the direction of the tests for overstatement is typically *from the recorded amount back to the supporting evidence.* When documents are involved, we call this process *vouching.*

Figure 6–4

The Audit Trail, Showing the Relationship between Vouching and Retracing

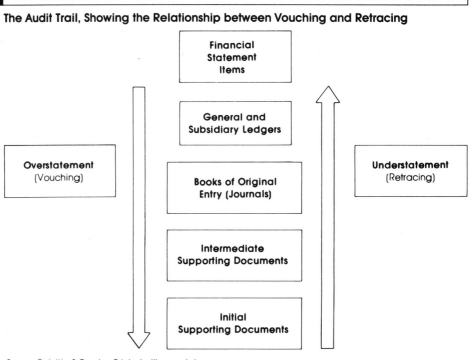

Source: Deloitte & Touche. Printed with permission.

On the other hand, tests for understatement cannot begin with the recorded amount because the objective in this case is to see that all existing items were actually recorded in the accounting records. For example, if accounts payable are understated, confirmation of recorded payables will not generally reveal the understatement. Therefore, we should begin with the *source documents supporting payables*, such as vendor invoices and receiving reports, and *follow them through to ascertain that they were properly recorded*. We call this process **retracing (or tracing)**.

Relating Audit Objectives to Auditing Procedures

☑ **Objective 3**
Write an audit program

Audit procedures are acts performed by the auditor to satisfy audit objectives. The third standard of audit field work lists four basic procedures by which evidence is gathered:

1. Inspection.
2. Observation.
3. Confirmation.
4. Inquiry.

The auditor also uses other procedures to supplement those listed in the field work standard. The supplemental procedures include

- Recomputation
- Reconciliation
- Analytical procedures (discussed in the previous section)

Procedures are always shown in written form in the audit program, and their results are documented in the audit working papers.

In gathering evidence we must always be concerned with two questions: (1) What things need to be investigated? (2) Which procedures produce the most competent evidence? The answer to both of these questions depends on two things: (1) the auditor's objective and (2) whether the tests are meant to verify a particular control practice (test of controls), a monetary transaction or balance (substantive test), or a combination of those two types of tests (a dual-purpose test). In this section, we explain the evidence-gathering procedures just listed and relate them to the questions raised in this paragraph.

Inspection

Like other evidence-gathering techniques, *inspection* can take various forms. For example, facilities of the client can be inspected to determine that they exist. Inventories can be inspected for physical condition to help determine their proper valuation. However, inspection is most often used in connection with documentary evidence.

As shown in Figure 5-4, competency of documentary evidence is a function of (1) point of origination of the document and (2) the party to whom the document is transmitted. Thus, externally generated documents (vendor invoices, bank statements, confirmations, etc.) are considered more competent than internally generated documents (sales invoices, receiving reports, etc.).

Observation

Observation is probably the most direct way of obtaining audit evidence. Almost any tangible phenomenon pertaining to the client may be observed. This auditing procedure is often used in meeting the audit objectives of transaction validity (internal control) and existence. Observations are made by comparing the observed phenomena with the client's records. For example, in testing of controls, the auditor observes whether the client's established and documented control procedures are actually being implemented. In substantive testing, the auditor observes many of the client's tangible assets to ascertain whether they exist and whether they correspond with the records of them. Similarly, cash and marketable securities are counted and compared with client detail records. The auditor observes the client's physical count of inventories and compares selected counts with client detail. The existence of land, buildings, machinery, and equipment can be corroborated through the auditor's observations. If, for example, as part of the preliminary tour of the client's premises, the auditor observes that certain new machinery and equipment is being used, he or she should ascertain that the equipment has been recorded on the books as purchased or leased. If it has been purchased, then the client's records should reflect proper charges to depreciation expense.

It should be noted that even though observation of tangible assets might provide valuable evidence that the assets exist, it will generally be of little or no usefulness in verifying the validity of other client assertions—such as proper valuation, proper cutoff, or validity of the transaction by which the asset was recorded on the books of the company. Other procedures, such as inspection of documents, recalculation of amounts, and inquiry of client personnel, are more useful to verify those assertions. All pertinent audit objectives must be satisfied, of course, before an opinion can be expressed regarding fairness of presentations of an account balance. Rarely, if ever, can the auditor reach a conclusion regarding fairness of a balance after only one audit objective has been met.

Confirmation

One of the most competent types of documentary evidence is provided by the audit **confirmation.** Confirmations are used most commonly to ascertain the existence of cash, accounts or notes receivable, accounts or notes payable, inventories, marketable securities, and capital stock issued and outstanding.

Confirmations vary in format and style according to the type of information needed. Generally, there are two types of audit confirmation requests:

- **Positive confirmation** requests, in which the confirming party is requested to communicate with the auditor regardless of whether the confirming party agrees that the information on the confirmation request is correct; and
- **Negative confirmation** requests, in which the confirming party is requested to communicate with the auditor only if the information supplied in the confirmation request is incorrect.

Typical positive and negative accounts receivable confirmation requests are shown in Figures 6–5 and 6–6, respectively.

Because of the nature of the negative confirmation request, the auditor assumes that an unanswered confirmation is an indication that the item is correctly stated. This is a tenuous assumption, because many confirming parties may simply ignore the confirmation request and never actually compare the information on it with their records. For that reason, negative confirmations are generally used when the auditor is seeking to confirm relatively small items from a relatively large audit population or when internal controls of the client are so effective that there is very little risk of errors or irregularities in the balances being confirmed. For example, negative confirmation requests are often used to confirm small customer demand deposit balances with banks or savings institutions or small customer accounts receivable, which are immaterial when considered individually.

Figure 6-5 ▰▬▬▬▬▬▬▬▬▬▬▬▬▬▬▬▬▬▬▬▬▬▬▬▬▬▬▬▬▬▬▬▬▬▬▬▬▬▬▬

Positive Accounts Receivable Confirmation Request

AUDITOR'S CONFIRMATION OF YOUR ACCOUNT WITH

Our auditors, Touche Ross & Co., are making their regular examination of our financial statements. Part of this examination includes direct verification of customer account balances. PLEASE EXAMINE THE DATA BELOW CAREFULLY AND EITHER CONFIRM ITS ACCURACY OR REPORT ANY DIFFERENCES TO OUR AUDITORS by completing and signing this form. Return it directly to our auditors in the enclosed envelope. They will advise us of any discrepancy reported. Do not send payments to the auditors. Your prompt reply will be appreciated.

ACCOUNT NUMBER	AS OF DATE	ACCOUNT DESCRIPTION	AMOUNT

PLEASE SIGN AND RETURN DIRECTLY TO

△ **TOUCHE ROSS & CO.**

Gentlemen: The information presented is (check one) CORRECT ☐ INCORRECT ☐ at the date shown. (Please explain any differences on the reverse side.)

Signature

Title   Date

KD-102

THIS IS NOT A REQUEST FOR PAYMENT

Source: Deloitte & Touche. Used with permission.

Figure 6-6 ▰▬▬▬▬▬▬▬▬▬▬▬▬▬▬▬▬▬▬▬▬▬▬▬▬▬▬▬▬▬▬▬▬▬▬▬▬▬▬▬

Negative Accounts Receivable Confirmation Request

AUDITOR'S CONFIRMATION OF YOUR ACCOUNT WITH

Our auditors, Touche Ross & Co., are making their regular examination of our financial statements. Part of this examination includes direct verification of customer account balances. PLEASE EXAMINE THE DATA BELOW CAREFULLY. If it agrees with your records, disregard this request. If it does NOT agree with your records, please report the differences directly to our auditors using the space provided on the reverse side, sign below and return in the enclosed envelope.

ACCOUNT NUMBER	AS OF DATE	ACCOUNT DESCRIPTION	AMOUNT

PLEASE REPORT ANY EXCEPTIONS DIRECTLY TO

△ **TOUCHE ROSS & CO.**

Gentlemen: The information presented is INCORRECT as explained on the reverse side

Signature

Title   Date

KD-103

THIS IS NOT A REQUEST FOR PAYMENT   **DO NOT RETURN IF THIS STATEMENT IS CORRECT**

Source: Deloitte & Touche. Used with permission.

Because of the nature of the positive confirmation request, the auditor must follow up on all positive requests not returned. In using a positive request, the auditor expects to get some response from the confirming party regardless of whether the party agrees with the information on the request. These requests are generally used when the auditor is seeking to *confirm relatively large or otherwise material items* from a relatively small audit population or when the understanding of the internal control structure reveals that there is a relatively high risk that errors or irregularities may exist in the balances being confirmed. Positive confirmation requests are typically used for such things as these:

- Verification of bank balances.
- Verification of marketable securities held by lenders.
- Verification of large, questionable, or past-due accounts receivable.
- Verification of inventories in public warehouses.
- Clearing matters of importance with the client's attorneys.
- Verification of long- and short-term notes receivable and notes payable.
- Verification of capital stock outstanding.

Confirmation is particularly useful in satisfying the audit objective of existence of key asset and liability accounts. Nevertheless, we should remember that it will not provide complete evidence as to valuation, cutoff, or transaction validity of accounts in many cases. For example, a positive account receivable request returned by a client customer and stating that the customer agrees with the client's balance constitutes evidence as to existence of the account receivable but does not constitute evidence as to its valuation (collectibility). For satisfaction of the valuation objective, the auditor must rely on recalculation and analysis of the allowance for doubtful accounts, as well as on discussions with the client regarding past-due accounts. Again, we must observe that all pertinent audit objectives must be satisfied with respect to an account balance before an unqualified audit opinion is justified.

Inquiry

An **inquiry** is a set of questions directed to persons having knowledge about a particular phase of the client's operations. It is *generally directed to client employees* and may be raised during virtually every phase of the audit, from preliminary planning to the final tests of account balances. Oral evidence produced by such inquiries is less competent than that produced by inspection, observation, or confirmations. However, the auditor does rely on it to some extent. Ultimately, even though these oral responses are incorporated into a **representation letter** (signed by managers and containing selected representations by them), the only real support for oral evidence is the integrity and reputation of the client. Since auditors, as a matter of policy, are strongly urged to avoid association with clients who lack integrity, they logically have some right to rely on the assertions made to them by their clients.

Although professional standards for independent auditors recognize the validity of oral evidence, these standards warn that the procurement of oral evidence should not be regarded as a substitute for other techniques, which provide more direct and more competent forms of evidence. In addition, SAS 19 (AU333) requires that all oral representations of management should be followed up in a representation letter to the auditor. Written representations from management thus confirm oral representations made by the client during the course of the engagement. The letters reduce the possibility of misunderstandings concerning matters that are the subject of the representation and emphasize the client's primary responsibility for the data included in the financial statements. Representation letters should be dated as of the last day of audit field work and, therefore, represent one of the last tasks that the auditor performs on the audit engagement. Such letters are addressed to the auditor and are signed by the appropriate official(s) of the company.

A variety of client assertions covering all aspects of financial statement disclosures appear in a representation letter. Among the assertions are such statements as these:

- Management is responsible for fairness of presentation in the financial statements.
- All financial records and related data have been made available to the auditor.
- To the extent of management's knowledge, no material errors or irregularities are contained in the financial statements.
- To the extent of management's knowledge, the company has complied with pertinent contractual arrangements.
- All information concerning related party transactions has been disclosed.
- All contingencies (liabilities, losses, illegal acts, unasserted claims, etc.) of which management has knowledge have been revealed to the auditor and adequately disclosed.
- All material events subsequent to the balance sheet date relating to the financial statements under audit have been properly disclosed.

We must realize that the preceding list is simply representative and does not include all items that may be covered in such a letter. Realistically, management and the auditor may agree on any item they feel is appropriate for disclosure in the representation letter. Those representations should generally be limited to the items considered either individually or collectively to be material. Such materiality limitations do not apply, however, to disclosures of illegal acts or irregularities, nor do they apply to management's assertions regarding completeness of accounting records.

Although representation letters are not considered to be highly competent evidence, they are often so important in corroborating oral evidence that management's refusal to furnish such a letter may prevent the auditor from providing an unqualified audit opinion. In such cases, the auditor would typically render a scope-qualified audit report or a disclaimer, whichever is more appropriate. Client representation letters are obtained as part of completing the audit engagement; they are illustrated and discussed further in Chapter 20.

Recomputation

The procedure of **recomputation** is used to provide evidence when verifying account balances determined by calculations. This evidence, sometimes called mathematical evidence, can provide proof toward fulfilling both the valuation and transaction validity audit objectives. Recomputations are performed throughout the audit as the details of account balances for such items as depreciation, bad debts, and accruals are tested. When the auditor uses a client-prepared working paper of any kind, one of the first procedures she or he will perform on it will be **footing and cross-footing** (readdition) to ascertain that the totals agree with the details included in the working paper. Recomputation often accompanies other evidence-gathering techniques, such as inspection of documents and confirmation.

Reconciliation

We have already observed the importance of evidence provided by parties outside the client organization. The specific amounts included in such information often may differ from the client's record of those data because of timing differences associated with increases or decreases in the item being proven. Because of these differences, the auditor must frequently perform **reconciliations** *to explain the differences between the balance of the item shown in the client's records and that provided by the outside party.* The reconciliation procedure is always used when the auditor is comparing the cash balance reported by the client's bank with the amount shown in the cash ledger account. Also, reconciliations are frequently necessary in comparing confirmed balances of individual accounts receivable with the balances shown for those accounts in the client's subsidiary ledger.

Reliance on the Work of Specialists

In some instances the financial statements may reflect disclosures that require evidential matter that an auditor is not capable of evaluating. For example, inventories of a jewelry manufacturer may include precious stones whose value depends on quality. A jeweler's appraisal is required in such situations to arrive at an appropriate valuation. The inventories of an energy company may include oil and gas reserves, which require a geologist's report. These professionals, as well as actuaries, engineers, and attorneys, among others, are commonly known as **specialists**.

   Auditing standards, in SAS 11 (AU336), allow the use of the work of specialists under certain conditions when it becomes necessary to obtain audit evidence that is outside the speciality field of accounting. In selecting a specialist, the auditor should examine the other professional's certification, reputation, and relationship with the client to ascertain whether the specialist is competent, honest, and objective. The auditor should then establish an understanding with the specialist (preferably documented) as to (1) the objectives and scope of the specialist's work; (2) the specialist's relationship, if any, to the client; (3) the methods or assumptions to be used in the specialist's work; (4) the specialist's understanding of the corroborative nature of his or her findings; and (5) the form and content of the specialist's report.

The auditor should make appropriate tests of the accounting data provided for the specialist. The report of the specialist should then be reviewed to ascertain that his or her findings support the related representations in the financial statements.

Ordinarily, if all of these procedures provide no inconsistencies or material errors, the auditor may conclude that sufficient evidence has been obtained from the specialist and make no reference to the specialist's work in the audit report. If, however, the auditor decides to modify (or qualify) the audit opinion based on either insufficient or inconsistent information from the specialist, the work of the specialist may be referenced in the audit report.

Timing of Audit Tests

In general, audit tests are performed during the *interim* (prior to year-end) and *final* field work stages of the audit. Decisions about timing of audit tests should be based partly on the audit objective and partly on other factors.

For example, if the audit objective is controls-related, it is desirable to perform the inquiry, observation, and inspection of documents at an interim date. In general, *tests should be performed as soon as practicable after audit objectives have been identified*, thus preventing rush and overtime during the final field work stages.

A significant part of the planning for the engagement, including preliminary analytical procedures, can also be performed at interim dates. This will help identify critical audit areas, where special audit effort should be concentrated. The understanding of the internal control structure should begin during this period. In many larger audits, some substantive tests may be performed before the end of the year, with the thought of extending those tests to the date of final field work as deemed necessary. Such tests include, for example, analyses of additions to and retirements from property and equipment accounts, income statement accounts, estimated liability for warranty, and clearing accounts that are not to be audited by testing items composing the ending balance. In general, *tests should be performed as soon as practicable after audit objectives have been identified.*

The auditor should recognize that applying substantive tests prior to the year end potentially increases the risk that errors that may exist at the balance sheet date will not be detected. The amount of that risk increases as the period between interim tests and the balance sheet date increases. Therefore, the auditor should take steps to control such risk by designing substantive tests over the remainder of the audit period (between the interim and balance sheet dates) that will provide a reasonable basis for extending interim conclusions to the balance sheet date.

Generally accepted auditing standards require that some updating of interim tests be done during the final stages of the audit to allow the auditor to extend his or her audit conclusions to cover the entire period. Furthermore, the auditor cannot rely solely on the internal control structure to justify the deletion of substantive tests. However, the year-end substantive tests may still be reduced substantially to include only analytical procedures (comparison of balance sheet accounts at interim and year-end periods with explanations of unexpected variances) or limited tests of details. These measures would be appropriate, for example, when the auditor has concluded that the system of internal control is adequate to detect or correct material errors and irregularities occurring during the period after interim tests were conducted.

If errors are discovered from substantive tests at interim dates, the auditor may be required either to modify the nature, timing, or extent of tests in the remaining period, or to re-perform interim auditing procedures as of the year end. Factors that may affect this decision are the possible implications of the errors, the nature and cause of the errors, their relationship to other phases of the audit, corrections subsequently made by the entity, and results of substantive tests during the remaining period.[2]

Working Papers

☑ **Objective 4**
Document evidence-gathering process in working papers

Working papers are the records brought together by the auditor to document the nature, timing, and extent of the testing carried out during the audit process. They show the procedures followed, the control and substantive tests performed, the information obtained, and the conclusions reached for each subsystem and for each account balance shown in the financial statements. The chief objectives of working papers are to *aid the auditor in conducting the examination* and to *provide evidence in support of the audit opinion.*[3] It is important that the auditor plan the form and content of working papers at the beginning of the audit. Such an arrangement leads to the most effective use of audit staff in the engagement, as well as of client personnel who might assist in working paper preparation.

In this section we first examine the guidelines for preparing working papers. Then we discuss their organization and content. After that, we consider the ownership and custody rights to working papers and relate their preparation to the planning phase of the audit.

Guidelines for Working Papers

Generally accepted auditing standards do not contain specific guidelines for preparing working papers. They do, however, state that the form and content of working papers should fit the needs and circumstances of the engagement to which the working papers apply. Indeed, the guidelines set forth in those standards are so broad that they apply to engagements for nonaudit (tax, MAS, and write-up) services as well as to those for audits. Factors that determine the desired quantity, type, and content of audit working papers for a particular engagement include the nature of the audit report expected to be rendered; the nature of the financial statements, schedules, or other information upon which the auditor is reporting; the condition of the client's records and internal controls; and the amount of supervision and review required for the assistants' work on a particular engagement.

Audit standards specify six broad guidelines for the organization and content of working papers:

1. The working papers must contain sufficient information to show that the audited information (financial statements or otherwise) agrees with the client's records.
2. The working papers must be organized to show that the engagement has been adequately planned and that the work of assistants has been supervised, in accordance with the first standard of audit field work.
3. The working papers must also show that the control structure of the client has been properly assessed, in accordance with the second standard of audit field work.
4. The auditing procedures followed and the tests performed in gathering sufficient competent evidential matter must be shown to meet the third standard of audit field work.
5. There must be evidence that the exceptions and unusual matters disclosed by auditing procedures were appropriately resolved or treated.
6. The working papers must also demonstrate that the conclusions reached by the auditor concerning significant aspects of the engagement (including client's compliance with internal controls and conformity of financial presentations with generally accepted accounting principles) are supported by the findings of the audit.[4]

Content of Working Papers

Audit working papers are generally divided into two parts: permanent files and current files. Permanent files are intended to show the history of the company and contain data of continuing interest to each succeeding examination. Current files, on the other hand, usually contain data pertinent only to the current year's examination.

The Permanent File.   The **permanent file** serves several purposes. First, it contains certain historical data of the company, which are used to reacquaint continuing auditors with the client from year to year and to provide new audit staff with an initial understanding of the client's affairs. Sometimes when one auditor succeeds another auditor on an engagement, the permanent file of the client can assist the successor in planning the engagement. Finally, many of the records in the permanent file do not change, or require only minor change, from year to year. Placing such papers in one location for easy reference eliminates the necessity for duplicating the repetitive (but necessary) information year after year.

The auditor constructs a permanent file for the client on the first audit engagement. As the years pass, elements are added, deleted, or modified as necessary. Contents of the permanent file include copies of the following items:

- The company charter, if applicable.
- The articles of incorporation and bylaws or partnership agreement.
- Organization charts and other data pertaining to internal control—such as flowcharts; questionnaires; narrative descriptions of pertinent systems; and observations concerning strengths, weaknesses, and actions taken by the company to eliminate weaknesses.
- Permanent financing arrangements of the company, such as bond indentures and stock issue agreements.
- Contracts with key employees, such as the company president; and other agreements—such as leases, stock options, pension plans, and contracts with major suppliers or customers that have continuing significance over the years.
- Analyses of key balance sheet accounts that have continuing significance. These include such accounts as capital stock, retained earnings, long-term debt, property and equipment, and intangible assets. These analyses provide vital information about the company history, which can be used in planning each successive engagement. Typically, they require only yearly update to remain current.
- The results of analytical procedures. These data include year-to-year changes in key operating and financing ratios—such as gross profit, current ratio, and rate of return on stockholder's equity. As pointed out earlier, year-to-year fluctuations in these accounts can assist the auditor in planning the audit by pinpointing areas in the financial statements requiring special attention. (Some CPA firms include results of analytical procedures in the current file rather than in the permanent file.)
- Revised and updated minutes of board of directors meetings, which serve as the auditor's permanent evidence that the client's major transactions over the years have been approved by appropriate company officials.
- **Time budgets**, which contain columns for estimated and total time spent on each of the various balance sheet and income statement categories. The time budget is a key factor in scheduling work to be done and in controlling the progress of the engagement (including supervision of assistants' work).

The Current File.   The **current file**, as mentioned previously, contains descriptions of auditing procedures performed on various accounting subsystems and account balances of the current period, plus adjustments to those accounts. These working papers in the current file help to document the evidence-gathering process. Appendixes to Chapters 13–20 contain segments of the audit working papers for JEP Manufacturing Company, whose financial statements are contained in Figure 5–1.

Figure 6–7 shows how parts of a typical current file of working papers relate to each other. The results of findings flow from supporting schedules to the working trial balance. These papers contain the auditor's record of all evidence-gathering procedures followed, tests performed, results of tests, and conclusions reached during the current audit. Since these papers are the only evidence that generally accepted auditing standards were followed and that conclusions reached were consistent with the evidence available, it is important that the papers be clearly and concisely written: complete enough to assure the validity of the conclusions reached (such as degree of client's compliance with internal controls); informative of material matters concerning the financial presentations

Figure 6–7

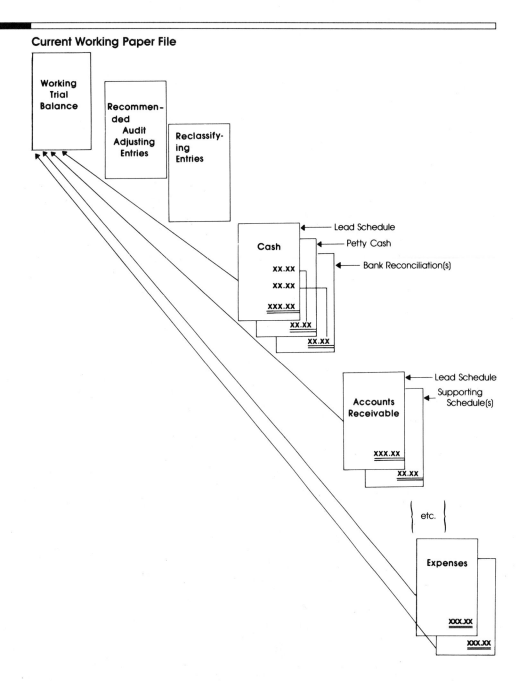

Current Working Paper File

(such as adequacy of disclosures, etc.); and cross-referenced in such a way as to facilitate greater understanding during the review process.

In accordance with the third standard of audit field work, sufficient competent evidential matter should be gathered by the auditor to support each material financial statement assertion. In terms of working papers, this means that each material account (and the systems supporting that account) in the financial statements should be supported by its own series of working papers. To ensure ease of understanding by reviewers, *each series of working papers should be treated as a unit*, showing the following:

- Book balances.
- Adjusting and reclassifying entries recommended.
- Pertinent audit objectives (discussed earlier in this chapter).
- Systems and balances to be audited and samples selected.
- Evidence gathered to support each assertion tested.
- Conclusions reached.

Because of the double-entry system of recordkeeping, financial statement accounts are interrelated. Because of these interrelationships, misstatements in one account are always offset by corresponding misstatements in other accounts. Therefore, each segment of the working papers and the conclusions related to them should be adequately cross-referenced to other financial statement segments that are interrelated so that reviewers can ascertain whether proper attention was given to all interrelated information.

. As Figure 6–7 shows, the current-file working papers are usually arranged in the following order:

Working Trial Balance. These show all financial statement account balances before adjustments, as well as recommended audit-adjustment and re-classification entries, relating those balances to the audited financial statements. Each account on the working trial balance should be cross-referenced to the appropriate lead schedule in the various segments of the working papers.

Recommended Audit-Adjusting Entries. These are entries the auditor has ascertained should be made by the client to make the financial statements conform to generally accepted accounting principles. Audit adjustments typically affect income, either individually or collectively, in a material way. They should be written neatly and concisely and should contain appropriate explanations and appropriate working paper cross-references.

Reclassifying Entries. In contrast to adjusting entries, reclassifying entries are made in the audit working papers and financial statements only. Since they typically do not affect income, there is usually no need for the client to incorporate them into company records. Reclassifications are often needed, however, for adequate informative financial statement disclosures. These entries should also be cross-referenced to appropriate segments of the working papers.

Financial Statement Segments. As discussed earlier, each important segment of the financial statements should have its own series of working papers, capable of showing individually the audit evidence gathered and the conclusions reached. Each segment should contain the following:

- A **lead schedule**, showing pertinent information about account balances before adjustment, plus recommended audit-adjustment and reclassification entries, and the final balance. The final balance should be cross-referenced directly to the working trial balance.
- **Supporting schedules**, showing audit evidence gathered and conclusions reached with regard to individual account balances and systems. These conclusions include those regarding propriety of client disclosures in conformity with generally accepted accounting principles and the extent of the client's adherence to prescribed internal controls.

Typically, the lead schedules and related supporting schedules are grouped by segments of the financial statement (current assets, noncurrent assets, liabilities, equities, revenues, and expenses) and, as shown in Figure 6–7, will generally follow the adjusting and reclassifying entries segments of the work papers. Figure 6–8 illustrates the format of a typical audit working paper lead schedule for cash. (The actual audit work performed with respect to cash, and reasons pertaining to it, are discussed in Chapter 19 and would be shown in the related supporting schedules.)

The current files may also contain a **general section**, which includes, among other things, the **audit program**. As stated earlier, the audit program contains a detailed listing of the audit procedures to be performed. The results of those procedures are then documented on the various lead schedules and supporting schedules. The client representation letter, the attorney's confirmation letter(s), other confirmation letters, and other documentary evidence of general importance to the current-year audit are also included in the general section of the audit working papers. Each audit firm will have its own specific guidelines for working-paper format. However, every working paper should include the following elements:

- Indexing numbers, so that an item can be located, removed, replaced, and used efficiently by reviewers.
- Cross-referencing numbers showing all important interrelated information found in other segments of the working papers.
- Heading, showing name of the client, title of the working paper, and date or period of time to which the audited information pertains.
- Signatures and initials of preparers so that persons responsible for performing the audit work can be easily identified if reviewers later question the evidence gathered or conclusions reached.
- Dates of the audit work, including interim field work, and initial and later review by supervisory personnel.
- Tick marks and legend. Audit **tick marks** are symbols placed on the working

Figure 6-8

Summary Type of Working Paper (Cash Lead Schedule)

	W. P. No.	A
J & P Manufacturing Co. Cash Dec. 31, 19X1	ACCOUNTANT	Cut
	DATE	2-1-X2

	W/P #	12/31/X1 Per Books	Adjustments & Reclassification DR (CR)	Final
Regular Account	B-1	10161632		
Payroll Account	B-2	1000000		
Special Account	B-3	31587316		
Petty Cash	B-4	30000		
Total Cash		42778948		

papers that explain the auditor's evidence-gathering procedures. Many firms have standard tick marks that are used uniformly throughout the firm for various procedures (footings, cross-footings, vouching, etc.). Other audit firms do not have such a policy. In the latter instances, a legend must be placed on each working paper, explaining the meaning of the tick marks to the reviewer.

Audited financial information relating to individual account balances is generally presented within one of two formats within the working papers. The **analysis format** is organized along the lines of a four-element equation showing the beginning balance, additions, removals, and the ending balance. This format is used when the auditor needs to retain all that information. Figure 6–9 shows a typical analysis type of working paper. The analysis format is generally used for notes receivable, notes payable, accrued receivables, accrued payables, property and equipment, accumulated depreciation, prepaid expenses and other assets, retained earnings, and capital stock. The **summary format** is used when the auditor determines that details of the ending balance in the accounts are more important than the elements associated with the accumulation of the account balance. Figure 6–8, the cash lead schedule, is an example of a summary type of working paper. The summary format is typically used for cash balances, accounts receivable, accounts payable, revenue, and expense accounts. These types of working papers are illustrated more completely in the appendixes to Chapters 13 through 20.

Ownership and Custody of Working Papers

Working papers are the property of the auditor or, more accurately, of the firm for whom the auditor works.[5] However, an audit firm's ownership rights to working papers are subject to certain ethical limitations. For example, when working papers are needed as an integral part of the client's records to make them complete, the auditor is required, under Rule 501 of the Code of Professional Conduct, to make copies available to the client. Auditing standards contain the warning that an auditor's working papers should not substitute for client records. Furthermore, information in the working papers is considered confidential under Rule 301 of the Code of Professional Conduct.

There are no explicit rules relating to the retention of working papers. In deciding on an appropriate records-retention policy, the accountant should be aware of pertinent legal requirements for records retention, such as the statute of limitations for examination of the client's tax returns, which is three years in most cases. Beyond that, the general guidelines require that the accounting firm should retain records for a period of time sufficient for the firm's needs. Most firms have adopted their own records-retention policies for working papers supporting the financial statements and for permanent file papers. Use of modern techniques, such as microfilming, makes storage easier and allows for extensive record retention when it is needed.

Figure 6–9

Analysis Type of Working Paper

JEP Manufacturing Co.

Notes Payable and Accrued Interest Principal

12-31-X6

W P No	M-1
ACCOUNTANT	JJ
DATE	1-22-X7

Bank	Date Issued	Due	Balance 12-31-X5	Principal Additions	Payments	Balance 12-31-X6
Fidelity Union Trust:						
	10-31-X5	1-31-X6	100000 – 2	–	100000 – M	–
	12-31-X5	4-30-X6	200000 – 2	–	200000 – M	–
	4-30-X6	8-31-X6	–	70000 – √ X	70000 – M	–
	8-31-X6	1-31-X7	–	150000 – √ X	–	150000 –
			300000 – 2	220000 –	370000 –	150000 – C
President Trust Company:						
	11-30-X5	2-28-X7	25000 – 2	–	25000 – M	–
	2-28-X6	5-31-X7	–	75000 – √ X	75000 – M	–
			25000 – 2	75000 –	100000 –	– C
	Total		325000 – 2	295000 –	470000 –	150000 –
			To A-2			To A-2

√ – Examined Bank advice for proceeds of the note

X – Examined copy of note, noting interest rate, principal amt., and
      Due date

M – Examined cancelled note and paid notice from bank

C – Agrees with Bank confirmation on B-2-1

C+ – Agrees with Bank confirmation on B-3-1

2 – Per prior year's working paper

∅ – Traced to cash disbursement journal

< – Verified Computation

Int. Rate / Collateral		Accrued 12-31-X5	Expense Interest 19X6	Payments	Accrued 12-31-X6	
8	3 mos	1333 33 ᵪ	666 67 <	2000 00	∅	—
8		—	5332 80 <	5332 80	∅	—
8¼		—	1924 81 <	1924 81	∅	—
8½		—	4250 00 <	—	C	4250 00 <
		1333 33 ᵪ	12174 28	9257 61		4250 00
8	3 mos	166 67 ᵪ	333 33 <	500 00	∅	—
8¼		—	1443 75 <	1443 75	∅	—
		166 67 ᵪ	1777 08	1943 75		—
		1500 00 ᵪ	13951 36	11201 36		4250 00
		To C	To A-3			To O

Automated Working Papers

In recent years, the advent of the microcomputer has revolutionized the preparation of audit working-papers. Computer software that automates much of the spreadsheet techniques used for audit working papers is now commercially available and in use by many firms. For example, it is common practice for many firms to develop software templates for columnar working papers such as those illustrated in Figures 6–8 and 6–9. The advantage of **automated working papers** lies in the speed and accuracy of the computer software. Mathematical computations of every kind can be made much more quickly and accurately than with traditional manual methods. In addition, the same templates can be used each year, making updating and editing much neater and faster than with manual methods. Adjustment entries posted to working trial balances (see Figure 6–7) are automatically posted to corresponding account numbers in the lead schedules and supporting schedules as well, providing the potential for increased internal consistency. Storage efficiency also is greatly improved, since vast amounts of data can be stored on one small computer diskette. We will discuss the use of the computer in the audit further in Chapter 10.

Planning and the Preparation of Working Papers

As mentioned previously in this chapter, it is advantageous for the auditor to be appointed as early during the client's fiscal year as possible. For one thing, such action will permit more complete documentation of audit work. Initial permanent file construction will begin and will continue through the planning phase of the audit because it is part of the work that needs to be done to acquaint the auditor with the client and the industry in which the client operates. Preliminary analytical procedures should also begin during the planning phase of the audit and be documented in the permanent file.

Early appointment of the auditor also permits an early decision about the extent to which client employees, including internal auditors, may be used by the independent auditor. Often, client employees can be used to prepare *pro forma working papers*, which include detailed analyses or summaries of accounts in the general ledger. These working papers can be included in the auditor's current file as part of the total evidence of audit work done. By using client employees to prepare some of these working papers, the amount of time the independent auditor spends can be reduced. This, in turn, results in lower fees and greater satisfaction for the client.

Summary

In this chapter we completed our discussion of the evidence-gathering process begun in Chapter 5. Starting with the financial statement assertions of management, the audit task is to identify the relevant audit objectives to be fulfilled.

Those objectives are (1) statement presentation; (2) transaction validity; (3) ownership; (4) cutoff; (5) valuation; (6) existence, and (7) internal control. The auditor's assessment of the nature, timing, and extent of the procedures necessary to satisfy those objectives for a particular account balance or class of transactions is a function of the inherent risk of misstatement as well as control risk for that particular account balance. Procedures such as inspection, observation, confirmation, inquiry, recomputation, reconciliation, and analytical tools are used to perform substantive audit tests. Such tests can involve any mixture of analytical procedures, direct tests of financial statement balances, or tests of transactions that the auditor deems most appropriate. Each of these types of procedures was discussed in some detail. Finally, the documentation of audit procedures in the form of working papers was discussed, and various types of working papers were illustrated.

Auditing Vocabulary

p. 211   **analysis format:**   A working paper organized to show beginning balance, additions, removals, and ending balance.

p. 187   **audit objectives:**   Objectives derived from the client's financial statements assertions that bridge the gap between the client's assertions and the procedures that are performed to verify those assertions.

p. 209   **audit program:**   A detailed listing of the audit procedures to be performed; a vital part in every audit engagement, because it assists in supervision of audit assistants.

p. 214   **automated working papers:**   Computer software templates that contain the same columnar headings as the analysis or summary-type working papers illustrated in the chapter.

p. 198   **confirmation:**   A letter to a third party, returned directly to the auditor, which verifies the existence of recorded amounts in the financial statements such as cash, accounts or notes receivable, accounts or notes payable, inventories, marketable securities, and capital stock.

p. 206   **current file:**   Working papers that contain descriptions of auditing procedures performed on various accounting subsystems and account balances of the current period, plus adjustments to those accounts; these working papers document the evidence-gathering process.

p. 192   **dual-purpose tests:**   Tests that serve the dual purpose of testing not only a specific internal control, but also the dollar amount of the account balance.

p. 202   **footing (and cross footing):**   Readdition to ascertain the totals agree with the details included in the working papers.

p. 209   **general section:**   The portion of the current files that includes correspondence and the audit program.

p. 200   **inquiry:**   Questions directed to persons having knowledge about a particular phase of the client's operations; generally regarded as the least competent procedure that can be performed, although it is extremely important and can give the auditor direction as to additional corroborating evidence to be obtained.

p. 209   **lead schedule:**   A working paper that shows pertinent information about account balances before adjustment, plus recommended audit adjustment and reclassification entries, and the final balance; typically, the working paper that links the working trial balance with the supporting schedules.

p. 198 **negative confirmation:** The type of confirmation in which the confirming party is requested to communicate with the auditor only if the information supplied in the confirmation request is incorrect; generally used in cases in which the population being confirmed consists of a large number of relatively small amounts and/or when internal controls are extremely strong.

p. 197 **observation:** A procedure by which the auditor observes tangible evidence. Observations are made by comparing the observed phenomena with client records, a procedure often used in determining whether client internal control is satisfactory, as well as whether tangible assets actually exist.

p. 205 **permanent file:** Working papers that contain historical data of the company, which are used to reacquaint continuing auditors with the client from year to year and to provide new audit staff with an initial understanding of the client's affairs.

p. 198 **positive confirmation:** The type of confirmation in which the confirming party is requested to communicate with the auditor regardless of whether the confirming party agrees that the information on the confirmation request is correct; generally used in cases in which the population being confirmed consists of a relatively small number of individually large amounts and/or when the internal control structure contains some weaknesses.

p. 202 **recomputation:** Mathematical recalculation of recorded amounts on the financial statements that provides proof of both valuation and transaction validity; performed for such items as depreciation, the allowance for doubtful accounts, and accruals.

p. 202 **reconciliation:** Comparison of client-recorded amounts to information provided by an outside party, and explanation of differences noted; frequently necessary in comparing confirmed balances of individual accounts receivable with the balances shown for those accounts in the client's subsidiary ledger.

p. 200 **representation letter:** A letter signed by managers and containing selected representations by them, dated as of the last day of audit field work, that has the purpose of corroborating the oral representations that have been given to the auditor during the course of the engagement. Representation letters are a requirement on all audit engagements.

p. 196 **retracing (or tracing):** The most common test of a transaction for understatement. To trace, begin with the source documents supporting the recorded amount and follow them through to the financial statements to ascertain that they were properly recorded.

p. 192 **sampling:** The application of an auditing procedure to less than 100 percent of the items within an account balance or class for the purpose of evaluating some characteristic of the balance or class.

p. 202 **specialists:** Professionals, other than accountants, from whom the auditor obtains evidence that he or she does not have sufficient expertise to provide.

p. 211 **summary format:** The working format used to describe the details of the ending balance in the accounts. Such working papers are generally used for cash, accounts receivable, accounts payable, revenue, and expense accounts.

p. 209 **supporting schedule:** The working paper that shows the details of audit evidence gathered and conclusions reached with regard to individual account balances and systems.

p. 194 **tests of balances:** Direct test of details that make up the ending balances that appear in the financial statements.

p. 194   **tests of details:**   Designed to detect specific misstatements in account balances that comprise the financial statements; can be categorized into two subclassifications: (1) tests of balances and (2) tests of transactions.

p. 194   **tests of transactions:**   Examination of documents that support the debit and credit entries to various accounts, such as vouching the details of the entries to the accounts receivable balances to underlying supporting documents or tracing the documentary support into the records to assure the transaction was recorded.

p. 209   **tick marks:**   Symbols placed on the working papers that explain the evidence-gathering procedures used.

p. 206   **time budget:**   A record of the budgeted and actual time spent on each engagement, by balance sheet account and by activity; a key factor in scheduling work to be done and in controlling the progress of the engagement (including supervision of assistants).

p. 195   **vouching:**   The most common test of a transaction for overstatement; starting with the recorded balance in the general or subsidiary ledger and obtaining evidence in the form of documentary support of that recorded amount.

p. 204   **working papers:**   The records brought together by the auditor to document the evidence-gathering process.

Appendix 6: The Evidence-Gathering Process for Cash in Banks

Audit objective	Financial statement assertion	Audit procedure*
Existence	Existence	1. Reconcile book and bank balances. 2. Confirm bank balance.
Transaction validity	Occurrence	1. Vouch entries in cash receipts journals to underlying deposit slips on a test basis. 2. Vouch entries in cash disbursements journals to underlying canceled checks. Note dates, payees, amounts, and endorsements.
Cutoff	Completeness, allocation	1. Trace deposits listed on reconciliation as in-transit to cutoff bank statement. Ascertain the reasonableness of time lag. 2. Vouch outstanding checks listed on the bank reconciliation to canceled checks received in cutoff bank statement. Inspect all checks returned with cutoff statement for possible omissions from outstanding check list.
Statement presentation	Presentation/disclosure	1. Inspect bank confirmation for restrictions on cash in bank. 2. Inquire of management about restrictions on the use of cash.
Valuation	Valuation	1. Foot cash receipts and disbursements records on a test basis. 2. Vouch postings in cash account to totals of cash receipts and disbursements journals. 3. Trace postings in cash receipts and disbursements journals to entries in the general ledger account.
Ownership		Usually not relevant.

*For more details, see Figure 19–2 and Appendix 19–A.

Notes

1. "Analytical Procedures," SAS 56 (New York: AICPA, 1988).
2. AU313, paragraphs .01–.09, (New York: AICPA, 1983).
3. AU339, paragraph .01 (New York: AICPA, 1982).
4. Ibid., paragraphs .04–.05.
5. Ibid., paragraph .06.

Questions for Class Discussion

Q6-1 Why does the auditor rely on testing procedures in gathering audit evidence? Explain.

Q6-2 What is meant by the *transactions validity audit objective*?

Q6-3 How does the auditor preserve the audit evidence gathered through the performance of auditing procedures?

Q6-4 What is meant by the terms *test of controls*, *substantive test*, and *dual-purpose test*?

Q6-5 Why do auditors often vouch elements of the account balances for assets to their underlying documentary support and trace such support to the account balances for liabilities? Explain.

Q6-6 The auditor discovers an overstatement of an asset; where should he or she logically look for the compensating error? Explain.

Q6-7 Can you list and briefly describe the four auditing procedures specifically mentioned in the third standard of field work? Are all of these procedures used in verifying each statement item? Explain.

Q6-8 Can you list and briefly describe four specific procedures that represent different ways of applying the inspection procedure?

Q6-9 Why is externally originated documentary evidence more competent than similar internally originated documentary evidence? Explain.

Q6-10 What is meant by the *audit trail*? List the formal records and documents normally appearing on the audit trail for accounts receivable, sequencing them in the order in which they are normally encountered in the vouching and tracing processes.

Q6-11 What is the difference between a positive and a negative confirmation request? When would each be likely to be used?

Q6-12 How are the results of oral inquiries preserved as evidence in an audit?

Q6-13 What is the meaning of the term *analytical procedures* as it is used in an independent audit? During which stages of a typical audit engagement are analytical procedures performed? How are the findings used in each of these stages?

Q6-14 Should any audit tests be performed before the end of the period under audit? Explain.

Q6-15 What types of information would an auditor expect to secure by examining a client's charter and bylaws? Contrast the procedures followed in examining those documents during a first-year engagement with the procedures followed in subsequent years.

Q6-16 What is an *audit program*? Describe its purposes. During which phase(s) of the audit examination should the audit programs be written?

Q6-17 What are *audit working papers*? Why are they important? Who owns them? Explain.

Q6-18 What are the guidelines provided by the AICPA relating to the organization and content of working papers? Discuss them.

Q6-19 What is the meaning and purpose of audit *tick marks*?

Q6-20 What is the difference between analysis-type working papers and summary-type working papers? In what circumstances would each be used?

Short Cases

C6-1 At the beginning of an audit engagement, Alice Robinson, the senior accountant in charge of the audit, takes Bryan Rosenberger, a staff accountant, to tour the client's plant. They observe the general condition of the equipment and specifically identify the new pieces of equipment acquired by the client during the year. After the tour, Alice asks Bryan to examine the documentary evidence in support of the new equipment observed during the plant tour. Bryan questions the wisdom of that assignment, suggesting that Alice is overauditing those items because they have already been observed during the plant tour.

Required: Tell how the senior accountant should respond to the staff accountant.

C6-2 In conferring with your audit staff prior to an audit engagement, you explain that the primary concern of the audit team will be the discovery of overstatements of assets and understatements of liabilities. A newly employed staff accountant states that he does not understand why the audit team is not equally concerned with both overstatements and understatements of assets and liabilities.

Required: Justify your position.

C6-3 Joanna Grove, a newly employed staff accountant, has observed from an auditing text that there are normally seven audit objectives to be met in performing the auditing procedures; she knows the procedures exist for the purpose of gathering sufficient competent evidential matter relating to the fairness of the financial statements. Joanna states that she presumes all these objectives will have to met in verifying all the account balances appearing in each of the accounting subsystems.

Required: Evaluate the position Joanna has taken.

C6-4 A staff accountant working under your supervision is vouching cash transactions to canceled checks and cash receipt vouchers. He states that he presumes that the canceled checks and cash receipt vouchers each constitute equally persuasive documentary evidence in support of cash disbursements and cash receipts, respectively.

Required: Comment on the staff accountant's assumption.

C6-5 You, as the senior accountant in charge of an audit engagement, have instructed Emilia Ciri, a staff accountant, to vouch, on a test basis, the debits in accounts receivable to the sales invoices. After she completed that task, you asked her to trace the purchase invoices to credits in the accounts payable ledger accounts. She asked you why she was required to work from the account balances back to the underlying documents in connection with accounts receivable and then was requested to work from the documents to the entries in the accounts in verifying items in the accounts payable accounts.

Required: Justify your instructions.

C6-6 Nino Parmakian, a staff accountant, observes that the audit program calls for a member of the audit team to inspect the cash receipts and cash payments journals for the months of January and February following the end of the audit period. The audit team has been cautioned against overauditing, and he, therefore, questions the wisdom of examining accounting records for those months because they are outside the period under audit. Nino feels that by eliminating those procedures the audit team could reduce the amount of time spent on the engagement and in that way reduce the likelihood of overauditing.

Required: Respond to the staff accountant's concerns.

C6-7 In August you are visiting with a prospective client regarding the possible performance of an audit for the calendar year ending December 31. The prospective client states that he presumes that he can make his decision at the end of the year, since the audit will be performed after that date.

Required: Respond to the prospective client.

C6-8 You are the senior accountant in charge of auditing a client whose management refuses to provide you with a client representation letter. The president states that he sees no reason for such a letter, since the audit team has the responsibility of discovering departures from generally accepted accounting principles, errors, and irregularities. Besides, he says, his firm has employed the auditors for those purposes.

Required: Explain to the client why the representation letter must be provided and the action that you will have to take in the event that he continues to refuse to provide the document. Justify your position.

C6-9 An important part of every examination of financial statements is the preparation of audit working papers. You are instructing an inexperienced staff member on his first auditing assignment. He is to examine an account. An analysis of the account has been prepared by the client for inclusion in the audit working papers.

Required:
a. Discuss the relationship of audit working papers to each of the standards of field work.
b. Prepare a list of the comments, commentaries, and notations that the staff member should make or have made on the account analysis to provide an adequate working paper as evidence of his examination. (Do not include a description of auditing procedures applicable to the account.)

(AICPA adapted)

C6-10 An auditor knows that analytical procedures are substantive tests that are extremely useful in the initial planning stages of the audit.

Required:

a. Explain why analytical procedures are called substantive tests.
b. Explain how analytical procedures may be useful to the auditor in the initial planning stages of the audit.
c. Identify the analytical procedures that a CPA would probably utilize during an examination performed in accordance with generally accepted auditing standards.

(AICPA adapted)

Problems

P6-1 Select the best answer for each of the following items.

a. The third standard of field work states that sufficient competent evidential matter may, in part, be obtained through inspection, observation, inquiries, and confirmations to afford a reasonable basis for an opinion regarding the financial statements under examination. The evidential matter required by this standard may, in part, be obtained through
   1. Analytical procedures.
   2. Audit working papers.
   3. Review of the system of internal accounting control.
   4. Proper planning of the audit engagement.

b. Audit programs generally include procedures necessary to test actual transactions and resulting balances. These procedures are primarily designed to
   1. Detect irregularities that result in misstated financial statements.
   2. Test the adequacy of internal control.
   3. Gather corroborative evidence.
   4. Obtain information for informative disclosures.

c. An abnormal fluctuation in gross profit that might suggest the need for extended audit procedures for sales and inventories would most likely be identified in the planning phase of the audit by the use of
   1. Tests of transactions and balances.
   2. A preliminary review of the client's control structure.
   3. Specialized audit programs.
   4. Analytical procedures.

d. Which of the following expressions is *least* likely to be included in a client's representation letter?
   1. No events have occurred subsequent to the balance sheet date that require adjustment to, or disclosure in, the financial statements.
   2. The company has complied with all aspects of contractual agreements that would have a material effect on the financial statements in the event of noncompliance.
   3. Management acknowledges responsibility for illegal actions committed by employees.
   4. Management has made available all financial statements and related data.

e. Pyle, CPA, accepted an engagement to perform the audit of the 19X5 financial

statements of ZYX Company. ZYX completed the preparation of the 19X5 financial statements on February 13, 19X6, and Pyle began the field work on February 17, 19X6. The field work was completed on March 24, 19X6, and the report was delivered to the client on March 28. The client's representation letter normally would be dated
1. February 13, 19X6.
2. February 17, 19X6.
3. March 24, 19X6.
4. March 28, 19X6.

f. An audit working paper that reflects the major components of an amount reported in the financial statements is referred to as a(an)
1. Lead schedule.
2. Supporting schedule.
3. Audit control account.
4. Working trial balance.

g. Which of the following factors most likely affects the auditor's judgment about the quantity, type, and content of working papers?
1. The degree of reliance on internal accounting control.
2. The content of the client's representation letter.
3. The timing of substantive tests completed prior to the balance sheet date.
4. The usefulness of the working papers as a reference source for the client.

h. Working papers that record the procedures used by the auditor to gather evidence should be
1. Considered the primary support for the financial statements being examined.
2. Viewed as the connecting link between the books of accounts and the financial statements.
3. Designed to meet the circumstances of the particular engagement.
4. Destroyed when the audited entity ceases to be a client.

i. Which of the following statements concerning the auditor's use of the work of a specialist is correct?
1. If the specialist is related to the client, the auditor is *not* permitted to use the specialist's findings as corroborative evidence.
2. The specialist may be identified in the auditor's report only when the auditor issues an unqualified opinion.
3. The specialist should have an understanding of the auditor's corroborative use of the specialist's findings.
4. If the auditor believes that the determinations made by the specialist are unreasonable, only an adverse opinion may be issued.

(AICPA adapted)

P6-2   Auditors frequently use the terms *standards*, *procedures*, and *objectives*.

Required:
a. Define *standards* as generally accepted in the auditing literature. You may want to refer to Chapter 2 of the text.
b. List the seven audit objectives discussed in this chapter. How do these objectives relate to the standards discussed in (a) and the assertions of the client in financial statements as discussed in Chapter 5?
c. Define the term *procedure* as generally accepted in auditing literature. List at least

eight different types of procedures that an auditor would use during an audit examination.

P6-3   A CPA accumulates various kinds of evidence on which he or she will base his or her opinion as to the fairness of financial statements he or she examines. Among this evidence are confirmations from third parties.

Required:
a. What is an audit confirmation?
b. What characteristics should an audit confirmation possess if a CPA is to consider it as valid evidence?

(AICPA adapted)

P6-4   As auditor of Texstar Manufacturing Company, you have obtained an unadjusted trial balance from the books of the company for the year ended February 28, 19X1. The following accounts are included on the trial balance:

	Dr. (Cr.)
Cash in bank, unrestricted	$ 37,245
Cash in bank, restricted	45,000
Marketable securities (at lower of cost or market) [2]	58,600
Accounts receivable, trade	86,295
Trade notes receivable [1]	55,000
Inventories [3]	220,000
Land	500,000
Building, less accumulated depreciation	595,000
Furniture and fixtures, net of accumulated depreciation	247,620
Patents, net of amortization	46,250
Trade accounts payable	(60,250)
Notes payable to banks, short terms	(76,480)
Mortgage payable	(795,000)
Capital stock	(250,000)
Retained earnings	(425,000)
Sales	(1,250,000)
Cost of sales	844,000
General and administrative expenses	162,000
Legal and professional fees	16,480
Interest expense	123,000

Additional information:
(1) All trade notes receivable are held by Texstar.
(2) Marketable securities are held in the company's safe deposit box at Texas National Bank.
(3) The company has $72,000 of inventory stored in a public warehouse in Houston.

Required:
a. To fulfill the *existence* audit objective, which of the accounts on the trial balance should you confirm from outside sources? Briefly explain from whom they should be confirmed and the information that should be confirmed. Organize your answer as follows:

Account name	From whom confirmed	Information to be confirmed

b. For the items that cannot be confirmed to determine existence, describe briefly the procedure that should be performed to satisfy this objective.

(AICPA adapted)

P6-5 For each of the items in the following list, describe (1) the auditor's primary auditing objectives in examining them; (2) one auditing procedure that will satisfy each objective; and (3) when these procedures should be performed (i.e., at interim periods or during final audit field work).

a. Recorded entries in the cash receipts journal.

b. Property plant and equipment.

c. Trademarks.

d. Accrued wages payable.

e. Investment in a subsidiary company.

f. Notes payable.

g. Retained earnings.

h. Miscellaneous expense.

P6-6 The types of tests that auditors perform can be subdivided into categories as (1) tests of controls, (2) substantive tests, and (3) dual-purpose tests. For each of the audit objectives in the following list, state which type of test would be most appropriate.

The audit objective is

a. To ascertain whether the credit department is approving all sales before goods are shipped.

b. To ascertain that all items shipped have been recorded properly in the sales journal.

c. To ascertain the proper valuation of recorded obsolete raw-materials inventory.

d. To ascertain whether all cash disbursements are made by serially numbered checks.

e. To ascertain that all major additions to property and equipment were approved by the board of directors.

f. To test pricing (valuation) of finished goods inventory.

g. To ascertain that proper rates were used for hourly employees in figuring payroll expense.

h. To determine that petty cash exists.

i. To determine whether all existing trade accounts payable are recorded.

j. To determine if mathematical checks were performed on sales invoices by departmental supervisors.

P6-7 In examining documentary support during substantive tests of balances, the direction of the audit test to be performed is quite important. In turn, the direction of test to be performed often depends on whether there is greater potential for client overstatement or understatement. On the other hand, for some audit tests, the direction of the test is less important because the audit objective may not be to detect client overstatements and understatements.

Required:

a. Explain the terms *vouch* and *trace* in the context of the preceding statement.

b. For each of the following audit objectives, state whether the test is for overstatement or understatement and whether either direction might be inferred. Also, state whether you would select vouching or tracing as the required auditing procedure. Then determine the client data file from which it would be most appropriate to select a sample; also, name the client data file to which the sample should be vouched or traced. Possible client data files for this problem include the following:

1. Sales invoice file.
2. Bill-of-lading file.
3. Credit files.
4. Purchase order file.
5. Accounts-receivable subsidiary ledger.
6. General ledger postings.
7. Receiving report file.
8. Purchase journal entries.
9. Vendor invoice file.
10. Sales journal entries.
11. Sales journal totals.
12. Materials requisition file.
13. Cost of production reports.
14. Perpetual inventory files.

Arrange your answer as follows (the first objective has been done for you as an example):

Audit objective	Overstatement, understatement, or either	Vouch or trace	From (data file)	To (data file)
(a)	Overstatement	Vouch	Sales journal entries	Sales invoice file, bill-of-lading file

The audit objectives are

a. To ascertain that recorded sales were actually made.
b. To ascertain that all purchases that were made were recorded.
c. To ascertain that sales invoices were recorded properly in the sales journal.
d. To ascertain that sales invoices were posted to the appropriate customer accounts receivable.
e. To ascertain that requisitions of raw materials inventory were recorded correctly as used in manufacturing work-in-process.
f. To ascertain that raw materials used were removed from perpetual inventory records.
g. To ascertain that general ledger postings for sales are adequately supported by a detailed summary of transactions.
h. To ascertain that sales journal entries were posted correctly in the company's general ledger.

For each of the following situations, assume that the auditor's preliminary tests indicate that there may be an error in a particular account; the error of primary concern is identified as either overstated (O) or understated (U). For each case presented, list one possible offsetting error of secondary concern—that is, the account that may be misstated and whether it would be overstated (O) or understated (U); also, name the substantive tests that may detect both the primary and secondary errors. The first case has been done for you as an example.

Case	Error of primary concern	Error of secondary concern	Substantive tests to detect
1.	Accounts receivable (O)	Sales (O)	Confirmation of accounts receivable Vouching sales invoices to shipping documents
2.	Inventories (O)		
3.	Accounts receivable (O)		
4.	Accounts payable (U)		
5.	Sales (U)		
6.	Notes payable (U)		
7.	Property and equipment (U)		

Case	Error of primary concern	Error of secondary concern	Substantive tests to detect
8.	Cash (O)		
9.	Cost of goods sold (O)		
10.	Depreciation expense (U)		

P6-9 During the examination of the annual financial statements of Amis Manufacturing, Inc., the company's president, R. Alderman, and Luddy, the auditor, reviewed matters that were supposed to be included in a written representation letter. On receipt of the following client representation letter, Luddy contacted Alderman to state that it was incomplete.

To E. K. Luddy, CPA

In connection with your examination of the balance sheet of Amis Manufacturing, Inc., as of December 31, 19X2, and the related statements of income, retained earnings, and changes in financial position for the year then ended, for the purpose of expressing an opinion as to whether the financial statements present fairly the financial position, results of operations, and changes in financial position of Amis Manufacturing, Inc., in conformity with generally accepted accounting principles, we confirm, to the best of our knowledge and belief, the following representations made to you during your examination. There were no

- Plans or intentions that may materially affect the carrying value or classification of assets and liabilities.
- Communications from regulatory agencies concerning noncompliance with, or deficiencies in, financial reporting practices.
- Agreements to repurchase assets previously sold.
- Violations or possible violations of laws or regulations whose effects should be considered for disclosure in the financial statements or as a basis for recording a loss contingency.
- Unasserted claims or assessments that our lawyer has advised are probable of assertion and must be disclosed in accordance with Statement of Financial Accounting Standards 5.

• Capital stock repurchase options or agreements or capital stock reserved for options, warrants, conversions, or other requirements.
• Compensating balance or other arrangements involving restrictions on cash balances.

R. Alderman, President
Amis Manufacturing, Inc.
March 14, 19X3

Required: Identify the other matters that Alderman's representation letter should specifically confirm. *(AICPA adapted)*

P6-10 Discuss the information you would expect to find in the permanent file section of a client's audit working papers. What *information relevant to the audit* would you expect to find in the following permanent file documents?
a. Minutes of board of directors and audit committee meetings.
b. Corporate charter and bylaws.
c. Organization charts.
d. Permanent financing arrangements, such as mortgage loan agreements, bond indentures, and stock issue agreements.
e. Employment contracts with key employees.
f. Time budget from previous year. *(AICPA adapted)*

P6-11 Below is a working paper for the Proof of Cash for Hupp Company for the month of July 19X6. Beside each number 1–9 (on page 228) supply the evidence-gathering procedure that provides the most competent evidence to support the information.

Hupp Company

P R O O F O F C A S H - T E S T M O N T H O F J U L Y

12/31/X6

	Reconciliation 6/30/X6	Receipts	July 19X6 Disbursements	Reconciliation 7/31/X6
Per bank statement	95,425 (1)	40,655 (1)	89,620 (1)	46,460 (1)
Deposits in transit:				
Beginning	550 (2)	(550) (2)		
Ending				-0-
Checks outstanding:				
Beginning	(1,645) (3)		(1,645) (3)	
Ending			2,523 (3)	(2,523) (3)
NSF check returned by bank in June redeposited in July	50 (4)	(50) (4)		
July bank service charge			(3) (5)	3 (5)
Bank error in July corrected in July		(45) (6)	(45) (6)	
		(7)	(7)	
	94,380 (7)	40,010 (8)	90,450 (9)	43,940 (7)

1.

2.

3.

4.

5.

6.

7.

8.

9.

Planning the Audit

Objectives

☐ **1.** Know the meaning and importance of audit planning.
☐ **2.** Know how to plan an audit.
☐ **3.** Know how to use analytical procedures during the planning stages of the audit.
☐ **4.** Know how to meet the standard for supervision of an audit.
☐ **5.** Know how to utilize the client's internal audit staff wisely in an independent audit engagement.

Adequate planning and supervision are vital prerequisites to a timely and successful completion of the audit engagement. As illustrated in the diagram on the next page, it is during the planning stages of the audit that business risk and inherent risk of misstatement in specific accounts and classes of transactions are assessed by the auditor.

The first standard of audit field work requires that the work is to be adequately planned, and assistants, if any, are to be properly supervised.[1] In this chapter, we discuss the importance of adequate planning and supervision, as well as the essential elements of the planning stage of the audit.

The Meaning and Importance of Planning

☑ **Objective 1**
Know the meaning and importance of audit planning

Planning is defined as the development of an overall *strategy* for the expected conduct and scope of the audit.[2] Successful audits are built upon the foundation of good planning. On the other hand, for most of the failed audits we discussed in Chapter 4, the root causes can be traced to poor planning.

Responsibility for planning the audit should be shared by the audit team. The engagement partner, who ultimately must sign the audit report, has the primary responsibility for planning the engagement. However, most of the operational details for planning are delegated to professionals at lower levels of the firm. Thus audit manager and senior or in-charge auditor assume primary roles in the planning process as well.

Figure 7–1 is a diagrammatical sketch of the chronological elements of the audit. Notice that each stage of the audit involves development of different strategies, based partially on the findings from the previous stage. The important

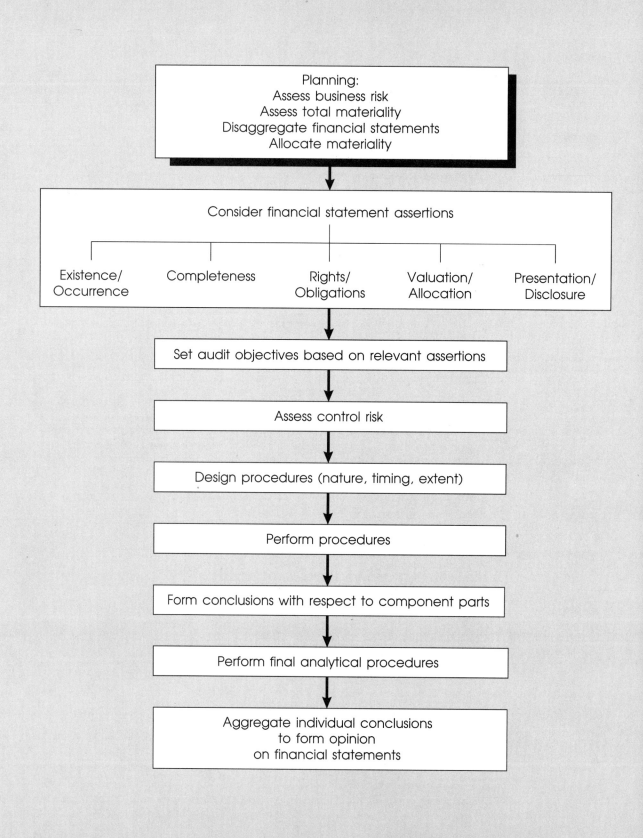

Figure 7–1

Chronological Order of the Elements of an Audit

Approximately 2-4 weeks	3-6 weeks		3-6 weeks		2-3 weeks	Until beginning of next audit
(2) Pre-engagement planning: business risk assessment	(4) Engagement planning, inherent risk assessment, audit area selection, control risk assessment (preliminary)	(5) Interim substantive tests	(7) Final control risk assessment, design of substantive tests	(8) Final tests of details, analytical procedures, subsequent events, representation letter	(10) Working paper review, drafting financial statements and audit report	(12) Postissuance review, subsequent discovery of facts existing at report date
(1) Engagement Acceptance	(3) Engagement letter		(6) End of fiscal year	(9) End of field work, date of audit report, representation letter	(11) Issuance of audit report and financial statements	

thing to remember is that all stages of the audit involve planning in some form. Planning begins before the audit engagement is accepted and continues throughout the entire process until, at the end of the current engagement, the audit team begins to plan the next year's engagement.

Approximate time frames provided in Figure 7–1 will vary widely from one engagement to another. The numbered elements in the figure indicate the following events:

1. The accountant is approached by a prospective client.
2. The accountant spends time obtaining knowledge about the business reputation and integrity of the prospective client, the industry in which the client operates, and the quality and completeness of the client's records, in order to assess business risk.
3. An engagement conference is held with the client. Agreement is reached as to the details of the audit. An engagement letter is originated.
4. Engagement planning continues; the financial statements are disaggregated; there is a preliminary assessment of inherent risk and materiality on an account-by-account basis; preliminary analytical procedures are performed, as well as a preliminary assessment of the control structure of the company; interim tests of controls are performed.
5. Interim tests of transactions creating financial statement balances are conducted.
6. The fiscal year ends.
7. There is a final assessment of control risk.
8. A program for the final stage of the audit of financial statement balances is developed and implemented. Subsequent events are examined. Audit risk and materiality are reevaluated.
9. The audit report date (last day of field work) occurs. The client representation letter is also dated as of this date.
10. Financial statements are drafted; there is an office review of working papers, and the audit report is drafted.
11. Financial statements and the audit report are delivered to the client.
12. Follow-up (including planning for following year).

Pre-Engagement Planning (1), (2)

Under optimal conditions, the prospective client should contact the accountant well in advance of the end of the fiscal year to be audited so that the accountant may have time to assess *overall business risk* of the client. **Business risk** includes factors related to the industry in which the client does business, as well as specific facts about the client, such as competitive position within the industry, financial structure, and the existence of related parties. Business risk is also associated with the integrity and reputation of the client. Quality control standards of the AICPA (Chapter 3) include standards for acceptance and continuance of clients; these standards exist to help auditors avoid association with clients who lack integrity.

The assessment of business risk is necessary for at least two reasons: First, if business risk factors related to the integrity and reputation of the client are found to exist, early identification of these factors will allow the auditor time to decide whether to accept the client. Second, if risk factors other than integrity are found to exist (such as highly volatile industry, much litigation, related party transactions, or a low level of auditor experience in the industry) such factors will affect the planning and staffing of the audit.

An auditor may investigate the industry, past history, integrity, and reputation of prospective clients by any of the following means:

1. Discussions with the potential client.
2. Reading past periods' financial statements.
3. Reading information about the client and the industry in trade journals and other media, such as *The Wall Street Journal* and *The Value Line Investment Survey*.
4. Performing preliminary analytical procedures on financial data of the company.
5. Contacting present and former business associates, banks, and attorneys, as well as various credit agencies.
6. Contacting the potential client's **predecessor auditor**.

SAS 7 (AU315) governs communication between predecessor and successor auditors. Because of the ethical rule regarding confidential client information, the successor auditor may contact the predecessor only with the client's permission. Once permission is granted, the successor's inquiry of the predecessor should include questions bearing on the integrity of the potential client, disagreements that may have arisen because of application of GAAP or GAAS, and, in general, the reason why the predecessor auditor is no longer engaged. The predecessor should respond promptly and fully to all of the successor's inquiries and should indicate areas of limited response. The successor auditor should take all of this information into account in deciding whether to accept an engagement.

If the results of these procedures do not raise serious doubts as to the business risks of being associated with the client, the engagement will generally be accepted.

Engagement Letter (3)

It is extremely important that the accountant and the client reach preliminary agreement concerning the work to be done and the responsibilities to be assumed by each. Most auditors recognize the importance of formalizing this agreement in the form of a written **engagement letter**. Although not required by generally accepted auditing standards, the written engagement letter has been widely used to avoid misunderstandings between auditors and clients regarding the nature, timing, and extent of audit or other professional services to be performed. The engagement letter (illustrated in Figure 7–2) is a written contract between the accountant and the client, which, among other things, may include

Figure 7–2 ■■■■■

Typical Engagement Letter

Best & Company
Certified Public Accounts

June 15, 19X2

Mr. Lane G. Collins, Chairman
JEP Manufacturing Co., Inc.
2140 Bryan Tower
Greensboro, Texas

Dear Mr. Collins:

This letter will confirm our understanding of the arrangements concerning our audit examination of the balance sheets of JEP Manufacturing Co., Inc., at December 31, 19X2 and X1, and the related statements of income, retained earnings, and cash flows for the years then ended.

Our examination will be made in accordance with generally accepted auditing standards. Accordingly, it is expected to include the tests and procedures that are necessary to express an opinion concerning the conformity of the financial statements with generally accepted accounting principles.

Generally accepted auditing standards require us to detect errors and irregularities that would have a significant impact upon the financial statements. However, since our examination is based on selected tests of the accounting records, it cannot provide absolute assurance that such errors and irregularities will be detected. Additionally, the audit examination should not be relied upon for detection of illegal acts that are related to the financial statements. Should errors, irregularities, or illegal acts that affect financial statements come to light during our examination, we will promptly bring them to your attention. Our findings regarding your system of internal control, including information about

- The nature of the work to be performed (auditing, MAS, tax, compilation, review, or any combination of those services).
- The period of time over which the engagement is expected to extend.
- Limitations of the engagement regarding the CPA's responsibility with respect to detection of errors, irregularities, or illegal acts.
- In the case of exclusively nonaudit services, a statement that the engagement is not to be construed as an audit.
- Responsibility of the accountant for communicating findings of the engagement.
- Time to be spent on the engagement and fee arrangements.

As indicated at the bottom of Figure 7–2, accountants who use written engagement letters typically request that clients sign and return a copy of the en-

Figure 7-2

(*continued*)

material weaknesses, will be communicated to you in a separate letter after the completion of our audit work.

At your request, we will perform the following nonaudit services: (1) timely preparation of all federal income tax returns; (2) review and analysis of your compliance with certain contractual loan arrangements with banks.

Our fees for the above work will be based on our regular rates for such services, plus actual out-of-pocket expenses. A billing will be rendered upon completion of our services, payable within 30 days from receipt. We will immediately notify you of any circumstances that could significantly affect our initial fee estimate in the amount of $54,000.

We expect to begin our preliminary field work on September 1, 19X2. The preliminary work should continue until approximately October 1, 19X2. Final field work should begin on February 20, 19X3, immediately after your expected year-end closing of February 15, 19X3.

Final field work should be complete by March 15, 19X3 and you should receive the audit report and report on internal control no later than March 31, 19X3.

If the foregoing is in accordance with your understanding, please sign below and return the duplicate copy of this letter to us. If you have further questions, please feel free to call me.

Very truly yours,

Robert C. Best, Partner

Accepted: _____

By: _____

Date: _____

gagement letter to indicate their acceptance of an agreement with the contents of the letter.

Since the engagement letter forms a written contract between the accountant and the client, adherence to the terms of the letter is part of the accountant's legal responsibility. Cases such as *1136 Tenants* (discussed in Chapter 4) have underscored the need for written agreements with clients concerning the nature, timing, and extent of professional services.

Engagement Planning (4)

Once the auditor and the client have reached an agreement, planning of the engagement enters a more detailed stage. Although the length of time required for the engagement may vary with its complexity, it is not uncommon for planning to cover several weeks. In planning an audit engagement, the auditor should develop an appropriate overall audit strategy. This strategy requires identification of areas of potential high risk of misstatement and the establishment of preliminary materiality thresholds for errors. In doing those things, the auditor relies on discussions with the client, observations, and analytical procedures using selected financial data of the client.

During this stage, the auditor must also obtain an understanding of the control structure of the client (the control environment, the accounting system, and critical control procedures). **Interim tests** of control procedures may also be performed during this period to ascertain whether the system is operating as it was designed. Details of these procedures will be discussed in Chapters 8 and 9. Other planning procedures will be discussed later in this chapter.

Interim Substantive Tests (5)

In many cases, the auditor may reach an early conclusion regarding the adequacy of the control structure and may begin performing substantive tests of transactions and balances at an interim date. Interim substantive tests may take several weeks to perform.

End of Fiscal Year (6)

Preliminary work can continue through the client's fiscal year end, but ideally it should end some time before that date, because the auditor must then be concerned with completing the audit on a timely basis. Adequate planning enables the auditor to schedule preliminary work so that it provides adequate time to decide on the nature, timing, and extent of final substantive tests of balances and other disclosures during final audit field work—when time deadlines for completing the audit are often critical. Properly timed communication of approximate time frames to the client's personnel will enable them to prepare physical facilities to accommodate the audit and to provide any client-prepared working papers that the auditor might be able to use in completing the examination on a timely basis. Client inventory counts should be observed, and cash funds on hand should be counted at the end of the period.

Final Audit Field Work (7), (8), and (9)

Final audit field work usually begins immediately after the client's books have been closed for the fiscal year. This will generally be approximately three to four weeks after the end of the fiscal year. It often takes several weeks to perform the final field work. The exact amount of time depends on the nature and extent of procedures remaining to be performed. It is during this time that a final evaluation is made of the client's internal control system, to determine the nature, timing, and extent of final substantive tests to be performed. The auditor may decide at this time that tests of internal controls, begun during interim work, should be extended to cover the time periods at or near the fiscal year end. This would occur, for example, when circumstances surrounding the client's system of internal controls have changed substantially since interim tests of transactions were performed.

Substantive tests include *both final analytical procedures using adjusted financial statement data and detailed tests of balances.* The time period to which substantive tests apply includes both the period under audit and the period after the balance sheet date, up to and including the last day of the field work (the date of the audit report). As part of the audit program, the auditor must review the events and transactions of the client between the close of the year being audited and the date of completion of the audit field work. These events and transactions, better known as *subsequent events*, are examined to provide the advantage of hindsight in evaluating the disclosures of various elements in the body of the financial statements and to determine whether disclosures relating to the activities of the subsequent period should be included in the footnotes to the financial statements. Subsequent events procedures are discussed at length in Chapter 20.

Review of Working Papers; Drafting of Financial Statements and Audit Report (10)

After the audit staff leaves the client's office, the working papers for the engagement are typically subjected to several reviews by supervisory personnel and, finally, by the partner in charge of the engagement. During this period, which can take two to three weeks, recommended adjustments and supplementary disclosures will be discussed with the client. As we have previously observed, management is primarily responsible for the financial statements, including footnote disclosures. Therefore, the auditor has no authority to change them without the permission of client management.

After completion of the final review, the auditor is ready to write the audit report. The nature of the report will depend on the nature and extent of audit evidence gathered and on the attitude of management toward accepting any proposed corrections to the financial statements. After that, the financial statements are proofread.

Issuance of Financial Statements and Audit Report (11)

The audited financial statements and the audit report are then delivered to the client. In addition, the auditor may have decided that significant deficiencies exist in the client's control structure. If so, these *reportable conditions* should be communicated to the client at this time. This may be done through a management letter, in which the auditor may communicate suggestions for improvements in operating efficiency as well as in internal controls.

Post-Issuance Review; Subsequent Discovery of Facts (12)

The auditor's responsibility does not end with the issuance of the audit report and the related letter on internal control. However, *the role of the auditor shifts at this time from an active to a passive one.* More specifically, after the issuance of the audit report, the auditor may discover facts that existed at the report date but were unknown to him or her at the time. If those previously undisclosed facts render the previously issued financial statements and audit report misleading, the auditor is required to take appropriate action to see that the newly discovered facts are made known as soon as possible. Responsibilities relating to post-issuance reviews [SAS 46 (AU390)] are covered in Chapter 20.

Procedures Involved in Planning the Audit

☑ **Objective 2**
Know how to plan
an audit

During the planning phase of the audit, the auditor should *assess business risk and inherent risk of misstatement* as well as *control risk* of various accounting systems and balances. These assessments will, in turn, help the auditor to decide the nature, timing, and extent of audit tests of balances as well as the number and quality of audit personnel required to perform those tests. The extent of planning necessary for an audit examination varies with the complexity of the engagement and the extent of the auditor's experience and knowledge of the client's affairs. Among the matters that should be considered by the auditor during the planning stage of the engagement are

- Understanding the entity's business and how it relates to the industry in which it operates.
- Understanding the entity's accounting policies and procedures.
- Understanding the accounting data processing system.
- Understanding the entity's control structure.
- Making preliminary judgments about materiality levels.
- Identifying financial statement items likely to require adjustment.
- Identifying conditions (such as material errors or irregularities or related-party transactions) that may require extension or modification of audit tests.
- Considering the nature of reports expected to be rendered (such as a report on consolidated statements, 10-K report for the Securities and Exchange Commission, etc.).[3]

Understanding the Client's Industry

It is impossible to perform an audit with due professional care without a thorough understanding of the industry in which the client operates. Such an understanding enables the auditor to place the engagement into proper perspective and to develop a proper assessment of business risk and planning materiality. Included in the auditor's set of information with respect to the client's industry should be the following:

- General economic conditions of the nation and the geographic region in which the client is located.
- Government regulations that might affect the industry.

- Changes in technology and the industry's sensitivity to those changes.
- Accounting practices that might be unique to the industry.
- Competitive conditions prevalent in the industry.
- Financial trends that prevail in the industry.

Knowledge of these and other matters is valuable in assessing *business risk* of the client. Such knowledge is usually obtained through experience with the entity or its industry and inquiry of client personnel. Working papers from prior years, whether they are from the auditor's own files or obtained through communication with predecessor auditors, can be a useful source of such information. In addition, the AICPA has published accounting and auditing guides for certain industries. Other valuable sources include industry publications, financial statements of other entities in the industry, textbooks, periodicals, and other individuals knowledgeable about the industry.[4] Figure 7–3 contains an industry summary page from a popular industrial reference series.

Figure 7–3

Industry Summary for Electrical Transformer Industry

Industry 3612, Transformers

This industry comprises establishments primarily engaged in the manufacture of power distribution, instrument, and specialty transformers. Establishments primarily engaged in the manufacture of radio frequency or voice frequency transformers, coils, or chokes are classified in industry 3677, and resistance welder transformers in industry 3623.

In the 19X2 Census of Manufacturers, Industry 3612, Transformers, recorded employment of 39.0 thousand. The total value of shipments for establishments classified in this industry was $2,916 million.

The value of shipments figure shown above is in current (19X2) prices. All dollar figures included in this report are at prices current for the year specified and, therefore, unadjusted for changes in price levels. Consequently, when making comparisons to prior years, users should take into consideration the inflation that has occurred.

Establishments in virtually all industries ship secondary products as well as products primary to the industry to which they are classified and have some miscellaneous receipts, such as resales and contract receipts. In current prices, industry 3612 shipped $2,669 million of products primary to the industry, $179 million of secondary products, and had $68 million of miscellaneous receipts. Thus, the ratio of primary products to the total of both secondary and primary products shipped by establishments in the industry was 94 percent (specialization ratio). In 19X7, this specialization ratio was 95 percent.

Establishments in this industry also accounted for 96 percent of products considered primary to the industry no matter where they actually were produced (coverage ratio). In 19X7, the coverage ratio was 97 percent. The products primary to industry 3612, no matter in what industry they were produced, aggregate $2,773 million in current prices.

The total cost of materials and services used by establishments classified in the transformers industry amounted to $1,422 million in current prices.

Source: U.S. Industrial Outlook (U.S. Dept. of Commerce, 1988)

Understanding the Client's Business

The auditor should become intimately familiar with the client's business, its organization, and its operating characteristics. Information vital in this regard includes the type of business in which the client is engaged, types of products and services, capital structure, related parties, locations, and production, distribution, and compensation methods. Like industry information, the auditor obtains knowledge of the client's business through experience with the entity, inquiry and observation of company personnel, and reading pertinent information about the company in industry periodicals.

Understanding the Accounting Information System

One of the first considerations of the auditor should be obtaining an *understanding of the entity's* **accounting information system**. The methods by which the client processes accounting information will affect the design of the accounting system and the internal control procedures. In addition, the extent to which the entity uses computer processing in significant accounting applications (those materially affecting the financial statements) and the complexity of that processing system will affect the nature, timing, and extent of the auditing procedures to be performed over those applications. Included among the factors that should influence the auditor's thinking in this area are the following:

- The extent to which the computer is used in each significant accounting application (e.g., cash receipts, cash disbursements, payroll, accounts receivable, inventories, property and equipment, etc.).
- The complexity of the entity's computer operations, including the use of an outside service center.
- The organizational structure of the computer processing activities.
- The availability of data in either machine-readable or hard copy. Since many, if not most, systems in larger entities involve on-line computer applications, hard copy either may not be available or may be available only for a short period of time. Some information may never be saved in human-readable form. If this is the case and if that information is needed in the audit, it will be necessary to use computer audit techniques to audit the information. These techniques are discussed in detail in Chapter 10. The use of computer-assisted audit techniques may increase audit efficiency and effectiveness by enabling the auditor to apply certain procedures to entire populations of accounts or transactions.
- If the auditor lacks the specialized skills required in auditing a computerized system, it may be necessary to seek the assistance of a professional who possesses such skills. This person may be on the auditor's own staff or an outside professional. If the use of another professional is planned, the auditor should have a sufficient computer-related knowledge to communicate the objectives of the other professional's work; to evaluate whether the work of the profes-

sional meets the auditor's objectives; and to evaluate the results of the procedures applied as they relate to key audit objectives. If the computer-audit specialist is a member of the audit staff, the rules pertaining to supervising work of assistants (discussed later in this chapter) apply.[5]

Understanding the Entity's Control Structure

A vital part of the planning of every engagement should be the understanding of the control structure of the client. Such an understanding allows the auditor to *assess control risk* and, when combined with information on the industry, business, and accounting policies and procedures, to design an appropriate audit program for the financial statement balances. Obtaining an understanding of the control structure of an entity is the subject of Chapters 8 and 9.

Making Preliminary Judgments about Materiality

It is during the planning stages of the audit that the auditor must develop preliminary estimates of *materiality*. As stated in Chapter 5, materiality is defined as a maximum amount of dollar error that is tolerable in the financial statements without affecting an informed financial statement user's judgments. The auditor must answer the following questions:

- Who are the primary users of the financial statements?
- What financial statement variables are most important to the primary financial statement users?
- How large an error could be accepted by the primary users before they would consider themselves to have made a financial mistake by investing, lending, or becoming otherwise involved with the client?

Answers to such questions involve much subjective judgment on the part of the auditor. Generally, the important financial statement variables to creditors or potential creditors are those that relate the entity's ability to pay (working capital, current and quick ratios, cash flow, etc.). On the other hand, the important financial statement variables to investors or potential investors are those that relate the entity's profitability (rates of return on assets and stockholders' equity, earnings per share, gross profit, etc.) When the relevant materiality variables have been decided, the auditor must then make a decision as to magnitude of misstatement that could affect the users' decisions. Although there are no written standards in this regard, some audit firms have set arbitrary levels such as 5 percent of the relevant variable (net income, for example). Although only an *educated guess*, quantitative materiality guidelines are important to the auditor during the planning stages. This is because materiality affects the nature, timing, and extent of planned audit procedures. Narrow materiality thresholds require more effective audit procedures, closer to year-end, and larger sample sizes on a given set of data than wide materiality thresholds.

Financial Statement Items Likely to Require Adjustment

In the diagram at the beginning of this chapter we illustrated that once overall business risk and materiality of the client has been assessed, the audit process involves *disaggregation of the financial statements* into their component systems and related accounts. Generally, those systems fall into the following categories:

- The revenue and collections system.
- The acquisition and expenditure system.
- The payroll system.
- The production and conversion system.
- The financing and investing system.

The *common denominator* account that is affected by each of these systems is cash. Once the process of disaggregation has taken place in the auditor's mind, he or she should use the preliminary judgment concerning materiality along with the assessment of **risk of misstatement** of specific accounts to select those accounts and other financial disclosures likely to require adjustment. Risk of misstatement, in this respect, refers to the *relative risk* that is characteristic of a particular account. Some accounts have a high risk of misstatement because of their ease of misappropriation and the amount of activity within the account during the operating cycle. Cash is an example of such an account. Other accounts have a high risk of misstatement because of significant and unexpected fluctuations that might have occurred in the recent past. To detect such fluctuations, the auditor must perform preliminary analytical procedures.

Preliminary Analytical Procedures

☑ **Objective 3**
Know how to use analytical procedures for audit purposes

One of the most important planning tools used by the auditor to identify potential areas of *high audit risk* of misstatement is *preliminary analytical procedures*. As described in Chapter 6, analytical procedures are the *study of plausible relationships* among financial and nonfinancial data.[6] The data may be in the form of absolute dollars, physical quantities, ratios, or percentages.

Analytical procedures involve comparisons of recorded amounts on the company's financial statements to *expectations* developed by the auditor from one or more of the following sources:

- Comparable information from prior periods for the same company.
- Anticipated results (budgets, forecasts, etc.).
- Relationships among elements of financial information within the period (usually in the form of ratios).
- Comparable information from the industry in which the client operates.

- Relationships of elements of the financial data to relevant nonfinancial information.

Analytical procedures are required to be performed during the planning stage of the audit. If recorded financial data of the client do not conform to the auditor's expectations, the auditor is alerted to potential high risk of misstatement in the accounts involved. Fluctuations that do not conform to a predictable pattern should cause the auditor to select those accounts and systems for primary audit attention.

Analytical Ratios

Ratios and percentage relationships are the devices most extensively used in the analytical process. These are calculated for the period under audit (or for portions of the period) and are then compared with the same ratios and percentages for prior periods or with industry averages for the current period. We now identify some of these ratios and relationships and explain their significance in the analytical process:

- *Inventory turnover* (cost of goods sold ÷ average inventory). This calculation and comparison is directly useful to the auditor in identifying obsolete or slow-moving merchandise. However, a significant change in turnover not explained by slow-moving merchandise can be an indication of a change in operational practices or errors in the determination of inventory. The auditor may also want to determine the average age of inventory in days (365 ÷ the turnover figure) to gain further insight into the client's inventory situation.
- *Accounts receivable turnover* (sales on account ÷ average accounts receivable) supplemented by the average collection period (days sales outstanding) for accounts receivable (365 ÷ turnover figure) can be used as a general check on the audited accounts receivable balance and on the collectibility of those accounts. Again, a significant change in this turnover figure could also be explained by a change in collections experience or possibly by an error in the accounts receivable balance.
- *Accounts payable turnover* (purchases on account ÷ average accounts payable) and the *average pay period* (365 ÷ turnover) can be used to help develop a general conclusion regarding the fairness of those account balances in the financial statements. These calculations, for example, can lead to the discovery of unrecorded accounts payable.
- The *gross margin percentage* (gross margin ÷ net sales) should be computed and compared with the percentages for prior years. An unexplained decrease in this percentage, for example, might suggest the possibility of unrecorded sales or overstated cost of sales.
- The auditor will want to compute the *net profit margin* (net operating income ÷ net sales) and compare it with prior-year percentages. If the gross margin percentage has been found to be consistent with that of prior years and the operating margin percentage has changed significantly, the auditor must seek

to explain that change in terms of one of the reasons cited later or entertain the possibility that some of the operating expense items are not fairly stated.

- The auditor will also want to calculate the *percentage relationship between net income from continuing operations and total assets*. That percentage in turn should be compared with the percentages for prior years. If the net operating income to sales percentage (see previous item) has been consistent with that of prior years and this percentage has changed significantly, the auditor will seek to explain such a change or look for possible errors in audited balances of related assets.

- The *percentage relationship between net income from continuing operations and equity capital* should be calculated and compared with that percentage for prior periods. If the other operating percentages cited above have been consistent with those of prior periods and this one has changed significantly, the auditor will be concerned with explaining that difference. The explanation could, for example, be significant new borrowings or repayments of debt.

- *Liquidity ratios* in the form of the current ratio (current assets ÷ current liabilities) and the quick assets ratio (liquid assets ÷ current liabilities) should be calculated primarily for the purpose of determining possible errors in the classifications of current assets or current liabilities. For example, assume that a company with $100,000 in current assets and $50,000 in current liabilities (a 2-to-1 current ratio) deliberately understated current assets and current liabilities in the amount of $10,000 for checks written but not released as of the balance sheet date. Current assets would appear as $90,000 and current liabilities as $40,000 on the balance sheet. Thus, the company's balance sheet shows an erroneous 2.25-to-1 current ratio. The misstatement of these ratios can be particularly important if the firm has been operating under significant net working capital constraints, such as long-term debt with restrictive covenants.

- *Leverage ratios* showing the relationships between debt and equity capital and between earnings and fixed interest charges should be calculated. Deviations from prior periods could show significant changes in the company's capital structure or ability to service its long-term debt.

Year-to-Year Fluctuations

One of the most common ways to develop expectations regarding the financial data of the company is to observe comparable data from prior years for the same company. Over a period of years, predictable patterns occur in financial statement accounts such as revenues, cost of goods sold, and certain expenses. In addition, relationships between certain other financial data such as gross margin percentage, current ratio, inventory turnover ratio, and days sales outstanding develop trends according to business fluctuations as well as management decisions of the company. Using prior years' figures on which to base expectations, the auditor compares the current year's data. If, during planning, the auditor detects unexpected fluctuations in these data, the affected accounts should be investigated for possible errors.

EXAMPLE
Auditors for the Bales Company are performing preliminary analytical procedures as part of planning for the 19X1 audit. The days sales outstanding for the company's receivables for 19X1 were 45.2 as opposed to 36.1 for 19X0. Such a fluctuation normally points to a slowdown in the collection process and an increased probability of uncollectibility of accounts receivable. Accordingly, the auditors should consider extending the tests of uncollectibility (valuation) over accounts receivable and the allowance for doubtful accounts.

It should be remembered that, when analytical procedures are performed during the planning stages of the audit, unaudited data (either annual or quarterly) must often be used. Therefore, there is an increased probability that the financial information being analyzed might contain errors or irregularities.

Anticipated Results

Another means of developing expectations for relationships among the client's data is the use of budgets and projections. If prepared carefully, based on sound principles and assumptions, such data often provide reasonably accurate predictions of the company's financial position and results of operations. Comparison of achieved results with budgeted results is often standard procedure for management of the client. Therefore, the auditor's work might consist of review of the client's budgetary process, including the client's responsibility accounting system and the actions that were taken by management to follow up on unexpected changes.

Comparable Industry Data

Comparisons of current financial data with comparable data from past periods and with projected results for the same company provides only an incomplete picture of how well the client is performing in relation to itself. A more complete picture can be obtained by comparison of current year data for the company with comparable data from the industry in which the client operates.

Moody's Investors Service, Dun and Bradstreet, Standard and Poor's, and other publishers gather financial information for thousands of companies. These data are classified into industries by standard industrial category (SIC) code numbers. Figure 7–4 presents industry financial data for the electronic transformer industry (SIC Category 3612).

It should be emphasized that, because data from industrial data bases are broad averages, comparisons of such data with that of a particular company are meaningful only up to a point. Differences in accounting methods, specific lines

Figure 7–4 ━━

Financial Data for the Electronic Transformer Industry

	SIC 3612 Transformers		
	19X1		
	$		%
Cash	113,275		9.8
Accounts receivable	314,397		27.2
Notes receivable	6,935		0.6
Inventory	344,449		29.8
Other current	67,040		5.8
Total current	846,097		73.2
Fixed assets	166,445		14.4
Other non-current	143,328		12.4
Total assets	1,155,870		100.0
Accounts payable	137,549		11.9
Bank loans	31,208		2.7
Notes payable	46,235		4.0
Other current	165,289		14.3
Total current	380,281		32.9
Other long term	193,030		16.7
Deferred credits	9,247		0.8
Net worth	573,312		49.6
Total liabilities & net worth	1,155,870		100.0
Net sales	2,219,224		100.0
Gross profit	681,302		30.7
Net profit after tax	97,646		4.4
Working capital	465,816		—

Ratios	UQ	MED	LQ
Quick ratio (times)	2.3	1.1	0.7
Current ratio (times)	3.9	2.5	1.5
Curr liab to NW (%)	27.0	52.4	154.6
Curr liab to inv (%)	58.4	110.6	182.8
Total liab to NW (%)	29.6	84.7	198.7
Fixed assets to NW (%)	17.3	37.6	58.0
Sales outstanding (days)	39.5	47.8	57.7
Cost of sales to inv (times)	10.7	6.5	4.9
Total asset turnover	2.56	1.82	1.36
Sales to NWC (times)	9.5	4.7	3.0
Acct pay to sales (%)	3.2	5.1	8.5
Return on sales (%)	5.3	2.5	0.6
Return on assets (%)	9.8	5.3	0.8
Return on NW (%)	15.9	9.0	3.0

UQ = Upper Quartile; MED = Median; LQ = Lower Quartile
Source: Copyright 1988 Dun & Bradstreet. Used with permission.

of business, and other factors may severely limit comparability. Nevertheless, industrial averages add information to the auditor's data set and should be used whenever possible.

The company data in Figure 7–5 are based on the financial statements of JEP Manufacturing Co., which is a company in the electrical transformer industry

Figure 7–5 ▬▬▬

Some Standard Financial Statement Ratios

Ratios	Ratio formulation	19X0	19X1	Industry average	Conclusion
Utilization					
Total asset turnover	$= \dfrac{\text{Net sales}}{\text{Total tangible assets}}$	1.65	1.72	1.82	Average but getting longer
Accounts receivable turnover	$= \dfrac{\text{Net sales on account}}{\text{Average accounts receivable}}$	11.69	7.71	N/A	Getting worse
Days sales outstanding	$= \dfrac{\text{Accounts receivable}}{\text{Daily sales}}$	31.2	47.36	47.8	Average but getting longer
Inventory turnover	$= \dfrac{\text{Cost of goods sold}}{\text{Average inventory}}$	6.79	6.39	6.5	Average but getting longer
Fixed asset turnover	$= \dfrac{\text{Net sales}}{\text{Net fixed assets}}$	6.23	7.35	N/A	Getting better
Liquidity					
Current ratio	$= \dfrac{\text{Current assets}}{\text{Current liabilities}}$	2.57	2.43	2.5	Adequate
Quick ratio	$= \dfrac{\text{Cash + marketable securities + accts. receivable}}{\text{Current liabilities}}$	.76	1.06	1.1	Adequate
Leverage					
Times interest earned	$= \dfrac{\text{Net income before tax + interest}}{\text{interest}}$	8.16	13.89	N/A	Improving
Debt ratio	$= \dfrac{\text{Current liabilities + noncurrent liabilities}}{\text{Total tangible assets}}$	.38	.38	N/A	Steady
Debt-equity ratio	$= \dfrac{\text{Current liabilities + noncurrent liabilities}}{\text{Tangible shareholders' equity}}$	.61	.60	.85	Better than average
Profitability					
Net profit margin	$= \dfrac{\text{Net operating income}}{\text{Net sales}}$	5.34%	5.76%	2.5%	Excellent
ROA (Return on assets)	$= \dfrac{\text{Net operating income}}{\text{Total tangible assets}}$	8.83%	9.93%	5.3%	Excellent
ROE (Return on equity)	$= \dfrac{\text{Net operating income}}{\text{Tangible shareholders' equity}}$	14.22%	15.91%	9.0	Excellent

Source: Terry S. Maness, *Introduction to Corporate Finance* (New York: McGraw-Hill Book Company, 1988), p. 60. Used with permission.

selected for illustrations throughout this text. Notice that we have transcribed the applicable data (column entitled "MED," or median) from Figure 7–4 into the column entitled "industry average" in Figure 7–5. Based on the available data, it appears that JEP Manufacturing Co.'s asset utilization figures are approximately average when compared to those of the industry, but perhaps not quite as good as they have been in prior years. On the other hand, it appears that JEP Manufacturing Co. has a lower-than-average debt-equity ratio (total liabilities to net worth in Figure 7–4) and is highly profitable when compared to other companies in the industry. Based on these comparisons, as well as materiality issues, the auditors will focus attention on inventories and receivables systems and balances, as pointed out in the planning memorandum later in this chapter.

Use of Nonfinancial Data

The auditor is always looking for nonfinancial data that can be used in developing general measurements of the client's expected volume of operations. For example, in auditing the records of a hospital, the number of patient days can be multiplied by the historical average revenue per patient day to arrive at an approximation of the expected revenue from patients. In auditing a hotel or motel, the percentage of occupancy multiplied by the maximum total room revenue, if the establishment was fully occupied, can be used in estimating revenues from room rentals. In auditing a college or university, the total number of student credit hours reported by the registrar can be multiplied by the tuition rate per hour to arrive at an approximation of tuition revenue. The number of members in a country club can be multiplied by the annual dues per member to arrive at an approximation of dues revenue. Other less directly related nonfinancial measures include such things as the relationship of energy usage in a manufacturing industry to the cost of goods manufactured or the relationship between the number of employees in a manufacturing firm and the cost of goods manufactured by the firm.

A more sophisticated technique for performing analytical procedures involves use of **regression analysis** to calculate an expected account balance. This technique calls for using one or more of the financial or nonfinancial variables mentioned above as independent predictor variables in the regression equation. A computer audit software program similar to those discussed in Chapter 10 can be used to perform the regression analysis. Advantages of this technique are (1) it provides an expected account balance based on logical relationships of business volume and other activity; (2) it automatically computes tolerances for variations from expectations; (3) it is more sensitive and, therefore, more precise, than ratio analysis; and (4) it can be programmed to automatically calculate statistically valid sample sizes for additional tests of details, if needed, to corroborate the findings of the analytical review procedures. Firms that use this type of extensive analysis rely heavily on it and, therefore, may greatly limit tests of details. Chapter 12 contains a brief discussion and illustration of regression analysis as a tool for prediction, as well as some simplified problems.

Use of the Computer for Data Analysis

The widespread use of advanced computer systems in processing accounting information has provided auditors with ways to analyze financial data that are not possible when manual systems are in use. Computer systems have the capability to store, retrieve, and analyze data for use in achieving a variety of management objectives. Such data may include detailed sales analyses, productivity reports, labor utilization studies, and detailed analyses of trends in other nonfinancial data. Although not directly related to the basic accounting records, these data bases may be valuable sources of information for the auditor to use in applying financial analytical review procedures, other substantive tests, and compliance testing.

Analyzing Variations from Expectations

Variations of company data from expectations can generally be explained in one of the following ways:

Business or Economic Changes.   In this case, it is likely that interrelated areas of the audit will be affected in a similar and logical fashion. For example, if sales have declined 30 percent due to a business or economic slowdown and commissions are based on sales volume, commissions should be down 30 percent as well. On the other hand, if sales are down and commissions are up, an unexpected and illogical fluctuation has occurred, and both of these accounts should receive further audit attention.

Accounting Changes.   In this case, the deviation from expectations has been produced by a change in accounting methods. Such changes must be disclosed in the footnotes to the financial statements. The effects of the change on financial statements should be isolated to a particular part of the financial statements and should be readily recognizable.

Errors or Irregularities.   If the deviation from expectation cannot be explained by economic events or accounting changes and appropriately corroborated by the findings from evidence-gathering, the auditor should consider the possibility that the data contain errors or irregularities. Such data should be the focus of more detailed audit procedures.

During the planning stages it is usually impossible to tell which of these factors is the primary cause of the deviation from expectations. The important thing at this stage is that the auditor be alerted to unexpected relationships among financial data and thus be enabled to design audit tests that are directed to these potential problem areas. More detailed tests on the systems and balances in those areas can then detect the exact cause of the unusual fluctuation.

Consideration of an Entity's Continued Existence

Analytical procedures can reveal significant trends over several years such as deteriorating cash flows, unprofitable operations, and inability to pay debts as they become due. If the client's data are recorded correctly, such trends could point to upcoming financial difficulty or the possibility that *the company might not continue as a going concern*.

SAS 59 (AU341) requires that the auditor *evaluate the aggregate results of audit procedures* for indications of substantial doubt about the entity's ability to continue as a going concern for a reasonable period of time (not to exceed one year beyond the date of the audited financial statements). The proper use of analytical procedures during the planning stages can sometimes provide early warning signals of impending financial problems for the company. Other procedures that might reveal potential going-concern problems at this stage of the audit include review of correspondence with creditors, reading the financial statements of prior periods, and discussions with client personnel. As the engagement progresses, the auditor should keep a detailed record in the working papers as to other evidence that points to going-concern problems. In Chapter 20 we will discuss other procedures, performed during later stages of the audit, that also help to identify potential going-concern problems for clients.

Other Planning Procedures

One of the procedures that the auditor should perform early in an audit engagement is to tour the client's facilities. During the **plant tour** the auditor should learn more about the client's business and industry, and the physical condition of inventories and plant assets. In addition, observations made during the plant tour can be useful later, during substantive test work, to refresh the auditor's memory about such things as obsolete inventory, extraordinary or routine maintenance and repairs, and fully depreciated assets.

Other procedures normally performed during the planning phase of the audit include a *review of past records* of the client and *discussions with other personnel of the accounting firm* who are (or have been) involved in work for the client. These persons may include members of the firm's MAS, tax, or accounting and review staffs. Client records for review include past correspondence with the client, prior years' working papers, if any, and prior audit reports. (See Figure 7–6.)

If the audit engagement of the previous year was performed by other independent auditors, the CPA may seek permission of the client to request a *review of the predecessor auditor's working papers*. Review of the predecessor auditor's working papers is useful and sometimes necessary for the current auditor to express an opinion on the financial statements of the current year, as well as to

Figure 7–6 ▰▭▭▭▭▭▭▭▭▭▭▭▭▭▭▭▭▭▭▭▭▭▭▭▭▭▭▭▭▭▭▭▭▭

Partial Audit Program

	Procedures	Procedures performed by	Comments or references
	1–Preliminary orientation		
1-1	Coordinate with the Supervising Partner and Manager concerning which preliminary orientation procedures and which preliminary discussions with principal officers will be performed by whom. Discuss any information based on their knowledge of or contacts with the client's operations that is pertinent to this program. If it is necessary to start audit tests concurrently with the performance of this program, establish tentative materiality and audit risk for such purpose after consultation with the Supervising Partner and Manager.	WLB	See Memo
1-2	Read the following:		
	a. The financial statements for the preceding year and the auditors' report thereon.	WLB	
	b. The commentary report for the preceding year.	WLB	
	c. Any reports issued since our last examination in connection with a transfer of interests, security registration, financing, or MAS engagement.	WLB	
	d. The Federal income tax returns for the preceding year, with particular emphasis on "Schedule M" items.	WLB	
	e. Any memorandums relating to unusual or complex tax matters, current or pending revenue agent's examinations, or significant changes in the tax law, regulations and decisions. (If the client is not subject to income taxes, or has special status for income tax purposes, this procedure should include familiarization with the applicable criteria for continuing such nontaxable or special status.)	WLB	See Memo
	f. Material in the correspondence file of current interest, including the engagement memorandum and supplements.	WLB	
	g. Any recent reports on the client or its industry distributed by a financial reporting service, such as Standard & Poor's or Value Line, or by a brokerage firm. (Such reports generally are obtainable from the client, a brokerage firm, or Executive Office.)	WLB	See Memo
	h. Any analyses prepared by the client comparing its operations with selected competitors or with industry statistics. (Statistics prepared by the trade association serving the client's industry generally are obtainable from the client, our Subject File Binder, or Executive Office.)	WLB	None prepared

(continued)

Figure 7–6 ▬▬▬▬▬▬▬▬▬▬▬▬▬▬▬▬▬▬▬▬▬▬▬▬▬▬▬▬▬▬▬▬▬▬▬▬

(continued)

	Procedures	Procedures performed by	Comments or references
	1–Preliminary orientation		
1-2	i. The most recent interim financial statements and internal reports for management. For later discussion (and for a more detailed investigation under the program for analytical review), note unusual or questionable items or trends and any significant changes in financial position or results of operations as compared with the same period for the preceding year and, if available, with the budget for the current year-to-date period (including any internal narrative reports relating to variances from budget). If the client does not prepare interim financial statements, scan the general ledger accounts to determine whether the amounts and relationships appear reasonable in comparison with the preceding year.	WLB	Through 6/30/X7
	j. Any quarterly reports to shareholders, current reports on Form 10-Q to the Securities and Exchange Commission, and periodic financial reports to any governmental agency having regulatory authority over the client's accounting. Note any unusual matters disclosed in such reports for later discussion.	WLB	No unusual items noted

Source: Deloitte & Touche. Used with permission.

assess the consistency of application of GAAP between the current and preceding years. Remember that audit evidence concerning the current year's beginning balance sheet accounts was obtained in previous years. A CPA auditing financial statements for the first time must obtain evidence regarding the fairness of presentation of beginning balances—such as inventories, property and equipment, accrued liabilities, capital stock, and retained earnings. The auditor may substantially reduce the audit effort in verifying these accounts and others by reviewing the working papers of the predecessor auditor.

The predecessor auditor should be available to the successor auditor for consultation and should make certain working papers available for the successor's review. The predecessor's working papers most often needed by the successor are those that will provide the successor with general information about the client's business and those that provide information of continuing accounting significance relating to the client. These typically include the corporate charter and bylaws, previous planning memoranda, and minutes of board of directors meetings. Information of continuing accounting significance may be obtained from analyses of both current and noncurrent balance sheet accounts, analytical summaries of past years, and analysis of contingencies.

The predecessor auditor may decide for valid business reasons (such as pending or threatened litigation) not to allow the successor auditor access to certain working papers. In such cases, the predecessor should provide the successor with an appropriate explanation of the circumstances.

The logistics of the audit work should be discussed with the client's management, board of directors, or audit committee during the planning phase of the audit. This helps prevent misunderstandings and inefficient use of client personnel. Current-year interim financial statements should be read for information that could be helpful in planning the engagement. New accounting or auditing pronouncements should be considered to determine how they will affect the scope of the audit. The senior or supervising auditor should also estimate the number of audit staff members and the number of client firm personnel that will be required for the engagement. After these actions have been completed, the auditor is ready to finalize the plans with the client for completing the audit.

The Audit Program: Relating Audit Objectives to Procedures

A vital part of planning an audit engagement should be an advance listing of expected procedures to be performed. This normally takes the form of a written *audit program*, in which the outlined procedures are designed primarily to direct the evidence-gathering process. The **audit program** aids in instructing assistants because it states in reasonable detail how audit objectives can be achieved.[7] The form of the audit program and the details included in it will vary, depending on the complexity of the engagement. Figure 7–6 illustrates a partial audit program for the preliminary planning phase of an audit. The complete and final audit program for a particular segment of the engagement should be developed after the auditor has finished the preliminary evaluation of the system of internal controls over that segment. The audit program for a particular segment of the audit will typically include all the procedures to be followed in that segment of the audit, including the understanding of the internal control structure as well as each account affected by that structure.

The Planning Memorandum

After the preliminary work has been completed, the accountant in charge of the field work typically summarizes in written form the results of the planning procedures. This summary is called the **audit planning memorandum**. It includes sections summarizing the auditor's preliminary orientation to the client's business; the discussions with principal officers concerning significant matters; the results of the preliminary understanding of internal controls; preliminary materiality estimates; the extent of dependence on client staff, including **internal auditors**; and a time budget and staff assignments for the audit. Figure 7–7 illustrates the planning memorandum for JEP Manufacturing Co.

Figure 7-7 ▰▰▰▰▰══

Planning Memorandum

JEP Manufacturing Co. and Subsidiaries
PLANNING MEMORANDUM
3-31-X1

JEP Manufacturing Company is a small specialty manufacturing company located in Greensboro, Texas. The company's common stock is approximately 90 percent owned by J. E. Coletrain, JEP's president and chairman; 9.9 percent of the remaining shares are owned by other members of the family.

JEP manufactures transformers, load break oil switches, vacuum interruptors, and sub-stations for the electric utility industry, oil industry, and other users of heavy electrical equip-ment. Transformers and switches compose the majority of JEP's sales volume and are sold primarily to Tarsit Co. and Indiana Electric. In the Switch Division, their primary competitors include Neverblow Electric, Sunpower Industries, and Light Equipment Company. The Transformer Division competes primarily with General Electric and Westinghouse. In order to remain competitive with mass producers such as G. E. and Westinghouse, JEP spe-cializes in made-to-order products, as opposed to standard models.

A five-year summary of earnings follows:

March 31,	19X6	19X7	19X8	19X9	19X0
Revenues	$4,809,744	$4,558,083	$5,126,796	$6,269,841	$6,600,945
Expenses	4,440,841	4,517,082	5,068,786	5,690,732	5,992,253
	92.3%	99.1%	98.9%	90.8%	90.8%
Net earnings before taxes	368,903	41,001	58,010	579,019	608,692
Taxes	166,479	8,179	16,375	240,603	260,592
Net earnings	202,424	32,822	41,135	338,506	348,100
Earnings per share	1.69	.19	.30	3.05	3.17

Planning Meeting

On March 30, 19X1, prior to commencement of field work on April 27, Mitchell Cloud, engagement manager, and John Hulme, in-charge accountant, met to discuss our audit and approach. On March 26, 19X1, the overall audit approach was discussed by Robert Best, engagement partner, and Mitchell Cloud, engagement manager.

Significant audit areas

Inventory is considered a critical audit area because of its material effect on the balance sheet. Also critical is management's estimation of percentage complete and the resulting completion of work-in-process and impact on earnings. The client will take a physical inventory at year end, which will be observed and test counted by Best & Co. (auditors). Percentage-of-completion estimates will be tested as to propriety, price allocations, and firm purchase commitments. A review of obsolete inventory will also be performed.

Figure 7–7 ▰▰▰▰

(continued)

Other audit areas

Accounts Receivable: standard procedures will be performed, including confirmation, aging analysis, and vouching subsequent collections.

The ratio of gross sales to expenses will be tested in sales and cash disbursements test work. Analytical procedures will also be performed at year end on material income statement accounts.

Other matters

The engagement is budgeted at approximately 300 hours with final field work beginning April 27. Completion of field work is scheduled for approximately May 29.

The audit staff will consist of the following individuals:

			Hours
In-charge	John Hulme	Sr.	190
Staff	Steve Golding	Ass't.	120
			310

Per discussion with client, final deadline is tentatively scheduled for conclusion of field work May 29 and final reports June 5.

The client has agreed to prepare working papers in the following areas:

• Percentage completion of work-in-process inventories.
• Federal income tax accruals.
• Year-end accruals.
• Management bonus plan.
• Pension and profit-sharing plan.

▰▰▰▰

Supervising the Audit

☑ **Objective 4**
Supervision of the audit

Supervision involves directing the work of assistants in accomplishing audit objectives.[8] We have observed that the auditor must evaluate her or his technical competence to handle particular audit tasks. In a similar manner, supervisors are responsible for determining that specific audit tasks are assigned only to persons who have the technical capability required to complete them. Other elements of supervision include (1) instructing assistants, (2) keeping informed about significant problems encountered on the engagement, (3) reviewing completed work, and (4) resolving differences of opinion among personnel. The extent of supervision required depends on the expertise of the audit personnel involved, as well as on the complexity of the audit task.

As a means of formalizing authority/responsibility relationships within a public accounting firm, individual accountants are generally designated as *partners*, *managers*, *seniors* (in-charge auditors), or *staff members*. The highest level of authority (and, therefore, the one having ultimate authority and supervisory responsibilities) is the partner. The next level is made up of managers, who typically have supervisory responsibilities for a designated group of in-charge auditors, or seniors. Staff members have no supervisory responsibilities. They are supervised by seniors assigned to specific audit engagements. Most large firms also have managers and partners who specialize in the audits of specific industries. In that capacity these persons are expected to help in resolving questions associated with the audits of clients in their fields of specialization.

Supervision involves day-by-day analysis of the work being done by assistants to judge whether they are meeting overall audit objectives. It is important that communications between the supervisor and assistants flow two ways. Assistants should be expected to communicate technical and other problems upward within the firm until those problems are effectively resolved. This communication is consistent with the consultation standard for quality control within a firm. On the other hand, overall audit objectives and progress should be continually communicated from the supervisor downward through the ranks to staff personnel. Good communication will help all persons involved in the engagement to feel that they have an important part in the overall effort and will also allow all persons involved to keep abreast of the pertinent activities as they happen.

One element of supervision that requires special consideration is that of resolving differences of opinion among personnel. On rare occasions, a staff member may feel, after appropriate consultation, that he or she disagrees with a conclusion reached by supervisors regarding a technical accounting or auditing issue. The CPA firm should establish procedures that will encourage the staff member to document her or his disagreement in such a situation. Only by doing so may staff members be encouraged to think for themselves as they will have to do in their move up the authority/responsibility ladder.

Reliance on the Work of Internal Auditors

☑ **Objective 5**
Wise use of client's
internal audit staff

In addition to providing assistance in preparing pro forma working papers, the client's internal auditors may be used to actually perform tests of controls and substantive tests for the independent auditor. SAS 9 (AU322) discusses the extent to which the independent auditor can rely on the work of internal auditors.

As explained in Chapter 1, the objective of the internal audit differs significantly from that of the independent audit. Internal auditors perform a number of *high-level monitoring services* for top management, including a continuing study and evaluation of internal control. Beyond that, they typically *review operating practices* of the client in order to promote increased efficiency and economy, and make inquiries of operating departments at management's direction. The effect of the internal audit function on the quality of the internal control system is discussed further in Chapter 8.

Although the client's internal audit staff may have complete organizational autonomy, it must be remembered that they are still client employees. Therefore, they do not have the level of independence required by generally accepted auditing standards to render an audit opinion on the client's financial statements. In some parts of the audit, however, internal auditors possess adequate objectivity, training, experience, and expertise to assist the independent auditor in the evidence-gathering process.

The auditor should evaluate the following attributes of the client's internal audit staff in deciding the extent to which their work can be replied upon:

- *The purpose served by the internal audit function.* If the internal audit function is truly an autonomous internal control-monitoring arm of top management, the internal audit staff may be used much more heavily than if the internal audit department is merely an element of the accounting department.
- *The competency of the internal audit staff.* Competency may be investigated by evaluating the professional credentials of the internal audit staff, their prior experience, and the client's practices for hiring, training, and supervising internal audit staff.
- *The objectivity of the internal audit staff.* In evaluating objectivity, the independent auditor should consider the organizational level to which the internal audit staff reports. This may be done by referring to the client's organization chart and by examining the internal auditor's recommendations in previously issued reports.
- *The work of the internal audit staff.* The independent auditor should examine, on a test basis, working papers that have been prepared by the internal audit staff in the past. In addition, the independent auditor should examine samples of the internal auditor's work and follow through the logic used by the internal audit staff in reaching conclusions.

If it is decided that the work of the internal audit staff can be relied upon, the independent auditor's activities may be affected in either or both of the following ways:

- Because the internal audit staff's work overlaps certain work of the independent auditor and improves the client's system of internal control, the nature and extent of the independent auditor's tests may be reduced.
- The independent auditor may actually use the client's internal audit staff to perform certain tests of controls and substantive tests. If this alternative is selected, it must be remembered that, although the internal auditor may perform the actual tests, the independent auditor is the only one qualified to

make the final audit judgments about the level of control risk and fairness of presentation of financial statement balances.

Summary

In this chapter, we have discussed the detailed procedures that are involved in planning and supervising the audit engagement. In terms of the audit risk model discussed in Chapter 5, effective planning is essential to properly assess the business risk of the client as well as the inherent risk of misstatement of specific accounts. Supervision involves directing the work of assistants in accomplishing audit objectives, and thus is an element to be considered in order to minimize detection risk.

We began our discussion of planning by illustrating the time sequence of the various elements of the typical audit. We pointed out that planning involves development of an audit strategy, which begins before the acceptance of the engagement and continues through its completion into the development of a strategy for the next year's engagement. We then discussed in detail the various matters that should be considered by the auditor in planning, such as understanding the client's industry and business, as well as the data processing and control structure. We emphasized that effective planning involves early establishment of materiality thresholds and identification of accounts that are likely to require adjustment. Analytical procedures are a required and effective tool to be used for this purpose during the planning stages of the audit. Various types of analytical tools were discussed. The documentation of the planning process, in the form of the engagement planning memorandum, was then discussed and illustrated. Finally, the use of internal auditors during the audit was discussed.

Auditing Vocabulary

p. 240   **accounting information system:**   The methods by which the client processes accounting information.

p. 243   **analytical procedures:**   The study of plausible relationships among financial and nonfinancial data.

p. 253   **audit program:**   A written list of procedures that satisfy the audit objectives and verify the financial statement assertions of the client. A partial audit program is illustrated in Figure 7-6.

p. 232   **business risk:**   The risk of an auditor being associated with financial statements that contain material misstatements, due to the industry in which the client operates, the business reputation and integrity of the client, and the quality and completeness of the client's records.

p. 233 **engagement letter:** The written contract between the accountant and client that clarifies the nature of the work to be performed, the period of time over which the engagement is expected to extend, any limitations of the engagement, the responsibility of the accountant for communicating findings of the engagement, and fee arrangements. The engagement letter is illustrated in Figure 7–2.

p. 236 **final field work:** The field work done between the end of the client's fiscal year and the date of the audit report.

p. 236 **interim tests:** Tests which are performed during the audit period, in order to save time and money at the end of the audit.

p. 253 **internal auditors:** Auditors who work within the client's organization to perform a high-level monitoring service for top management, including a continuing study and evaluation of internal control.

p. 229 **planning:** The development of an overall strategy for the expected conduct and scope of the audit.

p. 253 **planning memorandum:** A written summary of the results of planning procedures. The planning memorandum documents the auditor's compliance with the first standard of audit field work. Figure 7–7 illustrates a typical planning memorandum.

p. 250 **plant tour:** A tour of the client's facilities, usually conducted as one of the first procedures on the audit.

p. 233 **predecessor auditor:** The auditor who might have audited the financial statements of the client in previous years.

p. 248 **regression analysis:** A sophisticated statistical technique for developing expectations for balances in financial statement accounts. As computers are used more and more on the audit, regression analysis has become a more commonly used technique for performing analytical procedures.

p. 242 **risk of misstatement:** The relative risk that a particular account might contain errors or irregularities, due to the nature of the account and the ease of misappropriation of funds from that account.

p. 255 **supervision:** Directing the work of assistants and accomplishing audit objectives. Supervision includes instruction of assistants, keeping informed about significant problems encountered on the engagement, reviewing completed work of assistants, and resolving differences of opinion among personnel.

Notes

1. AU310.01
2. AU311.03
3. AU311.03
4. Ibid., paragraph .08
5. Ibid., paragraph .09
6. SAS 56 (AICPA, 1988), paragraph .02
7. AU311.05
8. AU311.11

Questions for Class Discussion

Q7-1 What does the term *planning* mean as it is used in generally accepted auditing standards?

Q7-2 What does the term *supervision* mean as it is used in generally accepted auditing standards?

Q7-3 What are the elements of a typical audit engagement, in chronological sequence?

Q7-4 Can you explain the concept of materiality as applied to auditing? Why is this concept important to the auditor during the planning stages of the audit?

Q7-5 What are the contents of a typical engagement letter? Explain why this document is important.

Q7-6 Why is it important to have communications between predecessor and successor auditors?

Q7-7 What are at least four things an auditor should do to determine whether a prospective client should be accepted?

Q7-8 What standards has the AICPA established to guide the CPA is deciding whether to accept a client? Why were those standards established?

Q7-9 What steps may an auditor take to identify areas of potentially high risk in an audit? Why should this be done? When should it be done?

Q7-10 Why is it essential that the auditor learn about the client's *industry*? What are some possible sources of this information?

Q7-11 Why is it essential that an auditor obtain an understanding of the client's *business* as a part of planning? What are some of the key elements of the client's business that the auditor should understand?

Q7-12 Why is the supervision of assistants such a vital part of a typical audit engagement? What activities are included in the supervision process?

Q7-13 What function(s) are typically performed by the client's internal audit department? To what extent can the work done by this department be (1) relied upon and (2) used by the independent auditor?

Q7-14 Describe the composition and usefulness of the following ratios during the audit and to which users those ratios would be useful: (a) quick ratio; (b) days sales outstanding; (c) times interest earned; (d) debt-equity; (e) return on assets.

Q7-15 How can industry averages for key financial ratios assist the auditor in planning the engagement? What are the sources of that data?

Q7-16 What is meant by the term *business risk*? How does the auditor go about assessing it?

Q7-17 What is meant by the term *risk of misstatement* at the individual account balance level?

Q7-18 How can nonfinancial data be used to develop expectations during preliminary analytical procedures? What are some examples?

Q7-19 What information can be obtained during a tour of the client's plant that can be vital to the planning of an audit?

Q7-20 What is the purpose of the planning memorandum? What are the contents of such a memorandum?

Short Cases

C7-1 A CPA has been asked to audit the financial statements of a publicly held company for the first time. All preliminary verbal discussions and inquiries have been completed between the CPA, the company, the predecessor auditor, and all other necessary parties. The CPA is now preparing an engagement letter.

Required: List the items that should be included in the typical engagement letter in these circumstances and describe the benefits derived from preparing an engagement letter.

(AICPA adapted)

C7-2 The auditor should obtain a level of knowledge of the entity's business—including events, transactions, and practices—that will permit the planning and performance of an examination in accordance with generally accepted auditing standards. Adhering to these standards enables the auditor's report to lend credibility to financial statements by providing the public with certain assurances.

Required:
a. How does knowledge of the entity's business help the auditor in the planning and performance of an examination in accordance with generally accepted auditing standards?
b. What assurances are provided to the public when the auditor states that the financial statements "present fairly . . . in conformity with generally accepted accounting principles"?

(AICPA adapted)

C7-3 Parker is the in-charge auditor with administrative responsibilities for the upcoming annual audit of FGH Company, a continuing audit client. Parker will supervise two assistants on the engagement and will visit the client before the field work begins.

Parker has started the planning process by preparing a list of procedures to be performed prior to the beginning of field work. The list includes

1. Review correspondence and permanent files.
2. Review prior years' audit working papers, financial statements, and auditor's reports.
3. Discuss with CPA firm personnel responsible for audit and nonaudit services to the client, matters that may affect the examination.
4. Discuss with management current business developments affecting the client.

Required: Complete Parker's list of procedures to be performed prior to the beginning of field work.

(AICPA adapted)

C7-4 In mid-summer of 19X1, you are given the in-charge responsibility for the Shop-Rite Corporation, a company that has been a client of your firm for six years. You have met the engagement partner, Richard Hamilton, who has advised you that you are to be in charge of planning and supervising the audit field work. The corporation has a fiscal year end of October 31.

Required: Discuss the necessary preparation and planning for the Shop-Rite Corporation annual audit before beginning audit field work at the client's office. Include in your discussion the sources of possible information you would consult, the kind of information you would seek, and the preliminary plans you would make for client assistance and staffing requirements. *Do not write an audit program.*

(AICPA adapted)

C7-5   When a CPA has accepted an engagement from a new client who is a manufacturer, one of the first things he or she may do is to tour the client's facilities.

Required:
   a. Name some of the things a CPA may observe during a plant tour.
   b. Discuss the ways in which these observations will be of help to the CPA in planning and conducting the audit.

(AICPA adapted)

C7-6   Jimmarc, Inc., a closely held company, wishes to engage Carlos Noro, CPA, to examine its annual financial statements. Although Jimmarc was in general satisfied with the services provided by its prior auditor, Delbert Killington, it thought the audit work that Killington performed was too detailed and interfered excessively with normal office routines. Noro has asked Jimmarc to inform Killington of the decision to change auditors, but Jimmarc does not wish to do so.

Required:
   a.   List and discuss the steps Noro should follow before accepting the engagement.
   b.   What additional procedures should Noro perform on this first-time engagement over and beyond those Noro would perform on the Jimmarc engagement of the following year?

C7-7   Joan Pimentel is a CPA who is conducting preliminary analytical procedures for the Broadaxe Manufacturing Company during the planning stages of the 19X3–X4 audit. During her review, Joan notices the following changes in relationships over the past three years. (You may assume that Joan is the continuing auditor for the years 19X0–X4.) Inventory turnover declined steadily over three years, from 18.3 times per year to 14.2 times per year. Average receivable collection period was twenty-three days in 19X1, and based on analysis of unadjusted financial statements, that comparative number was twenty-eight days in 19X4.

Required: Tell what each of these changes show Joan. How can she use them in planning the 19X3–X4 audit examination?

C7-8   Ben Talbert, CPA, has been engaged to perform the audit examination of the Huaco Resort Inn, the largest motor hotel in Arizona. The grounds of the hotel cover approximately forty acres and include swimming, tennis, golf, and racquetball facilities. There are 540 guest rooms, which have an average occupancy rate of 80 percent. The hotel also does extensive convention business through its convention center.
   There are a total of fifteen members on the inn's accounting staff, which is headed by

Mike Lively. Lively's official title is internal auditor, and his duties include supervision of the billing, cash receipts, and cash disbursements functions, as well as analysis of uncollectible accounts. Lively's staff performs all the major bookkeeping functions, which have included excellent internal controls in the past. Lively and his staff are very cooperative and have set aside 200 staff hours to assist Talbert in the audit.

Required:

a. Discuss the description and function of the internal auditor in terms of generally accepted auditing standards.

b. On the basis of your description in (a), does Lively fit the description of an internal auditor in terms of generally accepted auditing standards?

c. What audit work may Talbert use Lively and his staff to perform? For what audit work may they not be used?

d. How would Lively's duties need to be realigned, if at all, to permit Talbert to use him more extensively? What audit work may be performed by Lively and his staff in this case?

C7-9   You are the senior auditor on the audit engagement of Mixit Plastics, Inc., a large manufacturer of prefabricated plastic products. Your assistant on the job is Sue Smart, a recent honors graduate of So Hi University, who has never before worked on an audit. The areas of the audit examination that you have assigned to her are

a. Accounts receivable, sales, and the allowance for doubtful accounts.

b. Raw materials, work-in-process, and finished goods inventories and cost of goods sold.

c. Contingent liabilities.

Since you were deeply involved in completing another engagement when you learned you were to be in charge of the Mixit audit, you neglected to call Sue until two days before the audit was to begin. Feeling pinched for time, you told Sue to go to the file room, request the prior year's working papers, and begin her planning by reading them. You also told her to prepare pro forma current-year working papers using last year's papers as a model for her assigned areas. Since you followed prior year's working papers last year and had no problems when you audited these same areas, you feel that Sue can do the same this year. Besides, since she earned an A in auditing, you feel that she should have a firm grasp of what she should be doing without much help from you.

Required:

a. What problems might there be in your actions—on the basis of generally accepted auditing standards?

b. Should Sue be performing the audit of these financial statement areas? Why or why not?

c. List the audit objectives that were discussed in Chapter 6. How would you use these audit objectives in instructing Sue with respect to the audit of

1. Accounts receivables, sales, and the allowance for doubtful accounts?

2. Raw materials, work-in-process, and finished goods inventories and cost of goods sold?

3. Contingent liabilities?

C7-10   Arthur Olsen, CPA, is auditing the RCT Manufacturing Company as of February 28, 19X5. As with all engagements, one of Arthur's initial procedures is to make overall checks of the client's financial data by reviewing significant ratios and trends so that he has a better understanding of the business and can determine where to concentrate his audit efforts.

The financial statements prepared by the client with audited 19X4 figures and preliminary 19X5 figures are presented below in condensed form.

RCT Manufacturing Company

C O N D E N S E D   I N C O M E   S T A T E M E N T S

Years Ended February 28, 19X5 and 19X4

	19X5	19X4
Net sales	$1,684,000	$1,250,000
Cost of goods sold	927,000	710,000
Gross margin on sales	757,000	540,000
Selling and administrative expenses	682,000	504,000
Income before federal income taxes	75,000	36,000
Income tax expense	30,000	14,400
Net income	$ 45,000	$ 21,600

Additional Information: (1) The company has only an insignificant amount of cash sales; (2) The end-of-year figures are comparable to the average for each respective year.

RCT Manufacturing Company

C O N D E N S E D   B A L A N C E   S H E E T S

February 28, 19X5 and 19X4

Assets	19X5	19X4
Cash	$ 12,000	$ 15,000
Accounts receivable, net	93,000	50,000
Inventory	72,000	67,000
Other current assets	5,000	6,000
Plant and equipment, net of depreciation	60,000	80,000
	$242,000	$218,000

Liabilities and Equities	19X5	19X4
Accounts payable	$ 38,000	$ 41,000
Federal income tax payable	30,000	14,400
Long-term liabilities	20,000	40,000
Common stock	70,000	70,000
Retained earnings	84,000	52,600
	$242,000	$218,000

Required:
   a. For each year, compute the current ratio and a turnover ratio for accounts receivable. Using these ratios, identify and discuss auditing procedures that should be included in Olsen's audit of (1) accounts receivable and (2) accounts payable.
   b. Compute the ratios of cost of goods sold to sales, gross margin to sales, and expenses

to sales. On the basis of these comparative ratios, discuss whether any further audit attention might be advisable.

(AICPA adapted)

Problems

 P7-1 The following items pertain to planning the typical audit examination. Choose the best response for each item.

   a. Which of the following is an effective audit planning and control procedure that helps prevent misunderstandings and inefficient use of audit personnel?

     1. Arrange to make copies, for inclusion in the working papers, of those client supporting documents examined by the auditor.

     2. Arrange to provide the client with copies of the audit programs to be used during the audit.

     3. Arrange a preliminary conference with the client to discuss audit objectives, fees, timing, and other information.

     4. Arrange to have the auditor prepare and post any necessary adjusting or reclassification entires prior to final closing.

   b. Which of the following is the most likely first step an auditor would perform at the beginning of an initial audit engagement?

     1. Prepare a rough draft of the financial statements and of the auditor's report.

     2. Study and evaluate the system of internal administrative control.

     3. Tour the client's facilities and review the general records.

     4. Consult with and review the work of the predecessor auditor prior to discussing the engagement with the client management.

   c. The first standard of field work recognizes that early appointment of the independent auditor has many advantages to the auditor and the client. Which of the following advantages is *least* likely to occur as a result of early appointment of the auditor?

     1. The auditor will be able to plan the audit work so that it may be done expeditiously.

     2. The auditor will be able to complete the audit work in less time.

     3. The auditor will be able to plan better for the observation of the physical inventories.

     4. The auditor will be able to perform the examination more efficiently and will be finished at an early date after the year end.

   d. An auditor is planning an audit engagement for a new client in a business that is unfamiliar to the auditor. Which of the following would be the most useful source of information for the auditor during the preliminary planning stage, when the auditor is trying to obtain a general understanding of audit problems that might be encountered?

     1. Client manuals of accounts and charts of accounts.

     2. AICPA Industry Audit Guides.

     3. Prior-year working papers of the predecessor auditor.

     4. Latest annual and interim financial statements issued by the client.

   e. After preliminary audit arrangements have been made, an engagement confirmation letter should be sent to the client. The letter usually would *not* include

     1. A reference to the auditor's responsibility for the detection of errors or irregularities.

2. An estimate of the time to be spent on the audit work by audit staff and management.

3. A statement that management advisory services would be made available on request.

4. A statement that a management letter will be issued outlining comments and suggestions as to any procedures requiring the client's attention.

  f. In connection with the examination of financial statements by an independent auditor, the client suggests that members of the internal audit staff be utilized to minimize audit costs. Which of the following tasks could most appropriately be delegated to the internal audit staff?

1. Selection of accounts receivable for confirmation, based on the internal auditor's judgment as to how many accounts and which accounts will provide sufficient coverage.

2. Preparation of schedules for negative accounts receivable responses.

3. Evaluation of the internal control for accounts receivable and sales.

4. Determination of the adequacy of the allowance for doubtful accounts.

(AICPA adapted)

P7-2 The following items pertain to communication between predecessor and successor auditors. Choose the best response for each item.

  a. When a CPA is approached to perform an audit for the first time, the CPA should make inquiries of the predecessor auditor. This is a necessary procedure because the predecessor may be able to provide the successor with information that will assist the successor in determining

1. Whether the predecessor's work should be utilized.

2. Whether the company follows the policy of rotating its auditors.

3. Whether in the predecessor's opinion internal control of the company has been satisfactory.

4. Whether the engagement should be accepted.

  b. A CPA may reduce the audit work on a first-time audit by reviewing the working papers of the predecessor auditor. The predecessor should permit the successor to review working papers relating to matters of continuing accounting significance, such as those that relate to

1. Extent of reliance on the work of specialists.

2. Fee arrangements and summaries of payments.

3. Analysis of contingencies.

4. Staff hours required to complete the engagement.

  c. Prior to the acceptance of an audit engagement with a client who has terminated the services of the predecessor auditor, the CPA should

1. Contact the predecessor auditor without advising the prospective client and request a complete report of the circumstance leading to the termination with the understanding that all information disclosed will be kept confidential.

2. Accept the engagement without contacting the predecessor auditor since the CPA can include audit procedures to verify the reason given by the client for the termination.

3. Not communicate with the predecessor auditor because this would in effect be asking the auditor to violate the confidential relationship between auditor and client.

4. Advise the client of the intention to contact the predecessor auditor and request permission for the contact.

(AICPA adapted)

P7-3 The following items pertain to the meaning and use of the audit program. Choose the best response for each item.
  a. An audit program provides proof that
    1. Sufficient competent evidential matter was obtained.
    2. The work was adequately planned.
    3. There was compliance with generally accepted standards of reporting.
    4. There was a proper study and evaluation of internal control.
  b. Audit programs are modified to suit the circumstances on particular engagements. A complete audit program for an engagement generally should be developed
    1. Prior to beginning the actual audit work.
    2. After the auditor has completed an evaluation of the existing internal accounting control.
    3. After reviewing the client's accounting records and procedures.
    4. When the audit engagement letter is prepared.
  c. Which of the following is an aspect of scheduling and controlling the audit engagement?
    1. Include in the audit program a column for estimated and actual time.
    2. Perform audit work only after the client's books of account have been closed for the period under examination.
    3. Write a conclusion on individual working papers indicating how the results thereon will affect the auditor's report.
    4. Include in the engagement letter an estimate of the minimum and maximum audit fee.

(AICPA adapted)

P7-4 The following items pertain to analytical procedures in the audit examination. Choose the best response for each item.
  a. Significant unexpected fluctuations identified by analytical procedures will usually necessitate
    1. Consistency qualification.
    2. Review of internal control.
    3. Explanation in the representation letter.
    4. Auditor investigation.
  b. Which of the following is *not* a typical analytical procedure?
    1. Study of relationships of the financial information with relevant nonfinancial information.
    2. Comparison of the financial information with similar information regarding the industry in which the entity operates.
    3. Comparison of recorded amounts of major disbursements with appropriate invoices.
    4. Comparison of the financial information with budgeted amounts.
  c. An example of an analytical procedure is the comparison of
    1. Financial information with similar information regarding the industry in which the entity operates.

2. Recorded amounts of major disbursements with appropriate invoices.
3. Results of a statistical sample with the expected characteristics of the actual population.
4. EDP generated data with similar data generated by a manual accounting system.

d. The auditor's analytical procedures will be facilitated if the client

1. Uses a standard cost system that produces variance reports.
2. Segregates obsolete inventory before the physical inventory count.
3. Corrects material weaknesses in internal accounting control before the beginning of the audit.
4. Reduces inventory balances to the lower of cost or market.

(AICPA adapted)

P7-5   **T&H, Inc.—A Case Study**

Introduction:

The objective of this case study is to develop your analytical, problem-solving, and written communications skills. You will be performing risk and materiality analysis and writing a planning memorandum. You may use computers for the computations or perform the analysis by hand.

Completing the case should take approximately two hours and may be divided into as many separate sessions as you like. Your instructor may wish to assign the case to groups or individuals, at his or her option.

The case study continues in Chapter 8 (P8-12) and Chapter 20 (P20-13).

Case Background:

T&H, Inc. is a highly specialized, technologically oriented manufacturer of connectors consumed by the electronics industry. The industry is made up of relatively few companies and competition is based primarily on technological innovations and product improvements. Industry publications indicate that in the past two years, in most product lines, T&H has sharply increased its technological lead over its competitors.

The company was founded in the 1950s by Miles Nussy, president and owner of approximately 30 percent of the common stock. The board of directors, of which Mr. Nussy is chairman, consists of the members of management and four outside directors. The stock is traded on the New York Exchange.

T&H manufactures and sells various types of coaxial, cylindrical, and printed circuit connectors used for manufacturing electronic components. Most of T&H's customers are well-known, established firms in the electronics industry. The company's Cleveland headquarters and one of its two plants are located in a modern company-owned building on ten acres of land leased under an agreement expiring in 2X60. The second plant, leased under an agreement expiring in 19X3, is located in Skyline, Mississippi. T&H is currently negotiating with the building's owner to extend the lease twenty years.

T&H markets its products throughout the United States, using its staff of sales engineers who work on a salary plus commission basis. Marketing efforts are primarily related to serving existing customers, and advertising is minimal due to the restrictive market for T&H's products. Sales offices are maintained in Boston, Massachusetts; White Plains, New York; Falls Church, Virginia; Harrisburg, Pennsylvania; St. Louis, Missouri; Chicago, Illinois; Irving, Texas; and Los Angeles, California.

Financial Data Review:
This chart encapsulates selected financial data:

	Three Quarters Ended		Year Ended
	9/30/X7	9/30/X8	12/31/X7
Cash	$ 852	$ 1,052	$ 733
Accounts receivable (trade)	3,169	4,183	3,398
Inventories	2,920	4,028	3,272
Current liabilities	1,802	2,390	2,403
Sales	12,414	14,739	16,479
Cost of sales	9,492	9,919	11,864
% of sales	76.5%	67.3%	71.9%
Selling, G&A exp.	1,910	2,721	2,624
Current ratio	3.95:1	3.95:1	3.12:1
Debt/equity	.88:1	1.04:1	.90:1
Inventory Turnover	3.0 times	2.5 times	3.6 times

Discussion with the client revealed the following information:

• The increase in cash results from a payment for long-term debt due early in October 19X8.
• Trade receivables have increased due to increased sales. Days sales in receivables (assuming 270 sales days) have increased from fifty-nine to seventy-six days at September 30, 19X7 and 19X8, respectively, due to increased sales volume and a general slowdown in payments.
• Inventories have increased to meet increased demand. The increase, however, has adversely affected the inventory turnover ratio.
• Current liabilities have increased due to the increase in inventories and the current portions of long-term debt due in October. (See Inventories and Cash in the chart above.)
• Sales have increased due to improved volume and higher prices.
• Cost of sales (as a percentage of sales) continues to decline due to manufacturing efficiencies evolving from a standardization of the company's products. Management continues to eliminate unprofitable products. The increased sales volume has had the effect of spreading fixed costs over more units, thus reducing the per-unit cost of sales. (See Sales in the chart above.)
• Selling, general, and administrative expenses reflect an increase in the sales force.
• The company has entered into a new revolving credit agreement with Continental Bank, increasing the previous line by a total of $1,000,000 to $5,000,000.
• Historically, the response to confirmation has been poor, since many of the company's customers have accounting systems that do not enable them to confirm balances.
• The company often constructs fixed asset additions in-house and accounts for these items as inventory until completion.
• All general and subsidiary ledgers for T&H are kept on computer. Supporting documentation is generally good. Comparative financial statements will not be issued this year.

- The engagement is budgeted at approximately 300 hours with final field work beginning March 2. Completion of field work is scheduled for approximately April 5.

The audit staff will consist of the following individuals:

			Hours
In-charge	William Hines	Sr.	180
Staff	David Wilson	Asst.	120
			300

·Per discussion with client, final deadline is tentatively scheduled for conclusion of field work April 5 and final reports April 13.

The client has agreed to prepare working papers in the following areas:

- Percentage completion of work-in-process inventories
- Federal income tax accruals
- Year-end accruals
- Management bonus plan
- Pension and profit-sharing plan

T&H, INC.

T R I A L   B A L A N C E

Acc. #	Account	(12/31/X8) Current Period	(12/31/X7) Prior Period
100	Cash	1,199,887	732,982
101	Accounts receivable	4,220,082	3,412,351
102	Allowance for doubtful accts.	(49,963)	(14,562)
120	Inventory—raw materials	2,568,486	1,805,131
121	Inventory—WIP & FG	1,620,032	1,467,239
130	Prepaid expenses	150,491	89,396
140	Deferred income taxes	4,937	0
200	Property, plant, & equipment	4,096,802	3,933,191
201	Accumulated depreciation	(1,510,082)	(1,523,008)
220	Other assets	146,089	144,400
300	Accounts payable	(1,091,906)	(969,126)
301	Notes payable to bank	(535,817)	(205,771)
303	Current installment, l-t debt	(59,030)	(325,470)
310	Accrued payroll tax	(54,989)	(38,635)
311	Accrued pension costs	(99,786)	(66,787)
312	Other accrued liabilities	(944,506)	(797,250)
350	Long term debt	(3,645,987)	(2,287,494)
352	Deferred income tax payable	(59,291)	(66,123)
400	Common stock	(579,050)	(576,750)
401	Additional paid in capital	(1,731,252)	(1,722,914)
430	Retained earnings	(3,037,102)	(2,611,286)
435	Dividends paid	159,913	148,291
436	Cost of treasury stock	46,302	46,302
500	Sales	(19,531,097)	(16,478,997)

T&H, INC. (*continued*)

TRIAL BALANCE

Acc. #	Account	(12/31/X8) Current Period	(12/31/X7) Prior Period
510	Cost of goods sold	13,332,606	11,864,167
521	Rent expense	233,000	218,000
522	Salaries & employee benefits	1,783,947	1,196,114
523	Bad debt expense	30,600	8,859
530	Depreciation expense	372,621	372,463
535	Pension expense	99,600	74,500
540	Interest expense	274,527	256,816
550	Gain/Loss on sale of fixed assets	137,486	0
560	Miscellaneous—net	(44,643)	(113,027)
570	Other expenses	1,713,377	1,500,156
580	Income tax expense	794,000	558,300
600	Other income	(10,284)	(31,458)

Required:

a. Go to your college or university library and perform research on the electronics connector industry. Include in your information the long-term trends affecting the industry, as well as trends in standard financial data for the industry. Use Figures 7–3 and 7–4 as models.

b. Using the comparative trial balance provided for you, perform analytical procedures upon T&H, Inc.'s financial data. You are encouraged to use a generalized computer package such as LOTUS 1-2-3, or a proprietary software package such as Coopers and Lybrand's PRE-AUDIT for this purpose. Transcribe your results into a format similar to that of Figure 7–5.

c. Using the information from steps a. and b., in addition to the information provided in the introduction about T&H, Inc., assess the *business risk* for this client as high, medium, or low. Would you accept this company as a client? Why or why not?

d. Using the same information, assess the *inherent risk of misstatement* of each specific account in the company's trial balance as high, medium, or low. Which accounts would you select for further attention on the audit? Why?

e. Draft the planning memo for T&H, Inc. **Note**: You may want to defer this part of the case until you finish P8-12.

CHAPTER 8

The Effects of the Control Structure on the Audit

Objectives

☐ **1.** Know the meaning of the term *internal control structure* and its importance in the planning of the audit.

☐ **2.** Know the elements of an entity's internal control structure that should be considered in the financial audit.

☐ **3.** Know the control procedures that should characterize an effective internal control structure.

☐ **4.** Be able to explain the process by which control risk is assessed in an audit engagement.

The second standard of audit field work requires the auditor to obtain "a sufficient understanding of the internal control structure of the audit client to plan the audit and to determine the nature, timing, and extent of tests to be performed on the financial statement balances."[1] As illustrated in the diagram overleaf, that understanding must be obtained on a financial statement assertion-by-assertion basis, in order to provide a basis for the *assessment of control risk*. In this chapter we turn our attention to the general meaning and application of the second standard of audit field work.

Specific applications of the control risk assessment process to the various systems of the business are contained in Chapters 13 through 19.

The Control Structure

☑ **Objective 1**
Know the meaning of *internal control structure*

The internal control structure of an entity consists of the *policies and procedures* established by management to provide **reasonable assurance** that *specific objectives* of the entity will be achieved. The primary goal in establishing a strong internal control structure is to *synchronize employee actions and behavior patterns with the operating objectives of owners*. To operationalize that goal, more specific, subordinate *operating objectives* need to be considered.

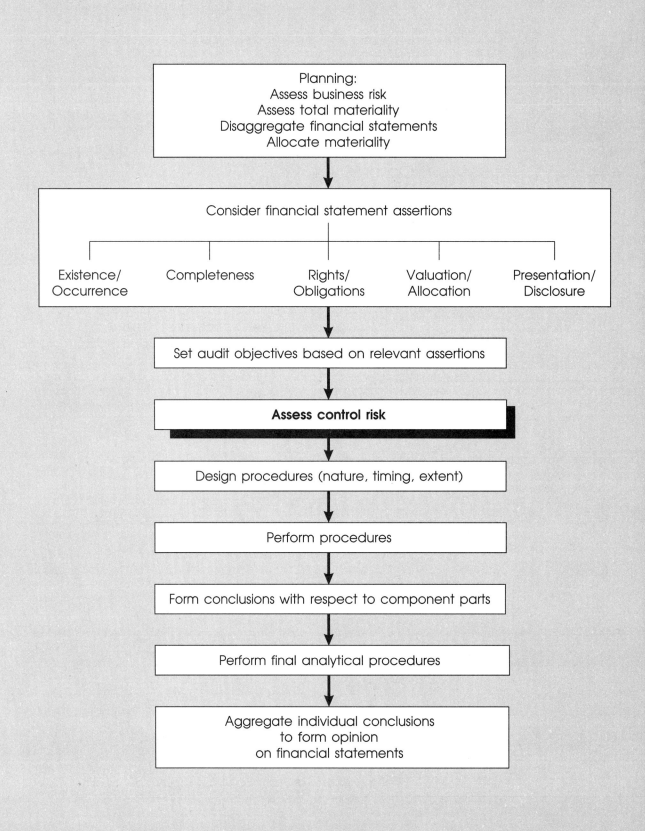

The operating objectives of an internal control structure generally include but are not limited to the following:

1. To assure that assets and business records are safeguarded against errors and irregularities.
2. To assure accuracy and reliability in the financial reporting process.
3. To promote operational efficiencies.
4. To encourage adherence to prescribed managerial policies and directives.
5. To encourage compliance with laws and regulations imposed by external parties such as governmental and other regulatory agencies.

While all of these objectives are critical to the long-range success of the entity, only (1) and (2) may be relevant to the auditor who examines the entity's financial statements. Control objectives (3), (4), and (5) pertain mostly to the efficiency of the entity and the effectiveness with which operating goals of the company are met. Those objectives would be more important to internal auditors who monitor those functions than to financial statement auditors.

Generally, the policies and procedures that are relevant to the financial audit relate to the entity's ability to *record, process, summarize, and report financial data* in a manner that accurately and fairly reflects the *assertions embodied in the financial statements*. Those assertions, discussed in previous chapters, are (1) existence or occurrence; (2) completeness; (3) rights or obligations; (4) valuation or allocation; and (5) presentation and disclosure.

Assessment of Control Risk

In a financial statement audit, the auditor considers the assertions listed in the preceding paragraph in the context of their relationship to a specific account balance or class of transactions (such as accounts receivable and revenues), in order to gather evidence to support the opinion on the financial statements. In so doing, the auditor must consider *audit risk*. As stated in Chapter 5, audit risk (RT) is made up of the following elements: (1) inherent risk, (2) control risk, and (3) detection risk. The purpose for the auditor's understanding of the control structure of the client is to enable him or her to assess the **control risk** associated with the financial statement assertions being verified. Control risk is defined as the risk that material errors or irregularities that might have occurred in the recording, processing, summarizing, and reporting process might have gone undetected by the entity's internal control structure.

Control risk should be assessed on an *assertion-by-assertion basis*. Figure 8–1 presents diagrammatically how the assessment of control risk affects the nature, timing, and extent of evidence to be gathered in support of financial statement assertions.

As shown in Figure 8–1, the assessment of control risk for a particular account balance or class of transactions serves as a *screening device* of sorts. First, the auditor decides which financial statement assertions are most relevant for the account balance or class of transactions. Second, the auditor develops a set

Figure 8–1 ▄▄▄▄▄

Relationship of Control Risk Assessment to Evidence

Financial statement assertions				
Existence/ occurrence	Completeness	Rights/ obligations	Valuation	Presentation/ disclosure

Audit objectives				
Existence/ transaction validity	Periodicity/ transaction validity	Ownership	Valuation	Statement presentation

Assessment of Control Risk

Detection risk audit procedures			
Confirmation	Observation	Inspection	Analytical Procedures
Inquiry		Recomputation	Reading

of audit objectives based on the relevant assertions. Third, the auditor obtains an understanding of the control structure, to arrive at a preliminary assessment of control risk for those assertions. This assessment may be expressed in quantitative terms, such as percentages, or in nonquantitative terms, such as a range (high, medium, low). If, for a particular assertion, the preliminary assessment of control risk is at the *maximum*, the auditor would likely use the following strategy for detection risk procedures:

- *Nature*: Detailed tests of balances and transactions, rather than analytical procedures.
- *Timing*: Procedures at or around year-end, rather than at an interim date.
- *Extent*: Large rather than small sample sizes.

If, for some assertions, the auditor desired to assess control risk at a level less than the maximum level, he or she would have to perform a more extensive review and tests of the controls. Should the results of that review be favorable, the auditor would infer that a more reliable system is associated with that assertion. Therefore, detection risk procedures for that assertion would be more analytical and less detailed, conducted at an interim date (as opposed to year-end), and would be composed of smaller sample sizes than would have been necessary under maximum control risk conditions.

In summary, there is a need for the financial statement auditor to consider the control structure of the audit client in order to assess control risk on an assertion-by-assertion basis. That assessment is used, in turn, to plan the nature, timing, and extent of detection risk procedures to be performed by the auditor on those financial statement assertions.

Elements of the Control Structure

☑ **Objective 2**
Know the elements
of the control
structure

The control structure of an entity generally consists of the *control environment, the accounting system, and control procedures.*

The Control Environment[2]

The **control environment** represents the aggregate effects of various conditions surrounding the audit client that influence the conduct of the audit engagement. Included in the control environment are the following elements:

- Management's philosophy and operating style.
- The entity's organizational structure.
- The functioning of the board of directors and its committees, particularly the audit committee.
- Methods of assigning authority and responsibility.
- Management's control methods for monitoring and following up on performance, including internal auditing.
- Personnel policies and practices.
- Various external influences that affect an entity's operations and practices, such as regulatory agencies of the federal or various state governments.

The *philosophy of management* sets the tone for the way in which most of the entity's business decisions are made. This philosophy includes management's attitude toward risk-taking and the emphasis on meeting projected results. Apathy on the part of management toward internal controls generally leads to eventual breakdown of the system, resulting in undetected errors and irregularities. Aggressiveness and goal orientation on the part of management are desirable business characteristics. However, overly aggressive management dominated by one or a few individuals with little or no accountability to others can lead to abuses of the entity and, in some cases, threaten its survival. Errors or irregularities perpetrated by such management are often most difficult to detect. The auditor should take an especially apathetic or aggressive style on the part of management into account when planning the audit.

The *organizational structure* of the entity includes the relationship that exists between the various operating units and the authority and responsibility assumed by various persons within those units. Figure 8–2 depicts the organization chart of JEP Manufacturing Co., which illustrates the company's organizational structure. To achieve effective controls, the entity should be organized along authority/responsibility lines, with the authority passing downward through the various levels of the organization and the responsibility flowing upward.

The *board of directors* or equivalent body should generally be charged with the ultimate authority for decision making. In Figure 8–2, the board of directors is depicted as occupying the highest position in the organization, with only the

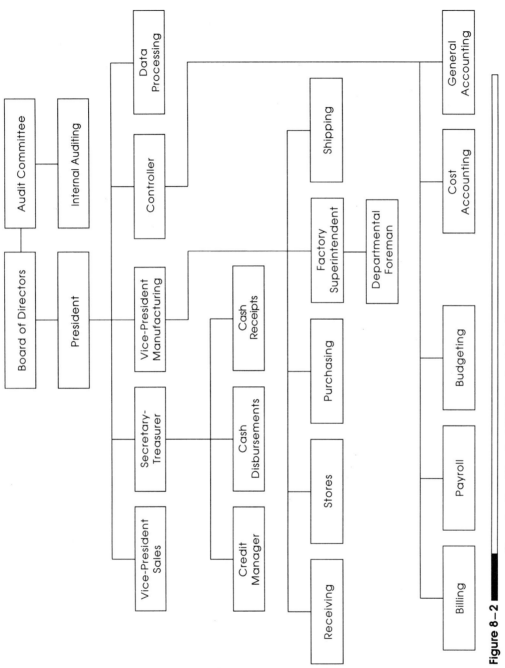

Figure 8–2 ■ **Organization Chart of JEP Manufacturing Co.**

audit committee as a peer group. As discussed in previous chapters, the audit committee is generally comprised of *outside directors* whose major job is oversight of the audit function and liaison with both internal and external auditors.

Methods of assigning authority and responsibility pertain to the policies of the company regarding overall conduct of employees, the jobs to which they are assigned, and the means by which transactions are authorized. For example, many corporations have established internal codes of corporate conduct defining acceptable business practices and advocating avoidance of conflict of interests. Responsibility for meeting company goals should be assigned to various managers within the entity. Authority should then be delegated to those persons to see that those goals are met. Procedures manuals should describe company policies and contain job descriptions of the various positions within the system, thus clarifying responsibilities of employees. Figure 8–3 represents a page from the procedures manual of JEP Manufacturing Co. listing the specific tasks to be performed by the cashier.

Management control methods pertain to the ability of management to direct the affairs of the entity, to effectively measure its performance, and to take remedial steps to assure that errors and inefficiencies are promptly detected and corrected. Included in management control methods should be an effective budgeting system that sets forth management's plans and effectively measures and compares its achieved results. A **responsibility accounting system** should delegate responsibility for meeting planned performance to line managers of various departments or divisions. Variances from expected performance levels should be promptly investigated and appropriate corrective measures taken. In the accounting function, one person should not be allowed to process a transaction completely from beginning to end without being checked by someone else. When computers are involved in authorizing transactions, controls should be integrated into the software to assure accuracy, completeness, and validity of the result.

An effective *internal audit function* should exist within the entity when size and cost justify it. In Figure 8–2, the internal audit function is shown as an autonomous unit in the organization chart, reporting directly to the audit committee. The purpose of the internal audit function is to monitor the compliance of other departments of the entity with the policies of the board of directors. The existence of an effective internal audit function within an entity can be a major step in achieving effective internal control.

An adequate system of internal control ultimately depends on the *personnel* who implement it. A system may have discrete responsibilities and clearly defined lines of authority and still be completely inadequate if the personnel are not appropriately qualified to run it. Therefore, the hiring and promotion practices of the client should give appropriate consideration to the qualifications required in each position as people are hired or promoted into those positions. In addition, it is appropriate to carry fidelity bond insurance on those persons who handle cash and other liquid assets. Such an arrangement should serve as a deterrent to fraud and also provide for recovery of losses in the event that fraud occurs.

Figure 8–3 ▬▬

Job Description in Procedures Manual: JEP Manufacturing Co.
Job title: Cashier

Responsible to: Treasurer

Summary of responsibilities: Responsible for receiving and depositing all cash (checks and currency) received by the company and for handling petty cash fund.

Detailed Responsibilities

1. The cashier shall receive all checks delivered by mail from mail clerk each day.
2. The cashier shall receive all cash (checks and currency) delivered to the cashier's window.
3. The cashier shall prepare a cash receipts voucher (Form C-1) in duplicate for each payment made through cashier's window. One copy of the voucher shall be delivered to the person making the cash payment. The other shall be kept for use by the cashier.
4. At the end of each day the cashier shall prepare a list in triplicate of all cash received (checks and currency) on Form C-2. One copy of this list shall be sent to the bookkeeper, another shall be attached to the deposit slip. The third copy shall be filed in chronological order in the cashier's office.
5. Cash received each day shall be deposited intact in the bank. A deposit form (Form C-3) shall be prepared in duplicate and reconciled with the list of cash receipts (Form C-2) as the deposit is made. One copy shall be included with the deposit. The other shall be filed with the office copy of Form C-2.
6. The cashier shall be responsible for the company's imprest petty cash fund in the amount of $500.
7. Payments shall be made from the petty cash fund on presentation of a validated voucher amounting to less than $10. Vouchers in excess of that amount should be routed to the Accounts Payable Department.
8. Any person receiving payment from the petty cash fund shall be expected to sign a petty cash voucher (Form C-4) for the amount of the payment.
9. At the end of each day, the cashier shall reconcile the petty cash fund (cash + petty cash vouchers) with the imprest balance. Any shortages shall be reported to the Treasurer on the Petty Cash Reconciliation form (Form C-5).
10. When the cash in the petty cash fund declines to $75, the cashier shall initiate a reimbursement request (Form C-6) in duplicate. One copy with attached supporting petty cash vouchers shall be sent to the controller for recording and approval. The approved voucher shall then be sent to the Treasurer for reimbursement. The other shall be filed chronologically in the cashier's office.

External influences such as government regulation can have a significant impact on the control policies and procedures of an entity. For example, financial disclosure and reporting requirements imposed by the SEC help to assure that reporting practices of a publicly traded company are proper. Some banking institutions are regularly examined by agencies such as the Federal Deposit Insurance Corporation (FDIC) as well as by independent auditing firms. Such external influences heighten the consciousness of management with regard to errors and irregularities and in some cases prompt management to institute more stringent internal control policies than would otherwise be considered necessary.

The Accounting System[3]

The auditor should understand the **accounting system** of the audit client sufficiently to plan the audit. A thorough understanding of the accounting system
involves the following:

- The types of transactions that are significant to the financial statements of
  the entity.
- How transactions are initiated.
- The accounting records, supporting documents, machine-readable information, and specific accounts in the financial statements involved in the processing and reporting of transactions.
- The processing involved from the initiation of a transaction to its inclusion in
  the financial statements, including the use of the computer in processing.
- The financial reporting process used to summarize and present the entity's
  financial statements, including significant accounting estimates and disclosures.

Figure 8–4 presents in narrative format a description of the accounting system for sales of JEP Manufacturing Co. The narrative description reflects an

Figure 8–4 ▪▪▪

Description of Sales and Accounts Receivable System: JEP Manufacturing Co.

A sales transaction is initiated by the sales department on the basis of a written customer purchase order. Multiple copies of a prenumbered sales invoice are prepared for
distribution to (1) and (2) the billing department, (3) the shipping department, (4) the
finished goods department, (5) the credit department, and (6) the customer as acknowl-
edgement of receipt of the order.

The credit department conducts a credit check of the customer. On approval of credit,
files for the customer are updated (either manually or on computer), and the shipping
department is notified of credit approval.

On receipt of the sales invoice, the finished goods department releases the goods to
the shipping department, where they are held pending credit approval. Once credit is
approved, goods are shipped, and the shipping department copy of the invoice is sent to
the billing department, where it is matched with the billing department copy. Prices and
quantities are checked for accuracy and completeness. The invoice is completed and
one copy is mailed to the customer. Another copy of the invoice is used as the source
document for entry of the transaction into the sales journal (manual or computer input
may be used). A copy of the sales invoice showing shipment and credit approval is then
sent to the accounts receivable bookkeeping department for posting to the customer's
account in the accounts receivable subsidiary ledger.

Sales summaries are prepared monthly in the billing department. These summaries
(either manual or computer) are sent to the general ledger bookkeeping department,
where a summary journal entry is made to the sales and accounts receivable accounts in
the general ledger.

Supervisory personnel in the general ledger department reconcile the sales and
accounts receivable accounts in the general ledger to the totals of the accounts receivable subsidiary ledger on a regular basis. The entire process is tested by internal auditors,
and errors are promptly corrected.

understanding of sales transactions, as well as the process involved from initiation to reporting of those transactions.

Control Procedures That Characterize an Effective System

☑ **Objective 3**
Know control
procedures

As the auditor obtains an understanding of the control environment and the accounting system, he or she will become knowledgeable of many of the **control procedures** performed by various departments within the entity. Because control procedures implemented by the client are integrated into the control environment and the accounting system, it is impossible to study the control environment and accounting system without obtaining some knowledge of the control procedures as well.

In general, the control procedures built into an effective control environment and accounting system should include the following characteristics:

• Segregation of responsibilities.
• Comparisons and compliance monitoring within the system.
• Adequate records and documentation.
• Limited access to assets and sensitive data.
• Execution of transactions in accordance with management's general or specific authority.

The inclusion of all or some combination of these characteristics in the control procedures of a system suggests strengths in the system. If any of these characteristics are missing from the controls of any system, there is probably a weakness in that system. Close examination of Figure 8–4 will reveal aspects of each of these vital characteristics. We now examine each of them in detail.

Segregation of Responsibilities

A firm should follow a practice of segregating responsibilities to reduce the probability of fraud and to reduce the likelihood of unintentional errors in the accounting data. Both of these anticipated results depend on the basic assumption that two or more employees will not work in collusion to perpetrate a fraud or to cover up an unintentional error.

The separation of *custodial*, *recordkeeping*, and *authorization responsibilities* is one of the fundamental requirements in appropriately segregating employee responsibilities. An employee who has access to an asset, such as the cashier receiving cash receipts, is characterized as having custodial responsibilities. However, those responsibilities also extend to persons charged with originating documents required for the acquisition or disposal of assets as well as for actually handling and holding assets. Within this definition, custodial employees include the treasurer of an organization and many of those who work under her or his jurisdiction—such as cashiers, cash disbursements personnel, and credit management personnel. The custodial designation also includes many employees involved in the manufacturing and payroll functions—such as persons charged with shipping, receiving, and storing inventories and with the payment of employees.

Recordkeeping personnel include the controller and those working under her or his jurisdiction—including all accounting and bookkeeping employees. If custodial and recordkeeping responsibilities are appropriately segregated, a recordkeeper and a custodial employee will have to collude for an intentional error to be committed and still have the physical asset agree with the record-keeper's record of it. Stated in another way, the recordkeeper shows what the custodial employee is charged with. This arrangement reduces the probability that the custodial employee will deliberately misappropriate assets unless there is collusion with the recordkeeper to cover the misappropriation. On the other hand, if these two functions are assigned to the same person, it would be relatively easy for that person to change the records to hide the theft of an asset.

Authorization personnel include those persons at every level of activity whose duty is to authorize transactions. The board of directors is usually charged with the ultimate authority in a corporation. They should approve most major transactions—such as major asset acquisitions, financing or borrowing arrangements, employment agreements with key officers, and purchase agreements with major suppliers. Other types of authority may be delegated by the board of directors to various organization personnel. For example, authority to purchase inventory will typically be vested in the purchasing agent; authority to sign checks may be assigned to the treasurer; authority to employ personnel may be delegated to the personnel department; and authority to approve write-offs of uncollectible accounts may be vested in the credit manager.

Within the custodial, recordkeeping, and authorization areas, the system should also provide for separation of responsibilities so as to allow one employee to check on the work of another employee. The client should try to do this with minimum duplication of effort. For example, in the custodial area, those persons authorized to acquire and dispose of assets should be separated from those having control over the assets. Such an arrangement involves at least two people in the acquisition or disposal of an asset; in that way, it reduces the probability that improper actions will be taken. Similarly, the same person should not authorize the payment of a vendor invoice and also sign the check paying the invoice. Neither should the authority for adding new employees or terminating existing employees be performed by the person distributing payroll checks.

In the recordkeeping area, it is always desirable to have subsidiary ledgers maintained by someone other than the person recording the transactions in the related control accounts to avoid the tendency to cover an error by changing one of the records. It is also desirable to assign transaction approval responsibilities to someone other than the person responsible for recording them.

Another device used to encourage employees in custodial, recordkeeping, and authorization positions to perform their tasks responsibly is a mandatory vacation policy. If all employees are required to take vacations, they know that their normal duties will be performed by someone else while they are away. The probability of thefts or bookkeeping errors occurring, for example, will be reduced by knowledge of the fact that such errors are likely to be discovered by the person temporarily handling the duties of the vacationing employee.

The effectiveness of segregating employee responsibilities depends on the basic assumption that two or more employees are unlikely to work in collusion to perpetrate a fraud or to cover up an unintentional error. However, such collusion might occur if the employees performing the separate tasks are related to each other. Therefore, it is desirable for a firm to follow a practice of not employing related personnel in positions vulnerable to collusion. It is also important to establish a policy relating to conflicts of interest to reduce the probability that an employee might collude with customers or suppliers to the detriment of the firm because of other relationships with those parties.

Comparisons and Compliance Monitoring

The entity should have an effective function of monitoring compliance with the controls built into the system. A vital part of such a system is the comparison of various records produced by the system for completeness and accuracy. In small businesses, the owner/manager may do this personally. In larger businesses, however, the responsibility for monitoring compliance may be delegated through separation of duties to either supervisory personnel within operating departments or the internal audit department. These persons, independent of both the recordkeeping and custodial functions, will compare the recorded accountability over assets (the books of the company) with the existing assets themselves, at intervals, and will take remedial action when necessary. In addition, when recordkeeping involves the keeping of both general and subsidiary ledgers, those records will be periodically compared and differences corrected.

For example, a supervisory person in the accounting department, independent of both the cash-handling function and the function of posting cash receipts to individual customer accounts, may prepare the monthly bank reconciliation. Alternatively, this function may be performed by the internal audit department, if the entity is of sufficient size to justify one. The overriding rule to follow in this respect is that no one person should have complete control of a transaction from beginning to end without being checked, in terms of accuracy and accountability, by another person or function within the system.

Adequate Records and Documentation

Records provide information about the past history of the entity. Unless proper records exist, it is impossible to obtain the audit evidence necessary to issue an unqualified audit opinion.

In Figure 5–3, we presented the *evidence tree* of a typical entity. The records system of an entity comprises its evidence tree. Those records consist of the general and subsidiary ledgers, books of original entry (journals), and intermediate and primary supporting documentation (invoices, receiving reports, deposit slips, etc.). In modern business entities, most of the records are maintained in the form of machine-readable files stored on magnetic tape or disk and are accessible only with the help of a computer.

Every system should have the capability of capturing the pertinent details of a transaction as it takes place. Those details should be retained either in the form of documents or machine-readable files for a sufficient amount of time to permit proper comparisons and cross checking for accuracy, validity, and completeness. Backup records should be retained for several periods to permit reconstruction of data bases should they be lost or damaged. Magnetic tape and disk records should be stored in an area where appropriate temperatures are maintained and should be protected from harmful magnetic fields.

Limited Access to Assets and Sensitive Data

Appropriate facilities must be provided to safeguard both assets and records from unnecessary deterioration, destruction, or misplacement. For example, perishable foods require appropriately refrigerated storage facilities to prevent unnecessary spoilage. Maintenance policies should be followed for fixed assets to prevent premature loss of usefulness.

In addition, unauthorized persons should be denied access to the assets of the entity. In general, persons who maintain the records (accountants) and persons who approve transactions should not be allowed direct access to assets. For example, persons who post customer payments to the accounts payable records should not be allowed to sign checks. Once checks are signed by persons in the treasurer's department, they should be mailed directly from that department and not be allowed to return to the department that prepared them. Materials and supplies should be stored in controlled-access facilities to prevent misuse or waste.

Records should be stored in facilities that reduce the probability of their alteration or destruction. Manually or electronically maintained accounts receivable records, for example, should be stored in a fireproof vault at the end of each day. Backup files maintained on magnetic tape or disk should be stored at an off-premises location. Records should be carefully checked in and out of the storage area by authorized personnel.

Execution of Transactions as Authorized

The transactions processed by each system within the entity should be subjected to proper approval before they are executed. Approval of transactions may occur at the highest levels of the business (the board of directors) or may be delegated to lower levels. Generally speaking, the materiality of the transaction dictates the level of approval required. For example, capital acquisition and financing decisions, because they are usually quite material and have long-lasting implications, are approved by the board of directors. On the other hand, purchase decisions for raw materials and for smaller items of property and equipment are generally delegated to the purchasing department. The important thing to remember is that each transaction, no matter how small, should be subjected either to management's general or specific authorization.

Budgets are also used as devices for subjecting the affairs of the entity to the approval process. Effective budgets help to control segments of operations and to measure the extent to which the segments have achieved the goals planned for them. In combination with a responsibility accounting system, budgets can be used as a very effective tool in controlling the financial affairs of the company and in strategizing for future profits and cash flows.

Special Considerations for Small Businesses

Effective internal controls are often more difficult to implement in small businesses than in large ones, due to one or more of the following factors:

1. Small businesses by definition have a very small number of employees, so it is often difficult to have appropriate segregation of recordkeeping, custodial, and authorization responsibilities.
2. Small businesses are often characterized by close personal relationships between owners and employees, sometimes placing employees in positions of unwarranted trust.
3. In many owner-managed small businesses, neither the owner nor the manager may possess the knowledge required to establish proper control procedures.

Control structure weaknesses caused by one or more of these conditions can render the accounting system so ineffective as to be unauditable in some cases.

Probably the most effective way to partially mitigate internal control problems in small businesses is to get the owner/manager involved in the process by which the financial statements are prepared and to keep him or her informed of all significant happenings in the business. For example, internal accounting controls can be dramatically improved in such cases by requiring the owner/manager to review support for all checks, sign them, and mail them without allowing them to return to the bookkeeper/preparer. All payments, except for very small cash disbursements, should be by check. All checks should be prenumbered, controlled, and accounted for as the owner/manager (or auditor) prepares the monthly bank reconciliation. Cash receipts might be controlled through a locked-box system at the bank instead of being handled by an employee who otherwise would have to maintain the cash receipts records and handle cash. These minimal procedures are simple and are not costly, but they can provide better control for the client and at the same time make the financial statements more auditable.

Internal Control Structure and the Audit Process

☑ **Objective 4**
Be able to assess
control risk

To fully understand how internal control affects the auditing process, we must refer again to the flowchart reproduced at the beginning of this chapter, which depicts the audit process. Recall that to plan the audit it is necessary to *disaggregate* the financial statements into the various subsystems which generate them. For purposes of our discussion, those subsystems are

- The revenue and collections system.
- The acquisition and expenditure system.
- The payroll system.
- The production and conversion system.
- The financing and investing system.

Figure 8–5 shows how these systems are interrelated. A business usually begins with infusions of cash through the financing system. Cash, which is labeled the *eye of the needle* in our diagram, is probably the most important single account in the financial statements to the auditor—not only because of its high relative risk but also because almost every other system's transactions eventually culminate in the disbursement or receipt of cash. Cash is used to acquire operating assets, to pay personnel, and to purchase raw materials inventories. These inputs are then used in production to convert raw materials into finished product.

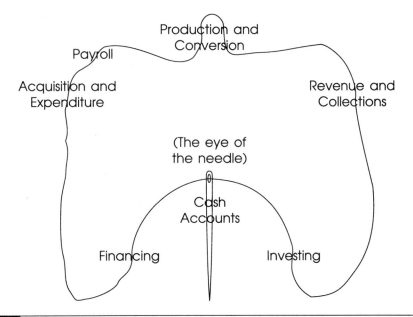

Figure 8–5

The Accounting Systems of a Business

The finished product is stored briefly until sold, when an appropriate cost-of-sales record must be made. Once sold, the product is exchanged for a receivable, which is held briefly until converted back to cash. If the process generates excess cash, it can either be paid out in dividends or invested in such things as income-earning securities or other near-cash assets. If the amount of cash generated is insufficient to meet the entity's operating and financing needs, additional funds must be obtained through borrowing or other financing arrangements.

As the auditor disaggregates the financial statements into component systems, he or she begins to understand the accounting system, a vital element of the control structure.

Obtaining the Initial Understanding

Figure 8–6 depicts diagrammatically the way in which the auditor assesses an entity's control structure. As shown in the diagram, the auditor obtains an understanding of the general features of the control structure (control environment, accounting system, and control procedures) as a part of engagement planning.

A conceptually logical approach to obtaining the initial understanding of the control structure requires the auditor to recognize that the purpose of the control structure of an entity is to *prevent, detect, or correct material errors and irregularities.* Therefore, the following sequence of steps should be taken:

1. Consider the types of errors and irregularities that could occur.
2. Consider the financial statement assertions that would be affected by those errors and irregularities, as well as the accounts that would be affected and in which direction (overstatement or understatement).
3. Determine the control attributes, policies, and procedures that should prevent or detect such errors and irregularities.
4. Determine whether the necessary attributes, policies, and procedures are prescribed by the client.

At least seven general types of material errors and irregularities may occur in any system. We will list and discuss each type, along with the financial statement assertions that are generally affected and the control procedures that should be in place to prevent, detect, or correct them.

Erroneously Recorded Transactions.   Transactions records may contain mathematical mistakes, or errors may result from misapplication of generally accepted accounting principles. Such errors may violate the financial statement assertions of valuation/allocation, rights/obligations, or disclosure. To prevent or detect such errors, responsible supervisory personnel should perform *compliance monitoring* and *comparison* functions, reviewing transactions for reasonableness, accuracy, and proper application of GAAP before they are processed. In addition, proper *segregation of duties* can assure that only persons who are in supervisory roles may authorize, or *execute*, transactions.

Figure 8–6

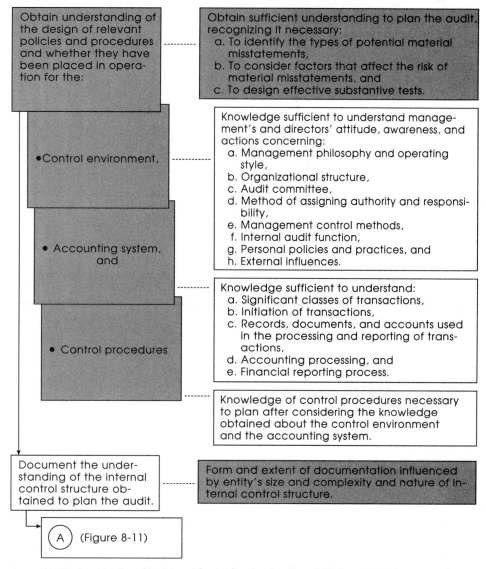

Consideration of the Internal Control Structure in a Financial Statement Audit

Obtain understanding of the design of relevant policies and procedures and whether they have been placed in operation for the:

Obtain sufficient understanding to plan the audit, recognizing it necessary:
a. To identify the types of potential material misstatements,
b. To consider factors that affect the risk of material misstatements, and
c. To design effective substantive tests.

• Control environment,

Knowledge sufficient to understand management's and directors' attitude, awareness, and actions concerning:
a. Management philosophy and operating style,
b. Organizational structure,
c. Audit committee,
d. Method of assigning authority and responsibility,
e. Management control methods,
f. Internal audit function,
g. Personal policies and practices, and
h. External influences.

• Accounting system, and

Knowledge sufficient to understand:
a. Significant classes of transactions,
b. Initiation of transactions,
c. Records, documents, and accounts used in the processing and reporting of transactions,
d. Accounting processing, and
e. Financial reporting process.

• Control procedures

Knowledge of control procedures necessary to plan after considering the knowledge obtained about the control environment and the accounting system.

Document the understanding of the internal control structure obtained to plan the audit.

Form and extent of documentation influenced by entity's size and complexity and nature of internal control structure.

(A) (Figure 8-11)

Source: SAS 55, Consideration of the Internal Control Structure in a Financial Statement Audit *(New York: AICPA, 1988), Appendix C. Used with permission.*

Invalid Transactions.   Recorded transactions may possess inadequate documentary support, or may be fictitious, thus violating the existence/occurrence assertion. To prevent or detect these errors, management should require *adequate records* (documentary support, preferably from outside sources) for all transactions before authorizing (*executing*) them. In addition, policies of the company should provide for appropriate *segregation of duties* involving custody of assets, recordkeeping, and authorization of transactions. Only authorized persons should be allowed *access* to assets or to records of the company.

Unrecorded Transactions. Transactions may have been omitted from the accounting records, by error or intent, thus violating the completeness assertion. To prevent this from happening, the client should have *prenumbered documents* supporting each system. Only authorized persons should have *access* to the documents. In addition, policies of the entity should require supervisory personnel in recording functions to account for the numerical sequence of the documents processed, following all documents through the system to the point of posting, and accounting for all documents voided.

Improperly Valued Transactions. Mathematical mistakes might have been made in recorded transactions, such as extension errors on sales invoices, or use of the wrong prices. Such errors violate the financial statement assertion of proper valuation. Control procedures should include *compliance monitoring* by supervisors, such as checking prices, quantities, and extensions on sales invoices.

Improperly Classified Transactions. Posting errors may result in misclassifications of amounts in balance sheet or income statement accounts (e.g., fixed assets vs. investments, or selling expense vs. general and administrative expenses). A more serious misclassification might be between balance sheet and income statement accounts, an error that affects net income. An example of such an error might be the misclassification of labor charges as inventory (an asset) rather than as expense. Such errors violate the financial statement assertion of proper disclosure. To prevent such errors, supervisory personnel in accounting functions should regularly *compare* and *monitor compliance* of bookkeepers with company accounting policies.

Transactions Recorded in the Wrong Period. This type of error could result in overstatement or understatement of an account balance through violation of the assertion of proper allocation. To prevent such errors, the client should use prenumbered documents (*adequate records*) in all systems such as sales, purchases, cash receipts, and cash disbursements. In addition, transactions occurring near the end of the period should be reviewed (*monitored*) to make sure that a proper cutoff of transactions has been achieved.

Improperly Summarized Transactions. Transactions may have been posted to the correct accounts, but a corresponding entry may not have been entered into the subsidiary records. Alternatively, persons preparing the financial statements may make errors in summarizing amounts for disclosures. To prevent such errors, the client's procedures should provide for preparation of control totals (*records*) of postings to subsidiary ledger accounts and for periodic *comparisons* of those totals with general ledger account balances.

You should notice that these errors and irregularities are common to all accounting systems. In addition, each error can generally be prevented, detected, or corrected by incorporating into the system one of the *control procedures* mentioned in the previous section. The auditor should be alert to the possibility of such errors, as well as the controls that would prevent, detect, or correct them, as the preliminary understanding of the control structure is obtained.

The knowledge necessary to understand the control structure is generally obtained in one or more of the following ways:

- Previous experience with the entity.
- Inquiries of management, supervisory and staff personnel.
- Inspection of documents produced by the system.
- Observation of activities and operations of the entity.

For example, the auditor may rely on previous experience with the entity, observation of employees and systems, and inquiry of management to obtain an understanding of the control environment. To understand the accounting system and control procedures, the auditor might read documentation manuals and narrative descriptions such as that shown in Figure 8–4. In addition, employees should be observed in the performance of their duties. Documents that evidence the performance of controls should be examined, as well as exception reports produced by the data processing system.

As an entity's operations and systems become more complex and sophisticated, it becomes more important for the auditor to understand the control structure before designing substantive tests. The same is true if the system is highly dependent on controls that are built into computer software. When these conditions are present, there are generally thousands of transactions involved in processing the accounts produced by the system. There may be many people, as well as computers, involved in implementing the system. In such cases, it is impossible for the auditor to reach a conclusion about the fairness of the balances without an understanding of the integrity of the system that produced them. For that reason, it is generally necessary to perform more extensive tests of controls on these systems, as described later in the chapter.

Documentation of Understanding

The documentation of the auditor's understanding of the control structure of a client, like all other audit procedures, is contained in the working papers for the engagement. The form and detail of documentation generally depends on the size and complexity of the entity, as well as on the nature of its control structure. For smaller entities, a narrative description of the system such as that contained in Figure 8–4 is generally sufficient. However, for larger systems, the auditor's understanding of the control structure is often enhanced by more elaborate documentation in the form of *questionnaires*, *decision tables*, or flowcharts.

Internal control questionnaires document the results of the auditor's inquiry into the features of the entity's control environment, system, and procedures.

Figure 8–7 ▰▰▰▰▰ ⊐

Partial Internal Control Questionnaire:
Sales and Accounts Receivable System, JEP Manufacturing Co.

Assertion: Existence/occurrence
Error: Invalid (fictitious) transactions

	Yes	No	Remarks
1. Is the shipping function performed by persons independent of credit and billing functions?	X		
2. Are written customer purchase orders required to support every sale?	X		
3. Are written shipping documents prepared for each sale?		X	A copy of sales invoice is used for this purpose.

Assertions: Completeness; Allocation
Errors: Unrecorded transactions
**   Transactions recorded in wrong period**

	Yes	No	Remarks
4. Is the use of prenumbered sales invoices required?	X		
5. Are sales invoices periodically checked for numerical sequence?		X	Account for the numerical sequence of a sample of sales invoices.
6. Are shipping documents matched with sales invoices before recording?	X		

Assertions: Valuation; Disclosure
Error: Improperly valued transactions

	Yes	No	Remarks
7. Do supervisors regularly review sales invoices for quantities, prices, extensions?	X		Sales supervisors review for quantities, prices. Accounting supervisors check extensions.
8. Is there a credit department separate from sales, shipping, and billing?	X		
9. Are all sales invoices reviewed for credit before shipment of goods?	X		

Assertions: Completeness; Disclosure
Errors: Improperly recorded transactions
**   Improperly classified transactions**
**   Improperly summarized transactions**

	Yes	No	Remarks
10. Are postings of invoices periodically checked on a test basis by accounting department supervisors?	X		
11. Are periodic sales summaries prepared?	X		
12. Is a reconciliation made between sales summary totals, general ledger, and subsidiary ledger control totals by persons who are independent of initial recording duties?	X		

Figure 8–7 illustrates a segment of an internal control questionnaire relating to a cash receipts system. Specific questions pertaining to each feature of the entity's control structure (environment, system, and procedures) should be included in the questionnaire. The questions should be designed to elicit responses from management as to whether specific control procedures (segregation of functions, comparisons, adequate records, limited access to assets, and proper approval of transactions) have been included in the entity's control environment and accounting system to prevent the specific types of errors discussed above.

Questions should be organized so that "yes" answers indicate system strengths and "no" answers indicate system weaknesses. Such an arrangement allows the auditor to isolate the weakness by simply looking at the "no" items. The weaknesses identified by "no" responses to questions should be accompanied by either a mitigating strength elsewhere in the system, or more extensive tests of the financial statement assertions affected. For example, it appears that, for JEP Manufacturing Co., written shipping documents are not required for every sale. However, written evidence of the sale is still provided because one copy of the sales invoice is used for this purpose. This represents a mitigating control. Perhaps a more serious weakness is that, even though prenumbered sales documents are prepared, there is no evidence that the numbers are accounted for. A mitigating control apparently does not exist for this weakness. Failure to account for prenumbered documents could cause transactions to be recorded in the wrong period, or perhaps not to be recorded at all. Therefore, the auditor should plan to perform more extensive substantive tests over the *completeness and allocation* assertions for sales at year-end, focusing on cutoff procedures. We will discuss these procedures in greater detail later in the chapter.

Flowcharts

Flowcharts are particularly helpful in understanding the sequences of relationships among activities involving documents within the internal control system. The charts are symbolic representations of a system or series of sequential processes and are designed to describe the flow of work in relation to a system of related activities. The auditor, while tracing the flow of documents and control procedures performed on them, should be able to obtain a thorough understanding of the control system. Once he or she achieves this understanding, the auditor can recognize strengths or weaknesses in the system by considering the types of material errors that could occur and by determining whether the controls necessary to prevent, detect, or correct those errors are prescribed by the client.

The steps in preparing a systems flowchart are as follows:

1. Obtain a thorough understanding of the duties performed, the documents handled, and the ways the documents flow as they are processed. This often will involve much time and discussion with client personnel as well as the completion of the internal control questionnaire.
2. Write a preliminary description of the system as it is understood to operate at this state. Some auditors use a **play script** such as the one illustrated in

Figure 8–8

Play Script of Sales and Receivables System

JEP Manufacturing Company

Actors	Functions performed
1. Sales clerks in sales department	1. Receives written customer purchase order. 2. Prepares 6-copy prenumbered sales invoice. 3. Distributes copies of sales invoice to (1) and (2) billing department; (3) shipping department; (4) finished goods department; (5) credit department; (6) customer as acknowledgement.
2. Credit department	1. Conducts credit check of customer. 2. Updates customer credit files. 3. Sends copy of approved sales invoice (5) to shipping.
3. Finished goods department	1. Upon receipt of sales invoice (4), pulls goods from inventory and releases to shipping.
4. Shipping department	1. Receives copy (3) of sales invoice. 2. Files temporarily pending credit approval. 3. Upon receipt of sales invoice copy (5) from credit, ships goods to customer. 4. Sends copy (5) to billing.
5. Billing department	1. Receives copies (1) and (2) from sales department; files temporarily, pending credit approval and shipping. 2. Upon receipt of approved invoice copy (5) from shipping, matches with copies (1) and (2). 3. Checks prices and quantities for accuracy and completeness. Completes extensions on invoice. 4. Copy (1) mailed to customer. Copy (2) used as source document for sales journal, then filed. 5. Sends copy (5) to accounts receivable bookkeeper. 6. (Monthly) Prepares sales summary. Sends copy to general ledger bookkeeping dept. Retains 1 copy and files.
6. Accounts receivable bookkeeper	1. Receives copy (5) of approved sales invoice showing shipment of goods from billing department. 2. Posts entry to customer account in accounts receivable subsidiary ledger.
7. General ledger bookkeeping	1. Receives sales summary from billing dept. 2. Makes general ledger entry to sales and accounts receivable. 3. (Supervisory personnel) Reconcile sales and accounts receivable accounts to subsidiary ledger totals.
8. Internal auditors	1. Test entire process on a regular basis. 2. Locate errors. 3. Resubmit transactions for error correction.

Figure 8–8 to initially document the description. Notice that the play-script working paper is organized in two columns. The one on the left is for the actors, showing the persons who perform each of the various tasks. The right-hand column shows the task performed and the documents prepared by each person.

3. Draw the flowchart, basing it on the knowledge obtained from the play script and from the client's answers to inquiries about the system. The play script described above is thus used as a tool in preparing the flowchart. Actors in the system are depicted (by department) as column headings in the flowchart. Actions taken by the various actors, documents generated, and direction of flow of those documents are shown by symbols on the flowchart. Figure 8–9 shows a few of the standard symbols, which will be used throughout this text and in problem solutions to depict processing functions, documents, and communication links. Standardization of symbols within a firm is important so that each flowchart can be readily understood by all persons reviewing it.

The following rules should be observed when drawing a systems flowchart:

1. Each chart should be properly labeled as to working paper reference numbers, company name, and type of system (cash receipts, inventory, purchases, etc.).
2. Departments and actors within the departments should be shown in column headings across the top of the chart.
3. Actions taken within a department, and documents generated by those

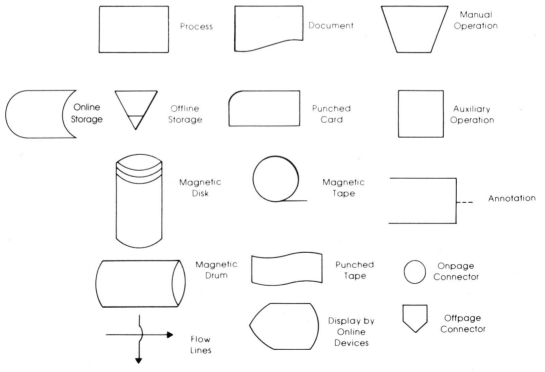

Figure 8–9

Standard Flowcharting Symbols

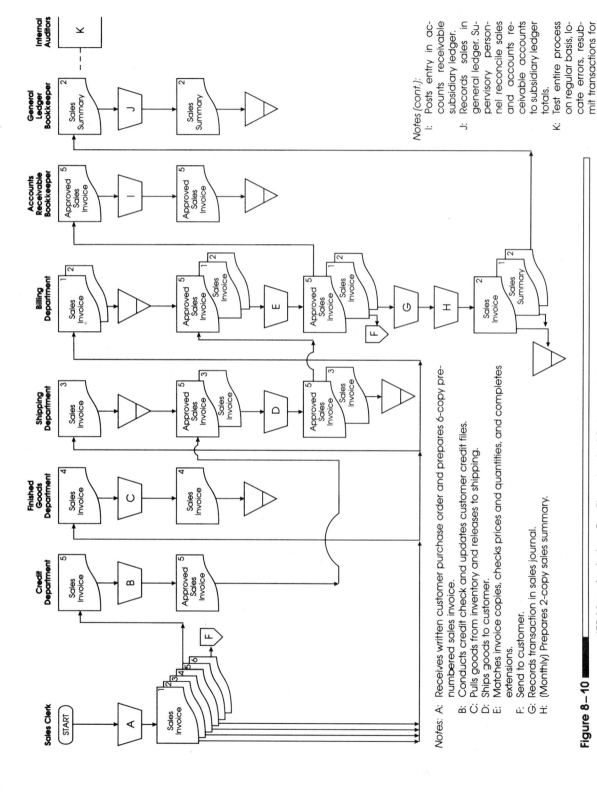

Notes: A: Receives written customer purchase order and prepares 6-copy pre-
       numbered sales invoice.
       B: Conducts credit check and updates customer credit files.
       C: Pulls goods from inventory and releases to shipping.
       D: Ships goods to customer.
       E: Matches invoice copies, checks prices and quantities, and completes
          extensions.
       F: Send to customer.
       G: Records transaction in sales journal.
       H: (Monthly) Prepares 2-copy sales summary.

Notes (cont.):
       I: Posts entry in ac-
          counts receivable
          subsidiary ledger.
       J: Records sales in
          general ledger. Su-
          pervisory person-
          nel reconcile sales
          and accounts re-
          ceivable accounts
          to subsidiary ledger
          totals.
       K: Test entire process
          on regular basis, lo-
          cate errors, resub-
          mit transactions for
          error correction.

Figure 8–10 ▬▬▬ JEP Manufacturing Co. Flowchart of Sales and Accounts Receivable System actions, should appear in the columns. The general flow of documents as they are handled by actors within a department should be depicted in a top-to-bottom-of-the-page sequence. Therefore, the document flow on the chart should be from left to right (by department) and from top to bottom within departments. Figure 8–10 depicts a flowchart for the sales and accounts receivable system; it was derived from the play script appearing in Figure 8–8.

4. Always use a flowchart template and ruler. A messy flowchart is difficult to read.

5. Narrative explanations should appear on the face of the chart in the form of annotations or at the bottom of the chart in a reference key.

Assessment of Control Risk[4]

After obtaining an understanding of the control structure of the client the auditor should be prepared to assess, on a system-by-system basis, the effects of the control structure on the financial statement assertions produced by the various systems. Figure 8–11 illustrates this process diagrammatically.

For some financial statement assertions, the auditor may assess control risk at its maximum level. Such an assessment would be appropriate (1) if results from consideration of the control structure indicated significant weaknesses in policies and procedures over the control environment and accounting system, or (2) if further investigation into policies and procedures affecting specific financial statement assertions would not be cost effective.

Recall from our earlier discussions of audit risk that *there is an inverse relationship between control risk and detection risk*. The planning objective of the auditor should be to control total audit risk at an acceptably low level. Therefore, at a specified level of inherent risk, if control risk is assessed as high, there must be a corresponding *reduction* in the maximum acceptable level of detection risk. Thus, after documenting the assessment of control risk, the auditor should plan to carry out extensive tests of balances and/or transactions on the related financial statement assertions.

EXAMPLE 1
Cargile, CPA, is auditing Dunhill, Inc.'s financial statements. As part of the investigation of the control environment of the company, Cargile learns that the company combines the duties of cash handling and recordkeeping for sales and accounts receivable. Because of this structural weakness, Cargile should set control risk at its highest level for the financial statement assertions of existence and valuation. No further tests of the accounting system are necessary. Rather, Cargile should perform extensive tests of balances (confirmation) and transactions (inspection of underlying documentation) for sales and accounts receivable. These tests would be conducted on the year-end balances, rather than at an interim date.

EXAMPLE 2
Assume the same facts as Example 1, except that there is proper segregation of cash handling and recordkeeping over sales and accounts receivable. However, further

Figure 8–11

Assessment of Control Risk on Assertion-by-Assertion Basis

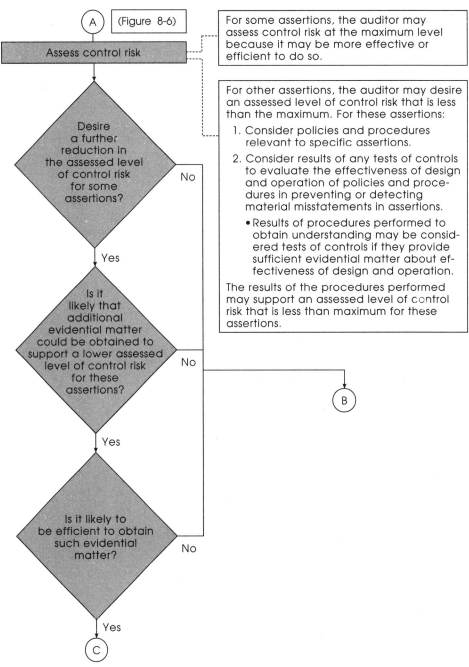

Source: SAS 55, *Consideration of the Internal Control Structure in a Financial Statement Audit* (New York: AICPA, 1988), Appendix C, used with permission.

Figure 8–11

(continued)

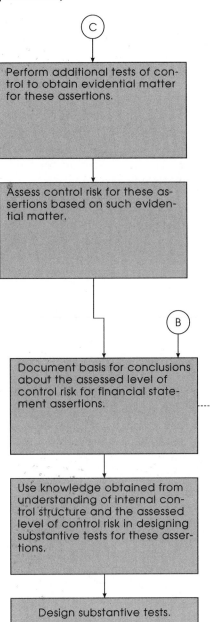

study of specific control procedures affecting the existence and valuation assertions is not expected to appreciably reduce the nature, timing, and extent of necessary tests of balances or transactions. In this case, Cargile should still set control risk over these assertions at its maximum and perform extensive tests of balances and/or transactions on the year-end balances.

For some financial statement assertions, the auditor may conclude that, if additional study and tests could be performed on the accounting system that supports the financial statement balances, control risk might be assessed at a level that is *less than the maximum level*. As a result, extensive tests on the balances and/or transactions might be curtailed in favor of analytical procedures, thus making the audit of balances more efficient and cost-effective. To proceed in this manner, as shown in Figure 8–11, the auditor must be able to answer "yes" to the following questions for a particular assertion:

1. Is a further reduction in the assessed level of control risk (from its preliminary assessment level) desirable?
2. Is evidential matter supporting such a reduction available?
3. Is it cost efficient to obtain such evidential matter?

To obtain the evidential matter necessary to support lower levels of control risk assessment, a detailed study of the underlying control structure, as well as tests of those controls, should be performed.

Tests of Controls

Figure 8–12 illustrates the transactions testing methodology for the sales and accounts receivable system for JEP Manufacturing Company. This figure summarizes the findings of the auditor's initial understanding of the internal control environment, accounting system, and control procedures for the company that have been documented in Figures 8–4 through 8–10. In addition, Figure 8–12 specifies the **tests of controls** that are appropriate for the system, as well as substantive tests that result from the process.

Tests of controls are designed to provide assurance that the policies and procedures prescribed by the client actually do exist and are functioning effectively. Some controls can be tested by merely *observing* client activities. An example of controls that can be tested by observation is segregation of the duties of authorization, recordkeeping, and custody of related assets. Transactions that leave a documented audit trail can be tested by *sampling* and inspection of documents from each of the various types of transactions and following them through the system to determine whether the company is complying with the provisions of the system as documented in the organization chart and procedures manuals.

Some tests of controls are, by their nature, also tests of balances. Thus, they are called **dual-purpose tests**. These tests are considered very efficient tests of transactions because they accomplish both controls and balance-related audit objectives. An example of a dual-purpose test would be inspection of documents in the sales system to ascertain if supervisors in the accounting department recheck extensions (price times quantity) on sales invoices before they are completed. Existence of this control helps assure proper *valuation* of sales and accounts receivable. To test the control, the auditor should recalculate the extensions on a sample of sales documents and examine the documents for the initials of a sales department supervisor. In so doing, the auditor simultaneously tests both the existence of the control and the existence and valuation of the transaction that is produced by the system.

The outcome of the detailed review and testing phases of the audit can produce three possible conclusions:

1. The system as represented to the auditor is both adequately prescribed and is operating as it should. In such a situation, the auditor would need to perform only limited substantive tests on the transactions and financial statement balances to justify the expression of an opinion on the statements.
2. The client is not complying with the prescribed procedures. This causes the auditor to ask a further question: Do other controls exist within the system to mitigate the discovered weakness? If so, we may disregard the lack of effectiveness and still not expand our substantive tests. On the other hand, if no mitigating controls exist, the auditor may extend substantive tests to compensate for the observed weaknesses.
3. If the tests of controls indicate that the system is not effective and there are no mitigating controls, it might be necessary in extreme cases either to withdraw from the audit or to issue a disclaimer of opinion.

For example, examine Figure 8–12. On the basis of our review of the control structure for Sales and Accounts Receivable for JEP Manufacturing, we may conclude the following:

1. There is adequate separation of duties between persons recording sales, authorizing sales, and handling assets. In addition, proper documentation of sales, in the form of written customer purchase orders and shipping documents, is required. These attributes, if working properly, strengthen the financial statement assertions of existence/occurrence and valuation. After testing these control attributes by observation and inspection of documents, the auditor may limit the substantive tests listed in the last column of Figure 8–12 and may perform more of those tests at an interim period (when less costly).
2. Sales invoices are prenumbered, but there is no evidence that they are accounted for on a regular basis. This potential weakness in the financial assertion of completeness should be mitigated by the auditor's test of sales invoices: selecting a block of prenumbered sales invoices, vouching for numerical sequence, and tracing the entries into the sales journal.
3. All sales are approved by the credit manager before goods are shipped, thus strengthening the assertion of proper valuation for accounts receivable. After testing this control by inspection of sales invoices and vouching the initials

Figure 8–12

Transactions Testing Methodology for Sales and Accounts Receivable System: JEP Manufacturing Co.

Financial statement assertion	Error or irregularity	Control that would prevent, detect, correct	Is control prescribed? (Figure 8–7)	Test of controls	Substantive test(s)
Existence/ occurrence	Invalid (fictitious) transactions	Require customer purchase orders and shipping documents for each recorded sale	Yes	Vouch recorded sales to copies of customer purchase orders and shipping documents	Confirmation of accounts receivable; vouching sales and cash receipts to supporting invoices and deposit slips
		Require separation of shipping and billing functions	Yes	Observation	
Completeness; allocation	Unrecorded transactions; transactions recorded in the period	Require prenumbered sales invoices and periodic accounting for numerical sequence	Yes	Trace copies of shipping documents to sales invoices and postings in sales journal	Same as test of controls (dual-purpose)
			No	Account for numerical sequence of sales invoices	
		Require matching of shipping documents with invoices	Yes		
Valuation	Invalid transactions (selling to customers who cannot pay)	Require approval of credit by separate credit department before shipment of goods	Yes	Vouch sales invoices for initials of credit manager	Recomputation of allowance for doubtful accounts Discussion of delinquent accounts with client Analytical procedures: Analysis of days' sales uncollected and accounts receivable turnover Recompute extensions on sales invoices
	Improperly valued transactions	Require supervisory review of sales invoices for prices, quantities, extensions	Yes	Vouch sales invoices for initials of sales, accounting supervisors	

Completeness; disclosure	Improperly recorded transactions; improperly classified transactions	Yes	Require supervisory review of sales invoices for quantities, price extensions, postings	Vouch sales invoices for initials of sales department supervisor and accounting supervisor	Trace postings of sales invoices into sales journal Recompute extension on sales documents Vouch quantities, prices to supporting documents
	Improperly summarized transactions	Yes	Require periodic sales summaries	Observation	Same as test of controls (dual purpose)
		Yes	Require reconciliation of sales summary totals to general and subsidiary ledgers by independent person	Trace sales summary totals to general ledger postings Trace postings of sales entries to accounts receivable subsidiary ledger on a test basis	Same as test of controls (dual purpose)

of the credit supervisor, the auditor may limit substantive tests of the allowance for doubtful accounts to the analytical procedures listed in the last column of Figure 8–12. These tests are less time-consuming (and less costly)
than the more detailed substantive tests of balances that are listed.

4. All sales invoices are thoroughly checked by supervisors in the billing
department for quantities, prices, and extensions before posting, thus
strengthening the assertions of completeness and disclosure. After testing
these controls by inspection of documents for initials of billing supervisors,
the auditor would greatly limit reperformance of these procedures (the
required substantive test of transactions), thus saving time and money.

5. Supervisors in the general ledger bookkeeping department regularly review
postings of sales journals to general and subsidiary ledger accounts and
regularly reconcile general ledger accounts to totals of subsidiary ledgers.
After testing these controls by observation and inspection of documentary
support, the auditor would greatly limit reperformance of these procedures
(the required substantive tests).

6. The entire process is tested and monitored on a regular basis by internal
auditors. The independent auditor should review the organization chart
to ascertain the autonomy of the internal audit department. In addition,
he or she should discuss the functions of the internal audit department
with supervisors, and perform tests of the internal auditors' work to determine the competence of the internal audit staff. After these tests are completed, the auditor may reduce the nature, timing, and extent of audit
procedures over all financial statement assertions that are tested by the
internal audit staff.

Communication of Internal Control Structure Deficiencies[5]

During the course of the audit, the auditor may become aware of deficiencies in
the design or operation of the internal control structure that, in the auditor's
judgment, could adversely affect the entity's ability to record, process, summarize, and report financial data consistent with the assertions of management
in the financial statements. Conditions such as the following are but a few
examples:

• Inadequate overall design of the control structure.
• Absence of any of the basic characteristics of effective control that were dis-
cussed earlier in this chapter (segregation of responsibilities, comparisons,
adequate records, limited access to assets, or approvals of transactions).
• Evidence that prescribed controls are not being followed by employees.
• Evidence of intentional override of the structure by those in authority.

These and other matters pointing to design or operational deficiencies constitute
reportable conditions that must be communicated to the audit committee of the
entity.

In some cases, reportable conditions may be of such magnitude as to be considered a **material weakness** in internal controls. In this context, a material weakness is defined as a condition in which the design or operation of an element of the control structure does not reduce to a relatively low level the risk that errors or irregularities in amounts that would be material to the audited financial statements may occur and not be detected within a timely period by employees acting in the normal course of their assigned functions. Material weaknesses may be identified separately, or they may be reported along with other less material reportable conditions.

Although the auditor is not required to do so, a vital part of the service that auditors perform for clients can be suggestions as to how deficiencies in the control structure can be corrected, or inefficiencies improved. Suggestions for improvement are generally communicated to the management of the company as a secondary objective of the audit.

If the entity does not have an audit committee, the auditor should report conditions of weakness to individuals with a level of authority and responsibility equivalent to the audit committee, such as the board of directors, trustees, or owners. The medium by which this is done is usually a written report on internal control. Such reports are discussed in detail in Chapter 22.

Summary

In this chapter we have discussed the effects of the auditor's understanding of the internal control structure on the financial audit. We first defined the meaning of the term *internal control structure* to include the control environment, accounting system, and control practices and procedures of an entity. We then outlined the general characteristics that effective control structures and systems should possess. Those are (1) segregation of responsibilities; (2) comparisons and compliance monitoring; (3) adequate records; (4) limited access to assets and records of the company; and (5) execution of transactions in accordance with management's general or specific authority. These characteristics should be used as criteria for judging the quality of the internal control structure of an entity.

The latter part of the chapter was devoted to the process by which the internal control structure is evaluated. In the first stage of the process, the auditor is required to evaluate the entity's control environment, accounting system, and control procedures sufficiently to form a preliminary assessment of control risk. The assessment may be quantitative or qualitative (high, medium, low) and must be made on a financial statement assertion-by-assertion basis.

For some assertions, the auditor may assess control risk at its highest level, requiring detection risk procedures that are both effective and extensive on the related financial statement assertions. The auditor may, however, identify control strengths for specific financial statement assertions which, if tested further, may cause control risk to be assessed at a lower level than originally planned, thus allowing detection risk procedures to be less extensive and less costly. A second and optional detailed testing stage is necessary for those controls. That stage, including related tests of controls, was discussed in detail.

Auditing Vocabulary

p. 281   **accounting system:**   The transactions that are significant to the financial statements of the entity, and the process by which those transactions are initiated, documented, processed, and reported.

p. 277   **control environment:**   The aggregate effects of various conditions surrounding the audit client that influence the conduct of the audit engagement.

p. 282   **control procedures:**   Those procedures built into an accounting system and control environment that help to assure the proper recording, summarization, classification, and reporting of transactions in accordance with generally accepted accounting principles.

p. 275   **control risk:**   The risk that material errors or irregularities might have occurred in the recording, processing, summarizing, and reporting process might have gone undetected by the entity's internal control system.

p. 300   **dual-purpose tests:**   Tests of transactions that serve the dual purpose of tests of controls and substantive tests of transactions.

p. 291   **internal control questionnaire:**   The vehicle which documents the auditor's inquiry into the features of the entity's control environment, accounting system, and control procedures. Questions on the questionnaire are organized so that a "yes" answer indicates a system strength and "no" answer indicates system weaknesses.

p. 305   **material weakness:**   A reportable condition in which the design or operation of an element of the control structure does not reduce to a relatively low level the risk that errors or irregularities in amounts that would be material to the audited financial statements may occur and not be detected in a timely period by employees acting in the normal course of their assigned functions. Material weaknesses are considered more serious than reportable conditions and must be reported to the audit committee.

p. 293   **play script:**   A working paper that may be prepared before drawing the flowchart, that facilitates the preparation of the flowchart.

p. 273   **reasonable assurance:**   The concept in auditing that recognizes that the cost of achieving internal control should not exceed the expected benefits to be derived.

p. 304   **reportable conditions:**   Deficiencies in the design or operation of the internal control structure that, in the auditor's judgment, could adversely affect the entity's ability to record, process, summarize, and report financial data consistent with the assertions of management in the financial statements. Reportable conditions must be communicated through the audit committee of the entity.

p. 279   **responsibility accounting system:**   A budgeting system that places the responsibility for achieving certain goals of the company on the managers of the various departments of the company.

p. 293   **systems flowchart:**   A pictorial description of the system, intended to aid in the auditor's understanding of the system.

p. 300   **tests of controls:**   Tests of transactions designed to provide assurance that the policies and procedures prescribed by the client actually do exist and that the system of internal control is functioning effectively.

Notes

1. SAS 55, *Consideration of the Internal Control Structure in a Financial Statement Audit* (New York: AICPA, 1988), footnote 1.
2. Ibid., Appendix A.
3. Ibid., paragraph 21.
4. Material for this section was adapted largely from SAS 55, *Consideration of the Internal Control Structure in a Financial Statement Audit* (New York: AICPA, 1988).
5. Material for this section was adapted from SAS 60, *Communication of Internal Control Structure Related Matters Noted in an Audit* (New York: AICPA, 1988).

Questions for Class Discussion

Q8-1 What is the relationship between a client's internal control structure and the substantive tests to be performed by the independent auditor?

Q8-2 What is the primary objective of the internal control structure? Discuss.

Q8-3 What are the operating objectives of an effective internal control structure? Which of these would the financial statement auditor be most concerned with?

Q8-4 What aspects of each material accounting system should be understood by the independent auditor?

Q8-5 What are the three basic risks associated with the expression of an opinion on financial statements? What is the relationship of the control structure of an entity to audit risk?

Q8-6 What are the elements of an entity's *control structure*? Explain each element.

Q8-7 What are the characteristics that should underlie an effective internal control structure? Discuss.

Q8-8 Which types of responsibilities should be separated in an effective internal control structure? Explain.

Q8-9 How can a mandatory vacation policy improve the reliability of an internal control structure?

Q8-10 Why is it important for a firm to have clearly defined lines of authority and responsibility? What are the means through which this is achieved?

Q8-11 How can an auditor judge whether or not a client has appropriately qualified personnel assigned to the various tasks to be performed?

Q8-12 What is the relationship among the control environment of the audited entity and the nature, timing, and extent of necessary audit procedures? Explain.

Q8-13 Why is it important to have appropriate authorization and approval procedures associated with the various transactions carried out by the client?

Q8-14 What effect do the following groups have on the independent audit: (1) the audit committee? (2) the internal audit staff?

Q8-15 What are some of the special problems associated with the establishment of an internal control structure for a small client?

Q8-16 What are the procedures used by the auditor to obtain an understanding of the client's internal control structure?

Q8-17 After a preliminary understanding is reached regarding the internal control structure of the client, how does the auditor proceed on a financial statement assertion-by-assertion basis?

Q8-18 What are the general types of material errors and irregularities that could occur because of a weak internal control structure? Discuss.

Q8-19 What is the purpose of an internal control questionnaire? How does it fit into the overall evaluation of internal control? Discuss.

Q8-20 How are flowcharts used in the evaluation of the internal control procedures for an accounting subsystem?

Q8-21 What is the relationship between tests of controls and substantive tests? Discuss this relationship.

Short Cases

C8-1 The town of Commuter Park operates a private parking lot near the railroad station for the benefit of town residents. The guard on duty issues annual prenumbered parking stickers to residents who submit an application form and show evidence of residency. The sticker is affixed to the auto and allows the resident to park anywhere in the lot for twelve (12) hours if four quarters are placed in the parking meter. Applications are maintained in the guard office at the lot. The guard checks to see that only residents are using the lot and that no resident has parked without paying the required meter fee.

Once a week the guard on duty, who has a master key for all meters, takes the coins from the meters and places them in a locked steel box. The guard delivers the box to the town storage building, where it is opened, and the coins are manually counted by a storage department clerk, who records the total cash counted on a "Weekly Cash Report." This report is sent to the town accounting department. The storage department clerk puts the cash in a safe, and on the following day, the cash is picked up by the town's treasurer, who manually recounts the cash, prepares the bank deposit slip, and delivers the deposit to the bank. The deposit slip, authenticated by the bank teller, is sent to the accounting department, where it is filed with the "Weekly Cash Report."

Required: Describe weaknesses in the existing system and recommend one or more improvements for each of the weaknesses to strengthen internal control over the parking lot cash receipts.

Organize your answer sheet as follows:

Weakness	Recommended Improvement(s)

(AICPA adapted)

C8-2 Jordan Finance Company opened four personal loan offices in neighboring cities on January 2, 19X0. Small cash loans are made to borrowers, who repay the principal with interest in monthly installments over a period not exceeding two years. Ralph Jordan, president of the company, uses one of the offices as a central office and visits the other offices periodically for supervision and internal auditing purposes.

Mr. Jordan is concerned about the honesty of his employees. He came to your office in December 19X0 and stated, "I want to engage you to install a system to prohibit employees from embezzling cash." He also stated, "Until I went into business for myself, I worked for a nationwide loan company with 500 offices, and I'm familiar with that company's internal control structure. I want to describe that structure so you can install it for me, because it will absolutely prevent fraud."

Required:
a. How would you advise Mr. Jordan on his request that you install the large company's internal control structure for his firm? Discuss.
b. How would you respond to the suggestion that the new structure would prevent embezzlement? Discuss.
c. Assume that in addition to undertaking the system's engagement in 19X1, you agreed to audit Jordan Finance Company's financial statements for the year ended December 31, 19X0. No scope limitations were imposed.
   1. How would you determine the scope necessary to satisfactorily complete your audit? Discuss.
   2. Would you be responsible for the discovery of fraud in this audit? Discuss.

(AICPA adapted)

C8-3 You were recently appointed the auditor for a private college. Your first assignment is to appraise the adequacy and effectiveness of the student registration procedures. You have completed your preliminary study. On the basis of your interviews and a walk-through of the student registration operation, you prepared the play script shown below.

Required:
a. Prepare a formal systems flowchart based on the following play script, using appropriate symbols and techniques.
b. Examine the flowchart and list five internal control weaknesses (such as omissions of certain steps or measures) in the student registration procedures. Use the characteristics of internal control discussed in this chapter as guidelines for your evaluation.

Admission—processing of registrations		
1 **Mail room**	**2** **Registration clerk**	**3** **Cashier**

• Opens all mail, prepares remittance advices and remittance listings
• Sends copies of advices and listings to:
  a. Cashier (with cash and checks)
  b. Accounts receivable clerk
  c. General bookkeeper
• Destroys other copies of advices and listings
	• Receives three copies of completed registration forms from students
	• Checks for counselor's or similar approval
	• Records appropriate fee from official class catalog
	• Approves forms, if completed properly, and sends students with registration forms to cashier
	• If forms not completed properly, returns forms to student for follow-up and reapplication
		• Collects funds or forwards two copies of registration forms to billing clerk
		• Records cash receipts in daily receipts record
		• Prepares and makes daily deposits
		• Forwards duplicate receipted deposit slips and daily receipts records to general bookkeeper
		• Destroys copies of daily receipts records

4 **Billing clerk**	5 **Accounts receivable** **clerk**	6 **General** **bookkeeper**
• Receives two copies of reg- istration form, prepares bill, and makes entries in regis- tration (sales) journal • Forwards copies of billings and registration forms to accounts receivable clerk and forwards copies of bill to general bookkeeper	• Posts accounts receivable subsidiary ledger detailed accounts from remittance listings • Matches billings and regis- tration forms and posts accounts receivable sub- sidiary ledger detailed accounts	• Journalizes and posts cash receipts and applicable registrations to general ledger • Enters registration (sales) journal data in general ledger

(CIA Examination adapted)

C8-4 Theresa Crane, administrator of Departure Haven Nursing Home, seeks your advice on a problem. Departure Haven employs three clerical employees who, among them, must perform the following functions. Mrs. Crane requests your advice as to how to assign the functions among the employees so as to achieve the highest degree of internal control.

   a. Maintains disbursements (payments) journal.
   b. Reconciles bank account.
   c. Prepares checks for signature.
   d. Opens mail and lists receipts.
   e. Deposits cash receipts.
   f. Maintains accounts receivable records.
   g. Determines when accounts receivable are uncollectible.
   h. Is responsible for petty cash fund.

X is custodial
Y is record keeping
Z has authorization
duties

Required:
   a. How would you distribute the various functions among clerks X, Y, and Z? Assume that all functions require approximately the same amount of time.
   b. List at least three unsatisfactory combinations of the functions.

(AICPA adapted)

C8-5 The following cases describe the internal control structures for different companies.
   a. When Sharon Fisher, purchasing agent for Cooper Cosmetics, orders materials, she sends a duplicate copy of the purchase order to the receiving department. When materials are received, Joe Ferguson, receiving clerk, records the date of receipt on the copy of the purchase order but does not count the goods received. The same copy of the purchase order is sent to accounting, where Lyle Brown uses it to support the purchase entry in the voucher register. The copy is then sent to raw materials stores, where William Potter uses it to update the perpetual inventory cards.
   b. At Halfiva Manufacturing Company, time cards of 450 employees are collected weekly by the foreman and delivered to the data processing department. There the cards are sorted and the hours worked are entered into the computer. These records are used to prepare individual payroll records, paychecks, and labor cost distribution records. The paychecks are compared with individual payroll records and signed by the treasurer, who returns them to the data processing supervisor for distribution.
   c. A sales branch of Rocklin Manufacturing Company has an office force consisting of the branch manager, I. C. Parama, and two assistants, Truett Beard and Jerry

Martinez. The branch has a local bank account in which it deposits cash receipts. Checks drawn on the bank account require Parma's signature or the signature of R. C. Timball, treasurer of the company. Bank statements and paid checks are returned by the bank to Parma, who retains them in his files after preparing the monthly bank reconciliation. Reports of disbursements are also prepared by Parma and submitted to Timball at the home office on scheduled dates.

Required: For each of the internal control structures described, point out
  a. The weaknesses, if any, that exist.
  b. The material errors or irregularities, if any, that might occur because of those weaknesses.
  c. Your recommendations for improvement in the structure.

(AICPA adapted)

Problems

P8-1 Select the best answer to each of the following items relating to the auditor's understanding of the control structure.
  a. An auditor obtains an understanding of the client's control structure primarily to
    1. Ascertain whether errors and irregularities exist.
    2. Determine the extent of tests of controls that should be performed.
    3. Determine the extent of substantive testing that should be performed.
    4. Make constructive suggestions to the client for improvement.
  b. In internal control, the basic concept recognizing that the cost of a control procedure should *not* exceed the benefits expected to be derived is known as
    1. Reasonable assurance
    2. Management responsibility
    3. Limited liability
    4. Management by exception
  c. Which of the following is an invalid concept of internal control?
    1. In cases where a person is responsible for all phases of a transaction there should be a clear designation of that person's responsibility.
    2. The recorded accountability for assets should be compared with the existing assets at reasonable intervals, and appropriate action should be taken if there are differences.
    3. Accounting control procedures may appropriately be applied on a test basis in some circumstances.
    4. Procedures designed to detect errors and irregularities should be performed by persons other than those who are in a position to perpetrate them.
  d. Internal controls are *not* designed to provide reasonable assurance that
    1. Transactions are executed in accordance with management's authorization.
    2. Irregularities will be eliminated.
    3. Access to assets is permitted only in accordance with management's authorization.
    4. The recorded accountability for assets is compared with the existing assets at reasonable intervals.

(AICPA adapted)

P8-2 Select the best answer for each of the following items relating to the characteristics of an internal control structure.

a. Which of the following activities would be *least* likely to strengthen a company's internal control structure?

1. Separating accounting from other financial operations
2. Maintaining insurance for fire and theft
3. Fixing responsibility for the performance of employee duties
4. Carefully selecting and training employees

b. Effective internal control in a small company that has an insufficient number of employees to permit proper division of responsibilities can *best* be enhanced by

1. Employing temporary personnel to aid in the separation of duties.
2. Direct participation by the owner of the business in the recordkeeping activities of the business.
3. Engaging a CPA to perform monthly write-up work.
4. Delegating full, clear-cut responsibility to each employee for the functions assigned to each.

c. Internal control is a function of management, and effective control is based upon the concept of charge and discharge of responsibility and duty. Which of the following is one of the overriding principles of internal control?

1. Responsibility for accounting and financial duties should be assigned to one responsible officer.
2. Responsibility for the performance of each duty must be fixed.
3. Responsibility for the accounting duties must be borne by the auditing committee of the company.
4. Responsibility for accounting activities and duties must be assigned only to employees who are bonded.

d. Proper segregation of functional responsibilities calls for separation of the

1. Authorization, approval, and execution functions.
2. Authorization, execution, and payment functions.
3. Receiving, shipping, and custodial functions.
4. Authorization, recording, and custodial functions.

e. The use of fidelity bonds may indemnify a company from embezzlement losses. The use also

1. Reduces the company's need to obtain expensive business interruption insurance.
2. Protects employees who made unintentional errors from possible monetary damages resulting from such errors.
3. Allows the company to substitute the fidelity bonds for various parts of internal accounting control.
4. Reduces the possibility of employing persons with dubious records in positions of trust.

(AICPA adapted)

P8-3 Select the best answer for each of the following items relating to the use of flowcharts in understanding a client's internal control structure.

a. Which of the following best describes the principal advantage of the use of flowcharts in reviewing internal control?

1. Standard flowcharts are available and can be effectively used for describing most company internal operations.

      2. Flowcharts aid in the understanding of the sequence and relationships of activities and documents.

      3. Working papers are not complete unless they include flowcharts as well as memoranda on internal control.

      4. Flowcharting is the most efficient means available for summarizing internal control.

  b. The normal sequence of documents and operations on a well-prepared systems flowchart is

      1. Top to bottom and left to right.

      2. Bottom to top and left to right.

      3. Top to bottom and right to left.

      4. Bottom to top and right to left.

  c. In connection with the study of internal control, an auditor encounters the following flowcharting symbols:

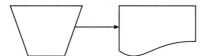

    The auditor would conclude that

      1. A document has been generated by a manual operation.

      2. A master file has been created by a computer operation.

      3. A document has been generated by a computer operation.

      4. A master file has been created by a manual operation.

  d. Which of the following flowchart symbols represents online storage?

1.
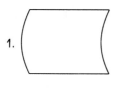

2.
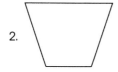

3.

4.

  e. Which of the following is *not* a medium that can normally be used by an auditor to record information concerning a client's internal control structure?

      1. Narrative memorandum

    2. Procedures manual

    3. Flowchart

    4. Decision table

(AICPA adapted)

P8-4 Select the best answer to each of the following items relating to the control risk assessment phase of the audit.

    a. Control risk must be evaluated on a(n)

        1. System-by-system, assertion-by-assertion basis.

        2. Company-by-company basis.

        3. Overall financial statement basis.

        4. Financial line item basis.

    b. After making a preliminary assessment of controls based on the understanding of the control structure, the auditor may decide to perform further tests of controls. This would be done only if

        1. Significant weaknesses exist in the system.

        2. Significant strengths exist in the system.

        3. It is cost-effective to proceed.

        4. Both (2) and (3).

    c. A conceptually logical approach to the auditor's detailed evaluation of internal accounting control consists of the following four steps:

        I. Determine whether the necessary procedures are prescribed and are being followed in an effective manner.

        II. Consider the types of errors and irregularities that could occur.

        III. Determine the internal control policies and procedures that should prevent or detect errors and irregularities.

        IV. Evaluate any weakness to determine its effect on the nature, timing, or extent of auditing procedures to be applied and suggestions to be made to the client.

    What should be the order in which these four steps are performed?

        1. III, IV, I, II

        2. III, I, II, IV

        3. II, III, I, IV

        4. II, I, III, IV

    d. Which of the following statements relating to tests of controls is most accurate?

        1. Auditing procedures cannot concurrently provide both evidence of effective control procedures and evidence required for substantive tests.

        2. Tests of controls include physical observations of the proper segregation of duties that ordinarily may be limited to the normal audit period.

        3. Tests of controls should be based on proper application of an appropriate statistical sampling plan.

        4. Tests of controls ordinarily should be performed as of the balance sheet date or during the subsequent period.

    e. Which of the following audit tests would be regarded as a test of controls?

        1. Tests of the specific items making up the balance in a given general ledger account.

        2. Tests of the inventory pricing to vendor's invoices.

        3. Tests of the signatures on canceled checks to board of directors' authorizations.

        4. Tests of the additions to property, plant, and equipment by physical inspections.

    f. After completing the detailed study of controls, the auditor should review the results and consider whether

1. The planned degree of reduction in control risk and the nature, timing, and extent of resulting substantive tests is justified.
2. The evidential matter obtained from the understanding of the internal control structure can provide a reasonable basis for an opinion on the financial statements.
3. Further study of the internal control structure is likely to justify any restriction of substantive tests.
4. Sufficient knowledge has been obtained about the entity's control structure.

(AICPA adapted)

P8-5   The internal control structure of an entity comprises the policies and procedures adopted by management to provide reasonable assurance that specific objectives of the entity will be achieved. Those objectives include safeguarding assets, assuring accuracy and reliability of accounting data, promoting operational efficiency, and encouraging adherence to prescribed managerial policies.

Required:
a. What is the purpose of obtaining an understanding of the control structure of an audit client?
b. What objective *must* be accomplished on every audit with respect to the client's control structure in order to comply with generally accepted auditing standards? How is that objective achieved?
c. What conditions would have to be present for the auditor to desire to perform a more detailed analysis of specific control procedures and policies than that performed during the preliminary review? Under what conditions would the auditor decide not to perform such an analysis?
d. How is the auditor's understanding of the internal control structure documented?
e. What is the purpose of tests of controls?
f. What are the by-products of the auditor's assessment of the control structure of an entity? Why are these important?

P8-6   As a CPA, you have been engaged to audit the financial statements of University Books, Incorporated. University Books maintains a large revolving cash fund exclusively for the purpose of buying used books from students for cash. The cash fund is active all year because the nearby university offers a large variety of courses with varying starting and completion dates throughout the year.

Receipts are prepared for each purchase and reimbursement vouchers are periodically submitted.

Required: Construct an internal control questionnaire to be used in documenting the understanding of the internal control structure of University Books' buying segments revolving cash fund. The internal control questionnaire should elicit a yes or no response. *Do not discuss the internal controls over books that are purchased.*

(AICPA adapted)

P8-7   The partially completed charge sales systems flowchart, following, depicts the charge sales activities of the Bottom Manufacturing Corporation.

A customer's purchase order is received and a six-part sales order is prepared therefrom. The six copies are initially distributed as follows:

Copy No. 1—Billing copy, to billing department.
Copy No. 2—Shipping copy, to shipping department.
Copy No. 3—Credit copy, to credit department.
Copy No. 4—Stock request copy, to credit department.
Copy No. 5—Customer copy, to customer.
Copy No. 6—Sales order copy, to a file in sales order department.

Specific internal control procedures and related documents are called for when each copy of the sales order reaches the applicable department or destination. Some of the procedures and related documents are indicated on the flowchart. Other procedures and documents on the flowchart are merely labeled with letters *a* to *r*.

Required: List the procedures or the internal documents that are labeled with letters *c* to *r* in the flowchart of Bottom Manufacturing Corporation's charge sales system.

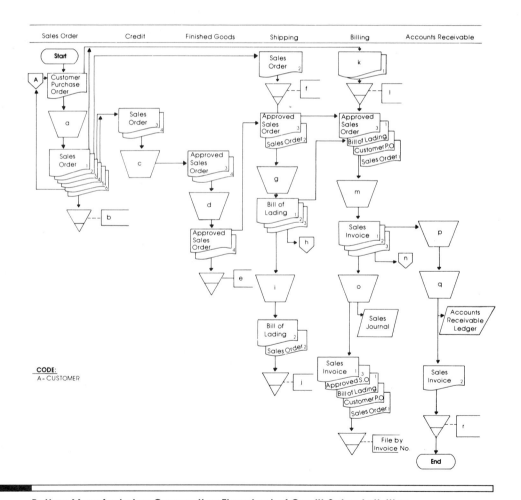

Bottom Manufacturing Corporation Flowchart of Credit Sales Activities

Organize your answer as follows (note that an explanation of the letters *a* and *b*, which appear in the flowchart, are entered as examples):

Flowchart Symbol Letter	Procedures or Internal Document
a	Prepare six-part sales order
b	File by order number

(AICPA adapted)

P8-8 Internal auditing is an important part of the control environment of an organization.

Required:
a. List five major operating objectives of internal control.
b. For each of the objectives listed, tell whether fulfillment of the objective is of primary concern for the internal auditor, the independent auditor, or both.

(IIA adapted)

P8-9 Each of the following situations describes a problem in internal control.
a. The accounts receivable bookkeeper, who was also the cashier, misappropriated a $1,000 check from a customer (A); the next day, when $1,000 was received on another customer's account (B), the bookkeeper credited customer (A)'s account instead.
b. Incorrect quantities are being used on receiving reports for goods received from vendors.
c. Goods are not being counted as they are received. Instead, receiving department personnel are using the quantities on a copy of the purchase order sent from the purchasing agent as the correct quantities received.
d. The purchasing agent has a brother-in-law who is the salesman/owner of a supplier of the company. The purchasing agent places orders with his brother-in-law but pays double the price that the brother-in-law normally charges. When payment is received by the brother-in-law, he splits the excess with the purchasing agent.
e. The factory foreman, who hires new employees, inserted a fictitious employee in the payroll records and has been submitting an extra time card for twenty-four months for the fictitious employee.

Required: Discuss each of the errors or irregularities described in the case situations in terms of
a. An internal control procedure that, if in operation, would have prevented the error or irregularity from occurring.
b. A test to ascertain if the control procedure was in place.
c. A substantive test that, depending on the strengths or weaknesses of the particular control procedure, would have to be expanded or limited.

P8-10 The division of the following duties should provide the best possible controls for Lazy J Enterprises, a small wholesale store.
*a. Assemble supporting documents for disbursements and prepare checks for signature.

　　*b. Sign general disbursement checks.

　　*c. Record checks written in the cash disbursements and payroll journal.

　　d. Mail disbursement checks to suppliers.

　　e. Cancel supporting documents to prevent their reuse.

　　*f. Approve credit for customers.

　　*g. Bill customers and record the invoices in the sales journal and subsidiary ledger.

　　*h. Open the mail and prepare a prelisting of cash receipts.

　　*i. Record cash receipts in the cash journal and subsidiary ledger.

　　*j. Prepare daily cash deposits.

　　*k. Deliver daily cash deposits to the bank.

　　*l. Assemble the payroll time cards and prepare the payroll checks.

　　*m. Sign payroll checks.

　　n. Post the journals to the general ledger.

　　o. Reconcile the accounts receivable subsidiary account with the control account.

　　p. Prepare monthly statements for customers by copying the subsidiary ledger account.

　　q. Reconcile the monthly statements from vendors with the subsidiary accounts payable account.

　　r. Reconcile the bank account.

Required: You are to divide the accounting-related duties *a* through *r* among Jill Thomas, Todd Robison, Lena Pini, and Bill Merck. Thomas, who is president of the company, is not willing to perform any functions designated by an asterisk and will do a maximum of two of the other functions. All the responsibilities marked with an asterisk are assumed to take about the same amount of time and must be divided equally between the two employees, Robison and Pini, who are equally competent.

(AICPA adapted)

P8-11 Adherence to generally accepted auditing standards requires, among other things, an understanding of the client's internal control structure. The most common approaches to obtaining this understanding include the use of a questionnaire, preparation of a memorandum, preparation of a flowchart, and combinations of these methods.

Required:

　　a. What is a CPA's objective in obtaining an understanding of the internal control structure for an audit?

　　b. Discuss the advantages to a CPA of using an internal control questionnaire and of using a flowchart.

　　c. If, after completing his or her evaluation of internal control for an audit, the CPA is satisfied that no material weaknesses in the client's internal control structure exist, is it necessary for him or her to test transactions? Explain.

(AICPA adapted)

P8-12 This problem is a continuation of T&H, Inc., the case study that began in Problem 7-5. We will continue the problem in Chapter 20, as we discuss completion of the audit.

　　As a part of planning the audit, assume that you have acquired the following knowledge as a part of your understanding of the control structure of the company, in addition to the facts as described in Problem 7-5:

1. Revenue and collections system:
    a. The cash receipts clerk is responsible for reconciling the monthly bank statements. There is no review of bank reconciliations by supervisors or internal auditors.
    b. Sales are recorded on the day the accounting department receives the invoice rather than on the day the item was shipped.
    c. Accounts receivable bookkeepers have access to the finished goods inventory in the warehouse.
2. Acquisitions and expenditure system:
    a. The company uses several different bank accounts in its operations. Schedules are not regularly prepared that show amounts transferred from one bank account to another.
    b. In recording purchases of raw materials, clerks use prices that are reflected in suppliers' (vendors') catalogs. No independent check is made to ascertain whether the most recent versions of vendors' catalogs are always used when purchases are recorded.
    c. There is no periodic review of property and equipment additions or deletions by accounting department supervisors.
    d. Accounts payable clerks are authorized to sign checks that do not exceed $500 in amount.

Required:
a. For each of the facts described above:
    1. Identify the control characteristic (segregation of duties, comparisons and compliance monitoring, records and documentation, limited access, execution of transactions as authorized) that has not been met.
    2. Suggest an error or irregularity that could occur due to the absence of the control.
    3. Suggest a substantive test (test of transactions or test of balances) that should be expanded to compensate for the control weakness.
b. What other action (if any) should be taken by the auditor with respect to the apparent weaknesses that exist in the system?

CHAPTER 9

The Computer Environment and the Control Structure

Objectives

☐ **1.** Describe the impact that the use of the computer has on the internal control structure of an audit client.
☐ **2.** Classify and analyze the types of computer controls that should exist in an internal control structure.
☐ **3.** Evaluate internal controls for a computer-based accounting system.

Because of its accuracy, speed, and adaptability to almost all business configurations, the computer has changed the way business is conducted throughout the world during the past three decades. In addition, changes in the marketplace have made computers cost-feasible for almost all business, personal, and classroom uses.

In recent years the capabilities of the computer have also changed the way that auditors think and the ways in which audit work is conducted. More specifically, the computer has affected the audit through its effects on the control structure and through its advancing use as an audit tool.

As we discussed internal control structure in Chapter 8, we considered the broad concepts and objectives of internal control that apply to all business environments. In that chapter, after identifying the objectives of internal control that apply to any business environment, we examined characteristics that should be present in an effective system of internal control. In this chapter we explain how the client's use of the computer to process financial data affects the control structure.

Appendixes to the chapter include examples of documentation for the auditor's understanding of the internal control structure, including program and systems flowcharts as well as internal control questionnaires.

Impact of the Computer on the Internal Control Structure

☑ **Objective 1**
Describe the impact of the computer on the control structure

Use of the computer does not in any way change the basic objectives of a sound internal control structure. However, the organization and procedures employed by the entity to implement those objectives *do* change. When the computer is used in significant accounting applications, the auditor must assess its impact and consider the computer activity in obtaining an understanding of the control structure. In addition, the auditor must obtain a sufficient understanding of the computer system to be able to identify and evaluate its essential control features. To help you understand the impact of computers on internal controls, we now examine the general environmental characteristics associated with computerized accounting records, as well as the component elements of a computer system. We also briefly consider the vulnerability of computerized accounting systems to fraud.

Environmental Characteristics

Inherent in a typical **electronic data processing** (**EDP**) system are certain unique features, which influence the procedures that should be followed to assure that the objectives of internal control (set forth in Chapter 8) are being met. These include the following:

Transaction Trails.   Parts of the traditional audit trail (financial statements, general and supporting ledgers, journals, supporting documents) that are important elements of a manual system are often nonexistent or exist for only a short time in human-readable form in a computerized system. Many businesses are finding ways to process transactions so that only one or two human-readable documents are generated. While this feature can be extremely beneficial and cost-effective for management, it can also be a source of great difficulty for the auditor. Thus, new ways of auditing the system (such as electronic monitoring) may need to be developed by both internal and external audit teams.

Uniform Processing of Transactions.   Once programmed, the computer will process all like transactions in exactly the same way. If programmed correctly, this means that computer processing virtually eliminates the occurrence of clerical errors normally associated with manual processing. If programmed incorrectly, this means that errors will be repeated as many times as there are transactions in the system, thus creating the potential for material misstatements in the financial statements.

Segregation of Functions.   A key element of internal control in a manual system is segregating the functions of custody over assets, recordkeeping, and authority for transaction approval. Elements of these functions generally will be concentrated into one department when a computer system is in use. Therefore, an individual who has access to the computer may be in a position to perform two or more functions that ideally should be separated. This places the individual in a position to both perpetrate and conceal errors or irregularities in the normal course of the duties assigned to him or her. For example, suppose one person in the company has the responsibility for both recording disbursements in the cash disbursements journal and reconciling the bank statement. That person could omit the recording of a check, either intentionally or unintentionally. The error could then be concealed by an improper reconciliation. If the client uses a computer to print checks and record cash disbursements, the computer may also generate information used to reconcile the account balance. If the same person entering information into the computer to execute the payment process also receives the output for the reconciliation process, a similar irregularity could be concealed. This example shows that procedures designed to detect errors and irregularities should be performed by persons other than those who are in a position to perpetrate them. To reduce the probability of such irregularities occurring, the procedures manual should include provisions for (1) adequate segregation of incompatible functions within the data-processing department, (2) segregation between computer (EDP) department personnel and personnel of other departments who review computer procedures, and (3) adequate control over access to data and computer programs.

Potential for Errors and Irregularities.   In computerized systems, there is greater potential for unauthorized persons to gain access to data and alter it without visible evidence or to gain access to records of assets. Also, in a computerized system, because there is decreased human involvement in handling transactions, there is less probability of persons observing errors and irregularities that would otherwise be obvious. If errors or irregularities are programmed into the system, either inadvertently or intentionally, they may remain undetected for long periods of time. Thus, when computer systems are in use, there may be a greater need for the auditor to concentrate more effort on the design of the system than when manually operated systems are in use.

Potential for Increased Management Supervision.   When the accounting and management system of a company is computerized, an ever-increasing amount of data can be made available in a very short time at reasonable cost to managers. In addition, computer systems offer management a wide variety of analytical tools that may be used to interpret financial and nonfinancial data and to make day-to-day managerial decisions. For example, computer programs that are readily available can compute key operating and financing ratios, as well as reconciliations of accounts. These data can be provided quickly and accurately by the computer. Some programmed applications even provide statistics regarding computer operations, which may be used to monitor the actual processing of transactions.

Initiation or Subsequent Execution of Transactions by the Computer.   In certain on-line computer systems, such as those found in large department stores or in the airline industry, the computer may be programmed to automatically initiate or execute transactions such as purchases or sales. The authorization of these transactions in an on-line system will not be documented in the same way as they would be in a manual accounting system. Thus, by accepting the design of a particular system, management may be implicitly authorizing the controls that are built into it. The audit in such cases may involve investigation into management's general or specific authorization policies, which are programmed into computer software during the design stages, to see whether they serve to check for data that fall outside predetermined limits and to test for overall reasonableness.

Dependence of Other Controls on Computer Processing. Inevitably, there will be manual control procedures within the client's organization that depend on the existence of computer controls for reliability and completeness. For example, it may be company policy to submit computer-processed error listings to manual review by a person in the company's EDP control group. The effectiveness of that person's review will depend on the accuracy and completeness of the computer-prepared error listing. Once again, to assure proper controls, it is imperative that both the company and the auditor be concerned about the design of the system.

Component Elements of a Computerized Accounting System

The components of a typical computerized system are shown in Figure 9–1. As you can see from that figure, the system includes software in the form of computer programs. A program, in addition to data, is entered into the system by various input devices. Notice that input media can include such devices as remote entry terminals, magnetic tape handlers, magnetic drums or disks, and punched tape or card handlers.

The microcomputer is a recent technological innovation, which can be either linked to the mainframe or other microcomputers (called a "network") or operated as a stand-alone unit. In Figure 9–1, we show the microcomputer as both a stand-alone unit and as part of the mainframe computer installation where the two are linked. Small amounts of data, which are stored in the memory of the mainframe unit, can be *downloaded* onto the microcomputer, where they can be modified as required by the user. Unlike the other input and output devices, the microcomputer has its own self-contained microprocessor contained on a single magnetic chip. Once data have been modified, they can be either returned to the memory of the mainframe computer for storage or stored on the microcomputer's own floppy or hard disk.

Data input through other devices must be processed by a compiler program, which converts them to machine language and then transmits them to the **central processing unit (CPU)**. There the data are processed as instructed by the program. After processing, the CPU transmits the processed data, again according to programmed instructions, to one of the output devices shown in Figure

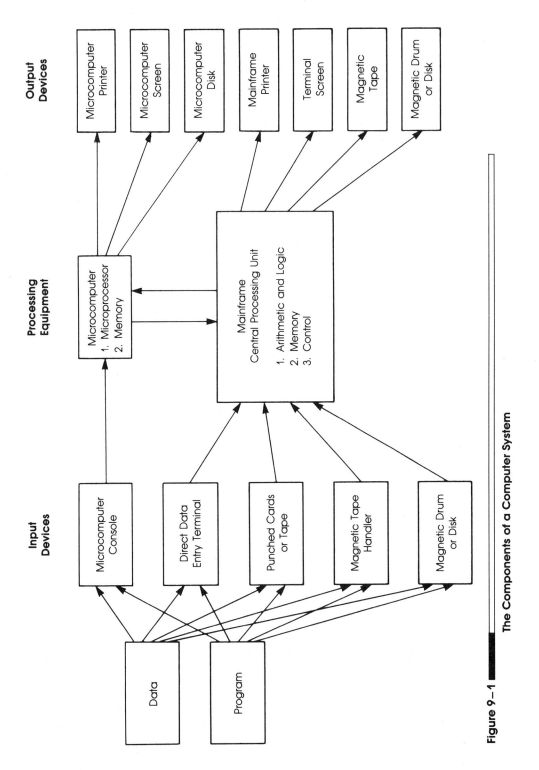

Figure 9–1

The Components of a Computer System

9–1. Output can appear on microcomputer printers or screens, direct-entry terminal screens, mainframe printers, punched tape or cards, magnetic tape, or magnetic disks. Output from microcomputer processing is stored on floppy or hard disks. For most mainframe installations, output is stored on magnetic tapes or disks.

If the accounting system simply calls for the accounting data (such as accounts receivable transactions) to be processed by the computer and conveyed back to persons in the system by means of hard copy printouts, the computer is basically being used as a sophisticated bookkeeping machine. In such a situation, the internal control problems, except for those relating to the computer software (programs), are little different from the ones described in Chapter 8 for a manually maintained accounting system. Such a system also can normally be audited without examining or directly testing the computer programs used in the system. In such situations, we are auditing *around the computer*.

In most instances, however, the use of the computer for accounting purposes involves much more than simply processing a series of transactions through to a printed document. In fact, many computer installations are being designed to use few if any printed documents at all. Most computerized recordkeeping systems call for the storage of data in machine-readable form. Any documents issued, such as invoices and checks, are issued by the computer. For example, the record of accounts receivable is accumulated and stored on either a magnetic tape or a magnetic disk, with balances updated each day, as shown in Figure 9–2. Such a system is generally programmed to have the computer print invoices and state-

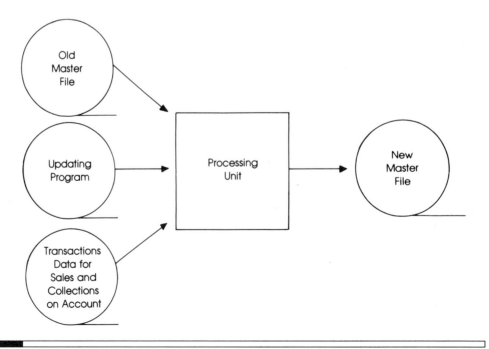

Figure 9–2

Systems Flowchart Showing the Updating of the Accounts Receivable Master File

ments to be sent to customers. The computer may also age the accounts receivable and provide a listing of past-due accounts automatically. In such a system, the human-readable audit trail often ceases at the point where the original documents are converted to machine-readable form and does not appear again until the final account balances are printed by the computer in the preparation of financial statements. Furthermore, in processing such things as collections on account or payments on account, the computer is performing both recordkeeping and custodial duties. Therefore, **integrated processing systems** such as these create special problems in implementing some of the internal control characteristics, such as proper segregation of duties and appropriate authorization procedures.

Fraud and the Computer[1]

Fraud has frequently been associated with computerized accounting systems, and in recent years computer fraud has been on the increase. A recent study conducted by a national CPA firm revealed that losses incurred as a result of computer fraud vary, but are considered to be between $3 billion and $5 billion annually for American business alone. In addition, undetected frauds continue to exist. Estimates of reported cases of computer fraud as a percent of computer frauds actually committed range from only 5 to as much as 20 percent. There are indications that the biggest, most successful schemes remain undetected.

There are three principal reasons for the increased frequency of computer fraud:

1. Increased opportunity. The number of knowledgeable users is increasing, as is the capability to access computerized data. Processing is becoming more and more decentralized, utilizing such tools as local area networks, telecommunications, and remote job entry.
2. Difficulty of detection. The vast quantities of data stored in a computer system make concealing a theft easier. Perpetrators seldom leave trails to follow, and most files may be instantaneously updated without leaving a record of having been altered.
3. Lucrative payoff. The average dollar amount of *reported* computer fraud is estimated by the Federal Bureau of Investigation to be $600,000, as compared with only $23,000 in the case of fraud that utilizes manual methods.

Studies of characteristics of computer fraud perpetrators have revealed three general patterns: (1) relationship to the organization; (2) level of computer expertise; and (3) motivation or intent. In 98 percent of the reported computer fraud cases, the person perpetrating the fraud has been an employee or officer of the company. The level of computer expertise of perpetrators of computer fraud has varied, but in most cases the frauds did not involve sophisticated schemes. Instead, they involved relatively simple schemes that took advantage of weaknesses in the existing system of internal controls.

Two predominant motives have emerged from the studies of reported computer fraud. Some frauds have as a direct goal the misappropriation of assets for the perpetrator's personal gain. Others are more concerned with delusion, misrepresentation, theft, or destruction of information. Both of these motives can have a significant impact on the entity's financial reporting system and on the financial statements.

Following are notable examples of computer fraud:

1. At Business Products Division of Saxon Industries, Inc. fraud was perpetrated using the computer to overstate inventories by $67 million over a 13-year period. In this case, the computer was used to maintain and process fictitious inventory quantities and prices.
2. A $21.3 million fraud at Wells Fargo Bank was made possible through weaknesses in the bank's interbranch transfer system.
3. More than $1 million in electronic communications supplies was stolen from the former Pacific Telephone Company as a result of weaknesses in the company's equipment-ordering system.
4. The Equity Funding fraud (see Chapter 4) resulted in losses of over $200 million. The computer aided managers of the company to process and maintain more than 64,000 fictitious insurance policies, thus vastly overstating assets and commissions income of the company. In this case, the computer was not used to commit the fraud, per se, but to create a mass of supporting detail designed to conceal the fraud.

Literally hundreds of other cases have been reported, and, as mentioned previously, we can only imagine the number of cases that are still undetected. In the meantime, computer technicians, systems designers, and auditors continue to wrestle with the problem of potential fraud associated with the use of the computer. The controls that are explained in the next section represent the present state of the art with regard to internal control and the computer. As technology changes, however, newer and more sophisticated controls will become necessary in the future.

Analysis of Computer Controls

☑ **Objective 2**
Classify and analyze computer controls

In Chapter 8, we described the elements of the control structure of a typical entity. Those elements include the control environment, the control system, and control procedures. In entities that utilize computers to process data, these same elements are applicable. In addition, the characteristics of internal control (proper segregation of duties, comparisons and monitoring, adequate records, limited access to assets, and proper approvals) that are vital for achieving control in manual systems are also essential in computerized systems. However, because of environmental differences, the way in which control is achieved in a computerized system is different from that of a manual system.

Where computer processing is used in significant accounting applications, there are generally two types of controls at work: *general controls* and *application controls*. The relationships among these controls are illustrated in Figure 9–3.

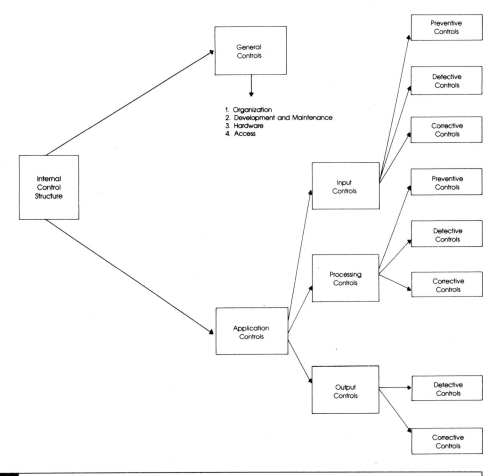

Figure 9–3

Relationships among Elements of the Computerized Control Structure

General Controls

General controls relate to all or many computerized accounting activities. They are designed to *contribute* to the achievement of specific control objectives and are considered to be interdependent with specific accounting control procedures. General controls include (1) organization controls within the computer department or between that department and others in the entity; (2) controls over the development, modification, and maintenance of computer programs and changes to data maintained on computer files; (3) hardware controls; and (4) controls over access to equipment and data files.

Organization Controls. In companies where mainframe computers are employed in significant accounting applications, **organization controls** within the computer department and between that department and others in the company are important. These controls are relied on to compensate for an operating arrangement that eliminates many of the records constituting the audit trail and many of the traditional segregations of duties. Also in the interest of appropriate independence within the firm, it is important for the computer department to have a high level of *organizational autonomy*. In particular, it should be separated organizationally from the accounting department. The company should also have an appropriate *segregation of responsibilities within the computer department*. The functions included among these responsibilities are defined briefly as follows:

- **Systems analysts** evaluate systems, analyze requirements for information, and design the systems for handling the data-processing needs of the company. They provide the system specifications that serve as guides for the programmers to follow in developing computer programs.
- **Programmers** prepare the computer programs to meet the specifications of systems analysts. They are responsible for coding the program logic to meet the requirements of specific processing problems and for documenting the programs in the form of flowcharts.
- **Computer operators** operate the equipment. The operators work from a set of operating procedures prepared by the systems analysts. Instructions for operations are documented in the *run manual*.
- **Data conversion operators** are equipment operators who convert human-readable documentary data into machine-readable form. These operators prepare the data for machine processing.
- **Librarians** in the electronic data-processing department are in charge of maintaining physical safeguards over the systems files (program files, data files, and program documentation). Such protection is necessary to provide adequate controls in design and redesign of systems as well as to maintain controls over data files and programs used in everyday processing.
- The **quality control group** acts as liaison between the data-processing center and the various user departments (such as accounting, production, etc.). They perform a function similar to that of internal auditors, because they continually test the processing accuracy of both hardware and software. They also review and follow up error messages from the computer, compare control totals to output, review document numbers, and distribute output to various user departments.

If the client has a comprehensive mainframe computer system, the computer department should be organized along the lines shown in Figure 9–4. As you can see from the organization chart, the systems and programming responsibilities of the data-processing system are completely segregated from the information-processing facility (IPF). This should mean that analysts and programmers are precluded from carrying out computer operations and that computer operators are precluded from changing the computer programs in any way. This segregation of responsibilities should be maintained, even within a very small computer facility. In sophisticated data-processing systems, it is also desirable to separate the library, data conversion, and quality control functions, as shown in the organization chart. Such a separation of responsibilities has several benefits:

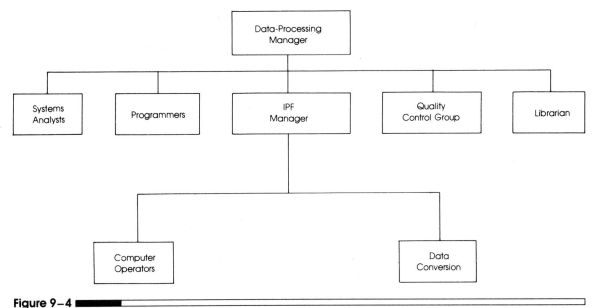

Figure 9–4 ■■■■

Organization Chart for Data-Processing Department

- An effective check on the accuracy and propriety of changes introduced into the system is provided.
- Operating personnel are prevented from implementing revisions without prior approval.
- Access to the equipment by nonoperating personnel and others who have knowledge of the system is eliminated.
- Efficiency is improved, because the capabilities, training, and skills required in carrying out each of these activities differ significantly.

In computer installations that lack proper separation of responsibilities (thus allowing programmers access to equipment) the use of a computer log can be a mitigating control. Computer logs and other documentation and maintenance controls are discussed in the next section.

Another provision that can help compensate for the lack of proper segregation of responsibilities is *required job rotation* among computer operators. All operators should also be *required to take vacations.*

As a means of checking on the separation of duties and on the existence of other organizational control characteristics in a computer department, the auditor should ask questions like those shown in Appendix 9-C. These questions suggest organizational characteristics that can help compensate for the lack of segregation of custodial, authorization, and recordkeeping responsibilities that is found in computer systems.

The organization controls described above are virtually impossible to implement if the company operates exclusively in a microcomputer environment. When using the microcomputer, it is probable that, to a certain extent, each user will perform most of the functions that can be separated in a mainframe environment. In fact, when microcomputers constitute the only equipment used, the company is unlikely to have a separate computer department. Instead, those persons performing each function (such as cash receipts, payroll, etc.) will have separate computer programs for their particular tasks. In such organizations, where computers are not linked together by a network using the same data base, traditional segregation of the duties (custody, recordkeeping, authorization) that are found in manual systems is sometimes possible. In such cases, it is necessary to limit access to critical programs to authorized personnel.

However, when microcomputers are linked together with the same data base and multiple users, care must be taken to ensure that users with incompatible functions are not given unauthorized access to the entire data base. In these cases, *it is necessary to control access to both equipment and programs*, as explained in the following paragraphs.

Development and Maintenance Controls.   Procedures for developing, maintaining, documenting, testing, and approving systems and changes thereto should be formalized in **procedure manuals**. Documentation is an important element of control and communication within the organization, because it generally provides an understanding of the system's objectives, concepts, and outputs, and is a source of information for the systems analysts and programmers who handle program maintenance and revision. Good documentation can help provide a basis for training new personnel, as well as continuity of operations in the event that experienced personnel leave the company.

The system should include *documentation controls* regardless of whether it contains purely mainframe or a mixture of mainframe and microcomputer technology. Planning is an integral part of software development. *Plans should be documented and approved* by appropriate supervisory personnel. Key users of a computer application (such as an accounts receivable file) should be involved in the planning, development, and testing of that application. Adequate audit trails and extensive testing should be provided for all computer programs as they are developed.

Procedure manuals should carefully describe the documentation required for each application. Ideally, such documentation should include information relating to the study of the data system, program and systems flowcharts, such as those illustrated in Appendixes 9–A and 9–B, as well as computer operator instructions. Changes in each application should be approved by supervisors. Extensive testing should be performed for each application to ensure that only authorized changes are made and that those changes are made properly.

When good documentation controls exist, the auditor can rely on them for an understanding of the control environment and accounting system for each significant application. In this way, the auditor can save time in obtaining an understanding of the client's internal control structure.

Documentation controls in an effective system often contain the following information:

- *Problem definition documentation* includes a description of the reasons for implementing the system, a description of the operations performed, the project proposals, evidence of initial approval of the system and subsequent changes thereto, and a listing of the assignment of various persons to project responsibilities.
- *Systems documentation* includes a description of the system, systems flow-charts showing the flow of data through the system and the interrelationships between processing steps and computer runs (see Appendix 9–B), input and output descriptions, file descriptions, control descriptions, and copies of authorizations and their effective dates for system changes that have been implemented.
- *Program documentation* is primarily used by systems analysts and programmers to control program corrections and revisions. It may be useful to the auditor in determining the current status of a program. Program documentation includes narrative descriptions of the program; program flowcharts (see Appendix 9–A), decisions tables, or detailed logic narratives; program instructions; listings of control features; detailed descriptions of file formats and record layouts; records of program changes, authorizations and effective dates; input and output formats; operating instructions; and descriptions of any special features.
- *Operations documentation* should be provided for the computer operator. It can be used by the auditor to obtain an understanding of the operator's functions and how data are processed on the machine. It should include a brief description of the program; description of the input and output forms required; sequences of files; set-up instructions and operating system requirements; operating notes listing program messages, halts, and action necessary to signal the end of a job; control procedures to be performed by operators; recovery and restart procedures; estimated normal and maximum run times; and emergency instructions.
- *User documentation* is provided for the users of the data. It usually contains a description of the system, the inputs and outputs of the system, a listing of control procedures and the persons performing those procedures, error correction procedures, cutoff procedures for submitting data to the EDP department, and a description of how the user departments should check reports for accuracy.
- *Operator documentation* should be prepared by the operator. It indicates the jobs that were run and any operator interaction in the process. This documentation takes the form of daily **computer logs**, usually prepared manually by the operator, listing the jobs run, the time required, and the operator who actually ran them. Also included are console logs, which list all interaction between the console and the CPU. This log is prepared by the computer as messages are entered from the console. It can be a valuable control for detect-

ing unauthorized intervention by the computer operator during processing of data. It also indicates how the operator responded to problems encountered during processing.[2]

Hardware Controls.   These are general controls built into the equipment to detect erroneous internal handling of data and to ensure the equipment's processing accuracy and reliability. **Parity check** is an example of such a **hardware control**. Other such controls are *dual circuitry* and *auxiliary power supplies*, which can help provide protection against errors that might otherwise occur as a result of a machine malfunction during power surges and outages. Although an auditor is not expected to be an engineering expert, he or she should at least be familiar with the basic controls built into the equipment. In evaluating the operating capabilities of a computer system, the auditor must always consider *downtime* caused by malfunctioning equipment. One way to be sure that the likelihood of errors from malfunctioning equipment is minimal is to examine the client's maintenance contract with the computer supplier. If scheduled maintenance is being performed, the auditor can be reasonably confident that hardware controls are working as they were designed to work. Other general evidence of hardware controls may be obtained by reviewing the client's computer downtime logs.

Access Controls.   Access to equipment and data files should be carefully controlled. Operating procedures should be adopted to protect files and programs from possible loss, destruction, or unauthorized use. **Access controls** should include the following:

- Provisions limiting access to the computer room.
- Controls over the use of library files.
- Qualitative standards to be met in the data-conversion phase of operations.
- Operational control procedures for scheduling use of the equipment and for controlling the use of files.
- Physical security for files and equipment; this should include provisions for backup facilities and plans for reconstruction of data that might inadvertently be destroyed.

File security, which relates to measures taken to safeguard files from total loss, is enhanced by such operating practices as the storage of backup files in fireproof vaults and in printed or microfilm form. *File retention policies* are related to file security and pertain to practices that protect against damage or minor loss to data files. One of the most important functions of a file retention policy is to provide for adequate reconstruction of data files if they are lost or destroyed. One of the most popular methods of providing for magnetic tape file reconstruction is the **grandfather, father, son** arrangement. In essence, this is a practice of retaining two generations of both master and transaction file data until a new master file is produced; thus, the current period's master file could be reconstructed if the original copy of that file were lost or destroyed.

When master files are maintained on magnetic disks rather than magnetic tape, updating files usually results in destruction of the previous generation's master file. The most efficient and least costly method of retaining the data in such a situation is to **dump** the file onto tape periodically (weekly or daily). In other instances the data on the disks may be printed out periodically. Either of those files can then be used along with the proper period transaction files in reconstructing the data in the same manner as are the backup tapes in the grandfather, father, son technique mentioned above.

Access Controls in Microcomputer or On-Line Environments[3]

Unauthorized access to data in a microcomputer or on-line terminal environment can create problems. Several of these problems, along with ways of dealing with them, are discussed below.

Data Obsolescence.   If microcomputers are used to **download** large volumes of data from the mainframe, there is a risk that users will create their own private data bases and management decisions might somehow be influenced by obsolete or inconsistent data. Accordingly, policies should be established to ensure that users delete from microcomputer data bases all data downloaded from the mainframe and that supervisors regularly review the work of subordinates to ensure that current data are being used.

Communications.   As data are moving between microcomputers and mainframes, outside influences, such as electrical interference or line noise, can alter or destroy the data being transmitted. High-quality communications software usually helps ensure the reliability of data transmission. Technical assistance should be provided by in-house experts who are knowledgeable about such problems to be sure that the proper software is used.

Data Security.   Linking microcomputers to mainframe computers gives all microcomputer users potential access to all information stored in the mainframe system, unless precautions are taken. Unlike most terminals used in on-line systems, microcomputers can store large volumes of data downloaded from the mainframe. *More important, microcomputers can be programmed to* **upload** *or change data in the mainframe.* Destruction, improper modification, and/or unauthorized disclosure of sensitive corporate data, whether intentional or not, can occur and have disastrous effects on the company. **Security software** offers the best protection against unauthorized microcomputer access to such data. Several mainframe hardware and software vendors have developed security software for use in on-line mainframe environments, including the micro-to-mainframe environments. Such software usually incorporates the following features:

1. **Passwords** that restrict access to authorized individuals.
2. *Computer logs* or journals that record each time a microcomputer or terminal

user gains access or attempts to access the mainframe. This log facility can be used to pinpoint attempted violation of the system.

3. *Terminal identification,* which is similar to passwords, restricts access to authorized specific microcomputers and terminals.

4. **Time-out facility** that automatically disconnects terminals that have not communicated with the mainframe within a specified period of time.

5. *Rules of use* that restrict what users can do once access to the mainframe has been granted. This facility can be used to limit access to certain files or records stored on the mainframe system and to prevent users from changing data on the mainframe system.

6. **Access attempt facility** that disconnects a particular terminal after a prescribed number of unauthorized attempts to gain mainframe access.

A method of accessing mainframes that is becoming increasingly popular in microcomputer or on-line terminal environments is the use of *dial-up* modems. In these installations, mainframes are configured to receive communications from microcomputers over telephone lines. In such systems, in addition to security software, **call-back** procedures are often used to protect mainframe-resident data. Such procedures require the mainframe to *call back* the terminal or microcomputer to ensure that communications are occurring via authorized telephones only. Call-back procedures can be performed manually or automatically by using a specialized device attached to the telephone lines, which disconnects all communication lines leading into the mainframe system. Another method often used to control unauthorized use of telephone lines is to disconnect all mainframe communication lines during periods when authorized users do not normally require access (after business hours, weekends, and holidays, for example). **Encryption of data** is a control that renders data useless to unauthorized individuals who might intercept data communications. This technique is not presently used on a wide scale because it adds to the level of complexity of the data. It should be considered, however, when highly sensitive data are transmitted over telephone lines.

Still another innovation in data processing is the **local area network (LAN)**. Networking involves linking microcomputers together to share and exchange information, such as budget or marketing statistics. In addition to the cable that connects the microcomputers, LANs typically include communication boards that are inserted into one of the expansion slots of the microcomputers, as well as a network-serving microcomputer and a large-capacity hard disk for data storage.

Data security becomes an issue in a LAN environment when users store their data files (including data downloaded from the mainframe) on the network's hard disk. Most LANs have some data security measures built into the networking software, but, unfortunately, these measures are not nearly as sophisticated or well developed as those available in the mainframe environment. As a result, *highly sensitive data generally should not be stored on a LAN's hard disk.* The same observation can be made for data storage on the floppy disks or hard disks of microcomputers.

In both LAN and stand-alone microcomputer environments, users should take precautions to regularly *back up data files* to decrease the risk of accidental or intentional destruction of those files. Duplicate disks generally should not be kept in the same place as ones that are used regularly. In addition, application software and data files should be protected when not in use to prevent unauthorized access to information. Particularly sensitive files should be locked in limited-access vaults or other protected facilities.

Application Controls

The auditor is always concerned with the accuracy and reliability of the accounting records. If those records are maintained on mainframe computer systems, the specific tasks to be performed by the computer department must be carefully monitored and controlled to make the records reliable. The practices followed in controlling these tasks are called **application controls**, and they are traditionally subdivided into three categories (listed in chronological order): input controls, processing controls, and output controls.

Input controls are of vital importance in a computerized system because this is the stage in the recordkeeping process at which most errors occur. These controls are designed to provide reasonable assurance that the data received by the computer department for processing have been (1) properly authorized, (2) properly converted to machine-readable form, and (3) properly accounted for subsequent to submission. Input controls also include controls associated with the rejection, correction, and resubmission of initially incorrect data.

Processing controls are designed to provide reasonable assurance that the computer has processed the data as it was intended to be processed in each individual application. By that we mean that all transactions are processed as authorized, that no authorized transactions are omitted, and that no unauthorized transactions are added.

Output controls are designed to ensure the accuracy of the processing result and to ensure that only authorized personnel receive the output.

Included in each of the previously cited categories of application controls are specific controls designed for specific functions:

- To prevent errors from occurring. These are characterized as *preventive controls*.
- To detect errors. These are characterized as *detective controls*.
- To correct errors. These are characterized as *corrective controls*.

The relationships among the various types of application controls are shown in Figure 9–3. Preventive controls generally are associated with input and processing controls only. Detective and corrective controls are implemented during all three stages of processing. These controls are listed by category in Figure 9–5.

Figure 9–5

Applications Controls

Input controls

Preventive	Detective	Corrective

1. Source data authorization
2. Data conversion controls
  a. Keypunch verification
  b. CRT verification
  c. Creation of machine-
    readable source
    documents
  d. Turnaround documents
3. Use of sequentially
  prenumbered forms
4. Programmed checks
  a. Validity tests
  b. Completeness checks
  c. Logic checks
  d. Limit tests
  e. Self-checking digits
	1. Batch control totals
	  a. Record counts
	  b. Control totals
	  c. Hash totals
	2. Data conversion controls
	  (same as preventive
	  controls)
	3. Machine-readable labels
	  a. Header labels
	  b. Trailer labels
	4. Programmed checks (same
	  as preventive controls)
		1. Error log
		2. Error input record

Processing controls

Preventive	Detective	Corrective

1. External identification labels
2. Programmed checks (same
  as for input controls)
	1. Batch control totals
	2. Machine-readable labels
	  (same as for input controls)
	3. Programmed checks (same
	  as for input controls)
		1. Error log

Output controls

	Detective	Corrective

	1. Reconciliations of output
	  data with control totals
	2. Review of output data
		1. Use of control group
		2. Error log
		3. Resubmission of erroneous
		  transactions through
		  identical process

Preventive Controls. Preventive controls are designed to detect mistakes that could occur in handling computerized accounting data—before they occur. These controls are located at various stages in the system but relate primarily to either the input or processing functions. The following preventive controls should be *associated with the input function*:

1. **Source data authorization.** All transactions should be processed in accordance with management's general or specific authorization. This normally calls for a visual audit of transactions (cash receipts, cash disbursements, sales, payrolls, etc.) by knowledgeable people in the various departments. Evidence of this review should be provided by notation (signature, initials, or stamped approval on the source document). When like transactions are as-

sembled into batches for processing, the appropriate supervisory personnel in the various departments should indicate their approval by attaching their signature, initials, or stamped approval to each batch. Visual audit at the department level can detect misspellings, invalid codes, unreasonable amounts, and other improper conditions to promote accuracy of input data.

2. **Data conversion controls.** These controls include such things as keypunch or cathode ray tube (CRT) verification of data, the creation of machine-readable source documents as a by-product of the manual recording of operations, and the use of turnaround documents. Keypunch or CRT verification is designed to make sure that the transaction data have been appropriately transferred from human-readable documents to machine-readable media. To ensure agreement between actual transaction data and input data, machine-readable source documents are often created as a by-product of a manual recording operation. For example, sales data, as it is recorded in the cash register, can be simultaneously recorded in punched tape or entered directly onto magnetic tape for purposes of providing machine-readable data for sales and removals from inventory. Turnaround documents are often used in billing for services such as those provided by a public utility. The billing may be in the form of a document that includes an electromagnetic code to be returned with the payment of the utility bill. The return segment is thus machine-readable to the same account, etc., contained in the original billing. Such procedures help to reduce the likelihood of erroneous input data.

3. **Use of sequentially prenumbered forms.** Use of such forms with full accountability established for all numbers is a traditional control technique, not only for computerized systems but also in manually maintained accounting systems. This practice helps prevent data from being omitted from computer inputs and also reduces the probability of unauthorized data being used.

4. **Use of the editing capability of the computer.** This capability can be used to validate input data after it has been converted to machine-readable form. The process requires that the computer be programmed to inspect and accept or reject transactions according to certain *validity or reasonable-limit tests* applied to quantities, amounts, codes, and other data contained in the input record. These often are referred to as *programmed checks* or programmed controls. They include

    a. **Validity tests**, designed to ensure that the transactions reflect transaction codes and valid characters and fit within a valid field size.

    b. **Completeness tests**, made to ensure that the input has the prescribed amount of data in all data fields.

    c. **Logic checks**, used when certain portions or fields of the record bear logical relationships to each other. The computer can be programmed to check for these relationships and to reject illogical combinations.

    d. **Limit tests**, designed to prevent amounts in excess of certain predetermined limits from being accepted by the computer. For example, a program for payroll can include a provision causing it to reject payroll rate changes greater than a specified percentage of the presently existing rate.

    e. **Self-checking digits**, used to ensure accuracy of identification numbers such as account numbers. To do this, the computer is programmed to perform an arithmetic operation in such a way that typical errors encountered in transcribing numbers can be detected.

Preventive controls *for the processing function* include external file identification labels and various programming checks:

1. **External identification labels** allow operators to visibly identify the type of data included on a magnetic tape. This helps ensure that the proper master files and data will be used by operators in processing transactions. By doing that, operators also minimize the possibility that data or program files will be destroyed through operator error.
2. **Programmed checks** include such things as checks for validity, for completeness, and for logic. These checks are accomplished by applying limit and reasonableness tests to the data during the processing function. These tests are designed to ensure that the program logic is consistent and that preprogrammed limits are not exceeded during processing.

Detective Controls.   Detective controls are designed to alert computer department personnel that a problem exists. They simply point out a problem once it has occurred. The problem must then be corrected to allow the production of correctly processed data. Detective controls *applied to the input and processing functions* often involve use of these elements:

1. **Batch control totals.** Batching involves the grouping of a specified number of transactions that are to be processed sequentially. **Batch control totals** should be established for each block of transactions. These totals should then be used to make certain that all transactions in the block are being processed. The totals may relate to **record counts** (the number of records included in each batch) or to *control totals* (the sum of a particular quantitative field of data, such as total sales or total net pay). **Hash totals** are another type of control total. They involve determining the sum of a series of numbers in the data file that would not ordinarily be added, such as account numbers in the accounts receivable file or social security numbers in the payroll file: As each batch of similar transactions is finished, control data for the input, processing, and output stages are compared; if the control total numbers for each of these stages agree, we are justified in assuming that the complete batch of transactions was processed.
2. **Data conversion controls.** Data conversion to machine-readable media, performed during the input stage, takes the form of keypunch verification or, more often, CRT verification. As explained earlier, this technique is designed to detect errors that may have occurred in transcribing the data from the original documents to machine-readable media. This verification should be performed on separate equipment and by operators other than the ones who created the original input media.
3. **Machine-readable labels.** The use of machine-readable labels on data-

recording media during the input and processing stages involves the use of computer-programming logic to help detect the use of improper file data. **Header labels** include such things as volume, file, and table of contents data. **Trailer labels**, typically containing one or more control totals that can be checked against the total accumulated when the file is read, are used to guard against failure to process any records in the file.

4. **Programmed checks.** Validity and reasonableness tests, discussed in the previous section, can be described as detective as well as preventive in nature. The presence of these controls in the client's programs alert operating personnel when a problem occurs or as soon as a programmed limit is exceeded or a validity test is violated. Errors in processing should be recorded in an error log and should be handled by the control group.

Detective controls *for the output function* include the following:

1. **Reconciliations of output data.** These reconciliations, particularly control totals, should agree with previously established control totals developed in the input phase or in the processing cycle.
2. **Review of output data.** This review looks for reasonableness and proper format. Basically, the functions of detective output controls are to determine that the processing function does not include unauthorized alterations by the computer operation section and that the data are substantially correct and reasonable.

Corrective Controls. Corrective controls are designed to assist individuals in investigating and correcting the causes of errors that have been detected as data are being processed. Like many of the preventive and detective controls previously discussed, corrective controls can be performed during the input, processing, or output stages of operations. Once errors have been detected, control techniques should be established to be sure that corrections are made to the transactions that are in error and to reenter the corrected transactions into the system. This is normally accomplished in three steps:

1. The *control group* should be required to enter all data rejected from the processing cycle in an *error log*. As the erroneous transactions are corrected and reentered, they should be checked off in the error log. The open (unresolved) items appearing in the log should be investigated periodically.
2. An *error input record* or *error log* (a report explaining the reason for each rejected item) should be prepared. Typically, each error should be returned to the department originating the data for correction and resubmission. The computer department should provide the source department with instructions for handling any such errors.
3. There should be a *resubmission of corrected transactions* to the error detection and input validation processes that were applied to the original transactions.

Microcomputer Software Controls

A principal cause of the proliferation of microcomputer applications in business has been the development of useful software. Microcomputer users, including both management and auditors, frequently develop their own software, writing programs in programming languages such as BASIC. In addition, sophisticated application software programs can be purchased from outside vendors, including CPA firms. Once tailored to the specific task, these programs are used repeatedly and may be shared among several users. For example, an electronic spreadsheet can be used to prepare a departmental budget. *An interesting adaptation of spreadsheet technology in the audit has been its use in developing electronic working papers.* Once created, the program is saved in the form of "templates" for repeated use in the future and/or given to others for the same task. Microcomputer audit software will be discussed further in Chapter 10.

The key control that should be emphasized in microcomputer software is *documentation*. The importance of documenting simple programs is highlighted when a change in responsibilities occurs. Suppose, for example, that a person using a particular software application is promoted within the firm. Those who follow might make critical errors in processing if they do not know exactly how to operate the package. Too often, personnel who use such packages without adequate knowledge of what they are designed to do adopt the attitude that since the computer is doing the task the end product must be correct—a conclusion that may prove to be incorrect. To illustrate this point, consider the following example. Suppose a payroll department employee has developed a template that will compute gross pay and deductions for a payroll application for a small company. As in all spreadsheet applications, each cell in the spreadsheet is programmed to accept values, labels, formulas, or, in some cases, very powerful *macro* commands. If the user fails to write the formulas for cell values correctly and inserts rows or columns in the spreadsheet without making corresponding changes in the formulas for the totals of those rows or columns, the work sheet can appear to foot and cross foot when, in fact, it does not. The developer, in this case, did not design the template to properly handle insertions of rows or columns. Although that person may be aware of the deficiency in the program and may never violate its parameters, others who are less knowledgeable might let the error pass without notice.

To prevent such errors from occurring, *at least three controls should be enforced* for microcomputer software. First, there should be a procedure for *testing all new microcomputer applications software* by knowledgeable users of those programs, to assure that they accomplish their desired objective in all users' hands. Second, the company *should enforce standards for adequate documentation of all microcomputer applications software used in significant accounting applications.* Third, there should be *provisions for adequate audit trails* in each stand-alone microcomputer application. For example, if an employee uses an electronic spreadsheet program to calculate the company's earnings per share, the output of that calculation (and related formulas) should be detailed enough to provide adequate review and approval by a supervisor. In addition, a log of transactions processed, transaction counts, and balancing/batch totals might be provided. A summary of daily transactions, generated by the computer, should be balanced with totals developed independently by a person other than the microcomputer operator. The balanced transactions log should be reviewed and approved by an appropriate supervisor.[4]

Understanding the Control Structure

☑ **Objective 3**
Be able to evaluate computer controls

Figure 9–6 presents a detailed sketch of the process followed in understanding the EDP control structure in a financial statement audit. The process described is theoretically the same as outlined in Figures 8–6 and 8–11 for a control structure in general. However, since the control environment, accounting system, and control procedures of the client (discussed in earlier parts of this chapter) are unique for a computerized system, the methods used by the auditor to understand and to test the system will be slightly different from those used in manual systems. It will be helpful for you to compare Figure 9–6 to Figures 8–6 and 8–11 as we review below the procedures typically followed by the auditor in understanding a computerized internal control system.

Initial Understanding of the System

The initial phase of the process provides an understanding of the control environment, the accounting system, the extent to which computers are used in each significant accounting application, and the basic internal control structure within the organization. The nature and extent of the procedures to be performed vary according to the complexity of the system. At the end of this phase, the auditor should understand the general controls that are built into the control structure (organization, hardware, documentation, and access controls). In addition, the auditor should have a general knowledge of the computerized accounting system, including how it generates the assertions that are included in the financial statements—from source documents through final distribution of output. Procedures used include

- Review of system documentation files, input preparation instructions, and users' manuals.
- Inquiry of client personnel, including systems analysts, programmers, and users.
- Inspection of records produced by the system.
- Completion of preliminary control checklists and questionnaires.

The auditor may inspect such documentation as flowcharts or narratives showing the flow of documents through the system. In all cases, he or she should take steps to thoroughly understand the meaning of terms used in those

Figure 9–6

Consideration of the EDP Internal Control Structure in a Financial Statement Audit

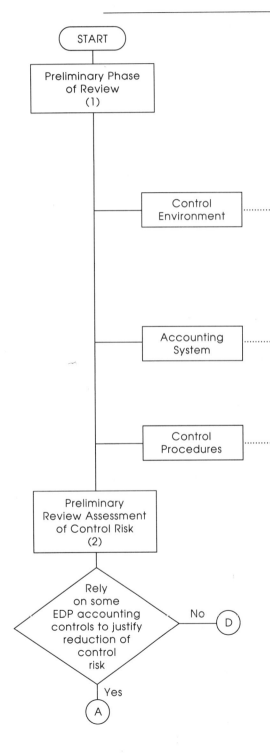

1. Initial Understanding of the System

Purpose

Obtain understanding of the design of relevant EDP policies and procedures and whether they have been placed in operation for the elements of the internal control structure. Also, obtain sufficient understanding to plan the audit, recognizing it necessary to

a. Identify types of potential material misstatements.
b. Consider factors that affect the risk of material misstatements.
c. Design effective substantive tests.

Obtain knowledge sufficient to understand management's and directors' attitudes, awareness, and actions concerning:

a. Management philosophy and operating style.
b. Organizational structure of EDP.
c. Methods of assigning authority and responsibility in both EDP and non-EDP segments.
d. Internal audit function.
e. EDP personnel policies and practices.

Obtain knowledge sufficient to understand:

a. The flow of transactions and significance of output, including initiation of transactions.
b. Records, documents, and accounts used in the processing and reporting of transactions.
c. Accounting processing by the computer.
d. Financial reporting processed by the computer.

Obtain knowledge of EDP control procedures necessary to plan after considering the knowledge obtained about the control environment and the accounting system.

Methods

Inquiry and discussion; observation; review of documentation; tracing of transactions; control questionnaires and checklists.

2. Initial Assessment of Control Risk

Purpose

Determine if there is enough basis in the EDP internal control structure for reliance to justify a reduction in the assessed level of control risk. Determine extent of any additional review within EDP.

Method

Judgment.

Figure 9–6 ▬▬▬▭▭▭▭▭▭▭▭▭▭▭▭▭▭▭▭▭▭▭▭▭▭▭

(continued)

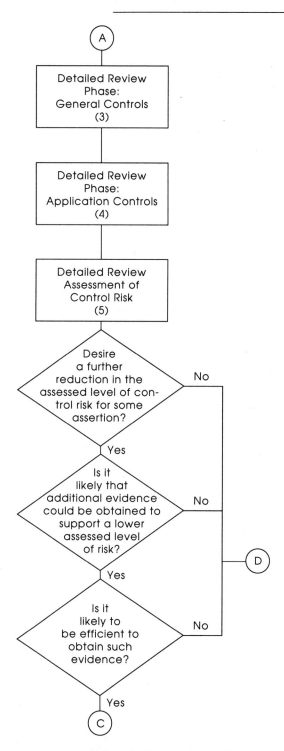

3. Detailed Review Phase—General Controls

Purpose

Identify those general controls on which reliance can be justified to support a reduction in the assessed level of control risk.

Determine how those controls operate and the effect such controls have on management's assertions.

Determine the effects of strengths and weaknesses on application controls.

Consider tests of controls that may be performed.

Methods

Detailed examination of documentation; interviewing internal auditors, EDP, and user department personnel; observing operation of general controls; completion of flowcharts, questionnaires, decision tables, etc.

4. Detailed Review Phase—Application Controls

Purpose

Identify those application controls on which reliance can be justified to support a reduction in the assessed level of control risk.

Determine how these controls operate and the effect such controls have on management's assertions.

Consider tests of controls that may be performed.

Consider the potential effect of identified strengths and weaknesses on tests of controls.

Methods

Detailed examination of documentation; interviewing internal auditors, EDP, and user department personnel; observing operation of application controls; completion of flowcharts, questionnaires, decision tables, etc.

5. Detailed Review Assessment of Control Risk

Purpose

For each significant accounting application and assertion, the auditor should consider if there is enough basis for reliance to justify an assessed level of control risk that is less than the maximum.

Consider policies and procedures relevant to specific assertions.

Consider the types of errors and irregularities that could occur.

continues

Figure 9–6 ▬▬▬▬

(continued)

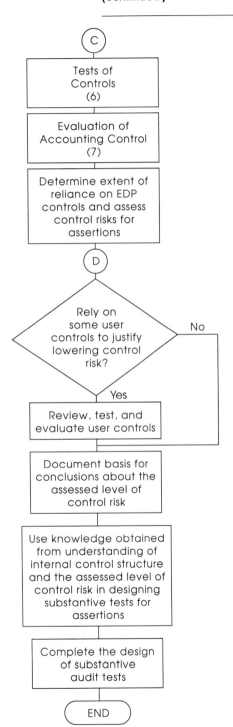

Determine the control procedures that prevent or detect such errors.

Assess effectiveness of EDP and non-EDP controls.

Method

Judgment.

6. Tests of Controls

Purpose

Determine whether the necessary control procedures that have been prescribed are being followed satisfactorily for specific assertions.

Provide reasonable assurance that controls are functioning properly.

Consider and, to the extent appropriate, document when, how, and by whom controls are provided.

Methods

Examination of records, tests of control procedures (test deck, ITF, etc.), inquiry, observation.

7. Evaluation of Control

Purpose

For each significant accounting application and assertion:

a. Consider the types of errors or irregularities that could occur.

b. Determine the controls that prevent or detect such errors and irregularities.

c. Determine whether the necessary control procedures are prescribed and followed satisfactorily.

d. Evaluate weaknesses and assess their effect on control risk and the nature, timing, and extent of substantive tests.

Method

Judgment.

Where the assessed level is less than the maximum, the basis for that conclusion should be documented.

Where the assessed level is the maximum, only that conclusion need be documented.

Source: "An Approach to Consideration of the Internal Control Structure for EDP-Based Applications in a Financial Statement Audit Under SAS 55." Reprinted from Journal of Accounting and EDP (New York: Auerbach Publishers). © 1990 Warren, Gorham & Lamont, Inc. Used with permission.

documents. This may include studying *record layouts* for descriptions of data elements and their positions in the data files.

As discussed in Chapter 8, in arriving at the initial understanding of the control structure, the auditor should consider (1) the types of errors and irregularities that could occur; (2) the financial statement assertions affected; (3) the control attributes that should prevent, detect, or correct the errors; and (4) whether those attributes are prescribed by the client. Documentation of the auditor's understanding should be in the form of flowcharts, such as those included in Appendixes 9–A and 9–B, and internal control questionnaires such as the ones illustrated in Appendixes 9–C and 9–D.

Initial Assessment of Control Risk

After completing the initial phase of the review, the auditor should be prepared to assess the significance of computer controls within each significant accounting application (revenues, payables, property and equipment, payrolls, etc.). In addition, within each application, the auditor should be able to assess control risk for each significant financial statement assertion (completeness, existence, valuation, rights, disclosure). That assessment might be made either on a quantitative basis (.10, .20, etc.) or informally (high, medium, low).

For some assertions, the auditor may assess control risk at the maximum level because the control structure contains deficiencies, or the cost of further testing would exceed the benefits to be derived in the form of reduced detection risk procedures. In these cases, the auditor must either plan to rely on user department controls (if they exist) or perform extensive detection risk procedures.

For other assertions, the auditor may conclude that, if additional tests were performed on the supporting control structure, a further reduction of control risk from its preliminary assessed level might be possible, thus reducing detection risk procedures. Assuming that further evidence regarding the controls exists and is cost effective to obtain, the auditor would continue with further review of both general and applications controls, as well as tests of those controls, as discussed in the sections that follow.

Detailed Review and Assessment: General Controls

The detailed general controls review is designed to provide an in-depth understanding of the general controls within the structure and to help the auditor identify the specific applications upon which he or she will rely. The principal procedures applied in this review include a detailed examination of documentation standards and manuals, interviews of client personnel such as internal auditors, and observation of operations. The documentation for such a review varies among auditing firms, but it often includes EDP controls questionnaires. Appendix 9–C shows part of a questionnaire used for this purpose by one major public accounting firm. The entire questionnaire contains sections pertaining to equipment and programming languages, organization chart, computer applications, and organization and operating controls. Within each of these sections are specific questions relating to segregation of duties, documentation, access to equipment, machine operations, program testing and changes, and file protection and retention.

At this point in the audit, the auditor should have a good idea of the accounting system and the control environment, plus the significant accounting applications that utilize computers. Supporting documentation has taken the form of systems and program flowcharts, narrative descriptions, and the EDP internal control questionnaire. All of this information is sufficient to indicate the following:

- The audit significance of the EDP system to the client's operations.
- The audit significance of specific applications within the system, indicating those applications to be reviewed in detail.
- Any weaknesses in organizational control and operating practices and the impact of those weaknesses on auditing procedures.

Remember that judgments made at this point can be extremely critical, because weaknesses in general controls are generally pervasive enough to affect the entire accounting system.

Detailed Review and Assessment: Application Controls

The next step in the detailed control risk assessment process is to review application controls. Application controls are often dependent on general controls. For this reason, it is appropriate to review general controls first before reviewing application controls. For example, if an application control procedure, such as matching shipping information with billing information, were to be performed by a customer-billing computer program, the auditor should review the controls over the access to and changing of computer programs before reviewing this programmed control procedure, because, in this case, the effectiveness of the application procedure is dependent on the general controls over access to and changing of programs.

A detailed review of application controls should encompass an understanding of both the details of the processing and the major controls over the phases of processing—input, processing, and output. Appendix 9–D contains specific questions that are typically asked in a detailed review of application controls. Other procedures included in completing the review are interviewing internal auditors and user department personnel, observing the operation of application controls, and inspecting documentation.

On the completion of the detailed review of each significant application, the auditor must determine if controls are adequate to prevent, detect, or correct material errors and irregularities in the financial statements. If those controls are not prescribed, the auditor might investigate whether there are user controls placed on processed data within the system that might mitigate the weaknesses in the accounting application. Such considerations will affect the nature, timing, and extent of the substantive tests to be performed on the related financial statement assertions.

Tests of Controls

As we learned in Chapter 8, the purpose of tests of controls is to provide reasonable assurance that the accounting controls prescribed by the client are actually being followed. In these tests, we are concerned with three basic questions:

- Were the necessary procedures performed?
- How were the procedures performed?
- By whom were the procedures performed?

The typical approach used in testing controls is to *observe the operation of the system* and to *inspect documentary evidence of* the controls being performed. This approach is appropriate for control procedures that leave *visible evidence* of having been performed, such as (1) files documenting program changes for each EDP application, along with approvals of those changes; and (2) EDP-generated error listings and exception reports.

For these controls, for example, the auditor would first vouch changes to approval signatures of appropriate personnel then ascertain that the control group followed up on error listings by returning the erroneous transactions to the proper personnel for corrections and resubmission.

Manual tracing and mapping is a technique used to analyze computer application programs. This helps identify the flows of transactions and the associated application controls within the program.

Computers that are directly involved in handling approvals and recording transactions often perform controls and leave *no visible evidence of those controls being performed*. This is the case, for example, with the *programmed checks* discussed earlier (i.e., validity tests, limit and reasonableness tests, etc.). Because of their critical importance to the presentation of the financial statements, when such controls are included and depended upon, the auditor should perform audit tests to ensure that unacceptable transactions are rejected by the computer and followed up for correction. The techniques used for testing such controls are part of *auditing through the computer* and include the use of test data, parallel simulation, integrated test facilities (ITFs), and continuous monitoring. These techniques will be discussed in Chapter 10 as we present the various ways in which the computer is used to perform audit work.

Final Assessment of Control Risk

If strong control attributes are present, the auditor may limit the nature, timing, and extent of substantive tests of financial statement assertions that are influenced by those controls. If weak internal controls are found, and if there are no mitigating controls to offset those weaknesses, the auditor must design substantive tests over affected assertions that will have a greater probability of detecting material misstatements in the financial statements.

Summary

In this chapter we have dealt with the general problem of understanding control structure and assessing control risk for firms that utilize the computer in significant accounting applications. We began by recognizing that such systems should have the same basic characteristics that were identified for all internal control systems in Chapter 8. As a matter of fact, when only microcomputers are used by various persons to process accounting data, traditional internal controls, supplemented by extra precautions to protect programs and data files, can be effective. However, when a firm uses a centralized computer system, a number of functions normally segregated in manual systems must be combined to allow the system to operate effectively. Therefore, responsibilities cannot be separated appropriately and must be compensated for by other control practices. In addition, specialized procedures must be developed to ensure adequate transaction trails; error detection in data; and physical protection of files from loss, destruction, or unauthorized use.

We subdivided the controls for computer systems into general controls and application controls. General controls are designed to contribute to the achievement of specific control objectives through their interdependence with specific control procedures. Application control procedures are designed to achieve specific control objectives and are often dependent on general controls for their effectiveness. We then discussed various types of general and application controls for mainframe installations and for on-line and microcomputer interface installations. Special general controls for stand-alone microcomputer installations were also discussed. Next, we discussed the process by which computer controls are typically evaluated by the auditor.

Auditing Vocabulary

p. 336 **access attempt facility:** Disconnects a particular terminal after a prescribed number of unauthorized attempts to gain mainframe access.

p. 334 **access controls:** Controls over access to equipment and data files.

p. 337 **application controls:** Programmed or software controls that provide accuracy and reliability of accounting records. Included in application controls are input controls, processing controls, and output controls.

p. 340 **batch control totals:** Totals of specific data fields within a batch. Control totals should be used to make sure that all transactions in the batch are being processed.

p. 336 **call-back:** Data security that is used for *dial up* installations. The mainframe is programmed to call back the terminal or microcomputer that accessed it to ensure that communications are occurring via authorized telephone lines only.

p. 324 **central processing unit (CPU):** That part of the hardware of a computer that contains the memory and the ability to perform arithmetic, logic, and control functions.

p. 339 **completeness tests:** Programmed controls made to ensure that the input has the prescribed amount of data in all data fields.

p. 333 **computer log:** Also called a console log. A written document that lists all interaction between the console and the CPU. It is prepared by the computer as messages are entered from the console, indicating how the operator responded to problems encountered during processing.

p. 330 **computer operators:** Persons who operate the computer equipment.

p. 330 **data conversion operators:** Equipment operators who convert human-readable documentary data into machine-readable form.

p. 335 **download:** Movement of data from mainframe files to smaller disk files so that data might be modified.

p. 335 **dump:** Periodic copying of files from disks to tape for review and permanent storage.

p. 322 **electronic data processing (EDP):** The type of information system that utilizes computers to record, summarize, classify, and report accounting information.

p. 336 **encryption of data:** A control that renders data useless to unauthorized individuals by reinterpreting it with other symbols.

p. 340 **external identification labels:** Visibly identifiable labels placed on disks or magnetic tapes.

p. 334 **file security:** Measures taken to safeguard files from total loss.

p. 329 **general controls:** Controls that relate to all or many computerized accounting activities; designed to contribute to the achievement of specific control objectives and considered to be interdependent with specific accounting control procedures. General controls will apply to all of an entity's application controls, and are thus considered to be pervasive with respect to the controls of the entity. Breakdowns in general controls are considered to affect the entity's ability to process all information, and are considered very serious.

p. 334 **grandfather, father, son:** A practice of retaining two generations of both master and transaction file data until a new master file is produced.

p. 334 **hardware controls:** General controls built into the equipment to detect erroneous internal handling of data.

p. 340 **hash total:** A type of control total that determines the sum of a series of numbers in the data file that would not ordinarily be added, such as account numbers in an accounts receivable file or social security numbers in the payroll file.

p. 341 **header labels:** Machine-readable labels that identify files.

p. 337 **input controls:** Controls designed to provide reasonable assurance that data received by the computer department for processing have been properly authorized, converted to machine-readable form, and properly accounted for subsequent to submission.

p. 327 **integrated processing system:** A system that coordinates a number of previously unconnected processes to improve overall efficiency by reducing or eliminating redundant data-entry or data-processing operations.

p. 330 **librarians:** Persons who are in charge of maintaining physical safeguards over systems files.

p. 339 **limit test:** Designed to prevent amounts in excess of certain predetermined limits from being accepted by the computer.

p. 336   **local area network (LAN):**   Linking microcomputers together to share and exchange information.

p. 339   **logic checks:**   Used when certain portions or fields of the record bear logical relationships to each other.

p. 349   **manual tracing and mapping:**   A technique used to analyze computer application programs that helps to identify the flows of transactions and the associated application controls within the program.

p. 329   **organization controls:**   General controls that pertain to the organization of the entity's EDP department and the autonomy of that department from other operating departments of the entity.

p. 337   **output controls:**   Designed to ensure the accuracy of the processing result and to ensure that only authorized personnel receive the output.

p. 334   **parity check:**   A type of hardware control that ensures the equipment's processing accuracy and reliability. A test as to whether the number of one-bits in an array is even (even parity check) or odd (odd parity check).

p. 335   **password:**   Special encodings that restrict access to sensitive data to authorized individuals.

p. 332   **procedure manuals:**   Documentation for development, maintenance, testing, and approving systems and changes thereto.

p. 337   **processing controls:**   Designed to provide reasonable assurance that the computer has processed the data as it was intended to be processed.

p. 340   **programmed checks:**   Controls built into software to utilize the computer's editing ability.

p. 330   **programmers:**   Persons who prepare the computer programs to meet specifications of systems analysts.

p. 330   **quality control group:**   Persons who continually test processing accuracy of both hardware and software.

p. 340   **record counts:**   A type of batch control total that sums the number of records being processed.

p. 335   **security software:**   Software written to provide access security.

p. 339   **self-checking digits:**   Used to ensure accuracy of identification numbers such as account numbers. The computer is programmed to perform an arithmetic operation in such a way that typical errors encountered in transcribing numbers can be detected.

p. 330   **systems analysts:**   Persons who evaluate systems, analyze requirements for information, and design systems.

p. 336   **time-out facility:**   Automatically disconnects mainframe terminals that have not communicated with the mainframe for a specified period of time.

p. 341   **trailer labels:**   Labels placed at the end of files to indicate end of processing and that contain one or more control totals that can be checked against the total accumulated when the file is read.

p. 335   **upload:**   Movement of data from disk files into the mainframe.

p. 339   **validity tests:**   Programmed controls that are designed to ensure that the transactions reflect transaction codes and valid characters and fit within a valid field size.

Appendix 9–A: Program Flowchart for Perpetual-Inventory-Records Updating Application

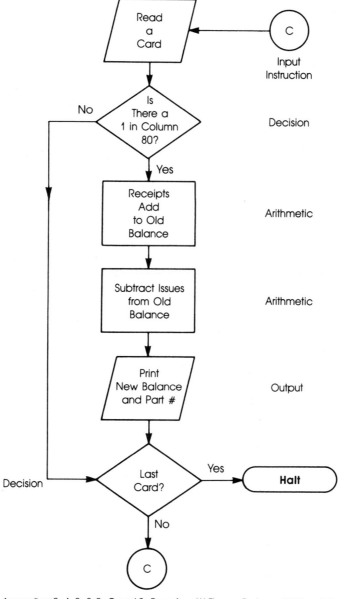

Appendixes 9–A, 9–B, 9–C, and 9–D are from W. Thomas Porter and William E. Perry, *EDP Controls and Auditing*, 4th ed. (Boston: Kent Publishing Company, 1984): 512–528.

Appendix 9–B: Systems Flowchart of Automated Processing for Purchase Order Procedures and Store Ledger-File Updating— Stores Department

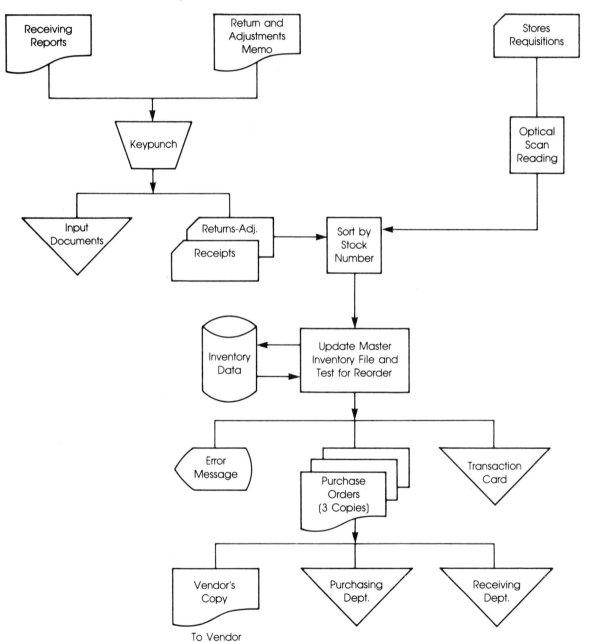

Appendix 9–C: General Controls Questionnaire (partial)

| Part I—System and Control Questionnaire | Accountant |
| | Date |

Company _____ Period ended _____

Branch, division, or subsidiary _____

			Answer
Question	**Yes**	**No**	**Remarks***
Organization and operating controls—(When applicable, all operating shifts are to be considered.)			
1. Does the internal auditor's program include a review of			
a. The arrangement of duties and responsibilities in the data processing department?			
b. Programs supplied by the data processing department that are used to prepare audit data?			
c. The controls of the serviced departments over the processing performed by the data processing department?			
2. Have procedures been established by which the qualifications of the Data Processing employees to perform their functions can be determined?			
3. Are all proof and control functions performed by personnel other than machine operators and programmers?			
4. Are the functions and duties of computer operators and programmers separate and distinct?			
5. Are the operators assigned to particular jobs or applications subject to periodic rotation?			
6. Are operators required to take vacations?			
7. Are the employees in data processing separated from all duties relating to the initiation of transactions and master file changes?			

continues

Appendix 9–C

(*continued*)

Question	Yes	No	Remarks*
8. Are departments that initiate changes in master file data or program data factors furnished with notices or a register showing changes actually made? (Examples of such changes are revisions in pay rates, selling prices, credit limits, and tax tables.)			
9. Are blank checks and other negotiable paper used by the data processing department controlled by someone independent of the machine operators?			
10. Have documentation procedures and standards been established?			
11. Is there supervisory review of documentation for adequacy, completeness and current status?			
12. Have standardized programming techniques and procedures (i.e., program formats, flowcharts, initialization routines, tape labeling, coding, etc.) been compiled in a programming manual and is the manual current?			
13. Are standardized operator instructions and run descriptions prepared and made available to the computer operators? *Note:* These instructions are generally incorporated into "run books."			

*Note: In the case of a "No" answer, the "Remarks" column should (1) cross-reference either to the audit program step (or steps) that recognizes the weakness or to the supporting permanent file memorandum on accounting procedures that explains the mitigating circumstances or lack of importance of the item, and (2) indicate whether the item is to be included in the draft of the letter to management on internal control.

Appendix 9–D: Applications Controls Questionnaire (partial)

| Part II—Specific Application Questionnaire | Accountant |
| | Date |

Company _____ Period ended _____

Branch, division, or subsidiary _____

| Question | Answer | | |
	Yes	No	Remarks*

A. Documentation
General
Documentation consists of work papers and records that describe the system and procedures for performing a data processing task. It is the basic means of communicating the essential elements of the data processing system and the logic followed by the computer programs. Preparing adequate documentation is a necessary, though frequently neglected, phase of computer data processing. A lack of documentation is an indication of a serious weakness within the management control over a data processing installation.
   Is the program or programs supported by an adequate documentation file?
   A minimum acceptable level of documentation should include
  1. Problem statement
  2. System flowchart
  3. Transaction and activity codes
  4. Record layouts
  5. Operator's instructions
  6. Program flowchart
  7. Program listing
  8. Approval and change sheet
  9. Description of input and output forms			

B. Input Controls General Input controls are designed to authenticate the contents of source documents and to check the conversion of this information into machine-readable formats or media. Normally these controls will not be designed to detect 100%			

continues

Question	Answer		
	Yes	No	Remarks*
of all input errors since such an effort would be either too costly or physically impractical. Therefore, an economic balance must be maintained between the cost of error detection and the economic impact of an undetected error. This should be considered when evaluating input control. Judgment must be used when identifying *essential information,* the accuracy of which *must* be verified. The following questions can also be used to evaluate internal control practices used in master file conversions.			
1. Are procedures adequate to verify that all transactions are being received for processing? (To accomplish this, there must be some systematic procedure to insure all batches that enter the machine room for processing or conversion are returned from the machine room. Basic control requirements are being met if the answer to *one* of the following questions is "yes.")			
a. Are batch controls (at least an item count) being established *before* source documents are sent to the machine room for keypunching or processing?			
b. If batch controls are established *in* the machine room, is there some other form of effective control (such as prenumbered documents) that provides assurance that all documents have been received?			
c. If no batch control is used, is there some other means of checking the receipt of all transactions? If yes, describe. (For example, in a payroll operation, the computer may match attendance time cards and corresponding job tickets for each employee as the master file is updated.)			
2. Are procedures adequate to verify the recording of input data on cards, magnetic tape, or disk? (Control is being maintained if the answer to *one* of the following questions is "yes.")			
a. Are important data fields subject to machine verification?			
b. If only some (or none) of the important data fields are verified, is an alternate checking technique employed? Some acceptable alternate techniques are			
1. Self-checking digits			
2. Control totals			
3. Hash totals			
4. Editing for reasonableness			

Appendix 9–D

(continued)

Question	Yes	No	Answer Remarks*
3. If input data is converted from one form to another (cards to tape, cards to disk) prior to processing on the computer system, are controls adequate to verify the conversion? Normal conversion controls include **a.** Record counts **b.** Hash totals **c.** Control totals			
4. If data transmission is used to move data between geographic locations, are controls adequate to determine transmission is correct and no messages are lost? Controls would normally include one or more of the following: **a.** Message counts **b.** Character counts **c.** Dual transmission			
5. Is the error correction process and the reentry of the corrected data subject to the same control as is applied to original data? (If control over corrections is lax, the correction process may be the largest source of error in the system.)			
6. Are source documents retained for an adequate period of time in a manner that allows identification with related output records and documents? (Failure to maintain documents may make it impossible to recreate files in the event they are damaged or destroyed.)			
C. Program and Processing Controls General Programs should be written to take the maximum advantage of the computer's ability to perform logical testing operations. In many cases, tests that could be employed are not used because the programmer does not know the logical limits of the data to be processed. Since the auditor will usually have a good knowledge of the proper limits of the data, he or she is in a position to detect weakness in program controls.			
1. Is adequate control exercised to insure that all transactions received are processed by the computer? (*Note:* The answer to one of the following two questions should be "yes.")			

continues

Appendix 9–D

(continued)

Question	Yes	No	Remarks*
a. If predetermined batch control techniques are being used, does the computer accumulate matching batch totals in each run wherein the corresponding transactions are processed, and is there adequate provision for systematic comparison of computer totals with predetermined totals? *(Note:* Having the computer internally match totals is more accurate than external visual matching. In addition, it should be noted that very often original batch totals are internally combined into pyramid summary totals as different types of input transactions are merged during progressive stages. This is acceptable if it does not create a serious problem in attempting to locate errors when the overall totals are compared.)			
b. If no batch total process is in use, is there an effective substitute method to verify that all transactions are processed? (Example: Any application where source documents are serially numbered and the computer system checks for missing numbers.)			
2. Is adequate use being made of the computer's ability to make logical data validity tests on important fields of information? These tests may include **a.** Checking code or account numbers against a master file or table. **b.** Use of self-checking numbers. **c.** Specific amount or account tests. **d.** Limit tests. **e.** Testing for alpha or blanks in a numeric field. **f.** Comparison of different fields within a record to see if they represent a valid combination of data. **g.** Checking for missing data.			
3. Is sequence checking employed to verify sorting accuracy of *each* of the following: **a.** Transactions that were presorted before entry into the computer (sequence check on first input run)? **b.** Sequenced files (sequence check incorporated within processing logic that detects out-of-sequence condition when files are updated or otherwise processed)?			

Appendix 9–D

(continued)

Question	Yes	No	Remarks*
4. Are internal header and trailer labels on magnetic media files (i.e., tape, disk, data cell) tested by the program? Such tests should include			
a. Input			
1. Correct file identification			
2. Proper date			
3. Correct sequence of files			
4. Record count check			
5. Control and hash total check			
b. Output			
Retention date has passed.			
5. If processing requires more than 30 minutes of computer time for any one program, are there adequate provisions for restarting the program if processing is interrupted?			
D. Output Control General Output control is generally a process of checking if the operation of input control and program and processing controls has produced the proper result. The following controls should be in effect in most data processing operations:			
1. Are internal header and trailer labels written on all magnetic media files created as output? Header labels consist of an identification record written as the first record on each file. The labels normally contain			
a. File identification (usually a code number)			
b. Date created			
c. File sequence number (for multiple reel or volume files)			
d. Retention date or period (used to determine the earliest date on which a file may be released for reuse) Trailer labels consist of a control record written as the last record on each file. These labels normally contain			
a. Record count			
b. Control or hash totals for one or more fields			
c. End-of-file or end-of-reel code			

*Note: In the case of a "No" answer, the "Remarks" column should (1) cross-reference either to the audit program step (or steps) that recognizes the weakness or to the supporting permanent file memorandum on accounting procedures that explains the mitigating circumstances or lack of importance of the item, and (2) indicate whether the item is to be included in the draft of the letter to management on internal control.

Notes

1. *Computer Fraud*, A Report presented to the National Commission on Fraudulent Financial Reporting by Ernst & Whinney, 1987.
2. *Audit and Accounting Guide—The Auditor's Study and Evaluation of Internal Control in EDP Systems* (New York, AICPA, 1977).
3. Price Waterhouse, *Managing Microcomputers: A Guide for Financial Policymakers.* (A report prepared under contract to the National Association of Accountants, 919 Third Avenue, New York, N.Y., 1984).
4. Price Waterhouse, ibid.

Questions for Class Discussion

Q9-1 What are the special internal control problems that must be recognized in auditing computerized accounting records?

Q9-2 Historically, in expressing an opinion on financial statements, the auditor has depended on the examination of documents supporting various items in the account balance for verification of account balances. How has the use of computerized accounting records affected this portion of the audit? Explain.

Q9-3 Why is the auditor so concerned with the organizational structure of the client's computer department?

Q9-4 Are you confident of the meaning of the following terms? Define.
   a. *Central processing unit*
   b. *Systems analyst*
   c. *Programmer*
   d. *Hardware controls*
   e. *Parity check*
   f. *Validity check*
   g. *Completeness check*
   h. *Logic test*
   i. *Limit test*
   j. *Self-checking digits*
   k. *Batch processing*
   l. *Machine-readable labels*
   m. *Validity and reasonableness test*

Q9-5 What is meant by the phrase *computer fraud*? Explain.

Q9-6 Can you distinguish between *general controls* and *application controls* as those terms are used in controlling a computerized accounting system?

Q9-7 What functions within the computer department should be separated in achieving appropriate internal control over the accounting process?

Q9-8 Can you list and describe the hardware controls that may be incorporated into computer equipment?

Q9-9   How does the grandfather, father, son arrangement for handling, processing, and storing computerized data help in protecting against the loss of data contained in computerized records?

Q9-10 Define and briefly describe each of the following: *input controls; processing controls; output controls.*

Q9-11 What is the difference between *preventive controls* and *detective controls*?

Q9-12 Can you describe four preventive controls associated with the input function?

Q9-13 What are two types of preventive controls associated with the processing function?

Q9-14 How are batch controls used as a detective control device?

Q9-15 How are machine-readable labels useful in exercising control over the input and processing functions?

Q9-16 What is meant by *corrective controls*? Explain.

Q9-17 How does the first general standard of GAAS relate to the auditor's responsibility in the audit of financial statements developed from computerized accounting data?

Q9-18 What are the possible conclusions that an auditor may reach after obtaining an understanding of the control structure associated with a computerized accounting system?

Q9-19 What are some of the special control problems associated with use of an on-line, real-time system for recording accounting data? Describe.

Q9-20 What are some of the special control problems associated with the use of microcomputers for recording accounting data? How should controls be implemented to deal with those types of problems?

Short Cases

C9-1   The McMillan Pharmaceutical Company's system for billing and recording accounts receivable is as follows:

   a. An incoming customer's purchase order is received in the order department by a clerk, who prepares a prenumbered company sales order form in which is inserted the pertinent information, such as the customer's name and address, customer's account number, quantity, and items ordered. After the sales order has been prepared, the customer's purchase order is stapled to it.

   b. The sales order form is then passed to the credit department for credit approval. Rough approximations of the billing values of the orders are made in the credit department for those accounts on which credit limitations are imposed. After investigation, approval of credit is noted on the form.

   c. Next the sales order form is passed to the billing department, where a clerk types the customer's invoice on a billing machine that cross-multiplies the number of items and the unit price, then adds the automatically extended amounts for the total amount of the invoice. The billing clerk determines the unit prices for the items from a list of billing prices.

   The billing machine has registers that automatically accumulate daily totals of customer account numbers and invoice amounts to provide *hash totals* and control amounts. These totals, which are inserted in a daily record book, serve as predetermined batch totals for verification of computer inputs.

The billing is done on prenumbered, continuous, carbon-interleaved forms having the following designations:

1. "Customer's copy."
2. "Sales department copy," for information purposes.
3. "File copy."
4. "Shipping department copy," which serves as a shipping order. Bills of lading are also prepared as carbon copy by-products of the invoicing procedure.

d. The shipping department copies of the invoices and the bills of lading are then sent to the shipping department. After the order has been shipped, copies of the bill of lading are returned to the billing department. The shipping department copy of the invoice is filed in the shipping department.

e. In the billing department, one copy of the bill of lading is attached to the customer's copy of the invoice, and both are mailed to the customer. The other copy of the bill of lading, together with the sales order form, is then stapled to the invoice file copy and filed in invoice numerical order.

f. A CRT device is connected to the billing machine so that the sales data are automatically entered into the computer as customers are billed. The data are processed in batches. At the end of the day, a printout of the sales transactions is produced. Printouts of daily sales are then filed by date in the sales department. These records are kept for two years before being destroyed.

Required: List the procedures that a CPA would employ in his or her examination of selected audit samples of the company's

a. Typed invoices, including the source documents.
b. CRT input.

(AICPA adapted)

C9-2   You will be examining for the first time the financial statements of the Central Savings and Loan Association for the year ending December 31. The CPA firm that examined the association's financial statements for the prior year issued an unqualified audit report.

During the current year, the association installed an on-line, realtime computer system. Each teller in the association's main office and seven branch offices has an on-line input/output terminal. Customers' mortgage payments and savings account deposits and withdrawals are recorded in the accounts by the computer from data input by the teller at the time of the transaction. The teller keys the proper account by account number and enters the information in the terminal keyboard to record the transaction. The accounting department at the main office has CRT input/output devices. The computer is housed at the main office.

Required: You would expect the association to have certain internal controls in effect because an on-line, realtime computer system is employed. List the internal controls that should be in effect solely because this system is employed, classifying them as

a. Those controls pertaining to input of information.
b. All other types of computer controls.

(AICPA adapted)

C9-3   Ted Leonardi, CPA, is examining the financial statements of the Georgetown Sales Corporation, which recently installed a computer. The following comments have been extracted from Ted's notes on computer operations and the processing and control of shipping notices and customer invoices.

To minimize inconvenience Georgetown converted without change its existing data-processing system. The computer company supervised the conversion and has provided training to all computer department employees (except input data operators) in systems design, operations, and programming.

Each computer run is assigned to a specific employee, who is responsible for making program changes, running the program, and answering questions. This procedure has the advantage of eliminating the need for records of computer operations because each employee is responsible for his or her own computer runs.

At least one computer department employee remains in the computer room during office hours, and only computer department employees have keys to the computer room.

System documentation consists of those materials furnished by the computer company—a set of record formats and program listings. These and the tape library are kept in a corner of the computer department.

The corporation considered the desirability of program controls but decided to retain the manual controls from its existing system.

Company products are shipped directly from public warehouses, which forward shipping notices to general accounting. There a billing clerk enters the price of the item and accounts for the numerical sequence of shipping notices from each warehouse. The billing clerk also prepares daily adding machine tapes (*control tapes*) of the units shipped and the unit prices.

Shipping notices and control tapes are forwarded to the computer department for data entry and processing. Extensions are made on the computer. Output consists of invoices (in six copies) and a daily sales register. The daily sales register shows the aggregate totals of units shipped and unit prices, which the computer operator compares to the control tapes.

All copies of the invoice are returned to the billing clerk. The clerk mails three copies to the customer, forwards one copy to the warehouse, maintains one copy in a numerical file, and retains one copy in an open invoice file that serves as a detailed accounts receivable record.

Required: Suppose that, as Ted's business partner, you are required to carry out this audit for him, because Ted has been appointed to a government position, effective immediately. Referring to Ted's notes, describe weaknesses in internal control over information and data flows and in the procedures for processing shipping notices and customer invoices. Recommend improvement in these controls and processing procedures. Organize your work sheet as follows:

Weakness	Recommended Improvement

(AICPA adapted)

C9-4   The following paragraphs are quoted from an article describing defects in the system of internal controls of Equity Funding Life Insurance Company, defects that resulted in one of the largest cases of computer fraud in history.

The EDP function ran in a mode that courted disaster but apparently left the EDP staff isolated from knowledge of the fraud. A central staff developed and ran the primary programs for the business, but programmers in other departments, such as actuarial, could also write and run their own programs, which had access to the live data base of insurance policies. The special processing required to carry out the fraud could have been done and, it is claimed, was done by the programmers outside of the central EDP staff. . . .

It is also claimed that EDP management had proposed on numerous occasions the establishment of an internal audit group for the EDP environment, but it was always rejected by top management. . . .

The EDP staff also observed the external auditors from a revealing point of view. The auditors were apparently handed EDP listings of policy records printed from the master files and accepted them as documents of record since the auditors had no capability or skills to directly access the master files in the system themselves. When the auditors happened to select a fake policy for confirmation, they were told that policy folder was in use by somebody in the company and would be available the next day. . . .

The way it worked was that Equity's head, Stanley Goldblum, set standards for growth in income, assets, and earnings. The desired quarterly and annual profits were relayed to Alan Green through Lewis and another executive. . . . Green would then go on the computer and crank out the necessary fictitious policies.*

Required:
a. What EDP controls were violated in this case?
b. As auditor of Equity Funding Life Insurance Company, how would you have reacted to these facts?

C9-5   Karen Hernandez, CPA, was engaged to examine the financial statements of Horizon Incorporated, which has its own computer installation. During the preliminary review, Karen found that Horizon lacked proper segregation of the programming and operating functions. As a result, she intensified the study and evaluation of the system of internal control surrounding the computer and concluded that the existing compensating general controls provided reasonable assurance that the objectives of the system of internal control were being met.

Required:
a. In a properly functioning EDP environment, how is the separation of the programming and operating functions achieved?
b. What are the compensating general controls that Karen most likely found? *Do not discuss hardware and application controls.*

(AICPA adapted)

C9-6   Rip van Longsleeper, a public accountant, has just emerged from a thirty-year siesta and is attempting to reactivate his public accounting practice. On his first audit engagement, he finds that his client's records are maintained on reels of magnetic tape. He examines one reel and, even by using a magnifying glass, is unable to read anything on it. He does not understand how he can audit financial data that he cannot see.

---

*Donn B. Parker, "Further Comment on the Equity Funding Insurance Fraud Case," *EDPACS* (January 1975): 16. Used with permission of *EDPACS, The EDP Audit, Control, and Security Newsletter*, 11250 Roger Bacon Drive, Suite 17, Reston, Va. 22090.

Required: Explain to Mr. Longsleeper how he should proceed with the audit of computerized accounting records.

C9-7   Talbert Corporation hired an independent computer programmer to develop a simplified payroll application for its newly purchased computer. The programmer developed an on-line, data base microcomputer system that minimized the level of knowledge required by the operator. It was based on typing answers to input cues that appeared on the terminal's viewing screen, examples of which follow:

   a. Access routine:
      1. Operator access number to payroll file?
      2. Are there new employees?

   b. New employees routine:
      1. Employee name?
      2. Employee number?
      3. Social security number?
      4. Rate per hour?
      5. Single or married?
      6. Number of dependents?
      7. Account distribution?

   c. Current payroll routine:
      1. Employee number?
      2. Regular hours worked?
      3. Overtime hours worked?
      4. Total employees this payroll period?

The independent auditor is attempting to verify that certain input validation (edit) checks exist to ensure that errors resulting from omissions, invalid entries, or other inaccuracies will be detected during the typing of answers to the input cues.

Required: Identify the various types of input validation (edit) checks the independent auditor would expect to find in the computerized payroll system. Describe the assurances provided by each identified validation check. Do not discuss the review and evaluation of these controls.

C9-8   Ajax, Inc., an audit client, recently installed a new EDP system to process more efficiently the shipping, billing, and accounts receivable records. During interim work, an assistant completed the review of the accounting system and the internal accounting controls. The assistant determined the following information concerning the new EDP system and the processing and control of shipping notices and customer invoices.

Each major computerized function (i.e., shipping, billing, accounts receivable, etc.) is permanently assigned to a specific computer operator who is responsible for making program changes, running the program, and reconciling the computer log. Responsibility for the custody and control over the magnetic tapes and system documentation is randomly rotated among the computer operators on a monthly basis to prevent any one person from having access to the tapes and documentation at all times. Each computer programmer and computer operator has access to the computer room via a magnetic card and a digital code that is different for each card. The systems analyst and the supervisor of the computer operators do not have access to the computer room.

The EDP system documentation consists of the following items: program listing, error listing, logs, and record layout. To increase efficiency, batch totals and processing controls are omitted from the system.

Ajax ships its products directly from two warehouses, which forward shipping notices to general accounting. There, the billing clerk enters the price of the item and accounts for the numerical sequence of the shipping notices. The billing clerk also prepares daily adding machine tapes of the units shipped and the sales amounts. Shipping notices and adding machine tapes are forwarded to the computer department for processing. The computer output consists of

1. A three-copy invoice that is forwarded to the billing clerk, and
2. A daily sales register showing the aggregate totals of units shipped and sales amounts that the computer operator compares to the adding machine tapes.

The billing clerk mails two copies of each invoice to the customer and retains the third copy in an open invoice file that serves as a detail accounts receivable record.

Required:

1. Describe the weaknesses and inefficiencies that you see in the above system.
2. For each weakness and inefficiency, describe one specific recommendation for improvement. Organize your answer as follows:

Weakness	Recommended Improvement

(AICPA adapted)

Problems

P9-1 Select the best answer for each of the following items relating to computerized accounting records.

a. An EDP technique that collects data into groups to permit convenient and efficient processing is known as
1. Document-count processing.
2. Multiprogramming.
3. Batch processing.
4. Generalized-audit processing.

b. Which of the following employees in a company's EDP department should be responsible for designing new or improved data-processing procedures?
1. Flowchart editor.
2. Programmer.
3. Systems analyst.
4. Control group supervisor.

c. Any assessment of the operational capabilities of a computer system must consider downtime. Even in a fully protected system, downtime will exist because of
1. Electrical power losses.
2. Unscheduled maintenance.
3. Unauthorized entry.
4. Keypunching errors.

d. Adequate technical training and proficiency as an auditor encompasses an ability to understand an EDP system sufficiently to identify and evaluate

1. The processing and imparting of information.
2. Essential accounting control features.
3. All accounting control features.
4. The degree to which programming conforms with the application of generally accepted accounting principles.

(AICPA adapted)

P9-2   Select the best answer to each of the following items relating to general controls over electronic data processing (EDP).

a. Which of the following *best* describes a fundamental control weakness often associated with EDP systems?
1. EDP equipment is more subject to systems error than manual processing is subject to human error.
2. EDP equipment processes and records similar transactions in a similar manner.
3. EDP procedures for detection of invalid and unusual transactions are less effective than manual control procedures.
4. Functions that would normally be separated in a manual system are combined in the EDP department.

b. An auditor's investigation of a company's EDP control procedures has disclosed the following four circumstances. Indicate which circumstance constitutes a weakness in internal control.
1. Machine operators do not have access to the complete run manual.
2. Machine operators are closely supervised by programmers.
3. Programmers do not have the authorization to operate equipment.
4. Only one generation of backup files is stored in an off-premises location.

c. Some EDP accounting control procedures relate to all electronic data-processing activities (general controls) and some relate to specific tasks (application controls). General controls include
1. Controls designed to ascertain that all data submitted for processing have been properly authorized.
2. Controls that relate to the correction and resubmission of data that was initially incorrect.
3. Controls for documenting and approving programs and changes to programs.
4. Controls designed to ensure the accuracy of the processing results.

d. When erroneous data are detected by computer program controls, such data may be excluded from processing and printed on an error report. The error report should most probably be reviewed and followed up by the
1. Supervisor of computer operations.
2. Systems analyst.
3. EDP control group.
4. Computer programmer.

e. One of the major problems in an EDP system is that incompatible functions may be performed by the same individual. One compensating control for this is the use of
1. Echo checks.
2. A self-checking digit system.
3. Computer generated hash totals.
4. A computer log.

    f. When an on-line, realtime (OLRT) electronic data-processing system is in use, internal control can be strengthened by

      1. Providing for the separation of duties between keypunching and error-listing operations.

      2. Attaching plastic file-protection rings to reels of magnetic tape before new data can be entered on the file.

      3. Making a validity check of an identification number before a user can obtain access to the computer files.

      4. Preparing batch totals to provide assurance that file updates are made for the entire input.

(AICPA adapted)

P9-3   Select the best answer for each of the following items relating to application controls within an EDP system.

    a. A procedural control used in the management of a computer center to minimize the possibility of data or program file destruction through operator error includes

      1. Control figures.

      2. Cross-footing tests.

      3. Limit checks.

      4. External labels.

    b. A customer inadvertently ordered part number 12368 rather than part number 12638. In processing this order, the error would be detected by the vendor with which of the following controls?

      1. Batch total.

      2. Key verifying.

      3. Self-checking digit.

      4. An internal consistency check.

    c. An advantage of manual processing is that human processors may note data errors and irregularities. To replace the human element of error detection associated with manual processing, a well-designed electronic data-processing system should introduce

      1. Programmed limits.

      2. Dual circuitry.

      3. Echo checks.

      4. Read after write.

    d. Which of the following is an example of application controls in electronic data-processing systems?

      1. Input controls.

      2. Hardware controls.

      3. Documentation procedures.

      4. Controls over access to equipment and data files.

    e. The grandfather, father, son approach to providing protection for important computer files is a concept that is most often found in

      1. On-line realtime systems.

      2. Punched-card systems.

      3. Magnetic tape systems.

      4. Magnetic drum systems.

(AICPA adapted)

P9-4 Select the best answer for each of the following items relating to more sophisticated computer systems.

  a. What is the computer process called when data processing is performed concurrently with a particular activity and the results are available soon enough to influence the particular course of action being taken or the decision being made?

   1. Realtime processing.

   2. Batch processing.

   3. Random-access processing.

   4. Integrated data processing.

  b. Which of the following is a characteristic of an integrated system for data processing?

   1. An integrated system is a realtime system, in which files for different functions with similar information are separated.

   2. A single input record describing a transaction initiates the updating of all files associated with the transaction.

   3. Parallel operations strengthen internal control over the computer processing function.

   4. Files are maintained according to organizational functions, such as purchasing, accounts payable, sales, etc.

  c. When an on-line, realtime (OLRT) electronic data-processing system is in use, internal control can be strengthened by

   1. Providing for the separation of duties between keypunching and other listing operations.

   2. Attaching plastic file-protection rings to reels of magnetic tape before new data can be entered on the file.

   3. Preparing batch totals to provide assurance that file updates are made for the entire input.

   4. Making a validity check of an identification number before a user can obtain access to the computer files.

  d. A management information system is designed to ensure that management possesses the information it needs to carry out its functions through the integrated actions of

   1. Data-gathering, analysis, and reporting functions.

   2. A computerized information retrieval and decision-making system.

   3. Statistical and analytical review functions.

   4. Production-budgeting and sales-forecasting activities.

  e. Which of the following is necessary to audit balances in an on-line EDP system in an environment of destructive updating?

   1. Periodic dumping of transaction files.

   2. Year-end utilization of audit hooks.

   3. An integrated test facility.

   4. A well-documented audit trail.

(AICPA adapted)

P9-5 When auditing an electronic data-processing (EDP) accounting system, the independent auditor should have a general familiarity with the effects of the use of EDP on the various characteristics of accounting control and on the auditor's study and evaluation of such control. The independent auditor must be aware of those control procedures commonly referred to as *general* controls and those commonly referred to as *application* controls. General controls relate to all EDP activities, and application controls relate to specific accounting tasks.

Required:
  a. What are the general controls that should exist in EDP-based accounting systems?
  b. What are the purposes of each of the following categories of application controls?
     1. Input controls.
     2. Processing controls.
     3. Output controls.

(AICPA adapted)

P9-6 The following topics are part of the relevant body of knowledge for CPAs having field work or immediate supervisory responsibility in audits involving a computer.
  a. Electronic data-processing (EDP) equipment and its capabilities.
  b. Organization and management of the data-processing function.
  c. Characteristics of computer-based systems.
  d. Fundamentals of computer programming.
  e. Computer center operations.
  CPAs who are responsible for computer audits should possess certain general knowledge with respect to each of these five topics. For example, on the subject of EDP equipment and its capabilities, the auditor should have a general understanding of computer equipment and should be familiar with the uses and capabilities of the central processor and the peripheral equipment.

Required: For each of topics **b–e** above, describe the general knowledge that should be possessed by those CPAs responsible for computer audits.

(AICPA adapted)

P9-7 When auditing the financial statements of a client who utilizes electronic data processing, it is important for the CPA to understand the essential characteristics of the client's system and the controls that are built into it.

Required:
  a. Describe how the client's EDP department should be organized to maximize internal control over processing activities. Include in your description how the EDP department should relate to the rest of the client's organization.
  b. An effective system of internal control also requires effective controls over source data as they flow into and out of the computer. These controls include input controls, processing controls, and output controls. List the characteristics of an effective system of input, processing, and output controls in a batch-controlled system.

(AICPA adapted)

P9-8 An extract from the problem statement section of the run manual for the pension fund accounting program of the Riley Insurance Company reads as follows:
  Persons who are 60 years of age or over when commencing employment are not eligible for the pension plan. All other employees automatically become members during the 37th month of continuous employment, and each employee's pension fund contribution will be deducted on the employee's payroll check each month thereafter.

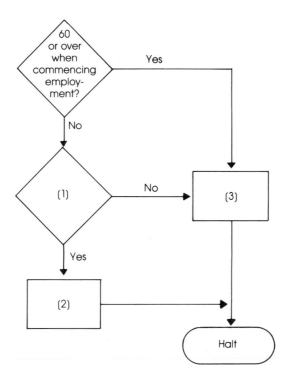

Required:
  a. Numbered symbol (1) in the above flowchart should be replaced by which of the following statements?
     1. Deduct pension fund contribution.
     2. Print ineligibility list.
     3. Employed more than 36 months?
     4. Employed more than 37 months?
  b. Numbered symbol (2) should be replaced by which of the following statements?
     1. Deduct pension fund contribution.
     2. Print ineligibility list.
     3. Employed more than 36 months?
     4. Employed more than 37 months?
  c. Numbered symbol (3) should be replaced by which of the following statements?
     1. Deduct pension fund contribution.
     2. Print ineligibility list.
     3. Employed more than 36 months?
     4. Employed more than 37 months?

(AICPA adapted)

P9-9   You are reviewing audit working papers containing a narrative description of the Tenney Corporation's factory payroll system. A portion of that narrative is as follows:
     Factory employees punch time-clock cards each day when entering or leaving the shop. At the end of each week, the timekeeping department collects the time cards and

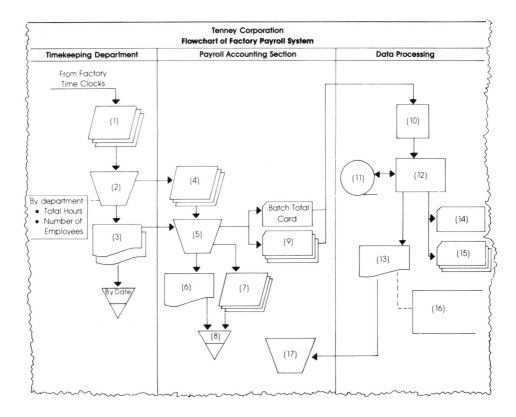

prepares duplicate batch-control slips by department showing total hours and number of employees. The time cards and original batch-control slips are sent to the payroll accounting section. The second copies of the batch-control slips are filed by date.

In the payroll accounting section, payroll transaction cards are keypunched from the information on the time cards, and a batch total card for each batch is keypunched from the batch-control slip. The time cards and batch-control slips are then filed by batch for possible reference. The payroll transaction cards and batch total card are sent to data processing, where they are sorted by employee number within batch. Each batch is edited by a computer program, which checks the validity of employee number against a master employee tape file and the total hours and number of employees against the batch total card. A detailed printout by batch and employee number, which indicates batches that do not balance and invalid employee numbers, is produced. This printout is returned to payroll accounting to resolve all differences.

In searching for documentation you found a flowchart of the payroll system, which included all appropriate symbols (American National Standards Institute, Inc.) but was only partially labeled. The portion of this flowchart described by the preceding narrative appears above.

Required:

a. Number your answer 1 through 17. Next to the corresponding number of your answer, supply the appropriate label (document name, process description, or file order) applicable to each numbered symbol on the flowchart.

b. Flowcharts are one of the aids an auditor may use to determine and evaluate a client's internal control system. List advantages of using flowcharts in this context.

(AICPA adapted)

P9-10 You are assigned to review the documentation of a data-processing function.

Required:

a. List three advantages of adequate documentation for a data-processing function.

b. Below are two columns of information. The left column lists six categories of documentation, and the right column lists eighteen elements of documentation related to the categories. Match each of the elements of documentation with the category in which it should be found. List letters **a** through **f** on your answer sheet. After each letter, list the numbers of the elements that best apply to that category. Use every element, but none more than once.

Categories

- **a.** Systems documentation.
- **b.** Program documentation.
- **c.** Operations documentation.
- **d.** User documentation.
- **e.** Library documentation.
- **f.** Data-entry documentation.

Elements

1. Flowcharts showing the flow of information.
2. Procedures needed to balance, reconcile, and maintain overall control.
3. Storage instructions.
4. Contents and format of data to be captured.
5. Constants, codes, and tables.
6. Verification procedures.
7. Logic diagrams and/or decision tables.
8. Report distribution instructions.
9. Message and programmed halts.
10. Procedures for backup files.
11. Retention cycle.
12. Source statement listings.
13. Instructions to show proper use of each transaction.
14. A complete history from planning through installation.
15. Restart and recovery procedures.
16. Rules for handling blank spaces.
17. Instructions to ensure the proper completion of all input forms.
18. List of programs in a system.

(CIA Examination adapted)

P9-11 General controls and applications controls are well-established principles in the accounting literature for companies that utilize mainframe computers. In these companies, EDP departments are organizationally autonomous, with each of the other departments acting as users. More and more companies, however, are beginning to utilize microcomputers as well as mainframe machines. The use of microcomputers has the effect of decentralizing, to some degree, the data-processing function, thus creating new challenges for the systems designer and the auditor with regard to general and applications controls.

Required:
a. Enumerate some *general controls* problems that face companies utilizing microcomputers.
b. Explain the concept of *networking*. What are its advantages for data processing? What are its disadvantages with respect to controls?
c. What specific *applications controls* are particularly useful when microcomputers are used in data processing? For each application control listed, briefly explain its purpose.

P9-12   We have stated in this chapter that the computer has changed the data-processing environment within which auditors must practice.

Required: What are the ways in which the control environment for a system that utilizes EDP differs from that of a manual system? What are the implications for the auditor and how is his or her work affected by these changes?

PART

Auditing Tools and Techniques

CHAPTER 10

The Computer as an Auditing Tool

Objectives

☐ **1.** Use computer for audit planning.
☐ **2.** Use computer to understand control structure.
☐ **3.** Use computer for substantive testing.
☐ **4.** Use computer for review and reporting phases of the audit.

When businesses first started using computers, two terms were used to describe the auditor's involvement with computer-generated records. These terms were **auditing around the computer** and **auditing through the computer**. Auditing around the computer basically calls for the auditor to perform auditing procedures (vouching, tracing, scanning, etc.) on the input and output data without the necessity of knowing what goes on inside the *black box*. Auditing around the computer is still done today in installations that involve relatively simple computer applications and that leave an extensive hard-copy (printout) trail of documentation. In such installations, the computer is used mostly as a high-speed calculator and bookkeeping machine, performing mostly clerical activities. The extensive hard copy that is generated can be audited in much the same way that manually prepared documents are audited.

Modern technological improvements have allowed computers to be involved in much more complex activities than merely processing data. Computers are now performing approval, recordkeeping, and asset-handling functions, often without leaving visible evidence of controls being performed or a hard-copy audit trail. In that kind of environment, it is essential to *audit through the computer* to obtain evidence relating to internal controls. Furthermore, in meeting the third standard of field work, auditors have learned to use the computer to gather evidence. The term we use for such usage is **auditing with the computer**.

Our discussion covers both the more established ways of using mainframe audit software and the more recently developed use of microcomputers in the audit. The techniques described in this chapter are used both by independent auditors and by internal auditors.

Use of the Computer during the Planning Stages of the Audit

Figure 10–1 describes and lists the advantages and disadvantages of some mainframe computerized techniques for audit planning and management.[1] Many of those techniques are used only by internal auditors, because the nature of their work is more detailed and extensive than that of the independent auditor. However, as technology improves and becomes more cost-feasible, such computerized methods could also be used in a typical financial-statement audit.

Audit area selection is used to identify high-risk areas among comparable units such as geographical areas. For example, suppose an internal or independent auditor for a casualty insurance company wished to examine loss claims for proper documentation. To be most effective the audit should focus on geographical regions where risk of loss is high. To identify those areas, a number of key indicators, such as number of claims filed, number of policyholder complaints, and other factors, should be examined. An audit package that has the ability to scan computerized files and to identify key data by specified criteria can then be used in planning the examination of the loss claims. Such techniques improve the efficiency and overall quality of the audit. However, similar operations are required in all geographical regions for data files to be appropriately computer accessible.

Simulation and modeling uses key indicators to build statistical models, which can be used to predict the level of an activity in an entity to be audited. If the actual activity deviates substantially from the model, the auditors should investigate to determine the causes of the deviation. For example, internal auditors for companies with branch sales activities might build a model to predict sales based on the number of past orders processed, economic trends, and so forth. Actual activity would then be compared with the model, and significant fluctuations from expectations would be examined. The key advantage of modeling for

Figure 10–1

Mainframe Computerized Planning Techniques

Technique	Description	Advantages	Disadvantages
Audit area selection	Examines key indicator information for location of areas to audit	Improves audit efficiency	Requires similar operations in all locations
Simulation/modeling	Compares expected values to actual values; identifies important differences	Uses live data for analysis	Costly
Scoring	Assigns scores to various systems; classifies by auditability	Sets audit priorities	Requires careful evaluation

Source: W. Thomas Porter and William E. Perry, *EDP Controls and Auditing.* 5th ed. (Boston: Kent Publishing Company, 1987). Used with permission.

planning purposes is that live data may be used for analysis. The chief disadvantage of the technique is its relatively high cost.

Scoring is a technique that helps the auditor select high-risk areas among unlike systems or activities, using external measurement characteristics. For example, internal auditors for an insurance company might use such a system to determine insurability of applicants. Life insurance applicants would be scored based on age, occupation, weight, and whether the person is a smoker, among other factors. The same concept can be applied in determining the areas to be audited. Characteristics such as the number of transactions processed, employee turnover, the number of customer complaints, and others can be used to score a particular area to determine whether it should be audited. The Internal Revenue Service uses this kind of system to identify particular tax returns for audit.

The microcomputer, with its advantages of power, speed, accuracy, and portability, is an indispensable audit tool. Almost all major CPA firms have developed microcomputer software for use in various phases of the audit. Typical uses during the planning stage of the audit are listed in Figure 10–2. The auditor may use the microcomputer to *perform preliminary analytical* procedures by computing key ratios for current and prior periods, making comparisons of those ratios and other data with similar data from other industries, and thus assisting in the assessment of inherent risk of the firm or particular account balances being audited.

Spreadsheet technology, such as LOTUS 1-2-3, SuperCalc, Excel, and others, are being developed for such critical audit tasks as time budgeting and control. In addition, spreadsheet technology is adaptable to the preparation of audit working trial balances, lead schedules, and supporting schedules. The advantage of this tool lies in the fact that, as audit adjustments are found and entries for those adjustments are prepared, the *software will post them not only to the working trial balance but also to all applicable working papers throughout the series*, thus saving time and effort.

The auditor of the twenty-first century will need to perform the role of business analyst more than ever before. Businesses, faced with high costs of capital, need assistance in planning for future expansion and growth. CPA firms, using the popular spreadsheet technology described above, have developed microcomputer software that will make necessary budget calculations for operating,

Figure 10–2

Microcomputer Software Used in Audit Planning

Planning function	Software capability
Preliminary risk analysis	Computes key ratios; makes comparisons over time and with average industry ratios to help determine audit risk
Time budget preparation	Spreadsheet template keeps track of audit time budgeted and spent by each area of activity
Automated working papers	Spreadsheet template prepares working trial balance, lead schedules, and adjusting entries

cash, and capital expenditure decisions. Thus, the accountant is better able to serve clients, as well as to evaluate risk in current audit situations, by using these technological improvements.

Appendix 10–A contains examples of time budget forms, proposed adjusting entry (scoresheet) work sheets, and other necessary audit information that can be prepared using the microcomputer. Some auditors have predicted that by the end of the 1990s most audit work will be documented in this way.

Use of the Computer to Obtain an Understanding of the Internal Control Structure

☑ **Objective 2**
Use computer to understand control structure

Our discussion in this section will focus on *auditing through the computer*. In Figure 10–3 we show the techniques used to perform tests on mainframe computers for *controls that leave no visible evidence of having been performed*. These controls were discussed in Chapter 9 and include *programmed checks* such as validity tests, limit and reasonableness tests, and other tests that utilize the editing capabilities designed into the computer software.

Figure 10–3

Techniques for Auditing *Through* the Computer: Controls

Technique	Description	Advantages	Disadvantages
Test-data method	Verifies processing accuracy of computer application systems by executing these systems using specially prepared sets of input data that produce preestablished results	Verifies processing logic and controls	Time-consuming if extensive tests performed
Parallel simulation	Use of one or more special computer programs to process "live" data through test programs	Uses the same data as the production run	Time and cost to develop
Integrated test facility	Uses auditor-developed fictitious or dummy entity within the framework of the regular application-processing cycle.	Evaluates system in normal operating environment	Difficult to back out test transactions
Continuous monitoring	Used in on-line, realtime systems to tag transactions as processed by the system	Effective for on-line operations. Auditors can supply their own criteria through on-line terminals	Unauthorized access to client data files

Source: Adapted from W. Thomas Porter and William E. Perry, *EDP Controls and Auditing*, 5th ed. (Boston: Kent Publishing Company, 1987): 426. Used with permission.

In the **test data approach**, the auditor first obtains duplicate copies of the client's master programs (usually on magnetic tape). The object of the test data is to test the controls included in each program (as shown in Figure 10–4). This is done by preparing a series of hypothetical transactions to be processed with the duplicate copy of the client's master program. Some of the transactions will be valid (i.e., no program checks, limits, or control amounts violated). Other transactions will violate the controls supposedly incorporated into the program. Thus, as the hypothetical transactions are run, the program checks should identify the invalid transactions and print them on an error listing or exception report. For example, suppose that the client's payroll master program prescribed a limit test of 60 hours a week. To test this program control, the auditor might insert in the test data a transaction that contains 60.5 hours in a pay period. If the control is performing as prescribed, the program should pinpoint the exception and include it in an error list or exception report. The use of test data is a relatively simple, fast, and inexpensive way to test programmed controls if only one or two controls are tested. However, the method can be time-consuming and, therefore, expensive if multiple tests are performed. In addition, this approach has the following other weaknesses:

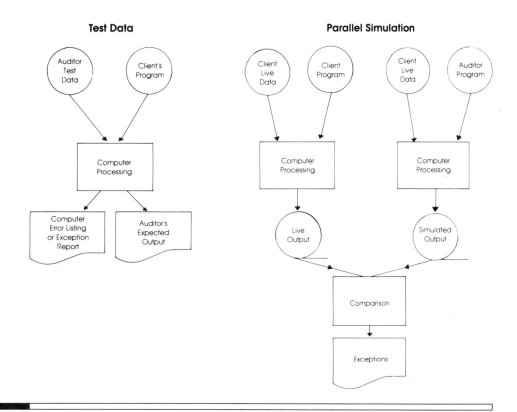

Figure 10–4

Comparison of Test Data and Parallel Simulation Approaches for Tests of Controls

- Since the program tested is usually a duplicate program supplied by the client, the auditor has no assurance that he or she is testing the program actually used by the client, unless the program is intercepted immediately after processing and duplicated at that point.
- Controls tested with test data are those that exist only at a point in time (i.e., when the test data is being processed). There is no provision for testing controls over the entire audit period unless repetitive tests are made.
- With test data, there is no opportunity to examine the documentation actually processed by the system.
- The scope of the test data approach is limited to the auditor's imagination. It is important, therefore, to be very careful in developing erroneous hypothetical transactions that would reveal material weaknesses in internal control.

Parallel simulation (sometimes called *controlled reprocessing*) utilizes *live* client data that is reprocessed with an auditor-controlled program (Figure 10–4). Usually the software used in parallel simulation is a generalized audit program prepared by the auditor. It consists of a series of specialized computer subroutines designed to perform the same process and produce the same result as the client's programs. The output of this system is then compared with the client's output from the same processing operation. Exception reports can then be prepared and investigated by the auditor.

Parallel simulation may be performed at various interim dates during the audit period. It may also be applied to the reprocessing of historical data. Parallel simulation has several advantages over the test data approach. For one thing, the auditor is using duplicate files of real client data, which can be verified by vouching transactions to source documents and approvals. Additionally, since the auditor's simulated system is separate from the client's, the simulated data can be processed at an independent facility. Furthermore, sample sizes in this approach can be greated expanded at relatively small costs.

The major disadvantage of parallel simulation is the time, effort, and expense of producing the program. Both the initial cost and the cost of the yearly update to keep the program current can be significant. Since the client will ultimately be billed for this cost, the auditor will have to convince the client that the program's ultimate benefits exceed those costs.

The **integrated test facility (ITF) approach** involves the creation of a *dummy* or fictitious subsystem (or *minicompany*) within the client's EDP system. The auditor then processes fictitious data for the minicompany simultaneously with client's live data and appends those records to the client's regular system. Test data specially coded to correspond with the *dummy* master files should contain all kinds of errors and exceptions, similar to the test data approach described earlier.

The ITF approach is the only advanced auditing technique that enables the auditor to *enter test data into a live computer run* for the purpose of tracking down errors in processing. Thus, the auditor has the assurance that he or she is testing the actual program that is being used to process live data. For example, an auditor could establish a dummy customer account receivable, which would be included in the client's customer account list. The auditor would then enter fictitious client sales in that account. The auditor could receive merchandise from the organization at a preestablished address, receive the invoice, pay the invoice (or elect not to pay), return merchandise and perform any other activity that might prove a fruitful area on which to test controls.

The major disadvantage of the ITF approach is that the results of dummy transactions might not be removed completely from the accounting records before financial statements are prepared, thus contaminating the client's master files. Some companies have provided for the removal of the extraneous data by inserting special routines into the application program to reverse the test transactions. Other companies have accomplished the task by letting the test transactions flow completely through the system and into hands of the internal auditor, who then makes the adjusting entries. In either case, it is necessary to let all dummy transactions be accumulated into a special account, for ease and completeness of processing when the reversing journal entries are made.

Controls testing in an on-line, realtime system can involve the use of test data. However, contamination of master files is especially hazardous in on-line options. To avoid such contamination, the computer must be programmed to reverse the *dummy* test transactions, which is often difficult. Usefulness of parallel simulation is also limited because of the great difficulty involved in simulating an on-line, realtime system.

Continuous monitoring is a technique that is often used in testing transactions entered into an on-line, realtime system. With this method, an audit routine is added to the client's master program. Transactions are sampled at random intervals, and output from the audit routine is used to test controls. To provide for such monitoring, *audit modules* or *audit hooks* must be built into the client's operating and applications programs. These modules provide a means for the auditor to select a transaction that exceeds certain limits (e.g., a dollar amount) for testing. Once the audit hook has identified the transaction, the computer can be programmed to *tag the transaction and to trace it through the system as it is processed*. The computer can then be programmed to provide a hard-copy printout of the paths followed by the transaction as well as the data with which the transaction interacts in processing. An alternative method to tagging is the use of an *audit log*, which records transactions selected for audit in a special file, available only to the auditor, for the purpose of making further audit tests.

Continuous monitoring is one of the few effective auditing control techniques that can be used in an on-line or micro/mainframe-interfaced system. This technique can be used without interfering with the client's normal processing routines. Some audit firms are developing the capability of hard-wiring terminals to clients' mainframe computers so that they can enter their own audit testing criteria directly into the system. One major disadvantage of this technique is that it can cause slowdowns in the normal processing of data, especially if many transactions are selected for audit. There is also a problem of possible access by unauthorized users with this method. For that reason, the auditor's edit criteria for the monitoring process should be kept confidential and should not be disclosed to client personnel except on a selected basis.

Auditing *with* the Computer: Use of the Computer during the Substantive Testing Phase of the Audit

☑ **Objective 3**
Use the computer for substantive testing

When significant accounting applications are performed using EDP equipment and accounting data are maintained only in machine-readable form (magnetic tapes; disks; etc.), it may be cost-effective to use the computer to perform auditing procedures. In those situations, the auditor may use either the client's computer or an auditor-controlled computer (such as a service center) to perform many of the tedious auditing procedures historically performed manually. The basic capabilities of computer software to perform the extraction and verification of balances procedures are summarized in Figure 10–5. These include special-purpose audit programs, generalized audit software, and terminal audit software.

Computer audit software may be used in performing a variety of auditing procedures, such as

- Recomputing data, such as depreciation charges, footing (addition) of sales, inventory, accounts receivable, and property and equipment files. Because of the computer's great speed and accuracy, most of these calculations can be 100 percent verified, often at lower cost than auditing a sample of them manually.
- Sorting various data files by any criteria selected by the auditor. As an example, inventory files may be sorted by location for use when performing inventory-observation procedures.
- Calculating sample sizes and selecting sample items, using various statistical techniques.

Figure 10–5

Auditing *with* the Computer: Techniques to Perform Audit Verification of Financial Statement Amounts

Techniques	Description	Advantages	Disadvantages
Special-purpose audit programs	Specially tailored programs to extract and present data from a specific application system's files, usually in an invariable format	Auditors learn intricacies of EDP operations	High level of EDP experience required
Generalized audit software	A set of computer programs that have the capability to process computer data files under the control of input parameters supplied by the auditor	Extract languages designed for auditors	Operational inefficiencies
Terminal audit software	Accesses, extracts, manipulates, and displays data from on-line data bases using remote-terminal inquiry commands	Terminal operation	Same as any on-line system

Source: W. Thomas Porter and William E. Perry, *EDP Controls and Auditing*, 5th ed. (Boston: Kent Publishing Company, 1987): 427. Used with permission.

- Performing analytical procedures, such as computation of ratios over a period of time or comparison of absolute dollar amounts with percentage fluctuations over time.
- Aging of accounts receivable, computing inventory turnover item-by-item, and performing other mathematical analyses that would be very cumbersome and time-consuming if performed manually.
- Making comparisons of book- and otherwise-determined data for various fields and calculating differences between those amounts. For example, inventory test counts can be compared with those listed on the client's final inventory listing, and a printout of differences can be generated for the auditor's review.
- Scanning the accounting records for unusual items, such as credit balances in accounts receivable or obsolete or slow-moving inventory items. Exceptional items can be printed out on hard copy for the auditor's further investigation.

Special-Purpose Audit Programs

Special-Purpose Audit Programs.   Programs may be written in the same programming language as that used by the client in the application program. Such languages include COBOL, RPG, BASIC, or FORTRAN. Sometimes the **special-purpose audit programs** are used because the objectives cannot be achieved using a generalized audit software language (discussed later). In other instances, the auditors may not have a generalized audit software package available. In some cases, such programs may be *written by the client*. For example, the client's internal audit staff may regularly age accounts receivable and perform various financial ratio analyses to effectively manage day-to-day activities of the company. As a result, the client may already have programs available that can be adapted for the auditor's use. However, if the programs are written by the client, there is a risk that the *auditor's independence may be compromised*. Therefore, if a client-prepared computer audit program is used, it will be necessary for the auditor to test the program thoroughly to determine whether it can be relied upon to produce the desired results. The extent of program verification will depend to some extent on the results of the study of controls over programs and operations. At a minimum, the auditor will need to review the client's program documentation and run book. It is generally also important for the auditor to perform tests to demonstrate that the program actually performs the required functions. Preferably, these tests should be performed at an independent data-processing facility.

The auditor can avoid the testing required in the use of client-prepared programs by having experts at his or her firm write the program. The procedures for doing this are the same as those required for the development of any other computer program. In general, this involves the following five steps, *for each application*:

1. Determining the required audit objectives and procedures, and preparing a document that defines, in detail, the required processing.

2. Developing a systems flowchart that includes all inputs, outputs, and major processing steps.
3. Developing program specifications using flowcharts, decision tables, and/or narratives that describe program logic and processing steps.
4. Coding, debugging, and testing.
5. Processing and reviewing results.

The extent to which the auditor can perform each of these functions varies from engagement to engagement and might depend on such factors as the auditor's knowledge of data processing and competence in developing computer programs, the complexity of the programs being developed, the source language being used, and the availability of client assistance. It is, in any event, a *time-consuming and expensive process*, particularly when we consider that the program's use will be limited to a specific client and that the audit program must be continuously monitored and revised for the client's program changes.

Generalized Audit Software

To overcome the disadvantages that are associated with the two sources of audit programs discussed above, most CPA firms have developed **generalized audit software**. These packages, when used with appropriate job control programs, can perform approximately the same wide range of computer audit functions that were discussed above without the disadvantages associated with tailored audit programs. Generalized audit software consists of a set of very powerful computer subroutines activated by a very simple user command language. Training is minimal, and, to the extent that the software is adaptable to several clients, the cost of using it over time is significantly less than for developing and using special-purpose programs.

One approach to developing generalized audit software is to create a series of programs, each of which is applicable to clients in a particular industry. For example, many CPA firms make extensive use of generalized audit software in audits of savings-and-loan or other financial institutions. Another approach has been to develop an audit software package that can be used for all clients with limited adaptations from client to client. For example, if a CPA firm has a computer-auditing package that can be used for accounts-receivable confirmation work, and the package is adaptable to several clients' hardware configurations, it can be used to confirm receivables for a hospital on one day and a manufacturing concern the next day.

The audit software packages used by the larger public accounting firms and selected corporations and agencies are listed in Appendix 10–B. These audit software packages are all written to perform a variety of functions, a partial list of which is shown in Figure 10–6. We also provide an example of the application of each function to the audit of inventories.

As shown here, generalized computer audit programs are designed to perform a wide range of audit functions on computerized records. Observe, however, that the computer *does not replace the auditor*. Rather, use of the computer to

Figure 10-6 ▬▬▬▬

Capabilities of Generalized Audit Software

Function	Inventory application
Scanning or examining computer records for exceptional or unusual conditions and listing items that violate those conditions	Scanning the inventory files for unusually slow-moving items, based on date of last sale or excessively long inventory turnover period
Making or checking computations and listing those items that are incorrect, based on criteria specified by the auditor	Calculation of inventory turnover; identification of items for which turnover is slow
Comparing data on different computer records or files, and listing unusual or irregular results	Test counts entered on computer input records can be compared with counts for same items listed on final inventory listing. Differences are then extended by unit cost
Selected samples of various types from computerized records	Computation of statistically valid sample size from auditor-specified criteria; selection of random sample; ordering of sample; printout of results
Checking computations and printouts of client computations that are incorrect	Recalculation of inventory extensions (units × cost); comparison with extended cost-per-client records; printout of amounts that are incorrect
Preparing various analyses and listings that facilitate the audit examination of the account	Analytical procedures, computation of gross profit percentage, inventory turnover ratios; comparison of percentages, ratios, and absolute dollar values with those of prior periods

perform the repetitive, mechanical tasks of the audit *frees the auditor* to perform the needed inquiries, make the necessary specifications, and perform the tasks that require judgments that only human beings can provide. The use of the computer should make the task of auditing more stimulating and challenging and should allow the auditor to obtain a higher level of satisfaction from the audit by knowing that the client has been served better.

In using mainframe generalized audit software, it is necessary to adapt the package to the specific application requirements of each individual audit. This requires the auditor to obtain knowledge in the following areas:

- The characteristics of the computer system being audited, including its input/output devices.
- The format desired for the work files (duplicate files of selected client data) produced by the software.
- The characteristics of the client's files (location of data records in the file, etc.).
- The functions to be performed.
- The calculations required.
- The characteristics of the required reports.[2]

The relationships between the client's files, the auditor's specifications, the generalized audit program, and the work file records produced by those inputs are illustrated in Figure 10-7.

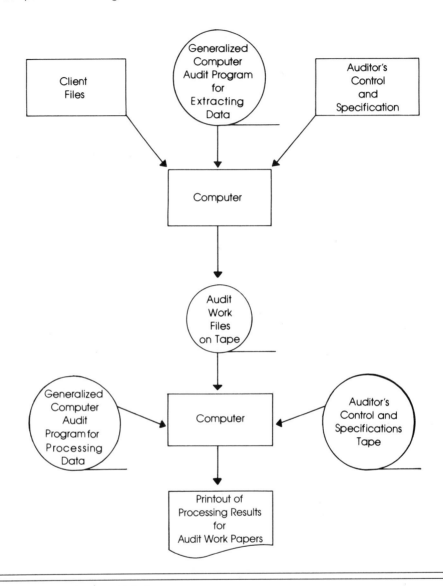

Figure 10–7

Use of Generalized Audit Software

Steps in Developing and Using Generalized Audit Software

We find at least four distinct steps followed by the auditor in developing and using generalized computer audit software packages. These steps include the following:

- A study and planning phase.
- Development of an overall flowchart and other documentary support for the audit software.

- Coding and testing the software package.
- Use of the software package in an actual audit situation.[3]

Planning the Software Package.   The first portion of the planning phase calls for a definition of the audit objective to be achieved by the software package. The computer is expected to carry out certain functions that assist the auditor in performing auditing procedures. That in turn requires the auditor to use a preliminary audit program including as much detail as possible. The objectives in using the computerized program should be consistent with the elements of that audit program.

   Next, the auditor should obtain information from clients about their computer and file characteristics, record layouts, and the availability of files. These data must then be evaluated to determine if they are compatible with the proposed audit software package. If so, the generalized auditing procedures can be finalized, and a working plan can be developed for the other steps described below.

Development of Underlying Documentary Support.   At this point, an overall flowchart should be developed, laying out the planned audit software applications. The audit software application requirements—including logic, calculations, format of reports, and procedures for controlling its application—should be appropriately defined. All these data should then be drawn together into appropriate documentary support in the form of a flowchart for the actual audit software application. After that, the generalized software program should be developed from the flowchart data.

Coding and Testing the Software Package.   The auditor is now ready to code the specification forms required to adapt the general software package to a specific application. Those specifications will be entered via CRT and placed on magnetic tape or disk to provide computer readability. After that, the full package—including the generalized audit software and the specification disk or tape—should be applied to a test file or to a portion of the client's file to prove that the auditor has correctly interpreted the client's file content and has specified the generalized software logic that creates the information necessary to achieve the audit objective.

Using the Computer Audit Package on an Element of the Audit.   After coding and testing, the auditor is ready to use the generalized audit software in combination with the specifications adapting it to the client's computer and records files in the performance of an element of the audit program. Such a software package is typically adaptable to a large number of functions in the actual performance of the audit. The package may be used, for example, to *create a work file* by having the computer read records from a client master file being audited and then create a new file consisting of selected data fields from the master file. The information on the work file may then be subjected to the various auditing procedures without risk of contamination of the client's master files. After processing, audited information from the work file may be printed out and actually become a part of the audit work papers.

The computer may also be used to *sort records* into a new sequence required for calculations, report printing, or other processing. For example, it may be used to resequence the work file into an ascending or descending sequence based on values in auditor-specified sort control fields.

The program can also call for the computer to *calculate certain additional values or to test existing file values.* In performing this function, the computer can, in effect, duplicate the procedures typically performed by the auditor working on human-readable records in verifying client calculations previously incorporated into the accounting records.

The program can also be used to *generate new files* within formats specified by the auditor. In a similar manner, the program can call for the *selection of certain records* or special processing of randomly selected test data from either the client or work records. For example, items recorded showing a value greater than a specified amount can be extracted from the client or work records and either processed in accordance with program specifications or printed out for manual use and for inclusion in the audit work papers.

Obviously, the results of the auditing procedures performed by the computer must, with our present level of audit expertise, ultimately be made available in human-readable form. At some stage, the data being processed by the computer or specified segments of it must be printed out to provide the auditor with visible proof of the results of the computerized auditing procedures.

Appendix 10–C contains an example showing how a typical generalized computer audit software package can be useful during the internal auditor's examination of inventory for accuracy, profitability, and obsolescence.

Terminal Audit Software

The computer audit software that has been discussed to this point in the chapter is designed to run on *batch processing* types of systems. These are systems in which multiple transactions of the same type (sales, purchases, payrolls, etc.) are grouped for processing, using a single program. In contrast, many modern systems call for on-line terminal or microcomputer interface with the mainframe. In such cases, **terminal audit software** can be used to perform substantive tests. Such software allows the auditor to access, extract, manipulate, and display data from the main data base by using remote terminal inquiry commands. This method has basically the same advantages and disadvantages as other on-line methods of auditing. The advantage comes from allowing the auditor to be connected directly to the client's mainframe computer without the inconvenience of having to read entire files of data to extract the needed information. The main disadvantage of the method is the possibility of unauthorized access to sensitive client data files.

Microcomputer Applications for Substantive Tests

As observed earlier, microcomputers can be used to perform a variety of audit functions. Among the substantive tests that can be performed by using appropriate microcomputer software are the following:

- *Statistical sampling*, including the calculation of sample sizes and sample results using mean-per-unit (MPU), difference, ratio, or monetary unit (dollar unit) sampling. These methods are discussed and illustrated in Chapter 12. Appendix 12–C illustrates this procedure using a microcomputer.
- *The preparation of the audit trial balance and lead schedules* with the microcomputer was discussed earlier as we explained how the microcomputer could be used during the planning stages of the audit. As the audit progresses and the auditor discovers errors in the client's records, he or she may also accumulate adjustments on a *scoresheet working paper* for later consideration as to whether the errors are material enough either individually or collectively to necessitate audit-adjusting entries. The scoresheet keeps track of the cumulative effect of the adjustments. The software usually has the capability of moving adjustments one by one into the computer-maintained working trial balance. As this is done, the adjustment is automatically entered on the lead schedules and any supporting schedules that contain the account number. An example of a scoresheet working paper is presented in Appendix 10–A.

Book and Tax Depreciation.   This package has the capability of building a data file of the client's detailed fixed assets. It will compute depreciation expense and accumulated depreciation for both book and tax purposes, as well as differences between book and tax income for purposes of the deferred tax computation and completion of the Schedule M–1 in the Corporate 1120 tax return.

Confirmation Control Systems.   These applications again use a spreadsheet technology (LOTUS 1-2-3, for example) to assist in preparing and monitoring confirmations for accounts receivable, accounts payable, cutoff statements, securities and cash held in trust, notes receivable, accounts with brokers, and notes payable.[4]

LIFO Work Paper Systems.   These LOTUS 1-2-3 packages help monitor the prior years' layers, calculate the current-year increment or decrement, and determine the adjustment and disclosure required for LIFO inventories.[5]

Foreign Currency Translation System.   This LOTUS 1-2-3 application helps translate or remeasure the effects of foreign currency translation on financial statements in accordance with FASB 52. A fluctuation report in local currency helps to analyze and review the financial statement fluctuations.[6]

Debt Analysis System.   This LOTUS 1-2-3 package helps perform overall and detail tests on debt. It *rolls forward* principal balances from the previous year, tests the interest expense and accrual, prepares amortization schedules, and calculates commonly required disclosures.[7]

New microcomputer applications for substantive tests are being developed continuously by most large CPA firms. This fact, coupled with increased portability and power for microcomputers, is fast revolutionizing the field work procedures performed during the modern audit. Executives of many large CPA firms predict that by the end of the 1990s the microcomputer will replace the calculator, pencil, and paper in the typical audit engagement.

Use of the Microcomputer during the Review and Reporting Stages of the Audit

☑ **Objective 4**
Use the computer for audit review and reporting

The person reviewing the working papers can use the same microcomputer audit programs that were used in the substantive testing phases of the audit to review the audit work. For example, final analytical review results may be stored on a hard disk instead of as hard-copy printouts, providing a far more efficient method of reviewing such data. The reviewer would then simply recall the data from the disk and decide on the basis of those data whether the balances appear to be fairly stated in light of the results seen in the remainder of the working papers.

Planning software can be used by audit partners and managers to compute forecasts of operating results, cash flows, and capital budgeting data. These projections can then be discussed with management of the company as it plans for the future. Such services are becoming more and more popular with clients. Thus, it is necessary for auditors to become familiar with them.

Word-processing and *desktop publishing software* can be used by the administrative staff of either the client or the auditing firm to prepare the draft or even the final product of the audited financial statements and the audit report. Such software allows the finished financial statements to be prepared quickly and accurately. It is paticularly useful in the editing process. Characters, words, and lines can be removed instantly by typing over them. Whole paragraphs and figures can be inserted and moved within the text of the draft, and many other useful functions can also be performed with this equipment.

Summary

In this chapter we have described how the computer is revolutionizing the way that modern audit work is performed. Computers are now being used in every phase of the audit, including planning, the assessment of internal control risk, substantive testing, and review and reporting. It is now possible to do a much more thorough job of auditing the financial statements, on a more cost-effective basis, through use of a combination of mainframe and microcomputer audit software packages.

The computer can be used during the planning stages of the audit to help identify high-risk areas that should be selected for further audit work. In addition, auditors have developed microcomputer packages to prepare time budgets and automated working papers, which have been shown to be tremendous time-savers in the audit. A variety of mainframe and microcomputer applications were discussed as part of the planning phase of the audit. Appendix 10–A contains examples of time budget forms, proposed adjustments working papers, and a working trial balance generated by microcomputer audit software.

The computer is very useful during the assessment of internal control risk. We discussed auditing *through* the computer by means of test data, parallel simulation, and the integrated test facility (ITF) for batch-processing systems. We then discussed the use of continuous monitoring for auditing controls through an on-line system. We also pointed out the advantages and disadvantages of each method.

Use of the computer during the substantive testing phase of the audit was discussed next. The uses of special-purpose audit programs, generalized audit software, and terminal audit software were discussed. An example of such a software package is described in Appendix 10–C.

Finally, special uses of microcomputer audit software for substantive tests and for the review and reporting phases of the audit were discussed.

Auditing Vocabulary

p. 379 **auditing around the computer:**   Performing auditing procedures on the input and output data without the necessity of knowing what goes on inside the computer.

p. 379 **auditing through the computer:**   Performing tests of the controls built into computer software in order to obtain assurance that those controls are working as planned. Auditing through the computer is typically done as the auditor obtains an understanding of the internal control structure of the client.

p. 379 **auditing with the computer:**   Using the computer in a cost-effective manner to perform audit procedures such as comparisons, confirmations, sampling, and other applications.

p. 385 **continuous monitoring:**   Tagging transactions processed by the system for audit as they are processed. See Figure 10–3.

p. 388 **generalized audit software:**   A set of computer programs that have the capability to process computer data files under the control of input parameters supplied by the auditor. See Figure 10–5.

p. 384 **integrated test facility:**   The use of auditor-developed fictitious or dummy entities within the framework of the regular application-processing cycle. See Figure 10–3.

p. 384 **parallel simulation:**   Use of one or more special computer programs to process "live" data through test programs. Parallel simulation is another way to audit through the computer. See Figure 10–3.

p. 381 **scoring:**   The technique that helps the auditor select high-risk areas among unlike systems or activities, using external measurement characteristics.

p. 380 **simulation and modeling:**   Uses key indicators to build statistical models, which can be used to predict the level of inactivity in an entity to be audited.

p. 387 **special-purpose audit programs:**   Specially tailored programs to extract and present data from a specific application system's files usually in an invariable format. See Figure 10–5.

p. 392 **terminal audit software:** Software that accesses, extracts, manipulates, and displays data from on-line data bases using remote-terminal inquiry commands. See Figure 10–5.

p. 383 **test data approach:** Obtaining duplicate copies of the client's master programs and running them with a series of hypothetical transactions. Some of the transactions will be valid and others will violate controls supposedly incorporated into the program. Test data is one of the ways to audit through the computer. See Figure 10–3.

Appendix 10–A: Coopers & Lybrand Computer Audit Programs*

Exhibit 1: Engagement Management Template (EMT)

One of the most demanding challenges faced by an engagement team is the process of planning and controlling the engagement. The Engagement Management Templates (EMT) are a series of interrelated spreadsheets designed to facilitate more effective budgeting, work scheduling, time reporting, time control, fee negotiations, and billings.

- **Time Management Budget (TMB) and TMB Supplements.** The TMB is used to budget field time by major audit category and by individual staff member. The basic template includes enough capacity to budget time for one supervisor, two seniors, and five staff auditors. By using one or more of the TMB Supplements, time can be budgeted for additional staff members. Time for other engagement team members (e.g., partner, manager, CAAG,† tax specialist) can also be entered.

  All budgeted time can be automatically priced at standard or other rates as specified by the user, thus providing much of the information necessary for preparing the client billing form. Projected rate per hour and realization percentage are computed based on billing information provided by the user.

- **Individual Time Management Summary (ITMS) and ITMS Supplements.** The ITMS summarizes, by major audit category, the actual time spent to date and the estimated time needed to complete for all persons assigned to the engagement. The basic template includes enough capacity to summarize time for one supervisor, up to two seniors, and five staff auditors. By using one or more of the ITMS Supplements, time can be summarized for additional staff members. Time spent to date and estimated time needed to complete can be automatically priced at standard or other rates as specified by the user.

---

*Used with permission.
†Computer Audit Assistance Group.

- **Time Management Overview (TMO).** The TMO summarizes, by major audit category, the completion status and the projected results for the entire engagement compared with the original budget. All hours and billing amounts at standard rates are summarized automatically from the TMB, ITMS, and any related supplements, and all variances and footings are computer-calculated. Revised projections of rate per hour and realization percentage are also computed, based on fee information supplied by the user for use in preparing progress or final billings.

  The EMT package includes several command files that speed both the budgeting and time summarization processes. These command files automatically carry appropriate data from one template to the next.

  These templates are equally effective in small and large engagement environments for controlling engagement profitability.

Exhibit 2: Adjustments Scoresheet (AJE)

The Summary of Unadjusted Differences (*scoresheet*) is an integral part of virtually every audit engagement's working papers. A scoresheet is difficult to maintain manually because it changes frequently and rapidly during the engagement. The Adjustments Scoresheet template (AJE) facilitates the preparation and maintenance of scoresheets by the auditor.

The most significant feature of AJE is its ability to monitor the status of proposed and recorded adjustments continuously throughout the audit. This feature enhances the timeliness and quality of discussions with clients concerning adjustments. When the client decides to record one or more of the adjustments, data can easily be moved from the "proposed adjustments" section to the "recorded adjustments" section of the scoresheet, and the relative significance of proposed adjustments is automatically recalculated.

The AJE template is an *electronic scoresheet* that

- Maintains running totals of proposed and recorded adjustments for four categories of adjustments (known errors, projected errors, estimated errors and debatable or *soft* items) and provides meaningful statistics regarding the materiality of each category of the proposed adjustments as the engagement progresses.
- Computes the impact of proposed adjustments on pretax and after-tax earnings, total assets, total liabilities, and equity.
- Facilitates recalculations of scoresheet totals and percentages as individual adjustments are recorded or proposals for them are withdrawn.

The AJE scoresheet will hold up to 100 proposed and recorded adjustments when used in a single-user, CP/M-based system, and about 55 adjustments when used on a multiuser, MP/M-based system.

```
:         A         ::  B  ::  C  ::  D  ::  E  ::  F  ::  G
1:TIME MANAGEMENT OVERVIEW(TMO)
2:VERSION 1.01
3:
4:    NAME OF CLIENT=========) TIME MGT.,INC.        ENGAGEMENT NO.==) 014-4684-
5:    PERIOD ENDING=========) 12/31/82               REPORTED BY=====) JP
6:********************************************************************************
7:                          BUDGETED  ACTUAL  EST. TO  TOTAL  VARIANCE
8:MAJOR AUDIT CATEGORIES     HOURS   TO DATE COMPLETE ESTIMAT. -UNDER-
9:                                                           HOURS   -OVER-
10:--------------------------------------------------------------------------
11:ENGAGEMENT PLANNING & STRATEGY:
12:-------------------------------
13:PRLM. UNDERSTANDING           15      10       0      10      5
14:PRLM. UNDERSTANDING-EDP. SYS. 10      12       0      12     -2
15:AUDIT SOFTWARE PLANNING       10      14       0      14     -4
16:ANALYTICAL REVIEW-PRLM.        8       6       0       6      2
17:ENG. PLANNING DOCUMENTATION    7       5       0       5      2
18:AUDIT PROGRAM                  5       6       0       6     -1
19:BUDGETS & STAFFING             5       8       0       8     -3
20:COORDINATE-OTHER OFFICES       2       1       0       1      1
21:COORDINATE-CLIENT              8       6       3       9     -1
22:-------------------------------
23:AUDIT PERFORMANCE:
24:-------------------------------
25:REVENUE CYCLE                 15      16       1      17     -2
26:PRODUCTION CYCLE              20      18       4      22     -2
27:PAYMENTS CYCLE-PURCHASES      10       8       0       8      2
28:PAYMENTS CYCLE-PAYROLL         6      10       0      10     -4
29:TAX PLANNING                   5       4       0       4      1
64:TRIAL BALANCE & SUB           11      13       4      17     -6
65:CONSOLIDATION                  5       0       5       5      0
66:REPORTS & STATEMENTS          20       6      14      20      0
67:F/S DISCLOSURE CHECKLIST       3       0       3       3      0
68:ANALYTICAL REVIEWS-YEAR END    4       3       5       8     -4
69:SUBSEQUENT EVENTS              3       1       1       2      1
70:MAP & ABCS                    12       5       8      13     -1
71:BOARD & OTHER MEETINGS        13       4       7      11      2
72:FILING & INDEXING              5       4       1       5      0
73:SEC REPORTS                            0       0       0      0
74:TAX RETURNS                   18       0      19      19     -1
75:STAFF PERFORMANCE REPORTS      6       0       5       5      1
76:TIME MANAGEMENT                8       5       8      13     -5
77:REVIEW & SUPERVISION          40      21      13      34      6
78:OTHER                                  0       0       0      0
79:CONTINGENCY                   25      22       5      27     -2
80:NEXT YEAR PLANNING            10       0       9       9      1
81:                            --------------------------------------
82:     TOTAL FIELD HOURS       530     380     183     563    -33
83:
84:MANAGER HOURS                 55      50      22      72    -17
85:PARTNER HOURS                 40      35      31      66    -26
86:                            --------------------------------------
87:  TOTAL GEN. PRACTICE HOURS  625     465     236     701    -76
88:
89:TAX PARTNER HOURS              7       5       0       5      2
90:TAX MANAGER HOURS              6       2       4       6      0
91:TAX SUPERVISOR HOURS          22      20      15      35    -13
92:TAX SENIOR HOURS                               0       0      0
93:CMAG MANAGER HOURS             5       5       1       6     -1
94:CMAG SUPERVISOR HOURS         25      19       9      28     -3
95:SUPPORT HOURS                  5       3               3      2
96:REPORT/STENO HOURS            30       5      27      32     -2
97:                            --------------------------------------
98:  TOTAL ENGAGEMENT HOURS     725     524     292     816    -91
99:                            ======================================
100:DOLLARIZED SUMMARY @ RATES
101:---------------------------
102:  PARTNER                 1400    1225    1085    2310   -910
103:  MANAGER                 1650    1500     660    2160   -510
104:  SUPERVISOR              3325    2175    1300    3475   -150
105:  SENIOR                  3380    2080    1300    3380      0
106:  STAFF A                 1980    1260     840    2100   -120
107:  STAFF B                  960    1050     100    1150   -190
108:  TAX PARTNER              245     175       0     175     70
109:  TAX MANAGER              180      60     120     180      0
110:  TAX SUPERVISOR           550     500     375     875   -325
111:  TAX SENIOR                 0       0       0       0      0
112:  CMAG MANAGER             150     150      30     180    -30
113:  CMAG SUPERVISOR          625     475     225     700    -75
114:  SUPPORT                  125      75       0      75     50
115:  REPORT/STENO             150      25     135     160    -10
116:                         --------------------------------------
117:     TOTALS              14720   10750    6170   16920  -2200
118:                         ======================================
119:
120:
121:                          FEE   RELIZ %  $/HR
122:                          ----  -------  ----
123:ORIGINALLY BUDGETED       7500     51    10.34
124:REVISED ESTIMATE          7500     44     9.19
125:VARIANCE(+BETTER+)(-WORSE-)  0     -7    -1.15
```

Time Management Overview from TMO Template

```
:.A.: B ::          C            :: D:: E    F  ::   G     ..  H   .   :    I    :   J   ::   K   .   L      M  .
1:IF YOU HAVE NOT ALREADY DONE SO, PRIOR TO USING THIS TEMPLATE, YOU
2:MUST READ THE PROPRIETARY NOTICE, LIMITATION OF LIABILITY CLAUSE,
3:AND COPYRIGHT NOTICE INCLUDED WITH THIS TEMPLATE PACKAGE.
4:*************************************************************************************************    VERSION 1.0
5:ADJUSTMENTS SCORESHEET
6:COMPANY                        PREPARER:LE            ENTER ORDINARY INCOME TAX RATE (CODE 1):     .47
7:B/S DATE                       RUN DATE:03/14/83      ENTER CAPITAL GAINS TAX RATE (CODE 2):       .?
8:-------
9:NOTE:  NEGATIVE AMOUNTS REPRESENT CREDITS AND POSITIVE AMOUNTS REPRESENT DEBITS
10:************************************************************************************************************
11:ENTRY   W/P                               CODE----PRE-TAX BAL.SHEET IMPACT----- ----PRE-TAX INCOME STATEMENT IMPACT--------------- NET INCOME
12:NO.     REF.      DESCRIPTION OF ENTRY     1,2    ASSETS   LIABS.    EQUITY    KNOWN  PROJECTED ESTIMATED DEBATABLE    TOTAL    IMPACT
13:-------
14:       PROPOSED ADJUSTMENTS:
15:-------
16:1   55-2  WRITE-OFF OBSOLETE MATERIAL IN INVENTORY  1  -500000                           500000           500000   265000
17:2   94-1  RECORD THEFT LOSS,INTEGRATED CIRCUITS     1  -275000          275000                             275000   .45750
18:3   64-8  RECORD GAIN ON SALE OF LAND HELD FOR INVE 2  1800000        -1800000                           -1800000 -1260000
19:    VAR. "LOTS OF OTHER STUFF TO BOOK             :        -100           100                               .000       55?
20:
21:
```

```
A1:*************************************************************************************************************
A2:
A3:-------
84.       RECORDED ADJUSTMENTS:
95:-------
85:6  50-6  UNRECORDED CASH RECEIPTS FROM CUSTOMERS   1  1423000                  -1423000                         -1423000  -754190
87:7  9-1   LOSS ON DISPOSAL OF A SEGMENT OF THE BUSI  1 -2230000                                   2230000          2230000  1181900
88:   VAR.  LOTS MORE STUFF GOT BOOKED                1          -190000    90000           100000                   100000    53000
89:   VAR.  LOTS MORE STUFF GOT BOOKED                :          -190000    90000           100000                   100000    53000
90:   VAR.  LOTS MORE STUFF GOT BOOKED                :          -190000    90000           100000                   100000    53000
91:   VAR.  LOTS MORE STUFF GOT BOOKED                1          -190000    90000           100000                   100000    53000
92:                                                                                                                       0        0
```

```
.A. B           C            :: D. E  ::   F    ::   G     ..  H   .   I    .   :    ::   K  ::  L   ::   M   :
125:                                                                                                              0        0
126:                                                                                                              0        0
127:                                                                      -------  -------  -------  -------  -------  -------
128:        TOTAL, RECORDED ADJUSTMENTS      -807000  -760000  360000  -1423000  400000  2230000     0    1207000  639710
129:                                         =======  =======  =======  =======  =======  =======  =====  =======  =======
130:
131:**********************************************************************************************************************
132:                                                                                    PRE-TAX     NET
133:                                           ASSETS   LIABILITIES   EQUITY   EARNINGS   INCOME
134:                                         -------  -------  -------  -------  -------
135:        TOTALS BEFORE AUDIT ADJUSTMENTS   20000000 -10000000 -10000000 -5000000 -2500000
136:        AUDIT ADJUSTMENTS RECORDED         -807000   -760000    360000  1207000   639710
137:                                         -------  -------  -------  -------  -------
138:        TOTALS AFTER AUDIT ADJUSTMENTS    19193000 -10760000  9640000 -3793000 -1860290
139:                                         =======  =======  =======  =======  =======
140:
141:        TOTALS OF PROPOSED ADJUSTMENTS    1025000    -3000        0 -1022000  -847000
142:                                         =======  =======  =======  =======  =======
143:
144:        % OF PROPOSED ADJUSTMENTS TO F/S AMOUNTS   5.34    .03     .00    26.94    45.5?
145:                                         =======  =======  =======  =======  =======
146:
147:                                           PROPOSED   % OF PRE-TAX
148:        IMPACT OF PROPOSALS ON PRE-TAX EARNINGS  ADJUSTMENT  EARNINGS
149:                                         -------  -------
150:                 KNOWN ADJUSTMENTS        -1525000  -40.21
151:
152:        MATHEMATICALLY PROJECTED AMOUNTS      3000     .08
153:
154:        JUDGMENTALLY ESTIMATED AMOUNTS      500000   13.18
155:
156:        DEBATABLE OR  SOFT  AMOUNTS             0     .00
157:                                         -------  -------
158:                 TOTALS                   -1022000  -26.94
159:                                         =======
160:
```

Adjustments Scoresheet from AJE Template

Exhibit 3: PRE-AUDIT

Financial statement preparation may be the most time-consuming, routine part of an audit. PRE-AUDIT is designed to speed up the processes of auditing, compilation, and review. This series of programs reduces the cost and complexity of preparing the trial balance worksheet, adjusting journal entries, fluctuation and ratio analysis, and financial statements, including the Statement of Changes in Financial Position in working capital and cash formats. It also interfaces with a number of other microcomputer products.

PRE-AUDIT will

- Group balance sheet and income statement lines under subheadings (e.g., cash grouped under current assets).
- Allow entry of account balances from general ledger; the user must enter all information for the first year; in subsequent years, only account balances are required.
- Group each account into a balance sheet or income statement line number.
- Process posting summaries to create a general ledger account total.
- Produce trial balance by account or by balance sheet and income statement line number; furnish year-to-year fluctuation percentage for each account or financial statement line.
- Generate lead schedules.
- Perform vertical fluctuation analysis.
- Display or print formatted balance sheet and income statement based on summarization of trial balance accounts plus adjusting journal entries.
- Produce a customized set of financial statements together with footnotes and ancillary schedules.
- Process adjusting journal entries.
- Instantly show effects of journal entries on net income.
- Show effect of adjustments on profit/loss and major balance sheet and income statement groupings; these can be calculated and displayed, or printed.
- Process scoresheet (unadjusted journal entries).
- Calculate and display common financial ratios.
- Provide formulas to customize many additional ratios.
- Accept entry of current and prior years' base amounts as a dollar amount or number, a financial line, or a range of financial lines, and produce a common size report of selected ranges of accounts.
- Transfer current balance to prior column and "zero out" current column.

```
FS31R-1                          PRE-AUDIT                        PAGE  001
REPORT DATE 01/06/84        MORGAN CHEMICAL CO.         PERIOD ENDED 12/31/81
(JOURNAL ENTRIES INCL)      * * * TRIAL BALANCE * * *

--------------------------------------------------------------------------------
ACT./FIN. NO.     ACCOUNT DESCRIPTION    CURRENT PERIOD  PRIOR PERIOD   FLUCT.
--------------------------------------------------------------------------------

  00101   01 PETTY CASH...................      1,500.00      1,500.00      0.00
  00102   01 CASH-COMMERCIAL ACCOUNT.......    312,620.00    232,420.00     34.51
  00103   01 CASH-PAYROLL ACCOUNT..........     78,000.00     72,000.00      8.33
  00104   02 ACCOUNTS RECEIVABLE OTHER.....          0.00          0.00      0.00
  00105   02 ACCOUNTS RECEIVABLE...........    434,862.00    468,311.00      7.14-
  00106   03 ALL.DOUBTFUL ACCOUNTS.........      9,147.00-    10,216.00-    10.46-
  00108   04 NOTES RECIEVABLE -CURRENT.....     15,000.00      9,000.00     66.67
  00109   15 NOTES RECEIVABLE..............     57,000.00     54,000.00      5.56
  00112   05 ACCRUED INT. RECEIVABLE.......      6,400.00      5,200.00     23.08
  00115   06 MARKETABLE SECURITIES.........    220,000.00    187,000.00     17.65
  00116   07 DIVIDENDS RECIEVABLE..........      2,450.00      3,000.00     18.33-
  00118   08 PREPAID INSURANCE.............     16,840.00     11,400.00     47.72
  00122   08 PREPAID TAXES.................      5,215.00      3,364.00     55.02
  00125   09 INVENTORY.....................    859,160.00    739,812.00     16.13
  00128   16 LAND..........................  1,200,000.00  1,200,000.00      0.00
  00130   17 BUILDINGS.....................  1,800,000.00  1,630,000.00     10.43
  00134   18 MACHINERY AND EQUIPMENT.......    532,669.00    429,830.00     23.93
  00137   19 ACCUMULATED DEPRECIATION......    211,336.00-   180,471.00-    17.10
  00139   25 GOODWILL......................     21,078.00     23,420.00     10.00-
  00140   26 PATENTS.......................      7,800.00     10,400.00     25.00-
  00141   27 ORGANIZATIONAL COSTS..........      6,874.00      8,250.00     16.68-
  00201   41 TRADE ACCOUNTS PAYABLE........    352,841.00-   267,621.00-    31.84
  00202   42 OTHER ACCOUNTS PAYABLE........    189,210.00-   115,423.00-    63.93
  00204   43 NOTES PAYABLE-CURR. PORTION...     40,000.00-    40,000.00-     0.00
  00205   50 NOTES PAYABLE.................    240,000.00-   280,000.00-    14.29-
  00207   44 ACCRUED INTEREST PAYABLE......      2,910.00-     3,400.00-    14.41-
  00208   44 ACCURED SALARY AND WAGES......     10,015.00-     8,315.00-    20.44
  00211   44 ACCURED UNEMPLOYMENT TAXES....      3,038.00-     2,495.00-    21.76
  00214   44 ACCURED LIABILITIES-OTHER.....    125,203.00-    49,040.00-   155.31
  00217   45 FEDERAL INCOME TAX PAYABLE....    132,321.00-    87,290.00-    51.59
  00218   45 STATE INCOME TAX PAYABLE......     19,380.00-     8,604.00-   125.24
  00223   43 BONDS PAYABLE-CURRENT PORTION.    120,000.00-   120,000.00-     0.00
  00224   51 BONDS PAYABLE.................    480,000.00-   600,000.00-    20.00-
  00230   60 COMMON STOCK-VOTING...........    760,000.00-   720,000.00-     5.56
  00231   60 COMMON STOCK-NON VOTING.......    280,000.00-   280,000.00-     0.00
  00234   61 PREFERRED STOCK...............    300,000.00-   300,000.00-     0.00
  00237   62 ADDITIONAL PAID IN CAPITAL....  1,000,000.00-   800,000.00-    25.00
                                                             0.00-    60.03
                                                             0.00-    11.19
                                                             0.00     20.70
                                                             0.00     18.94
                                                             0.00     14.95
```

```
* FS47S-2 *                      PRE-AUDIT
REPORT DATE 01/08/84        MORGAN CHEMICAL CO.         PERIOD ENDED 12/31/81
                          * * * COMMON SIZE REPORT * * *
--------------------------------------------------------------------------------
FIN.     FIN. LINE               CURRENT   FLUCT.      PRIOR    FLUCT.
NO.      DESCRIPTION             PERIOD      %         PERIOD     %
--------------------------------------------------------------------------------
BASE  ACCOUNT NUMBER:     101
      PETTY CASH               1,500.00    100.00    1,500.00    100.00

  01  CASH                   392,120.00    999.99  305,920.00    999.99
  02  ACCOUNTS RECEIVABLE    434,862.00    999.99  468,311.00    999.99
  03  ALLOW FOR DOUBTFUL A/C'S  9,147.00-  609.80   10,216.00-   681.07
  04  CURR PORT NOTES RECEIV  15,000.00    999.99    9,000.00    600.00
  05  INTEREST RECEIVABLE      6,400.00    426.67    5,200.00    346.67
  06  MARKETABLE SECURITIES  220,000.00    999.99  187,000.00    999.99
  07  DIVIDENDS RECEIVABLE     2,450.00    163.33    3,000.00    200.00
  08  PREPAID EXPENSE         22,055.00    999.99   14,764.00    984.27
  09  INVENTORY             859,160.00    999.99  739,812.00    999.99
```

Trial Balance and Common Size Report, Generated by PRE-AUDIT

```
* FS568-1 *                        PRE-AUDIT
REPORT DATE 01/08/84          MORGAN CHEMICAL CO.          PERIOD ENDED 12/31/81
                  * * * PROFIT/LOSS LISTING WITH NET EFFECT * * *

-------------------------------------------------------------------------------
SEQ                           OPENING    JOURNAL    CLOSING    SCORESHEET
NO.      DESCRIPTION          BALANCE    ENTRIES    BALANCE    ENTRIES    PCNT.
-------------------------------------------------------------------------------
    NET PROFIT/LOSS           116839-     30804      86035-     10680    12.41

  1 CURRENT ASSETS           1934550       8350    1942900      13180-    0.68
  2 NON-CURRENT ASSETS         57000          0      57000          0    0.00
  3 PROPERTY, PLANT & EQUIP  3321333          0    3321333       2500    0.08
  4 INTANGIBLE ASSETS          38911       3159-     35752          0    0.00
  5 CURRENT LIABILITIES       958923-     35995-    994918-         0    0.00
  6 NON-CURRENT LIABILITIES   720000-         0     720000-         0    0.00
  7 STOCKHOLDERS' EQUITY     3556032-         0    3556032-         0    0.00
  8 REVENUES                 8713244-         0    8713244-         0    0.00
  9 EXPENSES                 8596405      30804    8627209      10680    0.12
```

Selected Reports from PRE-AUDIT (continued)

```
FS46R-1                            PRE-AUDIT                   PAGE NO.   001
REPORT DATE 01/06/84          STANDARD RATIO REPORT      PERIOD ENDED 12/31/81
                              MORGAN CHEMICAL CO.

-------------------------------------------------------------------------------
RATIO NO.   RATIO TYPE   RATIO NAME          CURRENT PERIOD    PRIOR PERIOD
-------------------------------------------------------------------------------

    01         01        CURRENT RATIO             1.95            2.45
    02         12        QUICK RATIO               1.04            1.35
    03         03        RECEIVABLES TURNOVER     20.38           17.04
    04         08        AVERAGE COLL. PERIOD     17.65           21.12
    05         10        DAYS REC. UNCOLLECT      17.65           21.12
    06         01        INVENTORY TURN (RET)      6.94            6.68
    07         01        FINISHED GOODS TURN.      6.94            6.68
    08         04        DAYS ENDING INVENT       51.80           53.84
    09         01        WORKING CAPITAL TURN      8.89            7.64
    10         06        EQUITY TO TOT. ASSET      0.67            0.67
    11         01        LIAB. TO TOT. ASSETS      0.32            0.32
    12         05        LONG TERM DEBT RATIO      0.16            0.23
    13         03        RET. ON COMMON STOCK      0.11            0.45
    14         01        SALES TO EQUITY           2.44            2.72
    15         01        FIXED ASS. TO EQUITY      0.93            1.07
    16         01        SALES TO FIXED ASSET      2.61            2.53
    17         01        NET INCOME TO SALES       0.01            0.05
    18         06        INCOME TO TOT ASSETS      0.02            0.09
    19         07        GROSS MARGIN RATIO        0.31            0.36
    20         13        RETURN ON ASSETS          0.02            0.09
    21         09        INCOME TO INTEREST       16.03           42.95
    22         11        CASH FLOW TO CUR DEB      6.01            8.38
    23         01        SALES PER SQ. FOOT      434.01          390.31
    24         01        BOOK VALUE PER SHARE      7.11            5.71
    25         03        EARNINGS PER SHARE        0.23            0.91
```

Profit/Loss Listing with Net Effect and Standard Ratio Report, Generated by PRE-AUDIT

Appendix 10–B: Major Software Packages

The major audit software packages that have been developed are listed here.

Firm	Software	Firm	Software
Grant Thornton One First National Plaza Chicago, Ill. 60670	AUDASSIST	Dylakor Software Systems, Inc. 16255 Ventura Boulevard Encino, Calif. 91436	{ DYL-250 { DYL-260
Arthur Andersen and Company 69 West Washington Street Chicago, Ill. 60602	{ AUDEX { AUDEX 100		
U.S. Department of Commerce Springfield, Va. 22151	AUDIT		
Deloitte & Touche 1114 Avenue of the Americas New York, N.Y. 10036	AUDITAPE STRATA	Department of Health, Educa- tion and Welfare Audit Agency Office of the Assistant Secretary, Comptroller 330 Independence Avenue, S.W. Washington, D.C. 20201	HEWCAS
Dataskil Reading Bridge House Reading, England	AUDITFIND	Informatics, Inc. 21050 Vanowen Street Canoga Park, Calif. 91303	MARK IV AUDIT
Coopers & Lybrand 1251 Avenue of the Americas New York, N.Y. 10020	AUDITPAK II	Computer Resources Corp. 23 Leroy Avenue Darien, Conn. 06820	PROBE
Program Products, Inc. 95 Chestnut Ridge Road Montvale, N.J. 07645	AUDIT ANALYZER	Programming Methods, Inc. 1301 Avenue of the Americas New York, N.Y. 10019	SCORE-AUDIT
Ernst & Young 1300 Union Commerce Building Cleveland, Ohio 44115	{ AUTRONIC-16 { AUTRONIC-32		
John Cullinane Corporation 20 William Street Wellesley, Mass. 02181	{ CARS { EDP AUDITOR	KPMG Peat Marwick 3 Chestnut Ridge Road Montvale, N.J. 07645	S/2190

Source: W. Thomas Porter and William E. Perry, *EDP Controls and Auditing*, 5th ed. (Boston: Kent Publishing Company, 1987).

Appendix 10-C: Example of the Use of KPMG Peat Marwick's System 2190

An Example of System 2190 in Action

The internal auditor of XYZ company was examining inventory. He found that the inventory reports generated by his company's computer were voluminous and that it was time-consuming to reperform calculations because of the complexity of the programs. In addition, reperforming the calculations using the same programs did not provide an independent check on their validity. Finally, there was no data on inventory turnover by item, which he wanted for his evaluation of inventory obsolescence. He decided to use System 2190.

The first step was to prepare a statement describing his four objectives, as follows:

- Foot the inventory file, list subtotals by part number, and prepare a graph of inventory balances.
- Compute intercompany inventory profit by department.
- Verify and list inventory extensions and total any errors.
- Identify and list slow-moving items.

Next he prepared instructions on the System 2190 specification forms and entered the instructions into the computer. System 2190 read the specifications, checked their compliance with System 2190 coding rules, generated a COBOL program, printed it, and automatically began processing it.

The resulting reports accomplished each of the four objectives. In a short period of time, System 2190 had tested data that would have taken days to test manually, and the auditor had more time to investigate exceptions, evaluate slow-moving items for obsolescence, and make audit adjustments.

Notes

1. Discussions and illustrations in this section are taken from W. Thomas Porter and William E. Perry, *EDP Controls and Auditing*, 5th ed. (Boston: Kent Publishing Company, 1987), Chapters 10 and 13.
2. Ibid.
3. Ibid.
4. This is a description of the microcomputer software developed by Arthur Andersen and Company. "LOTUS 1-2-3" is a template for use with software developed by Lotus Development Corporation. Excel is a template developed by Microsoft Corporation.
5. See note 4 above.

6. See note 4 above.
7. See note 4 above.

Questions for Class Discussion

Q10-1   What is the relationship between the development of computerized accounting records and the use of the computer as an audit tool?

Q10-2   Has the use of the computer as an audit tool increased the cost of performing audits? Explain.

Q10-3   Can you name at least ten procedures that a typical computer software package can be expected to perform during the course of an audit?

Q10-4   What are the sources from which the auditor might be able to obtain a computer program that will allow use of the computer in the performance of an audit?

Q10-5   What are the advantages and disadvantages of using an audit program prepared by a client in performing an audit? If such a program is used, what must the auditor do before accepting the computer output produced by the program?

Q10-6   Is it practical for the auditing firm to prepare a separate computer program to be used in the performance of the audit for each client? Explain.

Q10-7   What are the five steps the auditor must carry out in the development of a computer audit program?

Q10-8   How can generalized audit programs overcome the disadvantages associated with the use of client-prepared programs and with the use of programs prepared by the auditor for each individual audit?

Q10-9   What is meant by *audit work files*? How are they created?

Q10-10   What are five functions that generalized audit software programs typically have the capability of performing?

Q10-11   What are four distinct steps normally followed by an auditor in developing and using a generalized computer audit software package?

Q10-12   How is a generalized computer software package typically adapted to the specific audit tasks to be performed during the audit of a client's financial statements?

Q10-13   Will computer printouts be included as part of the audit work papers when the computer is used as a tool in performing the audit? Explain.

Q10-14   What is meant by *automated work papers*?

Q10-15   Can you name at least five inventory auditing procedures that can be performed by the computer using a generalized computer audit program supplemented by appropriate job control language and specification cards?

Q10-16   What are at least five accounts receivable auditing procedures that the computer can perform using a generalized computer audit program?

Q10-17   What are some of the ways in which the microcomputer is being used to conduct the audit examination?

Q10-18 What is meant by the following terms: *auditing around the computer; auditing through the computer*? Under what circumstances might each of those auditing processes be followed? Explain.

Q10-19 What is the test data approach to the verification of computerized accounting data? Explain how that approach is carried out by the auditor. What is meant by the term *parallel simulation*? Explain.

Short Cases

C10-1 A CPA's client, Boos & Baumkirchner, Inc., is a medium-sized manufacturer of products for the leisure time activities market (camping equipment, scuba gear, bows and arrows, etc.). During the past year, a computer system was installed, and inventory records of finished goods and parts were converted to computer processing. The inventory master file is maintained on a disk. Each record of the file contains the following:

a. Item or part number.
b. Description.
c. Size.
d. Unit of measure code.
e. Quantity on hand.
f. Cost per unit.
g. Total value of inventory on hand at cost.
h. Date of last sale or usage.
i. Quantity used or sold this year.
j. Economic order quantity.
k. Code number of major vendor.
l. Code number of secondary vendor.

In preparation for year-end inventory, the client produces two identical sets of pre-printed inventory count cards. One set is for the client's inventory counts and the other is for the CPA's use to make audit test counts. Printed on the cards and interpreted on their face are the

1. Item or part number.
2. Description.
3. Size.
4. Unit of measure code.

In taking the year-end inventory, the client's personnel will write the actual counted quantity on the face of each card. When all counts are complete, the counted quantity will be coded onto the cards. The cards will be run through a scanner and processed against the disk file, and quantity-on-hand figures will be adjusted to show the actual count. A computer listing will be prepared to show any missing inventory count cards and all quantity adjustments of more than $100 in value. These items will be investigated by client personnel, and all required adjustments will be made. When adjustments have been completed, the final year-end balances will be computed and posted to the general ledger.

The CPA has available a general-purpose computer audit software package that will run on the client's computer.

Required:

   a. In general and without regard to the preceding facts, discuss the nature of general-purpose computer audit software packages and list the various types and uses of such packages.
   b. List and describe at least five ways a general-purpose computer audit software package can be used to assist in all aspects of the audit of the inventory of Boos & Baumkirchner, Inc. (For example, the package can be used to read the disk inventory master file and list items and parts with a high unit cost or total value. Such items can be included in the test counts to increase the dollar coverage of the audit verification.)

(AICPA adapted)

C10-2   In the past, the records to be evaluated in an audit have been printed reports, listings, documents, and written papers—all of which are visible output. However, in fully computerized systems employing daily updating of transaction files, output and files are frequently in machine-readable forms, such as tapes or disks. Thus, they often present the auditor with an opportunity to use the computer in performing an audit.

Required: Discuss how the computer can be used to aid the auditor in examining accounts receivable in such a fully computerized system.

(AICPA adapted)

C10-3   Regina Peters, CPA, has examined the financial statements of the Solt Manufacturing Company for several years and is making preliminary plans for the audit for the year ended June 30, 19X2. During this examination, Peters plans to use a set of generalized computer audit programs. Solt's EDP manager has agreed to prepare special tapes of data from company records for the CPA's use with the generalized programs.

The following information is applicable to Peters's examination of Solt's accounts payable and related procedures:

   a. The formats of pertinent tapes (see the accompanying four file formats).
   b. The following monthly runs are prepared:
      1. Cash disbursements by check number.
      2. Outstanding payables.
      3. Purchase journals arranged by account charged and by vendor.
   c. Vouchers and supporting invoices, receiving reports, and purchase order copies are filed by vendor code. Purchase orders and checks are filed numerically.
   d. Company records are maintained on magnetic tapes. All tapes are stored in a restricted area within the computer room. A grandfather, father, son policy is followed for retaining and safeguarding tape files.

Required:

   a. Explain the grandfather, father, son policy. Describe how files could be reconstructed when this policy is used.
   b. Discuss whether company policies for retaining and safeguarding the tape files provide adequate protection against losses of data.
   c. Describe the controls that the CPA should maintain over
      1. Preparing the special tapes.
      2. Processing the special tapes with the generalized computer audit programs.

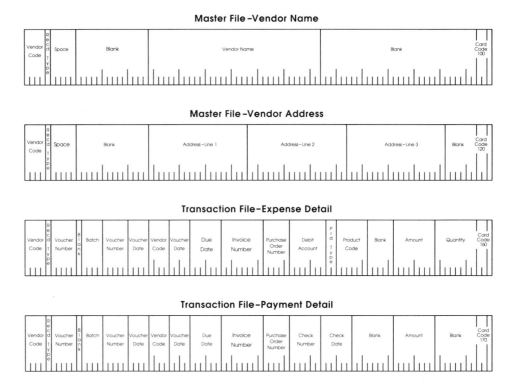

d. Prepare a schedule for the EDP manager, outlining the data that should be included on the special tape for the CPA's examination of accounts payable and related procedures. This schedule should show the
   1. Client tape from which the item should be extracted.
   2. Name of the item of data.

(AICPA adapted)

C10-4 Rip van Longsleeper, CPA, introduced to you in the Short Cases section of Chapter 9, has just completed his evaluation of the computerized accounting system in accordance with your earlier recommendations. He now needs to confirm a sample of his client's accounts receivable. He asks you to explain how he can select that sample and then best proceed with the confirmation of accounts receivable. He again complains that he cannot find the individual accounts on the reel of magnetic tape containing the accounts receivable balances.

Required: Explain to Mr. Longsleeper how he should proceed with the confirmation of accounts receivable.

Problems

P10-1   Select the best answer for each of the following items.

    a. Data Corporation has just completely computerized its billing and accounts receivable recordkeeping. You want to make maximum use of the new computer in your audit of Data Corporation. Which of the following auditing techniques could *not* be performed through a computer program?

        1. Tracing audited cash receipts to accounts receivable credits.

        2. Selecting on a random-number basis accounts to be confirmed.

        3. Examining sales invoices for completeness, consistency between different items, valid conditions, and reasonable amounts.

        4. Resolving differences reported by customers on confirmation requests.

    b. An auditor would be *least* likely to use a generalized computer audit program for which of the following tasks?

        1. Selecting and printing accounts receivable confirmations.

        2. Listing accounts receivable confirmation exceptions for examination.

        3. Comparing accounts receivable subsidiary files to the general ledger.

        4. Investigating exceptions to accounts receivable confirmations.

    c. The primary purpose of a generalized computer audit program is to allow the auditor to

        1. Use the client's employees to perform routine audit checks of the electronic data-processing records that otherwise would be done by the auditor's staff accountants.

        2. Test the logic of computer programs used in the client's electronic data-processing systems.

        3. Select larger samples from the client's electronic data-processing records than would otherwise be selected without the generalized program.

        4. Independently process client electronic data-processing records.

    d. An auditor can use a generalized computer audit program to verify the accuracy of

        1. Data-processing controls.

        2. Accounting estimates.

        3. Totals and subtotals.

        4. Account classifications.

    e. Auditors often make use of computer programs that perform routine processing functions such as sorting and merging. These programs are made available by electronic data-processing companies and others and are specifically referred to as

        1. User programs.

        2. Compiler programs.

        3. Supervisory programs.

        4. Utility programs.

    f. Processing data through the use of simulated files provides an auditor with information about the reliability of controls. One of the techniques involved in this approach makes use of

        1. Controlled reprocessing.

        2. Integrated test facility.

        3. Input validation.

        4. Program code checking.

    g. A primary advantage of using generalized audit packages in the audit of an advanced EDP system is that it enables the auditor to

1. Substantiate the accuracy of data through self-checking digits and hash totals.
2. Utilize the speed and accuracy of the computer.
3. Verify the performance of machine operations that leave visible evidence of occurrence.
4. Gather and store large quantities of supportive evidential matter in machine-readable form.

h. Which of the following is an advantage of generalized computer audit packages?
1. They are all written in one identical computer language.
2. They can be used for audits of clients that use differing EDP equipment and file formats.
3. They have reduced the need for the auditor to study input controls for EDP-related procedures.
4. Their use can be substituted for a relatively large part of the required compliance testing.

i. Smith Corporation has numerous customers, and a customer file is kept on disk storage. Each customer file contains the customer's name, address, credit limit, and account balance. The auditor wishes to test this file to determine whether credit limits are being exceeded. The best procedure for the auditor to follow would be to
1. Develop test data that would cause some account balances to exceed the credit limit and determine if the system properly detects such situations.
2. Develop a program to compare credit limits with account balances and print out the details of any account with a balance exceeding its credit limit.
3. Request a printout of all account balances so they can be manually checked against the credit limits.
4. Request a printout of a sample of account balances so they can be individually checked against the credit limits.

j. Auditing by testing the input and output of an EDP system instead of the computer program itself will
1. Not detect program errors which do *not* show up in the output sampled.
2. Detect all program errors, regardless of the nature of the output.
3. Provide the auditor with the same type of evidence.
4. Not provide the auditor with confidence in the results of the auditing procedures.

k. When testing a computerized accounting system, which of the following is *not* true of the test data approach?
1. Test data are processed by the client's computer programs under the auditor's control.
2. The test data must consist of all possible valid and invalid conditions.
3. The test data need consist of only those valid and invalid conditions in which the auditor is interested.
4. Only one transaction of each type need be tested.

(AICPA adapted)

P10-2   An auditor is conducting an examination of the financial statements of a wholesale cosmetics distributor with an inventory consisting of thousands of individual items. The distributor keeps its inventory in its own distribution center and in two public warehouses. An inventory computer file is maintained on a computer disk, and at the end of each business day, the file is updated. Each record of the inventory file contains the following:

a. Item number.
b. Location of item.
c. Description of item.
d. Quantity on hand.
e. Cost per item.
f. Date of last purchase.
g. Date of last sale.
h. Quantity sold during year.

   The auditor is planning to observe the distributor's physical count of inventories as of a given time. The auditor will have available a computer tape of the data on the inventory file on the date of the physical count and a general-purpose computer software package.

Required: The auditor is planning to perform basic inventory auditing procedures. Identify the basic inventory auditing procedures and describe how the use of the general-purpose software package and the tape of the inventory file data might be helpful to the auditor in performing such auditing procedures.

   Organize your answer as follows:

Basic Inventory Auditing Procedure	How General-Purpose Computer Software Package and Tape of the Inventory File Data Might Be Helpful
1. Observe the physical count, making and recording test counts where applicable.	Determining which items are to be test counted by selecting a random sample of a representative number of items from the inventory file as of the date of the physical count.

(AICPA adapted)

P10-3   The microcomputer has had a significant and permanent impact on the practice of auditing in recent years. Some even suggest that the audit of the future may even be performed without the use of paper and pencil.

Required:
   a. In what way is the use of the microcomputer complementary to the use of mainframe audit software? What are the relative advantages of microcomputer software compared to mainframe software? What are the limitations?
   b. Discuss at least five current uses of the microcomputer in the planning, execution, and reporting stages of the audit.

P10-4   CPAs may audit *around* the computer, but when the computer is used extensively in all processing applications, most CPAs prefer to audit *through* the computer. In still other applications it is possible to audit *with* the computer.

Required:
   a. Describe the auditing approach referred to as auditing around the computer. Why do auditors generally *not* use that approach?
   b. Under what circumstances would the CPA decide to audit through the computer instead of around it? What are some ways to audit through the computer?
   c. In auditing through the computer, the CPA may use a variety of methods.

1. What are test data? Why does the CPA use the test data approach? What are some of its disadvantages? How might those disadvantages be alleviated with proper planning?
2. What is the controlled processing approach? What are some of its advantages and disadvantages?
3. What is the ITF (minicompany) approach? What are some of the advantages of this method over other methods?

(AICPA adapted)

P10-5 Microcomputer software has been developed to improve the efficiency and effectiveness of the audit. Electronic spreadsheets and other software packages are available to aid in the performance of audit procedures otherwise performed manually.

Required: Describe the potential benefits to an auditor of using microcomputer software in an audit as compared to performing an audit without the use of a computer.

(AICPA adapted)

CHAPTER 11

Sampling Techniques and Internal Control Evaluation

Objectives

☐ **1.** Know how sampling fits into the overall audit process.
☐ **2.** Be able to explain how audit risk and materiality considerations affect the sampling process associated with the evaluation of controls.
☐ **3.** Develop the steps in the sampling process for both (a) judgmental and (b) statistical methods.

This chapter and the next provide an introduction to the use of audit sampling techniques. This chapter is concerned with audit sampling techniques useful in testing controls. Chapter 12 explains the use of sampling for substantive tests of details.

Whether applied to tests of controls or substantive tests of details, sampling is useful to the auditor because it provides an efficient means of reaching audit conclusions about certain characteristics of an entire class of transactions or an entire balance based on an examination of a representative subset of items selected from the class or balance. Standards of the profession allow the use of sampling rather than 100-percent verification. To assure the adequacy of samples, the auditor must consider both materiality and audit risk prior to establishing an appropriate sample size. Though never required, sampling is often relied upon for the accumulation of sufficient competent evidential matter as required by the third standard of field work.

This chapter explains how sampling is used in evaluating a system of internal control. Appendixes 11–A through 11–C include tables that can be used in determining the sample size for attributes sampling. Appendixes 11–D through 11–F include tables that can be used to evaluate the results of attributes samples. Appendix 11–G contains an example showing the use of the microcomputer in an attributes sampling application.

The Sampling Process and the Audit

☑ **Objective 1**
Know sampling as
part of audit
process

The term **sampling** as we use it in auditing is defined in SAS 39 (AU350) as "the application of an audit procedure to less than 100 percent of the items within an account balance or class of transactions for the purpose of evaluating some characteristic of the balance or class."[1] SAS 39 also prescribes the procedures that should be followed when sampling is used in an audit.

Audit sampling is commonly used to evaluate one or the other of two types of characteristics associated with a class of accounting transactions or an accounting balance. The first of these characteristics is the rate of occurrence of error from a particular documented control procedure. When used in this way, the auditor is performing a test of controls. Such tests are usually applied to a representative sample of all items from a class or balance that should have been subjected to the control procedure under study. These tests are the subject of this chapter.

The second characteristic of accounting data of common interest to auditors is the dollar value of (or dollar error in) a class of transactions or balance. The use of audit sampling to support conclusions about the dollar value of, or dollar error in, an account or balance is the subject of Chapter 12.

Conclusions reached on the basis of an audit sample are seldom considered in isolation. Usually, the auditor will find it necessary to combine the results of an audit sample with results from nonsampling procedures or other audit samples providing evidence related to the same audit objective. So, for example, the auditor may combine the results of one or more tests of documented controls conducted using audit sampling techniques with the results of nonsampling techniques employed to test undocumented controls, such as the segregation of duties. The results of nonsampling techniques are often based on auditing procedures such as inquiry and observation. The importance of the results of these tests in relation to the results of sampling are a matter of audit judgment. Neither is necessarily more important than the other.

The confirmation of accounts receivable may serve as an example in the case of substantive tests of details. The results of sampling techniques applied to accounts receivable will often be combined with results obtained from nonsampling procedures employed to assess the adequacy of the allowance for bad debts prior to reaching an audit conclusion about the valuation objective as concerns accounts receivable. Again, neither of these audit procedures is necessarily more important than the other. Just as different audit samples can lead to different conclusions about the fairness of various dollar values that appear as representations on financial statements, different audit sample results may assist the auditor in reaching different conclusions about the assessed level of control risk applicable to different types of financial statement assertions. For example, the auditor may conclude that evidence gathered in relation to controls over sales transactions supports a low level of controls risk for assertions related to sales events. Within the same engagement, the auditor may also reach the conclusion that available evidence does not support low levels of controls risk related to expenditures. Thus, control risk will be assessed as low for sales-related assertions but high for those related to expenditures.

It is important to observe that generally accepted auditing standards do not require the use of sampling. Rather, they require that the auditor plan procedures to ensure that all material disclosures on the financial statements receive some audit attention, whether through sampling or nonsampling procedures or some combination of both, and that all audit conclusions reached be properly documented.

This chapter begins with a discussion of the sampling process and the concepts that drive appropriate sample results in auditing. Professional standards (SAS 39) do not mandate statistical sampling. Neither statistical nor nonstatistical sampling is necessarily the preferred technique. There is no necessary reason to believe that the results of a judgmental technique should be different from or preferred to the results achieved from a well-designed statistical sample.

Because neither technique is necessarily preferable in all circumstances, this chapter begins with a discussion of concepts common to both nonstatistical and statistical sampling. Subsequently, attention is given to the typical use of statistical sampling techniques to support results in relation to tests of controls. The next chapter (Chapter 12) is similarly structured but deals with the use of audit sampling to support substantive tests of details useful in reaching conclusions about the dollar value of (or dollar error in) accounts or balances.

The Effects of Audit Risk, Materiality, and Auditor Expectations on the Sampling Process

☑ **Objective 2**
Explain effects of audit risk and materiality on the sampling process in relation to control assessment

In Chapter 6, we introduced the concepts of audit risk and materiality. As defined in SAS 47 (AU 312), audit risk is the risk of issuing an inappropriately unqualified audit report.[2] Materiality is the characteristic that an error in a financial statement item possesses when its disclosure, either alone or in aggregate with other similar errors, would affect the decision processes of an informed user of the financial statements. It is important for the auditor to consider audit risk and materiality as part of planning for the engagement, because of the effects they have on the nature, timing, and extent of audit tests. Since sampling refers to the extent of testing, we will now focus our attention on the effects of audit risk and materiality on sample sizes.

Audit Risk and Sampling

SAS 47 (AU 312) states the formula for audit risk as

$$RT = IR \times IC \times DR$$

where RT is total audit risk, IR is inherent risk, IC is internal control risk, and DR is detection risk.

All of these terms were defined in Chapter 5. Inherent risk and internal control risk are, respectively, the risk that material errors will occur because of factors inherent either in the company, industry, or account balance, and the risk that material errors that occur will not be detected and corrected by the internal control structure.

The client is primarily responsible for doing what is possible to control these two risks. It is the auditor's responsibility to develop conclusions or assessments regarding IR and IC. Those conclusions assist in establishing the nature, timing, and extent of tests for the detection risk element (DR) of the model. The auditor is responsible for controlling DR. This is done primarily in two ways:

1. The auditor should adhere to generally accepted auditing standards and to quality control standards such as professional development of staff, adequate consultation within the firm, and supervisory review of work performed by assistants, thus reducing nonsampling risk to an acceptable and low level.
2. When sampling is used, the auditor should carry out the sampling process so that the expected conclusion reached by auditing the sample will be the same as it would have been had the entire population of like items been examined for the same characteristic—that is, reduce the risk of sampling error to an acceptably low level.

Nonsampling Risk

Nonsampling risk involves parts of the audit process that are independent from sampling methods. These risks include the risk of forming incorrect conclusions because of failure to employ appropriate or effective auditing procedures, applying auditing procedures improperly, or drawing incorrect conclusions because of faulty reasoning by the auditor. For example, the most appropriate auditing procedure to determine existence of accounts receivable may be confirmation of those accounts with customers. The auditor may have examined sales invoices and, based on that procedure, concluded that the accounts receivable actually existed at the end of the period under audit. This is an example of failure to employ the appropriate auditing procedure. Auditing procedures may also be improperly applied, such as a failure to follow up on all differences found on accounts receivable confirmations. An example of improper reasoning would be concluding that an account receivable was collectible just because the client's customer returned the confirmation request to the auditor, as requested, with no exception noted. Neither the ability nor willingness to pay is confirmed by admission of the debt.

Nonsampling risk will exist even if the auditor examines 100 percent of the items in an account balance or system. Sample size is not a consideration in controlling nonsampling risk since it cannot be reduced by increasing the sample size. The auditor should, however, carefully conduct and plan each individual audit so that nonsampling error can be effectively controlled by adherence to quality control standards and generally accepted auditing standards.

Sampling Risk

Sampling error is the result of having selected a nonrepresentative sample. The risk of such an occurrence, called **sampling risk**, can be controlled but not necessarily detected. Sampling risk is the risk that the conclusion reached from examining and properly projecting results from a sample will be different from the conclusion reached by performing the same audit procedure on all items in the population before reaching a conclusion. The principal means of controlling sampling risk are to increase the size of a sample or to study a population characteristic with little variability among items within the population.

Since we are discussing the sampling process in this chapter, we will focus on the sampling element of detection risk in the equation for audit risk. In statistics, sampling risk is the mathematical complement of the reliability, or confidence percentage. Thus, if the auditor specifies acceptable risk of 5 percent, he or she is at the same time expressing desired **confidence** of 95 percent. Sampling risk is quantified and controlled in statistical sampling. In nonstatistical sampling, this risk is usually controlled qualitatively, as explained later.

The **acceptable risk of overreliance (ARO)** on internal control is the risk that the sample supports the auditor's planned assessment of control risk with respect to a particular financial statement assertion when the true population error rate does not justify such an assessment. For example, assume that, during the preliminary assessment of internal control risk for a company, the auditor is told by the client that all sales orders are approved by the credit department before goods are shipped and invoiced. The auditor plans to assess control risk at a low level so that substantive tests over the allowance for doubtful accounts can be reduced. Control risk can only be assessed at that level, however, if tests of the control reveal that the prescribed control is actually being carried out. Therefore, the auditor will conduct a test of controls, which consists of selecting a sample from the sales order file and examining those orders for the initials of the credit department supervisor. Suppose the auditor conducts the tests and, on the basis of sample results, estimates that the population deviation (error) rate for this control does not exceed 4 percent. The auditor may, in advance, have decided that the control would be judged as effective if deviation from it did not exceed a maximum tolerable rate of 5 percent. On the basis of the test, the auditor would conclude that control risk is, in fact, low and thus limit the substantive tests on the allowance for doubtful accounts. However, if (unknown to the auditor) the true deviation rate in the population was 10 percent for this control, the auditor would be overrelying on the control and thus overly limiting the related substantive tests.

The **risk of underreliance** is the risk that the sample results do not support the auditor's planned level of assessed risk for a control when the true occurrence rate for the control in fact supports such an assessment. In the above example, assume that the auditor, on the basis of the sample of sales orders chosen, concludes that the population deviation rate for credit approval of sales orders is 10 percent. With the maximum tolerable rate at 5 percent, the auditor would assess control risk as too high for the prescribed control and, thus, unnecessarily increase the substantive tests on the balance of the allowance for doubtful accounts. If the true rate of occurrence is, in fact, 4 percent, the auditor will have unnecessarily increased substantive tests.

The risk of underreliance on internal accounting control relates to the efficiency with which the audit is performed, not its effectiveness. For example, if the auditor erroneously concludes that internal control was not effective, he or she would usually extend substantive tests to compensate for the perceived inability to rely on internal accounting controls. In this case, the correct audit conclusion (the opinion) would not be jeopardized, because the auditing procedures would still be effective. The result would be inefficiency, perhaps resulting in a higher fee, lower profit, or both. Inefficiency in auditing must ultimately be corrected or it will result in loss of client goodwill and business. However, underreliance is generally of less concern to the auditor than overreliance.

If the auditor overrelies on internal controls and thus limits the scope of substantive tests that are related to those controls (for example, by using smaller sample sizes), those substantive tests will be less likely to detect material errors and irregularities in the financial statements than if larger samples were used. Thus, overreliance on internal controls can be a contributing factor in issuing an inappropriately unqualified audit report. Therefore, of the two types of risk, the auditor is usually more concerned with the risk of overreliance.

Sampling risk must be controlled by the auditor regardless of whether nonstatistical or statistical methods of sampling are employed. Examples later in the chapter illustrate how this is done with both nonstatistical and statistical sampling. SAS 39 states that because tests of controls are the primary source of evidence as to whether internal controls are being applied as prescribed, the auditor should specify low levels of acceptable risk of overreliance. If quantified, that risk might be as low as 1 to 10 percent. Tables for determination of sample size and evaluation of sample results in Appendixes A through F of the chapter specify levels of 10, 5, and 1 percent acceptable risk of overreliance (ARO), respectively.

Materiality

When related to the sampling process for tests of controls, materiality is expressed as the maximum rate of deviation from a prescribed control procedure that would be acceptable without altering the auditor's planned assessment of the effectiveness of a particular control. The term used to describe the maximum acceptable deviation is tolerable deviation rate (TDR). In our example above, the auditor specified a maximum tolerable deviation rate of 5 percent. This means that the auditor would tolerate as much as 5-percent deviation from the prescribed control and still conclude that the control was operating effectively. Statistically, we describe the maximum tolerable deviation rate as the desired upper precision limit. Factors that influence the auditor's assessment of the maximum tolerable deviation rate include

- The accounting records being tested. If the records are of critical importance to the presentations in the financial statements, a low tolerable deviation rate would be specified.
- Other related internal accounting control procedures. If there are other related controls that affect a single account balance on which the auditor intends to place some reliance, the auditor need not be quite so concerned with results relating to a single control as he or she would be if that control were the only one affecting reliance.
- The purpose of the auditor's evaluation. In the standard financial statement audit, the auditor's purpose is to assess internal control risk for the purpose of judging the nature, timing, and extent of detection risk procedures to be performed. The auditor should remember that although deviations from pertinent controls increase the risk of material errors in the accounting records, such deviations do not necessarily result in financial statement errors. In the example cited above, the fact that a credit supervisor forgot to sign one or more sales orders does not necessarily result in a misstated allowance for doubtful accounts.

Expected Population Deviation Rate

An important judgmental determinant of sample size for tests of controls is the auditor's expected population deviation rate (EPDR). This factor represents the auditor's "best guess" as to the deviation rate in the population. To determine a value for EPDR, the auditor generally begins with the rate of deviation from the particular control that was experienced in the previous year. This is usually a theoretically justifiable position. In auditing, as well as many other professions, we make the assumption that, in the absence of evidence to the contrary, what has held true in the past will hold true in the future. If the client has made no substantial changes in the system or in personnel who operate it, such a position can be justifiable. The expected error rate may be adjusted judgmentally, upward or downward, based on current-year improvement (or deterioration) in controls observed during the preliminary understanding of the internal control structure in the current year's engagement. In a new engagement, the auditor may take a preliminary sample of transactions, examine them, and use the observed rate as the expected rate.

EPDR is always specified at a level that is *less than TDR*, thus allowing for sampling error in making the judgment. For example, EPDR might be set at 1 percent for a particular control, based on prior experience. TDR for the same control might be set at 5 percent. In so doing, the auditor is stating that expected deviation from the control is 1 percent, but that he or she will be able to tolerate an actual deviation rate as high as 5 percent without altering the judgment about the effectiveness of the control.

The decision regarding sample size for tests of controls involves the assessment of acceptable risk of overreliance (ARO), as well as expected population deviation rate (EPDR) and tolerable deviation rates (TDR). The subjective judgment of the experienced auditor must be relied upon in establishing risk and materiality limits. Subjective probability judgments, although made quite frequently by auditors, have only recently been given attention in the auditing literature. As an example, an auditor may state "The maximum risk I desire to accept that the failure of a credit supervisor to approve a sale will cause a material misstatement in accounts receivable is 10 percent." The auditor is implying that he or she desires to have 90 percent confidence in the effectiveness of that control. Similarly, the auditor might determine by subjective judgment that the tolerable deviation rate is 5 percent, based on the relative importance of the control to the financial statements of the business. Also, based on the experience obtained in prior audits with the same client, the auditor might subjectively judge the expected population deviation rate to be the same as that experienced in the past.

Figure 11−1 illustrates the effects on sample sizes of changes in the various inputs regarding population size, tolerable deviation rate (TDR), acceptable risk of overreliance (ARO), and expected population deviation rate (EPDR). Although sample size does vary slightly with the size of the population sampled, when sampling large populations (in statistical sampling, generally those in excess of 1,000), such changes have only a very small effect on sample size. However, changes in the tolerable deviation rate, acceptable risk of overreliance, and expected population deviation rate will have a significant effect on sample size. For example, assume that we specify a 5-percent acceptable risk of overreliance and have a 2.5-percent expected error occurrence rate. If the maximum tolerable deviation rate is then decreased from 5 percent to 4 percent, the sample size would increase from 240 to 550 items, an increase of 120 percent (see Appendix 11−B).

Figure 11−1 ▰▰▰▰

Effect of Changes in Parameters on Sample Size

Factor (other factors constant)	Sample size
1. Population size	
a. Increase	a. Increase*
b. Decrease	b. Decrease*
2. Tolerable deviation rate (TDR)	
a. Decrease (smaller absolute number)	a. Increase
b. Increase (larger absolute number)	b. Decrease
3. Acceptable risk of overreliance (ARO)	
a. Increase	a. Decrease
b. Decrease	b. Increase
4. Expected Population deviation rate (EPDR)	
a. Increase	a. Increase
b. Decrease	b. Decrease

*The effect of changes in population size will be nominal if the size of the sample is proportionally small in relation to the total number of items in the population. Where sample sizes are 5 percent or less of the total number of items in the population, the size of the population can usually be ignored in determining an appropriate sample size.

Steps in the Sampling Process

☑ **Objective 3a**
Develop steps in
sampling process
for judgmental
methods

The steps to be followed in sampling for tests of controls are the same regardless of whether nonstatistical or statistical techniques are employed. We show those steps in Figure 11–2 as embedded in the control risk assessment process that was discussed in Chapter 8.

Determining the Objectives of the Tests of Controls

The broad objective of any test of controls is to determine whether internal controls, which have been prescribed by the client, are working as planned. Normally this involves specifying control attributes to be tested, as well as defining the conditions that constitute deviations from those controls.

Control **attributes** are prescribed by the management of the company through the organization chart and procedures manual and are designed to

Figure 11–2 ▰▬▭

The Sampling Process and Control Risk Assessment

Assess Control Risk

1. Consider errors and irregularities that could occur.
2. Consider the financial statement assertions affected.
3. Determine the control attributes that would prevent, detect, or correct the errors or irregularities.
4. Determine whether controls are prescribed by client.
5. **Perform Tests of Controls.**
6. **Evaluate results.**
7. **Assess control risk on an assertion-by-assertion basis.**

Steps in the Sampling Process

1. Determine the objective of the control test.
   a. Identify the specific control attribute(s) to be tested (see step 3 above).
   b. Define deviation conditions which would represent a departure from the desired control procedure.
2. Define the relevant data population(s) from which to sample, as well as the sampling unit and the sampling frame.
3. Determine the sample size.
4. Select the sample.
5. Audit the sample.
6. Evaluate the evidence from the sample.
7. Make conclusions based on sample results regarding:
   a. Assessed level of internal control risk.
   b. Modification of nature, timing, and extent of substantive tests.
   c. Conditions to be communicated to the client.

prevent, detect, or correct errors and irregularities. The following are examples of deviations that can be prevented by prescribed control procedures:

EXAMPLE 1

The auditor is concerned about the possibility of fictitious sales, an error or irregularity that could have a material impact on the financial statement assertion of *existence/occurrence* of accounts receivable and sales. A deviation would be sales recorded in the sales journal but not supported by the appropriate documents. A control attribute that would prevent the error from occurring is to require the use of prenumbered and controlled, written sales orders and shipping documents based on customer purchase orders for all sales.

EXAMPLE 2

The auditor is concerned about the possibility of invalid payments to employees for time not spent on the job (again, a violation of the *occurrence* assertion). A deviation would be to issue paychecks without the supporting evidence of approved time cards. A control attribute that would prevent such payments is the requirement that time cards be prepared for all employees on record and that those time cards be approved by supervisors before paychecks can be issued.

It is essential that the auditor begin the sampling process by defining the objective of the test of controls, because that determines what will be done in the other six steps of the sampling process. Occasionally, the auditor may wish to base a portion of his control risk assessment on procedures that can be observed, but which are not necessarily documented. Neither statistical nor nonstatistical sampling is normally an appropriate technique for the auditor to employ in gathering evidence about the effectiveness of such controls. For example, the auditor may wish to observe the preparation of payroll by clerks in the personnel section of a corporation. While the auditor may learn a great deal about the competency of the employees and whether they are referencing appropriate pay schedules and withholding tables, etc., such procedures do not usually result in a documented indication that the control procedure has been performed. Therefore, they are not susceptible to sampling. Nevertheless, such tests of controls can be useful in assessing control risk at something below the maximum level.

Sampling may be useful for tests of controls that are part of the internal control structure if an audit trail of documentary evidence is produced in the performance of the control procedures. Control procedures that must be tested without reliance on documentary evidence are generally not susceptible to audit sampling.

Defining the Relevant Data Population(s)

A **population** (universe, field) is a well-defined collection of objects or events. The auditor may specify any audit population that gives the highest probability of fulfilling the audit objective. Audit populations may consist of all entries in an account, customer account balances, sales invoices, or some other collection of objects or events.

To accomplish the desired audit objective, it is important that the correct audit population be sampled. For example, to test the control attribute in example (1) above, the correct audit population would be all sales recorded in the sales journal. If, instead, the auditor had defined the population as all sales orders written, the population would not have the possibility of including a control deviation, thus negating the objective of the test.

It is essential, according to SAS 39, that the sample be selected from the entire population, thus giving each item in the population a chance of being selected. In the case of example (1) above, the auditor should select the sample from all entries in the sales journal for the entire period under audit. The sampling process itself could probably be accomplished in part at an interim date, with completion being performed at the time of final audit field work, as discussed in Chapter 6.

The **sampling units** are the individual elements of the population. In example (1) above, the sampling unit would be one individual entry in the sales journal. The **sampling frame** is the physical representation of the sampling units. In our example, the sampling frame would be individual sales invoices. Defining the sampling unit and sampling frame helps the auditor to relate the audit objective to the sampling task.

Determining the Sample Size

The method of determining the sample size depends on whether the auditor decides to use strict judgmental or statistical sampling techniques. If strict judgmental sampling is used, the sample size is determined by the auditor's judgment, taking into account the following factors:

1. Acceptable risk of overreliance (ARO).
2. Expected population deviation rate (EPDR).
3. Maximum tolerable deviation rate (TDR).
4. Population size.

EPDR, TDR, and population size are all either known or specified in quantitative terms by the auditor. For example, an expected population deviation rate of 3 percent would be based on experience; a tolerable deviation rate of 5 percent would be based on the auditor's seasoned judgment; and population size of 10,000 entries would be determined by examining the universe. ARO is not quantified when strict judgmental sampling is used. Instead, it is usually set using qualitative levels, such as high, medium, or low. Thus, there are no mathematical formulas or tables to help the auditor evaluate sampling error in quantitative terms. This is a major difference between strict judgmental and statistical sampling. In statistical sampling, it is possible to evaluate mathematically the risk of sampling error based on the laws of probability.

Remember that all sampling requires the exercise of judgment by the auditor. Sampling results are not ends in themselves. They merely provide evidence that, when considered with other information collected by the auditor, provides the basis for making sound, judgment-based audit decisions. It is not possible, or even desirable, to eliminate judgment from any sampling plan. Generally accepted auditing standards do not require the auditor to use statistically valid sampling plans. Such plans do have an advantage over strict judgmental plans because of their unique ability to provide a mathematical measure of the uncertainty (risk) that results from basing an audit decision on what was found in a sample rather than in the entire population of data. Statistical plans also eliminate personal biases in choosing the elements of the sample and in establishing sample size. Since mathematical laws are used to determine the size of the statistical sample, it is possible for the auditor to specify and define in quantitative terms the extent of sampling risk that he or she is willing to take.

Selecting the Sample

Generally accepted auditing standards do not require any one particular sampling method. The auditor may, therefore, choose any one of several methods, depending on the objectives of the audit tests and the costs associated with drawing and examining the sample. However, since sampling by definition involves evaluating or estimating some characteristic of the population being audited, it is essential that the sample selection method allow the selection of a sample that is representative of the population from which it was chosen. In other words, the sample selection method should give each item in the audit population a chance (not necessarily an equal chance) of being selected for audit. It is also desirable to select samples in a way that gives reasonable assurance that the selection of any one item for the sample is independent of the selection of another. Therefore, the auditor should exercise caution if selecting, say, every hundredth item from a population. Systematically selecting each hundredth item can be undesirable because the selection of each item in the sample is dependent upon or determined by selection of the first item in the sample even when that first item itself is randomly selected. Systematic sampling is acceptable in audit practice, but only when the auditor can reasonably believe that the items within the population are randomly ordered prior to his or her selection of the first item in a systematic sample. Similarly, block sampling as described below can suffer from the lack of independent selection and must be used with caution.

Two nonstatistical sample selection techniques, which are simple, relatively inexpensive, and popular, are **haphazard sampling** and **block sampling**. Haphazard sampling, as the name suggests, follows no particular pattern. For example, an auditor might be vouching vendor invoices in support of accounts payable. Suppose these invoices were all in three file drawers. If the auditor opened each file drawer and, without any conscious bias toward selecting or omitting any item, selected fifty invoices, he or she would be following a haphazard selection process. While this method is convenient, there is no scientific basis of judging the representativeness of the sample. In addition, there may be an unconscious bias in the selection process, which may produce nonrepresentative sample results.

Block sampling calls for the selection of a block of sample items as a group for audit. Once the first item in the block is selected, the remainder of the block is chosen automatically. For example, the auditor might select four blocks of cash receipts data, one from each calendar quarter, to vouch totals to validated deposit slips. Test month selection, a special type of block sampling, is no longer permitted under generally accepted auditing standards. In this method, a test month was selected arbitrarily by the auditor and all items of the universe for that month were included in the sample. This method is no longer used because it is judged not to result in a representative sample. Block sampling is acceptable only if a sufficiently large number of blocks are used to produce a representative sample.

Random sampling is a form of sample selection that allows every item in the population an equal and independent chance of being selected. If we use unrestricted random sampling to draw a sample from a population of 10,000 items, each item would have a $\frac{1}{10,000}$ chance of being selected. The auditor using statistical sampling must use random sampling to select the items to be audited because the laws of probability are used to estimate sampling risk. To use the laws of probability correctly, a random selection technique must be followed.

Unrestricted random sampling, without replacement of the sample items selected (the selection method most often used by auditors), relies on two basic underlying properties for its usefulness: (1) each unit in the population has an equal chance of being selected, and (2) each possible group of n items has an equal chance of being selected. To use unrestricted random selection, the auditor must first be able to identify each item in the population with a specific number. Random number tables or computer programs with random number generators can then be used to select items by number to be included in the sample. Selection of sample items can be made either with or without replacement, although sampling without replacement is usually more appropriate for audit populations. Figure 11–3 illustrates a partial random number table. In using the table, the auditor begins by selecting a random starting number. This can be done by making a *blind stab* at a certain point on the table or by using some other arbitrary method to select the first number. Next, the auditor must decide the interval between items and the direction to proceed (top to bottom, left to right, etc.). The sample can then be selected by following that plan until items equaling the desired sample size have been selected.

Let's take a closer look at the use of a random number table. Suppose we want to select 360 sales invoices without replacement from a population of 25,000 items, numbered consecutively from 00001 to 25,000. We might first select an arbitrary starting point by making a blind stab with a pencil at the random number table. Assume that the point of the pencil falls on column (B), group 1, row 5 in Figure 11–3. We would then select invoice number 16856 as the first sample item. If we decide to proceed from that point down the columns of the random number table, selecting every tenth item, and from left to right by columns, the next sales invoice selected would be number 3651. We then continue that process until all 360 sample sales invoices have been selected. If duplicate numbers arise in the random number table, they are disregarded because we are sampling without replacement.

Figure 11–3 ▪

Selected Random Digits

	A	B	C	D	E	F	G
1	835431	206253	467521	029822	700399	554652	450184
	512651	743206	118787	587401	921517	015407	206860
	376187	189133	154812	828785	667020	998697	579598
	092530	869028	483691	165063	847894	041617	762973
	238036	(016856)	290105	538530	079931	412195	838814
	308168	717698	919814	092230	215657	469994	805803
2	773429	915639	900911	276895	149505	540379	224349
	171626	601259	009905	572567	441960	299704	313987
	180570	665625	424048	713009	830314	664642	521021
	558715	965963	494210	875287	488595	898691	713010
	345067	361180	989224	138905	355519	045847	746266
	583819	310956	174728	099164	118461	758000	496302
3	615026	599459	722322	555090	572720	826686	456517
	812358	389535	166779	441968	105639	632418	340890
	784592	(003651)	279275	055646	341897	510689	026160
	094619	636747	934082	787345	772825	603866	565688
	450908	919891	157771	114333	710179	062848	615156
	593546	728768	984323	290410	970562	906724	315005
4	873778	491131	209695	604075	783895	862911	772026
	965705	317845	169619	921361	315606	990029	745251
	311163	943589	540958	556212	760508	129963	236556
	454554	284761	269019	924179	670780	389869	519229
	124330	819763	596075	064570	495169	030185	866211
	920765	122124	423205	596357	469969	072245	359269
5	183002	540547	312909	389818	464023	768381	377241
	600135	865974	929756	162716	415598	878513	994633
	235787	023117	895285	027055	943962	381112	530492
	953379	655834	283102	836259	437761	391976	940853
	009658	521970	537626	806052	715247	808585	252503
	176570	849057	387097	311529	893745	450267	182626
6	747456	304530	931013	678688	270736	355032	400713
	486876	631985	368395	154273	959983	672523	210456
	987193	268135	867829	025419	301168	409545	131960
	358155	950977	170562	246987	884126	785621	467942
	021394	182615	049084	942153	278313	872709	693590
	735047	428941	630704	893281	716045	267529	427605

Source: Abridged with the permission of the author and publisher from H. N. Broom, "New Random Sampling Numbers," *Baylor Business Studies* No. 1 (Waco, Tex.: Hankamer School of Business, Baylor University, 1949).

Systematic sampling is another means of obtaining a randomly selected sample if the population units are already in random order. Once the sample size (n) is determined by the auditor, the interval k is calculated as follows:

$$k = N/n$$

where N is the number of items in the population. Using a random start as explained above, the auditor then selects every kth item for the audit sample. As an example, assume that we have decided on a sample size of 200 from an audit population containing 2,200 items. The interval $k = (2,200/200) = 11$. Using a random number table, we will then obtain a random start from within the first eleven items in the population. We will then choose every eleventh item from the random starting point until a total of 200 sampling units have been drawn.

A major advantage of systematic selection is that it can be used without numbers being assigned to the units in the population. Therefore, it may require less time than other random selection methods. However, the auditor should not assume that, because the population is not sequentially ordered, it must be randomly ordered. When the auditor is unsure as to exactly how the population is ordered, he or she can beneficially use several random starts instead of one. For example, in applying this method to the preceding example (seeking k), the auditor might plan to use ten random starts and a sampling interval of 110. That would produce ten subsamples of twenty items each (200 items in all).

Auditing the Sample

Auditing the sample for tests of controls usually involves inspection of documentary evidence. The documents examined and the manner of inspection depend on the audit objective involved and the population from which the sample is drawn. The following example illustrates how the sampling process is carried out.

Assume that the auditor has the objective of ascertaining whether credit department personnel approve all credit sales before goods are shipped to customers. Initials of credit supervisors should be written on one copy of the sales order, indicating approval of the credit sale. The correct audit population in this case is all sales entries made during the year. The sampling unit is one sales entry in the sales journal. The sampling frame is the sales invoice supporting the sales entry. Suppose the auditor determined that a sample size of 119 is sufficient for this purpose. He or she draws 119 sales entries randomly from the sales journal and then locates the sales documents that support those entries. The auditing procedure followed to determine whether the above control procedure has been followed would be inspection of each document in the sample for the initials of the credit department supervisor. Any of the following conditions would indicate a deviation from established controls:

1. A missing invoice.
2. An invoice without credit approval initials.
3. An invoice that is initialed, but not with the proper person's initials.

As the auditor inspects the sample, he or she should list each exception noted and follow up by asking client personnel for explanations and by examining documentary corroborative evidence where available. For example, on observing initials other than the credit supervisor's, the auditor might inquire and discover that the initials are those of the treasurer who supervises the credit department supervisor. Further investigation might reveal that the treasurer initialled during the credit department supervisor's absence for vacation. Such an explanation would generally be satisfactory. In such cases, the results of the tests would not result in a recorded deviation.

Evaluating Sample Results

After the sample documents have been audited, the auditor should tally and compute the error rate for the sample. In tests of controls, computation of results involves counting the number of deviations, calculation of the sample deviation rate, and extrapolation (estimation) of the population deviation rate.

In our example, suppose the auditor found a total of four sales invoices that were lacking initials of the credit department supervisor. In addition, suppose that one of the invoices chosen for audit could not be found and, therefore, could not be examined. The total number of exceptions in this case is five. The sample deviation rate is 4.2 percent ($5/119$). The auditor must then extrapolate this finding to the population taken as a whole. If this is a strict judgmental sample, the sample deviation rate becomes the auditor's point estimate of the population deviation rate. This percentage must be compared with the auditor's maximum tolerable deviation rate, as explained in the following paragraphs.

Making Conclusions Based on Sample Results

After the audit of the sample has been completed, three conclusions should be made on the basis of the sample results from tests of controls. These require judgments as to the following:

1. Assessed level of internal control risk.
2. Modifications of the nature, timing, or extent of substantive tests, if any.
3. Matters of internal control structure to be communicated to the client.

In assessing the level of control risk, the deviation (error) rate from the sample must be compared with the maximum tolerable deviation rate (TDR). Based on that comparison, we might reason as follows:

1. If the sample deviation rate is higher than the tolerable rate, the sample results do not support the auditor's planned risk level for the control being tested. In this case, the auditor would first look for mitigating controls in the same system, which might make up for the fact that the control being tested was weak. If such controls exist, the auditor would use judgment in deciding whether to extend substantive tests affected by the control. If no such controls exist, the auditor would extend the substantive tests of the balances. In addition, the auditor would probably communicate to the client the discovery of the internal control weakness, as discussed in Chapters 8 and 22.
2. If the sample deviation rate is lower than the tolerable rate, the auditor should consider how close the sample error rate is to the tolerable rate. If

the sample rate is substantially below tolerable rate, the auditor may conclude that results support the planned risk assessment. If the sample rate is almost equal to the tolerable rate, the auditor would probably modify the assessed risk level for the control and perform slightly more substantive tests for assertions associated with the control than if the control had been tested and found effective.

In our example the computed rate is 4.2 percent, and the tolerable deviation rate is assumed to be 7 percent. The auditor would, in this case, probably conclude that the control is effective. On the other hand, if the sample rate were 6.2 percent, the auditor would be less likely to conclude that the control is effective and might instead look for mitigating controls or extend substantive tests slightly.

Caution and professional judgment are required when assessments of control risk are made. For example, the auditor may have used sampling procedures for several elements of the control structure related to supporting documentation requirements for cash disbursements for purchases. He or she may also have observed segregation of purchasing, cash disbursements, and recording functions, as well as monthly reconciliations of subsidiary ledgers to control accounts. The auditor may have planned to rely on all three of these elements of the control structure in reducing the assessment of control risks to a level lower than the maximum. Professional judgment may be required to determine an appropriate final assessment of control risk with regard to the valuation or allocation assertions associated with these three elements of the control structure. If the last two of these three control elements are deemed satisfactory, the auditor may assess the final control risk at slightly below the maximum level, even though the tests of controls associated with the sample of amounts calculated and verified fails to support control risk at the initially planned level. Conversely, the auditor might conclude that the maximum control risk level (1.0) is appropriate because of failures in the nondocumented control procedures as they were observed even though the results of the sample from tests of controls projected satisfactory results.

Tests of Controls: Statistical Sampling for Attributes

☑ **Objective 3b**
Develop steps in sampling process for statistical methods of control evaluation

Attributes sampling is the statistical sampling method most often used by auditors to perform tests of controls. The population characteristic being estimated is usually deviation from established internal controls, expressed as percentages. For example, an auditor may wish to ascertain, with reasonable certainty, the rate at which a particular client system deviates from a procedure which requires evidence of management approval of prices and credit for charge sales.

Attributes sampling is not, however, limited to tests of controls in its application. It can also be used in substantive tests of account balances in estimating, for example, the percentage of overdue accounts receivable or the percentage of raw material inventory that is obsolete.

We will illustrate the process of statistical sampling for attributes in the same sequence as that followed for the sampling process in general, which was described in the previous section.

Determining the Audit Objective

To determine the audit objective, it is necessary to divide the control system into its various control attributes so that deviation from each attribute can be considered as a separate audit problem. For example, several critical control attributes may be included in the internal control structure for sales by JEP Manufacturing Co. Some of them are listed in Figure 11–4. These attributes have been identified from the auditor's understanding of the internal control structure, as discussed in Chapter 8. To improve efficiency in sampling for attributes, the sampling frame can often be defined in such a way that several different attributes can be tested by use of the same sample of items. When testing controls, it is important to select only those internal control attributes which, if missing, could result in material misstatements to one or more financial statement assertions. If these controls are found to be weak, the auditor must expand substantive tests over the related financial statement assertions to be able to express an unqualified audit opinion.

Of the key attributes, some will undoubtedly be more important than others. For example, in Figure 11–4 the auditor may determine that the absence of prenumbered sales orders (control attribute 1) is more critical to the assertion of

Figure 11–4 ▬▬▬

Attributes of Internal Control over Sales (and Related Financial Statement Assertions) for JEP Manufacturing Co.

1. Prenumbered sales orders are prepared and controlled numerically for each sale. (Completeness)

2. Each sales order must be approved by a supervisor in the credit department before the sales transaction may be completed. (Valuation)

3. Prenumbered shipping tickets should be originated when sales orders have been approved. (Existence/Occurrence)

4. Sales invoices are prepared only after a properly approved sales order is received by the sales department. (Existence/Occurrence)

5. Supervisors in the sales department should review each sales invoice for pricing and mathematical accuracy and indicate that fact by initialing the sales documents. (Valuation)

6. The shipping department should receive a copy of each approved shipping ticket as authority to release goods. (Existence/Occurrence)

7. The billing department should check each sales invoice for correct prices, quantities, and extensions before the invoice is mailed to the customer. (Completeness, Valuation, Disclosure)

8. The accounts receivable department should prepare a daily sales summary and a control total from the approved sales invoices issued each day. (Completeness, Disclosure)

9. A copy of the prenumbered shipping ticket and one copy of each sales invoice should accompany all merchandise shipped to customers. (Completeness, Existence/Occurrence)

existence/occurrence than the failure to have prenumbered shipping documents and sales invoices accompanying each order (attribute 9). More stringent requirements (lower maximum tolerable deviation rate and lower acceptable risk of overreliance) should be specified for samples that test the more critical internal control attributes, which would call for larger sample sizes for those attributes.

Once the attributes to be tested have been identified, we are ready to develop a testable hypothesis for each attribute. This is usually stated in terms of the maximum tolerable deviation rate (TDR) from the attribute that will be accepted. For example, if we want to test control attribute 1 in Figure 11–4, we might establish the following testable hypothesis:

The deviation for preparation of prenumbered sales orders does not exceed 5 percent.

Notice that the hypothesis is specific. It deals with a particular attribute—the preparation of prenumbered sales orders. An error condition would be defined as a sale for which no such document exists. If tests support the hypothesis, we can conclude that the control is effective and that there is a reasonably low risk that the financial statement assertion of completeness is materially in error. As a result, substantive tests of that assertion may be reduced. If tests lead to rejection of the hypothesis, we will conclude that the client is not complying with the control. In the absence of mitigating strengths in other related controls, that finding would logically lead to the extension of substantive tests of the completeness assertion related to sales. In other words, with other things being equal, the rejection of any one of the several hypotheses (one for each attribute tested) will normally lead the auditor to an assessment of control risks at a level closer to the maximum level than would have been the case if all tests had been successful.

Defining the Audit Populations

The relevant data population for control attributes 1 and 2 is all sales transactions. The sampling unit would then be an individual entry in the sales journal. The sampling frame, or physical representation of those sampling units, would be the sales invoice package, containing copies of the sales order and sales invoice. The attributes to be tested could be any one of those attributes in the list for which the population of sales transactions is appropriate. The relevant population, sampling unit, and sampling frame will change, depending on the objective of the audit test.

Determining the Sample Sizes

Although population size may be important in developing the overall sampling plan, it becomes less important in attribute sampling when the population exceeds 1,000 items. With populations of this size, changes in the size of the population have only minimal effect on sample size for a stated TDR and ARO. The sample size is determined primarily by (1) tolerable deviation rate (TDR), (2) maximum acceptable risk of overreliance (ARO), and (3) expected population deviation rate (EPDR).

As stated previously, the **maximum tolerable deviation rate (TDR)** is the quantitative specification of what constitutes a material deviation. Just as we described in the nonstatistical section, TDR is the maximum rate of deviation from a prescribed control procedure that the auditor is willing to accept without altering the planned level of risk assessment for the control element being tested. If the control attribute being tested is a critical element of the internal control structure, then the tolerable rate will be lower than in circumstances in which the control attribute was less critical. For example, if the control attribute is critical to the client's internal control structure, the auditor will probably establish a tolerable rate of around 5 percent or less. If the control attribute is less than critical, or if it is supported by complementary controls, then the auditor might choose a tolerable rate of between 5 and 10 percent.

The **maximum acceptable risk of overreliance** (ARO) is, as stated previously, the risk that sample results will support a lower assessed level of control risk than the initial assessment level when, in fact, the actual underlying rate of deviation in the population is too high to justify such an assessment. Once again, if the control attribute being tested is a critical control, ARO would be set at a lower level than if the control were less than critical or if it were complemented by other controls.

Expected population deviation rate (EPDR) is defined exactly as discussed previously in the chapter. That is, EPDR is the auditor's *best guess* judgment as to the true population deviation rate for the control. The auditor's expectation is based primarily on his or her past experience, tempered by any new facts about the client's control environment or accounting system that may have been learned during this year's preliminary assessment phase of the control structure.

Once the TDR, ARO, and EPDR rates have been judgmentally specified, tables such as those in Appendixes 11–A through 11–C may be consulted to determine sample size. Notice that there are separate tables for various levels of ARO—10, 5, and 1 percent. Various tolerable deviation rates (TDR) appear in the column headings across the top of the table. Expected population deviation rates (EPDR) appear in the far left column. The following example illustrates how the table is used.

Assume that the auditor specified a maximum tolerable deviation rate of 5 percent at a 5-percent risk of overreliance. If the expected population deviation rate were 2.5 percent, Appendix 11–B shows that the auditor should select a sample of 240 items. A computer audit program can be used to provide sample sizes if it is programmed to react to inputs of data included in these tables. When this is the case, computer files generally also contain a random number generator to select a representative sample in a random fashion. Figure 11–5 illustrates the process of sample selection for each control attribute in our hypothetical example, using the tables provided in Appendixes 11–A through 11–C.

Figure 11–5

Sample Sizes for Tests of Controls for JEP Manufacturing Co.

Attribute of interest	Acceptable Risk of Overreliance (ARO)	Expected Population Deviation Rate (EPDR)	Maximum Tolerable Deviation Rate (TDR)	Sample Size
1. Prenumbered written sales order prepared.	.05	2.5%	5%	240
2. All sales orders approved for credit.	.01	1.0%	4%	260
3. Prenumbered shipping tickets should be originated when sales orders have been approved.	.05	2.5%	5%	240
4. Sales invoices prepared for each sales order.	.05	2.5%	5%	240
5. Review of sales orders by supervisors.	.01	1.5%	4%	360
6. Shipping department receives copy of shipping ticket as authority to release goods.	.01	2.0%	5%	300
7. Billing department checks each sales invoice.	.01	1.5%	4%	360
8. Accounts receivable daily control total agrees with sales summary.	.01	0	0	260*
9. Prenumbered shipping tickets accompany all sales invoices.	.10	2.5%	5%	160

*Knowledge is required for the entire population. In this case, 260 control totals form the entire population of sales days of the year.

Selecting the Sample

After sample sizes have been determined, the auditor should next select representative sample items. The items selected depend on the population, the sampling unit, and the sampling frame. Because several (and, in some cases, all) critical control attributes may appear on documents supporting all transactions in the population, it is probable that the sampling frame and sampling unit will not change over the entire system. Therefore, the auditor may test several attributes using the same sample items. Such a practice improves audit efficiency and, therefore, reduces audit cost. However, different sample sizes may still be required for each attribute since the inputs for TDR and ARO levels may vary with the criticalness of the control attributes being tested. Generally, the more critical (material) the internal control attribute, the more likely the auditor is to increase the sample size by specifying lower risk of overreliance, or a lower tolerable deviation rate from the sample result.

As stated previously, the auditor must use a random selection technique in selecting the items to obtain a statistically valid sample. The most appropriate technique for a particular test depends on the homogeneity of the audit population and on whether the sampling units or frames of the audit population are sequentially numbered.

Homogeneity is the relative similarity of units included in the population insofar as the characteristic under consideration is concerned. For example, the client's audit population may be homogeneous with respect to control attribute 1 in Figure 11–4 if it is company policy to prepare written sales orders for all sales, regardless of individual amounts. On the other hand, the client's population of sales transactions may not be homogeneous with respect to control attribute 7 in Figure 11–4 if the billing department is expected to check prices, quantities, and extensions only on sales invoices in excess of a specified amount, such as $100. As we observed earlier, unrestricted random sampling is designed for use with populations that are homogeneous with respect to the characteristic being tested. Heterogeneous populations should be stratified, after which random sampling techniques can be applied within each of the various strata.

If the audit population is numerically sequenced, we can use a random number table and manual sample selection or a computer audit program with a random number generator to help assure proper selection of a random sample. If the audit population is randomly ordered, a random sample can be selected by systematic sampling.

Auditing the Sample

After choosing a representative sample, the auditor must next audit the items in the sample. In attribute sampling, this means that each unit in the sample must be examined for the presence or absence of the desired attribute. The auditor should be careful to note the number of sample units containing deviations from established controls. For example, assume that the auditor is examining a sample of 240 invoices selected from an audit population of sales invoices for compliance with control attribute 1 in Figure 11–4. Assume further that the auditor discovers one sales invoice in the sample not supported by a written sales order. This deviation from established internal control is regarded as a procedural error and may be expressed in terms of a percentage: $\frac{1}{240}$ or 0.42 percent.

Evaluating the Evidence

Once the results of the sample have been obtained, the auditor must evaluate the evidence. This requires a judgment as to the sufficiency and competency of the evidence obtained. Sufficiency of evidence is directly related to sampling risk, which is then expressed through the desired precision limits and level of acceptable sampling risk. For example, by specifying ARO of .05 in the sampling plan outlined above, the auditor expressed willingness to accept a 5-percent risk of overreliance. If this level of risk, coupled with the pertinent precision limits, is acceptable to the auditor, the 240-unit sample is large enough to meet the sufficiency test.

Competency of evidence is a qualitative decision. The auditor must decide whether the evidence obtained is, within the constraint of cost-effectiveness, the best obtainable in support of the conclusion regarding the attribute being tested in relation to the pertinent audit objectives and financial statement assertions. In our example, the most competent evidence available in support of the audit conclusion as to whether the client is preparing prenumbered sales orders for each sale would be a sample of sales invoices, which can be vouched to written sales orders.

Developing a Logical Conclusion

The final step in the sampling process requires the auditor to reach an audit conclusion regarding the item under investigation. In attribute sampling, the audit conclusion should be stated in terms of judgment as to whether the client has complied with the control attribute. Tables are available to assist the auditor in evaluating sample results and in making such judgments. Appendix 11–E can be used to make this audit decision with respect to our example. Observe that Appendixes 11–D through 11–F consist of three tables for ARO levels of 10, 5, and 1 percent respectively. Sample sizes, selected by the process described earlier, are listed in the extreme left-hand column. The numbers in the body of each table represent the number of deviations found in testing the attribute. Numbers across the top of the table represent the **achieved upper precision limits (AUPL)**: they show the maximum inferred population deviation rates, based on our findings as we examined the items in the sample.

Recall that the results for our example, with respect to control attribute 1, revealed one deviation in a sample of 240 items. Appendix 11–E shows that, with this result from the sample, the auditor may infer with 5-percent risk of overreliance (95-percent *confidence*) that the error rate for attribute 1 in the entire population does not exceed 2 percent. The auditor can then compare the AUPL (maximum inferred upper deviation rate) for attribute 1 with the tolerable deviation rate or TDR. If AUPL is less than or equal to TDR, the auditor may conclude, with measured confidence, that the client is, within specified limits, complying with the established control attribute. Appendix 11–G illustrates the use of a microcomputer audit program to evaluate results in a similar manner.

The existence of a company policy requiring this control attribute, coupled with actual compliance on the part of the client, supports the auditor's hypothesis that this element of the system of internal control is in place and is functioning as it should. If other elements considered important in the control system also are functioning as they should, the auditor is justified in performing limited substantive tests of details of assertions associated with this particular control attribute.

On the other hand, if AUPL is greater than TDR, the auditor must conclude that the client is not complying with established controls. In this case, even though the control attribute has been prescribed, noncompliance on the client's part indicates a weakness in control. Such noncompliance may lead to an extension of substantive tests of details. In our example, AUPL of 2 percent is less than TDR of 5 percent. The auditor may therefore conclude that controls over attribute 1 are in place and functioning as they should. This evidence, if consistent with results of control tests over other attributes in the system, will allow the auditor to conclude that the control structure over sales is effective and that it supports a lower assessment of control risk than if controls were not effective. Substantive tests of details of sales system assertions, then, may be limited.

Recall from Figure 11–2 that a full understanding of the internal control structure for a particular subsystem requires the auditor to follow a logical progression with respect to each material financial statement balance in the system. This progression requires the following steps:

1. Consider the errors and irregularities that could occur in those balances. For this purpose, transactions may
   a. Be erroneously recorded.
   b. Possess inadequate or invalid support.
   c. Be unrecorded.
   d. Be improperly valued.
   e. Be improperly classified.
   f. Be recorded in the wrong period.
   g. Be improperly summarized.
2. Consider whether those errors and irregularities could cause particular assertions to be materially misstated.
3. Determine the control attributes that should prevent or detect such errors and irregularities.
4. Determine whether the necessary attributes are being prescribed by the client.
5. Determine whether the prescribed procedures for these elements are being followed by the client (tests of controls).
6. Evaluate the results of tests of controls.
7. On the basis of steps 1 through 6, assess control risk and determine the nature, timing, and extent of audit tests on transactions and on balances emerging from the system (substantive tests).

The procedures in the paragraphs that follow are based on the understanding of the internal control structure over the sales and accounts receivable system for JEP Manufacturing Co. It is presumed that the auditor has already completed steps 1 through 4 by the process described in Chapter 8. The following discussion is concerned with tests of controls (step 5).

All significant control attributes pertaining to a particular financial statement assertion should be evaluated before proceeding to substantive tests of that assertion. For example, in Figure 11–4, assume that attributes 1 through 9 have been prescribed by the client as part of the system that created debits to accounts receivable, for both the control account and the subsidiary accounts, along with corresponding credits to the sales account.

Each control attribute should be evaluated in terms of the financial statement error or irregularity it was designed to detect or prevent. To illustrate this point, note that control attributes 1, 4, and 5 are designd to prevent errors related to completeness, valuation, and existence/occurrence in recording of sales invoices.

Deviations from these controls could result in a misstatement of the sales account through omission, or duplicate recording of sales invoices, or in mathematical mistakes in arriving at individual sales amounts. In Figure 11–6 we see that tests of controls reveal acceptable compliance with control attributes 1 and 4. Therefore, the auditor can infer that the system was operating effectively to ensure that all orders received were properly recorded on sales invoices. Substantive tests of details, such as recalculations of footings and extensions of sales invoices and tracing of invoice postings to journals and ledgers, may then be limited or curtailed, if there are no offsetting weaknesses in other controls in the process.

Tests of control attribute 5, a related control, reveal an unacceptably high rate of failure to have supervisor approval over mathematical accuracy of sales invoices. The lack of supervisor initials on a sales document, however, does not necessarily mean that the control procedure was not done. The supervisor may have merely forgotten to initial documents after they were reviewed. Neither does the lack of supervisor initials mean that an equivalent percentage of sales invoices were inaccurately prepared and, therefore, have caused a misstatement in the sales account balances. Nevertheless, due to the lack of acceptable

Figure 11–6

Results of Tests of Controls over Sales System: JEP Manufacturing Co.

(1) Attribute of interest	(2) Sample size	(3) Exceptions noted	(4) Error rate in sample [(3) ÷ (2)]	(5) Acceptable risk of over-reliance	(6) Evaluation AUPL	(7) Evaluation TDR	(8) Conclusion[a]
1. Prenumbered written sales orders prepared	240	1	.4%	.05	2%	5%	S
2. All sales orders approved for credit	260	5	1.9%	.01	5%	4%	N
3. Prenumbered shipping tickets originated when sales orders have been approved	240	1	.4%	.05	2%	5%	S
4. Sales invoices prepared for each sales order	240	2	.8%	.05	3%	5%	S
5. Review of sales order by supervisor	360	8	2.2%	.01	5%	4%	N
6. Shipping department receives copy of shipping ticket as authority to release goods	300	3	1%	.01	4%[b]	5%	S
7. Billing department checks each sales invoice	360	3	.8%	.01	3%	4%	S
8. Accounts receivable daily control total agrees with sales summary	260*	0*	0*	.01	0*	0*	S
9. Prenumbered shipping tickets accompany all sales invoices	160	1	.6%	.10	3%	5%	S

[a]S = supports lower assessed level of control risk than preliminary assessment; N = does not support lower assessed level of control risk than preliminary assessment.
[b]Rounded to next most conservative estimate per table.
*Represents entire population. Results represent known, not estimated error. Therefore, table is not used.

compliance in this area, there is a higher probability of sales misstatement than if the compliance rate had been acceptable. In this situation, the auditor may choose from alternative courses of action: (1) Look for a mitigating control that offsets the weakness; or (2) extend substantive tests over the assertion that is likely to be misstated because of the weakness (valuation).

In our example, control attribute 7 calls for the billing department to check the mathematical accuracy of sales invoices. Figure 11–6 reveals the AUPL was acceptably low in the billing department. This may persuade the auditor that there is sufficient mitigation over the weakness in control attribute 5 in the sales department to prevent the necessity for extension of tests of mathematical details over the sales account.

If the second alternative is elected, substantive tests of the valuation assertion should be expanded. In this case, a larger sample of sales invoices than otherwise necessary would be selected. Each sales invoice would then be extended and footed. Prices would be traced to applicable price lists and quantities would be vouched to appropriate shipping documents.

In any event, a thorough error analysis should be performed on each observed deviation from the prescribed procedures. This should give the auditor insight as to the underlying reasons for the errors and, in that way, help in formulating a judgment as to the quality of the system. Ultimately, however, the auditor's judgment must still prevail in determining the effects of the system of internal control on the extent, timing, and nature of the substantive audit tests.

Discovery Sampling

Although it is in some ways a form of attribute sampling, **discovery sampling** has a different audit objective from that of attribute sampling. The objective of discovery sampling is to select a sample size (n) that has a specified probability (x) of yielding at least one occurrence of a deviation within a given population size (P) with a critical rate of occurrence (p). The critical rate is equivalent to the tolerable rate of error. The deviation sought in this case is usually the existence of an irregularity.

Discovery sampling is most useful in these situations:

- When the auditor suspects that a particular kind of critical irregularity or fraud has occurred and would like to determine if it is an isolated case.
- When it is possible to estimate a critical rate of occurrence of an irregularity that would cause a material misstatement in the financial statements if not disclosed.
- When an audit population of high relative risk (such as cash or accounts receivable) reveals a breakdown in the segregation of duties (recordkeeping and cash handling, for example) after the preliminary assessment of internal control risk.

Figure 11–7 illustrates a discovery sampling table. With discovery sampling, the population size should be specified as a parameter. Therefore, we will have different tables for populations of different sizes. The table illustrated is for population sizes of 5,000 to 10,000. Sample sizes are shown in the first column of the table. Critical rates of occurrence appear across the top of the table. Probabilities of occurrence appear in the body of the table.

To illustrate the technique of discovery sampling, assume that the auditor suspects fraud may be occurring in the handling of cash receipts and the posting of credits to accounts receivable, both of which are done by the same client employee. Assume further that the audit population contains 10,000 credit postings to accounts receivable and that the auditor estimates that a material misstatement may result if as many as 100 transactions (1 percent) are improperly posted. The auditor, therefore, desires to know how large a sample would have to be drawn to be 99 percent confident of uncovering at least one occurrence of such a fraud. Using the table in Figure 11–7, we find that the auditor would have to examine a sample of 460 transactions.

As you can see in Figure 11–7, discovery sampling requires inordinately large sample sizes when critical rates of occurrence in a population are less than 0.5 percent and the required **confidence** is high. This sampling procedure is

Figure 11–7

Discovery Sampling Table: Probability of Including at Least One Occurrence in a Sample for Populations between 5,000 and 10,000

Sample size	Upper precision limit: Critical rate of occurrence							
	.1%	.2%	.3%	.4%	.5%	.75%	1%	2%
50	5%	10%	14%	18%	22%	31%	40%	64%
60	6	11	17	21	26	36	45	70
70	7	13	19	25	30	41	51	76
80	8	15	21	28	33	45	55	80
90	9	17	24	30	36	49	60	84
100	10	18	26	33	40	53	64	87
120	11	21	30	38	45	60	70	91
140	13	25	35	43	51	65	76	94
160	15	28	38	48	55	70	80	96
200	18	33	45	56	64	78	87	98
240	22	39	52	62	70	84	91	99
300	26	46	60	70	78	90	95	99+
340	29	50	65	75	82	93	97	99+
400	34	56	71	81	87	95	98	99+
460	38	61	76	85	91	97	99	99+
500	40	64	79	87	92	98	99	99+
600	46	71	84	92	96	99	99+	99+
700	52	77	89	95	97	99+	99+	99+
800	57	81	92	96	98	99+	99+	99+
900	61	85	94	98	99	99+	99+	99+
1,000	65	88	96	99	99	99+	99+	99+
1,500	80	96	99	99+	99+	99+	99+	99+
2,000	89	99	99+	99+	99+	99+	99+	99+

Source: Audit Sampling Reference Manual, © Ernst & Whinney, 1977. Used with permission.

designed to uncover only those irregularities that occur with some degree of frequency. Therefore, it cannot be expected to uncover rare occurrences of irregularities. Although discovery sampling has its place in the audit process, it is used much less frequently than basic attribute sampling.

Summary

In this chapter we have discussed the process of sampling as it relates to auditing in general and as it relates to testing for internal controls in particular. Sampling was defined as the application of an auditing procedure to less than 100 percent of the items within a universe (population) for the purpose of evaluating some characteristic of the universe. We emphasized that, although sampling is often a necessary part of auditing, it is not required by generally accepted auditing standards. Some audit processes were cited in which sampling, as contemplated by SAS 39 (AU350), is not applicable. We also emphasized that samples can be strictly judgmental or statistical. Statistical sampling, however, is more scientific because it is based on the laws of probability.

The risks involved in auditing were discussed in terms of the overall audit risk model of SAS 47 (AU312). That model was first described in Chapter 5. In this chapter we expanded the discussion of the model by developing the concepts of nonsampling and sampling risks. These were shown as component parts of the detection risk (DR) element of the overall audit risk model. Sampling risk was shown to be the element of the model that could be controlled by adjusting the size of the sample. The primary advantage of statistical sampling techniques over strict judgmental techniques is that we can express the sampling risk in quantitative terms when using statistical samples, whereas that cannot be done using nonstatistical samples. The concept of materiality, as defined in SAS 47, was also discussed. The sampling measure of materiality (tolerable deviation rate) was emphasized, as well as the effect of that factor on sample sizes.

Steps in the sampling process, as they apply to tests of controls during the detailed phase of the auditor's study and evaluation of the system of internal control, were then described. These steps, which are followed regardless of whether statistical or judgmental techniques are employed, include determining the objectives of the test; defining the relevant data population, sampling unit, and sampling frame; determining the sample size; selecting the sample; auditing the sample; evaluating the evidence from the sample; and making conclusions based on sample results. The auditor's responsibilities relating to each of these steps for both nonstatistical and statistical sampling for attributes were then described.

Appendixes to the chapter contain tables that can be used with statistical sampling to determine sample size and to evaluate sample results. A special appendix (Appendix 11–G), which briefly illustrates the use of a microcomputer in carrying out the sampling process, has also been included.

Auditing Vocabulary

p. 417   **acceptable risk of overreliance (ARO):**   The risk that the sample supports the auditor's planned assessment of risk for a control procedure when the true compliance rate does not justify such an assessment.

p. 435   **achieved upper precision limit (AUPL):**   The maximum inferred population error rate, based on the findings of the sampling process.

p. 421   **attribute:**   The control procedure or characteristic that is the objective of the test of controls.

p. 429   **attributes sampling:**   The statistical sampling method most often used by auditors to perform tests of controls. The population characteristic being estimated is usually deviation from a prescribed internal attribute or procedure.

p. 424   **block sampling:**   Selection of a block of sample items as a group for audit, most often by numerical sequence.

p. 417   **confidence:**   The mathematical complement of sampling risk.

p. 438   **discovery sampling:**   A form of attribute sampling, the objective of which is to select a sample (n) that has a specified probability (X) of yielding at least one occurrence of a deviation within a given population size (P) with a critical rate of occurrence (p).

p. 432   **expected population deviation rate:**   The rate of deviation from a prescribed control that the auditor expects, usually based on past experience.

p. 424   **haphazard sampling:**   Sampling that follows no particular pattern for selection of sample items.

p. 434   **homogeneity:**   Similarity of sampling units.

p. 432   **maximum tolerable deviation rate (TDR):**   The maximum percentage deviation from a prescribed control that the auditor can accept and still say that there is substantial compliance with that control.

p. 416   **nonsampling risk:**   The risk that is part of the audit process but is not associated with selecting a sample that is nonrepresentative of the population.

p. 422   **population:**   A well-defined collection of objects or events.

p. 425   **random sampling:**   A form of sample selection that allows every item in the population an equal and independent chance of being selected.

p. 417   **risk of underreliance:**   The risk that the sample results do not support the auditor's planned assessment of control risk when the true compliance rate, in fact, supports such an assessment.

p. 414   **sampling:**   The application of an audit procedure to less than 100 percent of the items within an account balance or class of transactions for the purpose of evaluating some characteristic of the balance or class.

p. 423   **sampling frame:**   The physical representation of the sampling units.

p. 417   **sampling risk:**   The risk of selecting a nonrepresentative sample, and thus making the wrong conclusions from the data examined.

p. 423   **sampling unit:**   The individual elements of the population.

p. 426   **systematic sampling:**   A means of taking every kth item from the population. In this case, k is an interval that equals $N \div n$, where N is the number of items in the population and n is the number of items in the sample.

Appendix 11–A: Determination of Sample Size—10 Percent Acceptable Risk of Overreliance (ARO)

Expected population deviation rate (EPDR)	Tolerable deviation rate (TDR)																				
	1	2	3	4	5	6	7	8	9	10	12	14	16	18	20	25	30	35	40	45	50
0		114	76	57	45	38	32	28	25	22	22	15	15	11	11	10	10	10	10	10	10
.25	400	200	140	100	80	70	60	50	50	40	40	30	30	20	20	20	20	10	10	10	10
.5	800	200	140	100	80	70	60	50	50	40	40	30	30	20	20	20	20	10	10	10	10
1.0		400	180	100	80	70	60	50	50	40	40	30	30	30	20	20	20	10	10	10	10
1.5			320	180	120	90	60	50	50	40	40	30	30	30	20	20	20	10	10	10	10
2.0		*	600	200	140	90	80	50	50	40	40	30	30	30	20	20	20	10	10	10	10
2.5			*	360	160	120	80	70	60	40	40	30	30	30	20	20	20	10	10	10	10
3.0				800	260	160	100	90	60	60	50	30	30	30	20	20	20	10	10	10	10
3.5				*	400	200	140	100	80	70	50	40	40	30	20	20	20	10	10	10	10
4.0					900	300	200	100	90	70	50	40	40	30	20	20	20	10	10	10	10
4.5					*	550	220	160	120	80	60	40	40	30	20	20	20	10	10	10	10
5.0						*	320	160	120	80	60	40	40	30	20	20	20	10	10	10	10
5.5						*	600	280	160	120	70	50	40	30	30	20	20	10	10	10	10
6.0							*	380	200	160	80	50	40	30	30	20	20	10	10	10	10
6.5							*	600	260	180	90	60	40	30	30	20	20	10	10	10	10
7.0								*	400	200	100	70	40	40	40	20	20	10	10	10	10
7.5								*	800	290	120	80	40	40	40	20	20	10	10	10	10
8.0									*	460	160	100	50	50	40	20	20	10	10	10	10
8.5									*	800	200	100	70	50	40	20	20	10	10	10	10
9.0										*	260	100	80	50	40	20	20	10	10	10	10
9.5										*	380	160	80	50	40	20	20	10	10	10	10
10.0											500	160	80	50	40	20	20	10	10	10	10
11.0											*	280	140	70	60	30	30	20	20	10	10
12.0											550	180	90	70	30	30	20	20	10	10	
13.0												*	300	160	90	30	30	20	20	10	10
14.0													600	200	100	40	30	20	20	10	10
15.0													*	300	140	40	30	20	20	10	10
16.0														650	200	50	30	20	10	10	
17.0														*	340	70	40	30	20	20	10
18.0															700	100	50	30	20	10	10
19.0															*	100	50	30	20	10	10
20.0																160	50	30	20	10	10
22.0																400	80	40	30	20	20
24.0																*	120	50	30	20	20
26.0																	260	80	30	30	20
28.0																	1000	100	50	30	20
30.0																		180	50	30	20
33.0																		1000	100	50	30
36.0																			280	80	40
39.0																			*	160	60
42.0																				500	90
46.0																					300

Note: * = more than 1000.
Source: Adapted from *Audit Sampling Reference Manual,* © Ernst & Whinney, 1977. Used with permission.

Appendix 11–B: Determination of Sample Size— 5 Percent Acceptable Risk of Overreliance (ARO)

Expected population deviation rate (EPDR)	Tolerable deviation rate (TDR)																				
	1	2	3	4	5	6	7	8	9	10	12	14	16	18	20	25	30	35	40	45	50
0		150	100	74	59	49	42	36	32	29	14	10	10	10	10	10	10	10	10	10	10
.25	650	240	160	120	100	80	70	60	60	50	40	40	30	30	30	20	20	20	10	10	10
.5	*	320	160	120	100	80	70	60	60	50	40	40	30	30	30	20	20	20	10	10	10
1.0		600	260	160	100	80	70	60	60	50	40	40	30	30	30	20	20	20	10	10	10
1.5		*	400	200	160	120	90	60	60	50	40	40	30	30	30	20	20	20	10	10	10
2.0			900	300	200	140	90	80	70	50	40	40	30	30	30	20	20	20	10	10	10
2.5			*	550	240	160	120	80	70	70	40	40	30	30	30	20	20	20	10	10	10
3.0				*	400	200	160	100	90	80	60	50	30	30	30	20	20	20	10	10	10
3.5				*	650	280	200	140	100	80	70	50	40	40	30	20	20	20	10	10	10
4.0					*	500	240	180	100	90	70	50	40	40	30	20	20	20	10	10	10
4.5					*	800	360	200	160	120	80	60	40	40	30	20	20	20	10	10	10
5.0						*	500	240	160	120	80	60	40	40	30	20	20	20	10	10	10
5.5						*	900	360	200	160	90	70	50	50	30	30	20	20	10	10	10
6.0							*	550	280	180	100	80	50	50	30	30	20	20	10	10	10
6.5							*	1000	400	240	120	90	60	50	30	30	20	20	10	10	10
7.0								*	600	300	140	100	70	50	40	30	20	20	10	10	10
7.5								*	*	460	160	100	80	50	40	30	20	20	10	10	10
8.0									*	650	200	100	80	50	50	30	20	20	10	10	10
8.5									*	*	280	140	80	70	50	30	20	20	10	10	10
9.0										*	400	180	100	70	50	30	20	20	10	10	10
9.5										*	550	200	120	70	50	30	20	20	10	10	10
10.0											800	220	120	70	50	30	20	20	10	10	10
11.0											*	400	180	100	70	40	30	20	20	20	20
12.0												900	280	140	90	40	30	20	20	20	20
13.0												*	460	200	100	50	30	20	20	20	20
14.0													1000	300	160	50	40	20	20	20	20
15.0													*	500	200	60	40	20	20	20	20
16.0														*	300	80	50	30	30	20	20
17.0														*	550	100	50	40	30	20	20
18.0															*	140	50	40	30	20	20
19.0															*	180	70	40	30	20	20
20.0																220	70	40	30	20	20
22.0																600	100	50	30	30	20
24.0																*	200	70	40	30	20
26.0																	400	100	50	30	30
28.0																	*	160	60	40	30
30.0																		280	80	40	30
33.0																		*	160	60	30
36.0																			460	100	50
39.0																			*	220	80
42.0																				800	140
46.0																					550

Note: * = more than 1000.
Source: Adapted from *Audit Sampling Reference Manual,* © Ernst & Whinney, 1977. Used with permission.

Appendix 11–C: Determination of Sample Size— 1 Percent Acceptable Risk of Overreliance (ARO)

Expected population deviation rate (EPDR)	1	2	3	4	5	6	7	8	9	10	12	14	16	18	20	25	30	35	40	45	50
.25	*	340	240	180	140	120	100	90	80	70	60	50	40	40	40	30	20	20	20	20	20
.5	*	500	280	180	140	120	100	90	80	70	60	50	40	40	40	30	20	20	20	20	20
1.0		*	400	260	180	140	100	90	80	70	60	50	40	40	40	30	20	20	20	20	20
1.5		*	800	360	200	180	120	120	100	90	60	50	40	40	40	30	20	20	20	20	20
2.0			*	500	300	200	140	140	100	90	70	50	40	40	40	30	20	20	20	20	20
2.5			*	1000	400	240	200	160	120	100	70	60	40	40	40	30	20	20	20	20	20
3.0				*	700	360	260	160	160	100	90	60	50	50	40	30	20	20	20	20	20
3.5				*	*	550	340	200	160	140	100	70	50	50	40	40	20	20	20	20	20
4.0					*	800	400	280	200	160	100	70	50	50	40	40	20	20	20	20	20
4.5					*	*	600	380	220	200	120	80	60	60	40	40	20	20	20	20	20
5.0						*	900	460	280	200	120	80	60	60	40	40	20	20	20	20	20
5.5						*	*	650	380	280	160	90	70	70	50	40	30	30	20	20	20
6.0							*	1000	500	300	180	100	80	70	50	40	30	30	20	20	20
6.5							*	*	800	400	200	120	90	70	60	40	30	30	20	20	20
7.0								*	*	600	240	140	100	70	70	40	30	30	20	20	20
7.5									*	800	280	160	120	80	70	40	30	30	20	20	20
8.0									*	*	400	200	140	100	70	50	30	30	20	20	20
8.5									*	*	500	240	140	100	70	50	30	30	20	20	20
9.0										*	700	300	180	100	90	50	30	30	20	20	20
9.5										*	1000	360	200	140	90	50	30	30	20	20	20
10.0											*	420	220	140	90	50	30	30	20	20	20
11.0											*	800	300	180	140	60	40	30	30	20	20
12.0												*	500	240	160	70	40	30	30	20	20
13.0												*	600	360	200	90	50	30	30	20	20
14.0													*	500	280	100	50	40	30	20	20
15.0													*	900	360	120	60	40	30	20	20
16.0														*	550	160	80	40	30	30	20
17.0														*	1000	180	80	40	40	30	20
18.0															*	240	100	50	40	30	20
19.0															*	300	100	60	40	30	20
20.0																420	120	60	40	30	20
22.0																*	200	90	50	40	30
24.0																*	340	120	70	40	30
26.0																	800	180	80	50	30
28.0																	*	280	100	60	40
30.0																		550	140	70	40
33.0																		*	300	100	60
36.0																			900	180	80
39.0																			*	400	140
42.0																				*	240
46.0																					900

Note: * = more than 1000.
Source: Audit Sampling Reference Manual, © Ernst & Whinney, 1977. Used with permission.

Appendix 11–D: Evaluation of Results—
10 Percent Acceptable Risk of Overreliance (ARO)

Sample size	Achieved upper precision limit: percent rate of occurrence (AUPL)																				
	1	2	3	4	5	6	7	8	9	10	12	14	16	18	20	25	30	35	40	45	50
10																0		1		2	
20											0				1	2		3	4	5	6
30								0				1		2		4	5	6	8	9	10
40					0					1		2	3		4	6	7	9	11	13	15
50				0				1			2	3	4	5		8	10	12	15	17	19
60			0			1		2			3	4	5	6	7	10	13	15	18	21	24
70			0			1		2		3	4	5	6	8	9	12	15	18	22	25	29
80			0		1		2		3	4	5	6	8	9	10	14	18	22	25	29	33
90			0		1	2			3	4	6	7	9	11	12	16	20	25	29	33	38
100			0	1		2	3	4		5	7	9	10	12	14	19	23	28	33	38	43
120		0		1	2	3	4	5	6	7	9	11	13	15	17	23	29	34	40	46	52
140		0	1	2	3	4	5	6	7	9	11	13	16	18	21	27	34	41	48	54	61
160		0	1	2	4	5	6	8	9	10	13	16	19	22	25	32	40	47	55	63	71
180		0	2	3	4	6	7	9	10	12	15	18	22	25	28	37	45	54	63	71	80
200		1	2	4	5	7	8	10	12	14	17	21	24	28	32	41	51	60	70	80	90
220		1	2	4	6	8	10	12	13	15	19	23	27	31	35	46	56	67	78	89	99
240	0	1	3	5	7	9	11	13	15	17	21	26	30	35	39	50	62	74	85	97	109
260	0	1	3	5	8	10	12	14	17	19	24	28	33	38	43	55	68	80	93	106	119
280	0	2	4	6	8	11	13	16	18	21	26	31	36	41	46	60	73	87	101	114	128
300	0	2	4	7	9	12	14	17	20	22	28	33	39	45	50	64	79	93	108	123	138
320	0	2	5	7	10	13	16	18	21	24	30	36	42	48	54	69	85	100	116	132	148
340	0	3	5	8	11	14	17	20	23	26	32	38	45	51	58	74	90	107	123	140	157
360	0	3	6	9	12	15	18	21	25	28	34	41	48	55	61	79	96	113	131	149	167
380	0	3	6	9	13	16	19	23	26	30	37	44	51	58	65	83	102	120	139	158	177
400	1	4	7	10	14	17	21	24	28	31	39	46	54	61	69	88	107	127	146	166	186
420	1	4	7	11	14	18	22	26	29	33	41	49	57	65	73	93	113	134	154	175	196
460	1	4	8	12	16	20	24	28	33	37	45	54	63	71	80	102	124	147	170	192	215
500	1	5	9	13	18	22	27	31	36	40	50	59	69	78	88	112	136	160	185	210	235
550	2	6	10	15	20	25	30	35	40	45	55	66	76	87	97	124	150	177	204	232	259
600	2	7	12	17	22	28	33	39	44	50	61	72	84	95	107	135	165	194	224	253	283
650	2	8	13	19	24	30	36	42	48	54	66	79	91	104	116	147	179	211	243	275	308
700	3	8	14	20	27	33	39	46	52	59	72	85	99	112	126	159	194	228	262	297	332
800	4	10	17	24	31	38	46	53	61	68	83	99	114	129	145	183	222	262	301	341	381
900	4	12	20	28	36	44	52	61	69	78	95	112	129	146	164	207	251	296	340	385	430
1000	5	13	22	31	40	49	59	68	77	87	106	125	144	164	183	232	280	330	379	429	479

Note: The number of observed occurrences are shown in the body of the table.
Source: *Audit Sampling Reference Manual*, © Ernst & Whinney, 1977. Used with permission.

Appendix 11–E: Evaluation of Results—
5 Percent Acceptable Risk of Overreliance (ARO)

Sample size	Achieved upper precision limit: percent rate of occurrence (AUPL)																				
	1	2	3	4	5	6	7	8	9	10	12	14	16	18	20	25	30	35	40	45	50
10																	0		1		
20												0				1	2	3		4	5
30										0			1		2	3	4	5	7	8	10
40								0			1		2		3	5	6	8	10	12	14
50					0					1	2	3	4		5	7	9	11	13	16	18
60				0				1			2	3	4	5	6	9	11	14	17	20	23
70				0			1		2		3	4	5	7	8	11	14	17	20	24	27
80			0			1		2		3	4	5	7	8	9	13	16	20	24	28	32
90			0			1	2		3	4	5	6	8	9	11	15	19	23	27	32	36
100		0		1				2	3	4	6	8	9	11	13	17	22	26	31	36	41
120		0	1		2	3	4	5	6		8	10	12	14	16	21	27	33	38	44	50
140		0	1	2	3	4	5	6	7		10	12	14	17	19	26	32	39	46	52	59
160		0	1	2	3	4	5	6	8	9	12	14	17	20	23	30	38	45	53	61	69
180		0	1	2	3	5	6	8	9	11	14	17	20	23	26	35	43	52	60	69	78
200		0	1	3	4	6	7	9	11	12	16	19	23	26	30	39	48	58	68	77	87
220		0	2	3	5	7	8	10	12	14	18	22	25	29	33	44	54	64	75	86	97
240		1	2	4	6	8	10	12	14	16	20	24	28	33	37	48	59	71	83	94	106
260		1	3	4	7	9	11	13	15	17	22	26	31	36	41	53	65	77	90	103	116
280		1	3	5	7	10	12	14	17	19	24	29	34	39	44	57	71	84	98	111	125
300	0	1	3	6	8	11	13	16	18	21	26	31	37	42	48	62	76	91	105	120	135
320	0	2	4	6	9	11	14	17	20	22	28	34	40	45	51	66	82	97	113	128	144
340	0	2	4	7	10	12	15	18	21	24	30	36	42	49	55	71	87	104	120	137	154
360	0	2	5	8	10	13	17	20	23	26	32	39	45	52	59	76	93	110	128	146	163
380	0	2	5	8	11	14	18	21	24	28	34	41	48	55	62	80	98	117	135	154	173
400	0	3	6	9	12	15	19	22	26	29	37	44	51	59	66	85	104	123	143	163	183
420	0	3	6	9	13	16	20	24	27	31	39	46	54	62	70	90	110	130	151	171	192
460	0	4	7	11	15	18	22	26	31	35	43	51	60	68	77	99	121	143	166	188	211
500	1	4	8	12	16	21	25	29	34	38	47	56	66	75	84	108	132	157	181	197	221
550	1	5	9	14	18	23	28	33	38	43	53	63	73	83	94	120	146	173	200	227	255
600	1	6	10	15	20	26	31	36	42	47	58	69	80	92	103	132	161	190	219	249	279
650	2	6	12	17	23	28	34	40	46	52	64	76	88	100	112	143	175	207	239	271	303
700	2	7	13	19	25	31	37	43	50	56	69	82	95	108	122	155	189	223	258	292	327
800	3	9	15	22	29	36	43	51	58	65	80	95	110	125	141	179	218	257	296	336	376
900	4	10	18	26	34	42	50	58	66	74	91	108	125	142	159	203	247	291	335	379	424
1000	4	12	20	29	38	47	56	65	74	84	102	121	140	159	178	227	275	324	374	423	473

Note: The number of observed occurrences are shown in the body of the table.
Source: Audit Sampling Reference Manual, © Ernst & Whinney, 1977. Used with permission.

Appendix 11–F: Evaluation of Results— 1 Percent Acceptable Risk of Overreliance (ARO)

Sample size	Achieved upper precision limit: percent rate of occurrence (AUPL)																				
	1	2	3	4	5	6	7	8	9	10	12	14	16	18	20	25	30	35	40	45	50
10																			0		
20																0	1		2	3	4
30													0			1	3	4	5	6	8
40											0		1		2	3	5	7	8	10	12
50									0			1	2		3	5	7	9	11	13	16
60								0			1	2	3		4	7	9	12	14	17	20
70							0				1	2	3	4	5	6	9	11	14	18	21	24
80						0				1		2	4	5	6	7	10	14	17	21	25	29
90					0				1	2	3	5	6	7	9	12	16	20	24	29	33
100					0			1	2	3	4	6	7	9	10	14	19	23	28	33	37
120				0		1	2		3	4	6	8	9	11	13	18	24	29	35	40	46
140				0		1	2	3	4	5	7	10	12	14	16	22	29	35	42	48	55
160			0	1	2	3		5	6	7	9	12	14	17	20	27	34	41	49	56	64
180			0	1	2	3	4	6	7	8	11	14	17	20	23	31	39	47	56	65	73
200			0	1	3	4	5	7	8	10	13	16	19	23	26	35	44	54	63	73	83
220			0	2	3	5	6	8	10	11	15	18	22	26	30	39	50	60	70	81	92
240		0	1	2	4	6	7	9	11	13	17	21	25	29	33	44	55	66	78	89	101
260		0	1	3	5	6	8	10	12	14	19	23	27	32	36	48	60	72	85	97	110
280		0	2	3	4	7	9	12	14	16	21	25	30	35	40	53	65	79	92	106	120
300		0	2	4	6	8	10	13	15	18	23	28	33	38	43	57	71	85	99	114	129
320		0	2	4	7	9	11	14	17	19	24	30	35	41	47	61	76	91	107	122	138
340		1	3	5	7	10	13	15	18	21	26	32	38	44	50	66	82	98	114	131	148
360		1	3	6	8	11	14	16	19	22	28	35	41	47	54	70	87	104	122	139	157
380		1	3	6	9	12	15	18	21	24	30	37	44	50	57	75	93	111	129	148	166
400		1	4	7	10	13	16	19	22	26	32	39	46	54	61	79	98	117	136	156	176
420		2	4	7	10	14	17	20	24	27	35	42	49	57	64	84	103	124	144	164	185
460	0	2	5	8	12	15	19	23	27	31	39	47	55	63	72	93	114	136	159	181	204
500	0	3	6	10	13	17	21	26	30	34	43	52	60	70	79	102	125	149	174	198	223
550	0	3	7	11	15	20	24	29	34	38	48	58	68	78	88	113	139	166	192	219	247
600	0	4	8	13	17	22	27	32	37	43	53	64	78	86	97	125	153	182	211	241	271
650	0	4	9	14	19	25	30	36	41	47	58	70	82	94	106	136	167	198	230	262	294
700	1	5	10	16	21	27	33	39	45	51	64	76	89	102	115	148	181	215	249	283	319
800	1	7	13	19	25	32	39	46	53	60	74	89	103	118	133	171	209	248	287	326	366
900	2	8	15	22	29	37	45	53	61	69	85	101	118	135	152	194	237	281	325	369	414
1000	2	9	17	25	34	42	51	60	69	78	96	114	133	151	170	218	266	314	363	412	462

Note: The number of observed occurrences are shown in the body of the table.
Source: Audit Sampling Reference Manual, © Ernst & Whinney, 1977. Used with permission.

Appendix 11–G: Computer-Assisted Statistical Sampling for Attributes—A Description of SAMPLE from Coopers & Lybrand

SAMPLE is a microcomputer program that can be used in controls testing in the following ways:

- To determine the required sample size for testing the deviation rate of a control, such as authorization of a disbursement.
- To analyze the results achieved in a sample.

Exactly the same techniques as those described in this chapter are used for computer-assisted statistical sampling for attributes. The only difference is that the sample size determination and sample results evaluation are performed by use of a microcomputer package rather than manual tables.

The microcomputer package is menu driven and designed for use by persons who have little training in use of the computer in the audit. We will describe Master Menu Option 1: Attribute Sampling, as shown in the following figure.

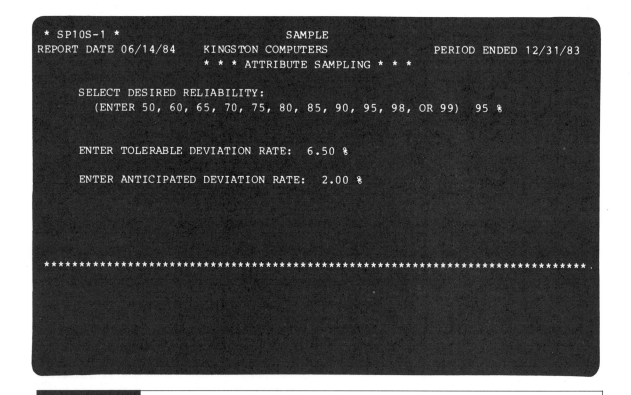

```
* SP10S-1 *                      SAMPLE
REPORT DATE 06/14/84    KINGSTON COMPUTERS            PERIOD ENDED 12/31/83
                    * * * ATTRIBUTE SAMPLING * * *

    SELECT DESIRED RELIABILITY:
       (ENTER 50, 60, 65, 70, 75, 80, 85, 90, 95, 98, OR 99)   95 %


    ENTER TOLERABLE DEVIATION RATE:   6.50 %

    ENTER ANTICIPATED DEVIATION RATE:   2.00 %



   ************************************************************************.
```

Attributes Sampling—Selection

You would use attribute sampling to estimate the true proportion of a defined characteristic within a population. In auditing, this characteristic is usually an error rate or control failure rate in areas such as authorization of disbursement checks.

To use the attribute sampling option, you supply

- A desired reliability level (1 − acceptable risk of overreliance) for your sample.
- A maximum tolerable deviation rate that you consider acceptable.
- An expected (anticipated) deviation rate that you reasonably expect.

In return, SAMPLE provides

- A required sample size.
- A critical number of deviations for the attribute within the sample.
- A chart showing the deviation percentage in the sample and the probability that the population rate falls below your specified tolerable error rate. Up to thirteen deviation values lower and higher than the critical number are provided. A broken line is drawn across the chart at the critical point.

```
* SP10S-2 *                        SAMPLE
REPORT DATE 06/14/84    KINGSTON COMPUTERS              PERIOD ENDED 12/31/83
                        * * * ATTRIBUTE SAMPLING * * *

    RESULTS ARE BASED ON THE FOLLOWING PARAMETERS:

    ONE SIDED RELIABILITY: 95 %
    TOLERABLE DEVIATION RATE: 6.50 %
    ANTICIPATED DEVIATION RATE: 2.00 %

    THE REQUIRED SAMPLE SIZE IS:    96
    THE CRITICAL NUMBER OF DEVIATIONS IS:    2

    EVALUATION OF THE RESULTS WILL DEPEND ON THE ACTUAL NUMBER
    OF DEVIATIONS IN THE SAMPLE, AS SHOWN IN THE FOLLOWING TABLE.

******************************************************************************

    ENTER
       1. TO CONTINUE PROCESSING AND DISPLAY RESULTS
       2. TO CONTINUE PROCESSING AND PRINT RESULTS
       3. TO ENTER NEW PARAMETERS
       9. TO RETURN TO MASTER MENU
```

Attributes Sampling—Sample Size Determination

A special application of this option is discovery sampling. This application is used to test an attribute so critical that even a single deviation detected in a sample may have a high audit significance. The following hypothetical example is used:

Client: Kingston Computers
One-sided **reliability** (risk of overreliance = 5%): 95%
Tolerable deviation rate: 6.50%
Anticipated deviation rate: 2.00%

From reports generated, it is shown that a required sample size of ninety-six items must be drawn, and the critical number of deviations for a reliability of 95 percent is two.

We now describe Master Menu Option 2: Evaluation of Attribute Sampling Results. This option produces one-sided (upper) and two-sided (upper and lower) precision limits for sample results at eleven reliability levels (from 99 to 50 percent). For a given reliability level, the reliability represents the probability that the population error rate or deviation rate exceeds the one-sided upper pre-

```
* SP10S-3 *                      SAMPLE
REPORT DATE 06/14/84       KINGSTON COMPUTERS              PERIOD ENDED 12/31/83
                           * * * ATTRIBUTE SAMPLING * * *


     NO. OF DEVIATIONS      PCT. DEVIATION      PCT. PROBABILITY THAT POPULATION
        IN SAMPLE             IN SAMPLE         DEVIATION RATE IS 6.50% OR LESS
             0                   0.00                     99.81
             1                   1.04                     98.65
             2                   2.08                     95.00
- - - - - - - - - - - - - - - - - - - - - - - - - - - - - - - - - - - - - - - - -
             3                   3.12                     87.33
             4                   4.16                     75.26
             5                   5.20                     60.06
             6                   6.25                     44.11
             7                   7.29                     29.76
*********************************************************************************
     ENTER:
     1. TO ENTER NEW PARAMETERS
     9. TO RETURN TO MASTER MENU
```

Attributes Sampling—Critical Error Level

```
* SP20S-2 *                          SAMPLE
REPORT DATE 06/14/84     KINGSTON COMPUTERS          PERIOD ENDED 12/31/83
            * * * EVALUATION OF ATTRIBUTE SAMPLING RESULTS * * *

    ATTRIBUTE SAMPLE CONDITIONS: SAMPLE SIZE = 300   NUMBER OF DEVIATIONS =  15
                                 DEVIATION RATE IN SAMPLE =   5.00 %

          ONE-SIDED             RELIABILITY      TWO-SIDED PRECISION LIMITS
    UPPER PRECISION LIMIT          LEVEL         LOWER              UPPER
            8.91 %                 99 %          2.30 %             9.39 %
            8.41 %                 98 %          2.49 %             8.91 %
            7.70 %                 95 %          2.80 %             8.25 %
            7.10 %                 90 %          3.08 %             7.70 %
            6.71 %                 85 %          3.28 %             7.36 %
            6.41 %                 80 %          3.43 %             7.10 %
            6.16 %                 75 %          3.58 %             6.99 %
            5.94 %                 70 %          3.69 %             6.71 %
            5.75 %                 65 %          3.79 %             6.55 %
            5.56 %                 60 %          3.89 %             6.41 %
            5.22 %                 50 %          4.08 %             6.16 %
*****************************************************************************

        ENTER:  1.  TO ENTER NEW PARAMETERS
                2.  TO PRINT ABOVE RESULTS
                9.  TO RETURN TO MASTER MENU
```

Attributes Sampling—Evaluation

cision limit and falls outside the two-sided precision range. In our example, we assume a sample size of 300 items and fifteen deviations from the prescribed internal control (a sample deviation rate of 5 percent). The figure above illustrates the results.

SAMPLE repeats the sample size and number of deviations we supplied at the top of the report. SAMPLE also provides the sample deviation rate ($^{15}/_{300}$). The chart provides a full range of values in which the population deviation rate should fall. For our example, look at the third line (reliability level 95). The column on the left, containing the upper precision limit, reads 7.70. This means that we can be 95 percent confident that the population has a deviation rate below 7.70 percent (equivalent to AUPL in Appendixes 11–D through 11–F). The columns on the right show lower and upper precision limits of 2.80 and 8.25. This means that we can be 95 percent confident that the population deviation rate falls between 2.80 percent and 8.25 percent.

Notes

1. Statement on Auditing Standards 39 (AU350), (New York: AICPA, 1983).
2. Statement on Auditing Standards 47 (AU312), (New York: AICPA, 1984).

Questions for Class Discussion

Q11-1 How is sampling defined in generally accepted auditing standards? Because of the nature of sampling, are there some instances in the audit that lend themselves to sampling more than others?

Q11-2 Does the auditor accept any risks in using sampling techniques in performing an audit? Discuss.

Q11-3 What is meant by a sampling error (also known as sampling risk)?

Q11-4 What is meant by a nonsampling error (also known as nonsampling risk)?

Q11-5 What is the difference between statistical and purely judgmental sampling? Discuss.

Q11-6 What are the advantages associated with using statistical sampling rather than judgmental sampling? Do those differences mean that the auditor should use statistical sampling techniques in performing all phases of the audit? Explain.

Q11-7 Because statistical sampling relies on the laws of probability in selecting sample data, the auditor is relieved from judgment decisions. Is the preceding statement true or false? Explain.

Q11-8 Is the auditor more concerned with risk of overreliance on internal control or risk of underreliance? Explain.

Q11-9 What is the meaning of the following terms?
a. Tolerable deviation rate.
b. Probability.
c. Sampling unit.
d. Unrestricted random sample.
e. Systematic sampling.
f. Population.

Q11-10 What are the steps in the sampling process? How do these steps differ, if at all, when statistical sampling is used rather than strict judgmental sampling?

Q11-11 What is unrestricted random sampling? How does it differ from other sampling techniques?

Q11-12 Under what circumstances might it be acceptable to use a systematic sampling technique rather than a random technique in selecting a sample of universe data for verification?

Q11-13 What is the purpose of attributes sampling?

Q11-14 What is the difference between discovery sampling and basic attributes sampling? Explain.

Q11-15 What functions are performed by the auditor after the sample items have been selected?

Q11-16 What is the relationship between precision (materiality) and reliability (1 − risk) in selecting and using the items included in a statistically valid sample?

Q11-17 The tolerable deviation rate established for a particular sample is stated at 6 percent. What is meant by that figure?

Q11-18 A particular sample has been selected to produce a desired confidence of 95 percent. What is meant by that statement?

Q11-19 What relationship exists between homogeneity of data in a universe and the use of stratified sampling techniques?

Q11-20 In working with statistically valid samples, can we have both stratified and random sampling techniques used in verifying the same universe? Explain.

Q11-21 An attribute sample indicates that a client has failed in some instances to implement a particular control procedure. Does that automatically mean that the substantive tests of those items must be expanded? Explain.

Q11-22 In what types of situations would an auditor be likely to use discovery sampling?

Q11-23 In what ways are the use of computer audit techniques assisting in the sampling process?

Q11-24 Explain how a single random sample can be used to test several different attributes or elements of the control system.

Q11-25 What three factors must the auditor establish prior to selecting an appropriate statistical attribute sample size? Explain how each of these factors is adjudged by the auditor as he makes these decisions.

Q11-26 Why is the acceptable risk of overreliance usually established for tests of controls at levels of 5–10 percent or lower?

Q11-27 Explain how the auditor can select an appropriate relevant range for the value of tolerable deviation rates when planning a test of controls.

Q11-28 Why will the auditor often select different tolerable deviation rates and/or different levels of acceptable risk of overreliance for various attributes when conducting control tests over a particular client application?

Short Cases

C11-1 Joe Caplin, CPA, is conducting the annual audit of the financial statements of the Monarch Corporation for the year ended December 31, 19X4. Mr. Caplin has decided to employ statistical sampling techniques in testing the effectiveness of internal control procedures over cash disbursements. All cash disbursements for Monarch Corporation are evidenced by sequentially numbered checks. In the three prior years, Monarch was audited by Schnook & Co., CPAs, who did not employ statistical techniques. When reviewing the previous year's working papers of Monarch, Caplin noticed that Schnook's audit program for cash disbursements controls (written twenty years ago) called for selection of February as a test month. All material controls were tested for February's transactions, and all errors found were resolved to Schnook's satisfaction.

Required:

a. Did Schnook & Co. follow generally accepted auditing standards on the previous year's audit? Explain.

b. Explain the progression of steps that Caplin should follow in assessing internal control risk over the cash disbursements system of the Monarch Corporation.

c. Explain how statistical sampling fits into the logical progression of steps as described in requirement (b) above.

d. Given his stated audit objective, which type of sampling methodology (i.e., attributes, discovery, variables) would Caplin be most likely to follow?

e. Explain how the items in the sample Caplin derives would be selected. Explain how the method used here is preferable to that used in prior years.

C11-2 You want to select a sample of 100 paid vouchers to be examined for appropriate supporting documents (invoices, purchase orders, receiving reports, and purchase requisitions). The paid vouchers range from number 1 to 10,000 for the period June 1, 19X2 to May 31, 19X3. The vouchers are listed on 400 pages of the client's voucher register, numbered from page 1 to page 400. Each page of the voucher register contains twenty-five items.

Required:

a. Describe three ways that a random sample of vouchers might be selected from the population of vouchers payable.

b. How could the computer be used in performing this task?

C11-3 In each of the following independent situations, design an unrestricted random sampling plan using the random number table in Figure 11–3. The plan should include identification of

a. The audit problem.

b. The audit population.

c. The sampling unit.

d. The sampling frame.

e. The attribute to be tested.

For each independent situation, after a sampling plan has been designed, select the first five items to be included in the sample from the table in Figure 11–3. Use a starting point of item 0925, Column A, for each situation. Continue down the table and from left to right by column, using the left-most digits in the columns.

Required:

a. Assume that you are examining sales invoices for approval signatures of departmental supervisors. Sales invoices for the audit period are consecutively numbered from 5,924 to 10,242.

b. Assume that you are examining cash disbursements for proper supporting documents. Cash disbursements for the audit period are all made by check, sequentially numbered from 32,115 to 46,851.

c. Assume that you are examining insurance claim forms to ascertain that proper supporting documents were filed for each claim and that those supporting documents were examined before the claim was paid. Insurance claims are recorded in a claims register by policyholder. The register contains 160 pages for the audit period with forty claims recorded on each page, except for the last page, which has only twenty-four claims on it.

d. Assume that you are examining prenumbered receiving reports in a receiving report register to ascertain whether the goods listed thereon were recorded in the perpetual inventory records as received during the audit period. The numbering of these receiving reports starts over at one each month. Each month's receiving reports are prefixed with a number one through twelve to designate the month of the year. There are 400 pages for the year and a maximum of forty pages per month. All pages have thirty entries, except for the last page for each month.

C11-4   Mavis Stores had two billing clerks during the year. Snow worked three months, and White worked nine months. As the auditor for Mavis Stores, Darren Lowe, CPA, uses attribute sampling to test clerical accuracy for the entire year. Because of the lack of internal verification, the system depends heavily on the competence of the billing clerks. The quantity of bills per month is constant.

Required:
  a. Lowe decided to treat the billing by Snow and White as two separate populations. Discuss the advisability of this approach, considering the circumstances.
  b. Lowe decided to use the same risk level, expected population deviation rate, and tolerable deviation rate for each population. Assuming he decided to select a sample of 200 to test Snow's work, approximately how large a sample is necessary to test White's?

(AICPA adapted)

C11-5   The Whitehall Company's principal activity is buying milk from dairy farmers, processing the milk, and delivering the milk to retail customers. You are engaged in auditing the sales transactions of the company and determine that
  a. The company has fifty retail routes; each route consists of 100 to 200 accounts, the number that can be serviced by a driver in a day.
  b. The driver enters cash collections from the day's deliveries to each customer directly on a statement form in record books maintained for each route. Mail remittances are posted in the route record books maintained for each route. These mail remittances are posted in the route record books by office personnel. At the end of the month, the statements are priced, extended, and footed. Photocopies of the statements are prepared and left in the customers' milk boxes with the next milk delivery.
  c. The statements are reviewed by the office manager, who prepares a monthly list for each route of accounts with 90-day balances or older. The list is used for intensive collection action.
  d. The audit program used in prior audits for the selection of sales transactions for tests of controls stated: "Select two accounts from each route, one to be chosen by opening the route book at random and the other as the third account on each list of 90-day or older accounts. For each account selected, choose the latest transaction for testing."
Your review of sales transactions leads you to conclude that statistical sampling techniques may be applied to their examination.

Required:
  a. Since statistical sampling techniques do not relieve the CPA of his or her responsibilities in the exercise of his or her professional judgment, of what benefit are they to the CPA? Discuss.
  b. Give the reasons why the auditing procedure previously used for selection of sales transactions [as given in (d) above] would not produce a valid statistical sample.
  c. Suggest two ways to select a valid statistical sample.

    d. Assume that the company has 10,000 sales transactions and that your statistical sampling disclosed six errors in a sample of 200 transactions. Is it reasonable to assume that 300 transactions in the entire population are in error? Explain.

(AICPA adapted)

C11-6   You have been assigned responsibility for planning statistical tests of controls for the revenue cycle of the ABC Corporation. One of the control elements to be tested involves credit approval. You have stipulated that the deviation condition will be a failure to properly approve the credit limit for each charge sale. You also decide to test an attribute whose deviation condition can be defined as a failure of the sales invoice to agree with the customer order.

Required:

    a. Which financial statement assertions are most clearly associated with these respective attributes?

    b. Assume that the appropriate approval of credit is more important given your audit objectives than is the second attribute. How will this affect your planning with regard to the acceptable risk of overreliance (ARO) and/or the tolerable deviation rate (TDR) for these respective attributes?

    c. Assuming that the anticipated or expected rate of error is the same for both of these control elements, which will require the larger sample size and why, given the assumptions stated above?

    d. Subsequent to completion of your plan a staff assistant comes to you with a question. The assistant wishes to know whether to examine for deviation from both attributes for all items in the sample of charged sales selected for examination in regard to these two tests. What is your advice?

Problems

P11-1   Select the best answer for each of the following items.

    a. What is the primary objective of using stratification as a sampling method in auditing?

      1. To increase the confidence level at which a decision will be reached from the results of the sample selected.

      2. To determine the occurrence rate for a given characteristic in the population being studied.

      3. To decrease the effect of variance in the total population.

      4. To determine the precision of the sample selected.

    b. For a large population of cash disbursement transactions, Arno Malchevsky, CPA, is testing the internal control structure by using attribute sampling techniques. Anticipating a deviation rate of 3 percent, he found from a table that the required sample size is 400, with a maximum tolerable deviation rate of 5 percent and reliability of 95 percent. If Malchevsky anticipated a deviation rate of only 2 percent but wanted to maintain the same maximum tolerable deviation rate and reliability, the sample size would be closest to

      1. 200.

      2. 400.

3. 533.
4. 800.
c. To satisfy the auditing standard relating to internal control, Tanya Jewett, CPA, uses statistical sampling to test control procedures. Why does Jewett use this technique?
  1. It provides a means of measuring mathematically the degree of reliability that results from examining only a part of the data.
  2. It reduces the use of judgment required of Jewett because the AICPA has established numerical criteria for this type of testing.
  3. It increases Jewett's knowledge of the client's prescribed procedures and their limitations.
  4. It is specified by generally accepted auditing standards.
d. How should an auditor determine the precision or materiality in estimating the tolerable deviation rate required in establishing a statistical sampling plan?
  1. By the materiality of an allowable margin of error the auditor is willing to accept.
  2. By the amount of reliance the auditor will place on the results of the sample.
  3. By reliance on a table of random numbers.
  4. By the amount of risk the auditor is willing to take that material errors will occur in the accounting process.
e. Which of the following is an advantage of systematic sampling over random number sampling?
  1. It provides a stronger basis for statistical conclusions.
  2. It enables the auditor to use the more efficient *sampling with replacement* tables.
  3. There may be correlation between the location of items in the population, the feature of sampling interest, and the sampling interval.
  4. It does not require establishment of correspondence between random numbers and items in the population.
f. An auditor makes separate control and substantive tests in the accounts payable area (which has good internal control). If the auditor uses statistical sampling for both of these tests, the confidence $(1 - ARO)$ level established for the substantive test is normally
  1. The same as that for tests of controls.
  2. Greater than that for tests of controls.
  3. Less than that for tests of controls.
  4. Totally independent of that for tests of controls.
g. An example of sampling for attributes would be estimating the
  1. Quantity of specific inventory items.
  2. Probability of losing a patent infringement case.
  3. Percentage of overdue accounts receivable.
  4. Dollar value of accounts receivable.
h. The purpose of tests of controls is to provide reasonable assurance that the accounting control procedures are being applied as prescribed. The sampling method that is most useful when testing controls is
  1. Judgment sampling.
  2. Attribute sampling.
  3. Unrestricted random sampling with replacement.
  4. Stratified random sampling.
i. Sampling generally may be applied to tests of controls when the client's internal accounting control procedures
  1. Depend primarily on appropriate segregation of duties.
  2. Are carefully reduced to writing and are included in client accounting manuals.

3. Leave an audit trail in the form of documentary evidence of controls performance.

4. Permit the detection of material irregularities in the accounting records.

j. Which of the following best describes what the auditor means by the rate of deviation in an attribute sampling plan?

1. The number of errors that can reasonably be expected to be found in a population.

2. The frequency with which a certain characteristic occurs within a population.

3. The degree of risk that the sample is not representative of the population.

4. The dollar range within which the true population total can be expected to fall.

k. Which of the following best describes the distinguishing feature of statistical sampling?

1. Statistical sampling requires the examination of a smaller number of supporting documents.

2. It provides a means for measuring mathematically the degree of uncertainty that results from examining only part of a population.

3. It reduces the problems associated with the auditor's judgment concerning materiality.

4. It is evaluated in terms of two parameters: statistical mean and random tests of controls.

l. If an auditor, planning to use statistical sampling, is concerned with the number of a client's sales invoices that contain mathematical errors, the auditor would most likely utilize

1. Random sampling with replacement.

2. Sampling for attributes.

3. Sampling for variables.

4. Stratified random sampling.

m. When using a statistical sampling plan, the auditor would probably require a smaller sample if the

1. Population increases.

2. Maximum tolerable deviation rate is lowered.

3. Desired reliability decreases, thus causing ARO to increase.

4. Expected deviation rate increases.

n. If certain forms are not consecutively numbered,

1. Selection of a random sample probably is not possible.

2. Systematic sampling may be appropriate.

3. Stratified sampling should be used.

4. Random number tables cannot be used.

o. Tim McCann, CPA, believes the industry-wide deviation rate of client billing errors is 3 percent and has established a maximum tolerable deviation rate of 5 percent. In the review of client invoices, McCann should use

1. Discovery sampling.

2. Attribute sampling.

3. Stratified sampling.

4. Variable sampling.   *(AICPA adapted)*

P11-2   Select the best answer for each of the following items.

a. An accounts receivable aging schedule was prepared on 300 pages, with each page containing the aging data for fifty accounts. The pages were numbered from 1 to 300, and the accounts listed on each page were numbered from 1 to 50.

Gunther Godla, an auditor, selected accounts receivable for confirmation using a table of numbers as illustrated in the following table.

Procedures performed by Godla

Select number from table of numbers	Separate 5 digits: 3 for page 2 for account	
02011	020-11	x
85393	853-93	*
97265	972-65	*
61680	616-80	*
16656	166-56	*
42751	427-51	*
69994	699-94	*
07942	079-42	y
10231	102-31	z
53988	539-88	*

x Mailed confirmation to account 11 listed on page 20.
y Mailed confirmation to account 42 listed on page 79.
z Mailed confirmation to account 31 listed on page 102.
* Rejected.

This is an example of which of the following sampling methods?
1. Acceptance sampling.
2. Systematic sampling.
3. Sequential sampling.
4. Random sampling.
   b. A CPA examining inventory may appropriately apply sampling for attributes in order to estimate the
   1. Average price of inventory items.
   2. Percentage of slow-moving inventory items.
   3. Dollar value of inventory.
   4. Physical quantity of inventory items.
   c. An advantage of using statistical sampling techniques is that such techniques
   1. Mathematically measure risk.
   2. Eliminate the need for judgmental decisions.
   3. Define the values of precision and risk required to provide audit satisfaction.
   4. Have been established in the courts to be superior to judgmental sampling.
   d. In estimation sampling for attributes, which one of the following must be known in order to appraise the results of the auditor's sample?
   1. Estimated dollar value of the population.
   2. Standard deviation of the values in the population.
   3. Actual occurrence rate of the attribute in the population.
   4. Sample size.
   e. If the size of the sample to be used in a particular test of attributes has not been determined by utilizing statistical concepts, but the sample has been chosen in accordance with random selection procedures, then
   1. No inferences can be drawn from the sample.

2. The auditor has committed a nonsampling error.

3. The auditor may or may not achieve desired precision at the desired level of risk.

4. The auditor will have to evaluate the results by reference to the principles of discovery sampling.

f. Assume that an auditor estimates that 10,000 checks were issued during the accounting period. If an EDP application control that performs a limit check for each check request is to be subjected to the auditor's test data approach, the sample should include

1. Approximately 1,000 test items.

2. A number of test items determined by the auditor to be sufficient under the circumstances.

3. A number of test items determined by the auditor's reference to the appropriate sampling tables.

4. One transaction.

(AICPA adapted)

P11-3   Evidential matter supporting the financial statements consists of the underlying accounting data (ledgers, journals, etc.) and all corroborating (documentary and other) information available to the auditor. In the course of performing an independent audit, the CPA is faced with the problems of deciding how to go about gathering this evidence and how much evidence to accumulate.

Required:

a. When is sampling an appropriate procedure for the auditor to use in the evidence-gathering process?

b. Describe strict judgmental sampling and explain when it would be more appropriate than using a more sophisticated statistical approach.

c. Describe statistical sampling and explain its advantages over strict judgmental sampling.

d. Do auditing standards require the use of statistical sampling? If not, what do they require?

P11-4   James Wilson, CPA, is planning the audit of Art Products Supply Company, a very large manufacturing corporation. Wilson is technically well trained and understands how to apply statistical sampling procedures in gathering audit evidence. He wants to use statistical sampling in the audit of Art Products Supply Company, particularly in the assessment of internal control risk.

Required:

a. Although statistical sampling during an audit allows for greater objectivity than purely judgmental sampling, there will be several areas in which Wilson must still exercise audit judgment in planning his statistical tests. Identify at least five of these judgments, and explain.

b. Assume that Wilson's sample of internal controls over inventory pricing for Art Products shows an unacceptable error rate. Describe the various actions that Wilson might take.

c. A nonstratified sample of 120 accounts payable vouchers is to be selected from a population of 3,200. The vouchers are numbered consecutively from 1 to 3,200 and are listed, forty to a page, in the computer printout of the voucher register. Describe two different techniques that Wilson may use to select a random sample of vouchers for review. Which of these techniques seems more appropriate? Why?

d. Describe in general how computer audit software can be used to assist Wilson in this portion of the audit.

(AICPA adapted)

P11-5 Levelland, Inc., a client of your firm for several years, uses a voucher system for processing all cash disbursements (about 500 each month). After carefully reviewing the company's internal controls, your firm decided to statistically sample the vouchers for eleven specific characteristics to test operating controls over the voucher system against the client's representations as to the system's operation. Nine of these characteristics are to be evaluated using attributes sampling, and two are to be evaluated using discovery sampling. The characteristics to be evaluated are listed on the voucher test work sheet (see accompanying illustration).

Pertinent client representations about the system are as follows:

a. Purchase orders are issued for all goods and services, except for recurring services such as utilities, taxes, etc. The controller issues a check request for the latter authorizing payment. Receiving reports are prepared for all goods received. Department heads prepare a services-rendered report for services covered by purchase orders. (Services-rendered reports are subsequently considered receiving reports.)

b. Copies of purchase orders, receiving reports, check requests, and original invoices are forwarded to accounting. Invoices are assigned a consecutive voucher number immediately on receipt by accounting. Each voucher is rubber stamped to provide spaces for accounting personnel to initial when (1) matching invoice with purchase order or check request, (2) matching invoice with receiving report, and (3) verifying mathematical accuracy of the invoice.

c. In processing each voucher for payment, accounting personnel match each invoice with the related purchase order and receiving report or check request. Invoice extensions and footings are verified. Debit distribution is recorded on the face of each invoice.

d. Each voucher is recorded in the voucher register in numerical sequence, after which a check is prepared. The voucher packets and checks are forwarded to the treasurer for signing and mailing the checks and canceling each voucher packet.

e. Canceled packets are returned to accounting. Payment is recorded in the voucher register, and the voucher packets are filed numerically.

The following are characteristics of the voucher population already determined by preliminary statistical testing. Assume that each characteristic is randomly distributed throughout the voucher population.

1. Of the vouchers, 80 percent are for purchase orders and 20 percent are for check requests.

2. The average number of lines per invoice is four.

3. The average number of accounts debited per invoice is two.

Appropriate statistical sampling tables appear in Appendixes 11–A through 11–C and in Figure 11–7. For values not provided in the tables, use the next value in the table that will yield the most conservative result.

Levelland, Inc.

V O U C H E R   T E S T   W O R K S H E E T

Years Ended December 31, 19X2

| | Year 1 | | | | Year 2 | | | |
Characteristics	Column A Sample size	Column B Expected population deviation rate (EPDR)	Column C Maximum tolerable deviation rate (TDR)	Column D Acceptable risk of overreliance (ARO)	Column E Required sample size	Column F Assumed sample size	Column G Number of errors found	Column H Achieved upper precision limit (AUPL)
For Attribute Sampling								
1. Invoice in agreement with purchase order or check request.		1.1%	3	5%		460	4	
2. Invoice in agreement with receiving report.		.4%	2	5%		340	2	
3. Invoice mathematically accurate.								
a. Extensions		1.4%	3	5%		1,000	22	
b. Footings		1.0%	3	5%		460	10	
4. Account distributions correct.		.3%	2	5%		340	2	
5. Voucher correctly entered in voucher register.		.5%	2	5%		340	1	
6. Evidence of accounting department checks.								
a. Comparison of invoice with purchase order or check request.		2.0%	4	5%		240	2	
b. Comparison of invoice with receiving report.		1.3%	4	5%		160	2	
c. Proving mathematical accuracy of invoice.		1.5%	3	5%		340	10	
For Discovery Sampling								
7. Voucher and related documents cancelled.		At or near 0	.75%	5%		600	5	
8. Vendor and amount on invoice in agreement with payee and amount on check.		At or near 0	.4%	5%		800	0	

Required:
   a. (Independently of items b, c, and d) Assume that an unrestricted random sample of 300 voucher numbers is to be drawn. Enter in column A of the work sheet the sample size of each characteristic to be evaluated in the sample.
   b. (Parts b, c, and d pertain only to Year Z) Given the expected population deviation rates, maximum tolerable deviation rates, and acceptable risk of overreliance in columns B, C, and D, respectively, enter in column E the required sample size to evaluate each characteristic.
   c. *Disregarding your answers in column E* and considering the assumed sample size and numbers of errors found in each sample as listed for each characteristic in columns F and G, respectively, enter in column H the AUPL for each characteristic.
   d. On a separate sheet, identify each characteristic for which the sampling objective was not met and explain what steps the auditor might take to meet his or her sampling or auditing objectives.

(AICPA adapted)

P11-6   Rebecca Resnick, an audit partner, is developing a staff training program to familiarize her professional staff with statistical decision models applicable to the audit of internal controls. She wishes to demonstrate the relationship of sample sizes to various statistical parameters. To do this, Resnick has prepared the following table using comparisons from two separate audit populations.

	Population 1 relative to population 2		Sample from population 1 relative to sample from population 2	
	Size	Expected deviation rate	TDR	Acceptable risk of overreliance (ARO)
Case 1	Larger	Equal	Lower	Equal
Case 2	Equal	Equal	Higher	Equal
Case 3	Equal	Smaller	Equal	Equal
Case 4	Smaller	Equal	Lower	Higher
Case 5	Equal	Smaller	Higher	Lower

Required: Given the characteristics of two separate populations and two samples (one drawn from population 1 and one from population 2), state whether, for each of the independent cases in the table, the planned sample size from population 1 should be
   a. Equal to the required sample size from population 2.
   b. Smaller than the required sample size from population 2.
   c. Greater than the required sample size from population 2.
   d. Indeterminate relative to the sample size from population 2.
      1. The required sample size from population 1 in case 1 should be _____.
      2. The required sample size from population 1 in case 2 should be _____.
      3. The required sample size from population 1 in case 3 should be _____.
      4. The required sample size from population 1 in case 4 should be _____.
      5. The required sample size from population 1 in case 5 should be _____.

(AICPA adapted)

P11-7 In the development of an audit program, it is determined that to achieve specified materiality and risk levels a sample of 254 items from a population of 5,000 is adequate on a statistical basis.

Required:
a. Briefly define each of the following terms used in the above statement:
 1. Population.
 2. Sample.
 3. Materiality.
 4. Risk levels.
b. If the population is 50,000 and the specifications for TDR and risk are unchanged from the situation above for a population of 5,000, which of the following sample sizes could be expected to be statistically correct for the larger population: 254, 260, 1,200, or 2,540? Justify your answer. (Your answer should be based on judgment and reasoning, rather than actual calculation.)
c. Statistical sampling techniques are being used in auditing. A sample is taken and analyzed to draw an inference or reach a conclusion about a population, but there is always a risk that the inference or conclusion may be incorrect. What value, then, is there in using statistical sampling techniques?

(AICPA adapted)

P11-8 As the auditor for the Gabbert Company, you have elected to use statistical sampling in performing tests of controls for the purchases and cost-of-sales systems. You have already studied and made a preliminary assessment of the control attributes that the client has said are prescribed to accomplish the objectives shown in the accompanying table.

Required:
a. Identify the financial statement assertions related to each of the control objectives (1)–(5) in column 1.
b. Prepare a sample plan work sheet similar to the one shown in Figure 11–5 that shows sample sizes determined for tests of controls.
c. For each of the samples state the
 1. Population from which you would draw the sample.
 2. The sampling unit.
 3. The sampling frame.
 4. The type of auditing procedure (vouching, tracing, recalculation, comparison, inspection, etc.).
 5. If vouching or tracing, the file to which the vouching or tracing would be done.
d. Assume that your sample results yielded, respectively, 1, 2, 1, 2, and 3 deviations from established internal control procedures. Prepare a sample evaluation work sheet similar to that shown in Figure 11–6. Statistically interpret the results of these samples. Which of the tests support a lower level of internal control risk than required (L) and which of the tests do not (N)?
e. What action do you recommend for the tests of controls that do not support a lower-than-maximum level of risk reliance for internal control? If the action includes expansion of substantive tests, which of those tests would you expand?

Objectives	Control Attribute	Maximum tolerable deviation rate (TDR)	Acceptable risk of overreliance (ARO) (%)	Expected population deviation rate (EPDR)
1. Only materials needed are ordered	Require prenumbered written purchase requisitions	5.0	10.0	1.0
2. Complete records of all goods ordered	Require prenumbered written purchase orders	5.0	5.0	1.0
3. Ordering at most economical prices	Require approval of prices by responsible officer	6.0	5.0	1.0
4. All goods paid for were, in fact, received	Require written receiving reports to be matched with all vendor invoices	4.0	1.0	.5
5. Accurate recording of all purchases	Require supporting documents comparison of quantities, prices, and recalculation of extended prices for all approved purchases invoices	4.0	1.0	1.0

P11-9   Jay Jiblum, CPA, is planning to use attribute sampling to determine the level of control risk associated with an audit client's internal control structure for sales. Jiblum has begun to develop an outline of the main steps in the sampling plan, as follows:

1. State the objective(s) of the audit test (e.g., to assess the control risk associated with internal accounting controls over sales).
2. Define the population (define the period covered by the test; define the sampling unit; define the completeness of the population).
3. Define the sampling unit (e.g., client copies of sales invoices).

Required:

a. What are the remaining steps in the outline above that Jiblum should include in the statistical test of sales invoices? Do not present a detailed analysis of tasks that must be performed to carry out the objectives of each step. Parenthetical examples need not be provided.

b. How does statistical methodology help the auditor to develop a satisfactory sampling plan?

(AICPA adapted)

P11-10 One of the generally accepted auditing standards states that sufficient competent evidential matter is to be obtained through inspection, observation, inquiries, and confirmation to afford a reasonable basis for an opinion regarding the financial statements under examination. Some degree of uncertainty is implicit in the concept of "a reasonable basis for an opinion," because the concept of sampling is well established in auditing practice.

Required:

a. Explain the auditor's justification for accepting the uncertainties that are inherent in the sampling process.

   b. Discuss the uncertainties that collectively embody the concept of audit risk.
   c. Discuss the nature of the sampling risk and nonsampling risk. Include the effect of sampling risk on substantive tests of details and on tests of controls.

(AICPA adapted)

P11-11 It is clear that auditing standards do not require the use of statistical sampling methods. In fact, auditing standards do not always advocate sampling.

   Required:
   a. Discuss at least two instances in a typical audit in which sampling is usually not appropriate.
   b. Define sampling as the term is used in the auditing literature.
   c. What are the basic requirements of Statement on Auditing Standards 39 (AU350) whenever sampling techniques are used?
   d. List the steps in the basic sampling process.
   e. When the objective of the audit test is to verify effectiveness on control structure elements through tests of controls, what are the determinants of sample size? What form do these determinants take when the audit plan specifies nonstatistical sampling?
   f. Describe the process by which a nonstatistical sample is drawn and evaluated.

CHAPTER 12

Sampling Techniques and Substantive Tests of Details

Objectives

☐ **1.** Understand the objectives of sampling for substantive tests of details.
☐ **2.** Use audit risk and materiality judgments when designing substantive tests of details.
☐ **3.** Understand the basic process of **substantive sampling** for tests of details.
☐ **4.** Execute substantive sampling procedures.
☐ **5.** Walk through the detailed execution of a classical statistical hypothesis test using two specific techniques (difference estimation and mean-per-unit estimation).
☐ **6.** Walk through the detailed execution of a statistical test based on the dollar-unit method.
☐ **7.** Realize the potential benefits of regression analysis as an auditor's tool.

Chapter 11 discussed the audit sampling process and its application to tests of controls. The principles developed in that chapter also apply to the use of sampling in substantive tests of details supporting transactions and account balances. However, the objectives of sampling for tests of dollar amounts are different from those for tests of controls. In this chapter we discuss the sampling processes used during the substantive tests of details phase of the audit.

Appendixes to this chapter include two tables. Each is useful in determining coefficients that assure an appropriate relationship between the auditor's judgments about sampling risks and the planned size of samples used in substantive tests of details. Also included is an appendix illustrating a microcomputer package that has been developed by one auditing firm for use in statistical sampling.

The Objectives of Sampling for Substantive Tests of Details

☑ **Objective 1**
Understand
substantive
sampling objectives
Sampling in conjunction with substantive tests of details may be used by the auditor for two fundamental reasons: first, to evaluate the accuracy of monetary amounts and second, to enhance the efficiency of audit procedures.

The Effectiveness of Substantive Sampling

The *primary objective of sampling for substantive tests of details is to evaluate whether the monetary amount reported for the balance or class of transactions of interest is fairly stated*. For example, the auditor's ultimate objective may be to develop evidence supporting the hypothesis that the total amount of error in the sales account does not exceed $50,000. This can be done by selecting a sample of sales transactions, auditing the items in the sample, and deriving a conclusion relating directly to a financial statement amount. This process involves the examination of documentary evidence for each item in the sample. These are tests of details from the class of sales transactions that support account balances such as accounts receivable. Other examples of such tests are

- Recalculation of amounts on individual client sales invoices.
- Sending, receiving, and compiling information from confirmation requests for accounts receivable to client customers.
- Vouching details of payroll records (hours, rates, etc.) to supporting time cards and personnel pay rate files.

Just as we observed for tests of controls, it is not always necessary to use sampling when the audit objective is related to the verification of dollar amounts. There are accounts that lend themselves to 100-percent verification. For example, in the audit of property and equipment, when there have been very few additions or retirements during the audit period, we will probably examine all additions and retirements. In other cases, the auditor might verify 100 percent of the items in a certain part of the class or balance, while verifying only a sample from another part. For example, in an audit population of accounts receivable that consists of a few very large accounts and many smaller accounts, the large accounts may be 100 percent verified while only a sample of the smaller accounts will be verified.

To reach a conclusion about the dollar value of the account balance, the auditor will combine results from auditing items in the 100-percent category with results projected from work done on the sample of smaller accounts. Generally, the tests of details employed to examine the items in the 100-percent verification group will be the same as procedures employed to examine items contained in the sample of smaller accounts. Combining results is necessary for effectiveness because the auditor is interested in whether the account balance in total is fairly presented. Tests of details applied to the larger accounts cannot alone be used to reach conclusions about the smaller accounts. Conversely, tests of details performed on the sample of smaller accounts can be used only to project results about the accounts from which the sample was drawn. The sampled items provide no information about the presence or absence of error in the larger accounts because those larger accounts were not included in the population of items from which the sample was drawn.

Sampling Efficiency

The combination of 100-percent verification of larger items from an account balance with projected results from a sample of smaller items in the account balance is quite common. Generally, such a combination is undertaken for reasons of **sampling efficiency**. Sampling is most efficient, that is, requires the smallest sample sizes for conclusions at a given level of risk, when the projected results from the sample apply to a group of detailed items whose range of values is small. For example, consider two different audit engagements involving the confirmation of accounts receivable. In one instance, the accounts receivable balances are relatively evenly distributed between the values of $10 and $10,000. In the other instance, the receivables values fall between $100 and $1,000 with the majority of accounts having values very close to $200. If a sample size of 100 is taken from each population, the risk of incorrect conclusions will be much higher for population 1 than for population 2.

Often, the variability of the dollar value of items in an account balance can be significantly reduced by setting aside a few larger accounts. By auditing every one of these few large items 100 percent, the total number of items to which tests of details must be applied (the large items plus the sample required for the smaller items) will be much less than the sample size required to reach similar conclusions based on sampling from the entire population.

In many instances, where audit sampling for substantive tests of details is to be employed, the auditor will also consider for inclusion in the 100-percent verification group: all items large enough to be individually material, items suspected to be unusual or out of the ordinary because of their complexity, timing, etc., and any other items considered especially risky. By including such items in the group for 100-percent verification, the auditor can confine sampling procedures to an environment in which they work best. Such an environment is one containing a large number of relatively small homogeneous items. For example, if an accounts receivable trial balance includes six customer accounts whose balances exceed $25,000, and 3,500 customer account balances of $500 or less, the auditor will find it more efficient to sample from the items whose value is less than $500 and combine these results with the results of a 100-percent examination of the six items in excess of $25,000. The potential impact on efficiency of such a decision can be illustrated as follows. If the auditor selects sixty items from the items whose value is less than $500 and also audits the six items above $25,000, the overall conclusion about the accounts receivable balance could be stated with a risk of error of 5 percent or less. Alternatively, should the auditor choose to randomly select sixty-six items from the entire balance regardless of the size of the items selected, and without necessarily auditing all of the larger accounts, the audit conclusion reached as a result might have risk of error as high as 20 percent or more.

Sometimes, the auditor will plan to reach conclusions about an account balance or class of transactions as a whole based on the application of sampling procedures but will not apply these procedures to very small accounts. This is usually done to reduce the range of variability in items subjected to sampling and can be acceptable. Generally, this should be done only if the *total* of smaller items not subjected to the possibility of inclusion in the sample is immaterial.

It is important to remember that the sample results apply only to those items given some opportunity to be selected in the sample. Conclusions about an entire account balance often require the combination of results from sampling and nonsampling procedures.

It is also important for results from a sample to be magnified or projected before reaching a conclusion about the total value of all the items from which the sample was chosen. For example, assume that the auditor discovers a $50 error in one sample item, a $100 error in a second item, and no other errors in a sample of 100 items from a subsidiary ledger containing 3,000 accounts. The auditor could project results by determining average error in the sample, $(50 + 100 + 0)/100 = \$1.50$, and multiplying by the number of items in the ledger, $\$1.50 \times 3,000 = \$4,500$. The conclusion drawn from this projection is that $4,500 is the most likely total error in the ledger of 3,000 items.

Statistical versus Nonstatistical Sampling

The concepts for sampling for substantive tests of details may be employed as guides to nonstatistical as well as statistical sampling applications. Professional standards allow use of either approach. Statistical sampling has the advantage of allowing quantification of allowances for sampling error in determination of appropriate sample sizes. On the other hand, statistical sampling requires quantitative expression of risk levels. Some believe this requires overly exact specifications to be provided by the auditor.

Some firms have developed hybrid approaches. Such approaches allow auditors to make qualitative judgments about appropriate risk levels and then use predefined algorithms or tables to translate these qualitative judgments into quantitative risk equivalencies for use in determining appropriate sample sizes. For example, an audit firm may develop an approach that asks the auditor to qualitatively assess the risk of control failure in relation to a particular system as low, moderate, or high. The auditor will then refer to a table or computer package that selects sample sizes based on this judgment and other judgments required to determine an appropriate sample size. These tools have been developed by audit firms with implicit quantitative risk levels associated with each of the qualitative levels available to the auditor. For example, the firm in constructing the table may have equated the qualitative judgment that risk of control failure is low with a quantitatively equivalent risk of 10 percent. The sample sizes recommended by the table are based on these quantitative equivalents. However, the auditor is not required to assess these quantities directly, and indeed, may not know that such equivalencies have been considered.

Supporting Concepts

Both statistical and nonstatistical substantive sampling procedures are tests of details that provide evidence in support of the audit opinion. The concepts that drive planning and analysis of such procedures should be employed to assure that the evidence provided by those procedures is sufficient to reduce the risk of failing to detect material misstatement to a professionally acceptable and low level. Properly employing these concepts will assure accomplishment of the auditor's sampling objectives.

The consideration of these concepts can be relatively complex and requires skill in applying professional judgment. However, the concepts are relatively few in number and are similar regardless of the substantive tests of details to which they are applied. These concepts are

1. Audit risk and its components, which include
   a. Specific component risks, associated with the account balance or class of transactions, that arise from the environment in which the client operates—that is, inherent risk and control risk.
   b. Specific component risks arising from the auditor's work in attempting to detect error—that is, detection risk and risk of incorrect rejection.
2. Materiality (tolerable error).
3. The logic of (statistical) sampling inference and its relationship to particular characteristics of the items in a class or balance.

These concepts are explained in the sections that follow.

Proper use will allow the auditor to be reasonably certain that there is an appropriately low level of risk of error in the conclusions reached about the fairness of the account value being audited. These concepts are the keys to (1) proper projection of a most likely value for the account under audit based on an examination of only a small number of items from that population, (2) assuring that the sample is indeed representative of the population, and (3) being certain that the risk of reaching an improper conclusion is low.

The Effects of Audit Risk and Materiality

☑ **Objective 2**
Use audit risk and materiality judgments in substantive test design

In earlier chapters and Chapter 11, we have discussed the concepts of audit risk and materiality. Those chapters defined audit risk as the risk of issuing an inappropriately unqualified audit opinion because of a material undetected error in the financial statements. The audit risk model as stated in those chapters is as follows:[1]

$$RT = IR \times IC \times DR \tag{1}$$

We stated in Chapter 11 that the responsibility of controlling inherent risk (IR) (to the extent that it can be controlled) and internal control risk (IC) belongs to the client. In substantive sampling, it is again the responsibility of the auditor to evaluate those risks and use those evaluations in deciding the nature, timing, and extent of tests of the details underlying the account balances shown in the financial statements. It is important for the auditor to form judgments regarding both *IR* and *IC* before conducting tests of details on the balances. These judgments are critical, because they are the basis for forming a conclusion regarding the maximum acceptable level of *detection risk, DR*, as we shall explain below.

Detection Risk

Detection risk is the component of the total audit risk model controllable by the auditor. Either of the two types of substantive audit tests, analytical procedures (*AP*) and tests of details (*TD*) can be used separately or in combination to reduce detection risk. Generally, the auditor can reduce detection risk by (1) increasing the size of the sample used for tests of details, or (2) using more extensive analytical procedures, or (3) altering the timing of substantive tests (e.g., performing the work nearer the balance sheet date), or by employing some combination of these three. The detection risk (DR) component of the audit risk model in (1) above is a product of the analytical procedures risk (AP) and tests of details risk (*TD*). Thus,

$$DR = AP \times TD \tag{2}$$

Analytical procedures can be quite useful in detecting material financial statement error. However, they are generally used to reach deductive conclusions rather than conclusions based on aggregating the results of numerous tests of details.[2] Therefore, analytical procedures do not fit the definition of sampling as described in SAS 39 (AU350).[3] Sampling procedures always rely on conclusions about the whole drawn from observations concerning individual tests of details. Since our concern is with audit sampling we will focus our discussion on the risks associated with tests of details rather than the risks associated with analytical procedures.

Sampling risks can be measured based on the laws of probability. However, the incorrect outcome associated with the occurrence of errors measured by sampling risk is often undetectable. Therefore, control of such risk during the planning for substantive tests of details is very important. Sampling risk exists any time the auditor reaches a conclusion about an account or class of transactions based on the application of audit procedures to less than 100 percent of those items. *Sampling risk* is the risk that conclusions reached about the class or balance based on examination of less than 100 percent of the items in that class or balance will be incorrect.

Nonsampling Risk and Tests of Details

As explained in Chapter 11, nonsampling risk is associated with errors that stem from incorrect conclusions by the auditor. Nonsampling risks are the result of the improper application of audit techniques and procedures, or the inappropriate selection or timing of procedures, or human error in reviewing results or conclusions derived by others. Nonsampling errors are almost always subject to detection. Therefore, they are controlled by adherence to appropriate quality control practices, generally accepted auditing standards, and personal professional vigilance. Although nonsampling risk is controllable and can usually be considered detectable, it can only be measured subjectively.

Sampling Risks and Tests of Details

In performing substantive tests of details, the auditor is concerned with two types of sampling risk.[4]

1. The **risk of incorrect acceptance** is the risk that the sample supports the conclusion that the recorded account balance is not materially misstated when, in fact, it is materially misstated.
2. The **risk of incorrect rejection** is the risk that the sample results support the conclusion that the recorded account balance is materially misstated when, in fact, it is not.

The risk of incorrect rejection, like the risk of underreliance on internal control (see Chapter 11), affects the efficiency of the audit. For example, if the evaluation of the audit sample leads to the conclusion that an account balance is materially misstated, the next step may be to obtain additional audit evidence relating to the balance. Examination of that evidence may lead to the conclusion that the balance is fairly stated after all, which is the correct conclusion in this case. Although the audit may be less efficient in such a case, it is nevertheless effective.

On the other hand, the risk of incorrect acceptance involves concluding that the account balance is fairly stated (thus leading to issuance of an unqualified audit opinion) when, in reality, it is materially misstated. The risk affects the *effectiveness* of the audit. Notice that this risk is directly related to the *TD* component of Equation (2)—it refers to the probability of issuing an inappropriately unqualified audit report. Thus, the risk of incorrect acceptance is of primary concern to the auditor in planning, performing, and evaluating samples.

Materiality and Substantive Tests of Details

Materiality has been previously defined as that characteristic possessed by a financial statement item when its disclosure, either alone or in combination with other similar items, would affect the decision processes of an informed user of the financial statements. In Chapter 11, we observed that the auditor's materiality judgment was expressed in terms of the maximum tolerable deviation rate that would be acceptable. That judgment in turn established the criterion for judging whether controls were effective. For substantive sampling for tests of details, the auditor's materiality judgment is expressed in terms of the maximum amount of dollar error that the auditor can accept and still conclude that the item is fairly presented in accordance with generally accepted accounting principles. For example, while auditing accounts receivable, the auditor might decide in advance of sampling to accept as much as a $300,000 error and still conclude that accounts receivable are not materially misstated.

As stated in Chapter 5, materiality decisions depend on judgment, experience, and the inherent risk associated with the particular account balance being audited. Therefore, it is necessary for the auditor to reach a conclusion regarding the measure of tolerable error for a specific account, as part of the planning process for auditing that account. This is so whether statistical or nonstatistical approaches are used in the tests of specific accounts.

Basic Logic of Audit Sampling Inference

The object of most substantive tests of details that employ sampling is to determine, based on the value of items in the sample, whether the population being tested should be declared to be materially in error or declared to be free of material error. This is a very different objective than simply determining the appropriate or true or average value of the items in the population being audited. The auditor interested in reaching conclusions based on sampling for substantive tests of details will certainly rely on the average value of items sampled. However, the auditor must determine whether it is reasonable to conclude that the appropriate value for the entire class or balance is fairly stated or materially in error based on the results of that sample. This requires some fundamental understanding of the relationship between the predictable behavior of a sample in relation to all possible samples of a given size from a given population (this relationship is described by the central limit theorem) and the associated concepts of projection from a sample to a population as a whole and allowance for sampling risk.

Sampling Results Have a Predictable Pattern

For random samples, the behavior of a sampling process will generally assure that the population of all possible sampling results (e.g., the average values for samples of a given size) will be approximately *normal* in shape. Normal means that approximately 50 percent of all possible sample results will fall above the actual average value or mean of the items in the population and 50 percent will fall below this average or mean value. Figure 12–12 (later) shows the typical shape for such a distribution of means. This distribution is often referred to as the sampling distribution and the shape of this distribution is referred to as normal.

The **central limit theorem** suggests that this distribution of the average value of items from samples of a given size for a given population will be located or centered at the average value of the population itself. The central limit theorem also suggests that the pattern of relative frequency of all possible *means*, which is the pattern graphed in Figure 12–12, will always be bell shaped, even though the pattern of population values (e.g., the population in Figure 12–1) is not. Significantly, the central limit theorem also suggests that the relative dispersion of the sampling distribution itself will depend upon and vary directly with the variability of the population being sampled. The statistical measure of this variability is referred to as the standard error. For sampling purposes, about two-thirds of all possible sample values will fall within one standard error of the mean of the population itself. **Standard error** is a measure of variability of the mean of samples from a given population. It is also called the standard deviation of a sampling distribution.

For example, the standard error of the average value obtained from any sample of size 100 drawn from the population in Figure 12–1, in which the particular characteristic observed is the book value of each account, might be $350. Changing the sample size, *or* the characteristic of interest (e.g., studying audited value rather than book value), *or* the population (e.g., excluding the larger items for separate study) will change the standard error.

Projection Determines Most Likely Effect

The auditor should not conclude that error in a population is less than the material or tolerable error established for that account or balance simply because the sample itself reveals errors that in total are less than the tolerable amount. Rather, the auditor must project a most likely total effect from the results of the sample itself. For example, an auditor who believes that a balance must be in error by $10,000 or more to be materially wrong would not conclude that the balance is fair simply because the sample of 100 items contains a total error of $1,000. Clearly, the appropriate inference or projection for most likely error based on the sample result is much larger than $1,000. If the sample of 100 that produced $1,000 in observed error comes from a population of 20,000 items, the auditor might appropriately conclude that the projected or most likely error is

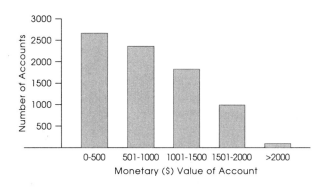

Figure 12–1

The Distribution of an Accounts Receivable Population

$200,000 (20,000/100 × 1,000). In these circumstances, it would be clear to the auditor that the risk of material error (error in excess of $10,000) is quite high, perhaps almost 100 percent.

Think about another circumstance based on the situation just described. This time, consider a sample whose most likely projected error is $10,000. In this circumstance, the risk of material error (error in excess of $10,000) is exactly the same as the likelihood that total error is less than $10,000. As in the previous example, the auditor would again conclude that the risk of material error in the balance as a whole is too high to adequately support a conclusion that the balance is fair. In fact, it is appropriate to conclude that error is as likely to be above $10,000 as below.

To reduce the risk of improperly concluding that the balance is fair, the auditor will employ the concept of an **allowance for sampling risk**. This will be done by accepting a balance as fair only if the projected error from a sample is significantly less than tolerable error. For example, in the illustration above, the auditor might determine that the balance can be declared fair based on sample results only if the total projected error from the sample is less than $7,500. The risk that the conclusion will be wrong depends on the variability of the sampling distribution. In our example, if the population is tightly distributed the risk of incorrect acceptance associated with the $7,500 limit might be 10 percent. However, if the items from the population being sampled are widely dispersed, the risk for the same $7,500 limit might be higher, say, 30 percent.

The difference between the $10,000 population error limit in our example and the $7,500 sample acceptance limit is referred to as an allowance for sampling risk. The allowance for sampling risk is used to assure that the risk of incorrect acceptance (type II, or β, sampling risk) will be (considerably) less than 50 percent. For a given sampling procedure and population, a larger allowance for sampling risk will ensure a lower risk of incorrect acceptance. These concepts are described more precisely and elaborately for statistical testing, but the fundamental concepts are employed in both statistical and nonstatistical substantive auditing testing.

Variability Influences Sample Size

There is another characteristic of a population that has significant impact on the auditor's consideration of an appropriate sample size. This characteristic is the dispersion or variability in the value of items of the population from which the sample will be taken. The variability of the value of items in a population or subpopulation can be measured and expressed in terms of **standard deviation**. This is a measure of the *average dispersion* of items in the population or stratification layer. A formal estimate of the variability of a population or stratification level is sometimes desirable. If so, the auditor will generally draw a preliminary sample from the population, audit that sample, and record the desired characteristics, such as dollar amount of the balance of each account selected for audit or the dollar amount of error in each account selected for audit. The average value for the sample, called the *sample mean*, is then computed. The estimated standard deviation is then computed using the following formula:

$$S_y = \sqrt{\frac{\sum\limits_{j=1}^{n} (Y_j - \bar{y})^2}{n - 1}}$$

where

S_y is the estimated population standard deviation.
Y is the value of the individual items in the sample, from $j=1$ to $j=n$.
$\bar{y}$ is the mean of the preliminary sample.
n is the number of items in the sample.

As discussed in the opening sections of the chapter, one effective way to reduce variation is to include the few largest items in a population in a group for 100-percent verification. The sample size required for remaining items can be reduced by stratifying the population as illustrated below. When stratification occurs, proportionately larger numbers of samples are selected from those accounts with greater dollar amounts.

Stratification for Sampling Efficiency

An estimation method is generally considered to be efficient if the desired results can be obtained by using a smaller sample than would be required by another method. The efficiency of a particular sampling process is affected by the *population standard deviation*, because this parameter has a significant effect on the sample size required to meet specified risk and materiality guides. Most audit populations are characterized by large standard deviations. As a result, the sample required would be larger than if the population had a smaller standard deviation. Because of that fact, **stratification** of the population can be a means of improving sampling efficiency.

In *stratifying* the audit population, the auditor in effect breaks the universe into several subpopulations, each of which will have a smaller standard deviation than that of the population taken as a whole. As a result, the combined samples from the various subpopulations from the various strata required to produce the desired statistical conclusions will often be smaller than the size of one large sample taken from the total population.

To illustrate, let's assume that an auditor wants to be satisfied that raw materials inventory is not overstated by more than $50,000. Part of the inventory examination involves price testing of raw materials inventory items to recent vendor invoices. The perpetual inventory records for raw materials (consisting of 5,000 items totalling $5 million) are scanned, and it is discovered that there are ten items that account for $2 million of the inventory value. Clearly, these ten items could and should be audited separately (perhaps 100 percent). By doing this, the variability in the remaining population of 4,990 items will be significantly smaller than for the complete universe of 5,000 items. The auditor will also have verified 40 percent of the total dollar value of inventory by auditing only ten of the 5,000 items. A sample can then be drawn from the subpopulation of 4,990 items to audit that universe. The sample drawn from that subpopulation plus the ten largest items should result in the need for a smaller total number of items being audited than would be the case if a sample was drawn from the entire population without regard to dollar amount.

Symmetry

The symmetry of the distribution of frequency of values in a population can also affect sample results. Consider, for example, the population in Figure 12–1; there are a very large number of accounts having individually small values, a moderate number of accounts having moderate values, and only a few accounts having large values. Such a population is unbalanced or asymmetric. A statistical measure of this lack of balance or uniformity of item counts across various values within a population is called **skew**. Typically, skewed populations can cause sample results to be biased, that is, to consistently overstate or understate slightly the true average value of a population.

Figure 12–2 depicts a general relationship between frequency of accounts and the size or dollar value of accounts that is typical of many audit populations (such as the population in Figure 12–1). Populations like that depicted in Figure 12–2 are *positively skewed*. This means that the tail to the right is flat and elongated in relation to the tail on the left.[5]

The distribution of the dollar amounts of error in an audit population can also have a bearing on the efficiency of particular audit sampling techniques. One typical shape for the distribution of errors in an audit population is shown by Figure 12–3. Another typical shape for the distribution of errors in a population is shown by Figure 12–4. Distributions of errors shown in Figures 12–3 and

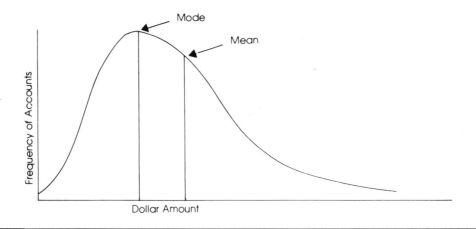

Figure 12–2

Positively Skewed Audit Population Distribution

12–4 are typical, in part, because they depict circumstances in which most accounts are correct or contain very little error. Both exhibit a tendency for errors, when they occur, to be relatively small, and for the likelihood of the error to be inversely related to the size of error. Figure 12–4 might be typical, for example, in a circumstance where customers are allowed one "free" item for every ten that are purchased in bulk. Such a pattern of errors might occur if customers are erroneously charged for the eleventh item.

When information about the distribution of account values and/or the dollar value of errors in accounts is available, it can often be utilized to assist the auditor in efficiently dividing the population into subpopulations or strata, to reduce the dispersion within each strata. For example, when facing a distribution of dollar errors such as that shown in Figure 12–4 the auditor might choose to take advantage of the natural clusters in accounts by developing separate estimates for (1) the dollar value of error in accounts with error greater than the amount A; (2) the dollar value error in accounts with error greater than the

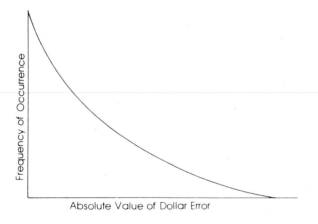

Figure 12–3

A Typical Shape for an Audit Population of Dollar Errors

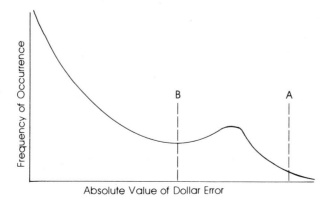

Figure 12–4

Another Typical Shape for an Audit Population of Dollar Errors

amount B, but less than the amount A; and (3) the dollar value of error in accounts with error less than the amount B. The variability in the results of the auditor's projection of the total value of dollar error for the account in total should be much smaller by using this procedure than would have been the case had the auditor chosen to estimate the total dollar value of error in the account without attempting stratified estimation.

So far we have discussed reducing variability by tailoring the specifications of subpopulations within the overall frame as related to the account balance under audit. Although these tailoring options can reduce variability in results, they will not eliminate it. Therefore, before completing the study of the population and before sampling, the auditor should attempt to study and estimate those characteristics of the subpopulations that will be subjected to sampling that greatly influence the variability of sample results. These factors are two: (1) the rate of expected error and (2) the relative size of expected errors. Estimating the standard deviation as described above is one way to study and obtain information about these two factors.

The Combined Impact of Risk, Materiality, and Population Characteristics on Sample Size Determination

As the size or frequency of error increases within a subpopulation, the size of a sample required to achieve the desired level of risk of incorrect acceptance will also increase. Experience with the application of sampling techniques to various populations is very useful to the auditor in making these judgments. Among factors useful in assessing populations in this regard are knowledge of prior years sample results, conclusions drawn concerning the strength of controls derived from tests of controls and other evidence concerning the control environment as it relates to the audit objective at hand, and the results of analytical procedures or other tests available at the time sample planning takes place.

The notions we have just discussed concerning appropriate ways for tailoring the sample to reduce dispersion, and the consideration of other factors about the population of interest that influence variability and hence sample size, should be considered by the auditor for use in planning for any substantive tests of details sample. These considerations are as applicable to nonstatistical or judgmental samples as they are to statistical samples.

Figure 12–5 summarizes the effects of factors that influence the size of the sample used to perform a substantive test. Notice that the factors of inherent risk, internal control risk, and risk of nondetection of error by other substantive tests, such as analytical procedures, have direct relationships to sample size. As these risks become greater, the allowable risk of incorrect acceptance for tests of details (TD) must be smaller. That, in turn, requires larger sample sizes. Conversely, as risks for internal control or other substantive tests decrease there is less need for reliance on substantive tests of details. This allows for greater risk of incorrect acceptance, which reduces the sample size necessary for substantive tests of details.

Figure 12–5 ■

Factors Influencing Sample Sizes for Substantive Tests of Details

| Factor | Risk (1 − Reliance) | Conditions leading to | | Related factor for substantive sample planning |
		Smaller sample size	Larger sample size	
IR	Inherent risk that material error will occur in client's transaction system without regard to controls	Greater reliance on client transaction environment	Lesser reliance on client transaction environment	Allowable risk of incorrect acceptance (TD)
IC	Internal control risk	Greater reliance on internal accounting controls	Lesser reliance on internal accounting controls	Allowable risk of incorrect acceptance (TD)
AP	Risk that nonsampling substantive tests (e.g., analytical procedures) related to the same objective as the sample will fail to detect error greater than the tolerable amount	Substantial reliance on substantive tests other than samples	Little or no reliance to be placed on other relevant substantive tests	Allowable risk of incorrect acceptance (TD)
TE	Measure of tolerable error for a specific account	Larger measure of tolerable error	Smaller measure of tolerable error	Tolerable error
E'	Expected size and/or frequency of errors	Smaller error or lower frequency	Larger error or higher frequency	Assessment of population characteristics
N	Number of items in population	Virtually no effect on sample size unless population is very small		

Figure 12–5 also shows that, as the measure of tolerable error (materiality threshold) becomes greater, allowing more variability in dollar estimates, the sample sizes for substantive tests become smaller. Of course, the opposite is also true. As the auditor reduces the amount of tolerable error, less variability can be allowed and (other things remaining the same) a larger sample will be necessary.

As the expected size or frequency of errors diminishes, smaller sample sizes are required. As they increase, larger samples are demanded. The absolute number of items in the population has little effect on sample size unless the population of items is small. These concepts will be illustrated mathematically when we discuss statistical sampling techniques later in the chapter. The concepts are applied only in a nonquantitative way when strict judgmental sampling is used.

■ ■

The Sampling Process for Substantive Tests of Details

☑ **Objective 3**
Understand the basic process of sampling for substantive testing

The appropriate steps for planning samples for substantive tests of details are essentially the same as those presented for attribute sampling, discussed in Chapter 11. Figure 12–6 lists steps that are followed in sampling where substantive tests of details are employed.

Figure 12–6 ▬▬▬▬

Steps in Sampling for Substantive Tests of Details

I. Planning the sample
  A. Determine the relevant audit objective for the specific substantive tests of details.
  B. Develop an estimate of tolerable error (*TE*) based on preliminary materiality level.
  C. Determine *TD*—the maximum allowable risk of incorrect acceptance for the specific substantive tests of details and consider an appropriate allowable risk of incorrect rejection.
  D. Study the population to which the results of substantive sampling will apply.
    1. Determine if 100 percent verification will apply to any portions of the population.
    2. Define that portion of the population to which sampling is to be applied, and estimate characteristics of that population which influence the efficiency of the sample and the selection of an appropriate sampling technique.
II. Selecting the sample
  A. Determine sample size, based on the factors in (I).
  B. Select a sample that is representative.
III. Examining and evaluating the sample
  A. Audit the sample, using appropriate tests-of-details procedures.
  B. Evaluate the evidence from the sample.
    1. Calculate the sample results.
    2. Project the results of the sample to the population.
    3. Combine sampling and nonsampling results.
    4. Form conclusion regarding related account balance or class of transaction using an appropriate allowance for sampling risk.

Planning the Sample

The auditor should consider the following factors when planning a particular sample for substantive tests of details, regardless of whether the sample is to be statistically valid or a judgmental sample.

- The audit objective to be met with the sample.
- Preliminary estimates of materiality and tolerable error.
- The allowable risks of incorrect acceptance and incorrect rejection.
- Relevant characteristics of the audit population.

Determining the Audit Objective.   In Chapter 6, we stated that the objectives of the substantive testing phase of the audit are to verify the client's financial statement assertions, including

- Appropriate statement presentation (disclosure).
- Transaction validity (occurrence).
- Completeness.
- Ownership.
- Periodicity (cutoff).
- Valuation/allocation.
- Existence.

When planning a sample for a substantive test, the auditor should begin by deciding which audit objectives are relevant to the population being sampled. Next, he or she should determine the auditing procedure, or combination of procedures, to be applied to achieve those objectives. For example, let us assume an audit client has a 2,000-item raw materials inventory, and that the auditor's objective is to determine whether the client's valuation for this inventory is fair (not materially in error). The auditor might then determine that procedures should include inspection of documents supporting unit costs, recalculation of extended costs for selected items, and recalculation of the client's final extended inventory totals.

Developing a Preliminary Estimate of Materiality and Establishing Tolerable Error.   The auditor should consider, as part of planning the sample, the maximum amount of monetary error that may exist without causing the financial statements to be materially misstated. Experience with the entity, knowledge of the company's industry, reporting practices, and both internal and external circumstances all affect the auditor's judgment in this matter. For example, in our inventory problem cited above, the auditor might typically begin by establishing an aggregate materiality threshold for error in a financial statement (say, $500,000). He or she would then allocate a proportionate amount (say 30 percent) to inventory based on the relative importance of the inventory balance to the overall financial statement presentation. In our case, the auditor may decide that he or she can accept as much as a $150,000 overstatement of inventories without judging them to be materially misstated. We call this the **tolerable error** (TE) for inventory.

Establishing the Maximum Allowable Risk of Incorrect Acceptance and the Risk of Incorrect Rejection.   The auditor must also reach a conclusion regarding the maximum tolerable risk of incorrect acceptance, as part of the planning process for substantive tests of details. In other words, the auditor must decide the level at which to set tests of details risk (TD) in Eq. (2). The following factors influence TD:

- The auditor's predetermined level of desired total audit risk (RT).
- The auditor's assessment of inherent risk (IR).
- The auditor's assessment of internal control risk (IC).
- The auditor's reliance on analytical procedures and hence the risk associated with such procedures (AP).

As depicted by Figure 12–7, several mechanisms are available that can act effectively to check otherwise undetected error equal to or in excess of tolerable error, should that error exist. As the figure suggests, there is always some inherent risk that such error will occur. Of course, this risk level varies with the nature of the class or balance for which substantive tests of details are being considered. For example, the inherent risk of significant or tolerable error in items such as cash may be much higher than the inherent risk associated with accounting and

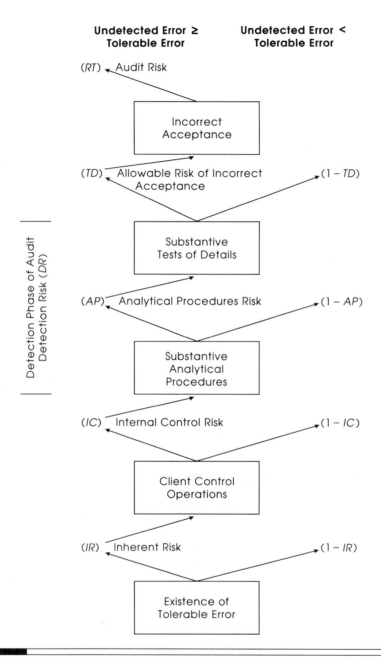

Figure 12–7

The Relationship among Audit Risk and Its Component Risks: $RT = IR \times IC \times AP \times TD$

reporting for inventories of bulky raw materials such as coal. Seasoned judgment may often be used by the auditor to appropriately assess the inherent risk associated with a particular class or balance.

The complement of that risk $(1 - IR)$ represents the likelihood that the total error occurring in the account or balance was less than tolerable error in the first place. If that is the case, then the financial statements associated with those accounts will be free of tolerable error in this respect. This will be the case whether the control system implemented by the client works well or not and regardless of whether tests and procedures employed in the audit might effectively detect tolerable error.

On the other hand, there will be some risk, IR, that in the absence of effective control operations or detection by the audit, error equal to or in excess of the tolerable error amount will indeed occur. Where this is the case, we will find ourselves still in the left column near the bottom of Figure 12–7. In this circumstance (which occurs with probability IR) the amount of undetected error in the account is greater than or equal to the tolerable error amount. Unless the client or the auditor detects and corrects the error, that error will continue to exist and incorrect acceptance will occur.

In our inventory example, we shall assume that the auditor is working with a very volatile inventory consisting of many different types of items. To be conservative, the inherent risk will be assessed at the maximum level; therefore, $IR = 1.0$.

In such circumstances, as Figure 12–7 suggests, the client's control operation may detect and correct the error. The likelihood of such an occurrence in the presence of tolerable error is equal to $1 - IC$. The complement of this probability, IC, is a measure of the risk that the internal control system of the client will fail to detect and correct the error.

In our inventory example, we shall assume that the client is well aware of the inherent risk associated with accounting for inventories and has devised an effective internal control structure to help reduce the risk of material error in accounting for inventories. Internal control risk is therefore set appropriately at $IC = .4$.

Should such a failure occur, then only the auditor's procedures are left to detect the error. The likelihood that the auditor will fail to do so is referred to as detection risk (DR), as discussed above. As Figure 12–7 suggests, there are two components of this risk. One of these is the risk (AP) that analytical procedures will fail to detect the presence of error equal to or greater than tolerable error. The other is the risk (TD) that tests of details will fail to detect such an error. The auditor assesses the likelihood of analytical procedures failing by considering the nature, extent, and timing of those procedures in relation to the audit objectives for which those tests are being planned. The likelihood that such procedures will detect the presence of tolerable error is $1 - AP$.

In our inventory example, it will be assumed that the auditor will conduct a detailed analytical procedures review of each of several product lines within the inventory. The review will include comparison of month-to-month profit margins on each line in the inventory as well as an analysis of inventory turnover statistics by product line for each month during the last three years. Therefore, because substantial reliance on analytical procedures will be attempted, $AP = .5$.

The likelihood of detection of any existing error greater than tolerable error by substantive tests of details is equal to $1 - TD$. Conversely, the likelihood that such tests will fail to detect the presence of amounts equal to or greater than tolerable error is TD.

The joint probability of tolerable error existing in the first place, along with a failure to detect and correct that error by the control system, as well as failure of analytical procedures to detect the error during the audit and a failure of substantive tests of details to detect that error during the audit is equal to audit risk, RT. This is the risk, as shown in Figure 12–7, of incorrectly accepting financial statements that include an amount equal to or greater than tolerable error in the financial statement balance or account for which the auditor is planning the substantive tests of details under consideration.

The practical use made of this joint risk equation is for planning the appropriate level for the allowable risk of incorrect acceptance when concerned about a particular sample plan for substantive tests of details. In this practical application, the auditor will solve the general equation for TD. Thus,

$$TD = RT/(IR \times IC \times AP) \tag{3}$$

In our inventory example, the auditor may determine that 5 percent is an appropriate level for audit risk. The other risks are as follows: inherent risk (IR), 100 percent; internal control risk (IC), 40 percent; and analytical procedures risk (AP), 50 percent. Therefore,

$$TD = .05/(1.0 \times .4 \times .5) = .25$$

Generally accepted auditing standards require that RT be kept at a reasonably low level. Levels of 5 percent or lower are common. By examining Eq. (3) we can see that if the auditor conservatively assumes error equal to or greater than tolerable error has indeed occurred ($IR = 1.0$), *and* that no reliance should be placed for planning purposes on the client's internal control system ($IC = 1.0$), *and* that no analytical procedures are to be employed with respect to the audit objective for which substantive tests of details are now being planned ($AP = 1.0$), then $TD = RT$. In such circumstances, the auditor would necessarily rely on very effective audit tests, conducted at or near year end, using a large sample size. Here, the auditor should establish an allowable risk of incorrect acceptance that, like RT, is commensurately low (5 to 10 percent). On the other hand, as can also be seen by examining Eq. (3), when the auditor reduces one or more of the component risks other than TD to less than 100 percent the allowable level of TD may be increased accordingly. This allows for

1. Less effective substantive tests of details.
2. Possibly more use of analytical procedures.
3. Performance of tests at interim rather than near year's end.
4. A smaller sample size.

For example, suppose that the auditor desires to hold total audit risk (RT) at .05. He or she has performed the necessary preliminary planning and internal control review procedures to have assessed inherent risk (IR) at 1.00 and internal control risk at .50. Because of the indicated high inherent risk in the account and low reliance on internal control, analytical procedures on potentially erroneous financial statement amounts have a .80 risk of nondetection of tolerable error. Thus, to maintain RT at the desired level of .05, the auditor must use substantive tests to accept a maximum tolerable rate of .125 risk of incorrect acceptance, or $[.05/(1.0 \times .50 \times .80)]$. This means that the auditor's desired confidence in substantive tests of details must be .875 $(1 - .125)$.

As Eq. (3) shows and the example illustrates, once an overall audit risk level (RT) has been established, the allowable risk of incorrect acceptance for substantive samples involving tests of details varies inversely with inherent risk, control risk, and analytical procedures risk. In circumstances where inherent risk, internal control risk, or analytical procedures risk are assessed as low, the allowable risk of incorrect acceptance can be increased. Put another way, as the auditor's reliance on control systems increases, *or* the auditor's confidence in substantive analytical procedures increases, *or* the underlying nature of the items associated with the class or balance of interest is perceived as less inherently risky, then the required level of confidence or reliability associated with the tests of details can be lowered.

Intuitively, it can be understood that smaller sample sizes are possible when the allowable risk of incorrect acceptance is increased because of the auditor's judgments that it is possible to rely on the results of analytical procedures performed by the auditor. Likewise, it is possible to rely on the control system based on prior assessments about that system. Similarly, where the inherent risk of an error equal to or in excess of tolerable error is not too high, the allowable risk of incorrect acceptance increases and sample size drops.

A statistical approach to substantive audit sampling for tests of details requires quantification of each element in the risk equation. Judgmental approaches do not. As mentioned above, either approach is acceptable. Using either approach, however, the auditor should carefully consider the relationships between the appropriate level for allowable risk of incorrect acceptance and the other risk components, as we have just discussed. As an illustration of how this can be done judgmentally, consider the inventory problem mentioned above. Suppose, as is usually the case, that the auditor decides that RT should be kept at a low level. Suppose, as well, that the auditor believes the inherent risk associated with these inventories is very high because the company (1) has only a few key customers; (2) has extremely elastic demand for its product; (3) is part of a very volatile industry; and (4) is extremely dependent on inventory for its financial position. In addition, suppose that the study and evaluation of internal control yielded the conclusion that several weaknesses exist in key areas affecting inventory quantities. Assume also that, because of those internal control weaknesses, the financial statement balances associated with inventory had a high probability of containing error in excess of tolerable error. Analytical procedures (AP) also had a very low probability of detecting material errors. All of these circumstances suggest very high levels for IR, IC, and AP. To keep the level of RT at an acceptably low level, the auditor would have to set TD at a low level, requiring a high level of confidence in tests of details procedures. This, in turn, requires larger sample sizes than would have been necessary if the auditor had established low levels for IR, IC, and AP.

The risk of incorrect rejection for substantive sampling purposes involving tests of details is usually determined independently of audit risk and its associated components. This risk is of lesser importance than is the risk of incorrect acceptance. Therefore it is frequently considered only informally or not at all when planning for substantive samples. It must be explicitly considered when using certain techniques for statistical sampling in auditing. With other techniques, it is considered only implicitly. Where explicitly considered, the risk of incorrect rejection is often set at low levels (5 to 10 percent). By establishing this risk at low levels, the auditor is able to avoid unnecessary embarrassment or confrontation involving the client. Low levels of the risk of incorrect rejection help avoid inefficiency in the initial performance of audit sampling activity. Factors commonly considered when this risk is explicitly assessed include (1) whether a large number of errors are expected to be uncovered as a result of the sampling process and (2) whether fallback procedures in case rejection of the balance as initially indicated would be difficult or costly to implement.

Defining and Studying the Relevant Data Population.   The auditor should determine that the data population for which the sample is drawn is appropriate for the specific audit objective. The correspondence between the population about which inferences are to be drawn and the physical representation of that population used to enumerate items from which the tests-of-details sample will be drawn is called a *frame*. In an audit, there are often alternative frames to consider. The auditor must select one before drawing sample items.

In our inventory example, the audit objective is to verify the value of the recorded amount of inventory. The relevant frame from which the sample must be drawn, therefore, should be the client's detailed list of 2,000 inventory items supporting the general ledger account for inventory being verified. If, on the other hand, the auditor were trying to verify completeness, he or she would select a sample from such supporting documents as purchase orders, receiving reports, vendor invoices, etc.

The size of the population has very little effect on the size of the sample to be drawn from the population unless the population is small. In most sampling applications, the sample size must be more than 5 percent of the population size for changes in the population to have a significant effect on sample size. We discuss this concept further when we illustrate statistical sampling techniques later in the chapter.

At this point, the auditor should consider the potential for stratification and 100-percent verification of large items. Potential error characteristics should be considered, and judgments made about appropriate risks and tolerable error in relation to sample size. Figure 12–5 summarizes these judgments.

Execution of Substantive Sampling for Tests of Details

☑ **Objective 4**
Execute substantive tests

After planning, the auditor must select sample items, examine those items, and evaluate the results. Let us assume for purposes of our nonstatistical example that the auditor has, after considering all of the relevant factors, subjectively determined that a sample of 100 items should be selected for audit, from the 2,000-item inventory.

Selecting the Sample. As observed for attributes sampling, either a non-statistical or a statistical sample, when properly applied, can provide sufficient evidence to support the audit conclusion if the sample is representative of the population. However, statistical sampling also helps the auditor to

- Design an efficient sample that meets the criteria shown in Figure 12–5.
- Quantitatively measure the sampling risk associated with the evidence obtained.
- Evaluate the sample results.

Nevertheless, statistical sampling involves additional costs of training auditors, designing individual samples to meet statistical requirements, and randomly selecting the items to be examined. Those costs must be weighed against the benefits to be derived from using statistical sampling. As discussed in Chapter 11, if statistical sampling is used, random sampling must be used to select the items for audit testing. A random sample is one that provides every item within a subpopulation equal opportunity for selection as a member of the sample to be audited. A random sample must also be selected in a manner that assures that the selection of any one item is independent of the selection of any other. Random selection generally requires use of either random-number tables or computer-generated item-selection patterns. We shall assume random selection for our inventory example.

Haphazard selection or interval selection are often used in selecting non-statistical samples. Some versions of block, or cluster sampling may also be used when appropriate. However, in all of these cases, care should be taken so that the requirements of SAS 39 (AU350) are met. Since the purpose of sampling for substantive tests of details is the acceptance or rejection of a population amount, a representative sample must be selected in all cases: every item in the population must have a chance (not necessarily an equal chance) of being selected.

Examining and Evaluating the Sample. Once the sample has been selected, *appropriate auditing procedures must be applied* to each item in the sample to fulfill the audit objective. In some instances it may not be possible to perform the desired procedure on one or more items in the sample. For example, in the process of inspecting documents supporting the cost of inventory, the auditor may not be able to locate appropriate supporting documents (recent vendor invoice, etc.). If considering such an item to be misstated would constitute a material error, alternative procedures should then be performed to resolve the item to the auditor's satisfaction.

The results of examining the sample should be expressed in terms of some monetary amount. This may be in the form of monetary error (aggregate dollar difference between the audited sample and the client's recorded value for that sample of items) or total monetary amount (aggregate dollar amount of the audited items in the sample). The auditor should then *project the results of the sample* to the population from which the sample was selected. If the auditor has stratified the population into relatively homogeneous groups for sampling, the results of each group should be projected separately for the group from which it was drawn and the results from all strata should be accumulated.

After auditing the sample we must project the sample result to the population. One method of projection is to multiply the results from the sample by a fraction, the numerator of which is the number of items in the population (or subpopulation) and the denominator of which is the number of items in the sample. For example, if the auditor discovers overstatement errors totaling $4,000 in a sample of 100 items drawn from an inventory population of 2,000 items, the total projected overstatement in the population would be $80,000 [$4,000 × (2,000/100)].

If sampling has been used on only a portion of the population, with the rest of the items in the population being 100-percent verified, the *projected error or total from the sample results should be added to the error total discovered in the group of items that was 100-percent verified.* For example, to arrive at the total estimated error, suppose that the audit population mentioned above had consisted of 2,050 items, 50 of which were extremely large and required 100-percent verification. Assume that we discovered a $4,000 overstatement error from our audit of the 50 very large items, plus the error projection of $80,000 calculated above for the sample. In this case, the total projected error in the population would be $84,000 ($80,000 from the population of sampled items plus $4,000 from the items that were 100-percent verified).

In forming a conclusion regarding the balance being audited by sampling, the estimated error should be compared with the auditor's *maximum tolerable error.* In addition, appropriate consideration should be given to the risk associated with the sampling process. If the total projected error is less than the tolerable error for the account balance or class of transactions, the auditor should still consider the possibility of incorrect acceptance of the amount derived from the sample. In monetary terms, an allowance for such a possibility is referred to as an *allowance for sampling risk.*

To illustrate, recall that in our inventory example the auditor has a maximum tolerable error of $150,000. If sampling and other results produce a total projected error of $84,000, the auditor may be reasonably assured that there is an acceptably low risk that the true monetary error in inventory exceeds $150,000. As illustrated by Figure 12–8, the allowance for sampling risk is $66,000. On the

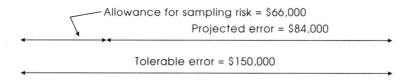

Figure 12–8

An Illustration Relating Tolerable Error, Projected Error, and Allowance for Sampling Risk

other hand, if the total projected error had been close to $150,000, the auditor might conclude that there is an unacceptably high risk that the total actual error in the population exceeds tolerable error. If the total projected error were quite close to $150,000 but still less than that amount, the auditor might be forced to conclude that the likelihood of error in excess of $150,000 is unacceptably high.

This circumstance makes an important point and one that may be counterintuitive. With a total projected error close to but less than $150,000, many are tempted to form the conclusion that the balance under audit is acceptable and need not be rejected. This is an incorrect conclusion because it fails to consider the necessity for an allowance for sampling risk. This allowance is necessary because of the variability of projection results inherent in sampling. A projected total error of just less than $150,000 may, with very high likelihood, be the result of sampling from a population in which the amount of error equals or exceeds that associated with tolerable error.

Assume, in our inventory example, that the variability of projected results based on the sample of 100 items is described by the distribution curve shown in Figure 12–9. The auditor does not know in advance whether error in excess of tolerable error ($150,000) exists. However, the auditor must guard against that possibility by *assuming that this could happen*. The risk of incorrect acceptance is reduced accordingly. Assuming that error equal to tolerable error ($150,000) is actually present, the pattern of all possible results for a sample of size 100 will cluster around the $150,000 value as shown in Figure 12–9. The probability of a projection of total dollar error just less than $150,000 (e.g., $148,000) will be very high. Concluding that error in excess of tolerable error is *not* present in such a circumstance is too risky. On the other hand, an allowance as great as $66,000

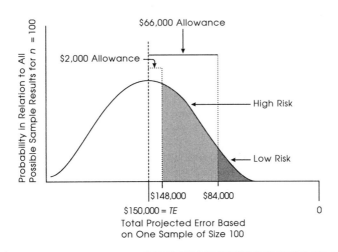

Figure 12–9

The Size of the Allowance for Sampling Risk Varies Inversely with the Level of Risk of Incorrect Acceptance

associated with the projected result of $84,000 of error assures the auditor that there is a relatively low risk of incorrect acceptance based on the projection of $84,000. As shown, the likelihood of a total projected error of $84,000 is very low if tolerable error (error of $150,000) is actually present. If the auditor concludes that sample results will *not* support a sufficiently large allowance for sampling risk, then appropriate fallback procedures should be considered.

Fallback procedures may include substantial expansion of the initial sample size to further reduce variance, and hence reduce the **allowance for sampling risk**, consistent with the planned level of allowance for the risk of incorrect acceptance. Other strategies are possible as well. One of these is to ask the client to rework the balance in question. Another is to plan for analytical procedures to be performed more extensively than originally planned—that is, at greater levels of detail than initially contemplated. As can be seen from Figure 12–5 or by study of Eq. (3), this will allow the auditor to increase the planned level for *TD* and therefore reduce the allowance for sampling risk. In some cases such a reduction may be sufficient to allow the difference between the original total projected error and the $150,000 tolerable error amount to exceed the appropriate allowance for sampling risk. If so, the auditor may accept the balance in question.

In addition to evaluating the frequency and amounts of monetary misstatements in the sample items, attention should be given to such factors as the nature and causes of the misstatements. These factors can include differences of opinion relating to the handling of an item, unintentional errors, irregularities, misunderstandings of instructions, or carelessness. The auditor should also consider the possible relationship of the causes of the misstatements to other phases of the audit. For example, the discovery of an irregularity usually necessitates a broader consideration of the possible implications for other elements of the financial statements than does the discovery of an unintentional error.

Other Conclusions from Results of Substantive Tests.   The results of substantive tests of details may suggest to the auditor that assumptions made during the planning stages of the audit or during the control risk assessment stage were in error. If that is the case, appropriate action should be taken. For example, suppose that we had assessed control risk at a low level and thus had reduced sample sizes for substantive tests of details. If those tests produce monetary errors that will not support acceptance of the financial statement amount, we may need to adjust our assessment of control risk upward. This adjustment, in turn, would cause us to expand our substantive tests of details in other accounts that are related to those controls. To illustrate this point, assume that in our inventory example we had employed a low control risk assessment and thus limited the detailed inspection of documents. If our detailed tests in this area cause us to project an error close to or in excess of $150,000, we would increase our control risk assessment, which, in turn, would cause us to take larger detailed samples when carrying out the substantive tests of cost of sales and cash disbursements.[6]

Statistical Sampling for Substantive Tests of Details

We will discuss three approaches to statistical sampling for substantive tests of details. Two of these are based on the classical statistical approach to hypothesis testing, and the third is based on the application of attribute sampling theory (as discussed in Chapter 11). The third approach, called probability-proportional-to-size sampling, analyzes the proportional errors occurring in the population of dollars that constitute a particular class or balance for which substantive testing objectives are specified.

The choice of whether to use one of these statistical approaches or a nonstatistical approach depends, as discussed above, on several factors. Statistical approaches allow quantification of risks and allowances for sampling error. Nonstatistical approaches rely on subjective judgments about sample sizes that are associated with professional judgments about audit risk and its components.

Using Statistical Hypothesis Testing in an Audit: Difference Estimation

This section illustrates and explains how to use difference estimation, a classical statistical hypothesis-testing approach, to conduct substantive tests of details in an audit. A second approach, mean-per-unit estimation, is illustrated in the next section. The steps followed are those listed in Figure 12–6. Each step is illustrated, but detailed explanations are limited to those features of the process uniquely associated with the **classical hypothesis-testing approach**.

1. *Determine the relevant audit objective.* The first step in a substantive sampling plan in an audit is the same regardless of the approach. The auditor must always begin by determining the relevant audit objective from the specific substantive tests of details under consideration. The objective(s) of a substantive test should be the same regardless of which of the statistical approaches is adopted. Indeed, it will be the same even if a nonstatistical approach is adopted.

To illustrate in a difference estimation situation, suppose that the control risk assessment over sales and receivables is complete. The client, Huaco Business Forms, Inc., has an aged trial balance of 5,000 customer accounts receivable having a recorded book value of $6 million. Total assets of Huaco are $75 million, and net earnings before tax are $5 million. The next phase of the audit calls for performance of substantive tests of details on the accounts receivable balances to determine that they do exist and that the balance shown for them is materially correct. The primary substantive test of details to achieve those objectives is confirmation of accounts receivable.

The relevant audit objectives are to determine the *existence* of accounts receivable and to establish their correct *valuation*. The two hypotheses in difference estimation may be stated in terms of the value of accounts receivable being either materially correct or materially misstated. *The hypothesis tested in this case is that the statement amount is in error by an amount equal to tolerable error.* This is sometimes called the alternative hypothesis or H_a.[7] If, as a result of the statistical tests, the auditor is able to reject this hypothesis it would be appropriate to conclude that the client's recorded book value (BV) is an appropriate GAAP value for the audit population. This second statement is usually associated with the null hypothesis or H_0. H_0 states that the financial statement amount is correct in accordance with GAAP.

2. *Determine the preliminary estimate of tolerable error.* The maximum acceptable dollar error can be influenced by both qualitative and quantitative factors. Qualitative factors include the *inherent risk* of misstatement of the item, as discussed earlier.

For example, if the auditor suspects the existence of an irregularity in handling receivables, inherent risk would be set at a high level. This in turn would result in a lower threshold of tolerable error in relation to materiality for that population than would be the case if only a few scattered inadvertent errors are anticipated. The quantitative factor would be the dollar amount of error that can be accepted by the auditor. Suppose, now, that you have discussed the situation of Huaco, Inc., with your superiors and can tolerate an error of $\pm\$30,000$ and still accept the balance as being fairly stated.

3. *Decide the maximum allowable risk of incorrect acceptance (TD) and an appropriate allowable risk of incorrect rejection.*

Suppose that you have judgmentally determined that reliance on the client's controls that are directly related to existence and valuation of accounts receivable balances (IC) is only 60 percent. In addition, results of preliminary analytical procedures (AP) that are related to the existence and valuation objectives have a 50-50 chance of detecting significant misstatement in the balance. Since receivables are susceptible to a high level of inherent risk, assume that IR, as discussed earlier, is to be set at 1.0. Therefore,

$IR = 1.0$

$IC = .40; (1.0 - .60)$

$AP = .50$

Assume that for this audit the limit on total audit risk (RT) is .01. Therefore, applying Eq. (3), we obtain the following result from the risk of incorrect acceptance as applied to tests of details (TD):

$$TD = RT/(IR \times IC \times AR)$$
$$= .01/(1.0 \times .40 \times .50)$$
$$= .01/.20$$
$$= .05$$

The auditor may then conclude that the total risk of failure of tests of details to detect a material misstatement should be .05.

The classical hypothesis-testing approaches are unique in that they *require* a quantification of the risk of incorrect rejection, α, as well as the risk of incorrect acceptance, *TD*. In predetermining α risk, the auditor must consider the *cost of resampling* should the population be rejected. If marginal cost is high, a low level of α risk should be prespecified, necessitating higher confidence levels and resultant larger original sample sizes. The procedure involved in additional sampling in our problem would be mailing second confirmation requests and vouching subsequent collections. The marginal cost of these procedures is high. Therefore, risk should be set low in the initial sample size. Presume that a .05 level of α has been selected as appropriate in this case.

The outcomes possible as a result of employing this approach are shown in Figure 12–10. If, *after sampling,* the auditor infers that the book value of the client is materially correct when in fact it is materially correct, he or she has made a correct audit decision. On the other hand, the auditor who infers that the book value is materially correct when in fact it is materially misstated, commits a **Type II sampling error**, and has incorrectly accepted the book value as fairly stated.

If, after sampling, the auditor infers that the book value of the population being audited is materially in error when in fact it is materially in error, he or she has made a correct audit decision. On the other hand, the auditor who infers that a book value is materially misstated, when in fact it is materially correct, commits a **Type I sampling error**, and has incorrectly rejected a fairly stated value.

4. *Define and describe the relevant data population.* Population size is determined by count. In this illustration, it consists of 5,000 customer accounts receivable. The sampling unit in this case is each account in the accounts

Figure 12–10

Possible Outcomes of Sampling

Sample-inferred state of the audit population	True state of the audit population	
	(1) Materially correct	(2) Materially misstated
(1) Materially correct	Correct decision	Type II (*TD*) risk Risk of incorrect acceptance
(2) Materially misstated	Type I (α) risk Risk of incorrect rejection	Correct decision

receivable subsidiary ledger. The sampling frame, or physical representation of these units, might be ledger cards in a manual system or individual records on an accounts receivable master file stored electronically in a computer system.

The choice of a classical hypothesis approach was made initially because this is an application in which, based on our analysis of controls and inherent risk, *numerous errors are expected.* Inspection of the detailed subsidiary accounts receivable ledger printout indicates that there are no unusually large balances. Therefore, all items will be subjected to the possibility of selection in our sample. No portion of the population will be subjected to 100-percent verification.

Had we expected few, if any errors, the classical hypothesis approach would probably not have been selected. Rather, the probability-proportional-to-size approach (discussed later) would probably have been selected, because it is usually more efficient in such circumstances.

When developing a statistical approach for implementation of a classical hypothesis test, the study of the variability of the population and its associated errors is necessary. Assume that you decide to take a preliminary sample of 30 accounts from the accounts receivable population for Huaco Corporation to learn about variability.[8]

We should audit the accounts in this preliminary sample and compare the audited value of each account with the client's book value to obtain a difference (d). Since we are only trying to get a preliminary estimate, confirmation will probably not be a necessary auditing procedure for this purpose. Instead, the alternative procedures of vouching subsequent collections and vouching charges in accounts to supporting documents will probably be sufficient. Suppose these procedures yielded the results shown in Figure 12–11.

Figure 12–11

Procedures for Calculating Estimated Standard Deviation of Errors

(1) Sampling unit (account)	(2) Book value x	(3) Audited value y	(4) Difference $d = x - y$ [(2) − (3)]	(5) $d - \bar{d}$	(6) $(d - \bar{d})^2$
1	470	500	−30	−65	4,225
2	400	370	+30	− 5	25
3	280	200	+80	+45	2,025
4	390	360	+30	− 5	25
5	560	480	+80	+45	2,025
6	2,720	2,640	+80	+45	2,025
7	500	500	0	0	0
.	.	.	.	.	. .
.	.	.	.	.	.
.	.	.	.	.	.
30	3,825	3,820	+5	−30	900
Totals	16,050	15,000	+1,050		26,100

$\bar{d}$ = average differences between audited and book value = $\dfrac{1,050}{30}$ = $35.

As inspection of Figure 12–11 reveals, seven of the thirty items in the pre-sample contain some error. In addition, both over- and understatements are revealed. Since a sufficient number of errors apparently exist in the population, the classical approach seems reasonable.

The determination of the size for the sample of confirmations of accounts receivable depends on the variability of the characteristic selected for audit from the population. Using the classical approach, there are several choices. Among these are the **difference** and the **ratio estimation** methods—and **mean-per-unit estimation** method, which is seldom used unless no book value is kept in support of a balance.

Ratio estimation is generally more efficient than the other classical methods when the size of the error in a book value is proportional to the book value itself. The **difference estimation** technique is usually more efficient when the size of error is relatively constant (unaffected by the size of the book value). Inspection of the results of the preliminary sample shown in Figure 12–11 indicates that the difference estimation technique is the better choice in this case. Due to their similarities the classical estimation techniques, which include ratio and difference estimation techniques, are subject to the same limitations. These estimation techniques should, therefore, not be applied in situations in which the error rate in a population is less than approximately 10 percent, nor when only overstated errors (or understated errors) are expected.

Because the difference estimation technique appears the best choice, you decide to plan accordingly. The preliminary sample provides knowledge about the expected size and frequency of errors. This information can now be put to use to study the variability of the populations of audited differences. This variability is measured by the **standard error**, or **standard deviation of the sampling distribution**. For populations containing a sufficient number of errors and sufficient numbers of both over- and understatements, the sampling distribution will be normally distributed. The sampling distribution for any population characteristic (in our case, differences between audited and book values or errors) can be used to measure the likelihood of any one particular sample outcome (the average error from an audited sample, or $35 in our case) in relation to all possible sample outcomes for samples of a given size and for a given population characteristic in a given population.

As mentioned previously, the sampling distribution behaves in accordance with the central limit theorem. This theorem from statistics assures us that if the population being considered has a finite mean and variance, then regardless of how the items in that population may be distributed across the range of values in that population, the distribution of sample means will be approximately normal for sufficiently sized samples (at least 30 items in most cases).

This means that for samples of sufficient size, the auditor can measure sampling risks α and TD associated with the sampling distribution by studying the relationship between the standardized normal distribution as described in tables such as those appearing as Appendixes 12–A and 12–B.

As can be seen from Figure 12–12, a normal distribution possesses two distinguishing characteristics. First, it is *symmetrical*, meaning that exactly 50 percent of the population items fall on either side of the mean. Statistical inferences

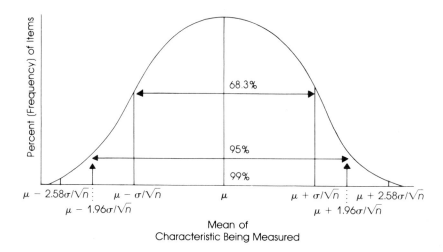

Note: μ = mean average value of the population.
σ = standard deviation of the population.
$\sigma/\sqrt{n}$ = standard deviation of the sampling distribution (Standard Error, or SE).

Figure 12–12 ▬▬

The Normal Sampling Distribution

made by auditors typically are based on the *assumption of a normally distributed population* with respect to its mean. Second, the normal distribution values congregate around the mean in such a way that 68.3 percent of them fall within plus-or-minus 1 standard deviation from the mean. Furthermore, 95 percent and 99 percent of the items fall within plus-or-minus 1.96 and 2.58 standard deviations from the mean, respectively.

The *general* relationship between standard deviation (σ) and standard error (SE) is another important consideration for the auditor. That relationship can be stated as follows:

$$SE = \sigma/\sqrt{n} \quad \text{or}$$

$$n = (\sigma/SE)^2$$

As the equations suggest, if the auditor can appropriately estimate the standard deviation of the population (σ) for which sample observations will be drawn, he can also estimate the standard error (SE or standard deviation of the sampling distribution). The sampling distribution is in turn important because it generates the value (the average or mean value of items observed) that will be used as illustrated later for the purpose of producing a projection about total error and reaching a conclusion about the presence or absence of tolerable error.

In our example the *specific population characteristic* selected for study *is the difference between audit value and book value*. The standard deviation of these differences is identified by the symbol SD. The specifically associated standard error of the sampling distribution for samples from this population is the standard error of differences, SED. In other words, for the specific characteristic chosen for study, $\sigma = SD$, and $SE = SED$. Therefore,

$$n = (SD/SED)^2$$

Any particular population characteristic has a unique distribution. In other words, every item in that population has one and only one value with respect to the characteristic chosen. Therefore, that population characteristic has a unique value for its standard deviation (e.g., *SD*). The value of *SED*, however, is not unique. It can be changed by changing the sample size. A larger *n* decreases *SED* and hence lowers the risks of sampling. Decreasing *n* has the opposite effect.

The *estimated standard deviation of differences (SDE)* is calculated as follows:

$$SDE = \sqrt{\frac{\sum_{j=1}^{n} (d_j - \bar{d})^2}{n - 1}} = \sqrt{\frac{26{,}100}{29}} = 30$$

where

d_j = the *j*th difference between audited and book values for sample items $j = 1$ through $j = n$.

5a. *Determine the sample size.* An **expected point estimate** of the population's dollar error (E') must be prespecified by the auditor when difference estimation is used. This expected dollar error estimate is similar to the expected occurrence rate for error in tests of controls.

The auditor may use experience gained from prior years in setting E'. Assume now that the previous year's audit of accounts receivable for Huaco Corporation revealed an estimated *overstatement* of accounts receivable in the amount of $3,000, which is expressed as E'.

Figure 12–13 shows how both α and *TD* are simultaneously controlled in the

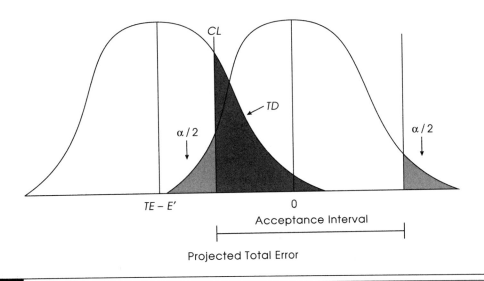

Figure 12–13 ▬▬

Risk Control for Audit Sampling

testing of hypotheses. The alternative hypothesis is established as the amount $TE - E'$ to account for expected existing overstatement error of \$3,000.

Also note that the Figure 12–13 is based on the sampling distribution for estimating the *total* error in accounts receivable. Hence, its variability is $N \cdot SED$ rather than SED. SED measures the standard error of the distribution of estimates of the *average error* of an account from the subsidiary ledger. The difference between the alternative hypothesis, $TE - E'$, and the critical limit, CL, is the *allowance for sampling risk*. The appropriate critical limit, CL, is computationally equivalent to *either*

$$TE - E' - (Z_{TD} \cdot SED \cdot N)$$
where $Z_{TD} \cdot SED \cdot N = $ the allowance for sampling risk

or

$$0 + Z_{\alpha/2} \cdot SED \cdot N$$

The first equation controls the risk of incorrect acceptance; the second equation controls the risk of incorrect rejection.

The sample-size equation computes the value of n, which simultaneously controls α and TD at planned levels. This is shown as follows:

$$TE - E' = Z_{TD} \cdot SED \cdot N + Z_{\alpha/2} \cdot SED \cdot N$$

or, since $n = (SD/SED)^2$ and using SDE to estimate SD,

$$TE - E' = Z_{TD} \cdot SDE/\sqrt{n} \cdot N + Z_{\alpha/2} \cdot SDE/\sqrt{n} \cdot N$$

Hence,[9]

$$n = \left[\frac{N(Z_{TD} + Z_{\alpha/2})SDE}{TE - E'} \right]^2$$

where

n = sample size

N = population size

Z_{TD} = one-tailed confidence coefficient for TD risk

$Z_{\alpha/2}$ = two-tailed confidence coefficient for α risk

SDE = estimated standard deviation of unreconciled differences in the audit population

TE = tolerable error

E' = expected error

This formula yields a sample size of 400 for the Huaco Corporation:

$$n = \left[\frac{5{,}000(1.64 + 1.96)30}{30{,}000 - 3{,}000} \right]^2 = 400$$

5b. *Select the sample.* After the sample size (n) has been determined, the auditor will select the sample on a random basis from the population of 5,000 accounts. To increase efficiency, the population may be stratified as discussed earlier, with the resultant advantages for audit populations with large variances.

6. *Audit the sample.* The auditor will next prepare and mail positive accounts receivable confirmation requests to all accounts included in the sample. The following auditing procedures would then be performed on the confirmation items.

   a. Receive the confirmation replies and follow up on those requests for which no replies were received. This generally involves sending second (and possibly third) requests.

   b. Perform alternative procedures (such as vouching subsequent collections to the cash receipts journal, vouching sales entries to invoices, shipping documents, etc.) for nonresponses.

   c. Reconcile differences between customer replies and the receivable amounts shown in the client's records.

After these procedures have been completed, the auditor will *determine the amounts* of all *errors* in the sample. Errors in this case are defined as the unreconciled differences between the verified balances and the balances shown on the client's records. An error value is then determined for each of the 400 units in the sample. When audited (customer-derived) values equal recorded values, the differences (error value) will be zero. Figure 12–14, step 2(d), shows the assumed findings of eighty unreconciled differences. The net *sum* of these differences (D) was $925 in the direction of overstatement.

7. *Evaluate the evidence.* Evaluating the evidence requires the steps shown in Figure 12–14. These steps include the following:

   a. Calculation of the point estimate of average dollar error ($\bar{d}$) and total dollar error ($\hat{D}$).

   b. Computation (or recomputation if preliminary estimate was made statistically) of the estimated population standard deviation of errors (SDE).

   c. Calculation of the size of the acceptance interval for errors (A).

   d. Computation of acceptance interval limits (UCL and LCL).

The **point estimate** of average dollar error per account ($\bar{d}$) is obtained by dividing the sum of all errors by the number of sampling units (accounts). The auditor then can project a point estimate of the dollar error in the population ($\hat{D}$) by multiplying ($\bar{d}$) by the number of items in the population (N). In our example, ($\bar{d}$) is $2.31 ($925/400). $\hat{D}$ is calculated as $11,550 ($2.31 $\times$ 5,000).

Since no statistical test can be made merely on the basis of a point estimate applied to the population, the auditor's next step is to construct an **acceptance interval** (A) around $\hat{D}$. This is done by statistical formulas in a series of steps. First, the standard deviation for error (SDE) must be estimated. This is the expected variability of dollar error around the true mean of the population. The

Figure 12–14 ■■■

Summary of the Difference Estimation Technique

Steps	Statistical formulas	Illustration for Huaco, Inc.
1. Develop a testable hypothesis.		H_0. The recorded value of accounts receivable ($6 million) is in error by less than the tolerable error of $30,000.

2. Gather the evidence by
  a. specifying TD, α, SD (or SDE if presample available), TE, N, and E'.
  b. drawing a random sample of size n.
  c. auditing the sample.
  d. determining the value of any unreconcilable error in the sample and summing the errors.
	$$n = \left[\frac{N(Z_{\alpha/2} + Z_{TD})SDE}{TE - E'} \right]^2$$
	
	 $$D = \sum_{i=1}^{n} d_i$$
	 where d_i = individual unreconciled error
		n = 400 customer accounts drawn at random from the population of 5,000 customer accounts and audited by noting unreconciled differences between audited amounts and book value for those amounts.
		330 accounts confirmed by customers, and 70 accounts audited by alternative procedures, with a total of 80 customers reporting differences that could not be reconciled; sum of these differences = $925 overstatement.

3. Evaluate the evidence by a. calculating the point estimate of the average dollar error ($\bar{d}$) and the projected population error ($\hat{D}$).	$$\bar{d} = \frac{D}{n}$$ $$\hat{D} = N \cdot \bar{d}$$	$\bar{d}$ = $925/400 = $2.31 $\hat{D}$ = 5,000 × 2.31 = $11,550
b. computing SDE.	$$SDE = \sqrt{\frac{\sum(d_i)^2 - n(\bar{d})^2}{n - 1}}$$ where d_i = error for ith item and $\bar{d}$ and n are defined as before.	Assume $\sum(d_i)^2 = $60,095 $$SDE = \sqrt{\frac{$60,095 - 400($2.31)^2}{399}}$$ $= $12.05
c. calculating the acceptance interval	$$A = N\left[Z_{TD} \cdot \frac{SDE}{\sqrt{n}} \cdot \sqrt{\frac{N - n}{N - 1}} \right]$$ where N, Z_{TD}, SDE, and n are defined as before. $$\sqrt{\frac{N - n}{N - 1}} = \text{finite correction factor}$$	$$A = 5,000\left[1.64 \cdot \frac{12.05}{\sqrt{400}} \cdot \sqrt{\frac{4,600}{4,999}} \right]$$ (assuming a level of .05 for TD risk). $= [5,000 \cdot 1.64 \cdot .6025 \cdot .9593]$ $= 4,739$

d. computing the acceptance limits:
    upper acceptance limit (UCL):
    lower acceptance limit (LCL).
	$UCL = \hat{D} + A$
	$LCL = \hat{D} - A$
		UCL = $11,550 + $4,739 = $16,289
		LCL = $11,550 - $4,739 = $6,811

distribution of errors is centered around a mean of $2.31 ($\bar{d}$), the estimated average error in the population.

The variability of errors in the population will generally be much less than the variability of values of the population items. This explains in large measure why sample sizes for difference estimation are usually more efficient than those for mean-per-unit estimation (discussed next). For example, suppose that our population of accounts receivable had a mean of $500, including equal numbers of items valued at $100, $400, and $1,000. That population would have a much larger standard deviation than would a population of errors (differences between audited and book values in accounts receivable), the average of which is $2.31 and individual differences of which were $12.00, (9.40), and 4.33, respectively. The smaller the variability of the error in population, as measured by the standard deviation, the more precise will be the estimate of the population error rate and the smaller (more efficient) will be the sample size required to make the estimate. In our example, SDE is calculated to be $12.05.

The next step in the evaluation process required computation of the acceptance interval (A) around $\hat{D}$, as shown in Figure 12–14, step 3(c). A represents the range of values around the sample result, $\hat{D}$, within which the true population error (expressed in dollars) is expected to fall.

A is measured by multiplying the coefficient ($Z_{TD} = 1.64$) for the desired level of TD by the estimated standard error, $N(SDE/\sqrt{n})$, for *total* unreconcilable error in the population.

Once **critical limits** (UCL, LCL) have been estimated, the auditor uses them to estimate an interval around $\hat{D}$. This interval consists of $\hat{D} \pm A$, as shown in Figure 12–14, step 3(d). In our illustration of Huaco, Inc., the upper limit (UCL) is $16,289, and the lower limit (LCL) is $6,811. This means that, given the auditor's acceptance of the population book value, there is a 5-percent sampling risk that the population is overstated by as much as $16,289 or as little as $6,811. Stated differently, the auditor may be 95 percent confident that the population is not overstated by more than $16,289 or less than $6,811.

8. *Developing the conclusion.* After applying the process described above, the auditor is ready to test the original hypothesis that the client's book value for accounts receivable is not misstated by an amount greater than tolerable error. If the interval UCL to LCL for total population error falls completely within the range formed by $\pm$ the original estimate of TE, accept the book value as not misstated by an amount greater than tolerable error (H_0). Otherwise, reject that hypothesis in favor of the alternate hypothesis (H_a) that the book value is misstated.

Of course, that decision rule can be applied only if the auditor is reasonably assured that nonsampling errors and other subjectively obtained evidence regarding the year-end balances of accounts receivable also point to fairness of presentation of those balances. In the case of Huaco, Inc., TE was originally estimated at $\pm$$30,000. As a result of the sampling process, total error was estimated at $6,811 to $16,289, a range completely within TE. If $\hat{D} \pm A$ had fallen out of the range set by TE (either on the understatement or overstatement side), H_0 would have been rejected in favor of H_a.

When an auditor rejects H_0 and concludes on the basis of sample results that an account balance is not acceptable, the following courses of action are available:

a. If the error is isolated to a particular type, such as sales cutoff, it may be desirable to expand audit work in the problem area. For example, extended tests may be performed on sales cutoff to determine more exactly the causes and extent of the error.

b. The account balance may be adjusted to an amount within the auditor's threshold of materiality. For example, if A had been $20,000, UCL would have been $31,550 and LCL would have been ($9,500). Assuming TE of $30,000, a minimum credit adjustment of $1,550 [(11,550 + 20,000) − 30,000] would bring UCL within the bounds of TE, and the auditor could then accept the population. If the client is unwilling to adjust the population on the basis of a sample, the auditor may have to develop more evidence to convince the client that this action is desirable. Also, if A is greater than TE, it is impossible for the book value to be adjusted to be within TE. This would have been the case for Huaco, Inc., if A had exceeded $30,000.

c. Sample size could be increased. When this happens, $\hat{D}$ and SDE remain the same if the number of errors and their amount is essentially the same in the expanded sample as in the original sample. However, referring to the formula in Figure 12−14, step 3(c), we see that A gets smaller as sample size increases. This, in turn, may cause the interval ($UCL − LCL$) to be narrower, to the point at which it is within the auditor's range for TE. The formula stated in Figure 12−11 may be used for the revised sample size (n), but the actual estimates for error $\hat{D}$ and standard deviation of error (SDE) from Figure 12−14 should be used in place of their presampling counterparts (E' and preliminary estimate of SDE, respectively) in the sample size formula stated earlier. The chief disadvantage of this approach is that it is often costly and offers no guarantee of a satisfactory result.

Regardless of which course of action is chosen, the auditor must realize satisfactory results (either acceptance of the hypothesis or adjustment of the account balance) before he or she can issue an unqualified audit opinion. If such results cannot be achieved, a qualified or adverse opinion will be necessary, since the account is presumed to contain material misstatement.

Mean-per-Unit Estimation

Description

☑ **Objective 5**
(continued)

The objective of mean-per-unit estimation is *to estimate the total value* of an audit population. This estimate is based on a precision range of values around a point estimate of the population total. That point estimate is the product of the mean of an audited sample and the number of items in the population. The precision range is calculated in a manner similar to that illustrated for the acceptance interval in difference estimation but based on α rather than TD. Once the precision range around the point estimate is calculated for the desired α risk, a decision may be made regarding the fairness of presentation of the population by comparing the accounts within the calculated precision range with the recorded book values.

The mean-per-unit estimation process can provide a highly reliable estimate of the population total, as long as the population values are not extremely skewed. Furthermore, mean-per-unit estimation is useful when the client does not have recorded book values for all items in the population. For example, suppose that the client has not taken a yearly physical count of inventory but, instead, has used a statistical technique to estimate, within specified precision limits, the value of inventory. The auditor could, after drawing a representative sample of inventory items, compute his or her own point estimate of inventory and construct a precision range (P) around that point estimate. If the client's recorded book value (BV) fell within $\pm P$ of the point estimate, the auditor would accept the book value as a fair statement of inventory. If, on the other hand, the recorded value fell outside that interval, the auditor would reject the book value as being a fair representation of the value of inventory. *Difference or ratio estimation could not be used in such a situation because both of those methods require a recorded value for each item in the population.*

The chief disadvantages of the mean-per-unit approach are its failure to yield a dollar estimate of error (which is often the desired audit objective) and the fact that unstratified mean-per-unit estimation techniques are often inefficient, especially in populations with large standard deviations.

An Illustration

Assume that Huaco, Inc., your client, had statistically estimated a value of $6 million for its 50,000-item, work-in-process inventory. Suppose further that a preliminary sample of the work-in-process inventory showed a standard deviation of $20 and that TE has been determined to be $\pm\$300,000$. Finally, assume the same facts for inherent risk (IR), internal control risk (IC), and analytical procedures risk (AP), as in the example for difference estimation. Using Eq. (3), we find TD risk to be .05. You may also assume that because of the high cost of additional sampling, you have set α risk at .05 as well. Figure 12–15 contains a step-by-step summary of the mean-per-unit estimation technique. It follows the same process as that illustrated earlier for difference estimation. The specific steps in the process, therefore, are not repeated here.

Notice that the initial hypothesis is the same as that stated under the difference estimation technique. The sample-size formula for mean-per-unit estimation differs from that of the difference estimation only by the characteristic being estimated. That is, with the mean-per-unit sampling, it is the actual value of the population being estimated, whereas difference sampling provides an estimate of the total error in the population. Notice further that, in the unstratified mean-per-unit technique, the standard deviation has the potential to be very

Figure 12–15 ▮▬▬▬▬▬

Summary of the Mean-per-Unit Estimation Technique

Steps	Statistical formulas	Illustration for Huaco, Inc.
1. Develop a testable hypothesis.		H_0: The recorded value of inventory ($6 million) is materially correct as stated
2. Gather the evidence by a. specifying Z_α, Z_{TD}, SDE, TE, and N. b. drawing a random sample. c. auditing the sample.	$n = \left[\dfrac{N(Z_{\alpha/2} + Z_{TD})\ SDE}{TE}\right]^2$	$= \left[\dfrac{50,000(1.96 + 1.64)20}{300,000}\right]^2$ = 144 items drawn at random. Perform counts of merchandise and vouch to client listing to verify quantities. Vouch price figures to vendors' invoices, labor reports, overhead summaries to verify unit pricing. Recalculate inventory extensions (number of units × unit price = extended price).
3. Evaluate the evidence by a. determining the average audited value of an item in the sample ($\bar{y}$) and calculating a point estimate of the population total therefrom (V).	$\bar{y} = \dfrac{\sum\limits_{i=1}^{n} y_i}{n}$ where y_i = value of each item in sample and n = number of sampling units $V = N \cdot \bar{y}$	Assume $\bar{y} = 118$ $V = 50,000 \cdot 118 = \$5,900,000$
b. computing the new estimated standard deviation from the sample (SDE).	$SDE = \sqrt{\dfrac{\Sigma(y - \bar{y})^2}{n - 1}}$‡	Assume $SD = 36$
c. calculating the precision interval.	$P = N\left(Z_{\alpha/2} \cdot \dfrac{SD}{\sqrt{n}}\right)^\dagger$	$= 50,000\left(1.96 \cdot \dfrac{36}{12}\right)$ = 294,000
d. computing the precision limits: upper precision limit (UPL);	$UPL = V + P$	$UPL = 5,900,000 + 294,000$ = 6,194,000
lower precision limit (LPL);	$LPL = V - P$	$LPL = 5,900,000 - 294,000$ = 5,606,000

†As in Figure 12–14 a finite population correction factor would be appropriately multiplied by the other factors in the formula if the sample size (n) relative to the population size (N) were greater than 5 percent.
‡If computed SDE is greater than initial estimate in 2, use acceptance interval approach to evaluation to assure proper control of TD.

large, causing this technique to be potentially less efficient than a stratified sampling technique.

After the sample has been selected and audited, a mean ($\bar{y}$) is calculated for the sample. This value becomes the auditor's point estimate of the true population mean. The point estimate (V) of the total value of the population can then be calculated as $N \times \bar{y}$, which, in the case of Huaco, Inc., is $5,900,000.

Since a statistical conclusion cannot be made on the basis of a point estimate, a precision range (P) must be constructed on either side of V. This is done in three steps (here and in Figure 12–15, SDE represents the estimated standard deviation of audited values, *not* audited differences):

1. Estimating a standard deviation (SDE) from the sample.
2. Estimating a standard error of the mean ($SDE/\sqrt{n}$).
3. Multiplying the standard error by the desired confidence coefficient ($Z_{\alpha/2}$) and the population size. Notice that, in contrast with the difference estimation technique, $Z_{\alpha/2}$ (and not Z_{TD}) is used as the appropriate confidence coefficient. This is because in mean-per-unit estimation, the objective, after sampling, is to *estimate the amount of, not the accountability of,* a population. It is based upon the hypothesis that the client's recorded amount is true, which leaves open the possibility of rejecting that hypothesis and, thus, incurring α risk.

For Huaco, Inc., P = $294,000. The upper and lower precision limits (UPL and LPL) can then be computed as $6,194,000 and $5,606,000, respectively.

The auditor must now *adopt a decision rule*, which can be stated as follows: Compare the recorded book value (BV) with the precision limits (UPL and LPL). Since BV falls within those limits, it will be accepted as a fair presentation.

If the auditor accepts BV as fairly presented, the risk of incorrect acceptance is present. In the case of Huaco, Inc., the auditor has calculated $5,900,000 as the best estimate of the population value and $118 as the best estimate of the mean of that population. Suppose that the true mean of the population of Huaco's inventory is not $118, but $114 (a value materially different from the hypothesized mean of $120, according to the original hypothesis.) The auditor can calculate the TD associated with the decision to accept $118 as the true value of the mean of the population. The formula is stated as follows:

$$Z_{TD} = \frac{\bar{y} - \mu}{SDE/\sqrt{n}}$$

where

$\quad Z_{TD}\qquad$ = confidence coefficient for TD risk.
$\quad \bar{y}\qquad\quad$ = the mean that was accepted.
$\quad \mu\qquad\quad$ = the hypothetical true mean.
$\quad SDE/\sqrt{n}$ = the standard error.

Substituting the assumed data in the formula, we find that the confidence coefficient for TD is 1.33, as shown below:

$$Z_{TD} = \frac{\$118 - \$114}{\$3} = \frac{\$4}{\$3} = 1.33$$

We see that Z_{TD} of 1.33 yields a risk (*TD*) of 9.2 percent (see Appendix 12–B). Thus, the auditor is assuming a sampling risk of 9.2 percent that the mean of the population was, in fact, $114 rather than the accepted figure of $118.

If the auditor rejects the book value as a fair presentation of the item, he or she incurs α risk. In our illustration, for example, suppose that the auditor had calculated a sample mean ($\bar{x}$) of $113, which was less than the amount considered as the lowest precision limit from the $120 *BV* mean of the population. If, in fact, $120 was the true mean, the auditor would have committed a Type I (α) statistical error. The calculation of the probability of this occurrence is

$$Z_{\alpha/2} = \frac{\mu - \bar{y}}{SDE/\sqrt{n}}$$

where

$$
\begin{aligned}
Z_{\alpha/2} &= \text{confidence coefficient for } \alpha \text{ risk.} \\
\mu &= \text{hypothesized true mean.} \\
\bar{y} &= \text{sample mean that was accepted as the true mean.} \\
SDE/\sqrt{n} &= \text{standard error of the mean.}
\end{aligned}
$$

Using the assumed data in the formula, we arrive at a Z value of 2.33 as shown below:

$$Z_{\alpha/2} = \frac{\$120 - \$113}{\$3} = \frac{\$7}{\$3} = 2.33$$

$Z_{\alpha/2}$ of 2.33 translates into an α sampling risk of 1.98 percent (see Appendix 12–A). Thus, there is a 1.98 percent chance that the auditor has decided that the book value is materially misstated when in fact the true population value is equal to the book value ($6 million).

Dollar-Unit (Probability-Proportional-to-Size) Sampling

☑ **Objective 6**
Walk through a dollar-unit sampling application

Dollar-unit sampling is a technique developed in recent years, combining certain features of attributes and variables estimation. It is unique in that it allows the auditor to make inferences regarding the dollar error in a population by using an attributes sampling evaluation table. Dollar-unit sampling is also characterized as *cumulative monetary sampling* and *sampling with probability proportional to size*, which are actually two separate but closely related methods. The dollar-unit sampling technique has been researched and used extensively by auditors in both the United States and Canada.[10]

The basic feature of dollar-unit sampling is that it defines the population in terms of *number of dollars* instead of number of items. The sampling unit thus becomes a dollar rather than an account, transaction, or document. Whereas in the difference estimation technique the accounts receivable population for Huaco, Inc., was defined as 5,000 accounts, with dollar-unit estimation the accounts receivable population is defined as six million dollar-units. The accounts to be drawn for the sample are then identified by relating the identified dollar sampling units to the accounts containing them. If the auditor takes a random sample of the population of $6 million, confirms the account balances included in the sample, and calculates the error in those balances, he or she can make statistical inferences about the *dollar error of the population* in much the same way as was done for percentage deviation from established attributes of internal control in Chapter 11. This procedure

- Allows a direct estimation of *maximum dollar error* in an audit population. This contrasts with the end result of attribute sampling, in which the auditor estimates the maximum percentage deviation from established internal control attributes. Thus, dollar-unit sampling is more suited to the auditor's ultimate objective than is pure attribute sampling.
- Includes *automatic stratification* of the population, which makes the sampling process more efficient. For example, if 500 of the dollars in a $6 million population were selected systematically for examination, every 12,000th dollar (6,000,000/500) would be selected. This means that, if systematic selection were used, then every account with an amount of $12,000 or more would be selected. Similarly, a $12,000 account would have twice the probability of being selected as a $6,000 account and three times the probability as a $4,000 account.
- Does not suffer the same problems of reliability as do the difference and ratio techniques, because it does not require specified differences between audited and book values in order to be useful.
- Provides a self-contained, quantitative model of the *linkage* between attribute sampling methods (used to judge the reliability of internal controls) and variables sampling methods (used to reach a conclusion about the fairness of presentation of account balances). Thus, with the same tests, it is possible to judge both the adequacy of internal controls and the fairness of balances that have emerged from the system. Thus, a high degree of audit efficiency may be achieved.

The dollar-unit sampling technique also has some disadvantages, especially when applied to certain types of populations.

- This technique requires that the population be *cumulatively totaled* so that the random dollar can be identified and related to specific accounts. This is often not possible without the aid of a computer.
- Large-value account balances (and, therefore, overstated accounts) have a greater chance of being selected for audit than smaller transactions (or understated accounts). Another statistical technique may be more appropriate, therefore, when the primary audit objective is to test for understatement.

- The technique cannot be used to select zero-value items for examination.
- Either credit balances must be sampled as a separate population or sample items must be selected on the basis of the absolute recorded values of population items.
- Dollar-unit sampling can often lead to large estimates of upper bounds on error when numerous errors occur in the population. Therefore, many auditors prefer to avoid use of this technique in such circumstances.

A discussion of dollar-unit sampling is not complete without a brief discussion of the selection methods used to draw a dollar-unit sample. Two basic selection methods are used: random selection based on random number tables or computer programs and systematic selection based on a recurring pattern. Both of these selection techniques utilize **probability-proportional-to-size** (PPS) **sampling**.[11] The systematic selection technique entails the following five steps:

1. Calculate the reported dollar value (X) of the population:

$$\sum_{i=1}^{N} x_i = X$$

2. Accumulate the reported account values such that there are as many accumulations as there are number of accounts (N).
3. For a specified sample size n, compute a **sampling interval** k according to the following formula:

$$\sum_{i=1}^{N} x_i/n = k$$

4. Select a random number between 1 and k; designate it as g.
5. Select the first account such that it contains the gth dollar, the second account such that it contains the $(g \pm k)$th dollar, the third account such that it contains the $(g \pm 2k)$th dollar, and so forth, until fewer than k dollars of cumulated population remain.

Consider the example in Figure 12–16. The reported dollar value of the population (X) is \$6 million consisting of 5,000 accounts (N). The sample size (n) of 150 accounts (discussed later) is divided into the population value (X) of \$6 million to obtain the interval (k) of \$40,000. A random number (g) between 1 and 40,000 is selected. Say this number is 22,416. The population, accumulated from 1 to 5,000 accounts, is then entered at the 22,416th dollar. The first account selected would be the account that contains the 22,416th dollar. The second account selected would contain the 62,416th cumulative dollar (40,000 + 22,416), and so forth until 150 accounts are selected, at which time fewer than 40,000 population dollars would be left.

It should be easy to see from the preceding example that the probability that

Figure 12–16 ■■■

Summary of the Dollar-Unit Sampling Technique

Steps	Statistical tables	Illustration for Huaco, Inc.
1. Develop a testable hypothesis		H_a: The recorded value of inventory ($6 million) is in error by less than the tolerable error, $120,000.
2. Gather the evidence by a. specifying *TD*, *TE*, and *E*.	Table for determining attribute sample size with reliability level corresponding to the required level for *TD* (i.e., if *TD* = .05 use the table appearing in Appendix 11–B).	*TD* = .05 *E*/*BV* = expected percentage rate of occurrence = 0. *TE*/*BV* = *TDR* = $120,000/ $6 million = 2%; *n* = 150 (table entry).
b. drawing a random sample.		A random sample of the accounts included in every 40,000th population dollar ($6,000,000/150) would be drawn.
c. auditing the sample.		Sample audited by noting unreconciled differences between audited amounts and book values for those amounts.
d. determining the value of each error in the sample and the percentage error to book value.		One account with 10% overstatement; one account with 25% over-statement.
3. Evaluate the evidence by a. using attribute sampling table to obtaining net upper error percentage limit.	Appropriate evaluation of results table from those contained in or similar to Appendixes 11–D, E, and F (e.g., for *TD* = 5% use Appendix 11–E).	*n* = 150, number of observed occurrences = .35 implying for reasons of conservatism use of table entry value equal to in number 1; (conservative) *UPL* = 4%.
b. converting percentage error limit to dollar limit. c. comparing dollar error limit with *TE*.		*UPL* × *BV* = .04 × $6,000,000 = $240,000 $240,000 > $120,000

any account of k or more dollars (40,000 in our example) will be included in the sample is 1.0. If an account is *larger* than k dollars in size, it may be included in the sample more than once. To handle this duplication, auditors often stratify the population into accounts of k or more dollars and all accounts of less than that amount. The accounts in the population of accounts in excess of k dollars are then 100-percent audited. The statistical analysis described in the paragraphs that follow is then applied only to accounts of fewer than k dollars. The results of the 100-percent audited items and sampled items are then aggregated, and appropriate inferences are made.

In Figure 12–16, we assume the same facts as those illustrated previously for Huaco, Inc., for the difference estimation technique, except that the auditor's preliminary threshold for error (TE) is ±$120,000, since greater reliance on controls is expected and, hence, far fewer errors (zero, in fact) are expected. Notice that the hypothesis tested in this technique is the same as for the difference technique. The sample size calculation, however, is different for the dollar-unit technique than for the others. Specifically, the difference technique requires an estimate of population standard deviation for error in order to calculate sample size. The dollar-unit sample size requires only *an estimate of TD, preliminary tolerable error, and expected dollar error (E) in the population.* In our illustration, $TD = 5$ percent, $TE = \$120,000$, and $E = 0$. Therefore, an attributes sampling table similar to the one illustrated in Appendix 11–B is appropriate for use in determining sample sizes ($ARO = .05$). The table entry is that associated with an expected percentage rate of occurrence ($EPDR$) of zero percent and TDR of 2 percent ($\$120,000/\$6,000,000$). The table entry for sample size is therefore $n = 150$. The auditor then performs tests of details on each of the 150 items included in the sample. The items selected for audit are selected systematically based on a random start and the sampling interval discussed above. This of course means that every account with a balance of at least $40,000 will be selected for inclusion in the sample.

The relationship between attribute sampling and dollar-unit sampling is illustrated by comparing the three characteristics that determine sample size in each case. The two approaches can be compared as follows:

Attribute Sampling Characteristic	Dollar-Unit Sampling	
	Characteristic	Huaco Example
Maximum tolerable devia- tion rate (*TDR*)	Maximum tolerable error (*TE*) Book value	$\$120,000/\$6,000,000 = 2\%$
Expected population devia- tion rate (*EPDR*)	*Expected error*/Book value	0%*
Acceptable risk of over- reliance (*ARO*)	Tests of details risk (*TD*) Acceptable risk of incorrect acceptance	5%

*usually assumed in dollar unit sampling

The tests of details applied to each item in the sample will determine whether there are unreconciled differences between audited amounts and book balances for each item sampled. Assume for illustrative purposes that the sample produces one account with a 10-percent overstatement and another account with a 25-percent overstatement. A conservative upper bound (*UPL*) on total error with 95 percent confidence ($TD = .05$) is $240,000 ($.04 \times \$6,000,000$). This is a conservative choice since the actual proportional number of whole errors observed is .35 ($.10 + .25$). The table is used by adjusting this amount upward to the next whole number, which in this case is the number 1, from the row for sample size of $n = 140$ (conservative estimate, since $n = 150$ is not shown) from Appendix 11–E, yielding AUPL of 4 percent.

Because the total net upper error limit of $240,000 is more than the tolerable error of $120,000, the auditor may conclude with at least 95-percent probability (risk of 5 percent or less) that Huaco, Inc.'s accounts receivable balance is overstated by as much as $120,000.

An alternative approach to dollar-unit sample evaluation is frequently employed in audit practice. This approach is more complex but also more precise. It is illustrated here using the facts from the Huaco example. Figure 12–17 shows how our results could be interpreted using such an approach.

Column (1) lists the "dollars sampled." In reality, *these are the individual accounts that encompass the 150 "dollars" in the dollar-unit sample*, assuming no duplication of items selected. Column (2) lists the errors that were found. Notice that no errors were found in 148 of the dollars sampled. Using tables based on the Poisson approximation of the binominal at 5 percent risk of incorrect acceptance, as shown in Figure 12–18, we may infer from the computations in Figure 12–18 that there is, *at worst*, a 2.01 percent misstatement that exists in the account *without considering* the two errors in the sample. This probability, in turn, is the product of the Poisson upper error limit incremental factor times 1 divided by sample size (column [3]). A similar calculation is made for the first and second errors found. In each case, the net upper error limit by value, shown in column

---

Figure 12–17 ▄▄▄

Calculation of Net Upper Error Limit for Dollar-Unit Sampling

(1) Dollars sampled	(2) Errors found	(3) Tainting percentage	(4) Worst allocation of total upper error limit frequency (%)	(5) Net upper error limit by value (%) [(3) × (4)]
148	0	100	2.01	2.01%
1	1	25	1.17	.29
1	1	10	1.04	.10
150	2			2.40%

Source: Adapted from R. Anderson and A. D. Tiettebaum, "Dollar Unit Sampling," Canadian Chartered Accountant (April 1973): 30–39.

Figure 12–18 ▄▄▄

Derivation of Allocation of Total Upper Error Limit Frequency

(1) Errors found in sample, ranked in declining percentages	(2) Upper error limit incremental factor[a]	(3) 1/Sample size	(4) Worst allocation of total upper error limit frequency [(2) × (3)][b]
0	3.0	1/150 = .0067	2.01%
1	1.75	1/150 = .0067	1.17
2	1.55	1/150 = .0067	1.04
3	1.46	1/150 = .0067	.98
4	1.40	1/150 = .0067	.93

[a]Based on the Poisson probability distribution at the 5-percent level of risk of incorrect acceptance (Figure 12–19).
[b]This table yields approximately the same results as those used to evaluate attribute samples (See Appendix 11–E).

Figure 12–19

Reliability Factors for Errors of Overstatement

Number of over-statement errors	Risk of incorrect acceptance				
	1%	5%	10%	15%	20%
0	4.61	3.00	2.31	1.90	1.61
1	6.64	4.75[a]	3.89	3.38	3.00
2	8.41	6.30[b]	5.33	4.72	3.28
3	10.05	7.76[c]	6.69	6.02	5.52
4	11.61	9.16[d]	8.00	7.27	6.73

[a] Incremental reliability = 1.75 (4.75 − 3.0)
[b] Incremental reliability = 1.55 (6.30 − 4.75)
[c] Incremental reliability = 1.46 (7.76 − 6.30)
[d] Incremental reliability = 1.40 (9.16 − 7.76)

(5) in Figure 12–17, is the product of the **tainting percentage** (3) times the worst allocation of total upper error limit frequency (4) from Figure 12–18.

The results of the example (Figure 12–17) show a total net upper error limit of 2.40 percent. The auditor may, therefore, conclude with 5 percent risk that Huaco, Inc.'s accounts receivable may be overstated by as much as $144,000 (2.4 percent × $6,000,000). If, as explained previously, the sample had included duplicated accounts, requiring the auditor to stratify the audit population and to select items in excess of the kth dollar for 100-percent audit, the amount of error from the 100-percent audited stratum would be added to the inferred error resulting from the sampling process at this point. The auditor must then compare this amount of error with the TE to determine whether the book value figure can be accepted. In this case, since $TE = \$120,000$, the auditor may conclude that the balance of accounts receivable is materially misstated.

A Note about Regression Analysis

The auditor may often wish to study the relationship between two variables. A convenient statistical tool for doing so is **regression analysis**.

The most obvious relationship between two variables of interest to the auditor is the one we have just been studying. That is, the relationship between the audited values of items in a population and the book values of those same items. Indeed, the classical hypothesis procedures for difference estimation, ratio estimation, and mean-per-unit estimation are special cases of general regression analysis.

A basic regression model considers the relationship between one *independent variable* and one *dependent variable*. As a convention in auditing, the dependent variable is often described as the *true value* or correct value, whereas the book value is described as the independent value.

A basic purpose of regression analysis is to produce a simple linear equation or line that best predicts the relationship between the dependent and independent variable based on the statistical analysis of a set of observations (e.g., sample observations) of actual occurrences between the two variables. As an example, consider the simple diagram shown in Figure 12–20.

This figure depicts the relationship between the dollar value of sales volume for eight different retail outlets and the floor space for each of those respective outlets. Since the scatter pattern produced by these eight points appears to conform to a linear pattern, regression analysis might be a useful tool to study the relationship. Assume that the auditor uses a computer-based program to compute a regression equation based on these data points. That equation is $y = \$10,000 + .66x$.

☑ **Objective 7**
Realize the benefits available from use of regression analysis

The general regression model has the form: $y = a + bx$. The value computed for a is $\$10,000$. This may be interpreted as the intercept of the regression line with the axis representing sales volume. The coefficient $b = .66$ may be interpreted as the slope of the regression line.

The auditor might use this relationship in several different ways. For example, it could be used as a basis for an analytical procedure to test the reasonableness of the sales in a ninth outlet. The floor space in that outlet, 6,000 sq. ft., is used as the value for the independent variable, x, in computing a predicted value for sales volume, y. The predicted value is $\$13,960$. This predicted value would then be compared with the actual book value of sales for that ninth outlet to test its reasonableness.

Another use of regression as an analytical procedure in auditing is to direct attention. For example, during the planning stage of the engagement the regression analysis involving sales volume and floor space might be used to determine whether there are any unusual or outlier observations associated with the points actually used to construct the regression equation. In the example in Figure 12–20 there are no such points. However, if one of the retail outlets had a sales volume associated with a point significantly above the regression line depicted in Figure 12–20, then the auditor might wish to extend special procedures to test the existence and valuation of sales and receivables emanating from that

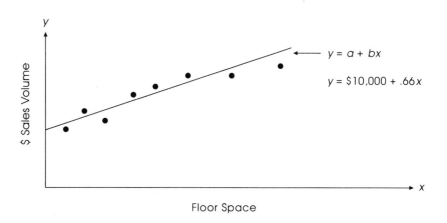

Figure 12–20 ▬▬▬▬▬▬▬▬▬▬▬▬▬▬▬▬▬▬▬▬▬▬▬▬▬▬▬▬▬▬▬

A Regression Line

particular location. These special procedures would be employed in addition to those regularly planned for all the units.

Regression analysis also has many administrative uses. For example, it may be used to estimate the relationship between audit fees and the size of audit clients. Size could be measured by sales volume or some other variables such as total assets. The director of audit services for a practice could utilize the regression equation to assist in developing new estimates for new proposals.

Summary

In this chapter we have focused on sampling techniques as they are applied to substantive tests of details. We began by discussing the objectives of sampling for substantive tests of details. We then discussed audit risk and materiality considerations as applied to classical hypothesis testing. These considerations should be seen as part of the auditor's overall audit risk and materiality model discussed in earlier chapters. The discussion of that model culminates in this chapter with numerical illustrations of the effects of inherent risk, internal control risk, and analytical procedures risk on the sample size for substantive tests of details.

The steps in the classical hypothesis-testing sampling process were then identified and illustrated. We first worked through an example of nonstatistical sampling to show how each step of the process is carried out. Then we described and illustrated the more sophisticated statistical sampling techniques, along with their relative strengths and weaknesses. Those included difference estimation, mean-per-unit estimation, and dollar-unit (PPS) estimation. The chapter also reviewed some of the potential uses of regression analysis in auditing.

Auditing Vocabulary

p. 501 **acceptance interval:** Region or range of values constructed to contain the true value of the population characteristic being studied with probability equal to one minus the risk of incorrect acceptance.

p. 476 **allowance for sampling risk:** The difference between tolerable error (materiality) and projected error. The amount by which tolerable error (materiality) must be reduced when the auditor is establishing the critical limit for a decision interval. The larger this value, the lower the risk of incorrect acceptance.

p. 474 **central limit theorem:** Statistical theory which states that, regardless of the shape of the distribution of population items, the means of samples chosen from those items will be normally distributed.

p. 493 **classical hypothesis testing:** A statistical approach to substantive testing that assists the auditor in choosing whether to conclude, based on statistical observations, that a financial statement amount is in error by an amount equal to tolerable error.

p. 503 **critical limits:** The maximum and minimum values included in the acceptance interval.

p. 497   **difference estimation:**   A classical variable technique based on study of the difference between audited values and book values. See Figure 12–10.

p. 508   **dollar-unit sampling:**   An approach to audit sampling that defines the population in terms of the number of dollars in a population rather than the number of items in that population. (See also, probability-proportional-to-size sampling, below.)

p. 499   **expected point estimate:**   Estimated actual dollar error in the population.

p. 504   **mean-per-unit estimation:**   A classical variables technique based on study of the average (mean) value of audited amounts in a sample.

p. 501   **point estimate:**   Mean value of sample observation.

p. 510   **probability-proportional-to-size (PPS) sampling:**   Selection of items for inclusion in a sample wherein the probability of selection is proportional to the dollar size of each item in the population.

p. 497   **ratio estimation:**   A classical variables technique based on study of the size of audit error in proportion to book value.

p. 514   **regression analysis:**   The statistical study of the relationship between paired observations of two (or more) variables.

p. 473   **risk of incorrect acceptance:**   The risk that a sample will support the conclusion that the recorded amount is not materially misstated when, in fact, it is materially misstated. See Type II error.

p. 473   **risk of incorrect rejection:**   The risk that a sample result supports the conclusion that the recorded amount is materially misstated when, in fact, it is not. See Type I error.

p. 469   **sampling efficiency:**   Study of the impact of sample design on sample size for given levels of risk in specific populations.

p. 510   **sampling interval:**   The dollar value of the difference between cumulative population dollars associated with the identification of items to be included in a sample.

p. 478   **skew:**   A characteristic describing any population that is not symmetrically distributed about its mean. For positively skewed distributions, the mean of the population will exceed the mode. The converse will be true for negatively skewed distributions.

p. 476   **standard deviation:**   The measure of average dispersion of items in a population from the population mean.

p. 497   **standard deviation of the sampling distribution:**   See standard error.

p. 475   **standard error:**   A measure of variability of the mean of samples from a given population—the standard deviation of the sampling distribution.

p. 477   **stratification:**   Division of a single population into several subpopulations based on relative size of the items involved.

p. 467   **substantive sampling:**   Sampling for the purpose of evaluating the monetary value of a balance or a class of transactions.

p. 514   **tainting percentage:**   Amount of observed error expressed as a percentage of the book value of the item being audited.

p. 483   **tolerable error:**   The planned maximum amount of monetary error that may exist without causing the financial statements to be materially misstated.

p. 495   **Type I error:**   Inferring that the book value of the client is materially in error when, in fact, it is materially correct. The risk of committing such an error is called Type I risk or the risk of incorrect rejection.

p. 495   **Type II error:**   Inferring that the book value of the client is materially correct when, in fact, it is materially misstated. The risk of such an outcome is referred to as Type II risk or the risk of incorrect acceptance.

Appendix 12–A: Areas in Two Tails of the Normal Curve of Selected Values of $Z_{\alpha/2}$ from the Arithmetic Mean

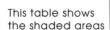 This table shows the shaded areas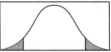

Z_α	.00	.01	.02	.03	.04	.05	.06	.07	.08	.09
0.0	1.0000	.9920	.9840	.9761	.9681	.9601	.9522	.9442	.9362	.9283
0.1	.9203	.9124	.9045	.8966	.8887	.8808	.8729	.8650	.8572	.8493
0.2	.8415	.8337	.8259	.8181	.8103	.8026	.7949	.7872	.7795	.7718
0.3	.7642	.7566	.7490	.7414	.7339	.7263	.7188	.7114	.7039	.6965
0.4	.6892	.6818	.6745	.6672	.6599	.6527	.6455	.6384	.0312	.6241
0.5	.6171	.6101	.6031	.5961	.5892	.5823	.5755	.5687	.5619	.5552
0.6	.5485	.5419	.5353	.5287	.5222	.5157	.5093	.5029	.4965	.4902
0.7	.4839	.4777	.4715	.4654	.4593	.4533	.4473	.4413	.4354	.4295
0.8	.4237	.4179	.4122	.4065	.4009	.3953	.3898	.3843	.3789	.3735
0.9	.3681	.3628	.3576	.3524	.3472	.3421	.3371	.3320	.3271	.3222
1.0	.3173	.3125	.3077	.3030	.2983	.2937	.2801	.2846	.2801	.2757
1.1	.2713	.2670	.2627	.2585	.2543	.2501	.2460	.2420	.2380	.2340
1.2	.2301	.2263	.2225	.2187	.2150	.2113	.2077	.2041	.2005	.1971
1.3	.1936	.1902	.1868	.1835	.1802	.1770	.1738	.1707	.1676	.1645
1.4	.1615	.1585	.1556	.1527	.1499	.1471	.1443	.1416	.1389	.1362
1.5	.1336	.1310	.1285	.1260	.1236	.1211	.1188	.1164	.1141	.1118
1.6	.1096	.1074	.1052	.1031	.1010	.0989	.0969	.0949	.0930	.0910
1.7	.0891	.0873	.0854	.0836	.0819	.0801	.0784	.0767	.0751	.0735
1.8	.0719	.0703	.0688	.0672	.0658	.0643	.0629	.0615	.0601	.0588
1.9	.0574	.0561	.0549	.0536	.0524	.0512	.0500	.0488	.0477	.0466
2.0	.0455	.0444	.0434	.0424	.0414	.0404	.0394	.0385	.0375	.0366
2.1	.0357	.0349	.0340	.0332	.0324	.0316	.0308	.0300	.0293	.0285
2.2	.0278	.0271	.0264	.0257	.0251	.0238	.0288	.0232	.0226	.0220
2.3	.0214	.0209	.0203	.0198	.0193	.0188	.0183	.0178	.0173	.0168
2.4	.0164	.0160	.0155	.0151	.0147	.0143	.0139	.0135	.0131	.0128
2.5	.0124	.0121	.0117	.0114	.0111	.0108	.0105	.0102	.00988	.00960
2.6	.00932	.00905	.00879	.00854	.00829	.00805	.00781	.00759	.00736	.00715
2.7	.00693	.00673	.00653	.00633	.00614	.00596	.00578	.00561	.00544	.00527
2.8	.00511	.00495	.00480	.00465	.00451	.00437	.00424	.00410	.00398	.00385
2.9	.00373	.00361	.00350	.00339	.00328	.00318	.00308	.00298	.00288	.00279

$Z_{\alpha/2}$	.0	.1	.2	.3	.4	.5	.6	.7	.8	.9
3	.00270	.00194	.00137	$.0^3967$	$.0^3674$	$.0^3465$	$.0^3318$	$.0^3216$	$.0^3145$	$.0^4962$
4	$.0^4413$	$.0^4413$	$.0^4267$	$.0^4171$	$.0^4108$	$.0^5680$	$.0^5422$	$.0^5260$	$.0^6159$	$.0^6958$
5	$.0^6573$	$.0^4340$	$.0^6199$	$.0^6116$	$.0^7666$	$.0^7380$	$.0^7214$	$.0^7120$	$.0^8663$	$.0^8364$
6	$.0^8197$	$.0^8106$	$.0^9565$	$.0^9298$	$.0^9155$	$.0^{10}803$	$.0^{10}411$	$.0^{10}208$	$.0^{10}105$	$.0^{11}520$

Source: Frederick E. Croxton, *Tables of Areas in Two Tails and in One Tail of the Normal Curve.* Copyright, 1949, by Prentice-Hall, Inc.

Appendix 12–B: Cumulative Standardized Normal Distribution

Area of shaded
region

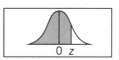

z	.00	.01	.02	.03	.04	.05	.06	.07	.08	.09
.0	.5000	.5040	.5080	.5120	.5160	.5199	.5239	.5279	.5319	.5359
.1	.5398	.5438	.5478	.5517	.5557	.5596	.5636	.5675	.5714	.5753
.2	.5793	.5832	.5871	.5910	.5948	.5987	.6026	.6064	.6103	.6141
.3	.6179	.6217	.6255	.6293	.6331	.6368	.6406	.6443	.6480	.6517
.4	.6554	.6591	.6628	.6664	.6700	.6736	.6772	.6808	.6844	.6879
.5	.6915	.6950	.6985	.7019	.7054	.7088	.7123	.7157	.7190	.7224
.6	.7257	.7291	.7324	.7357	.7389	.7422	.7454	.7486	.7517	.7549
.7	.7580	.7611	.7642	.7673	.7704	.7734	.7764	.7794	.7823	.7852
.8	.7881	.7910	.7939	.7967	.7995	.8023	.8051	.8078	.8106	.8133
.9	.8159	.8186	.8212	.8238	.8264	.8289	.8315	.8340	.8365	.8389
1.0	.8413	.8438	.8461	.8485	.8508	.8531	.8554	.8577	.8599	.8621
1.1	.8643	.8665	.8686	.8708	.8729	.8749	.8770	.8790	.8810	.8830
1.2	.8849	.8869	.8888	.8907	.8925	.8944	.8962	.8930	.8997	.9015
1.3	.9032	.9049	.9066	.9082	.9099	.9115	.9131	.9147	.9162	.9177
1.4	.9192	.9207	.9222	.9236	.9251	.9265	.9279	.9292	.9306	.9319
1.5	.9332	.9345	.9357	.9370	.9382	.9394	.9406	.9418	.9429	.9441
1.6	.9452	.9463	.9474	.9484	.9495	.9505	.9515	.9525	.9535	.9545
1.7	.9554	.9564	.9573	.9582	.9591	.9599	.9608	.9616	.9625	.9633
1.8	.9641	.9649	.9656	.9664	.9671	.9678	.9686	.9693	.9699	.9706
1.9	.9713	.9719	.9726	.9732	.9738	.9744	.9750	.9756	.9761	.9767
2.0	.9772	.9778	.9783	.9788	.9793	.9798	.9803	.9808	.9812	.9817
2.1	.9821	.9286	.9830	.9834	.9838	.9842	.9846	.9850	.9854	.9857
2.2	.9861	.9864	.9868	.9871	.9875	.9878	.9881	.9884	.9887	.9890
2.3	.9893	.9896	.9898	.9901	.9904	.9906	.9909	.9911	.9913	.9916
2.4	.9918	.9920	.9922	.9925	.9927	.9929	.9931	.9932	.9934	.9936
2.5	.9938	.9940	.9941	.9943	.9945	.9946	.9948	.9949	.9951	.9952
2.6	.9953	.9955	.9956	.9957	.9959	.9960	.9961	.9962	.9963	.9964
2.7	.9965	.9966	.9967	.9968	.9969	.9970	.9971	.9972	.9973	.9974
2.8	.9974	.9975	.9976	.9977	.9977	.9978	.9979	.9979	.9980	.9981
2.9	.9981	.9982	.9982	.9983	.9984	.9984	.9985	.9985	.9986	.9986
3.0	.9987	.9987	.9987	.9988	.9988	.9989	.9989	.9989	.9990	.9990
3.1	.9990	.9991	.9991	.9991	.9992	.9992	.9992	.9992	.9993	.9993
3.2	.9993	.9993	.9994	.9994	.9994	.9994	.9994	.9995	.9995	.9995
3.3	.9995	.9995	.9995	.9996	.9996	.9996	.9996	.9996	.9996	.9997
3.4	.9997	.9997	.9997	.9997	.9997	.9997	.9997	.9997	.9997	.9998

Note: TD risk = (1 − table value for Z_{TD} coefficient).
All entries from 3.49 to 3.61 equal .9998. All entries from 3.62 to 3.89 equal 9999. All entries
from 3.90 and up equal 1.0000.

Source: Alexander M. Mood et al., *Introduction to the Theory of Statistics.* Copyright © 1950. Used with permission of McGraw-Hill Book Company.

Appendix 12–C: Monetary Unit Sampling (MUS)—Coopers & Lybrand

Monetary (dollar) unit sampling is a statistical sampling technique that can be used to evaluate sample results when sample items have been selected on a probability-proportional-to-size (PPS) basis. It is often an efficient and effective sampling method in populations where few or no errors are expected. The primary audit objective is to detect and evaluate possible overstatements in the population being tested.

The Monetary Unit Sampling—Evaluation of Results (MUS) template handles several individual monetary unit sampling results, with a combined maximum of 100 errors, to be combined to produce a single overall evaluation. It can produce both one-sided and two-sided reliability statements at selected reliability levels. The MUS template will also provide either a one-sided or two-sided evaluation of a single sample.

This template can evaluate the results of a monetary unit sample and can also combine the results of two or more independent monetary unit samples (i.e., it can combine the results of separate samples of inventories and receivables and enable you to reach a statistical conclusion about the combined populations). This latter application can be very helpful when the auditor is trying to reach conclusions on the financial statements from separate sample results taken as a whole. Additionally, should you wish to stratify a population before PPS sampling in order to concentrate your sampling effort on a certain group of items within the population (e.g., to be sure that large dollar-value items or potentially misstated items are adequately represented), you can use this template to combine such strata results.

```
   :    A    ::    B    ::    C    ::    D    ::    E    ::    F    ::    G    ::    H    ::    I    :
 1:            COMBINED MONETARY UNIT ANALYSIS              VEP 1.01
 2:
 3:CLIENT:    COMBMUS, INC.                      RUN DATE:  5/11/83
 4:PREPARER:  JRT                                B/S DATE:  12/31/82
 5:***********************************************************************************************
 6:
 7:RESULTS:...............LOWER ERROR LIMIT           0
 8:                       POINT ESTIMATE          17000
 9:                       UPPER ERROR LIMIT       56885.05
10:
11:                                   *    TO OBTAIN BASIC FACTORS
12:INPUT:............................*  /LOAD, B:ONESIDXX,PARTIAL,A1:B105,D16
13:                                   *  OR   , B:TWOSIDXX,PARTIAL,A1:B105,D16
14:      ENTER IN DESCENDING          *      WHERE "XX" = RELIABILITY
15:            ORDER
16:              !                   BASIC FACTORS-ONE SIDED
17:              V      SAMPLING          95 % RELIAB
18:   ERROR    TAINTING  FRACTION    LOWER    UPPER              B / C      G * D      G * E
19: ---------- --------- --------- -------- ---------          --------- --------- ----------
20:     0         1       .0001        0     2.9958                                     29958
21:     1        .95      .0002        0     1.7481              4750        0        8303.475
22:     2        .9       .0001        0     1.552               9000        0         13968
23:     3        .4       .0002        0     1.458               2000        0          2916
24:     4        .1       .0001        0     1.3997              1000        0         1399.7
25:     5        .05      .0002        0     1.3595               250        0         339.875
26:     6                  1           0     1.3293                0         0            0
```

Combined Monetary Unit Analysis from the MUS Template

Notes

1. SAS 47 (AU312). *Audit Risk and Materiality*. (New York: AICPA, 1983).
2. SAS 56 (AU329). *Analytical Procedures*. (New York: AICPA, 1988).
3. SAS 39 (AU350). *Audit Sampling*. (New York: American Institute of Certified Public Accountants, 1981).
4. SAS 39 (AU350), para. 12.
5. J. Neter and J. K. Loebbecke, *Behavior of Major Statistical Estimators in Sampling Accounting Populations*, Auditing Research Monograph No. 2 (New York: AICPA, 1975).
6. SAS 39 (AU350), para. 42.
7. We usually express the recorded value as a mean (BV/N, where BV = book value and N = the number of items in the population). Alternatively, we may use as our statistic the mean (average) difference between audited and book values. In this case, the null hypothesis for the mean difference would be

$$H_0: \bar{D} = 0$$

That is, the average difference between the audited and book values is zero. The alternative hypothesis would be

$$H_a: \bar{D} = TE/N$$

That is, the average difference between the audited and book values is an amount different from zero by the amount TE/N. Another way of stating H_0 and H_a in this instance is that

H_0: The book balance is not misstated by more than TE.
H_a: The book balance is misstated by more than TE.

8. Charles T. Clark and Lawrence L. Schkade, *Statistical Analysis for Administrative Decisions*, 2nd ed. (Cincinnati: Southwestern, 1974): 240. Most authors agree that $n = 30$ constitutes a sufficiently large sample to make valid inferences using the central limit theorem.
9. This formula is usually adjusted by the small (finite) population correction factor whenever the sample size is more than 10 percent of the population size. The factor may be stated as follows:

$$\sqrt{\frac{N - n}{N - 1}}$$

Correction for small relative population sizes should also be made for estimated standard deviation and for precision range intervals whenever the population (relative to the sample size) is small (that is, when the sample size approaches 10 percent of the population size).

In addition, whenever SD is large, indicating a diverse population with accounts ranging from very large to very small, the population should be stratified to permit a more efficient sample size. In effect, stratification divides the audit population into several subpopulations, each of which has an SD smaller than that of the population taken as a whole. Larger samples are taken for higher dollar amounts, ensuring that the material individual accounts in the population will be examined.

10. R. Anderson and A. D. Tietlebaum, "Dollar Unit Sampling," *Canadian Chartered Accountant* (April 1973): 30–39.

11. For a more thorough presentation of this technique, see A. D. Bailey, Jr. *Statistical Auditing* (New York: Harcourt Brace Jovanovich, 1981): 177–201.

Questions for Class Discussion

Q12-1   What is the difference between attribute and classical hypothesis sampling techniques?

Q12-2   Is the completion of tests of controls an essential prerequisite for substantive sampling? Explain.

Q12-3   What is the relationship between classical hypothesis testing and substantive testing?

Q12-4   What effects do the assessment of inherent risk and internal control risk have on substantive tests?

Q12-5   Which characteristic of substantive tests (nature, timing, or extent) is affected by sampling?

Q12-6   What are the two aspects of sampling risk as it pertains to variables sampling techniques? Which of these is the auditor most concerned with? Explain.

Q12-7   How does the auditor's preliminary assessment of materiality affect the planning process in sampling for variables? What is the relationship between materiality and tolerable error?

Q12-8   What are the steps that are typically followed in sampling for substantive tests of details, regardless of whether statistical techniques are employed?

Q12-9   How do statistical techniques assist the auditor in substantive sampling?

Q12-10   What effect does stratification have on sample size? Why?

Q12-11   What are the requirements of SAS 39 (AU350) relating to sampling?

Q12-12   How can the auditor use nonstatistical sampling and meet the requirements of SAS 39 (AU350)?

Q12-13   What is meant by the term *normal distribution*? How is it related to the application of classical hypothesis testing?

Q12-14   What is meant by the term *estimated standard deviation*? How is it related to the application of classical hypothesis testing?

Q12-15   What is the relationship between the acceptance interval and the concept of tolerable error as it is applied to the audit?

Q12-16   What is meant by difference estimation sampling? Explain how this type of sampling is used. Explain its limitations.

Q12-17   What options are open to the auditor in the event that an extended point estimate is outside the auditor's acceptance interval? Explain.

Q12-18   What is meant by dollar-unit sampling? How is that technique used in auditing?

Short Cases

C12-1 You have been engaged to perform the annual examination of the financial statements of The Mountainview Corporation, a wholesale office supply business, for the year ended September 30, 19X4. You are currently in the process of auditing the client's inventory account, the largest current asset on the balance sheet, which has a book value of $5,560,000. The inventory consists of 5,000 individual stock items, which are kept in perpetual inventory files maintained by the company's computer. The file for each item of inventory consists of the following information:

  a. Item number
  b. Description
  c. Number of units on hand at year end
  d. Unit cost
  e. Extended cost (number of units × unit cost)
  f. Location
  g. Vendor code
  h. Date of most recent purchase
  i. Date of most recent sale

You decide that you would like to determine if the client's recorded book value of $5,560,000 is materially correct as of September 30. Your auditing procedures will include these steps:

  1. Observation of client inventory counts and the taking of test counts to determine if client counts are materially correct.
  2. Inventory pricing tests to determine if the client's unit cost is supported by adequate documentation.
  3. Recalculation of extensions and footings to ascertain that they are mathematically correct.

Your preliminary analytical procedures work and the results of your understanding of the internal control structure revealed the following:

  a. Numerous weaknesses existed in the client's inventory-taking procedures. You have concluded that controls in the area of quantities are only 60 percent reliable, although controls over pricing appeared to be good. Since all inventory records are kept by computer, all calculations are done internally by the computer.
  b. Your preliminary analytical procedures, while they are valuable in highlighting obvious mistakes, have only a 50-percent chance of detecting a single material misstatement. Because of the nature of the account you assign the highest possible value to inherent risk.
  c. You desire that total audit risk be no more than .01.
  d. You have decided, on the basis of the nature of this account, that tolerable error is $50,000. You are more concerned that the client might be trying to *overstate* inventories than understate them. Last year your tests revealed a $20,000 overstatement error in inventory quantities.
  e. A preliminary sample revealed an estimated standard deviation of the error in the population of $15 per item.
  f. Because of the high costs of additional sampling, you have set α risk at .05.

Required:

  a. Calculate the required *sample size* for difference estimation, basing it on the above assumptions.

b. Why is the difference estimation technique well suited to this type of audit problem?

c. What are some of the practical limitations of using the difference (or ratio) estimation technique?

d. How can computer audit software be used to perform auditing procedures 1, 2, and 3? (You may want to refer back to a previous chapter before answering this question.)

C12-2   Assume the same facts as stated in Case 12-1 and the following additional facts:

a. Your audited sample resulted in seventy differences between your test count and client-recorded count, for a net overstatement error of $500 in the sample.

b. Your revised estimate of the standard deviation of error (*SDE*) in the population based on your audited sample, is now $12.

Required:

a. What is your point estimate ($\hat{E}$) of the dollar overstatement in the inventory population due to client errors in physical counts?

b. On the basis of your original expectations and preliminary estimate of tolerable error, do you think the client's inventory is overstated by an amount greater than tolerable error?

c. Redo the problem, assuming a net $800 sample overstatement. What are your alternative courses of action based on this result?

NOTE: You may desire to use a computer program to solve this problem.

C12-3   In auditing the financial statements of Textron Plastics, Inc., you are currently in the process of confirming accounts receivable. At a recent staff training school, you learned of the advantages of dollar-unit sampling and have decided to apply the technique to Textron's accounts receivable population. You have gathered the following information:

a. Since you are dealing with an accounts receivable population, you are more concerned with errors of *overstatement* than of understatement. You are making the assumption that the maximum amount of overstatement is the complete amount of each account, but no more than the reported account value.

b. The company's accounts receivable population consists of 1,250 individual accounts, which total $1,350,000.

c. You have decided to accept a maximum risk of acceptance of overstatement error in excess of the tolerable amount of .05 and a maximum tolerable error in the population of $40,500.

Required:

a. What features of dollar-unit sampling make it desirable for use in an audit setting?

b. Discuss the relative benefits of the use of dollar-unit sampling (DUS) as opposed to difference estimation techniques.

c. Given the facts of the problem, calculate a sample size for the dollar-unit sample. Also, define the sampling unit and sampling frame for this technique.

d. Describe how you would go about selecting a sample using the DUS approach.

C12-4   Refer to Case 12-3. Suppose your sample results show ninety-seven accounts without error and three accounts overstated as follows:

Account name	Reported	Audited
Short Supply Co.	$500	$450
Small Circuit Co.	50	30
Rough Rider Co.	800	760

Required:
  a. On the basis of the findings above, what would you conclude about the maximum dollar error in the population of accounts receivable for Textron Plastics, Inc.?
  b. What further alternative courses of action would you take, considering the conclusion you reach in step (a) above?

C12-5 John Valle, president of Data Base, Inc., learns that Eileen Farley has verified the overall balance in the inventory account of his company by using a classical hypothesis-test sampling technique. He is surprised that an account would rely on estimates but at the same time insist that all accounting records be appropriately balanced out at the end of the period. Furthermore, he says he doubts that he can be sure that the inventory balance is correctly stated if the auditor only estimates what it should be. Ms. Farley explains that the estimate she has derived using the estimation sampling technique shows an inventory balance of $865,000 plus or minus $12,000.

Required: Respond to Mr. Valle's concerns. Include an explanation of what the $\pm\$12,000$ means.

C12-6 Paul Smith is a local practitioner CPA in Smalltown, Iowa. His clients include mostly small, family-owned businesses and are mostly tax or write-up clients. Last week, Paul was approached by Mr. I. M. Bigapple, president of the county's largest grain elevator operation, about the prospect of an audit. Mr. Bigapple explained that audited financial statements were needed to obtain a bank loan for planned expansion at the plant.

Yesterday, Paul visited Mr. Bigapple at his office to discuss the possibility of the audit. During his conversations with Mr. Bigapple, Paul discovered that the plant has 1,000 customers, located all across the state and in neighboring states. The company has issued warehouse receipts of approximately $5 million to these customers for grain stored on the company's premises. A percentage fee for storage is being charged to each of the customers, based on the ultimate selling price of the grain.

Although Paul keeps abreast of current auditing standards, he has had little opportunity to perform audit work due to the nature of his practice. He knows that in order to verify grain inventory, he will have to correspond with a sample of the company's 1,000 customers. Although the prospect of the audit presents an interesting challenge, he feels somewhat reluctant to proceed with such a big engagement without a thorough working knowledge of statistics.

Required:
  a. Is Smith's knowledge of auditing standards with regard to sampling adequate? Explain.
  b. Assume that Smith obtains sufficient knowledge of SAS 39 (AU350) to use a non-statistical sampling plan for estimation of the total dollar error in inventory (stated at $5 million on the financial statements of the company). Outline the steps that he should follow in his sampling plan.
  c. Suppose that Smith took a sample of 50 customers from the total population of 1,000 customers for *confirmation* of their grain balances. Confirmation requests were mailed to each of the 50 customers. The total amount of the accounts included in the 50-customer sample was $2 million. Customers were asked to respond directly to Smith as to whether they agreed to the amount of inventory stored in the warehouse. Of the 50 customers, 47 responded that they agreed to the total listed on the warehouse records. However, three customers responded as follows:

Customer	Amount per customer	Amount per Bigapple warehouse	Difference overstated (understated)
ABC Farms	$100,000	$110,000	$10,000
G. Haw Farms	25,000	30,000	5,000
Bar X Farms	35,000	40,000	5,000
Total difference			$20,000

If Smith had predetermined that a misstatement in inventories in the amount of $250,000 would be intolerable, how would he relate this finding to that criterion? (Assume there were no accounts in the population that were singled out for special consideration.)

d. What further procedures should Smith perform, if any, besides the estimate of dollar error in the balance?

e. With what confidence may Smith express his audit conclusion? Discuss.

Problems

P12-1 Select the best answer for each of the following items.

a. There are many kinds of statistical estimates an auditor may find useful, but basically every accounting estimate is either of a quantity or of an error rate. The statistical terms that roughly correspond to *quantities* and *error rate*, respectively, are
  1. Attributes and variables
  2. Variables and attributes
  3. Constants and attributes
  4. Constants and variables

b. An auditor selects a preliminary sample of 100 items out of a population of 1,000 items. The sample statistics generate an arithmetic mean of $120, a standard deviation of $12, and a standard error of the mean of $1.20. If the sample was adequate for the auditor's purposes and the auditor's desired acceptance interval range was ±$2,000, the *minimum* acceptable dollar value of the population would be
  1. $122,000
  2. $120,000
  3. $118,000
  4. $117,600

c. In classical hypothesis testing, which of the following must be known in order to estimate the appropriate sample size required to meet the auditor's needs in a given situation?
  1. The total amount of the population
  2. The desired standard deviation of the population
  3. The desired confidence level
  4. The desired standard deviation of the mean of the sampling distribution

d. Which of the following is *not* required in order to select an appropriate dollar-unit-sampling sample size?

   1. Expected dollar value of error in the population
   2. Maximum allowable risk of incorrect acceptance
   3. Maximum allowable risk of incorrect rejection
   4. Tolerable error
e. Use of the ratio estimation sampling technique to estimate dollar amounts is *inappropriate* when
   1. The total book value is known and corresponds to the sum of all the individual book values.
   2. A book value for each sample item is unknown.
   3. There are some observed differences between audited values and book values.
   4. The audited values are nearly proportional to the book values.
f. An auditor selects a preliminary sample of 100 items out of a population of 1,000 items. The sample statistics generate an arithmetic mean of $60, a standard deviation of $6, and a standard error of the mean of $.06. If the sample was adequate for the auditor's purposes and the auditor's desired acceptance range was ±$1,000, the *maximum* acceptable dollar value of the population would be
   1. $61,000
   2. $60,000
   3. $59,000
   4. $58,800
g. The major reason the difference and ratio estimation methods would be expected to produce audit efficiency is that
   1. The number of members of the populations of differences or ratios is smaller than the number of members of the population of book values.
   2. The risk of incorrect acceptance may be completely ignored.
   3. Calculations required in using difference or ratio estimation are less arduous and fewer than those required when using direct estimation.
   4. Variability of the populations of differences or ratios is less than that of the populations of book values or audited values.
h. The auditor's failure to recognize an error in tests of controls or a misstated account balance is described as
   1. A standard deviation
   2. A standard error of the mean
   3. A nonsampling error
   4. A sampling error
i. As the auditor for Miller Rubber Co., you have made separate statistical tests of controls and substantive tests of details for accounts payable. The system of internal control for Miller was found to be excellent. The confidence level $(1 - TD)$ established for substantive tests in this case will be
   1. Greater than that for tests of controls.
   2. Less than that for tests of controls.
   3. Equal to that for tests of controls.
   4. Unrelated to that for tests of controls.
j. When applying classical hypothesis testing for use with samples involving substantive tests of details, the auditor will normally establish an acceptance interval whose critical limit is
   1. Less than tolerable error.
   2. Equal to tolerable error.
   3. Greater than tolerable error.
   4. Unrelated to tolerable error.

k. Statement on Auditing Standards 47 (AU312) suggests a formula for determining the reliability level for substantive tests of details (*TD*) based on the risk assigned to internal accounting control (*IC*), inherent risk (*IR*), and analytical procedures (*AP*) and the desired combined reliability level (*RT*). This formula is

1. $TD = (1 - RT)/(IC \times AP + IR)$.
2. $TD = RT - IC - AP$.
3. $TD = RT/(IR \times IC \times AP)$.
4. $TD = (RT - 1)/(IC \times AP)$.

l. When planning for a classical hypothesis test in auditing, sample size should normally be planned so that

1. Precision and the allowance for sampling risk are equal.
2. Precision and the risk of incorrect acceptance are equal.
3. Tolerable error is equal to the sum of the allowance for sampling error plus precision.
4. None of the above.

(AICPA adapted)

P12-2 The following statements refer to the use of stratified sampling in auditing. For each one, select the best response.

a. Mr. Murray decides to use stratified sampling. The basic reason for using stratified sampling rather than unrestricted random sampling is to

1. Reduce as much as possible the degree of variability in the overall population.
2. Give every element in the population an equal chance of being included in the sample.
3. Allow the person selecting the sample to use his or her own judgment in deciding which elements to include in the sample.
4. Reduce the required sample size from a heterogeneous population.

b. In an examination of financial statements, a CPA will generally find stratified sampling techniques to be most applicable to

1. Recomputing net wage and salary payments to employees.
2. Tracing hours worked from the payroll summary back to the individual time cards.
3. Confirming accounts receivable for residential customers at a large electric utility.
4. Reviewing supporting documentation for additions to plant and equipment.

c. From prior experience, a CPA is aware that cash disbursements contain a few unusually large disbursements. In using statistical sampling, the CPA's best course of action is to

1. Eliminate any unusually large disbursements that appear in the sample.
2. Continue to draw new samples until no unusually large disbursements appear in the sample.
3. Stratify the cash disbursements population so that the unusually large disbursements are reviewed separately.
4. Increase the sample size to lessen the effect of the unusually large disbursements.

(AICPA adapted)

P12-3 During the course of an audit engagement, a CPA attempts to obtain satisfaction that there are no material misstatements in a particular account. Statistical sampling is a tool the auditor often uses to obtain representative evidence. On a particular engagement, an auditor determined that tolerable error in a population of accounts would be $35,000. To obtain satisfaction, the auditor had to be 97.5 percent confident that the population of accounts was not in error by more than $35,000 (risk of incorrect acceptance = 2.5 percent). The auditor decided to use unrestricted random sampling with replacement and took a preliminary random sample of 100 items (n) from a population of 1,000 items (N). The sample produced the following data:

Arithmetic mean of sample items ($\bar{x}$) = $4,000.
Standard deviation of sample items = SDE = $200.

The auditor also has available the following information:

Partial List of Reliability Coefficients	
If reliability coefficient ($Z_{\alpha/2}$) is	Then reliability is
1.70	91.086%
1.75	91.988
1.80	92.814
1.85	93.568
1.90	94.256
1.95	94.882
1.96	95.000
2.00	95.450
2.05	95.964
2.10	96.428
2.15	96.844

Standard error of the mean = $SDE/\sqrt{n}$
Population precision (P) = $N \times Z_{\alpha/2} \times SDE/\sqrt{n}$

Required:
  a. Define the statistical terms *reliability* and *precision* as applied here.
  b. If all necessary audit work is performed on the preliminary sample items and no errors are detected
     1. What can the auditor say about the total amount of accounts receivable at 97.5 percent confidence level with respect to the risk of incorrect acceptance?
  c. Assume that the preliminary sample was sufficient:
     1. Compute the auditor's extended point estimate of the population.
     2. Indicate how the auditor should relate this estimate to the client's recorded amount.

(AICPA adapted)

P12-4 Acme Corporation does not conduct a complete annual physical count of purchased parts and supplies in its principal warehouse but uses statistical sampling instead to estimate the year-end inventory. Acme maintains a perpetual inventory record of parts and supplies; management believes that mean-per-unit statistical sampling is highly effective in determining inventory values and is sufficiently reliable to make a physical count of each item of inventory unnecessary.

Required:
   a. Identify the audit evidence-gathering procedures used by the auditor that *change* or *are in addition to* normally required auditing procedures for inventories when a client utilizes statistical sampling to determine inventory value and does not conduct a 100-percent annual physical count of inventory items.
   b. Explain why mean-per-unit sampling is uniquely suited to this type of audit problem.
   c. Assume that you evaluated internal controls over physical counts of inventory and assessed the risk of overreliance on internal controls (*IC*) at 10 percent. In addition, assume that your analytical procedures in this area yielded a 40-percent chance of letting a material error pass undetected. Assuming that you desire an overall sampling risk of .01, compute *TD*, the allowable risk of incorrect acceptance for tests of details.
   d. Using the *TD* risk factor calculated in (c), calculate a sample size for the mean-per-unit sample (*n*) using the following additional assumptions:

   Population size (*N*) = 5,000
   Estimated standard deviation = $30
   α sampling risk = .05
   Preliminary tolerable error threshold = ±30,000

   e. Assume the same facts as above, except that after your assessment of internal controls, you assessed the risk of overreliance on internal controls (*IC*) to be .25 instead of .10. Calculate the effect that the finding has on sample size. What does it show about the relationship of the quality of the client's internal controls to the auditor's substantive tests of details (*TD*)?

P12-5   Assume the same facts as are established in Problem 12-4 through part (d). Suppose that you audited a sample of Acme Corporation's inventories and calculated the following:

   Mean of the audited sample ($\bar{x}$) = $110
   Standard deviation of the audited sample = $25

Required:
   a. What is your extended point estimate of the client's inventory based on these findings?
   b. What may your statistical conclusion be regarding the value of your client's inventory of purchased parts and supplies at the 95-percent confidence level?
   c. Suppose your client has a recorded value for inventories of purchased parts and supplies of $540,000. How will you relate this fact to your findings above? What type of sampling risk are you incurring in this decision?
   d. If the true value of your client's inventories were $500,000 and not the amount recorded on the books, what is the probability fo your reaching the conclusion you reached in parts (a) through (c) above?

P12-6   You want to evaluate the reasonableness of the book value of the inventory of your client, Draper, Inc. You satisfied yourself earlier as to inventory quantities. During the examination of the pricing and extension of the inventory, the following data were gathered using appropriate unrestricted random sampling with replacement procedures.

Total items in the inventory (N) = 12,700
Total items in the sample (n) = 400
Total audited value of items in the sample = $38,400
The sum of squares of the differences between item values and $\bar{x}$

$$\left(\sum_{j=1}^{j=400} (x_j - \bar{x})^2 \right) = 312,816$$

Formula for estimated population standard deviation (S_{xj})

$$S_{xj} = \sqrt{\dfrac{\displaystyle\sum_{j=1}^{j=n} (x_j - \bar{x})^2}{n - 1}}$$

Formula for estimated standard error of the mean:

$$\dfrac{S_{xj}}{\sqrt{n}}$$

Confidence level coefficient of the standard error of the mean at a 95 percent confidence (5 percent risk) level:

$$Z_{\alpha/2} = \pm 1.96$$

Required:
   a. On the basis of the sample results, what estimate can you make on the total value of the inventory? Show computations in good form where appropriate.
   b. What statistical conclusion can be reached regarding the estimated total inventory value calculated above at the confidence level of 95 percent? Present computations in good form where appropriate.
   c. Independent of your answers to (a) and (b), assume that the book value of Draper's inventory is $1,700,000, and based on the sample results, the estimated total value of the inventory is $1,690,000. As auditor, you desire a confidence (reliability) level of 95 percent. Discuss the audit and statistical considerations you must evaluate before deciding whether the sampling results support acceptance of the book value as a fair presentation of Draper's inventory.

(AICPA adapted)

P12-7   An audit partner is developing an office training program to familiarize his professional staff with statistical decision models applicable to the audit of dollar-value balances. He wishes to demonstrate the relationship of sample sizes to population size and variability and the auditor's specifications as to precision and confidence level. The partner prepared the following table to show comparative population characteristics and audit specifications of two populations.

	Characteristics of population 1 relative to population 2		Audit specifications as to a sample from population 1 relative to a sample from population 2	
Case	Size	Variability	Tolerable Error (TE)	Specified confidence level $(1 - TD)$
1	Equal	Equal	Equal	Higher
2	Equal	Equal	Larger	Equal
3	Larger	Equal	Tighter	Lower
4	Smaller	Smaller	Equal	Lower
5	Larger	Equal	Equal	Higher

Required: In each item (1) through (5) you are to indicate for the specified case from the above table the required sample size to be selected from population 1 relative to the sample from population 2. Your answer choice should be selected from the following responses.

a. Larger than the required sample size from population 2.
b. Equal to the required sample size from population 2.
c. Smaller than the required sample size from population 2.
d. Indeterminate relative to the required sample size from population 2.
　　1. In case 1 the required sample size from population 1 is _____.
　　2. In case 2 the required sample size from population 1 is _____.
　　3. In case 3 the required sample size from population 1 is _____.
　　4. In case 4 the required sample size from population 1 is _____.
　　5. In case 5 the required sample size from population 1 is _____.

(AICPA adapted)

P12-8　As auditor for the Roberts Publishing Company, you are auditing the balances of the work-in-process inventory account as of June 30, 19X0. The following information has been made available to you by the client, based on its estimates and records.

Number of items in work-in-process inventory $(N) = 5,000$
Book value of work-in-process inventory $(X) = \$1,500,000$
Mean of the population $= \$300 = (X/N)$
Standard deviation of the population $= \$75$

You selected a sample of thirty item numbers from the inventory, as shown in column (1) of the table shown below. Also shown in the table are the client's reported values (x_i) and the corresponding audited values (y_i) for each item examined in the inventory columns (3) and (4), respectively.

(1) Sample Item No. n_i	(2) Part No. #	(3) Reported Value x_i	(4) Audited Value y_i	(5) $(y_i - \bar{y})^2$	(6) Audit Differences $d_i = y_i - x_i$	(7) $(d_i - \bar{d})^2$
1	1786	$ 342.04	$ 325.93			
2	2714	210.53	236.77			
3	4870	259.62	321.13			
4	655	278.44	307.95			
5	2297	376.31	359.27			
6	1797	169.89	201.81			
7	3676	293.76	330.21			
8	2978	158.93	196.84			
9	4156	341.39	379.07			
10	3423	408.80	408.78			
11	3980	320.11	325.20			
12	4990	426.51	414.93			
13	381	368.26	373.79			
14	3713	336.98	344.33			
15	1937	291.82	321.19			
16	1630	233.46	272.90			
17	4653	353.86	367.36			
18	499	290.31	275.35			
19	1521	262.64	388.51			
20	380	312.47	377.30			
21	105	231.80	259.92			
22	612	257.39	271.58			
23	32	357.80	352.53			
24	3416	196.53	233.31			
25	4956	228.99	274.90			
26	118	303.16	323.49			
27	4927	228.16	271.07			
28	978	195.66	229.54			
29	1029	324.92	319.11			
30	3707	247.34	268.79			
		$8,607.88	$9,332.86			

Source: Andrew D. Bailey, Jr., *Statistical Auditing: Review, Concepts and Problems.* Copyright © 1981 by Harcourt Brace Jovanovich, Inc. Reprinted by permission of the publisher.

Required:

a. Complete columns (5) through (7) of the table. This will provide you with the needed information to compute the revised estimated standard deviation of the population (*SD*), the average difference between book values and audited values ($\bar{d}$), and the estimated standard deviation (*SDE*) as shown by the following formulas:

$$SD = \sqrt{\frac{\Sigma(y_i - \bar{y})^2}{n - 1}}$$

$$\bar{d} = \frac{\sum_{i=1}^{n} (y_i - x_i)}{n}$$

$$SDE = \sqrt{\frac{\Sigma(d_i - \bar{d})^2}{n - 1}}$$

Compute $\bar{x}$, $\bar{y}$, SD, $\bar{d}$, and SDE.

b. Without regard to TD and based on control of Type I (α) error alone construct a precision interval using the mean-per-unit estimation technique, assuming (1) 90 percent confidence and (2) 95 percent confidence. In each case, indicate what action you would take based on your sample results and the client's recorded amount.

c. Independent of your answers to step (b) above, compute the necessary sample size for the population based on the mean-per-unit formula in Figure 12–15 for the following two independent cases:

α risk	TD risk	Tolerable error
1. .20	.25	$135,000
2. .10	.05	$100,000

d. Construct the appropriate confidence interval using the *difference* estimation technique, assuming (1) 90 percent confidence and (2) 95 percent confidence. In each case, as in step (b) above, indicate what action you would take based on your sample results and the client's recorded amounts. Compare these results with those of step (b).

e. Independent of your answers to step (d) above, compute the necessary sample size for this population based on the difference estimation formula in Figure 12–14 for the following two independent cases:

α risk	TD risk	$(TE - E')$
1. .20	.25	$25,000
2. .10	.05	$100,000

Compare these results with those of step (c). *Note:* you must compute x, y, $\Sigma(y_i - y)^2$, d, and $\Sigma(d_i - d)^2$ in order to solve the problem.

P12-9 An appendix to SAS 39 (AU350) relates audit risk in the following way:

$$RT = IC \times AP \times TD$$

where

RT = The ultimate risk, with respect to a particular account balance or class of transactions, that there remain monetary errors greater than tolerable error after the auditor has completed all auditing procedures deemed necessary.

IC = The auditor's assessment of the risk that the system of internal control fails to detect errors equal to tolerable errors, given that such errors occur.

AP = The auditor's assessment of the risk that analytical procedures and other relevant substantive tests would fail to detect errors equal to tolerable error, given that those errors occur and are not detected by the system of internal control.

TD = The allowable risk of incorrect acceptance for the substantive test of details, given that errors equal to tolerable error occur and are not detected by the system of internal control or the auditor's other relevant substantive tests.

If the auditor wishes to determine TD, given that an assessment of IC and AP has been made for a specified level of UR, the above formula can be rearranged as follows:

$$TD = RT/(IC \times AP)$$

Required: What effect would the following factors have on sample size for substantive tests of details, all other factors remaining constant?
1. More risk related to internal control.
2. More reliance on analytical procedure and other substantive tests.
3. Less inherent risk of a particular account (e.g., less relative risk of misstatement).

P12-10 You have just been promoted to audit supervisor by the firm for which you have worked for the last several years. A manager for whom you worked on several engagements has expressed some concern about sample size selections as they relate to some of the audits that he manages. The standard approach in the past for substantive tests of details samples has been to select 200 items as a representative sample from populations that are subjected to substantive tests of details using audit samples. These items are usually selected without regard to their size. After auditing each item in the sample, an audit projection is calculated. This value is the product of the average audited value of items in the sample times the number of items in the population. This projected audit value for the account balance is then compared with the client's book value. If the projected audit value and the client's book value differ by an amount less than the tolerable error associated with the account, no adjustments are recommended and the account is considered to be acceptable.

Required:
a. Assume that the firm wishes to continue to use an approach that is nonstatistical. What factors should they consider before selecting a sample size and how does each of these factors influence the judgment about the appropriate size of the sample?
b. What control over the risk of incorrect acceptance is associated with the firm's current approach for reaching conclusions based on audit samples of substantive tests of details?
c. Can you recommend an approach to reaching a conclusion about an account or balance based on a sample of substantive tests of details that would improve the firm's ability to control the risk of incorrect acceptance?
d. Someone has suggested that rather than select items for nonstatistical samples without regard to size, that the selection of items for nonstatistical sampling purposely or consciously be done in a manner which emphasizes the selection of more larger items than smaller items without excluding from selection some small items. As-

sume that, since this approach allows each item in the population some chance of selection, it is not an inappropriate method for selecting a sample. What is the likely impact of such a sample selection alternative on the auditor's determination of an appropriate sample size?

e. Assume that the approach to nonstatistical sample selection outlined in item (d) is to be adopted. How might the table from Appendix 11–E for evaluation of results be used as a rough guide for comparing results from nonstatistical samples with similar results that might be obtained using a more formal statistical approach?

P12-11 For a particular substantive audit sample, an auditor has determined that an appropriate level for *TD* is 10 percent. The auditor anticipates a few errors in the account to which audit procedures are to be applied for sampling purposes. Most errors are likely to be overstatements. Total error in the population is estimated to be about 1 percent of the total book value. The auditor believes that error of as much as 7 percent in the account balance could be tolerated without materially affecting the financial statements as a whole when considering the impact of such potential error in aggregation with errors being considered in other accounts.

Required: Recommend an appropriate size for a statistical sample using the dollar unit (PPS) approach.

P12-12 In planning for a statistical sample for substantive testing purposes using a dollar unit approach, an auditor makes the following observations:

Tolerable error = $200,000
Book value = $2,000,000
Estimated or expected total error = $60,000
TD = .10

Required: Determine the appropriate sample size.

P12-13 An auditor completing a monetary-unit-sampling application in conjunction with substantive tests of details observes the following based on a sample of 80 items:

One item is overstated by 45%.
One item is overstated by 28%.
One item is overstated by 2%.
77 items contain no error.

The desired risk of incorrect acceptance has been established at 10%.

Required: Employ the appropriate table from the appendixes in Chapter 11 to evaluate the sample result. If necessary, provide a more conservative response rather than rely on interpolation between values within the table you select.
Note: A standard statistical software package (e.g., SAS, SPSS, or some LOTUS packages) can be used in solving P12–14, P12–15, and P12–16.

P12-14 Estimating audit hours would enable a CPA firm to control actual audit time, estimate audit fee, or submit quotations to prospective clients. A CPA firm would consider a variety of factors to estimate audit hours, such as, potential audit risk, strength of internal controls, assets, average level of accounts receivable, average level of inventory.

Assume that you are given the following data relating to ten audit engagements completed in 19X8.

Assets	Internal audit hours	External audit hours
000		
$3,200	200	700
3,000	150	900
4,700	290	880
5,000	400	850
6,000	310	1000
4,500	300	830
7,500	550	1100
8,000	600	1120
9,000	500	1500
8,500	550	1200

Required:
a. Find a simple linear regression equation using *Assets* as the independent variable to predict external audit hours.
b. Find a multiple linear regression equation to predict external audit hours. Explain how the internal audit hours are related to external audit hours in the equation.
c. Which one of the above linear regression equations would you recommend for adoption? Explain.
d. Given that assets are $8,200,000, and internal audit hours are 400, for a potential client, estimate the audit hours required to complete the engagement.

P12-15 CPA firms charge clients for audit services based on actual audit hours elapsed by various levels of professional staff at their respective predetermined hourly rates. In addition, actual out-of-pocket expenses are also added for billing the clients. Prospective clients, before engaging a CPA firm, may obtain audit fee estimates from two or more CPA firms. CPA firms, before submitting a fee estimate to a prospective audit risk, may consider a variety of factors, such as potential audit risk, total assets, average level of accounts receivable, average level of inventory, tentative assessment of internal control strength, and audit hours elapsed on similar audit client situations in the preceding period. Consideration of these factors enable a CPA firm to estimate audit hours by level of professional staff (e.g., partners, managers, supervisors, senior accountants, etc.) and estimate audit fees by application of the appropriate hourly rates.

Assume that you are given audit fee data for ten clients obtained in 19X8, and you are asked to find an appropriate linear regression equation for estimating audit fees for new clients for 19X9. Consider the ten client engagements to be typical of the clients the CPA firm expects to submit audit fee estimates to in competitive bidding in 19X9. The audit fee data for the ten clients consist of partner and manager's (PM) audit hours, audit hours of other accountants (OA), out-of-pocket expenses, and the total amount billed, which are as follows:

Job #	PM hours	OA hours	Out-of-pocket expenses	Total billed
101	50	280	$1,250	$12,700
102	70	700	540	26,090
103	40	270	250	10,800

(continued)

Job #	PM hours	OA hours	Out-of-pocket expenses	Total billed
104	120	1090	900	40,800
105	100	500	2,200	24,200
106	85	500	600	18,200
107	140	900	1,250	36,650
108	65	220	450	10,950
109	30	60	300	3,900
110	190	1240	1,400	50,200

Two prospective clients, Alpha Co. and Delta Inc., have asked the CPA firm to submit fee estimates for the current year's audit. As a result, the following information was gathered after a visit to the clients' locations and tentative review of the relevant documentation and discussion with the clients' key personnel:

	Alpha Co.	Delta Co.
PM hours	150	95
OA hours	980	190
Out-of-pocket expenses	$500	$450

Delta's size of operation, product, process, etc., appear to be substantially identical to Omega Corporation's, an audit client serviced under Job #108 during 19X8, and is estimated to take about the same number of audit hours (285) as for Omega in 19X8.

Required:

a. Find the simple linear regression equation for estimating audit fees using total audit hours (PM + OA) as the independent variable.

b. Find the multiple linear regression equation for estimating audit fees. Use PM and OA as separate independent variables.

c. Using the equations found under (a) and (b) above, determine the estimated price for audit services for the two potential clients.

d. Which equation do you consider should be used? Explain.

e. A staff accountant suggests that an overall hourly rate based on the ten audits could be used to estimate the audit fees for the two potential clients. Do you agree with the staff accountant? Justify your answer.

f. Make recommendations, if any, to improve the reliability of audit fee estimates.

P12-16 Beta Paint Manufacturing Company (BPMC) manufactures paints and sells its products through 300 retail outlets. Of the 300 stores, 20 are very large, 30 are very small, and the remaining 250 stores are substantially of similar size, layout, and have similar fixtures. The location manager's responsibilities include monitoring of the day-to-day operation of the store, authorizing disbursements for location operating expenses, hiring of part-time help as needed, and coordination of location activities with the Home office. All other activities (e.g., inventory control, establishing selling price, sales promotion, etc.) are controlled by the Home office.

The internal audit manager is considering using a linear regression model for predicting the overall reasonableness of operating expenses at each of the 250 locations. For the other 50 locations the internal audit manager decides to follow the traditional approach for testing operating expenses. He is not certain as to which independent variable(s) he should include in the model; however, he believes that "gallons of paint sold" and "part-time help in hours" are associated with the incurrence of operating expenses.

Further, data relating to operating expenses, gallons of paint sold, and part-time help in hours by location are readily available. Therefore, he asks his assistant to gather these data for 19X8. Consider the following scaled-down data for 20 locations:

Operating expenses	Gallons of paint sold	Part-time help in hours
$3,200	1,800	300
2,400	1,000	250
2,700	1,700	250
4,700	2,800	350
3,500	2,200	300
1,700	800	250
5,200	3,600	400
2,000	1,100	250
3,800	2,000	250
4,500	2,600	350
4,400	2,300	350
1,900	900	250
2,500	1,200	250
5,000	3,400	400
3,000	1,700	250
4,300	2,500	350
2,700	1,400	300
5,000	3,300	350
3,700	2,200	300
2,800	1,500	250

Required:
a. Find an appropriate linear regression equation (simple or multiple). Justify your choice.
b. Based on the following data, determine the expected operating expenses:

Gallons of paint sold	3,000
Part-time help in hours	300

The Application of Audit Theory in Practice

CHAPTER 13

The Revenue and Collections System

Objectives

☐ **1.** Identify the relevant audit objectives for the revenue and collections system based on the client's financial statement assertions.
☐ **2.** Assess materiality and inherent risk for the revenue and collections system.
☐ **3.** Obtain an understanding of the control structure and assess control risk for the revenue and collections system.
☐ **4.** Design and perform detection risk procedures for accounts receivable, sales, and related account balances emerging from the revenue and collections system.

The first twelve chapters of this text were devoted to the theory underlying the audit function. We began by defining auditing as a process of gathering evidence regarding the economic assertions of another party, ascertaining the correspondence of those assertions with established criteria, and communicating the results of the process to interested users. Our discussions in Chapters 1 through 12 explained the meaning of that definition. We studied generally accepted auditing standards, which are the rules by which the evidence-gathering process takes place. In addition, we explored the ethical and legal foundations for those standards. We discussed the concepts of audit risk and materiality, which determine the nature, timing, and extent of the procedures necessary to formulate an audit opinion. We studied evidence and learned that it must be both sufficient and competent to support the auditor's opinion. We presented the theory of internal control, and the way in which the auditor's assessment of control risk affects the evidence-gathering process. Finally, we learned the value and necessity of evidence-gathering tools, such as sampling and the use of the computer. In Chapters 13 through 20 our focus is on the application of these theoretical concepts in practice, with special emphasis on the financial statement audit.

At this point, it would be useful to refer again to Figure 5–2, which depicts the model for the financial statement audit. In this chapter, we shall apply that evidence-gathering process to the revenue and collection system of a typical entity.

Appendixes to the chapter illustrate audit programs for sales, accounts receivable, and cash receipts transactions, as well as control attributes that should be tested during the auditor's assessment of control risk. In addition, we illustrate working papers that support the evidence-gathering process for the revenue and collections system of JEP Manufacturing Co.

Audit Objectives

☑ **Objective 1**
Identify audit
objectives for the
revenue and
collections system

As discussed in Chapter 6, audit objectives for the revenue and cash collections system are logical extensions of the client's financial statement assertions for the accounts produced by the system. It will be helpful for you to visualize audit objectives as client assertions that must be verified before the auditor can express an opinion as to whether the various account balances associated with the revenue and collection system are presented in accordance with GAAP. Those objectives are

1. Existence/occurrence.
2. Valuation.
3. Ownership rights.
4. Completeness and proper cutoff.
5. Proper statement presentation.

A useful question to ask when contemplating the evidence-gathering process is *What errors or irregularities are most likely in this system or account balance?* Experience has shown that errors of *overstatement* of assets and revenues have been a major contributing factor in failed audits of the past. Notable examples of litigation involving overstated receivables and revenues are *McKesson & Robbins* and *Equity Funding.* These cases are summarized in Chapter 4. Overstatement of receivables and revenues may occur either through the inclusion of fictitious receivables or the failure to reduce existing receivables for amounts that have been collected. The audit objective involved in testing revenue and receivables for overstatement is that of *existence or occurrence.*

On the other hand, it is also possible for errors of *understatement* to occur in the form of unrecorded transactions. Certain audit procedures, designed as tests of understatement for revenue, receivables, and collections, verify the assertion of completeness. The going concern convention (discussed in Chapter 1) requires that trade receivables be disclosed at their net realizable value. A failure to do so is another source of error in the financial statements. Therefore, the auditor is concerned with verifying that appropriate provision has been made for anticipated losses from uncollectible receivables. We characterize this audit objective as the verification of *valuation.*

Another possible source of error can arise from the client's continuing to account for factored or pledged receivables as if full ownership rights still existed in those receivables. Certain auditing procedures discussed later in the chapter are designed to verify that the client has full ownership rights to all recorded accounts and notes receivable. This audit objective can be characterized as verification of *ownership rights.*

Increases in receivables (and revenues) or collections on account (and cash inflows resulting from those collections) and cash sales that occur near the end of a fiscal period can be recorded in the wrong period. This type of error would be a violation of the matching concept discussed in Chapter 1, as well as the *com-*

pleteness and *allocation* assertions in the financial statements. The auditor, therefore, must be concerned with the audit objective of verifying *proper cutoff*.

Revenue and receivables must also be properly *disclosed* in the financial statements. That includes proper classification, proper labeling, and appropriate parenthetical and footnote disclosures. Therefore, a distinction should be made between (1) notes and accounts receivable, (2) trade and nontrade receivables, and (3) current and noncurrent receivables. In addition, once a proper net realizable value of receivables (gross amount less allowance for doubtful accounts) is determined, that value should be disclosed in the financial statements. Furthermore, the statements must properly disclose any information relating to the assignment or pledging of accounts receivable. The audit objective in this case can be characterized as the verification of appropriate *statement presentation*.

Planning for the Audit of the Revenue and Collections System

☑ **Objective 2**
Establish risk and materiality thresholds

During the planning stages of the audit, it is necessary for the auditor to consider the *relative risk* of misstatement of the various accounts in the financial statements. In this sense, relative risk involves the ease of misappropriation of the assets involved in a particular system. Cash, of course, is the asset that has the highest risk of misappropriation among assets on the balance sheet. When defalcations of cash occur (whether caused by poor internal controls, collusion, or management fraud), the accounts that most often contain the offsetting irregularities are either revenue or accounts receivable. Therefore, the revenue and cash collection system generally has the highest inherent risk of misstatement among all systems. Ordinarily, assessment of high inherent risk in a system requires low materiality thresholds, thus necessitating very effective and extensive year-end detection risk procedures.

Because of the high inherent risk of misstatement that exists, the only way in which the nature, timing, and extent of detection risk procedures can be diminished in the revenue and collections system is by assessment of control risk at very low levels. Thus, it is necessary for the auditor to obtain a thorough understanding of the internal control structure of the revenue and collections system before planning detection risk procedures.

Understanding the Control Structure

☑ **Objective 3**
Understand the control structure and assess control risk

A proper understanding of the control structure underlying the revenue and collections system involves an understanding of (1) the control environment, (2) the accounting system, and (3) control procedures prescribed by the client. As outlined in Chapter 8, as the auditor obtains the initial understanding of the control environment and the accounting system, he or she must

1. Consider the errors and irregularities that could occur.
2. Consider the results of undetected errors and irregularities on related financial statement assertions.
3. Consider the control attributes that would prevent, detect, or correct such errors.
4. Ascertain whether those control attributes are prescribed.

The Control Environment

As we pointed out in Chapter 8, the control environment represents the conditions that surround the client and influence the conduct of the audit engagement. Those conditions include management's philosophy and operating style, its organizational structure, the functioning of its board of directors and audit committee, methods of assigning authority and responsibility, methods for monitoring day-to-day activities (including internal auditing), personnel policies and practices, and the effects of various external influences, such as governmental regulatory agencies. The auditor generally learns of these conditions through prior experience with the entity, as well as discussions with client personnel and observation of the entity's operations.

The Accounting System

It is essential that the auditor obtain an understanding of the accounting system that is in place for revenue and collections in order to effectively plan the audit of the financial statement assertions produced by the system. Among the things that an auditor should learn is the *flow of transactions* through the system, as well as the *documents and other records that support those transactions*. Figure 13–1 illustrates the flow of transactions through a typical entity's system of revenues and collections, and the accounts generated by those transactions. By nature, some transactions (such as cash or credit sales) involve *exchanges* between the entity and third parties. The primary balances generated are accounts receivable, sales, and cash. For example, in Figure 13–1, a sales transaction (1) involves exchange of goods or services with third parties for either cash or a right to receive cash in the future (account receivable). A cash receipts transaction (2) involves the collection of cash from third parties either from a cash sale or a customer account. Documents that evidence exchanges between the entity and third parties, or *boundary documents,* are generally considered the most competent part of the audit evidence trail. Other *supporting documents* provide corroborating evidence of the validity of the transaction through approvals, cross-checks, recalculations, and follow-up. Figure 13–2 lists the various exchange transactions, along with boundary and supporting documents, for a typical entity's revenue and collection system.

Some supporting documents, while critical to the functioning of the system, are internally generated and retained internally. Thus, they are generally considered less competent documentary evidence than supporting documents from external sources. Nevertheless, even internal documents may be part of the

Figure 13-1

Flow of Transactions through Revenue and Collections System

Cash			Sales	
Beginning bal. xxx				xxxx (1)
Cash Sales xxxx (1)				
Receipts xxxx (2)				

Accounts Receivable			Sales Discounts	
Beginning bal. xxxx			xx (2)	
Credit sales xxxx (1)	xxxx (2)			
	xx (3)			
	xx (5)		**Sales Returns and Allowances**	
Ending bal. xxxx			xx (3)	

Allowance for Doubtful Accounts			Bad Debts Expense	
	Beginning bal. xxx		xx (4)	
xx (5)	xxx (4)			
	Ending bal. xxx			

(1) Sales; (2) Cash receipts and sales discounts; (3) Sales returns and allowances; (4) Adjustment of allowance for doubtful accounts; (5) Write-offs of uncollectible accounts.

Figure 13–2

Exchange Transactions and Documents

Exchange transaction	Boundary documents	Supporting document(s)
Sales for cash	Customer order form	Customer order approval form
	Sales ticket or sales invoice	Cash register tape or duplicate sales ticket
Sales on account	Sales invoices	Shipping document
		Bill of lading
Collection of cash	Statement of amount owed	Remittance lists, remittance advice forms
	Customer remittance advice	Validated bank deposit slips
Sales return	Credit memo	Receiving report

company's internal monitoring process and thus may be a vital part of controls. Examples of such documents are *credit department reports* and *write-off memorandums* evidencing credit department monitoring and approval of additions to the allowance for doubtful accounts and write-offs of accounts receivable (transactions 4 and 5 in Figure 13–1).

The auditor should understand the process involved from the initiation of these transactions to their inclusion in the financial statements. Such an understanding may be accomplished through previous experience with the entity, inquiry of client personnel, observation of employees in the normal course of performing their assigned functions, and reading narrative descriptions of the system in the client's procedures manuals. The auditor's understanding is generally documented in one or a combination of three ways: (1) internal control questionnaires, (2) narrative descriptions, and (3) systems flowcharts. Appendix 13–A contains an illustrative internal control questionnaire (Figure A–1) and flowcharts (Figures A–2 through A–4), which help to document the auditor's understanding of the accounting system.

Control Procedures

Both the control environment and the accounting system for revenues and collections should contain policies and procedures that enhance the entity's ability to *record, process, summarize, and report financial data* in a manner that accurately and fairly reflects the assertions embodied in the financial statements. To be effective, policies and procedures prescribed by the company should include (1) appropriate segregation of responsibilities, (2) an effective system of comparisons and compliance monitoring, (3) adequate records and documentation, (4) limited access to assets and sensitive data, and (5) proper execution of transactions in accordance with management's general or specific authority.

Appendix 13–B of this chapter contains figures that describe the steps in control risk assessment for the revenue and collection system. Figures B–1, B–2, and B–3 in that appendix evaluate possible errors or irregularities, results, and control attributes on an assertion-by-assertion, function-by-function basis. We now discuss each of these attributes as they apply to the revenue and collections system.

Appropriate Segregation of Responsibilities

The functions that are typically performed in the revenue and collections cycle generally include the following:

- *Exchange functions* are those performed in carrying out exchange transactions. These include processing customer orders, evaluating credit risk, shipping goods, billing customers, processing cash receipts, and processing sales returns and allowances.
- *Processing functions* are designed to establish accountability and provide reliable financial data. These include recording sales, cash receipts, and sales returns and allowances, as well as establishing an appropriate provision for uncollectible accounts.
- *Safeguard functions* are performed to provide appropriate custodial controls over assets and records associated with the system.

The flowcharts in Appendix 13–A (Figures A–2 through A–4) illustrate appropriate division of responsibilities within these functions, which includes segregation of the duties of custody over assets, recordkeeping, and approval of transactions.

In *processing customer orders,* the credit function should be separated from the handling of cash receipts and from the recordkeeping function and the sales function. This segregation of critical duties reduces the likelihood that the system will contain errors or irregularities. If, for example, the credit function was performed by the same person handling cash receipts, that person could take cash paid by a customer and initiate an authorization to write the customer's account off as a bad debt to cover the defalcation. If the credit and bookkeeping functions were performed by the same person, it would be possible for that person to cover up mistakes in granting credit to customers by improperly recording the write-off of uncollectible accounts as sales returns and allowances. The primary reason for separating the credit function from the sales function is to reduce the probability of the firm accepting undesirable credit risks to improve sales volume. The sales manager, for example, is unlikely to be as concerned with the collectibility of accounts as he or she would be with showing a larger volume of sales.

In *processing and recording cash receipts,* it is important that the person handling cash receipts does not have access to the accounts receivable records. This arrangement is designed to prevent the person receiving cash from taking cash and introducing changes into the accounting records to cover the defalcation.

The *billing function* should be separated from the handling of cash receipts. It is important to observe that any system of internal control relies on the assumption that the parties to a transaction will always act in their own self-interest. Therefore, we count on customers objecting to receiving bills for amounts already paid as part of our control system. If the person handling cash receipts also bills customers, he or she could take cash and temporarily prevent discovery of the defalcation by not billing the customer whose payment was taken.

Any *special discount concessions* to customers should be approved by a responsible supervisor. Without this provision, it would be possible for a person handling cash receipts to remove cash equal to the discount associated with an account paid after the discount period and cover the defalcation by showing a debit to sales discounts rather than to cash.

The *accounts receivable ledger clerk recording sales and cash collections* should be someone other than the general ledger bookkeeper. This separation of responsibilities is designed to force two individuals to check their records with each other in recording the sales and cash receipts transactions. The general ledger bookkeeper will have a control account balance that should equal the sum of the subsidiary ledger account balances. If each of these records is maintained by a different person, it will be necessary for the two persons to periodically check their records against each other.

Persons having the *authority to originate noncash credits* to receivables should not have access to cash. Failure to separate these responsibilities could allow the theft of cash to be covered by the origination of a noncash debit (sales return, sales discount, etc.) to balance the credit to receivables. Similarly, the authority to initiate write-offs of uncollectible accounts should be vested in an independent person, subject to the approval of a responsible official.

Comparisons and Compliance Monitoring

Within the system of revenues and collections, no one person should be allowed to process a transaction completely without being cross-checked by someone else. Use of proper comparisons and sales involves the following:

In processing customer orders, supervisors in the sales department should compare unit prices on invoices with company catalogs for accuracy. Units entered on the sales invoice should be compared with units ordered per the customer purchase order. Extensions on the sales invoices (price × quantity) should be recalculated by supervisors and checked on a test basis for accuracy by internal auditors.

In the billing department, units billed should be compared to units shipped as noted on the shipping department copy of the sales invoice. Prices should be double-checked against company catalogs or price lists as the invoices are completed.

In the recording functions, general ledger entries should be compared to totals of monthly sales summaries from the billing department. Supervisory personnel should perform periodic reconciliation of sales journal, sales summary, and sales invoices posted to individual customer accounts. The general ledger balance of accounts receivable should be periodically reconciled to the total of the accounts receivable subsidiary ledger.

In the cash receipts function, supervisors should make regular comparisons of the amounts of cash deposited to the totals of credits to cash sales and accounts receivable, less discounts. Individuals independent of the cash handling function, such as internal auditors, should perform regular reconciliations of the entity's bank accounts.

Adequate Records and Documentation

In general, documents shown in Figure 13–2, supplemented by normal accounting records, will provide an adequate system of records if they are organized and processed as follows:

Proper credit investigation and approval procedures should be performed and documented on the *customer order approval form.*

Sales invoices should be sequentially numbered and a procedure should be established to account for the use of the invoice forms.

Credit memos should also be sequentially numbered and controlled in the same manner as are sales invoices. Appropriate authorization and approval procedures should be performed and documented in connection with the issuance of each credit memo.

Sequentially numbered **remittance advice forms** should be prepared when cash is received by the company.

Authorization and approval procedures, including the approval by a responsible official within the company, should be performed and documented before an account receivable is allowed to be written off as uncollectible. Formal procedures should be established for a continuing review for possible collection of accounts written off. Failure to establish such procedures would make cash receipts from such accounts especially vulnerable to defalcation.

Formal procedures should be established for carrying out the billing function.

Properly controlled *sequentially prenumbered bills of lading* should be used to authorize shipments. The document used should be appropriately accounted for and reconciled with customer orders and sales invoices. In this way, a firm makes sure that all goods or services are billed as they are delivered.

Accounts receivable records should include both an accounts-receivable control account and a subsidiary ledger.

Formal procedures should be established for authorizing and approving the acceptance of notes receivable.

Access to Assets and Data

The major assets involved in the revenue and collection system are cash and accounts receivable. Access to cash should be limited to only those persons in the system who have custodianship duties. As shown in the flowchart in Figure A–4 of Appendix 13–A, only two persons have custodianship duties in a mail cash receipts system: the mail clerk who opens the mail and the cashier. All other departments perform their duties based on a cash receipts list prepared by the mail clerk. Since accounts receivable records and billing are handled by others in the system, the customer acts as the monitor of the mail clerk. Supervisors who reconcile deposits to total credits in accounts receivable and sales act as the monitors of the cashier.

Access to accounts receivable records should be limited to only the accounts receivable bookkeeping department. Records should be stored in fireproof locked facilities when not in use.

For cash sales, access to cash should be limited by use of cash registers and other mechanical devices. Persons who have access to register tapes should not be the same persons who operate the equipment. After each shift, an independent employee should reconcile the amount of sales per the register tapes in the machine with the amount of cash deposited.

Daily deposits of cash should be made. Large amounts of cash should not be allowed to remain overnight in company safes or other locations.

Execution of Transactions as Approved

In the revenue and collections system, the primary authority for approval of transactions rests with the credit department. As shown in Figure A–2 of Appendix 13–A, shipment of goods to customers cannot occur without proper credit approval. Although not shown on the flowchart, the credit department should receive a copy of the aged accounts receivable listing. Persons in the credit department should follow up with slow or nonpaying accounts for collection. Supervisory personnel in the credit department should prepare the support for the periodic entry to the allowance for doubtful accounts, based on company accounting policies. As individual accounts become uncollectible, the credit department should authorize write-offs.

Computer Controls

In most entities, batch processing of sales and cash receipts transactions is performed through a separate EDP department. In these environments, control procedures should be designed to prevent, detect, or correct errors at the point of input, processing, and output. In addition, file controls should provide accuracy checks, as well as proper physical protection against damage and unauthorized access. Control procedures for a computerized revenue system are detailed in Appendix 13–A, Figure A–5.

Detailed Control Risk Assessment Procedures

After obtaining an understanding of the entity's control structure, as outlined above, the auditor should be in a position to form a preliminary assessment of control risk. As stated in Chapter 8, this assessment should be made on a financial statement assertion-by-assertion basis. The measurement technique used for assessment may be quantitative, in which the auditor assigns percentages to control risk for the various assertions. Alternatively, the assignment of risk levels may be ordinal (such as high, medium, or low).

For those assertions supported by weak controls, or in cases in which it is not cost effective to proceed with control assessment, the auditor will assign the highest level of control risk. This decision will necessitate selection of low-detection risk procedures—procedures that are very effective, performed at or around year-end, using large sample sizes—on the related financial statement assertions.

For those financial statement assertions supported by effective prescribed controls, the auditor may desire to assess control risk at a lower level than the preliminary assessment level, if costs of obtaining the necessary evidence are not too high. For these assertions, the auditor would enter the detailed stage of control risk assessment.

As explained in Chapter 8, the detailed stage of control risk assessment involves three steps (steps 5, 6, and 7 of the 7-step process begun in the initial assessment phase):

5. Conduct tests of prescribed controls to ascertain if they are performing effectively.
6. Evaluate results of tests of controls.

7. Assess control risk, and design substantive tests for affected financial statement assertions accordingly.

Appendix 13–C describes the methodology that should be used for tests of the control attributes identified in Figures B–1, B–2, and B–3 of Appendix 13–B.

Detection Risk Procedures

☑ Objective 4
Design and perform detection risk procedures

After control risk has been assessed, the auditor should be enabled to design the nature, timing, and extent of detection risk procedures that provide sufficient, competent evidential matter in support of the financial statement assertions for the revenue and collection system. Theoretically, if the control structure of the entity were judged by the auditor to be extremely strong, providing little or no risk of material errors or irregularities remaining undetected, an opinion on the financial statements could be based on the strength of the system of controls alone. However, reality takes account of both the sampling and nonsampling risk associated with the audit process, so some substantive tests of material account balances in the system will always be necessary. Substantive tests are designed to determine whether the accounts associated with the revenue and collection system are stated in accordance with GAAP. The results of these tests, as well as tests of controls over the system, are accumulated as evidence in working papers similar to those shown in Appendixes 13–E through 13–J. An audit program for transactions and accounts in the system is illustrated in Appendix 13–D.

As we deal with the substantive testing phase of the audit in this chapter and in the chapters to follow, we will be developing the auditing procedures normally followed in verifying the balance sheet and income statement accounts most directly associated with each subsystem being evaluated. For the revenue and collection system, that includes

- accounts and notes receivable
- the allowance for doubtful accounts
- revenues

Substantive tests of the cash account balance are included in Chapter 19.

The auditing procedures associated with the revenue and collection system are designed to meet the following audit objectives:

- Verification of *existence* and completeness.
- Verification of *ownership rights*.
- Verification of proper *cutoff* (also includes completeness).
- Verification of proper *valuation*.
- Verification of appropriate *statement presentation*.

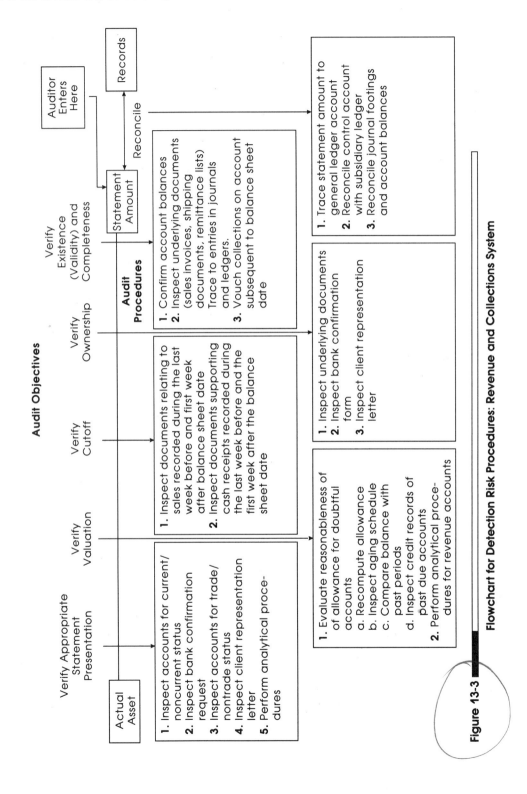

Figure 13-3   **Flowchart for Detection Risk Procedures: Revenue and Collections System**

Figure 13–3 illustrates diagrammatically the substantive tests generally performed for the revenue system. We will discuss each audit objective in detail in the sections that follow.

Reconciliation of Account Balances with Underlying Accounting Records

As shown in Figure 13–3, we begin our verification of receivables and their related valuation accounts by tracing the statement amount to the general ledger accounts for accounts receivable and notes receivable. It is also important to balance the accounts and notes receivable subsidiary ledgers against their control accounts. During the reconciliation process, we also recompute ledger and special journal column totals by footing and cross-footing those records. If the underlying records support the statement balances, the auditor is ready to carry out the procedures necessary to meet the audit objectives cited earlier in the chapter. The reconciliation, footing, and cross-footing procedures are illustrated in Appendix 13–E.

Verification of Existence

The actual existence of a receivable as an asset depends on the client's having a valid claim for the amount shown in the account.

Confirmation.   Confirmation of accounts receivable from various customers is the *primary auditing procedure used in verifying existence.* This procedure is judged to be so important that it is required by generally accepted auditing standards, unless confirmation is impossible or impractical to perform. Chapter 6 included illustrations of both the negative and positive types of accounts-receivable confirmation requests. As a means of improving the dependability of these requests, the mailing should be carefully supervised by the auditor, and all responses to confirmation requests should come directly to the auditor. Appendixes 13–E and 13–H illustrate the statistics kept regarding both the number and percentage of confirmation requests sent and received with no exceptions, as well as those received with exceptions. All confirmations returned with exceptions noted by customers require follow-up procedures by the auditor to ascertain whether the client or the customer has recorded the proper amount receivable. If the client has recorded an erroneous amount receivable, an adjusting journal entry may be required. An example of a confirmation request returned by the customer with no exceptions noted is shown in Appendix 13–G.

The confirmation of notes receivable often takes the form of a letter to the maker of the note, confirming such details as the original balance, unpaid balance as of the balance sheet date, interest rate, accrued interest receivable as of the balance sheet date, and any collateral held by the client as security for the note. When the signed notes themselves are available for the auditor's examination, there would logically be less need for confirming them than for confirming accounts receivable. Nevertheless, notes receivable, too, are often confirmed in the same manner as accounts receivable. Because of their negotiability, they should be inspected at the time cash is counted and should be controlled until the cash count has been completed. Notes owned but not on hand for inspection should always be confirmed with the parties holding them.

The accounts and notes to be confirmed will be chosen either by using judgment or by statistical sampling techniques. Because material errors are more likely to occur in recording large receivables, auditors generally use a stratified sample. A stratified sample requires the auditor to divide the receivables into two or more groups, or strata, on the basis of amounts shown in the accounts. The sample is then drawn to include a higher percentage of accounts with large balances and a lower percentage of the smaller ones.

The replies to confirmation requests should be appropriately processed by the auditor. This requires a careful investigation of all replies that suggest balances different from the ones shown on the client's books. As we have observed, **negative accounts receivable confirmation** *requests* are typically used in confirming small account balances; the presumption is that an unanswered confirmation request validates the account balance. In the case of **positive accounts receivable confirmation** *requests,* however, the auditor must follow up on all unanswered confirmation requests until satisfied that the balance shown on the client's books is correct or that it needs to be adjusted to make it correct. In situations where debtors cannot confirm account balances, these confirmation procedures may be applied to individual open invoices.

Differences between the account balances shown on the client's books and the balances reported in the confirmation requests can often be explained by shipments of goods or by collections in transit. In these instances, the auditor should be particularly concerned with delays in recording credits resulting from customer payments on account. Significant delays of this type suggest possible **lapping** of the accounts. Lapping occurs when the person receiving cash temporarily takes cash and covers that act by delaying the credit to the receivable account. Later, when payment is received from another customer, a credit is entered to the account that should have been credited for the cash that was stolen rather than to the account that was actually being paid. The person committing such an act generally intends to reimburse the company for the cash temporarily stolen but often may be unable to do so. One way of protecting against lapping is to have customer payments sent directly to the company's bank, where they can be picked up by persons who have no recordkeeping responsibilities for cash collections.

In other instances, the differences between the book and confirmation balances may bring to light *disputed account balances or client errors* in recording sales. In such instances, appropriate audit adjustments must be made to allow the receivables, sales, or sales returns and allowances balances to be fairly presented in the financial statements.

Alternative Procedures. In some cases, it may be impractical or impossible to confirm accounts receivable as of the balance sheet date. For example, some of the client's customers may have voucher systems for payment of accounts incompatible with the client's receivables system. The federal government is another example of a customer with which accounts receivable confirmation is virtually impossible. In the event that it is impractical or impossible to confirm the accounts receivable, the auditor may rely on alternative procedures in rendering an opinion on the financial statements. These include the following:

1. Vouching **subsequent collections** of accounts receivable.
2. Inspection of underlying documentation for charges and credits to accounts receivable.

Vouching of collections on account subsequent to the balance sheet date is probably the most useful alternate procedure, because it allows the auditor the benefit of hindsight in the verification of receivables. Keep in mind that the audit field work will be performed after the close of the period being audited. That allows the auditor to apply this procedure for verifying the validity of receivables by inspecting the cash receipts journal for a period of time following the end of the fiscal period under audit. The collection of a receivable following the end of the period provides strong evidence in support of the existence and validity of the receivable as of the end of that period. In vouching subsequent collections, however, the auditor must be sure that the collections being vouched pertain to sales and related receivables that actually occurred before the balance sheet date and not in the intervening period between the balance sheet date and collection date.

For this reason, the auditor should also inspect on a test basis the documents underlying the entries to the accounts-receivable subsidiary ledger accounts: the sales invoices, shipping tickets, bills of lading, credit memos, and the documents supporting receipts from customers. As these documents are inspected, they should be properly *matched* to individual transactions and *traced* through the accounting records to the appropriate receivable account, noting the dates of the transactions. If the auditor is concerned with the possible overstatement of sales and receivables, the appropriate auditing procedure generally is to *vouch* the debit entries to customer accounts receivable back to the sales invoices. This procedure shows that the debit entries are properly supported by sales invoices. On the other hand, if we were concerned with a possible understatement of these items, we would trace the invoices to the debits in customer accounts receivable. Alternative procedures performed on accounts receivable are illustrated in Appendix 13–F.

It is important to observe that if receivables are material and the auditor can perform neither confirmation nor alternative procedures, a limitation is considered imposed on the scope of the audit, which will *usually preclude the expression of an unqualified audit opinion*. Furthermore, a client-imposed restriction on such procedures is usually regarded as a more serious matter than a restriction attributed solely to the auditor in an unrestricted client environment. In cases of client-imposed restrictions, the auditor might contemplate more seriously a disclaimer of opinion, depending on the amount of receivables to which the scope limitation pertains. However, if the auditor can satisfactorily verify the existence of the receivables balances by expanding the alternate procedures, an unqualified opinion may still be rendered on the financial statements.

Verification of Ownership

In the case of receivables, the existence of typical documentary support in the form of sales invoices, shipping documents, notes, etc., provides evidence of ownership. However, the auditor is always concerned with contingencies that may cloud the ownership rights of a client. For example, accounts receivable are sometimes assigned or pledged for the purpose of securing cash during the time they would normally be outstanding and awaiting collection. Quite logically, the primary source of funds in such a situation would be the client's banker. Therefore, as we shall see in Chapter 19, the *bank confirmation request* used in verifying cash also requests the banker to indicate whether or not the bank has any contingent claims against the client's receivables, either as a result of pledged receivables or discounted notes receivable. The auditor will also typically request a *representation letter* from the client stating that all such contingent claims against receivables have been disclosed in the financial statements. Shipments of goods on consignment, for example, are sometimes incorrectly recorded as sales; the auditor must be concerned with discovering such errors. This type of error is often suggested by unusually large debits and credits to accounts receivable at certain times of the year.

Verification of Cutoff

Because of the matching convention associated with the financial reporting process, it is important for the auditor to verify that transactions have been appropriately cut off at the end of each period. The point at which revenues should be recognized is determined by reference to the *realization convention*. In the case of sales, the earning process is generally presumed to have been completed and a legal claim against the purchaser established at the point where title passes. *Title passage*, in turn, is generally determined by the *FOB point*. For example, merchandise sold FOB shipping point should be recognized as a sale on the date of shipment. On the other hand, merchandise sold *FOB destination* should be recognized as a sale only when it reaches its destination. Therefore, in verifying the cutoff of sales transactions, it is important for the auditor to inspect the shipping documents associated with merchandise shipped around the end of the fiscal period to determine whether those sales have been recorded in the proper period.

The auditor is often more concerned with overstatement than with understatement of the client's sales. Thus, he or she should be particularly sensitive to *sales recorded before the cutoff date but not shipped until after the cutoff date*. The most appropriate test for this kind of overstatement, therefore, is vouching the last several entries in the client's sales journal to shipping documents. Assuming the client's shipping terms are FOB shipping point, sales entries dated before the cutoff date accompanied by shipping documents dated after the cutoff date generally indicate sales overstatements, except in unusual circumstances such as the sale of custom-made goods.

In the case of *income from services*, the earning process is presumed to have been completed as services are performed. Therefore, the auditor should examine the documents supporting the service efforts rendered near the end of the period to appropriately verify the cutoff of that type of income. *In the nonprofit area*, taxes and contributions received as revenues are generally designated for use over specific periods of time. It is important for the auditor to identify those designations and to verify that revenues have been recognized in the reporting period during which the resources provided by them are expected to be used.

In connection with the collection of accounts receivable, it is important for the auditor to inspect the documents associated with cash receipts near the end of the period to determine that they have been recorded as credits to accounts receivable in *the appropriate fiscal period*. The client, in an effort to improve the firm's current ratio, may keep the cash record open and record both cash received after the end of the fiscal period and payments on account after the end of the period as though they occurred at the end of the period under audit. If the client holds only the cash receipts book open, cash will be overstated and accounts receivable will be understated. This obviously will have no effect on the current ratio. On the other hand, if the cash disbursements book is also held open and if current assets are in excess of current liabilities, the current ratio will be overstated. There is usually a higher risk of this type of cutoff error when the client has long-term debt with a restrictive current-ratio covenant. Therefore, the auditor must give particular attention to such possibilities if he or she discovers such covenants during the planning phase of the audit.

We have observed the effect of an improper cash cutoff in the preceding paragraph. If sales are improperly cut off, both the net income and accounts receivable balances will be incorrect. The extent of the error, however, depends on whether or not the sales cutoff error is consistent or *inconsistent with the cost of sales cutoff*. If, for example, a sale properly associated with the period following the one being audited is improperly recorded in the period under audit, both sales and accounts receivable will be overstated. Net income will, therefore, be overstated by the amount of the sales price of the goods. However, if at the same time the cost of the goods associated with the sale is also inappropriately recorded as cost-of-sales for the period under audit, the distortion in net income and retained earnings will be equal to the gross margin on the sale of the goods. For that reason, it is extremely important for the auditor to be sure not only that the sales and cost-of-sales cutoffs are individually proper but also that they are consistent with each other.

Verification of Valuation

Under generally accepted accounting principles, management of the entity is responsible for reporting short-term receivables at net realizable value. Therefore, auditing procedures to meet the valuation objective are directed toward evaluating whether the client's provision for uncollectible accounts and notes is reasonable. The provision for bad debts is generally determined on the basis of past experience and is typically calculated either as a percentage of sales or as a percentage of receivables. The auditor generally begins by recomputing the client's allowance for uncollectible accounts, based on whichever of these procedures has been followed by the client. In addition, he or she may compute either or both of the following key analytical ratios over several years: (1) accounts receivable turnover (sales ÷ average accounts receivable) or (2) days' sales to collection (365 ÷ accounts receivable turnover). Examining these trends over time gives the auditor an idea of the success of the client's continuing collection efforts for accounts and notes receivable.

For the purpose of more precisely evaluating the reasonableness of the allowance for uncollectible accounts, the auditor will generally **age** *the accounts receivable*. That procedure involves listing the individual amounts receivable as current or, if past due, by the number of days they are past due, as is illustrated in the aging schedule shown in Appendix 13–E. This schedule allows the auditor to give special attention to the past-due accounts in evaluating the adequacy of the allowance for uncollectible accounts. In so doing, the auditor typically will inspect the records of past-due accounts and correspondence developed in attempts to collect them. Another procedure for verifying the reasonableness of the allowance account includes a comparison of the allowance provision in the current period with those of prior periods. Just as in the case of the procedures discussed earlier, this evaluation may show that an audit adjustment should be made to establish an appropriate provision for estimated losses in the collection of receivables. If accounts receivable have increased due to slow collection, the tests of collectibility should be expanded. Sometimes a client will hold securities as collateral for certain receivables. When that is the case, the auditor should examine the securities to ascertain their value in judging any possible loss in collecting the receivables.

Accrued interest on notes receivables should be *recomputed*. It is also necessary to recompute the unearned discount on noninterest-bearing or low-interest-bearing notes to be sure that those items are appropriately valued in the financial statements. The value assigned to sales revenue is often verified by comparison. More specifically, the auditor may compare year-to-year totals in sales accounts by category (see Appendix 13–I) or by month (see Appendix 13–J). If unusual fluctuations are noted in these accounts, the auditor will need to obtain explanations from the client and to corroborate the client's explanations by further inspection of documentary support. Unusual fluctuations in sales may be explained by any one or a combination of the following factors:

- Unusual changes in operations caused by such external factors as strikes, recessions, increased competition, and so on.
- Exceptional circumstances that greatly increase or decrease demand for the client's product.
- Accounting changes in method of accounting for sales.
- Cutoff errors for sales and shipments.

If sales fluctuations are caused by either of the first two factors and corroborative audit tests support the client's explanations, no further audit tests usually need to be performed. On the other hand, major sales fluctuations caused by accounting changes generally need to be disclosed by the client. Material cutoff errors need to be corrected by means of an adjusting journal entry.

Ascertaining Appropriate Statement Presentation

The procedures just discussed are primarily concerned with verifying the balances that should be shown for receivables and the related valuation accounts. In presenting those receivables in the balance sheet, it is important to verify that an appropriate distinction has been made between current and noncurrent receivables and that appropriate disclosures have been made relating to any contingent claims against the receivables. In distinguishing between current and noncurrent receivables, we should recall that a current receivable should, in the normal course of business operations, be expected to be collected within one year or the operating cycle; whichever is longer. The operating cycle provision, for example, allows installment accounts receivable that are due within the normal collection period, even though longer than twelve months, to be classified as current receivables.

To meet the requirement of full disclosure, accounts receivable assigned to a financing agency should be so labeled. It is also important to disclose parenthetically or in a footnote information relating to pledged accounts receivable. In making judgments regarding these disclosures, the auditor relies on the findings from procedures followed in the verification of ownership as discussed earlier in this section. It is also important to distinguish between trade and nontrade receivables. Receivables from officers and employees, for example, should be presented in a separate account in the balance sheet. Notes receivable should be separated from accounts receivable in the balance sheet.

Supplemental Auditing Procedures for an Initial Audit

Because the substantive tests rely on the double-entry accounting relationships between the balance sheet and income statement accounts, the auditor must perform supplemental auditing procedures during an initial audit engagement in order to express an opinion on the operating statements (income statement, statement of changes in financial position, and statement of retained earnings). Those procedures are designed to satisfy the auditor that the beginning-of-the-period balance-sheet account balances were fairly presented. Again the auditor relies heavily on the proof of transaction validity in expressing an opinion on the income statement in an initial audit. Beyond that, however, the auditor must reconcile individual beginning-of-the-period balance-sheet account balances with their end-of-the-period audited balances by *analyzing the increases and decreases to the accounts during the year* and fitting them into a basic four-element equation, stated as follows:

Beginning-of-the-period balance + increases to the account during the period − decreases in the account during the period = ending balance in the account

This equation reflects the basic format for the analysis type of work paper typically prepared as evidence in support of long-term asset balances. If the supplemental procedures show that the beginning-of-the-period account balance fits into the four-element equation for that account, the auditor can express an opinion on the financial statement in an initial audit through the medium of a normal, unqualified audit report. However, in an initial audit, the auditor can express an opinion on the *end-of-the-period balance sheet only*, without performing the supplemental procedures described in this paragraph. If such procedures cannot practicably be performed, the auditor must disclaim an opinion on the operating statement and statement of changes in financial position for the period.

Audit Adjustments

The substantive tests described in the preceding pages can result in the discovery of material errors that must be corrected by adjusting or reclassifying entries, such as those reflected in the appendix to Chapter 20. You must depend on your background in intermediate accounting in determining what those adjusting entries should be. However, as an auditing student, you should recognize that the objective of such entries is to correct the account balances reflected in the statements for the period under audit. To illustrate this point, suppose that your cutoff procedures disclose a sale recorded in the period under audit that should have been recorded in the next period. Such a situation simply requires a reversal of the sales entry in the audit work papers. You will leave the recording of the sale in the next period to the client's accountants.

It is also important for you to recognize that all audit adjustments must be approved by the client before they can be incorporated into the audited statements. However, if the client refuses to permit an adjustment that is necessary for fair presentation of the financial statements to be recorded, the auditor will have to appropriately modify his or her audit report to reflect either a qualified or adverse opinion relating to the fairness of presentation of the financial statements.

Using the Computer in Auditing the Revenue System

As we observed in Chapters 9 and 10, computers are generally used today in the maintenance of revenue system records. When a completely computerized system involving the maintenance of accounts receivable and sales data in machine-readable form is used, the auditor can advantageously use the computer to select the various sample data required for the performance of audit tests. For example, the computer can be programmed to *calculate an appropriate sample size* and to *select the accounts to be confirmed*. Furthermore, it can be programmed to *print out all pertinent details on each of the confirmation requests*.

The computer also can be programmed to scan the accounts-receivable records for the purpose of *testing the aging of those accounts*. The scanning capability of the computer can also be used to identify unusual conditions in the files, such as credit balances in accounts receivable created by improper recording practices. The computer's mathematical capability can be used to *recalculate* such important numerical fields as the totals of all categories in the client's aged accounts-receivable listing. To test appropriate sales cutoff, the computer can be programmed to *extract and print out* the sales and cash-collection transactions for the last few days of the period under audit and the first few days of the next period. The printout can then be checked against the documentary support for those transactions to verify the appropriateness of cutoff in connection with both types of transactions. Test transactions to be verified against documentary support can also be selected from the machine-readable records by the computer. The printout of those transactions then can be verified against the documents from which they originated. These are some examples, but not a complete list, of the ways in which the computer can be used as an audit tool in the audit of computerized records for revenues, receivables, and cash receipts.

Summary

In this chapter we have applied the audit process discussed throughout Section II of the text to the revenue and collections system of a typical business entity. That process involves (1) recognition of the relevant audit objectives for the revenue and collections system, (2) planning the audit for this system, (3) understanding the control structure as it relates to revenue and collections, and (4) design and implementation of detection risk procedures.

The relevant audit objectives for the revenue and collection system are existence, completeness, ownership, cutoff, valuation, and appropriate statement presentation. These audit objectives are the result of the need to verify the assertions contained in the financial statements of the audited entity.

We stated that planning of the audit of the revenue and collection system is necessary in order to evaluate inherent risk of the accounts associated with the system and to develop a proper concept of materiality. In this respect, inherent risk refers to the relative risk of misstatement of the accounts in the system: cash, accounts receivable, and sales. We stated that, because of their natures, these three accounts have among the highest risks of misstatement of any accounts in the financial statements.

We emphasized that it is important for the auditor to reach an understanding of the control structure underlying the financial statement assertions. This is done to assess control risk. The auditor's assessment of control risk, along with his or her assessment of inherent risk, is then used to determine the nature, timing, and extent of necessary detection risk procedures on the assertions. We discussed the characteristics that comprise an effective control structure for the revenue and collection system. These include (1) appropriate separation of responsibilities, (2) adequate comparison and compliance monitoring, (3) adequate records systems, (4) limited access to assets and records, and (5) execution of transactions in accordance with proper authority. We discussed the application of each of these concepts to the revenue and collection system. We then discussed the process by which the auditor obtains an understanding of the control environment, the accounting system, and various control policies and procedures that are applied by the entity.

In the last part of the chapter, we described the auditing procedures that must be performed to verify existence, completeness, ownership, cutoff, valuation, and appropriate statement presentation of the balances produced by the revenue and collection system. These procedures are characterized as substantive tests of account balances. Finally, we described briefly how the computer can be used to perform some of the substantive tests when the revenue and collection system data are maintained in computerized files.

Auditing Vocabulary

p. 560   **aging:**   A procedure that involves listing the individual accounts receivable from individual customers in order of age as determined by the date of the underlying sale or collection. See the working paper in Appendix 13–E for an illustration.

p. 551   **bill of lading:**   Document (internal or external) used to verify shipment of goods.

p. 550   **credit memo:**   An internal document whereby approval is granted to credit a customer account receivable for such things as sales discounts or sales returns and allowances.

p. 556   **lapping:**   An irregularity that occurs when the person receiving cash temporarily misappropriates the cash and covers that act by delaying the credit to the customer's account in the accounts receivable subsidiary ledger.

p. 556   **negative accounts receivable confirmation:**   A confirmation that is requested to be returned from the customer only if the customer disagrees with the balance being confirmed.

p. 556   **positive accounts receivable confirmation:**   A confirmation that is requested to be returned from the customer regardless of whether the customer agrees that the amount confirmed is correct.

p. 550   **remittance advice form:**   An internal document that serves as a turnaround document, mailed to customers and returned with their checks (remittances).

p. 557   **subsequent collections:**   Collections of accounts receivable that are received between the end of the fiscal year and the last day of audit field work.

Appendix 13–A: Illustrative Questionnaires, Flowcharts, and Other Devices Used in Understanding the Internal Control Structure for Revenue and Collections

Figure A–1

Internal Control Questionnaire

1. Are all credit sales approved by the Credit Department prior to shipment?
2. Is the Credit Department independent of the Sales Department?
3. Are sales priced on the basis of approved price lists?
4. Are prenumbered sales invoice forms used?
5. Are all sales invoice forms properly controlled?
6. Are prenumbered shipping orders used to authorize shipments to customers?
7. Are prenumbered shipping order forms properly controlled?
8. Is a prenumbered bill of lading prepared in the Shipping Department prior to release of goods to the common carrier?
9. Are prenumbered bill-of-lading forms properly controlled?
10. Are shipping orders, bills of lading, and invoices properly matched before sales are recorded in the accounting records?
11. Are sales invoices properly checked for mathematical and billing accuracy?
12. Are sales data reported independently to the general ledger bookkeeper and the accounts-receivable bookkeeper?
13. Are sales returns, sales credits, and other credits properly supported by prenumbered documentation forms?
14. Are all sales returns, sales credits, and other credits approved by a responsible officer?
15. Is the mail opened by someone other than the cashier or bookkeeper?
16. Are daily remittance lists prepared by the person opening the mail?
17. Is the daily remittance list reconciled with the daily deposit of cash?
18. Are the daily remittance lists and deposit slips regularly compared to the cash debits and accounts-receivable credit entries?
19. Are prelists of receipts on account reported independently to the general ledger bookkeeper and the accounts-receivable bookkeeper?
20. Is the subsidiary accounts-receivable ledger reconciled regularly with the accounts-receivable control account balance?

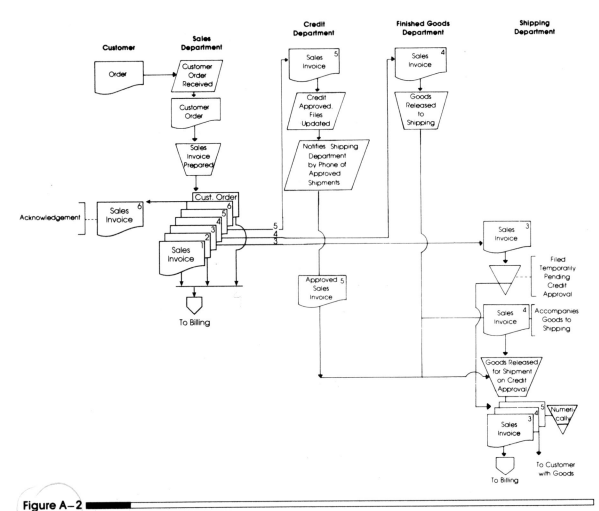

Flowchart for Processing Customer Orders and Shipping

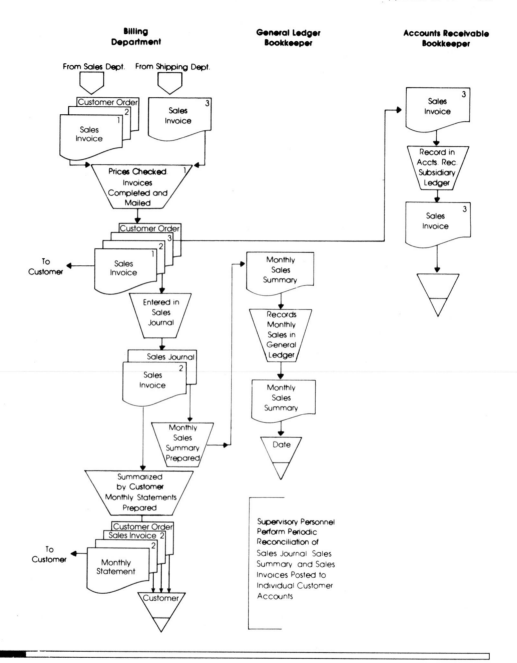

Flowchart for Recording Sales and Accounts Receivable

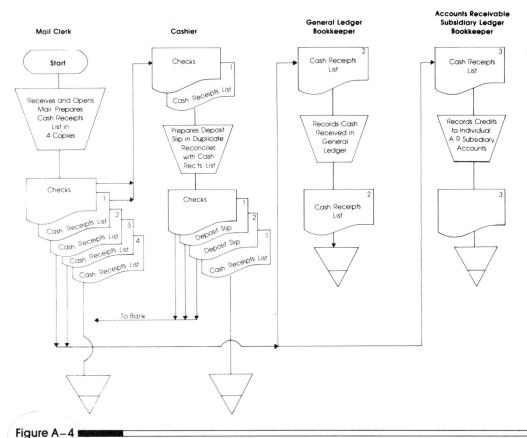

Figure A–4

Flowchart for Mail Cash-Receipts System

Figure A–5

Material Control Procedures for Computerized Revenue System

Input Controls

- The system should include provisions designed to account for and control all revenue system transaction data from their origin to the time they are submitted to the EDP department. These procedures should be directed toward assuring that all transactions reach that department.
- Within the EDP department, the company should have an appropriate verification process designed to make sure that the revenue system input data are correctly converted to machine-readable media.
- The error correction and resubmission process for revenue system data should be properly controlled within the EDP department.

Figure A–5 ▬▬▬▭▬▭▭▭▭▭▭▭▭▭▭▭▭▭▭▭▭▭▭▭▭▭▭▭▭▭▭▭▭▭▭▭▭▭▭▭

(continued)

Processing Controls

- After the revenue system's transactions have been converted to machine-readable media, the EDP department should provide controls that will ensure that all transactions are processed. Control totals over sales, sales returns, and cash collections should be developed at the point where transaction data are received. These should subsequently be reconciled with totals placed in process.
- The computer should be programmed to make logical validity tests on the important fields of information transmitted to the computer's processing unit. These might include, for example, field validity tests to ensure that numerical information is in the proper fields and the use of check digits to see that transactions are posted to the proper individual customer accounts.
- Provisions should be made for sequence checking of revenue system input data by accounting for all invoice or other document numbers.
- Header and trailer labels should be included on magnetic media files and should be tested as those files are used.

Output Controls

- Header and trailer labels should be placed on all media files created as output to reduce the probability of those files being misused.
- Control totals for output should be produced by the computer and should be reconciled with predetermined totals for various revenue system data by someone independent of the department originating the information.
- Error corrections and adjustments to master files should be properly reviewed and approved prior to being incorporated in those files.
- Authorized and approved corrections to master files should be followed up to see that they are promptly and properly incorporated in those files.

File Controls

- Control totals should be maintained on all files and should be verified each time a file is processed.
- All files containing revenue system data should be adequately supported by backup data that will allow the files to be reproduced if they are damaged or destroyed. The grandfather, father, son technique is an example of this capability.
- The files containing revenue system account data should be physically protected against damage from fire or other accidental damage.
- The EDP department should make adequate provisions for periodically checking the contents of master files by having them printed out and reviewed against underlying data.

The auditor typically determines whether these application controls are in place by using an applications controls questionnaire similar to the one that is shown in Appendix 9-A.

Figure B–1

Appendix 13–B: Functions Requiring Specific Controls

Exchange Functions Requiring Specific Controls

Financial statement assertion	Functions	Possible errors or irregularities	Results of undetected errors	Control attributes to prevent, detect, or correct errors or irregularities
Valuation	Processing customers' orders Evaluation of credit risk	Invalid transactions: Sales to customers who will be unable to pay for merchandise	Excessive losses from bad debts Inadequate provisions for bad debts	Proper evaluation of credit risk before approval of shipment (evidenced by approval signature) by separate credit department
Completeness	General processing	Erroneous transactions: Orders lost and, therefore, not shipped Shipment that is duplicated	Loss of revenue Customer dissatisfaction Errors in sales and receivables	Prenumbered written sales orders to be originated from customer orders Accounting for all sales orders
Completeness; existence	Shipping	Transactions recorded in wrong period: Items recorded as sold, not shipped Items shipped but not recorded as sold	Sales and receivables overstated Unrecorded or fictitious sales and receivables Loss of inventory Cost of sales understated	Proper approval and matching of prenumbered shipping documents with sales orders and sales invoices Segregation of shipping and billing functions
Completeness; existence	Billing customers	Erroneous transactions: Customers billed for unordered merchandise Customers not billed for merchandise shipped	Receivables and sales improperly stated Failure to collect for goods shipped	Matching of approved sales orders with bills of lading for all billings Use of prenumbered sales invoices and accounting for all numbers Matching of sales invoices with bills of lading

Completeness	Processing cash receipts Cash sales receipts	Unrecorded transactions: Misappropriation of cash Unrecorded sales	Loss of cash Sales understated	Use of cash registers with daily reconciliation by supervisors
Existence	Mail receipts	Invalid transactions: Misappropriation of cash Improperly recorded collections on account	Loss of cash Delay in receiving cash Cash or accounts receivable misstated	Prelisting of all cash received Proper segregation of responsibilities Periodic reconciliation of cash bank accounts with book records of cash
Disclosure	Processing sales returns and allowances	Improperly classified transactions: Improper credits to receivables Returned merchandise improperly recorded	Loss of merchandise Misappropriation of cash Receivables or sales returns and allowances misstated	Prenumbered and properly controlled credit memos Receiving report for goods returned in support of credit memo Approval of all returns

Figure B–2

Processing Functions Requiring Specific Controls

Financial statement assertion	Functions	Possible errors and irregularities	Possible results of undetected errors and irregularities	Control attributes to prevent, detect, or correct errors or irregularities
Completeness; valuation; existence	Recording sales Accuracy of journalizing and posting	Unrecorded or improperly recorded transactions: Unrecorded sales Improperly recorded sales Fictitious sales	Sales and receivables misstated	Use of prenumbered sales invoices and accounting for all numbers Periodic mathematical proof of invoices against records by supervisor or other independent employee
Disclosure; valuation	Proper updating of subsidiary ledger accounts	Improperly summarized transactions: Inaccurate balances in customer accounts	Receivables control not in agreement with subsidiary ledger	Review of postings by independent person Periodic reconciliation of control account with subsidiary ledger Segregation of general and subsidiary ledger duties
Completeness	Recording cash receipts	Unrecorded or improperly valued transactions: Unrecorded cash receipts Inaccurate recording of cash receipts	Lack of accountability: Misappropriation of cash and receivables or sales misstated	Use of clearly defined procedures for accounting for cash receipts from specifically identified and controlled documents Periodic and continuing reconciliation of inflows of cash with cash receipts records
Disclosure; valuation	Recording sales returns and allowances	Improperly recorded transactions: Improperly recorded sales returns and allowances	Lack of accountability: Loss of merchandise Sales returns and allowances and receivables misstated	Use of clearly defined procedures for accounting for sales returns and allowances from specifically identified and controlled documents
Valuation	Recording allowances for bad debts and write-off of bad accounts	Improperly valued transactions: Improper provision for bad debts Improper write-offs of receivables	Possible defalcation: Receivables improperly valued Bad debt expense misstated	Use of clearly defined procedures for providing for bad debts Use of clearly defined procedures for determining when receivables should be written off, including appropriate approval procedures Periodic aging of receivables

Figure B–3

Safeguard Functions Requiring Specific Controls

Financial statement assertion	Functions	Possible errors and irregularities	Possible results of undetected errors and irregularities*	Control attributes to prevent, detect, or correct errors or irregularities
Existence	Custodial care of cash receipts	Failure to maintain appropriate custodial care over cash received	Loss of cash Theft of cash	Custodial accountability for cash at point of receipt All receipts deposited intact each day Safe storage facilities for undeposited cash
Existence/completeness	Storage and care of records	Failure to maintain appropriate custodial care over accounting records	Loss of records Alteration of accounting data	Custodial responsibility for accounting records Appropriately protected storage areas for records when not being used Back-up capability to allow records to be reconstructed if lost or damaged

*Errors and irregularities in safeguarding functions can lead to any of the seven general types of material errors or irregularities involving transactions (listed in Chapter 8).

Appendix 13–C: Methodology for Tests of Controls—Sales, Accounts Receivable, and Cash Receipts

Figure C–1   Transactions Testing Methodology: Sales and Accounts Receivable

Attribute of interest	Data field (population)	Sample size[a]	Auditing procedure	Description of test	
				From	**To**
Sales orders are:					
Numerically controlled	Sales order file	240	Inspect numerical sequences	N/A	
Recorded on sales invoices, shipping documents, sales journals	Sales order file	240	Trace	Sales order file	Sales invoice file
Reviewed for approvals of prices, extensions, footings, credit check	Sales order file	240	Recompute extensions; Vouch	N/A; Sales order file	Price lists; Credit files
Shipping documents are:					
Numerically controlled	Shipping document files	Judgmental	Inspect numerical sequences	N/A	
Required for all sales	Shipping document files	Judgmental	Vouch	Shipping files	Sales invoice file
Sales invoices are:					
Numerically controlled	Sales invoice files	Judgmental	Inspect numerical sequences	N/A	
Received by inventory control as authority to release goods	Sales invoice files (copy #_____)	300	Inspect for approval: Stamp of inventory control supervisor	N/A	
Supported by shipping reports and sales orders	Sales invoice files	160	Vouch	Sales invoice file	Shipping document file; Sales order files
Sales journal entries are:					
Supported by documentation	Sales journal entries	240	Vouch	Sales journal	Sales orders, sales invoices, shipping documents

Control	Sample unit	Sample size	Procedure	From	To
Entered properly in subsidiary ledgers	Sales journal entries	240	Trace	Sales journal	Accounts receivable ledger
Entered properly in general ledger	Summary postings in sales journal	Judgmental	Reconcile	Sales journal	General ledger account
General ledger entries are supported by monthly journal totals	General ledger debit and credit postings	Judgmental	Reconcile	General ledger	Sales journal
Subsidiary ledger postings agree with entries in sales journal	Subsidiary ledger debit postings	Judgmental	Reconcile	Subsidiary ledger	Sales journal entries

[a] Sample sizes in these examples were selected using the attribute sampling methodology discussed in Chapter 11. The following parameters were prespecified for applicable cases, for simplicity: ARO = 5 percent; expected population deviation rate (EPDR) = 2.5%; TDR = 5%. In practice, each sample size must differ, depending on the precision and risk the auditor is seeking.

Figure C–2

Transactions Testing Methodology: Cash Receipts

Attribute of interest	Data field (population)	Sample size^a	Auditing procedure	Description of test	
				From	**To**
Cash sales slips/register tapes are: Controlled numerically	Cash sales slips/ register tapes	Judgmental	Inspect numerical sequence	N/A	
Used as posting medium for cash sales	Cash sales slips/ register tapes	240	Trace	Sales slips/ register tapes	Sales journal
Balanced daily to cash received and deposited	Cash sales slips/ register tapes	Judgmental	Reconcile	Sales slips/ register tapes	Cash summary and deposit slips
Subsidiary ledger credit postings: For cash, are supported by remittance advices	Credit postings to subsidiary ledger	240	Vouch	Ledger entries	Remittance advices
For noncash credits, are supported by credit memoranda	Credit postings to subsidiary ledger	240	Vouch	Ledger entries	Credit memoranda and write-off memoranda
Write-off memoranda properly approved by credit manager Total credits posted to subsidiary ledgers agree with credits posted to control accounts	Credit postings to subsidiary ledger	Judgmental	Reconcile	Subsidiary ledgers	General ledger
Credit memoranda are: Accounted for numerically	Credit memoranda file	Judgmental	Inspect numerical sequence	N/A	
Posted properly to accounts	Credit memoranda file	240	Trace	Credit memoranda file	Subsidiary ledger postings
Reviewed for calculations	Credit memoranda file	240	Recompute discounts, etc.	N/A	
Daily remittance lists are: Supported by remittance advices	Remittance list file	Judgmental	Vouch	Remittance list	Remittance advices

Properly posted to individual accounts and control accounts	Remittance list file	160	Trace	Remittance list	Subsidiary ledger credit postings
Reconciled to daily deposit	Remittance list file	160	Reconcile	Remittance list	General ledger postings deposit slips
Cash receipts journal postings are: For cash sales, supported by sales	Cash receipts journal entries	160	Vouch	Journal postings	Sales tickets/ receipts tapes
Posted properly to individual and control accounts	Cash receipts journal entries	160	Trace	Journal postings	Subsidiary and control accounts
Supported by validated deposit slips	Cash receipts journal entries	160	Vouch	Journal postings	Validated deposit slips
Daily deposits are supported by remittance lists	Deposit slip file	Judgmental	Vouch	Deposit slips	Remittance lists
General ledger cash account debits are supported by validated deposit slips	Cash account postings	Judgmental	Vouch	Postings	Validated deposit slips

[a]Sample sizes in these examples were selected using the attribute sampling methodology discussed in Chapter 11. The following parameters were prespecified for applicable cases, for simplicity: ARO = 5 percent; expected population deviation rate (EPDR) = 2.5%; TDR = 5%. In practice, each sample size must differ, depending on the precision and risk the auditor is seeking.

Appendix 13–D: Audit Programs for Sales and Accounts Receivable and for Cash Receipts Transactions

Figure D–1

Selected Audit Program Procedures for Transactions Testing:
Sales and Accounts-Receivable Charges

Audit Program for Sales and Accounts-Receivable Transactions

1. Select a sample from the sales order file.
   a. Account for numerical sequence of sales orders.
   b. Trace sales orders to matching sales invoices, shipping documents, and entries into sales journal.
   c. Review sales orders and matching invoices for approval of credit department supervisor, noting that prices, quantities, extensions, and footings were checked and that credit was properly approved before sale.
2. Select a sample of shipping documents from shipping department files.
   a. Account for numerical sequence of shipping documents.
   b. Vouch shipping documents to sales invoice files.
3. Select a sample from sales invoice file.
   a. Account for numerical sequence of sales invoices.
   b. Inspect invoices for stamp indicating that inventory was relieved.
   c. Vouch invoices to shipping department files and sales order file.
4. Select a sample of individual entries to sales journal.
   a. Vouch entries to supporting documents (sales invoice, sales order, shipping documents).
   b. Trace entries to postings in accounts-receivable subsidiary ledgers.
5. Select a sample of sales journal monthly totals. Compare totals to postings in general ledger for sales and accounts receivable for agreement.
6. Select a sample of general ledger postings to sales and accounts receivable. Compare debit and credit postings to sales journal monthly totals for agreement.
7. Select a sample of postings to accounts-receivable subsidiary ledger accounts. Vouch postings to individual entries in sales journal.

Figure D–2 ▬▬▬

Selected Audit Program Procedures for Transactions Testing:
Cash Receipts and Accounts-Receivable Credits

Audit Program for Cash Receipts Transactions

1. Select a sample of cash sales slips or register tapes.
   a. Reconcile register readings with recorded sales and trace to sales journal postings.
   b. Reconcile register readings with cash deposit and vouch to deposit slip.
   c. Account for numerical sequence of cash sales tickets, if applicable.
2. Select a sample of credit postings to the accounts-receivable subsidiary ledger.
   a. Vouch the credits to remittance advice file.
   b. Vouch noncash credits to credit memo file or write-off file in credit department. Note any undocumented credits.
3. Reconcile total credit postings per subsidiary ledger with total credit to accounts receivable control account for selected months.
4. Select a sample from the credit memo file.
   a. Account for numerical sequence of credit memos.
   b. Trace postings of credit memos to individual and control accounts.
   c. Recalculate sales discounts and verify sales returns to receiving reports.
5. Select a sample of daily remittance lists.
   a. Vouch entries to remittance advices.
   b. Trace individual postings by date to specific subsidiary ledger accounts. Trace total posting to general ledger account entries (cash debit, accounts-receivable credit).
   c. Reconcile total of remittance list to daily cash deposit. Vouch to bank-validation deposit slip by date.
6. Select a sample of cash-receipts journal postings.
   a. Vouch to cash sales tickets or remittance advices.
   b. Trace credit postings to individual accounts receivable and total posting to accounts receivable and cash control.
   c. Reconcile daily cash summaries to daily deposit slips validated by bank.
7. Select a sample of deposits per bank statement. Vouch to remittance list totals and cash-receipts journal totals.
8. Select a sample of postings to cash, accounts receivable, and sales in the general ledger. Vouch to bank deposits.

Appendix 13–E: Accounts Receivable Aged Trial Balance

JEP Manufacturing Co.
Accounts Receivable
Aged Trial Balance
3/31/X1

	W. P. No.	E
	ACCOUNTANT	SMG
	DATE	5/8/X1

Confirmation Number	Customer	Current	30–60 Days	60–90 Days	Over 90 Days
	Amco Production	562 30			
	Am East Well and Pump	1012 23			
①	Alabama Power	105 46			
	Aaco Services Co.		5731 87	989 94	
	City of Federal Heights		300 47		
	City Public Service Board		613 30		
	Cabrillo Services		566 22		
②	Consolidated Edison	30120 00	232 52 E-1-1		
	D & L Tool, Inc.		407 07		
	Dallas Power Co.	21525 00	1 05		
	Duke Powell	7364 00			
	Elliott Central	14499 25			
	Florida Power & Light	62752 00			2550 00
	Florida Power Corporation	14200 00			
	Other (Details Omitted)	640865 66	207706 49	<346 17>	<3588 19>
	Totals 3-31-X1	793005 90	215558 98	643 77	<1138 19>
	Percentage of total	78.6	21.4	0.1	<0.1>
	Totals 3-31-X0	327268 ▽	176305 ▽	16592 ▽	15727 ▽
	Percentage of total	61.1	32.9	3.1	2.9

C-Q Confirmation sent; received
◡ ✱ Footed, Cross-footed
© No reply received to confirmation, or customer not able to reply.
    See alternative procedures performed on E-1 and E-1-1
▽ Per prior year working papers
✓ Agreed to 3-31-X1 general ledger
✱ Tested aging to accounts receivable billings. No exceptions noted.

		Total	*		

	562	30	
	1012	23	
	105	46	ꝗ
	672	81	
	300	47	
	613	30	
	566	22	
E-1	30352	52	Ⓒ
	407	07	
	21526	05	ꝗ
	7364	00	
	14499	25	
E-1	65202	00	Ⓒ
	14200	00	
	84463	79	

Note: The large increase in the total accounts receivable balance over prior years (primarily in the over-30 days category) is due largely to end-of-year sales in 19X1 to many customers, including [details deleted]. Considering these increases in individual receivable accounts as well as the large increase in the over-30 day category and subsequent collections by JEP of these balances, the increase in accounts receivable at 3-31-X1 appears reasonable.

Note: No allowance for doubtful accounts is used by JEP since their business is strictly a special order-type operation and all their customers are reliable. Past collection experience indicates that this is reasonable.

	100807	047	⋇ √
	⋇ A-1		
	100.0		
	53588	7	√
	100.0		

Conclusion: Based on the audit work performed as documented in the E-series working papers, which was considered adequate to meet the objectives of the audit for receivables, accounts receivable appear to be fairly stated at 3-31-X1 in accordance with generally accepted accounting principles.

Appendix 13–F: Alternative Procedures Performed on Accounts Receivable

	Invoice #	Amount			
JEP mfg. Co.			W. P. No.		E-1
Alternative Procedures Performed on A/R			ACCOUNTANT		Smb
3-31-X1			DATE		5/8/X1

SEE TICK LEGEND ON E-1-2

	Invoice #	Amount			
Consolidated Edison				E	
Receivable @ 3-31-X1				30402 52	E-2-1 ③
Cash rec'd subsequent to 3-31-X1	19084	30120 00 ✓			
Unpaid invoice	18972	282 52 ✓		30402 52	
Amount unconfirmed				-0-	
Florida Power & Light					
Receivable @ 3-31-X1				65202 00	E-2-1 ④
Cash rec'd subsequent to 3-31-X1	19057	14400 00 ✓			
	19090	4388 00 ✓			
	19091	7200 00 ✓			
	19119	13164 00 ✓			
	19120	7200 00 ✓			
	19058	16400 00 ✓			
Unpaid invoice	18560	2450 00 ⊗		65202 00	
Amount unconfirmed				-0-	
Houston Lighting & Power				E	
Receivable @ 3-31-X1				89730 00	E-2-1 ⑤
Cash rec'd subsequent to 3-31-X1	18970	49850 00 ✓			
Unpaid invoice	19093	39880 00 ⊕		89730 00	
Amount unconfirmed				-0-	
Texaco				E	
Receivable @ 3-31-X1				26337 00	E-2-1
Unpaid invoice	19092	26337 00			
Amount unconfirmed				-0-	

				Invoice #	Amount					

JEP Mfg. Co.

Alternate Procedures performed on A/R

3-31-X1

W. P. No.   E-1-2

ACCOUNTANT   Smts

DATE   5/11/X1

Westinghouse Electric – Houston

  Receivable @ 3-31-X1 .... 2942446 E-2-1 ⑬

Cash rec'd subsequent to 3-31-X1 ... 19029 ... 2942446 ✓

  Amount unconfirmed .... -0-

✓ Agreed amount of payment and invoice # to appropriate invoice, noting that invoice date was prior to 4-1-X1 and therefore appropriately classified as a receivable @ 3-31-X1. Traced receipt of this payment to validated daily deposit slip subsequent to 3-31-X1. Amounts do appear to be receivable @ 3-31-X1.

✗ Agreed amount to invoice #18972 dated 2-13-X1. Noted that goods were shipped 2-13-X1 per shipping order. Agreed description of goods shipped to customer's P.O. # 1650324 dated 1-5-X1. Amount appears to be a receivable @ 3-31-X1.

✗ Agreed amount to invoice #19092 dated 3-20-X1. Agreed description of goods per invoice to customer's P.O. # HL-169247-1M and to shipping documents dated prior to 3-31-X1 and signed as rec'd by Texaco personnel. Amounts appear to be properly classified as a receivable @ 3-31-X1. 1 month lag appears reasonable considering client.

Ⓧ Agreed amount to invoice #18560 dated 9-25-X0. Agreed description of goods per invoice to customer's P.O.# 37956 - 14475 and to shipping documents due 9-25-X0. Amount appears to be properly classified as a receivable @ 3-31-X1. Receivable still has yet to be collected because of a rework performed on the goods that were still in transport at this date.

Agreed amount to invoice # 19093 dated 3-20-X1. Agreed description of goods per invoice to customer's P.O. # M-46477 dated 7-31-X0. Goods were shipped 3-20-X1. Amount does appear to be a receivable @ 3-31-X1.

Appendix 13–G: Accounts Receivable Confirmation

JEP MANUFACTURING COMPANY
P.O. Box 1000
Greensboro, Texas 75401

E-2-1
S MG
5/11/X1

April 10, 19X1

Dallas Power Co.
15 Providence
Dallas, Tx. 75201

Gentlemen:

Best and Company, Suite 4500, Byron Building, Dallas, Texas 75201 are making their usual examination of our accounts; therefore, would you confirm directly to them the amount of your indebtedness to us as of the close of business on March 31, 19X1.

According to our records, you were indebted to us as follows: $21,526.05.

E

Yours truly,

L. Philip Neeson

L. Philip Neeson
Financial Vice-President

LN:gr

The above information is correct, except as noted:

_____

_____

_____

J. F. Wagner   5/01/X1
‾‾‾‾‾‾‾‾‾‾‾‾‾‾‾‾‾‾‾‾‾‾‾‾‾‾‾‾‾‾‾‾‾
Signature

Supervisor, Accounts Payable
‾‾‾‾‾‾‾‾‾‾‾‾‾‾‾‾‾‾‾‾‾‾‾‾‾‾‾‾‾‾‾‾‾
Title

Appendix 13–H: Accounts Receivable Confirmation Statistics

	W. P. NO.	E-3
JEP Mfg. Co	ACCOUNTANT	Smg
A/R Confirmation Stats		
3-31-X1	DATE	5/11/X1

		Number		Amount	
		19X0 ◊	19X1	19X0 ◊	19X1
Year-End Balance		31	34	53588719	100847047
Confirmations Requested		11	13 E-0	51369534	92160537 E-2-1
% of Total		35%	38%	96%	91%
Confirmations Received					E-2
w/o exception		6	4	31418946	43534465
w/ exception - cleared		0	0	—	—
		6	4	31418946	43534465
% of Total		36.4%	32.1%	61.2%	47.2%
Alternate Procedures					E-2-1
Nonresponding A/C's		5	6	10190546	33325088
Unable to Confirm		2	3	9760042 E-2	15300984
		7	9	19950588	48626072
% of Total		63.6%		38.8%	
Total Verified		11	13	51369534	92160537
% of amt. mailed		100%	100%	100%	100%

◊ Per prior year's w/p's.

Appendix 13–I: Sales

	JEP Mfg. Co.	W. P. No.	X
	Sales	ACCOUNTANT	Smith
	3-31-X1	DATE	5/21/X1

A/C #	Description			Year Ended 3-31-X0	Year Ended 3-31-X1	
302	Liquid Dist. Transformers through 100 KVA			7798449 05	3874548 73	①
304	Liquid Dist. Transformers above 100 KVA			1870680 40	252364 00	②
307	Potheads / Parts			6790 22	1136008 0	③
306,308, 309	Oil Fuel Circuits, Disconnect Assemblies			1138466 25	-0-	④
310	Purchased Parts			5039451	1576 62	③
311	Manufactured Parts			1041081 81	220 50	③
312	Repair Sales			3815056	137678 9	
315	Cancellation Sales			10150 0	36850 0	
316-324	Load Break Switches			3451410 76	3908748 53	⑤
325	Adjustments & Allowances			⟨19938 60⟩	⟨19769 30⟩	
330	Freight			⟨164669 49⟩	⟨182811 36⟩	
350-360	Other (Compensators, Motor Controls)			4227349	6714895	⑥
				6273930 96	8033080 36	
	AJE ⟨1⟩ To reverse prior year % completion				⟨1158372 00⟩	
	AJE ⟨2⟩ To record current year % completion				964886 05	
				6273930 36	7839589 41	
					A-3	

Explanation of Significant Fluctuations

Conclusion: Based on the audit work performed, which was considered adequate to meet the objectives per the Audit program (APG), it appears that sales for 19X1 are fairly stated.

① Sales are up in the A/c due to increased orders from REOA for this type of transformer. REOA is developing large oil field in Saudi Arabia and in China, therefore the large increase in this particular pump. When REOA develops a field in this way, they require many of these transformers because of the tremendous expense of the undertaking. Fluctuation appears reasonable.

② Sales here are down because a competitor, Southwest Transformer, is currently offering a product in this class that is much less expensive.

③ Sales formerly charged to Accounts 310 & 311 are now being charged to A/c 307, now entitled "Parts", explaining the significant increase in this account and the decreases in the other two. Overall decrease appears reasonable as JEP now concentrates in completed units.

④ Sales formerly charged to 306, 308, & 309 are now being spread to other, more appropriate sales A/c's, especially "Load Break Switches."

⑤ Most significant customer of Load Break Switches from JEP is So. California Edison. Sales this year have remained relatively constant while JEP has been able to increase its margin from 24% to 29%.

⑥ Motor controls sales have shown an increase in both gross sales and margin, although it is difficult to allocate the costs of this category, since is so closely associated with the activity in R & D. Increase does appear reasonable.

Appendix 13–J: Analysis of Sales

	JEP Manufacturing Corporation		W. P. No.	X-1
	Analysis of Sales		ACCOUNTANT	Client / CMS
	12-31-X6		DATE	2-20-X7

	∅ 19X6	∅ 19X5	Increase ⟨Decrease⟩
January	188390 ✓ ¥	206720	⟨18330⟩
February	126240	110460	15780
March	290530	290520	⟨9990⟩
April	452410 ✓ ¥	450690	1720
May	774890	829460	⟨54570⟩
June	1057410	957670	99740
July	923890 ✓ ¥	964290	⟨40400⟩
August	544580	763240	⟨218660⟩
September	311620	401240	⟨89620⟩
October	433050 ✓ ¥	384290	48760
November	313720	247360	66360
December	234970 —	214170 —	20800
Total	5641700	5820110	⟨178410⟩

T/B-2

ͷ Footings checked.
∅ Agreed to general ledger. No exceptions noted.
✓ Priced, extended, and totaled 240 invoices. No exceptions noted.
— Compared invoices and shipping records for last 10 days of period. Cutoff proper at 12-31.
¥ Tested postings to customer accounts. No exceptions noted.

Note: Decline in sales for 19X6 due largely to labor strike in July, August and September 19X6. Examined union correspondence to corroborate work stoppage. Explanation agrees to details in inventory and labor statistics.

Questions for Class Discussion

Q13-1   What is meant by the term *audit objectives*?

Q13-2   What audit objectives should be achieved in verifying the account balances included in the revenue and collection system?

Q13-3   What does the auditor depend on as the primary evidence supporting the strength or weakness of the control structure?

Q13-4   Is it conceptually possible for an auditor to express an opinion on the financial statements without performing substantive tests? Explain.

Q13-5   What is meant by *boundary documents*?

Q13-6   What are the boundary documents that support revenue and collection system transactions?

Q13-7   What is meant by the following: *exchange functions; processing functions; safeguard functions*?

Q13-8   What tasks, typically performed in handling revenue and collection system activities, should be separated from each other? Cite the reasons for each of these separations.

Q13-9   Why is it inappropriate to have the billing function performed by the cashier?

Q13-10   Why is it important to have special discount concessions approved by responsible supervisors?

Q13-11   Why is it important to have specific responsibilities associated with the operations of the revenue system assigned to specific persons?

Q13-12   Why is it important to use sequentially numbered invoices and shipping tickets? Explain how these documents are used as control devices.

Q13-13   What problems are associated with the identification and handling of uncollectible accounts?

Q13-14   How does the auditor evaluate the system of internal control for a revenue system that is computerized?

Q13-15   What are the audit objectives typically met by substantive testing procedures in the audit of revenue system accounts?

Q13-16   How does the auditor rely on the double-entry system and beginning- and end-of-period asset balances in the verification of revenue account balances?

Q13-17   How does the auditor verify the existence of accounts receivable? Explain.

Q13-18   What does the auditor do when it is impractical or impossible to confirm accounts receivable as of the balance sheet date? Explain.

Q13-19   What evidence does an auditor gather in verifying the ownership of receivables?

Q13-20   Why is it important for the auditor to verify the cutoff of sales and cash receipts transactions? What procedures are used in verifying the cutoff of those transactions?

Q13-21   How does the auditor verify the valuation of accounts receivable? Explain.

Q13-22   What are the primary concerns of the auditor in verifying the appropriate statement presentation of receivables?

Q13-23 What supplemental procedures must the auditor perform in an initial audit to express an opinion on all the financial statements for the period under audit? Explain why those procedures must be performed.

Q13-24 Is it possible for an auditor to express an opinion on the end-of-period balance sheet only in an initial audit, without performing the supplemental procedures discussed in the preceding question? Explain.

Q13-25 What (briefly) are the ways in which the computer can be used in performing the audit of revenue and collection system transactions and acount balances?

Short Cases

C13-1 Darlene Dodge, CPA, is examining the financial statements of a manufacturing company with a significant amount of trade accounts receivable. Dodge is satisfied that the accounts are properly summarized and classified and that allocations, reclassifications, and valuations are made in accordance with generally accepted accounting principles. Dodge is planning to use accounts-receivable confirmation requests to satisfy the third standard of field work as to trade accounts receivable.

Required:
a. Identify and describe the two forms of accounts-receivable confirmation requests and indicate what factors Dodge will consider in determining when to use each.
b. Assume Dodge has received a satisfactory response to the confirmation requests. Describe how Dodge could evaluate collectibility of the trade accounts receivable.

(AICPA adapted)

C13-2 After determining that computer controls are valid, Janis Hastings is reviewing the sales system of Rosco Corporation in order to determine how a computerized audit program may be used to assist in performing tests of Rosco's sales records.

Rosco sells crude oil from one central location. All orders are received by mail and indicate the preassigned customer identification number, desired quantity, proposed delivery date, method of payment, and shipping terms. Since price fluctuates daily, orders do not indicate a price. Price sheets are printed daily and details are stored in a permanent disk file. The details of orders are also maintained in a permanent disk file.

Each morning the shipping clerk receives a computer printout that indicates details of customers' orders to be shipped that day. After the orders have been shipped, the shipping details are input into the computer, which simultaneously updates the sales journal, perpetual inventory records, accounts receivable, and sales accounts.

The details of all transactions, as well as daily updates, are maintained on disks that are available for use by Hastings in the performance of the audit.

Required:
a. How may a computerized audit program be used by Hastings to perform substantive tests of Rosco's sales records in their machine-readable form? *(Do not discuss accounts receivable and inventory.)*
b. After having performed these tests with the assistance of the computer, what other

auditing procedures should Hastings perform to complete the examination of Rosco's sales records?

Prob 2

(AICPA adapted)

C13-3 The Art Appreciation Society operates a museum for the benefit and enjoyment of the community. During hours when the museum is open to the public, two clerks positioned at the entrance collect a $5 admission fee from each nonmember patron. Members of the Art Appreciation Society are permitted to enter free of charge on presentation of their membership cards.

At the end of each day, one of the clerks delivers the proceeds to the treasurer. The treasurer counts the cash in the presence of the clerk and places it in a safe. Each Friday afternoon the treasurer and one of the clerks deliver all cash held in the safe to the bank and receive an authenticated deposit slip, which provides the basis for the weekly entry in the cash receipts journal.

The board of directors of the Art Appreciation Society has identified a need to improve their system of internal control over cash admission fees. The board has determined that the cost of installing turnstiles, sales booths, or otherwise altering the physical layout of the museum will greatly exceed any benefits that may be derived. However, the board has agreed that the sale of admission tickets must be an integral part of its improvement efforts.

Hubert Smith has been asked by the board of directors of the Art Appreciation Society to review the internal control over cash admission fees and provide suggestions for improvement.

Required: Indicate weaknesses Smith should find in the existing system of internal control over cash admission fees and recommend one improvement for each of the weaknesses identified.

Organize the answer as indicated in the following illustrative example:

Weakness	Recommendation
1. There is no basis for establishing the documentation of the number of paying patrons.	1. Prenumbered admission tickets should be issued upon payment of the admission fee.

(AICPA adapted)

C13-4 Your client is the Spring Valley Shopping Center, Inc., a shopping center with thirty store tenants. All leases with the store tenants provide for a fixed rent plus a percentage of sales, net of sales taxes, in excess of a fixed-dollar amount computed on an annual basis. Each lease also provides that the landlord may engage a CPA to audit all records of the tenant for assurance that sales are being properly reported to the landlord.

You have been requested by your client to audit the records of the Bali Pearl Restaurant to determine that the sales totaling $390,000 for the year ended December 31, 19X1 have been properly reported to the landlord. The restaurant and the shopping center entered into a five-year lease on January 1, 19X1. The Bali Pearl Restaurant offers only table service. No liquor is served. During meal times there are four or five waitresses in attendance who prepare handwritten prenumbered restaurant checks for the customers. Payment is made at a cash register, manned by the proprietor, as the customer leaves. All sales are for cash. The proprietor also is the bookkeeper. Complete files are kept of restaurant checks and cash register tapes. A daily sales book and general ledger are also maintained.

Required:
   a. List the audit objectives that would be of primary concern to you in auditing the sales system of Bali Pearl Restaurant.
   b. List the auditing procedures you would employ to verify the total annual sales of the Bali Pearl Restaurant. (Disregard vending machines sales and counter sales of chewing gum, candy, etc.)

(AICPA adapted)

C13-5 You are auditing the Alaska branch of Far Distributing Co. This branch has substantial annual sales, which are billed and collected locally. As a part of your audit you find that the procedures for handling cash receipts are as follows:

Cash collections on over-the-counter sales and COD sales are received from the customer or delivery service by the cashier. On receipt of cash, the cashier stamps the sales ticket "paid" and files a copy for future reference. The only record of COD sales is a copy of the sales ticket given to the cashier to hold until the cash is received from the delivery service.

Mail is opened by the secretary to the credit manager, and remittances are given to the credit manager for his review. The credit manager then places the remittances in a tray on the cashier's desk. At the daily deposit cutoff time, the cashier delivers the checks and cash on hand to the assistant credit manager, who also takes them to the bank. The assistant credit manager also posts remittances to the accounts-receivable ledger cards and verifies the cash discount allowable.

You ascertain that the credit manager obtains approval from the executive office of Far Distributing Co., located in Chicago, to write off uncollectible accounts. You also learn that he has retained in his custody as of the end of the fiscal year some remittances that were received on various days during the last month.

Required:
   a. From the narrative above, construct a systems flowchart for the cash receipts system of the Alaska branch.
   b. Describe the material internal control weaknesses under the procedures now in effect for handling cash collections and remittances.
   c. List procedures that you would recommend to strengthen internal control over cash collections and remittances.

(AICPA adapted)

C13-6 The flowchart on page 593 depicts the activities relating to the shipping, billing, and collecting processes used by Smallco Lumber, Inc.

Required: Identify weaknesses in the system of internal accounting control relating to the activities of (1) warehouse clerk, (2) bookkeeper #1, (3) bookkeeper #2, and (4) collection clerk. *(AICPA adapted)*

C13-7 You have been engaged by Gibraltar Savings and Loan Association to audit its financial statements for the year ended December 31, 19X2. The CPA who audited last year's financial statements rendered an unqualified opinion.

In addition to servicing its own mortgage loans, the association acts as a mortgage-

C13-6

Smalles Lumber, Inc.

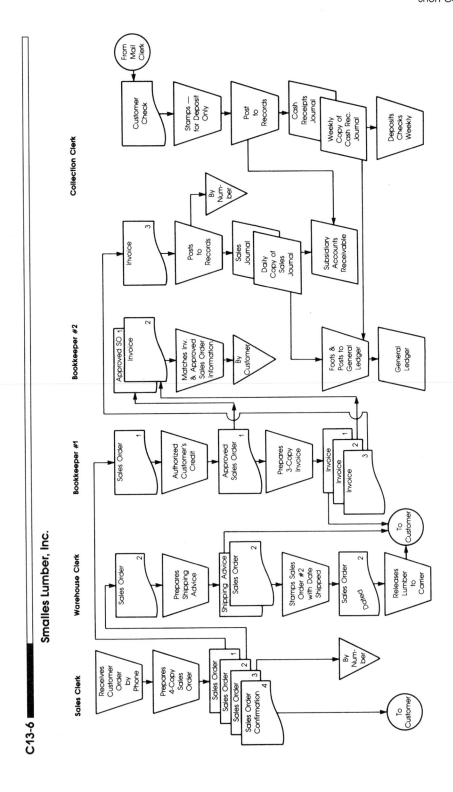

servicing agency for three life insurance companies. In this activity, the association maintains mortgage records and serves as the collection and escrow agent for the mortgagees (the insurance companies), who pay a fee to the association for these services.

Cash collections (all by mail) on the serviced mortgages are batched daily and entered in an EDP system through an input terminal located in the association's main office. The operator keys the proper mortgage number and enters the receipt information on the terminal keyboard. (This information is obtained from a remittance advice enclosed with the payment.) By this operation, magnetic master files are updated and the transaction data is stored on a random-access disk; once each month a hard copy transcript of the account is printed out as a report to the mortgagee. Cash disbursements from the escrow accounts are keypunched on cards, merged monthly with the magnetic master file, also stored on disk, and printed out on the monthly hard copy report. All disk-stored records are erased after the monthly report is printed. The remittance advices and disbursement authorization documents are filed by mortgage account number.

Required: You would expect the association to have certain internal controls in effect in the EDP system with respect to input controls, processing controls, and output controls. What controls unique to the EDP system described above should be in effect? You may classify controls as

a. Those controls pertaining to input of information.

b. All other types of computer controls.

(AICPA adapted)

C13-8 The customer billing and collection functions of the Nash-Robinson Company, a small paint manufacturer, are attended to by a receptionist, an accounts-receivable clerk, and a cashier who also serves as a secretary. The company's paint products are sold to wholesalers and retail stores.

The following describes all the procedures performed by the employees of the Nash-Robinson Company pertaining to customer billings and collections:

a. The mail is opened by the receptionist, who gives the customer's purchase orders to the accounts-receivable clerk. Fifteen to twenty orders are received each day. Under instructions to expedite the shipment of orders, the accounts-receivable clerk at once prepares a five-copy sales invoice form, which is distributed as follows:

  1. Copy 1 is the customer billing copy and is held by the accounts-receivable clerk until notice of shipment is received.

  2. Copy 2 is the accounts-receivable department copy and is held for ultimate posting of the accounts-receivable records.

  3. Copies 3 and 4 are sent to the shipping department.

  4. Copy 5 is sent to the storeroom as authorization to release the goods to the shipping department.

b. After the paint order has been moved from the storeroom to the shipping department, the shipping department prepares the bills of lading, then labels the cartons. Sales invoice copy 4 is inserted in a carton as a packing slip. After the trucker has picked up the shipment, the customer's copy of the bill of lading and copy 3, on which are noted any undershipments, are returned to the accounts-receivable clerk. The company does not back-order in the event of undershipments; customers are expected to reorder the merchandise. The Nash-Robinson Company's copy of the bill of lading is filed by the shipping department.

c. When copy 3 and the customer's copy of the bill of lading are received by the accounts-receivable clerk, copies 1 and 2 are completed by numbering them and inserting quantities shipped, unit prices, extensions, discounts, and totals. The accounts-receivable clerk then mails copy 1 and the copy of the bill of lading to the customer. Copies 2 and 3 are stapled together.

d. The individual accounts-receivable ledger cards are posted by the accounts-receivable clerk by a bookkeeping machine procedure whereby the sales register is prepared as a carbon copy of the postings. Postings are made from copy 2, which is then filed, along with staple-attached copy 3, in numerical order. Every month, the general ledger clerk summarizes the sales register for posting to the general ledger accounts.

e. Since the Nash-Robinson Company is short of cash, the deposit of receipts is also expedited. The receptionist turns over all mail receipts and related correspondence to the accounts-receivable clerk who examines the checks and determines that the accompanying vouchers or correspondence contain enough detail to permit posting of the accounts. The accounts-receivable clerk then endorses the checks and gives them to the cashier who prepares the daily deposit. No currency is received in the mail, and no paint is sold over the counter at the factory.

f. The accounts-receivable clerk uses the vouchers or correspondence that accompanied the checks to post the accounts-receivable ledger cards. The bookkeeping machine prepares a cash receipts register as a carbon copy of the postings. Monthly, the general ledger clerk summarizes the cash receipts register for posting to the general ledger accounts. The accounts-receivable clerk also corresponds with customers about unauthorized deductions for discounts, freight or advertising allowances, returns, etc., and prepares the appropriate credit memos. Disputes involving large amounts are turned over to the sales manager for settlement. Each month the accounts-receivable clerk prepares a trial balance of the open accounts receivable for the accounts-receivable listing.

Required:

a. Discuss the internal control weaknesses in the Nash-Robinson Company's procedures related to customer billings and remittances and the accounting for these transactions. In your discussion, in addition to identifying the weaknesses, explain what could happen as a result of each weakness.

b. For each weakness, list one substantive auditing procedure for testing the significance of the potential error.

(AICPA adapted)

C13-9   You are auditing the accounts-receivable account of Rob Roy Plastics, Inc. As part of that examination, you mailed 280 positive accounts-receivable requests to confirm trade receivables directly with Rob Roy's customers. Several accounts receivable confirmations have been returned with the notation that "verification of vendors' statements is no longer possible because our data-processing system does not accumulate each vendor's invoices."

Required: What alternative auditing procedures could be used to audit these accounts receivable?

(AICPA adapted)

C13-10 Finney, CPA, was engaged to conduct an audit of the financial statements of Clayton Realty Corporation for the month ending January 31, 19X4. The examination of monthly rent reconciliations is a vital portion of the audit engagement.

The following rent reconciliation was prepared by the controller of Clayton Realty Corporation and was presented to Finney, who subjected it to various auditing procedures:

Clayton Realty Corporation

R E N T   R E C O N C I L I A T I O N

For the month ended January 31, 19X4

Gross apartment rents	
(Schedule A)	$1,600.800*
Less vacancies	
(Schedule B)	20,500*
Net apartment rents	1,580,300
Less unpaid January rents	
(Schedule C)	7,800*
Total	1,572,500
Add prepaid rent collected	
(Apartment 116)	500*
Total cash collected	$1,573,000*

Schedules A, B, and C are available to Finney but have not been illustrated. Finney has obtained an understanding of the internal control structure and found that it could be relied upon to produce reliable accounting information. Cash receipts from rental operations are deposited in a special bank account.

Required: What substantive auditing procedures should Finney employ during the audit in order to substantiate the validity of each of the dollar amounts marked by an asterisk (*)?

(AICPA adapted)

C13-11 Jerome Paper Company engaged you to review its internal control system. Jerome does not pre-list cash receipts before they are recorded and has other weaknesses in processing collections of trade receivables, the company's largest asset. In discussing the matter with the controller, you find he is chiefly interested in economy when he assigns duties to the fifteen office personnel. He feels the main considerations are that the work should be done by people who are most familiar with it, capable of doing it, and available when it has to be done.

The controller says he has excellent control over trade receivables because receivables are pledged as security for a continually renewable bank loan, and the bank sends out positive confirmation requests occasionally, based on a list of pledged receivables furnished by the company each week.

Required:

a. Explain how pre-listing of cash receipts strengthens internal control over cash.

b. Assume that an employee handles cash receipts from trade customers before they are recorded. List the duties that employee should not do to withhold from him or her the opportunity to conceal embezzlement of the receipts.

(AICPA adapted)

C13-12 You have been assigned to the first examination of the accounts of The Chicago Company for the year ending March 31, 19X8. The accounts receivable were confirmed at December 31, 19X7, and at that date, the receivables consisted of approximately 200 accounts with balances totaling $956,750. Seventy-five of these accounts with balances totaling $650,725 were selected for confirmation. All but twenty of the confirmation requests have been returned; thirty were signed without comments, fourteen had minor differences, which have been cleared satisfactorily, while eleven confirmations had the following comments:

a. We are sorry, but we cannot answer your request for confirmation of our account as the PDQ Company uses an accounts-payable voucher system.

b. The balance of $1,050 was paid on December 23, 19X7.

c. The above balance of $7,750 was paid on January 5, 19X8.

d. The above balance has been paid.

e. We do not owe you anything at December 31, 19X7 as the goods, represented by your invoice dated December 30, 19X7, number 25,050, in the amount of $11,550, were received on January 5, 19X8 on FOB destination terms.

f. An advance payment of $2,500 made by us in November 19X7 should cover the two invoices totalling $1,350 shown on the statement attached.

g. We never received these goods.

h. We are contesting the propriety of this $12,525 charge. We think the charge is excessive.

i. Amount okay. As the goods have been shipped to us on consignment, we will remit payment upon selling the goods.

j. The $10,000, representing a deposit under a lease, will be applied against the rent due to us during 19X9, the last year of lease.

k. Your credit dated December 5, 19X7, in the amount of $440, cancels the above balance.

What steps would you take to clear satisfactorily each of the above eleven comments?

(AICPA adapted)

C13-13 Harris, CPA, has been engaged to audit the financial statements of the Spartan Drug Store, Inc. Spartan is a medium sized rental outlet that sells a wide variety of consumer goods. All sales are for cash or check. Cashiers utilize cash registers to process these transactions. There are no receipts by mail and there are no credit card or charge sales.

Required: Construct the "Processing Cash Collections" segment of the internal accounting control questionnaire on "Cash Receipts" to be used in understanding the internal control structure for the Spartan Drug Store, Inc. Each question should elicit either a yes or no response. Do not discuss the internal controls over cash sales.

(AICPA adapted)

Problems

P13-1 Select the best answer for each of the following items relating to internal control within the revenue system.

a. A company policy should clearly indicate that defective merchandise returned by customers is to be delivered to the

1. Salesclerk.

    2. Receiving clerk.

    3. Inventory control clerk.

    4. Accounts-receivable clerk.

b. In a properly designed internal control structure, the same employee may be permitted to

    1. Receive and deposit checks, and also approve write-offs of customer accounts.

    2. Approve vouchers for payment, and also sign checks.

    3. Reconcile the bank statements, and also receive and deposit checks.

    4. Sign checks, and also cancel supporting documents.

c. Which of the following is an effective internal control over accounts receivable?

    1. Only persons who handle cash receipts should be responsible for the preparation of documents that reduce accounts-receivable balances.

    2. Responsibility for approval of the write-off of uncollectible accounts receivable should be assigned to the cashier.

    3. Balances in the subsidiary accounts-receivable ledger should be reconciled to the general ledger control account once a year, preferably at year end.

    4. The billing function should be assigned to persons other than those responsible for maintaining accounts-receivable subsidiary records.

d. Which of the following internal control procedures will *most* likely prevent the concealment of a cash shortage resulting from the improper write-off of a trade account receivable?

    1. Write-offs must be approved by a responsible officer after review of credit department recommendations and supporting evidence.

    2. Write-offs must be supported by an aging schedule showing that only receivables overdue several months have been written off.

    3. Write-offs must be approved by the cashier, who is in a position to know if the receivables have, in fact, been collected.

    4. Write-offs must be authorized by company field sales employees, who are in a position to determine the financial standing of the customers.

e. The most likely result of ineffective internal controls in the revenue cycle is that

    1. Fictitious transactions could be recorded, causing an understatement of revenues and overstatement of receivables.

    2. Irregularities in recording transactions in the subsidiary accounts could result in a delay in goods shipped.

    3. Omission of shipping documents could go undetected, causing an understatement of inventory.

    4. Final authorization of credit memos by personnel in the sales department could permit an employee defalcation scheme.

f. Which of the following would be the *best* protection for a company that wishes to prevent the "lapping" of trade accounts receivable?

    1. Segregate duties so that the bookkeeper in charge of the general ledger has *no* access to incoming mail.

    2. Segregate duties so that *no* employee has access to both checks from customers and currency from daily cash receipts.

    3. Have customers send payments directly to the company's depository bank.

    4. Request that customers' payment checks be made payable to the company and addressed to the treasurer.

g. After the auditor has prepared a flowchart of the internal controls over sales and formed an initial assessment, the auditor would perform tests on all internal control procedures

1. Documented in the flowchart.
2. Considered to be weaknesses that might allow errors to enter the accounting system.
3. Considered to be strengths that the auditor plans to rely on.
4. That would aid in preventing irregularities.

h. To conceal defalcations involving receivables, the experienced bookkeeper would probably charge which of the following accounts?
1. Miscellaneous income.
2. Petty cash.
3. Miscellaneous expense.
4. Sales returns.

i. To safeguard the assets through proper internal control, accounts receivable that are written off are transferred to a(n)
1. Separate ledger.
2. Attorney for evidence in collection proceedings.
3. Tax deductions file.
4. Credit manager, since customers may seek to reestablish credit by paying.

j. To achieve good internal control, which department should perform the activities of matching shipping documents with sales orders and preparing daily sales summaries?
1. Billing.
2. Shipping.
3. Credit.
4. Sales order.

k. To determine whether the internal control structure operated effectively to minimize errors of failure to invoice a shipment, the auditor would select a sample of transactions from the population represented by the
1. Customer order file.
2. Bill of lading file.
3. Open invoice file.
4. Sales invoice file.

P13-2 Select the best answer to each of the following items relating to the confirmation of receivables.

a. The auditor obtains corroborating evidential matter for accounts receivable by using positive or negative confirmation requests. Under which of the following circumstances might the negative form of the accounts-receivable confirmation be useful?
1. A substantial number of accounts are in dispute.
2. Internal control over accounts receivable is ineffective.
3. Client records include a large number of relatively small balances.
4. The auditor believes that recipients of the requests are unlikely to give them consideration.

b. In determining validity of accounts receivable, which of the following would the auditor consider *most* reliable?
1. Documentary evidence that supports the accounts-receivable balance.
2. Credits to accounts receivable from the cash receipts book after the close of business at year end.
3. Direct telephone communication between auditor and debtor.

4. Confirmation replies received directly from customers.

c. The confirmation of the client's trade accounts receivable is a means of obtaining evidential matter and is specifically considered to be a generally accepting auditing
1. Principle.
2. Standard.
3. Procedure.
4. Practice.

d. It is sometimes impracticable or impossible for an auditor to use normal accounts-receivable confirmation procedures. In such situations the *best* alternative procedure the auditor might resort to would be
1. Examining subsequent receipts of year-end accounts receivable.
2. Reviewing accounts-receivable aging schedules prepared at the balance sheet date and at a subsequent date.
3. Requesting that management increase the allowance for uncollectible accounts by an amount equal to some percentage of the balance in those accounts that *cannot* be confirmed.
4. Performing an overall analytic review of accounts receivable and sales on a year-to-year basis.

e. Confirmation of individual accounts-receivable balances directly with debtors will, of itself, normally provide evidence concerning the
1. Collectibility of the balances confirmed.
2. Ownership of the balances confirmed.
3. Validity of the balances confirmed.
4. Internal control over balances confirmed.

f. Jacob Hirsch is engaged in the audit of a utility that supplies power to a residential community. All accounts-receivable balances are small, and internal control is effective. Customers are billed bi-monthly. In order to determine the validity of the accounts-receivable balances at the balance sheet date, Hirsch would most likely
1. Examine evidence of subsequent cash receipts instead of sending confirmation requests.
2. Send positive confirmation requests.
3. Send negative confirmation requests.
4. Use statistical sampling instead of sending confirmation requests.

g. During the first part of the current fiscal year, the client company began dealing with certain customers on a consignment basis. Which of the following auditing procedures is *least* likely to bring this new fact to the auditor's attention?
1. Tracing of shipping documents to the sales journal.
2. Test of cash receipts transactions.
3. Confirmation of accounts receivable.
4. Observation of physical inventory.

h. During the process of confirming receivables as of December 31, 19X2, a positive confirmation was returned indicating the "balance owed as of December 31 was paid on January 9, 19X3." The auditor would most likely
1. Determine whether there were any changes in the account between January 1 and January 9, 19X3.
2. Determine whether a customary trade discount was taken by the customer.
3. Reconfirm the zero balance as of January 10, 19X3.
4. Verify that the amount was received.

(AICPA adapted)

P13-3 Select the best answer to each of the following items relating to the verification of cutoff of sales.

a. A sales-cutoff test of billings complements the verification of
   1. Sales returns.
   2. Cash.
   3. Accounts receivable.
   4. Sales allowances.

b. To determine that sales transactions have been recorded in the proper accounting period, the auditor performs a cutoff review. Which of the following *best* describes the overall approach used when performing a cutoff review?
   1. Ascertain that management has included in the representation letter a statement that transactions have been accounted for in the proper accounting period.
   2. Confirm year-end transactions with regular customers.
   3. Examine cash receipts in the subsequent period.
   4. Analyze transactions occurring within a few days before and after year end.

c. A CPA is engaged in the annual audit of a client for the year ended December 31, 19X1. The client took a complete physical inventory under the CPA's observation on December 15 and adjusted its inventory control account and detailed perpetual inventory records to agree with the physical inventory. The client considers a sale to be made in the period that goods are shipped. Listed below are four items taken from the CPA's sales-cutoff test work sheet. Which item does *not* require an adjusting entry on the client's books?

	Date (month/day)		
	Shipped	Recorded as sale	Credited to inventory control
1.	12/10	12/19	12/12
2.	12/14	12/16	12/16
3.	12/31	1/2	12/31
4.	1/2	12/31	12/31

d. Which of the following might be detected by an auditor's cutoff review and examination of sales journal entries for several days prior to and subsequent to the balance sheet date?
   1. Lapping year-end accounts receivable.
   2. Inflating sales for the year.
   3. Improper cutoff of bank balances.
   4. Misappropriating merchandise.

e. An auditor is reviewing sales cutoff as of March 31, 19X0. All sales are shipped FOB destination, and the company records sales three days after shipment. The auditor notes the following items:

		(Amounts in thousands)	
Date shipped	Month recorded	Selling price	Cost
March 28	March	$192	$200
March 29	March	44	40
March 30	April	77	81
April 2	March	208	220
April 5	April	92	84

If the client records the required adjustment, the net effect on income in thousands of dollars for the period ended March 31, 19X0 is
1. An increase of 12.
2. An increase of 8.
3. A decrease of 12.
4. A decrease of 8.

(AICPA adapted)

P13-4 Select the best answer to each of the following items relating to the valuation of receivables.
   a. The audit working papers often include a client-prepared, aged trial balance of accounts receivable as of the balance sheet date. This aging is *best* used by the auditor to
   1. Evaluate internal control over credit sales.
   2. Test the accuracy of recorded charge sales.
   3. Evaluate the reasonableness of the allowance for doubtful accounts.
   4. Verify the validity of the recorded receivables.
   b. Once a CPA has determined that accounts receivable have increased due to slow collections in a "tight money" environment, the CPA would be likely to
   1. Increase the balance in the allowance for bad debts accounts.
   2. Review the going concern ramifications.
   3. Review the credit and collection policy.
   4. Expand tests of collectibility.
   c. In determining the adequacy of the allowance for uncollectible accounts, the *least* reliance should be placed on which of the following?
   1. The credit manager's opinion.
   2. An aging schedule of past-due accounts.
   3. Collection experience of the client's collection agency.
   4. Ratios calculated showing the past relationship of the valuation allowances to net credit sales.
   d. Some firms that dispose of only a small part of their total output by consignment shipments fail to make any distinction between consignment shipments and regular sales. Which of the following would suggest that goods have been shipped on consignment?
   1. Numerous shipments of small quantities.
   2. Numerous shipments of large quantities and few returns.
   3. Large debits to accounts receivable and small periodic credits.
   4. Large debits to accounts receivable and large periodic credits.

(AICPA adapted)

P13-5 Select the best answer to each of the following miscellaneous items relating to sales and receivables.
   a. Madison Corporation has a few large accounts receivable that total $1 million. Nassau Corporation has a great number of small accounts receivable that also total $1 million. The importance of an error in any one account is, therefore, greater for Madison than for Nassau. This is an example of the auditor's concept of
   1. Materiality.
   2. Comparative analysis.

3. Reasonable assurance.

4. Relative risk.

b. A CPA auditing an electric utility wishes to determine whether all customers are being billed. The CPA's best direction of test is from the

1. Meter department records to the billing (sales) register.

2. Billing (sales) register to the meter department records.

3. Accounts-receivable ledger to the billing (sales) register.

4. Billing (sales) register to the accounts-receivable ledger.

c. Which of the following auditing procedures is most effective in testing credit sales for understatement (completeness)?

1. Age accounts receivable.

2. Confirm accounts receivable.

3. Trace sample of initial sales slips through summaries to recorded general ledger sales.

4. Trace sample of recorded sales, from general ledger to initial sales slip.

d. An auditor is testing sales transactions. One step is to trace a sample of debit entries from the accounts-receivable subsidiary ledger back to the supporting sales invoices. What would the auditor intend to establish by this step?

1. All sales have been recorded.

2. Debit entries in the accounts-receivable subsidiary ledger are properly supported by sales invoices.

3. All sales invoices have been properly posted to customer accounts.

4. Sales invoices represent bona fide sales.

e. An auditor reconciles the total of the accounts-receivable subsidiary ledger to the general ledger control account, as of October 31, 19X2. By this procedure, the auditor would be most likely to learn of which of the following?

1. An October invoice was improperly computed.

2. An October check from a customer was posted in error to the account of another customer with a similar name.

3. An opening balance in a subsidiary ledger account was improperly carried forward from the previous accounting period.

4. An account balance is past due and should be written off.

f. A corporation is holding securities as collateral for an outstanding account receivable. During the course of the audit engagement the CPA should

1. Verify that title to the securities rests with the corporation.

2. Ascertain that the amount recorded in the investment account is equal to the fair market value of the securities at the date of receipt.

3. Examine the securities and ascertain their value.

4. Refer to independent sources to determine that recorded dividend income is proper.

(AICPA adapted)

P13-6   Items (a) through (i) below are questions excerpted from a typical internal control questionnaire for the purpose of understanding internal controls over processing of customer orders and shipping. As explained in the text, a "yes" response to such a question indicates a potential strength in the system while a "no" response indicates a potential weakness.

a. Are all credit sales approved by the credit department prior to shipment?

b. Is the credit department independent of the sales department?

    c. Are prices based on approved price lists?
    d. Are prenumbered sales invoice forms used?
    e. Are all sales invoice forms numerically controlled?
    f. Are prenumbered shipping orders used to authorize shipments to customers?
    g. Are shipping orders used to authorize shipments to customers?
    h. Are prenumbered bills of lading prepared in the shipping department prior to release of goods to the common carrier?
    i. Are bills of lading numerically controlled?

Required: For each question above, list
    a. The error or irregularity that item was designed to detect.
    b. The effect that the absence of the control could have on the financial statements, and the financial statement assertion affected.
    c. The test that would be necessary in order to ascertain whether the control was actually being implemented if the answer to the internal control question were "yes." When sampling of documents is involved, indicate the data file from which a sample would be chosen and the appropriate auditing procedure (e.g., vouching, tracing, recalculation, etc.). You may want to refer to Figure C-1.
    d. The substantive test (see Figure 13-3) that would have to be extended, if any, if that control were missing or if the client demonstrated a low level of compliance.

Organize your answer according to the following format. The first question has been answered as an example.

Item	Error or irregularity	Effect on financial statements	Test of controls	Substantive test
(a)	Invalid transaction	Excessive losses from bad debts (valuation)	Vouch from sales invoice files to credit files	Inspect credit records for past-due accounts

P13-7 Items (a) through (k) below are questions excerpted from a typical internal control questionnaire for the purpose of understanding internal controls over the billing, sales returns and allowances, and cash receipts systems. As explained in the text, a "yes" response to such a question indicates a potential strength in the system while a "no" response indicates a potential weakness.

    a. Are shipping orders, bills of lading, and invoices properly matched before sales are recorded in the accounting records?
    b. Are sales invoices properly checked for mathematical and billing accuracy?
    c. Are sales data reported independently to the general ledger bookkeeper and the accounts-receivable bookkeeper?
    d. Are sales returns, sales credits, and other credits properly supported by pre-numbered documentation forms?
    e. Are all sales returns, sales credits, and other credits approved by a responsible officer?
    f. Is the mail opened by someone other than the cashier or bookkeeper?
    g. Are daily remittance lists prepared by the person(s) opening the mail?
    h. Is the daily remittance list reconciled with the daily deposit of cash?
    i. Are the daily remittance lists and deposit slips compared to the cash debits and accounts-receivable credit entries regularly?
    j. Are pre-lists of receipts on account reported independently to the general ledger bookkeeper and the accounts-receivable bookkeeper?

k. Is the accounts-receivable subsidiary ledger reconciled regularly with the accounts-receivable control account balance?

Required: For each question above, list
a. The error or irregularity which that control attribute was designed to detect.
b. The effect that the absence of the control would have on the financial statements.
c. The test that would be necessary to ascertain whether the control were actually being implemented if the answer to the internal control question were "yes." When sampling of documents is involved, indicate the data file from which a sample would be selected and the auditing procedure (e.g., vouching, tracing, recalculation, etc.) most appropriate for the sample (see Figures C-1 and C-2).
d. The substantive test (see Figure 13-3) that would have to be extended, if any, if that control were missing or if tests indicated inadequate compliance.
Organize your answer in the same format as that shown above for Problem 13-6.

P13-8 Items (a) through (i) below list procedures typically performed by the auditor as part of the audit of the revenue and collections systems.
a. Trace a sample of sales orders to the sales invoice file.
b. Reconcile the total amount of accounts receivable per the general ledger account with the total of the accounts-receivable subsidiary ledger.
c. Vouch totals from the daily deposit slips to daily remittance lists.
d. Recompute extensions and footings on a sample of sales invoices.
e. Trace a sample of sales invoices or cash register tapes to entries in the sales journal.
f. Inspect a sample of sales invoices for evidence of credit approval.
g. Trace entries in sales journal to corresponding entries in accounts-receivable subsidiary ledger (individual customer accounts).
h. Vouch entries in general ledger for write-offs of accounts receivable to credit memoranda and write-off memoranda.
i. Confirm individual accounts receivable directly with customers.

Required: For each item above, state
a. Whether the test is a test of controls, a substantive test, or possibly both (a dual-purpose test).
b. The audit objective(s) being fulfilled by the test: statement presentation, transaction validity, ownership, periodicity, valuation, or existence. *Note*: A particular procedure may satisfy one or more audit objectives simultaneously.

P13-9 In connection with your receivables-confirmation work for the January 31 audit of Black & Co., you receive the following exceptions to confirmation requests:
a. A customer returned the confirmation request with the notation: "We do not owe the above amount because it was paid by our check dated January 30."
b. Another customer returned the confirmation request with the notation: "We do not owe the above amount because it was paid by our check dated January 20."

Required: What would you do in following up on each exception? Explain and justify any differences between your two answers.

P13-10 Prior to your confirmation of accounts receivable, the credit manager shows you five accounts totaling $2,500, out of total accounts receivable of $350,000, that he asks you not to confirm. He indicates that there have been disputes regarding the amounts owed in all five cases. A significant correspondence file has been developed relating to whether or not merchandise delivered had been in accordance with customer's specifications in each case. For that reason, he feels that confirmation requests would merely agitate the customers and yield no useful information.

Required: How would you, as an auditor, handle this situation during your audit of accounts receivable?

P13-11 The Installment Jewelry Company has been in business for five years but has never had its financial statements audited. Engaged to make an audit for 19X7, you find that the company's balance sheet carries no allowance for bad accounts, because bad accounts have been expensed as written off. Recoveries have been credited to income as collected. The company's policy is to write off at December 31 of each year those accounts on which no collections have been received for three months. The installment contracts generally are for two years.

On your recommendation, the company agrees to revise its accounts for 19X7 to give effect to bad-account treatment on the reserve basis. The reserve is to be based on a percentage of sales, that is to be derived from the experience of the past five years. Statistics for the past five years are shown on the following table.

Required: Prepare the adjusting entry or entries to set up the allowance for bad accounts. Assume that the books have not been closed for 19X7. (Support each item with organized computations; income tax implications should be ignored.)

	Charge sales	Accounts written off and year of sale				Recoveries and year of sale
19X3	$100,000	(19X3) $ 550				
19X4	$250,000	(19X3) $1,500	(19X4) $1,000			(19X3) $ 100
19X5	$300,000	(19X3) $ 500	(19X4) $4,000	(19X5) $1,300		(19X4) $ 400
19X6	$325,000	(19X4) $1,200	(19X5) $4,500	(19X6) $1,500		(19X5) $ 500
19X7	$275,000	(19X5) $2,700	(19X6) $5,000	(19X7) $1,500		(19X6) $ 600

Accounts receivable at December 31, 19X7 were as follows:

19X6 sales	$ 15,000
19X7 sales	135,000
	$150,000

CHAPTER 14

The Acquisitions and Expenditures System

Objectives

☐ **1.** Identify relevant audit objectives for the acquisitions and expenditures system based on the client's financial statement assertions.
☐ **2.** Assess materiality and inherent risk for the system.
☐ **3.** Obtain an understanding of the control structure and assess control risk for the various assertions produced by the system.

In the course of doing business, a retail or manufacturing company must spend cash or incur trade debt to acquire inventory, property and equipment, and supplies necessary to operate the company. In addition, the entity might make expenditures for present or future services such as utilities, insurance, or rent. In this chapter we turn our attention to the audit process for the system and account balances associated with the acquisitions and expenditures system. As in the previous chapter, our discussion will follow the format for the audit process outlined in Figure 5–2.

Appendixes to this chapter illustrate questionnaires and system flowcharts typically used to document the auditor's understanding of the control structure for the acquisitions and expenditures system. Also included are illustrations of the transactions testing methodology used to perform tests of controls over the system.

Audit Objectives

☑ **Objective 1**
Identify audit
objectives for the
acquisitions and
expenditures
system

As discussed in earlier chapters, audit objectives are developed from the financial statement assertions associated with the accounts produced by the system. For the acquisitions and expenditures system, the primary asset accounts are cash, inventories, and property and equipment. Asset accounts that are often secondary in importance are supplies inventory and prepaid expenses, such as insurance and rent. A multitude of expense accounts may be produced by the expenditures system, categorized as manufacturing, selling, and general and administrative expenses. The primary liability accounts associated with the acquisitions and expenditures system are trade accounts or vouchers payable; secondary are accrued liabilities. The audit objectives that pertain to these accounts include

1. Transaction validity, existence, and occurrence.
2. Valuation.
3. Proper cutoff (related to the allocation assertion).
4. Ownership rights for assets; obligation for liabilities.
5. Completeness.
6. Proper statement presentation or disclosure.

Audit Planning for the Acquisitions and Expenditures System

☑ **Objective 2**
Assess materiality
and inherent risk for
the accounts in the
acquisitions and
expenditures
system

Inventories are often the largest and most important of current assets on the balance sheets of manufacturing or commercial business enterprises. It is not uncommon for raw materials inventory balances for a medium-sized manufacturing business to consist of millions of individual transactions. In addition, because of the many different (and sometimes unique) methods used, accounting for them can often be quite complex.

Inventories are vulnerable to potential material errors of many types, including errors of valuation, completeness, existence, and disclosure. Errors in accounting for inventories often have pervasive effects because they affect income statement as well as balance sheet accounts. For example, an overstatement of inventory is often offset by an understatement of the cost-of-goods-sold account on the income statement, thus overstating current assets as well as gross profit and net income. Thus, in terms of the audit risk model of Chapter 5, inherent risk for inventory accounts should generally be set at a relatively high level. In addition, relatively low materiality thresholds are generally necessary, because of the pervasiveness of potential errors.

Fixed assets generally constitute the largest single asset group in the financial statements of a business enterprise. Because of the size of the account balances, they are material. However, although subject to the same types of errors as inventories, fixed assets are usually not easily movable and, therefore, are not subject to the high levels of risk of misappropriation as are the more liquid assets. Also, except for the period during which the entity originated, it is probable that only a relatively small number of fixed asset transactions will occur within any one fiscal period. Under these circumstances, it is possible to examine most, if not all, of the transactions that produced the end-of-period balances. Thus, the independent auditor rarely spends much time focusing on controls that are unique to fixed assets. It should be understood, however, that the same control structure that applies to the acquisition of inventory also applies to the acquisition of property and equipment.

In contrast, prepaid expense accounts, which are also produced by the disbursements system, are in many instances not material to the company's overall financial position and results of operations. Accounting methods for these accounts are typically straightforward and relatively simple. Thus, prepaid expenses are generally not subject to a high level of inherent risk of misstatement. Generally, since relatively few transactions of this type occur in the typical business, it is often possible to audit the financial statement balances for these accounts quite cost-effectively without much detailed consideration of the control structure that surrounds them.

When we shift our attention from assets to trade and accrued liabilities, the financial statement assertion that generally produces the greatest risk is *completeness*—that is, the risk that the client will *understate liabilities.* Therefore, procedures used to accomplish audit objectives for payables must include those designed to detect unrecorded amounts as well as those that verify recorded amounts. Since payment of trade and accrued payables and operating expenses involves cash handling, inherent risk of misstatement is generally considered to be high for these current liability and expense accounts.

In the section that follows, we will consider the control structure over the acquisition and expenditures system, with particular emphasis to those controls that pertain to purchases of inventories and fixed assets as well as to accounts payable and cash disbursements.

Understanding the Control Structure

☑ **Objective 3**
Assess control risk for the acquisitions and expenditures system

The activities involved in the acquisition and expenditures system include the following:

1. Requisitioning.
2. Ordering.
3. Receiving.
4. Storing.
5. Cash disbursements.

The processing functions designed to establish accountability and provide reliable financial data over the acquisitions and expenditures system are

1. Recording acquisitions, returns, and cash payments.
2. Maintaining records over perpetual inventories.
3. Maintaining subsidiary ledgers for fixed assets and depreciation.
4. Maintaining subsidiary ledgers for accounts payable.

To understand the control structure over the acquisitions and expenditures system, it is necessary to study and evaluate the following elements: (1) control environment; (2) accounting system; and (3) control procedures prescribed by the client.

The Control Environment

Because of the high inherent risk of misstatement that typically exists in a cash disbursements system involving numerous transactions and sometimes thousands of account balances, management's attitude and operating style should be one of diligence toward preventing, detecting, and correcting errors and irregularities. The organizational structure of the company should be well-defined and should include effective methods of assigning authority and responsibility throughout the system. All personnel who handle the responsibilities of requisitioning, ordering, receiving, and accounting for the assets and liabilities involved in the system should be qualified technically and experientially for their respective duties.

The data processing environment should contain adequate general controls to assure organizational autonomy and proper segregation of functions within the computer department. Documentation of programs, including changes, should be complete. Controls should prevent unauthorized access to assets, data files, and computer programs.

The presence of a properly trained and organizationally autonomous internal audit staff who report to an audit committee is a valuable enhancement to the control environment. Internal auditors can provide effective day-to-day monitoring of the operational effectiveness of the acquisitions and expenditures system, making sure that prescribed company policies for such controls as approval of transactions, proper records, and safeguarding of assets are being followed.

The independent auditor generally learns of these and other environmental conditions through prior experience with the entity, as well as discussions with client personnel and observation of the entity's operations.

The Accounting System

Figure 14–1 presents diagrammatically the typical flows of transactions through the acquisitions and expenditures system. For simplification, we have assumed that all acquisitions are made on account. Thus, we assume that a credit entry is first made to accounts payable or to vouchers payable for each eventual disbursement of cash.

The auditor must obtain an understanding of the flow of these transactions

Figure 14-1 ▬▬▬

Flow of Transactions through the Acquisitions and Expenditures System

Raw Materials Inventory		
Beginning bal. xxx		
xxx (1)	xxx (4)	

Cash in Bank	
xxx (8)	xxx (2)
	xxx (5)

Fixed Assets		
Beginning bal. xxx		
xxx (1)	xxx (4)	
	xxx (8)	
Ending bal. xxx		

Accounts or Vouchers Payable	
	Beginning bal. xxx
xxx (4)	xxx (1)
xxx (5)	xxx (3)
	Ending bal. xxx

Gains (losses) on Disposals	
xxx (8)	xxx (8)

Depreciation Expense
xxx (7)

Accumulated Depreciation	
xxx (8)	Beginning bal. xxx
	xxx (7)
	Ending bal. xxx

Manufacturing Expenses
xxx (3)

Prepaid Expenses	
Beginning bal. xxx	xxx (6)
xxx (2)	
Ending bal. xxx	

Selling Expenses
xxx (3)

Accrued Liabilities	
xxx (5)	Beginning bal. xxx
	xxx (3)
	Ending bal. xxx

Administrative Expenses
xxx (3)
xxx (6)

Notes: (1) Acquisitions. (2) Prepayments. (3) Incurrence of manufacturing, selling, and administrative expenses. (4) Purchase returns. (5) Payments of accounts payable and accrued liabilities. (6) Expensed portion of prepaid expenses for period. (7) Recognition of depreciation. (8) Retirements of fixed assets.

from the point of initiation to the point of inclusion in the financial statements. Such an understanding may begin with the auditor's previous experience with the entity. Understanding is enhanced through inquiry of client personnel, observation of employees in the normal course of their assigned functions, and reading narrative descriptions of the system in the client's procedures manuals.

As explained in Chapter 8, the following sequence of steps is required:

1. Consider the errors and irregularities that could occur.
2. Consider the results of undetected errors on the related financial statement assertions.
3. Consider the control attributes that would prevent, detect, or correct those errors or irregularities.
4. Ascertain whether the necessary control attributes are prescribed.

Appendixes 14–B through 14–F contain figures that outline these steps for the acquisitions and expenditures system.

The auditor's understanding is documented in one or a combination of the following ways: (1) internal control questionnaires, (2) narrative descriptions, and (3) systems flowcharts. Appendix 14–A contains an illustrative internal control questionnaire (Figure A–1) and flowcharts (Figures A–2 through A–4), which help to document the auditor's understanding of the accounting system for acquisitions and expenditures.

Control Procedures

The control environment and the accounting system for acquisitions and expenditures should contain policies and procedures that enhance the entity's ability to *record, process, summarize, and report financial data* in a manner that accurately and fairly reflects the assertions embodied in the financial statements. Policies and procedures that should be prescribed by the company include (1) appropriate segregation of responsibilities, (2) adequate records and documentation, (3) an effective system of comparisons and compliance-monitoring, (4) limited access to assets and sensitive data, and (5) proper execution of transactions in accordance with management's general or specific authority.

Appropriate Segregation of Responsibilities

Appropriate segregation of responsibilities requires that exchange functions, processing functions, and safeguard functions be handled by different persons or departments within the entity. Thus, the duties of custody of assets, purchasing, receiving, accounting, and cash disbursements should be kept separate. Among the many controls that should be carried out in the system to protect resources and to assure accuracy in the recording process are the following:

- The stores department should be kept separate from the purchasing and disbursing functions.
- The stores ledger clerk should not have access to the storeroom or to the handling of inventory items.

- A centralized purchasing department should be responsible for making all purchases of inventories and fixed assets. Persons having responsibility for purchases should have no access to cash.
- A separate receiving department should be responsible for all items of inventory and equipment entering the business.
- In processing purchase orders and the vouchers authorizing cash disbursements, the persons preparing and approving the vouchers for payment should have no other responsibilities relating to cash payments.
- The authority to borrow should be separated from the cash-handling function. Normally, this authority would be vested in the treasurer or a special committee of the client's board of directors.
- Persons authorized to sign checks should have no responsibilities relating to the preparation of vouchers and should have no access to cash receipts or cash records.
- Checks should be mailed directly from the cash disbursements section of the treasurer's department and should not be allowed to return to the accounting department where vouchers were originally prepared.
- Bank reconciliations should be performed by internal auditors or by other personnel who have no other cash-handling or recordkeeping duties.

The questionnaires and flowcharts in Appendix 14–A illustrate appropriate division of responsibilities for the acquisition and expenditures system, as well as typical inquiries that are made of management to assure that segregation of critical functions is prescribed by management.

Adequate Records and Documentation

The primary *exchange transactions* in the system involve (1) acquisitions of inventory and fixed assets (including leasing of equipment); (2) returns of defective, unsalable, or unusable items purchased; and (3) payments on account. Figure 14–2 illustrates these exchange transactions, along with the related boundary and supporting documents that should accompany them.

Figure 14–2 ▬▬

Exchange Transactions and Supporting Documents

Exchange transaction	Boundary document	Supporting document(s)
Acquisition of inventory or fixed assets	Vendor's invoice; lease agreement	Purchase requisition; acquisition work order; purchase order; receiving report; voucher
Purchase returns	Debit memorandum	Receiving report; shipping document
Payment of trade payables	Canceled check	Paid voucher and documents

Comparisons and Compliance Monitoring

As with all systems in the entity, no one person in the acquisitions and expenditures system should be allowed to process a transaction completely without being cross-checked by someone else.

In the purchasing function, the purchasing agent should compare records of items received with vendor invoices and purchase orders for completeness. Invoice terms and details should be matched to receiving reports and purchasing department records before vendor invoices are approved for payment. A "blind" copy of the purchase order (quantities omitted) should be sent to the receiving department to notify them that an order will soon be arriving.

In the receiving department, all items received should be counted and inspected for quality before they are accepted. Items should be received only from vendors for whom the purchasing department has forwarded a copy of the purchase order. Damaged items should be forwarded to the shipping department for return to vendors, with proper notification in the form of a debit memorandum.

Stores department personnel should receive copies of both the purchase order and receiving report. On receipt of inventory into the department, quantities and descriptions of materials listed on these documents should be compared with those listed on the purchase requisition for completeness and accuracy, before the goods are placed into inventory.

Supervisors in operating departments who requisition fixed assets should compare items received with work orders to assure that model numbers are correct and that the equipment is in proper working order.

The accounts payable section of the accounting department should receive copies of all documents produced in the system: the purchase requisition, purchase order, work order (in the case of fixed assets), receiving report, and vendor invoice. No voucher should be prepared until all of these documents are produced. Before preparing the voucher, all supporting documents should be examined for completeness and accuracy. Later in the process, as vouchers are approved for payment, persons in the accounts payable section should check the account distribution on the voucher before entering it into the voucher register as paid.

When computers are in use, control totals such as batch totals, hash totals, and record counts should be used to assure completeness and accuracy of processing. Periodically, general and subsidiary ledger account balances for raw materials inventories should be reconciled, and all differences should be accounted for. These procedures should be performed either by the internal audit department or by other persons who are independent of both the general and subsidiary ledger functions. In addition, internal auditors should prepare monthly bank reconciliations. As they do, they should examine canceled checks for date, payee, signature and endorsement. Amounts of checks should be compared with entries in the check register and voucher register.

Access to Assets and Data

As stated previously, the major assets involved in the acquisitions and expenditures system are cash, inventories, and fixed assets. Access to cash should be limited only to persons in the cash disbursements section of the treasurer's department. Except for petty cash, all cash balances should be maintained in banks. Disbursements should be made only by means of prenumbered and properly authorized checks.

Access to inventories should be limited to personnel in the stores department or warehouses. Warehouses and production areas should be kept properly maintained to avoid damage or deterioration from the elements. During non-business hours, all facilities should be locked, and, if necessary, guarded by authorized personnel. Burglar and fire alarms should be used.

General and subsidiary ledgers, whether maintained manually or by computer, should be kept in properly locked facilities protected from fire and other casualties. Access to those ledgers should be allowed only to persons in the general ledger and subsidiary ledger sections of the accounting department. Sensitive files kept on computer records should be accessible only by means of proper passwords or user identification numbers.

Execution of Transactions as Approved

In the acquisitions system, the primary authority for approval of transactions is usually delegated to the purchasing agent. As shown in Figure A–2 of Appendix 14–A, the purchasing agent is authorized to obtain competitive bids for all major inventory and fixed assets. In addition, he or she approves invoices as to quantities received, requisitioned, and ordered, as well as prices and shipping terms. The purchasing agent should also authorize all returns of items found to be defective or erroneously shipped to the company.

For material fixed asset acquisitions, a work order should be initiated by the operating department requesting the purchase. The work order should be properly approved by a responsible official before a purchase order is issued. As shown in Figure A–3 of the appendix, the treasurer's department approves work orders for large fixed asset acquisitions, after consulting a capital budget. The work order is then submitted to the board of directors, where the proposal is reviewed, approved or disapproved, and documented in the minutes.

In the cash disbursements system, the treasurer's department normally has authority to approve payment of vouchers and notes. As shown in Figure A–4, approval is granted for payment only after all of the supporting documentation is examined. As checks are signed, the voucher and all supporting documents are marked "paid" to prevent resubmission.

Detailed Control Risk Assessment Procedures

After obtaining an understanding of the entity's control structure, as outlined above, the auditor should make a preliminary assessment of the internal control risk associated with each financial statement assertion. This should be done in a manner similar to that outlined in Chapter 8. As we have stated previously, the level of control risk may be expressed either quantitatively (in terms of percentages) or qualitatively (high, medium, low).

For those financial assertions supported by weak controls, or in cases in which it is not cost effective to proceed with control assessment, the auditor will assign the highest level of control risk. This decision will necessitate selection of low-detection risk procedures—those that are very effective, performed at or around year-end, using large sample sizes—on the related financial statement assertions.

On the other hand, if certain financial statement assertions are supported by effective prescribed controls, and if it is cost-effective to proceed, the auditor may desire to assess control risk at a lower level than the preliminary assessment level. For these assertions, the auditor should enter the detailed stage of control risk assessment.

As explained in Chapter 8, the detailed stage of control risk assessment involves these steps, which complete the 7-step process begun during the initial assessment phase:

5. Conduct tests of prescribed controls to ascertain if they are performing effectively.
6. Evaluate results of tests of controls.
7. Reach conclusion as to control risk, and design substantive tests for affected financial statement assertions accordingly.

Appendix 14–G contains a diagram and Appendix 14–H contains the related audit program that illustrate the methodology that should be used for tests of the control attributes identified in Appendixes 14–B through 14–F.

Summary

In this chapter we have concentrated attention on the planning and control risk assessment stages of the audit process for the system of acquisitions and expenditures. Planning for the audit of this system involves recognition of relevant audit objectives and assessment of audit risk and materiality. Assessment of control risk requires understanding the client's control structure. That, in turn, involves becoming familiar with the client's control environment and accounting system, along with the control procedures that are prescribed in each.

Audit objectives for the system are extensions of the financial statement assertions of the client. They include verification of existence, ownership/obligation, completeness (including proper cutoff), valuation, and appropriate statement presentation (disclosure).

We established that inherent risk for the acquisitions and expenditures system is relatively high due to the nature of some of the accounts involved and the potential that exists for misstatement of those accounts. Any reduction in planned substantive tests for these accounts should be dependent on a relatively low assessment of control risk. Thus, it is important that the control structure surrounding these accounts be evaluated thoroughly. We discussed and illustrated the attributes that a sound control structure for acquisitions and expenditures should possess. In addition, we discussed tests that may be performed on these attributes to assure that they are working as prescribed.

Appendix 14–A: Illustrative Questionnaires, Flowcharts, and Other Devices Used in Understanding the Control Structure for the Acquisitions and Expenditures System

Figure A–1

Selected Internal Control Questionnaire Items

	Yes	No	Comments
Processing of purchase orders			
1. Are purchases of goods and services so authorized that persons who approve and execute transactions can determine whether the authorization was issued by persons acting within the scope of their authority?	____	____	
2. Are prenumbered purchase orders prepared and approved for conformity with general or specific authorization as to vendor, goods or services ordered, prices, and other elements?	____	____	
3. Are all major purchases made on the basis of competitive bids or some other scheme to ensure that the company obtains the most economical price?	____	____	
Receipt of goods and services			
4. Are prenumbered receiving reports prepared for all receipts of goods or services?	____	____	
5. Are vendor invoices and purchase orders compared with receiving records for quantity, prices, amounts back-ordered, etc.?	____	____	
Recording acquisitions of goods and services			
6. Is the preparation of initial purchase records performed by persons who do not also:			
a. Prepare supporting documents required for payment?	____	____	
b. Sign checks?	____	____	
c. Handle signed checks?	____	____	
d. Handle cash receipts after initial recording?	____	____	
7. Is proper documentation (purchase orders, receiving reports, purchase requisitions, vendor invoices) required before any purchase is recorded?	____	____	
8. Are supporting records (purchase orders, receiving reports, etc.) compared to vendor invoice for prices, quantities, terms, etc.?	____	____	

(continues)

Figure A–1

(continued)

Payments on account	Yes	No	Comments
9. Are subsidiary records maintained of trade payables by persons who do not also:			
a. Prepare supporting documents required for payment of vouchers?	____	____	
b. Issue checks?	____	____	
c. Handle cash receipts after initial recording?	____	____	
10. Are recorded disbursements matched individually or adequately tested with initial credits in the subsidiary records, and are the balances of individual vendor accounts computed or adequately tested by persons who do not also:			
a. Prepare supporting documents required for payment of vendors?	____	____	
b. Issue checks?	____	____	
c. Handle signed checks?	____	____	
d. Handle cash receipts after initial recording?	____	____	

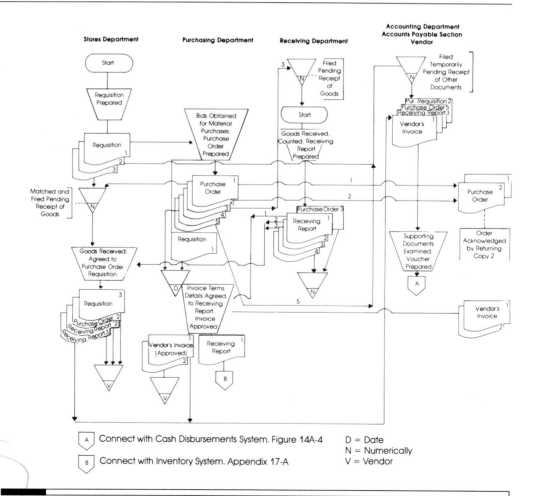

| A | Connect with Cash Disbursements System. Figure 14A-4 |

| B | Connect with Inventory System. Appendix 17-A |

D = Date
N = Numerically
V = Vendor

Figure A–2

Inventory Purchasing, Receiving, and Vouchers Preparation

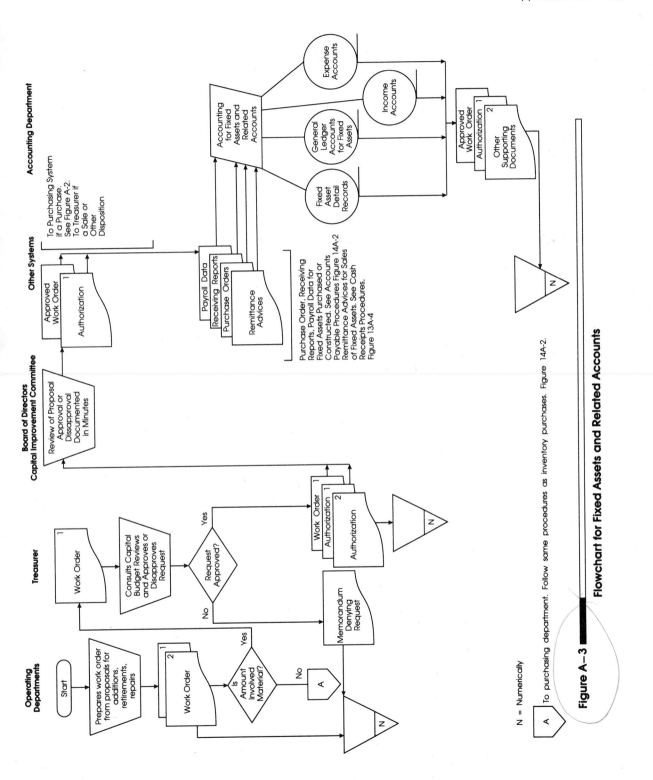

Figure A–3

Flowchart for Fixed Assets and Related Accounts

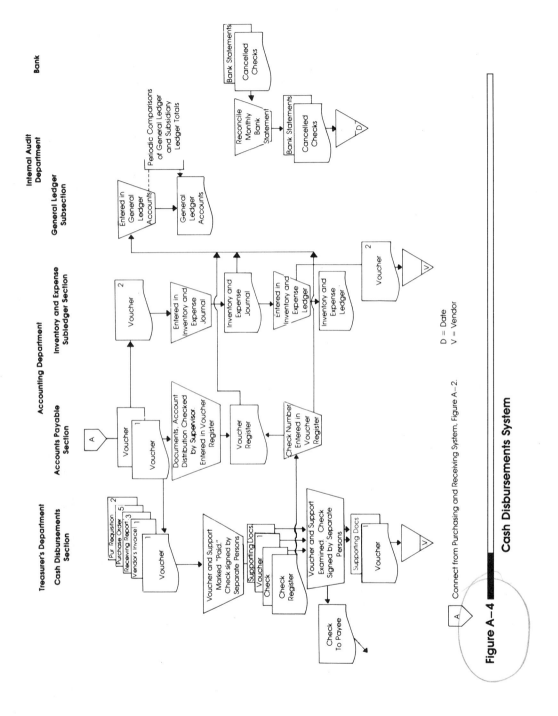

Figure A–4 Cash Disbursements System

Appendix 14–B: Exchange Functions and Specific Controls—Inventory and Accounts Payable

Financial assertion	Functions	Possible errors or irregularities	Results of undetected errors	Control attributes to prevent, detect, or correct errors or irregularities
Completeness	Processing purchase orders: Requisitions of goods, services	Invalid transactions: Ordering material not needed; duplicate purchase	Oversupplies or short supplies; work inefficiencies	Require the use of economic order quantity (EOQ) calculations for all significant orders purchased Require prenumbered written requisitions from stores department personnel for all goods ordered Receiving department should accept merchandise only if a purchase order or other approval has been issued by the purchasing department Systematic reporting of product changes that affect raw materials needs
Completeness	Ordering of goods or services	Invalid transactions: Incomplete records of goods ordered	Understatement of accounts payable and cost of sales	Require prenumbered written purchase orders for all goods ordered
Valuation		Ordering at uneconomical prices	Inefficient usage of funds; possible illegal kickbacks for employees from suppliers	Require all purchases to be made by competitive bids in order to get the most economical prices Require approval of prices by responsible officer
Existence	Payments on account	Invalid transactions: Misappropriation of cash payments by employees	Misstatements in cash or accounts payable balances	Separation of accounting, check preparation, and check-signing functions Require checks to be signed by responsible official with no recordkeeping or preparation responsibilities; dual signatures on checks; check protector devices, etc. Require checks to be mailed under supervision of the signer without being returned to preparer Checks should be sequentially numbered and should be accounted for by person preparing bank reconciliation Check preparation should be based on properly authorized and approved vouchers that are mutilated (stamped paid) when check is signed

(continues)

Appendix 14–B (continued)

Financial assertion	Functions	Possible errors or irregularities	Results of undetected errors	Control attributes to prevent, detect, or correct errors or irregularities
		Resubmission of supporting documents for payment a second time	Overstatement of accounts payable	Require cancellation of all supporting papers (invoices, purchase orders, receiving reports, requisitions) as checks are signed
Existence	Receipt of goods and services	Invalid transactions: Paying for goods not received Unauthorized delivery of goods to other employee-controlled locations	Overstatement of accounts payable	Require prenumbered receiving reports for all purchases approved Separation of purchasing and receiving functions Require employee purchases to be made through regular purchasing channels
Completeness		Unrecorded transactions: Transactions recorded in the wrong period Invalid transactions: Receiving inferior quality or inaccurate quantity of goods	Understatement of accounts payable and cost of sales Loss of production time; reorders of merchandise	Require follow-up on receiving reports, purchase orders, or vendor invoices for which there is no support Require receiving personnel to count all quantities of goods received; send one copy of receiving report to purchasing department Require purchasing department to review all major purchases for quality and quantity, then recalculate footing and extensions on vendor invoices and other supporting papers
Valuation	Payments on account	Improperly valued transactions: Inaccuracies in recording amounts payable, and payments thereon	Overstatement or understatement of payables	Require verification of recorded amounts, such as account distributions and extended amounts on vouchers, etc.
			Discrepancies between subsidiary ledger total and control accounts	Use of control totals in posting routines, periodic reconciliation of general and subsidiary ledger totals

Appendix 14–C: Inventories—Processing Functions and Related Controls

Financial assertion	Functions	Possible errors or irregularities	Results of undetected errors	Control attributes to prevent, detect, or correct errors or irregularities
Valuation, completeness	Recording acquisitions of goods and services	Improperly valued, classified, summarized transactions: Transactions recorded in the wrong period Inaccurate or incomplete accounting for goods requisitioned, ordered, or received	Understatement of accounts payable and cost of sales	Require prenumbered purchase requisitions, purchase orders, and receiving reports; require accounting department to receive copies of all of these before voucher is prepared Require all purchases to be routed through accounts payable and not directly through cash disbursements Require checking of all vendors' invoices for mathematical accuracy, quantity, prices, and terms Require reconciliation of invoices with supporting documents Require use of accounting manuals and employee approval for determining distribution of invoice charge to general ledger Require double-checking of distribution of charges on vouchers payable Require periodic balancing of accounts payable subsidiary ledger or open voucher register items with the general ledger control account Require follow-up on receiving reports, purchase orders or vendors' invoices for which there is no support
Existence, valuation, completeness, ownership		Erroneous transactions: Recording purchases of goods and services not requisitioned, purchased, or received	Overstatement of accounts payable; paying for goods not received	Separation of accounting function from purchasing and receiving Require proper documentation for all approved purchases: purchase requisitions, purchase orders, receiving reports, vendor invoices Copy of purchase orders going to receiving department should omit quantities to force receiving clerk to count goods

(continues)

Appendix 14–C (continued)

Financial assertion	Functions	Possible errors or irregularities	Results of undetected errors	Control attributes to prevent, detect, or correct errors or irregularities
		Unrecorded or improperly valued transactions: Unrecorded or inaccurate recording of goods purchased	Overstatement or understatement of accounts payable, inventories	Require verification of recorded amounts, such as account distributions and extended amounts on vouchers, etc. Use of control totals in posting routines, periodic reconciliation of general and subsidiary ledger totals
Valuation	Recording payments on account	Erroneous transactions: Inaccurate record of payment	Misstatements of cash, accounts payable	Require use of prenumbered checks Require prenumbered vouchers to support each check written Require all disbursements to be made by check Require checking of the numerical sequence of cancelled checks during the reconciliation process
Completeness, disclosure		Invalid or unrecorded transactions: Incomplete record of payments	Misstatements of cash, accounts payable	Require voided checks to be mutilated and retained for inspection Require monthly reconciliation of bank accounts by person independent of cash custody or recordkeeping functions Require that checks be examined and compared to cash disbursements records in the bank reconciliation process Require check signee to examine all supporting documents Require effective accounting control over interbank transfers to prevent or detect kiting (improper use of bank clearing procedure)
Disclosure, valuation, completeness, ownership	Recording purchase returns and allowances	Erroneous or invalid transactions: Failure to record items returned Failure to accurately record items returned	Misstatements of book inventories and accounts payable	Require approval by responsible official of purchase returns and allowances Require purchase returns to be cleared through proper receiving department procedures Require the accounts payable department to be notified of all goods returned

Appendix 14–D: Exchange Functions Requiring Specific Controls—Fixed Assets

Financial assertion	Functions	Possible errors or irregularities	Effect of errors and irregularities on financial statements	Control attributes to prevent, detect, or correct errors and irregularities
Existence; ownership	Purchase of property and equipment	Purchase of property and equipment that are not needed, inefficient, or ineffective	Failure to maximize profits or cash flows	Require capital budgeting techniques Segregate functions of custody of assets and approval of transactions Require review and approval of all major property and equipment purchases by board of directors
		Purchase of property and equipment for personal use	Misappropriation of cash Understatement of property and equipment	Segregate functions of custody of assets and recordkeeping Require a work order system for all property and equipment additions
	Leasing property and equipment as lessee	Unauthorized or uneconomical lease agreements	Failure to maximize profits or cash flow	Require capital budgeting techniques Require use of proposals, approval, and analysis techniques for leased property by qualified officials
	Sales of property, plant, and equipment	Unauthorized sale or trade-in of assets	Misappropriation of cash Failure of detail records to agree with general ledger control	Segregate functions of custody of assets, recordkeeping, and approvals Require a work order system for all property and equipment sales and trade-ins
	Trade-ins of property, plant, and equipment	Sale or trade-ins of assets and retention of proceeds by operating personnel	Misappropriation of cash Failure of detail records to agree with general ledger control	Require all such transactions to be approved by board of directors, if material Require periodic observation of property and equipment and reconciliation of counts with fixed assets detail records Allow only designated officials to sell property and equipment Subject all sales to the same cash receipts controls as described in Chapter 13 for cash receipts from operations

Appendix 14—E: Processing Functions Requiring Specific Controls—Fixed Assets

Financial assertion	Functions	Possible errors or irregularities	Effect of errors and irregularities on financial statements	Control attributes to prevent, detect, or correct errors and irregularities
Completeness; valuation; ownership rights	Recording purchases of property and equipment	Improperly recorded transactions: Capitalizing items that should be expensed; Expensing items that should be capitalized	Overstatement of income; Overstatement of assets; Understatement of income; Understatement of assets	Require a policy on capitalization for all fixed asset purchases; Require full documentation (work orders, purchase orders, receiving reports, vendor reports) before approval of voucher
Existence		Unauthorized transactions: Recording unauthorized or fictitious purchases	Overstatement of assets	Require periodic reconciliation of fixed asset detail records with general ledger control account by responsible official
Completeness; disclosure		Erroneous transactions: Erroneous recording of purchases	Misstatement of assets; Failure of detail records to agree with control accounts	
Ownership	Recording lease transactions	Improperly recorded transactions: Expensing items that should have been capitalized	Understatement of assets and liabilities; Misstatement of income	Require review of all lease transactions for requirements of capitalization under FASB Statement 13
Completeness	Recording depreciation expenses	Inaccurate or untimely recording of transactions: Erroneous or inaccurate records of depreciation	Misstatement of assets; Misstatement of income	Require formal depreciation policy for all assets; Require periodic review of accounting for depreciation by supervisory personnel
Completeness	Recording sales and trade-ins of property and equipment	Erroneous recording of sales and trade-ins	Misstatement of assets; Failure of detail records to agree with control accounts	Require review and double-checking of all sales transactions by supervisory personnel; Require periodic reconciliation of fixed asset detail records with general ledger control account

Appendix 14–F: Safeguard Functions Requiring Specific Controls—Fixed Assets

Financial assertion	Functions	Possible errors or irregularities	Effect of errors and irregularities on financial statements	Control attributes to prevent, detect, or correct errors and irregularities
Existence; valuation	Custody of property and equipment	Undue abuse and subjection to the elements, wear and tear, etc. Carelessness leading to accidents	Mechanical failures leading to unanticipated repairs and lower profits Losses due to casualties such as fire; lower profits	Require physical protection of machinery and equipment in storage buildings, warehouses, sheds, etc. Establish appropriate maintenance policy Conduct an adequate training program on equipment and building safety Maintain adequate fire and casualty insurance coverage

Appendix 14—G: Transactions Testing Methodology for Acquisitions and Expenditures System

Attributes of interest	Data field (population)	Sample size[a]	Auditing procedure	From	To
1. Purchase requisitions are:					
a. Numerically controlled.	Purchase requisition file	Judgmental 240	Inspect num. sequence		N/A
b. Followed up with proper procedures.	Purchase requisition file	240	Trace	Purchase requisition file	Purchase orders, receiving reports, vendor invoices, vouchers payable, posting
c. Approved by supervisory personnel.	Purchase requisition file	240	Inspect for approval signature or initials		N/A
2. Purchase orders are:					
a. Numerically controlled.	Purchase order file	Judgmental 240	Inspect num. sequence		N/A
b. Supported by purchase requisitions, competitive bids.	Purchase order file	240	Vouch	Purchase order file	Purchase requisition file, vendor files
c. Approved properly.	Purchase order file	240	Inspect for approval signatures or initials		N/A
3. Receiving reports are:					
a. Numerically controlled.	Receiving report file	Judgmental 240	Inspect num. sequence		N/A
b. Matched with other papers supporting purchases as to quantity, quality of goods.	Receiving report file	240	Vouch	Receiving report file	Purchase orders, requisition file, vendor files
c. Posted accurately to perpetual inventory records.	Receiving report file	240	Reconcile quantities; check for verification of goods received in salable condition; trace	Receiving report file	Entries in perpetual inventory records
4. Vendor invoices are:					
a. Reviewed and approved by purchasing agent.	Vendor invoice, vouchers payable files	240	Inspect for purchasing agent signature		N/A
b. Recalculated and prices checked.	Vendor invoice, vouchers payable files	240	Recalculate, vouch	Vendor invoice	Recent vendor catalog price list
c. Compared to receiving reports for quantity.	Vendor invoice, vouchers payable files	240	Compare quantities	Invoice	Receiving report

5. Purchase and expense journal entries are:

a. Supported by documentation.	Purchase and expense journal entries	240	Vouch	Purchase and expense entries	Purchase requisitions, purchase orders, receiving reports, vendor invoices
b. Entered properly in subsidiary ledgers.	Purchase and expense journal entries	240	Trace	Purchase and expense journal entries	Accounts payable and inventory ledgers
c. Entered properly in general ledger.	Purchase and expense journal entries	Judgmental	Reconcile	Purchase and expense journal entries	General ledger accounts

6. Vouchers payable are:

a. Checked by accounts payable personnel for proper amounts, account distributions.	Vouchers payable file (unpaid and paid)	240	Recalculate extensions, verify accuracy of account distribution		N/A
b. Supported by adequate documentation.	Vouchers payable file (unpaid and paid)	240	Vouch	Vouchers	Supporting documents
c. Posted accurately to accounts when prepared.	Vouchers payable file (unpaid and paid)	240	Trace	Vouchers	Entries in voucher register, general ledger, subsidiary ledgers
d. Recorded properly as paid.	Paid vouchers	240	Reconcile check numbers	Voucher register	Check register

7. Payments on account are:

a. All supported by prenumbered checks.	Voucher register entries	240	Vouch	Voucher register	Check register and cancelled checks
b. Supported by adequate documentation.	Check register	240	Vouch	Check register	Vouchers, invoices, receiving reports, purchase orders, purchase requisitions
c. Accompanied by cancellation of supporting documents.	Paid vouchers (see 6(d))	240 (see 6(d))	Inspect for cancellation of documents		N/A
d. Posted to proper accounts in general and subsidiary ledgers.	Check register (see 7(b))	240 (see 7(b))	Trace	Check register	Postings to general ledger accounts

a Sample sizes in these examples were selected using the attribute sampling methodology discussed in Chapter 11. The following parameters were prespecified for applicable cases, for simplicity; desired risk of overreliance (ARO) 5%; expected deviation rate = 2.5%; desired TDR = 5%. In practice, each sample size must differ, depending on the precision and risk the auditor is seeking.

Appendix 14–H: Illustrative Audit Program Procedures for Transactions Testing of Cash Disbursements

Selected Audit Program Procedures for Transactions Testing

1. **a.** Inspect a series of purchase requisitions and account for proper numerical sequence.
   Select a sample from the purchase requisition file.
   b. Trace the sample through the system to its posting in the general ledger, and match with purchase orders, receiving reports, and vendor invoices.
   c. Inspect for proper approval signatures of store's supervisors.
2. **a.** Account for the numerical sequence of a series of purchase orders.
   Select a sample of purchase orders.
   b. Vouch quantities to purchase requisitions from stores department.
   c. Inspect for approval signatures of purchasing agent.
3. **a.** Account for the numerical sequence of a series of receiving reports.
   Select a sample of receiving reports.
   b. Vouch to purchase orders and requisitions, reconciling quantities received and placed in stores to quantities requisitioned and ordered. Trace to vendor invoices and to posting to vouchers payable. For sales returns and allowances, ascertain proper recording.
   c. Trace quantities to postings in perpetual inventory records.
4. Select a sample of vendor invoices from the vouchers payable file.
   a. Inspect for approval signatures of purchasing agent.
   b. Recalculate extensions, footings.
   c. Trace prices to vendor price lists or catalogs. Compare quantities with receiving reports, purchase orders.
5. Select a sample of entries to the purchases and expense journal.
   a. Vouch to purchase requisitions, purchase orders, receiving reports, vendor invoices.
   b. Trace postings to inventory and accounts payable ledgers, if available.
   c. Reconcile summary postings to general ledger accounts for inventories, accounts payable, and expenses.
6. Select a sample of vouchers payable.
   a. Inspect for approval signatures indicating verification of amounts, account distribution, etc. Recalculate extensions, footings.
   b. Vouch to supporting documents.
   c. Trace entries to voucher register.
   d. For paid vouchers, reconcile check numbers to voucher register and check register. Examine documents for cancellation.
7. Select a sample of entries from the voucher register.
   a. Vouch entries for paid vouchers to check register and cancelled checks.
   b. Foot voucher register for one or more periods and trace postings to general ledger and subsidiary ledgers, if appropriate.
8. Select a sample of entries to the check register.
   a. Vouch to cancelled checks, paid vouchers, and related supporting documents.
   b. Select a sample of paid vouchers. Inspect the documents included in the vouchers for proper cancellation.
   c. Foot and cross-foot the check register for one or more periods and trace postings to general ledger.

Note: Auditing procedures in this program generally correspond with the procedures outlined in Appendix 14–G.

Questions for Class Discussion

Q14-1   What financial statement assertions of the client are associated with the acquisitions and expenditures system? How do those assertions relate to the auditor's objectives?

Q14-2   What is the process by which the audit of the acquisitions and expenditures system takes place?

Q14-3   What decisions must the auditor make during the planning stages of the audit concerning the acquisitions and expenditures system? How do those decisions relate to the evidence-gathering process?

Q14-4   Why is the auditor less concerned with internal controls over fixed assets and prepaid expenses than for inventories or trade payables?

Q14-5   What features should be included in a sound control environment over acquisitions and expenditures?

Q14-6   What are the boundary documents typically found in the acquisitions and expenditures system? Relate each to a specific exchange transaction.

Q14-7   What exchange functions are typically found in the acquisitions and expenditures system?

Q14-8   Why is it important to have sequentially numbered purchase orders and to control the use of those documents?

Q14-9   What elements of the control system are designed to protect a company from paying for merchandise it did not receive?

Q14-10   What control attributes should be present to reduce the probability of an improper purchase of fixed assets?

Q14-11   What responsibilities should be segregated in the acquisitions and expenditures system? Why?

Q14-12   How do capital budgeting techniques fit into the control structure for fixed assets?

Q14-13   What errors or irregularities should be prevented by safeguard controls for the acquisitions and expenditures system?

Q14-14   What EDP controls should be present in the system of acquisitions and expenditures?

Q14-15   What is the process that the auditor would follow in assessing the level of control risk that is applicable to the acquisitions and expenditures system? How does that assessment affect the nature, timing, and extent of detection risk procedures to be performed on related financial statement assertions?

Short Cases

C14-1   Paul Mathis, CPA, is performing an examination of the financial statements of Tommy Tucker Plastics, Inc., for the year ended March 31, 19X8. Tommy Tucker Plastics is on Mathis's firm list of "emerging businesses," having just begun to manufacture a single product from a patented process two years ago. Although the past two years for the company have been (in the president's words) "touch and go," the attitude of the twenty employees is positive toward the future. Business has been brisk, and new orders are coming in from the company's thirty customers. However, the company has only one major supplier of raw materials, and demand has sometimes caused stock shortages. The corporation borrowed $1,500,000 for working capital from First Republic Bank last year, pledging inventory and receivables against the note, which bears interest at prime rate plus 2 percent. The note is due at the end of the current year but is renewable, according to the loan officer at the bank. A restriction in the note agreement requires that the company maintain a 1.5 to 1 current ratio and .75 to 1 quick ratio for the term of the note. Results from preliminary analytical procedures, based on unaudited quarterly data, showed that the company had maintained a 1.52 to 1 current ratio, but that quick ratio had fallen to .6 to 1 several times during the past 6 months.

Required:

a. Without considering internal control, at what level (high, medium, or low) should Mathis set inherent risk for cash and trade accounts payable at Tommy Tucker Plastics, Inc.? Justify your response, based on the facts given.

b. Prepare an outline of steps in the audit process for the acquisitions and expenditures system for Tommy Tucker Plastics, Inc., and discuss the strategy that Mathis should take in planning for this part of the engagement.

c. What is the level of understanding Mathis must gain of the control structure of Tommy Tucker Plastics, Inc.? What circumstances would necessitate a deeper understanding than the required level? Do you think Mathis will strive to attain a deeper level of understanding of controls than required? Why or why not?

C14-2   Campus Casuals, a popular clothing store for both male and female students at State University, has hired Heather Simmons, CPA, to perform an initial audit on the store's financial statements for the year ended August 31, 19X8. The purpose of the audit is to qualify the company for a working capital loan from the First State Bank. The store personnel consists of the owner/manager, an assistant manager, two clerks, and a bookkeeper. The principal business of Campus Casuals consists of purchasing several lines of clothing from approximately twenty-five vendors and selling at retail prices to the public. The store has an excellent reputation among students and young professionals in the city and has experienced steady growth since opening two years ago.

Required:

a. Outline the plan that Simmons should follow in understanding the control structure of Campus Casuals.

b. What attributes or characteristics should be present in the system of acquisitions and expenditures for Campus Casuals?

c. Construct the internal control questionnaire that Simmons should use in studying the acquisitions and expenditures system of Campus Casuals.

C14-3   In 19X4 XY Company purchased over $10 million of office equipment under its "special" ordering system, with individual orders ranging from $5,000 to $30,000. "Special" orders entail low-volume items that have been included in an authorized user's budget. Department heads include in their annual budget requests the types of equipment and their estimated cost. The budget, which limits the types and dollar amounts of office equipment a department head can requisition, is approved at the beginning of the year by the board of directors. Department heads prepare a purchase requisition form for equipment and forward the requisition to the purchasing department. XY's "special" ordering system functions as follows:

Purchasing: On receiving a purchase requisition, one of five buyers verifies that the person requesting the equipment is a department head. The buyer then selects the appropriate vendor by searching the various vendor catalogs on file. The buyer then phones the vendor, requesting a price quotation, and gives the vendor a verbal order. A prenumbered purchase order is then processed with the original sent to the vendor, a copy to the department head, a copy to receiving, a copy to accounts payable, and a copy filed in the open requisition file. When the buyer is orally informed by the receiving department that the item has been received, the buyer transfers the purchase order from the unfilled file to the filled file. Once a month the buyer reviews the unfilled file to follow up and expedite open orders.

Receiving: The receiving department receives a copy of the purchase order. When equipment is received the receiving clerk stamps the purchase order with the date received, and, if applicable, in red pen prints any differences between quantity on the purchase order and quantity received. The receiving clerk forwards the stamped purchase order and equipment to the requisitioning department head and orally notifies the purchasing department.

Accounts payable: On receipt of a purchase order, the accounts payable clerk files the purchase order in the open purchase order file. When a vendor invoice is received, the invoice is matched with the applicable purchase order, and a payable is set up by debiting the equipment account of the department requesting the items. Unpaid invoices are filed by due date and, at due date, a check is prepared. The invoice and purchase order are filed by purchase order number in a paid invoice file, and then the check is forwarded to the treasurer for signature.

Treasurer: Checks received daily from the accounts payable department are sorted into two groups: those over $10,000 and those $10,000 and less. Checks for $10,000 and less are machine-signed. The cashier maintains the key and signature plate to the check-signing machine, and maintains a record of usage of the check-signing machine. All checks over $10,000 are signed by the treasurer or the controller.

Required: Describe the internal accounting control weaknesses relating to the purchases and payments of "special" orders of XY Company for each of the following functions:
  a. Purchasing
  b. Receiving
  c. Accounts payable
  d. Treasurer

(AICPA adapted)

C14-4   Questions 1 through 8 below are frequently found in internal control questionnaires used by auditors to obtain an understanding of the control structure over the system of acquisitions and expenditures of a company. A "yes" response to the question indicates a potential strength and a "no" response indicates a potential weakness.
  1. Are prenumbered receiving reports required for all approved purchases?
  2. Is the purchasing function performed by persons who are independent of the receiving, accounting, and cash-handling functions?
  3. Are control totals used in posting routines to vendor accounts?
  4. Are checks signed by persons who are independent from persons who prepared them?
  5. Are all supporting documents required to be canceled on payment of an invoice?

6. Are all checks serially numbered and accounted for?
7. Are all purchase returns required to be approved by a responsible official?
8. Are quantities left blank on the copy of purchase order sent to receiving department?

Required: For each question listed above, state
   a. The internal control characteristic (segregation of responsibilities, comparisons, adequate records, limited access to assets, execution of transactions as authorized) that is embodied.
   b. The test that should be performed in order to test the effectiveness of the control if the answer to the question is "yes."
   c. The financial statement error that the control attribute was designed to detect.
   d. The financial statement assertion that is related to the control attribute listed (existence/occurrence, valuation, completeness, rights/obligations, disclosure).
   e. The substantive test that might need to be expanded on the related assertion if the answer to the question is "no."

C14-5   You have been engaged by the management of Alden, Inc., to review its internal control over the purchase, receipt, storage, and issue of raw materials. You have prepared the following notes to describe Alden's procedures:

Raw materials, which consist mainly of high-cost electronic components, are kept in a locked storeroom. Storeroom personnel include a supervisor and four clerks. All are well trained, competent, and adequately bonded. Raw materials are removed from the storeroom only on written or oral authorization of one of the production supervisors.

There are no perpetual inventory records; hence, the storeroom clerks do not keep records of goods received or issued. To compensate for the lack of perpetual records, a physical inventory count is taken monthly by the storeroom clerks who are well supervised. Appropriate procedures are followed in making the inventory count.

After the physical count, the storeroom supervisor matches quantities counted against a predetermined reorder level. If the count for a given part is below the reorder level, the supervisor enters the part number on a materials-requisition list and sends this list to the accounts-payable clerk. The accounts-payable clerk prepares a purchase order for a predetermined reorder quantity for each part and mails the purchase order to the vendor from whom the part was last purchased.

When ordered materials arrive at Alden, they are received by the storeroom clerks. The clerks count the merchandise and reconcile the counts to the shipper's bill of lading. All vendors' bills of lading are initialed, dated, and filed in the storeroom to serve as receiving reports.

Required: Describe the weaknesses in internal control and recommend improvements of Alden's procedures for the purchase, receipt, storage, and issue of raw materials. Organize your answer sheet as follows:

Weaknesses	Recommended Improvements

C14-6   Items 1 through 4 indicate errors or irregularities that occurred in Redbird Corporation's system of acquisitions and expenditures.
   1. Over a period of months, a clerk in the accounting department prepared a large number of individually small vouchers from a fictitious vendor, using a post office box number as an address. Checks were issued to the fictitious vendor and mailed to the post office box, where they were received by the clerk and cashed.

2. Supplies expense, account number 4204, was incorrectly debited for a charge to repairs and maintenance expense, account number 4240, in the amount of $1,245.
3. The company ordered 3,560 units of raw material from Trent Company at a price of $3.00 per unit, less a 15 percent trade discount. Only 3,160 units were received and placed in inventory. Trent erroneously invoiced Redbird for 3,560 units at $3.00 per unit. The voucher was approved and the check was prepared for the full amount.
4. A clerk in the accounts payable department submitted to the treasurer's department a prepared check and a voucher containing a purchase requisition, purchase order, receiving report, and vendor invoice from Riteway, Inc. After the treasurer's department approved payment and signed the check, it was returned to the clerk. The clerk deposited the check in a fictitious account controlled by him, and resubmitted the documents for payment to Riteway, Inc.

Required: For each error or irregularity listed,
a. Discuss an internal control attribute that would have prevented the error or irregularity.
b. Discuss a test of controls that would verify the effectiveness of the internal control attribute.
c. Discuss a substantive test that would need to be extended to discover the error or irregularity.

Problems

P14-1   Select the best answer for each of the following items relating to internal control within the acquisitions and expenditures system.
a. Sandra Jackson, the purchasing agent of Judd Hardware Wholesalers, has a relative who owns a retail hardware store. Jackson arranged for hardware to be delivered by manufacturers to the retail store on a COD basis, thereby enabling her relative to buy at Judd's wholesale prices. Jackson was probably able to accomplish this because of Judd's poor internal control over
1. Purchase orders.
2. Purchase requisitions.
3. Cash receipts.
4. Perpetual inventory records.
b. Which of the following is a primary function of the purchasing department?
1. Authorizing the acquisition of goods.
2. Ensuring the acquisition of goods of a specified quality.
3. Verifying the propriety of goods acquired.
4. Reducing expenditures for goods acquired.
c. Effective internal control over the purchasing of raw materials should usually include all the following procedures *except*
1. Systematic reporting of product changes that will affect raw materials.
2. Determining the need for the raw materials prior to preparing the purchase order.
3. Obtaining third-party written quality and quantity reports prior to payment for the raw materials.
4. Obtaining financial approval prior to making a commitment.
d. An effective internal accounting control measure that protects against the

preparation of improper or inaccurate disbursements would be to require that all checks be

1. Signed by an officer after necessary supporting evidence has been examined.
2. Reviewed by the treasurer before mailing.
3. Sequentially numbered and accounted for by internal auditors.
4. Perforated or otherwise effectively canceled when they are returned with the bank statement.

e. Based on observations made during an audit, the independent auditor should discuss with management the effectiveness of the company's internal procedures that protect against the purchase of

1. Required supplies provided by a vendor who offers *no* trade or cash discounts.
2. Inventory items acquired based on an economic order quantity (EOQ) inventory management concept.
3. New equipment that is needed but does *not* qualify for special tax treatment.
4. Supplies individually ordered, without considering possible volume discounts.

f. To avoid potential errors and irregularities, a well-designed system of internal accounting control in the accounts payable area should include a separation of which of the following functions?

1. Cash disbursements and invoice verification.
2. Invoice verification and merchandise ordering.
3. Physical handling of merchandise received and preparation of receiving reports.
4. Check signing and cancellation of payment documentation.

g. Which of the following is a standard internal control for cash disbursements?

1. Checks should be signed by the controller and at least one other employee of the company.
2. Checks should be sequentially numbered and the numerical sequence should be accounted for by the person preparing bank reconciliations.
3. Checks and supporting documents should be marked "Paid" immediately after the check is returned with the bank statement.
4. Checks should be sent directly to the payee by the employee who prepares documents that authorize check preparation.

h. Which of the following is an effective internal control measure that encourages receiving department personnel to count and inspect all merchandise received?

1. Quantities ordered are excluded from the receiving department copy of the purchase order.
2. Vouchers are prepared by accounts-payable department personnel only after they match item counts on the receiving report with the purchase order.
3. Receiving department personnel are expected to match and reconcile the receiving report with the purchase order.
4. Internal auditors periodically examine, on a surprise basis, the receiving department copies of receiving reports.

i. A good system of internal control over purchases will give proper evaluation to the time for ordering merchandise. When making this evaluation, the purchasing company should give primary consideration to

1. The price differences that exist between various vendors who will supply the merchandise at the required time.
2. The borrowing cost of money (interest), which the company must incur as a consequence of acquiring the merchandise.
3. The trade-off between the cost of owning and storing excess merchandise and the risk of loss by *not* having merchandise on hand.

    4. The flow of funds within the company, which indicates when money is available to pay for merchandise.

j. To strengthen the system of internal control over the purchase of merchandise, a company's receiving department should

    1. Accept merchandise only if a purchase order or approval granted by the purchasing department is on hand.

    2. Accept and count all merchandise received from the usual company vendors.

    3. Rely on shipping documents for the preparation of receiving reports.

    4. Be responsible for the physical handling of merchandise but *not* the preparation of receiving reports.

k. A client's materials-purchasing cycle begins with requisitions from user departments and ends with the receipt of materials and the recognition of a liability. An auditor's primary objective in reviewing this cycle is to

    1. Evaluate the reliability of information generated as a result of the purchasing process.

    2. Investigate the physical handling and recording of unusual acquisitions of materials.

    3. Consider the need to be on hand for the annual physical count if this system is *not* functioning properly.

    4. Ascertain that materials said to be ordered, received, and paid for are on hand.

l. Which of the following is an internal control procedure that would prevent a paid disbursement voucher from being presented for payment a second time?

    1. Vouchers should be prepared by individuals who are responsible for signing disbursement checks.

    2. Disbursement vouchers should be approved by at least two responsible management officials.

    3. The date on a disbursement voucher should be within a few days of the date the voucher is presented for payment.

    4. The official signing the check should compare the check with the voucher and should deface the voucher documents.

m. Which of the following is an effective internal control over cash payments?

    1. Signed checks should be mailed under the supervision of the check signer.

    2. Spoiled checks that have been voided should be disposed of immediately.

    3. Checks should be prepared only by persons responsible for cash receipts and cash disbursements.

    4. A check-signing machine with two signatures should be utilized.

n. When there are few property and equipment transactions during the year, the continuing auditor usually makes a

    1. Complete review of the related internal controls and performs compliance tests of those controls being relied upon.

    2. Complete review of the related internal controls and performs analytical review tests to verify current year additions to property and equipment.

    3. Preliminary review of the related internal controls and performs a thorough examination of the balances at the beginning of the year.

    4. Preliminary review of the related internal controls and performs extensive tests of current year property and equipment transactions.

o. Property acquisitions that are misclassified as maintenance expense would most likely be detected by an internal control system that provides for

    1. Investigation of variances within a formal budgeting system.

    2. Review and approval of the monthly depreciation entry by the plant supervisor.

3. Segregation of duties of employees in the accounts payable department.
4. Examination by the internal auditor of vendor invoices and canceled checks for property acquisitions.

(AICPA adapted)

P14-2 Properly designed and utilized forms facilitate adherence to prescribed internal control policies and procedures. One such form might be a multicopy purchase order, with one copy intended to be mailed to the vendor. The remaining copies would ordinarily be distributed to the stores, purchasing, receiving, and accounting departments.

The following purchase order is currently being used by National Industrial Corporation:

PURCHASE ORDER

SEND INVOICE ONLY TO:

297 Hardingten Dr., Bx., NY 10461

TO _____   SHIP TO _____

_____   _____

_____   _____

Date to be shipped	Ship via	Disc. terms	Freight terms	Adv. allowance	Special allowance
Quantity		Description			

PURCHASE CONDITIONS

1. Supplier will be responsible for extra freight cost on partial shipment, unless prior permission is obtained.

2. Please acknowledge this order.

3. Please notify us immediately if you are unable to complete order.

4. All items must be individually packed.

Required:
- a. In addition to the name of the company, what other necessary information would an auditor recommend be included in the illustrative purchase order?
- b. What primary internal control functions are served by the purchase order copies that are distributed to the stores, purchasing, receiving, and accounting departments?

(AICPA adapted)

P14-3 Brown, CPA, has been engaged to audit the financial statements of Star Manufacturing, Inc. Star is a medium-sized company that produces a wide variety of household goods. All acquisitions of materials are processed through the purchasing, receiving, accounts payable, and treasury functions.

Required: Prepare the following segments of the internal accounting control questionnaire to be used in obtaining an understanding of Star's internal accounting control structure. Each question should elicit either a "yes" or a "no" response.
- a. Purchases
- b. Receiving
- c. Accounts payable
- d. Treasury

(AICPA adapted)

P14-4 Tralor Corporation manufactures and sells several different lines of small electric components. Its Internal Audit Department completed an audit of the expenditure cycle for the company. Part of the audit involved a review of the internal controls for payables including the controls over the authorization of transactions, the accounting for transactions, and the protection of assets. The following comments appear in the internal audit staff's working papers.
1. Routine purchases are initiated by user activities on authorized purchase requests. Such purchases are actually made by the Purchasing Department using prenumbered purchase orders approved by authorized purchasing agents. The original of the five-part purchase order goes to the vendor, a copy is retained in Purchasing, a copy is sent to the user department, a copy is sent to the Receiving Department to be used as a receiving report, and a copy is sent to the accounts payable section of the Accounting Department.
2. Because of complex technical and performance criteria, purchases of specialized goods and services are negotiated directly between the user department and the vendor. Established procedures require that the specialist-user and the Purchasing Department approve invoices for such purchases prior to recording and payment. Strict budgetary control of such purchases is maintained at the specialist-user level.
3. The accounts payable section maintains a list of persons in Purchasing authorized to approve purchase orders and of persons in operating departments authorized to approve invoices for specialized purchases. The list was last updated two years ago and is seldom used by accounts payable clerks.
4. All vendor invoices are numbered upon receipt and recorded in a pre-voucher register. The register is annotated to indicate the dates invoices involving special purchases are forwarded to operating departments for approval, and the dates they are returned. Review of the register indicated that there were seven open invoices for

special purchases which had been forwarded to operating departments for approval over thirty days ago and had not yet been returned.

5. Prior to making entries in accounting records, a transaction audit is performed by an accounts-payable clerk. This involves matching the accounts payable copy of the purchase order with a copy of a properly authorized receiving report and the vendor's invoice, or obtaining departmental approval of invoices for special purchases. Other aspects of the transaction audit involve checking the mathematical accuracy of all documents and determining the appropriate accounting distribution.

6. After invoices are recorded in the approved voucher register, they are filed in alphabetical order. Unpaid invoices are processed for payment on the 5th and 20th of each month, and all cash discounts are taken whether or not earned.

7. Supporting documents are cancelled upon payment by an authorized person in the treasurer function who signs the checks. Payments are made based upon original documents only.

8. Pre-numbered blank checks are kept in a locked safe and access is limited to authorized persons. Other documents and records maintained by the accounts payable section are readily accessible to all persons assigned to the section and to others in the accounting function.

Required: Review the eight comments that appear in the internal audit staff's working papers. Determine whether the internal audit staff's findings indicate that a strength or weakness exists in the controls of the expenditure cycle.

1. For each internal control **strength** identified, explain how the described procedure contributes toward achieving good authorization, accounting, or asset protection controls.

2. For each internal control **weakness** identified, explain why it is a weakness and present a recommendation to correct the weakness.

Use the following format to present your answer.

Comment number	Strength(s) or weakness(es)	Explanation as to why finding is a strength or weakness	Recommendation to correct weakness

(Adapted from CMA Examination)

P14-5 Anthony, CPA, prepared the accompanying flowchart, which portrays the raw materials purchasing function of one of Anthony's clients, a medium-sized manufacturing company, from the preparation of initial documents through the vouching of invoices for payment in accounts payable. The flowchart was a portion of the work performed on the audit engagement to evaluate internal control.

Required: Identify and explain the systems and control weaknesses evident from the flowchart. Include the internal control weaknesses resulting from activities performed or not performed. All documents are prenumbered.

MEDIUM-SIZED MANUFACTURING CO.
RAW MATERIALS PURCHASING FUNCTION

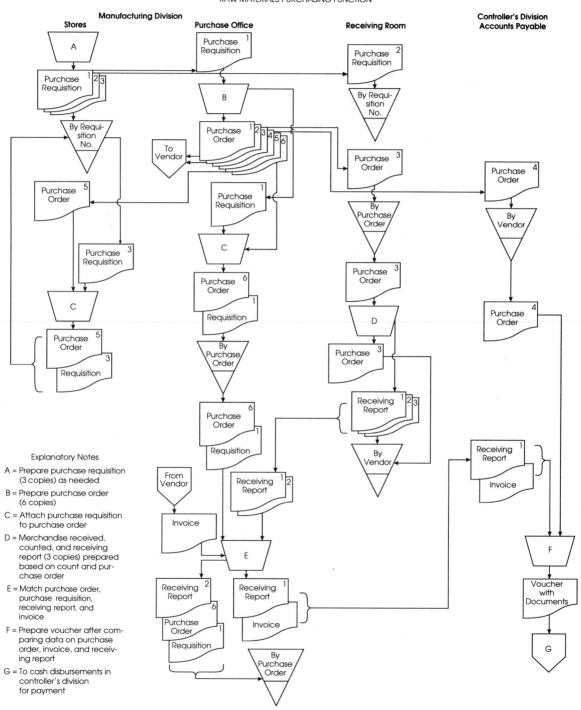

Explanatory Notes

A = Prepare purchase requisition
(3 copies) as needed

B = Prepare purchase order
(6 copies)

C = Attach purchase requisition
to purchase order

D = Merchandise received,
counted, and receiving
report (3 copies) prepared
based on count and pur-
chase order

E = Match purchase order,
purchase requisition,
receiving report, and
invoice

F = Prepare voucher after comparing data on purchase
order, invoice, and receiving report

G = To cash disbursements in
controller's division
for payment

P14-6   Dunbar Camera Manufacturing, Inc., is a manufacturer of high-priced precision motion picture cameras in which the specifications of component parts are vital to the manufacturing process. Dunbar buys valuable camera lenses and large quantities of sheetmetal and screws. Screws and lenses are ordered by Dunbar and are billed by the vendors on a unit basis. Sheetmetal is ordered by Dunbar and is billed by the vendors on the basis of weight. The receiving clerk is responsible for documenting the quality and quantity of merchandise received.

A preliminary review of the system of internal control indicates that the following procedures are being followed:

1. *Receiving Report*:   Properly approved purchase orders, which are prenumbered, are filed numerically. The copy sent to the receiving clerk is an exact duplicate of the copy sent to the vendor. Receipts of merchandise are recorded on the duplicate copy by the receiving clerk.
2. *Sheetmetal*:   The company receives sheetmetal by railroad. The railroad independently weighs the sheetmetal and reports the weight and date of receipt on a bill of lading (waybill), which accompanies all deliveries. The receiving clerk only checks the weight on the waybill to the purchase order.
3. *Screws*:   The receiving clerk opens cartons containing screws, then inspects and weighs the contents. The weight is converted to number of units by means of conversion charts. The receiving clerk then checks the computed quantity to the purchase order.
4. *Camera lenses*:   Each camera lens is delivered in a separate corrugated carton. Cartons are counted as they are received by the receiving clerk and the number of cartons are checked to purchase orders.

Required:

a. Explain why the internal control procedures as they apply individually to receiving reports and the receipt of sheetmetal, screws, and camera lenses are adequate or inadequate. *Do not discuss recommendations for improvements.*
b. What financial statement distortions may arise because of the inadequacies in Dunbar's system of internal control and how may they occur?

(AICPA adapted)

P14-7   Items (a) through (j) are internal control questions designed to be used in the audit of property and equipment. A "yes" answer to such a question would indicate a potential strength in the system, while a "no" answer indicates a potential weakness.

a. Are review and approval required by responsible officials for all major property and equipment purchases and disposals?
b. Are capital budgeting techniques required before the decision is made to purchase new property and equipment?
c. Are all purchases of movable fixed assets required to be made through the same purchasing channels as all other cash disbursements?
d. Are all fixed asset disposals required to go through the same channels and cash receipts controls as sales of inventory?
e. Is a work order system required for all property and equipment purchases and sales, as well as repair and maintenance?
f. Does the company have a capitalization policy for fixed assets that allows for proper recording of assets and expenses?

g. Are periodic reconciliations made between fixed assets detail records and general ledger control accounts for fixed assets and depreciation?

h. Are all lease agreements reviewed by a responsible official prior to being recorded?

i. Is periodic review of the depreciation records performed by supervisory personnel?

j. Is the company required to maintain adequate fire and casualty insurance coverage?

Required: For each question (a) through (j), indicate

a. The error or irregularity, if any, which that control attribute is designed to prevent, detect, or correct.

b. The possible effect on the financial statements if that control attribute were missing.

c. The test of controls that would be performed if the answer to the question were "yes" (indicating a potential strength in the system). If inspection of documents is appropriate, indicate the file from which the sample of documents would be selected and the file to which the sample would be vouched or traced.

d. Whether the test mentioned in (c) is also a substantive test.

e. The substantive test that would need to be expanded if the answer to the question is "no" (indicating a potential weakness in internal control).

Use the following format for your answer. The first item has been answered as a model.

Item	Error or irregularity	Effect on financial statements	Test of controls	Also a substantive test?	Expansion of substantive test
(a)	Invalid transaction	Misappropriation of cash and fixed assets	Inspection of documents: vouch a sample of property and equipment additions to supporting documentation and approval per board of directors' minutes	Yes	Same as test of controls

P14-8   For each error or irregularity in property, equipment, and depreciation, name the internal control attribute that, if prescribed by the client, would prevent, detect, or correct it.

a. Repairs and maintenance expense has been much higher this year than in the past three years. Analysis of the account reveals charges that should have been capitalized.

b. The purchasing agent purchased a large amount of small tools for his own use and caused the company to pay for them.

c. The depreciation expense program for computer-maintained fixed assets records does not allow for appropriate cost recovery, according to the most recent Internal Revenue Service regulations.

d. The computer programmer, writing the program for fixed asset retirements, caused "net book value" to be removed from the "cost" category and failed to remove accumulated depreciation from the records for all retirements.

e. A lease that should have been capitalized was recorded as a month-to-month lease.

f. The company is still using in everyday operations property and equipment that were fully depreciated five years ago.

g. In reviewing computerized records for property and equipment, you find that a number of individual assets have been depreciated to negative carrying values (accumulated depreciation exceeds cost).

    h. Printout of computer-prepared depreciation records reveals nonsensical information in important data fields.

    i. Computerized fixed-asset ledger detail does not agree with computer-prepared general ledger totals for property and equipment and accumulated depreciation.

P14-9   Items (a) through (g) are questions excerpted from a typical internal control questionnaire for the purpose of evaluating internal controls over the accounting for purchases, accounts payable, and inventory. As explained in the text, a "yes" response indicates a potential strength in the system while a "no" response indicates a potential weakness.

    a. Is the preparation of initial purchase records performed by persons who do not also prepare purchase requisitions, sign checks, and otherwise handle cash?

    b. Is proper documentation (in the form of purchase orders, receiving reports, purchase requisitions, and vendor invoices) required before vouchers are prepared?

    c. Are supporting records (purchase orders, receiving reports, etc.) compared to vendor invoices for prices, quantities, terms, etc., before vouchers are approved for payment?

    d. Are subsidiary records maintained of trade payables by persons independent of cash disbursements and purchasing functions?

    e. Are recorded cash disbursements matched individually or adequately tested against initial credits in the subsidiary accounts-payable records?

    f. Are perpetual records maintained over quantities and unit prices for all material inventory items?

    g. Are perpetual records of inventories periodically reconciled with physical counts and with general ledger account totals?

Required: For each question above, list:

    a. The error or irregularity that the control attribute was designed to detect.

    b. The effect that the absence of the control attribute could have on the financial statements.

    c. The test that would be necessary to ascertain whether the control were actually being implemented if the answer to the internal control question were "yes." When sampling of documents is involved, indicate the data file from which a sample would be selected and the auditing procedure (e.g., vouching, tracing, recalculation, etc.) most appropriate for the sample.

CHAPTER 15

The Audit of Selected Accounts in the Acquisitions and Expenditures System

Objectives

☐ **1.** Perform detection risk procedures for fixed assets.
☐ **2.** Perform detection risk procedures for accounts and trade notes payable.
☐ **3.** Perform detection risk procedures for prepaid items.
☐ **4.** Perform detection risk procedures for accrued liabilities.
☐ **5.** Perform detection risk procedures for operating expenses.

In this chapter we continue our discussion of the acquisitions and expenditures system. The sole learning objective for you is to be able to perform the detection risk procedures which are typically performed in order to verify the assertions of management that are embodied in the financial statements. As stated in Chapter 14, the audit objectives derived from management's assertions include verification of

1. Transaction validity, existence, and occurrence.
2. Ownership rights for assets; obligation for liabilities.
3. Proper cutoff (allocation).
4. Valuation.
5. Completeness.
6. Proper statement presentation or disclosure.

Our discussion will focus on the audit of the following account balances: (1) fixed assets, (2) accounts and trade notes payable, (3) prepaid expenses, (4) accrued liabilities, and (5) selected operating expense accounts.

Fixed Assets

☑ **Objective 1**
Be able to perform
detection risk
procedures for
fixed assets

As we observed in Chapter 14, as a general rule, most clients will have only a limited number of fixed-asset-related transactions during each fiscal period. Therefore, after the initial audit—during which the auditor should verify the existence, ownership, cutoff, valuation, and statement presentation for all fixed tangible assets held by the client—the auditor will be concerned primarily with verifying *acquisitions and disposals during the period.* The evidence relating to those transactions is typically incorporated into an analysis-type working paper similar to the working paper shown in Appendix 15–A. As you can see, that working paper is organized around the basic four-element equation, which reconciles the beginning-of-period balances for each of the various types of fixed assets with acquisitions, disposals, and end-of-period balances. Similar information is also shown for accumulated depreciation. The tick-mark legend for fixed assets is contained in Appendix 15–C.

Figure 15–1 shows us that the auditor begins the *substantive verification* of fixed assets by reconciling the amounts shown on the balance sheet with the data in the underlying accounting records. Again, the statement amount should be vouched to the ledger account, and the balance in the ledger account should be recomputed. Furthermore, the trial balance of the fixed-asset subsidiary ledgers should be reconciled with their respective control accounts.

Verifying Acquisitions and Disposals

Verification of Existence. After the statement amounts have been reconciled with the underlying accounting records, the auditor will next verify the existence of the assets. In doing this, he or she will be primarily concerned with inspecting records of major assets acquired during the year. All or a sample of the fixed assets acquired should be selected from the fixed-asset subsidiary ledger; the auditor should then list these items (by location, if possible) and then observe these assets in the plant. Each major fixed asset will normally be assigned an equipment identification number when it is purchased. That number should be recorded in the accounting records and stamped or printed on the machine to identify it specifically.

The auditor may also, on touring the plant during physical inventory observation, select a sample of fixed assets and trace them into the subsidiary ledger to ascertain that they were recorded properly.

Verification of Ownership. The verification of ownership is important in the audit of fixed assets. In recent years it has become even more important because of the extensive use of leased assets. As shown in Appendix 15–B, the auditor should begin by inspecting the documents underlying acquisitions and retirements during the year. He or she should also inquire about possible liens on fixed assets. Furthermore, the accounting records should be inspected for evidence of rental payments, which might indicate that an asset was actually leased

Audit Objectives

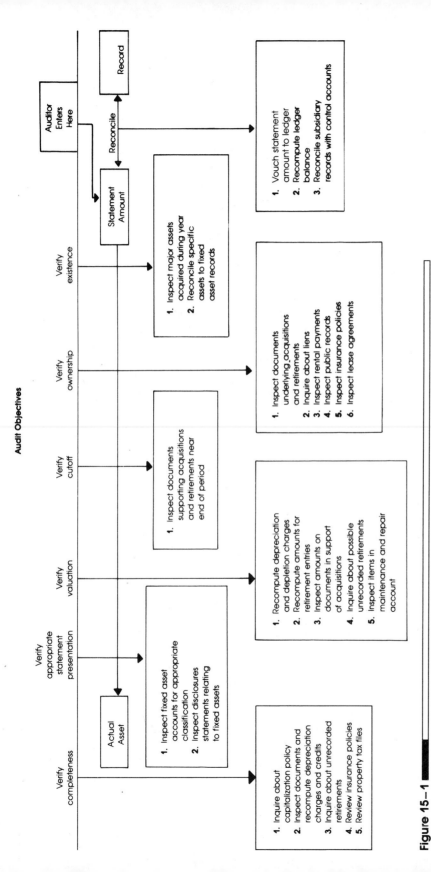

Figure 15–1 Flowchart for Substantive Tests of Fixed Assets

647

rather than owned. In the case of land, the auditor may want to inspect the public records or tax records to verify ownership. Paid real estate tax receipts also provide good evidence of ownership. As a general rule, the auditor will also inspect insurance policies in the process of meeting this audit objective, with the expectation that all owned assets will be insured.

As we observed in the preceding paragraph, present-day business practices often call for fixed assets to be leased on a long-term basis. FASB 13 requires that those leases, which are in substance installment purchases, should be recognized as asset acquisitions with both the fixed asset and the related obligation being shown in the balance sheet. Therefore, if the client is using leased assets, it is important for the auditor to *inspect and analyze all lease agreements to determine whether they should be recognized as fixed assets or treated as normal operating leases.*

Verification of Cutoff (Allocation). The verification of cutoff is less important for fixed asset transactions than it is for transactions involving current assets. Nevertheless, an improper cutoff of a transaction involving cash and fixed assets can cause both fixed assets and current assets to be misstated. Fixed asset transactions that involve the incurrence of long-term debt and that are recorded in the wrong period can also cause both fixed assets and noncurrent liabilities to be misstated. In addition, depreciation can be improperly recorded or omitted from the company's records for some assets. Therefore, the auditor normally will give some attention to inspecting the underlying documents relating to acquisitions and retirements occurring near the end of the year to determine whether they have been recorded in the appropriate fiscal period. Also, depreciation expense should be recalculated to ensure that it was recorded in the proper period.

Verification of Valuation. The verification of valuation is another important objective to be met in the audit of fixed assets. In meeting this audit objective, the auditor is primarily concerned with inspecting documents supporting acquisitions and retirements. Valuations assigned to assets acquired by exchange should be in accordance with the provisions of APB 29. Such transactions are also often between related parties and thus require special attention. In the case of depreciable assets, the valuation audit objective also requires verification of the valuation base for the asset and recomputation of depreciation expense. The working paper in Appendix 15–D illustrates audit work performed on accumulated depreciation and depreciation expense. This auditing procedure also extends to the recomputation of depletion of wasting assets.

In *inspecting* the documents underlying fixed asset acquisitions, it is important for the auditor to verify that these acquisitions have been recorded at cost. In the verification of the valuations of capitalized leases, cost is defined as the present value of lease payments. Since this procedure involves using an imputed interest rate, the auditor must evaluate the propriety of the rate used.

In verifying valuation, the auditor must also be satisfied that the client has appropriately distinguished between assets and expenses in accounting for fixed-asset-related transactions. Maintenance and repair accounts include fixed-asset-related expenditures. Therefore, it is important for the auditor to inspect the larger entries in those accounts and to vouch them to supporting documents for the purpose of discovering expenditures that should have been capitalized rather than charged to expense. In the process of making this inspection, the auditor will also be developing substantive evidence to support the balance in the maintenance and repairs expense accounts. Construction work orders issued during the year should be examined to learn of *possible erroneous capitalizations of expenditures*. Also, as the auditor is inspecting fixed asset acquisitions, she or he will also be concerned with determining whether they should be expensed rather than capitalized. The auditor should be concerned about the possibility that assets have not been adequately maintained, and she or he relies on observations during the plant tour and conferences with the plant manager to judge whether or not provisions should be made for deferred maintenance.

Completeness. The auditor must be alert for items included as asset acquisitions that should have been charged to maintenance and repairs expense. He or she should inspect the documents and recompute the amounts credited to fixed assets and debited to accumulated depreciation in connection with the retirements of fixed assets. In so doing, it is important for the auditor to inquire about possible unrecorded retirements, particularly if the control structure is such that retirements could be accomplished without an entry in the accounting records. That could occur, for example, if the client does not require appropriate authorization and approval actions prior to the retirement of each fixed asset. The auditor may learn of retirements of equipment by reviewing depreciation charges, analyzing debits to accumulated depreciation, and reviewing insurance policy changes. Unrecorded disposals can also be discovered by reviewing the property tax files and scanning invoices for fixed asset additions. In that process the auditor is trying to determine whether assets retired are being replaced.

Verification of Appropriate Statement Presentation. The appropriate statement presentation for fixed assets requires that they be shown in the noncurrent section of the balance sheet at their acquisition costs, offset by accumulated depreciation or depletion. Fully depreciated assets should be disclosed separately. Depletable assets may be shown net of accumulated depletion. It is also desirable to have the financial statements include a parenthetical or footnote disclosure of the method(s) of depreciation used by the client. In achieving this objective, the auditor will be inspecting the fixed asset elements of the balance sheet to see that those items are appropriately presented.

Using the Computer in Auditing Fixed Assets

When fixed assets and depreciation records are maintained on machine-readable media, the auditor can utilize computer audit software to perform many of the auditing procedures on the systems and accounts discussed in the previous section. Both tests of controls and substantive tests may be performed by using the computer. *Tests of controls* may be performed by use of test data, parallel simulation, or some of the other approaches discussed earlier in the text.

Assuming that detailed fixed-asset records, including all the information specified earlier, are kept on magnetic tape files, the *substantive auditing procedures*

Figure 15–2 ▬▬

Use of Computer Audit Software for Substantive Auditing Procedures

Audit objective	Auditing procedure
Existence	Selecting sample from detail records for observation
	Sorting the sample by plant location
	Printing sample items
Ownership; transaction validity	Printing vendor information for use in vouching purchases to vendor invoices
	Printing out lease information for use in determining proper capitalization
Cutoff	Scanning and printing from vendor files for last receiving reports so that underlying documents may be examined
Valuation	Recomputing footings for the subsidiary ledger showing cost, accumulated depreciation, and depreciation expense, and comparing the total with control accounts
	Scanning the file to identify fully depreciated items, and printing results so that they can be discussed with the client

shown in Figure 15–2 can be performed by the computer, with appropriate audit software.

Accounts and Trade Notes Payable

☑ **Objective 2**
Be able to perform detection risk procedures for accounts and trade notes payable.

The relationships between the audit objectives for accounts payable and the procedures used to meet those objectives are shown in Figure 15–3. The working papers that illustrate the performance of these procedures are contained in Appendixes 15–E and 15–F. Audit objectives for trade notes payable are similar to those of accounts payable and will be discussed along with related audit procedures.

We begin our verification of payables by reconciling the financial statement balance with the underlying accounting records. This involves vouching the financial statement amount to the general ledger account, recomputing (on a test basis) the totals of the purchases and cash disbursements journals, recomputing ledger account balances, and reconciling control accounts with the appropriate subsidiary records.

Verification of Existence, Completeness, and Valuation

To verify the assertion of existence for trade payables, the auditor generally performs tests for *overstatement.* To verify the assertion of completeness, the auditor must perform tests for *understatement.* Each of these tests helps the auditor to verify proper monetary valuation of trade payables.

As stated in Chapter 6, tests for overstatement typically begin by taking samples of recorded transactions or balances and *vouching* for them either by

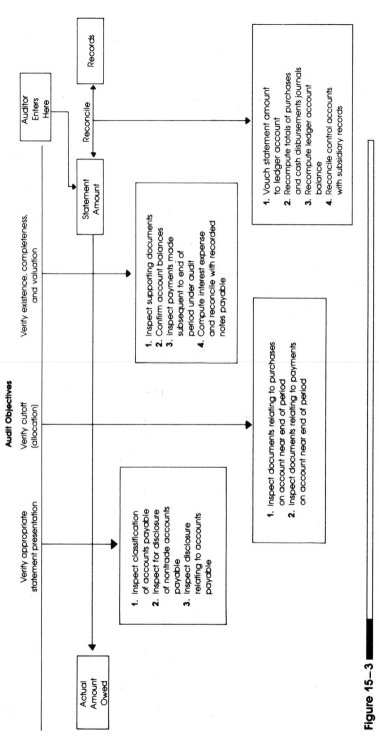

Figure 15–3

Flowchart for Substantive Tests of Accounts Payable

confirmation or inspection of documents. The working paper illustrated in Appendix 15–E shows that a sample of balances from recorded trade accounts payable has been *confirmed* with vendors. Confirmation of trade payables can also consist of requesting copies of year-end statements from vendors and reconciling the details of those statements with the client's year-end balances of accounts payable. Short-term notes payable, including those with banks, are typically confirmed with the lenders, along with interest rates, terms of repayment, due dates, and collateral.

Although confirmation is considered a very effective audit procedure, it is often not considered as necessary to ascertain the existence and proper valuation of recorded payables as it is for receivables. The reason for this can be discovered by comparing the underlying documentary evidence for accounts and notes receivable with that of accounts and notes payable. The primary source documents for an account or trade note receivable are sales invoices and internally generated note agreements. Such documents are often relatively easy to fabricate. Thus, they are not considered highly competent evidence (see Chapter 5). On the other hand, the source documents for tests of transactions for accounts payable are vendor invoices and canceled checks. For notes payable the source documents are externally generated note agreements. These documents are considered very competent. Furthermore, inspection of documentary evidence on file with the client is often less costly than confirmation, making it the preferred procedure in many cases.

In ascertaining *completeness* of recorded payables, the auditor typically performs tests of understatement. As stated in Chapter 6, tests for understatement begin by selecting samples of documentary support for transactions and tracing them into the accounting records. One of the most effective procedures for discovering unrecorded or understated payables is the inspection of payments made subsequent to the end of the period under audit. This process is called the *search for unrecorded liabilities*. It allows the auditor the benefit of hindsight in identifying and valuing the liabilities outstanding at the end of the period. It is also helpful in the verification of *cutoff*.

As illustrated in Appendix 15–F, the search for unrecorded accounts payable typically begins in the cash disbursements journal subsequent to the end of the year under audit. Using a predetermined materiality threshold, the auditor selects a sample of canceled checks indicating payments on account. The underlying support for these payments is located (vendor invoices, purchase orders, receiving reports). In the case of merchandise or raw materials inventory, the date on the receiving report is examined. If that date predates the end of the year, the vendor invoice should be included in accounts payable, since the inventory was on hand and was likely included in client counts. In the case of services, the date of the invoice is controlling. Invoices paid subsequent to year-end that predate the end of the year should also be included in accounts payable. After examining canceled checks, the auditor typically completes the search for unrecorded liabilities by examining unmatched receiving report files and unpaid vendor invoice files, performing the same procedures for those documents as performed on the paid items discussed above.

In searching for unrecorded notes payable, the auditor typically analyzes the interest expense account for the period under audit and vouches each entry in the account to the underlying note documents. Charges to interest expense not supported by underlying notes payable signal an unrecorded note payable.

Statement Presentation (Disclosure)

Verification of appropriate statement presentation requires procedures to ascertain that all existing trade payables are properly disclosed at their materially correct values. The verification of proper statement presentation requires the auditor to inspect the classifications of payables in the balance sheet to see that a proper distinction has been made between trade and nontrade (employee, etc.) payables and between current and noncurrent items. In the case of trade notes payable, details of all material notes should be disclosed, including interest rates, due dates, and client collateral pledged as security. Disclosures (including financial statement footnotes) relating to trade payables should be read for accuracy and clarity.

A letter of representation, including client assertions relating to completeness of payables, should be obtained by the auditor to remind management that the primary responsibility for overall fairness of presentation of these items rests with them.

Prepaid Expenses

☑ **Objective 3**
Be able to perform detection risk procedures for prepaid items.

Prepaid expenses may include such items as prepaid rent, prepaid taxes, and other deferred charges. The inclusion of prepaid expenses among assets results more from the operation of the matching concept than from their intrinsic value. In most audits, the amounts shown for prepaid expenses will be relatively immaterial and, therefore, will require only a limited amount of the auditor's attention. Also, as explained earlier, little attention is usually given to the assessment of control risk associated with these items. We will confine our discussion to the audit of prepaid insurance, which is very similar to that of all other such items.

The major audit objectives for prepaid insurance are verification of existence, proper valuation, cutoff, and financial statement presentation. A working paper that illustrates the audit procedures typically performed to verify these objectives is contained in Appendix 15–G.

The auditor generally begins the audit of prepaid insurance by inspecting and listing the fire and casualty insurance policies in existence as of the end of the period being audited. In the process of listing those policies, it is important for the auditor to relate them to the specific assets covered by each of the policies, to help evaluate the adequacy of the client's insurance coverage. Details of insurance policies in force will often be confirmed with the client's insurance agent. Such details include the insuring company, policy number, type of coverage, amount of premium, and period covered by the premium. Using this information, the auditor also will recompute the amount of prepaid insurance and the premiums expired during the year as part of the verification of both insurance expense and prepaid insurance accounts. Both of these account balances can be reconciled to premium payments for the period by using the following four-element equation:

Beginning balance + payments − expense = ending balance

As illustrated in Appendix 15–G, the beginning balance is usually verified by vouching to the ending balance from the prior year's audited working papers. Premiums paid are vouched to cash disbursements. Insurance expense is re-calculated based on the term of the policy and the elapsed time during the audit period. By providing this type of analysis, the auditor is, in effect, providing substantive evidence in verification of both prepaid insurance and insurance expense.

Accrued Liabilities

☑ **Objective 4**
Be able to perform detection risk procedures for accrued liabilities

Accrued liabilities are estimated obligations of the company that arise through accounting recognition of unpaid costs due to past services received, past contractual commitments, or operation of the tax laws. Payments of accrued liabilities arise in the expenditure system, which explains their inclusion in this part of the text. The *matching concept* of accounting requires that expenses incurred but which remain unpaid as of the end of an accounting period be estimated and recognized in the financial statements. Examples of accrued liabilities are

- Accrued salaries and wages (covered in Chapter 16).
- Accrued commissions.
- Accrued income taxes.
- Other accrued taxes, such as franchise or sales taxes.
- Accrued pension costs.
- Accrued professional fees.
- Accrued rent.
- Accrued warranty costs.

Often accrued liabilities are aggregated and reported as a lump-sum on the financial statements, because the individual accounts are immaterial.

The audit objectives for accrued liabilities include existence, verification of transaction validity, completeness (including proper cutoff), valuation, and financial statement presentation.

The audit work performed on accrued property taxes is illustrated in Appendix 15–H. As illustrated on the working paper, there is an inverse relationship between the accrued liability account and the prepaid account. The disbursements for prepaids and accruals can be viewed as taking place at the opposite ends of the expenditure cycle. The audit procedures for verification of accrued liabilities are very similar to those performed for prepaid expenses. Notice that the working paper is prepared in the *analysis* format. Thus, it has columns for beginning balance, additions, retirements, and ending balance.

The *existence* and proper *valuation* of the liability account is generally verified by inspecting the documents that produced the liability. In the case of accrued property taxes payable, the property tax receipts are inspected and the details are agreed to the client's computational working paper. Agreement of the beginning balance for each property tax account to the ending balance per the prior year's audited working papers also provides evidence that the liability or prepaid amount exists and that it is properly valued.

Proper *transaction validity* for accrued liabilities is verified by recomputing the expense, based on the details of the supporting documentation (in this case, the property tax receipts). In addition, the auditor inspects the underlying documentation for cash disbursement transactions by vouching the entries in the general ledger to the cash disbursements journals and to canceled checks.

Verification of *completeness* for accrued liabilities involves performance of tests of *understatement,* much like those performed for accounts payable. Thus, the auditor's tests for completeness of accrued liabilities are generally performed as a part of the *search for unrecorded liabilities* discussed earlier in this chapter.

Verification of appropriate *statement presentation* for accrued liabilities involves comparisons of current-year accruals and related expenses with those for the prior year for reasonableness. Since, in many cases, accrued expenses tend to be based on the passage of time, the auditor's best estimate of the balance in one of these accounts is often the balance per the prior year's audited working papers. In addition, the auditor should spend time reading the financial statements, including the footnotes, for appropriate disclosures. In this regard, the auditor should pay particular attention to prescribed disclosure policies of the Financial Accounting Standards Board and other authoritative bodies. Examples of FASB pronouncements that apply in the area of accrued liabilities include FASB Statement No. 5, "Accounting for Contingencies" (discussed in Chapter 20) and FASB Statement No. 87, "Employers' Accounting for Pension Plans." In both of these instances, the auditor must rely on evidence provided by specialists, such as attorneys and actuaries, to make decisions as to adequacy of disclosure.

Operating Expenses

☑ **Objective 5**
Be able to perform detection risk procedures for operating expenses

An extremely important result of the acquisitions and expenditures system is the generation of a multitude of operating expense accounts. The fairness of presentation of these accounts is of critical importance to investors and potential investors, whose primary use of the financial statements necessitates an accurate measurement of income.

Due to their interrelationship with asset and liability accounts, the audit of operating expenses related to those accounts is often performed simultaneously with *tests of transactions.* Examples included in this chapter are depreciation expense, insurance expense, and property tax expense. However, other tests are typically performed on these account balances to assure that the assertions embodied in them are a fair representation of the true operating results of the entity and that revenues have been appropriately matched with expenses. These tests include *analytical procedures* and *detailed analysis of account balances*.

Analytical Procedures

Recall that in Chapter 7 we defined analytical procedures as comparisons of recorded amounts on the company's financial statements to *expectations* developed by the auditor from various sources. Financial data, and particularly income statement data, can be expected to conform to rather predictable patterns over time. During the audit of the financial statements, analytical procedures may be used as *corroborative tests* to other substantive tests of balances or details, to detect particular errors or irregularities in the financial statements. For example, the commissions expense account for the current year might be compared with that of the prior year. If sales have increased by 10 percent, and if commissions are based on sales, commissions expense might be expected to increase by 10 percent. If the commissions expense account has increased by, say, 20 percent, the auditor might expect an error to have occurred in the account.

Gross margin percentages and inventory turnover ratios might be compared with prior years to detect misstatements of cost of goods sold. Individual expense accounts might be compared with budgets. If budgets are properly prepared, then unexplained variations from those figures might represent undetected errors in the accounts. Nonfinancial data might be used to develop expectations in balances of expense accounts as well. For example, if the auditor learned during the audit of property and equipment that the amount of square footage in the plant had doubled over the past year, he or she might reasonably expect the utilities expense for the year to have approximately doubled as well, if similar equipment and capacity were utilized in both the new and existing facilities.

Analytical procedures for expenses are typically performed by examining year-to-year fluctuations between expense account balances on the financial statements. If fluctuations in the accounts exceed predetermined materiality levels (either on an absolute or percentage basis), the auditor must investigate the cause of the fluctuations. This is usually done by inquiry of the client and by performing tests of transactions to corroborate the client's responses.

Detailed Analysis of Expense Accounts

Certain expense accounts are so critical to the audit that analytical procedures are not sufficient to assure their fairness of presentation. Often these accounts are related to very important asset or liability accounts, and a detailed analysis of them is necessary to reach an opinion as to the financial statements. A detailed analysis consists of *inspection of documents* such as invoices, canceled checks, and other support to verify the existence, proper valuation, and disclosure of the expense. For example, a detailed analysis of the repairs and maintenance expense account is an integral part of the audit of fixed assets, as discussed earlier in the chapter. Analysis of this account is necessary to determine whether the company followed a proper policy for capitalization of fixed asset expenditures. The account entitled "miscellaneous expense" is usually analyzed if it approaches materiality, to ascertain the nature of the charges in the account and whether they should be classified into other expense or asset accounts. Still other important expense accounts that are typically analyzed separately by the auditor include interest expense, and legal and professional fees. We will discuss the audit of these accounts in later chapters.

Summary

In this chapter we have discussed the audit procedures that are necessary to verify the financial assertions embodied in selected accounts in the acquisitions and expenditures system. Audit objectives for these accounts typically include verification of existence, transaction validity, valuation, completeness (including proper cutoff), and statement presentation. We discussed the primary audit objectives and related them to appropriate procedures for fixed assets, accounts payable, prepaid expenses, accrued liabilities, and operating expense accounts.

In Chapter 16 we will explore the audit objectives and related procedures for a system that is closely related to expenditures: the payroll system.

Appendix 15–A: Lead Schedule for Fixed Assets

JEP Manufacturing Co.
Fixed Assets
3-31-X1

W. P. No.	I		
ACCOUNTANT	SmG		
DATE	5/5/X1		

A/c #	Description	W/P Reference	Adjusted Balance △ 3-31-X0	Additions	Retirements
131	Purchased Shop Mach. + Equip.	I-2	415943 33	23065 15	
132	Constructed Shop Mach. + Equip.	I-2	74624 82	932 01	
133	Patterns and Dies	I-4	55024 54	13769 38	
			545592 69	37766 54	
134	Truck and Auto				
135	Land				
136	Building				
137	Building Annex				
139	Office Furniture + Fixtures				
140	Building Roof				
141	Sky Point Leasehold		Details Deleted		
142	Sky Point House				
143	Sky Point Furniture + Fixtures				
144	Sky Point Caretaker's house				
145	Landscaping				
146	Computer Equipment				
147	R & D Machinery				
	Total Fixed Assets		1733767 36	106128 16	
	Less Accumulated Depreciation				
	Net Amount Per Trial Balance				

See Tick mark legend and conclusions on I a (Appendix 15-C)

Balance per B/S ✓ 3-31-X1	Rate ⑤ / Method	Accumulated Depreciation			
		Balance ✓ 3-31-X0	Provision	Retirements	Balance 3-31-X1
4390084 8 ⎞	10% ⎞	3017810 1	I-1 3053299		3323140 00
755568 3 ⎠	10% ⎠				
6877392	20%	4438254 ✓	I-1 415556		4853810
5833592 3		3461635 5	3468855		3808521 0
A-1					
					✓
1839899 52		6875917 5	I-1 8545799		① 7730500 00 ✓
7730500 20 ①					A-1
10668495 52					
A-1					

Appendix 15–B: Schedule for Additions
to Shop Machinery and Equipment

JEP Manufacturing Co.				W. P. No.		I-2
Additions – Shop Machinery and Equipment				ACCOUNTANT		PBC / Smith
3-31-X1				DATE		5/5/X1

	Month Ended			Cost	
	4-30-X0			1361 23	✓ˣ
	5-31-X0			913 60	
	6-30-X0			704 53	
	7-31-X0			775 53	
	8-31-X0			3445 10	✓ˣ
	9-30-X0			227 48	
	10-31-X0			961 92	
	11-30-X0			892 55	
	12-31-X0			1108 08	✓ˣ
	1-31-X1			5087 90	
	2-28-X1			6580 61	✓ˣ
	3-31-X1			1938 63	
				23997 16	
Constructed		I	932 01		
Purchased		S	23065 15		
				23997 16	

See tick mark legend and conclusions I a (Appendix 15-C)

Appendix 15–C: Auditor's Tick-Mark Legend for Fixed Assets

			W. P. No.	I a
	JEP Mfg. Co.		ACCOUNTANT	Smℓ
	Tick Legend re: Fixed Assets		DATE	5/5/X1
	3-31-X1			

△ Agreed to prior year auditors' W/P's

√ Agreed to 3-31-X1 B/L

∧∗∗ Footed; Crossfooted

ⅎ Recomputed by auditors - appears reasonable - no material exceptions were noted.

⊗ Depreciation method and rate appear reasonable and consistent with prior year's. Current treatment appears comparable to prior year's treatment and depreciable lives are consistent.

✗ Agreed to paid invoice (s) noting that cost was properly recorded as a depreciable asset. Done a test basis w/o exception.

Note: Examined a listing of operating leases, noting proper classification of the leases as operating leases. No exceptions were noted.

Conclusion: Based on the audit work performed which was considered adequate to meet the objectives per the APG, it appears that the balances in Fixed Assets and related Depreciation accounts are fairly stated as of 3-31-X1.

Note: Reviewed Repairs & Maintenance expenses for the period, noting no unusual items. Amts. charged appeared reasonable & proper.

Appendix 15–D: Depreciation Schedule

	W. P. No.	I-1
JEP Manufacturing Co.	ACCOUNTANT	PBC/SmS
Depreciation Schedule	DATE	5/5/X1
3/31/X1		

Description	Date Acquired	Original Cost	Est. Life (X) (years)	Depr. Rate (X) (%)
Machinery and Equipment:				
Acquisitions to 4-1-X0				
(details not shown)	19X7-X8	297234 04	10	10%
Machinery & Equipment				
Current year additions				
Machinery & Equipment	19X1	23997 16	10	10%
		321231 20		
Patterns and Dies:				
Acquisitions to 4-1-X0	19X7-X8	15313 34	5	20%
Current year additions	19X1	13769 38	5	20%
		29082 72		
Other Property and Equipment	}	Details Deleted		
Totals		1839895 52		
		I		

See Tick mark legend and conclusions on Ia. (Appendix 15-C).

Thru 3-31-X0	Current Yr.	Remaining Cost				
1365722 44	2972342 ⁊	13093818				
	80957 ⁊	2318759				
1365722 44	3053299	15412577				
	I					
573490	270466 ⁊	687378				
	1450 90 ⁊	1231848				
573490	415556	19192 36				
	I					
77305000	8545799					
I	I					

Appendix 15–E: Trade Accounts Payable

			W. P. No.	N-1
JEP Manufacturing Co.			ACCOUNTANT	PBC/Smt
Trade Accounts Payable			DATE	5/11/X1
3-31-X1				

Name	Amount		
Allegheny Ludow	30421 20		
Altec Corporation	75 55		
American Packing	2709 00		
Amco, Inc.	26093 48		
Arrow Electronics	5 88		
Austin Hardware	991 37		
B & B Supply	339 72		
Centaur Metals Supply	22972 24	¢
Clemtex, Ltd.	2583 7	
Colt Industries	867 00	© ✓
Dal Air Investment	16055 02	¢
Decco, Inc.	594 00	
East Texas Distributors	262406 43	
Elastimold Division	3789 70	© ✓
Ex-Cel Steel	19030 86	© ✓
Exxon Co.	16953 22	
General Electric Co.	3691 29	
Other [Details Omitted]	115336 50		
Total	501915 83	✓	
	⋀		
Less: RJE ⟨B⟩ To reclassify			
payable to East Texas Distributors			
as intercompany (payable to			
wholly-owned subsidiary)	⟨262506 43⟩		
	239409 40		
	A-2		

⋀ Footed
C ¢ Confirmations sent, received on N-2 (not shown)
© No reply. Alternative procedures performed. See ✓ below
✓ Examined copy of check dated subsequent to 3-31-X1 with supporting invoices attached. Noted that amount was properly included as account payable at 3-31-X1
✓ Agreed to 3-31-X1 general ledger

Conclusion: Based on audit work performed which was considered adequate to meet the audit objectives, accounts payable is fairly stated at 3-31-X1. Smt

Appendix 15—F: Search for Unrecorded Liabilities

JEP Mfg. Co.
Search for Unrecorded Liabilities
3-31-X1

W. P. No.	N-3
ACCOUNTANT	SmG
DATE	5/12/X1

SCOPE > #1000

Check # ✓	Payee	Amount	Applicable to 19X1	Properly Recorded in A/P or Accrued in 19X1	Applicable to 19X2
6941	Wyoming Valley Machinery	4950 00			✓
6995	Gen'l Life Ins. Co.	8249 81			✓
7033	X Systems	4175 08	4175 08	✓	
7037	JC Ross Truck Line	1482 56			✓
7231	X Systems	2527 08	2527 08	✓	
7251	Gen'l Life Ins. Co.	10257 11			✓
7264	ABC	1256 90			✓
7280	J. Hughes Co.	2522 53			✓
7286	P J N	5000 00	5000 00	✓	
	Total applicable to 19X1		11702 16	Immaterial. Pass further investigation. SmG	

✓ Per check register for the period beginning 4-1-X1, through 5-12-X1 (end of audit field work).

✓ Applies to column heading.

Note: This search for unrecorded liabilities was conducted through 5/12/X1 and check # 7291 with a scope of #1000. No unrecorded liabilities were noted. In consideration of the above results, continuation of the search past 5/12/X1 is not considered necessary.

Note: The above search included payments to East Texas Dist. as well.

Appendix 15–G: Prepaid Insurance Schedule

JEP Mfg. Co.
Prepaid Insurance
3-31-X1

W. P. NO.	G-1
ACCOUNTANT	HB
DATE	5/5/X1

| | | | Term | |
Coverage	Policy No.	From	To	
Fleet Auto & Truck	540-4398-7 ⦟	12-1-X0	12-1-X1	
'79-Mack & Lufkin Trailer	1300 641-23 ⦟	12-1-X0	12-1-X1	
'79-Mack & Lufkin Trailer	CXTPE-26994 ⦟	12-1-X0	12-1-X1	
Blanket Crime	FBB-135607 ⦟	10-6-X0	10-6-X1	
Building - Fire & E.C.	8-56-59-46 ⦟	6-30-X9	6-30-X2	
Contents (excluding stock)	C-56-98-72 ⦟	3-20-X0	6-20-X2	
Business Interruption	C-56-98-71 ⦟	1-30-X0	4-30-X1	
Commercial Umbrella	UL-67-46-77 ⦟	3-30-X0	3-30-X3	
General Liability	540-4398126 ⦟	12-1-X0	12-1-X1	
Directors & Officers Liability	9524-84 ⦟	5-20-X0	5-20-X1	
Sky Point Lodge	241-795187 ⦟	7-14-X0	7-14-X1	
Business Travel & Commuting insurance	640 39064 ⦟	3-9-X1	3-9-X2	

⅄ Footed

⦟ Agreed amount and information on policy coverage to insurance policy from appropriate company

⦟ Agreed to prior year's audited working papers

✚ Recomputed insurance expense. Appears reasonable.

Issuing Company	Total Premium	Balance 3-31-X0	Payments	Expenses	Balance 3-31-X1
Intern. Ins. Co.	2693 00		2693 00	896 77 †	1796 23
U. S. Fire Ins. Co.	1267 00	—	1267 00	422 29 †	844 71
Can. Union Ins.	534 83	—	534 83	178 10 †	356 73
Ins. Co. of N. Amer.	636 00	—	636 00	318 00 †	318 00
Commonwealth	8559 52	6419 88 ×		5478 00 †	941 88
" "	1963 00	1963 00 ×		817 87 †	1145 13
" "	5912 08	4386 55 ×		3863 89 †	522 66
Puritan Ins. Co.	13500 00	13500 00 ×		4500 00 †	9000 00
N. Prince Ins. Co.	18355 00	—	18355 00	13618 74 †	4736 26
Nat. Union Fire	3696 00	—	3696 00	3080 00 †	616 00
U. S. Fire Ins. Co.	624 00	—	624 00	468 00 †	156 00
Fed. Ins. Co.	2680 86	—	2680 86	223 32 †	2457 54
		26269 43 ᴎ	30486 69 ᴎ	33864 98 ᴎ	22891 14 ᴎ
Difference – immaterial -- pass					⟨328 72⟩
					22562 42
					G

Appendix 15–H: Accrued Property Taxes Payable

TEP Manufacturing Co.
Prepaid and Accrued Property Taxes Payable
3-31-X1

Client/SME
5/6/X1

Due Dates	Authority	Property	Assessed valuation	Total tax	Period covered
(√)					
1/1	Greensboro I.S.D.	Plant and warehouse	500000 √	7500 √	19X0 √
				8000 √	19X1 √
6/1/X1	City of Greensboro	" "	450000 √	4500 √	6/1/W9-6/1/X0 √
6/1/X2				4500 √	6/1/X0-6/1/X1 √
1/1	Collins County	" "	450000 √	4500 √	19X0 √
				4500 √	19X1 √
	Greensboro I.S.D.	Office Building	400000 √	6000 √	19X0 √
				6400 √	19X1 √
6/1/X1	City of Greensboro	" "	350000 √	3500 √	6/1/W9-6/1/X0 √
6/1/X2				3500 √	6/1/X0-6/1/X1 √
1/1	Collins County	" "	350000 √	3500 √	19X0 √
				3500 √	19X1 √

√ ⨉ Footed, cross-footed

√ Agreed details to property tax receipts.

✓ Agreed to prior years working papers.

⨉ Vouched payments to cash disbursements and cancelled checks.
(No exceptions noted.)

✗ Recomputed expense. (No exceptions noted.)

6 Balance 3-31-X0	7 Prepaid Payments	8 Expense	9 Balance 3-31-X1	10 Balance 3-31-X0	11 Accrued Additions	12 Payments	13 Balance 3-31-X1
5625		5625	–0–				
–0–	8000	2000	6000				
				3375	1125	4500	–0–
					3375		3375
3375		3375	–0–				
	4500	1125	3375				
4500		4500	–0–				
–0–	6400	1600	4800				
				2625	875	3500	–0–
					2625		2625
2625		2625	–0–				
	3500	875	2625				
16125	22400	21725	16800	6000	8000	8000	6000

Questions for Class Discussion

Q15-1   What is meant by *fixed assets*?

Q15-2   What accounts, other than tangible fixed assets, are typically verified in connection with the audit of fixed asset accounts?

Q15-3   Why is the auditor generally less concerned about the internal control procedures for the fixed assets system than for the other systems we have discussed to this point?

Q15-4   Why does the auditor concentrate on the examination of acquisitions and disposals in verifying the existence of fixed assets? Explain.

Q15-5   What procedures are followed in verifying the ownership of fixed assets? Describe them briefly.

Q15-6   Why is it important to inspect lease agreements in verifying the ownership of fixed assets? Explain.

Q15-7   Why does the auditor analyze the items in the maintenance and repairs account during the audit of fixed assets?

Q15-8   How does the examination of insurance policies relate to the verification of fixed assets?

Q15-9   How and for what reason does the auditor verify depreciation expense?

Q15-10   What procedures would the auditor apply to determine that all property and equipment retirements had been recorded on the books?

Q15-11   Why is the confirmation of accounts receivable generally performed more frequently than is the confirmation of accounts payable?

Q15-12   What procedures does the auditor follow in the search for unrecorded liabilities?

Q15-13   How is the completeness of trade accounts payable verified?

Q15-14   How is the completeness of notes payable verified?

Q15-15   What are the audit objectives that pertain to prepaid expenses?

Q15-16   What procedures are followed in verifying the objectives set out in Q15–15?

Q15-17   What is the relationship between prepaid expenses and accrued liabilities?

Q15-18   What are the audit objectives for accrued liabilities?

Q15-19   How does the analysis-type working paper help to explain the audit work performed on prepaid expenses and accrued liabilities?

Q15-20   What are some expense accounts that are audited along with tests of transactions of prepaid expense accounts? Accrued liability accounts?

Short Cases

C15-1   Carl Rivera, CPA, is the auditor for a manufacturing company with a balance sheet that includes the caption "Property, Plant, and Equipment." Rivera has been asked by the company's management if audit adjustments or reclassifications are required for the following material items that have been included in or excluded from "Property, Plant, and Equipment."

a. A tract of land was acquired during the year. The land is the future site of the client's new headquarters, which will be constructed in the following year. Commissions were paid to the real estate agent used to acquire the land, and expenditures were made to relocate the previous owner's equipment. These commissions and expenditures were expensed and are excluded from "Property, Plant, and Equipment."

b. Clearing costs were incurred to make the land ready for construction. These costs were included in "Property, Plant, and Equipment."

c. During the land-clearing process, timber and gravel were recovered and sold. The proceeds from the sale were recorded as other income and are excluded from "Property, Plant, and Equipment."

d. A group of machines was purchased under a royalty agreement that provides royalty payments based on units of production from the machines. The cost of the machines, freight costs, unloading charges, and royalty payments were capitalized and are included in "Property, Plant, and Equipment."

Required:

a. Describe the general characteristics of assets, such as land, buildings, improvements, machinery, equipment, fixtures, etc., that should normally be classified as "Property, Plant, and Equipment," and identify audit objectives (i.e., how an auditor can obtain audit satisfaction) in connection with the examination of "Property, Plant, and Equipment." *Do not discuss specific auditing procedures.*

b. Indicate whether each of items (a)–(d) above requires one or more audit adjustments or reclassifications, and explain why such adjustments or reclassifications are required or not required.

Organize your answer as follows:

Item no.	Is audit adjustment or reclassification required? Yes or No	Reasons why audit adjustment or reclassification is required or not required

(AICPA adapted)

C15-2 In connection with a recurring examination of the financial statements of the Louis Manufacturing Company for the year ended December 31, 19X9, you have been assigned the audit of the accounts of the manufacturing equipment, manufacturing equipment: accumulated depreciation, and repairs of manufacturing equipment. Your review of Louis's policies and procedures has disclosed the following pertinent information:

a. The manufacturing equipment account includes the net invoice price plus related freight and installation costs for all the equipment in Louis's manufacturing plant.

b. The manufacturing equipment and accumulated depreciation accounts are supported by a subsidiary ledger that shows the cost and accumulated depreciation for each piece of equipment.

c. An annual budget for capital expenditures of $1,000 or more is prepared by the budget committee and approved by the board of directors. Capital expenditures over $1,000 that are not included in this budget must be approved by the board of directors, and variations of 20 percent or more must be explained to the board. Approval by the supervisor of production is required for capital expenditures under $1,000.

d. Company employees handle installation, removal, repair, and rebuilding of the machinery. Work orders are prepared for those activities and are subject to the same budgetary control as other expenditures. Work orders are not required for external expenditures.

Required:

a. Cite the major objectives of your audit of the accounts of the manufacturing equipment, manufacturing equipment: accumulated depreciation, and repairs of manufacturing equipment. Do not include in this listing the auditing procedures designed to accomplish these objectives.

b. Prepare the portion of your audit program applicable to the review of 19X9 additions to the manufacturing equipment account.

(AICPA adapted)

C15-3 Henri Mincin, CPA, is the auditor of the Raleigh Corporation. Mincin is considering the audit work to be performed in the accounts payable area for the current year's engagement.

The prior year's working papers show that confirmation requests were mailed to 100 of Raleigh's 1,000 suppliers. Mincin's sample was designed to select accounts with large dollar balances. A substantial number of hours were spent by Raleigh and Mincin in resolving relatively minor differences between the confirmation replies and Raleigh's accounting records. Alternate auditing procedures were used for those suppliers who did not respond to the confirmation requests.

Required:

a. Identify the accounts payable audit objectives that Mincin must consider in determining the auditing procedures to be followed.

b. Identify situations when Mincin should use accounts payable confirmations and discuss whether Mincin is required to use them.

c. Discuss why the use of large dollar balances as the basis for selecting accounts payable for confirmation might not be the most efficient approach; indicate what more efficient procedures could be followed when selecting accounts payable for confirmation.

(AICPA adapted)

C15-4 Taylor, CPA, is engaged in the audit of Rex Wholesaling for the year ended December 31, 19X2. Taylor obtained an understanding of the internal control structure relating to the purchasing, receiving, trade accounts payable, and cash disbursement cycles and has decided not to proceed with tests of controls. Based upon analytical procedures Taylor believes that the trade accounts payable balance on the balance sheet as of December 31, 19X2, may be understated.

Taylor requested and obtained a client-prepared trade accounts payable schedule listing the total amount owed to each vendor.

Required: What additional substantive audit procedures should Taylor apply in examining the trade accounts payable?

(AICPA adapted)

C15-5 During an examination of the financial statements of Gole, Inc., Elsa Robbins, CPA, requested and received a client-prepared property casualty insurance schedule, which included appropriate premium information.

Required:

a. Identify the type of information, in addition to the appropriate premium information, that would ordinarily be expected to be included in a property casualty insurance schedule.

b. What are the basic auditing procedures Robbins should perform in examining the client-prepared property casualty insurance schedule?

(AICPA adapted)

Problems

P15-1 Select the best answer to the following items relating to substantive verification of plant assets and their related accounts.

a. Once the initial audit of a newly constructed industrial plant has been performed, which of the following is of *least* concern, with respect to *consistency*, to the continuing auditor in the following year?
  1. Prior year's capitalization policy.
  2. Prior year's capitalized costs.
  3. Prior year's depreciation methods.
  4. Prior year's depreciable life.

b. An auditor would be *least* likely to use confirmations in connection with the examination of
  1. Inventories.
  2. Long-term debt.
  3. Property, plant, and equipment.
  4. Stockholders' equity.

c. The auditor is *least* likely to learn of retirements of equipment through which of the following?
  1. Review of the purchase return and allowance account.
  2. Review of depreciation.
  3. Analysis of the debits to the accumulated depreciation account.
  4. Review of insurance policy riders.

d. The auditor may conclude that depreciation charges are insufficient by noting
  1. Insured values greatly in excess of book values.
  2. Large amounts of fully depreciated assets.
  3. Continuous trade-ins of relatively new assets.
  4. Excessive recurring losses on assets retired.

e. Which of the following auditing procedures would be *least* likely to lead the auditor to find unrecorded fixed-asset disposals?
  1. Examination of insurance policies.
  2. Review of repairs and maintenance expense.
  3. Review of property tax files.
  4. Scanning of invoices for fixed asset additions.

f. A normal auditing procedure is to analyze the current year's repairs and maintenance accounts to provide evidence in support of the audit proposition that
   1. Expenditures for fixed assets have been recorded in the proper period.
   2. Capital expenditures have been properly authorized.
   3. Noncapitalizable expenditures have been properly expensed.
   4. Expenditures for fixed assets have been capitalized.

g. Which of the following *best* describes the independent auditor's approach to obtaining satisfaction concerning depreciation expense in the income statement?
   1. Verify the mathematical accuracy of the amounts charged to income as a result of depreciation expense.
   2. Determine the method of computing depreciation expense and ascertain that it is in accordance with generally accepted accounting principles.
   3. Reconcile the amount of depreciation expense to those amounts credited to accumulated depreciation accounts.
   4. Establish the basis for depreciable assets and verify the depreciation expense.

h. Which of the following explanations might satisfy an auditor who discovers significant debits to an accumulated depreciation account?
   1. Extraordinary repairs have lengthened the life of an asset.
   2. Prior years' depreciation charges were erroneously understated.
   3. A reserve for possible loss on retirement has been recorded.
   4. An asset has been recorded at its fair value.

i. Which of the following is the *best* evidence of real estate ownership at the balance sheet date?
   1. Title insurance policy.
   2. Original deed held in the client's safe.
   3. Paid real estate tax bills.
   4. Closing statement.

j. Which of the following is a customary auditing procedure for the verification of the legal ownership of real property?
   1. Examination of correspondence with the corporate counsel concerning acquisition matters.
   2. Examination of ownership documents registered and on file at a public hall of records.
   3. Examination of corporate minutes and resolutions concerning the approval to acquire property, plant, and equipment.
   4. Examination of deeds and title guaranty policies on hand.

k. An auditor determines that a client has properly capitalized a leased asset (and corresponding lease liability) as representing, in substance, an installment purchase. As part of the auditor's procedures, the auditor should
   1. Substantiate the cost of the property to the lessor and determine that this is the cost recorded by the client.
   2. Evaluate the propriety of the interest rate used in discounting the future lease payments.
   3. Determine that the leased property is being amortized over the life of the lease.
   4. Evaluate whether the total amount of lease payments represents the fair market value of the property.

l. In connection with a review of the prepaid insurance account, which of the following procedures would generally *not* be performed by the auditor?
   1. Recompute the portion of the premium that expired during the year.
   2. Prepare excerpts of insurance policies for audit working papers.

   3. Examine support for premium payments.
   4. Confirm premium rates with an independent insurance broker.
m. Tennessee Company violated company policy by erroneously capitalizing the cost of painting its warehouse. The CPA examining Tennessee's financial statements would most likely learn of this error by
   1. Discussing Tennessee's capitalization policies with its controller.
   2. Reviewing the titles and descriptions for all construction work orders issued during the year.
   3. Observing, during the physical inventory observation, that the warehouse has been painted.
   4. Examining in detail a sample of construction work orders.
n. The auditor interviews the plant manager. The auditor is most likely to rely on this interview as primary support for an audit conclusion on
   1. Capitalization vs. expensing policy.
   2. Allocation of fixed and variable costs.
   3. The necessity to record a provision for deferred maintenance costs.
   4. The adequacy of the depreciation expense.
o. In the examination of property, plant, and equipment, the auditor tries to determine all of the following except the
   1. Adequacy of internal control.
   2. Extent of property abandoned during the year.
   3. Adequacy of replacement funds.
   4. Reasonableness of the depreciation.
p. The auditor is most likely to seek information from the plant manager with respect to the
   1. Adequacy of the provision for uncollectible accounts.
   2. Appropriateness of physical inventory observation procedures.
   3. Existence of obsolete machinery.
   4. Deferral of procurement of certain necessary insurance coverage.

(AICPA adapted)

P15-2 In the past, the records to be evaluated in an audit have been printed reports, listings, documents, and written papers—all of which are visible output. However, in fully computerized systems, which employ daily updating of transaction files, output and files are frequently in machine-readable forms, such as cards, tapes, or disks. Thus, they often present the auditor with an opportunity to use the computer in performing an audit.

Required:
   a. List the major audit objectives for fixed assets and accumulated depreciation.
   b. For each objective listed in (a), describe one or two auditing procedures that would satisfy that objective.
   c. For each auditing procedure listed in (b), describe how computer audit software can be used, if at all, to assist the auditor.
Organize your answer as follows:

Audit Objective	Auditing Procedure(s)	Ways Computer Audit Software May Be Used

(AICPA adapted)

P15-3   In connection with the annual examination of Johnson Corporation, a manufacturer of janitorial supplies, you have been assigned to audit the fixed assets. The company maintains a detailed property ledger for all fixed assets. You prepared an audit program for the balances of property, plant, and equipment, but have yet to prepare one for accumulated depreciation and depreciation expense.

Required:
a. Prepare a separate comprehensive audit program for the accumulated depreciation and depreciation expense accounts.
b. For each procedure listed in (a), suggest ways that computer audit software can be utilized to assist in the audit, if possible.

(AICPA adapted)

P15-4   You are engaged in the examination of the financial statements of The Smoky Mountain Manufacturing Company and are auditing the machinery and equipment account for the year ended December 31, 19X2. Your permanent file contains the schedule shown on the accompanying figure.

Your examination reveals the following information:

a. The company uses a ten-year life for all machinery and equipment for depreciation purposes. Depreciation is computed by the straight-line method. Six months' depreciation is recorded in the year of acquisition or retirement. For 19X2, the company recorded depreciation of $2,800 on machinery and equipment.

b. The Burnham grinder was purchased for cash from a firm in financial distress. The chief engineer and a used machinery dealer agreed that the machine, which was practically new, was worth $2,100 in the open market.

c. For production reasons the new air compressor was installed in a small building that was erected in 19X2 to house the machine and for general storage. The cost of the building, which has a twenty-five-year life, was $2,000 and is included in the $4,500 voucher for the air compressor.

d. The power lawnmower was delivered to the home of the company president for his personal use.

e. On June 1, the battery in a battery-powered lift truck was accidentally damaged beyond repair. The damaged battery was included at a price of $600 in the $4,200 cost of the lift truck purchased 2½ years ago. The accumulated depreciation on the battery was $180. The company decided to rent a replacement battery rather than buy a new battery. The $320 expenditure is the annual rental for the battery paid in advance, net of a $40 allowance for the scrap value of the damaged battery, which was returned to the battery company.

f. The Rockwood saw sold on August 1 had been purchased twelve years ago for $1,500. It was fully depreciated. The saw was in use until it was sold.

g. On September 1, the company determined that a production-casting machine was no longer needed and advertised it for sale for $1,800 after determining from a used machinery dealer that this was its market value. The casting machine had been purchased for $5,000 five years ago. It had been assumed to have no salvage value for depreciation purposes.

h. On November 1, a baking oven was purchased for $10,000. A $2,800 down payment was made, and the balance will be paid in monthly installments over a three-year period. The December 1 payment includes interest charges of $36. Legal title to the oven will not pass to the company until the payments are completed.

Required:
a. Prepare the auditor's adjusting journal entries required at December 31, 19X2, for machinery and equipment and accumulated depreciation.
b. Prepare the working paper for the machinery and equipment account.
Note: You may prepare a computerized spreadsheet for this problem, if you wish.

Machinery and equipment			
Balance 12/31/X0	19X1 retirements	19X1 additions	Balance 12/31/X1
$21,800	$2,100	$5,700	$25,400

A transcript of the machinery and equipment account for 19X2 follows:

19X2	Machinery and equipment	Ref.	Debit	Credit
Jan 1	Balance forward	VR	$25,400	
Mar 1	Burnham grinder	VR	1,200	
May 1	Air compressor	VR	4,500	
June 1	Power lawnmower	VR	600	
June 1	Lift truck battery	VR	320	
Aug 1	Rockwood saw	CR		$ 150
Nov 1	Electric spot welder	VR	4,500	
Nov 1	Baking oven	VR	2,800	
Dec 1	Baking oven	VR	236	
			39,556	150
Dec 31	Balance forward			39,406
			$39,556	$39,556

P15-5 In the course of a regular annual audit of the Bean Manufacturing Corporation, you are assigned to the audit of machinery and equipment. A transcript of the ledger account appears below:

Machinery and Equipment—Acct. 83

Jan. 1	Balance	209,628.12	Apr. 25	CR 12	75.00
Apr. 18	VR 23	31,994.45			
July 28	JV 8	10,436.26			
Sept. 9	VR 41	14,189.00			
Nov. 11	VR 52	7,261.88			

You have examined the invoices for September 9 and November 11, and you have no questions concerning them. In support of the entry of April 18, you find an invoice, reproduced below. In support of the entry of July 28, you find a journal voucher, which is also reproduced here.

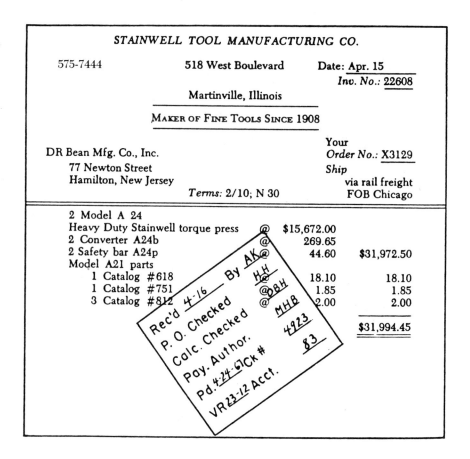

JOURNAL VOUCHER 8
Construction of conveyor

Machinery and equipment	$10,436.26	
Drafting department salaries		$ 792.00
Repair department wages		2,401.00
Factory direct labor		1,758.00
Purchases		5,485.26
To record cost of conveyor, as follows:		
John Redfield, draftsman, 43 hours @ $8	$ 344.00	
Wm. White, draftsman, 56 hours @ $8	448.00	
	$ 792.00	
Repairmen assigned to construction:		
D. Baker, 94 regular hours @ $9	846.00	
42 overtime hours @ $13.50	567.00	
E. Miller, 71 regular hours @ $8	568.00	
35 overtime hours @ $12	420.00	
	$2,401.00	

(continued)

Factory workers assigned to construction:

R. Fischer,	94 regular hours @ $6		$ 564.00
	35 overtime hours @ $9		315.00
J. Smith,	94 regular hours @ $6		564.00
	35 overtime hours @ $9		315.00
			$1,758.00
Purchases VR 34–18			$ 921.85
VR 35–4			2,876.50
VR 35–13			235.42
VR 35–37			689.17
VR 36–11			319.40
VR 36–22			442.92
			$5,485.26

Required: After applying the usual auditing procedures to the information available, state the adjustments to be made to the machinery and equipment account or questions for further investigation that are suggested by the ledger transcript and supporting documents. Assume all amounts are material. Dollar amounts of adjustments are not required.

(AICPA adapted)

P15-6   You are examining the financial statements of the Aby Company, a retail enterprise, for the year ended December 31, 19X9. The client's accounting department presented you with an analysis of the Prepaid Expenses account balance of $31,400 at December 31, 19X9 as shown in the accompanying account analysis.
Additional information includes the following:
1. Insurance policy data:

Type	Period covered	Premium
Fire	12/31/X8 to 12/31/Y0	$1,000
Liability	6/30/X9 to 6/30/Y0	9,500

2. The postage meter machine was delivered in November and the balance due was paid in January. Unused postage of $700 in the machine at December 31, 19X9 was recorded as expense at time of purchase.
3. Bond discount represents the unamortized portion applicable to bonds maturing in 19Y0.
4. The $9,600 paid and recorded for advertising was for the cost of an advertisement to be run in a monthly magazine for six months, beginning in December 19X9. You examined an invoice received from the advertising agency and extracted the following description:

   "Advertising services rendered for store opened in November 19X9. . . . $6,900"

5. Aby has contracted to purchase Skyhigh Stores and has been required to accompany its offer with a check for $1,000 to be held in escrow as an indication of good faith. An examination of canceled checks revealed the check had not been returned from the bank through January 19Y0.

Aby Company

ANALYSIS OF PREPAID EXPENSES ACCOUNT

December 31, 19X9

Description	Balance December 31, 19X9
Unexpired insurance:	
Fire	$ 750
Liability	4,900
Utility deposits	2,000
Loan to officer	500
Purchase of postage meter machine, one half of invoice price	400
Bond discount	3,000
Advertising of store opening	9,600
Amount due for overpayment on purchase of furniture and fixtures	675
Unsaleable inventory—entered June 30, 19X9	8,300
Contributions from employees to employee welfare fund	(275)
Book value of obsolete machinery held for resale	550
Funds delivered to Skyhigh Stores with purchase offer	1,000
Total	$31,400

Required: Assuming that you have examined acceptable underlying audit evidence, prepare a worksheet to show the necessary adjustments, corrections, and reclassifications of the items in the Prepaid Expenses account. In addition to the information shown in the above analysis, the following column headings are suggested for your worksheet:

Adjustments and Reclassifications		Prepaid Expenses Adjusted Balance December 31, 19X9	Disposition of Adjustments and Reclassifications				
					General		
Debit	Credit		Expense Debit (Credit)	Accts. Rec.— Other	Account	Debit	Credit

Note: You may use a computerized spreadsheet to prepare this working paper, if you wish.

(AICPA adapted)

CHAPTER 16

The Payroll System and Related Accounts

Objectives

☐ **1.** Identify the relevant audit objectives for the payroll system, as well as perform other planning procedures.

☐ **2.** Understand the attributes of an effective internal control structure in the payroll system.

☐ **3.** Perform the detection risk procedures necessary to fulfill the audit objectives pertaining to payroll-related financial statement balances.

One of the most important elements of the expenditures system of an entity is the payroll system. In this chapter we give special attention to the audit of the payroll system and related account balances.

We include, as appendixes to the chapter, diagrams that depict key internal control attributes, systems flowcharts, and transactions testing methodology for the payroll system.

Audit Objectives and Planning Considerations

☑ **Objective 1**
Identify audit objectives for payroll system

A number of accounts are associated with the payroll system. They include officers' salaries, sales-related salaries and commissions, direct and indirect labor expenses, vacation and other fringe benefits expense, pension expense, payroll tax expense, and related accrued liability accounts. Payroll and labor-oriented costs generally constitute a major portion of inventories and cost of goods sold for manufacturing entities. In addition, payroll expenses often constitute the major component of expenses on the operating statements of service-oriented or not-for-profit entities.

The audit of the payroll system is important for at least two reasons. First, because of the pervasive impact on the financial statements of labor-related expenses and liabilities, payrolls are generally considered material. Second, the relative risk of misstatement for payroll-related accounts is often high, in comparison with other systems of the entity. This is because of the direct connection of payrolls with the cash disbursements system.

Payroll systems for various entities may range from simple to very complex. However, a payroll system will always include the functions of *employment, accumulation and distribution of payroll costs, and disbursements of cash*. When internal controls over a payroll system are weak, several types of major errors or irregularities may occur. Possible errors include (1) insertion of fictitious employees into the system; (2) insertion of erroneous or fraudulent hours into the system; (3) errors in allocation of payroll-related costs to work-in-process and finished goods inventories, causing those accounts to be misstated; and (4) failure to properly accrue and pay federal and state payroll taxes. The audit objectives for the payroll system must be designed to detect these types of errors and irregularities. Therefore, the primary audit objectives for the payroll system are

1. Existence or occurrence (transaction validity).
2. Completeness.
3. Proper valuation.
4. Cutoff of expenses and liabilities related to payrolls (allocation).
5. Proper statement presentation or disclosure.

Understanding the Control Structure

☑ **Objective 2**
Understand the attributes of an effective internal control structure for payrolls

Because of the relatively large number of transactions that must be processed by a typical payroll system, and because payroll costs affect so many other accounts in the financial statements, the auditor must obtain a thorough knowledge of the control structure of the entity to effectively plan the nature, timing, and extent of audit tests on payroll-related financial statement balances. As is the case for other systems, the three major components of the control structure for payrolls include the control environment, the accounting system, and control procedures.

The Control Environment

Since the payroll system is considered a part of the cash expenditures system, the same observations that we made in Chapter 14 concerning the control environment surrounding cash disbursements also apply to payrolls. Specifically, management's attitude toward controls should be serious regarding the design and operations of the system for prevention, detection, and correction of errors and irregularities. The organizational structure of the entity should provide for proper segregation of duties with respect to payrolls. This generally requires the organizational separation of the functions of employment, accounting, and cash disbursements. In addition, personnel who handle these responsibilities should be qualified technically and experientially for their respective duties.

In most entities, extensive use is made of computers in all phases of payroll processing: employment, accounting, and cash disbursements. General EDP controls over payrolls should provide for the following: (1) organizational autonomy of the computer department; (2) proper segregation of duties within the computer department; (3) proper documentation of programs and changes; and (4) physical protection of files, to prevent unauthorized access to assets, data files, and computer programs.

As in the case of other systems, the control environment over payrolls is enhanced by the presence of an effective internal audit function. Internal auditors not only provide an effective day-to-day monitoring function for the accounting over payrolls, but they may also assist in protecting assets by performing such duties as periodic reconciliation of payroll bank accounts and observation of the distribution of paychecks to employees.

The independent auditor obtains an understanding of the control environment of the entity by prior experience, as well as inquiry of client personnel and observations of employees carrying out their assigned functions.

There are several built-in incentives for an entity to maintain effective controls over the payroll system that do not exist for other systems. First, the employees themselves are highly likely to monitor the system on their own behalfs, for underpayments of salaries and wages. In addition, an integral part of the payroll system involves preparing periodic tax returns to federal and state payroll and unemployment tax authorities. Payrolls are subject to audit by these authorities, and monetary penalties and fines may be levied against the company for underreporting of wages. Although these incentives often make the control environment less risky, they do not mitigate the fact that control weaknesses may exist in the accounting system.

The Accounting System

Figure 16–1 presents diagrammatically the typical flows of transactions through the payroll system, as well as the interrelationships of the various accounts involved. The accounting process itself is usually simple and straightforward. It begins with the accrual of various labor-related expenses, continues through the payment of those expenses from a separate imprest bank account, and

Figure 16–1

Flow of Transactions: Payroll System

Cash in Bank—Payroll		Accrued Salaries and Wages	
Beginning balance xxx	xxx (4)		Beginning balance xxx
xxx (5)		xxx (4)	xxx (1)
Ending balance xxx			Ending balance xxx

Direct/Indirect Labor Expense	
xxx (1)	

Withholding Taxes Payable	
	Beginning balance xxx
xxx (4)	xxx (1)
	Ending balance xxx

Salaries and Wages Expense	
xxx (1)	

Accrued Payroll Taxes	
	Beginning balance xxx
xxx (4)	xxx (2)
	Ending balance xxx

Payroll Tax Expense	
xxx (2)	

Accrued Employee Benefits	
	Beginning balance xxx
xxx (4)	xxx (3)
	Ending balance xxx

Employee Benefits Expense	
xxx (3)	

Notes: (1) Accrued wages and salaries; (2) Accrued payroll taxes; (3) Accrued employee benefits; (4) Payment of accrued liabilities; (5) Reimbursement of payroll bank account (from acquisitions and expenditures system, Chapter 14).

culminates with the reimbursement of that account from the general cash accounts through the cash disbursements process described in Chapter 14. Along the way, the company obtains services from employees and incurs obligations to them for accrued salaries and wages. In addition, the company incurs obligations to governmental taxing authorities for payroll taxes and unemployment taxes.

The auditor should obtain a thorough understanding of the flow of labor-related transactions from the point of initiation to the point of their inclusion in the financial statements. As is the case with other systems, this understanding is normally obtained through a combination of methods, including prior experience with the entity, inquiry of client personnel, observation of employees in the normal course of performing their assigned functions, and reading of client documentation such as procedures manuals. The auditor's understanding of the control structure is documented by means of internal control questionnaires, narrative descriptions, and systems flowcharts.

Control Procedures

The payroll system should embody policies and procedures over recording, processing, summarizing, and reporting functions that provide for accurate and fair reflection of the financial statement accounts produced by the system. As is the case with other systems in the entity, control procedures over the payroll system should provide for the following characteristics: (1) appropriate segregation of responsibilities, (2) adequate records and documentation, (3) an effective system of comparisons and compliance-monitoring, (4) limited access to assets and sensitive data, and (5) proper execution of transactions in accordance with management's general or specific authority. To achieve these characteristics, the management of the entity should adopt controls that are designed to prevent, detect, or correct specific errors and irregularities across various functions in the system. Appendix 16–A summarizes the functions that are central to the payroll system, the errors or irregularities that could occur in those functions, results of those errors, and control attributes that should be present in the system to prevent, detect, or correct them. Appendixes 16–B and C illustrate the application of those control attributes in a flowchart format.

Appropriate Segregation of Responsibilities

As shown in Appendixes 16–A through C, the duties involving exchange, processing, and safeguard functions should be segregated within the entity. With respect to payrolls, exchange functions involve the hiring and termination of employees. Processing functions involve the accumulation, processing, summarization, and reporting of payroll-related accounting data, and safeguard functions involve cash handling and monitoring. Thus, the duties of employment, accounting, cash handling, and internal auditing should be performed by different persons or departments.

In large entities, the employment function should be performed by a separate personnel department. The personnel department should receive requisitions for either rate changes or personnel changes from the operating departments. On receiving general or specific authority to fill positions from the board of directors, the personnel department should advertise positions, screen applicants, and process employment files for new hirees. No employee should be allowed to terminate employment without processing through the personnel department. At that time, the employee's name should be removed from the active payroll files.

The accounting function for payrolls should be handled through a separate payroll department. That department should be responsible for accumulating the data needed to prepare periodic payrolls, including hours worked, rates of pay, and deductions. As shown in Appendix 16–B, in larger entities, hours worked may be prepared by a separate timekeeping section within the payroll department. Paychecks are typically prepared in the department. Payroll journals or registers should be maintained by the department, as well as individual employee earnings records. In smaller entities, payroll preparation may be performed by an independent payroll preparation service. In these cases, employee time cards and other supporting documents are submitted to the payroll service. All payroll records are processed and kept by the service. Employee paychecks are returned to the company along with supporting documentation, for review by supervisory personnel before checks are distributed. Such payroll services are a cost-effective source of control over payrolls for companies that cannot afford to maintain a separate payroll department.

There may also be separate cost accounting, accounts payable, and general ledger departments. The cost accounting department has the responsibility of allocating labor to inventories and cost of goods sold, in accordance with the entity's cost accounting system. The accounts payable department has the responsibility of receiving a copy of the payroll register from the payroll department and preparing the voucher to reimburse the payable bank account. The general ledger department receives copies of documentation from both the payroll and cost accounting departments, and uses that documentation to prepare general ledger entries.

The safeguard function of cash handling should generally be handled through a separate treasurer's department. Internal auditors provide an important safeguard as well, by preparing the monthly bank reconciliations over payroll bank accounts and by performing day-to-day tests of transactions.

Records and Documentation

The primary exchange transactions involving payroll include the accrual of payroll and withholding taxes, and the payment of accrued liabilities. Figure 16–2 depicts the boundary and supporting documents for these transactions. We discuss a few of these documents below.

- **Employee time cards.** Documents prepared daily by hourly personnel that indicate the time the employee started and stopped and the number of hours worked. Most often, time is accumulated automatically by time clocks. Time cards are usually submitted weekly by hourly personnel.
- **Job-time tickets.** Records used in a job-order cost system to allocate gross labor costs to work-in-process inventories by job. As time is accumulated on time cards, it should be allocated to various jobs by means of job-time tickets. These are periodically extended by applicable rates and posted into the labor distribution summary.
- **Employment files.** Records that include date of employment, character references, rates of pay, authorized deductions, performance evaluations, and termination notices.
- **Rate authorization slips.** Documents generally prepared by management,

Figure 16-2 ■■■■

Exchange Transaction and Documents: Payrolls and Related Costs

Exchange transaction	Boundary document	Supporting document
Accrual of payroll, with-holding taxes	Employee time cards	Employment files Rate authorization
	Salaried payroll: Employment records	Employee exemption certificates (W-4) Deduction slips Labor distribution sheets Individual payroll records Job-time tickets
Payment of accrued liabilities	Employee paychecks	Individual payroll records Summary voucher to reimburse payroll account
	Checks in payment of other accrued liabilities	Vouchers in support of disbursements Payroll tax returns

based on union or other labor contracts with employees. In the case of upper-level management, authorization to hire and recommendations for salary generally must come from the board of directors.

- **Employee exemption certificates.** Otherwise known as Form W-4 of the federal government, these certificates are prepared by the employee and authorize the number of exemptions that the employee claims for withholding of federal income taxes. Similar documents may be obtained from state and local governments whenever local law prescribes withholding of those income taxes. Federal and state laws require that these records be kept for all employees.
- **Deduction slips.** Forms prepared by employees authorizing payroll deductions, including income taxes, insurances, savings or retirement plan deductions, and other deductions such as United Way contributions.
- **Labor distribution sheets.** Records that summarize the way in which the gross payroll charges should be distributed among the accounts in the general ledger (e.g., work-in-process inventories, expenses, etc.).
- **Individual payroll records.** Records maintained for each employee by time period, showing gross pay, withholdings from all sources, net pay, check number, and date.
- **Payroll tax returns.** Quarterly federal tax returns for income and social security (FICA) taxes (Form 941) as well as yearly unemployment tax returns (Form 940). In addition, state and local governments have similar returns for withholding of income taxes. These tax returns must be filed completely and on a timely basis to avoid possible penalties and fines against the company.

Comparisons and Compliance Monitoring

Like all other systems, to be effective, there should be a proper system of checks and balances within the payroll system that requires comparisons of key records and monitoring of compliance with managerial policies and directives on an ongoing basis. For example, as shown in Appendixes 16–B and C, foremen in the production department should regularly review job-time tickets and compare them with time cards before forwarding them to the timekeeping department. In the timekeeping department, hours worked as shown on the time cards should be reconciled to job-time tickets before they are approved. In the payroll department, rates for hourly personnel should be compared to payroll records by supervisors before approval is given to process the checks. In the treasurer's department, checks issued should be verified against the payroll register. If checks or cash are issued in person rather than through the mails, identification should be required. Separate imprest payroll bank accounts should be reconciled by the internal auditing department. Unclaimed wages, held by the treasurer's department, should be periodically compared to the accounting department's records of those checks.

With respect to payroll taxes, the company should have well-established policies that clearly set forth the procedures and timing for filing payroll tax returns. Competent persons should periodically review the payroll tax files and compare the returns with payroll and deposit records for completeness and accuracy.

Access to Assets and Data

As in other areas of the cash expenditures system, access to cash should be limited to persons in the treasurer's department. Access to personnel data files should be limited to persons in the personnel and payroll departments. The flowcharts in Appendixes 16–B and C illustrate proper limitation of access to assets and personnel data files.

Execution of Transactions as Authorized

The board of directors or equivalent authoritative body of the enterprise has the ultimate authority to approve payroll transactions. With respect to hiring, the personnel committee of the board of directors generally exercises its authority to specifically approve the hiring of executive management personnel. However, a significant amount of that authority is delegated to the personnel department to hire lower-level employees, and to terminate them on the basis of recommendations of supervisory personnel in the operating departments.

As shown in Appendixes 16–A and B, to prevent erroneous or deliberately misstated time records, departmental supervisors in the operating departments should review and approve all regular and overtime hours worked and should supervise clock punching. To prevent or detect the use of incorrect rates in the preparation of payrolls, rates and hours worked should be approved through the personnel office.

Terminations of hourly and lower-level administrative employees should be approved by supervisory personnel in the operating departments. For highly-paid salaried employees such as management, terminations should be approved by the board of directors. All changes should be properly documented in the files of the personnel department.

Detailed Tests of Transactions

Because of the tremendous volume of transactions that typically flow through the payroll system, it is not uncommon for the auditor to seek a high level of assurance (low level of control risk) with regard to controls. As we have stated previously, some built-in incentives already exist for clients to maintain effective controls over payrolls. Nevertheless, after reaching a preliminary understanding of the control structure and making an initial assessment of control risk, the auditor may desire to assess that risk at even lower levels. To do this, it will be necessary to conduct a detailed study of the control system and to perform tests of prescribed controls. The steps for the detailed study are the same as those outlined in Chapter 14 for the cash expenditures system.

Appendix 16–D contains details of a transactions-testing methodology for testing controls in the payroll system. Notice that the control attributes listed in Appendix 16–D are related to audit objectives. For example, to assist in satisfying the audit objective of transaction validity, changes in the employment structure of the company (new hires, terminations, etc.) should be subjected to proper approvals. To test this control, the auditor would select a sample from the population of employee earnings records showing new hirees, terminations, and rate changes and vouch those changes to authorization slips, board of directors' minutes, or personnel committee minutes.

Also notice that many of the tests of transactions listed in Appendix 16–D involve dual-purpose tests. In other words, because of the nature of the procedure being performed, it is both a test of controls and a substantive test. For example, to test for existence of personnel being paid, as well as transaction validity, the auditor selects a sample from the population employee earnings records (probably the same sample as that used in the preceding paragraph) and vouches the names and rates to the personnel files of the company. Since the rates of pay are used in the calculation of gross pay per the employee earnings records, the auditor, in testing these rates, is verifying proper valuation of wages and salaries expense in the financial statements. After performing all of the tests listed in Appendix 16–D, the auditor would probably need to perform very few, if any, detailed tests of payroll balances that are discussed in the next section. Instead, a great deal of reliance would be placed on corroborative analytical tests of expense and accrued liability accounts.

Detection Risk Procedures

☑ **Objective 3**
Perform detection risk procedures for payroll-related accounts

The relationship between audit objectives and procedures necessary to verify them is shown in Figure 16–3. Extensive detection risk procedures such as these are often not necessary if the control risk associated with the client's control structure is low. Detection risk procedures for payrolls are designed to detect payments to fictitious employees, to ascertain the validity and proper valuation of recorded transactions, to ascertain completeness, proper cutoff and existence of accrued liabilities, and to verify proper statement presentation or disclosure.

Figure 16-3

Detection Risk Procedures for Payroll-Related Accounts

Audit Objectives

Existence of employees	Transaction validity, completeness, and appropriate valuation	Existence and cutoff of liabilities	Completeness and statement presentation
1. Vouch signatures of endorsees on payroll checks to W-4s and time cards.	1. Recalculate gross pay and deductions for sample of employees.	1. Recompute accrued salaries and other payroll-related liabilities.	1. Read payroll-related disclosures for proper classification and disclosure.
2. Scan endorsements on canceled payroll checks for unusual items.	2. Recalculate footings and extensions of payroll journal.	2. Inspect payroll tax returns.	2. Compare with prior year accrued liabilities.
3. Inspect voided checks.	3. Trace postings of payroll journal to general ledger account postings.		
4. Vouch charges and credits in payroll journal to supporting documents in personnel files.	4. Vouch net pay total from payroll journal to transfers from general bank account to payroll bank account.		
5. Vouch sample from terminated employees file to payroll records from subsequent periods.	5. Reconcile labor costs per payroll summary to charges in labor accounts.		
6. Perform surprise payroll observation.	6. Reconcile payroll summary totals with labor distribution summary totals.		
	7. Trace totals in labor distribution summary to general ledger account postings.		
	8. Vouch entries in labor distribution summary to supporting documents.		
	9. Perform analytical procedures on payroll expense and accrued liability accounts.		
	10. Recompute accrued salaries payable; other payroll-related accruals.		

Existence of Fictitious Employees

If internal controls are weak, it may be possible to insert a fictitious employee into the system. For example, assume that a foreman has the following responsibilities: (1) keeps the supply of unused time cards, (2) notifies the personnel office of terminations, (3) approves hours worked, and (4) distributes paychecks to employees. When employee X resigns, the foreman may fail to notify the personnel office of X's action. He may insert a fictitious time card for X, continue to clock X in as if nothing had happened, and intercept X's paychecks for his own use.

To detect fictitious employees in the payroll, the auditor often begins with a sample of paid (canceled) paychecks returned in the company's payroll bank statement. Signatures of endorsees on the checks are vouched to W-4 forms in the payroll records and to time cards. Endorsements on the checks are scanned for unusual items and double endorsements (in this case, the fictitious paycheck would bear the forged endorsement of employee X as well as that of the foreman). Voided checks are inspected to make sure that they have, in fact, not been used.

Charges and credits in the payroll journal for selected employees are vouched to supporting documents (employment authorization forms, W-4s, etc.) in the employment files of the company. A sample of employees from the terminations file may also be vouched to payments in the subsequent period to see if any such payments appear.

Under unusually poor conditions of internal controls, the auditor might observe a payroll distribution on a surprise basis. In this case, the auditor would accompany the company paymaster as the distribution of paychecks is made. As the employees pick up their paychecks, they must present identification and sign for the check in the presence of the paymaster and the auditor. If any checks remain unclaimed, they must be investigated extensively as possible fraudulent items.

Tests of Transactions

Many of the tests which were described in the preceding section as tests of controls are dual-purpose tests and thus also serve the purpose of verifying the balances underlying payroll-related expense accounts. Items (1) through (8) in the second column of Figure 16–3 are dual-purpose tests, which serve the purpose of verifying the validity and proper valuation of various charges and credits in the ledgers, journals, and supporting documentation. Appendix 16–E contains details of transactions-testing methodology for a small company that uses an independent payroll service to process payrolls. In these cases, input and output records are reviewed for reasonableness. Rates and time are matched to supporting documents, and check amounts are matched to payroll check registers and to canceled checks. Dates, employee names and numbers, and endorsements are verified against supporting documents.

Analytical Procedures

If tests of controls have been performed and the auditor has concluded that control risk is low, the auditor may be satisfied to forego tests of transactions in favor of analytical procedures for payroll expense and related accrued liability accounts. Examples of analytical procedures are

- Balances for payroll expenses may be compared with prior years' balances.
- Direct and indirect labor may be computed as a percentage of sales and compared with similar figures from the prior year to detect unusual or unpredicted relationships.
- Commissions expense from the current year can be recomputed based on average commission percentages and sales figures. The recomputed balance should then be compared with the actual commissions expense, and material differences should be explained.
- Payroll tax expense can be computed as a percentage of salaries and wages

and compared with the same relationship from the previous year to detect misstatements in payroll tax expense.

- Accrued payroll tax liability accounts can be compared with those of the prior year, and unusual fluctuations investigated.

Completeness, Cutoff, and Existence of Liabilities

Proper cutoff, completeness, and existence of liabilities related to the accrued liability accounts are generally verified by recomputing the accrued salaries and other payroll-related liability accounts. For example, accrued salaries might be calculated by multiplying total gross pay for the pay period that extends through the client's year end by the fraction of that period that falls within the fiscal year. FICA taxes withheld can be recomputed for a sample of employees by multiplying the applicable rate by the base wages for those employees. Withholding taxes can be recomputed for the same sample by use of appropriate payroll tax tables. Accrued payroll taxes payable can be recomputed for the final pay period as follows:

$$\left(\begin{array}{l}\text{FICA taxes withheld per pay} \\ \text{period} \times 2) + \text{withholding} \\ \text{taxes for pay period}\end{array}\right) \times \frac{\text{Days in pay period prior to fiscal year end}}{\text{Days in pay period}}$$

Unemployment tax accruals should also be recomputed using proper rates and salary bases. The recomputed accruals should be compared with those recorded in the accounts and significant differences should be resolved. The client's payroll tax forms should be examined to ascertain whether they were filed in a timely and correct manner.

Appropriate Statement Presentation

When the other detection-risk procedures have been performed, the auditor should read payroll-related disclosures in the financial statements for proper classification and disclosure. In addition, final analytical procedures, comparing balances with prior years' figures after adjustments have been made, provide additional assurance that payroll expense and accrual accounts are fairly presented.

Using the Computer to Perform Payroll Audit Procedures

When records are computerized, the computer can be used to assist the auditor in performing any of the tests of controls or detection-risk procedures listed in the preceding sections, if they are repetitive or mechanical. For example, the computer can be used to perform a 100-percent recomputation of the gross pay, deductions, and net pay for all employees. It can also be programmed to verify the footings and extensions in payroll-related records and to trace postings of accounting summaries into the related general ledger accounts. We can also use the computer to trace related input documents to the payroll records and to print out register entries that correspond to canceled checks. Those entries can then be used in the auditor's manual vouching procedures. The computer can also be programmed to perform analytical procedures and to scan the accounts for unusual transactions. Unusual items can be printed out and used in discussions with the client.

Summary

In this chapter, our discussion focused on the audit of the payroll system and its related account balances. We began by outlining the major audit objectives applicable to the system. Those include existence/occurrence (transaction validity), completeness, proper valuation, cutoff, and proper statement presentation or disclosure. We then discussed planning considerations for the audit of the payroll system. We stated that, under most conditions, the inherent risk of misstatement for the payroll system is relatively high, given its connection with the disbursement of cash.

The major part of the chapter was devoted to a discussion of the control structure that should exist in payroll systems. If that structure is intact and is working as planned, the auditor may rely on the system (set control risk at a low level). Thus, the auditor may perform fewer and less effective detection risk procedures on payroll-related financial statement balances.

The latter part of the chapter focused on detection risk procedures. We first discussed the more detailed procedures that should be performed when control risk is assessed at high levels due to major weaknesses in the system. Then we presented a brief discussion of analytical procedures that are appropriate if control risk is assessed at low levels. The chapter concluded with a discussion of ways in which the computer could be used to perform both tests of controls and substantive tests.

Auditing Vocabulary

p. 687 **deduction slips:**   Forms prepared by employees that authorize various types of payroll deductions.

p. 687 **employee exemption certificates (Form W-4):**   Certificates prepared by employees that authorize the number of exemptions that the employee claims for withholding of federal income taxes.

p. 686 **employee time cards:**   Documents prepared by hourly personnel to accumulate the total number of hours worked.

p. 686 **employment files:**   Separate records for each employee that include date of employment, character references, rates of pay, authorized deductions, performance evaluations, and termination notices.

p. 687 **individual payroll records:**   Records maintained for each employee by time period.

p. 686 **job-time tickets:**   Records used in a job-order cost system to allocate gross labor costs to work-in-process inventories by job.

p. 687 **labor distribution sheets:**   Records that summarize the way gross payroll charges are distributed among the accounts in the general ledger.

p. 684 **payroll tax returns:**   Quarterly federal tax returns for income and social security taxes.

p. 686 **rate authorization slips:**   Documents prepared by management to approve rates of pay for certain types of jobs.

Appendix 16–A: Exchange Processing and Safeguard Functions Requiring Specific Controls

Function	Possible errors or irregularities	Results of undetected errors	Control attributes to prevent, detect, or correct errors or irregularities
Hiring and termination of employees; authorization of pay rates, deductions	Invalid or erroneous transactions: Hiring an unauthorized employee or paying an employee the wrong amount	Misappropriation of cash through payrolls	Require a separate personnel department through which is approved job descriptions; authorization of new hirees and terminations; rate changes; deductions.
	Recording the hiring of a fictitious employee	Misappropriation of cash through payrolls	Require authorization of salaried personnel through board of directors or personnel committee. Require operating departments to requisition all new hirees, terminations, and changes. Require documentation for all wage data in personnel files. The names of persons on the payroll should be traced to the personnel department records to be sure that they were employees of the company during the period.
Timekeeping	Invalid transactions: Erroneous or deliberately misstated time records (punching more than one time card or misstating time tickets)	Overpayments or misappropriation of cash through overstatement of payroll liability	Require use of timeclocks and time cards for all hourly personnel. Require departmental supervisors to approve all regular and overtime hours worked and to supervise clock punching. Control the supply of unused time cards. Require preparation of time tickets for job costing system. Require reconciliation of time tickets with time cards. Daily time reports or job-time cards should be reconciled with total hours worked as shown on employee timeclock cards.

	Invalid or improperly recorded transactions:	Misstatement of payroll liability	Separate the duties of payroll preparation, timekeeping, and cash disbursements. Require approval of rates and hours worked.
Preparation of payroll and taxes	Insertion of fictitious employee by person preparing payroll; using incorrect rates (regular, overtime, incentive), hours		
	Improperly valued transactions: Checks issued for incorrect amounts	Misappropriation of cash	Require verification of checks issued with payroll register.
Paying the payroll and taxes	Invalid transactions: Checks mailed or distributed to unauthorized persons	Misappropriation of cash	Require checks to be mailed without being returned to preparer. Require identification for distributees of paychecks.
	Transactions not timely recorded: Tax returns filed and paid late	Inefficient use of cash	Require timely filing and payment of payroll taxes.
	Improperly recorded and summarized transactions: Inadequate control over unclaimed wages and cash disbursements for payroll	Inaccuracies in recording payroll liability and cash disbursements	Require separate imprest payroll bank account, reconciled by persons independent from other payroll functions. Require follow-up for unclaimed wages, including restoration of unclaimed checks to cash along with establishment of current liability. Unclaimed payroll checks, held by the treasury department, should be periodically checked by the accounting department against their record of those checks.

Appendix 16–B: Employment and Payroll Cost Accumulation

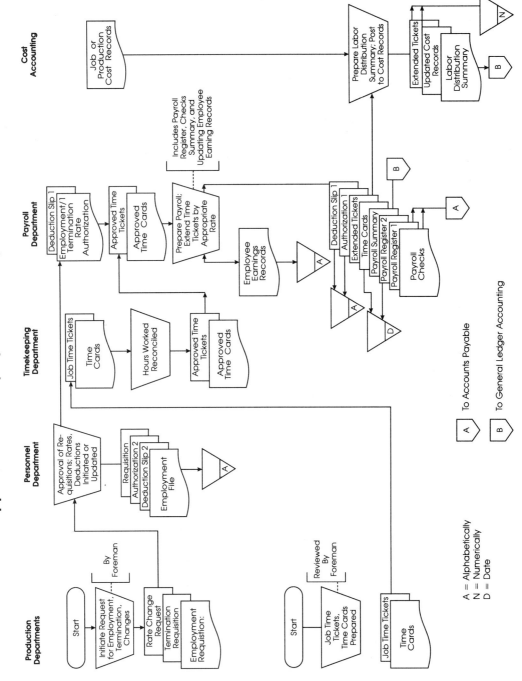

Appendix 16–C: Cash Disbursements and General Ledger Accounting for Payrolls

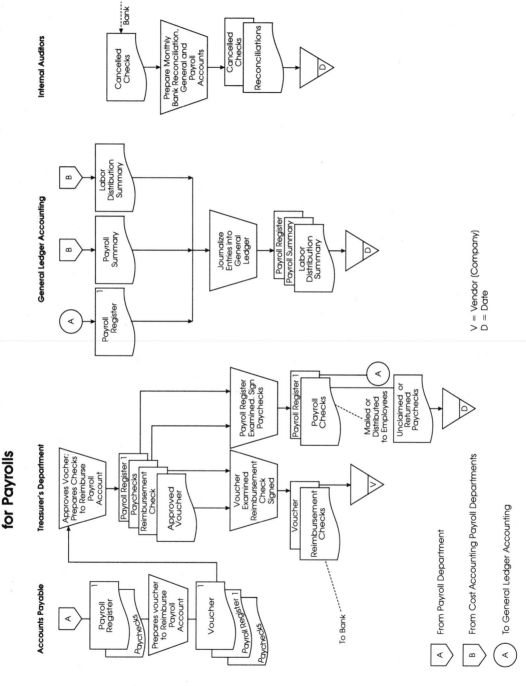

Accounts Payable

Treasurer's Department

General Ledger Accounting

Internal Auditors

V = Vendor (Company)
D = Date

A — From Payroll Department

B — From Cost Accounting Payroll Departments

A — To General Ledger Accounting

Appendix 16–D: Transactions Testing Methodology—Payroll System

Audit objective	Attribute of interest	Data field (population)	Audit procedure*	From	To
Transaction validity	New hires, termination, rate changes, and other changes are subjected to proper approvals	Employee earnings records: new hirees, terminations, rate changes	Vouch	Employee earnings records	Authorization slips, board of directors, or personnel committee minutes
Existence; transaction validity; valuation	Personnel being paid are both existent and authorized	Employee earnings records (names, rates)	Vouch	Employee earnings records	Personnel files
Completeness; transaction validity	Personnel actions (new hires, rate changes, terminations) are appropriately processed	Employment requisitions, terminations, rate change files	Trace	Employment requisition files in personnel departments	Employee earnings records
	Payroll deductions are properly authorized by employees	Employee earnings records: deductions	Vouch	Employee earnings records	Supporting data in employment file (W-4s, union contracts, etc.)
Valuation	Payroll deductions are processed correctly	Deductions slips	Trace	Deduction slips	Employee earnings records, payable journals, ledgers
Transaction validity	Timekeeping data about employees are adequately supported	Payroll journal (hours worked)	Vouch	Payroll journal	Time cards
Transaction validity	Timekeeping data about each job or department are adequately supported and in agreement with employee data	Job or production cost records	Vouch	Job or production cost records	Extended time tickets
			Reconcile	Job or production cost records	Payroll summary and payroll journals
			Reconcile	Time cards	Job-time tickets

Transaction validity	Regular and overtime hours worked are approved by departmental supervisors	Time cards	Vouch hours worked	Time cards	Management approval signatures
Existence; completeness	Checks issued to employees are verified to net pay per payroll register	Canceled checks per bank statement	Trace	Canceled checks	Entries in payroll register, employee earnings records
Existence; completeness	Entries in payroll register are supported by canceled checks	Entries in payroll register	Vouch	Payroll register	Canceled checks
Existence	Identification is required of all distributees of paychecks	Canceled checks	Vouch / Observe a surprise distribution of payroll checks†	Canceled checks	Employment files (W-4s, etc.)
Existence; completeness; transaction validity	Follow-up is required for unclaimed wages	Outstanding checks from payroll bank account	Trace	Outstanding check list	Subsequent entry to restore to cash and set up current liability account

*Sample sizes should be determined judgmentally or statistically, according to methodology discussed in Chapter 11.
†Should be performed by the auditor only if other attributes of internal control are missing.

Appendix 16–E: Payroll Testwork

			W. P. No.	Z-4
JEP Mfg. Co.			ACCOUNTANT	Smdy
Memo re: Payroll Testwork				
3-31-X1		✓	DATE	5/14/X1

All non-exempt, hourly employees are paid through
a computer payroll service on a weekly basis. We
reviewed these payroll procedures with Shirley Stevens,
payroll clerk. The following guidelines are in effect:
All employee time cards are reviewed and initialed by
the appropriate foreman. All time cards are submitted
to Mrs. Stevens who reviews for reasonableness. Any
changes to the employee's standard pay are entered on a
payroll change worksheet. All hours worked and
any authorized pay changes are submitted to National
Bank of Commerce (payroll service) who processes the
information per JEP's master control file and prints
the checks which are returned to Mrs. Stevens the
following week, along with a printout of all checks,
employees, employee #, and all appropriate deductions.
We reviewed Mrs. Stevens's payroll and employment
records noting that no employee was making more than
the authorized union wage. We then selected 10
employees from throughout the year and traced their

			W. P. No.	
			ACCOUNTANT	
			DATE	

wage from their authorized amount per the union
agreement, through their time cards, agreeing wage,
employee name, no., and hours to the printout from
NBC and finally agreeing the check amount per NBC
to the paid check, noting date, proper employee name,
employee number and endorsement. No exceptions
were noted in the above procedures. Finally, we
reviewed the weekly payroll for reasonableness,
noting no unusual fluctuations in the period under
review.

Conclusion: Based upon the audit procedures performed
as outlined above, which were considered adequate
to meet the objectives per the APG, it appears that
payroll procedures are being adequately adhered to
and that the payroll expense for the year ended 3-31-X1
is fairly stated.

Questions for Class Discussion

Q16-1 Explain the relationship between the expenditures system and the payroll system.

Q16-2 What are some of the accounts that are associated with the payroll system?

Q16-3 Why is the audit of the payroll system considered important?

Q16-4 What are the primary functions that are typically included in the payroll system?

Q16-5 What are the major errors or irregularities that could occur in a payroll system?

Q16-6 What are the primary audit objectives pertaining to the payroll system?

Q16-7 Why is it necessary for the auditor to obtain an understanding of the control structure pertaining to payrolls?

Q16-8 What are the basic elements of the control structure pertaining to payrolls?

Q16-9 What are the auditor's primary concerns considering the control environment of the business concerning payrolls?

Q16-10 What are some EDP controls that should be exercised in the control environment pertaining to payrolls?

Q16-11 Of what benefit can an internal audit department be in the payroll system?

Q16-12 What are the built-in incentives for a typical entity to maintain effective controls over payrolls?

Q16-13 Describe the flow of transactions through a typical payroll system.

Q16-14 What are the procedures that the auditor uses to obtain an understanding of the control environment for payrolls?

Q16-15 What are the procedures that the auditor uses to obtain an understanding of the accounting system for payrolls?

Q16-16 What controls do entities typically employ to prevent the hiring of a "fictitious employee?"

Q16-17 What controls do entities typically employ to assure that all employees are paid the correct amounts?

Q16-18 What controls should be exercised in the preparation of periodic payroll tax returns?

Q16-19 What duties should typically be separated in a good system of internal control over payrolls?

Q16-20 What duties are typically performed by the timekeeping department? The paymaster?

Q16-21 Why is an effective cost accounting system a central element in achieving control over payrolls?

Q16-22 Who should provide the "safeguard" function in a system of internal controls over payrolls?

Q16-23 What purpose do the following documents serve in a payroll system: time cards; job-time tickets; employment files; exemption certificates; labor-distribution sheets?

Q16-24 What records are typically compared in an accounting system over payrolls?

Q16-25 What departments or individuals within an entity should have authority to approve transactions?

Q16-26 In choosing a mixture of analytical procedures, tests of transactions, and direct tests of balances, which combination of the three is best suited for payrolls? Why?

Q16-27 Why would the auditor, when given a choice, generally choose a dual-purpose test over payrolls? Explain.

Q16-28 Under what conditions would an auditor generally ask to observe a distribution of employee paychecks for an audit client?

Q16-29 What are some particularly useful analytical procedures for payroll-related balances? What are the purposes of those procedures?

Q16-30 What are the procedures that are particularly effective in helping the auditor decide the proper valuation and disclosure of payroll-related accrued liability accounts?

Short Cases

C16-1 The Wacker Company employs about 50 production workers and has the following payroll procedures:

The factory foreman interviews applicants and on the basis of the interview either hires or rejects the applicants. When the applicant is hired he or she prepares a W-4 form (Employee's Withholding Exemption Certificate) and gives it to the foreman. The foreman writes the hourly rate of pay for the new employee in the corner of the W-4 form and then gives the form to a payroll clerk as notice that the worker has been employed. The foreman verbally advises the payroll department of rate adjustments.

A supply of blank time cards is kept in a box near the entrance to the factory. Each worker takes a time card on Monday morning, fills in his name, and notes in pencil on the time card his daily arrival and departure times. At the end of the week the workers drop the time cards in a box near the door to the factory.

The completed time cards are taken from the box on Monday morning by a payroll clerk. Two payroll clerks divide the cards alphabetically between them, one taking the A to L section of the payroll and the other taking the M to Z section. Each clerk is fully responsible for her or his section of the payroll. The clerk computes the gross pay, deductions, and net pay, posts the details to the employee's earnings records, and prepares and numbers the payroll checks. Employees are automatically removed from the payroll when they fail to turn in a time card.

The payroll checks are manually signed by the chief accountant and given to the foreman. The foreman distributes the checks to the workers in the factory and arranges for the delivery of the checks to the workers who are absent. The payroll bank account is reconciled by the chief accountant, who also prepares the various quarterly and annual payroll tax reports.

Required:
a. List the material weaknesses in the system of internal control and state the financial statement errors that are likely to result from those weaknesses.
b. For each weakness noted in (a), suggest an internal control procedure that would improve the system.

c. For each weakness noted in (a), list a substantive audit procedure that will have to be extended to check on it.

(AICPA adapted)

C16-2 Items (a) through (k) are questions excerpted from a typical internal control questionnaire for the purpose of understanding the internal control structure over preparation and payment of payrolls. As explained in the text, a "yes" response to such a question indicates a potential strength in the system and a "no" response indicates a potential weakness.

a. Are personnel files maintained for all employees by a separate personnel department?

b. Are new hires, terminations, and rate changes subjected to approvals by authorities in the personnel and operating departments?

c. Are personnel action forms for new hires, rate changes, and terminations appropriately processed by the payroll department?

d. Are all payroll deductions based on authorization by the employees?

e. Are all payroll deductions being processed correctly?

f. Are timekeeping data used in payroll preparation adequately supported by time cards and time tickets?

g. Are all regular and overtime hours worked by employees approved by departmental supervisors?

h. Are checks issued to employees verified to net pay per the payroll register by persons who reconcile the payroll book account?

i. Are entries in the payroll register supported by canceled checks?

j. Is proper identification required of all persons who distribute pay checks?

k. Is proper follow-up performed for all unclaimed wages by restoring such items to cash and making an equivalent entry to a current liability account?

Required: For each question above, list

a. The error or irregularity which that control attribute was designed to detect.

b. The effect that the absence of the control attribute would have on the financial statements.

c. The test necessary to ascertain whether the controls were actually being implemented if the answer to the question is "yes." When sampling of documents is involved, indicate the data file from which a sample would be chosen and the audit procedure (vouching, tracing, recalculation, etc.) that is appropriate (see Appendix 16–D).

d. Whether the test of controls listed in (c) is also a substantive test of transactions. If not, indicate the substantive test (Figure 16–3), that would be extended, if any, if that control attribute were missing or if the test of controls results demonstrated a low level of compliance.

Organize your answer according to the format specified below. The first question has been answered as an example.

Item	Error or irregularity	Effect on financial statements	Test of controls	Also a substantive test or substantive test extended
(a)	Insertion and paying fictitious employees	Misappropriation of cash	Observation	Surprise payroll observation to detect fictitious employees

C16-3   In connection with his examination of the financial statements of the Olympia Manufacturing Company, a CPA is reviewing procedures for accumulating direct-labor hours. He learns that all production is by job order and that all employees are paid hourly wages, with time-and-one-half for overtime hours.

Olympia's direct-labor-hour input process for payroll and job-cost determination is summarized in the flowchart below.

Steps A and C of the process are performed in timekeeping, step B in the factory operating departments, step D in payroll audit and control, step E in data preparation (keypunch), and step F in computer operations.

Required: For each input processing step A through F
a. List the possible errors or discrepancies that may occur.
b. Cite the corresponding control procedure that should be in effect for each error or discrepancy.
c. Briefly discuss the most appropriate test for the control.

Note: Your discussion of Olympia's procedures should be limited to the input process for direct-labor hours, as shown in steps A through F in the flowchart. Do not discuss personnel procedures for hiring, promotion, termination, and pay-rate authorization. In step F do not discuss equipment, computer program, and general computer operational controls.

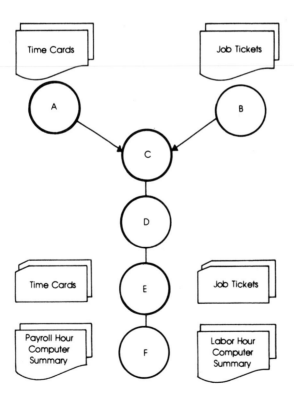

Organize your answer for each input-processing step as follows:

Step	Possible errors or discrepancies	Control procedures	Most appropriate test of controls

(AICPA adapted)

C16-4   The Gibraltar Loan Company has 100 branch loan offices. Each office has a manager and four or five subordinates who are employed by the manager. Branch managers prepare the weekly payroll, including their own salaries, and pay employees from cash on hand. The employee signs the payroll sheet signifying receipt of his or her salary. Hours worked by hourly personnel are inserted in the payroll sheet from time cards prepared by the employees and approved by the manager.

The weekly payroll sheets are sent to the home office along with other accounting statements and reports. The home office compiles employee earnings records and prepares all federal and state salary reports from the weekly payroll sheets.

Salaries are established by home office job evaluation schedules. Salary adjustments, promotions, and transfers of full-time employees are approved by a home office salary committee based on the recommendations of branch managers and area supervisors. Branch managers advise the salary committee of new full-time employees and terminations. Part-time and temporary employees are hired without referral to the salary committee.

Required:
a. On the basis of your review of the payroll system, how do you think funds for payroll might be diverted?
b. Prepare a payroll audit program to be used in the home office to audit the branch office payrolls of the Gibraltar Loan Company.

(AICPA adapted)

C16-5   You are engaged in auditing the financial statements of Henry Beasley, a large independent contractor. All employees are paid in cash because Beasley believes this arrangement reduces clerical expenses and is preferred by his employees.

During the audit you find in the petty cash fund approximately $200, of which $185 is stated to be unclaimed wages. Further investigation reveals that Beasley has installed the procedure of putting any unclaimed wages in the petty cash fund so that the cash can be used for disbursements. When the claimant to the wages appears, he or she is paid from the petty cash fund. Beasley contends that this procedure reduces the number of checks drawn to replenish the petty cash fund and centers the responsibility for all cash on hand in one person inasmuch as the petty cash custodian distributes the pay envelopes.

Required:
a. Does Beasley's system provide proper internal control of unclaimed wages? Explain fully.
b. Because Beasley insists on paying salaries in cash, what procedures would you recommend to provide better internal control over unclaimed wages?

(AICPA adapted)

Problems

P16-1 Select the best answer for each of the following items relating to the internal controls over payroll.

a. In the audit of which of the following types of profit-oriented enterprises would the auditor be most likely to place special emphasis on testing the internal controls over proper classifications of payroll transactions?
1. A manufacturing organization.
2. A retailing organization.
3. A wholesaling organization.
4. A service organization.

b. A CPA reviews a client's payroll procedures. The CPA would consider internal control to be less than effective if a payroll department supervisor was assigned the responsibility for
1. Reviewing and approving time reports for subordinate employees.
2. Distributing payroll checks to employees.
3. Hiring subordinate employees.
4. Initiating requests for salary adjustments for subordinate employees.

c. For internal control purposes, which of the following individuals should preferably be responsible for the distribution of payroll checks?
1. Bookkeeper.
2. Payroll clerk.
3. Cashier.
4. Receptionist.

d. Which of the following is an effective internal control used to prove that production department employees are properly validating payroll time cards at a time-recording station?
1. Time cards should be carefully inspected by those persons who distribute pay envelopes to the employees.
2. One person should be responsible for maintaining records of employee time for which salary payment is *not* to be made.
3. Daily reports showing time charged to jobs should be approved by the supervisor and compared to the total hours worked on the employee time cards.
4. Internal auditors should make observations of distribution of paychecks on a surprise basis.

e. During 19X9, a bookkeeper perpetrated a theft by preparing erroneous W-2 forms. The bookkeeper's FICA withheld was overstated by $500, and the FICA withheld from all other employees was understated. Which of the following is an auditing procedure that would detect such a fraud?
1. Multiplication of the applicable rate by the individual gross taxable earnings.
2. Utilizing form W-4 and withholding charts to determine whether deductions authorized per pay period agree with amounts deducted per pay period.
3. Footing and crossfooting of the payroll register, followed by tracing postings to the general ledger.
4. Vouching canceled checks to federal tax forms 941.

f. Effective internal control over the payroll function would include which of the following?
1. Total time recorded on time-clock cards should be reconciled to job reports by employees responsible for those specific jobs.

2. Payroll department employees should be supervised by the management of the personnel department.

3. Payroll department employees should be responsible for maintaining employee personnel records.

4. Total time spent on jobs should be compared with total time indicated on time-clock cards.

g. Which of the following individuals is the most appropriate person to be assigned the responsibility of distributing envelopes that include employee payroll checks?

1. The company paymaster.

2. A member of the accounting department.

3. The internal auditor.

4. A representative of the bank where the company payroll account is maintained.

h. A CPA reviews a client's payroll procedures. The CPA would consider internal control to be less than effective if a payroll department supervisor was assigned the responsibility for

1. Distributing payroll checks to employees.

2. Reviewing and approving time reports for subordinate employees.

3. Hiring subordinate employees.

4. Initiating requests for salary adjustments for subordinate employees.

i. It would be appropriate for the payroll accounting department to be responsible for which of the following functions?

1. Approval of employee time records.

2. Maintenance of records of employment, discharges, and pay increases.

3. Preparation of periodic governmental reports as to employees' earnings and withholding taxes.

4. Temporary retention of unclaimed employee paychecks.

j. Effective internal control over the payroll function should include procedures that segregate the duties of making salary payments to employees and

1. Controlling unemployment insurance claims.

2. Maintaining employee personnel records.

3. Approving employee fringe benefits.

4. Hiring new employees.

(AICPA adapted)

P16-2   Select the best answer for each of the following items related to the audit of payroll transactions.

a. A surprise observation by an auditor of a client's regular distribution of paychecks is primarily designed to satisfy the auditor that

1. All unclaimed payroll checks are properly returned to the cashier.

2. The paymaster is *not* involved in the distribution of payroll checks.

3. All employees have in their possession proper employee identification.

4. Names on the company payroll are those of bona fide employees presently on the job.

b. In testing the payroll of a large company, the auditor wants to establish that the individuals included in a sample actually were employees of the company during the period under review. What will be the *best* source to determine this?

1. Telephone contacts with the employees.

2. Tracing from the payroll register to the employees' earnings records.

    3. Confirmation with the union or other independent organization.

    4. Examination of personnel department records.

c. Which of the following procedures would normally be performed by the auditor when making tests of payroll transactions?

    1. Interview employees selected in a statistical sample of payroll transactions.

    2. Trace number of hours worked as shown on payroll to time cards and time reports signed by the supervisor.

    3. Confirm amounts withheld from employees' salaries with proper governmental authorities.

    4. Examine signatures on paid salary checks.

d. Which of the following is the *best* reason why an auditor should consider observing a client's distribution of regular payroll checks?

    1. Separation of payroll duties is less than adequate for effective internal control.

    2. Total payroll costs are a significant part of total operating costs.

    3. The auditor did *not* observe the distribution of the entire regular payroll during the audit in the prior year.

    4. Employee turnover is excessive.

e. If a control total were to be computed on each of the following data items, which would *best* be identified as a hash total for a payroll EDP application?

    1. Gross pay.

    2. Hours worked.

    3. Department number.

    4. Number of employees.

f. When examining payroll transactions an auditor is primarily concerned with the possibility of

    1. Overpayments and unauthorized payments.

    2. Posting of gross payroll amounts to incorrect salary expense accounts.

    3. Misfootings of employee time records.

    4. Excess withholding of amounts required to be withheld.

g. Which of the following is the *best* way for an auditor to determine that every name on a company's payroll is that of a bona fide employee presently on the job?

    1. Examine personnel records for accuracy and completeness.

    2. Examine employees' names listed on payroll tax returns for agreement with payroll accounting records.

    3. Make a surprise observation of the company's regular distribution of paychecks.

    4. Visit the working areas and confirm with employees their badge or identification numbers.

h. An auditor decides that it is important and necessary to observe a client's distribution of payroll checks on a particular audit. The client organization is so large that the auditor *cannot* conveniently observe the distribution of the entire payroll. In these circumstances, which of the following is *most* acceptable to the auditor?

    1. Observation should be limited to one or more selected departments.

    2. Observation should be made for all departments regardless of the inconvenience.

    3. Observation should be eliminated and other alternative auditing procedures should be utilized to obtain satisfaction.

    4. Observation should be limited to those departments where employees are readily available.

i. A common audit procedure in the audit of payroll transactions involves vouching selected items from the payroll journal to employee time cards that have been approved by supervisory personnel. This procedure is designed to provide evidence in support of the audit proposition that

1. Only bona fide employees worked and their pay was properly computed.
2. Jobs on which employees worked were charged with the appropriate labor cost.
3. Internal controls relating to payroll disbursements are operating effectively.
4. All employees worked the number of hours for which their pay was computed.

j. One of the auditor's objectives in observing the actual distribution of payroll checks is to determine that every name on the payroll is that of a bona fide employee. The payroll observation is an auditing procedure that is generally performed for which of the following reasons?

1. The professional standards that are generally accepted require the auditor to perform the payroll observation.
2. The various phases of payroll work are *not* sufficiently segregated to afford effective internal accounting control.
3. The independent auditor uses personal judgment and decides to observe the payroll distribution on a particular audit.
4. The standards that are generally accepted by the profession are interpreted to mean that payroll observation is expected on an audit unless circumstances dictate otherwise.

k. To check the accuracy of hours worked, an auditor would ordinarily compare clock cards with

1. Personnel records.
2. Shop job-time tickets.
3. Labor variance reports.
4. Time recorded in the payroll register.

(AICPA adapted)

P16-3   Bonnie James, who was engaged to examine the financial statement of Talbert Corporation, is about to audit payroll. Talbert uses a computer service center to process weekly payroll. James learns how the system works.

Each Monday, Talbert's payroll clerk inserts data in appropriate spaces on the preprinted, service-center-prepared input form and sends it to the service center via messenger. The service center extracts new permanent data from the input form and updates master files. The weekly payroll data are then processed. The weekly payroll register and payroll checks are printed and delivered by messenger to Talbert on Thursday.

Part of the sample selected for audit by James includes the input form and payroll register shown below.

Required:

a. Describe how James should verify the information in the preceding payroll input form.

b. Describe (but do *not* perform) the procedures that James should follow in the examination of the November 23, 19X2, payroll register.

Talbert Corporation

P A Y R O L L   I N P U T

Week Ending Friday, Nov. 23, 19X2

	Employee Data—Permanent File					Current Week's Payroll Data			
			W-4		Hours		Special deductions		
Name	Social security		infor-mation	Hourly rate	Reg	OT	Bonds	Union	Other
A. Bello	999-99-9991		M-1	10.00	35	5	18.75		
B. Cardinal	999-99-9992		M-2	10.00	35	4			
C. Dawn	999-99-9993		S-1	10.00	35	6	18.75	4.00	
D. Ellis	999-99-9994		S-1	10.00	35	2		4.00	50.00
E. Frank	999-99-9995		M-4	10.00	35	1		4.00	
F. Gillis	999-99-9996		M-4	10.00	35			4.00	
G. Huvos	999-99-9997		M-1	7.00	35	2	18.75	4.00	
H. Jones	999-99-9998		M-2	7.00	35			4.00	25.00
J. King	999-99-9999		S-1	7.00	35	4		4.00	
New employee									
J. Siegal	999-99-9990		M-3	7.00	35				

Talbert Corporation

P A Y R O L L   R E G I S T E R

Nov. 23, 19X2

		Hours		Payroll			Taxes withheld			Other		
Employee	Social security	Reg	OT	Regular	OT	Gross payroll	FICA	Fed	State	with-held	Net pay	Check no.
A. Bello	999-99-9991	35	5	350.00	75.00	425.00	26.05	76.00	27.40	18.75	276.00	1499
B. Cardinal	999-99-9992	35	4	350.00	60.00	410.00	25.13	65.00	23.60		296.27	1500
C. Dawn	999-99-9993	35	6	350.00	90.00	440.00	26.97	100.90	28.60	22.75	260.78	1501
D. Ellis	999-99-9994	35	2	350.00	30.00	380.00	23.29	80.50	21.70	54.00	200.51	1502
E. Frank	999-99-9995	35	1	350.00	15.00	365.00	22.37	43.50	15.90	4.00	279.23	1503
F. Gillis	999-99-9996	35		350.00		350.00	21.46	41.40	15.00	4.00	268.14	1504
G. Huvos	999-99-9997	35	2	245.00	21.00	266.00	16.31	34.80	10.90	22.75	181.24	1505
H. Jones	999-99-9998	35		245.00		245.00	15.02	26.40	8.70	29.00	165.88	1506
J. King	999-99-9999	35	4	245.00	42.00	287.00	17.59	49.40	12.20	4.00	203.81	1507
J. Siegal	999-99-9990	35		245.00		245.00	15.02	23.00	7.80		199.18	1508
	Total	350	24	3,080.00	333.00	3,413.00	209.21	540.90	171.80	159.25	2,331.84	

(AICPA adapted)

P16-4   A CPA's audit working papers contain a narrative description of a *segment* of the Croyden Factory, Inc., payroll system and an accompanying flowchart as follows:

The internal control system with respect to the personnel department is well-functioning and is *not* included in the accompanying flowchart.

Croyden Inc.,
Factory Payroll System

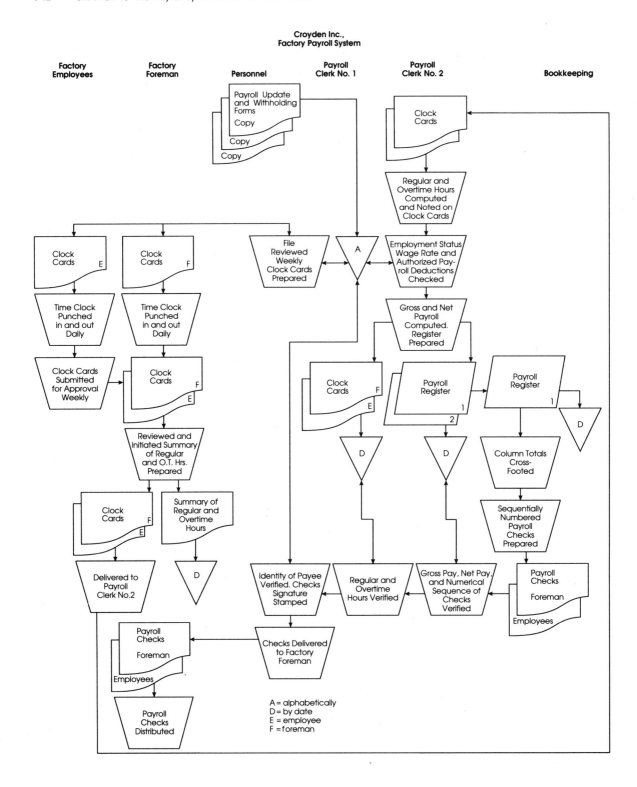

At the beginning of each work week, payroll clerk No. 1 reviews the payroll department files to determine the employment status of factory employees and then prepares time cards and distributes them as each individual arrives at work. This payroll clerk, who is also responsible for custody of the signature stamp machine, verifies the identity of each payee before delivering signed checks to the foreman.

At the end of each work week the foreman distributes payroll checks for the preceding work week. Concurrent with this activity, the foreman reviews the current week's employee time cards, notes the regular and overtime hours worked on a summary form, and initials the aforementioned time cards. The foreman then delivers all time cards and unclaimed payroll checks to payroll clerk No. 2.

Required:
  a. On the basis of the narrative and accompanying flowchart, what are the weaknesses in the system of internal control?
  b. On the basis of the narrative and accompanying flowchart, what inquiries should be made with respect to clarifying the existence of *possible additional weaknesses* in the system of internal control?
  (*Note*: Do not discuss the internal control system of the personnel department.)
  c. What substantive tests on payroll balances, if any, should be extended because of the weaknesses pointed out in requirements (a) and (b)?

(AICPA adapted)

CHAPTER 17

The Production and Conversion System

Objectives

☐ **1.** Identify the relevant audit objectives for the production and conversion system.
☐ **2.** Plan the audit of the production and conversion system.
☐ **3.** Obtain an understanding of the control structure in the production and conversion system.
☐ **4.** Perform the detection risk procedures necessary to fulfill the audit objectives for the production and conversion system.

In the previous three chapters, we have discussed the audit of systems in which the costs of raw materials and labor are accumulated in manufacturing entities. Once accumulated, raw materials inventories flow into the production system. Labor and overhead are allocated to the job or process as raw materials are converted to finished-goods inventories. In time, those inventories are sold, and the cost of goods sold is matched against revenue from sales. In this chapter, we focus our attention on the audit of this process, which we refer to as the production and conversion system. We will follow the same audit process that was illustrated in Figure 5–2. It might be helpful to refer to that figure again as you study the chapter.

In the appendixes to the chapter, we include diagrams that depict systems flowcharts, key control attributes, and working papers that illustrate detection risk procedures over inventory and cost-of-goods-sold accounts in the financial statements of JEP Manufacturing Co.

Audit Objectives

☑ **Objective 1**
Identify the audit objectives for the production and conversion system

The accounts included in the production and conversion system include raw materials, work-in-process, and finished-goods inventories, as well as cost of goods sold. The audit objectives that are of importance include

1. Existence or occurrence (related to transaction validity).
2. Proper valuation.
3. Ownership rights/obligations.
4. Cutoff of both purchases and sales (related to the assertion of allocation).
5. Completeness.
6. Proper statement presentation or disclosure.

These objectives are developed from the financial statement assertions of management regarding inventories and represent the most important sources of error in the financial statements.

The auditor is concerned with ensuring that the inventory accounts are not overstated to include nonexistent inventory and, perhaps to a lesser degree, that inventory might exist that is not included. Additionally, transactions might be recorded in the system, but in the wrong periods. Thus, *existence*, *completeness*, and proper *cutoff* are considered primary audit objectives.

An important objective of the auditor is to verify that the debit and credit transactions that produced the inventory and cost-of-goods-sold balances in the financial statements are adequately supported by competent documentary or machine-readable evidence. *Transaction validity* is thus considered an important audit objective that must be verified.

Many different means of *valuation* might be used in the *disclosure* of inventories within the boundaries of generally accepted accounting principles. For example, several different costing methods (FIFO, LIFO, weighted-average, etc.) are acceptable. Within each of these, the lower-of-cost-or-market rule must be applied. The management of the entity, with the auditor's concurrence, must choose the most appropriate disclosure alternatives that present financial position and results of operations in the fairest manner possible. These factors make *valuation* and *statement presentation* primary objectives of verification for the auditor.

It is possible for inventories to exist and not to be owned. Many wholesale or retail businesses utilize *consignment* as a means of facilitating sales and conserving cash. Thus, when the auditor considers inventories that exist, he or she must conduct proper tests to verify that, if they are listed as assets on the balance sheet, they are actually *owned* by the business.

Planning Considerations

As we discussed in Chapter 14, there is often a high level of inherent risk associated with the audit of the systems that surround inventories. This is because inventory errors often have pervasive effects on income as well as balance sheet variables. In addition, depending on the cost accounting system, the computation of certain types of work-in-process or finished-goods inventories can be quite complex.

The cost accounting systems in certain industries can have unique features that necessitate a high level of understanding. For example, the inventories for oil and gas refiners and other companies in the extractive industries often require certain unique estimates and accounting methods. In these cases, the supervisory-level auditor should make sure that the audit senior and all staff persons have the proper level of industry audit training. In-charge and staff persons should read industry periodicals and perform other research on the company to understand the intricacies of accounting for inventories in the industry before audit field work begins.

Because of the materiality and relatively high inherent risk of inventories, the auditor generally spends a proportionately large amount of time in the audit of the production and conversion system of a manufacturing business enterprise. Additionally, the field work supervisor will probably assign the more experienced staff persons to the audit of the production and conversion system.

Just as with receivables, the auditor is inclined to believe that, if an intentional misstatement in inventories were to occur, the client would be more likely to *overstate inventories* than to understate them. Consequently, many of the procedures used to meet the audit objectives for inventory balances are designed to verify recorded amounts. It is worth noting, however, that perpetual inventory records are often kept over inventories and are adjusted periodically to conform to physical counts. The offsetting entry to record an unexplained inventory adjustment is most often made to cost of goods sold. Therefore, inventory balances might be correctly stated as of the balance sheet date, while purchases of that inventory might be unrecorded. The result of such an error is an understatement of both cost of goods sold and accounts payable. For this reason, the *search for unrecorded liabilities*, which was discussed in detail in Chapter 14, is also an important audit procedure for cost of goods sold.

One of the most important elements of planning the audit of inventories is the planning of the observation of year-end physical counts of inventories. Observation of physical counts is the most effective way of ascertaining that inventories exist and that accounting over them is proper. The auditor should inquire of the client as to the days on which counts are to be conducted. Client inventory-taking instructions should be reviewed for completeness. The location of storage facilities for inventories should be ascertained, and the in-charge auditor should plan to have competent, well-informed staff persons at every site to observe the counts. We will discuss the procedures involved in inventory observation later in the chapter.

Another vital part of planning the audit of the production and conversion cycle is the use of analytical procedures such as calculation of gross profit and inventory turnover ratios. Comparison of these figures with those of the company for the prior year and those of the industry can help pinpoint such potential errors as inventory obsolescence, valuation, and cutoff problems. Analytical procedures can also be useful in helping the auditor to decide on the reasonableness of accounting estimates used for valuation disclosure of inventories.

Understanding the Control Structure

☑ **Objective 3**
Understand control structure and assess control risk for the production and conversion system

In most accounting systems involving inventories, thousands or even millions of transactions are processed annually. This makes it necessary for the auditor to obtain a thorough understanding of the control structure of the production and conversion system before proceeding with the audit of the assertions embodied in the financial statement balances. As is the case with all other systems, the control structure for inventories consists of the control environment, the accounting system, and control procedures.

The Control Environment

Management's attitude should be serious toward maintaining a system that is capable of preventing, detecting, or correcting specific errors or irregularities. The operating style of management should reflect this attitude. The organizational structure of the business should provide for adequate separation of critical duties. Larger entities should have internal audit departments that regularly monitor compliance with company policies and procedures and report directly to audit committees of the board of directors. Job descriptions should be provided for all employees, and duties of employees at various levels should reflect proper authority-responsibility relationships. A responsibility accounting system should be employed within the company, which places responsibility for meeting various portions of the operating budget on the shoulders of various department heads.

The auditor learns about the control environment surrounding an entity by prior experience, discussions with firm personnel, inquiries and observation of company management and employees, and reading pertinent system documentation, including organization charts and procedures manuals.

The Accounting System

Figure 17–1 presents diagrammatically the typical flow of costs through the production and conversion system. It is important that the accounting system over these costs match as closely as possible the *physical flow of the goods*. Initiation of the production system occurs in the production department. Raw materials are generally released to production on the basis of a bill of materials that prescribes the standard amount of materials to be used in the product. The production de-

Figure 17–1

Flow of Transactions: Production and Conversion System

Raw Materials Inventory

Beginning inventory xxx	xxx (1)
From expenditures	
system xxx	
xxx	xxx
Ending inventory xxx	

Direct Labor

From payroll system xxx	xxx (2)

Manufacturing Overhead

From expenditures	xxx (3)
system xxx	

Work-in-Process Inventory

Beginning inventory xxx	xxx (4)
(1) xxx	
(2) xxx	
(3) xxx	
xxx	xxx
Ending inventory xxx	

Finished Goods Inventory

Beginning inventory xxx	xxx (5)
(4) xxx	
xxx	xxx
Ending inventory xxx	

Cost of Goods Sold

(5) xxx	

Notes: (1) Raw material used in production; (2) direct labor used in production; (3) manufacturing overhead allocation; (4) transfer of completed goods; (5) cost-of-goods-sold entry.

partment documents the requisitioning of materials by means of a **raw-materials-issue slip**, which is sent to the raw materials stores department. The raw materials stores department uses the issue slips along with receiving reports (from the acquisition system in Chapter 14) as the documentation for updating raw material perpetual inventory files.

From this point in the system, there is a great divergence in practice among different manufacturing companies. As we mentioned earlier, the cost accounting system of a particular entity should be tailored to fit the needs of the production and conversion system, and of the product. The process that we present below is merely one example.

As the goods move through the production department, labor and overhead are introduced. Direct and indirect labor charges are processed through the payroll system (Chapter 16) and are documented by time cards and rate slips in that system. The cost accounting department receives a copy of the **labor distribution summary** from the payroll department. This summary distributes labor charges between jobs or processes, depending on the type of cost accounting system that is utilized. The labor distribution summary becomes the source document for labor charges to inventory in the cost accounting department. Then, using a standard cost system, the cost accounting department generally applies overhead to the job or the process based on predetermined formulas. Thus, the cost accounting department accumulates costs in the work-in-process inventory accounts.

As the process is completed, the production department prepares **production reports** that show the number of units completed and transferred to finished goods. One copy of that report is forwarded to the cost accounting department and one copy to the finished goods department along with the goods. In the finished goods department, production reports are used along with copies of sales invoices from the revenue system (Chapter 13) to post **perpetual inventory records** of finished goods inventories. In the cost accounting department, a copy of the production report is used as the basis for the preparation of the journal entry to transfer work-in-process to finished goods inventories. The cost accounting department also gets a copy of the sales summary from the revenue system, and uses this to prepare the journal entry transferring costs from finished goods inventory to cost of goods sold.

As is the case with other systems, the auditor's understanding of the control system is documented by means of internal control questionnaires, narrative descriptions, and systems flowcharts. Appendix 17–A contains a flowchart depicting the production and conversion system.

Control Procedures

The control environment and the accounting system over inventories and cost of goods sold should embody policies and procedures over recording, processing, summarizing, and reporting functions that provide for accurate and fair reflection of the financial statement assertions of management. Control procedures for the production and conversion system include (1) proper segregation of responsibilities, (2) adequate records and documentation, (3) an effective system of comparisons and compliance-monitoring, (4) limited access to assets and sensitive data, and (5) proper execution of transactions in accordance with management's general or specific authority.

Proper Segregation of Responsibilities

As with all systems, the functions of custody of assets, recordkeeping, and approval of transactions should be kept separate. As shown in Appendix 17–A, this is usually accomplished in the production and conversion system by separating the purchasing, receiving, storage, production, shipping, and cost accounting functions. Actually, since the production and conversion system is linked through inventories and cost of goods sold with the acquisitions and expenditures, payroll, and revenue and collections systems discussed in previous chapters, it is clear that good accounting control is enhanced by requiring all of these functions to be performed by separate departments.

Adequate Records and Documentation

Figure 17–2 lists the documentation that should be included in the production and conversion system. We have discussed these documents along with the accounting system in the previous section or in previous chapters.

Unlike the other systems of the business, most of the documentation in the production and conversion system is internally generated and held internally. According to the guidelines that were set out in Chapter 5 for competency of evidence, at first glance these documents would not be considered very competent. It should be pointed out, however, that more competent externally generated documents are generated only with exchange transactions. The movement of goods from one department to another within the entity, as is the case in the production and conversion system, does not constitute an exchange transaction with an external entity. Thus, it is not possible to generate external documents from such activities. Furthermore, in the production and conversion system, documentation is considered adequate if it properly tracks the movement of goods within the system, and if the integrity of the system is protected by other control attributes, such as proper segregation of duties, proper use of comparisons and compliance monitoring, proper authorizations, and other measures. In addition, it should be recalled from previous chapters that the acquisition of raw materials, the incurrence of labor and overhead charges, and the sales of inventory (all involving boundary transactions) are all documented by more competent externally generated evidence. If all of these controls are in place and are operating as prescribed, documentation of the production and conversion system is considered sufficient as well as competent.

Figure 17–2

Documentation for the Production and Conversion System

Function or transaction	Primary document	Supporting documents
Raw materials issues	Issue slips	Perpetual inventory records
Application of labor to inventories	Job-time tickets	Time cards, labor distribution summary
Application of overhead to inventories	Standard cost records	
Transfer of work-in-process to finished goods	Production reports	Scrap reports
Transfer of finished goods to cost of goods sold	Sales invoices	Sales summaries

Comparisons and Compliance Monitoring

The best example of the use of comparisons in the production and conversion system is the use of a production budget and a standard cost system. Standard costs are set for labor, materials, and overhead for each item of inventory produced. Records of standard costs are usually kept in computer files. As the production process takes place, variances from standard costs are computed for raw materials, labor, and overhead. Generally both usage and efficiency variances are produced for these factors of production. **Scrap reports** are also produced as a by-product of the system. The production control department or internal audit department should compare actual performance with the operating budget, and follow up with recommendations for improvements in the process. Scrap reports should be examined for trends, and if excessive scrap is continuously produced, causes should be found and ways devised to reduce it.

Perpetual inventory records are generally kept on computer files by personnel in both the raw materials and finished goods stores departments. Work-in-process inventory records may be maintained by the cost accounting department. General ledger accounts for inventories may be maintained in still another department. Periodically, physical counts should be taken of raw materials and finished goods, and an estimate made of work-in-process inventories. These counts and computations should be compared to the records maintained at all locations, and all differences reconciled. Material discrepancies between book and physical counts should be thoroughly investigated. Then, all records should be adjusted to reflect quantities of inventories at proper physical count levels.

The internal audit division should regularly compare cost per unit of inventory with underlying documentary support. For example, raw material costs should be compared with recent vendor invoices if the FIFO pricing system is being used for inventories. Work-in-process and finished-goods cost per unit should be compared with underlying cost records to assure that unit cost of these inventories is reasonable in the records of the entity.

Adjusting journal entries should be made in the books of the entity to reflect adjustments for either quantities or unit cost of inventories. Losses from scrap should be analyzed, and causes identified and corrected.

Access to Assets and Data

As we mentioned in Chapter 14, access to inventories should be limited to personnel in the stores department or warehouses. Warehouses and production areas should be kept properly maintained to avoid damage or deterioration from weather and other elements. All facilities should be kept locked and, if necessary, guarded during nonbusiness hours. Depending on the nature of the business, facilities may be locked and guarded even during business hours. Burglar and fire alarms should be utilized as well.

All accounting records, including cost accounting records, should be kept safely locked in protected areas while not in use. If sensitive cost accounting data is stored in computer files, only authorized personnel should be allowed access to that data. Controls such as access codes, passwords, and other user identification should be utilized to prevent improper access to data files.

Execution of Transactions as Approved

The primary approval function in the production and conversion system rests with the production control department, who monitors and controls the standard cost system, and who follows up variances from standards for materials, labor, and overhead. As we discussed in Chapter 14, approvals over acquisition of raw materials rests with the purchasing agent. The credit department serves the primary approval function at the other end of the system by approving credit for customers who purchase finished-goods inventories.

Control Risk Assessment Procedures

If the auditor desires to rely on controls to reduce the nature, timing, and extent of detection risk procedures (discussed in the next section) he or she will need to perform control risk assessment procedures on the system. The purpose of these procedures is to determine (1) whether specific controls discussed in the preceding section are prescribed by the client; and (2) whether prescribed controls are actually being followed. Figure 17–3 presents an internal control questionnaire that is designed to facilitate the process of eliciting, in "yes-no" (strength-weakness) format, from the client, whether specific controls are in place to strengthen or weaken particular financial assertions. The related assertions are listed in the right-hand margin of the figure. For example, to strengthen the financial assertion that stated inventory exists, the client should prescribe the control that requires that inventories be physically safeguarded in restricted-access areas. The auditor, concerned about the control, asks whether the specific control is prescribed. A "yes" response to the question indicates a strength in the system.

To obtain evidence regarding that attribute, the auditor would *observe* the physical facilities. If, in fact, inventories are kept under these safeguard controls, the auditor has evidence that justifies restriction of inventory observation procedures (the required detection risk procedure for determining existence). It must be noted, however, that there are other controls that should be in place in addition to this to assure that inventories exist (see numbers 2, 5, and 7a). Before restriction of inventory observation procedures can actually be done, the other controls must also be tested and found effective.

Appendix 17–B summarizes, by financial statement assertion, the functions that are involved in the production and conversion system, the errors and irregularities that may be involved in performing those functions, the financial statement effects of those errors, and the control attributes that should prevent, detect, and correct them. Figure 17–4 shows some of the tests performed on various data populations to ascertain whether prescribed controls are working as planned.

Figure 17–3 ▰▰▰▰

Internal Control Questionnaire (partial): Production and Conversion System

	Yes	No	Financial assertion
Storage processing and recordkeeping of inventory			
1. Are inventories physically safeguarded (e.g., by using fenced compounds and similar areas with restricted access)?	___	___	Existence
2. Are the following duties regarding inventories separate?			Existence; completeness
a. Receiving?	___	___	
b. Handling and storing?	___	___	
c. Shipping?	___	___	
d. Perpetual recordkeeping?	___	___	
3. Is the following documentation required for entries to perpetual records?			Completeness; transaction validity
a. Materials issues (issue slip)?	___	___	
b. Materials purchases (receiving reports)?	___	___	
4. Is some form of perpetual recordkeeping employed over:			Transaction validity; valuation
a. Quantities?	___	___	
b. Unit prices?	___	___	
5. Are perpetual records of inventories reconciled periodically to physical counts?	___	___	Existence; completeness
6. Are perpetual records of inventories reconciled periodically to general ledger accounts?	___	___	Disclosure
7. As to counting of inventory quantities:			Existence; completeness
a. Are all participants given proper written instructions and adequately supervised during the making of counts?	___	___	
b. Are there procedures ensuring that all goods are counted and that none is double-counted?	___	___	Completeness
c. Are there procedures to ensure an adequate cutoff of			Cutoff
1. Sales?	___	___	
2. Purchases?	___	___	
3. Movement of inventories between areas?	___	___	
d. Are differences between counts and records of inventory quantities investigated and recorded immediately upon discovery?	___	___	Completeness
e. Is work-in-process inventory inspected, and is adequate effort made to ascertain stage of completion?	___	___	Valuation; completeness
f. Are slow-moving, obsolete, or damaged inventories appropriately identified?	___	___	Valuation
g. Are goods on consignment-in or consignment-out appropriately identified?	___	___	Ownership rights
h. Are there procedures for preventing alteration, omission, or duplication of inventory counts?	___	___	Completeness

If proper controls are not prescribed, or if the auditor discovers that prescribed controls are not being followed, then control risk must be set at the maximum level, and a more effective detection risk audit program must be developed for the assertions involved.

The auditor must combine the results of the understanding of the control structure over the production and conversion system with those of the acquisition and expenditure system, before deciding the nature, timing, and extent of detection risk procedures to be performed on the inventory and cost-of-goods-sold accounts, described in the next section.

Figure 17–4

Transaction Testing Methodology: Production and Conversion System

Control attribute	Sampling involved?	Population	Procedure	From	To
1. Documentation is required for receipt of inventory.	Yes	Purchase orders	Vouch	Purchase orders	Receiving reports
Documentation is required for issues of raw materials inventories	Yes	Materials entries to work in process	Vouch	Journal entries	Raw materials issue slips
Documentation is required for inventory on consignment and inventory in public warehouses.	Yes	Sales invoices	Vouch	Sales invoices	Vendor invoices
		Perpetual inventory records	Vouch	Inventory records	Confirmation from warehouse
2. Periodic reviews are made by responsible officials for overstocked, obsolete, or slow-moving inventory	No		Inspect	Inventory records	
3. Perpetual records are kept and updated periodically for purchases and issues	Yes	Perpetual inventory records	Observe	Officials performing their duties	
			Vouch	Perpetual inventory records	Receiving reports and materials issue slips
4. Numerical sequence of receiving reports and issue slips is checked	Yes	Receiving reports	Reconcile numerical sequence		
		Issue slips	Reconcile numerical sequence		
5. Periodic spot checks of inventories are taken, perpetual records are adjusted, and errors are corrected	No	Perpetual records	Scan for adjusting entries		
6. General ledger entries are supported by monthly journal totals	Yes	General ledger account postings	Reconcile	General ledger	Appropriate journals
7. Subsidiary ledger postings agree with entries in journals	Yes	Subsidiary ledger account postings	Reconcile	Subsidiary ledgers	Appropriate journals

Detection Risk Procedures for Inventories and Cost of Goods Sold

☑ **Objective 4**
Design and
perform detection
risk procedures

Detection risk procedures are designed to determine whether the financial statement assertions embodied in the inventory and cost-of-goods-sold balances are free from material misstatements. Figure 17–5 illustrates the substantive tests performed to verify the audit objectives over inventories.

The auditor begins the substantive-testing phase of the inventory audit by *reconciling* the amounts shown in the balance sheet for various inventory items with the underlying accounting records. This procedure helps verify the accuracy of recorded values and is thus related to the valuation assertion. The first step in this reconciliation process involves vouching the statement amounts back to the respective ledger account balances. Those balances should in turn be reconciled with the subsidiary ledgers (perpetual inventory records) for merchandise inventory, raw materials, work in process, or finished goods. This procedure is illustrated in Appendix 17–C, the lead schedule for inventories.

In a merchandising firm, selected debits to the perpetual inventory records can also be traced to purchase invoices. Receiving reports may also be tested to verify the accuracy of additions to inventory. The totals in the voucher register, inventory and expense journal, purchase returns and allowances journal, and cash disbursements journal should also be *recomputed* and balanced in the reconciliation process. The pertinent items should be traced to their respective ledger accounts. Some of these procedures will have been carried out during the tests of controls as illustrated in Figure 17–4. These are examples of *dual-purpose tests*, designed to verify both effectiveness of internal controls and details of balances.

Verification of Existence and Completeness

The verification of existence and completeness of inventories involves gathering evidence regarding the quantity of inventory on hand as of the balance sheet date. Although it is the client, not the auditor, who is responsible for determining inventory quantities, usually by physical count, the auditor is responsible for ascertaining that client counts were made effectively and that they accurately and completely reflect quantities on hand as of the balance sheet date. The predominant auditing procedure used to satisfy the existence and completeness objectives is *observation of client inventories.*

Observation.   It is important to remember that, when inventories exist and are material to the financial statements taken as a whole, the auditor must generally be present to observe and to take some **test counts** when the client physically counts the inventory, to justify the issuance of an unqualified audit opinion. The auditor usually traces the details of test counts to the final inventory schedule to be sure the items observed are included in that schedule. The extent of observation and test counting necessarily varies with the design and quality of the client's system of internal accounting control, as well as external circumstances facing

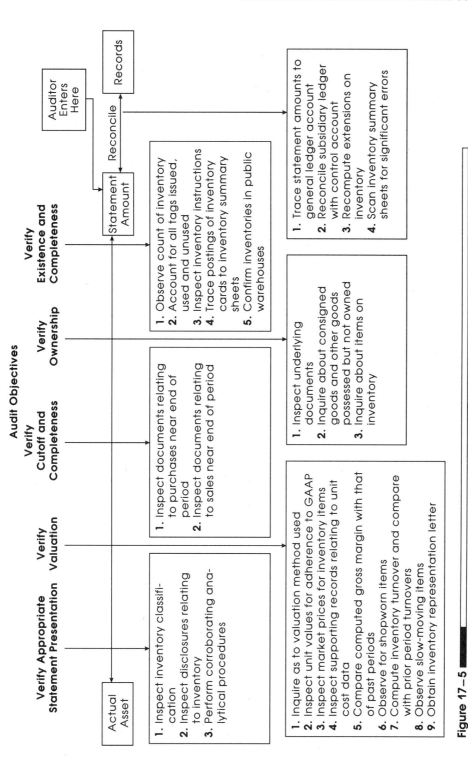

Audit Objectives

Verify Appropriate Statement Presentation

1. Inspect inventory classification
2. Inspect disclosures relating to inventory
3. Perform corroborating analytical procedures

Verify Valuation

1. Inquire as to valuation method used
2. Inspect unit values for adherence to GAAP
3. Inspect market prices for inventory items
4. Inspect supporting records relating to unit cost data
5. Compare computed gross margin with that of past periods
6. Observe for shopworn items
7. Compute inventory turnover and compare with prior period turnovers
8. Observe slow-moving items
9. Obtain inventory representation letter

Verify Cutoff and Completeness

1. Inspect documents relating to purchases near end of period
2. Inspect documents relating to sales near end of period

Verify Ownership

1. Inspect underlying documents
2. Inquire about consigned goods and other goods possessed but not owned
3. Inquire about items on inventory

Verify Existence and Completeness

1. Observe count of inventory
2. Account for all tags issued, used and unused
3. Inspect inventory instructions
4. Trace postings of inventory cards to inventory summary sheets
5. Confirm inventories in public warehouses

Statement Amount — Reconcile — Records

Auditor Enters Here

Actual Asset

1. Trace statement amounts to general ledger account
2. Reconcile inventory subsidiary ledger with control account
3. Recompute extensions on inventory
4. Scan inventory summary sheets for significant errors

Figure 17–5   **Flowchart for Substantive Tests of Inventory**

the client. Figure 17–6 summarizes some of these variables and the resultant procedures necessary to verify the existence and completeness of inventories. Appendix 17–D illustrates the inventory observation memorandum that is typically required in order to explain the results of the inventory observation procedure. Appendix 17–E illustrates the inventory observation questionnaire that often serves as a checklist to make sure that counts were properly taken by the client. It also may serve as the basis for writing the observation memorandum.

Observation of inventory ordinarily begins with an inspection of the client's physical inventory instructions. In making this inspection, the auditor should be alert for weaknesses that could allow particular elements of the inventory to be counted twice or possibly be omitted during the inventory-taking process. One of the procedures the auditor would expect to find incorporated in the instructions to prevent such errors is the use of *prenumbered inventory tags* with detachable segments. The instructions should include a provision requiring that all inventory tags be accounted for, both when they are issued to the inventory counting teams and when the detachable segments are returned and listed on the inventory summary sheets. In this way, the auditor can be assured that all inventory is included in the final count, thus verifying completeness.

The auditor should observe the client's inventory-taking process for the purpose of determining adherence to the inventory instructions and for evaluating

Figure 17–6

Circumstances Affecting Inventory-Auditing Procedures to Verify Existence and Completeness

Situation	Auditing Procedure
Inventories determined periodically by physical count	Observation imperative: extensive test counts
Perpetual records kept, adjusted periodically for physical counts	Observation imperative: test counts may be limited if client internal controls are good
Extremely good client internal control: rotational counts made at interim periods or client uses statistical sampling method to estimate year-end inventories	Perform limited observation procedures at interim dates when counts are made and ascertain validity of sampling plan if that method of estimation is used
Impossible or impracticable for auditor to observe year-end counts because not engaged until after client's fiscal year end	Perform alternative procedures; however, must still make such test counts as deemed necessary
Client requests auditor not to observe inventories	Qualify or disclaim audit opinion and state reason
Goods stored in public warehouses; amount not material to financial statements	Confirm amounts with warehouse manager
Goods stored in public warehouses; amount material to financial statements	Confirmation and supplemental procedures (including test counts)
First year of audit, so auditor unable to obtain satisfaction with respect to opening inventories	Perform alternative procedures; if not possible, disclaim an opinion on the income statement, retained earnings statement, and statement of changes in financial position, along with unqualified opinion on balance sheet

the competency of the inventory teams. He or she should then *test count* certain items and *reconcile* those counts with the amounts shown on the inventory summary sheets. This also has the effect of verifying the clerical accuracy of transferring amounts from individual inventory tags to the inventory summary sheets. The physical count of inventory should be compared with the perpetual inventory. If the physical count is higher than the perpetual inventory, the auditor should be concerned with such errors as the possibility that credit memos may not have been prepared for items returned by customers. A variance in the opposite direction could be caused by unrecorded cost of sales or thefts of inventories. Test counts of raw materials and finished goods inventories are illustrated in Appendixes 17–F and 17–G.

Some clients may maintain such excellent controls of perpetual inventories that they do not take physical counts of all goods. Instead, they may take only periodic, rotational, spot checks of quantities at selected storage locations at interim dates. In such cases, the auditor should be on hand to observe the interim counts and to take such test counts as he or she deems necessary.

In other cases, the client may estimate year-end inventories by means of statistical sampling, as illustrated in Chapter 12. In such cases, the auditor should always, among other procedures, ascertain the validity of the statistical sampling plan and the representativeness of the sample used to estimate the inventory balance.

Alternative Procedures.   In some situations, it may be impossible or impracticable for the auditor to observe and test-count inventories at the balance sheet date. This may be the case, for example, when the auditor has not been engaged until after the balance sheet date. In these situations, if the client has maintained proper perpetual records, the auditor may still be able to verify the existence of year-end inventories by the use of alternative procedures. These procedures must be performed as soon as possible after the balance sheet date and include the following:

1. Review of client inventory instructions.
2. Inquiry of the client as to how counts were made.
3. Inspection of physical inventory records, noting that the proper procedures were performed and adjustments were made where necessary.
4. Test-counting of selected items, tracing the movement of inventories back through the perpetual records by use of issue slips and receiving reports, then reconciling the resultant calculations with amounts shown on the perpetual records as of the balance sheet date.

Notice that alternative procedures usually require more audit effort than ordinary observation of the inventory-taking process and that they still require such test counts as the auditor deems necessary to verify goods on hand as of the balance sheet date. Furthermore, the longer the time span between the balance sheet date and the date the test counts are actually made, the more cumbersome and, therefore, costly these procedures become. When the auditor concludes that performing such procedures is too costly to justify them, a scope-qualified audit report is appropriate.

There may also be circumstances in which the client specifically requests the auditor not to observe the inventory counts. Such client-imposed scope restrictions on the audit are usually sufficient to preclude the expression of an unqualified opinion, especially when inventories are material. In most cases, the auditor should evaluate the client's reasoning carefully and issue a disclaimer of opinion.

Working papers have been provided in the appendixes of this chapter to illustrate inventory observation questionnaires and memoranda that are written as a part of a typical inventory observation. In addition, inventory test-count sheets are illustrated, showing auditor test counts vouched to client final inventory listings. All these procedures are performed to ascertain that inventory exists and that it is being accounted for properly.

When *inventories are held in public warehouses and are not material* to the financial statements, the physical observation requirement does not apply. Instead, the auditor is expected to confirm with the independent custodians the amounts of such inventory items. This procedure, however, cannot be substituted for the observation of inventories *held in company-operated warehouses located away from the client's main office* because of the lack of independence of the warehouse operator. In those situations the auditor must either visit the warehouses or engage a public accounting firm in that locality to perform the observation procedure. Additionally, when goods stored in independent warehouses are material to the financial statements, the auditor should perform supplemental procedures on the inventory, which include such test counts as the auditor deems necessary.

In an *initial audit* for a client whose inventories have not been observed in previous years, the auditor may not be able to obtain satisfaction with regard to opening-inventory quantities. Since opening inventories affect the income statement and statement of cash flows, the auditor may issue a disclaimer of opinion for those statements while expressing an unqualified opinion on the end-of-period balance sheet, for which inventory quantities have been verified by observation. However, if the client has maintained perpetual inventory records with appropriate controls, the auditor may still be able to express an opinion on all statements.

Valuation

The verification of inventory valuation generally begins when the auditor *investigates the valuation method* used by the client. The auditor must then determine whether that method produces, within the limits of materiality, a valuation that is in accordance either with one of the generally accepted cost-flow assumptions or with the lower of cost or market valuation procedures. The second method (valuation at the lower of cost or market value) is the more conservative method and is, therefore, generally preferred by accountants.

Inspection and Vouching. Having ascertained that the valuation method in use is in accordance with GAAP, the auditor will then, on a test basis, *inspect the values assigned* to various inventory items to determine whether the valuation method ostensibly being used by the client has been followed. The costs assigned to inventory should be the invoice cost less cash discounts taken. Discounts taken can be verified by comparing, on a test basis, cash disbursements with their respective purchase invoices. The auditor verifies that proper costing has been used by the client by vouching raw material prices to vendor invoices, as shown in the working papers in Appendixes 17–H and 17–J.

In addition to ascertaining that proper historical costing has been used, the principle of conservatism suggests that the auditor *compare the values assigned to inventory with replacement cost,* for the purpose of determining whether they are significantly lower than cost. If that has occurred, the auditor will have to calculate the lower of cost or market values for inventories. This procedure also involves obtaining selling price and selling cost data, as well as costs to complete work in process and normal profit margin. These data would then be used to calculate the cost-or-market ceiling and floor limitations.

In verifying the valuation of work in process and finished goods inventories, it is important for the auditor to *inspect the supporting records* found within the cost accounting subsystem. This will include job order sheets (if the firm is using a job order cost system), cost-of-production reports (when a process cost system is being used), and standard cost cards (where inventories are valued at standard costs). The inspection of such cost data should include tests of the procedures for allocating material, labor, and overhead costs to the individual units of the product, where historical costs are used. When standard costs are used, the auditor should *analyze and recompute variance account balances* on a test basis. The auditor is primarily interested in determining that costs have been properly assigned to finished goods, work in process, and cost of goods sold. It is important to recognize that these inventories should be valued at amounts not significantly different from those derived from generally accepted full-absorption cost accounting procedures.

If the client is a retail store, valuation of inventories involves vouching not only the unit costs of goods but also the retail price. In this case, the best evidence to support retail price would be current client catalogs or price lists. Markups and markdowns would be vouched to appropriate documents indicating management approval. Finally, the retail estimation method used by the client would be recalculated by the auditor.

During the observation of inventory, it is important for the auditor to give special attention to *inventory items that may be damaged, shopworn, or obsolete.* Slow-moving (obsolete) items are most likely to be discovered by examining the perpetual inventory records. Attribute sampling may appropriately be used in estimating the percentage of slow-moving inventory items. The valuation of such items should be reduced to provide for probable losses on their disposal.

Analytical Procedures. Some overall checks are important in helping the auditor determine whether or not inventory and cost of sales have been valued in accordance with GAAP. The first of these general checks requires computation of the *gross margin percentage* realized during the audit period and a comparison of that percentage with the percentages realized historically. It is also important for the auditor to compute the *turnover of inventory* for the purpose of helping determine whether the inventory includes obsolete or slow-moving items that may be improperly valued. A significant decline in turnover, one that is not appropriately accounted for by changes in operating practices, would suggest the possibility that obsolete or slow-moving items are included in inventory. Appendix 17–J illustrates the computation and comparison of historical trends in inventory turnover.

It is also desirable for the auditor to secure an *inventory representation letter* from the client stating that a particular generally accepted method of inventory valuation has been followed and that appropriate provisions have been made for obsolete and slow-moving inventory items. This representation letter should also include a statement to the effect that inventory held on a consignment has been excluded from the inventory balance.

In verifying the valuation of inventories, it is also important to *recompute the footings and extensions* on the physical inventory summary sheets and to *scan* those sheets for unusual amounts. Entries required to adjust the perpetual inventory account balances to amounts shown on the inventory sheets summarizing the results of the physical inventory should be traced to the inventory accounts.

Ownership

The verification of ownership requires the auditor to *inspect*, on a test basis, the documents underlying the acquisition of individual inventory items, including purchase orders, receiving reports, and vendor invoices. If these documents are in order and can be properly related to inventory possessed by the client, the auditor has good evidence in support of client ownership of inventory. Notice that vouching of documents was also the recommended procedure for verification of valuation. The same procedure used to achieve that objective can be used to ascertain ownership. The price-testing working papers, which appear as Appendixes 17–H and 17–J, illustrate the vouching process.

With respect to consigned goods, the auditor should inquire about them and secure an inventory representation letter stating that such goods have been excluded from the inventory accounts. He or she can then examine the final inventory listing to verify that such goods have, in fact, been excluded from inventories.

Cutoff

Cutoff (periodicity) errors occur near the beginning or end of the audit period when entries involving the acquisition or disposal of merchandise are included as transactions in the wrong period. In verifying proper cutoff, the auditor must *inspect the underlying documents relating to both purchases and sales* made near the end of the period under audit and during the first few days of the succeeding period. This procedure is performed to determine completeness, proper allocation of costs to reporting period, and that the client held legal title to the goods as of the balance sheet date. Ordinarily, merchandise acquisitions should be recorded as of the date the title to the goods passes to the purchaser. Generally, this is the FOB point, but there are some exceptions. For example, the title to custom-made merchandise passes to the purchaser when the production process has been completed. From a practical point of view, a firm may follow a practice of recognizing all merchandise acquisitions as additions to inventory when they are received at the client's receiving dock. If this practice is followed consistently, and does not have a material effect on the financial statements from period to period, such an arrangement would be considered acceptable.

As we observed in Chapter 13, it is also important to verify the cutoff of shipments for the purpose of seeing that the cost of inventory going out to customers is transferred to cost of sales in the appropriate period. Again, the auditor will inspect the documents underlying the sales transactions occurring near the end of the period under audit and during the first few days of the next period, giving particular attention to the dates of the shipping tickets and the terms of sale to determine when each shipment should have been transferred from inventory to cost of sales. Entries from the sales journal should be selected for dates up to and including the balance sheet date. Each entry should be vouched to shipping documents indicating that the goods were, in fact, shipped and not on hand (and counted) at the balance sheet date.

Sometimes **inventory in transit** will exist at the balance sheet date. In these cases, the auditor must ascertain that inventory has been properly recorded as purchased at the date the goods were shipped FOB shipping point. The working paper in Appendix 17–K illustrates the audit work typically performed on in-transit inventory.

Statement Presentation

The verification of appropriate statement presentation primarily involves seeing that the disclosure requirements relating to inventory have been met. The auditor must inquire of the client as to *whether any part of the inventory has been pledged* as security against creditor claims. If so, the auditor must ascertain that the amount of the pledged inventory has been appropriately disclosed in the balance sheet. It is also necessary for the financial statements to disclose *the method used in valuing the inventory*. Furthermore, in the case of a manufacturing firm, appropriate distinction should be made between inventories of raw materials, work in process, and finished goods. The client representation letter mentioned earlier in this section should include information regarding any amount of inventory pledged and the valuation practices followed by the client.

In cost-of-sales systems that utilize perpetual inventories, clients will usually make individual *entries to cost of goods sold* as each sale is made. To verify these amounts, the auditor should select samples of sales invoices, recompute the cost of sales on each invoice, and trace those amounts to the amounts recorded in the books. The auditor should also match the amount of cost-of-goods-sold on each invoice with the sales amount and ascertain that the two amounts were both recorded in the same accounting period. In situations where cost-of-goods-sold is not recorded for individual transactions, the auditor would verify the various elements of the cost-of-goods-sold formula stated earlier in this section. Beginning inventories would be traced to the prior year's audit work papers, and appropriate auditing procedures would be performed on purchases and ending inventories. Cost-of-goods-sold would then be verified as the mathematical result of the formula.

As a final overall check on the reasonableness of the inventory, the auditor will perform *analytical procedures on key financial statement ratios relating to inventory.* After ratios have been calculated, explanations of material fluctuations should be obtained from the client and should be followed up with further documentation when the auditor considers it necessary. Relationships shown between inventory turnover, ending inventory levels, and sales volume, for example, should all corroborate the results of the tests of details we have discussed in this section. The working paper in Appendix 17–I illustrates some of the analytical procedures that can assist the auditor in deciding whether the pieces of the puzzle actually fit together to form a coherent and consistent picture concerning the presentation of inventories.

Interrelationship of Inventory and Cost of Sales Balances

If detection risk procedures over inventory balances (described above) lead the auditor to conclude that inventories are fairly presented, the cost-of-goods-sold figure can be estimated by means of *analytical procedures.* The following familiar formula can be used:

  Beginning-of-period finished-goods inventory
  + cost of goods manufactured
  − end-of-period finished-goods inventory
  = cost of goods sold.

Cost of goods manufactured can also be estimated as follows:

  Beginning-of-period work-in-process inventory
  + cost of materials, labor, and overhead
  − end-of-period work-in-process inventory
  = cost of goods manufactured.

Likewise, cost of raw material used in the manufacturing process can be approximated as

  Beginning-of-period raw-materials inventory
  + purchases of raw materials
  − end-of-period raw-materials inventory
  = raw materials issued into production.

As you can see from these equations, the various inventory accounts are the "fences" at both ends of the fiscal period defining the cost-of-goods-sold figure in the financial statements. Therefore, in ascertaining the reasonableness of the cost-of-sales data, it is important to verify the various inventory balances as well as the transactions that record the flow of costs into and out of the system.

Using the Computer in Auditing the Production and Conversion System

The computer is used extensively in many inventory, cost of sales, cash disbursements, and payroll systems. Applications include maintenance of perpetual inventory files, cost accounting systems, and the related subsidiary ledgers and journals, including payroll records. In such cases, the auditor can, with appropriate computer audit software, use the computer in both the controls and substantive testing phases of the audit.

In the controls testing phase, for example, the auditor might apply the test data approach to ascertain whether certain control attributes (listed in Appendix 17–B) were, in fact, being applied to transactions processed. Alternatively, the auditor might use parallel simulation or other approaches to reprocess live client data and compare results with those obtained by the client.

In the substantive testing phase of the audit, the computer can be used extensively to verify inventory, cost of sales, and trade payables balances. For example, the computer can be used *in the initial reconciliation of accounting records* by comparing totals of general and subsidiary ledger accounts. *In verifying the existence of inventories*, the computer can stratify master files of inventory, contained on magnetic tape, by dollar amount; then select a sample for inventory observation; and print the sample items, including listings of locations, to facilitate the test counting process. Auditor test counts may then be recorded on computer input documents. The computer can be used to compare test counts with client perpetual inventories and print out an exceptions report.

In verifying valuation, the auditor can utilize the computer audit software to foot and extend all master files of inventory. The computer can also be used *to compute ratios, such as inventory turnover, by item*. Alternatively, the sorting capability of the computer can be used *to identify inventory by date of last sale or shipment* to help determine if certain items are slow-moving or obsolete.

To help verify proper cutoff of inventory and trade payables, the computer can be used to print lists of the last shipping documents or receiving reports processed during the period. The auditor can then vouch or trace the items to the appropriate accounting records. These are some examples, rather than a complete list, of ways in which the computer can be used in this part of the audit. Remember that the computer, with proper software, in general can be used to perform the mechanical, repetitive procedures of the audit and can perform these tasks in a fraction of the time required to perform them manually.

Summary

In this chapter, we have described the audit process for the production and conversion system. We began by stating the audit objectives for the system, which include existence/occurrence, completeness, valuation, cutoff, ownership rights/obligations, and proper statement presentation. We briefly reviewed the significance of each of these audit objectives. In addition, we discussed other planning considerations for the audit, including the necessity for making early arrangements for the observation of physical inventory counts.

We then described the process by which the auditor obtains an understanding of the control structure surrounding the production and conversion system. The process includes obtaining a thorough knowledge of the control environment and the accounting system, as well as control procedures instituted by the entity at various stages of the production process.

In the latter part of the chapter, we discussed detection risk procedures for inventories and cost of goods sold. These procedures, designed to satisfy the various audit objectives, are natural extensions of the financial statement assertions. The nature, timing, and extent of the necessary detection risk procedures depend on the results of the auditor's assessment of the control structure of the entity, and the resultant assessment of control risk for the various financial statement assertions.

Auditing Vocabulary

p. 733 **inventory in transit:** Inventory that has been purchased or sold and is still in the hands of the carrier as of the balance sheet date.

p. 720 **labor distribution summary:** A summary of labor charges prepared by the payroll department that distributes labor costs between jobs or processes.

p. 720 **perpetual inventory records:** Records prepared by the inventory stores department that show levels of various types of inventories on hand on a continuous basis.

p. 720 **production reports:** Reports prepared by the production department that show the number of units completed and transferred to finished goods inventory.

p. 719 **raw-materials-issue slips:** Documents prepared by the raw materials inventory department that show raw materials issued to work in process.

p. 722 **scrap reports:** Reports that show damaged or ruined inventories in the production process.

p. 726 **test counts:** Counts of client inventories that are taken on a test basis by the auditor. Such counts are reconciled with the client's physical counts of inventories for accuracy and reliability.

Appendix 17 –A: Inventory Accounting System

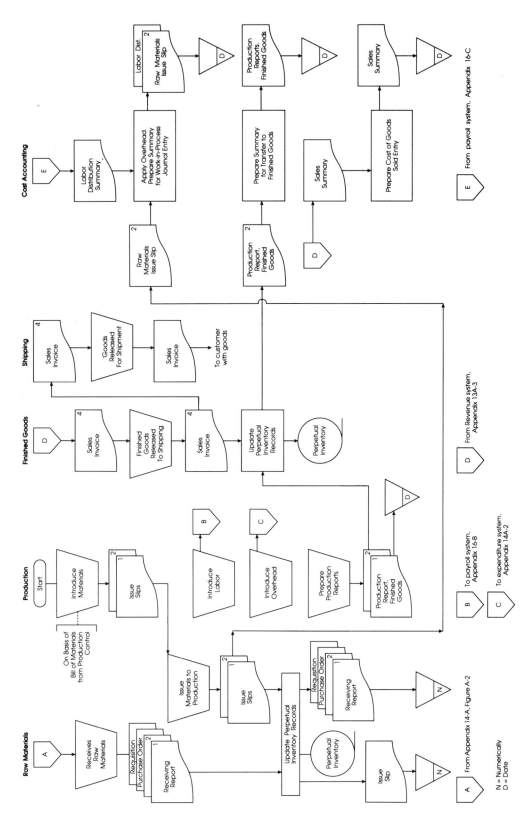

Appendix 17–B: Summary of Errors, Results, and Control Attributes by Financial Statement Assertion—Production and Conversion System

Related financial statement assertion(s)	Functions	Possible errors and irregularities	Results of undetected errors	Control attribute to prevent, detect, or correct error
Valuation, completeness, existence	Storage processing and record-keeping of inventory	Improperly valued transactions: Incomplete or inaccurate records of movement of goods	Discrepancies between control accounts and subsidiary ledgers	Require documentation of receipts (receiving reports) and issues (bills of materials, issue slips)
		Thefts of merchandise	Discrepancies between physical counts and amounts per books	
		Ineffective control of inventory on consignment out or in:	Discrepancies in records; over-statement or understatement of inventory, cost of sales	Require documentation of inventory on consignment-out or consignment-in
		Ineffective control of inventory in public warehouses		Require proper controls over inventory stored in public warehouses
		Inaccurate records of obsolete, over-stocked, slow-moving inventory	Overstatement of inventory	Require periodic review by responsible officials for obsolete, overstocked, or slow-moving inventory
	Shipment of merchandise	See Appendixes 13–A and 13–B		

Assertions	Function	Possible misstatement	Error/condition	Control procedures
Valuation, existence, completeness	Recording the transfers and processing of raw materials	Invalid transactions or improperly valued, classified, summarized transactions: Failure to record items purchased or used; Inaccurate recording of items purchased or used	Misstatements of inventories, cost of sales	Require separate inventory accounting procedures, including documentation of materials received (receiving reports) and used (bill or materials and issue slip). Require posting to perpetual records from prenumbered receiving reports and raw materials issue slips. Require accounting of numerical sequence of documents by inventory. Require periodic spot checks of inventory quantities and comparison with perpetual records
Valuation, existence, completeness, disclosure	Custody of inventory	Mishandling of physical inventories; waste and pilferage	Deterioration of inventory	Require storage facilities that protect goods from physical deterioration
			Wastage and pilferage of inventory	Require designated inventory custodians, who are held responsible for physical control over various categories of inventories
			Errors in physical counts	Require periodic counts by teams with one person counting and one person recording counts; persons counting should be independent of inventory custodians. Require tagging or other identification system that adequately identifies goods counted. Require spot checks by supervisory personnel of goods counted
			Discrepancies between physical counts and records	Require perpetual records of inventories. Require reconciliation or adjustment of perpetual inventories to physical counts

Appendix 17−C: Inventory Summary

			W. P. No.	F
JEP Manufacturing Co.			ACCOUNTANT	JB
Inventory Summary				
3-31-X1			DATE	5-5-X1

		Adjusted Balance 3-31-X0	Balance Per Books 3-31-X1	
Costs & Estimated Earnings on Income Contracts	A-1	1104937 12		
#130 Obsolete	A-1	—	55798 89	
#125 Raw Materials		591516 96	4064686 83	
#127 Work-in-Process		111142 90	927741 61	
#129 Inventory in Transit		24300 77	31306 01	
		727923 63	5079533 34	

Note: See F-50 Raw materials bulk file.

Conclusion: Based upon the work performed which was adequate to acheive the audit objectives as stated in the APG; it appears that inventories & estimated costs and earnings on incomplete contracts are fairly stated @ 3-31-X1 and on a basis consistent with prior years.

∨ : Per prior years workpapers.

△ : Per 3-31-X1 general ledger

	Adjustments		Adjusted Balance 3-31-X1	Final Adjustments		Final Balance 3-31-X1
	DR.	CR.		DR.	CR.	
				(2) 904138.95		904138.95
						A-1
	F-50		F-50			
	(104) 34288.63	(104) 55798.89	34288.63		(3) 34288.63	-0-
	(103) 647417.23	(105) 405476570	F-50			
		(102) 9921.13	647417.23			
			F-1			
	(103) 900577.33	(103) 927741.61	900577.33		(2) 706082.52	194494.81
						A-1
			F-6			
			31306.31			31306.01
						A-1
			161358920			873218.05
			F-a			F-a

Appendix 17–D: Observation of Inventory

JEP Manufacturing Co. Inventory Observation 3-31-X1		W. P. No.	F-21
		ACCOUNTANT	TB
		DATE	3-31-X1

Our representative, Todd Burnett, arrived at JEP Mfg. Co. Greensboro, Texas at approx. 8:30 a.m. on 3-31-X1 to observe client's physical inventory. We accompanied inventory control mgr., Elvis Rizor (who had all responsibility for physical inventory), on a tour of the warehouse & premises. The warehouse was well arranged and in good order; it appeared that all goods were being tagged & counted. Scrap & obsolete material appeared to be properly identified (which was immaterial to total inventory).

After a tour of the plant facilities, we made several test counts of raw materials, work-in-process, & a small amt. of finished goods in the various depts. See work paper F-24 → F-26.

Subsequently, we went to East Texas Distributors, a wholly owned subsidiary of JEP Mfg. Co. We toured the facility with Burt Andrews, President, who had over-all responsibility for the count of both East Texas Distributors inventory and the JEP Mfg. inventory located

		W. P. No.
		ACCOUNTANT
		DATE

there. The plant appeared in good order and JEP Mfg. Co.
inventory was appropriately segregated.

We made several test counts as documented on
East Texas F-11 & F-24-6 (JEP Mfg. Co. Inventory held @ E. Texas).

We supervised the pulling of tags and it appeared
that the East Texas Dist. Client was following prescribed
inventory procedures.

Upon returning to JEP Mfg. Co., we commenced our
test counts of work-in-process, going through all
depts. and stages of completion, including finished
goods.

After sufficient test counts were made, we supervised the pulling of tags and accounted for all tags
issued, used, & voided. See F-23. Based on the above,
the physical inventory performed by the client &
under our observation, appeared adequate @ 3-31-X1 to
properly reflect inventory quantities.

Appendix 17–E: Inventory Observation Questionnaire

JEP MANUFACTURING COMPANY
INVENTORY OBSERVATION QUESTIONNAIRE
3-31-X1

F-20
JB
3-31-X1

CLIENT JEP Manufacturing Co.

LOCATION Greensboro, Texas

INVENTORY OBSERVATION as of 3-31-X1

QUESTION	ANSWER
1. Did the company issue printed inventory instructions?	*Yes*
2. If so, have we obtained a copy for our files?	*Yes see F-22*
3. Was the plant shut down for inventory taking?	*Yes*
4. If plant was not shut down, how was proper control exercised over quantities?	*N/A*
5. State the following dates and hours that the inventory: Was started Was completed	*3/31/X1 730 AM* *3/31/X1 — PM*
6. Who was in overall charge of the inventory taking (give name and title)?	*Elvis Reisor* *Mgr. – INVENTORY CONTROL*
7. Was he present during the entire time?	*Yes*
8. State the date and time that auditors' representatives were present.	*9:00 AM* *PM*
9. Were all items actually counted, weighed or measured?	*Yes*
10. Perpetual inventory records:	
(a) Have been or will they be adjusted to the physical count?	*Yes*
(b) If required, have you checked your test count to perpetual inventor records?	*N/A*
(c) Are adjustments to count material?	*NO*
11. How is merchandise not belonging to the company shown on the inventory?	*None*
12. How were the following classes of items indicated so as to be properly priced: Obsolete Discontinued	*Counted + Identified by Elvis Reisor, Inv. Mgr.*

Damaged
Overstocked

13. Were all physical counts:

   (a) Subject to adequate supervision?

   (b) Subject to dual control in which
      at least one person is independent
      of the regular storekeeper?

   (c) Based on numbered tag (or other
      controllable system). If not,
      explain.

   (d) If numbered tags were used, did
      you account for all numbers used,
      voided and not used?

   (e) Subject to clerical checking where
      necessary?

14. Were there any machinery or materials
charged to property accounts included
in the inventory count?

15. How was merchandise in "cars on track"
accounted for?

16. Was warehouse or storeroom orderly and the
stock adequately protected against the
weather or other losses?

17. In your opinion have all merchandise and
supplies been properly inventoried, and
if not, why?

18. Are we to receive a complete copy of the
company's inventory; if so, is it
attached?

19. Obtain last receiving record number(s)
for checking cutoff. (If not numbered,
list last few receivers.)

20. Obtain last shipping or sales record
number(s) for checking cut-off. (If not
numbered, list last few shippers and
sales invoices.)

21. If the inventory observation is on the
balance sheet date the following
procedures should be followed:

   (a) List the number of the last
      check(s) issued.

   (b) Count cash on hand including
      undeposited receipts.

   (c) Examine securities.

   (d) Mail all possible confirmations.

22. Consider confirmation or observation of the
company's inventories located to suppliers
or with others.

23. Other comments: (Reverse side if necessary).

Appendix 17–F: Test Count of Raw Materials

	JEP Manufacturing Co.	W. P. No.	F-24
	Test Counts – Raw Materials	ACCOUNTANT	JB
	3-31-X1	DATE	3-31-X1

#	Description	Item #	Count	Unit of Measure	
505	100×160 Copper		1170 ∨	LBS	
509	Copper 9 sq. HF		201 ∨	LBS	
514	Copper 182 × 325		59 ∨	LBS	
602	Copper 10HF		518 ∨	LBS	
736	Core Steel		98030 ∨	LBS	
743	Core Steel		8720 ∨	LBS	
710	Core		40 ∨	EA.	

∨ Agreed to final inventory listing F-50 (not reproduced)

Appendix 17–G: Test Count of Finished Goods

	JEP Manufacturing Co.				W. P. NO.	F-26	
	Test Counts – Finished Goods				ACCOUNTANT	JB	
	3-31-X1				DATE	3-31-X1	

	#	Description	Work Order #	Count	Unit of Measure	
Dolden	198	Transformer	80-01-065	6 √	each	
Dolden	196	Switches	80-10-025	2 √	each	

√ Agreed to final inventory listing F-3 (not reproduced)

Appendix 17–H: Raw Materials Price Testing

JEP Manufacturing Co.

Raw Materials – Pricing Testwork

3-31-X1

	W. P. No.	F-4-1
	ACCOUNTANT	PBC/LB
	DATE	4-30-X1

	Inventory Page No.	Description	Quantity	Unit Cost	(A) Extended Value	Supplier
1	24	# 9F524 Fuse	147	4 75	698 25	General Elec. Co.
2	26	# 7200-66 Bushings	38	41 66	1583 08	Central Maloney
3	26	# 600-54 Bushings	79	24 65	1947 35	Elastimold Spec.
4	28	# 3009-1 Bushing Assembly	73	30 16	2201 68	Wasco Co.
5	32	# 662 Core	40	131 33	5253 20	S&M Mfg.
6	66	1007 × ¾" Cotton Tape	543.5	2 82	1532 27	Hisco Co.
7	94	# K24-4814 Relay	124	4 75 Ea.	589 00	Potter + Brumfield
8	105	# 1925 Thermometer with Brass Wheel	189	18 51 Ea.	3498 39	Rochester Gauges
9	105	Type T-2 Thermometer Spec.	19	12223 Ea.	2322 37	Marshalltown Mfg.
10	144	# 164 Pivot Arm Aux. Switch	123	7 50 Ea.	741 69	Lindale Precision
11	164	# 41268 Body J2CX	42	36 84 Ea.	1547 28	ETD Machinery
12	164	# 443 Stud. Bushing Comp.	22	36 58 Ea.	804 76	Midland Casting

Note ① Item selected per work paper F-4 judgementally in compliance with SAS 39.

Note ② Inventory is priced at lower of cost or market. Cost is determined on FIFO Basis and replacement cost is market. Methods are consistent with prior years.

Note ③ #167583.81 price tested which is approximately 24% of total inventory.

∨ – Agreed to paid invoice for applicable FIFO layer quantity and/or recalculated based on paid invoice and freight charges.

✗ – Per final inventory listing F-50 for items judgementally selected.

◢ – Per client maintained perpetual records.

Conclusion – Based upon the audit work performed which was considered adequate to obtain the audit objectives as stated in the audit programs, raw materials inventory appears to be fairly valued at 3-31-X1. /LB

Quantity Per Layer	Purchase Order	Invoice Date	FIFO Price Per Layer	(B) Extended FIFO Value	(A) - (B) Difference
125	39745	12/12/X9	4 74 ✓	696 78	1 47
205	41676	3/3/X1	41 26 ✓	1567 85	15 20
112	39923	1/24/X0	24 65 ✓	1947 33	- 0 -
13	39378	2/26/X0	30 16 ✓	2201 68	- 0 -
6	39922	2/5/X0	131 50 ✓	5260 00	(6 80)
500	40498	10/2/X0	2 78 ✓	1510 93	2 34
150	28649	7/24/X4	4 75 ✓	589 00	- 0 -
36	41580	2/16/X1	18 51 ✓	3498 39	- 0 -
2	41414	1/22/X1	122 23 ✓	2322 37	- 0 -
194	39490	2/25/X0	6 23 ✓	741 69	- 0 -
48	18880	3/31/X6	36 84 ✓	1547 28	- 0 -
48	1498	3/5/X1	36 58 ✓	804 76	= 0 -
					31 21

Pass - Due Minly to Rounding and minor clerical Inaccuracy

Appendix 17–I: Inventory Turnover

	JEP Manufacturing Co. Inventory Turnover 3-31-X1				W. P. No.	F-A
					ACCOUNTANT	JB
					DATE	5-4-X1

	3-31-X9			3-31-X0	
Cost of Sales	4767149			4817446 before adjustment 4939060 after adjustment	
(%)	80.1%			82.7% after adjustment	
Before work-in-process adj.					
Beg. Inventory	976972			1322969	
End. Inventory	1322969			1563873 Ⓐ	
Total	2299941			2886842	
Divide by 2	÷ 2			÷ 2	
Average	1149971			1443421	
Related Turnover	4.15			3.34	
(%)					
After work-in-process adj.					
Beg. Inventory	658148			610950	
End. Inventory	610950			727240 Ⓑ	
Total	1269098			1338190	
Divide by 2	÷ 2			÷ 2	
Average	634549			669095	
Related Turnover	7.51			7.38	

ᴸ Per prior year work papers

Note: Per discussion with Phil Neeson, V. P. of Finance, slight decrease in turnover is attributable to increase in production and size of backlog. Inspected production + backlog reports and noted that these explanations reflected actual facts.

			Adjusted & Reclassified Balance 3-31-X1				
3-31-X1							
5717336 Before adjustment							
5596840 after adjustment		5579933					
81.4% after adjustment							
Ⓐ 1563873							
1613589							
3177462							
÷ 2							
1588731							
.360							
Ⓑ 727240		727240					
F 907507		F 873218					
1634747		1600458					
÷ 2		÷ 2					
817374		800729					
6.85		6.97					

Appendix 17–J: Inventory Price Testing

		W. P. No.	F-4-0
JEP Manufacturing Co. Memo Re: Inventory Price Testing 3-31-X1		ACCOUNTANT	JB
		DATE	5-4-X1

We examined several items for inventory costing (pricing) on F-4-1 & F-4-2 based on a sample selection determined in compliance with our firm's sampling policy. The FIFO quantity layers were obtained for each item selected from the clients perpetual inventory system. The related supporting documents (purch. order, paid invoice) were examined, the calculated FIFO price per layer determined, & inventory values extended. Small immaterial differences were noted attributable mainly to rounding error.

In addition, we noted invoice date relating to the inventory layers to determine the presence of slow-moving or obsolete items. None of a significant nature were noted on items price tested. See raw materials BULK F-50, where we reviewed for obsolescence - and amounts adjusted.

Appendix 17–K: In-Transit Inventory

JEP Manufacturing Co.
In-Transit Inventory
3-31-X1

W. P. No.	F-6
ACCOUNTANT	JB
DATE	5-12-X1

Company		Invoice #	Amount
Ayar Mach. Production		207	1125 70
Boyle's Galvanizing		7717	308 92
Delair Investment	✓	4314	2445 57
"		4315	1054 26
"	✓	4321	1285 00
Detroit Coil Co.		3-1203	894 31
"		3-1204	900 20
Electromagnetic Ind.	✓	88-1094	82 48
"	F-25-3	35-8934	108 07
General Electric	✓	086-11209-3	14000 10
Gould-Brown		46-00167	617 76
"		46-92870	31 19
Hisco Corp.		5-2453	651 00
Murray Industrial	F-25-3	1-39724	116 60
Newark Electronics		142574	85 23
Parmeli Inc.	✓	81-360	2135 00
Potter & Brumfield		F-47932	379 33
Qualitex Corp.	✓	00897	2087 67
J & M Manufacturing	✓	0215	9620 64
L. V. Weatherford		529143	8 12
Texas Precision Investment		1829	5968 96
Note: Per JEP Mfg. Co. purchase journal			31306 11

✓ Vouched to invoice & receiver indicating goods rec'd after 3-31-X1 but should have been included in inventory.

Questions for Class Discussion

Q17-1 Explain what is meant by the production and conversion system.

Q17-2 How does the auditor's attitude when verifying inventory differ from his or her attitude when verifying accounts payable? Explain.

Q17-3 What relationship exists between the verification of inventory and the verification of cost of goods sold?

Q17-4 What are the audit objectives for the production and conversion system?

Q17-5 What are the planning considerations for the auditor with respect to the production and conversion system? Discuss.

Q17-6 When inventories and cost of sales are material, why is it imperative that the auditor obtain an understanding of the control structure of the entity? Explain.

Q17-7 What are the elements of the control structure over the production and conversion system that must be considered by the auditor?

Q17-8 Explain the elements of the control environment as they relate to the production and conversion system.

Q17-9 Explain the flow of transactions through the accounting sytem of a typical production and conversion system.

Q17-10 What control attributes should be present in an effective system of controls over the production and conversion system?

Q17-11 What duties should be segregated within the production and conversion system to achieve effective controls?

Q17-12 Are the documents generated by the production and conversion system internally or externally generated? Does this necessarily prevent effective controls? Explain.

Q17-13 What comparisons are generally made within the production and conversion system to assure proper controls?

Q17-14 What are the key access controls in the production and conversion system? What is their purpose?

Q17-15 What persons within the production and conversion system serve the purpose of approval of transactions? Which transactions require approvals?

Q17-16 Explain the process by which the auditor obtains an understanding of the control procedures within the production and conversion system.

Q17-17 What is the purpose of tests of controls over the production and conversion system? Explain ways that tests of controls can be performed most efficiently.

Q17-18 What auditing procedures are performed to verify the existence and completeness of inventory?

Q17-19 How does the auditor verify the valuation of inventory? Explain.

Q17-20 How does the auditor react to significant differences between physical and perpetual inventory balances?

Q17-21 What differences are there between the procedures followed in verifying the existence and completeness of inventory stored in public warehouses in another city and inventory stored in company warehouses in another city? Justify those differences.

Q17-22 Why is the auditor concerned with calculating the gross margin percentage and inventory turnover in the verification of inventory? Discuss fully.

Q17-23 Why does the auditor obtain a representation regarding inventory in the representation letter from the client?

Q17-24 What are the effects on net income of the client of an improved cutoff of inventory at the end of the audit period?

Q17-25 What are some of the ways in which the computer may be used in auditing elements of the production and conversion system?

Short Cases

C17-1 Alicia Decker, CPA, is performing an examination of the financial statements of Allright Wholesale Sales, Inc., for the year ended December 31, 19X0. Allright has been in business for many years and has never had its financial statements audited. Decker has gained satisfaction with respect to the ending inventory and is considering alternative auditing procedures to gain satisfaction with respect to management's representations concerning the beginning inventory, which was not observed.

Allright sells only one product (bottled Brand X beer), and maintains perpetual inventory records. In addition, Allright takes physical inventory counts monthly. Decker has already confirmed purchases with the manufacturer and has decided to concentrate on evaluating the reliability of perpetual inventory records and performing analytical procedures to the extent that prior years' unaudited records will enable such procedures to be performed.

Required:
1. What observations would you make about inherent risk for this engagement, based on the facts as stated?
2. Outline an audit plan for Allright Wholesale. Include a discussion of the process that you would follow, and the chronological sequence of events.
3. What mixture of audit tests (analytical, tests of transactions, tests of balances) would you choose for the audit of the inventory and cost of goods sold for Allright? What would the timing of those tests be? Would sample sizes tend to be large or small? Discuss.

(AICPA adapted)

C17-2 Retail Corporation, a ten-store men's haberdashery chain, has a written company policy stating that company buyers may not have an investment in nor borrow money from an existing or potential supplier. Robert Chan, the independent auditor, learns from a Retail employee that Ira Williams, a buyer, is indebted to Hubert Park, a supplier, for a substantial amount of money. Retail's volume of business with Park increased significantly during the year. Chan believes the debtor/creditor relationship of Williams and Park constitutes a conflict of interest that might lead Williams to perpetrate a material fraud.

Required:
a. Discuss what immediate actions Chan should take on discovery of the above facts.
b. Discuss what additional actions Chan should take to be satisfied that Retail has no significant inventory or cost-of-sales problems as a result of the weakness in internal control posed by the apparent conflict of interest. Identify and discuss in your answer the specific problems, such as overstocking, which Chan should consider.

(AICPA adapted)

C17-3 Ace Corporation does not conduct a complete annual physical count of purchased parts and supplies in its principal warehouse but uses statistical sampling instead to estimate the year-end inventory. Ace maintains a perpetual inventory record of parts and supplies and believes that statistical sampling is highly effective in determining inventory values and is sufficiently reliable to make a physical count of each item of inventory unnecessary.

Required:
a. When a client utilizes statistical sampling to determine inventory value and does not conduct a 100-percent annual physical count of inventory items, the auditor must proceed differently. Identify the auditing procedures the independent auditor will be using that change or are in addition to normal required auditing procedures.
b. List at least ten normal auditing procedures that should be performed to verify physical quantities whenever a client conducts a periodic physical count of all or part of its inventory.

(AICPA adapted)

C17-4 In an annual audit at December 31, 19X1, you find the following transactions near the closing date:
a. Merchandise costing $1,822 was received on January 3, 19X2, and the related purchase invoice recorded January 5. The invoice showed the shipment was made on December 29, 19X1, FOB destination.
b. Merchandise costing $625 was received on December 28, 19X1, and the invoice was not recorded. You located it in the hands of the purchasing agent; it was marked "on consignment."
c. A packing case containing product costing $816 was standing in the shipping room when the physical inventory was taken. It was not included in the inventory because it was marked "hold for shipping instructions." Your investigation revealed that the customer's order was dated December 18, 19X1, but that the case was shipped and the customer billed on January 10, 19X2. The product was a stock item of your client.
d. Merchandise received on January 6, 19X2, costing $720, was entered in the purchase register on January 7, 19X2. The invoice showed shipment was made FOB supplier's warehouse on December 31, 19X1. Since it was not on hand at December 31, 19X1, it was not included in inventory.
e. A special machine, fabricated to order for a customer, was finished and in the shipping room on December 31, 19X1. The customer was billed on that date and the machine excluded from inventory, although it was shipped on January 4, 19X2.

Required:

    a. State whether each of the above items of merchandise should be included in the client's inventory.

    b. Give your reason for your decision in each case.

C17-5   An auditor is conducting an examination of the financial statements of a wholesale cosmetics distributor with an inventory consisting of thousands of individual items. The distributor keeps its inventory in its own distribution center and in two public warehouses. An inventory computer file is maintained on a computer disk, and at the end of each business day the file is updated. Each record of the inventory file contains the following data:

    a. Item number.

    b. Location of item.

    c. Description of item.

    d. Quantity on hand.

    e. Cost per item.

    f. Date of last purchase.

    g. Date of last sale.

    h. Quantity sold during year.

    The auditor is planning to observe the distributor's physical count of inventories as of a given date. The auditor will have available a computer tape of the data on the inventory file on the date of the physical count and a general purpose computer software package.

Required: The auditor is planning to perform basic inventory auditing procedures. Identify the basic inventory auditing procedures and describe how the use of the general purpose software package and the tape of the inventory file data might be helpful to the auditor in performing such auditing procedures.

    Organize your answer as follows:

Basic Inventory Auditing Procedure	How General Purpose Computer Software Package and Tape of the Inventory File Data Might be Helpful
1. Observe the physical count, making and recording test counts where applicable.	Determining which items are to be test counted by selecting a random sample of a representative number of items from the inventory file as of the date of the physical count.

(AICPA adapted)

Problems

P17-1   Select the best answer for each of the following items relating to internal control in the production and conversion system.

    a. The objectives of internal accounting control for a production cycle are to provide assurance that transactions are properly executed and recorded, and that

        1. Custody of work in process and of finished goods is properly maintained.

2. Production orders are prenumbered and signed by a supervisor.
3. Raw materials purchases are authorized by the purchasing department.
4. Independent internal verification of activity reports is established.

b. Which of the following is a question that the auditor would expect to find on the production cycle section of an internal accounting control questionnaire?

1. Are vendors' invoices for raw materials approved for payment by an employee who is independent of the cash disbursements function?
2. Are signed checks for the purchase of raw materials mailed directly after signing without being returned to the person who authorized the invoice processing?
3. Are all releases by storekeepers of raw materials from storage based on approved requisition documents?
4. Are details of individual disbursements for raw materials balanced with the total to be posted to the appropriate general ledger account?

c. Which of the following internal control procedures could best prevent direct labor from being charged to manufacturing overhead?

1. Reconciliation of work in process inventory with cost records.
2. Comparison of daily journal entries with factory labor summary.
3. Comparison of periodic cost budgets and time cards.
4. Reconciliation of unfinished job summary and production cost records.

d. Sanbor Corporation has an inventory of parts consisting of thousands of different items of small value individually, but significant in total. Sanbor could establish effective internal control over the parts by requiring

1. Approval of requisitions for inventory parts by a company officer.
2. Maintenance of inventory records for all parts included in the inventory.
3. Physical counts of the parts on a cycle basis rather than at year end.
4. Separation of the storekeeping function from the production and inventory recordkeeping functions.

e. A well-functioning system of internal control over the inventory/production functions would provide that finished goods are to be accepted for stock only after presentation of a completed production order and a(n)

1. Shipping order.
2. Material requisition.
3. Bill of lading.
4. Inspection report.

(AICPA adapted)

P17-2 Select the best answer for each of the following items relating to verifying the existence and completeness of inventory.

a. An auditor will usually trace the details of the test counts made during the observation of the physical inventory taking to a final inventory schedule. This auditing procedure is undertaken to provide evidence that items physically present and observed by the auditor at the time of the physical inventory count are

1. Owned by the client.
2. *Not* obsolete.
3. Physically present at the time of the preparation of the final inventory schedule.
4. Included in the final inventory schedule.

b. The physical count of inventory of a retailer was higher than shown by the perpetual records. Which of the following could explain the difference?

1. Inventory items had been counted but the tags placed on the items had *not* been taken off the items and added to the inventory accumulation sheets.
2. Credit memos for several items returned by customers had *not* been taken off the items and added to the inventory accumulation sheets.
3. *No* journal entry had been made on the retailer's books for several items returned to its suppliers.
4. An item purchased "FOB shipping point" had *not* arrived at the date of the inventory count and had *not* been reflected in the perpetual records.

c. When outside firms of nonaccountants specializing in the taking of physical inventories are used to count, list, price, and subsequently compute the total dollar amount of inventory on hand at the date of the physical count, the auditor will ordinarily
1. Consider the report of the outside inventory-taking firm to be an acceptable alternative procedure to the observation of physical inventories.
2. Make or observe some physical counts of the inventory, recompute certain inventory calculations and test certain inventory transactions.
3. *Not* reduce the extent of work on the physical count of inventory.
4. Consider the reduced audit effort with respect to the physical count of inventory as a scope limitation.

d. The auditor tests the quantity of materials charged to work in process by tracing these quantities to
1. Cost ledgers.
2. Perpetual inventory records.
3. Receiving reports.
4. Material requisitions.

e. From which of the following evidence-gathering auditing procedures would an auditor obtain *most* assurance concerning the existence of inventories?
1. Observation of physical inventory counts.
2. Written inventory representations from management.
3. Confirmation of inventories in a public warehouse.
4. Auditor's recomputation of inventory extensions.

f. Which one of the following procedures would *not* be appropriate for an auditor in discharging his or her responsibilities concerning the client's physical inventories?
1. Confirmation of goods in the hands of public warehouses.
2. Supervising the taking of the annual physical inventory.
3. Carrying out physical inventory procedures at an interim date.
4. Obtaining written representation from the client as to the existence, quality, and dollar amount of the inventory.

g. The primary objective of a CPA's observation of a client's physical inventory count is to
1. Discover whether a client has counted a particular inventory item or group of items.
2. Obtain direct knowledge that the inventory exists and has been properly counted.
3. Provide an appraisal of the quality of the merchandise on hand on the day of the physical count.
4. Allow the auditor to supervise the conduct of the count so as to obtain assurance that inventory quantities are reasonably accurate.

h. A client's physical count of inventories was lower than the inventory quantities shown in its perpetual records. This situation could be the result of the failure to record

    1. Sales.
    2. Sales returns.
    3. Purchases.
    4. Purchase discounts.
  i. An auditor has accounted for a sequence of inventory tags and is now going to trace information on a representative number of tags to the physical inventory sheets. The purpose of this procedure is to obtain assurance that
    1. The final inventory is valued at cost.
    2. All inventory represented by an inventory tag is listed on the inventory sheets (completeness).
    3. All inventory represented by an inventory tag is bona fide.
    4. Inventory sheets do *not* include untagged inventory items.

(AICPA adapted)

P17-3 Select the best answer for each of the following items relating to the verification of valuation of inventory.
  a. Which of the following is the *best* auditing procedure for the discovery of damaged merchandise in a client's ending inventory?
    1. Compare the physical quantities of slow-moving items with corresponding quantities of the prior year.
    2. Observe merchandise and raw materials during the client's physical inventory taking.
    3. Review the management's inventory representation letter for accuracy.
    4. Test overall fairness of inventory values by comparing the company's turnover ratio with the industry average.
  b. A CPA examining inventory may appropriately apply sampling for attributes in order to estimate the
    1. Average price of inventory items.
    2. Percentage of slow-moving inventory items.
    3. Dollar value of inventory.
    4. Physical quantity of inventory items.
  c. In verifying debits to perpetual inventory records of a nonmanufacturing firm, the auditor would be *most* interested in examining the purchase
    1. Journal.
    2. Requisitions.
    3. Orders.
    4. Invoices.
  d. Raider, Inc. uses the last-in, first-out method of valuation for half of its inventory and the first-in, first-out method of valuation for the other half of its inventory. Assuming the auditor is satisfied in all other respects, under these circumstances the auditor will issue a(n)
    1. Opinion modified due to inconsistency.
    2. Unqualified opinion with an explanatory middle paragraph.
    3. Qualified or adverse opinion depending upon materiality.
    4. Unqualified opinion.
  e. When an auditor tests a client's cost-accounting system, the auditor's tests are *primarily* designed to determine that
    1. Quantities on hand have been computed based on acceptable cost-accounting techniques that reasonably approximate actual quantities on hand.

2. Physical inventories are in substantial agreement with book inventories.
3. The system is in accordance with generally accepted accounting principles and is functioning as planned.
4. Costs have been properly assigned to finished goods, work-in-process, and cost of goods sold.

f. An auditor would be *most* likely to learn of slow-moving inventory through
1. Inquiry of sales personnel.
2. Inquiry of stores personnel.
3. Physical observation of inventory.
4. Review of perpetual inventory records.

g. An inventory turnover analysis is useful to the auditor because it may detect
1. Inadequacies in inventory pricing.
2. Methods of avoiding cyclical holding costs.
3. The optimum automatic reorder points.
4. The existence of obsolete merchandise.

h. Which of the following would detect an understatement of a purchase discount?
1. Verify footings and crossfootings of purchases and disbursement records.
2. Compare purchase invoice terms with disbursement records and checks.
3. Compare approved purchase orders to receiving reports.
4. Verify the receipt of items ordered and invoiced.

(AICPA adapted)

P17-4 Your client, whose fiscal year ends on December 31, takes a physical inventory on November 30 and, at that time, adjusts the perpetual inventory control account to the physical inventory balance. Your cutoff of tests on November 30 and December 31 reveal the following facts relating to two invoices:

Amount	Date	Invoice terms FOB	Date goods shipped	Date goods received	Date invoice entered in voucher register
$1,350	11/28	Shipping point	11/28	12/3	11/29
$ 850	12/27	Destination	11/27	12/30	1/2

Required: Assuming all errors are material, give any adjusting entries that you would make in your audit working papers as of 12/31.

P17-5 During your first audit of Apex Company, you find that the client's income statement shows cost of sales in the amount of $200,000. The company maintains a perpetual inventory system but adjusts the book balance to the amount determined by physical count at the end of each year.

In the course of your examination of the inventory balances, both at the beginning and end of the year, you discover the following facts:

Beginning of the year

a. Invoices totalling $3,640 were entered in the voucher register in January, but the goods were received during December.

b. December invoices totalling $8,000 were entered in the voucher register in December, but goods were not received until January.

End of the year

c. Sales of $5,000 (cost: $4,000) were made on account on December 31, and the goods were delivered at that time, but all entries relating to the sales were made on January 2.

d. Invoices totalling $6,000 were entered in the voucher register in January, but the goods were received in December.

e. December invoices totalling $4,000 were entered in the voucher register in December, but the goods were not received until January.

f. Invoices totalling $1,500 were entered in the voucher register in January, and the goods were received in January, but the invoices were dated December. The terms are FOB shipping point.

Required: (Make corrections to prior year's income directly to retained earnings.)

a. List the adjusting entries to be made in your work papers.

b. Calculate the corrected cost of sales for the current year. All inventory adjustments have been and should be reflected as part of cost of sales.

P17-6   As part of a test of inventory control, you examined the perpetual inventory records of stockroom M. A full set of records (subsidiary and control) is maintained in the factory, and a controlling account is also kept in the accounting department.

The following facts are discovered relating to the two sets of records for stockroom M:

a. Receipts of materials in stockroom M, entered properly on factory records but treated by the accounting department as stockroom N, $240.

b. Correction was made by the accounting department of an error in a prior period. The error was the recording of an $800 withdrawal of materials as $500. The original item had been correctly entered by the factory record clerk.

c. A shortage of item M-143, amounting to $45, was noted and entered as an issuance during the period on the factory records, but the information had not been transmitted to the accounting department.

d. The initial inventory, according to factory records, was $11,000 in stockroom M. Receipts of $14,000 and withdrawals of $13,000 are reflected in the records of the accounting department.

Required: From the preceding information, calculate the beginning inventory, receipts, issuances, and ending inventory balances shown on the factory records.

P17-7   Your client took his physical inventory on December 31, at the close of the firm's fiscal year, and adjusted the perpetual inventory for the difference between physical and book inventory. During your audit, you discover that goods costing $10,000 and selling for $12,000 were shipped on December 29, FOB shipping point. However, the entries relating to this transaction were not recorded until January 5.

Required: Assuming that all amounts reflected above are material, what adjustments should you record in your working papers?

P17-8   In the course of your examination of your client's records as of November 30, end of the fiscal year, you discover the following items relating to inventory:

a. Merchandise costing $12,000 was received on November 20 and counted in the physical inventory taken on November 30. However, the invoice relating to this acquisition was not entered in the voucher register until December 5.

b. An invoice for $5,000 was recorded in the voucher register on November 27 (when shipped FOB shipping point). The merchandise reflected on this invoice was not received until December 6.

Required: Assuming that the perpetual inventory account has been adjusted to agree with the physical inventory taken on November 30, without considering the two items stated above, what adjusting entries should you make?

P17-9 Your client's fiscal year closes on November 30, but the physical inventory was taken on October 31. The perpetual inventory account was adjusted downward at that date to bring it into agreement with the physical inventory amount. The client gave no consideration at either October 31 or November 30 to unmatched receiving reports in the accounts-payable department files. The total amounts were:

October 31	$34,000
November 30	$40,000

Required: Give the adjusting entries, if any, that you would make in your audit working papers. Assume all amounts are material.

P17-10 Your client has a perpetual inventory system. A physical inventory was taken December 31 of the year under audit, and the book inventory was adjusted to agree with the physical inventory. The following items were not taken into consideration.
  a. There was a file of unmatched receiving reports at December 31.
  b. The client subtracts purchase discounts from invoice cost and records the net amount in the inventory account. The physical inventory was valued by using the prices shown on vendor invoices.
  c. No cost-of-sales entry was made for goods sold and shipped to a customer on December 31.
  d. Vendor invoices were on hand at December 31 but had not been recorded because the goods had not been received. The invoice terms were all FOB shipping point.
  e. At the close of the preceding year, goods had been received but the entries to record the purchases were not made until the current year.

Required: For each of the above items, indicate whether the error would cause net income to be overstated, understated, or would have no effect. Justify your answer in each instance.

CHAPTER 18

The Financing and Investing System

Objectives

☐ **1.** Recall the ways businesses are financed, and the nonoperating investment alternatives that are generally available.
☐ **2.** Be able to state and to activate the audit objectives for the financing and investing system.
☐ **3.** Understand and be able to critically assess elements of the control structure for the financing and investing system.
☐ **4.** Design and perform a program of detection risk procedures for account balances contained in this system.

All business entities, whether large or small, must determine ways to arrange the capital structure that best suits the needs and desires of the owners. Once capital is raised, the managers of the business must determine the optimal manner in which to invest funds. Obviously, most of the capital of the business will be invested in operating assets and inventory. However, excess funds will often be invested in nonoperating assets, such as equity and debt securities. Using the same basic format that was first illustrated in Figure 5–2, this chapter focuses attention on the audit of the system by which capital is raised and invested.

Appendixes to the chapter include illustrated working papers for the financing and investing system for JEP Manufacturing Co.

Financing Business Operations

☑ **Objective 1**
Recall ways in
which a business
is financed

Financing a business through debt essentially involves a three-element cycle beginning with the issuance of the debt obligation in exchange for cash or other assets. This phase is followed by the periodic payment of interest on the obligation while it is outstanding. Ultimately, the principal amount of the obligation will also be paid, either in installments or as a lump sum. The accounts involved in this part of the system include the following:

- Cash.
- Notes or mortgages payable.
- Installment contracts payable.
- Bonds payable.
- Interest expense.
- Accrued interest payable.

Financing through the use of equity capital primarily involves the recognition of new capital interests in exchange for cash or other assets. Periodic distributions of resources may then be made to owners, either as withdrawals or as dividends, depending on the capital structure of the business. Capital interests may also be redeemed or repurchased. Accounts involved in this part of the system include the following:

- Cash.
- Common stock.
- Preferred stock.
- Paid-in capital in excess of par or stated value.
- Donated capital.
- Unappropriated retained earnings.
- Appropriated retained earnings.
- Treasury stock.
- Dividends declared.
- Dividends payable.
- Sole proprietor's capital account.
- Partners' capital accounts.

Investments

☑ **Objective 1 (cont.)**
Recall
nonoperating
investment
alternatives

Investments are made up of nonoperating assets. Although most of these assets will be in the form of equity and debt securities, land and other assets held for incremental gains, rather than for use in operations, are also classified as investments. Investments may be included in both the current and noncurrent sections of the balance sheet.

The investments included in current assets represent temporary commitments of excess cash. They are the most liquid noncash assets and may include any or all of the following items:

- Marketable equity securities of unaffiliated companies (less than 20-percent owned).
- Marketable debt securities.
- Savings accounts.
- Certificates of deposit.

Noncurrent investments are held for the long-term production of income, for incremental gains, or for the purpose of preserving operational relationships with other companies. A client's portfolio of noncurrent investments might include any or all of the following items:

- Equity or debt securities of affiliated or unaffiliated companies.
- Mortgages or notes receivable.
- Loans or advances to affiliated companies.
- Fixed assets not used in business operations.
- Cash value of life insurance policies of which the company is the beneficiary.
- Investments in partnerships or other nonstock companies.

Audit Objectives

☑ **Objective 2**
Activate audit objectives for the financing and investing system

As in all other systems, the audit objectives for the financing and investing system are logical extensions of management's financial statement assertions. Those include

1. Existence or occurrence (related to transaction validity)
2. Completeness
3. Proper valuation
4. Cutoff
5. Ownership rights/obligations
6. Proper statement presentation or disclosure

In the case of investments, the auditor is concerned that the client might have included amounts in the financial statements that did not exist, or transactions that did not occur. In the case of debt financing, on the other hand, the auditor's concern might be more toward existing debt that is not recorded. Tests in the financing and investing cycle must, therefore, include those that detect overstatements as well as those that detect understatements. In addition, tests must be performed to assure that transactions are recorded in the proper period (*cutoff*).

For both the financing and investing sides of the system, four distinguishing characteristics help shape the evidence-gathering process:

- Typically, the auditor encounters only a *limited number of transactions* involving accounts in a given audit period.
- Any given transaction is likely to be *material* in amount. As a result, the exclusion or improper recognition of a single transaction could be the source of a material error.
- Legal or regulatory requirements are often associated with the transactions; for example, a registration statement must be filed with the SEC before a new issue of stock or bonds can be marketed. These requirements are very important, and *client records must be complete*.
- A contractual relationship always exists between the investor and the investee, and will usually provide for an amount to be returned to the investor in the form of interest or dividends.

Because of these distinguishing characteristics, *transaction validity* is one of the most important audit objectives that must be met. This objective is typically fulfilled by performing tests of the transactions that make up the account balances in the system. Documentary evidence that supports the validity of the transaction also generally supports the assertion of *ownership*, in the case of investments, and of *obligation* in terms of liabilities.

One of the most important *disclosures* that must be made of investment or financing accounts is their proper *valuation*. This includes use of the proper accounting methods, the mathematical accuracy of accounts, and the proper use of estimates and accruals. The properly planned audit must include procedures that assure that all of the assertions of management relating to valuation and disclosure are proper.

Because of the close proximity of the financing and investing systems with the cash account, inherent risk can be considered relatively high for the system. In planning the engagement, therefore, the auditor should spend time studying the control environment surrounding the system. Control procedures such as proper segregation of duties of cash handling and recordkeeping, and limited access to cash, should be the focus of the auditor's attention, as discussed in the next section. However, because of the distinguishing characteristics of these accounts, the relatively high inherent risk associated with them makes it necessary to perform substantive tests of balances and transactions rather than extensive tests of controls.

Understanding the Control Structure

☑ **Objective 3**
Understand and evaluate the control structure

The control structure over the financing and investing system consists of the following elements: the control environment, the accounting system, and control procedures.

Control Environment

Much useful information can be gathered about management's overall philosophy and operating style by studying the control environment in the financing and investing system. Management's operating philosophy is often reflected in the ways the entity is financed and in the types of investments that appear in the financial statements of the company. The auditor should spend time analyzing the financial statements of the entity to become familiar with its debt/equity structure, as well as the character and stability of its investments.

The organizational structure of the entity should provide for proper segregation of functional duties of cash handling, recordkeeping, and authority to approve transactions. Since some investments are near-cash items, their physical custody is generally handled by the treasurer's department. Recordkeeping duties, as in all systems, generally fall under some branch of the controller's department. Since relatively few (but material) transactions occur in these systems, authority to approve financing and investing transactions should generally be vested in the board of directors. As in other systems, the control environment may be enhanced by the existence and proper functioning of internal auditors, who perform regular tasks of comparing physical assets (investments) and liabilities with company records, and who monitor compliance with company policies.

The Accounting System

Figures 18–1 and 18–2 present diagrammatically the typical flow of transactions through the financing system and the investing system. In Figure 18–1, we see that cash flows into the entity either through the issuance of long-term debt or capital stock. Over time, the long-term debt is repaid, along with accrued interest. Dividends may be declared and paid on capital stock. If the circumstances require it, capital stock may be redeemed. Figure 18–2 shows that excess cash in the business may be invested (the types of instruments were described earlier in the chapter). From time to time, investments may be sold as needed and the proceeds used in the business to buy operating assets, or to repay debt. Sales of investments for amounts greater than or less than carrying value will produce realized gains or losses, respectively.

Figures 18–3 and 18–4 depict systems flowcharts for the financing and investing systems, respectively. These charts depict the proper flow of transactions through the system, as well as the control procedures that should be in place, as discussed in the next section.

Control Procedures

The control environment and the accounting system over financing and investing activities should include policies and procedures for recording, processing, summarizing, and reporting of transactions that provide reasonable assurance

Figure 18–1

Flow of Transactions: Financing System

Long-Term Debt			
xxx (3)			xxx (1)
		Ending bal.	xxx

Cash		
xxx (1)		xxx (3)
xxx (2)		xxx (5)
		xxx (7)
		xxx (8)

Capital Stock			
xxx (8)			xxx (2)
		Ending bal.	xxx

Interest Expense

xxx (4)	
xxx (5)	

Additional Paid-In Capital			
xxx (8)			xxx (2)
		Ending bal.	xxx

Accrued Interest Payable

xxx (5)			xxx (4)
		Ending bal.	xxx

Retained Earnings			
Losses	xxx	Earnings	xxx
	xxx (6)		
		Ending bal.	xxx

Dividends Payable

xxx (7)			xxx (6)
		Ending bal.	xxx

(1) Additional debt financing; (2) Additional equity financing; (3) Repayment of debt; (4) Accrual of interest; (5) Payment of interest; (6) Declaration of dividends; (7) Payment of dividends; (8) Redemptions of stock.

Figure 18–2

Flow of Transactions: Investing System

Investments			
Beginning bal. xxxx		Retirements	xxxx (3)
	xxxx (1)		
Ending bal.	xxxx		

Cash		
xxxx (3)	xxxx (1)	
xx (2)		

Gain/Loss from Investments

	xx (3)

Investment Income

	xx (2)

(1) New acquisitions; (2) Investment income; (3) Dispositions.

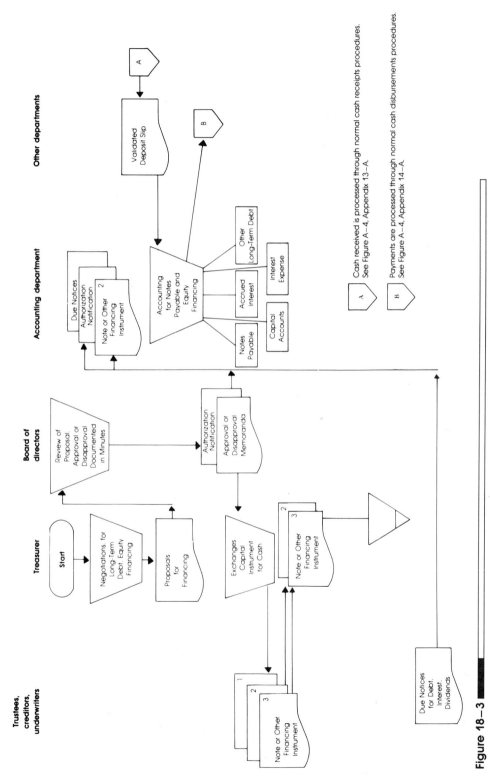

Figure 18—3   Flowchart for the Financing System

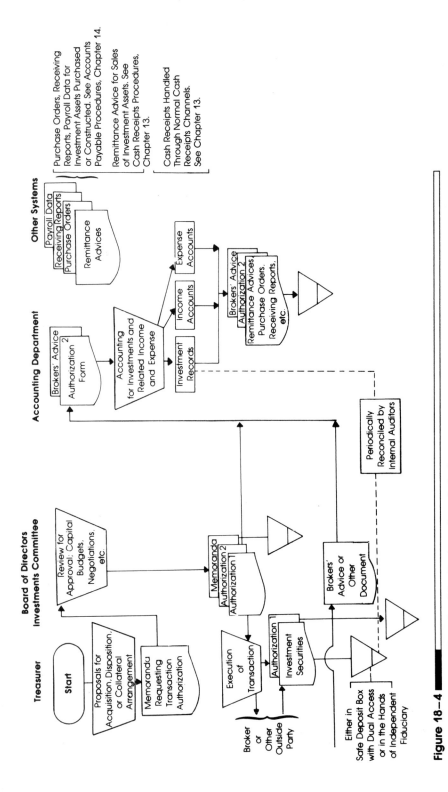

Figure 18–4 ━━━ Flowchart for the Investments System

that financial assertions produced by the system are fairly and accurately presented. As with all other systems, these policies and procedures should include (1) proper segregation of responsibilities; (2) adequate records and documentation; (3) an effective system of comparisons and compliance-monitoring; (4) limited access to assets and records; and (5) proper execution of transactions in accordance with management's general or specific authority.

Proper Segregation of Duties

The duties of custody of assets, recordkeeping, and approval of transactions over financing and investing activities should be kept separate. As shown in Figures 18–3 and 18–4, the treasurer's department usually handles the function of custody of assets, whereas the board of directors must give approval for transactions. The accounting department receives documentary support for all transactions, allowing them to perform the recordkeeping function for both financing and investing activities.

In a publicly held corporation, an independent registrar or transfer agent exercises control over the issuances and transfers of stock. If bond financing is used, the company may employ an independent bond trustee and an independent interest-paying agent. The corporation, in turn, holds these parties responsible for carrying out their respective fiduciary responsibilities and for submitting periodic reports to the company's board of directors.

Adequate Records and Documentation

Figures 18–5 and 18–6 list the boundary and supporting documents included in the financing and investing systems. Many of these documents and their functions have already been discussed in previous chapters, along with our discussions of the cash receipts and cash expenditures systems. Other documents are illustrated in the flowcharts in Figures 18–3 and 18–4.

For the financing system, forms should be used to provide formal authorization and approval of all transactions. The forms and documents for these transactions are typically nonstandard but are usually available for the auditor's review on request. They might include registration statements with the SEC, bond **trust indentures, underwriters' agreements** for capital stock, internal memoranda, and, of course, board of directors' minutes, which show actions taken by that body.

The form supporting the authorization to issue capital stock should include a description of the type of stock and the number of shares being issued, as well as spaces for authorization signatures. The basic stock certificate should require the signature of a responsible company official who does not have direct access to the proceeds from the issuance of the stock. The authorization to reacquire capital stock should show the number of shares, the description of the stock, and the amount to be paid for the shares. Dividend declaration resolutions should be recorded in the minutes of the board of directors and should show the amount of

Figure 18–5

Exchange Transactions, Boundary and Supporting Documents, Financing System

Exchange transaction	Boundary document	Supporting document
Borrowing under note arrangements	Cash receipts	Note agreement; board of directors' approval
Borrowing under bond or other arrangements	Cash receipts	Bond indenture; registration statement; board of directors' approval; lease agreements
Payment of interest on debt obligations	Canceled checks	Due notices for interest; note agreements; bond trustee records
Repayment of debt principal	Canceled checks	Due notices for principal; note agreements; bond trustee records
Issuance of stock	Cash receipts	Underwriters agreement; registration statement; stock certificate stubs; board of directors' approval
Payment of dividends	Canceled checks	Board of directors' approval
Redemption of stock	Canceled checks	Board of directors' approval
Acquisition of treasury stock	Canceled checks	Board of directors' approval
Sale of treasury stock	Cash receipts	Board of directors' approval

Figure 18–6

Exchange Transactions and Documents: Investments

Exchange transaction	Boundary document	Supporting document
Purchase of marketable equity or debt securities	Canceled check Broker's advice	Authorization-to-buy form; cash disbursement voucher; board of directors' minutes
Purchase of other investments	Canceled check Purchase agreement	Board of directors' minutes
Sale of marketable equity or debt securities	Remittance advice Broker's advice	Authorization-to-sell form; validated deposit slip; board of directors' minutes
Sale of other investments	Remittance advice Sales agreement	Validated deposit slip; board of directors' minutes
Receipt of Income from investments	Remittance advice	Dividend records of various investment services; interest contract

the dividend per share, the date of record, and the date on which payment is to be made. A voucher system, or some similar arrangement, should be used to assemble the necessary supporting data for the approval of interest and dividend payments and for the retirement of debt and equity instruments.

The records underlying capital stock accounts of a corporation should be designed to make sure the actual owners of stock are properly recognized in the corporate records or in the records of the independent registrar and transfer agent, so that the correct amounts of dividends will be paid to the stockholders owning the stock as of the dividend record date. When no transfer agent is employed, the company should maintain well-defined policies and develop appropriate documentary support for preparing and issuing stock certificates, reacquiring stock certificates, and recording capital stock transactions. This ordinarily requires a capital stock book that provides a record of the issuances and reacquisitions of capital stock over the life of the corporation and a shareholder's ledger showing the number of shares held by each individual stockholder at any point in time. When stock is redeemed, the canceled stock certificates should be defaced to prevent reissuance and then filed with their corresponding stock issuance stubs. If an independent registrar and transfer agent is used, that party will have the responsibility of issuing stock in accordance with the authorization of the board of directors, as well as the responsibility for maintaining the stockholder records.

For the *investing system*, supporting documents usually include the following:

- An *authorization-to-buy form* that includes a specific description of the security to be purchased plus spaces for authorization signatures or initials.
- **Broker's advice forms** (invoices provided by securities brokers as evidence of purchase and sale transactions) appropriately matched with the authorizations to buy or sell securities.
- A *cash disbursement voucher* properly supported by the documents listed above and having spaces for the initials of various persons charged with checking documents, extensions, and accounting treatment of the payment (see Chapter 14).
- A *cash remittance advice form* to be used as the company's first evidence of cash received from interest, dividends, or sales of securities (see Chapter 13).
- An *authorization-to-sell form* having spaces for specific identification of the securities being sold plus authorization signatures or initials.
- *Schedules showing reconciliation* of the periodic independent calculation of interest and dividend incomes with the amounts shown for those items in the accounting records.

The results of investment activities normally will be recorded in the cash disbursements and cash receipts journals. If a significant number of investments are held, it is also important to have *subsidiary records*, showing the individual securities held, that are periodically reconciled with the general ledger control accounts for investments. The records of a company should be organized to properly account for investment income and for gains and losses from the sales of investments.

Comparisons and Compliance Monitoring

The system should provide for effective oversight by independent persons who regularly compare the recorded accountability of assets and liabilities with their physical substance at regular intervals. For the *financing* system, the detailed debt and equity records should be reconciled with their respective general ledger account balances on a regular basis. This procedure should be performed by persons who have no responsibility relating to the detailed records. Internal audit personnel are ideal for the task. Interest expense on debt also should be calculated independently from the provisions of the individual note and bond agreements and reconciled with the balance in the general ledger accounts. A similar procedure may be performed for dividend records, recalculating the dividends on various issues of stock, comparing them with authorization in board of directors' minutes, and tracing them to both cash disbursements records and appropriate entries in the retained earnings account.

For *investments*, detailed records of marketable securities should be reconciled with general ledger accounts on a regular basis by employees who do not have responsibility for the detailed records. Interest income should be recalculated independently and the proceeds traced to cash receipts and to the investments records.

Access to Assets and Data

In the *financing* system, the major asset is cash. Therefore, the same controls apply as were discussed in Chapter 13 for the revenue and collections system.

In the *investments* system, the assets at major risk of misappropriation are marketable equity and debt securities. Adequate provisions should be made to safeguard such assets from misappropriation. This usually involves implementation of the following controls:

- Persons having custodial responsibility for investments should not have access to the accounting records and should be bonded.
- To properly protect the securities from theft or misuse, a bank safe deposit box should be used to store the company's negotiable securities. Two persons should be required to be present to access the safe deposit box.
- If large amounts of securities are kept in the company's investment portfolio, the company should consider using an independent firm such as a brokerage house or investment banking firm as custodian.
- The records associated with investments and investment income should be appropriately stored in a safe or vault designed to protect them from damage or alteration when not in use.
- All cash receipts from interest or dividends or from the disposal of securities should be promptly deposited in the bank.

Execution of Transactions as Approved

Because of the materiality of the individual transactions involved, the primary authority over approvals of financing and investing activities should rest with the board of directors or equivalent group. Generally, they will delegate authority to borrow within established guidelines, and authority to make purchases and sales of investments to the treasurer's department.

Authorization to borrow money on behalf of the company or to issue stock should be subject to the specific approval of the board of directors. Policies and procedures should be set up within bond indentures to provide prompt payment of interest and repayment of principal. All dividends on all classes of stock should be approved by the board of directors, as should stock redemptions.

Authorization to borrow against securities should rest with a responsible official of the company having no custodial responsibilities for those securities. The authorization to dispose of securities should be vested in a responsible official other than the person having custodial responsibility for them. The investments committee of the board of directors should periodically review the investment activities of the company.

Control Risk Assessment Procedures

Appendix 18–A contains a chart that shows the major functions of the investments system, the possible errors and irregularities that could occur, results on specific financial statement asssertions, and the control attributes that should prevent, detect, or correct them. For the financing system, these functions and controls are much the same as those for the revenue and collections system, described in Chapter 13.

As we discussed earlier in the chapter, because of the distinguishing characteristics of these systems, the auditor may spend a relatively small amount of time conducting tests of control attributes. Audit evidence for these transactions is often relatively easy and inexpensive to obtain. Thus, it is more cost effective to conduct audit tests of the transactions and balances, once the major features of the internal control structure are understood.

Detection Risk Procedures for Long-Term Debt Accounts

☑ **Objective 4**
Design and perform detection risk procedures for long-term debt accounts

Debt capital is obtained most frequently through issuance of mortgage notes or bonds payable, or by use of installment contracts to acquire assets. Resources anticipated to be needed for only a short period of time may be acquired through the issuance of short-term notes. The auditing procedures used to verify such notes are essentially the same as those described in Chapter 14 for trade notes payable. Large amounts for long-term capital expenditures may be acquired through the issuance of long-term notes, generally secured by specific client assets. This type of debt capital is called **mortgage notes payable**.

Accountants apply a substance-over-form interpretation to some building and equipment lease arrangements, causing them to be treated as installment purchases. Therefore, we may find another type of debt capital characterized as *obligation under capital lease*. Corporations may also issue *bonds*, in which case the bond indenture becomes the contract through which long-term debt capital is obtained. Because of the similarities between these types of debt, we shall deal with the substantive verification of these account balances as a group.

The normal starting point for verification of debt accounts is the preparation of the analysis-type working paper, showing beginning balances, additions, retirements, and ending balances for both the principal amount and accrued interest. Such a working paper is illustrated in Appendix 18–B. As you examine this working paper, notice that it follows the typical flow of transactions into and out of the notes payable account, which was illustrated in Figure 18–1.

As shown in Figure 18–7 and illustrated in the working paper, we begin our substantive verification of debt accounts by reconciling the respective liability accounts with their underlying accounting records. In so doing, we trace the balances shown in the financial statements to the general ledger accounts and recompute the balances in those accounts.

Verification of Existence and Completeness

In verifying the existence of debt in an initial audit, the auditor must inspect the documents underlying each individual debt item. These typically will include vouching authorization for new borrowing to the board of directors' minutes and obtaining copies of agreements for notes payable, installment contracts for installment contracts payable, and bond indentures for bonds payable. Pertinent data, such as the issue and maturity dates and the rates of interest, should be extracted from the bond indenture agreement. In auditing publicly held companies, the contents of the bond indenture should be confirmed with the trustee. The auditor should also ascertain that the opinion of legal counsel has been secured on the legality of the issue. Copies of these documents or confirmations should be obtained and placed in the auditor's permanent file of working papers for later reference on subsequent audit engagements. The auditor should also inspect the journal entries made in recognizing debt capital obligations and trace the resources (cash, for example) received in exchange to the appropriate asset accounts.

In subsequent audits, *only the documentation supporting changes in debt capital items occurring during the fiscal period under audit need be inspected*. These items include evidence of new borrowings, as well as canceled checks issued in repayment of principal and in payment of interest.

Because the auditor is especially concerned about unrecorded obligations (completeness), it is important to reconcile the interest expense shown in the income statement with the interest expense computed on the basis of the contractual obligations outstanding during the year. If the recorded interest expense is in excess of the computed amount, it is possible that a note payable may not have been recorded. Where the debt account balance is composed of a number of different elements, such as a number of different notes payable, it is important to reconcile the list of notes payable with the balance shown in the financial statements.

Confirmation can also play an important role in verifying the existence of recorded notes and bonds payable. For short-term notes payable, the auditor should refer to the standard bank confirmation (see Appendix 19–D). This confirmation calls for the bank to provide detailed information regarding the existence, amount, dates, interest rates, and collateral for notes payable to the bank. For long-term notes and mortgages payable, a letter of confirmation should be sent to all creditors. Appendix 18–D illustrates a long-term note payable confirmation that has been received and compared to client records with no exceptions noted. The confirmation should request creditors to provide all pertinent data, such as issue date, principal amount, interest rate, terms of repayment, and

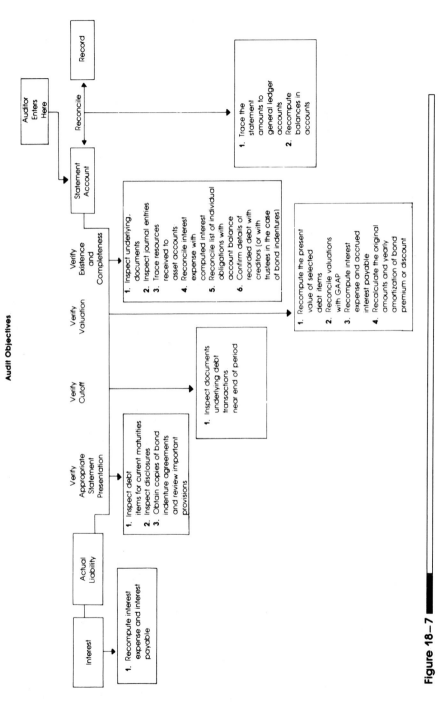

Figure 18—7 Flowchart for Substantive Verification of Long-Term Debt Accounts

collateral pledged. For bonds payable, a confirmation request should be sent to the trustee, who should be asked to provide the terms of the bond indenture, plus information regarding the client's compliance with those terms during the audit period.

Verification of Valuation

Although the value to be assigned to most liabilities can be ascertained by simply examining the documents supporting the obligations, the valuations assigned to some debt items must be *recomputed* to determine whether they are reflected in accordance with GAAP. For example, noninterest-bearing and low-interest notes should be reflected in the financial statements at their discounted present values. The same is true for installment contracts payable. In the case of bonds, unamortized premiums should be added to the bonds payable account and any unamortized discount should be subtracted from that account in order to establish the values to be assigned to those items in the balance sheet. The amortization schedules for these items and for mortgages payable should be examined. Acquisition costs associated with new mortgages should be verified by examining the related cancelled checks and closing statements.

Verification of Cutoff

Although the verification of cutoff is not as important for long-term debt items as for certain current assets and liabilities, it should still be verified. This requires the auditor to inspect duplicate copies of new note agreements as well as vouchers payable for principal and interest payments occurring near the end of the audit period to determine whether they have been recorded in the appropriate fiscal period. New notes should be included as liabilities in the body of the financial statements when dated on or before the balance sheet date.

Verification of Appropriate Statement Presentation

Appropriate statement presentation calls for most long-term debt items to be shown as noncurrent liabilities. Generally accepted accounting practices, however, require that current maturities of long-term debt be reflected as current liabilities unless they are to be liquidated from noncurrent assets, such as resources contained in a sinking fund account. For that reason, the auditor must inspect the outstanding debt obligations and recalculate any amounts that should be moved from noncurrent liabilities to the current liability classification in the balance sheet (see Appendix 18–C).

The auditor must also inspect disclosures relating to long-term debt accounts. These include such things as footnotes describing the terms of the debt items outstanding and the assets pledged as collateral against them. Furthermore, debt agreements frequently include restrictions on the activities of the companies, such as compensating balance provisions, restrictions on the payment of dividends, or the maintenance of a specified current ratio or balance in retained earnings. The auditor must make the necessary corroborative tests to ensure that such restrictions have been adhered to and that they are appropriately disclosed in the footnotes. Such tests include confirmation of compensating-balance arrangements with creditor banks and the *recomputation* of critical ratios and amounts to ensure that they are within prescribed limits.

The amount shown in the balance sheet for accrued interest payable must also be recomputed from the contractual arrangements associated with each of the debt items. This is usually done from duplicate copies of the notes. After the accrued interest payable has been recomputed, it should be reconciled to the respective liability and expense account balances shown in the financial statements. Payments of interest expense are vouched to cash disbursements journals and to canceled checks. A four-element equation, including the beginning-of-period accrual balance, plus interest expense, less interest payments, and the resulting end-of-period accrual balance, should be the format of the reconciliation and should be reflected in the audit working papers.

Audit of Pension Plan Accounts

A special type of audit problem exists when the client has adopted a pension plan for its employees. Most employee pension plans in existence today are qualified under the provisions of the Employee Retirement Income Security Act of 1974 (ERISA). Employee pension plans regulated under ERISA must satisfy a variety of criteria in order to obtain favored tax treatment for the employer and employee. Among these criteria are (1) minimum funding levels, (2) the treatment of past service costs, (3) minimum vesting rights for participating employees, (4) minimum disclosure requirements for the employer, and (5) minimum requirements for the trustees. The auditor, in preparation for auditing an employee pension plan, should review and become familiar with all of the preceding legal requirements as well as the related income tax laws.

The auditor's main concerns in auditing a client's pension plan are to ascertain the propriety of transactions involving the plan in terms of compliance with applicable laws and regulations and to ascertain that the provisions of the plan have been properly disclosed. A copy of the client's pension plan should be obtained and studied to identify all its pertinent features. That copy should be placed in the auditor's permanent file and retained for reference on future audits. The auditor should review all material transactions involving the plan and ascertain that its provisions were carried out in compliance with ERISA. If there is currently an excess of the actuarially computed value of vested pension benefits over retirement funds and related balance sheet accruals, less prepayments and deferred charges, it should be disclosed fully in the footnotes of the financial statements and on the balance sheet as a long-term liability. In addition, if any material changes have occurred in the method of accounting for pension costs during the period, they should be evaluated by the auditor for possible effect on the audit opinion.

Amounts contributed to the plan by both the client and employees should be vouched to appropriate cash disbursements and payroll records. These may also be confirmed with the trustee of the pension plan. Entries recording pension costs should be vouched to appropriate underlying documents, such as trustee and actuarial reports. Pension plan data relating to funding levels and various other actuarially determined amounts should be confirmed with the trustee or actuary, reviewed for reasonableness, and scrutinized for compliance with applicable laws. In cases of complex actuarial computations, the auditor may engage and rely on the report of an actuarial specialist to evaluate those computations.

Disclosure requirements for pension plans include (1) a brief statement that the plan exists and identification of employee groups covered; (2) a description of the accounting and funding methods employed; (3) the current provision for pension costs; (4) the excess of any of the actuarially computed value of vested benefits over retirement funds and balance sheet accruals, less prepayments and deferred charges; and (5) the nature of any matters that might affect comparability of disclosures, such as changes in accounting methods or significant amendments to the plan.

Detection Risk Procedures for Equity Accounts

☑ **Objective 4**
Design and perform detection risk procedures for equity accounts

The fundamental accounting equation (assets − liabilities = capital) suggests that if the auditor has appropriately verified all assets and liabilities at both the beginning and the end of the period under audit, the total equity capital balance and its net change during the year will have to be correct. For that reason the audit of owners' equity requires substantially less audit time than is devoted to verifying other types of account balances. However, the auditor is still concerned with verifying these items independently of the amounts that might be calculated by use of the accounting equation.

As shown in Figure 18–8, the primary objectives to be met in auditing owners' equity are verification of the existence, valuation, cutoff, and appropriate statement presentation of equity capital account balances.

Verification of Existence

The existence objective is easily satisfied when an independent registrar or transfer agent is used. In such cases the transfer agent should be asked to confirm directly to the auditor the shares of capital stock outstanding, the transactions occurring during the audit period, and the values assigned to those transactions. It is also important to review the minutes of the board of directors' meetings for evidence that equity capital transactions, including declarations of dividends, new issuances of stock, and repurchases of stock, have been approved by that body. When an independent registrar or transfer agent is not used, it is important for the auditor to inspect the client's stock record books in the initial audit. Details of capital stock outstanding are then recorded in the

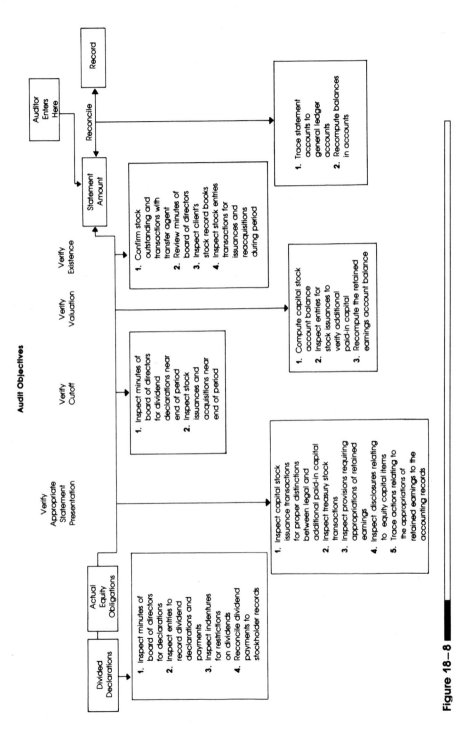

Figure 18–8 ▮ **Flowchart for Substantive Verification of Equity Capital Accounts**

auditor's permanent file of working papers. In subsequent audits, the emphasis should be on *inspecting new issuances and repurchases during the period*. If new capital stock has been issued for cash or to bring about a merger with another company, the evidence supporting those transactions should also appear in the minutes of the board of directors' meetings and should be examined by the auditor. If the client holds treasury stock certificates, they should always be examined and counted.

Verification of Valuation

The value assigned to each capital stock account balance is normally verified by determining the number of shares outstanding at the balance sheet date (see the procedures just outlined for determining existence) and multiplying that amount by the par, or stated, value of the stock. The auditor will rely either on the confirmation reply from the independent registrar or transfer agent or on an inspection of the capital stock record book to secure that information. The auditor will also need to inspect entries recording the issuance of stock to determine that the appropriate amount has been recorded in the paid-in capital in excess of par value account. Entries to record treasury stock transactions should also be examined by the auditor. The value assigned to retained earnings can be verified by recomputing the balance, using the beginning-of-period balance plus additions during the period less the deductions during the period. Entries to the retained earnings account that have not been examined in connection with the other parts of the audit should be vouched to underlying documentary support. This may be the case, for example, when prior period adjustments have been made by the client.

Verification of Cutoff

Although the problem of verifying the appropriate cutoff of equity capital transactions is not as important as verification of cutoff of current items, some attention should be given to that phase of the audit, particularly insofar as dividend obligations are concerned. In examining the retained earnings account, the auditor should inspect the minutes of the board of directors' meetings to determine the dates as of which all dividends have been declared, so that the appropriate liability can be recognized for cash dividends payable. In some instances, stock issuances or acquisitions may occur near the end of the period, in which case it will be necessary for the auditor to verify that they have been recorded in the appropriate accounting period.

Appropriate Statement Presentation

Perhaps the most important objective to be met in auditing the equity capital accounts is to verify that those accounts have been appropriately presented in the financial statements. The auditor must inspect all capital stock issuance and reacquisition transactions during the year to be sure that an appropriate distinction has been made between legal capital and paid-in capital in excess of par or stated value. Treasury stock transactions must be inspected to determine whether an appropriate distinction has been made between additional paid-in capital and noncontributed capital as those transactions were recorded.

Actions originating with the board of directors (or taken because of requirements imposed by the state or bond indenture) relating to the appropriation of retained earnings must be traced to the accounting records to ensure that an appropriate distinction is made between appropriated and unappropriated retained earnings. It is also important for the auditor to inspect disclosures relating to capital stock—such as those for stock options, stock warrants, and convertible securities—to ascertain whether such items have been appropriately disclosed in accordance with applicable APB opinions or FASB statements.

As you saw in Figure 18–8, the auditor must also verify the various transactions involving dividend declarations and payments. The procedures for meeting this audit requirement begin with an inspection of the minutes of the board of directors' meetings for the amounts and dates of dividend declarations. Each amount should then be traced to the retained earnings account. In implementing this procedure, the auditor will be particularly concerned with the possibility of discovering unrecorded dividends. It is also important in this connection to inspect long-term debt contractual agreements, such as bond indentures and preferred stock indentures, to determine whether there are restrictions on the company insofar as the payment of dividends is concerned.

The valuations assigned to dividends will be determined by the amounts per share for cash dividends and by either the fair market value or the par value of the stock in the case of stock dividends. At this point it is important to recognize that the declaration of *a stock dividend creates a special stockholders' equity account rather than a liability account*. It is also important for the auditor to determine that the additional shares issued as a stock dividend conform to the authorization provided by the board of directors. The auditor should also make certain that the dividend distributions (both cash and stock) have been made to the stockholders of record as of the record date. In so doing, the auditor will want to inspect a sample of recorded dividend payments by tracing the payee's name on the cancelled check to the stockholder's record as of the date of record.

An analytical schedule for each equity capital account reconciling beginning-of-period balances, additions, reductions, and end-of-period balances, should be prepared to summarize the evidence gathered in the verification of those accounts. Appendix 18–E illustrates this process for capital stock, treasury stock, additional paid-in capital, and retained earnings.

As noted in Appendix 18–E, one of the primary additions to retained earnings normally will be net income for the period. The auditor should trace the credit entry in retained earnings for that item to the net income figure shown in the income statement. This procedure should be done late in the audit period, after all adjusting entries affecting net income have been recorded. In addition, the auditor should trace all audit-adjusting entries affecting retained earnings to postings in the account. Notice that this procedure has also been reflected in Appendix 18–E. Other additions to be verified in retained earnings may include prior period adjustments, which should be verified individually.

The primary reduction of retained earnings will be the dividends declared during the period. Debit entries in the retained earnings account for dividends should be vouched to board of directors' minutes. Dividends paid should be vouched to the cash disbursements records, while dividends declared but unpaid should be reconciled with the dividends payable account balance. This audit work is illustrated in Appendix 18–G. Other debits may include prior-period adjustments that should be verified individually or operating losses that should be traced to the income statement. The auditor should also inspect all debits and credits to retained earnings (other than those for net income, net losses, and dividends) to determine whether they should have been included in the income statement.

Detection Risk Procedures for Investments

☑ **Objective 4 (cont.)**
Design and perform detection risk procedures for investments

Auditing procedures for marketable equity securities and for cash surrender value of officers' life insurance are illustrated in Appendixes 18–F, 18–H, and 18–I. As we observed in earlier chapters, the audit objectives applicable to the investments subsystem can be identified by asking what could cause the account balances shown for investments owned by the client to be incorrect. For example, a difference would occur if the client included in the investment account items that do not really exist. Perhaps the difference is caused by the disposal of investments that were not credited to the appropriate investment account. The audit objective in proving or disproving this point can be characterized as the *verification of existence* (validity).

Closely associated with verification of existence is *verification of the ownership* of investments held by the client. In meeting this objective, the auditor is concerned with ascertaining that the investments included in the accounts belong to the client. He or she also seeks to discover the extent to which outside parties may hold claims against those investments.

The going-concern convention logically requires that current marketable securities be valued at their cash-realizable value. On the other hand, this same convention logically requires that long-term investments be valued at cost (amortized in certain cases) or on the equity method. Therefore, the auditor must perform the procedures required to determine that those valuation practices have been followed. In meeting the *verification of valuation* objective, the auditor is concerned with ascertaining that all securities are recorded in the investment accounts at values established by generally accepted accounting principles.

Although the auditor is concerned with seeing that the acquisitions and disposals of investments, as well as the income from those investments, are recorded in the proper period, the *verification of cutoff* is much less important in auditing these accounts than it is in the verification of revenues and cost of sales. An error in cutoff would generally involve offsetting errors in cash and investments. Therefore, such an error would be significant only if a material gain or loss on sale were involved or if the error involved cash and noncurrent investments. For that reason, some attention should be given to verifying that transactions occurring near the end of the audit period and the beginning of the following period have been recorded in the proper period.

Investments must also be properly presented in the financial statements. This includes proper classification, proper labeling, and appropriate parenthetical and footnote disclosures. It is especially important that an appropriate distinction be made between current or temporary investments and those investments that should be classified as noncurrent assets on the balance sheet. Furthermore, because of the valuation procedures established by GAAP, it is also necessary to distinguish between investments in marketable equity securities and other securities. Among long-term investments, it is also important to disclose separately any investments held for the purpose of significantly influencing or controlling the operations of another company; these investments should be disclosed separately from investments that do not involve such relationships. Statements must also appropriately disclose information relating to the pledging of investments as collateral. The audit objective covering all these elements can be characterized as *appropriate statement presentation*.

We show the relationship of these audit objectives to the appropriate auditing procedures that satisfy them in Figure 18–9. As we have observed before, the objective of substantive verification is to gather evidence to support the proposition that the investment accounts are fairly presented in accordance with GAAP. The number of transactions in this area is often small, but the size of transactions individually or collectively may be large. Therefore, the auditor often will determine transaction validity by verifying all acquisitions, disposals, and other changes occurring in the investment accounts during the current year. This involves *vouching* the recorded acquisitions and disposals to supporting documents—such as broker's advices, cancelled checks, bank drafts for officers' life insurance premiums, remittance lists and advices, etc. By combining these amounts with beginning balances, which have been verified by *tracing* them to corresponding ending balances from the prior year's audit working papers, the auditor *recalculates* the ending balance for each investment account. This process is illustrated in the working papers that appear in Appendixes 18–F and 18–H.

After the recalculation of balances just described, the process of verifying the ending investment account balances and their related accounts begins. The initial step in this process is to *reconcile* the end-of-period statement account balances with the underlying accounting records. The financial statement balances should first be reconciled to the balances in the general ledger accounts. After that, the investment control accounts should be reconciled with their respective subsidiary records, and the account balances should be recomputed.

Verification of Existence

As shown in Appendix 18–F, the existence of securities is verified by *inspecting and listing the securities on hand*. The pertinent details of each security, such as serial number, type, interest rate, face amount, number of shares, etc., should be listed. Although the auditor is not responsible for verifying the authenticity

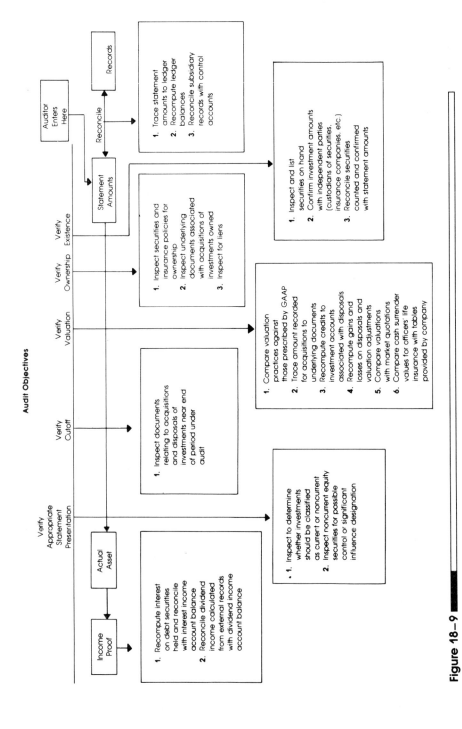

Figure 18–9

Flowchart for Substantive Verification of Investments

of the securities being examined, he or she should be alert for obvious forgeries. This auditing procedure should be performed in the presence of the client employee(s) charged with the custodial responsibility for securities and should be carried out at the same time that cash is being counted. If it is impossible to perform those procedures simultaneously, the securities storage box should be sealed at the time of the cash count and remain sealed until the securities can be inspected. The custodian of the securities should be asked to sign an acknowledgment for the return of the securities when the inspection is finished.

In instances in which investments owned by the client are held by independent custodians such as brokers or trustees, they should be confirmed with those parties. Securities in a bond sinking fund, for example, generally will be held by the bond trustee and should be confirmed with that party. Such confirmation requests should contain the same details as would be required if the auditor had inspected and listed the securities, as discussed above. After the inspection and confirmation procedures have been completed, the list of securities verified to be in existence as of the end of the fiscal period should be reconciled with the statement balances for securities owned. The list is then used as the basic working paper on which the evidence associated with the verification of valuation, ownership, cutoff, and statement presentation is recorded. Details of insurance policies owned by the client should be confirmed with insurance companies as of the end of the audit period. As shown in Appendix 18–I, such details include policy number, name(s) of insured persons, beneficiaries, face amount, any policy loans outstanding, and selected other information.

Verification of Ownership

The ownership of investments should be verified by inspecting them for outstanding liens as the other auditing procedures are performed. For securities, the auditor examines individual certificates for endorsements and inspects confirmation replies for securities held by agents and others. Also, as shown in Appendix 18–G, the broker's advices, which are issued as evidence of acquisitions and disposals of securities, should be inspected to determine whether the company is the registered owner of the securities. For insurance policies, the confirmation reply from the insurance company (Appendix 18–I) gives information as to the owner of the policy in the upper right-hand portion of the form.

Verification of Valuation

The verification of valuation is a critical objective in the audit of investments. Typically, the procedures followed in verifying valuation appear on the working paper that contains the list of investments prepared at the time they were inspected and confirmed (see Appendixes 18–F and 18–H). The auditor generally begins by *comparing* the valuation practices followed with those prescribed by GAAP. He or she will also want to *vouch* the amounts recorded in the investment accounts back to the underlying documents associated with acquisitions to see that they have been properly recorded in the accounts. In meeting the valuation objective, it is also necessary to *recompute* the credits to the accounts associated with the sales of investments and to vouch details of disposition transactions to underlying documents (broker's advices, cash receipts, etc.). At this time, realized gains and losses on disposals of marketable equity securities, as well as unrealized valuation adjustments, should be *recomputed* in accordance with the provisions of FASB 12. As a last overall auditing procedure, the market quotations for securities held should be compared with their recorded values. These procedures are illustrated in Appendix 18–F.

Verification of Cutoff

Transactions recording acquisitions and disposals of securities that have occurred near the end of the period should be identified and traced to the underlying documents to determine that they were recorded in the appropriate fiscal period. Here again, appropriate cutoff is not as important as it is for revenues and cost of sales, but some attention should be given to it.

Verification of Appropriate Statement Presentation

Another important consideration in the audit of investments involves determining how the various investments should be disclosed in the balance sheet. For investments to be classified as a *current asset*, they *should be readily convertible to cash*. Also, in the normal course of operations, they should be *expected to be converted to cash* within a year, or within the operating cycle, whichever is longer. All other investments should be classified in the noncurrent assets section. The attitude of conservatism requires that questionable items be classified as noncurrent. A careful distinction should also be made between noncurrent investments held for the purpose of controlling or significantly influencing the operations of another company and those held only for the purpose of realizing investment income or an increment in value.

With respect to *long-term investments*, APB 18 requires use of the *equity method of accounting* if the investment gives the client the ability to exercise significant influence over the operating and financial policies of an investee. Among other things, such as representation on the investee's board of directors, participation in management decisions, and significant intercompany transactions, APB 18 states that an investment representing 20 percent or more of the voting stock of an investee should lead to a presumption of the ability to exercise significant influence.[1] The equity method requires that the client increase the carrying value of its investment in the investee by its proportionate share of earnings and decrease it by the proportionate share of losses and dividend distributions from the investee. Therefore, the auditor must be satisfied that the earnings, losses, and dividends of investee companies have been appropriately recognized. GAAP also requires that investors recognize nontemporary declines in carrying value of investments as losses.[2] That requires the auditor to determine whether such declines have occurred and, if so, whether they have been recorded.

Audited financial statements of the investee are considered sufficient evidence to enable the auditor to determine whether the equity method has been applied properly by the client. These statements may have been audited by another auditor as long as the report of the other auditor is acceptable to the auditor seeking the evidence. We discuss reliance on the work of other auditors more thoroughly in the reporting chapters of this text. Audited statements of investees are also considered competent (but not necessarily sufficient) evidence to assist the auditor of the investor in determining the proper carrying value of other investments. Other evidence may include market price quotations of actively traded securities of investees, as well as independent appraisals of investee asset values when securities are not actively traded.

Unaudited financial statements of the investee company can also provide some evidence as to proper application of the equity method and as to the carrying value of nonaffiliated long-term investments, but they are not considered sufficient evidence by themselves. In cases in which unaudited financial statements are used as evidence in support of significant investments, the auditor should either apply the auditing procedures deemed necessary or request the investee's independent accountant to apply those procedures. The extent of the auditing procedures necessary in this case depends on the materiality of the investment in relation to the financial statements of the client investor.[3]

With respect to nonaffiliated investments in marketable equity securities, FASB 12 requires that the client's portfolio be divided into current and noncurrent components for financial reporting purposes. Each of these portfolios must then be evaluated at the lower of aggregate cost or market. Balance sheet valuation accounts should be set up for each portfolio for this purpose. Offsetting charges or credits must be made to (1) unrealized gain or loss accounts on the income statement for current investments, and to (2) similar accounts in owners' equity for noncurrent investments. The auditor should obtain evidence regarding these valuations by *comparing market quotations* with those used by the client, *recalculating* the adjustments to the valuation accounts, and *examining the journal* entries to ascertain that the client's portfolio adjustments were appropriately recorded. Appendix 18–F is organized to facilitate disclosures for marketable equity securities in accordance with FASB 12 and to illustrate the auditing procedures discussed above.

As we could observe in Figure 18–9, the audit of investments requires an extension of auditing procedures beyond verifying that the statement account balances fairly reflect the values of investment assets owned. The auditor should also develop an *independent verification of investment income.* Typically this involves two procedures, as shown in Appendix 18–F. The first requires the auditor to independently *recompute* the interest or dividends that should have been earned on securities owned by the client and to verify per share amounts by reference to appropriate outside sources (Standard & Poors, Value Line Investment Survey, etc.). The second is to *reconcile* that amount with the interest or dividend income account balance. This verification for equity securities valued under the equity method will already have been accomplished by auditing procedures previously described for meeting the valuation objective.

Other Types of Investments

In some instances, land, mineral deposits, or other properties may be purchased and held as investments. Such investments are held partly for the purpose of realizing an increment in value during the holding period. Therefore, such investments should be valued at their initial costs plus carrying costs, such as taxes and interest, incurred in holding them. Carrying value should also be periodically adjusted for decrements in value. The auditor will be concerned with analyzing such investment accounts to see that GAAP valuation practices have been followed. He or she should also document all auditing procedures performed on these investments in a manner similar to that described above for investments in securities and life insurance policies.

Summary

This chapter has focused on the audit process for the financing and investing system. We began by describing the audit objectives for the system. Those objectives include existence or occurrence, completeness, proper valuation, cutoff, ownership rights/obligations, and proper statement presentation or disclosures. We then briefly described the types of transactions that comprise the financing and investing system, and we discussed planning considerations for the audit.

The necessity of obtaining an understanding of the control structure for the system was considered next. Elements of the control structure include the control environment, the accounting system, and control procedures embodied in them. Each of these elements were discussed in detail.

In the latter part of the chapter, detection risk procedures for key financial statement accounts emerging from the system were discussed. Working papers included in Appendixes 18–B through 18–I illustrate these procedures.

Auditing Vocabulary

p. 775   **broker's advice forms:**   The invoice from the broker that shows the purchase or sale of marketable equity or debt securities.

p. 766   **financing:**   The means by which a business organizes its affairs in order to provide capital for its operations.

p. 766   **investments:**   Nonoperating uses of the financial resources of an entity.

p. 777   **mortgage notes payable:**   Notes generally secured by mortgages on specific client assets.

p. 773   **trust indenture:**   The written agreement between the company and the bond trustee that sets forth the duties and obligations of both the company and the trustee on behalf of the bondholders of the company.

p. 773   **underwriters' agreement:**   The contract with the underwriters, who are the parties entrusted with the initial sale of the company's stock or bonds.

Appendix 18–A: Devices Used to Evaluate Internal Controls for Investments

Figure A–1

Exchange Functions Requiring Specific Controls

Financial assertions	Functions	Possible errors or irregularities	Possible results of undetected errors	Control attributes to prevent, detect, or correct errors or irregularities
Existence/ occurrence	Purchase of securities and other investments	Investments could be acquired without the knowledge or approval of the company; Acquisition of securities for personal use with company funds	Unexpected shortages in cash from making unsound business investments	Require approval of all major investment acquisitions by board of directors or investment committee; Require registered securities to be held in the name of the client or in the name of a custodian who has proper power of attorney
Existence/ occurrence; completeness	Pledging of securities as collateral for firm obligations	Use of company-owned securities as collateral for personal loans of custodian	Shortages in working capital; Misappropriation of assets	Require securities held as collateral to be physically segregated from other securities; Require approval of such transactions by appropriate officials
Existence/ occurrence	Receipt of interest and dividend checks	Misappropriation of cash to personal use	Understatement of cash and income; Misappropriation of cash	Require separation of recording and custodial duties associated with investments; Require periodic reconciliation of records and physical assets by persons having no other recordkeeping or custodial duties
Existence/ occurrence	Sale of securities and other investments	Investments could be sold without the knowledge or approval of the company and without being removed from the books	Overstatement of assets; Misappropriation of cash	Require approval of all major investment disposals by board of directors or investment committee; Require segregation of custodial and recordkeeping functions; Require periodic reconciliation of records and physical assets by persons independent of custodial functions

Figure A–2 ■■■■■■

Processing Functions Requiring Specific Controls

Financial assertions	Functions	Possible errors or irregularities	Possible results of undetected errors	Control attributes to prevent, detect, or correct errors or irregularities
Valuation; disclosure; completeness	Recording purchases of investment	Inaccurate or improper recording of acquisitions	Misstatement of assets	Require the accounting department to maintain an independent record of each investment or security, including serial or other identification numbers, number of shares, face amounts, dates of purchase, interest rates, etc. Require inspection and periodic reconciliation of purchase documents with accounting records
Valuation; disclosure; completeness	Recording interest and dividend income	Inaccurate or improper recording of income from investments	Misstatement of assets and income	Require proper accounting over investment income by persons independent of custodianship duties Require periodic reconciliation of investment income with dividend records; recalculation of interest accrued, etc., by independent persons
Valuation	Adjusting the carrying value of investments	Improper values of assets	Misstatement of asset portfolio	Require periodic review of proper carrying value of investment portfolio by a responsible official, and adjust when necessary
Completeness; disclosure	Recording sale of securities and other investments	Failure to record a disposal of securities and other investments Improperly recorded disposals	Overstatement of assets	Require inspection and periodic reconciliation of securities and investments with accounting records Require approval of write-downs and disposals by board of directors or investment committee Require proper control to be exercised over securities sold or written down

Figure A–3

Safeguard Functions Requiring Specific Controls

Financial assertions	Functions	Possible errors or irregularities	Possible results of undetected errors	Control attributes to prevent, detect, or correct errors or irregularities
Existence/ occurrence	Custodianship of securities	Unauthorized personal access to assets	Unauthorized sale or use of assets as collateral	Require dual custodianship over assets held in safe deposit boxes at financial institutions; for large portfolios of assets, require independent custodian such as trust department of a bank or other fiduciary Require bonding of all custodians of investment securities Require segregation of custodianship from recordkeeping duties Require periodic reconciliation of physical assets with accounting records by independent persons

Appendix 18-B: Notes Payable

						W. P. No.	m
	JEP Manufacturing Co.					ACCOUNTANT	*SmG*
	Notes Payable					DATE	5/12/X1
	3-31-X1						

A/c	Description	Balance 3-31-X0	Principal Additions	Principal Retirements	Balance 3-31-X1 ✓
206	J.E. Coletrain - 11-30-X8 Payable in 4 annual installments of $29,825 beginning 1-2-X9; Interest @ Prime rate, Payable quarterly	5965000		2982500 ⊗	M-1 2982500 R A-2
207	Xerox	–	738600 #	49230	689370 C A-2
209	Prudential Insurance Co. 6-8-X3 - Payable in annual installments of $50,000 beginning on 10-1-X0 Original Amount $715,000 Interest Rate 8.70%	40000000		5000000 ⊗	M-1 35000000 ✓ A-2
205	FNB Greensboro 11¾%	17500000	50000000 ✗	67500000 ✗	-0- 9
		63465000	50738600	75561730	38671870

C & Confirmations sent; received
⊘ Agreed to prior year working papers
✓ Agreed to 3-31-X1 general ledger
7 Recomputed amount. Appears reasonable.
✗ Agreed amount to paid checks. No exceptions noted.
See copy of purchase agreement in PF-14-4
✗ Agreed to cancelled note. Appears proper.

Current Portion Reclassified Balance	Interest Reasonableness Test		
	$59650 \times 12\% \times \frac{1}{4}$ =	1784 60	
	$59650 \times 13\% \times \frac{1}{4}$ =	1938 62	
	$59650 \times 21\frac{1}{2}\% \times \frac{1}{4}$ =	3231 96	
RJE ⟨298250 0⟩	$29825 \times 17\% \times \frac{1}{4}$ =	1250 10	
-0-			8205 28 ⊤
A-2			
⟨1477 20⟩	Total interest expense		2543 4 ⊤
5416 50			
A-2			
⟨f⟩	$400000 \times .0870 \times \frac{6}{12}$ =	17400 00	
RJE ⟨500000 0⟩	$350000 \times .0870 \times \frac{6}{12}$ =	15225 00	
300000 00			32625 00 ⊤
A-2			
			19333 01 ⊤ ⊗
305416 50	Total interest expense		60417 63
A-2	Amortization of debt expense		1125 84 K
			61543 47
	AJE ⟨6⟩		1916 00
			63459 47
			A-3

Appendix 18–C: Reclassification of Current Maturities

		W. P. No.	Ma
JEP Mfg. Co.		ACCOUNTANT	SmS
Reclassification of L-T Debt		DATE	5/12/X1
3-31-X1			

For F/S purpose, L-T Debt must be broken down
into two components: that portion payable w/in one
year and that portion payable in periods beyond the upcoming
year. The current portion of JEP's L-T Debt is calculated
as follows:

Xerox – monthly installments of #123.10	(12 × 123.10) =	1477.20	
Prudential next payment due 10-1-X1		50000.00	
JE Coletrain next payment due 1-2-X2		29825.00	
Current portion L-T Debt		81302.20	
		A-2	

RJE (c) A-6	Dr.	Cr.
Xerox N/P	1477.20	
Prudential N/P	50000.00	
Coletrain N/P	29825.00	
Current Portion L-T Debt		81302.20
(To reclassify current portion of Long-Term Debt.)		

✓ Per appropriate agreement

Appendix 18-D: Notes Payable Confirmation Received

JEP MANUFACTURING COMPANY
P.O. Box 1000
Greensboro, Texas 75401

M-1
SMG
5/12/X1

April 2, 19X1

Mrs. J. E. Coletrain
2612 S. 8th Avenue
Greensboro, Texas 75401

Dear Mrs. Coletrain:

Best and Company, Suite 4500, Byron Building, Dallas, Texas 75201, are making their usual examination of our accounts. Please confirm directly to them the amount of our indebtedness to you as of the close of business on March 31, 19X1. According to our records, our indebtedness to you on that date was as follows:

Original Balance	$119,300
Unpaid Balance at March 31, 19X1	$29,825.00
Interest Rate	Prime rate of Mercantile National Bank
Date of Note	November 3, 19X8
Date Due	
Interest paid to Date	Jan. 1, 19X1
Collateral	Unsecured

A return envelope is enclosed for your convenience.

Very truly yours,

JEP Manufacturing Co.

L. Philip Neeson

L. Philip Neeson
Financial Vice President

The above information is correct except as noted:

Elizabeth L. Coletrain   *4-21-X1*
Signature   Title   Date

Appendix 18–E: Lead Schedule for Equity Capital Accounts

	W. P. No.	4
JEP Manufacturing Corporation	ACCOUNTANT	SmL
Analysis of Equity Accounts	DATE	5/19/X1
3-31-X1		

	Preferred Stock		Common Outstanding	
	Amount	Shares	Amount	Shares
Balance per 3-31-X0 Financial Statements	6020000 ✓	1204 ✓	7599476 ✓	109664 ✓
Prior Period Adjustments:				
To reverse prior year percentage-of-completion entry				
To adjust investment in subsidiary to equity method				
To amortize excess cost of subsidiary				
To record year-end deferred tax adjustment				
Net income - statement effect of 3-31-X0 "Off-Ledger" entries				
Beginning retained earnings per general ledger, 3/31/X0				
① Preferred Stock Sinking Fund	<6020000> ✓	<1204> ✓		
② Quarterly Dividends:				
6/30/X0, Preferred Stock (1204 shares @ .75/sh)				
8/14/X0, Preferred Stock (1204 shares @ .375/sh)				
Adjustment for tax treatment of obsolete inventory				
End-of-year adjustments:				
To reverse prior year percentage-of-completion entry (AJE <4>)				
To adjust investment in subsidiary to equity method (AJE <4>)				
To amortize excess cost of subsidiary (AJE <5>)				
To record year-end deferred tax adjustment (AJE <6>)				
To eliminate adjustment for tax treatment of obsolete inventory (AJE <3>)				
To adjust deferred taxes payable for obsolete inventory (AJE <7>)				
Net income for year				
	-0-	-0-	7599476 ⨍	109664 ⨍
			A-2	

✓ Per Prior Year working papers

✗ Per Prior Year working papers; Certificate #13 for 1599 shares issued to JEP Manufacturing inspected; held in safe deposit box at bank. No exceptions noted.

① Per Board of Directors Minutes dated 6-9-X0. See PF-4 for copy of minutes. Authorized retirement of 1204 shares at $50/share. (1204 × 50 = 60,200)

② Vouched authorization to Board of Directors' Minutes of 6-9-X0.

✓ Vouched payment to cancelled checks. No exceptions noted.

⨍ Reviewed account; noted no activity for year.

Stock Treasury Amount	Shares	Paid-in Capital		Retained Earnings	
‹101216 7›	‹1599›	3463850		2287255 22	
				‹157280 95›	
				‹152354 00›	
				5987 00	
				72529 00	
				‹92704 57›	
				1963431 70	
				‹ 903 00› ✓	
				‹ 451 55› ✓	
				1437 036	
				276358 36	
				187022 00	
				‹ 7903 00›	
				‹123599 66›	
				‹ 1437036›	
				‹ 8054 63›	
			A-3	451677 97	
‹101216 7› ᵀ	‹1599› ᵀ	3463850 ᵀ		2737578 19	
A-2		A-2		A-2	

Conclusion: Based on audit work performed, which was considered adequate to meet the audit objectives for owners' equity accounts, they are fairly stated in accordance with generally accepted accounting principles @ 3-31-X1.   SmS

Appendix 18–F: Marketable Equity Securities

			W. P. No.	C-1
JEP Manufacturing Co.			ACCOUNTANT	Client / Cut
Marketable Equity Securities				
3-31-X1			DATE	4/29/X1

Purchase Date	Description	Balance 3-31-X0	Cost		Balance 3-31-X1
			Purchases	Sales	
	General Motors (1000 shares) Common (Cert. # 2604)	33700 00	0		33700 00 ✗
	Sears Roebuck + Co Common (4000 shares) (Cert # 4583)	80400 00	0		80400 00 ✗
	General Electric (1600 shares) Common (Cert # 3695)	34848 00	0		34848 00 ✗
	Union Carbide (1000 shares) Common (Cert # 4586)		50125 00 Ⓔ		50125 00 ✗
	IBM Common (1000 shares) (Cert # 26032)		52000 00 Ⓔ		52000 00 ✗
	ITT preferred H series (1000 shares) (Cert # 24211)		50250 00 Ⓔ		50250 00 ✗
	Xerox Common (1000 shares) (Cert # 211462)		51768 00 Ⓔ	9819 00 ✗	41949 00 ✗
		148948 00 ⌄	204143 00 ⌄	9819 00 ⌄	343272 00 A-1

⌄ Footed   ✗ Cross-footed
✗ Inspected certificate on safe deposit box, First National Bank. Agreed total with subsidiary ledger.
✓ Traced to cash receipts records. No exceptions noted.
0 Details agreed to prior year audited working papers. No exceptions noted.
✗ Computation checked.
Ⓔ Examined brokers' advice. Traced to cancelled check and cash disbursements records. Examined records for evidence of transactions occurring at or near year-end cut off date. None noted.
ϕ Vouched to market price per Wall Street Journal on March 31, 1981.
Ⓣ Vouched per share dividend to Value Line Investment Survey, Summary and Index. Traced dividend proceeds to cash receipts. No exceptions noted.

Net Sales Proceeds	Gain (Loss) on Sales	Dividend Income	Market Value		
			Per Share	Total	
		4265 Ⓣ	46 3/8 ¢	46375 00	
		16240 Ⓣ	16 3/8 ¢	65500 00	
		5600 Ⓣ	55 2/8 ¢	89400 00	
		2400 Ⓣ	51 7/8 ¢	51875 00	
		2600 Ⓣ	55 1/8 ¢	55125 00	
		2800 Ⓣ	48 ¢	43000 00	
79030 0 ✓	⟨19160 0⟩ ✗	3800 Ⓣ	46 ¢	46000 00	
79030 0	⟨19160 0⟩	37205 00		402275 00 ✗	
	A-3	X-7			

Note: Ascertained that the above securities are all properly accounted for as current assets under provisions of FASB Statement No. 12. In my opinion, marketable equity securities and related income are fairly presented at 3-31-X1. CW

Appendix 18–G: Dividends Declared and Paid

	JEP Mfg. Co.		W. P. No.	Y-1
	Dividends Declared and Paid per Review of the		ACCOUNTANT	Smith
	Minutes of the Board of Directors & Exec. Committee		DATE	5/21/X1
	3-31-X1			
	Description	Amount per share	Declaration Date	Date Paid
	Board of Directors	$ .75 ①	6-9-X0	7-31-X0
	Board of Directors	$ .375 ②	6-9-X0	3-14-X0
① For quarter ended 6-30-X0 (75 × 1204 = $903 Ⓐ)			
② For ½ quarter ended 8-14-X0 - the date on which all			
	preferred stock was retired. (.375 × 1204 = 451.55 Ⓐ)			
	Σ Ⓐ's = 1354.55 = (903 + 451.55)			
	ᵤ			

Appendix 18–H: Cash Surrender Value

				Total Payment	Premium Expense	Increase in Cash Value	Cash Surrender Value
			JEP Mfg. Co.				L
			Cash Surrender Value				L.B.
			3-31-X1			↓	5/13/X1
			Great West Policy #1729-197				
			L-1 #500,000 on James C. Proctor				
			Cash Surrender Value 3-31-X0				1 22 000 00 △
			Payments (1277.43 per mo.)	15 329 16	3 329 16	12 000 00	12 000 00
			#1000 increase in CSV w/				
			each payment				L-1
			CSV 3-31-X1				C 13 400 000
			Great West Policy #2190 171				
			#300,000 on Anita Proctor				
			Cash Surrender Value 3-31-X0				4 000 00 △
			Payments (793.49 per mo.)	9 527 88	1 727 88	7 800 00	7 800 00
			#400 increase in CSV w/				
			1st 2 payments - #700				
			increase - thereafter				
			CSV 3-31-X1				⊗ 11 800 00
			Gross Cash Surrender Value @ 3-31-X1				145 800 00
			Difference - pass				< 500 00 >
			Balance per G/L @ 3-31-X1		5 051 04		145 300 00 ✓
					X-7		A-1
			Less : Policy Loan				C < 76 500 00 >
							A-1
			Net Value 3-31-X1				68 800 00 ✓
							A-1

Conclusion : Based on the audit work performed, which was considered
adequate to meet the objectives per the APG, it appears that the
balance in CSV - Life Insurance Policies is fairly stated @ 3-31-X1.

△ Per prior year's W/P's
✓ Agreed to 3-31-X1 G/L
C C Confirmation sent - rec'd. See L-1
∠ Examined bank draft on a test basis - no exceptions noted
⊗ Examined table of CSV from insurance company and noted that CSV @ 3-31-X1
   appeared reasonable and proper per their computation. Traced confirmation.

Appendix 18–I: Life Insurance Confirmation

**STANDARD CONFIRMATION INQUIRY
FOR LIFE INSURANCE POLICIES**
Developed by
AMERICAN INSTITUTE OF CERTIFIED PUBLIC ACCOUNTANTS
LIFE OFFICE MANAGEMENT ASSOCIATION
MILLION DOLLAR ROUND TABLE

L - L
C ωT
5/1/X1

_____ April 2, 19X1 _____

Dear Sirs:

Please furnish the information requested below in items 1 through 9 (and also in items 10 through 12 if any of those items are checked) for the policies identified on lines A, B and C. This information is requested as of the date indicated. IF THE ANSWER TO ANY ITEM IS "NONE," PLEASE SO STATE. The enclosed envelope is provided for the return of one copy of this form to the accountant named below.

(Ins. Co.) <u>The Great Life Assurance Co.</u>
      c/o Mrs. Debrah Burn, Denver Policy Values
      <u>Suite 12, 16 Fifth Ave.</u>
      Denver, Colorado 80202

JEP Manufacturing Company, Inc.
(Name of owner as shown on policy contracts)

Information requested as of <u>March 31, 19X1</u>

(Accountant) Best and Company
      Suite 4500, Bryon Building
      Dallas, Texas 75201

Request authorized by

		Col. A	Col. B
A.	Policy number	1729-197	
B.	Insured James E. Proctor		
C.	Beneficiaries as shown on policies (if verification requested in item 11) Col. A— *J EP Manufacturing Co* Col. B—		
1.	Face amount of basic policy	$ *500,000* 4	$
2.	Values shown as of (insert date if other than date requested)		
3.	Premiums, including prepaid premiums, are paid to (insert date)	*May 21 X1*	
4.	Policy surrender value (excluding dividends, additions and indebtedness adjustments)	$ *134,000 L*	$
5.	Surrender value of all dividend credits, including accumulations and additions	$ *NPAR*	$
6.	Termination dividend currently available on surrender	$	$
7. Other surrender values available to policyowner	a. Prepaid premium value	$	$
	b. Premium deposit funds	$	$
	c. Other	$	$
8.	Outstanding policy loans, excluding accrued interest	$ *76,500*	$ *L*
9. If any loans exist, complete either "a" or "b"	a. Interest accrued on policy loans	$	$
	b. 1.) Loan interest is paid to (enter date)	*Jul. 21 X0*	
	2.) Interest rate is (enter rate)	*.5 %*	

The accountant will indicate by a check (✔) which if any of items 10-12 are to be answered

☐	**10.** Is there an assignee of record? (enter Yes or No)		
☐	**11.** Is beneficiary of record as shown in item C above? (enter Yes or No*)	*	*
☐	**12.** Is the name of policyowner (subject to any assignment) as shown at the top of the form? (enter Yes or No) _____. If No, enter name of policyowner of record. _____		

*If answer to 11 is No, please give name of beneficiary or date of last beneficiary change._____

Date <u>4-7-X1</u>   By<u>*Diane McCarthy*</u>   Title <u>*Policy Values*</u>
             For the insurance company addressed

Additional copies of this form are available from the American Institute of CPAs, 666 Fifth Avenue, New York, N. Y. 10019

Notes

1. APB Opinion No. 18 (New York: AICPA, 1972).
2. FASB 12, *Accounting for Certain Marketable Securities* (Stamford, CT, Financial Accounting Standards Board, 1975).
3. SAS No. 1, Section 332 (New York: AICPA, 1973).

Questions for Class Discussion

Q18-1 What are the three elements of the cycle associated with financing through debt?

Q18-2 What distinguishes noncurrent investments from plant assets? Explain.

Q18-3 What are the exchange functions associated with the investments subsystem? Describe them.

Q18-4 What are the four distinguishing characteristics that help shape the evidence-gathering process for the financing and investing system? Describe briefly.

Q18-5 What functions should be separated within the financing and investing system?

Q18-6 What are the forms and authorization procedures that should be maintained in support of the exchange and processing functions within the financing and investing system?

Q18-7 What responsibilities should the board of directors have relating to financing and investing activities?

Q18-8 What safeguard controls should be present in the system of control for investments?

Q18-9 What control attributes should be present to prevent the person having custody of a company's securities from acquiring securities for personal use? Explain.

Q18-10 What control attributes are used to prevent misappropriation of cash received from interest and dividends? Explain.

Q18-11 Why should a company insist that persons having custody of securities be bonded? Is it also necessary to bond personnel handling the accounting records for investments? Explain.

Q18-12 Why is it desirable to require two persons to be present to open the bank safe deposit box where securities are kept?

Q18-13 How will the fact that a firm employs a transfer agent to handle capital-stock-related transactions, rather than having company employees handle such transactions, affect the evidence-gathering process? Explain.

Q18-14 Which documents should be examined by the auditor in verifying the existence of long-term debt? Describe them.

Q18-15 Under what circumstances would the auditor use confirmation procedures in verifying notes and bonds payable? Explain.

Q18-16 Under what circumstances would the auditor use confirmation procedures in the verification of equity capital? Explain.

Q18-17 What procedures should the auditor follow in verifying the valuation of debt securities?

Q18-18 What is the relationship between the verification of interest expense and the verification of debt securities outstanding? Discuss.

Q18-19 Why does the audit of owners' equity typically require substantially less audit time than is required in the verification of other types of account balances?

Q18-20 What auditing procedures should be performed in the verification of treasury stock held by a client?

Q18-21 How does the auditor verify the record of dividends declared during the year?

Q18-22 What is a broker's advice form? What functions does it serve in connection with securities transactions?

Q18-23 How does the auditor verify existence (validity) of securities included in the investment account?

Q18-24 How does the auditor verify the ownership of securities held by a client?

Q18-25 How does the auditor verify the valuation of securities included in the client's investment account?

Q18-26 Under what circumstances should noncurrent investments in equity securities be valued by use of the equity method of accounting? Explain.

Q18-27 How should marketable equity securities be valued in the balance sheet?

Q18-28 Why is it important to verify independently both interest and dividend income received from investments held by the client? Explain.

Short Cases

C18-1 You are a CPA engaged in an examination of the financial statements of Pate Corporation for the year ended December 31, 19X9. The financial statements and records of Pate Corporation have not been audited by a CPA in prior years.

The stockholders' equity section of Pate Corporation's balance sheet at December 31, 19X9, follows:

Stockholders' equity

Capital stock—10,000 shares of $10 par value authorized; 5,000 shares issued and outstanding	$ 50,000
Capital contributed in excess of par value of capital stock	32,580
Retained earnings	47,320
Total stockholders' equity	$129,900

Pate Corporation was founded in 19X1. The corporation has ten stockholders and serves as its own registrar and transfer agent. There are no capital stock subscription contracts in effect.

Required:

a. Prepare the detailed audit program for the examination of the three accounts comprising the stockholders' equity section of Pate Corporation's balance sheet. (Do not include in the audit program the verification of the results of the current year's operations.)

b. After every other figure on the balance sheet has been audited, it might appear that the retained earnings figure is a balancing figure and requires no further verification. Why do you, as a CPA, verify retained earnings as you do the other figures on the balance sheet? Discuss.

(AICPA adapted)

C18-2   You were engaged to examine the financial statements of Ronlyn Corporation for the year ended June 30, 19X7.

On May 1, 19X7, the corporation borrowed $500,000 from the Second National Bank to finance plant expansion. The long-term note agreement provided for the annual payment of principal and interest over five years. The existing plant was pledged as security for the loan.

Due to unexpected difficulties in acquiring the building site, the plant expansion had not begun at June 30, 19X7. To make use of the borrowed funds, management decided to invest in stocks and bonds, and on May 16, 19X7, the $500,000 was invested in securities.

Required:
a. What are the audit objectives in the examination of long-term debt?
b. Prepare an audit program for the examination of the long-term note agreement between Ronlyn and Second National Bank.

(AICPA adapted)

C18-3   The following covenants are extracted from the indenture of a bond issue. The indenture provides that failure to comply with its terms in any respect automatically advances the due date of the loan to the date of noncompliance (the regular date is twenty years hence). Give any audit steps or reporting requirements you feel should be taken or recognized in connection with each one of the following.
   a. "The debtor company shall endeavor to maintain a working capital ratio of 2 to 1 at all times, and in any fiscal year following a failure to maintain said ratio, the company shall restrict compensation of officers to a total of $100,000. Officers for this purpose shall include chairman of the board of directors, president, all vice-presidents, secretary, and treasurer."
   b. "The debtor company shall keep all property that is security for this debt insured against loss by fire to the extent of 100 percent of its actual value. Policies of insurance comprising this protection shall be filed with the trustee."
   c. "The debtor company shall pay all taxes legally assessed against property that is security for this debt within the time provided by law for payment without penalty and shall deposit receipted tax bills or equally acceptable evidence of payment of same with the trustee."
   d. "A sinking fund shall be deposited with the trustee by semiannual payments of $300,000, from which the trustee shall, in his discretion, purchase bonds of this issue."

(AICPA adapted)

C18-4   Jimmack Corporation adopted a pension plan for its employees on January 1, 19X8. Provisions of the plan were as follows:
   a. The corporation shall contribute 10 percent of its net income before deducting

income taxes and the contribution, but not in excess of 15 percent of the total salaries paid to the participants in the plan who are in the employ of the corporation at year end. The employees make no contribution to the plan.

b. An employee shall be eligible to participate in the plan on January 1 following completion of one full year of employment.

The following data pertain to the corporation and its employees for 19X9:

Corporate income before income taxes and contribution to pension plan: $7,325,000

Employment records:

Name	Date employed	Date terminated	Salary paid in 19X9
Jimmack	12/08/X3	—	$179,000
Baker	02/01/X5	—	141,000
Cohen	02/08/X5	04/09/X9	35,000
Delman	09/15/X6	—	80,000
Jarman	09/21/X9	12/22/X9	30,000
Zibranek	05/06/X9	—	55,000
			$520,000

Required:

a. What are the detailed audit objectives for the corporation's liability accrual to the corporate pension plan?

b. What audit evidence needs to be obtained to satisfy the objectives listed in (a)? Include in your answer the detailed procedures needed to verify the information given above for corporate income and employment records.

c. Recalculate the corporation's contribution accrual for 19X9.

d. Based on the information provided, what deficiencies, if any, do you see in the company's accounting practices? What other information might you need to determine if the company's accounting methods comply with GAAP?

e. How might the company's accounting policies, or lack of them, affect your audit opinion, considering your perceived materiality of the pension fund liability disclosures?

(AICPA adapted)

C18-5   The Ford Corporation leased equipment from the Nixon Company on October 1, 19X1. You have learned through conversations with the controller of Ford Corporation, your client, that the transaction was accounted for as a purchase. Terms of the lease are as follows:

a. The lease is for an eight-year period expiring September 30, 19X9.

b. Equal annual lease payments are to be made in the amount of $600,000, due October 1 of each year. The first payment was made on October 1 of 19X1.

c. The equipment has an estimated useful life of eight years, with no residual value expected.

d. Ford has adopted the straight-line method of depreciation and takes a full year's depreciation in the year of purchase.

e. The rate of interest contemplated by Ford and Nixon is 10 percent. (Present value of an annuity of $1 in advance for eight periods at 10 percent if $5.868.)

Required:
   a. What audit evidence would you obtain with regard to the above facts? Be specific in terms of audit objectives and procedures.
   b. What expense(s) should Ford record as a result of the above facts for the year ended December 31, 19X1? Show supporting computation in good form.

(AICPA adapted)

C18-6   You have been engaged to examine the financial statements of the Elliott Company for the year ended December 31, 19X3. You performed a similar examination as of December 31, 19X2.

Following is the trial balance for the company as of December 31, 19X3:

	Dr. (Cr.)
Cash	$128,000
Interest receivable	47,450
Dividends receivable	1,750
6½% secured note receivable	730,000
Investments at cost:	
Bowen common stock	322,000
Investments at equity:	
Woods common stock	284,000
Land	185,000
Accounts payable	(31,000)
Interest payable	(6,500)
8% secured note payable to bank	(275,000)
Common stock	(480,000)
Paid-in capital in excess of par	(800,000)
Retained earnings	(100,500)
Dividend revenue	(3,750)
Interest revenue	(47,450)
Equity in earnings of investments carried at equity	(40,000)
Interest expense	26,000
General and administrative expense	60,000

You have obtained the following data concerning certain accounts:
   a. The 6½ percent note receivable is due from Tysinger Corporation and is secured by a first mortgage on land sold to Tysinger by Elliott on December 21, 19X2. The note was to have been paid in twenty equal quarterly payments beginning March 31, 19X3, plus interest. Tysinger, however, is in very poor financial condition and has not made any principal or interest payments to date.
   b. The Bowen common stock was purchased on September 21, 19X2, for cash in the market where it is actively traded. It is used as security for the note payable and held by the bank. Elliott's investment in Bowen represents approximately one percent of the total outstanding shares of Bowen.
   c. Elliott's investment in Woods represents 40 percent of the outstanding common stock that is actively traded. Woods is audited by another CPA and has a December 31 year end.
   d. Elliott neither purchased nor sold any stock investments during the year other than that noted above.

Required: For the following account balances, discuss (1) the types of evidential matter you should obtain and (2) the auditing procedures you should perform during your examination.

   a. 6½ percent secured note receivable.
   b. Bowen common stock.
   c. Woods common stock.
   d. Dividend revenue.

(AICPA adapted)

C18-7 In auditing the financial statements of Associated Milk Products, Inc., a manufacturer of ice cream and other dairy products, you find the following item on the balance sheet as of June 30, 19X6:

Cost of patents $120,000

Referring to the ledger accounts, you note the following items regarding a patent on a soft ice cream machine acquired in 19X0:

19X0	Legal costs incurred in defining the validity of the patent	$14,000
19X1	Attorney fees for prosecuting an infringement suit	26,000
19X1	Additional legal fees in infringement suit	1,250
19X5	Improvements (unpatented) on machine	12,250

There are no credits in the account and no allowance for amortization has been set up in the books. There are three other patents issued in 19X2, 19X3, and 19X4, all of which were developed by the staff of the client. All patented machines are presently very marketable. However, they are expected to be in demand for only the next three years.

Required:
   a. As auditor, what are your primary audit objectives concerning patents?
   b. What auditing procedures should you apply to the Associated patent account in light of the facts?
   c. What audit adjustments, generally, would you recommend, if any? (Do not discuss dollar amounts.)

(AICPA adapted)

C18-8 As a result of highly profitable operations over a number of years, Western Manufacturing Corporation accumulated a substantial long-term investment portfolio. In the examination of the financial statements for the year ended December 31, the following information came to the attention of the corporation's CPA:
   a. The manufacturing operations of the corporation resulted in an operating loss for the year.
   b. The corporation has placed the securities making up the investment portfolio with a financial institution that will serve as custodian of the securities. Formerly the securities were kept in the corporation's safe deposit box in the local bank.

Required:
   a. List the objectives of the CPA's examination of the long-term investment account. For each objective, discuss the auditing procedures that would satisfy it.
   b. Under what conditions would the CPA accept a confirmation of the securities on hand from the custodian in lieu of personally inspecting and counting the securities?

(AICPA adapted)

C18-9 You were engaged to examine the financial statements of Ronson Corporation for the year ended July 31, 19X9.

On May 1, 19X9, the Corporation borrowed $500,000 from First City National Bank to finance plant expansion. Due to unexpected difficulties in acquiring the building site, the construction starting was delayed until July 1, 19X9. To make use of the borrowed funds, management decided to invest in marketable equity securities. The investment was made on May 5, 19X9.

Required:
  a. What are the audit objectives for short-term investments in marketable equity securities?
  b. In your audit, how would you do the following:
   1. Verify the dividend income recorded for the stocks?
   2. Determine proper valuation for the portfolio at July 31, 19X9?
   3. Establish the authority for the investment transaction?
   4. Determine the validity of the purchase transaction?
   5. Determine proper statement presentation for the investment account?

(AICPA adapted)

Problems

P18-1 Select the best answer for each of the following items relating to the verification of long-term debt.
  a. The auditor's program for the examination of long-term debt should include steps that require the
   1. Verification of the existence of the bondholders.
   2. Examination of any bond trust indenture.
   3. Inspection of the accounts-payable subsidiary ledger.
   4. Investigation of credits to the bond interest income account.
  b. During an examination of a publicly held company, the auditor should obtain written confirmation regarding debenture transactions from the
   1. Debenture holders.
   2. Client's attorney.
   3. Internal auditors.
   4. Trustee.
  c. Several years ago, Conway, Inc., secured a conventional real estate mortgage loan. Which of the following auditing procedures would be *least* likely to be performed by an auditor examining the mortgage balance?
   1. Examine the current year's cancelled checks.
   2. Review the mortgage amortization schedule.
   3. Inspect public records of lien balances.
   4. Recompute mortgage interest expense.
  d. During its fiscal year, a company issued, at a discount, a substantial amount of first-mortgage bonds. When performing audit work in connection with the bond issue, the independent auditor should
   1. Confirm the existence of the bondholders.
   2. Review the minutes for authorization.

3. Trace the net cash received from the issuance to the bonds-payable account.
4. Inspect the records maintained by the bond trustee.

e. During the year under audit, a company has completed a private placement of a substantial amount of bonds. Which of the following is the *most* important step in the auditor's program for the examination of bonds payable?
   1. Confirming the amount issued with the bond trustee.
   2. Tracing the cash received from the issue to the accounting records.
   3. Examining the bond records maintained by the transfer agent.
   4. Recomputing the annual interest cost and the effective yield.

f. During the course of an audit, a CPA observes that the recorded interest expense seems to be excessive in relation to the balance in the long-term debt *account*. This observation could lead the auditor to suspect that
   1. Long-term debt is understated.
   2. Discount on bonds payable is overstated.
   3. Long-term debt is overstated.
   4. Premium on bonds payable is understated.

g. A company issued bonds for cash during the year under audit. To ascertain that this transaction was properly recorded, the auditor's *best* course of action is to
   1. Request a statement from the bond trustee as to the amount of the bonds issued and outstanding.
   2. Confirm the results of the issuance with the underwriter or investment banker.
   3. Trace the cash received from the issuance to the accounting records.
   4. Verify that the net cash received is credited to an account entitled "Bonds Payable."

(AICPA adapted)

P18-2 Select the best answer to each of the following items relating to the verification of owners' equity.

a. An audit program for the examination of the retained earnings account should include a step that requires verification of the
   1. Gain or loss resulting from disposition of treasury shares.
   2. Market value used to charge retained earnings to account for a two-for-one stock split.
   3. Authorization for both cash and stock dividends.
   4. Approval of the adjustment to the beginning balance as a result of a write-down of an account receivable.

b. Florida Corporation declared a 100 percent stock dividend during 19X5. In connection with the examination of Florida's financial statements, Florida's auditor should determine that
   1. The additional shares issued do not exceed the number of authorized but previously unissued shares.
   2. Stockholders received their additional shares by confirming year-end holdings with them.
   3. The stock dividend was properly recorded at fair market value.
   4. Florida's stockholders have authorized the issuance of 100-percent stock dividends.

c. Which of the following is the *most* important consideration of an auditor when examining the stockholders' equity section of a client's balance sheet?
   1. Changes in the capital stock account are verified by an independent stock transfer agent.

   2. Stock dividends or stock splits during the year under audit were approved by the stockholders.

   3. Stock dividends are capitalized at par or stated value on the dividend declaration date.

   4. Entries in the capital stock account can be traced to a resolution in the minutes of the board of directors' meetings.

d. All corporate capital stock transactions should ultimately be traced to the

   1. Minutes of the board of directors.

   2. Cash receipts journal.

   3. Cash disbursements journal.

   4. Numbered stock certificates.

e. Where *no* independent stock transfer agents are employed and the corporation issues its own stocks and maintains stock records, cancelled stock certificates should

   1. Be defaced to prevent reissuance and attached to their corresponding stubs.

   2. *Not* be defaced, but segregated from other stock certificates and retained in a cancelled certificates file.

   3. Be destroyed to prevent fraudulent reissuance.

   4. Be defaced and sent to the secretary of state.

f. If a company employs a capital stock registrar and/or transfer agent, the registrar or agent, or both, should be requested to confirm directly to the auditor the number of shares of each class of stock

   1. Surrendered and cancelled during the year.

   2. Authorized at the balance sheet date.

   3. Issued and outstanding at the balance sheet date.

   4. Authorized, issued, and outstanding during the year.

g. When a company has treasury stock certificates on hand, a year-end count of the certificates by the auditor is

   1. Required when the company classifies treasury stock with other assets.

   2. Not required if treasury stock is a deduction from stockholders' equity.

   3. Required when the company had treasury stock transactions during the year.

   4. Always required.

(AICPA adapted)

P18-3 Select the best answer for each of the following items.

a. In order to avoid the misappropriation of company-owned, marketable securities, which of the following is the *best* course of action that can be taken by the management of a company with a large portfolio of marketable securities?

   1. Require that one trustworthy and bonded employee be responsible for access to the safekeeping area, where securities are kept.

   2. Require that employees who enter and leave the safekeeping area sign and record in a log the exact reason for their access.

   3. Require that employees involved in the safekeeping function maintain a subsidiary control ledger for securities on a current basis.

   4. Require that the safekeeping function for securities be assigned to a bank that will act as a custodial agent.

b. Which of the following is *not* one of the auditor's primary objectives in an examination of marketable securities?

   1. To determine whether securities are authentic.

   2. To determine whether securities are the property of the client.

      3. To determine whether securities actually exist.

      4. To determine whether securities are properly classified on the balance sheet.

  c. The auditor should insist that a representative of the client be present during the physical examination of securities in order to

      1. Lend authority to the auditor's directives.

      2. Detect forged securities.

      3. Coordinate the return of all securities to proper locations.

      4. Acknowledge the receipt of securities returned.

  d. A company has additional temporary funds to invest. The board of directors decided to purchase marketable securities and assigned the future purchase and sale decisions to a responsible financial executive. The best person(s) to make periodic reviews of the investment activity should be

      1. The investment committee of the board of directors.

      2. The treasurer.

      3. The corporate controller.

      4. The chief operating officer.

  e. The auditor can *best* verify a client's bond sinking fund transactions and year-end balance by

      1. Recomputation of interest expense, interest payable, and amortization of bond discount or premium.

      2. Confirmation with individual holders of retired bonds.

      3. Confirmation with the bond trustee.

      4. Examination and count of the bonds retired during the year.

  f. If the auditor discovers that the carrying amount of a client's investments is overstated because of a loss in value that is *other than a temporary decline* in that market value, the auditor should insist that

      1. The approximate market value of the investments be shown on the face of the balance sheet.

      2. The investments be classified as long term for balance sheet purposes, with full disclosure in the footnotes.

      3. The loss in value be recognized in the financial statements of the client.

      4. The equity section of the balance sheet separately show a charge equal to the amount of the loss.

  g. In a manufacturing company, which one of the following auditing procedures would give the *least* assurance of the validity of the general ledger balance of investment in stocks and bonds at the audit date?

      1. Confirmation from the broker.

      2. Inspection and count of stocks and bonds.

      3. Vouching all changes during the year to brokers' advices and statements.

      4. Examination of paid checks issued in payment of securities purchased.

(AICPA adapted)

P18-4 Items (a) through (e) are questions typically found in an internal control questionnaire for notes payable. A "yes" answer indicates a potential strength in the system, and a "no" answer indicates a potential weakness.

  a. Are subsidiary records over debt and equity securities maintained by persons who are independent of the cash receipts and disbursements function?

  b. Are periodic reconciliations made between general ledger accounts and their respective supporting records for notes payable, bonds payable, and interest expense by persons who are independent of the custodianship function?

c. Are recorded amounts for debt, capital stock, and other liabilities checked or adequately tested periodically (by comparison with independent records, reference to subsequent settlements, independent computation and confirmation) by persons independent of the cash-handling and recording functions?

d. Are unissued bonds, notes, capital stock, warrants, and other unissued debt securities accessible only to the custodian and to those who prepare and issue such securities?

e. Are there procedures for determining that debt and equity financing transactions are recorded at the amounts and in the accounting periods in which they were executed?

Required: For each item (a) through (e) listed above, state

a. The error or irregularity which that control was designed to prevent, detect, or correct.

b. The test of controls, if any, that would be necessary if the answer to the question were "yes," indicating a potential strength in the system.

c. The substantive auditing procedure that would have to be extended if the answer to the question were "no," indicating a potential weakness in the system of internal control.

P18-5 Discuss the audit objectives for each of the following procedures over long-term debt, accrued interest payable, and owners' equity accounts.

a. Recompute interest expense and accrued interest payable.

b. Confirm details of notes payable with creditors.

c. Obtain copies of bond indenture agreements and review the important details.

d. Reconcile interest expense per books with recomputed interest expense per procedure (a).

e. Vouch new issues of capital stock to approval in minutes of board of directors' meetings.

f. Inspect client's stock record books.

g. Scan the general ledger account for retained earnings and vouch all material entries to documentary support. Investigate any unusual transactions.

h. Inspect note and stock issuances and retirements near the end of the period.

i. Recalculate the amounts and yearly amortization of bond discount or premium.

P18-6 In performing the audit of a large corporation that has a bond issue outstanding, the trust indenture is typically reviewed and a confirmation letter is obtained from the trustee.

Required:

a. What are the major audit objectives to be considered in examination of bonds payable?

b. Name at least eight matters of importance to the auditor that can be found either in the bond trust indenture or in the letter of confirmation with the trustee. For each item named, associate it with an audit objective.

(AICPA adapted)

P18-7 You have the following information relating to the capital accounts of Acco Bear Company. You audited Acco's financial statements last year.

		Debit	Credit	Balance
Capital stock, authorized 50,000 shares @ $10 par value				
Jan. 1, 19X1	Balance forward			250,000
July 1, 19X1	Stock dividend		125,000	375,000
Capital paid in on capital stock in excess of par value				
Jan. 1, 19X1	Balance forward			37,500
July 1, 19X1	Stock dividend		18,750	56,250
Retained earnings				
Jan. 1, 19X1	Balance forward			364,208
Mar. 31, 19X1	Dividend paid	25,000		339,208
July 1, 19X1	Stock dividend	143,750		195,458
Sep. 30, 19X1	Dividend paid	37,500		157,958
Dec. 31, 19X1	Net income		60,000	217,958

Excerpts from minutes of board of directors' meetings:

Meeting date	Action taken
March 5	Approved cash dividend of one dollar per share payable March 31 to stockholders of record March 25.
July 15	Approved stock dividend at rate of one share for two shares held payable August 1 to stockholders of record August 25.
September 5	Approved cash dividend of one dollar per share payable September 30 to stockholders of record September 25.
December 5	Approved cash dividend of one dollar per share payable January 31 to holders of record January 25.

Required:

a. Prepare working papers showing the work performed in the audit of these accounts.

b. Prepare any required audit adjustments. Assume all amounts are material.

Note: You may use a computer spreadsheet for this problem.

P18-8 Questions (a) through (g) below are questions from a typical internal control questionnaire designed to assist in the understanding of internal controls over a company's portfolio of marketable equity securities. A "yes" response indicates a potential strength in the system of internal control, while a "no" response indicates a potential weakness.

a. Are all major acquisitions and disposals required to be approved by the investment committee of the board of directors?

b. Are all registered securities held in the name of the client or in the name of a custodian who has proper power of attorney?

c. Are all securities held as collateral physically segregated from other securities, and is board-of-director approval required for such transactions?

d. Does the company require segregation of the recordkeeping and custodial duties over investments, and is periodic reconciliation made of records and the physical assets by persons independent of both of these duties?

e. Is the accounting department required to maintain an independent record of each investment or security, including serial numbers, number of shares, face amounts, dates of purchase, interest rate, etc.?

f. Is periodic review of the carrying value of the investment portfolio required by a responsible official who is independent of the day-to-day recordkeeping and custodial functions?

g. Is proper accounting required over investment income by persons independent of custodianship duties, and is periodic verification made of investment income per books with dividend and interest records of investee companies?

Required:

a. For each question (a) through (g), indicate
 1. The error or irregularity which that control attribute was designed to prevent, detect, or correct.
 2. The possible financial statement effects if that control attribute were missing, resulting in a "no" response in the internal control questionnaire.
 3. The substantive test that would be extended if there were no mitigating controls and the attribute of interest were missing, according to client response to the questionnaire. (See Figure 18–9.)

b. Why do controls such as those over investments in marketable equity securities not often require tests to ascertain whether they are working as planned?

P18-9 List the audit objectives for the following substantive tests of details over investments:

a. Inspect and list the securities on hand.

b. Compare valuation practices to those required by GAAP for the investment.

c. Vouch acquisitions and disposals of investments to underlying documentation.

d. Reconcile subsidiary records over investments with control account totals.

e. Confirm the details of life insurance policies on key personnel with the insurance company.

f. Confirm details of securities held with independent custodians, such as brokers or trustees.

g. Recalculate interest on debt securities held and reconcile with interest income account balance in the general ledger.

P18-10 You are in charge of the audit of the financial statements of the McIver Corporation for the year ended December 31. The corporation has had the policy of investing its surplus funds in marketable securities. Its stock and bond certificates are kept in a safe deposit box in a local bank. Only the president or the treasurer of the corporation has access to the box.

You were unable to obtain access to the safe deposit box on December 31 because neither the president nor the treasurer was available. Arrangements were made for your assistant to accompany the treasurer to the bank on January 11 to examine the securities. Your assistant has never examined securities that were being kept in a safe deposit box and requires instructions. Your assistant should be able to inspect all securities on hand in an hour.

Required:

a. List the instructions you would give your assistant regarding the examination of the stock and bond certificates kept in the safe deposit box. Include in your instructions the details of the securities to be examined and the reasons for examining these details.

b. After returning from the bank, your assistant reported that the treasurer had entered the box on January 4 to remove an old photograph of the corporation's original building. The photograph was loaned to the local chamber of commerce for display purposes. List the additional auditing procedures required because of the treasurer's action.

(AICPA adapted)

P18-11 During your audit of the 19X9 financial statements of Longwood, Inc., you find a new account titled "Miscellaneous Assets." Your examination reveals that, in 19X9, Longwood, Inc., began investing surplus cash in marketable securities and the corporation's bookkeeper entered all transactions she believed related to investments in this account. Information summarized from the miscellaneous assets account appears at the end of this problem.

All security purchases include brokers' fees and sales are net of brokers' fees and transfer taxes when applicable. The fair market values (net of brokers' fees and transfer taxes) for each security as of the 19X9 date of each transaction were

Security	3/31	6/30	7/31	11/15	11/30
Compudata common	48		60	61¼	62
Standard Atomic common	26	30			
Standard Atomic preferred		16⅔	17		
Interstate Airlines bonds		102			101
Longwood, Inc., common			82		

Longwood, Inc.

INFORMATION SUMMARIZED FROM THE MISCELLANEOUS ASSETS ACCOUNT

For the Year Ended December 31, 19X9

Date 19X9		Folio	Debit	Credit
Compudata Common Stock				
Mar. 31	Purchased 500 shares @ 48	CD	24,000	
July 31	Received cash dividend of $2 per share	CR		1,000
July 31	Sold 100 shares @ 60	CR		6,000
Nov. 15	Pledged 100 shares as security for $4,000 bank loan payable the following February 15	CR		4,000
Nov. 30	Received 150 shares by donation from stockholder whose cost in 19X1 was $10 per share	JE	1,500	
Standard Atomic Common Stock				
Mar. 31	Purchased 900 shares @ 26	CD	23,400	
June 30	Received dividend ($.25 per share in cash and 1 share Standard Atomic preferred for each 5 shares common owned)	CR		225

Standard Atomic Preferred Stock

| June 30 | Received 180 shares as stock dividend on Standard Atomic common | MEMO | | |
| July 31 | Sold 80 shares @ 17 | CR | | 1,360 |

Interstate Airlines Bonds *(due ten years from November 30, 19X9, with interest at 6 percent payable May 31 and November 30)*

June 30	Purchased 25 $1,000 bonds @ 102	CD	25,625	
Nov. 30	Received interest due	CR		750
Nov. 30	Accumulated amortization	JE		25
Nov. 30	Sold 25 bonds @ 101	CR		25,250

Other

July 31	Sold 40 shares of Longwood, Inc., treasury stock @ 82 (purchased in 19X5 at $80 per share—carried at cost)	CR		3,280
Dec. 29	Prepaid 19X0 rental charge on safe deposit box used for investments	CD	35	
	Totals		74,560	41,890

Required:
   a. For each of the transactions described above, list the evidence-gathering procedure (vouching, retracing, recalculation, confirmation, inspection, etc.) that is most appropriate and the most appropriate and valid source document for the evidence.
   b. Prepare adjusting entries, if any, that you consider appropriate.

(AICPA adapted)

P18-12 You are to make an examination of the bond investment account of the Sanders Company in connection with an examination of the financial statements as of December 31, 19X6. This is the first time such an examination has been made. Your working papers should include provisions for analyzing all 19X6 transactions, including those affecting profit and loss. Transcripts of the account and a summary of pertinent information on brokers' advices of purchase or sale are given below. All accruals of interest income have been properly recorded at the end of 19X5 and 19X6.

Required: **a.** Set up a worksheet to analyze the year's transactions, beginning with the book balance at 1/1/X6, and showing all book entries and audit adjustments for 12/31/X6. You may use a computer spreadsheet for this portion of the problem, if you desire.

| | | Investment account | | |
Date	Description	Debit	Credit	Balance
Jan. 1	Balance			29,950.00
	10M Underhill Co. (10,550.00)			
	20M Carlyle, Inc. (19,400.00)			
Feb. 15	20M Arthur Corp.	20,550.00		50,500.00
Sept. 1	Carlyle, Inc.		9,817.00	40,683.00

			Brokers' advices		
Date	**Quantity**	**Description**	**Price**	**Interest**	**Amount**
Purchases					
11/30/X4	10M	Underhill Co.			
		July 1, 19X9	103	$250	10,550
1/1/X5	20M	Carlyle, Inc.			
		February 1, 19X9	97	–	19,400
3/1/X6	20M	Arthur Corp.			
		July 1, 19X9	102½	50	20,550
Sales					
10/1/X6	10M	Carlyle, Inc.			
		Feb. 1980	98	17	9,817

Use the following column headings:
1. Balance (1/1/X6).
2. Purchases.
3. Sales.
4. Amortization.
5. Corrections.
6. Audited balance (12/31/X6).

b. Prepare adjusting entries to correct the books at December 31, 19X6, to agree with your worksheet, assuming the books have not been closed. Explanations for each entry should show clearly how the amounts were determined. Correct income of prior years through retained earnings.

P18-13 The following long-term debt working paper (indexed K-1) was prepared by client personnel and audited by AA, an audit assistant, during the calendar year 19X8 audit of American Widgets, Inc., a continuing audit client. The engagement supervisor is reviewing the working papers thoroughly.

Required: Identify the deficiencies in the working paper that the engagement supervisor should discover.

American Widgets, Inc.
W O R K I N G   P A P E R S

December 31, 19X8

Lender	Interest rate	Payment terms	Collateral	Balance 12/31/X7	19X8 borrowings	19X8 reductions	Balance 12/31/X8	Interest paid to	Accrued interest payable 12/31/X8	Comments
φ First Commercial Bank	12%	Interest only on 25th of month, principal due in full 1/1/Y2; no prepayment penalty	Inventories	$ 50,000 ✓	$300,000 A 1/31/X8	$100,000 ⊕ 6/30/X8	$ 250,000 CX 12/31/X8	12/25/X8	$2,500 NR	Dividend of $80,000 paid 9/2/X8 (W/P N-3) violates a provision of the debt agreement, which thereby permits lender to demand immediate payment; lender has refused to waive this violation
φ Lender's Capital Corp.	Prime plus 1%	Interest only on last day of month, principal due in full 3/5/Y0	2nd Mortgage on Park St. Building	100,000 ✓	50,000 A 2/29/X8	—	200,000 C	12/31/X8	—	Prime rate was 8% to 9% during the year
φ Gigantic Building & Loan Assoc.	12%	$5,000 principal plus interest due on 5th of month, due in full 12/31/Y9	1st Mortgage on Park St. Building	720,000 ✓	—	60,000 ⊕	660,000 C	12/5/X8	5,642 R	Reclassification entry for current portion proposed (See RJE-3)
φ J. Lott, majority stockholder	0%	Due in full 12/31/Y1	Unsecured	300,000 ✓	—	100,000 N 12/31/X8	200,000 C	—	—	Borrowed additional $100,000 from J. Lott on 1/7/X9
				$1,170,000 ✓ F	$350,000 F	$260,000 F	$1,310,000 T/B F		$8,142 T/B F	

Interest costs from long-term debt

Interest expense for year	$ 281,333 T/B R
Average loan balance outstanding	$1,406,667 R

Five year maturities (for disclosure purposes)

Year end	12/31/X9	$ 60,000
	12/31/Y0	260,000
	12/31/Y1	260,000
	12/31/Y2	310,000
	12/31/Y3	60,000
	Thereafter	360,000
		$1,310,000 F

Tickmark Legend

F	Readded, foots correctly
C	Confirmed without exception, W/P K-2
CX	Confirmed with exception, W/P K-3
NR	Does not recompute correctly
A	Agreed to loan agreement, validated bank deposit ticket, and board of directors' authorization, W/P W-7
⊕	Agreed to canceled checks and lender's monthly statements
N	Agreed to cash disbursements journal and canceled check dated 12/31/X8, clearing 1/8/X9
T/B	Traced to working trial balance
✓	Agreed to 12/31/X7 working papers
⊕	Agreed interest rate, term, and collateral to copy of note and loan agreement
⊕⊕	Agreed to canceled check and board of directors' authorization, W/P W-7

Overall conclusions

Long-term debt, accrued interest payable, and interest expense are correct and complete at 12/31/X8

CHAPTER 19

The Audit of Cash

Objectives

☐ **1.** Assess inherent risk and perform other planning procedures for the cash account.
☐ **2.** Understand the control structure and assess control risk for cash balances.
☐ **3.** Design and perform procedures to verify the major audit objectives over cash balances, including unique procedures to detect errors and irregularities that may occur.

The primary objective of this chapter is to enable you to develop a logical program for detection risk procedures for the cash account. Chronologically, most of the procedures required for the audit of cash would be performed prior to all of the others we discussed in Chapters 13 through 18. That might prompt you to ask why we discuss the audit of cash at the end of the series rather than at the beginning. In answering that question, it might be helpful to refer to Figure 8–5, in which we depict all of the interrelated systems of the business. In that figure, the cash account is referred to as "the eye of the needle." As discussed in Chapters 13 through 18, all of the other systems of the business relate to the *flows* of cash into and out of the business. The audit of *cash transactions* is accomplished as we audit those related systems. In this chapter, however, we focus on the audit of *cash balances*. Observe that the ending cash balance is part of the following four-element equation:

1. Beginning balance
2. + Cash receipts (see Chapters 13 and 18)
3. − Cash disbursements (see Chapters 14 through 16)
4. = Ending balance.

The procedures developed in this chapter are designed to show how the audited balance for cash fits into the equation.

Assessing Inherent Risk for Cash

In quantitative terms, cash account balances are generally small in relation to such things as accounts receivable, inventory, and fixed assets. Nevertheless, auditors have historically spent more than a proportionate amount of time in auditing cash transactions and end-of-period cash balances. As Figure 8–5 shows, all business activities are oriented toward the conversion of resources to cash and the settlement of obligations in cash. Therefore, at some point in the life of the business, *the results of all business activities will pass through cash.* This is evident as we refer to the *"cash back to cash"* cycle. The *operating cycle,* for example, is characterized as the average period elapsing between the commitment of cash to the acquisition of merchandise and the collection of receivables from the sale of the merchandise. Similarly, the time elapsing between the purchase of a fixed asset and the ultimate consumption of that asset in operations is called the *cash to fixed assets to cash cycle.* Therefore, because all business activities eventually clear through cash, the verification of cash transactions over a period of many years helps us prove not only the appropriateness of cash inflows and outflows, but also the fairness of other asset and various liability accounts.

Another characteristic making the verification of cash so important to the auditor is the *relative risk* associated with the cash balance. Because of its universal usability and the auditor's inability, from a practical point of view, to identify specific units of cash, this resource is *more vulnerable to theft, fraud, and embezzlement* than any other resource owned by a business entity. Some types of cash receipts realized from transactions not having built-in accountability controls, such as sales of scrap, are especially vulnerable to diversion from their intended uses. Furthermore, a small difference between the amount of actual cash held by an entity and the amount shown in the cash account can be the clue leading to the discovery of much more significant irregularities in the handling of cash transactions. Consistent with this fact, the *client typically expects greater precision* (lower materiality thresholds) in the verification of the cash balance than in the verification of other assets, such as inventory or fixed assets.

Audit Objectives

Audit objectives directly related to cash balances include the *verification of existence, proper cutoff,* and *appropriate statement presentation.* Because of the vulnerability of cash to fraud and embezzlement, the auditor should also identify and develop auditing procedures specifically directed toward searching for errors and irregularities. Chapter 13 contained an explanation of how cash receipts, in the absence of appropriate internal controls, might be misappropriated. We also saw how cash received in the collection of receivables might be temporarily misappropriated through a *lapping procedure.* In Chapter 14, we saw how, in the absence of appropriate internal control procedures, cash could be misappropriated through false or inappropriate disbursements. Additional procedures designed to discover such errors and irregularities, as well as the irregularity of *kiting*, are developed in the last section of this chapter.

Understanding the Control Structure

The Control Environment

☑ **Objective 2**
Understand the control structure for cash

A client may have only one general cash account, but the cash item in the balance sheet often will include balances from three types of accounts. There will always be one or more *general cash account(s)*. If the firm has a significant number of employees, it should have an *imprest payroll account* against which payroll checks will be drawn. Also, because most firms will need to make some small payments in currency, we will generally find an *imprest petty cash account* on most clients' books.

The Accounting System

If a firm handles all general cash receipts and disbursements through one bank, the accounting records will contain only one general cash account. However, if the client uses more than one bank, the records typically will include a ledger account for each bank account used. All of the cash receipts and disbursements shown in Figure 19–1 will be recorded in this (these) account(s). For the reasons stated earlier in the chapter, we give attention to the accounting system associated with the handling of cash and the recording of cash transactions as we specifically verify the cash balances.

Because our assessment of internal control risk for cash is primarily concerned with determining the effectiveness of the structure in preventing or detecting irregularities, it is important for us to begin by recognizing that an embezzlement involves both a theft of cash and an alteration of records to "cover up" the theft. This points up the fact that we *rely on the records of cash to establish accountability for cash as it is handled by custodial personnel.* In addition to this accountability, we also rely on customers and vendors to call attention to any errors that are detrimental to them. It will be helpful to recognize that cash is most vulnerable to theft as it is received and as it is disbursed.

A theft of cash receipts can be "covered" by introducing one or more of the following errors into the cash collection procedures and records:

• Avoiding billing a customer whose payment was stolen.
• Billing a customer at a "special" price and sharing the difference with the customer.
• Charging an account off to bad debts after the customer's payment has been stolen.

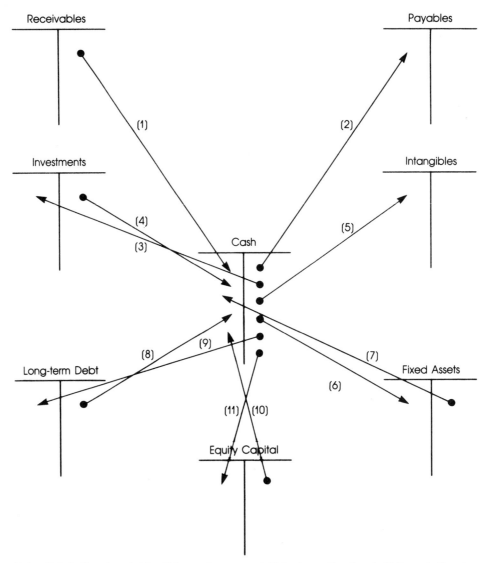

Receivables

Payables

(1)

(2)

Investments

Intangibles

(4)

(5)

(3)

Cash

Long-term Debt

(8)

(9)

(7)

Fixed Assets

(6)

(11) (10)

Equity Capital

Notes: (1) Collection of receivables; (2) Payments on account; (3) Purchase of investments; (4) Disposal of investments; (5) Purchase of intangibles; (6) Purchase of fixed assets; (7) Disposal of fixed assets; (8) Issuance of debt securities; (9) Retirement of debt; (10) Issuance of stock; (11) Dividends and retirement of stock.

Figure 19–1

The Accounting System for Cash

- Debiting sales discounts for an amount equal to cash receipts stolen.
- Overstating cash disbursements by an amount equal to cash receipts stolen.
- Continuous delaying of credits to customer accounts equal to the amount of cash "borrowed" from cash receipts. This is generally called **lapping.**

Also, if the control structure does not place special checks on cash receipts from accounts written off and scrap sales, the receipts from these items often can be stolen without the theft being discovered.

A theft of cash through cash disbursements can be covered by introducing the following errors into the cash disbursements procedures and records:

- Duplicate payment of a vendor's invoice and "sharing" the second payment with the vendor.
- Fictitious or overstated documents supporting expense reimbursement vouchers.
- Payment to an outside party for goods or services not received, with the check being "shared" with the outside party.
- Inflated payroll checks with excess being "shared" with the check recipient.
- Fictitious payroll checks with a forged endorsement.
- Shifting payroll tax deductions so as to allow the embezzler to recover more from the Internal Revenue Service than was actually withheld from his or her checks.
- Payment of interest or dividends in excess of amount the firm is liable for and "sharing" the difference with the recipient.
- Exclusion from the bank reconciliation of an outstanding check equal to the amount of cash stolen.
- The introduction of fictitious or overstated petty cash vouchers to cover a theft of currency from petty cash.
- Transferring from one bank account to another cash equal to the cash shortage at the end of the year, and recording only the deposit. We refer to this practice as *kiting* the cash account.
- Omission from client records of charges made by the bank against the client's account equal to the amount of the shortage.

Control Procedures

Although the above lists do not include all possible defalcation practices, they do show the need for a strong control structure for cash. Such a structure will include the characteristics of control discussed in Chapter 8. Those characteristics call for the practices shown below to be followed in handling cash, recording cash transactions, and periodically relating the accountability for cash to the amount of cash actually held by the client. The latter of these is accomplished by periodic reconciliations of bank and book cash balances, as described later in the chapter.

- *Segregation of responsibilities* requires that custodianship, recordkeeping, and authorization functions for both cash receipts and cash disbursements should all be assigned to different employees at the highest level within a company. This generally involves the complete separation of the controller's (recordkeeping) responsibilities from those of the treasurer (custodial officer).

- *Assignment of responsibility* for those functions to specific employees. For example, the chief custodial officer is generally the treasurer of the company. In that capacity, he or she has custodial responsibility for all company cash. The person in that position should be responsible for opening and monitoring the bank accounts and should exercise custodial authority over all bank accounts held by the company. The treasurer should also have control over the check-signing process, including control over check signature machines and plates.

- *Properly qualified personnel* should be used in the cash-handling, recordkeeping, and approval functions. This requirement extends to bonding custodial employees. Bonding not only protects against loss from embezzlement but also minimizes the risk of employing in positions of trust persons who are of questionable integrity.

- An *adequate records and approval system* should be maintained for all transactions by persons who do not have access to the asset itself. Approval procedures that should be associated with cash disbursements were described in Chapter 14.

- Appropriate provision should be made for *limited access to cash*. This involves the mandatory use of checking accounts for all material cash transactions and daily deposits of cash receipts intact in the bank. Such an arrangement reduces the amount of currency and checks kept on the client's premises, where they are vulnerable to misappropriation. It also involves the use of petty cash funds for small disbursements. Responsibility for such funds should be vested in specific individuals, who should keep them in a safe location pending disbursement.

- Provisions should be made for *monitoring compliance* with established policies and for checking custodial accountability. This will normally include preparation of monthly bank reconciliations and other monitoring activities by internal auditors.

These elements of internal control were discussed in Chapters 13 and 14. You should review them before proceeding with the rest of this chapter.

Imprest Petty Cash

Businesses and other organizations generally find it impractical to pay many small obligations by check. As a result, an **imprest** petty cash fund is generally established to handle such payments. As the name suggests, a check for a stated amount, such as $500 or $1,000, will be drawn and converted to currency to establish such a fund. As small bills are paid from the fund, petty cash disbursement vouchers are prepared, signed by the recipient, and placed in the petty cash box. When the currency in the fund has been reduced to a nominal amount, a reimbursement request supported by the petty cash disbursement vouchers is prepared. At that time, a check is drawn on the general cash account to bring the fund back up to its imprest balance. As the reimbursement request is recorded, the various expense accounts shown on the petty cash disbursement vouchers are debited and cash is credited.

To properly control petty cash, it is important to make one employee specifically accountable for it. Also, the firm should establish appropriate controls over all petty cash disbursement vouchers. This requires the use of sequentially numbered forms and approval by a responsible official as each disbursement is made.

Incidentally, the use of an imprest petty cash fund within the arrangements described above provides an additional element of control by permitting the company to have a "dual" record of cash inflows and outflows. It allows all cash receipts to be deposited intact and requires all cash disbursements (including reimbursements of petty cash) to be made by check. Thus, the elements of the bank's record of cash (balances, receipts, and disbursements) can be reconciled with those elements of the book record of cash. This is accomplished through the preparation of a four-column *proof of cash* described later in the chapter.

Imprest Payroll Account

As the name suggests, an **imprest** payroll account regularly contains either a fixed balance, such as $1,000, or a zero balance. Immediately preceding the issuance of payroll checks against this account, an amount equal to the total payroll is transferred from the general cash account to the imprest account. As a result of this practice, if checks in excess of the transfer are cashed against the account, the firm will quickly discover that checks in excess of the amount reflected for the payroll have somehow been issued to payees. Because the effective control of the volume of checks required for payroll payments is often difficult, the imprest payroll account can be used to provide such a much-needed additional control over payroll disbursements.

Detection Risk Procedures

After having assessed control risk, we may turn our attention to the substantive tests associated with the verification of the end-of-period cash balances. First, we look at the audit objectives that should be achieved in the verification process. Then we develop the procedures the auditor should follow in meeting those objectives, including procedures designed to document the auditor's search for errors and irregularities involving cash.

As the auditor begins verifying the amount shown for cash in the balance sheet, he or she will first want to reconcile that amount with the underlying accounting records. This reconciliation process as well as the auditing procedures followed to accomplish the audit objectives are shown in the *cash working papers* in the chapter appendixes. When the client has more than one cash account, a *lead schedule* working paper may be necessary to summarize the balances in the cash accounts. Notice that working paper B (Appendix 19–A) contains a lead schedule, which is a summary of the details of cash balances for the JEP Manufacturing Company. The schedule shows, for example, that cash for the company totals $37,814.93 and is made up of three bank accounts—regular, mercantile, and payroll—all of which are *supported* by **bank reconciliations** (supporting schedules B-1, B-2, and B-3, respectively). B-1 is the only reconciliation included in the appendixes (see Appendix 19-C). The company also has a petty cash fund (B-4) and a time deposit (B-5).

If the client already has reconciled the bank and book balances and has made appropriate adjustments to the ledger accounts, the auditor's first step in relating the statement to the accounting records is to compare the financial statement amount with the amount shown in the cash ledger account. This amount should be the same as the adjusted balance per books on the bank reconciliation. It is also important at this time to recompute (foot) both the cash receipts and cash disbursements journals and to trace the journal entries to the ledger accounts. Having completed this phase of the verification of cash, the auditor is ready to perform the auditing procedures required to meet the three audit objectives cited earlier. Figure 19–2 shows the relationships between the audit objectives and the procedures required to meet those objectives. (Note that the tick marks used in the appendixes to show procedures followed are explained in Appendix 19–B).

Verification of Existence

The cash account balance typically will include both cash on hand and cash in the bank. The auditor should physically count the cash on hand, which may include both change funds and petty cash, to verify its existence. This is normally done at the close of business on the last day of the fiscal period under audit. The auditor should take at least two precautions in performing the count of cash.

First, *the cash count should be made simultaneously with the inspection of investments and negotiable instruments.* If this arrangement is impractical, those documents must be controlled from the time the cash count is initiated until it is finished and the documents can be inspected. This requirement prevents the auditor from double-counting the assets. Without this provision, the auditor could be misled into counting cash temporarily acquired by using the negotiable instruments as collateral and, later, also counting the instruments themselves as investments and negotiable instruments after they have been returned to their files. Furthermore, *all cash should be controlled throughout the time of the cash count* to avoid the possibility of the auditor again being misled into counting a specified amount of cash more than once. A common way of achieving this control is to seal each container of cash immediately after it has been counted. After the count of all cash has been completed, the auditor should retrace the counting cycle to verify that the individual seals were not broken after the cash in them was counted.

The second major precaution is that the *count should always be made in the presence of the custodian of each of the funds,* and he or she should be asked to sign a receipt for the return of cash after the count has been completed. This arrange-

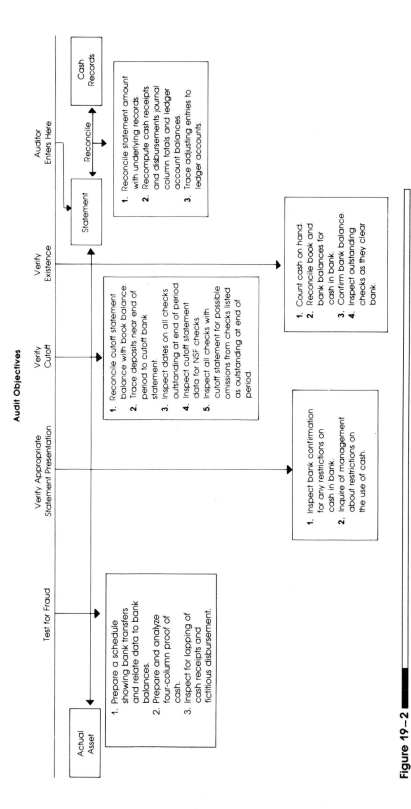

Figure 19–2   **Substantive Tests of Balances for Cash**

ment is designed to prevent the custodian from alleging that all the cash charged to his or her custody was there prior to the auditor's count but not returned after the audit. Such a claim might otherwise be made if the auditor had found a shortage in the fund.

The *cash in the bank should be confirmed* directly with the bank. In so doing, the auditor should use the standard AICPA **bank confirmation** form shown in Appendix 19–D. The confirmation request must be signed by an appropriate representative of the client to allow the bank to provide the information requested by the auditor. However, the auditor should supervise the mailing of the request and arrange to have the bank's reply returned directly to the auditing firm. The balance shown on the confirmation form should be reconciled with the bank reconciliation schedule previously prepared by the client. Notice that this is done on working paper B-1 (Appendix 19–C) through cross-referencing. Also, checks shown to be outstanding as of the date of the bank reconciliation should be inspected as they clear the bank after the end of the period under audit. The procedure is illustrated in Appendix 19–C.

Verification of Cutoff

In Chapters 13 and 14, we described the error that could be introduced into the financial statements by improperly cutting off cash receipts and cash disbursements. As a means of more directly verifying that these transactions have been recorded in the appropriate accounting periods, the auditor should, with appropriate authorization from the client, request a **bank cutoff statement** some fifteen to twenty days after the end of the period under audit. That statement should include deposit slips and canceled checks clearing the bank between the end of the fiscal period and the cutoff date. The cutoff statement should be sent directly to the auditor to prevent changes or extractions of documents by client personnel.

The auditor should reconcile the bank cutoff statement with the client's record of cash in bank. Deposits made near the end of the period should be inspected. The auditor will be particularly concerned with the dates on the outstanding checks. All should, of course, be dated prior to the end of the fiscal period. The auditor will also be concerned with the dates on which the checks have cleared the bank. If an unusually long period of time has elapsed between the date shown on a check and the date on which the check cleared the bank, the auditor should raise questions as to whether the cash payment record may have been improperly cut off at the end of the fiscal period. Management should be expected to provide an explanation for the delay in clearance of outstanding checks. Kiting (which we take up in the section on errors and irregularities) is also detectable by examining paid checks returned with the cutoff bank statement and tracing them to cash disbursements records to see if they were recorded properly.

Charges against the account for nonsufficient funds (NSF) checks will also be of particular interest to the auditor in working with the cutoff bank statement. These are customers' checks that have been deposited but have been charged back against the client's account because the customers did not have sufficient funds to cover them. Because the NSF checks did not represent cash as of the end of the fiscal period, the auditor usually recommends adjustment for them by crediting cash and debiting a receivables account. **Postdated customer checks** are also receivables rather than cash. The client should follow a practice of restrictively endorsing such checks to provide proper accounting control over them.

The auditor should inspect all checks returned with the bank cutoff statement. He or she should identify the checks shown as outstanding at the end of the fiscal period and clearing with the cutoff statement to see that they have been properly listed in the end-of-period bank reconciliation. Of perhaps even greater importance is the attention that should be given to any checks dated before the end of the period under audit but omitted from the list of outstanding checks in the end-of-period bank reconciliation. Since this is a technique that could be used to cover a cash shortage, the auditor must secure a complete explanation of all such items. All of the above procedures are illustrated in Appendixes 19–A through 19–D. Appendix 19–E describes the audit work typically performed to ascertain proper cutoff of cash receipts and cash disbursements as of the balance sheet date.

Verification of Appropriate Statement Presentation

As you examine the bank confirmation form shown on working paper B-6 (see Appendix 19–D), you will observe that the bank is expected to disclose any restrictions on the use of cash—such as a minimum balance required under a loan agreement. The auditor should be certain that any such restrictions are appropriately disclosed in presenting cash on the audited balance sheet. It is important to recognize that cash shown in the balance sheet without any reference to restrictions is interpreted to be cash available for use at the discretion of management. The auditor should see that any required adjustments or disclosures relating to the presentation of cash in the balance sheet are appropriately reflected in the audited financial statements. It is also appropriate to observe at this point that *savings account balances are appropriately reflected as current investments rather than as cash.*

The Search for Errors and Irregularities

The procedures listed in the preceding paragraphs are designed to verify *whether the statement account balance for cash fairly represents the actual amount of cash held by the client.* Because cash is highly susceptible to fraud and embezzlement, the auditor must also carry through some auditing procedures designed to help judge whether or not irregularities, in the form of defalcations of cash, may have occurred during the period under audit. We have already mentioned certain precautionary measures and follow-up procedures that should be performed in connection with cash receipts and cash disbursements (Chapters 13 and 14). Those are designed to determine whether cash has been improperly extracted through the medium of the receipts and disbursements processes. We now describe procedures typically followed as the auditor tests the cash accounts for possible irregularities of different types.

The first of these checking procedures involves the preparation of a **bank transfer schedule** such as the one shown on working paper B-8 in Appendix 19–F. This schedule, normally incorporated into the working papers any time the client has more than one bank account, is designed to trace transfers between banks and, in that way, discover kiting.

Kiting occurs when an amount is withdrawn from one bank and deposited in another without the withdrawal being shown in the book record for the first bank. To implement kiting, the perpetrator makes the deposit on the last day of the fiscal period, in a bank located in a different city from the one on which the check was written. Then, the perpetrator omits the check from the disbursement record of the period under audit, thus inflating the total cash balance by the amount of the deposit. Such an action can be undertaken by upper-level management as a means either of covering a theft of cash equal to the amount of the deposit or of improperly inflating the cash balance as of the balance sheet date.

Notice in Appendix 19–F that columns are provided for dates on which the cash transfer was recorded per books and per bank for both the disbursing and receiving bank accounts. A kiting situation would show *the cash receipt in the books before the balance sheet cutoff* and *the cash disbursement recorded after the balance sheet cutoff*. If the cash disbursement is not recorded, the check for the disbursing bank would not appear at all in the cash disbursements record for the period either before or after the balance sheet date. The auditor should detect the unrecorded disbursement as he or she examines the cancelled checks returned with the cutoff bank statement and traces them to the cash disbursements records of the period under audit.

The second checking procedure involves the preparation and analysis of a **four-column proof of cash.** An example of this schedule is shown in Figure 19–3. This working paper can be prepared in either of two ways. The more common practice is to reconcile the book balances for the beginning of the period, receipts and disbursements for the period, and the end-of-period cash balance with the same four elements of bank data. However, *it is generally preferable to work from the unadjusted data from both records to adjusted figures for both the bank and book data.* This latter refinement is the type of four-column proof reflected in Figures 19–3 and 19–4. It has at least two advantages over the more conventional one.

First, it is generally easier to think through a correction process when trying to change a previously incorrect figure to a correct one than it is to think through an adjustment of one figure to another, neither of which may be correct. Observe, as you look at Figure 19–3, that the *beginning balances as well as all adjustments to those balances have to balance across the working paper.* The previously cited advantage recognizes, for example, that it is easier to think through the addition of outstanding checks at the end of the period to the bank disbursements column and a simultaneous subtraction from the end-of-period bank balance than

Figure 19-3

Four-Column Proof Schedule

	Balance at beginning of period	Receipts	Disbursements	Balance at end of period
Balances from bank statement	$ 8,400	$21,000	$23,500	$ 5,900
Undeposited receipts at beginning of period	+1,200	−1,200		
Undeposited receipts at end of period		+1,800		+1,800
Outstanding checks at beginning of period	−2,500		−2,500	
Outstanding checks at end of period			+3,000	−3,000
Check improperly charged to account			− 800	+ 800
NSF checks charged to account		− 200	− 200	
Adjusted bank balances	$ 7,100	$21,400	$23,000	$ 5,500
Balances from books	$ 7,100	$20,200	$22,985	$ 4,315
NSF checks (see above)		− 200		− 200
Note collected by bank not recorded on books		+1,400		+1,400
Bank service charges			+ 15	− 15
Adjusted book balances	$ 7,100	$21,400	$23,000	$ 5,500

it is to work the same data into a conventional statement that simply reconciles bank and book figures.

A second very important advantage of using the illustrated four-column proof is the fact that the adjusted cash receipts and disbursement data can be used to provide additional evidence that the sales and purchases figures are properly reflected in the financial statements. For example, sales for the period can be computed by using a modified four-element equation, stated as follows:

End-of-period receivables balance + cash receipts from customers (adjusted cash receipts from four-column proof total less nonsales-related receipts) − receivables balance at the beginning of the period + noncash credits to accounts receivable (sales discounts allowed, sales returns and allowances, and accounts receivable written off during the period) = sales for the period.

The figure so calculated can be compared with the recorded amount for sales to provide additional evidence in support of the nominal account balance. Because the auditor will have independently verified the parts of the equation that deal with receivables balances, this amounts to an additional independent verification of sales. This is another example of the jigsaw puzzle types of relationships that exist among the accounting data.

Figure 19–4

Four-Column Proof Schedule Disclosing Defalcation of Cash Receipts

	Balance at beginning of period	Receipts	Disbursements	Balance at end of period
Balances from bank statement	$ 8,400	$20,000	$23,500	$ 4,900
Undeposited receipts at beginning of period	+1,200	−1,200		
Undeposited receipts at end of period		+1,800		+1,800
Outstanding checks at beginning of period	−2,500		−2,500	
Outstanding checks at end of period			+3,000	−3,000
Check improperly charged to account			− 800	+ 800
NSF checks charged to account		− 200	− 200	
Adjusted bank balances	$ 7,100	$20,400	$23,000	$ 4,500
Balances from books	$ 7,100	$20,200	$23,985	$ 3,315
NSF checks (see above)		− 200		− 200
Note collected by bank not recorded on books		+1,400		+1,400
Bank service charges			+ 15	− 15
Adjusted book balances	$ 7,100	$21,400	$24,000	$ 4,500

A similar equation can be developed for the verification of the purchases account balance independent of the amount shown in the ledger for purchases. That equation is stated as follows:

End-of-period payables balance + cash payments to vendors (adjusted cash payments from four-column proof less nonpurchase-related payments) − payables balance at the beginning of the period + noncash charges to payables (purchase discounts allowed and purchase returns and allowances) = purchases for the period.

The four-column proof is, however, most directly useful in helping the auditor discover situations in which *the book record of cash disbursements may have been deliberately overstated* to cover *an embezzlement* of cash receipts or where *cash receipts may have been deliberately understated* to cover *a theft* of cash through an improper cash disbursement. The first of these, for example, could occur if the person handling cash receipts had access to the cash disbursement record. In Figure 19–4, we have reproduced the source data shown in Figure 19–3 (except for the assumed theft of cash receipts in the amount of $1,000 and the overstatement of cash disbursements by the same amount to cover the theft) to show how the four-column proof schedule helps the auditor in discovering such a defalcation. You will observe that both the beginning-of-period and end-of-period balances reconcile in Figure 19–4. Therefore, a simple bank reconciliation would not disclose the defalcation. The four-column proof of cash should be prepared by the auditor when internal control over cash is weak.

Summary

In this chapter we have described the auditing procedures followed in auditing the balance shown for cash. We began by observing that as we audit the various subsystems we indirectly verify cash receipts and cash disbursements. We then explained that because the relative risk associated with an opinion on the cash balance is much greater than for other items on the balance sheet, the auditor must spend more time on the audit of this item than the size of the cash balance would seem to justify. Next, we showed how the accounting records and cash-related documents could be altered to "cover" a theft of cash.

In the last part of the chapter, we explained how cash balances are verified. Since auditing procedures for verifying cash receipts and disbursements have been described previously, we focused most of our attention on the substantive tests required to meet the audit objectives of proving existence, cutoff, and proper statement presentation for cash balances. Some attention was also given to the auditing procedures that should be performed in searching for errors and irregularities in cash balances.

Auditing Vocabulary

p. 834   **bank confirmation:**   A confirmation request signed by an appropriate representative of the client, mailed to the bank for completion, and returned directly to the auditor showing the bank's record of amounts on deposit as well as amounts borrowed and other pertinent business transacted between the company and the bank. For an example of the bank confirmation, see Appendix 19–D.

p. 834   **bank cutoff statement:**   A bank statement for a portion of the period immediately after the balance sheet date (15 to 20 days). That statement should include deposit slips and canceled checks clearing the bank between the end of the fiscal period and the cutoff date. Those deposit slips and canceled checks should constitute most of the reconciling items on the client's end-of-period bank reconciliations.

p. 832   **bank reconciliation:**   The supporting schedule showing the reconciliation of the difference between cash per banks and cash per books. See Appendix 19–C for an example.

p. 836   **bank transfer schedule:**   A schedule designed to trace transfers between banks and, in that way, discover kiting. The transfer schedule shows dates per books and per bank of transfers occurring between bank accounts.

p. 836   **four-column proof of cash:**   A working paper that shows a total reconciliation of the beginning balance, receipts, disbursements, and ending balance in a bank account for both books and bank. To be correct, all four of these fields should be equal. Four-column proofs of cash should always be prepared when internal control over cash is weak.

p. 830 **imprest accounts:** Accounts that are reimbursed from time to time in the normal course of business. Typically, clients should utilize imprest accounts for petty cash and for payroll.

p. 836 **kiting:** The defalcation that occurs when an amount is withdrawn from one bank account and deposited in another without the withdrawal being shown in the book record for the first bank. A kiting situation is best detected by preparing a schedule of bank transfers.

p. 828 **lapping:** For an explanation of this term, see Chapter 13.

p. 835 **postdated checks:** Checks dated after the period in which they are actually written, with the intention of the client not cashing the checks. Such checks represent receivables and not a valid claim to cash as of the balance sheet date.

Appendix 19–A: Cash

	JEP Manufacturing Co.		W. P. No.	B
	Cash		ACCOUNTANT	JnG
	3-31-X1		DATE	4/28/X1

	#		W/P Reference		Adjusted Balance 3-31-X0	Balance per G/L 3-31-X1	
	1	Cash on Deposit - Regular	B-1		21333 51	1398 14	
	3	Cash on Deposit - Mercantile	B-2	*	500 00	500 00	
	4	Cash on Deposit - Payroll	B-3	*	1200 00	500 00	
		Petty Cash	B-4	*	687 50	687 50	
	7	Time Deposit	B-5	*	60798 71	33843 29	
					84519 72	36928 93	
						A-1	
		RJE ⟨D⟩			0	886 00	
						37814 93	
						A-1	

✓ Agreed to prior year auditors' w/p's

✗ Agreed to 3-31-X1 G/L

See explanation of tick marks and conclusion on Ba

* Not reproduced

Appendix 19–B: Tick Legend Regarding Cash

	JEP Mfg. Co. Tick Legend re: Cash. 3-31-X1		W. P. No.	Ba
			ACCOUNTANT	SmS
			DATE	5/4/X1

✓ Agreed amount to paid check returned with cutoff statement received unopened by auditors from Bank. Traced o/s checks to cutoff statement and into cash disbursements book prior to year-end. We noted that checks were properly signed and endorsed and that check cleared the bank within a reasonable period of time. Checks do appear to be o/s as of 3-31-X1

⊲ Traced deposit-in-transit per bank reconciliation to deposit credited per bank cutoff statement. We noted that the time lag was reasonable.

∅ Agreed amount to 3-31-X1 Beginning Balance per bank cutoff statement.

⋈ Footed

⊠ Agreed amount to 3-31-X1 G/L

Ɋ Confirmation sent; received.

⌗ These checks had not cleared the bank as of 4-30-X1. Pass further investigation as amount is immaterial.

< Performed same ~~procedures~~ as in ✓ above to checks returned w/ 4-30-X1 Bank statement. Checks do appear to be o/s @ 3-31-X1.

Note: Compared receipts per cash receipts book with credits per bank statements for March 23, 19X1 through April 7, 19X1. All receipts matched appropriate credits.

Conclusion: Based upon the audit work performed, which was considered adequate to meet the objectives per the APB it appears that cash is fairly stated @ 3-31-X1.

Appendix 19–C: Bank Reconciliation

JEP MANUFACTURING COMPANY
Bank Statement Reconciliation
G. L. Account # _____

B-1
PBC/SMG
5/4/X1

Month Ended _March 31_ , 19 _X1_

General Ledger Balance
Prior Month < 224,531.19 > X

Balance per Bank Statement *B-6*
as of _____ ¢ 166,642.66¢

Add Debits

_____ _____
_____ _____
_____ _____
_____ _____

Add Deposits in Transit
3-31-X1   258.16 /
_____ _____
_____ _____

Total Debits   1,115,744.57 X

258.16

Less Credits

_____ _____
_____ _____
_____ _____

Less Checks Outstanding
Per List below Ø 165,502.68
Other / _____

Total Credits   889,815.24 X

Balance per General Ledger 1,398.14 X

Balance per Reconciliation 1,398.14
"B /

Checks Outstanding:*

⊕	✓	✓	✓	✓
✓	✓	✓	✓	✓
⊕	✓	✓	✓	✓
✓	✓	✓	✓	✓
✓	✓	✓	✓	✓
✓	✓	✓	✓	✓
✓	✓	✓	✓	✓
✓	✓	✓	✓	✓
✓	✓	✓	✓	✓
✓	⊕	✓	✓	✓
X	✓	✓	✓	✓
✓	✓	✓	✓	✓
✓	✓	X	✓	✓
✓	✓	✓	✓	✓
✓	✓	✓	✓	✓
✓	✓	✓	✓	✓

TOTAL 165,502.68 ⊙
⋁

**Includes listing
of checks on p. 2.**

*Details omitted.

Appendix 19–D: Standard Bank Confirmation Inquiry

STANDARD BANK CONFIRMATION INQUIRY B-6

Approved 1966 by

AMERICAN INSTITUTE OF CERTIFIED PUBLIC ACCOUNTANTS

and

BANK ADMINISTRATION INSTITUTE (FORMERLY NABAC)

ORIGINAL
To be mailed to accountant

March 31, 19X1

Your completion of the following report will be sincerely appreciated. IF THE ANSWER TO ANY ITEM IS "NONE," PLEASE SO STATE. Kindly mail it in the enclosed stamped, addressed envelope *direct* to the accountant named below.

Report from

Yours truly,

JEP Manufacturing Co., Inc.

(ACCOUNT NAME PER BANK RECORDS)

By C. Paul Snelson

Authorized Signature

(Bank) First Greensboro National Bank

P.O. Box 1044

Greensboro, Texas 75000

Bank customer should check here if confirmation of bank balances only (item 1) is desired.

☐

NOTE—If the space provided is inadequate, please enter totals hereon and attach a statement giving full details as called for by the columnar headings below.

Accountant   Best and Company
Suite 4500, Byron Building
Dallas, Texas 75201

1. At the close of business on March 31, 19X1 our records showed the following balance(s) to the **credit** of the above named customer. In the event that we could readily ascertain whether there were any balances to the credit of the customer not designated in this request, the appropriate information is given below.

AMOUNT	ACCOUNT NAME	ACCOUNT NUMBER	Subject to With-drawal by Check?	Interest Bearing? Give Rate
$ 166,642.66 B-1 21,129.18 B-3	JEP Manufacturing Co. General Fund Payroll	00-210-5 00-001-8	Yes Yes	No No

2. The customer was directly liable to us in respect of loans, acceptances, etc., at the close of business on that date in the total amount of $ none , as follows:

AMOUNT	DATE OF LOAN OR DISCOUNT	DUE DATE	INTEREST Rate	INTEREST Paid to	DESCRIPTION OF LIABILITY, COLLATERAL, SECURITY INTERESTS, LIENS, ENDORSERS, ETC.
$					

3. The customer was contingently liable as endorser of notes discounted and/or as guarantor at the close of business on that date in the total amount of $ none , as below:

AMOUNT	NAME OF MAKER	DATE OF NOTE	DUE DATE	REMARKS
$				

4. Other direct or contingent liabilities, open letters of credit, and relative collateral, were

5. Security agreements under the Uniform Commercial Code or any other agreements providing for restrictions, not noted above, were as follows (if officially recorded, indicate date and office in which filed):

Yours truly, (Bank) First Greensboro National Bank

Date April 30, 19X1

By Robert S Goldsboro

Authorized Signature Vice President

Additional copies of this form are available from the American Institute of CPAs, 1211 Avenue of the Americas, New York, N.Y. 10036

Appendix 19—E: Proper Period Cutoff on Cash

	JEP Mfg. Co.		W. P. No.	B-7-2
	Memo re: Proper Period Cutoff on Cash		ACCOUNTANT	Smith
	3-31-X1	JM	DATE	5/5/X1

To determine that there was proper cutoff of all cash receipts and disbursements we performed the following procedures:

① Obtained a copy of the last check issued in FYE 19X1 (ck # 66934) and noted that all checks issued prior to that check were dated prior to 3-31-X1 and cleared the bank within a reasonable time subsequent to 3-31-X1. In addition, we examined the first 15 checks issued after 3-31-X1, noting that none of the checks had been endorsed by any bank prior to 4-1-X1.

② Examined all interbank transfers of a significant amount (see W/P B-8) noting the proper recording of all transactions.

③ Examined all deposits made 5 days before and after FYE to determine that they were properly recorded in the correct period.

No exceptions were noted in the above procedures - it appears that there was a proper cutoff of cash receipts & disbursements.

Appendix 19–F: Bank Transfers Schedule

		W. P. No.	B-8
JEP mfg.		ACCOUNTANT	SmS
Bank Transfers Schedule		DATE	5/4/X1
3-31-X1			

All Transactions 3-23-X1 — 4/9/X1 From / To	Check #	TRANSFERRED FROM Date		
		Per Check	Per Books	Per Bank
General A/C – Savings A/C	66727	3-23-X1	3-23-X1	3-23-X1 ✓
General A/C – Payroll A/C	66894	3-26-X1	3-26-X1	3-26-X1 ✓
General A/C – Payroll A/C	66932	3-31-X1	3-31-X1	3-31-X1 ✓
General A/C – East Texas Dist	66934	3-31-X1	3-31-X1	3-31-X1 ✓
General A/C – Savings A/C	66946	4-6-X1	4-6-X1	4-6-X1 ✓
General A/C – Savings A/C	66982	4-9-X1	4-9-X1	4-10-X1 ✓
Savings A/C – General A/C	N/A	N/A	3-31-X1	3-31-X1 ✓
Savings A/C – General A/C	N/A	N/A	3-30-X1	3-31-X1 ✓
East Texas Dist. – General A/C	7863	3-31-X1	3-31-X1	4-3-X1 ✓

Note: The above information was obtained from a review of cash receipts and disbursements journals and bank statements.

✓ Agreed to bank statement and validated deposit slip/cancelled check.

ⓧ Not recorded - payroll account remains at a constant #500. Expense is recorded when the reimbursement check is prepared. Appears to be properly treated and is consistent w/ prior years.

See conclusion on B₈

TRANS. TO

Date			Amount	
Per Books	Per Bank			
3-23-X1	3-23-X1 ✓		12000000	
3-26-X1 ⊗	3-26-X1 ✓		16934 37	
3-31-X1 ⊗	3-31-X1 ✓		31528 57	
3-31-X1	3-31-X1 ✓		30452 23	
4-6-X1	4-6-X1 ✓		30000 00	
4-9-X1	4-10-X1 ✓		B-6 A ③ 140000 00	
3-31-X1	3-31-X1 ✓		B-6 P ③ 50000 00	
3-31-X1	3-31-X1 ✓		B-6 P ③ 190000 00	
4-2-X1	4-2-X1 ✓		✗ ✓ 886 00 B (ETDC)	

✗ This deposit-in-transit has been properly removed
from East Texas' Cash A/c but was Dr. to
Accrued liability A/c by Sharon Spencer
so that A/R could be relieved. The amount
should be reclassed to Cash. See ⑧ and
RJE ⑩ on 0-1.

Questions for Class Discussion

Q19-1 The procedures required for the audit of cash will be performed prior to those discussed in the preceding chapters. What, then, is the justification for delaying our discussion of the audit of cash until those other procedures have been discussed? Explain.

Q19-2 Explain the four-element equation as it relates to the audit of cash.

Q19-3 What is the difference between a theft of cash and an embezzlement of cash?

Q19-4 Why are cash receipts from written-off accounts and scrap sales especially vulnerable to theft or embezzlement? Explain.

Q19-5 List five procedures that might be used to cover a theft of cash through cash disbursements. What internal control procedures should be present within the client's control system to help prevent these embezzlements?

Q19-6 How does the use of an imprest petty cash fund improve a client's control over small cash disbursements? Explain.

Q19-7 Why should a firm use an imprest payroll bank account? Explain.

Q19-8 For what reasons do auditors typically spend more than a proportionate amount of time in auditing cash transactions and end-of-year cash balances? Explain.

Q19-9 What is the audit risk associated with expressing an opinion regarding a firm's cash balance?

Q19-10 The treasurer of the company is generally its highest ranking custodial officer; what are his or her typical responsibilities?

Q19-11 What responsibilities should be separated in an appropriately organized system of internal control for cash?

Q19-12 What is meant by *lapping*?

Q19-13 What is meant by *kiting*?

Q19-14 What procedures should be followed when verifying the existence of cash?

Q19-15 Why does the auditor prepare a schedule showing bank transfers during the period under audit? Explain.

Q19-16 Why does the auditor prepare a four-column proof in connection with the audit of cash? Explain.

Q19-17 What are the auditor's primary concerns in determining that cash has been appropriately presented in the financial statements?

Short Cases

C19-1 The following client-prepared bank reconciliation is being examined by Kautz, CPA, during an examination of the financial statements of Cynthia Company:

Cynthia Company

BANK RECONCILIATION: VILLAGE BANK ACCOUNT 2

December 31, 19X2

Balance per bank **(a)**		$18,375.91
Deposits in Transit **(b)**		
12/30	$1,471.10	
12/31	2,840.69	4,311.79
Subtotal		22,687.70
Outstanding checks **(c)**		
837	6,000.00	
1941	671.80	
1966	320.00	
1984	1,855.42	
1985	3,621.22	
1987	2,576.89	
1991	4,420.88	(19,466.21)
Subtotal		3,221.49
NSF check returned 12/29 **(d)**		200.00
Bank charges		5.50
Error Check No. 1932		148.10
Customer note collected by the bank		(3,025.00)
($2,750 plus $275 interest) **(e)**		
Balance per books **(f)**		$ 550.09

Required: Indicate one or more auditing procedures that should be performed by Kautz in gathering evidence in support of each of the items (a) through (f) above.

(AICPA adapted)

C19-2 The flowchart on page 850 illustrates a manual system for executing purchases and cash disbursements transactions.

Required: Indicate what each of the letters (A) through (L) represent. Do not discuss adequacies or inadequacies in the system of internal control.

(AICPA adapted)

C19-3 Toyco, a retail toy chain, honors two bank credit cards and makes daily deposits of credit card sales in two credit card bank accounts (Bank A and Bank B). Each day Toyco batches its credit card sales slips, bank deposit slips, and authorized sales return documents, and keypunches cards for processing by its electronic data-processing department. Each week detailed computer printouts of the general ledger credit card cash accounts are prepared. Credit card banks have been instructed to make an automatic weekly transfer of cash to Toyco's general bank account. The credit card banks charge back deposits that include sales to holders of stolen or expired cards.

The auditor conducting the examination of the 19X6 Toyco financial statement has obtained copies of the detailed general ledger cash account printouts, a summary of the bank statements, and the manually prepared bank reconciliations, all for the week ended December 31, 19X6 (see pages 851 and 852).

Flowchart for C19-2

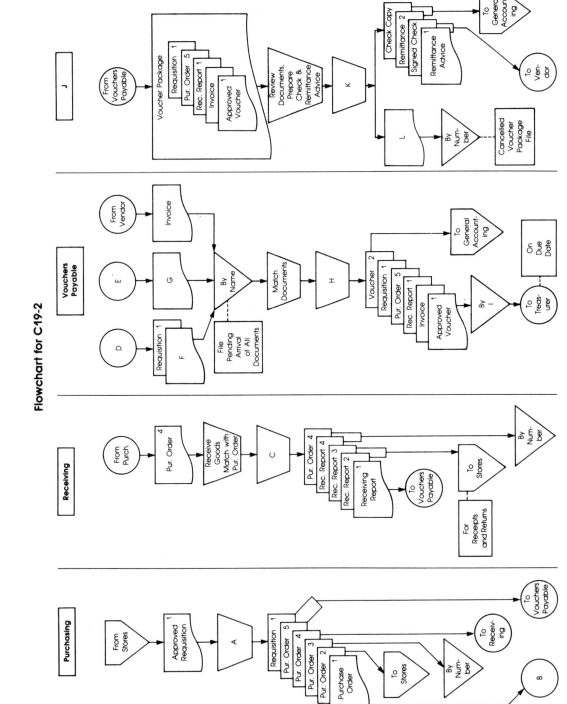

For C19-3

Toyco

DETAILED GENERAL LEDGER CREDIT CARD CASH ACCOUNT PRINTOUTS

For the Week Ended December 31, 19X6

	Bank A	Bank B
	Dr. or (Cr.)	Dr. or (Cr.)
Beginning Balance		
December 24, 19X6	$12,000	$ 4,200
Deposits		
December 27, 19X6	2,500	5,000
December 28, 19X6	3,000	7,000
December 29, 19X6	0	5,400
December 30, 19X6	1,900	4,000
December 31, 19X6	2,200	6,000
Cash transfer		
December 27, 19X6	(10,700)	0
Chargebacks		
Expired cards	(300)	(1,600)
Invalid deposits (physically deposited in wrong account)	(1,400)	(1,000)
Redeposit of invalid deposits	1,000	1,400
Sales returns for week ending		
December 31, 19X6	(600)	(1,200)
Ending Balance		
December 31, 19X6	$ 9,700	$29,200

Toyco

SUMMARY OF THE BANK STATEMENTS

For the Week Ended December 31, 19X6

	Bank A	Bank B
	(Charges) or Credits	
Beginning Balance		
December 24, 19X6	$10,000	$ 0
Deposits dated		
December 24, 19X6	2,100	4,200
December 27, 19X6	2,500	5,000
December 28, 19X6	3,000	7,000
December 29, 19X6	2,000	5,500
December 30, 19X6	1,900	4,000
Cash transfers to general bank account		
December 27, 19X6	(10,700)	0
December 31, 19X6	0	(22,600)
Chargebacks		
Stolen cards	(100)	0
Expired cards	(300)	(1,600)
Invalid deposits	(1,400)	(1,000)
Bank service charges	0	(500)
Bank charge (unexplained)	(400)	0
Ending Balance		
December 31, 19X6	$ 8,600	$ 0

For C19-3

Toyco

BANK RECONCILIATIONS

For the Week Ended December 31, 19X6

Code No.	Bank A	Bank B
		Add or (Deduct)
1. Balance per bank statement December 31, 19X6	$8,600	$ 0
2. Deposits in transit December 31, 19X6	2,200	6,000
3. Redeposit of invalid deposits (physically deposited in wrong account)	1,000	1,400
4. Difference in deposits of December 29, 19X6	(2,000)	(100)
5. Unexplained bank charge	400	0
6. Bank cash transfer not yet recorded	0	22,600
7. Bank service charges	0	500
8. Chargebacks not recorded— stolen cards	100	0
9. Sales returns recorded but not reported to the bank	(600)	(1,200)
10. Balance per general ledger December 31, 19X6	$9,700	$29,200

Required: On the basis of a review of the December 31, 19X6, bank reconciliation and the related information available in the printouts and in the summary of bank statements, describe what procedures the auditor should perform to obtain audit satisfaction for each item on the bank reconciliations.

Assume that all amounts are material and all computations are accurate.

Organize your answer sheet as follows, using the appropriate code number for each item on the bank reconciliations:

Code No.	Procedures to Be Performed by the Auditor to Obtain Audit Satisfaction

(AICPA adapted)

Problems

P19-1 Select the best answer for each of the following items related to general internal controls over cash.

    a. Which of the following auditing procedures is the *most* appropriate when internal control over cash is weak or when a client requests an investigation of cash transactions?

    1. Proof of cash.

    2. Bank reconciliation.

    3. Cash confirmation.

    4. Evaluate ratio of cash to current liabilities.

b. Which of the following is one of the best auditing techniques that might be used by an auditor to detect kiting between two or more banks used by the client?

    1. Review composition of authenticated deposit slips.

    2. Review subsequent bank statements received directly from the banks.

    3. Prepare a schedule of bank transfers.

    4. Prepare year-end bank reconciliations.

c. Kiting is a technique that might be used to conceal a cash shortage. The auditor can *best* detect kiting by performing which of the following procedures?

    1. Examining the details of deposits made to all bank accounts several days subsequent to the balance sheet date.

    2. Comparing cash receipts records with the details on authenticated bank deposit slips for dates subsequent to the balance sheet date.

    3. Examining paid checks returned with bank statements subsequent to the balance sheet date.

    4. Comparing year-end balances per the standard bank confirmation forms with like balances on the client's bank reconciliations.

d. The use of fidelity bonds protects a company from embezzlement losses and also

    1. Protects employees who make unintentional errors from possible monetary damages resulting from such errors.

    2. Allows the company to substitute the fidelity bonds for various parts of internal accounting control.

    3. Reduces the company's need to obtain expensive business interruption insurance.

    4. Minimizes the possibility of employing persons with dubious records in positions of trust.

e. An unrecorded check issued during the last week of the year would most likely be discovered by the auditor when the

    1. Check register for the last month is reviewed.

    2. Cutoff bank statement is reconciled.

    3. Bank confirmation is reviewed.

    4. Search for unrecorded liabilities is performed.

f. Internal control over cash receipts is weakened when an employee who receives customer mail receipts also

    1. Prepares initial cash receipts records.

    2. Records credits to individual accounts receivable.

    3. Prepares bank deposit slips for all mail receipts.

    4. Maintains a petty cash fund.

g. Contact with banks for the purpose of opening company bank accounts should normally be the responsibility of the corporate

    1. Board of Directors.

    2. Treasurer.

    3. Controller.

    4. Executive Committee.

h. The cashier of Safir Company covered a shortage in the cash working fund with cash obtained on December 31 from a local bank by cashing but not recording a check drawn on the company's out-of-town bank. How would the auditor discover this manipulation?

    1. Confirming all December 31 bank balances.

    2. Counting the cash working fund at the close of business on December 31.

    3. Preparing independent bank reconciliations as of December 31.

    4. Investigating items returned with the bank cutoff statements.

i. For an appropriate segregation of duties, journalizing and posting summary payroll transactions should be assigned to

    1. The treasurer's department.

    2. General accounting.

    3. Payroll accounting.

    4. The timekeeping department.

j. To establish illegal "slush funds," corporations may divert cash received in normal business operations. An auditor would encounter the greatest difficulty in detecting the diversion of proceeds from

    1. Scrap sales.

    2. Dividends.

    3. Purchase returns.

    4. COD sales.

k. Operating control over the check signature plate normally should be the responsibility of the

    1. Secretary.

    2. Chief accountant.

    3. Vice-president of finance.

    4. Treasurer.

l. As an in-charge auditor you are reviewing a write-up of internal control weaknesses in cash receipt and disbursement procedures. Which one of the following weaknesses, standing alone, should cause you the *least* concern?

    1. Checks are signed by only one person.

    2. Signed checks are distributed by the controller to approved payees.

    3. Treasurer fails to establish *bona fides* of names and addresses of check payees.

    4. Cash disbursements are made directly out of cash receipts.

(AICPA adapted)

P19-2 Select the best answer for each of the following items relating to auditing procedures followed by verification of cash. Items (a), (b), and (c) are based on the following information:

    Listed below are four interbank cash transfers, indicated by the numbers (1), (2), (3), and (4), of a client for late December 19X4 and early January 19X5. Your answer choice for each item of (a), (b), and (c) should be selected from this list.

	Bank Account One Disbursing Date (Month/Day)		Bank Account Two Receiving Date (Month/Day)	
	Per Bank	Per Books	Per Bank	Per Books
1.	12/31	12/30	12/31	12/30
2.	1/2	12/30	12/31	12/31
3.	1/3	1/2	1/2	12/31
4.	1/3	12/31	1/2	12/31

a. Which of the cash transfers indicates an error in cash cutoff at December 31, 19X4?

b. Which of the cash transfers would appear as a deposit in transit on the December 31, 19X4, bank reconciliation?

  c. Which of the cash transfers would *not* appear as an outstanding check on the December 31, 19X4, bank reconciliation?

  d. The auditor should ordinarily mail confirmation requests to all banks with which the client has conducted any business during the year, regardless of the year-end balance, since

    1. The confirmation form also seeks information about indebtedness to the bank.

    2. This procedure will detect kiting activities which would otherwise not be detected.

    3. The mailing of confirmation forms to all such banks is required by generally accepted auditing standards.

    4. This procedure relieves the auditor of any responsibility with respect to nondetection of forged checks.

  e. With respect to contingent liabilities, the Standard Bank Confirmation Inquiry form approved jointly by the AICPA and the Bank Administration Institute requests information regarding notes receivable

    1. Held by the bank in a custodial account.

    2. Held by the bank for collection.

    3. Collected by the bank.

    4. Discounted by the bank.

  f. The auditor's count of the client's cash should be coordinated to coincide with the

    1. Study of the system of internal controls with respect to cash.

    2. Close of business on the balance sheet date.

    3. Count of marketable securities.

    4. Count of inventories.

  g. The standard bank cash confirmation form requests all of the following *except*

    1. Maturity date of a direct liability.

    2. The principal amount paid on a direct liability.

    3. Description of collateral for a direct liability.

    4. The interest rate of a direct liability.

  h. An internal management tool that aids in the control of the financial management function is a cash budget. The principal aim of a cash budget is to

    1. Ensure that sufficient funds are available at all times to satisfy maturing liabilities.

    2. Measure adherence to company budgetary procedures.

    3. Prevent the posting of cash receipts and disbursements to incorrect amounts.

    4. Ensure that the accounting for cash receipts and disbursements is consistent from year to year.

  i. To gather evidence regarding the balance per bank in a bank reconciliation, an auditor would examine all of the following *except*

    1. Cutoff bank statement.

    2. Year-end bank statement.

    3. Bank confirmation.

    4. General ledger.

  j. A CPA obtains a January 10 cutoff bank statement for his client directly from the bank. Very few of the outstanding checks listed on his client's December 31 bank reconciliation cleared during the cutoff period. A probable cause for this is that the client

    1. Is engaged in kiting.

    2. Is engaged in lapping.

    3. Transmitted the checks to the payees after year-end.

    4. Has overstated its year-end bank balance.

k. Two months before year-end the bookkeeper erroneously recorded the receipt of a long-term bank loan by a debit to cash and a credit to sales. Which of the following is the most effective procedure for detecting this type of error?

1. Analyze the notes payable journal.
2. Analyze bank confirmation information.
3. Prepare a year-end bank reconciliation.
4. Prepare a year-end bank transfer schedule.

(AICPA adapted)

P19-3 In connection with your audit of the ABC Co. at December 31, 19X6, you were given a bank reconciliation by a company employee, which shows

Balance per bank	$15,267
Deposits in transit	18,928
	$34,195
Checks outstanding	21,378
Balance per books	$12,817

As part of your verification you obtain the bank statement and canceled checks from the bank on January 15, 19X7. Checks issued from January 1 to January 15, 19X7 per the books were $11,241. Checks returned by the bank on January 15th amounted to $29,219. Of the checks outstanding December 31st, $4,800 were not returned by the bank with the January 15th statement, and of those issued per the books in January 19X7, $3,600 were not returned.

a. Prepare a schedule showing the above data in proper form.
b. Suggest four possible explanations for the condition existing here and state what your action would be in each case, including any necessary journal entry.

(AICPA adapted)

P19-4 State the reasons for the following procedure requirements, all of which help to strengthen internal control.

a. The ticket-taker of a motion picture theatre is required to tear each ticket presented for admission in two and present the stub to the patron.
b. The clerks of a department store are instructed to give the customer her or his cash register receipt along with the proper change.
c. The waitresses of the Elite Restaurant prepare the customer's check, which the customer then pays to the cashier. The waitresses are instructed not to make corrections on the check but, if an error is made, to void the check and issue a new check. All voided checks are to be given to the manager at the end of the day.
d. The Larson Manufacturing Co. prepares six copies of each purchase order. The third copy is sent to the receiving department to be used as a receiving report, but the form is so designed that the quantity ordered does not print on this copy.
e. After the treasurer of the Ardent Co. signs disbursement checks, the supporting data are returned to the accounting department, but the checks are given to his secretary for mailing.

P19-5 The Pembrook Company had poor internal control over its cash transactions. Facts about its cash position at November 30 were the following:

The cash books showed a balance of $18,901.62, which included undeposited receipts. A credit of $100 on the bank statement did not appear on the books of the company. The balance, according to the bank statement, was $15,550.

When the auditor received the cutoff bank statement on December 20, the following cancelled checks were enclosed: No. 62 for $116.25, No. 183 for $150.00, No. 284 for $253.25, No. 8621 for $190.71, No. 8623 for $206.80, and No. 8632 for $145.28. The only deposit was in the amount of $3,794.41 on December 7.

The cashier handles all incoming cash and makes the bank deposits personally. He also reconciles the monthly bank statement. His November 30 reconciliation is shown below:

Balance, per books, November 30		$18,901.62
Add: Outstanding checks:		
8621	$190.71	
8623	206.80	
8632	145.28	442.79
		$19,344.41
Less: Undeposited receipts		3,794.41
Balance per book, November 30		$15,550.00
Deduct: Unrecorded credit		100.00
True cash, November 30		$15,450.00

Required:
a. You suspect that the cashier may have misappropriated some money. Prepare a schedule showing your estimate of the loss.
b. How did the cashier attempt to conceal his theft?
c. On the basis of only the information above, name two specific features of internal control that were apparently missing.
d. If the cashier's October 31 reconciliation is known to be in order and you start your audit on December 10, what specific auditing procedures could you perform to discover the theft?

(AICPA adapted)

P19-6 Explain the objective(s) of each of the following substantive tests performed in verifying cash balances:
a. Count cash on hand in the presence of the custodian.
b. Trace adjusting journal entries to cash accounts from journals to postings in the general ledger account.
c. Trace deposits near the end of the period according to the bank reconciliation to cutoff bank statement and ascertain whether the time lag for clearing the bank is proper.
d. Inspect bank confirmation for any restrictions on cash in bank—such as time deposits, compensating balances, etc.
e. Confirm "cash per bank" on the client's bank reconciliation directly with the bank.
f. Inspect all checks clearing with the bank cutoff statement for payee, date, and amount.

   g. Compare checks clearing the bank with amounts per the outstanding check list for omitted checks or errors in amounts on the outstanding checks list.
   h. Prepare a schedule of interbank transfers for approximately three days before and after the balance sheet date.
   i. Prepare and analyze a four-column proof of cash.

P19-7 An auditor obtains a July 10 bank statement directly from the bank.

   Required: Explain how this cutoff bank statement will be used
   a. In the auditor's review of the June 30 bank reconciliation.
   b. To obtain any other audit information.

(AICPA adapted)

P19-8 The following information was obtained in an audit of the cash account of Tuck Company as of December 31, 19X7. Assume that the CPA is satisfied as to the validity of the cash book, the bank statements, and the returned checks, except as noted.
   a. The bookkeeper's bank reconciliation at November 30, 19X7:

Balance per bank statement		$ 19,400
Add deposit in transit		1,100
Total		$ 20,500
Less outstanding checks		
#2540	$140	
1501	750	
1503	480	
1504	800	
1505	130	2,300
Balance per books		$ 18,200

   b. A summary of the bank statement for December 19X7:

Balance brought forward	$ 19,400
Deposits	148,700
	$168,100
Charges	132,500
Balance, December 31, 19X7	$ 35,600

   c. A summary of the cash book for December 19X7 before adjustments:

Balance brought forward	$ 18,200
Receipts	149,690
	$167,890
Disbursements	124,885
Balance, December 31, 19X7	$ 43,005

   d. Included with the canceled checks returned with the December bank statement were the items shown on the list on the next page.
   e. The Tuck Company discounted its own sixty-day note for $9,000 with the bank on December 1, 19X7. The discount rate was 6 percent. The bookkeeper recorded the proceeds as a cash receipt at the face value of the note.

f. The bookkeeper records customers' dishonored checks as a reduction of cash receipts. When the dishonored checks are redeposited, they are recorded as a regular cash receipt. Two NSF checks for $180 and $220 were returned by the bank during December. The $180 check was redeposited, but the $220 check was still on hand at December 31. Cancelations of Tuck Company checks are recorded by a reduction of cash disbursements.

g. December bank charges were $20. In addition, a $10 service charge was made in December for the collection of a foreign draft in November. These charges were not recorded on the books.

h. Check #2540 listed in the November outstanding checks was drawn in 19X5. Since the payee cannot be located, the president of Tuck Company agreed to the CPA's suggestion that the check be written back into the accounts by a journal entry.

Information about Canceled Checks Returned with Bank Statement

Number	Date of check	Amount of check	Comments
#1501	November 28, 19X7	$ 75	This check was in payment of an invoice for $750 and was recorded in the cash book as $750.
#1503	November 28, 19X7	$580	This check was in payment of an invoice for $580 and was recorded in the cash book as $580.
#1523	December 5, 19X7	$150	Examination of this check revealed that it was unsigned. A discussion with the client disclosed that it had been mailed inadvertently before it was signed. The check was endorsed and deposited by the payee and processed by the bank even though it was a legal nullity. The check was recorded in the cash disbursements.
#1528	December 12, 19X7	$800	This check replaced #1504, which was returned by the payee because it was mutilated. Check #1504 was not canceled on the books.
___	December 19, 19X7	$200	This was a counter check drawn at the bank by the president of the company as a cash advance for travel expense. The president overlooked informing the bookkeeper about the check.
___	December 20, 19X7	$300	The drawer of this check was the Tucker Company.
#1535	December 20, 19X7	$350	This check had been labeled NSF and returned to the payee because the bank had erroneously believed that the check was drawn by the Luck Company. Subsequently the payee was advised to redeposit the check.
#1575	January 5, 19X8	$10,000	This check was given to the payee on December 30, 19X7, as a postdated check with the understanding that it would not be deposited until January 5. The check was not recorded on the books in December.

i. Outstanding checks at December 31, 19X7, totalled $4,000, excluding checks #2540 and #1504.

j. The cutoff bank statement disclosed that the bank had recorded a deposit of $2,400 on January 2, 19X8. The bookkeeper had recorded this deposit on the books on December 31, 19X7, and then mailed the deposit to the bank.

Required: Prepare a four-column proof of cash of the cash receipts and cash disbursements recorded on the bank statement and on the company's books for the month of December 19X7. The reconciliation should agree with the cash figure that will appear in the company's financial statements.

(AICPA adapted)

P19-9 MLG Company's auditor received, directly from the banks, confirmations and cutoff statements with related checks and deposit tickets for MLG's three general-purpose bank accounts. The auditor determined that internal accounting control over cash was satisfactory and will be relied upon. The proper cutoff of external cash receipts and disbursements was established. No bank accounts were opened or closed during the year.

Required: Prepare the audit program of substantive procedures to verify MLG's bank balances. Ignore any other cash accounts.

(AICPA adapted)

CHAPTER 20

Completing the Audit

Objectives

☐ **1.** Search for and verify estimated and contingent liabilities.
☐ **2.** Perform final analytical procedures.
☐ **3.** Review supplementary data.
☐ **4.** Ascertain existence and proper disclosure of subsequent events.
☐ **5.** Review working papers, summarize audit evidence, and draw conclusions from the evidence presented.
☐ **6.** Respond appropriately to information that comes to your attention subsequent to the issuance of financial statements.

As shown by the diagram on the following page, after evidence-gathering procedures have been performed on the component systems of the financial statements, the evidence-gathering process is completed. Completion of the audit is accomplished by performing overall analytical procedures, and by pulling together remaining loose ends of the audit to form conclusions with respect to the component systems and balances. In this phase of the audit, you may think of the auditor as making some final checks to see that the pieces of the "jigsaw puzzle" fit together in the form of fairly presented financial statements.

Chapter appendixes include illustrated working papers for the working trial balance as well as for adjusting and reclassifying entries for JEP Manufacturing Company.

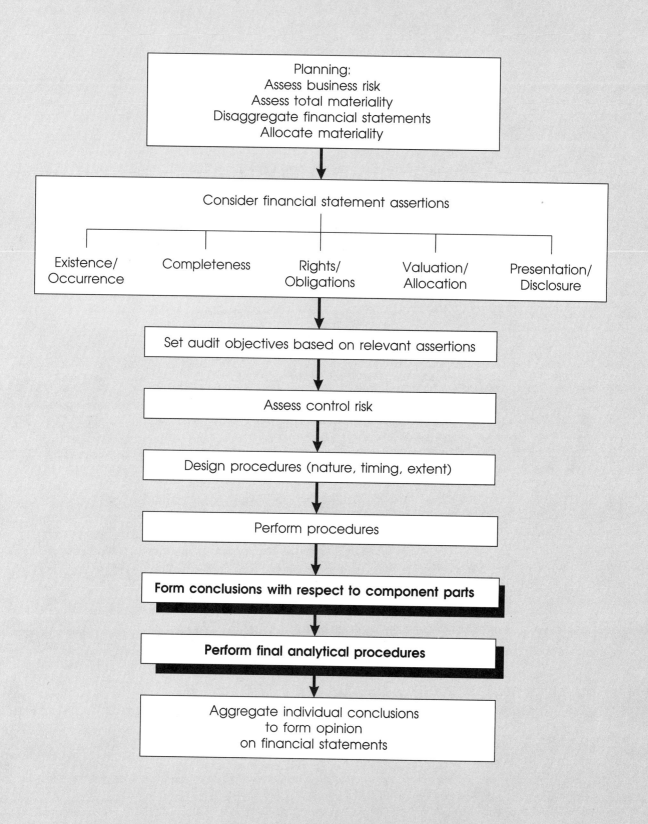

Search for and Verification of Estimated and Contingent Liabilities

Before completing the evidence-gathering phase of the audit, the auditor must verify that *estimated liabilities* and *contingent liabilities* have been fairly presented. We give particular attention to the verification of *existence, valuation,* and *appropriate statement presentation* in this phase of the audit. In meeting those audit objectives, the auditor must direct much of his or her efforts toward the discovery of omitted or understated items.

It is important to begin our discussion of this area by emphasizing the difference between an estimated liability and a contingent liability. An **estimated liability** is a future obligation to an outside party resulting from activities that have already occurred. It is different from other such obligations, however, in that the *precise amount of the obligation is unknown.* The estimated amount of the obligation is recorded in the accounting records and reflected in the financial statements. A **contingent liability,** on the other hand, is a *potential future obligation* resulting from past activities. As you can see, the word *potential* is the primary difference between the two definitions. A contingent liability is one that may or may not actually exist, depending on the future resolution of some uncertainty. The amount of a contingent liability may be either known or unknown, depending on the nature of the potential obligation.

The auditor, in distinguishing between estimated and contingent liabilities, must be guided by the provisions of FASB 5, which state that if a potential obligation meets three criteria—(1) it exists, (2) it is both highly probable and reasonably estimatable, and (3) it is the result of events that occurred prior to the balance sheet date—it should be treated as an estimated liability rather than as a contingent liability. *GAAP requires that estimated liabilities be accrued and be included in the liability section of the balance sheet, while contingent liabilities (which are considered "reasonably possible" to occur) generally are disclosed through the medium of financial statement footnotes.* A point estimate or range of amount should be given, if possible, and if no estimate is possible, disclosures should indicate that fact.

Estimated Liabilities

Obligations for income taxes, product warranty agreements, and purchase commitments are typical examples of estimated liabilities. After the auditor has reconciled the statement amounts for these items with the underlying accounting records, he or she should inspect the documents (such as the tax return, the warranty agreement, or the purchase commitment contract) to verify the existence of the respective estimated liabilities. It is also important to review the minutes of the board of directors' meetings in the search for unrecorded estimated liabilities.

The *valuation* of estimated liabilities should be verified by recomputing the probable obligation from available documentation or related account balances. It is important, for example, to examine the client's tax return and the reports of internal revenue agents relating to the client's tax obligations in determining whether the estimated liability for income taxes is properly valued. The estimated liability for warranty should take into consideration the past experience of the company in establishing the percentage relationship between sales and product warranty costs. Accrued sales commissions payable should be verified against sales. Prices on purchase commitment contracts should be inspected and compared with end-of-period market quotations in determining whether an estimated liability for purchase commitments has been properly valued. The existence of open commodity futures contracts, for example, can be verified by direct confirmation with the client's commodity traders.

Estimated liabilities should be presented in the liability section of the balance sheet. They should be classified as current or noncurrent, depending on the nature of the respective obligations. Parenthetical and footnote disclosures should be added to explain uncertainties relating to the estimated liability account balances.

Contingent Liabilities

Contingent liabilities include such things as possible obligations from pending litigation, notes receivable discounted and guarantees of obligations of others, ongoing tax disputes, and open letters of credit at banks. Because of their nature, the auditing procedures for verifying contingencies are not as well defined as are the procedures for verifying other elements of the financial statements. The primary auditing objective, however, is *to verify their existence.* Because they are potential liabilities, the auditing literature continues to focus attention on the discovery of undisclosed contingent obligations. The following auditing procedures are designed to accomplish that objective:

- *Inquire of management* regarding their procedures for identifying, evaluating, and accounting for contingencies. A primary task of the auditor in carrying out this procedure is to let management know the different kinds of contingencies that may be associated with the client's operating environment. Obviously, this procedure will not be useful in discovering intentional failures to disclose contingencies. It will, however, be useful if management has a basic commitment to the fair presentation of the financial data.
- Closely associated with the preceding auditing procedure is the requirement that the *letter of representation* from a client contain a statement that management is aware of no undisclosed contingent liabilities.
- The auditor should *analyze the legal expense account* and invoices for professional services for the period. This analysis is directed toward the discovery of possible lawsuits and tax assessments associated with legal fees paid by the client.
- The auditor should *obtain a confirmation letter* similar to the one shown in Figure 20–1 from all attorneys performing major legal services for the client during the year.[1] The precise form and content of this **attorney's letter** are discussed later in this section. For this purpose, the client may provide the auditor with a list of pending or threatened litigation and other claims and

Figure 20-1

Typical Attorney Confirmation Letter

CLIENT COMPANY
Anywhere, USA

January 26, 19X3

Attorney for the Client
Anywhere, USA

Gentlemen:

(1) —   Our auditors, James Brown & Co., CPAs, are auditing our financial statements for the fiscal year ending 12/31/19X2. In connection with that audit, we have provided them with the attached list describing and evaluating certain contingencies to which you have devoted substantial attention on behalf of the company in the form of legal consultation or representation. We have also provided an estimate of potential losses where those could be provided. These contingencies are regarded by management as material for financial reporting purposes.

(3) —   We ask you to furnish to our auditors such information regarding the nature of the litigation, the progress of each case to date, how management is responding or intends to respond to the litigation, and an evaluation of the likelihood of an unfavorable outcome along with an estimate, if one can be made, of the amount or range of potential loss. Please furnish our auditors any other information you consider necessary to supplement the information already provided, including an explanation of those matters as to which your views may differ from those stated in the attached documents. Also

(4) — please advise the auditors of any pending or threatened litigation, claims, or assessments you know of that have been omitted from this list. In the absence of omissions, please state that the list provided for the auditor is complete.

(2) —   We have also provided the auditors with the attached list of unasserted claims, along with our proposed responses if those claims are asserted and our judgment as to the likelihood of an unfavorable outcome. In connection with the unasserted claims

(5) — listed in the attached document, please furnish our auditors with such explanations if any, as you consider necessary to supplement the information included in the list, including an explanation of those matters as to which your views may differ from those

(6) — stated in our list. It is our understanding that you are also responsible for informing the management of our firm when in your judgment an unasserted claim requires disclosure in the financial statements.

(7) —   We also request you to state the nature of any reasons you may have for limiting your response to this confirmation request.

    Your reply to this confirmation request should be sent directly to our auditors in the attached, postage-paid envelope addressed to them.

Sincerely yours,

Management, Client Company

---

assessments. Alternatively, the client's lawyer may be asked to furnish the required information with respect to pending or threatened litigation.
- The auditor should *inspect letters of credit in force* as of the balance sheet date and obtain a confirmation of the used and unused portions of the balances shown in those letters.

Other procedures performed throughout the audit, although primarily for different purposes, may disclose contingent liabilities arising because of claims, litigation, or assessments. Examples of these other procedures are

- *Reading the minutes* of directors', stockholders', and other appropriate committees' meetings held during and subsequent to the period being examined; this is done to discover contingent commitments, such as guarantees of the debt of an affiliate.
- *Reading contracts, loan agreements, leases, and correspondence* from taxing or governmental agencies for evidence of liabilities.
- *Inspecting the working papers* prepared to this point in the audit for any indication of potential contingencies. For example, the bank confirmation (illustrated in Appendix 19–D) should be inspected for potential contingent liabilities associated with notes receivable discounted or loan guarantees.

Pending or threatened litigation is among the most important of contingent liabilities. As indicated in the preceding paragraph, the auditor relies heavily on the client's legal counsel for information relating to these matters. Each attorney who has provided legal service for the client during the year should be requested to reply to a confirmation letter similar to the one shown in Figure 20–1 to secure that information. You will observe that the letter is signed by client management and asks the company's legal counsel to provide information regarding contingencies that existed as of the end of the audit period or that may have developed during the period between the balance sheet date and the date of the audit report.

The standard letter of confirmation as shown in Figure 20–1 should include the following items:

1. The client's list of material *pending or threatened litigation.*
2. The client's list of any material unasserted claims with which the attorney has been involved. For this purpose, an **unasserted claim** is a cause for legal action, which someone may have against the client but which has not been filed as of the date of the confirmation letter.
3. A request that the attorney furnish information regarding the status of each of the listed items of pending or threatened litigation. This response should provide indications as to the *probability* of an unfavorable outcome and a *range of potential loss* in the event of an unfavorable outcome.
4. A request that the attorney identify any pending or threatened legal actions of which he or she is aware that may not be included in the client's list.
5. A request that the lawyer comment on unasserted claims for which his or her views differ from management's.
6. A direct statement that the attorney is responsible for informing management when, in his or her judgment, there is an unasserted claim requiring disclosure in the financial statements.
7. A statement requiring the attorney to identify the nature of any reasons for limitations in response to the confirmation request.[2]

The references to each of the listed items in the illustrated confirmation letter are identified by their respective numbers in the margin of the letter shown in Figure 20–1. You should also observe that the letter requires that the confirmation reply be sent *directly to the auditors.*

In 1975, an agreement was reached between the American Bar Association and the American Institute of Certified Public Accountants as to the form and content of lawyers' confirmation letters. This agreement took into account the importance of maintaining the confidentiality of attorney/client communications. However, it also recognized the importance of client/auditor communications, which essentially require waiver of the attorney/client privilege with respect to the information in the confirmation letter. The letter format illustrated in Figure 20–1 is the product of this agreement. In spite of the agreement, however, auditors sometimes have difficulty securing satisfactory responses from clients' attorneys. In some cases, an unsatisfactory response consists of an inadequate reply and, in other instances, a refusal by the attorney to provide the information. Although reluctance to provide information can be justified either by a lack of knowledge or by what the attorney construes to be a confidential relationship between attorney and client, the auditor must have a satisfactory reply to enable the expression of an unqualified opinion on the financial statements. Therefore, if the unavailable information could directly affect the fairness of presentation of the financial statements, the auditor, in accordance with SAS 12 (AU337), would have to modify her or his audit opinion to reflect the lack of available evidence. This requirement has the effect of placing pressure on the client's attorneys to cooperate with the auditor by providing contingent liability information.

Frequently, the auditing firm will seek a separate evaluation of a potential liability from its own legal counsel to supplement the responses of the client's attorneys. This can be particularly helpful in evaluating contingent liabilities because of the fact that the client's attorney is an *advocate of the client* and in that capacity may lose some of her or his objectivity in evaluating the potential liability associated with the pending legal action. For that reason, for example, an auditor should be concerned about the possibility of undisclosed unasserted claims if a client's attorney resigns shortly after delivering a letter indicating no significant disagreements with the client's assessment of contingent liabilities.

Inquiries in the lawyer's confirmation letter may be limited to matters that are considered individually or collectively material, provided that the client and the auditor have reached an understanding on the limits of materiality for this purpose. Likewise, the lawyer may limit her or his response to matters considered individually or collectively material, provided that the lawyer and the auditor have reached an understanding on the limits of materiality for this purpose.

Analytical Procedures

☑ **Objective 2**
Perform final
analytical
procedures

As we have observed earlier in the text, the evidence-gathering process involves two types of substantive tests: (1) tests of details, consisting of inspection, confirmation, and observation of evidence of all kinds; and (2) analytical procedures. We now turn our attention to how the final analytical phase of the audit is used to gather evidential matter required by the third standard of field work.[3]

We perform final *analytical procedures* to test the overall reasonableness of the financial data. These procedures are carried out primarily by making independent computations and by comparison of account balance and ratio data for a number of periods. The purpose of final analytical procedures is to identify *unusual items* and *unexpected fluctuations* that may remain *after* tests of details have been performed, which may lead to the discovery of undetected material misstatements of the financial data that still exist after the detailed substantive tests have been performed.

Analytical procedures are defined as a study of plausible relationships among recorded financial data. Analytical procedures are *required* during this final phase of the audit. At this stage, we depend primarily on a *comparison of the current period data with past periods' data.* For most entities, recorded data can be expected to conform to a predictable pattern over time. Deviations from this pattern may be caused by significant changes in circumstances, which need to be disclosed in the financial statements. Thus, analytical procedures are one means of *auditing by exception.* The implication is that any significant changes in account balances or in operating results should be explained in terms of changing circumstances existing during the audit period. Because of the periodic nature of these comparisons and because extensive tests of details have been performed on balance sheet data, final analytical procedures tend to be *concentrated on the income statement accounts.* Year-to-year comparisons are divided into three subcategories.

1. *Overall analytical procedures* of the general financial condition and profitability trends. The procedure used most frequently by the auditor in making an overall review of the income statement is the comparison of current year revenues and expenses with the corresponding figures for the previous year.
2. *Detailed analytical procedures* involving comparisons of elements of financial statement data, including operating and financial ratios.
3. *Direct tests of some account balances* or classes of transactions for reasonableness.

The basic assumption underlying the analytical process is that the financial data and operational relationships should be consistent with those of prior periods for the client and with the client's industry. Thus, the auditor should become familiar with the client's operations, the environment in which the firm operates, and the client's industry—all this for the purpose of identifying the expectations for the financial data. This means that the primary procedures followed in analytical procedures will be *recomputation* of client-recorded amounts and *comparisons* using nonfinancial data, industry statistics, and analytical ratios. The most important phase of analytical procedures often is the investigation of significant variations and unusual relationships. As discussed in Chapter 7, significant deviations from expectations can usually be related to one of the following causes:

- Changes in operations, which may involve both profitability and cash flow.
- Exceptional circumstances surrounding the client's operations.
- Accounting changes.

If the auditor is unable, after performing substantive tests of details, to explain differences in terms of one of these characteristics, the possibility of undetected errors remaining in the financial data should be considered.

Regardless of the method used to develop the auditor's expectation of the proper account balance, an important element of final analytical procedures is the *comparison of the recorded amount with an expected amount*. The auditor should obtain an explanation from the client for any account showing a material deviation from expectations. He or she should then follow up with corroborative tests (i.e., inspection of documents, further inquiry, etc.) to ascertain that the client's explanation is reasonable.

Consideration of an Entity's Continued Existence

In most of the legal cases discussed in Chapter 4, the business failed shortly after the auditor had expressed an unqualified audit opinion. This fact, perhaps more than any other, led the Dingell Commission to ask the penetrating question, "Where were the auditors?"

In response to the concerns of the public over this issue, the Auditing Standards Board has issued SAS 59 (AU341), entitled *The Auditor's Consideration of an Entity's Ability to Continue as a Going Concern*. For purposes of this statement, an entity ceases to be a going concern when it loses the ability to sustain its operations without entering into bankruptcy.

It is a required procedure on all audits to evaluate the aggregate results of audit procedures for indications of substantial doubt about the entity's ability to continue as a going concern for a reasonable period of time, not to exceed one year beyond the date of the audited financial statements.[4] The audit procedures that are prescribed for such an evaluation include

- Analytical procedures on the relationships between recorded data in the financial statements and elsewhere.
- Reviewing events that occurred subsequent to the balance sheet date and before the date of issuance of the audit report.
- Reviewing compliance of the company with the terms of debt and loan agreements.
- Reading minutes of meetings of stockholders, board of directors, and other important committees.
- Inquiring of the company's legal counsel regarding litigation, claims, and assessments.
- Confirming with related and third parties details of arrangements to provide
- or maintain financial support to those parties.
- Obtaining written representations from management.

When indications (negative trends in operations or cash flows, recurring losses, default on loans, etc.) are that the entity may not remain a going concern, other factors should be considered by the auditor. Specifically, he or she should begin to investigate possibilities for disposal of assets, availability of new credit, cost-cutting factors, and possibilities for obtaining additional equity capital. Management's plans with respect to each of these alternatives should be evaluated. If substantial doubt regarding the continued existence of the entity still remains, the auditor should take steps to determine that the financial statements include adequate disclosure about possible discontinuance of operations. In addition, the audit report should be modified to include an explanation of the situation. Figure 21–13 is an example of this type of report.

Review of Supplementary Data

☑ **Objective 3**
Review
supplementary
data

The evidence we have gathered to this point has been designed to help the auditor determine whether he or she can express an opinion that the basic financial statements (balance sheet, income statement, statement of cash flows and statement of retained earnings) have been fairly stated. This is interpreted to include the parenthetical comments and footnotes associated with those statements. A typical annual report for a corporation or a 10-K report filed under the Securities Exchange Act of 1934 may include, in addition to the financial statements, a narrative report by management describing the year's operations (see Figure 5–1 for JEP Manufacturing Co.), consolidating information, historical summaries, or projections of anticipated future trends for the company. Some of this information may be from sources outside the accounting system of the entity. The auditing profession has for some time been concerned about possible inconsistencies between the audited financial data and data outside the basic financial statements in a client's annual report.

Several auditing standards have addressed this issue. SAS 8 (AU550) applies to information contained in annual reports, 10-K reports, and other *documents submitted to investors or creditors by the client;* it requires no auditing procedures for this information. Instead, this standard requires the auditor merely to read the other information for inconsistencies with the information in the audited financial statements. If the auditor concludes that there is a material inconsistency, he or she should consider whether the financial statements or the auditor's report, or both, require revision. If the auditor concludes that neither the statements nor the report requires revision, the client should be requested to revise the other information. If the client declines to do so, the auditor may revise the audit report to include an explanation of the inconsistency. Of course, the more extreme option of withdrawal from the engagement and disassociation of the auditor's name with the statements is always available as well.[5]

If the **supplemental data** appear in an *auditor-submitted document,* as discussed in SAS 29 (AU551), the auditor has the option of auditing the other information. If this option is taken, the auditor's report should be extended to express an opinion as to whether the accompanying information is fairly stated in all material respects in relation to the basic financial statements. If the other information is not audited, then the auditor's responsibility is limited to reading the accompanying information for obvious mistakes or inconsistencies with the audited information. If none are found, the auditor's disclaimer of opinion on the supplemental data should accompany the audit report on the basic financial statements.[6]

In some instances, the FASB or Government Accounting Standards Board (GASB) may require disclosure of supplementary information outside the basic financial statements. For example, GASB Statement No. 5 requires presentation of certain historical trend information relating to pension activities outside the basic financial statements of certain government entities. These types of information differ from other supplemental disclosures because the FASB or GASB considers the information to be a vital part of the reporting process, and because authoritative guidelines for measurement and disclosure have been established. In these cases, the auditor should *apply limited procedures* to the information *and* should *report deficiencies in, or omissions of* the information. The following are among the procedures that the auditor should apply in these cases:

1. *Inquire of management* concerning the methods of preparing and disclosing the information, whether it is within prescribed guidelines, whether any changes have been made in methods, and any significant assumptions or interpretations made.
2. *Read* and *compare* the information for consistency with management's responses to inquiries in (1), with audited financial statements, and with other information obtained during the engagement.
3. Consider whether management's response in (1) should be included in the management representation letter (illustrated in Figure 20–3).[7]

If the results of the preceding inquiries and other procedures indicate that the client has fulfilled necessary disclosure requirements of the FASB or GASB, the auditor need make no mention of the supplementary information in the audit report. However, if management's disclosures appear to depart from the FASB or GASB guidelines, if the required information is omitted, or if the auditor is unable to complete the prescribed procedures, the auditor should expand the audit report to describe the nature of the misstatement, omission, or limitation in procedures.

Subsequent Events

☑ **Objective 4**
Ascertain existence and proper disclosure of subsequent events

The third standard of reporting states that adequate disclosures are presumed to exist in the financial statements unless otherwise stated in the audit report. This means in part that, in fulfilling the *cutoff* and *statement presentation* objectives, the auditor must be satisfied that all elements in the financial statements relate to the audit period and that all significant financial facts are disclosed. Transactions or events may occur after the balance sheet date and before the issuance of the audit report, which, because of the hindsight they provide, affect the disclosures on the client's financial statements. We call these **subsequent events.** The search for unrecorded liabilities continues through an examination of events subsequent to the balance sheet date; the discovery of an unrecorded liability may be identified by a subsequent event. The auditor may need to request that the account balances be adjusted or the nature of the events be disclosed for any of these transactions or events that have a material effect on the balances shown in the financial statements or on the interpretation of those data to meet the requirements of generally accepted accounting principles. Therefore, the auditor's *formal review of subsequent events should be extended through the date of the auditor's report.*

There are generally two types of subsequent events requiring the auditor's consideration. The level of disclosure that each demands depends on two things: the date of the causal event and the date of the culminating transaction. In Figure 20–2 we relate the two types of subsequent events to the level of disclosure required for them.

The first type of subsequent event provides additional evidence with respect to conditions that existed as of the balance sheet date. By this we mean that the cause of the *change in the financial picture was present before the end of the period under audit.* Therefore, the change should show up in the financial statements. When the auditor learns after the balance sheet date that a culminating transaction or event has occurred that affects the financial statements under audit, the client should be asked to *adjust the financial statements* to reflect the more recent (and more accurate) information. Examples of Type 1 subsequent events include

- Bankruptcy of a client's customer, whose now uncollectible balance is included in accounts receivable as of the balance sheet date. Accounts receivable as of the end of the audit period should be reduced by the amount of the uncollectible account.
- Settlement of an estimated liability, such as pending litigation or an income tax liability, after the balance sheet date for an amount different from that shown on the balance sheet. Again, the liability account should be adjusted to show the final settlement figure.

Figure 20–2

Subsequent Events and the Auditor's Responsibilities for Disclosure

	Date of causal event	Date of culminating transaction	Level of disclosure necessary
Type 1	Before balance sheet date	After balance sheet date	Adjust financial statements
Type 2	After balance sheet date	After balance sheet date	Disclose in footnotes

- Payment of a claim disclosed as a contingent liability at the balance sheet date. For example, a charge to notes receivable in the cash disbursements journal during the period subsequent to the balance sheet date could reflect the settlement of an endorser's contingent liability. In that case, the contingent liability should be recognized as an accrued liability.
- Discovery of an unrecorded liability.

The second type of subsequent event consists of events *whose causal and culminating factors both occurred after the balance sheet date.* If the nature of the event is of such importance that it would affect user interpretations of the financial data, the events should be disclosed in the footnotes to the financial statements. Occasionally an event such as this might be so significant that disclosure can best be accomplished by presenting pro forma statements in the footnotes. However, only narrative footnote disclosure generally is required. Type 2 subsequent events that may require disclosure (but not adjustment) in the financial statements are these:

- Sale of bond or capital stock issue.
- Purchase of a business.
- Settlement of litigation in which the event giving rise to the claim occurred subsequent to the balance sheet date.
- Loss of plant or inventories as a result of casualty.
- Losses of receivables resulting from conditions such as a customer's major casualty arising subsequent to the balance sheet date.

Subsequent events of the types described in the preceding paragraphs are typically discovered by performing the following procedures during final stages of the audit field work:

1. *Inspecting* the client's latest available interim financial statements and comparing them with disclosures made in the audited financial statements.
2. *Inquiring* of officers and other persons in authority as to whether
   a. any substantial contingent liabilities or commitments existed either at the balance sheet date or at the date the inquiry is made;
   b. any substantial changes were made in the capital structure of the company between the balance sheet date and the date of the audit report;
   c. there has been any change in the current status of items in the financial statements that were originally accounted for on the basis of tentative or inconclusive data or any unusual adjustments that were made during the subsequent events period.
3. *Inspecting* the minutes of meetings held between the end of the audit period and the date of completion of field work.
4. *Inquiring* of client's legal counsel concerning claims, litigation, and assessments.
5. *Obtaining a client representation letter* with regard to subsequent events.

Review and Summarization Process

☑ **Objective 5**
Review working
papers, summarize
evidence, and
draw conclusions

The results of the evidence-gathering process are all contained in working papers such as those included as appendixes to the various chapters of this book. It is important to remember that, after the audit of a particular system and related account balances (including final analytical procedures) has been completed, the section of the working papers reflecting the findings relating to that system should stand on its own and the auditor should be able to draw appropriate conclusions from it. For example, after the audit of the sales and accounts receivable system has been completed (including analysis of ratios and trends, as well as all compliance and substantive tests), the auditor should be able to state whether all the related accounts (sales, accounts receivable, allowance for doubtful accounts, bad debts expense, etc.) are fairly presented in accordance with GAAP. To the extent possible, all appropriate procedures applied to a system (from development of audit objectives through final analytical procedures) should be completed as a unit so that the audit work can then be subjected to a timely review by audit supervisory personnel.

The audit process almost always generates the need for certain adjusting entries that the auditor feels should be made to allow the financial statements to be fairly presented in accordance with GAAP. Such entries typically are recorded in the working trial balance and in a separate list of auditor's adjustments prepared primarily for the client. We should point out that the *client must approve these adjustments* before they can be incorporated in the financial statements. Adjusting journal entries should also be posted to the lead schedules and individual working papers so that their totals will agree with adjusted amounts for each account balance on the adjusted trial balance.

The relationships among the different elements of the working papers were depicted in Figure 6–7. The lead schedules and supporting schedules included in that figure have been presented as appendixes to various preceding chapters of the text. Illustrations of working trial balances for the balance sheet and income statement items, adjusting entries, and reclassifying journal entries are included in appendixes to this chapter. After the working trial balance has been completed, formal statements should be prepared from the adjusted data. *Those are the statements on which the auditor expresses an opinion.*

The working papers should also include a *letter of representation* from the client, documenting management's oral representations during the audit. This document is required by SAS 19 (AU333), which suggests twenty specific matters that should be included.[8] The primary purposes of this letter are to *impress upon management its responsibilities for the data included in the financial statements and to document the oral responses to auditors' inquiries from management* relating to the various parts of the audit. A management representation letter must be included as part of the audit working papers; however, it should not be regarded as a substitute for more direct and reliable evidence. The letter does, however, provide some evidence and it documents the fact that the auditor has asked management certain questions relating to the financial statements. Figure 20–3 contains an example of a typical **client representation letter.**[9] The letter should be dated to coincide with the date of the audit report.

After the working papers have been summarized, they are subjected to a series of reviews. Usually, at least three reviews are conducted by separate persons, starting with the accountant in charge of the audit engagement and culminating with the partner supervising the audits of the industry in which the client

Figure 20–3

Illustrative Client Representation Letter

CLIENT COMPANY
Anywhere, USA

(Date of auditor's report)

Client's Independent Auditor
Anywhere, USA

Gentlemen:

    In connection with your audit of our financial statements for the fiscal year ending 12/31/19X2, for the purpose of expressing an opinion as to whether those statements present fairly the financial position, results of operations, and cash flows of our company in conformity with generally accepted accounting principles, we confirm to the best of our knowledge and belief the following representations made to you during your examination:

1. We are responsible for the fair presentation in the financial statements of financial position, results of operations, and cash flows in accordance with generally accepted accounting principles.

2. We have made available to you all
   a. Financial records and related data.
   b. Minutes of the meetings of stockholders, directors, committees of directors, or summaries of actions of recent meetings for which minutes have not yet been prepared.

3. There have been no
   a. Irregularities involving management or employees who have significant roles in the system of internal accounting control.
   b. Irregularities involving other employees that could have a material effect on the financial statements.
   c. Communications from regulatory agencies concerning noncompliance with or deficiencies in financial reporting practices that could have a material effect on the financial statements.

4. We have no plans or intentions that may materially affect the carrying values or classifications of assets and liabilities.

5. The following have been properly recorded or disclosed in the financial statements: [Here will be listed the various items covered in SAS 19] .

Sincerely,

Chief Executive Officer

Chief Financial Officer

operates. The relationship between authority and the review processes is shown in Figure 20–4. The review process is directed toward three goals, namely,

- Evaluating the performance of audit staff.
- Making sure that the audit meets the accounting firm's standard of performance.
- Counteracting any bias that may enter into the auditor's judgment.

As the working papers move through the review process, from the initial review by the immediate supervisor of the audit staff toward final review by the partner supervising audits in the industry, they typically proceed from a review of particulars at the lowest level to a review for general reasonableness at the partner level. For example, the first review will be concerned with checking such things as mathematical accuracy, the appropriate identification of various working papers, and the adequacy of the content of individual working papers. As the review process moves toward the partner level, attention must be given to the overall adequacy of the evidence, the reasonableness of the conclusions reached, and the adequacy of disclosure in the financial statements.

Because the working papers reflect the auditor's documentation of the evidence in support of the audit report, attention must ultimately be given to judging *whether the data included in the working papers make the auditor's opinion legally and ethically defensible.* It is important, for example, that the reviewers make sure that there are no unanswered questions, ambiguous conclusions, or inconsistent evaluations that would make the legal defense of the audit opinion vulnerable.

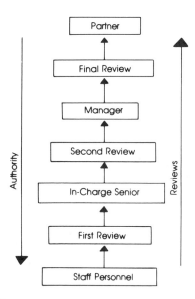

Figure 20–4

Relationship between Authority and the Review Process

Events Subsequent to the Issuance of Financial Statements

☑ **Objective 6**
Respond
appropriately
to subsequent
discovery of facts
existing at audit
report date

The procedures discussed to this point are *overt auditing procedures,* which must be performed before the issuance of the audit report. They are typically completed as of the date the audit field work is finished. *After the audit report has been signed, the role of the auditor shifts from an active to a passive one.* This means that the auditor no longer has a responsibility for actively seeking additional audit evidence after the last day of audit field work. However, he or she must still be alert for subsequent discovery of facts that existed at the date of the audit report and that would have affected the financial statements had they been known at that time.

Events Discovered before the Issuance of the Audit Report

The responsibility for events that come to the auditor's attention after the last day of field work depends on whether the events occur (1) during the brief period after the last day of field work and before the actual issuance of the audit report or (2) after the issuance of the audit report. In the first situation, there is still time to intervene in the process before the report is issued if new information comes to the auditor's attention. If such information is, in the auditor's judgment, material enough to warrant inclusion in the financial statements, it must be identified as either a Type 1 or Type 2 event. If it is a Type 1 event, the financial statements should be adjusted and the audit report will bear the same date as the original report.

If it is a Type 2 event requiring only footnote disclosure, the auditor may follow either of two courses of action. If the event is isolated, and no other events of importance have transpired since the last day of field work, the report may be dual dated. Within this arrangement, the opinion as to the newly discovered event disclosed in the footnote is dated as of the date of discovery of that event. The opinion as to the remainder of the disclosures will carry the original date. In this case, the auditor's responsibility for events occurring in the period subsequent to the end of the audit field work is limited to the event referred to in the footnote. On the other hand, if the auditor feels there is a strong possibility that other events may have occurred since the conclusion of field work, subsequent-events field work procedures may be performed up to the date of discovery of the new information. In this case, the entire audit report will be dated as of the date of discovery of the new information,[10] and the auditor's responsibility for events occurring in the subsequent period is extended to the date of discovery of the new information.

Consideration of Omitted Procedures after the Report Date

After the audit report has been issued, the working papers may be subjected to a **post-issuance review** in connection with the auditing firm's quality control program or a peer review by another accounting firm. During this time, it may come to the attention of the auditor that a necessary procedure has been omitted. Examples of such an occurrence might include post-issuance discovery that certain accounts receivable that should have been confirmed were not, in fact, confirmed or that the auditor failed to obtain all of the necessary copies of board of directors' minutes. In these cases there is no indication that omission of auditing procedures failed to detect material misstatements or, indeed, that any misstatement exists. However, the due professional care standard dictates that the auditor should assess the importance of the omitted procedure and, in light of all of the known facts, decide whether the procedure should be performed. A review of working papers, discussion of the circumstances with engagement personnel and others, and a reevaluation of the overall scope of the examination may be helpful in making this assessment. For example, the results of other related procedures that were applied may compensate for the omitted procedure or make its omission less important. Also, if such an omission is discovered in a later year's audit, evidence gathered at the later date may support the previously expressed opinion.

If the auditor concludes that, in fact, the omitted procedure should have been performed and that there are persons currently relying or likely to rely on the previously issued audit opinion, he or she should try to apply the omitted procedure (or acceptable alternative procedure).[11] Such a procedure may lead to the action suggested below for subsequent discovery of facts existing at the audit report date.

Subsequent Discovery of Facts Existing at Audit Report Date

After the completed financial statements and auditor's report are released to the public, the auditor *continues to have a passive responsibility* with respect to material facts existing at the audit report date, but which were not disclosed because they were not known to the auditor at the time the report was issued. Responsibility for subsequent discovery of facts existing at the date of the audit report is governed by the provisions of SAS 1, Section 561.

Under this standard, the auditor has no responsibility for actively searching for erroneous or omitted financial statement disclosures after the report date. However, he or she cannot ignore material facts that come to light after that date if these facts would have had to be disclosed had they been known. Investors and other financial statement users are in possession of information the auditor now knows to be erroneous. Furthermore, they may be relying on such information to make important financial decisions regarding the client. Therefore, the auditor must take steps to correct the disclosures.[12]

Once the auditor determines that the information about erroneous or omitted facts is reliable and that it existed at the date of the audit report, he or she should request that the client make appropriate disclosures of the newly discovered facts, along with the financial statement impact, to persons who are known to be currently relying or who are likely to rely on the financial statements and audit report.[13]

If effects can be promptly determined, revised disclosures should consist of revised financial statements and audit report. When issuance of audited financial statements of a subsequent period is close at hand, revised disclosures may be made in those statements. If effects of misstatements cannot be promptly determined, the client should be asked to notify relying parties that the erroneous financial statements and audit report are not to be relied upon and that revised financial statements and audit report will be issued upon completion of an investigation. Where annual reports or registration statements of publicly traded companies are involved, appropriate disclosure would include notification of the SEC.

If the auditor learns that client management refuses to make the appropriate disclosure of facts as described in the preceding paragraphs, he or she should undertake the following actions:

1. Notify each member of the client's audit committee or board of directors of management's refusal to disclose important facts.
2. Notify the client that the audit report should no longer be associated with the financial statements.
3. Notify regulatory agencies having jurisdiction over the client that the audit report should no longer be relied upon.
4. Notify each party known by the auditor to be relying on the financial statements that the audit report should no longer be relied upon.

In all cases in which subsequent discovery of important facts existing at the audit report date arises, the auditor would be well advised to consult with legal counsel because of the possible legal implications of those events.

Summary

In this chapter we have discussed the completion of the evidence-gathering phase of the audit, in which the auditor finishes field work tests and prepares to issue the audit report. We began with a discussion of the search for and verification of estimated and contingent liabilities, including those arising from possible claims, litigation, or assessments. Then we discussed the post-balance-sheet analytical procedures, during which the auditor forms conclusions about the relationships between findings from tests of details and the more general overview of relationships between audited account balances and the adequacy of footnotes.

The auditor's responsibilities with respect to supplementary data—such as historical summaries, statistical summaries, and other data outside the basic financial statements—were taken up next. The review process for working papers, including procedures directed at evaluating the sufficiency and competency of evidence, was also examined in this section.

In the last part of the chapter, we defined subsequent events and discussed their effects on the audited financial statements and the audit report. Finally, we described the auditor's reactions to the subsequent discovery of facts existing at the date of the audit report. In that section we considered the difference between the auditor's responsibilities while performing an active role in the evidence-gathering process and while assuming a passive role after the audit report date.

Auditing Vocabulary

p. 864 **attorney's letter:** A confirmation letter obtained from the client's attorney that verifies pending or threatened litigation and unasserted claims.

p. 875 **client representation letter:** A letter that documents management's oral representations made during the audit, having the primary purposes of impressing upon management its responsibilities for the data included in the financial statements and for documenting managements' oral responses to the auditors' inquiries during the audit.

p. 863 **contingent liability:** A potential future obligation resulting from past activities.

p. 863 **estimated liability:** A future obligation to an outside party resulting from activities that have already occurred.

p. 877 **post-issuance review:** A review conducted in connection with the auditing firm's quality control program, after issuance of audit reports for particular financial periods.

p. 872 **subsequent event:** Transactions or events that may occur after the balance sheet date and before the issuance of the audit report that affect the disclosures on the client's financial statements.

p. 870 **supplementary data:** Data that are outside the basic financial statements (including footnotes) of the company.

p. 866 **unasserted claims:** A cause for legal action that someone may have against the client but that has not been filed as of the date of the attorney's confirmation letter.

Appendix 20–A: Adjusting Journal Entries

					Balance	Sheet	Income	Statement
					DR.	CR.	DR.	CR.

Mfg. Co.
Adjusting Journal Entries
3-31-X1

W. P. No. A-5
ACCOUNTANT SmL
DATE 5/11/X1

Description	Balance Sheet DR.	Balance Sheet CR.	Income Statement DR.	Income Statement CR.
AJE ⟨1⟩ Prior yr. ⟨2⟩				
Sales			118100749 ✓	
Retained Earnings		27635836 ✓		
Cost of Sales				8285787 6 ✓
Freight				2262749 ✓
Commission				5343988 ✓
To reverse prior year % of completion ADJ				
AJE ⟨2⟩ F-5				
Contract Rev. Earned – not billed 9041389 5 ✓				
Cost of Sale			706082 52 ✓	
Freight			2226430 ✓	
Commissions			607471 0 ✓	
Sales				9871150 35 ✓
WIP		706082 52 ✓		
to record current yr. % completion				
AJE ⟨3⟩ See ⟨104⟩				
Deferred Income	368253 6 ✓			
Retained Earnings	143703 6 ✓			
Obsolete Inventory		3428863 ✓		
Cost of Sales				1169070 9 ✓
(To eliminate Def. Inc. & Obsolete Inv. for F/S Report purposes) (Set up for tax purposes)				
AJE ⟨4⟩ AA-9				
Invest. in Sub.	204143 ✓			
Earning of Sub.				17121 ✓
Retained Earnings		187022 ✓		
To record equity in subsidiary				
AJE ⟨5⟩ AA-9				
Retained Earnings	7903 ✓			
Earning in Sub.			1916 ✓	
Investment in Sub.		9819 ✓		
To amortize excess cost of Sub.				
✓ Posted to T/B				

Note: Other adjusting journal entries have been omitted.

Appendix 20–B: Working Trial Balance—Assets

JEP Manufacturing Co.		
Working Trial Balance – Assets		
3-31-X1		

W. P. No.	A-1
ACCOUNTANT	SmG
DATE	4/28/X1

Assets	Adjusted Balance 3-31-X0	Balance per B/L✓ 3-31-X1	Adjustments DR.	CR.
Cash	845197 2	369289 3		
Marketable Securities	1489480 0	343272 00		
Accounts Receivable				
Trade	5353139 6	10080704 7		
Other (Details Deleted)	227392 5	91179 7		
Notes Receivable	64000 00	54000 00		
Costs + Estimated Earnings	11049371 2	—	(2) 904138 95	
Deposits	57612 5	63112 5		
Prepaid Expenses	2893506	2681855	(100) 10832 8	
Inventory:				
Raw Materials	5915169 6	40646868 3	(103) 647417 23 (102) 99211 3	(103) 105476590
Work in Process	1114219 0	9277416 1	(103) 9005177 33	(2) 706082 52 (103) 9277416 1
In-Transit	2430077	313060 1		(3) 342886 3
Obsolete		557988 9	(104) 342886 3	(104) 557988 9
Total Current Assets	26647840 9	65154525 1	24875054 2	57885984 8
Property, Plant and Equipment				
Machinery and Equipment	5455926 9	5833592 3		
Other (Details Deleted)	11881746 7	12565362 9		
Less: Accumulated Depreciation	(6875920 1)	(77305000 7)		
Net Property, Plant + Equip.	1046175 35	1066845 52		
Investment in Subsidiary	1791119 00	—	(4) 204143 00	(5) 98199 00
Cash Surrender Value of Life Ins.	1255000 0	1453000 0		
Less: Policy Loan	(765000 0)	(765000 0)		
Deferred Debt Expense	48273 0	37014 6		
Total Assets	39439057 4	76547994 9	26916484 2	57984174 8

✓ Agreed to prior year working papers.
✓ Agreed to 3-31-X1 general ledger.

Adjusted Balance 3-31-X1	Reclassifications DR.	Reclassifications CR.	Reclassified Balance 3-31-X1	Working Paper Reference
3692893 (D)	88600		3781493	B
34327200			34327200	C-1
100807047			100807047	E
911797		(E) 215550	696247	(omitted)
540000			540000	(omitted)
90413895			90413895	F
631125			631125	G
2790183			2790183	G
64741723			64741723	F
19449481			19449481	∫
3130601			3130601	
—				
321435945	88600	215550	321308995	
58335923			58335923	I
125653629			125653629	
⟨77305000⟩			⟨77305000⟩	I
106684552			106684552	
19432400			19432400	(omitted)
14530000			14530000	L
⟨7650000⟩			⟨7650000⟩	L
370146			370146	(omitted)
454803043	88600	215550	454676093	

Appendix 20–C: Working Trial Balance— Liabilities and Stockholders' Equities

JEP Manufacturing Co.
Working Trial Balance
Liabilities and Stockholder Equity
3-31-X1

W. P. NO.	A-2
ACCOUNTANT	Smds
DATE	4/28/X1

Liabilities	Adjusted Balance 3-31-X0	Balance Per B/L 3-31-X1	Adjustments DR.	Adjustments CR.
Current:				
Accounts Payable	50041055	50191583		
Intercompany Payable (net)	—	—		
Notes Payable – Banks	17500000	—		
Current Maturities of Long-Term				(105) 4578300
Accrued Expenses	23226904	15213231		(107) 3530288
				(108) 4870000
				(106) 6500000
Reserve Allowance		19432400		
Federal Income Taxes Payable				
Current	410668	(19333132)		(109) 40637662
Deferred	12359966			(6) 58847 32
				(7) 805463
Dividends Payable – Preferred	90300			
Total Current	103628893	65504032		66806475
Deferred Income	—	4177853	(101) 23332	
			(104) 460317	
			(3) 3682536	
Notes Payable				
Coletrain	5965000	2982500		
Xerox	—	689370		
Prudential	40000000	35000000		
Total Liabilities	149593893	108353805	4166185	66806445
Stockholders' Equity:				
Treasury Stock	(1012167)	(1012167)		
Preferred Stock	6020000	—		
Common Stock	7599476	7599476		
Additional Paid-in Capital	3463850	3463850		
Retained Earnings	23872552 22	197644751	(7) 805463	(4) 18702200
			(5) 790300	(1) 27635836
			(6) 12359966	
			(3) 1437036	
Current year earnings – Net		449430234	404262437	
Total Stockholders' Equity	24479668 81	657126144	419655202	46338036
Total liabilities + Stockholder Equity	394390574	765479949	423821387	113144481

✓ Agreed to prior year's working papers.
✓ Agreed to 3-31-X1 general ledger.

Adjusted Balance 3-31-X1	Reclassifications DR.	Reclassifications CR.	Reclassified Balance 3-31-X1	Working Paper Reference
50191583	(E) 26240643		23950940	N-1
		(E) 26025093	26025093	N-1
—			—	M
		(C) 8130220	8130220	Ma
34691819		(D) 88600	34780419	Omitted
19432400			19432400	Omitted
21304530	(F) 1031600		20272930	
6690175		(F) 1031600	7721775	
—			—	
132310527	26240643	34243913	140313797	
11668			11668	Omitted
2982500	(C) 2982500		-0-	M
689370	(C) 147720		541650	M
35000000	(C) 5000000		30000000	M
170994065	34370863	34243913	170867115	
⟨101267⟩			⟨101267⟩	U
—			—	
7599476			7599476	U
3463850			3463850	U
228590022			273757819	U
45167777				U
283808978			283808978	
454803043	34370863	34243913	454676093	

Appendix 20-D: Working Trial Balance—Income Statement

JEP Manufacturing Co.
Trial Balance -- Income Statement
3-31-X1

W. P. NO.	A-3
ACCOUNTANT	Smith
DATE	4-28-X1

	Adjusted Balance ◢ 3-31-X0	Balance per Gen. Ledger 3-31-X1	Adjustments DR.	Adjustments CR.
			(2) 2226430	(1) 2262749
Net Sales	652289605	803308036	(1) 18100449	(2) 98715035
			(2) 70608252	(3) 1690709
Cost of Sales	493906041	226791653	(104) 1690709 (103) 37024293	(103) 226791653 (1) 82857876
Gross Profit	158383564	576516383	76286876	412318022
			(106) 6500000 (105) 4573300	(100) 108328
Selling, Administrative Expenses	96915119	121032921	(102) 992113 (107) 3550288 (103) 4870000 (2) 6074710	(1) 53439888
Motor Control Devices	4050120	5092152		
Operating Income	57418325	450391310	789414179	41777038
Interest and Other Income	5131278	5193271		(101) 23332
Equity in Earnings of Subsidiary	3466800	—	(5) 191600	(4) 1712100
Interest and Debt Expense	8088760	6154347		
Earnings before F.I.T.	57927643	449430234	789605779	419505770
Federal Income Taxes: Current	18010701	—	(109) 4063766 2	
Federal Income Taxes: Deferred	5107066	—		(6) 6475234
	23117767	—	40637662	6475234
Net Earnings	34809876	449430234	830243441	425981004

◢ Agreed to prior year's working papers.
√ Agreed to 3-31-X1 general ledger.

Adjusted Balance 3-31-X1	Reclassifications DR.	CR.	Reclassified Balance 3-31-X1		W/Paper Reference
7839589 41			7839589 41		X
5579933 04			5579933 04		X-4
2259656 37			2259656 37		
1421260 16			1421260 16		X-2
509215 2			509215 2		X-4-1
7874746 9			7874746 9		
521660 3			521660 3		X-7-1
152050 0			152050 0		AA-9
615434 7			615434 7		M
7933022 5			7933022 5		
4063766 2		(F) 80540 0	3983226 2		P-4
⟨ 6475234 7⟩ (F) 80540 0			⟨ 566983 4⟩		P-4
3416242 8	80540 0	80540 0	3416242 8		
4516777 97	80540 0	80540 0	4516777 97		

Appendix 20–E: Reclassifying Journal Entries

JEP mfg. Co.
Reclassifying Journal Entries
3-31-X1

W. P. No. A-6
ACCOUNTANT SmB
DATE 5/11/X1

	Balance Sheet		Income Statement	
	DR.	CR.	DR.	CR.
RJE ⟨A⟩ E-4				
Receivable from East Texas	2155.50			
Misc. Receivables		2155.50 ②		
(To properly reflect receivable from				
East Tex. for consolidating purposes)				
RJE ⟨B⟩ N-1-2				
Accounts Payable	262406.43 ①			
Intercompany Pay to ET		262406.43		
(To reclass A/P to East Tx. Dist.)				
RJE ⟨C⟩ Ma				
Xerox N/P	14772.0 ✓			
Prudential N/P	50000.00 ✓			
Caldwell N/P	29825.00 ✓			
Current Portion L-T Debt		81302.20 ✓		
(to reclassify the current				
portion of Long-Term Debt				
RJE ⟨D⟩ 0-1				
Cash	886.00 ✓			
Accrued Expenses		886.00 ✓		
(To properly reflect deposit-in-				
transit from East Texas)				
RJE ⟨E⟩ Net of ⟨A⟩+⟨B⟩				
Accounts Payable N-1	262406.43 ①			
Intercompany Payable		260250.93 ✓		
Misc. Receivables		2155.50 ②		
late RJE ⟨F⟩ P-4				
Deferred tax expense			8054 ✓	
Current tax liability	10316 ✓			
Current tax expense				8054 ✓
Def. tax liability		10316 ✓		
to properly classify current & def.				
FIT provision at 3-31-X1				
✓ Posted to T/B.				

Notes

1. Developed from appendix to Statement on Auditing Standards (SAS) 12 (New York: AICPA, 1976): 8, 9.
2. Developed from requirements set out in SAS 12.
3. Materials in this section were developed from AU318 (New York: AICPA, 1978, revised 1988), with some direct quotations from that statement.
4. SAS 59 (New York: AICPA, 1988).
5. SAS 8 (New York: AICPA, 1975).
6. SAS 29 (New York: AICPA, 1980).
7. SAS 49 (AU558), *Required Supplementary Information* (New York: AICPA, 1988).
8. SAS 19, paragraph 4 (New York: AICPA, 1977).
9. Developed from illustration in SAS 19 (New York: AICPA, 1977).
10. Ibid., Section 530.
11. "Consideration of Omitted Procedures After the Report Date," SAS 46 (AU390), (New York: AICPA, 1983).
12. Ibid., Section 561.
13. This section does not apply to situations arising from developments or events occurring after the date of the auditor's report. Neither does it apply to ultimate resolutions or final determinations of matters that were contingent on some future event as of the date of the issuance of the report (such as litigation) or to other matters that had been adequately disclosed in the financial statements as of the report issuance date.

Questions for Class Discussion

Q20-1 What is meant by the term *analytical procedure*?

Q20-2 What is the difference between an estimated liability and a contingent liability?

Q20-3 Why does the auditor analyze the client's legal expense account? Explain.

Q20-4 What are some procedures that, even though performed primarily for the other purposes, may disclose contingent liabilities? What liabilities would you expect to discover in performing each of these procedures?

Q20-5 What is the purpose of the attorney's confirmation letter? What items are included in that letter?

Q20-6 How should the auditor react to a failure of the client's attorney to reply to the attorney's confirmation letter? Explain.

Q20-7 What is the basic assumption underlying the analytical process? Explain.

Q20-8 How does the auditor use nonfinancial data in the analytical process?

Q20-9 What does the auditor do in the event that significant variations or unusual relationships are discovered in the analytical process?

Q20-10 How are industry statistics used in the analytical process? Explain.

Q20-11 What are the analytical ratios typically calculated during the performance of analytical procedures? Explain how each of those ratios is used in making judgments regarding the fairness of presentation of the financial data.

Q20-12 What is the auditor's responsibility relating to supplementary data provided by management in the annual report containing audited financial statements? Explain.

Q20-13 What is the general content of the letter of representation that the auditor secures from the client? What purposes does such a letter serve?

Q20-14 What steps are included in the typical public accounting firm's working paper review process? Describe them.

Q20-15 What is the auditor's responsibility relating to transactions and events occurring in the client's business between the end of the audit period and the date of the issuance of the audit report? How does the auditor react to the discovery of these events?

Q20-16 What are at least two subsequent events that could occur between the end of the period under audit and the date of the audit report, requiring the auditor to recommend adjustment of the financial statements?

Q20-17 What three or more actions might the client take between the end of the period under audit and the date of the audit report that would require disclosure in the end-of-period financial statements? Justify your action in each situation.

Q20-18 How do the auditor's responsibilities relating to subsequent events change after the audit report has been issued? Explain.

Q20-19 Facts existing prior to the date of the audit report that significantly affect the audited financial statements of the client are discovered after the audit report has been issued; how should the auditor react to this situation? Explain.

Short Cases

C20-1 Julie Hollingsworth, CPA, is auditing the financial statements of Hobart, Inc. In the process of her audit, she discovers the following information:

a. Litigation involving a patent infringement lawsuit, filed against the company in the prior year, is about to be settled out of court for $75,000.

b. A disgruntled employee has notified the company that she plans to file a wage discrimination suit against the company next month (after the balance sheet date but before the issuance of the audit report).

c. The company has been in violation of the "Clean Air Act" for a period of six years. To date, no claims have arisen, but the president of the company has a note on his desk to return the call of the state director of environmental protection.

d. The company has guaranteed the debt of an affiliate in the amount of $2,000,000.

e. Delinquent payroll taxes are due because the payroll clerk became ill and has been on sick leave for a month.

Required:

a. Define the term "loss contingency" as it is used in FASB Statement Number 5.

b. Which, if any, of the items above meet the definition of loss contingency? Explain.

c. What audit procedure(s) would have brought each of the above situations to light?

    d. Discuss other audit procedures that are typically used to test for loss contingencies related to claims, litigation, and assessments.

    e. Do you think that any of the above items, if properly disclosed, should have an impact on the auditor's report?

C20-2 Dan Peters, CPA, is finishing the audit work of Nolen Plastics, Inc. He is considering performing analytical procedures as a part of his wrap-up work for the engagement.

    Required:

    a. Are analytical procedures required at this stage of the audit? Why or why not?

    b. Discuss the types of analytical procedures that would be useful for a medium-sized manufacturing concern during this stage of the audit.

    c. What are the possible explanations of material fluctuations between accounts or items of the financial statements? Which ones of those explanations should have been accounted for by this stage? Why?

    d. Describe the actions that Peters should take if he should discover an unusual unexpected fluctuation in an account balance or relationship at this stage of the audit.

C20-3 In connection with his examination of Flowmeter, Inc., for the year ended December 31, 19X3 Hirsch, CPA, is aware that certain events and transactions that took place after December 31, 19X3, but before he issues his report dated February 28, 19X4, may affect the company's financial statements.

    The following material events or transactions have come to his attention:

    1. On January 3, 19X4, Flowmeter, Inc., received a shipment of raw materials from Canada. The materials had been ordered in October 19X3 and shipped FOB shipping point in November 19X3.

    2. On January 15, 19X4, the company settled and paid a personal injury claim of a former employee as the result of an accident which occurred in March 19X3. The company had not previously recorded a liability for the claim.

    3. On January 25, 19X4, the company agreed to purchase for cash the outstanding stock of Porter Electrical Co. The acquisition is likely to double the sales volume of Flowmeter, Inc.

    4. On February 1, 19X4, a plant owned by Flowmeter, Inc., was damaged by a flood resulting in an uninsured loss of inventory.

    5. On February 5, 19X4, Flowmeter, Inc., issued and sold to the general public $2,000,000 in convertible bonds.

    Required: For each of the above events or transactions, indicate the audit procedures that should have brought the item to the attention of the auditor, and the form of disclosure in the financial statements including the reasons for such disclosures.

    Arrange your answer in the following format.

Item No.	Audit Procedures	Required Disclosure and Reasons

(AICPA adapted)

C20-4 You are examining the financial statements of Moderate Manufacturing Corporation in connection with the preparation of financial statements to be issued with an unqualified opinion. There are some strengths in internal control, but the office and bookkeeping staff comprises only three persons. You have tested a random sample of acquisition transactions in detail and found no significant exceptions.

Required:

a. Set up a detailed audit program, explaining the steps you consider necessary in connection with the following expense accounts (the total of one year's charges in each account is set forth opposite each item):

Advertising	$60,000
Rent	$ 8,000
Salesman's commission	$39,000
Insurance	$ 4,000

b. State what documents or evidence you as an auditor would examine in the verification of each of the following:
1. Advertising expense, where advertising is placed through an agency.
2. Advertising expense, where advertising is placed directly in newspapers by the client.
3. Royalty expense.
4. Repair expense.

c. Under what circumstances would you forego analytical procedures on the above accounts?

(AICPA adapted)

Problems

P20-1 Select the best answer to each of the following items relating to analytical procedures of income statement account balances.

a. Auditors sometimes use comparison of ratios as audit evidence. For example, an unexplained decrease in the ratio of gross profit to sales may suggest which of the following possibilities?
1. Unrecorded purchases.
2. Unrecorded sales.
3. Merchandise purchases being charged to selling and general expense.
4. Fictitious sales.

b. Of the following procedures, which is the *most* important for an auditor to use when making an overall review of the income statement?
1. Select sales and expense items, and trace amounts to related supporting documents.
2. Compare actual revenues and expenses with the corresponding figures of the previous year and investigate significant differences.
3. Obtain from the proper client representatives, inventory certificates for the beginning and ending inventory amounts (used to determine cost of sales).
4. Ascertain that the net income amount in the statement of changes in financial position agrees with the net income amount in the income statement.

   c. Overall analysis of income statement accounts may bring to light errors, omissions, and inconsistencies *not* disclosed in the overall analysis of balance sheet accounts. The income statement analysis can *best* be accomplished by comparing monthly

      1. Income statement ratios to balance sheet ratios.

      2. Revenue and expense account balances to the monthly reported net income.

      3. Income statement ratios to published industry averages.

      4. Revenue and expense account totals to the corresponding figures of the preceding years.

   d. An auditor is reviewing changes in sales for two products. Sales volume (quantity) declined 10 percent for product A and 2 percent for product B. Sales prices were increased by 25 percent for both products. Prior-year sales were $75,000 for A and $25,000 for B. The auditor would expect this year's total sales for the two products to be approximately

      1. $112,500.

      2. $115,000.

      3. $117,000.

      4. $120,000.

(AICPA adapted)

P20-2 Select the best answer to each of the following items relating to clients and client/attorney relationships.

   a. As part of an audit, a CPA often requests a representation letter from his client. Which one of the following is *not* a valid purpose of such a letter?

      1. To provide audit evidence.

      2. To emphasize to the client his or her responsibility for the correctness of the financial statements.

      3. To satisfy himself or herself by means of other auditing procedures when certain customary auditing procedures are not performed.

      4. To provide possible protection to the CPA against a charge of knowledge in cases where fraud is subsequently discovered to have existed in the accounts.

   b. Management furnishes the independent auditor with information concerning litigation, claims, and assessments. Which of the following is the auditor's primary means of initiating action to corroborate such information?

      1. Request that client lawyers undertake a reconsideration of matters of litigation, claims, and assessments with which they are consulted during the period under examination.

      2. Request that client management send a letter of audit inquiry to those lawyers with whom management consulted concerning litigation, claims, and assessments.

      3. Request that client lawyers provide a legal opinion concerning the policies and procedures adopted by management to identify, evaluate, and account for litigation, claims, and assessments.

      4. Request that client management engage outside attorneys to suggest wording for the text of a footnote explaining the nature and probable outcome of existing litigation, claims, and assessments.

   c. A CPA has received an attorney's letter in which *no* significant disagreements with the client's assessments of contingent liabilities were noted. The resignation of the client's lawyer shortly after receipt of the letter should alert the auditor that

      1. Undisclosed, unasserted claims may have arisen.

    2. The attorney was unable to form a conclusion with respect to the significance of litigation, claims, and assessments.

    3. The auditor must begin a completely new examination of contingent liabilities.

    4. An adverse opinion will be necessary.

d. A lawyer's response to a letter of audit inquiry may be limited to matters that are considered individually or collectively material to the financial statements if

    1. The auditor has instructed the lawyer regarding the limits of materiality in financial statements.

    2. The client and the auditor have agreed on the limits of materiality and the lawyer has been notified.

    3. The lawyer and auditor have reached an understanding on the limits of materiality for this purpose.

    4. The lawyer's response to the inquiry explains the legal meaning of materiality limits and establishes quantitative parameters.

e. An auditor will ordinarily examine invoices from lawyers primarily in order to

    1. Substantiate accruals.

    2. Assess the legal ramifications of litigation in progress.

    3. Estimate the dollar amount of contingent liabilities.

    4. Identify possible unasserted litigation, claims, and assessments.

(AICPA adapted)

P20-3 Select the best answer to each of the following items relating to subsequent events.

a. Which event that occurred after the end of the fiscal year under audit but prior to issuance of the auditor's report would *not* require disclosure in the financial statements?

    1. Sale of a bond or capital stock issue.

    2. Loss of plant or inventories as a result of fire or flood.

    3. A major drop in the quoted market price of the stock of the corporation.

    4. Settlement of litigation, when the event giving rise to the claim took place after the balance sheet date.

b. A client has a calendar year-end. Listed below are four events that occurred after December 31. Which one of these subsequent events might result in adjustment of the December 31 financial statements?

    1. Adoption of accelerated depreciation methods.

    2. Write-off of a substantial portion of inventory as obsolete.

    3. Collection of 90 percent of the accounts receivable existing at December 31.

    4. Sale of a major subsidiary.

c. The auditor's formal review of subsequent events normally should be extended through the date of the

    1. Auditor's report.

    2. Next formal interim financial statements.

    3. Delivery of the audit report to the client.

    4. Mailing of the financial statements to the stockholders.

d. In connection with the annual audit, which of the following is *not* a "subsequent events" procedure?

    1. Review available interim financial statements.

    2. Read available minutes of meetings of stockholders, directors, and committees, and inquire about matters dealt with at meetings for which minutes are *not* available.

3. Make inquiries with respect to the financial statements covered by the auditor's previously issued report if new information that might affect that report has become available during the current examination.
4. Discuss with officers the current status of items in the financial statements that were accounted for on the basis of tentative, preliminary, or inconclusive data.

e. Jerry Jones, CPA, examined the 19X3 financial statements of Ray Corp. and issued an unqualified opinion on March 10, 19X4. On April 2, 19X4, Jones became aware of a 19X3 transaction that may materially affect the 19X3 financial statements. This transaction would have been investigated had it come to Jones's attention during the course of the examination. Jones should

1. Take *no* action because an auditor is *not* responsible for events subsequent to the issuance of the auditor's report.
2. Contact Ray's management and request their cooperation in investigating the matter.
3. Request that Ray's management disclose the possible effects of the newly discovered transaction by adding an unaudited footnote to the 19X3 financial statements.
4. Contact all parties who might rely upon the financial statements and advise them that the financial statements are misleading.

(AICPA adapted)

P20-4 Select the best answer to each of the following items relating to the search for contingent and unrecorded liabilities.

a. When auditing contingent liabilities, which of the following procedures would be *least* effective?
1. Abstracting the minutes of the board of directors' meetings.
2. Reviewing the bank confirmation letter.
3. Examining customer confirmation replies.
4. Examining invoices for professional services.

b. A company sells a particular product only in the last month of its fiscal year. The company uses commission agents for such sales and pays them 6 percent of their *net sales* thirty days after the sales are made. The agents' sales were $10 million. Experience indicates that 10 percent of the sales are usually *not* collected and 2 percent are returned in the first month of the new year. The auditor would expect the year-end balance in the accrued commissions payable account to be
1. $528,000.
2. $540,000.
3. $588,000.
4. $600,000.

c. The auditing procedures used to verify accrued liabilities differ from those employed for verification of accounts payable because
1. Accrued liabilities usually pertain to services of a continuing nature, while accounts payable are the result of completed transactions.
2. Accrued liability balances are less material than accounts payable balances.
3. Evidence supporting accrued liabilities is nonexistent, while evidence supporting accounts payable is readily available.
4. Accrued liabilities at year-end will become accounts payable during the following year.

    d. A company guarantees the debt of an affiliate. Which of the following *best* describes the auditing procedure that would make the auditor aware of the guarantee?

      1. Review minutes and resolutions of the board of directors' meetings.

      2. Review prior year's working papers with respect to such guarantees.

      3. Review the possibility of such guarantees with the chief accountant.

      4. Review the legal representation letter returned by the company's outside legal counsel.

P20-5 During an audit engagement, Rick Harper, CPA, has satisfactorily completed an examination of accounts payable and other liabilities and now plans to determine whether there are any loss contingencies arising from litigation, claims, or assessments.

Required: What are the auditing procedures that Harper should follow with respect to the existence of loss contingencies arising from litigation, claims, and assessments? Do not discuss reporting requirements.

(AICPA adapted)

P20-6 Saul Windek, a CPA, is nearing the completion of an examination of the financial statements of Jubilee, Inc., for the year ended December 31, 19X0. Windek is currently concerned with ascertaining the occurrence of subsequent events that may require adjustment or disclosure essential to a fair presentation in conformity with generally accepted accounting principles.

Required:

    a. Briefly explain what is meant by the phrase *subsequent event*.

    b. How do those subsequent events that require financial statement adjustment differ from those that require financial statement disclosure?

    c. What procedures should be performed in order to ascertain the occurrence of subsequent events?

(AICPA adapted)

P20-7 During 19X2, Waldron Company introduced a new line of machines that carry a two-year warranty against manufacturer's defects. Based on industry experience, the estimated warranty costs related to dollar sales are as follows:

Year of sale   4%
Year after sale   6%

Sales and actual warranty expenditures for the years ended December 31, 19X2, and December 31, 19X3, were as follows:

	Sales	Actual warranty expenditures
19X2	$ 500,000	$15,000
19X3	700,000	47,000
	$1,200,000	$62,000

Assume that sales and warranty expenditures have occurred evenly over the two years.

Required:
  a. Based on the data provided above, what amount is shown in the estimated liability for warranty account on 12/31/X3?
  b. Evaluate the adequacy of the recorded balance for estimated liability for warranty. Show supporting calculations.

P20-8 In connection with his examination of the financial statements of the Time Corporation, Henry Burrell is reviewing the federal income taxes payable account.

With the approval of its board of directors, the Time Corporation made a sizable payment for advertising during the year being audited. The corporation deducted the full amount in its federal income tax return. The controller acknowledges that this deduction probably will be disallowed because it relates to political matters. He has not provided for this disallowance in his federal income tax provision and refuses to do so because he fears that this will cause the revenue agent to believe that the deduction is not valid.

Required:
  a. Discuss reasons why Burrell should review federal income tax returns for prior years and the reports of internal revenue agents. What information will these reviews provide? (Do not discuss specific tax return items.)
  b. What is the CPA's responsibility in the tax provision issue? Explain.

(AICPA adapted)

P20-9 The Lewis Company, a manufacturer of heavy machinery, grants a four-year warranty on its products. The estimated liability for product warranty account shows the following transactions for the year:

Opening balance	$45,000
Provision for current year sales	20,000
	65,000
Cost of servicing claims	12,000
Ending balance	$53,000

A review of unsettled claims and the company's experience indicates that the required balance at the end of the year is $80,000, including claims likely to be made against current-year sales.

The balance in estimated income taxes payable is $27,000, which adequately covers any additional liability for prior years' income taxes and includes a $25,000 provision for the current year. For income tax purposes only the cost of servicing claims may be deducted as an expense.

The following additional information is available from the company's records at the end of the current year. Cost of sales includes the $20,000 provision for warranty expense.

Gross sales	$2,040,000
Sales returns and allowances	40,000
Cost of goods sold	1,350,000
Selling and administrative expense	600,000
Net income before income taxes	50,000

Required: Prepare the necessary adjusting journal entries, giving effect to the proper accounting treatment of product warranty and federal income taxes. Support each entry with clearly detailed computations. The books have not been closed. Assume a rate of 50 percent for income tax calculations.

(AICPA adapted)

P20-10 You secure the following information from City Gas Company relating to your client's operations for the year under audit.

	Last year	This year	Increase (decrease)
Average number of customers	27,000	26,000	(1,000)
MCF sales	486,000	520,000	34,000
Revenue	$1,215,000	$1,274,000	$59,000

Required: Explain this year's increase in operating revenues by preparing an analysis showing the effect of changes in
a. Average number of customers.
b. Average gas consumption per customer.
c. Average rate per MCF sold (MCF = thousand cubit feet).

P20-11 The Borow Corporation is an importer and wholesaler. Its merchandise is purchased from a number of suppliers and is warehoused by Borow Corporation until sold to consumers.

In conducting an audit for the year ended June 30, 19X1, the company's CPA determined that the internal control structure was good. Accordingly, the physical inventory was observed at an interim date, May 31, 19X1, instead of at year-end.

The following information was obtained from the general ledger:

Inventory, July 1, 19X0	$ 87,500
Physical inventory, May 31, 19X1	95,000
Sales for eleven months ended May 31, 19X1	840,000
Sales for year ended June 30, 19X0	960,000
Purchases for eleven months ended May 31, 19X1 (before audit adjustments)	675,000
Purchases for year ended June 30, 19X1 (before audit adjustments)	800,000

The CPA's audit disclosed the following information:

Shipments received in May and included in the physical inventory but recorded as June purchases	$7,500
Shipments received in unsaleable condition and excluded from physical inventory. Credit memos had not been received nor had chargebacks to vendors been recorded	
Total at May 31, 19X1	1,000
Total at June 30, 19X1 (including May unrecorded chargebacks)	1,500
Deposit made with vendor and charged to purchases in April 19X1. Product was shipped in July 19X1	2,000
Deposit made with vendor and charged to purchases in May 19X1. Product was shipped FOB destination, on May 29, 19X1, and was included in May 31, 19X1 physical inventory as goods in transit	5,500
Through the carelessness of the receiving department a June shipment was damaged by rain. This shipment was later sold at its cost of $10,000 in June	

Required: A frequently used auditing procedure is to test the reasonableness of the year-end inventory by the application of gross profit ratios. Prepare in good form the following schedules:

a. Computation of the gross profit ratio for eleven months ended May 31, 19X1.
b. Computation by the gross profit ratio method of cost of goods sold during June 19X1.
c. Computation by the gross profit ratio method of June 30, 19X1 inventory.

(AICPA adapted)

P20-12 The Bell Co. asks your help in determining the amount of loss in connection with a fire that destroyed part of the company's inventory and some of the accounting records. You are able to obtain the following information from the records available:

a. The fire occurred on July 15.
b. The last physical inventory was taken on the previous January 31, and the inventory at that time, at cost, was $23,000.
c. The face amount of the insurance policy covering inventory is $15,000, and the policy carries an 80 percent coinsurance clause.
d. Accounts payable were $12,000 on January 31, and $14,000 at the time the fire occurred.
e. Payments to vendors from January 31 to the date of the fire amounted to $71,000.
f. All sales are on account, and accounts receivable were $15,000 at January 31 and $12,000 at the date of the fire.
g. Collections on receivables from January 31 to the date of the fire amounted to $97,000.
h. Most articles sell at approximately 25 percent in excess of cost. An inventory of merchandise not destroyed by the fire amounted to $16,000 at cost on July 15.

Required:
a. Determine the estimated value of inventory lost due to the fire.
b. How much can the company recover from the insurance company?

P20-13 This problem completes the case study of T&H, Inc., which began in Problem 7-5 and continued in Problem 8-12.

You are the audit senior in charge of the field work for T&H, Inc. During your review of the detailed audit working papers, you discover that your three audit staff persons have proposed a number of adjusting entries for your consideration. These proposed adjustments are the result of audit procedures developed based on our understanding of the control structure and assessment of control risk for T&H, Inc., in Problem 8-12. The proposed adjusting entries are as follows:

1. T&H, Inc. uses several different bank accounts in its operations. As mentioned in Problem 8-12 (2)(a), bank transfer schedules are not regularly prepared. Consequently, a $40,000 transfer made by the treasurer on December 31 from one account to another was recorded only as a receipt and not a disbursement. The account credited to offset the charge to cash was account 560, Miscellaneous-Net.
2. The cash receipts clerk is responsible for reconciling the bank statements. Recall from Problem 8-12 (1)(a) that there is no review of monthly bank reconciliations by supervisors. Not being able to account for a $86,583 increase in the account, the clerk creates a "reconciling item" of $86,583 to make the reconciliation balance. When the auditors recomputed interest expense, it is discovered that a note payable for $86,583 to the bank was not recorded.
3. Sales are recorded on the day the accounting department receives the invoice

[Problem 8-12 (1)(b)], rather than the date of shipment. A shipment in the amount of $170,097 was shipped on December 31. The invoice was received by the bookkeeper on January 4 and recorded that same day.

4. Historically, the percentages of accounts receivable that were provided for as doubtful accounts has been adequate in terms of the accounts that subsequently have had to be written off. Those percentages were

0–30 days	0.00%
30–60 days	5.00%
60–90 days	10.00%
over 90 days	20.00%

The company's aging schedule of accounts receivable, audited by one of the assistants, showed the following amounts in the various categories for accounts receivable:

Category	Amount	Subsequent collections
0–30 days	$2,608,957	$2,003,259
30–60 days	1,063,008	875,987
60–90 days	365,987	309,886
over 90 days	232,093	47,463
Allowance	46,963	
Net	4,220,082	

5. During the price testing of raw-materials inventory (Account No. 120) the assistant accountant assigned to inventory vouched the prices of raw-materials inventory purchases to vendor invoices. Recall from Problem 8–12 (2)(b) that purchases are recorded based on the catalog price, rather than the price on the invoice. A total of 112 items of inventory were price tested. In these items, the assistant discovered a total of $1,355.33 net overstatement. Raw-materials inventory consists of 11,000 items. The 112-item sample was selected on the basis of a statistical sampling plan that utilized the difference estimation technique. The confidence level for estimation of total error was 95%. The standard error of the difference was valued at $1.03. Assume that your materiality threshold for error for raw-materials inventory is $40,000.

6. During the audit of cash account 100, an NSF check from a customer was discovered in the amount of $23,789.

7. During the audit of accounts receivable, a number of confirmation requests were not returned by customers. It was discovered, after noting the weakness identified in Problem 8-12 (1)(c), that one of the bookkeepers was stealing inventory and making fictitious journal entries for the sales of inventory on account. The amount of the theft totalled $154,500.

8. The examination of property and equipment [prompted by internal control weakness (2)(c) in Problem 8-12] revealed that the fixed assets accounting clerk had made a mistake in writing off a building that had been sold during the year. The building had a cost value of $64,000, a useful life of twenty years, zero salvage value, and was being depreciated on the straight-line method. It was sold at the beginning of its eleventh year of usage. The clerk removed the net carrying value from the building account and nothing from the accumulated depreciation account. The building was sold for $75,000.

9. Also during the audit of property and equipment, the assistant analyzed the rent expense account (No. 521 in the trial balance). In that account he found twelve monthly charges of $18,166.67 for rent expense on a very large warehouse that had been used for the past five years for storage. The lease agreement was a month-to-month lease with no option to purchase. In addition to those charges, the assistant found in the current year, five monthly charges of $3,000 each for rent on equipment. On examination of the lease agreement, the assistant discovered the lease transfers ownership of the equipment to the lessee during the 48th month (the last month of the lease) for a total consideration of $10,000. The economic life of the equipment is four years. The market rate of interest is currently 11% and is expected to remain at that level during the term of the lease. The cash price of the machinery was $120,000. T&H, Inc. uses the straight-line depreciation method for manufacturing equipment.

10. The confirmation letter from the company's actuarial expert regarding the pension plan indicated that the company accrued $15,000 too much in pension costs to meet this year's contribution to the plan.

Required: Analyze each of the proposed adjusting entries using the accompanying LOTUS program (MATERIAL.WKS). Instructions for this program follow this problem.

Using the financial data provided by the computer program, the knowledge of T&H, Inc. that you have gained from Problems 7-5 and 8-12, and other relevant factors (e.g., nature of the account), decide whether to post or pass each proposed adjustment. Be prepared to discuss the reasoning behind each decision.

Computer Instructions for Problem 20-13

Use the LOTUS command "/ File Retrieve" to load the program. The file to be loaded is named MATERIAL.WKS.

A menu will appear after the program has been loaded. You can select a menu option in one of two ways. One way is to press the key corresponding to the first letter of your menu choice. For example, to select the menu option *Input,* simply press the letter '*I.*' The other way to select a menu option is to use the arrow keys to position the cursor over your choice and then to press the *Enter* key.

Step 1. Input the data

Select the *Input* option. Enter the proposed adjustments in journal entry form. Begin the first entry in the first available line. Skip *one* line between each entry. Use a positive number for a debit, and a negative number for a credit. For example, a $50,000 sale on credit and the cash payment of $7,000 rent would be recorded as follows:

Entry #	Acc.#	Account	Amount
1	101	Accounts Receivable	50,000
	500	Sales	−50,000
2	521	Rent Expense	7,000
	100	Cash	−7,000

To erase an entry press the space bar and then press the *Enter* key.

After you have entered the data, press the *Enter* key to return to the main menu. If nothing happens, press the *Enter* key a second time, and you will return to the main menu.

Step 2. Post the entries

After entering the proposed adjustments, select the *Post* option. The computer will post your entries to the trial balance. This process is somewhat lengthy (about 10 minutes), so please be patient.

Selecting the *Post* option more than once will *not* double-post the entries. Thus, to add, change, or delete an entry, simply repeat Steps 1 and 2.

Step 3. Analyze the entries

After the adjustments have been posted, select the *Analyze* option. This option will calculate the effect of each proposed adjustment, as well as the total effect of all of the proposed adjustments, on several financial measurements.

You may look at the analysis on the screen by using the *View* option or get a printout of the output by selecting the *Print* option.

Step 4. Save the data

Select the *Save* option to save your work on the disk. If you do not save the file, it will remain as it was when you first booted it up.

Troubleshooting

Selecting the *Print* option when the printer is not turned on will cause the program to "crash," and the menu will not work. Normally, the letters CMD will be highlighted at the bottom of the screen. If the program crashes, these letters will disappear. If this happens, do not worry because you have *not* lost your data. Press *Alt* and *P* simultaneously to restart the program. The letters CMD will then reappear at the bottom of the screen, and the menu will work properly.

PART V

Reports and
Other Services

CHAPTER **21**

The Audit Report

Objectives

☐ **1.** Be able to differentiate the reporting responsibility of management from the reporting responsibility of the independent auditor.
☐ **2.** Know the meaning of the phrase *association with financial statements.*
☐ **3.** Know the auditor's standard unqualified report.
☐ **4.** Recognize situations requiring departures from the unqualified audit report.
☐ **5.** Recognize situations that may require the addition of explanatory language to the unqualified audit report.
☐ **6.** Be able to update and reissue audit reports on comparative financial statements.

In Chapter 1, we defined auditing as the systematic process of gathering objective evidence regarding economic assertions, ascertaining correspondence of those assertions with established criteria, and *communicating the results* to interested users. As shown in the illustration on the following page, the culmination of the audit process and, therefore, the ultimate goal of the independent audit, is the aggregation of the conclusions from the various segments of the audit to form the audit report on the financial statements.

To meet the requirements for clear and unambiguous communications, the accounting profession has adopted four generally accepted standards that the auditor must meet in reporting the findings of the audit. Those standards were listed in Figure 2–1 and were discussed briefly in Chapter 2. It would be helpful to familiarize yourself with them again before proceeding. In this chapter, we examine the criteria that must be met in fulfilling the requirements of the reporting standards of auditing.

Appendixes to the chapter contain information on more specialized reporting topics, such as reports on segment information, supplementary information, reports on information accompanying the basic financial statements in auditor-submitted documents, and reports on condensed financial statements and selected financial data.

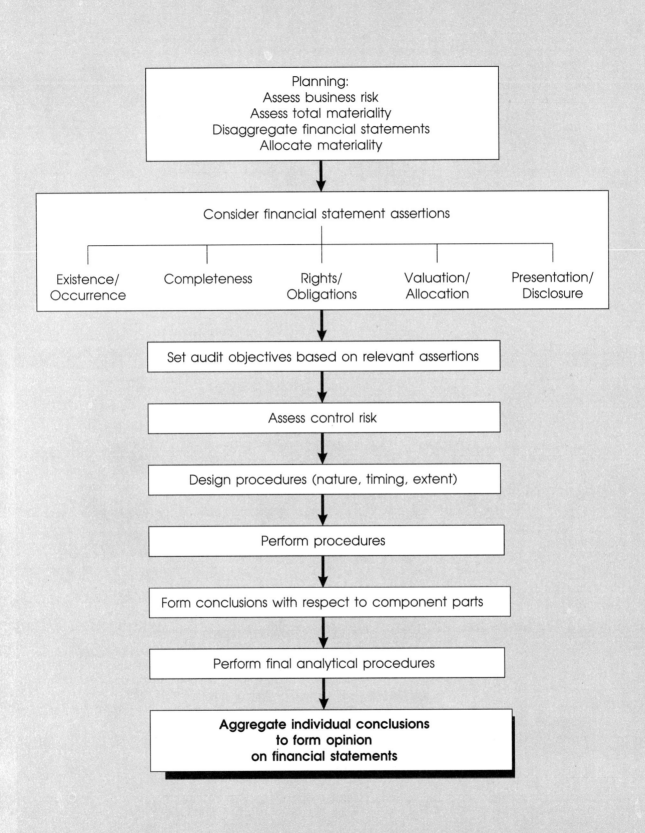

Reporting Responsibilities of Management and the Auditor

☑ **Objective 1**
Differentiate
management
and auditor
responsibilities

Financial statements belong to the client company. Management of the company, therefore, has the primary responsibility for the fairness and completeness of all disclosures contained in them. That fact is clearly stated in the unqualified audit report contained in Figure 1–3, as well as the report of management of JEP Manufacturing Company in Figure 5–1. If the auditor finds that the financial statements contain uncorrected errors or irregularities, financial statements may be adjusted to reflect GAAP *only with the client's permission*.

The responsibility to express an opinion on the financial statements, however, belongs to the independent auditor. Thus, the auditor controls the content of the audit report. It must be written to communicate clearly and effectively the following things:

1. The responsibilities of both management and auditor.
2. The nature and scope of audit activities performed and the results of those activities.
3. The degree of assurance that the auditor is providing regarding the fairness of presentation of the financial statements.

If management declines to make essential financial disclosures, the third reporting standard requires that the auditor provide them in the audit report and appropriately modify the opinion to recognize the omission.

Association with Financial Statements

☑ **Objective 2**
Know the meaning
of *association*

The fourth standard of reporting is probably the most complex of all the reporting standards. It requires that the audit report contain either an expression of opinion regarding the financial statements taken as a whole or an assertion that an opinion cannot be expressed and the reasons therefor. Furthermore, any time an accountant's name is *associated* with financial statements, the report is required to contain a clear indication of the character of the accountant's examination, if any, and the degree of responsibility taken.

A professional accountant may be required to wear any or all of several hats in service to clients, depending on the complexity of their business and their individual needs. A CPA's services can range from bookkeeping for smaller, nonsophisticated businesses to audits of major corporations. Some of the services rendered by CPAs require no representation as to the quality of the client's financial statements. An example of such services is the preparation of tax returns. However, all services that require the accountant to be associated with the financial statements, whether as an auditor or in other capacities, require an accountant's report or letter that meets the requirements of the fourth reporting standard.

A key element, therefore, in understanding the accountant's reporting obligation is understanding what it means to be **associated with financial statements**. Figure 21–1 depicts the possible levels of an accountant's association with financial statements and serves as a preview of our discussion in Chapters 21, 22, and 23.

Generally, the clients of CPA firms may be classified into two broad categories: public entities and nonpublic entities. For this purpose, a **public entity** is defined as

> . . . any entity (a) whose securities trade in a public market either on a stock exchange (domestic or foreign) or in the over-the-counter market, including securities quoted only locally or regionally; (b) that makes a filing with a regulatory agency in preparation for the sale of any class of its securities in a public market; or (c) that is a subsidiary, corporate joint venture, or other entity controlled by an entity covered in (a) or (b).[1]

The financial reporting practices of public entities are governed by the Securities Exchange Commission (SEC). Among the requirements of the SEC for a public company is that an annual report be issued to stockholders containing the company's audited financial statements. By far, the most common association that an independent accountant can have with the financial statements of a public entity is as an auditor. However, the accountant's *association* with financial statements can include at least two more superficial levels. At the minimum, an accountant is considered associated with financial statements when he or she has consented to the use of his or her name in a report, document, or written communication (except tax returns) containing the statements. This is true whether or not the accountant appends his or her name to the statements.

The most remote level of association for public entities is with unaudited financial statements. The most remote level of association for nonpublic entities is the **compilation** of a client's financial statements. In this type of engagement, the accountant merely prepares unaudited financial statements from the books and records of the client. The next level of association for both public and nonpublic entities involves reviews of either annual or interim financial information. A review consists largely of *inquiry and analytical* procedures, which, while they are

Figure 21–1

Levels of Auditor's Association with Financial Statements

	Public entities			Nonpublic entities		
	(1) Unaudited statements	(2) Review*	(3) Audit	(1) Compilation	(2) Review	(3) Audit
Level of association						
Degree of assurance given by accountant	None	Negative	Positive	None	Negative	Positive
Primary authoritative documents	SAS 26	SAS 36	SAS 58	SSARS 1**	SSARS 1**	SAS 58

*May be performed for public or nonpublic entities.
**Statements on Standards for Accounting Review Services.

auditing procedures, are not sufficient for the expression of an audited opinion. Compilations and reviews are discussed at length in Chapter 23. The closest level of association possible for the accountant for either type entity is the *audit*. Notice that as the level of association becomes closer, the level of assurance expected from the accountant increases from none at the most remote level to a positive expression of an opinion on the financial statements at the closest level.

Again observe that the fourth standard of reporting applies to any financial statement with which the accountant is associated. In this chapter we concentrate our discussion on reporting responsibilities for the *audit level of association (level 3) for both public and nonpublic entities and for unaudited financial statements (level 1)* of public entities. Reporting responsibilities for the other levels of association are discussed in Chapters 22 and 23.

The Unqualified Audit Report

☑ **Objective 3**
Know the auditor's
standard report

The report with an unqualified opinion (Figure 1–3, page 12) is the type of report most frequently found in corporate annual reports. Following are brief highlights of the features of an **unqualified audit report**:

1. It has a title that includes the word *independent*.
2. It has three paragraphs: introductory, scope, and opinion.
3. The *introductory paragraph* begins with a statement that the financial statements were audited, and then lists very specifically the financial statements involved and the dates covered. It also contains statements that outline and differentiate the responsibilities of management and those of the auditor.
4. The *scope paragraph* begins with the statement that the audit was conducted in accordance with generally accepted auditing standards (GAAS). It contains an explanation that GAAS require that the auditor plan and perform the audit to obtain *reasonable assurance* about whether the financial statements are free from *material misstatement*. It also contains a brief description of the audit, and the auditor's statement as to whether he or she believes that the audit provides a reasonable basis for the opinion.
5. The *opinion paragraph* contains the statement as to whether, in the auditor's opinion, the financial statements are presented fairly, in all material respects, in accordance with GAAP.
6. The manual or printed signature of the firm is attached.
7. The date of the report, which is the end of field work, is attached.

The audit report must always be issued on the "**financial statements taken as a whole**." This phrase refers to the four basic financial statements for the *current period as well as all prior years presented for comparative purposes*. Therefore, the number of financial statements that are referenced in the audit report is controlled by the number of statements that are included in the company's annual report.

Typically, auditors remain associated with their clients over a period of years. When that occurs they become known as **continuing auditors**. If the annual report of a company includes comparative statements for two years, the audit report must cover both years if the auditor has performed the audits for both years. In essence, then, by issuing an unqualified audit report with comparative financial statements, the continuing auditor is issuing two separate opinions:

1. An unqualified audit opinion on the financial statements of the current year; and
2. An *updated* unqualified audit opinion on the financial statements for the preceding year, if that type opinion was issued in the previous year.

If the prior-year statements are unaudited, they should be marked "unaudited," and the auditor should limit his or her opinion to the audited statements. A separate paragraph describing the responsibility assumed for the statements of the prior period should be included.

The report with an unqualified audit opinion can be issued only if the following circumstances are present:

*   The auditor has gathered *sufficient competent evidence* to assure that the three standards of audit field work have been met.
*   Audit evidence has revealed no significant uncorrected departures from GAAP.
*   The auditor is independent.

Reports with Other Than Unqualified Opinions

☑ **Objective 4**
Recognize situations requiring qualified or extreme reports

In this section, we discuss circumstances that require reports with other than unqualified opinions.[2] These represent the *absence* of one or more of the essentials for the unqualified opinion in the list in the previous section. The presence of one of these circumstances requires the issuance of a **qualified audit opinion**. Figure 21–2 presents the range of qualification alternatives that are available to the auditor.

As shown in Figure 21–2, if the effects of the qualification are *pervasive* (i.e., if they have a material impact on the financial statements taken as a whole), a more extreme type of opinion than the qualified is appropriate. As Figure 21–2 shows, the extreme audit opinion for the limitation of audit scope (circumstance 1) is the *disclaimer*. The extreme opinion for the failure of the financial statements to conform to GAAP is the *adverse opinion*.

In determining the type of opinion to be rendered, the auditor begins by determining whether a qualifying circumstance exists. If one or more reasons to qualify the opinion exist, the auditor must *make a judgment as to whether the financial statement effects of the circumstance would affect the decision of an informed user of*

Figure 21-2

Opinion Qualification Alternatives

	Effects of deviation	
Deviation	Material but not pervasive*	Pervasive*
1. Limitation of scope	"Except for" qualification	Disclaimer
2. Failure to conform with GAAP	"Except for" qualification	Adverse

*Pervasive means having a material impact on fairness of presentation of the *financial statements taken as a whole* (not limited to an isolated account balance or class of transactions).

the financial information. If so, it is *material* and the audit report must at least be qualified. Beyond that, however, the auditor must decide whether the circumstances of qualification produce a *pervasive* (very material) effect on the fairness of presentation of the financial statements taken as a whole. If they do, a qualified opinion would no longer be appropriate; instead, an extreme opinion should be issued.

The most commonly used determinant of reporting materiality is the relative magnitude or dollar effect of an item on an important financial statement variable, such as total assets or net income. For example, if the client has failed to adhere to GAAP in one or more disclosures and refuses to correct the financial statements, the auditor should, as part of completion of the evidence-gathering phase of the audit, combine the dollar effects of all adjusting entries that the client has failed to make. The aggregate error should then be compared with a judgmentally predetermined cutoff level for materiality. If the dollar effect of the errors is *material* (important enough to affect users' decisions) *but isolated* to, say, one or a relatively few elements of the financial statements taken as a whole, a qualified opinion should be issued. If, however, the effect of errors on key financial statement variables is so material (pervasive) that it affects the fairness of presentation of the financial statements taken as a whole, an adverse opinion would be required.

Other determinants of materiality include consideration of these factors:

- *The user group.* Investors are usually more interested in items that affect income or ability to pay dividends. Creditors, on the other hand, usually are more concerned with balance sheet items, because these reflect the client's ability to meet creditor's claims. The auditor does not always know the primary user group but should be more sensitive to the effects of disclosures on certain selected variables when he or she does know the user group.
- *The nature of the item.* For example, where *fraud or irregularities* or other illegal acts have taken place, the materiality threshold for disclosure is lower than for inadvertent errors. Similarly, items involving *related parties* would be more sensitive to materiality standards than those arising from transactions among unrelated entities.

Reports Accompanying Scope Limitations

A scope limitation occurs when, for some reason, the auditor is *unable to obtain access to existing sufficient evidence* to support one or more of the disclosures in the financial statements. Such limitations can arise because of (1) restrictions caused by underlying conditions, or (2) restrictions imposed by the client. *When a client imposes restrictions on the scope of the audit, it is generally regarded as a more serious mater than when the restrictions result from other conditions;* this is because such restrictions limit the auditor's investigative independence. The AICPA encourages use of a disclaimer in such situations. Examples of client-imposed scope restrictions are those that deny the auditor the opportunity to observe physical inventory counts or to confirm certain accounts receivable. Clients may impose such scope restrictions because they want to limit the amount of audit fees, or in the case of receivables confirmation, to avoid annoying any of their customers who may be particularly averse to receiving confirmation requests. Other types of client-imposed restrictions are refusal to provide copies of board of directors' minutes and refusal to provide a client representation letter. In all cases, the reasons for the restrictions should be evaluated by the auditor prior to deciding whether to issue a qualified opinion or a disclaimer of opinion. However, professional standards require a disclaimer when clients refuse to supply such vital evidence as the representation letter (Chapter 20). The auditor's main concern in such situations is that the client may be trying to conceal a misstatement.

In other cases, the client may have imposed no restrictions but, because of unusual circumstances beyond the client's control, the auditor is nonetheless unable to obtain necessary evidence. Following are examples:

- Inability to confirm accounts receivable or to perform alternative procedures because of poor customer response to confirmation requests and inadequate subsequent collection information (Chapter 13).
- Inability to observe the physical count of inventories or to perform alternative inventory verification procedures because the client has no perpetual inventory system; this could happen if the auditor was hired only after the end of the client's fiscal year (Chapter 17).
- Refusal of the client's attorney to furnish a lawyer's letter (Chapter 20).
- Inability to obtain access to audited financial statements of an investee.

An example follows (Figure 21-3) in which the auditor was not hired until after the client's fiscal 19X2 year-end and thus was unable to observe physical inventories. Inventories in this situation are considered material but not pervasive to the financial statements taken as a whole, and alternative procedures (outlined in Chapter 17) were not possible.

Qualifying language in a scope-restricted audit report should appear in three places. In the scope paragraph, the first sentence (referring to application of generally accepted auditing standards) should be preceded with the qualifying phrase, "except as explained in the following paragraph." A middle

Figure 21–3 ■

Report with Qualified Opinion—Scope Limitation

<hr>

Independent Auditor's Report

INTRODUCTORY PARAGRAPH: (Same first paragraph as the standard report)

SCOPE PARAGRAPH:
 Except as discussed in the following paragraph, we conducted our audits in accordance with generally accepted auditing standards. Those standards require that we plan and perform the audit to obtain reasonable assurance about whether the financial statements are free of material misstatement. An audit includes examining, on a test basis, evidence supporting the amounts and disclosures in the financial statements. An audit also includes assessing the accounting principles used and significant estimates made by management, as well as evaluating the overall financial statement presentation. We believe that our audits provide a reasonable basis for our opinion.

EXPLANATORY PARAGRAPH:
 We were unable to observe the taking of physical inventories as of December 31, 19X2 (stated at $X,XXX,XXX) and December 31, 19X1 (stated at $X,XXX,XXX), since those dates were prior to the time we were engaged as auditors for the company. Due to the nature of the company's records, we were unable to satisfy ourselves as to the inventory quantities by means of other auditing procedures.

OPINION PARAGRAPH:
 In our opinion, *except for the effects of such adjustments, if any, as might have been determined to be necessary had we been able to observe the physical inventories,* the financial statements referred to in the first paragraph present fairly, in all material respects, the financial position of ABC Company as of December 31, 19X2 and 19X1, and the results of its operations and its cash flows for the years then ended in conformity with generally accepted accounting principles.

<hr>

paragraph should then be inserted, containing the *facts* associated with the qualification as well as the *effects* on the financial statements of the items to which the scope limitation pertains. Finally, the first sentence of the opinion paragraph should be modified with the qualifying phrase, beginning with the words "except for." Notice that the reference in the opinion paragraph should be to the *possible effects, if any* of potential financial statement adjustments and not to the qualification itself.

Disclaimer of Opinion

A **disclaimer of opinion** states that the auditor does not express an opinion on the financial statements. The fourth standard of audit reporting requires that, in cases in which a disclaimer is appropriate, the reason for the disclaimer should be clearly set forth in the report. A disclaimer of opinion would have been justified if the inventories of ABC, Inc., at December 31, 19X2 and 19X1 had been *pervasive* (very material) with respect to the financial statements taken as a whole.

Alternatively, there may have been more than one scope limitation on the audit, such as failure to obtain evidence regarding other accounts in addition to inventories. Although a scope limitation pertaining to a single account may not be pervasive, the combined effects of scope limitations on several accounts might be. An example of a disclaimer due to multiple scope limitations follows (Figure 21–4).

If a pervasive scope limitation exists with respect to one or more of the financial statements taken as a whole, but not to the others, the auditor may **split the opinion** by disclaiming an opinion on the effected statements and expressing an unqualified opinion on the remainder of the statements. For example, if the auditor had been hired in 19X2 so that only the beginning inventories for that year (assumed pervasive) could not be observed or adequately audited by means of alternative procedures, the auditor would use qualifying language as in Figure 21–5.

Figure 21–4 ▬▬

Disclaimer—Scope Limitation

Independent Auditor's Report

INTRODUCTORY PARAGRAPH:

We were engaged to audit the accompanying balance sheets of ABC Company as of December 31, 19X2 and 19X1, and the related statements of income, retained earnings, and cash flows for the years then ended. These financial statements are the responsibility of the Company's management.

SCOPE PARAGRAPH: (Omitted from this report)

EXPLANATORY PARAGRAPH:

The Company did not make a count of its physical inventories in 19X2 or 19X1, stated in the accompanying financial statements at $X,XXX,XXX as of December 31, 19X2 and at $X,XXX,XXX as of December 31, 19X1. Furthermore, evidence supporting the cost of property and equipment acquired prior to December 31, 19X1 is no longer available. The company's records do not permit the application of other auditing procedures to inventories or property and equipment.

OPINION PARAGRAPH:

Since the company did not take physical inventories and we were not able to apply other auditing procedures to satisfy ourselves as to inventory quantities and the cost of property and equipment, the scope of our work was not sufficient to enable us to express, and we do not express, an opinion on these financial statements.

Figure 21-5 ▰▰

Split Opinion: Balance Sheet Only, Single Year

INTRODUCTORY PARAGRAPH:
We have audited the accompanying balance sheet of ABC Company as of December 31, 19X2. We were engaged to audit the related statements of income, retained earnings, and cash flows for the year then ended. These financial statements are the responsibility of the Company's management. Our responsibility is to express an opinion on the balance sheet based on our audit.

SCOPE PARAGRAPH: (Same as scope qualified report, above)

EXPLANATORY PARAGRAPH:
We did not observe the taking of physical inventories as of December 31, 19X1 (stated at $X,XXX,XXX) since that date was prior to the time we were engaged as auditors for the company. Furthermore, perpetual inventory records supporting inventories were not sufficient to permit the application of alternative audit procedures regarding the existence of inventories. Accordingly, we are unable to express, and do not express, an opinion regarding the statements of income, retained earnings, and cash flows for the ABC Company for the year ended December 31, 19X2.

OPINION PARAGRAPH:
In our opinion, the balance sheet presents fairly, in all material respects, the financial position of ABC Company at December 31, 19X2, in conformity with generally accepted accounting principles.

Other Reasons for Disclaimer of an Audit Opinion

There are many reasons for disclaiming an audit opinion. One of these, for the pervasive scope limitation, was discussed above. Still other reasons for the disclaimer include *association with unaudited financial statements of a public entity* and *nonindependence of the auditor.*

We have stated previously in this chapter that an accountant is associated with financial statements when consent has been given to use the CPA's name in a report, document, or other written communication containing the statements, whether or not the accountant prepares the statements or appends his or her name to them. When an auditor is associated with the statements of a public entity, but *has not audited or reviewed* the statements, a disclaimer of opinion is appropriate (Figure 21-6).

Such a disclaimer may accompany the unaudited financial statements, or it may be placed directly on them. In addition, each page of the financial statements should be clearly and conspicuously marked as unaudited. In such a case, the accountant has no responsibility to apply audit procedures beyond reading the financial statements for obvious material errors. Also, no reference should be made to any procedures applied because of this might lead to misunderstanding

Figure 21–6

Disclaimer: Unaudited Financial Statements

The accompanying balance sheet of ABC Company as of December 31, 19X2 and 19X1, and the related statements of income, retained earnings, and cash flows for the year then ended were not audited by us and, accordingly, we do not express an opinion on them.[3]

---

on the part of readers. The accountant, however, is still required to disclose any departures from GAAP that are discovered during the reading of the financial statements and that the client refuses to disclose. In such cases, the above disclaimer should be modified to include the necessary disclosures and their effects on the financial data, if readily determinable. *The accountant is never justified in simply disclaiming an opinion if evidence exists that the financial statements are misleading.* If the client will not agree to a revision of the financial statements or to a modified disclaimer, the accountant should withdraw from the engagement and refuse to be associated with the financial statements.

If it becomes apparent that the accountant's name is to be included in a *client-prepared written communication* of a public entity containing financial statements that have not been audited or reviewed, the accountant should request (a) that his or her name not be included, or (b) that the financial statements be marked unaudited and be accompanied by a disclaimer of opinion. Failing that, the accountant should advise the client that consent was not given and should take other measures, such as consultation with an attorney.

When the auditor is *not independent* of the client, any auditing procedures that might be performed would not be in conformity with generally accepted auditing standards. The nonindependence disclaimer overrides all other disclaimers, and when other reasons to disclaim besides nonindependence exist, they should not be mentioned. Even when auditing procedures are performed, they should not be mentioned. In addition, each page of the financial statements should be marked as unaudited. The following disclaimer is recommended when an accountant is not independent (Figure 21–7).

Figure 21–7

Disclaimer: Nonindependence

We are not independent with respect to ABC Company, Inc., and the accompanying balance sheets as of December 31, 19X2 and 19X1, and the related statements of income, retained earnings, and cash flows were not audited by us, and accordingly, we do not express an opinion on them.

Notice that the reason for lack of independence, as specified in Rule 101 of the Code of Professional Conduct of the AICPA (Chapter 3), need not be disclosed in the disclaimer.

Reports Accompanying Financial Statements That Contain Departures from GAAP

When the client has (1) made material disclosures that do not conform to GAAP, or (2) omitted material disclosures necessary for compliance with GAAP, *either a qualified or an adverse opinion is necessary.* This conforms to the first auditing standard of reporting (which requires that the audit report shall state whether the financial statements are in conformity with GAAP) and with the third reporting standard (which provides for a presumption of adequate informative disclosures in the financial statements unless otherwise specified in the audit report). Whether a qualified or an adverse opinion is required *depends on the materiality of the effects on financial statements of the departure* from GAAP.

These types of reports are regarded as requiring the most serious kind of qualification, because they deal with a willful violation of GAAP by the client. The SEC will not allow clients to submit 10-K annual reports under the Securities Exchange Act of 1934, or registration statements under the Securities Act of 1933, that contain material departures from GAAP that are known to the auditors. That is one reason why these types of reports are so rarely seen in practice. The following (Figure 21–8) is an example of an audit report *qualified* because of the failure to capitalize a long-term lease obligation.

Figure 21–8

Qualified Opinion: Departure from GAAP

INTRODUCTORY PARAGRAPH: (Unchanged from the unqualified report)

SCOPE PARAGRAPH: (Unchanged from the unqualified report)

EXPLANATORY PARAGRAPH:

   The Company has excluded from property and debt in the accompanying balance sheet as of December 31, 19X2, certain lease obligations, which, in our opinion, should be capitalized in order to conform with generally accepted accounting principles. If these lease obligations were capitalized, property would be increased by $X,XXX,XXX; long-term debt by $X,XXX,XXX; and retained earnings by $X,XXX,XXX as of December 31, 19X2. Net income and earnings per share would be increased (decreased) by $XXX,XXX and $X.XX, respectively, for the year ended.

OPINION PARAGRAPH:

   In our opinion, except for the effect of not capitalizing lease obligations, as discussed in the preceding paragraph, the financial statements present fairly, in all material respects, the financial position of the ABC Company at December 31, 19X2 and 19X1, and the results of its operations and its cash flows for the years then ended, in conformity with generally accepted accounting principles.

Notice that the report qualified for departures from GAAP contains the following characteristics:

- No change in the introductory or scope paragraphs from the unqualified report—because the scope requirements of GAAS have been met.
- An explanatory paragraph that discloses the *fact* of the departure(s) from GAAP and the related *dollar effects* on all affected financial statement components.
- The qualifying language beginning with the phrase *"except for"* in the opinion paragraph.

One exception to the practices just cited occurs when the auditor can show that the departure from GAAP was necessary to keep the financial statements from being misleading. In such a rare situation, an unqualified opinion may be issued.

Adverse Opinion

Whenever uncorrected departures from GAAP have an effect that is so material that a qualified opinion is not justified, or whenever an intentional misstatement has occurred (an *irregularity* as defined in Chapter 4), an *adverse opinion* should be issued. An **adverse opinion** states that the financial statements, taken as a whole, are not fairly presented in accordance with GAAP. An adverse opinion may be issued, for example, when one pervasive departure from GAAP has been discovered or when there are several uncorrected departures from GAAP, the combined effects of which are pervasive to the financial statements taken as a whole. From the preceding illustration, for example, if the effects of the failure to capitalize the lease were pervasive to the financial statements taken as a whole, the audit report would be changed as follows (Figure 21–9).

Figure 21–9 ▬▬▬

Adverse Opinion

INTRODUCTORY PARAGRAPH: (Same as above)

SCOPE PARAGRAPH: (Same as above)

EXPLANATORY PARAGRAPH: (Same as above. If multiple departures from GAAP are noted, the facts and financial statement effects should be placed in as many paragraphs as necessary to adequately explain them. If the effects are not reasonably determinable, the report should state that fact.)

OPINION PARAGRAPH:
   In our opinion, *because of the effects of the matters discussed in the preceding paragraph(s),* the financial statements referred to above *do not present fairly,* in conformity with generally accepted accounting principles, the financial position of ABC Company as of December 31, 19X2 and 19X1, or the results of its operations or its cash flows for the years then ended.

Notice the distinctive features of the adverse opinion:

- It contains no introductory or scope paragraph modifications—again, because the scope requirements of GAAS have been met.
- Like its qualified counterpart, it contains an explanatory paragraph or paragraphs, disclosing the facts of the departures from GAAP and the effects of those departures on the financial statements.
- The opinion is adverse because of the material effects of the departures from GAAP on the financial statements taken as a whole.

Adding Explanatory Language to the Standard Report

☑ **Objective 5**
Recognize situations requiring explanatory language

There are several situations in which, in spite of the fact that special circumstances require audit **report modification**, an unqualified report is still issued. In these cases, the auditor should be careful not to use qualifying language such as "except for" to avoid confusing the reader. Figure 21–10 lists the circumstances that may require the addition of a separate explanatory paragraph or other explanatory language, although not constituting qualified reports. We will discuss selected reports in this group in the sections that follow.

Reports Accompanying Material Accounting Changes

One of the generally accepted accounting principles requires that methods of accounting adopted by companies be followed consistently from period to period, so that comparability between financial data of successive years may be

Figure 21–10

Circumstances That May Require Modification of Standard Report Wording

- Material changes in accounting principles.
- Material uncertainties concerning future events, the outcome of which are not susceptible of reasonable estimation.
- Uncertainty as to whether the company may be a going concern.
- Reliance on the work and reports of other auditors.
- Emphasis of a matter.
- Departure from a promulgated accounting principle in order to prevent the financial statements from being misleading (discussed in the preceding section).
- Omission of supplemental information required by the FASB or government accounting standards board (GASB); or failure to remove substantial doubt about conformity.
- Material inconsistency of other information in documents containing audited financial statements with information appearing in the financial statements themselves.
- Updated report on comparative financial statements of prior periods differs from those previously expressed.
- Report of a successor auditor on comparative financial statements when a predecessor auditor has refused to reissue the opinion of the prior year.

maintained. The standard unqualified audit report, in stating the GAAP have been followed, *implies that comparability between successive years' financial data have not been materially affected by accounting changes*, although no direct reference to consistency is made. If, however, accounting changes have occurred that affect consistency of application of GAAP in the financial statements, the auditor should modify the language of the standard report to contain a reference to the financial statement footnote that describes the change.

Accounting changes are defined in APB Opinion 20 as *changes in accounting principles or methods of applying those principles, changes in reporting entities, or correction of prior periods' errors*. These changes may occur at the client's discretion if it can be shown that the newly adopted accounting principle is the preferable way of reporting. Also, such changes may be mandated by the FASB or other authoritative bodies and the client may be forced to adopt the change for financial statements to continue to comply with GAAP. The auditor is required by the second standard of reporting to modify the audit report for material accounting changes that affect consistency, regardless of whether the changes are made at the discretion of the client.

Changes that are deemed to affect consistency, and, therefore, to *require modification of the audit report*, include the following:

- Changes in reporting entities (such as the inclusion of subsidiary companies in consolidated financial statements of the current year that were not included in a previous year, even though owned during that year).
- Changes in an accounting principle, or in the method of applying a principle, or changes in an estimate that are inseparable from changes in principle.
- Corrections of prior-period errors involving principles, such as the correction of the prior period's improper application of an inventory accounting method.

Changes deemed *not to affect consistency* and, therefore, not requiring mention in the unqualified audit report include

- Changes in accounting estimate, such as changes in the estimated lives of fixed assets for depreciation purposes.
- Error corrections that do not involve principle, such as the correction of a mathematical mistake from a prior period.
- Variations in format of financial statements, including classifications.
- Changes arising because of substantially different transactions or events, such as the purchase or sale of product lines or services, or the purchase or sale of subsidiaries.
- Changes expected to have a material future effect, but having an immaterial effect on current financial statements.

According to generally accepted accounting principles, there are certain changes that require a *retroactive restatement of prior periods' financial statements* in

Figure 21–11 ■

Modification: Inconsistent Application of GAAP

As discussed in Note X to the financial statements, the Company changed its method of computing depreciation in 19X2.

order to meet the comparability standard. APB Opinion 20 lists the following as examples of circumstances requiring such restatement:

- Changes in reporting entity.
- Changes from the LIFO method of inventory costing to another method.
- Change to or from the full-cost method of accounting in the extractive industries.
- Changes in method of accounting used for long-term construction contracts.[4]

The report modification for an accounting change is quite simple. An explanatory paragraph is *added to the standard report* as follows (Figure 21–11).

The addition of this explanatory paragraph is required as long as the financial statements for the year of the accounting change continue to be included in the financial statements. However, if the accounting change is accounted for by the retroactive restatement method, as discussed above, the explanatory paragraph need only appear in the year in which the change is made, since after that time, all financial statements presented will reflect consistent application of GAAP.

The auditor's concurrence with the accounting change is implied. Whenever the client indicates a desire to make accounting changes that affect comparability, the auditor should evaluate the proposed change, focusing on the following: (a) the general acceptability of the newly adopted principle; (b) whether the method of accounting for the effects of the change is in conformity with GAAP; and (c) management's justification for the change. If all of these conditions are not met, then the auditor should issue either a qualified or adverse opinion for the client's failure to comply with GAAP.

Reports Relating to Material Uncertainties

All financial statements include some disclosures that involve some degree of **uncertainty**. For example, the allowance for doubtful accounts, the allowance for depreciation, and various liability accounts are all estimates. Therefore, the measurement of these amounts must make allowances for reasonable uncertainty. However, since these items are susceptible to estimation, they can be supported by various types of *existing evidence*. There are other uncertainties for which *no evidence exists* as of the date of the audit. These matters *may not be susceptible to reasonable estimation* as of the date of the audit report because their outcome is contingent on the future occurrence of some event. A matter that is expected to be resolved in the future when sufficient evidence becomes available is called an *uncertainty.* Such matters require a report *modification.* Examples of such uncertainties include the following:

- The outcome of pending or threatened litigation, the effects of which are not estimable by the client or the client's attorney.
- The resolution of a pending tax investigation involving a possible claim for refund or deficiency.
- Potential recoverability of a deferred cost.
- Probability of realization of certain receivables, such as those from officers and directors whose financial resources are not known.
- The possibility that the company may not be able to continue as a going concern.

The decision as to whether to modify the audit report when uncertainties exist depends principally on two things: (1) the materiality of the item and (2) the probability that the event may occur.

In the case of the uncertainty, materiality sometimes does not depend on the relative dollar amount of the uncertainty. This is because the distinguishing characteristic of the uncertainty is the fact that it cannot be estimated. Qualitative factors such as relative importance of the item and number of uncertainties facing the company must also be considered.

When the company faces an uncertainty that is material, management is required to report the uncertainty in accordance with the provisions of Statement of Financial Accounting Standards (SFAS) No. 5, *Accounting for Contingencies.* This standard defines a contingency as a condition giving rise to possible future gain or loss that may occur in the future as one or more events occurs or fails to occur.[5] The standard prescribes the following criteria for accrual of a loss contingency:

1. It must be *probable.*
2. It must be *estimable.*

Since such items are susceptible of estimation, they do not fit the definition of uncertainty.

The criterion prescribed by SFAS No. 5 for *disclosure* of a loss contingency is that it be *reasonably possible* of occurring. The accounting standard defines "reasonably possible" as "less than likely but more than remote." A range of loss may or may not be possible to estimate.

SAS 58 defines situations involving uncertainties that may require an explanatory paragraph. Specifically, the following guidelines apply:

1. If there is a *remote likelihood of a material loss* the auditor would *not* add a separate explanatory paragraph to the report.
2. If there is a *reasonable possibility of a material loss,* the auditor must subjectively decide whether to add an explanatory paragraph, based on the magnitude of the item and the likelihood of its occurrence.

Figure 21–12

Report Modification: Litigation

As discussed in Note X to the financial statements, the company is a defendant in a lawsuit alleging infringement of certain patent rights and claiming royalties and punative damages. The company has filed a counteraction, and preliminary hearings and discovery proceedings on both actions are in progress. The ultimate outcome of the litigation is not presently determinable.

3. If there is a *probable chance of material loss,* but if management has not been able to make a reasonable estimate of the loss, an explanatory paragraph should be added to the report.

Figure 21–12 illustrates the explanatory paragraph added to the standard unqualified report for the uncertainty involving litigation. Figure 21–13 illustrates the modifying paragraph whenever the company appears not to be a going concern.

Figure 21–13

Report Modification: Going Concern

The accompanying financial statements have been prepared assuming that the Company will continue as a going concern. As discussed in Note X to the financial statements, the Company has suffered recurring losses from operations and has a net capital deficiency that raise substantial doubt about its ability to continue as a going concern. Management's plans in regard to these matters are also described in Note X. The financial statements do not include any adjustments that might result from the outcome of this uncertainy.

Source: SAS 59 (New York: AICPA, 1988). Used with permission.

If the auditor concludes that a material uncertainty is *not properly disclosed, or that it is based on inappropriate accounting principles or inappropriate accounting estimates,* a *qualified or adverse opinion* should be issued, since these represent departures from generally accepted accounting principles.

Reliance on the Work of Other Auditors

Sometimes an auditor will be engaged to audit a parent company, or a subsidiary, or a branch of a consolidated or combined group of entities, while other accountants are auditing the other components concurrently. In such cases, the first thing an auditor should decide is whether or not he or she can serve as the **principal auditor**. Factors to be considered in this decision include the following:

- The materiality of the portion of the financial statements he or she has examined, compared to the materiality of the components examined by others.

- The extent of his or her knowledge of the overall financial statements, compared to that possessed by the other auditors.
- The relative importance of the component that he or she is auditing to the overall financial statements of the combined group.[6]

If the auditor decides, on the basis of these and other factors, that he or she cannot serve as the principal auditor, then on completion of the audit, the auditor should submit his or her audit report to the principal auditor. The principal auditor then relies on that report in the issuance of an opinion on the financial statements of the consolidated entity.

The principal auditor should ordinarily make inquiries of appropriate business associates concerning the professional reputation of the other auditor(s). Additionally, he or she should obtain a *representation letter* from each other auditor stating that person's independence of the client under the rules of the AICPA and, if applicable, the rules of the SEC. The principal auditor should also ascertain

- That the auditor is aware that the financial statements of the component are to be included in financial statements upon which the principal auditor is reporting and that the report of the contributing auditor will be relied upon by the principal auditor.
- That the auditor is familiar with GAAP in the United States, or accounting practices required by the SEC, where appropriate.
- That the auditor is aware that a review will be made of matters affecting elimination of intercompany transactions and the uniformity of accounting practices among components included in the combined financial statements.

When other auditors are involved, the principal auditor must *decide whether to make reference* in the audit report to the work of the other auditor(s). Such references are generally omitted when the examination is made by an associated or correspondent firm (such as an international affiliate) or when the other auditor was retained by the principal auditor, who closely supervised the work. Also, the contributing auditor might be unacknowledged if the portion of the financial statements he or she examined is immaterial to the financial statements covered by the principal auditor's report and the principal auditor takes steps to ascertain the adequacy of the other auditor's examination.

In cases of no reference, barring other circumstances, the standard unqualified audit report would be rendered by the principal auditor. All auditors must still be responsible, of course, in the event of lawsuit or action by the SEC, for the work that each did individually. The following *additional auditing procedures* should be performed by the principal auditor when the decision is made not to make reference to the work of other auditors:

1. Visit the other auditors and discuss the auditing procedures followed and the results thereof.

2. Review the other auditors' programs and, perhaps, issue instructions for the other auditors to follow.
3. Review the working papers of the other auditors, including the assessment of internal control risk and the audit conclusions reached.

If, on the other hand, the principal auditor decides to *make reference* to the work of the other auditors, the additional procedures in the preceding list need not be performed. Instead, the principal auditor expands the introductory paragraph of the standard report to include a reference to the portion of the financial statements examined by other auditors. The language of the scope and opinion paragraph is also modified to disclose that the principal auditor's report, insofar as it relates to the entity audited by the other auditor, is based on that auditor's report. Such a modification does not constitute a qualified audit report.

An audit report that makes reference to the work of other auditors follows in Figure 21–14. A less frequently applied alternative to the above presentation is to present both the report of the principal auditor and that of the other auditor, after obtaining permission from the other auditor to do so.

Figure 21–14 ▬▬▬

Opinion Based in Part on Report of Another Auditor

Independent Auditor's Report

We have audited the consolidated balance sheets of ABC Company as of December 31, 19X2 and 19X1, and the related consolidated statements of income, retained earnings, and cash flows for the years then ended. These financial statements are the responsibility of the Company's management. Our responsibility is to express an opinion on these financial statements based on our audits. We did not audit the financial statements of B Company, a wholly-owned subsidiary, which statements reflect total assets of $_____ and $_____ as of December 31, 19X2 and 19X1, respectively, and total revenues of $_____ and $_____ for the years then ended. Those statements were audited by other auditors whose report has been furnished to us, and our opinion, insofar as it relates to the amounts included for B Company, is based solely on the report of the other auditors.

SCOPE PARAGRAPH: (Same as unqualified, except for last sentence, as follows)
We believe that our audits *and the report of other auditors* provide a reasonable basis for our opinion.

OPINION PARAGRAPH: (Same as unqualified report, except first phrase)
In our opinion, *based on our audits and the report of other auditors,* the consolidated financial statements referred to above present fairly . . .

Emphasis of a Matter

In rare instances the auditor may wish to emphasize certain circumstances even though issuing an unqualified audit report. Normally, such information should be included in a separate explanatory middle paragraph of the audit report. The following are examples of items that may be so emphasized:

- The entity is a component of a larger business enterprise.
- The entity has had significant transactions with related parties.
- An unusually important subsequent event has occurred.
- An unusually important accounting matter affects the comparability of current financial statements with those of the preceding period.[7]

Piecemeal Opinions

The term **piecemeal opinion** was historically used to define the situation in which the auditor disclaimed an opinion or issued an adverse opinion on the financial statements taken as a whole, while expressing an unqualified opinion on specified accounts in the statements. Although such reports were once used, *they are now generally considered inappropriate,* since it is feared that the piecemeal opinion on the specified accounts might tend to contradict or overshadow the disclaimer or adverse opinion on the financial statements taken as a whole.[8]

Updating and Reissuing Audit Reports

☑ **Objective 4**
Be able to update and reissue audit reports

When a continuing auditor issues an opinion on comparative financial statements, he or she should update the opinion issued on the previous year's financial statements. **Updating** the opinion of a previous year can take the form of either (1) reexpression of the opinion previously expressed (as illustrated in Figure 1–3) or (2) issuing a different opinion from that previously expressed. In the latter case, the auditor may decide to issue a report with an updated opinion different from a previous opinion because he or she has become aware, during the current examination, of circumstances or events that affect the prior period. For example, the auditor may have qualified his or her opinion for a departure from GAAP in the prior period. If the error is corrected during the current period, that fact should be recognized in the updated version of the report, and the opinion on the comparative financial statements should be unqualified.

In an updated opinion, if an auditor expresses an opinion on prior-period financial statements that is different from the one previously expressed, he or she should disclose all the reasons for the different opinion in a separate explanatory paragraph of the audit report. Also, if the updated report is other than unqualified, the auditor should include in the opinion paragraph an appropriate reference to the explanatory paragraph. The explanatory paragraph should contain the following disclosures:

- The date of the auditor's previous report.
- The type of opinion previously expressed.
- The circumstances or events that caused the auditor to express a different opinion.
- The fact that the auditor's updated opinion is different from the previous opinion on those statements.

Reissuance of an audit report involves merely the reproduction of a previously issued audit report in a subsequent period. Reissuance might occur if, for example, the client was requested by a prospective creditor to provide copies of the most recent audited financial statements in connection with a bank loan subsequent to the original issuance date of the audit report. It might also occur if a *predecessor auditor* were requested by a former client to reissue or to consent to the reuse of a previously issued audit report. In these situations, the auditor may presently have no revised information with respect to the financial statements covered by the previously issued audit report. Therefore, it is important that the *original report date be used* to avoid any confusion to the reader as to the date of the auditor's representations.

A predecessor auditor, before consenting to the reissuance of a report, should take steps to ascertain that the previously issued report is still appropriate. These steps include the following:

1. Reading the financial statements of the current period.
2. Comparing the financial statements of the prior period with those of the current period.
3. Obtaining a letter of representation from the successor auditor as to whether the successor auditor's examination revealed any matters that, in the successor's opinion, might have a material effect on the financial statements reported on by the predecessor auditor.

Successor Auditors' Reports on Comparative Statements

If a *successor auditor is reporting on comparative financial statements* and the *report of the predecessor is not presented*, the successor auditor's report should indicate in the scope paragraph that the financial statements of the prior period were examined by other auditors (names need not be presented), along with the date of the predecessor auditor's report and the type of opinion expressed by the predecessor. The scope paragraph should also give the reasons if the predecessor's report was other than unqualified.

After the scope paragraph, the successor's report should express an opinion on the financial statements of the *current period only*. A successor auditor, in meeting the consistency standard, should adopt procedures that are practical and reasonable in the circumstances to obtain assurance that the principles employed are consistent between the current and preceding years. The successor auditor may review the predecessor's working papers and in that way reduce the scope of auditing tests of opening balances. This, of course, must be agreed to by both the client and predecessor auditor. If the successor auditor becomes aware of information that indicates a need for revising the prior period statements, he or she should ask the client to arrange a meeting of the three parties to resolve the matter.

An example of a successor auditor's report on comparative financial statements when the unqualified report of the predecessor is not reissued is shown in Figure 21–15.

Figure 21–15

Predecessor Auditor's Report Not Presented

Independent Auditor's Report

INTRODUCTORY PARAGRAPH: (Same as standard report, *single year, (19X2)* in addition to this sentence)

The financial statements of ABC Company as of December 31, 19X1, were audited by other auditors whose report dated March 31, 19X2, expressed an unqualified opinion on those statements.

SCOPE PARAGRAPH: (Same as standard report)

OPINION PARAGRAPH: (Standard opinion paragraph for one year (19X2) only)

Summary

In this chapter we have focused on meeting the standards of reporting, with particular emphasis on the requirements imposed by the fourth reporting standard. We began by defining *association with financial statements* as that phrase is used in the fourth reporting standard. We then reviewed the full spectrum of audit reports available under generally accepted auditing standards and gave examples of various types of reports. We explored the reasons for disclaimers, such as unaudited financial statements of a public entity and lack of independence.

We also discussed other departures from the wording of the standard unqualified audit report that do not constitute qualifications, such as accounting changes, uncertainties, reliance on the work of other auditors and emphasis of certain important matters. Finally, we discussed the updating and reissuance of previously issued audit reports.

In Chapter 22 we will extend our discussion of the other levels of association with financial statements and illustrate the reports that should be rendered with each type of association. Other special reporting topics will also be addressed.

Auditing Vocabulary

p. 918   **adverse opinion:**   The opinion that is rendered whenever uncorrected departures from GAAP have an effect that is so material that a qualified opinion is not justified, or whenever an intentional misstatement has occurred (an irregularity).

p. 908   **association with financial statements:**   Consent to the use of the CPA's name in a report, document, or written communication (except tax returns) containing the financial statements, or submission to the client or others, financial statements that the CPA has prepared or assisted in preparing.

p. 931   **basic financial statements:**   Generally contained the balance sheet, statement of income, statement of retained earnings, statement of cash flows, financial statements prepared according to a comprehensive basis of accounting of other than GAAP, descriptions of accounting policies, and notes to financial statements.

p. 908   **compilation:**   See Chapter 23.

p. 933   **condensed financial statements:**   Financial presentations in considerably less detail than those provided in the basic audited financial statements.

p. 910   **continuing auditor:**   An auditor who remains associated with a client over a period of years.

p. 913   **disclaimer of opinion:**   A statement by the accountant that no opinion can be issued on the financial statements of the client.

p. 909   **financial statements taken as a whole:**   All of the financial statements for the current period as well as those of all prior years presented for comparative purposes.

p. 908   **negative assurance:**   See definition in Chapter 22.

p. 926   **piecemeal opinion:**   The issuance of a disclaimer or an adverse opinion on the financial statements taken as a whole, while expressing an unqualified opinion on specified accounts in the financial statements. Such reports are considered inappropriate.

p. 923   **principal auditor:**   The auditor who audits the principal components of a consolidated or combined group of entities while other accountants are auditing the other components concurrently.

p. 908   **public entity:**   Any entity whose securities trade in a public market or who makes a filing with a regulatory agency in preparation of the sale of any class of its securities in a public market, or a subsidiary of such an entity.

p. 910   **qualified audit opinion:**   Circumstances that represent the absence of one or more of the essentials for the unqualified opinion. Qualified opinions may be given for two reasons: (1) limitations of scope in the engagement and (2) failure of the client to conform with disclosure requirements of GAAP. See Figure 21–2.

p. 927   **reissuance:**   The reproduction of a previously issued audit report in a subsequent period.

p. 919   **report modification:**   A departure from the standard wording of the unqualified audit report that does not constitute a qualified report. See Figure 21–10 for circumstances that may require modification of standard report wording.

p. 930   **segment information:**   Information required by FASB Statements 14 and 21 that includes disclosures about the company's operations in different industries, its foreign operations and export sales, and its major customers.

p. 914   **split opinion:**   The expression of one type of opinion on certain financial statements and another type of opinion on other financial statements. See Figure 21–5 for an illustration.

p. 931   **supplementary information:**   Information presented outside the basic financial statements.

p. 921 **uncertainty:** An event giving rise to possible future gains or losses that, at the time of issuance of the audit report, is not susceptible to reasonable estimation.

p. 909 **unqualified audit report:** The standard opinion on financial statements. To issue an unqualified audit opinion means that (1) the auditor has gathered sufficient competent evidence, (2) audit evidence has revealed no significant uncorrected departures from GAAP, and (3) the auditor is independent.

p. 926 **updating:** Either (1) reexpression of the opinion previously expressed in a former year or (2) issuing a different opinion from that previously expressed.

Appendix 21: Specialized Reporting Situations

Reports on Segment Information

FASB Statements 14 and 21 require that publicly traded companies include certain **segment information** in their annual reports. This required information comprises disclosures about the company's operations in different industries, its foreign operations and export sales, and its major customers. Disclosure of segment information requires *disaggregation of certain significant financial statement components*—such as revenue, operating profit or loss, identifiable assets, depreciation, and capital expenditures.

The auditor must seek evidence that the segment information is *presented in conformity with GAAP in relation to the financial statements taken as a whole.* He or she is not required to narrow the application of the concept of materiality with respect to any errors or misstatements in the segment information, or to issue a separate opinion on the segment information. Auditing procedures for segment information should include the following procedures, where applicable:

1. Consideration of whether the entity's revenue, operating expenses, and identifiable assets are appropriately classified among industry segments or geographic areas.
2. Inquiry of management concerning methods used in deriving segment information, and judgments as to the reasonableness of those methods when evaluated against the criteria of FASB 14.
3. Inquiry as to the practices followed in accounting for sales and transfers between industry segments and between geographic areas and tests of those transactions.
4. Tests of the disaggregation of the entity's financial statements into segment information to verify whether it is in accordance with GAAP.
5. Inquiry as to the methods (and reasonableness thereof) of allocation of expenses between segments or geographic areas.
6. Determination of whether segment information has been consistently prepared from period to period.[9]

The audit report on the overall financial statements applies to segment information as well as all other audited information. As such, the report would not normally refer to the segment information or to audit procedures performed on the information. However, the following situations would call for an opinion qualification, if the segment information is material to the financial statements taken as a whole:

- A misstatement or omission of the segment information.
- A change in the accounting principle relating to the segment information.
- Inability to apply adequate auditing procedures to the segment information.

In such instances, the same considerations apply as those stated earlier for the various types of qualified reports.

Reports on Information Accompanying the Basic Financial Statements in Auditor-Submitted Documents

The auditor may submit to the client or to others documents that contain, in addition to the basic financial statements and the auditor's standard report thereon, certain supplemental information. SAS 29 (AU551), which deals with reports on such supplemental information, states that the auditor's standard report covers the basic financial statements.[10] The **basic financial statements** contain the following elements:

- Balance sheet(s).
- Statement(s) of income
- Statement(s) of retained earnings.
- Statement(s) of cash flows.
- Financial statement(s) prepared according to a comprehensive basis of accounting other than GAAP.
- Descriptions of accounting policies.
- Notes to financial statements.
- Other schedules identified as being a part of the basic financial statements.

Supplementary information, on the other hand, is presented outside the basic financial statements and is not considered a necessary part of compliance with GAAP. It may include such things as:

- Additional details of accounts (such as general and administrative expenses) included in the basic financial statements.
- Consolidating information.
- Historical summaries of items, such as incomes and earnings per share, extracted from the basic financial statements.
- Statistical data.
- Other material, perhaps from sources outside the accounting system of the entity.
- A description of auditing procedures applied to specific items in the financial statements.

When the auditor submits a document including both the basic financial statements and supplemental data, he or she *must*, in accordance with the fourth auditing standard of reporting, *report on all information included in the document*. This means that the auditor's report must do the following:

1. State that the examination has been conducted for the purpose of forming an opinion on the basic financial statements.
2. Identify the supplemental data.
3. State that the accompanying information is presented for purposes of additional analysis and is not a required part of the basic financial statements.
4. Include either an opinion as to whether the accompanying information is fairly presented in all material respects in relation to the financial statements taken as a whole, or a disclaimer of opinion on that information if sufficient auditing procedures were not applied to the supplemental data.

If auditing procedures have been performed on the supplementary data, the auditor's concept of materiality should again be directed toward items that are material to the financial statements taken as a whole and not to the individual disclosures in the supplemental information. The audit report, if any, on the supplemental information may be presented separately or added to the auditor's standard report on the basic financial statements.

Where the audit report includes descriptions of additional auditing procedures applied to specific elements supporting financial statement items, these procedure descriptions should not contradict or detract from the description of the scope of the examination in the standard audit report on the basic financial statements. They should also be set forth separately so as to maintain a *clear distinction between management's representations and the auditor's representations*.

An example of a report on supplementary information follows, in which the other information was not audited. The following paragraph should be added to the audit report on the basic financial statements:

> Our examination was made for the purpose of forming an opinion on the basic financial statements taken as a whole. The accompanying information is presented for purposes of additional analysis and is not a required part of the basic financial statements. Such information has not been subjected to the auditing procedures applied in the examination of the basic financial statements, and accordingly, we express no opinion on it.

Reports on Condensed Financial Statements and Selected Financial Data

Special rules apply when the auditor reports on the following information:

- Condensed annual or interim financial statements that are derived from audited financial statements of a public entity that is required to file, at least annually, complete audited financial statements with a regulatory agency.

- Selected financial data that are derived from audited financial statements of either a public or a nonpublic entity and that are presented in a document that includes audited financial statements (or, in the case of a public entity, that incorporates audited financial statements by reference to information filed with a regulatory agency).

SAS 42 (AU552) governs the specific presentation of these types of financial information under the general reporting guidelines of SAS 29 (AU551). **Condensed financial statements** are defined for purposes of this statement as financial presentations in considerably less detail than those provided in the basic audited financial statements. Condensed financial statements may not include all of the necessary disclosures for full conformity with GAAP and should be read in conjunction with the complete financial statements in order to gain a complete picture of the client's financial position and results of operations. Therefore, if an auditor is engaged to report on condensed financial statements that are derived from audited financial statements, the report on those statements should be different from the audit report on the basic financial statements. Specifically, the report on the condensed financial statements should indicate

- That the auditor has examined and expressed an opinion on the complete financial statements.
- The date of the audit report on the complete financial statements.
- The type of opinion expressed on those statements.
- Whether, in the auditor's opinion, the information set forth in the condensed financial statements is fairly stated in all material respects in relation to the complete financial statements from which it has been derived.

If the auditor is engaged to report on selected financial data, the report should be limited to data that are derived from *audited financial statements*. This may include data calculated from amounts presented in the financial statements, such as working capital. If the financial data presented includes both data derived from the financial statements and other information (such as number of employees or square footage of buildings), the auditor's report should specifically identify the data upon which he or she is reporting. The report should appear as follows:

> We have audited, in accordance with generally accepted auditing standards, the consolidated balance sheet of X Company and subsidiaries as of December 31, 19X0, and the related consolidated statements of income, retained earnings, and cash flows for the year then ended (not presented herein); and in our report dated February 15, 19X1, we expressed an unqualified opinion on those consolidated financial statements. In our opinion, the information set forth in the accompanying condensed consolidated financial statements is fairly stated in all material respects in relation to the consolidated financial statements from which it has been derived.

Sometimes a client might make a statement in a *client-prepared document* that names the auditor and also states that condensed financial statements or other financial data have been derived from audited financial statements. Such statements do not in themselves require the auditor to report on the condensed financial statements or other selected financial data, provided that these disclosures are included in a document that contains audited financial statements (or, as is the case with public entities, that incorporates such statements by reference to information filed with a regulatory agency). However, *if such statements are made in a document that does not include (or incorporate by reference) audited financial statements, the auditor should request that neither his nor her name nor reference to the work be associated with the information.* Alternatively, the auditor may disclaim an opinion on the information and request that the disclaimer be included in the document. If the client does not comply with this request, the auditor should advise the client of denial of consent to association. Additionally, he or she should consider what other actions might be appropriate, such as consultation with legal counsel.

Notes

1. SAS 26 (AU504) (New York: AICPA, 1979).
2. Material in this section is largely derived from SAS 58 (AU508) (New York: AICPA, 1988).
3. SAS 26 (AU504) (New York: AICPA, 1979).
4. APB Opinion No. 20, *Accounting Changes* (New York: AICPA, 1971).
5. SFAS No. 5, *Accounting for Contingencies* (New York: AICPA, 1975).
6. SAS 1, Section 543.
7. SAS 58 (AU508), paragraph 37.
8. Ibid.
9. SAS 21 (AU435) (New York: AICPA, 1977).
10. Material in this section is derived from SAS 29 (AU551) (New York: AICPA, 1980) and from SAS 42 (AU552) (New York: AICPA, 1982).

Questions for Class Discussion

Q21-1 What recourse does an auditor have when he or she discovers that the client has omitted a footnote disclosure that, in the auditor's judgment, must be included to have the financial statements be fairly presented? Explain.

Q21-2 What recourse does the auditor have if she or he discovers a material departure from generally accepted accounting principles that the client refuses to change? Discuss.

Q21-3 What levels of association may an accountant have with a client's financial statements?

Q21-4 How does an accountant disclose his or her association with unaudited financial statements? With audited financial statements? Explain.

Q21-5 To whom should the audit report be addressed? Why?

Q21-6 How does one distinguish between an adverse opinion and a disclaimer of opinion?

Q21-7 Under what circumstances may an auditor issue a disclaimer of opinion?

Q21-8 How does the auditor determine whether to issue a qualified opinion or an adverse opinion? Explain.

Q21-9 What is meant by a scope limitation in an audit report? Does such a limitation always require a qualification in the opinion paragraph? Explain.

Q21-10 What is typically included in the middle paragraph of a qualified audit report? Under what circumstances would a middle paragraph be included in an audit report?

Q21-11 In what situation might a client have a departure from generally accepted accounting principles and still receive an unqualified report? Explain.

Q21-12 What are the types of accounting changes that would require a report modification for lack of consistency?

Q21-13 What types of accounting changes do not require a consistency modification in the audit report?

Q21-14 What accounting changes require a retroactive restatement of prior periods' financial statements? Explain.

Q21-15 How does the auditor modify his or her audit report when material uncertainties relating to the operations of the client are discovered? Explain.

Q21-16 How does an auditor who is not independent report on his or her association with financial statements?

Q21-17 What three possible positions might a principal auditor engaged in the audit of consolidated financial statements take regarding the work of another auditor who had examined the financial statements of a subsidiary?

Q21-18 What factors should be considered in determining whether an auditor can serve as a principal auditor for a firm's consolidated financial statements?

Q21-19 How does the principal auditor associated with consolidated financial statements decide whether the work of another auditor, relating to the subsidiary's financial statements, can be accepted? Explain.

Q21-20 What is the auditor's responsibility relating to segment information included with the financial statements to make them conform to the requirements of FASB 14?

Q21-21 What is the auditor's responsibility for supplementary information included in the financial statements? Explain.

Q21-22 What date should be shown as the date of issuance of the audit report?

Q21-23 What is meant by the reissuance of an audit report? What date should be shown on such a reissued audit report? Explain.

Q21-24 What three steps should a predecessor auditor take before allowing his or her audit report to be reissued with the audit report of a successor auditor?

Q21-25 What steps should be taken by the successor auditor if the report of the predecessor auditor is not presented with comparative financial statements?

Short Cases

C21-1 Patricia Leer, CPA, has discussed various reporting considerations with three of her audit clients. The three clients presented the following situations and asked how each would affect the audit report.

a. In prior years, when Leer issued an unqualified report on the client's comparative financial statements, this statement showed the net change in working capital, whereas in the current year the statement shows net change in cash balance. The client agrees with Leer that the change is material but believes the change is obvious to readers and need not be discussed in the footnotes to the financial statements or in Leer's report. The client is issuing comparative statements but wishes only to restate the prior year's statement to conform to the current format.

b. A client has a loan agreement that restricts the amount of cash dividends that can be paid and requires the maintenance of a particular current ratio. The client is in compliance with the terms of the agreement, and it is not likely that there will be a violation in the foreseeable future. The client believes there is no need to mention the restriction in the financial statements because such mention might mislead the readers.

c. During the year, a client correctly accounted for the acquisition of a majority-owned domestic subsidiary but did not properly present the minority interest in retained earnings or net income of the subsidiary in the consolidated financial statements. The client agrees with Leer that the minority interest presented in the consolidated financial statements is materially misstated but takes the position that the minority shareholders of the subsidiary should look to that subsidiary's financial statements for information concerning their interest therein.

Required: Each of the situations above relates to *one or more* of the four generally accepted auditing standards of reporting.

Identify and describe the applicable generally accepted auditing standard (GAAS) of reporting in each situation and discuss how the particular client situation relates to the standard and to Leer's report.

Organize your answer sheet as follows:

Situation	Applicable GAAS of reporting	Discussion of relationship of client situation to standard of reporting and to Leer's report

(AICPA adapted)

C21-2 Tamara Rose, CPA, has satisfactorily completed the examination of the financial statements of Bale & Booster, a partnership, for the year ended December 31, 19X9. The financial statements were prepared on the basis of GAAP and include footnotes that indicate that the partnership was involved in continuing litigation of material amounts relating to alleged infringement of a competitor's patent. The amount of damages, if any, resulting from this litigation could not be determined at the time of completion of the engagement. The prior years' financial statements were not presented.

Required: On the basis of the information presented, prepare an auditor's report that includes appropriate explanatory disclosure of significant facts.

(AICPA adapted)

C21-3 Lila Roscoe, CPA, has completed the examination of the financial statements of Excelsior Corporation as of and for the year ended December 31, 19X5. Roscoe also examined and reported on the Excelsior financial statements for the prior year. She drafted the following report for 19X5.

> March 15, 19X6
> We have audited the balance sheet and statements of income and retained earnings of Excelsior Corporation as of December 31, 19X5. Our examination was made in accordance with generally accepted accounting standards and, accordingly, included such tests of the accounting records as we considered necessary in the circumstances.
>
> In our opinion, the above-mentioned financial statements are accurately prepared and fairly presented in accordance with generally accepted accounting principles in effect at December 31, 19X5.
>
> *Lila Roscoe, CPA*
> *(Signed)*

Other information:
a. Excelsior is presenting comparative financial statements.
b. Excelsior does not wish to present a statement of cash flows for either year.
c. During 19X5, Excelsior changed its method of accounting for long-term construction contracts and properly showed the effect of the change in the current year's financial statements and restated the prior-year statements. Roscoe is satisfied with Excelsior's justification for making the change. The change is discussed in footnote number 12.
d. Roscoe was unable to perform normal accounts-receivable confirmation procedures, but alternate procedures were used to satisfy her as to the validity of the receivables.
e. Excelsior Corporation is the defendant in a litigation, the outcome of which is highly uncertain. If the case is settled in favor of the plaintiff, Excelsior will be required to pay a substantial amount of cash, which might require the sale of certain fixed assets. The litigation and the possible effects have been properly disclosed in footnote number 11.
f. Excelsior issued debentures on January 31, 19X4, in the amount of $10,000,000. The funds obtained from the issuance were used to finance the expansion of plant facilities. The debenture agreement restricts the payment of future cash dividends to earnings after December 31, 19X9. Excelsior declined to disclose this essential data in the footnotes to the financial statements.

Required: Consider all facts given and rewrite the auditor's report in acceptable and complete format incorporating any necessary departures from the standard report.

Do not discuss the draft of Roscoe's report but identify and explain any items included in *"Other Information"* that need not be part of the auditor's report.

(AICPA adapted)

C21-4 Various types of "accounting changes" can affect the second reporting standard of the generally accepted auditing standards. This standard reads, "The report shall identify those circumstances in which such principles have not been consistently observed in the current period in relation to the preceding period."

Assume that the following list describes changes which have a material effect on a client's financial statements for the current year.
a. A change from the completed-contract method to the percentage-of-completion method of accounting for long-term construction-type contracts.

b. A change in the estimated useful life of previously recorded fixed assets, based on newly acquired information.

c. Correction of a mathematical error in inventory pricing made in a prior period.

d. A change from prime costing to full-absorption costing for inventory valuation.

e. A change from presentation of statements of individual companies to presentation of consolidated statements.

f. A change from deferring and amortizing preproduction costs to recording such costs as an expense when incurred because future benefits of the costs have become doubtful. The new accounting method was adopted in recognition of the change in estimated future benefits.

g. A change to including the employer share of FICA taxes as "Retirement benefits" on the income statement from including it with "Other taxes."

h. A change from the FIFO method of inventory pricing to the LIFO method of inventory pricing.

Required: Identify the type of change described in each item above, state whether any modification is required in the auditor's report *as it relates to the second standard of reporting*, and state whether the prior year's financial statements should be restated when presented in comparative form with the current year's statements. Organize your answer sheet as shown in the following illustration.

For example, a change from the LIFO method of inventory pricing to the FIFO method of inventory pricing would appear as shown.

Item No.	Type of Change	Should Auditor's Report Be Modified?	Should Prior Year's Statements Be Restated?
Example	An accounting change from one generally accepted accounting principle to another generally accepted accounting principle	Yes	Yes

(AICPA adapted)

C21-5 Sturdy Corporation owns and operates a large office building in a desirable section of New York City's financial center. For many years the management of Sturdy Corporation has modified the presentation of their financial statements by

a. Showing a write-up to appraisal values in the building accounts.

b. Accounting for depreciation expense on the basis of such valuations.

Warren Wyley, a successor CPA, was asked to examine the financial statements of Sturdy Corporation for the year ended December 31, 19X0. After completing the examination, Wyley concluded that, consistent with prior years, an adverse opinion would have to be expressed because of the materiality of the apparent deviation from the historical-cost principle.

Required:

a. *Describe* in detail the form of presentation of the middle paragraph of the auditor's report on the financial statements of Sturdy Corporation for the year ended December 31, 19X0, clearly identifying the information contained in the paragraph. *Do not discuss deferred taxes.*

b. *Write a draft* of the opinion paragraph of the auditor's report on the financial statements of Sturdy Corporation for the year ended December 31, 19X0.

(AICPA adapted)

C21-6 John Darden, CPA, was asked to submit to his client, the Dundee Corporation and con-solidated subsidiaries, a report that contained the following information:
- **a.** Audited comparative consolidated balance sheets, income statements, statements of retained earnings, and statements of cash flows for the years 19X2 and 19X1.
- **b.** Complete description of the company's accounting policies.
- **c.** Consolidating information.
- **d.** A ten-year summary of earnings and earnings-per-share for the consolidated entity.
- **e.** Complete footnotes to consolidated financial statements.
- **f.** A description of auditing procedures applied to specific items in the financial statements.
- **g.** Additional details of general and administrative expenses.

Required:
- **a.** Label each of the preceding listed items of information with a (B) if it is part of the basic financial statements or with an (S) if it is considered supplementary information of the kind sometimes included in auditor-submitted documents.
- **b.** Outline the CPA's investigative and reporting responsibility for items in the basic financial statements and for items included in supplementary information.

Problems

P21-1 Select the best answer to each of the following items relating to audit reports.
- **a.** The fourth generally accepted auditing standard of reporting requires an auditor to render a report whenever an auditor's name is associated with financial statements. The overall purpose of the fourth standard of reporting is to require that reports
  1. Ensure that the auditor is independent with respect to the financial statements under examination.
  2. State that the auditor's examination of the financial statements has been conducted in accordance with generally accepted auditing standards.
  3. Indicate the character of the auditor's examination and the degree of responsibility assumed.
  4. Express whether the accounting principles used in preparing the financial statements have been applied consistently in the period under examination.
- **b.** The auditor's report makes reference to the basic financial statements, which are customarily considered to be the balance sheet and the statements of
  1. Income and cash flows.
  2. Income, changes in retained earnings, and cash flows.
  3. Income, retained earnings, and cash flows.
  4. Income and retained earnings.
- **c.** An investor is reading the financial statements of the Sundby Corporation and observes that the statements are accompanied by an unqualified auditor's report. From this the investor may conclude that

    1. Any disputes over significant accounting issues have been settled to the auditor's satisfaction.

    2. The auditor is satisfied that Sundby is operationally efficient.

    3. The auditor has ascertained that Sundby's financial statements have been prepared accurately.

    4. Informative disclosures in the financial statements but not necessarily in the footnotes are to be regarded as reasonably adequate.

d. Which of the following *best* describes the reference to the expression "taken as a whole" in the fourth generally accepted auditing standard of reporting?

    1. It applies equally to a complete set of financial statements and to each individual financial statement.

    2. It applies only to a complete set of financial statements.

    3. It applies equally to each item in each financial statement.

    4. It applies equally to each material item in each financial statement.

e. When comparative financial statements are presented, the fourth reporting standard, which refers to financial statements "taken as a whole," should be considered to apply to the financial statements of the

    1. Periods presented plus the one preceding period.

    2. Current period only.

    3. Current period and those of the other periods presented.

    4. Current and immediately preceding period only.

f. When the audited financial statements of the prior year are presented together with those of the current year, the continuing auditor's report should cover

    1. Both years.

    2. Only the current year.

    3. Only the current year, but the prior year's report should be presented.

    4. Only the current year, but the prior year's report should be referred to.

g. When an auditor submits a document containing audited financial statements to a client, the auditor has a responsibility to report on

    1. Only the basic financial statements included in the document.

    2. The basic financial statements and only that additional information required to be presented in accordance with provisions of the Financial Accounting Standards Board.

    3. All of the information included in the document.

    4. Only that portion of the document that was audited.

h. Which of the following would be an *inappropriate* addressee for an auditor's report?

    1. The corporation whose financial statements were examined.

    2. A third party, even if the third party is a client who engaged the auditor for examination of a nonclient corporation.

    3. The president of the corporation whose financial statements were examined.

    4. The stockholders of the corporation whose financial statements were examined.

i. On February 13, 19X8, Celia Fox, CPA, met with the audit committee of the Gem Corporation to review the draft of Fox's report on the company's financial statements as of and for the year ended December 31, 19X7. On February 16, 19X8, Fox completed all remaining field work at the Gem Corporation's headquarters. On February 17, 19X8, Fox typed and signed the final version of the auditor's report. On February 18, 19X8, the final report was mailed to Gem's audit committee. What date should have been used on Fox's report?

    1. February 13, 19X8.

    2. February 16, 19X8.

   3. February 17, 19X8.
   4. February 18, 19X8.

(AICPA adapted)

P21-2 Select the best answer for each of the following items relating to the audit report when the client has *changed auditors.*

   a. Before reissuing a report that was previously issued on the financial statements of a prior period, a predecessor auditor should
   1. Review the successor auditor's working papers.
   2. Examine significant transactions or events since the date of previous issuance.
   3. Obtain a signed engagement letter from the client.
   4. Obtain a letter of representation from the successor auditor.

   b. Jerry Jerome has completed an examination of the financial statements of Bold, Inc. Last year's financial statements were examined by Tom Smith, CPA. Since last year's financial statements will be presented for comparative purposes without Smith's report, Jerome's report should
   1. State that the prior year's financial statements were examined by another auditor.
   2. State that the prior year's financial statements were examined by Smith.
   3. *Not* refer to the prior year's examination.
   4. Refer to Smith's report only if the opinion was other than unqualified.

   c. After performing all necessary procedures, a predecessor auditor reissues a prior period report on financial statements at the request of the client without revising the original wording. The predecessor auditor should
   1. Delete the date of the report.
   2. Dual-date the report.
   3. Use the reissue date.
   4. Use the date of the previous report.

   d. Elizabeth Rusk, CPA, succeeded Fenwick Boone, CPA, as auditor of Moonlight Corporation. Boone had issued an unqualified report for the calendar year 19X5. What can Rusk do to establish the basis for expressing an opinion on the 19X6 financial statements with regard to opening balances?
   1. Rusk may review Boone's working papers and thereby reduce the scope of auditing tests Rusk would otherwise have to do with respect to opening balances.
   2. Rusk must apply appropriate auditing procedures to account balances at the beginning of the period so as to be satisfied that they are properly stated and may *not* rely on the work done by Boone.
   3. Rusk may rely on the prior year's financial statements since an unqualified opinion was issued and must make reference in the auditor's report to Boone's report.
   4. Rusk may rely on the prior year's financial statements since an unqualified opinion was issued and must refer in a middle paragraph of the auditor's report to Boone's report of the prior year.

(AICPA adapted)

P21-3 Select the best answer to each of the following items relating to audit reports on consolidated financial statements.

   a. Thomas Feiner, CPA, has examined the consolidated financial statements of Kass

Corporation. Ezra Jones, CPA, has examined the financial statements of the sole subsidiary material in relation to the total examined by Feiner. It would be appropriate for Feiner to serve as the principal auditor, but it is impractical for him to review the work of Jones. Assuming an unqualified opinion is expressed by Jones, one would expect Feiner to

1. Refuse to express an opinion on the consolidated financial statements.
2. Express an unqualified opinion on the consolidated financial statements and not refer to the work of Jones.
3. Express an unqualified opinion on the consolidated financial statements and refer to the work of Jones.
4. Express an "except for" opinion on the consolidated financial statements and refer to the work of Jones.

b. Hedy Nielsen, CPA, is the principal auditor who is auditing the consolidated financial statements of her client. Nielsen plans to refer to another CPA's examination of the financial statements of a subsidiary company but does *not* wish to present the other CPA's audit report. Both Nielsen's and the other CPA's audit reports have noted no exceptions to generally accepted accounting principles. Under these circumstances, the opinion paragraph of Nielsen's audit report should express

1. An unqualified opinion.
2. A modified opinion.
3. An "except for" opinion.
4. A principal opinion.

c. When a principal auditor decides to make reference to the examination of another auditor, the principal auditor's report should clearly indicate the

1. Principal auditor's qualification on the overall fairness of the financial statements, taken as a whole, "except for" the work and report of the other auditor.
2. Procedures that were performed by the other auditor in connection with the other auditor's examination.
3. Division of responsibility between that portion of the financial statements covered by the examination of the other auditor.
4. Procedures that were performed by the principal auditor to obtain satisfaction as to the reasonableness of the examination of the other auditor.

d. Heather Halsey is the independent auditor examining the consolidated financial statements of Rex, Inc., a publicly held corporation. Jeffrey Lincoln is the independent auditor who has examined and reported on the financial statements of a wholly owned subsidiary of Rex, Inc. Halsey's *first* concern with respect to the Rex financial statements is to decide whether Halsey

1. Can serve as the principal auditor and report as such on the consolidated financial statements of Rex, Inc.
2. Can make reference to Lincoln's work in Halsey's report on the consolidated financial statements.
3. Should review Lincoln's workpapers with respect to the examination of the subsidiary's financial statements.
4. Should resign from the engagement since a qualified opinion is the only type that could be rendered on the consolidated financial statements.

e. Which of the following is the *least* important consideration when an auditor is deciding whether he or she can act as principal auditor for consolidated financial statements and utilize the work and reports of other independent auditors?

1. Whether the portion of the financial statements he or she has examined is

material compared with the portion examined by other auditors.
2. Whether the components he or she examined are important relative to the enterprise as a whole.
3. Whether he or she has examined the parent company statements.
4. Whether he or she has sufficient knowledge of the overall financial statements.

(AICPA adapted)

P21-4 Select the best answer for each of the following items relating to audit reports qualified because of departures from GAAP and scope limitations.

a. An auditor is confronted with an exception considered sufficiently material as to warrant some deviation from the standard unqualified auditor's report. If the exception relates to a departure from generally accepted accounting principles, the auditor must decide between expressing
   1. An adverse opinion and an explanatory opinion.
   2. An adverse opinion and an "except for" opinion.
   3. An adverse opinion and a disclaimer of opinion.
   4. A disclaimer of opinion and an "except for" opinion.

b. A company issues audited financial statements under circumstances that require the presentation of a statement of cash flows. If the company refuses to present a statement of cash flows, the independent auditor should
   1. Disclaim an opinion.
   2. Prepare a statement of cash flows and note in a middle paragraph of the report that this statement is auditor prepared.
   3. Prepare a statement of cash flows and disclose in a footnote that this statement is auditor prepared.
   4. Qualify his opinion with an "except for" qualification and a description of the omission in a middle paragraph of the report.

c. When financial statements are prepared on the basis of a going concern and the auditor believes that the client may *not* continue as a going concern, the auditor should issue
   1. An unqualified opinion with modifying language.
   2. An unqualified opinion with an explanatory middle paragraph.
   3. An "except for" opinion.
   4. An adverse opinion.

d. If the auditor believes that required disclosures of a significant nature are omitted from the financial statements under examination, the auditor should decide between issuing
   1. A qualified opinion or an adverse opinion.
   2. A disclaimer of opinion or a qualified opinion.
   3. An adverse opinion or a disclaimer of opinion.
   4. An unqualified opinion or a qualified opinion.

e. Limitation on the scope of the auditor's examination may require the auditor to issue a qualified opinion or to disclaim an opinion. Which of the following would generally be a limitation on the scope of the auditor's examination?
   1. The unavailability of sufficient competent evidential matter.
   2. The engagement of the auditor to report on only one basic financial statement.
   3. The examination of a subsidiary's financial statements by an auditor other than the one who examines and reports on the consolidated financial statements.
   4. The engagement of the auditor after year end.

 f. In which of the following circumstances would an auditor be required to issue a qualified report with a separate explanatory paragraph?
  1. The auditor satisfactorily performed alternative accounts receivable procedures because scope limitations prevented performance of normal procedures.
  2. The financial statements reflect the effects of a change in accounting principles from one period to the next.
  3. A particular note to the financial statements discloses a company accounting method that deviates from generally accepted accounting principles.
  4. The financial statements of a significant subsidiary were examined by another auditor, and reference to the other auditor's report is to be made in the principal auditor's report.

 g. Under the AICPA Code of Professional Conduct, a CPA may issue an unqualified opinion on financial statements that contain a departure from generally accepted accounting principles if he or she can demonstrate that due to unusual circumstances the financial statements would be misleading if the departure were not made. Which of the following is an example of unusual circumstances that could justify such a departure?
  1. New legislation.
  2. An unusual degree of materiality.
  3. Conflicting industry practices.
  4. A theoretical disagreement with a standard promulgated by the Financial Accounting Standards Board.

 h. In determining the type of opinion to express, an auditor assesses the nature of the reporting qualifications and the materiality of their effects. Materiality will be the primary factor considered in the choice between
  1. An "except for" opinion and an adverse opinion.
  2. An "except for" opinion and a modified opinion.
  3. An adverse opinion and a disclaimer of opinion.
  4. A qualified opinion and a piecemeal opinion.

 i. When restrictions that significantly limit the scope of the audit are imposed by the client, the auditor generally should issue which of the following opinions?
  1. "Except for."
  2. Disclaimer.
  3. Adverse.
  4. Modified.

(AICPA adapted)

P21-5 Select the best answer for each of the following items relating to accounting changes and consistency modifications in the standard audit report.
 a. Which of the following four events may be expected to result in a consistency modification in the auditor's report?
  1. The declining balance method of depreciation was adopted for newly acquired assets.
  2. A revision was made in the service lives and salvage values of depreciable assets.
  3. A mathematical error in computing the year-end LIFO inventory was corrected.
  4. The provision for bad debts increased considerably over the previous year.

 b. When comparative financial statements are presented and a change in accounting principle is made in the current year, the financial statements of the prior year should be restated *except* when the change is
  1. From the completed-contract to the percentage-of-completion method of accounting for long-term construction-type contracts.

   2. From the LIFO to the FIFO method of inventory pricing.
   3. From the FIFO to the LIFO method of inventory pricing.
   4. From the "full-cost" to another acceptable method of accounting used in the extractive industry.

c. A company has changed its method of inventory valuation from an unacceptable one to one in conformity with generally accepted accounting principles. The auditor's report on the financial statements of the year of the change should include
   1. No reference to consistency.
   2. A reference to a prior period adjustment.
   3. A middle paragraph explaining the change.
   4. A justification for making the change and the impact of the change on reported net income.

(AICPA adapted)

P21-6 Select the best answer to each of the following items relating to a disclaimer of opinion.

a. In which one of the following situations must the CPA issue a disclaimer of opinion?
   1. He or she owns stock in the company.
   2. Some portion of the client's financial statements does not conform to generally accepted accounting principles.
   3. He or she has omitted a normally required auditing procedure.
   4. Generally accepted accounting principles have not been applied on a basis consistent with that of the preceding year.

b. An auditor is unable to determine the amounts associated with certain illegal acts committed by the client. In these circumstances the auditor would *most* likely
   1. Issue either a qualified opinion or a disclaimer of opinion.
   2. Issue only an adverse opinion.
   3. Issue either a qualified opinion or an adverse opinion.
   4. Issue only a disclaimer of opinion.

c. When are an auditor's reporting responsibilities *not* met by attaching an explanation of the circumstances and a disclaimer of opinion to the client's financial statements?
   1. When he or she believes the financial statements are misleading.
   2. When he or she was unable to observe the taking of the physical inventory.
   3. When he or she is not independent.
   4. When he or she has performed insufficient auditing procedures to express an opinion.

(AICPA adapted)

P21-7 Select the best answer to each of the following items relating to miscellaneous aspects of audit reports.

a. In which of the following circumstances would an adverse opinion be appropriate?
   1. The auditor is not independent with respect to the enterprise being audited.
   2. An uncertainty prevents the issuance of an unqualified opinion.
   3. The statements are *not* in conformity with GAAP regarding pension plans.
   4. A client-imposed scope limitation prevents the auditor from complying with generally accepted auditing standards.

b. When an adverse opinion is expressed, the opinion paragraph should include a direct reference to
   1. A footnote to the financial statements, which discusses the basis for the opinion.

2. The scope paragraph that discusses the basis for the opinion rendered.
3. A separate paragraph that discusses the basis for the opinion rendered.
4. The consistency or lack of consistency in the application of generally accepted accounting principles.

c. When auditing a public entity's financial statements that include segment information, the auditor should
1. Make certain the segment information is labeled "unaudited" and determine that the information is consistent with audited information.
2. Make certain the segment information is labeled "unaudited" and perform only analytical review procedures on the segment information.
3. Audit the segment information and, if the information is adequate and in conformity with GAAP, do *not* make reference to the segment information in the auditor's report.
4. Audit the segment information and, if the information is adequate and in conformity with GAAP, refer to the segment information in the auditor's report.

d. An auditor's examination reveals a misstatement in segment information that is material in relation to the financial statements taken as a whole. If the client refuses to make modifications to the presentation of segment information, the auditor should issue
1. An "except for" opinion.
2. A "subject to" opinion.
3. An unqualified opinion.
4. A disclaimer of opinion.

e. If management chooses to place supplementary information required by the FASB in footnotes attached to the financial statements, this information should be clearly marked as
1. Unaudited.
2. Supplementary information required by the FASB.
3. Disclosures required by the FASB.
4. Audited financial data required by generally accepted accounting principles.

(AICPA adapted)

P21-8 On September 30, 19X5, White & Co., CPAs, was engaged to audit the consolidated financial statements of National Motors, Inc., for the year ended December 31, 19X5. The consolidated financial statements of National had not been audited the prior year. National's inadequate inventory records precluded White from forming an opinion as to the proper or consistent application of generally accepted accounting principles to inventory balances on January 1, 19X5. Therefore, White decided not to express an opinion on the results of operations for the year ended December 31, 19X5. National elected not to present comparative financial statements.

Rapid Parts Company, a consolidated subsidiary of National, was audited for the year ended December 31, 19X5, by Green & Co., CPAs. Green completed its field work on February 28, 19X6, and submitted an unqualified opinion on Rapid's financial statements on March 7, 19X6. Rapid's statements reflect total assets and revenues constituting 22 and 25 percent, respectively, of the consolidated totals of National. White decided not to assume responsibility for the work of Green. Green's report on Rapid does not accompany National's consolidated statements.

White completed its field work on March 28, 19X6, and submitted its auditor's report to National on April 4, 19X6.

Required: Prepare White and Company's auditor's report on the consolidated financial statements of National Motors, Inc.

(AICPA adapted)

P21-9 The following tentative auditor's report was drafted by a staff accountant and submitted to a partner in the accounting firm of Better & Best, CPAs:

**To the audit committee
American Widgets, Inc.**

INTRODUCTORY PARAGRAPH:

We have audited the consolidated balance sheets of American Widgets, Inc., and subsidiaries as of December 31, 19X2 and 19X1, and the related consolidated statements of income, retained earnings, and cash flows for the years then ended. Other auditors examined the financial statements of certain subsidiaries and have furnished us with reports thereon containing no exceptions. Our opinion expressed herein, insofar as it relates to the amounts included for those subsidiaries, is based solely on the reports of the other auditors.

SCOPE PARAGRAPH:

We conducted our audits in accordance with generally accepted auditing standards. As such, we included such tests of the accounting records and such other tests as we considered necessary in the circumstances.

MIDDLE PARAGRAPH #1:

As discussed in note 4 to the financial statements, on January 8, 19X3, the company halted the production of certain medical equipment as a result of inquiries by the Food and Drug Administration, which raised questions as to the adequacy of some of the company's sterilization equipment and related procedures. Management is not in a position to evaluate the effect of this production halt and the ensuing litigation, which may have an adverse effect on the financial position of American Widgets, Inc.

MIDDLE PARAGRAPH #2:

As fully discussed in note 7 to the financial statements, in 19X1 the company extended the use of the last-in, first-out (LIFO) method of accounting to include all inventories. In examining inventories, we engaged Dr. Irwin Same (Nobel Prize winner 19X0) to test check the technical requirements and specifications of certain items of equipment manufactured by the company.

OPINION PARAGRAPH:

In our opinion, except for the effects, if any, on the financial statements of the ultimate resolution of the matter discussed in the second preceding paragraph, the financial statements referred to above present fairly the financial position of American Widgets, Inc., as of December 31, 19X1, and the results of its operations for the year then ended, in conformity with generally accepted accounting principles.

To be signed by
Better & Best, CPAs

March 1, 19X3, except for Footnote 4, which is January 8, 19X3

Required: Identify deficiencies in the staff accountant's tentative report.

(AICPA adapted)

P21-10 Ben Maddox, CPA, was engaged to audit the financial statements of Baby Doe Mining Company and Consolidated Subsidiaries for the two years ended June 30, 19X8. Following are the results of Maddox's audits:

1. The financial statements for Rocky Bottom Corporation, a Colorado subsidiary whose total assets and revenues constituted 28 percent and 30 percent, respectively, of the consolidated totals for each year, were audited by Taylor and Company of Gunnison, Colorado. Unqualified opinions were issued to Maddox by Taylor and Company for both 19X7 and 19X8.

2. The financial statements of Baby Doe (the parent corporation) for 19X7 failed to capitalize certain lease obligations which, in Maddox's opinion, should have been capitalized. The error resulted in a $5,600,000 understatement of both fixed assets and long-term debt in 19X7. Net income and retained earnings were understated by $350,000, and earnings per share were understated by $1.01 per share for that year. The misstatement resulted in the issuance of a qualified opinion (issued September 15, 19X7) on the consolidated financial statements. After lengthy negotiations with the controller of Baby Doe, Maddox convinced him to correct the error in 19X8.

3. One of the consolidated subsidiaries of Baby Doe, First Strike Mining of Durango, Colorado, is the defendant in a lawsuit alleging negligence in a 19X7 mining accident in which two employees were seriously injured and one was killed. The company carries $1 million in liability insurance. The case is in trial, but the attorney is not presently able to reasonably estimate the loss, if any, or the probability of an unfavorable outcome. The contingency is described in Footnote 12 to the consolidated financial statements.

4. On August 3, 19X8, Baby Doe acquired a new subsidiary, Silver Dollar Mine, Inc. This event was properly disclosed in Footnote 10 to the consolidated financial statements.

5. Field work for the 19X8 audit ended on September 15, 19X8.

   Required: Prepare the draft of the audit report on the consolidated comparative financial statements of Baby Doe Mining Company and Consolidated Subsidiaries for the two years ended June 30, 19X8.

CHAPTER 22

Other Types of Reports

Objectives

☐ **1.** Recognize the difference between a review of interim financial statements and an audit.
☐ **2.** Recognize situations that require the use of a special report.
☐ **3.** Understand the auditor's responsibility for letters to underwriters.
☐ **4.** Be able to draft various types of reports on internal controls.

In this chapter we resume our discussion of reports rendered by accountants. In Chapter 21, our discussion centered around the audit report that accompanies audited financial statements. That report is designed to disclose whether an entity's financial position, results of operations, and cash flows are presented in conformity with GAAP. We also discussed briefly the report that should be included with the unaudited financial statements of a public entity when the accountant has been associated with those statements. But accountants also issue other types of reports, some of which we examine in this chapter.

The specific content of those reports depends primarily on the following factors: the level of association the accountant has had with the financial statements (look again at Figure 21–1); the nature of the financial statement data being reported on; and the type of service being performed by the accountant.

The term *association with financial statements* was defined in Chapter 21. This term should not be confused with a CPA's preparation of financial statements as an employee of a firm or as a member of an organization. Because of an employee CPA's nonindependence, any statement prepared in that capacity should be signed as an employee or organization member, and not as a CPA.

Recall that there are basically three levels of association for outside accountants providing services to both public and nonpublic entities. Besides the audit level of association, there are the *review and compilation levels for unaudited financial statements of nonpublic entities.* The reports associated with those services are covered in Chapter 23. There are also *reviews of interim financial information* and association with *unaudited financial statements* for public entities. Each of these levels of association requires a specific type of report.

Some special reports of accountants may be classified on the basis of the *nature of the financial data* covered by the report. Audited financial statements may, for example, be prepared in accordance with a comprehensive basis of accounting other than GAAP. If a full-scope audit is not required, the accountant may be engaged to audit only specific elements or accounts of a financial statement. In other instances, the accountant may be asked to apply only selected auditing procedures to certain elements or accounts of a financial statement. In other cases, the auditor may be asked to report on client compliance with contractual agreements or regulatory requirements. Finally, the auditor may be associated with financial information presented in prescribed forms or schedules, such as those required by state insurance boards.

Still other reports by independent auditors can better be described by relating them to *types of services* performed to produce them. Such reports include letters to underwriters and reports on internal control.

Reports on Reviews of Interim Financial Information

☑ **Objective 1**
Recognize the difference between interim reviews and audits

Publicly held corporations issue interim financial information to shareholders. The period of time covered by this information may be a quarter or a month ending on a date other than the entity's fiscal year end. Interim financial information *may be presented alone or may be included in a note to audited financial statements*. The SEC requires the inclusion of selected quarterly data with audited annual financial statements. Such data include net sales, gross profit, and income from continuing operations. Per-share data for the above income statement items must also be disclosed for each full quarter within the two most recent fiscal years and any subsequent interim period for which income statements are presented.

The independent accountant may be involved with a client's interim financial information in a variety of ways. At the lowest level, this involvement may take the form of *informal consultation* on matters that arise as the interim financial information is being prepared. At the other extreme, the accountant may perform an *audit* of the interim financial statements in accordance with generally accepted auditing standards. The most common type of involvement, however, can be characterized as a **review** of the interim financial information; SAS 36 (AU722) states that "the objective of a review of interim financial information is to provide the accountant, based on objectively applying his (or her) knowledge of financial reporting practices to significant accounting matters of which he (or she) becomes aware through inquiries and analytical procedures, with a basis for reporting whether material modifications should be made for such information to conform with generally accepted accounting principles."[1] It is important to recognize that a review *itself does not provide the basis for the expression of an audit opinion* because it does not require an understanding of the internal control structure, tests of accounting records, or other corroborating evidential matter obtained through inspection, observation, or confirmation of the *interim* information. However, this standard applies only to public entities and the SEC requires that all of these entities issue annual audited financial statements.

Hence, in all cases in which the accountant is associated as a reviewer of interim financial statements, he (or she) will have been associated with the audited annual financial statements of the entity as well.

Timeliness is a very important element in interim financial reporting. Such information must be made available to interested parties more promptly than the annual financial statements. For that reason, some expenses included in interim financial reports are estimated. Furthermore, each interim period is viewed primarily as an integral part of an annual period calling for the application of the *annualization concept* in presenting deferrals, accruals, and estimations.

Procedures for the Interim Review

The procedures associated with the interim review can be summarized from SAS 36 (AU722) as follows:

1. *Inquiry* concerning the accounting system to obtain an understanding of the manner in which transactions were recorded, classified, and summarized in the preparation of interim financial information, and inquiry into any significant changes in the system of internal accounting control to ascertain their potential effect on the preparation of interim financial information.
2. *Analytical procedures* on interim financial information by reference to internal financial statements, trial balances, or other financial data to help in the identification of unusual relationships and individual items that appear to be unusual. This involves
   a. A systematic comparison of current financial information with that anticipated for the current period, that of the immediately preceding interim period, and that of the corresponding interim period of the previous fiscal year.
   b. A study of the interrelationships of the elements of the financial information that would be expected to conform to a predictable pattern based on the entity's past experience.
   c. A consideration of the types of matters that in the preceding year or quarters required accounting adjustment.
3. *Reading the minutes* of meetings of stockholders, board of directors, and committees of the board of directors to identify actions that might affect the interim financial information.
4. *Reading the interim financial information* to consider, on the basis of information coming to the accountant's attention, whether the information being reported conforms with generally accepted accounting principles.
5. *Obtaining letters from other accountants,* if any, who have been engaged to perform a review of the interim financial information of significant segments of the reporting entity, its subsidiaries, or other significant investees.
6. *Inquiry of officers and other executives* having the responsibility for financial and accounting matters concerning
   a. Whether the interim financial information has been prepared in conformity with generally accepted accounting principles.
   b. Changes in the entity's business activities or accounting practices.

    c. Matters as to which questions have arisen in the course of applying the foregoing procedures.

    d. Events subsequent to the date of the interim financial information that would have a material effect on the presentation of such information.

Factors Affecting the Use of the Interim Review

The extent to which these procedures should be applied varies with the nature of the engagement. SAS 36 (AU722) cites the following variables that should be considered in making that judgment.

- The accountant's knowledge of the accounting and reporting practices of the entity. Since the accountant will usually have audited the firm's most recent annual financial statements, his or her knowledge of these practices will be extensive and may permit the application of limited procedures to the interim data.
- The accountant's knowledge of weaknesses in internal control. This knowledge, also, should have been acquired during the audit of the most recent annual financial statements. The accountant should then direct interim procedures toward discovering changes in the system during the interim period and differences between controls underlying the interim and annual information. Material accounting control weaknesses could prevent preparation of interim financial information in conformity with GAAP, and may thus require a scope limitation on the review procedures sufficient to preclude the issuance of a review report.
- The accountant's knowledge of changes in the nature or volume of the client's activities. Examples include business combinations, disposal of a segment of the business, or extraordinary items.
- Issuance of accounting pronouncements during the interim period. Such pronouncements may affect the client's reporting practices and, therefore, need to be covered in the accountant's review procedures.
- Accounting records maintained at multiple locations. This situation may call for performing review procedures at both corporate headquarters and other locations selected by the accountant.

Reporting Requirements

Reporting requirements for reviews of interim financial information depend on whether the interim financial information is presented (1) alone or (2) in a footnote to audited financial statements.

    If the information is *presented alone*, and appropriate review procedures have been performed, permission is generally given for the accountant's name to be associated with a review report. If the scope of procedures performed does not permit the completion of a review, the accountant should not permit the use of his or her name. Scope restrictions might be caused by such circumstances as timing of the review work, inadequate accounting records, or a material weakness in internal control. If the client subsequently presents, in a document issued to stockholders, third parties, or the SEC, interim financial information that the accountant has reviewed, the accountant should request that the review report be included. If the client will not agree to the accountant's request, or if the scope of the review has been limited, the accountant should request that neither his or her name nor reference to work performed be associated with the information. Also, if the accountant concludes that the interim financial information does not conform to GAAP, he or she should advise the board of directors of the respects in which the information does not conform. The report should be modified if the accountant finds disclosures to be inadequate.

The accountant's *report associated with the interim financial information presented alone* should be addressed to the company, its board of directors, or stockholders and should be dated as of the completion of the review. It should, according to SAS 36 (AU722), include the following elements:

- A statement that the review of interim financial information was made in accordance with the standards for such reviews.
- An identification of the interim financial information reviewed.
- A description of the procedures for a review of interim financial information.
- A statement that a review of interim financial information is substantially less in scope than an audit and a disclaimer of opinion regarding fairness of presentation.
- A statement indicating whether the accountant is aware of any material modifications that should be made to the interim information to make it conform to GAAP.

Each page of the interim financial information should be marked clearly as "unaudited." Notice that, except for identification of the type of financial statements being reviewed and the time periods covered, the elements included in the review report for interim information are the same as those included in the review report for annual financial statements of a nonpublic entity, discussed in Chapter 23.

Circumstances that require deviations from the standard report format include *departures from GAAP* and *inadequate disclosures*. Normally no modifications are required for uncertainties affecting the interim information or the lack of consistency in application of GAAP, as long as these items are adequately disclosed in the interim information.

If interim financial information is presented with audited annual financial statements, as is usually the case for publicly traded companies reporting under SEC regulations, the interim data are ordinarily regarded as supplementary information. As such, this information will not have been subjected to the auditing procedures applied to the basic financial statements. Management should, therefore, *clearly mark the information as unaudited.*

If the auditor has performed the review procedures discussed previously, no separate report on that information is ordinarily necessary. In addition, the auditor ordinarily need not modify the report on the audited financial statements. However, the audit report *should be expanded* to include appropriate disclosures when any of the following four circumstances exists:

- Selected quarterly *data required by SEC regulations are omitted or have not been reviewed.* The audit report in this case would include expanded disclosures of the omission or lack of review.
- Interim financial information included in the note to audited financial statements has *not been clearly marked as unaudited.* In this case, the audit report should be expanded to disclaim an opinion on the interim information.
- Interim financial information is *not presented in conformity with GAAP.* In this case the audit report would contain a separate paragraph setting out the facts and explaining the effects of any departures from GAAP.
- Interim financial information includes an indication that a review was made but *fails to include the statement that the review is substantially less in scope than an audit examination and a disclaimer of opinion.* In this case, the audit report should contain a separate paragraph disclosing those facts.

Engagement Letter and Working Papers

An *engagement letter* is recommended for reviews of interim financial information, so that the accountant and the client may avoid any misunderstanding as to the nature of the work performed or the degree of responsibility accepted by the accountant. The letter would normally include (1) a description of procedures to be performed; (2) an examination that such procedures do not constitute an audit; and (3) a description of the form of the report to be rendered, if any.

There are no formal guidelines for *working papers* in support of reviews of interim financial information. However, the accountant should logically follow the general guidelines set forth in Chapter 6 in this case, which states that the working papers should be adapted to the needs of the particular engagement.

Special Reports

☑ **Objective 2**
Recognize special
reporting situations

Certified public accountants are sometimes asked to

1. Perform audits of financial statements prepared in accordance with the *cash basis or some other basis of accounting that is not in accordance with GAAP.*
2. Perform audits of specified elements, accounts, or items of financial statements.
3. Perform procedures that lead to reports on compliance with aspects of contractual agreements or regulatory requirements related to audited financial statements.
4. Prepare financial information presented in prescribed forms or schedules that require a prescribed form of audit report.[2]

In addition, they may be asked to apply *selected auditing procedures* not constituting a full audit to specified elements or accounts of a financial statement.

All such engagements require **"special reports."** SAS 62 sets out the guidelines for these special types of reports.

Audits of Financial Statements Prepared in Accordance with a Comprehensive Basis of Accounting Other Than GAAP

Generally accepted auditing standards must be met for the audit examination and report anytime an opinion is to be expressed on **financial statements**. SAS 62 defines a financial statement as

> a presentation of financial data, including accompanying notes, derived from accounting records and intended to communicate an entity's economic resources or obligations at a point in time or the changes therein for a period of time in accordance with a comprehensive basis of accounting.[3]

SAS 62 also describes four types of comprehensive bases of accounting other than GAAP.

- A basis of accounting that the reporting entity uses to comply with the requirements or financial reporting provisions of *a government regulatory agency* to whose jurisdiction the entity is subject. An example is the uniform system of accounts prescribed by the Interstate Commerce Commission for railroad companies.
- A basis of accounting that the reporting entity uses or expects to use to file its income tax return for the period covered by the financial statements. This may be characterized as the *tax basis.*
- The *cash receipts and disbursements* basis of accounting, including modifications of the cash basis having substantial support, such as capitalizing fixed assets and recording depreciation on fixed assets or accruing only income taxes.
- *Any other basis* involving a definite set of criteria having substantial support and applied to all material items appearing in the financial statements. (An example of this basis of accounting is the *price-level-adjusted basis of accounting.*)

Normally, fairness of presentation must be judged by the auditor in terms of compliance of the financial statements with GAAP. The use of GAAP presumes that the financial statements purport to present financial position and results of operations. However, some financial statements are not intended to present financial position and results of operations. These include

- Statements of assets and liabilities arising from cash transactions that do not include owners' equity accounts.
- Statements of cash receipts and disbursements.
- Summaries of operations.
- Statements of operations by product lines.

The definition of financial statements is broad enough to cover all the above examples, as well as the balance sheet, income statement, statement of retained earnings, and statement of cash flows. The auditor is allowed to change the guidelines against which fairness of presentation is measured from GAAP to another comprehensive basis of accounting, *as long as that basis is one of the four listed above.* This means that the auditor can render any one of the types of reports discussed earlier, ranging from an unqualified report through a disclaimer of opinion (see Figures 21–2 and 21–10), with financial statements presented in accordance with an acceptable comprehensive basis of accounting other than GAAP.

Figure 22–1 illustrates the typical report prepared in accordance with one of these bases of accounting. Such a report should include

1. A title that includes the word *independent.*
2. An introductory paragraph that is the same as the standard audit report, except for the terminology used to describe the financial statements.

Figure 22–1

Financial Statements Prepared on the Entity's Income Tax Basis

Report of Independent Certified Public Accountants

The Partners
ABC Partnership

We have audited the accompanying statements of assets, liabilities, and capital—income tax basis of ABC Partnership as of December 31, 19X2 and 19X1, and the related statements of revenue and expenses—income tax basis and changes in partners' capital accounts—income tax basis for the years then ended. These financial statements are the responsibility of the Partnership's management. Our responsibility is to express an opinion on these financial statements based on our audits.

We conducted our audits in accordance with generally accepted auditing standards. Those standards require that we plan and perform the audit to obtain reasonable assurance about whether the financial statements are free of material misstatement. An audit includes examining, on a test basis, evidence supporting the amounts and disclosures in the financial statements. An audit also includes assessing the accounting principles used and significant estimates made by management, as well as evaluating the overall financial statements presentation. We believe that our audits provide a reasonable basis for our opinion.

As described in Note X, these financial statements are prepared on the accounting basis used for income tax purposes, which is a comprehensive basis of accounting other than generally accepted accounting principles.

In our opinion, the financial statements referred to above present fairly, in all material respects, the assets, liabilities, and capital of ABC Partnership as of December 31, 19X2 and 19X1, and its revenue and expenses and changes in partners' capital accounts for the years then ended, on the basis of accounting described in Note X.

To be signed by
Firm name

City, State
Date

Source: From Grant Thornton, *Accounting and Auditing Bulletin* 88-40 (October 18, 1988).

3. A scope paragraph similar to that of the standard audit report on GAAP-based financial statements.

4. An explanatory paragraph that
   a. States (and refers to a note in the financial statements that describes) the *basis of presentation* used in the financial statements.
   b. States that the basis of presentation is a comprehensive basis of accounting other than GAAP.

5. A paragraph that expresses the auditor's opinion (or disclaims an opinion) on whether the financial statements are presented fairly, in all material respects, in conformity with the basis of accounting described. If the statements are not presented fairly, or if there has been a scope limitation on the engagement, all of the circumstances should be adequately described in separate explanatory paragraphs, and the opinion paragraph should be appropriately modified.

6. A paragraph that restricts the distribution of the report to those within the entity or regulatory agency, if the financial statements are prepared in accordance with the requirements of financial reporting provisions of a governmental regulatory agency.

7. The manual or printed signature of the auditor.

8. The date, which should be the last day of audit field work.

As you can see in Figure 22–1, the introductory, scope, and opinion paragraphs generally differ from the standard audit report only in referring to the comprehensive basis of accounting rather than to generally accepted accounting principles. However, such a report must include a paragraph (see item 2 of the list) that informs the reader about the basis of accounting followed, and specifically about the fact that the comprehensive basis of accounting followed is other than GAAP.

In some instances, the auditor is forced to consider whether the financial statements being reported on are *suitably titled*. For example, a cash-basis financial statement containing asset, liability, and capital accounts is not appropriately referred to as a balance sheet. If the auditor believes that the financial statements are not suitably titled, the report should be modified to disclose that fact. For example, the cash-basis financial statement purporting to be a balance sheet might be titled "Statement of Assets and Liabilities Arising from Cash Transactions."

Reports on Specified Elements of Financial Statements

In rare instances, a client may request an accountant to issue a report on specified elements, accounts, or items in a financial statement. Such reports normally fall into one of two categories:

• Reports expressing an *audit opinion* on one or more specified elements or accounts (such as an opinion regarding the fairness of presentation of a rental or royalty schedule or a provision for federal income taxes); or
• Reports relating to the results of *applying agreed-upon procedures* to one or more specified elements or accounts (such as confirmation of trade accounts receivable).

An audit geared to express an opinion on specified elements or accounts requires the auditor to meet the general and field work auditing standards, plus the second, third, and fourth reporting standards. The first reporting standard need not be met because it pertains to the financial statements taken as a whole, which is not a part of the scope of audit work in engagements such as these. In auditing only the provision for federal income taxes of an entity, for example, the auditor's procedures (recomputation, inspection of documents, etc.) are narrowed to a single account and the related accounts, such as the federal income tax accrual. Therefore, the auditor should not mention the financial statements taken as a whole in the audit report. Neither should the report be allowed to accompany the financial statements of the entity—even with a disclaimer of opinion on them. In most cases, issuing a disclaimer of opinion or an adverse opinion on the financial statements taken as a whole while expressing an opinion on a specified element or account is tantamount to expressing a *piece-meal opinion*, which is no longer permitted under generally accepted auditing standards.

Since the audit report in this instance is narrowed to a specified element or account in the financial statements, the *auditor's judgment regarding materiality should be narrowed*, as well, to that element or account alone. Thus, disclosures, or lack of them, which ordinarily would not be material, might become material in this context.

Figure 22–2 illustrates an audit report on a specified element of financial statements that relates to royalties. Notice from the illustration that the report includes

1. A title that includes the word *independent*.
2. A paragraph that
   a. States that the specified elements or items identified in the report were audited. If applicable, the report would state that the audit was made in conjunction with an audit of the company's financial statements.
   b. Differentiates the responsibilities of management and the auditor.
3. A scope paragraph that includes the same elements as those in the standard audit report.
4. A paragraph that describes the basis on which the specified elements, accounts, or items are presented and, when applicable, any agreements specifying such basis, if the presentation is not prepared in conformity with generally accepted accounting principles or another comprehensive basis of accounting.
5. An opinion paragraph that expresses the auditor's opinion (or disclaims an opinion) on whether the specified elements, accounts, or items are presented fairly, in all material respects, in conformity with the basis of accounting described.
6. A paragraph that restricts the distribution of the report to those within the entity or those parties that would otherwise understand the nature of the engagement.
7. The auditor's manual or printed signature.
8. The date.

Figure 22–2 ▬▬▬

Report Related to Royalties

Report of Independent Certified Public Accountants

Board of Directors
XYZ Corporation

We have audited the accompanying schedule of royalties applicable to engine production of the Q Division of XYZ Corporation for the year ended December 31, 19X2, under the terms of a license agreement dated May 14, 19XX, between ABC Company and XYZ Corporation. This schedule is the responsibility of the XYZ Corporation's management. Our responsibility is to express an opinion on this schedule based on our audit.

We conducted our audit in accordance with generally accepted auditing standards. Those standards require that we plan and perform the audit to obtain reasonable assurance about whether the schedule of royalties is free of material misstatement. An audit includes examining, on a test basis, evidence supporting the amounts and disclosures in the schedule. An audit also includes assessing the accounting principles used and significant estimates made by management, as well as evaluating the overall schedule presentation. We believe that our audit provides a reasonable basis for our opinion.

We have been informed that, under XYZ Corporation's interpretation of the agreement referred to in the first paragraph, royalties were based on the number of engines produced after giving effect to a reduction for production retirements that were scrapped, but without a reduction for field returns that were scrapped, even though the field returns were replaced with new engines without charge to customers.

In our opinion, the schedule of royalties referred to above presents fairly, in all material respects, the number of engines produced by the Q Division of XYZ Corporation during the year ended December 31, 19X2, and the amount of royalties applicable thereto, under the license agreement referred to above.

This report is intended solely for the information and use of the board of directors and management of XYZ Corporation and ABC Company.

To be signed by
Firm name

City, State
Date

Source: From Grant Thornton, *Accounting and Auditing Bulletin* 88-40 (October 18, 1988).

Engagements to report on the results of applying agreed-upon procedures to specified elements or accounts [see SAS 35 (AU622)] require the auditor to meet only the general standards and the first standard of field work. These engagements may include the application of selected auditing procedures (not constituting a full audit) to specified accounts in connection with a proposed acquisition or claims of creditors. Because of their limited nature, such engagements may be accepted only if the following conditions are met:

• *The parties involved must have a clear understanding* of the specific auditing procedures being performed. This may be accomplished through (1) discussions with the client; (2) review of correspondence with the named parties; (3) comparisons of the procedures to be applied with the written requirements of a supervisory agency, when applicable; or (4) distributing a draft of the report or client engagement letter to the parties involved with a request for their reply before the report is issued.

- *Distribution of the report must be restricted to the parties* involved and named in the engagement letter.

The accountant's report should indicate the specified elements or accounts to which procedures were applied as well as the intended distribution of the report. It should enumerate the procedures performed and state the accountant's finding while disclaiming an opinion on the specified elements or accounts. It should also state that the report relates only to the specified elements of the financial statements and not to the financial statements taken as a whole.

Reports on Compliance with Contractual Agreements or Regulatory Requirements

Companies may be required by contractual agreement or by regulatory agencies to furnish compliance reports prepared by independent auditors. For example, loan agreements may impose on borrowers a variety of covenants involving matters such as payments into a sinking fund, payment of interest, maintenance of current ratio, restriction of dividend payments, and use of the proceeds from the sale of property. The lenders in such a situation may request assurance from the independent auditor that the borrower has complied with the covenants of the agreement.

A report in this type of situation *generally gives* **negative assurance** *relative to the applicable covenants.* Such assurance may be given in a separate report or in one or more paragraphs of the auditor's report accompanying the financial statements. *However, it should not be given unless the auditor has audited the financial statements* to which the contractual agreement or regulatory requirements relate. In this case, a negative assurance statement could read as follows:

> In connection with our audit, nothing came to our attention that caused us to believe that the company was not in compliance with any of the terms, covenants, provisions or conditions of. . . . However, our audit was not directed primarily toward obtaining knowledge of such noncompliance.[4]

Financial Information Presented in Prescribed Forms or Schedules

The accountant is often expected to use printed forms or schedules, provided by the bodies with which they are to be filed, that prescribe the wording of an auditor's report. *Many of these forms are not acceptable to the independent auditor* because the prescribed form of auditor's report does not conform with the applicable professional reporting standards. For example, the prescribed language may call for assertions that are not consistent with the auditor's function or responsibility. In some instances, the special report forms can be made acceptable by inserting additional wording; others can be made acceptable only by complete revision. When a printed report form calls for an independent auditor to make an assertion that cannot be justified within professional standards, the *form should be reworded or a separate report should be attached.* The reporting provisions in such instances should conform to those described earlier for reporting on financial statements that are prepared in accordance with a comprehensive basis of accounting other than generally accepted accounting principles.

Other Reports Classified by Type of Service Rendered

Letters to Underwriters

☑ **Objective 3**
Recognize
the auditor's
responsibility
for letters to
underwriters

Certified public accountants may provide still other types of reports for clients. In connection with the audit examination of financial statements and schedules contained in registration statements filed with the Securities and Exchange Commission under the Securities Act of 1933, the public accountant is frequently asked, but is not required, to issue **letters to underwriters** (commonly called **comfort letters**). These letters provide additional information relating to both audited and unaudited elements of the registration statement, including

1. A statement as to the independence of the accountant.
2. An opinion as to whether the audited financial statements and schedules included in the registration statement comply as to form in all material respects with the applicable accounting requirements of the Securities Act of 1933 and the published rules and regulations thereunder.
3. Negative assurances as to whether unaudited financial statements and schedules included in the registration statements
   a. *Comply as to form* with the applicable accounting requirements of the Securities Act of 1933 and the published rules and regulations thereunder;
   b. Are fairly presented in conformity with generally accepted accounting principles on a *basis substantially consistent with that of the audited financial statements and schedules* included therein.
4. Negative assurances as to whether, during a specified period following the date of the latest financial statements in the registration statement and prospectus, there have been *any significant changes* in capital stock or long-term debt or any significant changes in other specified financial statement items.

Each individual letter should be tailored to meet the needs of the underwriter. However, the CPA should avoid phrases such as "examined" and "made a limited review" to describe the work performed, because they might mislead the reader to infer that an audit or review was made of the information. To avoid a misunderstanding as to the purpose and intended use of the comfort letter, it should conclude with a paragraph reading somewhat as follows:

This letter is solely for the information of, and assistance to, the underwriters in conducting and documenting their investigation of the affairs of the company in connection with the offering of the securities covered by the Registration Statement and is not to be used, circulated, quoted, or otherwise referred to within or outside the underwriting group for any other purpose, including but not limited to the registration, purchase, or sales of securities, nor is it to be filed with or referred to in whole or in part in the Registration Statement or any other document except that reference may be made to it in the underwriting agreement or in any list of closing documents pertaining to the offering of the securities covered by the Registration Statement.[5]

The comfort letter should also contain a statement saying that the accountant has not examined the financial statements of the company as of any date or for any period subsequent to dates of the last audited statements. That statement should be followed by another that the accountant is unable to, and does not, express an opinion on the unaudited data presented subsequent to the date of the last audited statements.

The addressee of the comfort letter is typically the underwriter, with a copy being sent to the client. The date of the letter is ordinarily on or shortly before the **closing date,** which is the date on which the issuer (client) delivers the securities to the underwriter in exchange for the proceeds of the securities offering.

Reports on Internal Control

☑ **Objective 4**
Know the contents and format of reports on internal control

An independent accountant may be engaged to report on an entity's internal control structure in at least four ways:

a. Expressing an *opinion* on the adequacy of an entity's internal control structure in effect as of a specified date.
b. Communication of internal control structure related matters (called *reportable conditions*) to the audit committee or equivalent authoritative body within the client's organization that are noted during an audit of the financial statements.
c. Reporting on all or part of an entity's structure for the *restricted use of management or regulatory bodies based on the regulatory agency's prescribed criteria.* In making such a report, however, if a weakness is discovered that is outside the prescribed criteria, it should also be included in the report.
d. Making *other special-purpose reports* on all or part of an entity's internal control structure for the restricted use of management, specified regulatory agencies, or other specified third parties.[6]

The procedures required in the evidence-gathering process vary with the nature of the report. In all instances, however, the accountant will be concerned with assessing risk control and verifying that the control procedures are in conformity with the provisions of the organization chart and procedures manual.

Report types (c) and (d) relate to studies of internal control made as part of very limited-purpose engagements, which are relatively infrequent. As such, they are considered beyond the scope of this text and are not included in our discussion.

Reports That Express an Opinion on Internal Control

We now turn our attention to the accountant's report rendered in connection with an engagement to *express an opinion* on the adequacy of an entity's internal control structure in which the accountant places no restrictions on the use of the report (report type a). Such reports may be useful to regulatory agencies, management, or internal auditors but should be of little value to some other users (such as creditors). In the final analysis, regulatory agencies, directors, and officers of the corporation have the responsibility of deciding whether such reports would be useful to the general public.

An internal control audit engagement should involve planning the scope of the engagement, reviewing the design of the system, testing prescribed procedures, and evaluating the results of the review and tests. The accountant should obtain from management the following written representations:

- Acknowledgment of management's responsibility for establishing and maintaining the internal control structure.
- A statement that management has disclosed to the accountant all material internal control weaknesses of which it is aware, including those for which management believes the cost of corrective action may exceed the benefits.
- Descriptions of any irregularities involving managers or employees who have significant roles in the internal control structure.
- A statement as to whether there are any changes subsequent to the date being reported on that would significantly affect the internal control structure, including any corrective actions taken by management with regard to material weaknesses.

The accountant should also *document the work done* to express an opinion on the internal control structure. The working papers should include documents prepared by the entity to describe its internal control structure. Other documents should provide evidence regarding the planning of the examination, the review of the system, and the testing phases of the examination.

On completion of the examination, the accountant's report expressing an opinion on an entity's internal control structure should contain the following elements:

- A description of the scope of the engagement.
- The date to which the opinion relates.
- A statement that the establishment and maintenance of the system is the responsibility of management.
- A brief explanation of the broad objectives and inherent limitations of internal control.

- The accountant's opinion as to whether the structure taken as a whole is sufficient to meet the broad objectives of internal control insofar as those objectives pertain to the prevention or detection of errors and irregularities in amounts that would be material in relation to the financial statements.

The report should be dated as of the date of completion of field work and may be addressed to the entity whose structure is being studied or to its audit committee, its board of directors or stockholders.[7]

Communication of Internal Control Structure Related Matters Noted in an Audit[8]

When an accountant is engaged to audit a client's financial statements, the procedures that he or she applies to obtain an understanding of the entity's control structure are restricted to those that will enable the auditor to meet the second standard of audit field work. These procedures are, in many respects, not considered adequate for expressing an opinion on the entity's control structure, such as was discussed in the previous section. However, during the course of an audit, the auditor may become aware of matters relating to the internal control structure that may be of interest to the audit committee, or equivalent body of the company. These matters, referred to as **reportable conditions,** might adversely affect the organization's ability to record, process, summarize, and report financial data consistent with the financial statement assertions that were discussed in earlier chapters.

Deficiencies may be discovered by the auditor in the control environment, the accounting system, or in the procedures employed by the company. Such deficiencies may include inadequate design of the system, absence of appropriate segregation of duties, lack of appropriate documentation, absence of proper comparisons and compliance monitoring, or inadequate provisions for safeguarding of assets. In addition, reportable conditions would include evidence of failure to comply with established policies and procedures that are designed to prevent, detect, or correct errors and irregularities, or evidence of intentional override of the system by those in authority.

Generally accepted auditing standards *do not require the auditor to search for reportable conditions* in the control structure. However, if the auditor's procedures that were performed to obtain an understanding of the control structure (outlined in previous chapters) uncover reportable conditions, the auditor should report these to the audit committee. In deciding whether a particular condition should be reported, the auditor should consider the entity's size, the complexity and diversity of its activities, its organizational structure, and its ownership characteristics.

Generally accepted auditing standards *do not require that internal control structure matters be reported in writing*. If information is communicated orally, however, the auditor should document the communication of these conditions in the working papers. As a practical matter, and usually as a service to clients, the

Figure 22–3 ▪▪▪▪▪

Auditor's Letter Citing Reportable Conditions in Control Structure

B R O W N   A N D   S M I T H

Certified Public Accountants

February 20, 19X2
Audit Committee
Client Company
Address

Gentlemen:

We have audited the financial statements of XYZ Company for the year ended December 31, 19X1, and have issued our report thereon dated February 15, 19X2. In planning and performing our audit, we considered the company's internal control structure in order to determine our auditing procedures for the purpose of expressing our opinion on the financial statements. The purpose of our audit was not to provide assurance on the internal control structure. However, we noted certain matters involving the internal control structure and its operation that we consider to be reportable conditions under standards established by the American Institute of Certified Public Accountants. Reportable conditions involve matters coming to our attention relating to significant deficiencies in the design or operation of the internal control structure that, in our judgment, could adversely affect the organization's ability to record, process, summarize, and report financial data consistent with the assertions of management in the financial statements.

1. Purchase invoices are paid without an independent verification of the receipt of materials included on the invoices.
2. Purchase invoices are not stamped "paid" when checks are issued in payment of them.

This report is intended solely for the information and use of the audit committee, management, and others within the organization.

Sincerely yours,

BROWN AND SMITH, CPAs

communication of reportable conditions will be in the form of a letter similar to that illustrated in Figure 22–3.

The report should

1. Indicate that the purpose of the audit was to report on the financial statements and not to provide assurance on the internal control structure.
2. Include the definition of reportable conditions.
3. Include a comment on restriction of the distribution to the audit committee, management, and other company insiders.

Some reportable conditions may be of such importance as to be considered **material weaknesses.** For this purpose, a material weakness is defined as follows:

> A reportable condition in which the design or operation of the specific internal control structure elements do not reduce to a relatively low level the risk that errors or irregularities in amounts that would be material in relation to the financial statements being audited may occur and not be detected within a timely period by employees in the normal course of their assigned functions.[9]

At the auditor's discretion, and sometimes at the client's request, the auditor may choose to separately identify material weaknesses in the report.

The auditor should retain a copy of the letter and follow up on it in subsequent audits, to ascertain whether the weaknesses observed in the preceding audit have been corrected.

The timing of the report may be critical, because in some cases immediate corrective action may be necessary. For this reason, the communication of reportable conditions may occur during or at the completion of interim field work.

Although the auditor is not required to communicate suggestions regarding corrective action of reportable conditions, this is often a vital part of service to clients. Generally accepted auditing standards permit the communication of suggestions in the letter.

In addition, in most engagements, the auditor may communicate to the client a variety of observations and suggestions that go beyond internal control structure issues. These matters may deal with operational or administrative efficiencies, business strategies, and other items of short or long-range benefit of the client.[10] Usually, these matters are covered in a *management letter,* which is a separate communication.

Summary

In this chapter we have discussed and illustrated various reports that auditors may render in connection with engagements other than an independent audit of financial statements. The contents of these reports depend primarily on the level of association the auditor has with the information, the nature of the data being reported on, and the types of services being performed. A report must be rendered in any situation in which the accountant is associated with a client's financial statements. He or she is presumed to be associated with a client's financial statements anytime he or she has consented to the use of his or her name in connection with a report, document, or written communication containing the client's financial statements.

We described reports rendered in connection with the review of interim financial information. Here we observed the similarity between these reports and the review report for unaudited statements of nonpublic entities, which will be discussed in Chapter 23.

In the last section of the chapter we described various special reports issued by public accountants performing audits of statements prepared in accordance with a basis of accounting other than GAAP and providing other services for clients. Reports on other services include letters to underwriters and reports on internal control.

Auditing Vocabulary

p. 962 **closing date:** The date on which the issuer of stock or debt delivers the securities to the underwriter in exchange for the proceeds of the securities offering.

p. 961 **comfort letter:** Another name for a letter to underwriters.

p. 955 **financial statement:** A presentation of financial data, including accompanying notes, derived from accounting records and intended to communicate an entity's economic resources or obligations at a point in time, or the changes therein for a period of time, in accordance with a comprehensive basis of accounting.

p. 961 **letters to underwriters:** A letter written to the underwriter of the company's initial stock or debt offerings that provides additional information relating to both audited and unaudited elements of a registration statement.

p. 966 **material weakness:** A reportable condition in internal control in which the design or operation of the specific internal control structure elements do not reduce to a relatively low level the risk that errors or irregularities in amounts that would be material in relation to the financial statements being audited may occur and not be detected within a timely period by employees in the normal course of their assigned functions.

p. 960 **negative assurance:** A lesser form of assurance than positive audit assurance. Negative assurance, used in review reports, letters to underwriters, and certain types of special reports, generally states that the accountant, based on procedures performed, is not aware of any material modifications or adjustments that should be made in financial presentations to make them conform with GAAP or another comprehensive basis of accounting. Wording varies slightly for different types of reports.

p. 964 **reportable conditions:** Deficiencies in the internal control structure of the company that affect the organization's ability to record, process, summarize, and report financial data consistent with the financial statement assertions of management. Such matters should generally be reported to the audit committee or equivalent body of the company.

p. 950 **review:** A form of association with financial statements, the objective of which is to provide the accountant with a basis for reporting whether material modification should be made for such information to conform with generally accepted accounting principles.

p. 955 **special report:** A report falling into one of the following categories:
1. Audits of financial statements prepared in accordance with a basis of accounting other than GAAP.
2. Audits of specified elements, accounts, or items of financial statements.
3. Reports on compliance with aspects of contractual regulatory requirements.
4. Financial information presented in prescribed forms or schedules.

Notes

1. Statement on Auditing Standards (SAS) 36 (AU722) (New York: AICPA, 1981).
2. SAS 62 (AU621) (New York: AICPA, 1989). We have summarized segments of that publication in this section of the chapter.
3. Ibid., paragraph 2.
4. Ibid., paragraph 19.
5. Statement on Auditing Standards (SAS) 49 (New York: AICPA, 1984).
6. SAS 30 (AU642) paragraph 2 (New York: AICPA, 1980).
7. Ibid., paragraphs 35–38.
8. Material from this section is summarized from SAS 60 (AU325) (New York: AICPA, 1988).
9. Ibid., paragraph 15.
10. Ibid., paragraph 19.

Questions for Class Discussion

Q22-1 What is meant by *other types of reports rendered by accountants*?

Q22-2 What four types of presentations are typically characterized as special reports?

Q22-3 What are two reports that can best be described by relating them to the types of services rendered?

Q22-4 What analytical procedures are used in performing a review of financial statements?

Q22-5 Which inquiries should the accountant make in performing a review of financial statements?

Q22-6 What are the contents of the accountant's report on a review of the financial statements?

Q22-7 What questions should be asked of officers and other executives during an engagement calling for the review of interim financial data? Indicate the reasons for each of the questions asked.

Q22-8 What are two ways in which the interim financial information reviewed by the accountant may be used by the client?

Q22-9 How does the standard audit report compare with an audit report rendered in connection with an audit of financial statements prepared in accordance with a comprehensive basis of accounting other than GAAP?

Q22-10 What special concerns will the auditor have in writing a report on financial statements prepared by using the cash basis of accounting?

Q22-11 What are the special characteristics associated with an accountant's report on the examination of specified elements or accounts appearing in a client's financial statements? Should such a report include a disclaimer of opinion on the financial statements taken as a whole? Explain.

Q22-12 How would an auditor react to an engagement requiring that his or her report be presented on printed forms or schedules provided by regulatory bodies? Explain.

Q22-13 What is meant by a *comfort letter*? What is typically included in such a letter?

Q22-14 Under what four circumstances may an independent accountant be engaged to report on an entity's internal control structure?

Q22-15 What interested groups might logically find an accountant's report on internal control useful?

Short Cases

C22-1 Grace Collins, CPA, has been the auditor for Murbank Enterprises, a medium-sized publicly traded company, for the past five years. Recently Murbank requested that Collins perform quarterly reviews of the company's interim financial statements. Collins has agreed to perform those reviews and to issue a quarterly report based on the review procedures.

Required:
  a. What is the purpose of a review of interim financial information?
  b. How does the nature of a review of interim financial information differ from an audit?
  c. How does the nature of a review of interim financial information differ from a review of yearly information for nonpublic entities?
  d. Describe the procedures Collins should follow in conducting her review.
  e. Describe the report that Collins should render to Murbank's audit committee, based on the above circumstances.
  f. How would Collins's reporting responsibility differ if, instead of being issued alone, the interim financial statements were included in footnotes to the company's annual audited financial statements?

C22-2 Middleboro Corporation, a company with which you have not previously been associated, has been having a great deal of trouble in valuing its end-of-period finished goods inventory as of June 30, 19X2. The production and accounting branches of the company are currently in disagreement as to the exact value to place on an end-of-period finished goods inventory. They have asked if you could perform an audit examination of the finished goods inventory account and render an opinion as to the fairness of its presentation in the company's financial statements, which they have agreed to accept as an arbitrated value for finished goods. Middleboro Corporation has not previously been audited.

Required:
  a. Do generally accepted auditing standards allow such engagements? If so, under what conditions, if any, may the audit of the inventory account be performed?
  b. Outline some special considerations for this audit that would not otherwise be as important (such as materiality guidelines, reporting considerations, etc.).
  c. Describe the report that would be rendered in an engagement such as this.
  d. How would your reporting responsibility differ if, instead of being asked to audit the finished goods inventory account, you had been asked to give your opinion regarding the company's compliance with a contractual arrangement with a vendor, an arrangement that involved finished goods inventories?

C22-3 The board of directors of Walenda Associates, a large, local building supply concern in your city, has recently elected an audit committee for the first time. Up to this year the company has never been audited. The board of directors has also decided that the company does not need a financial statement audit for the current year because they are convinced that your firm's review services are sufficient to meet Walenda's immediate needs. They approach you with a request that you conduct a thorough audit of the company's internal control structure for the past year; they theorize that a competent professional accountant like you can surely discover the system's major weaknesses and communicate them. The audit of internal controls, they feel, should improve efficiency of operations and enhance future profitability of the company—if they choose to follow your suggestions.

Required:

a. How does an engagement such as this one differ in objective from obtaining an understanding of the internal control structure as part of a financial statement audit?

b. Describe how auditing procedures for this engagement differ from auditing procedures performed while obtaining an understanding of the internal control structure as part of a financial statement audit.

c. What representations should be obtained from Walenda's management in regard to the engagement described?

d. How will the report rendered by the auditor for this engagement differ from a standard report on internal control based on a study conducted as part of a financial statement audit?

C22-4 Loretta Loman is a CPA who has examined the financial statements of the Broadwall Corporation, a publicly held company, for the year ended December 31, 19X1. Loman was asked to perform a review of the financial statements of Broadwall Corporation for the period ending March 31, 19X2. The engagement letter stated that a review does not provide a basis for the expression of an opinion.

Required:

a. Explain why Loman's review will not provide a basis for the expression of an opinion.

b. What are the review procedures Loman should perform, and what is the purpose of each procedure? Structure your response as follows:

Procedure	Purpose of Procedure

c. Assuming that Loman's review procedures do not reveal any material departures from generally accepted accounting principles, draft the typical report that Loman should issue.

(AICPA adapted)

Problems

P22-1 Select the best answer to each of the following items relating to the review of interim financial information.

a. If, as a result of a review of interim financial information, a CPA concludes that such information does *not* conform with generally accepted accounting principles, the CPA should

1. Insist that the management conform the information with generally accepted accounting principles, and if this is not done, resign from the engagement.
2. Adjust the financial information so that it conforms with generally accepted accounting principles.
3. Prepare a qualified report that makes reference to the lack of conformity with generally accepted accounting principles.
4. Advise the board of directors of the respects in which the information does *not* conform with generally accepted accounting principles.

b. The objective of a review of the interim financial information of a publicly held company is to

1. Provide the accountant with a basis for the expression of an opinion.
2. Estimate the accuracy of financial statements based on limited tests of accounting records.
3. Provide the accountant with a basis for reporting to the board of directors or stockholders.
4. Obtain corroborating evidential matter through inspection, observation, and confirmation.

c. A report based on a review of interim financial statements would include all of the following elements *except*

1. A statement that an examination was performed in accordance with generally accepted auditing standards.
2. A description of the procedures performed or a reference to procedures described in an engagement letter.
3. A statement that a limited review would *not* necessarily disclose all matters of significance.
4. An identification of the interim financial information reviewed.

d. In a review of interim financial information, the auditor's work consists primarily of

1. Studying and evaluating limited amounts of documentation supporting the interim financial information.
2. Scanning and reviewing client-prepared interim financial statements.
3. Making inquiries and performing analytical procedures concerning significant accounting matters.
4. Confirming and verifying significant account balances at the interim date.

e. A modification of the CPA's report on a review of the interim financial statements of a publicly held company would be necessitated by which of the following?

1. An uncertainty.
2. Lack of consistency.
3. Reference to another accountant.
4. Inadequate disclosure.

(AICPA adapted)

P22-2 Select the best answer to each of the following items relating to reports on internal control.

a. A CPA should *not* issue a report on an entity's internal control structure related to a financial statement audit if

1. The report is to be sent to stockholders with unaudited financial statements.
2. The CPA has not audited the company's financial statements.

3. The report is not to be given to creditors.
4. The report is to be given to management.

b. Because of the technical nature and complexity of internal accounting control and the consequent problem of understanding reports thereon, questions have been raised as to the benefits of such reports prepared by independent auditors. Which of the following groups probably would find a report on internal control *least* useful?

1. Regulatory agencies.
2. General creditors.
3. Management.
4. Internal auditors.

c. Dey, Knight, & Co., CPAs, has issued a qualified opinion on the financial statements of Adams, Inc., because of a scope limitation. Adams, Inc., requested a report on internal control, which it intends to give to one of its major creditors. What effect, if any, would the qualified opinion have on the internal control report that Dey, Knight, & Co. intends to prepare based on its audit engagement?

1. The audit scope limitation should be indicated in the report on internal control.
2. A report on internal control cannot be issued based on a qualified opinion.
3. The audit scope limitation has no effect, but Dey, Knight, & Co. should not issue the report if it will be given to a creditor.
4. The audit scope limitation has no effect on a report on internal control.

d. Ramirez Corp. has received a government grant and asked you, as a CPA, to prepare a report on internal control, which is required by the terms of the grant. The governmental agency responsible for the grant has prepared written criteria, including a questionnaire, for such a report. During your study to prepare the report you find what you consider a material internal-control weakness in accounting for the grant. This weakness was not covered by the criteria established by the governmental agency. What action should you take in your report to the governmental agency?

1. Include the weakness in the report even though not covered by the agency's criteria.
2. Do not include the weakness in the report because it is outside the criteria established by the agency.
3. Advise Ramirez Corp.'s management but do not include the weakness in the report.
4. Include a comment in the report that you do not believe the criteria established by the agency are comprehensive but do not include the weakness in the report.

(AICPA adapted)

P22-3 Select the best answer to each of the following items relating to special reports and letters to underwriters.

a. An auditor's report would be designated as a special report when it is issued in connection with which of the following?

1. Financial statements for an interim period that are subjected to a review.
2. Financial statements prepared in accordance with a comprehensive basis of accounting other than generally accepted accounting principles.
3. Financial statements that purport to be in accordance with generally accepted accounting principles but do *not* include a presentation of the statement of changes in financial position.

    4. Financial statements that are unaudited and are prepared from a client's accounting records.

  b. One example of a *special report,* as defined by Statements on Auditing Standards, is a report issued in connection with

    1. A feasibility study.

    2. A review of interim financial information.

    3. Price-level-basis financial statements.

    4. Compliance with a contractual agreement *not* related to the financial statements.

  c. The term *special reports* may include all of the following *except* reports on financial statements

    1. Of an organization that has limited the scope of the auditor's examination.

    2. Prepared for limited purposes, such as a report that relates to only certain aspects of financial statements.

    3. Of a nonprofit organization that follows accounting practices differing in some respects from those followed by business enterprises organized for profit.

    4. Prepared in accordance with a cash basis of accounting.

  d. In a comfort letter to underwriters, the CPA should normally avoid using which of the following terms to describe the work performed?

    1. Examined.

    2. Read.

    3. Made inquiries.

    4. Made a limited review.

  e. A CPA should *not* normally refer to which one of the following subjects in a comfort letter to underwriters?

    1. The independence of the CPA.

    2. Changes in financial statement items during a period subsequent to the date and period of the latest financial statements in the registration statement.

    3. Unaudited financial statements and schedules in the registration statement.

    4. Management's determination of line of business classifications.

  f. When asked to perform an examination in order to express an opinion on one or more specified elements, accounts, or items of a financial statement, the auditor

    1. May *not* describe auditing procedures applied.

    2. Should advise the client that the opinion will result in a piecemeal opinion.

    3. May assume that the first standard of reporting with respect to generally accepted accounting principles does *not* apply.

    4. Should comply with the request only if they constitute a major portion of the financial statements on which an auditor has disclaimed an opinion based on an audit.

(AICPA adapted)

P22-4 Select the best answers to the following items.

  a. The accountant's report expressing an opinion on an entity's internal control structure should state that the

    1. Establishment and maintenance of the system of internal control are the responsibility of management.

    2. Objectives of the client's system of internal accounting control are being met.

    3. Study and evaluation of the system of internal control was conducted in accordance with generally accepted auditing standards.

    4. Inherent limitations of the client's system of internal accounting control were examined.

  b. When an auditor performs a review of interim financial statements, which of the following steps would not be part of the review?

    1. Review of computer controls.

    2. Inquiry of management.

    3. Review of ratios and trends.

    4. Reading the minutes of the stockholders' meetings.

  c. The accountant's report expressing an opinion on an entity's internal control structure would *not* include a

    1. Description of the scope of the engagement.

    2. Specific date that the report covers, rather than a period of time.

    3. Brief explanation of the broad objectives and inherent limitations of internal control.

    4. Statement that the entity's internal control structure is consistent with that of the prior year after giving effect to subsequent changes.

  d. When reporting on financial statements prepared on a comprehensive basis of accounting other than generally accepted accounting principles, the independent auditor should include in the report a paragraph that

    1. States that the financial statements are in conformity with a comprehensive basis of accounting other than generally accepted accounting principles.

    2. States that the financial statements are *not* intended to have been examined in accordance with generally accepted auditing standards.

    3. Refers to the authoritative pronouncements that explain the comprehensive basis of accounting being used.

    4. Justifies the comprehensive basis of accounting being used.

  e. An auditor's report on financial statements that are prepared in accordance with a comprehensive basis of accounting other than generally accepted accounting principles should preferably include all of the following, *except*

    1. A title that includes the word "independent."

    2. An opinion as to whether the use of the disclosed method is appropriate.

    3. An opinion as to whether the financial statements are presented fairly in conformity with the basis of accounting described.

    4. An explanatory paragraph that describes the basis of accounting used.

(AICPA adapted)

P22-5 Young and Young, CPAs, completed an examination of the financial statements of XYZ Company, Inc., for the year ended June 30, 19X3, and issued a standard unqualified auditor's report dated August 15, 19X3. At the time of the engagement, the board of directors of XYZ requested a special report attesting to the adequacy of the provision for federal and state income taxes and the related accruals and deferred income taxes as presented in the June 30, 19X3, financial statements.

    Young and Young submitted the appropriate special report on August 22, 19X3.

Required: Prepare the special report that Young and Young should have submitted to XYZ Company, Inc.

(AICPA adapted)

P22-6 In early September the Sharp Corporation retained you to make an examination of its financial statements for the current year ending December 31. Your appointment occurred shortly after the death of the CPA who had audited the company in prior years. Assume that you completed your examination during the following February and prepared a draft of your audit report containing an unqualified opinion on the financial statements. Your report, as required by your engagement letter, was addressed to the board of directors. You also drafted a report describing weaknesses in the system of internal control observed during your examination and setting forth your recommendations for the correction of these weaknesses.

During your review of the drafts of these reports with the president of Sharp Corporation, he expressed his satisfaction with the unqualified report on the financial statements but indicated that the report on internal control was unnecessary. The president stated that he was aware of the weaknesses in internal control and that he would personally take steps to remedy them. Finally, the president instructed you not to render the internal control report. He explained that he felt the board of directors should deal with major policy decisions and not be burdened with day-to-day management problems.

Required:
   a. Enumerate at least five separate factors that should be considered before reaching a decision whether to render the internal control report.
   b. In the event that you decide to render the internal control report to Sharp Corporation, would you render it to the audit committee of the board of directors or to the president? Explain fully.

(AICPA adapted)

P22-7 Martin, CPA, has been engaged to express an opinion on Beta Manufacturing Company's system of internal control in effect as of June 1, 19X7.

Required:
   a. Compare Martin's examination of the internal control structure for the purpose of expressing an opinion on it with the understanding of internal accounting control obtained as part of an examination of the financial statements in accordance with generally accepted auditing standards. The comparison should be made as to the (1) scope, (2) purpose, and (3) timing of the engagements, and (4) users of the reports.
   b. Identify the major contents of Martin's report expressing an opinion on Beta's internal control structure. Do **not** draft the report.

(AICPA adapted)

CHAPTER 23

Nonaudit Services and Reports

Objectives

When you finish this chapter, you should have a basic knowledge of the standards that govern

- ☐ **1.** Tax services.
- ☐ **2.** Management advisory services.
- ☐ **3.** Attestation services.
- ☐ **4.** Accounting and review services.
- ☐ **5.** Financial forecasts and projections.

There are approximately 20,000 firms of certified public accountants operating within the United States. Of these, six firms, commonly known as the "Big Six" as a group, bill the majority of professional fees. These firms have offices in all the major cities across the country and in many foreign countries. The size of an individual office may range from fewer than twenty to more than 1,000 professional accountants. Other multiple-office firms are also referred to as international firms, because they, like the Big Six, have offices throughout the world. In addition, there are hundreds of local and regional CPA firms with professional staff sizes ranging from one to 100. All of these firms provide a variety of services in addition to auditing.

Tax Services

☑ **Objective 1**
Know statements
on responsibilities
in tax practice

Because income taxes are so directly related to the accounting data, tax services constitute an important part of the total services performed by CPA firms. These range from the preparation of tax returns of all types to providing tax advice and tax planning services. Some firms and individual CPAs may specialize in tax services to the extent that these services compose the majority of the firm's billings. The AICPA has established the Division of Federal Taxation to monitor the tax practice of certified public accountants. This body has issued statements defining the accountant's responsibilities in tax practice, which serve as qualitative guidelines for rendering tax services. These statements are summarized in Appendix 23–A.

A CPA, in performing tax services, is permitted to take an advocacy position in support of a client's position relating to tax matters. He or she is not expected to maintain an appearance of independence as is the case in the performance of an audit. However, the CPA is expected to adhere to Ethics Rule 102 in tax practice. This rule requires that the accountant exhibit integrity and objectivity in the exercise of his or her duties and that professional judgment decisions not be delegated to the client. In taking the position as an advocate for the client, the CPA must be able to show that there is reasonable basis for the position taken. Also, it is important to observe that the CPA is expected to meet the general standards of technical proficiency and due professional care in providing tax services.

In Chapter 3, we observed that the CPA is prohibited from receiving fees contingent on his or her findings in the performance of an attest engagement. In the performance of tax services, we have an exception to the contingent fee provision when the fees are fixed by court or when they are based on the findings of a governmental agency or as a result of judicial proceedings.

The declaration that must be signed by the preparer of a tax return reads as follows:

> Under penalties of perjury, I declare that I have examined this return and accompanying schedules and statements, and to the best of my knowledge and belief, it is true, correct, and complete. Declaration of Preparer (other than taxpayer) is based on all information of which the preparer has any knowledge.

It is important to observe that the CPA signing this statement has no duty to conduct examinations to determine the correctness of the data but must ask questions relating to any errors that come to his or her attention.

A CPA may, in the process of preparing a client's tax return, learn of an error in a previous year's tax return. In those instances the CPA should inform the client of the error (preferably in writing) and advise the client regarding the appropriate action to be taken. The CPA is not obligated to inform taxing authorities. In fact, under Ethics Rule 301, it would be wrong to do so without the client's permission. However, if the client does not correct the error, the accountant should seriously question the advisability of continuing a professional relationship with the client.

In advising a client regarding tax matters, the accountant must again meet the competency and due professional care standards. In the event that there are new developments, such as a change in the tax law subsequent to advice given to a client, the CPA has no responsibility for disclosing such developments unless he or she assists the client in implementing the advice previously given or has an agreement calling for him or her to keep the client informed regarding future developments relating to the advice given.

Management Advisory Services

☑ **Objective 2**
Know standards for management advisory services

The CPA, because of her or his professional exposure to the operations of many different types of clients and because of his or her professional expertise in designing accounting systems and interpreting financial data, is especially well equipped to provide **management advisory services (MAS)**. Indeed, this is a very rapidly expanding area of practice for most CPA firms. Such services can include systems analysis, advice on improvements of existing systems, the installation of accounting systems, and in some instances assistance to clients in finding qualified management personnel.

Management advisory services are sanctioned and encouraged by the AICPA as long as they are consistent with the professional competence, ethical standards, and responsibilities of accountants. Although an accountant is expected to be professionally competent to perform such services, he or she is not expected to have technical training as a management consultant. Management advisory services staffs are typically found only within the organizations of larger CPA firms and may well consist of people trained in nonaccounting fields, such as computer science or management. Because the nature of some management advisory services is so different from pure auditing and accounting, MAS staffs often have little or no contact with the audit, tax, or other nonaudit service staffs of the same firm.

The AICPA has established a Management Advisory Services Executive Committee to provide technical support and guidance to practitioners in this area of practice. This committee has issued a series of statements on standards for management advisory services, which are summarized in Appendix 23–B.

Management advisory services (MAS) are divided into two general categories: **MAS consultations** and **MAS engagements**. MAS consultations consist of informal business advice given to a client based mostly, if not entirely, on existing personal knowledge of the client's circumstances, the technical matters involved, and the mutual intent of the parties. MAS consultations usually take relatively little time and the accountant's responses to the client are usually oral. MAS engagements, on the other hand, involve an analytical approach and process applied in a more formal study or project. They typically involve more than an incidental amount of time and effort. The process involves determination of the client's objectives, fact-finding opportunity or problem-definition, evaluation of alternatives, formulation of proposed action, communication of results, implementation, and follow-up.

We should observe, just as we did in discussing tax services, that the CPA does not need to meet the ethical standard of independence in performing management advisory services. However, Ethics Rule 102, which relates to integrity and objectivity as well as the general standards of *technical competence* and *due professional care*, must still be met. In cases where a public accounting firm provides management advisory services and also audits the financial statements of the firm, the question repeatedly has been raised as to whether such a firm could appear to be independent in performing the audit. The present position taken by the AICPA is that *independence is not impaired as long as the CPA simply recommends the actions to be taken*. The CPA may also assist in the implementation of those actions, as long as he or she does not assume the role of a manager or employee. The CPA must, however, leave the *final decision* relating to all aspects of implementation to client management. This matter is treated more completely in Appendix 23–B.

Within Appendix 23–B we present a summary of management advisory services standards. One element of those standards gives particular attention to the responsibility of the accountant for communicating the results of a management advisory services engagement to the client. No specific report format is suggested, but the standards state that the report is expected to be a *statement of the consultant's principal findings, conclusions, recommendations, accomplishments, and major assumptions*—together with any limitations, reservations, or qualifications. Although the report may be presented orally, in most cases it is presented in written form. If an oral report is rendered, the practitioner should prepare a memorandum for his or her files documenting recommendations and other information discussed with the client.

Attestation Standards

☑ **Objective 3**
Know attestation services

In Chapter 1, we defined an "attest engagement" as one in which an accountant is engaged to issue a written statement that expresses a conclusion regarding the assertions of another party. The most common attest engagements are audits of historical financial statements, which have been the focus of our discussion throughout the text to this point. However, attest engagements may also include *reviews* and *engagements to apply agreed-upon procedures* to either historical or prospective financial assertions of others. Financial assertions may be presented in the form of financial statements, or in some form other than financial statements, such as a statement of performance of a particular investment fund. In addition, financial assertions may purport to present GAAP or some other comprehensive set of established criteria for fairness other than GAAP, such as the cash basis of accounting.

To establish a broad framework for the variety of attest services increasingly demanded of accountants, the Auditing Standards Board and the Accounting and Review Services Committee of the AICPA have issued a set of attestation standards. **Attestation** standards are a *natural extension of generally accepted auditing standards*. Although these standards encompass all attestation services including auditing, they were designed to apply to nonaudit services in which accountants may be engaged to express some conclusion other than positive audit assurance to the assertions provided by others. Examples of such engagements include reports on descriptions of systems of internal accounting control; on descriptions of computer software; on compliance with statutory, regulatory, and contractual requirements; on investment performance statistics, and on information supplementary to the basic financial statements. Thus, rather than supersede GAAS for audited financial statements, attestation standards are intended to enhance both consistency and quality in the performance of all attest services, including audits.

Figure 23–1 presents the attestation standards. Notice that there are eleven

Figure 23–1

Attestation Standards

General Standards

1. The engagement shall be performed by a practitioner having adequate technical training and proficiency in the attest function.
2. The engagement shall be performed by a practitioner having adequate knowledge in the subject matter of the assertion.
3. The practitioner shall perform an engagement only if he or she has reason to believe that the following two conditions exist:
   a. The assertion is capable of evaluation against reasonable criteria that either have been established by a recognized body or are stated in the presentation of the assertion in a sufficiently clear and comprehensive manner for a knowledgeable reader to be able to understand them.
   b. The assertion is capable of reasonably consistent estimation or measurement using such criteria.
4. In all matters relating to the engagement, an independence in mental attitude shall be maintained by the practitioner or practitioners.
5. Due professional care shall be exercised in the performance of the engagement.

Standards of Field Work

1. The work shall be adequately planned and assistants, if any, shall be properly supervised.
2. Sufficient evidence shall be obtained to provide a reasonable basis for the conclusion that is expressed in the report.

Standards of Reporting

1. The report shall identify the assertion being reported on and state the character of the engagement.
2. The report shall state the practitioner's conclusion about whether the assertion is presented in conformity with the established or stated criteria against which it is measured.
3. The report shall state all of the practitioner's significant reservations about the engagement and the presentation of the assertion.
4. The report on an engagement to evaluate an assertion in conformity with agreed-upon criteria or on an engagement to apply agreed-upon procedures should contain a statement limiting its use to the parties who have agreed upon such criteria or procedures.

Figure 23–2

Report Resulting from Application of Agreed-upon Procedures

To ABC Inc. and XYZ Fund:

We have applied the procedures enumerated below to the accompanying Statement of Investment Performance Statistics of XYZ Fund for the year ended December 31, 19X1. These procedures, which were agreed to by ABC Inc. and XYZ Fund, were performed solely to assist you in evaluating the investment performance of XYZ Fund. This report is intended solely for your information and should not be used by those who did not participate in determining the procedures.

(Paragraph to enumerate the procedures and findings.)

These agreed-upon procedures are substantially less in scope than an examination, the objective of which is the expression of an opinion on the Statement of Investment Performance Statistics. Accordingly, we do not express such an opinion.

Based on the application of the procedures referred to above, nothing came to our attention that caused us to believe that the accompanying Statement of Investment Performance Statistics is not presented in conformity with the measurement and disclosure criteria set forth in note 1. Had we performed additional procedures or had we made an examination of the Statement of Performance Statistics, other matters might have come to our attention that would have been reported to you.

Date and *Signature*

standards, arranged, like the generally accepted auditing standards, into three broad categories: general standards, standards of field work, and reporting standards. Many of the attestation standards are very similar to the generally accepted auditing standards, and may be regarded as having the same general meaning. Those standards include general standards 1, 4, and 5, as well as both field work standards. Thus we confine our discussion in this chapter to attestation standards that do not have a specific referent in generally accepted auditing standards. Those include general standards 2 and 3, as well as the reporting standards.

Figure 23–2 illustrates a report resulting from the application of agreed-upon procedures (not an audit) to the investment performance statistics of a government securities mutual fund. This report will help illustrate the differences between attestation standards and generally accepted auditing standards.

General Standards

Knowledge of Practitioner and Verifiability of Assertions

The second and third general attestation standards help to establish appropriate *boundaries around the attest function*. Specifically, they require that the attestor have adequate knowledge of the subject matter of the assertion, and that the assertion be capable of reasonably consistent estimation or measurement using established or stated criteria. Whenever the assertions being attested to pertain to financial or other related disclosures, the attestor is required to possess the knowledge needed to verify the assertion. Whenever the assertion involves expertise in a field that is outside of accounting (such as the performance of the investment fund referred to in Figure 23–2) it is not necessary that the accountant obtain all of the necessary knowledge to judge the reliability of the assertion. In that case, the requirement may be met, in part, through the use of one or more specialists (for example, a government securities specialist).

The third general attestation standard pertains to the assertions that are the subject of the attestation engagement. In the report illustrated in Figure 23–2, the assertion to be attested to is the investment performance of the XYZ Fund. Two conditions must be present regarding assertions of a client before an attest engagement can be performed:

1. *The assertions must be capable of evaluation against some reasonable criteria* that have been established by a recognized authority, or are stated in the presentation of assertions in a sufficiently clear manner to avoid confusion in interpretation. When the assertions pertain to financial statements, the criteria against which they are evaluated are often generally accepted accounting principles. On the other hand, when the assertion is (as illustrated in Figure 23–2) the investment performance of a fund, the criteria may be set by the users (in this case, ABC, Inc.). Whenever the criteria for evaluation are set by groups that do not follow due process or do not as clearly represent the public interest as the AICPA, FASB, or other official bodies, criteria should be critically evaluated by the attestor for both *relevance and reliability*.

2. The assertions must be capable of *reasonably consistent estimation or measurement* using the criteria that have been selected. Consistency will insure comparability of presentations in succeeding time periods. If inconsistencies exist, the measurement methods should be disclosed and changes therein explained or reconciled with former methods to permit proper interpretation over time. In Figure 23–2, we would expect that ABC Inc.'s criteria for investment performance would be consistent over time, and, if it were not, that the company would justify and properly disclose changes in those criteria.

Reporting Standards

Identification of Assertions and Character of Engagement

The first reporting standard requires that the report identify the assertion(s) being reported on and state the character of the engagement. In Figure 1–3 (Chapter 1), the assertions being reported on in the standard audit report are those included in the balance sheets of ABC Company as of December 31, 19X2 and X1, and the related statements of income, retained earnings, and cash flows for the years then ended. The financial statements themselves, which contain the assertions, should accompany the audit report. In Figure 23–2, the assertion identified is the investment performance of the XYZ Fund for the year ended December 31, 19X1. The Statement of Investment Performance Statistics for the fund for that year will accompany the attestor's report.

Communication of the character of the engagement involves both a description of the nature and scope of the work performed and a reference to the professional standards governing the engagement. In Figure 1–3, the nature of the work performed is an audit examination. The scope of such an engagement involves the examination of evidence, on a test basis, that supports the amounts included in the financial statements. Also involved is assessment of the appropriateness of the accounting principles used, the significance of estimates made by management, and the appropriateness of the overall financial statement presentation and disclosures. In Figure 23–2, the character of the engagement is the application of agreed-upon procedures between the attestor and ABC Company to the Statement of Investment Performance Statistics of XYZ Fund for the year ended December 31, 19X1. These procedures were substantially less in scope than an audit. Thus, they did not include the application of evidence-gathering procedures that would have been necessary to verify all of the relevant financial statement assertions (listed above), which would have allowed the expression of an audit opinion on the Statement of Investment Performance Statistics. Notice that Figure 23–2 contains a paragraph in which this fact is explained and in which an audit opinion is disclaimed.

The Practitioner's Conclusion

The second reporting standard requires that the practitioner state his or her conclusions about whether the assertion is presented in conformity with the established or stated criteria against which it was measured.

The nature of the stated conclusions in the attest report should match the level of service performed. Figure 23–3 presents the various levels of attest services that can be performed for clients, along with the corresponding levels of assurance that should be provided for each.

The audit is the highest level of service that can be provided, requiring a reduction of attestation risk to a low level. Thus, the highest level of assurance must be provided by the auditor, which is "positive." Positive assurance is usually expressed by stating that, in the auditor's opinion, the financial statements referred to in the opening paragraph of the report are, in all material respects, fairly presented in conformity with generally accepted accounting principles.

Review reports constitute a lower level of service than audits, allowing the practitioner to increase controlled attestation risk to a moderate level, and necessitating only "negative assurance." Review reports are discussed in the next section. Similarly, reports based on the results of applying agreed-upon procedures, such as illustrated in Figure 23–2, express negative assurance. Notice that negative assurance may be expressed as follows: "nothing came to our attention

Figure 23-3 ▰▰▰

Levels of Attestation Services and Assurances Given

Level of service	Attestation risk	Assurance given
General Distribution Reports		
Audit examination	Low	Positive
Review	Moderate	Negative
Limited Distribution Reports		
Engagements to apply agreed-upon procedures		Negative

that caused us to believe that . . . (the assertions) . . . are not presented in conformity with . . . (the agreed-upon criteria). . . ."

It is important to note that, even on engagements in which full-scope audits are not conducted, the lack of consistent application of GAAP or other criteria, or the omission of necessary information, would still necessitate modification of the report.

Reservations about the Engagement

Sometimes the practitioner may encounter unresolved problems on the engagement that may prevent the expression of an unqualified attest report. Such problems may include restrictions on the scope of the engagement that prevent the practitioner from obtaining sufficient evidence to support the conclusions in the report. The problems may also include reservations that an accountant might have about the client's presentation of the assertion in accordance with the criteria that have been established. In such cases, the practitioner should issue either a *qualified report*, *an adverse report*, *or a disclaimer*, depending on the nature of the unresolved problem. In all cases in which other than an unqualified report is expressed, the reasons for the qualification should be stated in a separate paragraph of the report.

Restricted Use Reports

Whenever, as illustrated in the report in Figure 23–2, the attest engagement requires the practitioner to evaluate an assertion in accordance with a set of agreed-upon criteria, or whenever the engagement involves limited procedures to be performed strictly under an agreement between the attestor and a named third party, the use of the report should be limited to only those parties who have agreed to the criteria or procedures. The reason for this standard is to prevent misunderstandings that might occur if the report were to be allowed to be distributed to persons who might have no knowledge of the agreement between the practitioner and the client.

Accounting and Review Services

The rendering of accounting and review services to small, nonpublic companies is a growing element of public accounting practice. These services may even be a major part of the practice of many small local firms. Some large firms have established separate emerging business divisions to provide these services to their clients. In performing these services, the accountant simultaneously functions as financial advisor, tax consultant, and bookkeeper. In some cases, there may also be a need for the CPA to prepare the client's financial statements for presentation to management, creditors, or investors.

In 1977, the Accounting and Review Services Committee was established by the AICPA to regulate accounting and review services. Formed in response to external criticism alleging that too little attention had been given to setting standards in the area of nonaudit services, the Committee has issued several Statements on Standards for Accounting and Review Services (SSARS). In addition, the Committee was instrumental in the issuance of the attestation standards mentioned in the preceding section.

Statements on Standards for Accounting and Review Services cover two basic types of engagements for *nonpublic entities* (see Figure 21–1): (1) compilations of financial statements and (2) reviews of financial statements. We give an overview of these services and the types of reports produced by them in the sections that follow.

Compilation of Financial Statements

The **compilation** of financial statements is defined by SSARS 1 (AR100) as presenting, in the form of financial statements, information that is the representation of management (owners) without undertaking to express any assurance on the statements.[1] Because the users of such financial statements should be readily able to identify the degree of responsibility, if any, the accountant is taking with respect to such statements, the public accountant compiling such statements is required to present a report providing that information. That report should state these three facts:

- A compilation has been performed.
- A compilation is limited to presenting, in the form of financial statements, information that is the representation of management (owners).
- The financial statements have not been audited or reviewed, and accordingly, the accountant does not express an opinion or any other form of assurance on them.

The standard report that is appropriate for a compilation is shown in Figure 23–4. Each page of the financial statements should include a reference, such as "See Accountant's Compilation Report." The compilation report should be dated as of the date of completion of the compilation engagement.

Figure 23–4

Accountant's Compilation Report

I (we) have compiled the accompanying balance sheet of XYZ Company as of December 31, 19XX, and the related statements of income, retained earnings, and cash flows for the year then ended, in accordance with standards established by the American Institute of Certified Public Accountants.

A compilation is limited to presenting, in the form of financial statements, information that is the representation of management (owners). I (we) have not audited or reviewed the accompanying financial statements and, accordingly, do not express an opinion or any other form of assurance on them.

Date and Signature

The accountant may be asked to issue a compilation report on one financial statement, such as the balance sheet, and not on the other related financial statements. There is no regulation prohibiting the accountant from accepting such an assignment.

The acceptance of an engagement to compile financial statements carries with it certain implied *capabilities of the accountant* accepting such an appointment. The accountant is expected to have knowledge of accounting principles and practices of the industry in which the entity operates. To obtain this knowledge, publications such as AICPA industry audit guides and industry periodicals should be consulted. The accountant should also possess a general understanding of the nature of the entity's transactions, the form of its accounting records, the stated qualifications of its accounting personnel, the accounting basis on which the financial statements are to be presented, and the form and content of the financial statements. On the basis of that understanding, the accountant should consider whether it is necessary to perform other accounting services, such as assistance in adjusting the books of account or consultation on accounting matters, in the process of compiling financial statements.

The accountant is *not required to make inquiries* or perform other procedures to verify, corroborate, or review information supplied by the entity. The accountant should read the financial statements and ascertain to the best of his or her knowledge that they are free from obvious material errors, such as arithmetical or clerical mistakes, misapplication of accounting principles, and inadequate disclosures. If inquiries or other contacts with the client have shown the information supplied by the client to be incorrect, incomplete, or otherwise unsatisfactory, the accountant should insist on providing the additional or revised information. If the client refuses to provide the needed information, the accountant should withdraw from the compilation engagement.

In some cases, a client may ask the accountant to compile financial statements that contain only information needed to make specific decisions. In these instances, it may be impracticable to spend the time necessary to pull together substantially all the informative disclosures necessary for conformity with GAAP. Omitted disclosures might include selected footnotes or the statement of cash flows. Compilation standards permit the association of the CPA's name with such statements, provided that the omission of substantially all disclosures is indicated in the report and is not, to the CPA's knowledge, made with the intent to deceive users of the financial statements. The compilation report should be modified in these cases (1) to cite the election of management to omit substantially all disclosures that, if included, might influence users' conclusions, and (2) to state that the financial statements are not designed to be used by those who are not informed about the missing disclosures. However, if the client should later provide a copy of the statements to an outside party who expects full disclosures, the statements should be revised to include the appropriate footnotes and a revised compilation report.

A nonindependent accountant is not prohibited from compiling the financial statements for an entity. In such situations, the accountant's report should carry a statement informing the users of the financial statements that he or she is not independent with respect to the client company. That statement should not include the reason for lack of independence.

An accountant may also compile financial data in conformity with a comprehensive basis of accounting other than GAAP, such as the cash basis of accounting. In such cases, the accountant's compilation report should be expanded to include disclosure of the basis of accounting that was used.

Although not required by SSARS 1, it is wise to obtain a letter from the client listing the work that will be performed and, perhaps more importantly, the work that will not be performed. The *1136 Tenants* case, reviewed in Chapter 4, illustrates the peril that can result from not obtaining such a letter. Appendix 23–C shows an illustrative engagement letter for a compilation engagement. A similar letter should be written for a review engagement, containing an exact description of the work to be performed as well as the responsibilities assumed.

Review of Financial Statements

Earlier in this chapter, we discussed standards for *attestation services*. We defined an *attest engagement* as one in which the accountant is engaged to *express a conclusion* regarding the assertions of another party. In audit engagements, that conclusion is stated positively, in the form of an audit opinion. However, as illustrated in Figure 21–1, for nonpublic clients, a less costly attestation alternative is the **review**.

The accountant may be asked either to review the financial statements in connection with compiling them or to review financial statements already compiled by the client. The *purpose of a review* is to provide the accountant with a basis for giving *negative assurance* to the client as to whether material modifications need to be made to financial statements in order to make them conform to GAAP or another comprehensive basis of accounting. It should be noted that this is the same purpose as that of the review of interim financial information for a public company, discussed in Chapter 22.

The review engagement assumes the same background knowledge relating to the industry as that described for a compilation engagement. In addition, however, SSARS 1 prescribes the following *inquiry and analytical procedures* that the accountant should perform in such an engagement:

1. Inquiries should be made concerning the entity's
   a. Accounting principles and practices and the methods followed in applying them;
   b. Procedures for recording, classifying and summarizing transactions and accumulating information for disclosure in the financial statements.

   Appendix 23–D includes a list of illustrative inquiries that may be used in meeting these two review requirements.
2. Analytical procedures, designed to identify relationships and individual items that appear to be unusual, should be performed during the reviewing process. These consist of
   a. Comparison of the financial statements with statements for comparable prior periods;
   b. Comparison of the financial statements with anticipated results, such as budgets and forecasts, if they are available;
   c. A study of the relationships of the elements of the financial statements that would be expected to conform to a predictable pattern based on the entity's experience. Examples are the relationships between changes in sales and changes in accounts receivable; between sales and expenses, such as commissions, which ordinarily fluctuate with sales; and between changes in property, plant, and equipment and changes in the repairs and maintenance expense accounts.
3. Inquiries should be made concerning actions taken at meetings of the stockholders, board of directors, committees of the board of directors, and other similar meetings that may affect the financial statements.
4. The accountant should read the financial statements to consider, on the basis of information coming to his or her attention, whether the financial statements appear to conform with generally accepted accounting principles.
5. The accountant should obtain reports from other accountants, if any, who have been engaged to audit or review the financial statements of significant components of the reporting entity, such as its subsidiaries and investees.
6. Inquiry should be made of persons having responsibility for financial and accounting matters concerning the following points:
   a. Whether the financial statements have been prepared in conformity with generally accepted accounting principles;
   b. Changes in the entity's business activities or accounting principles and practices during the year;
   c. Any matters as to which questions have arisen in the course of applying the foregoing procedures;
   d. Events subsequent to the date of the financial statements that would have a material effect on the financial statements.

It is important to observe that a review of financial statements does not involve obtaining an understanding of the client's internal control structure; nor does it involve tests of accounting records, responses to inquiries by obtaining corroborating evidential matter, and certain other procedures ordinarily performed during an audit. Therefore, a review does not provide assurance that the accountant will become aware of all significant matters that would be disclosed in an audit. On the other hand, *a review is intended to provide greater assurance to users than the compilation.* This is evidenced by the fact that a nonindependent CPA is prohibited from issuing a review report, which is in contrast to the nonindependent CPA's association with compiled financial statements. In this respect, the review engagement is more similar to an audit engagement than to a compilation. Moreover, *a CPA is prohibited from issuing a review report on financial statements that omit substantially all disclosures,* a requirement that is similar to audit standards. If the accountant performing the review becomes aware that information in the financial statements is incorrect, incomplete, or otherwise unsatisfactory, he or she should perform additional procedures that will allow the expression of negative assurance on the financial statements. The accountant may also wish to *obtain a representation letter,* similar to the one shown in Chapter 20, from the owner, manager, or executive officer.

If the review suggests no need for modifying the financial statements, a report should accompany the statements, declaring the following:

- A review was performed in accordance with standards established by the American Institute of Certified Public Accountants.
- All information included in the financial statements is the representation of management (owners) of the entity.
- A review consists primarily of inquiries of company personnel and analytical procedures applied to financial statements.
- A review is substantially less in scope than an audit, the objective of which is the expression of an opinion regarding the financial statements taken as a whole, and accordingly, no such opinion is expressed.
- The accountant is not aware of any material modification that should be made to the financial statements in order for them to be in conformity with generally accepted accounting principles other than those modifications, if any, indicated in the report.

As with a compilation, the report should be dated as of the completion of the review engagement, and each page of the financial statements should include a reference such as "See Accountant's Review Report." The standard report shown in Figure 23–5 illustrates how these reporting requirements can be met.

If for some reason the accountant is *unable to perform the inquiry and analytical procedures* considered necessary to achieve the limited assurance expressed in the preceding report, he or she *has no adequate basis for issuing a review report.* In such a situation, the accountant should consider whether the circumstances resulting in an incomplete review also preclude the issuance of a compilation report (the next-lower level of assurance). If the accountant concludes that there is reasonable justification for the limitation of review procedures, an appropriate compilation report can be issued.

If inquiry and analytical procedures reveal material misstatements or omissions in the financial statements, then the accountant should insert a paragraph that adequately explains the misstatements or omissions and the effects on the financial statements. The accountant's review report would then be modified appropriately.

Figure 23–5 ▬▬▬

Accountant's Review Report

We have reviewed the accompanying balance sheet of XYZ Company as of December 31, 19X2, and the related statements of income, retained earnings, and cash flows for the year then ended in accordance with standards established by the American Institute of Certified Public Accountants. All information included in those financial statements is the representation of management (owners) of XYZ Company.

A review consists primarily of inquiries of company personnel and analytical procedures applied to financial data. It is substantially less in scope than an examination in accordance with generally accepted auditing standards, the objective of which is the expression of an opinion regarding the financial statements as a whole. Accordingly, we do not express such an opinion.

On the basis of our review, we are not aware of any material modifications that should be made to the accompanying financial statements in order for them to be in conformity with generally accepted accounting principles.

Date and Signature

Documentation Associated with Compilation and Review Processes

Although professional standards do not prescribe specific content for working papers, the accountant should provide supporting documentation for both compilation and review engagements. The elements of the working papers that are suggested for each of these types of engagements are shown in Figure 23–6. These include the engagement letter, various checklists showing that the accountant obtained the required knowledge of the client's business and industry,

Figure 23–6 ▬▬▬

Suggested Working Paper Documentation for Compilation and Review Engagements

	Compilations	Reviews
1. Engagement letter	yes	yes
2. Checklist showing accountant's knowledge of business and industry	yes	yes
3. Checklist in support of inquiries and analytical procedures	N/A	yes
4. Working trial balance, including adjustments and other data connecting the client's accounting records to the financial statements	yes	yes
5. Indication that CPA has read the compiled financial statements	yes	N/A
6. Summary of data in support of notes to financial statements	yes	yes
7. Reasons for omissions of disclosures	yes	N/A
8. Summaries of discussions of unusual matters encountered	yes	yes
9. Representation letters	optional	yes
10. Copies of reports from other accountants associated with subsidiary entities included in consolidated financial statements	yes	yes
11. Reasons for step-down from higher level engagement, if applicable	yes	yes

working trial balance and adjustments, summary of data in support of footnote disclosures, summaries of key discussions with the client, and other evidence in support of the work that was done.

Financial Forecasts and Projections[2]

☑ **Objective 5**
Understand standards for forecasts and projections

The services of preparing and reporting on financial forecasts and projections were, for years, confined to the realm of management advisory services. However, in recent years the financial community has shown increasing interest in such services causing them to currently have a higher level of importance than ever before. In fact, attestation services (discussed earlier in this chapter), once confined to audits of historical financial statements, have now been expanded to include audit examinations as well as application of agreed-upon procedures to prospective financial statements.

Prospective financial statements currently are being used in many different types of business situations by a host of different user groups. The advent of the microcomputer and the related "spreadsheet" software has made the process of preparing financial projections faster and easier than ever before. These projections include cash-flow studies, capital-budgeting studies, and long-range and short-range operating budgets, as well as forecasted results of operations for target companies in connection with possible mergers or acquisitions. The external users of financial forecasts and projections include the Securities and Exchange Commission and other agencies of the federal or state governments, financial institutions considering financial backing of proposed ventures, and present or prospective investors in new or emerging business enterprises. In recent years a significant amount of financial forecasting and projecting has been performed in connection with syndicated, tax-oriented investments (tax shelters) relating to real estate, oil and gas, research and development projects, farming transactions, and equipment leasing.

Guidelines for Financial Forecasts and Projections

Because of the increased demand for financial projections from the financial community, the AICPA has issued a number of documents over the past decade that provide guidance for the preparation and presentation of financial forecasts and projections. In 1985 the *Statement on Standards for Accountants' Services on Prospective Financial Information* was issued. Entitled "Financial Forecasts and Projections," this statement provides that an accountant who either (1) submits to clients or others prospective financial statements that he or she has assembled or (2) reports on prospective financial statements should either *compile, examine,* or *apply agreed-upon procedures* to the prospective financial statements, if it is expected that those statements are to be used by a third party.

Specifically, the Statement

- Defines a "financial forecast" and a "financial projection."
- Establishes procedures and reporting standards for a compilation service on prospective financial statements.
- Establishes procedures and reporting standards for an examination service on prospective financial statements.
- Establishes standards for services to apply agreed-upon procedures to prospective financial statements.

Prospective financial statements are defined as either financial forecasts or financial projections including summaries of significant assumptions and accounting policies. The preferred format for presentation of prospective financial statements is the same as for historical financial statements, since this presentation facilitates comparisons of past results with projected results. Prospective financial statements may take the form of complete basic financial statements or may be limited to the following minimum items:

a. Sales or gross revenues.
b. Gross profit or cost of sales.
c. Unusual or infrequently occurring items.
d. Provision for income taxes.
e. Discontinued operations or extraordinary items.
f. Income from continuing operations.
g. Net income.
h. Primary and fully diluted earnings per share.
i. Significant cash flows.
j. A description of what management intends the prospective financial statements to present, a statement that the assumptions are based on information about circumstances and conditions existing at the time the prospective information was prepared, and a caveat that the prospective results may not be achieved.
k. Summary of significant assumptions.
l. Summary of significant accounting policies.

Any presentation that omits one or more of the applicable minimum items (a) through (i) is a *partial presentation*, which would not ordinarily be appropriate for general use. The provisions of the statement do not apply to partial presentations. Additionally, the statement does not apply to *pro forma presentations* (historical financial statements adjusted for a prospective transaction) or to *prospective financial statements covering wholly expired periods* (such as last year's budget).

Financial forecasts are defined as prospective financial statements that present, to the best of the responsible party's knowledge and belief, an entity's expected financial position, results of operations, and cash flows. A forecast is to be based on assumptions reflecting conditions expected to exist and the course of actions that management expects to take. It may be expressed in specific monetary amounts as a single point estimate or as a range within which the financial information is expected to fall, based on specific assumptions that are neither biased nor unreasonable.

Financial projections are prospective financial statements that present, to the best of the responsible party's knowledge and belief, given one or more *hypothetical assumptions*, an entity's expected financial position, results of operations, and cash flows. A financial projection can be thought of as the answer to the hypothetical question "What would happen if . . . ?" Projections, like forecasts, may contain ranges of values.

Uses of Prospective Financial Statements

Prospective financial statements may be either for "general use" or for "limited use." "General use" refers to the use of the statements by persons with whom the **responsible party** (either management or others) is not directly negotiating, for example, in an offering statement of an entity's debt or equity interests. Recipients of general use prospective financial statements are unable to ask the responsible party direct questions about the presentation. These persons are not in an advantageous position to ask "What if . . . ?" Therefore, the most beneficial projection to them is the responsible party's best estimate of projected results (i.e., the financial forecast). *Thus, only a financial forecast is appropriate for general use.*

"Limited use" refers to use of prospective financial statements by the responsible party alone or by the responsible party and third parties in negotiating for bank loans, submissions to regulatory agencies, and other internal uses. Third parties are in the position to ask "What if . . . ?" Therefore, *either financial forecasts or financial projections are appropriate for limited use.*

Because a financial projection is not appropriate for general use, an accountant should not consent to the use of his or her name in conjunction with the projection that he or she believes will be distributed to those who will not be negotiating directly with the responsible party, unless the projection is used to supplement a financial forecast.

Compilation of Prospective Financial Statements

Earlier in this chapter we defined the term *compilation* as it applies to historical financial statements. When applied to prospective financial statements, a compilation is defined as a professional service that involves

a. Assembling, to the extent necessary, the prospective financial statements based on the responsible party's assumptions.
b. Performing required compilation procedures, such as reading the prospective financial statements with their summaries of significant assumptions and accounting policies and considering whether they appear to be (1) presented in conformity with AICPA presentation guidelines and (2) not obviously inappropriate.
c. Issuing a compilation report.

As in the case of the compilation of historical financial statements, a compilation of prospective financial statements is not intended to provide assurance on the prospective financial statements or the assumptions underlying such statements. Thus, the report on the compilation of prospective financial statements expresses no opinion or any other form of assurance.

Rule 201 of the Code of Professional Conduct applies to compilation engagements for historical as well as prospective financial statements. Thus, the accountant who performs the compilation must possess adequate technical training and proficiency and exercise due professional care in the engagement. Additionally, the work should be adequately planned, and assistants, if any, should be appropriately supervised. Adequate compilation procedures should be performed on the prospective financial statements. These include

a. Establishing an understanding with the client, preferably in writing, regarding the services to be performed.

b. Inquiring about the accounting principles used in the preparation of the prospective financial statements, giving consideration to principles used in preparation of comparable historical financial statements, or to principles applicable in the industry.

c. Asking how the responsible party identifies the key factors and develops its assumptions.

d. Obtaining a list of key assumptions providing the basis for the prospective financial statements and considering whether there are any obvious omissions in light of the key factors upon which the prospective results of the entity appear to depend.

e. Considering whether there appear to be any obvious internal inconsistencies in the assumptions.

f. Performing, or testing the mathematical accuracy of, the computations that translate the assumptions into the prospective financial statements.

g. Reading the prospective financial statements, including the summary of significant assumptions, and considering whether they appear to be in conformity with AICPA presentation guidelines for prospective financial statements, and whether they are not obviously inappropriate in relation to the accountant's knowledge of the entity and its industry.

h. If a significant portion of the prospective period has expired, the accountant should consider the projected financial information in light of actual results.

i. Obtaining written representations from the responsible party concerning the prospective financial statements (including assumptions). The responsible party should indicate responsibility for the assumptions. For financial forecasts, the representation should include a statement that the forecast presents, to the best of the party's knowledge and belief, the expected financial position, results of operations, and cash flows, based on present circumstances and present expected courses of action. For the financial projection, the representation should include a statement that the projection presents, to the best of the party's knowledge and belief, the expected financial position, results of operations, and cash flows, based on the given hypothetical assumptions and present expected courses of action.

j. If, after applying any of the above procedures, the accountant believes he or she has received representations that are incomplete, inappropriate, or misleading, an attempt should be made to obtain revised information. Failure to become satisfied after this point should result in withdrawal from the engagement.

The *report on the compiled prospective financial statement* should include

a. An identification of the prospective financial statements presented by the responsible party.
b. A statement that the accountant has compiled the prospective financial statements in accordance with standards established by the AICPA.
c. A statement that a compilation is limited in scope and does not enable the accountant to express an opinion or any other form of assurance on the prospective financial statements or the assumptions.
d. A caveat that the prospective results may not be achieved.
e. A statement that the accountant assumes no responsibility to update the report for events and circumstances occurring after the date of the report.

Examination of Prospective Financial Statements

The CPA is permitted by the *Financial Forecasts and Projections* statement to examine a prospective financial statement. That examination is considered to be an *attestation* service that involves

a. Evaluating the preparation of the prospective financial statements.
b. Evaluating the support underlying the assumptions.
c. Evaluating the presentation of the prospective financial statements for conformity with AICPA presentation guidelines.
d. Issuing an examination report.

The report associated with the examination expresses whether, in the accountant's opinion, (1) the prospective financial statements are presented in conformity with AICPA guidelines; and (2) the assumptions provide a reasonable basis for the responsible party's forecast, or whether the assumptions provide a reasonable basis for the responsible party's projection given the hypothetical assumptions.

The accountant performing the examination of the prospective financial statements should be independent. In addition, he or she should possess adequate technical training and proficiency to examine prospective financial statements; adequately plan the engagement and supervise the work of assistants, if any; and obtain sufficient competent evidence to provide a reasonable basis for his or her examination report.

The first step in examining the prospective financial statements should be to reach an understanding between the accountant and the responsible party regarding the services to be performed. Ordinarily, this is done in the form of a written engagement letter. The accountant's overall objective in such an examination is to limit *attestation risk* (i.e., risk of attesting to a misleading forecast) to a level that is, in the accountant's judgment, appropriate for the level of assurance that may be imparted in the examination report. The same risk model as that proposed for historical financial statements (see Chapter 2) is also appropriate in the case of prospective financial statements. However, in this case, *assurance is limited to whether the financial statements are in conformity with AICPA presentation guidelines and whether the assumptions provide a reasonable basis for management's forecast, or in the case of a projection, whether the hypothetical assumptions are reasonable.*

Procedures followed in the examination should be essentially the same as those followed in an audit examination of historical financial statements, insofar as the nature of the examined financial information will permit. Procedures should be chosen that assess inherent and control risk and that restrict detection risk. Any combination of appropriate procedures—inquiry, inspection of documents, or other procedures—may be applied. The most important information that the accountant examines in this case is the *underlying support for the assumptions in the forecast or the hypothetical assumptions in the projection.* In so doing, the accountant should consider

a. Whether sufficient pertinent sources of information about the assumptions have been considered. Examples of external sources include government and industry publications, economic forecasts, existing or proposed legislation, and reports of changing technology. Internal sources include budgets, labor agreements, patents, royalty agreements and records, sales backlog records, debt agreements, and actions of the board of directors involving the plans of the entity.

b. Whether the assumptions are consistent with the sources from which they were derived.

c. Whether the assumptions are consistent with each other.

d. Whether historical information used in developing the assumptions is sufficiently reliable.

e. Whether historical information used in developing the assumptions is comparable over the periods specified.

f. Whether logical arguments or theory used in developing the assumptions are reasonable.

In evaluating the preparation and presentation of the prospective financial statements, the accountant should select procedures that will provide reasonable assurance of the following:

a. The presentation reflects the identified assumptions.

b. Computations that translate assumptions into prospective amounts are mathematically accurate.

c. Assumptions are internally consistent.
d. Accounting principles used in
- financial forecasts are consistent with those expected to be used in the historical financial statements covering the prospective period and those used in the most recent historical statements, if any.
- financial projections are consistent with the accounting principles expected to be used in the prospective period and those used in the most recent historical financial statements, if any, or that they are consistent with the purpose of the presentation.
e. Presentation of the prospective financial statements follows the AICPA guidelines set forth in its *Guide for Prospective Financial Statements*.
f. Assumptions have been adequately disclosed based on AICPA presentation guidelines for prospective financial statements.

In addition, the accountant should consider whether the prospective financial statements should be revised because of mathematical errors, unreasonable or internally inconsistent assumptions, inappropriate or incomplete presentation, or inadequate disclosure. A representation letter should be obtained from the responsible party that acknowledges responsibility for both the financial presentation and the underlying assumptions.

The accountant's standard report on an examination of a forecast is illustrated in Figure 23–7. Notice that the report includes the following disclosures:

a. An identification of the prospective financial statements presented.
b. A statement that the examination of the prospective financial statements was made in accordance with the AICPA standards and a brief description of the nature of such an examination.

Figure 23–7

Accountant's Report on a Forecast

We have audited the accompanying forecasted balance sheet, statements of income, retained earnings, and cash flows of XYZ Company as of December 31, 19XX, and for the year then ending. Our examination was made in accordance with standards for an examination of a forecast established by the American Institute of Certified Public Accountants and, accordingly, included such procedures as we considered necessary to evaluate both the assumptions used by management and the preparation and presentation of the forecast.

In our opinion, the accompanying forecast is presented in conformity with guidelines for presentation of a forecast established by the American Institute of Certified Public Accountants, and the underlying assumptions provide a reasonable basis for management's forecast. However, there will usually be differences between the forecasted and actual results, because events and circumstances frequently do not occur as expected, and those differences may be material. We have no responsibility to update this report for events and circumstances occurring after the date of this report.

c. The accountant's opinion that the prospective financial statements are presented in conformity with the AICPA's presentation guidelines as set forth in its *Guide for Prospective Financial Statements* and that the underlying financial assumptions provide a reasonable basis for the forecast or a reasonable basis for the projection given the hypothetical assumptions.

d. A caveat that the prospective results may not be achieved.

e. A statement that the accountant assumes no responsibility to update the report for events and circumstances occurring after the date of the report.

The accountant's standard report may be modified in the following circumstances:

a. If, in the accountant's opinion, the prospective financial statements depart from AICPA presentation guidelines, a qualified opinion or an adverse opinion may be issued.

b. If the accountant believes that one or more significant assumptions do not provide a reasonable basis for the forecast, or a reasonable basis for the projection given the hypothetical assumptions, an adverse opinion should be issued.

c. If the accountant's examination is limited so as to preclude him or her from applying one or more procedures considered necessary in the circumstances, a disclaimer of opinion should be issued.

d. The report can be modified to emphasize a matter or to report an evaluation based in part on a report of another accountant.

Applying Agreed-Upon Procedures to Prospective Financial Statements

An accountant may decide to apply agreed-upon procedures to prospective financial statements provided that (a) the specified users involved have participated in establishing the nature and scope of the engagement and take responsibility for the adequacy of the procedures performed, (b) distribution of the report is to be restricted to specified users involved, and (c) the prospective financial statements include a summary of significant assumptions. The accountant who accepts such an engagement should be independent, since it, too, falls under the definition of *attestation services*. In addition, the accountant should possess adequate technical training and proficiency to apply those procedures. The engagement should be adequately planned and assistants properly supervised. Finally, sufficient evidence to provide a reasonable basis for the accountant's report should be gathered. Procedures may be as limited or extensive as the specified users desire, as long as the users take responsibility for their adequacy. The accountant's report on the results of applying agreed-upon procedures should

a. Indicate the prospective financial statements covered by the accountant's report.

b. Indicate that the report is limited in use, intended solely for the specified users, and should not be used by others.

c. Enumerate the procedures performed and refer to conformity with the arrangements made with the specified users.

d. If the agreed-upon procedures constitute less than a full audit, state that the work performed was less in scope than an examination of prospective financial statements in accordance with AICPA guidelines and disclaim an opinion on whether the prospective financial statements are in conformity with AICPA presentation guidelines.

e. State the accountant's findings.

f. Include a caveat that the prospective results may not be achieved.

g. State that the accountant assumes no responsibility to update the report for events and circumstances occurring after the date of the report.

Pro Forma Statements

The CPA may assist the client in preparing, and also may attest to, various types of pro forma financial statements. These are *adjusted historical statements that give effect to contemplated transactions*, such as mergers and acquisitions, divestitures, recapitalizations, or other types of corporate reorganizations. **Pro forma statements** may be included in prospectuses, proxy statements, and other public documents, as well as in less widely-circulated documents.

The auditor's responsibilities and reporting obligations with respect to pro forma financial information depend on how the information itself is presented. If the pro forma information is presented *outside the basic financial statements* but within the same document as the audit report, and the auditor is *not engaged to report* on it, then the auditor should merely *read the pro forma information* for substantial consistency with the information in the basic financial statements and audit report. If the pro forma information is consistent with the information in the basic financial statements and audit report, no reference need be made to it in the audit report. However, if the pro forma financial information is inconsistent with the representations in the financial statements and audit report, then the CPA should take steps to assure that either the pro forma information, the basic financial statements or the audit report are changed to provide a consistent communication to the reader.[3]

If the CPA is *engaged to either audit or review* the pro forma financial information, he or she may do so if the following conditions are met:

a. The document that contains the pro forma financial information includes complete historical financial statements of the most recent year (or shorter period);

b. The historical financial statements of the entity have either been audited or reviewed; and

c. The accountant who is reporting on the pro forma financial information has an appropriate level of knowledge of the accounting and financial and reporting practices of each significant part of the combined entity.

The CPA should obtain an understanding of the underlying pro forma transaction. For example, if a business combination is being considered, the CPA should read relevant contracts and minutes of meetings of the board of directors and inquire of knowledgeable officials of the company. In addition, he or she should obtain a sufficient level of knowledge of each significant constituent part of the combined entity. Discussions should be conducted with management regarding the assumptions they are making on the proposed transactions. Other procedures should also be performed, such as obtaining written representations from management concerning their responsibility for the underlying assumptions, their reasonableness, and the appropriateness of their disclosures. The CPA should then read the pro forma financial information and evaluate its proper disclosure before issuing the attestation report.[4]

Summary

In this chapter we have briefly described the nonaudit and atypical audit services that may be provided by certified public accountants, as well as the standards that govern those services. Included are tax services, management advisory services, attestation standards, accounting and review services, and projected financial statements.

We began by observing that the preparation of tax returns and the provision of tax advice and planning services are a logical part of services provided by CPA firms, because the data required for those services are directly related to accounting data. In performing tax services, the CPA is not required to be independent and, therefore, may take an advocacy position in support of the client's position relating to tax matters. Also, because of this relationship, fees for tax work may be contingent on findings of a court, governmental agency, or judicial proceedings. We also observed that the CPA must sign any tax return that he or she prepares even if no compensation is received for preparing the return.

Another rapidly growing segment of public accounting practice is that of providing management advisory services. These services include systems analysis, installation of accounting systems, operational advice to clients, and a number of other services. Such services are generally divided into two categories, which are characterized as management consultation and management advisory service engagements. The first of these is somewhat informal, but the second involves investigation and analysis to arrive at alternative courses of action and communicates the recommended action to the client through a formal report. Again, in performing this type of service, the CPA is not required to be independent but is expected to meet the general and technical standards of the Code of Professional Conduct.

We briefly reviewed the attestation standards of the AICPA, which, although they apply to audits, were intended to apply more directly to nonaudit attest services. We illustrated a report that results from such services and discussed the attestation standards that have no direct referent in generally accepted auditing standards, in order to contrast the two groups of standards.

Next, we described accounting and review services for nonpublic entities. We defined the two basic types of such services (compilations and reviews), and differentiated them from each other as well as from an audit engagement. We also outlined the scope of both the compilation and the review engagement and illustrated the reports that accompany them.

In the last section we dealt with the CPA's association with prospective financial statements, otherwise known as financial forecasts and financial projections. In discussing these types of services, we emphasized the fact that the CPA whose name is associated with a forecast must carefully avoid wording the attest statement to give the impression that he or she may be vouching for the achievability of the forecast. We also discussed the meaning of the term "pro forma financial statements," as well as the CPA's association with them.

Auditing Vocabulary

p. 980   **attestation:**   Attest engagement. See Chapter 1.

p. 986   **compilation:**   Presenting, in the form of financial statements, information that is the representation of management without undertaking to express any assurance on the statements.

p. 993   **financial forecast:**   Prospective financial statements that present, to the best of the responsible party's knowledge and belief, an entity's expected financial position, results of operations, and cash flows.

p. 994   **financial projection:**   A prospective financial statement that presents, to the best of the responsible party's knowledge and belief, given one or more hypothetical assumptions, an entity's expected financial position, results of operations, and cash flows.

p. 979   **management advisory services (MAS):**   Systems analysis, advice on improvements of existing systems, installation of accounting systems, and rendering advice and assistance to clients in finding qualified management personnel. Management advisory services are divided into two general categories: MAS consultations and MAS engagements.

p. 979   **MAS consultation:**   Consists of informal business advice given to a client based mostly on existing personal knowledge of the client's circumstances.

p. 979   **MAS engagement:**   Involves an analytical approach and process applied in a formal study or project, to determine the client's objectives, to define their problems, to evaluate alternative solutions, to formulate proposed actions, to communicate results, to implement, and to follow up. MAS engagements are far more detailed than MAS consultations.

p. 1000   **pro forma statement:**   Adjusted historical statements that give effect to contemplated transactions.

p. 992   **prospective financial statements:**   Financial statements that present an entity's prospective financial position, results of operations, and cash flows for future periods.

p. 994   **responsible party:**   Client management or others who have responsibility for making assertions in prospective financial statements.

p. 988   **review:**   The form of attestation service that provides the accountant with a basis for giving negative assurance to the client as to whether material modifications need to be made to financial statements to make them conform to GAAP or other comprehensive basis of accounting.

Appendix 23–A: Tax Practice Standards

The practice of public accounting related to taxation in the United States is regulated by the U.S. Treasury Department and the AICPA Code of Professional Conduct, as interpreted by the Committee on Responsibilities in Tax Practice. This committee, through the authority of the AICPA's Division of Federal Taxation, has issued standards of responsibilities in tax practice for members of the AICPA, which are more restrictive in some respects than those established by the Treasury Department or by the Code of Professional Conduct. These standards are actually a body of advisory opinions as to what constitutes good tax practice; to the extent that they are more restrictive than the Code of Professional Conduct or Treasury Department rules, their authority depends on the general acceptability of the opinions expressed on the statements. Hence, they do not have the force of authority that the Treasury Department rules have. Nevertheless, they do carry the weight of general acceptability for what are considered to be appropriate responsibilities of the CPA engaged in tax practice.

As of 1991, eight Statements on Responsibilities in Tax Practice were in effect. These statements are summarized briefly in the following paragraphs.

Answers to Questions on Returns

A CPA should sign the preparer's declaration on a federal tax return only if the taxpayer has made a reasonable effort to provide all the answers to applicable questions on the return. Whenever a question is left unanswered by the taxpayer, the reason for the omission should be stated. The possibility that an answer to a question might prove disadvantageous to the taxpayer does not justify omitting an answer or a statement of the reason for such an omission.

Recognition of Administrative Proceedings of Prior Year

An "administrative proceeding" can be an examination (audit) by an internal revenue agent, a district conference, or an appellate conference relating to a taxpayer's return on a claim for refund. A "waiver" can be a waiver of restrictions upon the Internal Revenue Service (IRS) of a deficiency on tax; the acceptance of the IRS's findings by a partnership, fiduciary, or Subchapter S corporation; or the acceptance of an overassessment.

The selection of the treatment of an item (income, deduction, credit, etc.) in a tax return should be based on the facts and rules as of the time the return is prepared. Normally, the disposition of an item in a later year as part of an administrative proceeding by the execution of a waiver from a prior year does not govern that item's treatment in a later year's return, unless the taxpayer is bound by agreement with the IRS to a certain treatment. A CPA may, therefore, sign a return as preparer in a later year if the return contains a departure from the prior year's treatment, if he or she has reasonable grounds for doing so. He or she may do this without disclosing the departure.

Use of Estimates

A CPA may prepare tax returns involving estimates if the use of such estimates is generally acceptable or if it is impracticable, under the circumstances, to obtain exact data. When estimates are used, the CPA should present them in such a manner that greater accuracy than exists is not implied. The CPA should be satisfied with the reasonableness of all estimates used in a taxpayer's return before signing the return as preparer.

Knowledge of Error

A CPA is required to advise the tax client promptly when errors or omissions are discovered in a previously filed return or when it is learned that a client has failed to file a required return. The CPA's advice should include a recommendation of the measures to be taken (usually, an amended return for the prior year is advisable). The CPA is not obligated to inform the IRS of the error and, in fact, may not do so without the client's permission.

If the CPA has knowledge of an uncorrected error in a client's prior-year return that results in an understatement of tax liability, he or she should consider this fact in deciding whether to proceed with preparation of any subsequent returns. If such returns are prepared, steps should be taken by the CPA to ensure that the error is not repeated.

Knowledge of Error: Administrative Proceedings

When a CPA is representing a client in an administrative proceeding concerning a return in which the CPA is aware of an error resulting in a material understatement of tax liability, she or he should request that the client agree to disclose the error to the IRS. If the client refuses to agree to disclose the error, the CPA's recourse may be withdrawal from the engagement.

Advice to Clients

In providing advice to a client, the CPA must use judgment to ensure that such advice reflects adequately informed professional competence and that it suits the client's needs. When subsequent developments (such as changes in the law) affect advice previously provided to a client, the CPA is not obligated to inform the client of such developments unless (1) the CPA is assisting the client in implementing plans associated with the advice previously provided, or (2) a specific agreement exists to inform the client of new developments.

Certain Procedural Aspects of Preparing Returns

A CPA is normally allowed to rely on information provided by the client without examining or reviewing any documents or other supporting evidence. However, the client should be encouraged to provide supporting data where appropriate.

The CPA should make use of prior year's returns of the client whenever feasible. Whenever information provided by the client appears to be incorrect or incomplete, the CPA should make enough inquiries to resolve doubts and take measures to correct the information before signing the return as preparer.

If a CPA prepares a federal tax return, he or she should always sign it without modifying the preparer's declaration.

Positions Contrary to the Government

A CPA may take positions contrary to the Internal Revenue Code or Treasury Regulations in the preparation of a federal tax return—if there is reasonable support for this position. Reasonable support might exist, for example, when two Internal Revenue Code provisions conflict or when the Internal Revenue Code and Treasury Regulations are silent on a matter. When a position taken is contrary to the Internal Revenue Code (expected to be a rare circumstance), the CPA should disclose the treatment in the tax return. Positions contrary to Treasury Regulations or IRS interpretations may be taken without disclosure in the return. In no event may a CPA take a position that lacks reasonable support.

Appendix 23–B: Management Advisory Services

CPAs historically have served as business advisors and consultants, performing functions that are described as management advisory services (MAS). In general, management advisory services consist of advice and assistance concerning such matters as an entity's organization, personnel, finances, operations, systems, controls, and other aspects of current or proposed activities. Such services are often closely related to the auditing, tax, and accounting and review services that CPAs provide.

Management advisory services may range from the provision of business advice based only on the knowledge and experience of the accountant to engagements involving extensive fact-finding and analysis. The form of MAS that is based on personal knowledge about the client, the circumstances, the technical matters involved, and the mutual intent of the parties is known as an *MAS con-*

Appendix 23–B has been summarized from *Statements on Management Advisory Services* (New York: AICPA, 1991). Copyright © 1991 by the American Institute of Certified Public Accountants, Inc. Reprinted with permission.

sultation. The form that requires an analytical approach and process is known as an *MAS engagement.* Regardless of the form taken, management consulting serves the purpose of helping clients to improve the use of their capabilities and resources and to achieve their objectives. This may involve such activities as

1. Counseling management in its analyzing, planning, organizing, operating, and controlling functions.
2. Conducting special studies, preparing recommendations, proposing plans and programs, and providing advice and technical assistance in their implementation.
3. Reviewing and suggesting improvement of policies, procedures, systems, methods, and organization relationships.
4. Introducing new ideas, concepts, and methods to management.

The ethical standards set forth in Rule 201 of the Code of Professional Conduct require that the work be performed with professional competence and due professional care, that adequate planning and supervision be performed, and that sufficient relevant data be gathered to support the practitioner's conclusions and recommendations. In addition, technical standards have been developed under Ethics Rule 204 for both MAS engagements and MAS consultations. These standards relate to the following:

1. *The role of the MAS practitioner.* An MAS practitioner should not assume the role of management or take any positions that might impair his or her objectivity.
2. *Understanding with client.* An oral or written understanding should be reached with the client concerning the nature, scope, and limitations of the work to be performed.
3. *Client benefit.* Since the potential benefits to be derived by the client are a major consideration in MAS practice, such potential benefits should be viewed objectively, and the client should be notified if the practitioner has reservations concerning them. In offering and providing MAS, results should not be explicitly or implicitly guaranteed. When estimates of quantifiable results are presented, they should be clearly identified and the support for such estimates should be disclosed.
4. *Communication of results.* Significant information pertinent to the results of the MAS engagement or consultation should be appropriately communicated to the client, together with any limitations, qualifications, or reservations needed to assist the client in making its decision.

By its nature, an MAS engagement is more formally structured than an MAS consultation, taking more time and requiring more detailed documentation. Thus, the rules for meeting the general and practice standards for MAS engagements are more detailed and specific than those for MAS consultations.

Appendix 23–C: Illustrative Engagement Letter: Compilation

(Appropriate Salutation)

    This letter is to confirm our understanding of the terms and objectives of our engagement and the nature and limitations of the services we will provide.
We will perform the following services:

1. We will compile, from information you provide, the annual and interim balance sheets and related statements of income, retained earnings, and cash flows of XYZ Company for the year 19XX. We will not audit or review such financial statements. Our report on the annual financial statements of XYZ Company is presently expected to read as follows:

>   I (we) have compiled the accompanying balance sheet of XYZ Company as of December 31, 19XX, and the related statements of income, retained earnings, and cash flows for the year then ended, in accordance with standards established by the American Institute of Certified Public Accountants.
>   A compilation is limited to presenting in the form of financial statements information that is the representation of management. I (we) have not audited or reviewed the accompanying financial statements and, accordingly, do not express an opinion or any other form of assurance on them.

Our report on your interim financial statements, which statements will omit substantially all disclosures, will include an additional paragraph that will read as follows:

>   Management has elected to omit substantially all of the disclosures required by generally accepted accounting principles. If the omitted disclosures were included in the financial statements, they might influence the user's conclusions about the company's financial position, results of operations, and cash flows. Accordingly, these financial statements are not designed for those who are not informed about such matters.

If, for any reason, we are unable to complete the compilation of your financial statements, we will not issue a report on such statements as a result of this engagement.

2. We will also . . . (discussion of other services).

    Our engagement cannot be relied upon to disclose errors, irregularities, or illegal acts, including fraud or defalcations, that may exist. However, we will inform you of any such matters that come to our attention.
Our fees for these services. . . .
We shall be pleased to discuss this letter with you at any time.
If the foregoing is in accordance with your understanding, please sign the copy of this letter in the space provided and return it to us.

                                Sincerely yours,

_____

Acknowledge: (Signature of accountant)
XYZ Company

_____

President

_____

Date

_____

Appendix 23–C is from Statements on Standards for Accounting and Review Services (SSARS) 1 (New York: AICPA), pp. 23–24.

Appendix 23–D: Review of Financial Statements— Illustrative Inquiries

The inquiries to be made in a review of financial statements are a matter of the accountant's judgment. In determining inquiries, an accountant may consider (1) the nature and materiality of the item, (2) the likelihood of misstatement, (3) knowledge obtained during current and previous engagements, (4) the stated qualifications of the entity's accounting personnel, (5) the extent to which a particular item is affected by management's judgment, and (6) inadequacies in the entity's underlying financial data. The following list of inquiries is for illustrative purposes only. The inquiries do not necessarily apply to every engagement, nor are they meant to be all-inclusive. This list is not intended to serve as a program or checklist in the conduct of a review; rather, it describes the general areas in which inquiries might be made. For example, the accountant may feel it is necessary to make several inquiries to answer one of the questions listed below, such as item 3(a).

1. *General*
   a. What are the procedures for recording, classifying, and summarizing transactions (relates to each section discussed below)?
   b. Do the general ledger control accounts agree with subsidiary records (for example, receivables, inventories, investments, property and equipment, accounts payable, accrued expenses, noncurrent liabilities)?
   c. Have accounting principles been applied on a consistent basis?
2. *Cash*
   a. Have bank balances been reconciled with book balances?
   b. Have old or unusual reconciling items between bank balances and book balances been reviewed and adjustments made where necessary?
   c. Has a proper cutoff of cash transactions been made?
   d. Are there any restrictions on the availability of cash balances?
   e. Have cash funds been counted and reconciled with control accounts?
3. *Receivables*
   a. Has an adequate allowance been made for doubtful accounts?
   b. Have receivables considered uncollectible been written off?
   c. If appropriate, has interest been reflected?
   d. Has a proper cutoff of sales transactions been made?
   e. Are there any receivables from employees and related parties?
   f. Are any receivables pledged, discounted, or factored?
   g. Have receivables been properly classified between current and noncurrent?
4. *Inventories*
   a. Have inventories been physically counted? If not, how have inventories been determined?

Appendix 23–D is from Statement on Standards for Accounting and Review Services (SSARS) 1 (New York: AICPA, 1991), pp. 20–23.

    b. Have general ledger control accounts been adjusted to agree with physical inventories?

    c. If physical inventories are taken at a date other than the balance sheet date, what procedures were used to record changes in inventory between the date of the physical inventory and the balance sheet date?

    d. Were consignments in or out considered in taking physical inventories?

    e. What is the basis of valuation?

    f. Does inventory cost include materials, labor, and overhead where applicable?

    g. Have write-downs for obsolescence or cost in excess of net realizable value been made?

    h. Have proper cutoffs of purchases, goods in transit, and returned goods been made?

    i. Are there any inventory encumbrances?

5. *Prepaid expenses*

    a. what is the nature of the amounts included in prepaid expenses?

    b. How are these amounts amortized?

6. *Investments, including loans, mortgages, and intercorporate investments*

    a. Have gains and losses on disposal been reflected?

    b. Has investment income been reflected?

    c. Has appropriate consideration been given to the classification of investments between current and noncurrent and to the difference between the cost and market value of investments?

    d. Have consolidation or equity accounting requirements been considered?

    e. What is the basis of valuation of marketable equity securities?

    f. Are investments unencumbered?

7. *Property and equipment*

    a. Have gains or losses on disposal of property or equipment been reflected?

    b. What are the criteria for capitalization of property and equipment? Have such criteria been applied during the fiscal period?

    c. Does the repairs and maintenance account only include items of an expense nature?

    d. Are property and equipment stated at cost?

    e. What are the depreciation methods and rates? Are they appropriate and consistent?

    f. Are there any unrecorded additions, retirements, abandonments, sales, or trade-ins?

    g. Does the entity have material lease agreements? Have they been properly reflected?

    h. Is any property or equipment mortgaged or otherwise encumbered?

8. *Other assets*

    a. What is the nature of the amounts included in other assets?

    b. Do these assets represent costs that will benefit future periods? What is the amortization policy? Is it appropriate?

    c. Have other assets been properly classified between current and noncurrent?

    d. Are any of these assets mortgaged or otherwise encumbered?

9. *Accounts and notes payable and accrued liabilities*
   a. Have all significant payables been reflected?
   b. Are all bank and other short-term liabilities properly classified?
   c. Have all significant accruals, such as payroll, interest, and provisions for pension and profit-sharing plans, been reflected?
   d. Are there any collateralized liabilities?
   e. Are there any payables to employees and related parties?

10. *Long term liabilities*
    a. What are the terms and other provisions of long-term liability agreements?
    b. Have liabilities been properly classified between current and noncurrent?
    c. Has interest expense been reflected?
    d. Has there been compliance with restrictive covenants of loan agreements?
    e. Are any long-term liabilities collateralized or subordinated?

11. *Income and other taxes*
    a. Has provision been made for current and prior-year federal income taxes payable?
    b. Have any assessments or reassessments been received? Are there tax examinations in process?
    c. Are there timing differences? If so, have deferred taxes been reflected?
    d. Has provision been made for state and local income, franchise, sales, and other taxes payable?

12. *Other liabilities, contingencies, and commitments*
    a. What is the nature of the amounts included in other liabilities?
    b. Have other liabilities been properly classified between current and non-current?
    c. Are there any contingent liabilities, such as discounted notes, drafts, endorsements, warranties, litigation, and unsettled asserted claims? Are there any unasserted potential claims?
    d. Are there any material contractual obligations for construction or purchase of real property and equipment and any commitments or options to purchase or sell company securities?

13. *Equity*
    a. What is the nature of any changes in equity accounts?
    b. What classes of capital stock have been authorized?
    c. What is the par or stated value of the various classes of stock?
    d. Do amounts of outstanding shares of capital stock agree with subsidiary records?
    e. Have capital stock preferences, if any, been disclosed?
    f. Have stock options been granted?
    g. Has the entity made any acquisitions of its own capital stock?
    h. Are there any restrictions on retained earnings or other capital?

14. *Revenue and expenses*
    a. Are revenues from the sale of major products and services recognized in the appropriate period?
    b. Are purchases and expenses recognized in the appropriate period and properly classified?

c. Do the financial statements include discounted operations or items that might be considered extraordinary?

15. *Other*

a. Are there any events that occurred after the end of the fiscal period that have a significant effect on the financial statements?

b. Have actions taken at stockholder, board of directors, or comparable meetings that affect the financial statements been reflected?

c. Have there been any material transactions between related parties?

d. Are there any material uncertainties? Is there any change in the status of material uncertainties previously disclosed?

Notes

1. Statement on Standards for Accounting and Review Services (SSARS) 1 (New York: AICPA, 1979). We have summarized segments of that publication in this section of the chapter.
2. Extensive use was made in this section of material included in *Statement on Standards for Accountants' Services on Prospective Financial Information* (New York: AICPA, 1985). Copyright © 1985 by the American Institute of Certified Public Accountants.
3. "Reporting on Pro Forma Financial Information," *Statement on Standards for Attestation Engagements* (AICPA, September 1988). See also SAS No. 8, *Other Information in Documents Containing Audited Financial Statements*, and SAS No. 37, *Filings Under Federal Securities Statutes*.
4. Ibid., "Reporting on Pro Forma Financial Information," paragraph 10.

Questions for Class Discussion

Q23-1 What nonaudit services are provided by public accountants? Which of these constitute *attest* services?

Q23-2 Why is the public accountant particularly well suited to provide clients with management advisory services?

Q23-3 What are the services typically provided in management advisory services engagements?

Q23-4 What are the differences between an accountant's reports on unaudited financial statements of public entities and those on unaudited financial statements of nonpublic entities? Explain.

Q23-5 What is meant by the term *compilation of financial statements*?

Q23-6 How is a review of financial statements different from the compilation of financial statements? Explain. Why is a review considered an attest service?

Q23-7 In a compilation engagement, how should the accountant react to information supplied by the client that appears to be incomplete or otherwise unsatisfactory? Explain.

Q23-8 What analytical procedures are used in performing a review of financial statements?

Q23-9 What inquiries should the accountant make in performing a review of financial statements?

Q23-10 What are the contents of the accountant's report on a review of the financial statements?

Q23-11 How should the accountant react to a request by the client to perform specific auditing procedures on some element of the accounting records in connection with a review engagement?

Q23-12 Suppose that an audit client wants to change that engagement to an engagement to review the financial statements: how should the auditor react to such a request? Explain.

Q23-13 What, briefly, is the accountant's general responsibility in reporting to a client the findings on a management advisory services engagement?

Q23-14 Compare and contrast the qualitative standards that the public accountant is expected to meet in performing tax services with those expected to be met in performing audit services.

Q23-15 Under what circumstances should a CPA sign the tax return for another party? Discuss.

Q23-16 What is the distinction between forecasts and projections in the preparation of prospective financial statements? Explain.

Q23-17 What is meant by *pro forma statements*?

Q23-18 What are the constraints within which a CPA may allow his or her name to be associated with prospective financial statements?

Short Cases

C23-1 Your CPA firm has been approached by Lazy Acres, a small local real estate operation in Butte, Montana, about the possibility of performing auditing or some other type of service for them. You have determined that the company is in need of the following:
   a. Monthly assistance in posting entries from the cash receipts and disbursements records to their general ledger.
   b. Preparation of monthly cash-basis financial statements to submit to the First State Bank of Helena, an institution that has extended the real estate firm a $200,000 line of credit.
   c. Preparation of quarterly payroll tax returns.
   d. Preparation of the company's annual partnership tax return.

The president of the company, J. R. Thomas, is not certain as to the types of services he needs you to perform. He asks your advice as to the kinds of services you are qualified to perform.

Required:
   a. Of each of the services listed above, discuss the ones you feel qualified to perform.
   b. What additional information, if any, might you want to obtain before advising Mr. Thomas?
   c. On the basis of the facts listed above, what services would you recommend?

C23-2 Irving Brown, CPA, received a telephone call from Leo Calhoun, the sole owner and manager of a small corporation. Calhoun asked Brown to prepare the financial statements for the corporation and told Brown that the statements were needed in two weeks for external financing purposes. Calhoun was vague when Brown inquired about the intended use of the statements. Brown was convinced that Calhoun thought Brown's work would constitute an audit. To avoid confusion Brown decided not to explain to Calhoun that the engagement would only be to prepare the financial statements. Brown, with the understanding that a substantial fee would be paid if the work were completed in two weeks, accepted the engagement and started the work at once.

During the course of the work, Brown discovered an accrued expense account labeled "professional fees" and learned that the balance in the account represented an accrual for the cost of Brown's services. Brown suggested to Calhoun's bookkeeper that the account name be changed to "fees for limited audit engagement." Brown also reviewed several invoices to determine whether accounts were being properly classified. Some of the invoices were missing. Brown listed the missing invoice numbers in the working papers with a note indicating that there should be a follow-up on the next engagement. Brown also discovered that the available records included the fixed asset values at estimated current replacement costs. Based on the records available, Brown prepared a balance sheet, income statement, and statement of stockholder's equity. In addition, Brown drafted the footnotes but decided that any mention of the replacement costs would only mislead the readers. Brown suggested to Calhoun that readers of the financial statements would be better informed if they received a separate letter from Calhoun explaining the meaning and effect of the estimated replacement costs of the fixed assets. Brown mailed the financial statements and footnotes to Calhoun with the following note included on each page: "The accompanying financial statements are submitted to you without complete audit verification."

Required: Identify the inappropriate actions of Brown and indicate what Brown should have done to avoid each inappropriate action. Organize your answer sheet as follows:

Inappropriate Action	What Brown Should Have Done to Avoid Inappropriate Action

(AICPA adapted)

Problems

P23-1 Select the best answer for each of the following items relating to reports on unaudited financial statements.

   a. When an independent CPA is associated with the financial statements of a nonpublicly held entity but has *not* audited or reviewed such statements, the appropriate form of report to be issued must include a (an)
   1. Negative assurance.
   2. Compilation report.

3. Disclaimer of opinion.
4. Explanatory paragraph.

b. Which of the following procedures is *not* included in a review engagement of a nonpublic entity?
1. Inquiries of management.
2. Inquiries regarding events subsequent to the balance sheet date.
3. Any procedures designed to identify relationships among data that appear to be unusual.
4. An understanding of the internal control structure.

c. Which of the following would *not* be included in a CPA's report based on a review of the financial statements of a nonpublic entity?
1. A statement that the review was in accordance with generally accepted auditing standards.
2. A statement that all information included in the financial statements is the representation of management.
3. A statement describing the principal procedures performed.
4. A statement describing the CPA's conclusions based on the results of the review.

d. You are a CPA retained by the manager of a cooperative retirement village to do "write-up work." You are expected to prepare unaudited financial statements, with each page marked "unaudited" and accompanied by a disclaimer of opinion stating no audit was made. In performing the work, you discover that there are no invoices to support $25,000 of the manager's claimed disbursements. The manager informs you that all the disbursements are proper. What should you do?
1. Submit the expected statements, but omit the $25,000 of unsupported disbursements.
2. Include the unsupported disbursements in the statements since you are not expected to make an audit.
3. Obtain from the manager a written statement that you informed him of the missing invoices and that he assured you that the disbursements are proper.
4. Notify the owners that some of the claimed disbursements are unsupported and withdraw if the situation is not satisfactorily resolved.

e. Carson Jeffries, CPA, had prepared unaudited financial statements for a client, the Gold Company. Since the statements were only to be used internally by the client, Jeffries did *not* include any footnotes and so noted this in the accompanying disclaimer of opinion. Three months after the statements were issued, the Gold Company asked Jeffries if it would be all right to give a copy of the statements to its banker who had requested financial statements. How should Jeffries respond?
1. Jeffries should revise the statements to include appropriate footnotes and attach a revised disclaimer of opinion before they are released to the banker.
2. Gold may give the statements to the banker as long as Jeffries's disclaimer of opinion accompanies the statements.
3. Gold should retype the statements on plain paper and send them to the banker without Jeffries's report.
4. Gold may let the banker review the statements and take notes but should not give the banker a copy of the statements.

f. Which of the following best describes the responsibility of the CPA when he or she prepares unaudited financial statements for his or her client?
1. He or she should make a proper study and evaluation of the existing internal control as a basis for reliance thereon.
2. He or she is relieved of any responsibility to third parties.

    3. He or she does not have the responsibility of applying auditing procedures to the financial statements.

    4. He or she has only to satisfy himself or herself that the financial statements were prepared to conformity with generally accepted accounting principles.

g. A CPA has a financial interest in a corporation and is associated with that corporation's unaudited financial statements. Under such circumstances the CPA's report should state that the CPA is *not* independent with respect to the corporation and should include

    1. The other elements of a compilation report, since that is the only appropriate report to render in this situation.

    2. A description of the reasons for the CPA's lack of independence and a disclaimer of opinion on the financial statements.

    3. A statement that each page of the financial statements is "unaudited" and a qualified opinion on the financial statements.

    4. A description of the reasons for the CPA's lack of independence and a qualified opinion on the financial statements.

h. When engaged to compile or review financial statements, the CPA's responsibility to detect fraud

    1. Is limited to informing the client of any matters that come to his or her attention that cause the auditor to believe an irregularity exists.

    2. Is the same as the responsibility that exists when the CPA is engaged to perform an audit of financial statements in accordance with generally accepted auditing standards.

    3. Arises out of the CPA's obligation to apply procedures designed to bring to light indications that a fraud or defalcation may have occurred.

    4. Does *not* exist unless an engagement letter is prepared.

i. Which of the following must accompany unaudited financial statements prepared by a CPA?

    1. Only a disclaimer of opinion.

    2. Either a disclaimer of opinion or adverse opinion.

    3. Either a disclaimer of opinion or a qualified opinion.

    4. Either a disclaimer of opinion, adverse opinion, or qualified opinion.

j. Richard Loeb, CPA, has completed a review of the Bloto Company's unaudited financial statements and has prepared the following report to accompany them:

> The accompanying balance sheet of the Bloto Company as of August 31, 19X5, and the related statements of income, retained earnings, and cash flows for the year then ended were not audited by us and, accordingly, we do not express an opinion on them.
>
>   The financial statements fail to disclose that the debentures issued on July 15, 19X2, limit the payment of cash dividends to the amount of earnings after August 31, 19X3. The company's statements of income for the years 19X4 and 19X5, both of which are unaudited, show this amount to be $18,900. Generally accepted accounting principles require disclosure of matters of this nature.

    Which of the following comments best describes the appropriateness of this report?

    1. The report is satisfactory.

    2. The report is deficient because Loeb does not describe the scope of the review or give reference to the CPA's reservations regarding presentation.

3. The report is deficient because the second paragraph gives the impression that some audit work was done.

4. The report is deficient because the explanatory comment in the second paragraph should precede the opinion paragraph.

k. Which of the following is the *least* important factor a CPA should consider in determining whether financial statements with which the CPA is associated may be issued as unaudited?

1. The restrictions a client might place on observing inventories or confirming receivables.

2. The intended use of the financial statements.

3. The procedures actually performed.

4. The needs of the client.

l. Sharon Reed, a partner in a local CPA firm, performs free accounting services for a private club of which Reed is treasurer. In which of the following manners should Reed issue the financial statements of the club?

1. On the firm's letterhead with a disclaimer for lack of independence.

2. On the firm's letterhead with a disclaimer for unaudited financial statements.

3. On plain paper with no reference to Reed so that Reed will not be associated with the statements.

4. On the club's letterhead with Reed signing as treasurer.

(AICPA adapted)

P23-2 Select the best answer for each of the following items.

a. In which of the following reports should a CPA *not* express negative or limited assurance?

1. A standard compilation report on financial statements of a nonpublic entity.

2. A standard review report on financial statements of a nonpublic entity.

3. A standard review report on interim financial statements of a public entity.

4. A standard comfort letter on financial information included in a registration statement of a public entity.

b. Inquiry of the entity's personnel and analytical procedures are the primary bases for the issuance of a (an)

1. Compilation report on financial statements for a nonpublic company in its first year of operations.

2. Auditor's report on financial statements supplemented with price-level information.

3. Review report on comparative financial statements for a nonpublic company in its second year of operations.

4. Management advisory report prepared at the request of the client's audit committee.

c. A CPA who is *not* independent may issue a

1. Review report.

2. Comfort letter.

3. Qualified opinion.

4. Compilation report.

d. During a review of financial statements of a nonpublic entity, the CPA would be *least* likely to

1. Perform analytical procedures designed to identify relationships that appear to be unusual.

2. Obtain written confirmation from management regarding loans to officers.
3. Obtain reports from other accountants who reviewed a portion of the total entity.
4. Read the financial statements and consider conformance with generally accepted accounting principles.

e. Compiled financial statements should be accompanied by a report stating all of the following *except*
   1. The accountant does *not* express an opinion or any other form of assurance on them.
   2. A compilation has been performed.
   3. A compilation is limited to presenting in the form of financial statements information that is the representation of management.
   4. A compilation consists principally of inquiries of company personnel and analytical procedures applied to financial data.

f. When an accountant is *not* independent, the accountant is precluded from issuing a
   1. Compilation report.
   2. Review report.
   3. Management advisory report.
   4. Tax planning report.

g. Under which of the following circumstances could an auditor consider rendering an opinion on pro forma statements that give effect to proposed transactions?
   1. When the pro forma statements include amounts based on financial projections.
   2. When the time interval between the date of the financial statements and consummation of the transactions is relatively long.
   3. When certain subsequent events have some chance of interfering with the consummation of the transactions.
   4. When the CPA has audited the historical financial statements that are included in the same document as the pro forma information.

h. A CPA's report on a forecast should include all of the following *except*
   1. A description of what the forecast information is intended to represent.
   2. A caveat as to the ultimate attainment of the forecasted results.
   3. A statement that the CPA assumes *no* responsibility to update the report for events occurring after the date of the report.
   4. An opinion as to whether the forecast is fairly presented.

i. When the financial statements of a nonpublic entity for a prior period have *not* been audited and are presented, for comparative purposes, with current-period statements that have been audited,
   1. The auditor should request removal of the unaudited statements since it is improper to present them for comparative purposes with audited statements.
   2. The auditor should identify the financial statements that were *not* examined in a separate paragraph in the auditor's report accompanying the current statements.
   3. The unaudited statements do *not* need to be marked "unaudited" as this may confuse the users of the statements.
   4. The auditor's report accompanying the statements should *not* mention that the prior period statements are unaudited, but the unaudited statements should be marked "unaudited."

j. A CPA should *not* undertake a management advisory service engagement that includes continued participation through implementation, unless
   1. The CPA accepts overall responsibility for implementation of the chosen course of action.
   2. The CPA acquires an overall knowledge of the client's business that is equivalent to that possessed by management.

3. Upon implementation, the client's personnel will have the knowledge and ability to adequately maintain and operate such systems as may be involved.

4. Upon implementation, a new study and evaluation of the system of internal control is performed.

k. Which of the following is a Management Advisory Service Engagement Practice Standard only?

1. In performing management advisory service, a practitioner must act with integrity and objectivity and be independent in mental attitude.

2. The management advisory service engagement is to be performed by a person or persons having adequate technical training as a management consultant.

3. Management advisory service engagements are to be performed by practitioners having competence in the analytical approach and process and in the technical subject matter under consideration.

4. Before undertaking a management advisory service engagement, a practitioner is to notify the client of any reservations regarding anticipated benefits.

(AICPA adapted)

P23-3 Select the best answer for each of the following questions. (Refer to the appendixes.)

a. As part of your annual audit of a client, you prepare the federal income tax return. What modifications, if any, should you make to the preparer's declaration when signing the return?

1. You should make no modification.

2. You should modify the declaration to conform with the wording of your audit report.

3. You should add a sentence to the declaration that the information contained herein was taken from audited financial statements covered by your report dated _____.

4. You should add a sentence to the declaration that some of the information contained herein was furnished by the client without audit.

b. A CPA firm's primary purpose for performing management advisory services is to

1. Prepare the CPA firm for the changing needs and requirements of the business community.

2. Establish the CPA firm as a consultant, which will enable the CPA firm to ensure future viability and growth.

3. Provide advice and technical assistance that will enable a client to conduct its business more effectively.

4. Enable staff members of the CPA firm to acquire the necessary continuing education in all areas of business.

c. The AICPA Committee on Management Services has stated its belief that a CPA should *not* undertake a management advisory service engagement for implementation of the CPA's recommendations unless

1. The client does not understand the nature and implications of the recommended course of action.

2. The client has made a firm decision to proceed with implementation based on his or her complete understanding and consideration of alternatives.

3. The client does not have sufficient expertise within his or her organization to comprehend the significance of the changes being made.

4. The CPA withdraws as independent auditor for the client.

d. In tax practice, which of the following would *not* be considered reasonable support for taking a position contrary to the Internal Revenue Code?

1. Proposed regulations advocated by the IRS.
2. Legal opinions as to the constitutionality of a specific provision.
3. Possible conflicts between two sections of the Internal Revenue Code.
4. Tax court decisions *not* acquiesced to by the IRS.

e. Juanita Adams, CPA, is preparing a federal tax return for Ralph Evans. In an interview to gather the necessary data, Evans stated he had given about $100 to charitable organizations soliciting at the door such as the local volunteer fire department and March of Dimes. What should Adams do with this information when preparing the tax return?
1. She should ignore it because Statements on Responsibility in Tax Practice issued by the AICPA prohibit the use of estimates.
2. She should identify $100 as "Other miscellaneous contributions."
3. She should identify as contributions "volunteer fire department—$50; and March of Dimes—$50."
4. She should increase one of Evans's other specifically named contributions by $100.

f. Tim Cortney has moved to a distant city but desires to continue to retain Hugo Blake, CPA, to prepare his personal federal tax return. Blake telephones Cortney after receiving his written list of information to be used in the preparation of the tax return because it appears to contain an understatement of interest expense. From the conversation Blake learns that the interest expense should be double the amount indicated on the written list. Blake, who asked Cortney to send a photocopy of the supporting evidence indicating the correct amount of the interest expense, has not received the correspondence and the filing deadline is five days away. Under the circumstances Blake should
1. Prepare the return based on the written information received and *not* sign the preparer's declaration.
2. Prepare the return based on the written information received, clearly indicating that an amended return will follow.
3. Prepare the return based on the written and oral information received.
4. Send Cortney a telegram indicating that no tax return will be prepared until all requested data are received.

g. When a CPA prepares a federal income tax return for an audit client, one would expect
1. The CPA to take a position of client advocacy.
2. The CPA to take a position of independent neutrality.
3. The taxable net income in the audited financial statements to agree with taxable net income in the federal income tax return.
4. The expenses in the audited financial statements to agree with the deductions in the federal income tax return.

h. In accordance with the AICPA Statements on Responsibilities in Tax Practice, if after having provided tax advice to a client there are legislative changes that affect the advice provided, the CPA
1. Is obligated to notify the client of the change and the effect thereof.
2. Is obligated to notify the client of the change and the effect thereof if the client was not advised that the advice was based on existing laws which are subject to change.
3. Can *not* be expected to notify the client of the change unless the obligation is specifically undertaken by agreement.
4. Can *not* be expected to have knowledge of the change.

i. In accordance with the AICPA Statements on Responsibilities in Tax Practice, where a question on a federal income tax return has not been answered, the CPA should sign the preparer's declaration only if

1. The CPA can provide reasonable support for this omission upon examination by the IRS.
2. The information requested is *not* available.
3. The question is *not* applicable to the taxpayer.
4. An explanation of the reason for the omission is provided.

j. While performing tax services for a client, a CPA may learn of a material error in a previously filed tax return. In such an instance the CPA should

1. Prepare an affidavit with respect to the error.
2. Recommend compensating for the prior year's error in the current year's tax return where such action will mitigate the client's cost and inconvenience.
3. Advise the client to file a corrected return regardless of whether or not the error resulted in an overstatement or understatement of tax.
4. Inform the IRS of the error.

(AICPA adapted)

P23-4 Judd Hanlon, CPA, was engaged to prepare the federal income tax return for the Guild Corporation for the year ended December 31, 19X2. This is Mr. Hanlon's first engagement of any kind for the Guild Corporation.

In preparing the 19X2 return, Mr. Hanlon finds an error on the 19X1 return. The 19X1 depreciation deduction was overstated significantly—accumulated depreciation brought forward from 19X0 to 19X1 was understated, and thus the 19X1 base for declining balance depreciation was overstated.

Mr. Hanlon reported the error to Guild's controller, the officer responsible for tax returns. The controller stated: "Let the revenue agent find the error." He further instructed Mr. Hanlon to carry forward the material overstatement of the depreciable base to the 19X2 depreciation computation. The controller noted that this error also had been made in the financial records for 19X1 and 19X2 and offered to furnish Mr. Hanlon with a letter assuming full responsibility for this treatment.

Required:
a. Evaluate Mr. Hanlon's handling of this situation.
b. Discuss the additional action that Mr. Hanlon should now undertake.

(AICPA adapted)

P23-5 The CPA firm of Blank, Miller & Tage prepares a significant number of individual and corporate income tax returns. G. DeFilippo is a newly hired junior accountant. This is DeFilippo's first job since graduation from school. His initial assignment is to work with the tax department in the preparation of clients' 19X2 income tax returns. DeFilippo was instructed that he was not required to examine supporting data and that he could use the 19X1 returns of all clients in preparing the 19X2 returns. Further, he was instructed to sign all returns he prepared.

Required: Answer the following, setting forth reasons for any conclusions stated.
a. What is the professional responsibility of the CPA firm and DeFilippo to clients in connection with the preparation of income tax returns, examining supporting data, and signing the return?

b. Give some examples of performance that would result in violation of these responsibilities.

(AICPA adapted)

P23-6 The following report on the basic financial statements was drafted by a staff assistant at the completion of the review engagement of GLM Company, a continuing client, for the year ended September 30, 19X8. The 19X7 basic financial statements for the year ended September 30, 19X7, which were also reviewed, contained a departure from generally accepted accounting principles that was properly referred to in the 19X7 review report dated October 26, 19X7. The 19X7 financial statements have been restated.

To the Board of Directors of GLM Company:

We have reviewed the accompanying balance sheets of GLM Company as of September 30, 19X8 and 19X7, and the related statements of income and retained earnings for the years then ended, in accordance with generally accepted auditing standards. Our review included such tests of the accounting records as we considered necessary in the circumstances.

A review consists principally of inquiries of company personnel. It is substantially less in scope than an audit, but more in scope than a compilation. Accordingly, we express only limited assurance on the accompanying financial statements.

Based on our reviews, with the exception of the matter described in the following paragraph, we are not aware of any material modifications that should be made to the accompanying financial statements in order for them to be in conformity with generally accepted accounting principles applied on a consistent basis.

In its 19X7 financial statements the company stated its land at appraised values. However, as disclosed in note X, the company has restated its 19X7 financial statements to reflect land at cost.

November 2, 19X8

Required: Identify the deficiencies in the draft of the proposed report on the comparative financial statements. Group the deficiencies by paragraph. Do not redraft the report.

(AICPA adapted)

P23-7 John Cox, CPA, has been approached to perform work on the prospective financial statements of Newtone, Inc., for the use of third parties who might be interested in buying the company.

Required:
1. Describe the kinds of work that CPAs are qualified to perform on prospective financial statements.
2. Of the types of services described in (1), which constitute "attest" services? Why?
3. Describe the difference between a financial forecast and a financial projection. Which of these types of prospective financial statements would be acceptable for "general" as opposed to "limited" use? Why?

4. If Cox performs an audit of the prospective financial statements of Newtone, Inc., what are the limits of his engagement, if any? Why?
5. Describe the contents of Cox's standard audit report on Newtone's financial forecast.

P23-8 In some circumstances, a certified public accountant may be associated with *pro forma financial statements*.

Required:
1. What business circumstances of the client can cause a CPA to become associated with pro forma financial statements?
2. How do pro forma financial statements differ from prospective financial statements?
3. Describe the CPA's responsibilities with respect to pro forma financial statements.
4. Under what conditions may the CPA attest to pro forma financial statements?

CHAPTER 24

Internal, Operational, and Governmental Auditing

Objectives

☐ **1.** Understand the major differences between internal auditing and financial auditing.
☐ **2.** Be able to define the "operational audit" and to understand how it differs from the financial audit.
☐ **3.** Have a working knowledge of audits of governmental programs, organizations, activities, and functions.

In Chapter 1, we defined auditing as a systematic process of gathering evidence concerning economic assertions, ascertaining their correspondence with established criteria, and communicating the results to interested users. That definition is broad enough to cover all types of auditing: independent (external) audits, internal audits, and audits of governmental entities. It is important to realize that financial statement audits comprise only a part of the audit work that must be done in our society. In this chapter we focus our attention on other types of audits besides the financial statement audit.

Appendixes to the chapter cover the following:
1. Statement of responsibilities of internal auditing.
2. Summary of general and specific standards for the professional practice of internal auditing.
3. General accounting office (GAO) auditing standards.

Internal Auditing

Within an economic entity, management is always concerned with the extent to which employees are adhering to its policies and directives and with the efficiency of operations and effectiveness of the recordkeeping system. Accountants employed for the purpose of evaluating internal operations and recordkeeping activities are called internal auditors. Such people are, in effect, extensions of the arm of management, employed for the purpose of verifying what other key employees are doing and evaluating the efficiency and effectiveness of their work. As we have explained the various elements of the independent audit of financial statements, we have often referred to the role of internal auditors in ensuring compliance with internal control procedures and in providing assistance to the independent auditor during the audit. We now turn our attention to a more complete description of the work performed by this segment of the accounting profession.

Internal auditors are employees of the company being audited. However, because they are expected to evaluate performance, effectiveness, and compliance of various activities and departments against prescribed managerial policies, they should be members of an autonomous group that is free to objectively investigate and evaluate what other departments are doing. Because of the need for *internal independence*, the internal auditing department should report to the audit committee of the board of directors or an upper-level management official. The important thing in determining exactly the position within the organization that the internal auditing staff will occupy is to be sure that the individual or group to whom they report has sufficient authority within the organization and that the audit objectives are not compromised. That person or group should also be in position to see that changes recommended by the internal auditor are implemented.

The organizational requirements described in the preceding paragraph are designed to ensure the internal auditing staff of *independence within the firm*, which allows the internal auditors to be objective in evaluating the operations of all segments and to report operations without fear of reprisals for the discovery and reporting of weaknesses. We should recognize that this type of independence within the firm is different from, but comparable to, the kind of external independence required for independent auditors.

In their early history, internal auditors were primarily concerned with improving compliance with managerial objectives and procedures. In recent years, however, the functions performed by these accountants have been broadened to include an analysis and evaluation of operating efficiency and effectiveness commonly characterized as operational auditing. In some instances, internal auditors also perform a more sophisticated type of operational auditing characterized as *management auditing*. In performing this service they are in fact evaluating the performance of managers.

As the internal auditing segment of the accounting profession has become more important in the operations of enterprise units, they have organized into a professional association called the Institute of Internal Auditors (IIA). Through the medium of this organization, internal auditors have adopted a *code of ethics* (included as an appendix to Chapter 3). In addition, the organization has adopted a *statement of responsibilities of internal auditing* and a *summary of standards for the professional practice of internal auditing*. These documents are reflected in Appendixes 24–A and 24–B, respectively.

The IIA has also implemented a certification program, which allows an accountant to be designated as a Certified Internal Auditor (CIA) upon passing an examination administered by the association. This examination covers principles of internal auditing, internal auditing techniques, principles of management, and disciplines related to internal auditing.

To appropriately serve management, internal auditing should include the following activities:

1. Reviewing and appraising the soundness, adequacy, and application of accounting, financial, and operating controls.
2. Ascertaining the extent of compliance with established policies, plans, and procedures.
3. Ascertaining the extent to which company assets are accounted for and safeguarded from losses of all kinds.
4. Ascertaining the reliability of accounting and other data developed within the organization.
5. Appraising the quality of performance in carrying out assigned responsibilities.[1]

Operational Auditing

☑ **Objective 2**
Define operational auditing and differentiate from a financial audit

Operational auditing may be defined as "a comprehensive examination and appraisal of business operations for the purpose of informing management whether or not the various operations are performed in a manner which complies with established policies directed toward management's objectives. Included in the audit is an appraisal of the efficient use of both human and physical resources as well as an appraisal of various operating procedures. The audit should also include recommendations for solutions to problems and for increasing efficiency and profits."[2] Observe from this definition that the objective of such an audit is to provide information that will be of service to management. These audits, then, can be described as an organized search for ways to improve the efficiency and effectiveness of an organization's operations. For business entities, an operational audit should be designed to increase profitability by discovering more efficient ways of allocating and using resources and improving communications within the firm.

Operational auditing differs in several ways from financial (external) auditing. Among the major differences between operational and external auditing are (1) the nature of the assertions being audited, (2) the criteria against which those assertions are evaluated, and (3) the intended users of the auditor's report.

Nature of the Assertions

The assertions verified by the financial statement auditor are the basic financial statement assertions of SAS 31 (AU326); they include existence/occurrence, completeness, rights/obligations, valuation/allocation, and presentation/disclosure. The auditor is required under GAAS to obtain an *understanding* of the control structure of the entity sufficient to plan the nature, timing, and extent of procedures to be performed on these assertions. In contrast, the primary assertions that are to be verified by the operational auditor (often implied in the nature of the work rather than expressed in a contract or other agreement) are

1. *Effectiveness*, which refers to the ability of the management team of the entity to produce a desired result. An example might be the development and implementation of a new data base management system for a university that integrates the processes of registration, enrollment, tuition collection, and financial aid. Another example might be the development of an automated internal control system for a food distribution corporation that eliminates a substantial portion of the work that must be performed by humans.
2. *Efficiency*, which is the ability to produce the desired results with the least cost. For example, in automating the food distribution process, the company might be saved millions of dollars in labor expenditures over the next 5 years.

Whereas the understanding of the control structure is a *means to an end* in the financial statement audit, improving the effectiveness and efficiency of the internal control structure of an entity are generally *ends unto themselves* in the operational audit.

Criteria for Evaluation

Whereas the criteria for evaluation of financial statement assertions is GAAP, the criteria for evaluation of the assertions of effectiveness and efficiency for the operational audit must be set internally by top management of the entity, and will generally vary from project to project. For example, the vice president for university operations, working closely with the registrar, cashier, and the director for student financial aid, should set the objectives for the data base management system for the university referred to in the above illustration. Similarly, the vice president for operations of the food distributor should set the criteria for the new internal control system, working closely with the heads of engineering, the audit committee, and the internal audit department. These criteria should be used by the internal audit team in evaluating the effectiveness of the activity and the efficiency with which the desired result was achieved.

Operational audits might be performed at several levels within the entity. Generally, those levels may be categorized as follows: (1) functional; (2) organizational; and (3) special assignments. Functionally, an entity might be subdivided by *systems*. For example, the functions in the accounting system of a business might include financing and investing, production, billing, cash receipts and disbursements, and payrolls. An operational audit might focus attention on the effectiveness and efficiency of any one of these functions, such as payrolls. Such an audit would require a specific set of criteria against which effectiveness and efficiency of the payroll function could be measured.

Organizationally, an entity might be divided into divisions or segments, each with a complete set of functions (billing, production, payroll, etc.). An operational audit might focus attention on the effectiveness and efficiency of the control structure of a particular division or segment of the business.

Special assignments include audits of activities that cut across functions and organizational units. Examples are special audit projects involving the effectiveness of the EDP system of the entire organization, and special investigations into fraud or violations of the Foreign Corrupt Practices Act of 1977. Each of these types of operational audits require a unique set of criteria, specified by top management, and clearly communicated to the audit team.

Another major contrast between criteria of financial and operational auditors is the time period to which they relate. Whereas the financial audit emphasizes whether GAAP have been followed in past financial statements, the operational audit focuses on the implementation of present and future plans and expectations. Although some operational audit tasks might be related to the historical financial statements, the primary focus of the operational audit would more likely be the operating, cash, or capital budgets of the company.

Still another difference between criteria of financial and operational auditors is that the criteria used by operational auditors may involve *nonfinancial* as well as financial activities. In the illustration of the university data base system above, for example, the effectiveness of the system concerns its ease of operation, reliability of reporting class sizes and enrollments, and acceptance by faculty, administration, and student body, as well as its impact on revenues of the institution.

Users of Operational Reports

Whereas the users of the report of the financial statement auditor are generally external investors and creditors, the intended users of most operational audit reports are members of the entity's top management, audit committee, or other internal policy-setting group.

The work performed in carrying out the operational audit can be divided into the following elements:

1. Planning the work to be performed.
2. Gathering the evidence relating to performance.

3. Evaluating the evidence.
4. Formally reporting the results of the audit to management.

Planning an Operational Audit

The basic concept underlying the operational audit is that efficiency and effectiveness should be measured by *evaluating the extent to which management objectives are being achieved*. Therefore, as a first step in planning an operational audit, the auditor must determine and become thoroughly familiar with those objectives and the plans and procedures that management has established to achieve those objectives. It will be helpful for you to think of these criteria against which efficiency and effectiveness will be measured as being made up of the following:

1. Long-range goals for the company.
2. Short-term objectives designed to achieve the long-range goals.
3. Specific plans, policies, procedures, and strategies that management has identified to be followed in achieving short-term objectives.

It is important to observe at this point that, while the auditor generally will not question the first two of these items, he or she will be evaluating the plans and procedures and the ways in which those plans and procedures are being implemented.

Operational audits of necessity will involve separate evaluations of various segments of a firm's operations. In most instances the specific segments to be evaluated will be determined by management. In some instances, however, the specific area to be evaluated may be left to the discretion of the auditor (in most cases, the internal auditing department).

After the operating objectives, plans and procedures, and specific segment of the business to be evaluated have been identified, the auditor is ready to proceed with planning and organizing the audit. He or she will begin by arranging a preliminary meeting with the supervisor of the operating segment being audited. In this meeting it is important for the auditor to establish rapport with the supervisor and employees of the segment to be audited to help ensure a cooperative attitude by the personnel of the segment. Because of the nature of such an audit (evaluation of efficiency and effectiveness), it is important for the auditor to use tact and diplomacy in this meeting with segment personnel. It is also important for the auditor to make some judgments at this point as to the general nature of the problems that may be encountered in performing the audit.

Having carried out the preliminary contact described in the preceding paragraph, the auditor is now ready to organize the audit assignment. This includes the following steps:

1. Selection of the right type and level of personnel to perform the work.
2. Determination of the work plan, including development of review programs to serve as the "road maps" of the work to be done.

3. Identification of the purpose of the review and the expected benefits to be derived from the examination.
4. Projection of the time schedule for the work up through issuance of the report. This will include man-hour estimates for each phase of the work (e.g., preliminary work, actual data development and field review, analysis of data collected, and drafting and issuing of the report—including review of the report with management).
5. Estimation of cost, direct and indirect, to complete all aspects of the assignment.[3]

Steps 2 and 4 should be formalized into an audit program that can be used as a guideline in gathering and evaluating evidence. Such a program can take the form of a checklist on which the auditor can efficiently summarize the findings during the evidence-gathering phase of the audit.

Gathering the Evidence

The internal auditor, just as with an independent audit of financial statements, is concerned with securing evidence. However, in an operational audit, he or she will be seeking evidence with regard to the extent to which the segments being evaluated are meeting their operating objectives. We may think of this phase of the operational audit as being somewhat similar to work done in meeting the third standard of field work in an independent audit of financial statements.

Because of the nature of an operational audit, the most important evidence-gathering procedure generally will be *interviews with personnel* involved in the operations of the segment being audited. It is important that the auditor be prepared to raise appropriate questions in these interviews. Therefore, prior to scheduling the interviews, the various documents and other data (such as budgets) relating to the segment being audited must be assembled and studied to permit more efficient use of the interview time. A checklist should be used by the auditor to quickly and effectively record the answers to the questions raised.

In addition to the interview procedure, the auditor performing an operational audit will want to knowledgeably *observe* the people and things associated with the segment being audited. General impressions and, in some instances, tentative conclusions can be developed from these observations. At a minimum, these observations should help the auditor in making judgments regarding the validity of the interview evidence.

Some of the data gathered from documents and from the interviews will need to be *analyzed*. This involves a detailed examination of those data with the intent of discovering or uncovering qualities, causes, effects, motives, and possibilities that can be a springboard to further research or as a basis for judgment. For example, an auditor examining the operations of a purchasing department may want to list a sample of purchase orders and analyze them in terms of bids, source procurements, approvals, past history of particular purchases, and other matters.

In some instances it may be necessary for the auditor performing an operational audit to *verify data* collected during the evidence-gathering process. Verification involves corroborating the data to determine its truth, accuracy, genuineness, or validity. This typically calls for comparing data, such as an accounting entry, with supporting details or documents.

As the data are gathered, it may be necessary to further investigate some of the data with the objective of discovering hidden facts, particularly when the auditor feels that the conditions surrounding the operations may be suspect. In connection with this procedure, we should observe that, in most situations, the auditor will be able to depend on the integrity of the supervisors of the segment being audited just as the independent auditor depends on the integrity of management in an audit of the financial statements. However, there may be exceptions, and when the operational auditor finds himself or herself in such a situation, some of the accumulated evidence must be critically evaluated by further investigation.

After the auditing procedures have been carried out, the operational auditor should summarize his or her findings in working papers that are designed to facilitate the final evaluation and reporting phases of the audit.

Evaluating the Evidence

The next step in an operational audit involves a careful *study and analysis of the evidence* gathered for the purpose of determining what recommendations should be made to management. In making this evaluation, the *evidence gathered should be related to the operating objectives of the segment being audited*. Evaluation implies the use of professional judgment in determining the existence of operating inefficiencies and the corrective actions necessary to overcome those inefficiencies.

In developing recommendations, it is important for the auditor to consider the costs of implementing the recommendations as well as the benefits that are expected to be derived from them. In other words, there must be a positive cost-benefit relationship associated with the recommendations. In making the recommendations, various alternatives may have to be considered, with the ultimate choice being the one that is expected to have the largest positive cost-benefit effect on operations.

As a last step in the evaluation processs, it is important that the auditor *discuss, on an informal basis, the findings and possible recommendations with the supervisors of the segment being investigated*. The comments and recommendations from these persons can be important considerations in arriving at the final recommendations to be included in the operational audit report. These discussions should also help promote a more cooperative attitude in implementing the recommendations.

Reporting the Results of the Operational Audit

The internal auditor, acting as an arm of management, may develop a report recommending specific changes to be made in the operations of the audited segment to allow it to adhere more closely to prescribed procedures and ultimately to improve profits. In other situations the internal auditor will simply report his or her evaluations of the evidence gathered and allow top management to develop its own course of action. The precise nature of the report will depend on the technical capabilities of the internal auditor and the desires of management relating to the particular segment of the business that has been audited.

If changes are recommended by the auditor, it is extremely important that the report be diplomatic in stating those recommendations. That means that each word must be considered carefully, with the ultimate objective of realizing the cooperation of the segment supervisors to implement recommended changes.

The formal report should be organized to include the *purpose, goal, scope,* and *limitations* of the audit as well as the auditor's *findings; opinions; evaluations;* and, if desired by management, *recommendations*. It should be written in language that the segment supervisor can be expected to understand. As a general rule, it is desirable to begin the findings, opinions, evaluations, and recommendations section of the report by *citing the things that are being done effectively before bringing attention to the inefficiencies discovered during the audit*. A report organized in this manner has a greater possibility of securing the cooperation and support of the operating personnel. In Figure 24–1 we show elements of an operational audit report.

Operational audits may also include a *follow-up phase,* in which the auditor revisits the segment to discuss the corrective actions taken in response to prior recommendations. In some instances this phase of the audit may be directed toward making sure that personnel of the segment previously audited understood fully the recommendations included in the formal audit report. In this way the auditor will be available to discuss any problems that may have arisen as the audited segment attempts to implement the recommendations.

Audits of Governmental Programs, Organizations, Activities, and Functions

☑ **Objective 3**
Understand the nature and purpose of audits of governmental programs, organizations, activities, and functions

Over $100 billion in financial assistance is given by the federal government each year to more than 100,000 entities (both public and private) in the form of grants.[4] Such grants may range in size from a few thousand dollars to millions of dollars, and may involve projects ranging from educational assistance to farm and military subsidies. To assure that these grant funds are used effectively and efficiently to accomplish the desired result, the federal government requires that certain entities who receive funds have annual audits. Those audits may be conducted by employees of the general accounting office (GAO) of the federal government, or by independent CPAs.

The Single Audit Act of 1984[5]

The decades of the 1960s through the 1980s witnessed massive growth in expenditures of federal funds to state and municipal governments and to private entities administering federal programs. Currently, this assistance involves all 50 states, over 80,000 local governments, and hundreds of different federal

Figure 24–1

Illustrative Operational Audit Report

Audit Highlights

Highway Transportation Department
(A regularly scheduled review)

Prior audit:	No deficiency findings.
Audit coverage:	1. Equipment maintenance and vehicle dispatching
	2. Fuel, parts, and repair services
	3. General administrative activities.
Overall opinion:	In general, the operation was functioning in a reasonably satisfactory manner.
	We did find some control weaknesses. The most serious involved the lack of separation of duties in the procurement of parts and services. Steps are being taken to correct these weaknesses.
	Despite the weaknesses, however, the department's activities were being performed satisfactorily.
Executive action required:	None.

Summary Report

Foreword This report covers the results of our regularly scheduled review of the activities of the Highway Transportation Department. Our last review of the department's activities disclosed no deficiencies.

The department's primary responsibilities are (1) to transport personnel and materials, and (2) to maintain and repair automobile equipment.

At the time of our review, there were about fifty employees assigned to the department. Operating costs (not including labor) for equipment rental, repair parts and services, and fuel and oil, are projected to reach about $900,000 for 19XX. Mileage for the year will total about 5 million miles.

During this review we issued one progress report to bring to management's attention certain matters requiring prompt corrective action.

Purpose We have made an examination of the Highway Transportation Department's principal activities to determine whether they were being controlled adequately and effectively. In performing our review, we examined the system of controls concerned with the following activities:

1. Equipment maintenance and vehicle dispatching, including (a) scheduling preventive maintenance inspections, (b) performing regular maintenance and repairs, and (c) dispatching cars and trucks.
2. Ordering, receiving, and disbursing fuel and parts and obtaining automotive repair services.
3. General administrative activities concerned with (a) property accountability, (b) plant protection, (c) accident reporting, (d) insurable value reporting, (e) gasoline credit cards, and (f) petty cash.

Opinions and Findings We formed the opinion that adequate controls had been provided over the activities we reviewed, except for a lack of separation of duties in the

Figure 24-1 ▰▰▰▰▰

(continued)

procurement of parts and services. Three other matters of lesser significance likewise involved control weaknesses.

We also formed the opinion that, despite the control weaknesses we had detected, the functions we reviewed were being performed in a generally satisfactory manner.

Our conclusions and findings on each of the three groups of activities covered in our examination are summarized in the following paragraphs.

Equipment Maintenance and Vehicle Dispatching

Adequate controls have been provided that were designed to make sure that (1) automotive equipment would receive inspection and preventive maintenance in accordance with the manufacturers' recommendations, and (2) truck and car dispatching would be accomplished in accordance with established procedures.

We examined preventive maintenance reports and related control records and satisfied ourselves that maintenance was being properly scheduled, monitored, and performed. We also examined documentation supporting vehicle dispatching and observed the dispatching operations; we concluded that dispatching was being adequately controlled and performed.

Ordering, Receiving, and Disbursing Fuel and Parts, and Obtaining Vehicle Repair Services

Controls had been provided that were designed to make sure that fuel, parts, and outside repair services were (1) ordered when needed, (2) recorded upon receipt, and (3) properly approved for payment.

Summary of Findings Requiring Corrective Action

The four matters requiring corrective action are summarized as follows:
1. There was no separation of functional authority in the procurement of parts and services, and effective administration of labor-hour agreements was beyond the Highway Transportation Department's resources.
2. Gasoline and oil were being withdrawn by company employees without adequate surveillance.
3. The area in which the Highway Transportation Department is located was not adequately protected.
4. The insurable value of repair parts on hand was not being reported.

Finding 1 is referred jointly to the manager of the Procurement Department and the manager of the Highway Transportation Department for completion of corrective action. Findings 2 and 3 are referred to the manager of the Highway Transportation Department for completion of corrective action. Finding 4 has been corrected.

Source: Adapted from *The Practice of Modern Internal Auditing* by Lawrence B. Sawyer (Altamonte Springs, Florida: Institute of Internal Auditors): 468–472. Used with permission.

programs. State governments also include the District of Columbia, Puerto Rico, and any Indian tribe. Local governments include cities, towns, counties, school districts, and housing and airport authorities. Federal programs include a multitude of transportation, welfare, education, health, and job training activities. This increase in federal expenditures has given rise to the need for increased accountability on the part of recipients, and also an increased demand for audit services.

In the beginning, because the funds were granted on an individual basis by different federal government entities, each grant that exceeded a certain size was required to be audited. In addition, different agencies had specific requirements for audits, and no one agency required comprehensive audit coverage of the entity receiving assistance, thus leaving gaps in audit coverage. If, for example, a community health clinic received grants from six different government agencies for the purpose of prenatal care for expectant mothers, it was possible for the clinic to undergo six separate audits of that particular activity during a fiscal period, with no audit coverage over other needed areas. It soon became apparent that cost-effective audit coverage on a grant-by-grant basis would be impossible to achieve.

To achieve greater effectiveness and efficiency in audits of federally assisted funding programs, Congress passed the Single Audit Act of 1984. Applicable to audits of federally assisted programs conducted by both employees of the general accounting office (GAO) and independent CPAs, the Single Audit Act has four major purposes:

1. To improve the financial management of state and local governments with respect to federal financial assistance programs.
2. To establish uniform requirements for audits of federal financial assistance provided to state and local governments.
3. To promote the efficient and effective use of audit resources.
4. To ensure that federal departments and agencies, to the maximum extent practicable, rely on and use audit work done pursuant to . . . the Act.

The **single audit** is designed to encompass the entire financial operations of each applicable government agency or program (entity) to determine and report whether

1. The financial statements of the entity present fairly its financial position and the results of its operations in accordance with generally accepted accounting principles *and whether the entity has complied with laws and regulations that may have a material effect on the financial statements.*
2. The entity has *internal control systems* to provide reasonable assurance that it is managing federal financial assistance programs in *compliance with applicable laws and regulations.*
3. The entity has *complied with laws and regulations* that may have a material effect on each major federal program.

The Act requires a single annual audit with these objectives for each government agency or program that receives $100,000 or more in annual federal support. Entities with between $25,000 and $100,000 in assistance may elect to have single audits or audits of individual programs. Entities with less than $25,000 in support are exempt from the Act.

At least three separate audit reports are required as the result of the single audit: (1) the standard audit report on the financial statements of the entity; (2) a report on the study and evaluation of internal controls; and (3) a report on the results of the testing of the entity's compliance with laws and regulations pertaining to each major federal assistance program.

Government Auditing Standards

Audits of governmental programs, organizations, activities, and functions are generally governed by *Standards for Audit of Governmental Organizations, Programs, Activities, and Functions,* (otherwise known as the *yellow book*) published by the Comptroller General of the United States. These standards govern not only the audits of state and local governments and programs receiving funds under the Single Audit Act of 1984 (see previous section), but also audits of federal government organizations, agencies, programs, activities, and functions.

Figure 24–2 presents an overview of generally accepted government auditing standards (GAGAS). These standards *include the standards prescribed by the AICPA for financial audits.* However, they go beyond AICPA standards in several respects. A detailed discussion of the standards is in Appendix 24–C.

GAO standards govern not only **financial audits** but also **performance audits**. In this context, financial auditing includes the traditional function of providing an independent opinion on whether an entity's financial statements present fairly the results of financial operations, and whether other financial information is presented in conformity with GAAP or other stated criteria. In the case of the governmental entity, GAAP includes financial reporting requirements of the Governmental Accounting Standards Board (GASB), the FASB, and the GAO. Some state and local governments and regulatory bodies also have established specific accounting principles. However, besides providing reasonable assurance regarding fair presentation of financial statements, the financial audit prescribed by the GAO also encompasses procedures designed to determine whether the entity has adhered to specific financial *compliance requirements,* such as those prescribed by contracts.

Performance auditing, on the other hand, provides an independent view of the extent to which government officials are faithfully, efficiently and effectively carrying out their responsibilities as required by law.[6] **Performance audits** include two separate subcategories: (1) **economy and efficiency audits** and (2) **program audits**. Audits of economy and efficiency are designed to determine (a) whether the entity is acquiring, protecting, and using its resources economically and efficiently; (b) the causes of inefficiencies or uneconomical practices; and (c) whether the entity has complied with laws and regulations concerning economy and efficiency. Economy and efficiency audits may focus on issues such as whether the entity is following sound procurement practices, whether it is acquiring needed resources at the lowest cost, whether it is properly protecting and maintaining

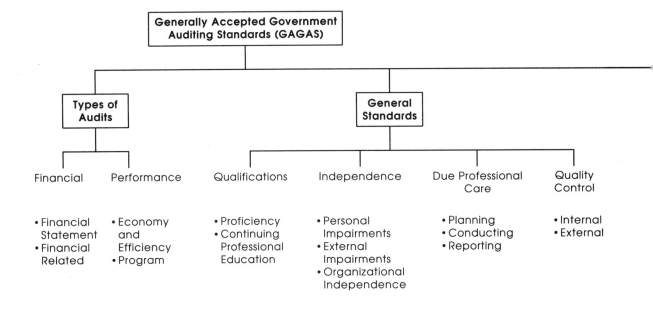

Source: Copyright 1988, General Accounting Office. Reprinted with permission.

its resources, or whether it is avoiding idleness, overstaffing, or other inefficient operating procedures.

Program audits are designed to assess whether the objectives of a proposed or ongoing program are proper, to determine the effectiveness of the entity in achieving desired results, to identify factors inhibiting satisfactory performance, and to determine whether effectiveness and efficiency have been properly balanced as goals of the program.

You should see by this discussion that the comprehensive audit prescribed by government auditing standards encompasses features of both the financial audit described earlier in the text and elements of the operational audit, discussed earlier in this chapter. However, the comprehensive audit goes further in each respective category to include monitoring of compliance with applicable laws and regulations of the federal government.

The General Standards

As shown in Figure 24–2, general standards of the GAO cover both financial audits and performance audits. The standards provide the foundation for the competently performed government audit. Four areas are emphasized: (1) qualifications; (2) independence; (3) due professional care; and (4) quality control.

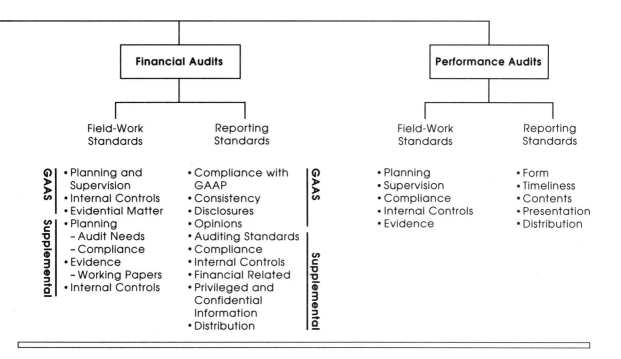

The purpose of the *qualifications* section is to provide assurance that the audit team, individually and collectively, possesses proficiency needed to conduct the audit. Like the AICPA standards, GAO auditing standards require the auditor to obtain adequate training and proficiency. However, the GAO standards *add a stringent requirement for continuing education*. Specifically, every two years, all persons who work on government audits must complete at least 80 hours of continuing professional education (CPE). For those who are in supervisory positions, at least 24 of the 80 hours must be in government-audit-related subjects. Auditing firms who conduct GAO-related audits are expected to maintain records to document the CPE of all affected personnel.

The general standard relating to *independence* is very much like its counterpart under GAAS of the AICPA. In all matters relating to the audit, both individual auditors and the firms or government organizations of which they are a part should be free from personal and external influences that might impair independence. Relationships to be avoided include, but are not limited to

- Official, professional, personal, or financial relationships that might cause the auditor to limit the extent of inquiry or disclosure, or to bias the findings in any way.
- Preconceived ideas toward individuals, groups, organizations, or objectives of a particular program.

- Previous managerial or director relationships with the entity that would bias the auditor.
- Political or social convictions that might bias the auditor.

External factors that might unduly influence the auditor or impair independent judgment include

- Interference by an external party that limits the scope of the audit.
- External interference in the selection of audit procedures or transactions examined.
- Unreasonable time restrictions.
- Restrictions on funding of the audit.

The GAO employee or other government auditor and his or her agency is expected to remain organizationally independent while performing the GAO audit. This requires that the auditing function be sufficiently independent of the audited entity within the government organizational structure to allow complete freedom to plan and conduct the audit, and to report the findings to applicable authorities.

The *due professional care standard* for GAO audits, like independence, is similar to its AICPA counterpart. However, the due care standard for the GAO audit requires that the auditor consider *materiality* or significance in deciding on the items to be selected for audit as well as those that need to be reported. Both qualitative and quantitative dimensions of materiality need to be considered (see Chapter 5). In government audits, the materiality level, as well as the acceptable level of audit risk may be *lower* than for similar-type audits in the private sector because of the public accountability of the entity, the various legal and regulatory requirements, and the visibility and sensitivity of government programs and activities. Criteria for determining materiality include amount of revenues and expenditures of the entity, newness of the activity or changes in conditions, adequacy of internal controls, and results of prior audits.

Due care in the government audit also involves proper *follow-up* on known findings and recommendations from previous audits that could have an effect on the current audit. Examples could include internal control weaknesses noted in previous years' audits that remain uncorrected. The auditor's report should disclose the status of known but uncorrected deficiencies. The audit procedures should include those designed to track the status of management's actions on significant material recommendations from previous audits.

The GAO standards add a section on *quality controls* to general audit standards. Under these standards, both internal and external quality reviews are required. Internal reviews must be conducted by the CPA firms who perform GAO audit work. In addition, at least once every three years, firms must submit to external quality control reviews by unaffiliated organizations. Procedures for these reviews are similar to those outlined in Chapter 3 for quality reviews of firms of independent auditors.

Financial Audit Standards

For the financial audit, GAO standards supplement AICPA standards of field work in the areas of *planning* and *working papers*. In the area of planning, to avoid overauditing and duplication of work, the auditor should consider the levels of government involved, as well as the legal and regulatory requirements of each level. Then, *tests should be made of compliance* with all applicable laws and regulations. The goal is to detect both intentional and unintentional instances of noncompliance that could have an impact on the financial statements of the entity. The auditor should become aware, in advance, of the types of errors and irregularities that are common to the government program being audited, and plan to conduct tests designed to detect these errors and irregularities.

There are six supplemental requirements for *working papers* on GAO financial audits. These requirements are very similar to those outlined in Chapter 6 for audit working papers under AICPA standards.

For financial audit *reporting*, GAO standards supplement the AICPA standards in six areas. Specifically added to the AICPA standards are the following:

1. A requirement that the report state that the audit was made in accordance with generally accepted *government auditing standards.*
2. A written report should be prepared concerning the *results of tests of compliance with applicable laws and regulations.* The report should contain a statement of *positive assurance* on the items tested for compliance and a statement of *negative assurance* regarding the items not selected for compliance testing. It should report all material instances of noncompliance, as well as all instances or indications of illegal acts that could result in criminal prosecution.
3. The auditors should prepare a written report on their understanding of the entity's internal control structure and their assessment of control risk. This report may be incorporated into the report on the financial statements, or prepared as a separate report. Such a report would be similar to that described in Chapter 23.
4. Written audit reports are to be prepared giving the results of each financial related audit.
5. If certain information is prohibited from general disclosure (as might be the case for classified information in audits of certain agencies), the report should state the nature of the information omitted and the requirement that makes the omission necessary.
6. Written audit reports are to be submitted to appropriate authorities within the audited entity as well as to other officials who might have legal oversight authority over the entity. Unless restricted by law or regulation, copies should be made available for public inspection.

Performance Audit Standards

Performance audits of the GAO are similar to operational audits discussed earlier in the chapter. As shown in Figure 24–2, *field-work standards* for these audits are very similar to those of the AICPA. However, it must be remembered that the focus of the audit procedures in GAO audits is primarily to verify that the entity has been both effective and efficient in achieving the desired results of the government program, rather than to determine whether financial statements are fairly presented. Thus, as explained for operational audits, the criteria for desired results should be adquately explained to members of the audit team.

The *report* for the performance audit of the GAO is similar in content to that of the operational audit, illustrated in Figure 24–1. However, GAO audit standards are more specific than those of the IIA regarding contents. GAO standards for performance audits require that written reports be prepared on a timely basis for each performance audit. Specifically, the performance audit report should contain

- A statement of the audit objectives and a description of the audit scope and methodology.
- A full discussion of the audit findings and, where applicable, the auditor's conclusions.
- The cause of problem areas noted in the audit, as well as recommendations for actions to correct the problems.
- A statement that the audit was made in accordance with generally accepted government auditing standards.
- All significant instances of noncompliance and abuse, and indications or instances of illegal acts that could result in criminal prosecution.
- Pertinent views of responsible officials of the entity concerning audit findings and planned corrective actions, if applicable.
- A description of any significant noteworthy accomplishments of the management of the entity.
- A listing of any significant issues needing further study and consideration.
- A statement about any pertinent information that was omitted due to confidentiality. The nature of the information and the reasons for omission should be noted.

The performance audit report should be complete and accurate, and should be as clear and concisely written as the subject matter permits. Like financial audit reports, distribution of the performance audit report should be to responsible entity officials, as well as to those in charge of oversight functions over the entity. Unless restricted by law or regulation, copies should also be made available for public inspection.

Coordination with GAAS

In recognition of the issuance of updated GAO standards for financial audits, the AICPA issued SAS 63 in 1989 to help interpret the independent financial auditor's responsibilities under traditional generally accepted auditing standards to the expanded GAO standards that require tests and reports of compliance with applicable laws and regulations as well as reports on presentation of financial statements in accordance with GAAP. There are generally four responsibilities of independent CPAs under GAAS that are interpreted by SAS 63 in light of GAO standards: (1) illegal acts that have a direct and material impact on governmental programs or entities; (2) reports on compliance with laws and regulations and on the internal control structure in GAO-related audits; (3) tests and reports on compliance on the part of federal financial assistance programs in audits conducted in accordance with the Single Audit Act of 1984; and (4) establishment of an understanding with management regarding the type of engagement when engaged to test and report on compliance with other laws and regulations in connection with a governmental entity's financial statements.[7]

SAS 63 recognizes that GAO audits or audits under the Single Audit Act of 1984 require an expanded responsibility beyond that recognized in a financial audit, to the process of monitoring and reporting compliance with applicable laws and regulations on the part of the entity. Thus, it bridges the gap between GAO standards and GAAS for the compliance aspect of financial audits, providing help in interpreting the independent auditor's responsibilities in such engagements.

Summary

In this chapter we have described what the accountant does in performing the operational audit and the audit of governmental organizations, programs, activities, and functions. These audits may be performed by internal auditors, GAO auditors, or independent CPAs. In the first part of the chapter, we focused our discussion on the work of the internal auditor. We observed that the internal auditor is, in reality, an extension of the arm of management charged primarily with reviewing and evaluating operating controls, including ascertaining the extent of compliance with prescribed policies; ascertaining the reliability of accounting and other data; and evaluating the quality of management's performance in carrying out assigned responsibilities.

Operational auditing was then discussed as a comprehensive examination and appraisal of operations for the purpose of informing management as to compliance with established policies designed to achieve the objectives of management. This includes an appraisal of both the effectiveness of various functions, organizational units, or programs within the entity, as well as the efficiency with which plans of management are carried out.

Audits of governmental organizations, programs, activities, and functions were then discussed. Particularly, we discussed the impact that the Single Audit Act of 1984 had on audits in this category, as well as details of the auditing standards of the GAO for both employees of the government and independent CPAs who perform such audit work.

Auditing Vocabulary

p. 1035   **economy and efficiency audits:**   Performance audits that are designed to determine (1) whether the entity is acquiring, protecting, and using its resources economically and efficiently; (2) the causes of inefficiencies or uneconomical practices; and (3) whether the entity has complied with laws and regulations concerning economy and efficiency.

p. 1035   **financial audits:**   In the context of GAO standards, financial audits include the traditional function of providing an independent opinion on whether an entity's financial statements present fairly the results of financial operations, and whether other financial information is presented in conformity with GAAP or other stated criteria. In addition, financial audits also encompass procedures designed to determine whether the entity has adhered to specific financial compliance requirements, such as those prescribed by law or contract.

p. 1024   **internal auditors:**   Auditors employed for the purpose of evaluating internal operations and recordkeeping activities within a business.

p. 1025   **operational auditing:**   A comprehensive examination and appraisal of business operations for the purpose of informing management as to whether or not the various operations are performed in a manner that complies with established policies directed toward management's objectives.

p. 1035   **performance audits:**   In the context of GAO standards, provides an independent view of the extent to which government officials are faithfully, efficiently, and effectively carrying out their responsibilities as required by law.

p. 1035   **program audits:**   Performance audits that are designed to assess whether the objectives of a proposed or ongoing program are proper, to determine the effectiveness of the entity in achieving desired results, to identify factors inhibiting satisfactory performance, and to determine whether effectiveness and efficiency have been properly balanced as goals of the program.

p. 1034   **single audit:**   An audit performed under the Single Audit Act of 1984, applicable to audits of federally assisted programs, designed to encompass the entire financial operations of each applicable governmental program. The purpose of the single audit is to determine and report whether (1) the financial statements of the government are presented fairly in accordance with GAAP and whether the government has complied with laws and regulations; (2) the government has internal control systems to provide reasonable assurance that it is managing federal financial assistance programs in compliance with applicable laws and regulations; and (3) the government has complied with laws and regulations that may have a material effect on each major financial program.

Appendix 24–A

STATEMENT OF RESPONSIBILITIES
OF INTERNAL AUDITING

The purpose of this statement is to provide in summary form a general understanding of the role and responsibilities of internal auditing. For more specific guidance, readers should refer to the *Standards for the Professional Practice of Internal Auditing*.

NATURE

Internal auditing is an independent appraisal activity established within an organization as a service to the organization. It is a control which functions by examining and evaluating the adequacy and effectiveness of other controls.

OBJECTIVE AND SCOPE

The objective of internal auditing is to assist members of the organization in the effective discharge of their responsibilities. To this end, internal auditing furnishes them with analyses, appraisals, recommendations, counsel, and information concerning the activities reviewed. The audit objective includes promoting effective control at reasonable cost.

The scope of internal auditing encompasses the examination and evaluation of the adequacy and effectiveness of the organization's system of internal control and the quality of performance in carrying out assigned responsibilities. The scope of internal auditing includes:

- Reviewing the reliability and integrity of financial and operating information and the means used to identify, measure, classify, and report such information.

- Reviewing the systems established to ensure compliance with those policies, plans, procedures, laws, and regulations which could have a significant impact on operations and reports, and determining whether the organization is in compliance.

- Reviewing the means of safeguarding assets and, as appropriate, verifying the existence of such assets.

- Appraising the economy and efficiency with which resources are employed.

- Reviewing operations or programs to ascertain whether results are consistent with established objectives and goals and whether the operations or programs are being carried out as planned.

RESPONSIBILITY AND AUTHORITY

Internal auditing functions under the policies established by management and the board. The purpose, authority and responsibility of the internal auditing department should be defined in a formal written document (charter), approved by management, and accepted by the board. The charter should make clear the purposes of the internal auditing department, specify the unrestricted scope of its work, and declare that auditors are to have no authority or responsibility for the activities they audit.

The responsibility of internal auditing is to serve the organization in a manner that is consistent with the *Standards for the Professional Practice of Internal Auditing* and with professional standards of conduct such as the *Code of Ethics* of The Institute of Internal Auditors, Inc. This responsibility includes coordinating internal audit activities with others so as to best achieve the audit objectives and the objectives of the organization.

INDEPENDENCE

Internal auditors should be independent of the activities they audit. Internal auditors are independent when they can carry out their work freely and objectively. Independence permits internal auditors to render the impartial and unbiased judgments essential to the proper conduct of audits. It is achieved through organizational status and objectivity.

Organizational status should be sufficient to assure a broad range of audit coverage, and adequate consideration of and effective action on audit findings and recommendations.

Objectivity requires that internal auditors have an independent mental attitude, and an honest belief in their work product. Drafting procedures, designing, installing, and operating systems, are not audit functions. Performing such activities is presumed to impair audit objectivity.

The *Statement of Responsibilities of Internal Auditors* was originally
issued by The Institute of Internal Auditors in 1947. The
current *Statement*, revised in 1981, embodies the concepts
previously established and includes such changes as are deemed
advisable in light of the present status of the profession.

Appendix 24–A used with permission of The Institute of Internal Auditors, Inc.

Appendix 24–B Summary of General and Specific Standards for the Professional Practice of Internal Auditing

100 *INDEPENDENCE*—INTERNAL AUDITORS SHOULD BE INDEPENDENT OF THE ACTIVITIES THEY AUDIT.

    110 *Organizational Status*—The organizational status of the internal auditing department should be sufficient to permit the accomplishment of its audit responsibilities.

    120 *Objectivity*—Internal auditors should be objective in performing audits.

200 *PROFESSIONAL PROFICIENCY*—INTERNAL AUDITS SHOULD BE PERFORMED WITH PROFICIENCY AND DUE PROFESSIONAL CARE.

The Internal Auditing Department

    210 *Staffing*—The internal auditing department should provide assurance that the technical proficiency and educational background of internal auditors are appropriate for the audits to be performed.

    220 *Knowledge, Skills, and Disciplines*—The internal auditing department should possess or should obtain the knowledge, skills, and disciplines needed to carry out its audit responsibilities.

    230 *Supervision*—The internal auditing department should provide assurance that internal audits are properly supervised.

The Internal Auditor

    240 *Compliance with Standards of Conduct*—Internal auditors should comply with professional standards of conduct.

    250 *Knowledge, Skills, and Disciplines*—Internal auditors should possess the knowledge, skills, and disciplines essential to the performance of internal audits.

    260 *Human Relations and Communications*—Internal auditors should be skilled in dealing with people and in communicating effectively.

    270 *Continuing Education*—Internal auditors should maintain their technical competence through continuing education.

    280 *Due Professional Care*—Internal auditors should exercise due professional care in performing internal audits.

300 *SCOPE OF WORK*—THE SCOPE OF THE INTERNAL AUDIT SHOULD ENCOMPASS THE EXAMINATION AND EVALUATION OF THE ADEQUACY AND EFFECTIVENESS OF THE ORGANIZATION'S SYSTEM OF INTERNAL CONTROL AND THE QUALITY OF PERFORMANCE IN CARRYING OUT ASSIGNED RESPONSIBILITIES.

    310 *Reliability and Integrity of Information*—Internal auditors should review the reliability and integrity of financial and operating information and the means used to identify, measure, classify, and report such information.

Appendix 24–B is from *Summary of Standards for the Professional Practice of Internal Auditing* (Altamonte Springs, Fla.: Institute of Internal Auditors, 1978). Copyright 1978 by The Institute of Internal Auditors, Inc. Reprinted with permission.

320 *Compliance with Policies, Plans, Procedures, Laws, and Regulations*—Internal auditors should review the systems established to ensure compliance with those policies, plans, procedures, laws, and regulations which could have significant impact on operations and reports and should determine whether the organization is in compliance.

330 *Safeguarding of Assets*—Internal auditors should review the means of safeguarding assets and, as appropriate, verify the existence of such assets.

340 *Economical and Efficient Use of Resources*—Internal auditors should appraise the economy and efficiency with which resources are employed.

350 *Accomplishment of Established Objectives and Goals for Operations or Programs*—Internal auditors should review operations or programs to ascertain whether results are consistent with established objectives and goals and whether the operations or programs are being carried out as planned.

400 *PERFORMANCE OF AUDIT WORK*—AUDIT WORK SHOULD INCLUDE PLANNING THE AUDIT, EXAMINING AND EVALUATING INFORMATION, COMMUNICATING RESULTS, AND FOLLOWING UP.

410 *Planning the Audit*—Internal auditors should plan each audit.

420 *Examining and Evaluating Information*—Internal auditors should collect, analyze, interpret, and document information to support audit results.

430 *Communicating Results*—Internal auditors should report the results of their audit work.

440 *Following Up*—Internal auditors should follow up to ascertain that appropriate action is taken on reported audit findings.

500 *MANAGEMENT OF THE INTERNAL AUDITING DEPARTMENT*—THE DIRECTOR OF INTERNAL AUDITING SHOULD PROPERLY MANAGE THE INTERNAL AUDITING DEPARTMENT.

510 *Purpose, Authority, and Responsibility*—The director of internal auditing should have a statement of purpose, authority, and responsibility for the internal auditing department.

520 *Planning*—The director of internal auditing should establish plans to carry out the responsibilities of the internal auditing department.

530 *Policies and Procedures*—The director of internal auditing should provide written policies and procedures to guide the audit staff.

540 *Personnel Management and Development*—The director of internal auditing should establish a program for selecting and developing the human resources of the internal auditing department.

550 *External Auditors*—The director of internal auditing should coordinate internal and external audit efforts.

560 *Quality Assurance*—The director of internal auditing should establish and maintain a quality assurance program to evaluate the operations of the internal auditing department.

Appendix 24–C Summary of Statement on Government Auditing Standards

I. Introduction

  A. Purpose

   1. This statement contains standards for audits of government organizations, programs, activities, and functions, and of government funds received by contractors, nonprofit organizations, and other nongovernment organizations.

   2. The standards are to be followed by auditors and audit organizations when required by law, regulation, agreement or contract, or policy.

II. Types of Government Audits

  A. Purpose

   1. This chapter describes the types of audits that government and nongovernment audit organizations conduct, and that government organizations arrange to have conducted. This description is not intended to limit or require the types of audits that may be conducted or arranged.

   2. In conducting these types of audits, auditors should follow the applicable standards included and incorporated in this statement.

  B. Financial audits

   1. Financial statement audits determine (a) whether the financial statements of an audited entity present fairly the financial position, results of operations, and cash flows or changes in financial position in accordance with generally accepted accounting principles, and (b) whether the entity has complied with laws and regulations for those transactions and events that may have a material effect on the financial statements.

   2. Financial related audits include determining (a) whether financial reports and related items, such as elements, accounts, or funds are fairly presented, (b) whether financial information is presented in accordance with established or stated criteria, and (c) whether the entity has adhered to specific financial compliance requirements.

  C. Performance audits

   1. Economy and efficiency audits include determining (a) whether the entity is acquiring, protecting, and using its resources (such as personnel, property, and space) economically and efficiently, (b) the causes of inefficiencies or uneconomical practices, and (c) whether the entity has complied with laws and regulations concerning matters of economy and efficiency.

   2. Program audits include determining (a) the extent to which the desired results or benefits established by the legislature or other authorizing body are being achieved, (b) the effectiveness of organizations, programs, activities, or functions, and (c) whether the entity has complied with laws and regulations applicable to the program.

  D. Understanding the audit objectives and scope

   1. Audits may have a combination of financial and performance audit objectives, or may have objectives limited to only some aspects of one audit type.

2. Auditors should follow the appropriate standards in this statement that are applicable to the individual objectives of the audit.

E. Other activities of an audit organization

1. Services other than audits: The head of the audit organization should establish policy on which audit standards from this statement should be followed by the auditors in performing such services. However, as a minimum, auditors should collectively possess adequate professional proficiency and exercise due professional care for the service being performed.

2. Investigative work: The head of the audit organization should establish policy on whether the audit standards in this statement, or some other appropriate standards, are to be followed by the employees performing this work.

3. Nonaudit activities: The head of the audit organization should establish policy on what standards in this statement are to be followed, or whether some other appropriate standards are to be followed, by the employees in performing this type of work.

III. General Standards

A. Qualifications: The staff assigned to conduct the audit should collectively possess adequate professional proficiency for the tasks required.

B. Independence: In all matters relating to the audit work, the audit organization and the individual auditors, whether government or public, should be free from personal and external impairments to independence, should be organizationally independent, and should maintain an independent attitude and appearance.

C. Due professional care: Due professional care should be used in conducting the audit and in preparing related reports.

D. Quality control: Audit organizations conducting government audits should have an appropriate internal quality control system in place and participate in an external quality control review program.

IV. Field Work Standards for Financial Audits

A. Relationship to AICPA standards

1. The standards of field work for government financial audits incorporate the AICPA standards of field work for financial audits, and prescribe supplemental standards of field work needed to satisfy the unique needs of government financial audits.

2. The field work standards of the AICPA and the supplemental standards in chapter 4 of this statement apply to both financial statement audits and financial related audits.

B. Planning:

1. Supplemental planning field work standards for government financial audits are:

a. Audit requirements for all government levels: Planning should include consideration of the audit requirements of all levels of government.

b. Legal and regulatory requirements: A test should be made of compliance with applicable laws and regulations.

(1) In determining compliance with laws and regulations:

(a) The auditor should design audit steps and procedures to provide reasonable assurance of detecting errors, irregularities, and illegal acts that could have a direct and material effect on the financial statement amounts or the results of financial related audits.

(b) The auditor should also be aware of the possibility of illegal acts which could have an indirect and material effect on the financial statements or results of financial related audits.

C. Evidence (working papers)

1. The AICPA field work standards and this statement require that: A record of the auditors' work be retained in the form of working papers.

2. Supplemental working paper requirements for financial audits are that working papers should:

a. Contain a written audit program cross-referenced to the working papers.

b. Contain the objective, scope, methodology and results of the audit.

c. Contain sufficient information so that supplementary oral explanations are not required.

d. Be legible with adequate indexing and cross-referencing, and include summaries and lead schedules, as appropriate.

e. Restrict information included to matters that are materially important and relevant to the objectives of the audit.

f. Contain evidence of supervisory reviews of the work conducted.

D. Internal control

1. The AICPA field work standards and this statement require that: A sufficient understanding of the internal control structure is to be obtained to plan the audit and to determine the nature, timing, and extent of tests to be performed.

V. Reporting Standards for Financial Audits

A. Relationship to AICPA standards

1. The standards of reporting for government financial audits incorporate the AICPA standards of reporting for financial audits, and prescribes supplemental standards of reporting needed to satisfy the unique needs of government financial audits.

2. The reporting standards of the AICPA and the supplemental standards in chapter 5 of this statement apply to both financial statement audits and financial related audits.

B. Supplemental reporting standards for government financial audits are:

1. Statement on auditing standards: A statement should be included in the auditors' report that the audit was made in accordance with generally accepted government auditing standards. (AICPA standards require that public accountants state that the audit was made in accordance with generally accepted auditing standards. In conducting government audits, public accountants should also state that their audit was conducted in accordance with the standards set forth in chapters 3, 4, and 5.)

2. Report on compliance: The auditors should prepare a written report on their tests of compliance with applicable laws and regulations. This report, which may be included in either the report on the financial audit or a separate report, should contain a statement of positive assurance on those items which were tested for compliance and negative assurance on those items not tested. It should include all material instances of noncompliance, and all instances or indications of illegal acts which could result in criminal prosecution.

3. Report on internal controls: The auditors should prepare a written report on their understanding of the entity's internal control structure and the assessment of control risk made as part of a financial statement audit, or a financial related audit. This report may be included in either the auditor's report on the financial audit or a separate report. The auditor's report should include as a minimum: (a) the scope of the auditor's work in obtaining an understanding of the internal control structure and in assessing the control risk, (b) the entity's significant internal controls or control structure including the controls established to ensure compliance with laws and regulations that have a material impact on the financial statements and the results of the financial related audit, and (c) the reportable conditions, including the identification of material weaknesses, identified as a result of the auditor's work in understanding and assessing the control risk.

4. Reporting on financial related audits: Written audit reports are to be prepared giving the results of each financial related audit.

5. Privileged and confidential information: If certain information is prohibited from general disclosure, the report should state the nature of the information omitted and the requirement that makes the omission necessary.

6. Report Distribution: Written audit reports are to be submitted by the audit organization to the appropriate officials of the organization audited and to the appropriate officials of the organizations requiring or arranging for the audits, including external funding organizations, unless legal restrictions, ethical considerations, or other arrangements prevent it. Copies of the reports should also be sent to other officials who have legal oversight authority or who may be responsible for taking action and to others authorized to receive such reports. Unless restricted by law or regulation, copies should be made available for public inspection.

VI. Field Work Standards for Performance Audits

A. Planning: Work is to be adequately planned.

B. Supervision: Staff are to be properly supervised.

C. Legal and regulatory requirements: An assessment is to be made of compliance with applicable requirements of laws and regulations when necessary to satisfy the audit objectives.

1. Where an assessment of compliance with laws and regulations is required: Auditors should design the audit to provide reasonable assurance of detecting abuse or illegal acts that could significantly affect the audit objectives.

2. In all performance audits: Auditors should be alert to situations or transactions that could be indicative of abuse or illegal acts.

D. Internal control: An assessment should be made of applicable internal controls when necessary to satisfy the audit objectives.

E. Evidence: Sufficient, competent, and relevant evidence is to be obtained to afford a reasonable basis for the auditors' judgments and conclusions regarding the organization, program, activity, or function under audit. A record of the auditors' work is to be retained in the form of working papers. Working papers may include tapes, films, and discs.

VII. Reporting Standards for Performance Audits

A. Form: Written audit reports are to be prepared communicating the results of each government audit.

B. Timeliness: Reports are to be issued promptly so as to make the information available for timely use by management and legislative officials, and by other interested parties.

C. Report contents

1. Objectives, scope, and methodology: The report should include a statement of the audit objectives and a description of the audit scope and methodology.

2. **Audit findings and conclusions:** The report should include a full discussion of the audit findings, and where applicable, the auditor's conclusions.

3. **Cause and recommendations:** The report should include the cause of problem areas noted in the audit, and recommendations for actions to correct the problem areas and to improve operations, when called for by the audit objectives.

4. **Statement on auditing standards:** The report should include a statement that the audit was made in accordance with generally accepted government auditing standards and disclose when applicable standards were not followed.

5. **Internal controls:** The report should identify the significant internal controls that were assessed, the scope of the auditor's assessment work, and any significant weaknesses found during the audit.

6. **Compliance with laws and regulations:** The report should include all significant instances of noncompliance and abuse and all indications or instances of illegal acts that could result in criminal prosecution that were found during or in connection with the audit.

7. **Views of responsible officials:** The report should include the pertinent views of responsible officials of the organization, program, activity, or function audited concerning the auditors' findings, conclusions, and recommendations, and what corrective action is planned.

8. **Noteworthy accomplishments:** The report should include a description of any significant noteworthy accomplishments, particularly when management improvements in one area may be applicable elsewhere.

9. **Issues needing further study:** The report should include a listing of any significant issues needing further study and consideration.

10. **Privileged and confidential information:** The report should include a statement about any pertinent information that was omitted because it is deemed privileged or confidential. The nature of such information should be described, and the basis under which it is withheld should be stated.

D. **Report presentation:** The report should be complete, accurate, objective, and convincing, and be as clear and concise as the subject matter permits.

E. **Report distribution:** Written audit reports are to be submitted by the audit organization to the appropriate officials of the organization audited, and to the appropriate officials of the organizations requiring or arranging for the audits, including external funding organizations, unless legal restrictions, ethical considerations, or other arrangements prevent it. Copies of the reports should also be sent to other officials who may be responsible for taking action on audit findings and recommendations and to others authorized to receive such reports. Unless restricted by law or regulation, copies should be made available for public inspection.

VIII. **AICPA Generally Accepted Auditing Standards**

A. General standards

1. The examination is to be performed by a person or persons having adequate technical training and proficiency as an auditor.

2. In all matters relating to the assignment, an independence in mental attitude is to be maintained by the auditor or auditors.

3. Due professional care is to be exercised in the performance of the examination and the preparation of the report.

B. Standards of field work

1. The work is to be adequately planned and assistants, if any, are to be properly supervised.

2. A sufficient understanding of the internal control structure is to be obtained to plan the audit and to determine the nature, timing, and extent of tests to be performed.

3. Sufficient competent evidential matter is to be obtained through inspection, observation, inquiries, and confirmations to afford a reasonable basis for an opinion regarding the financial statements under examination.

C. Standards of reporting

1. The report shall state whether the financial statements are presented in accordance with generally accepted accounting principles.

2. The report shall identify those circumstances in which such principles have not been consistently observed in the current period in relation to the preceding period.

3. Informative disclosures in the financial statements are to be regarded as reasonably adequate unless otherwise stated in the report.

4. The report shall either contain an expression of opinion regarding the financial statements, taken as a whole, or an assertion to the effect that an opinion cannot be expressed. When an overall opinion cannot be expressed, the reasons therefor should be stated. In all cases where an auditor's name is associated with financial statements, the report should contain a clear-cut indication of the character of the auditor's examination, if any, and the degree of responsibility he or she is taking.

Notes

1. William T. Thornhill, *Complete Handbook of Operational and Management Auditing.* (Englewood Cliffs, N.J.: Prentice-Hall, Inc., 1981): 42.
2. John W. Cook and Gary M. Winkle, *Auditing* (Boston: Houghton Mifflin Company, 1984): 383–384.
3. Thornhill, pp. 92–93.
4. John R. Miller and Frederick D. Wolf, "A New Look at the Yellow Book: Tomorrow's Government Audits," *Journal of Accountancy* (November 1988): 64–80.
5. Excerpted from W. A. Broadus, Jr. and Joseph D. Comtois, "The Single Audit Act: A Needed Reform," *Journal of Accountancy* (April 1985): 62–70.
6. Excerpted from Comptroller General of the United States, *Standards for Audit of Governmental Organizations, Programs, Activities and Functions.* (Washington, D.C.: U.S. General Accounting Office, 1988).
7. SAS 63, *Compliance Auditing Applicable to Government Entities and Other Recipients of Governmental Financial Assistance.* (AICPA, April 1989).

Questions for Class Discussion

Q24-1 Define operational auditing.

Q24-2 Who performs operational audits? Explain.

Q24-3 What is the relationship between the internal auditor and management?

Q24-4 How does the concept of independence within the firm relate to the internal auditing function?

Q24-5 What activities are performed by internal auditors?

Q24-6 What are the criteria against which efficiency and effectiveness are measured in performing an operational audit? What are the special problems associated with the measurement of efficiency and effectiveness?

Q24-7 What is the most important evidence-gathering procedure in performance of an operational audit? What other procedures are typically performed in an operational audit?

Q24-8 What are the elements of a typical report developed from an operational audit?

Q24-9 What are the purposes of the Single Audit Act of 1984? Briefly explain why the Act was passed by Congress.

Q24-10 In general, describe the three major components of a typical single audit and the report(s) which emerge therefrom.

Q24-11 Briefly compare and contrast the GAO Auditing Standards with generally accepted auditing standards.

Q24-12 Compare and contrast the two general types of GAO audits.

Short Cases

C24-1 You are performing an operational audit of the procedures followed in handling the sale of scrap metal in a metal fabrication firm. You learn that all scrap material is delivered to the shipping area at the end of each day. The shipping clerk is then responsible for the sale of the scrap at the end of each week. The scrap is sold for cash, which is remitted to the cashier.

Required:
  a. What additional information would you seek in completing your audit of scrap sales procedures?
  b. What would be your special points of concern in connection with this audit?
  c. Suggest procedures that might be implemented to meet those concerns.

C24-2 As an internal auditor, you have been asked to perform an operational audit of the procedures followed in arriving at standard cost variances.

Required: Discuss the major steps you would take in performing this examination.

C24-3 To function effectively, the internal auditor must often educate auditees and other parties about the nature and purpose of internal auditing.

Required:
a. Define "internal auditing."
b. Briefly describe *five* possible benefits of an internal auditing department establishing a program to educate auditees and other parties in the nature and purpose of internal auditing.

(IIA adapted)

C24-4 You are an internal auditor preparing for an exit conference. The auditee manager has been very defensive, has refused to participate in interim discussions of findings, has discouraged discussions with lower-level supervisors, and has cooperated as little as possible during the audit.

Below are ten statements that relate to your actions as auditor in conducting and controlling the exit conference:
a. You should also invite his subordinate supervisors to attend the exit conference.
b. It is important that you match the manager's firm attitude in order to impress him.
c. The conference should be conducted in such a manner that the manager will be discouraged from injecting his opinions.
d. If a case arises when you and the manager do not agree as to audit report language, ask him to suggest a revision.
e. Ask the manager if he would like to provide written comments for inclusion in the audit report.
f. Ask the manager if there are any areas that he would like you to audit as an extension of the field work.
g. Orally present the audit findings in the least offensive manner so as to create no waves, even though the findings may be presented more forcefully in the report.
h. If the manager suggests another area of audit, tell him that your report will identify the audit as being done at his suggestion.
i. In an effort to overcome the manager's anticipated strong antagonism, identify findings as management's omission.
j. Advise the manager that any corrective measures taken to resolve audit findings should be cleared with you.

Required: List the identifying number of each of the actions above that would adversely affect rather than improve auditor/auditee relations. Explain why you selected each response.

(IIA adapted)

C24-5 An accountant in the treasury department of Health Plans, Inc., was disturbed by changes made by management affecting the work in the department. The changes were the result of recommendations made during a recent internal audit but were never explained to the accountant. The changes were as follows:
a. New responsibilities were assigned to the accountant for performing proofs of quarterly accruals of investment interest on securities.
b. The accountant must now prepare weekly proofs of cash receipts and disbursements.
c. The accountant will no longer have access to the security vault, the imprest cash fund, and the incoming mail.
d. Periodic review will be made of the accountant's work by the supervisor.

The accountant has expressed dissatisfaction with the above changes because of the constraints and dilution of job responsibilities and an indication of lack of trust.

You have been asked to discuss the rationale for the changes with the accountant.

Required: Give a reasonable explanation for each of the changes listed above based on internal control considerations. Do not use the same reason for more than one change.

(IIA adapted)

Problems

P24-1 Select the best answer for each of the following items relating to principles of internal auditing.

    a. Which of the following would contribute least to the independence of the internal auditing department?

        1. Having the director of internal auditing report directly to the chief operating officer of the organization.

        2. Requiring the internal auditing staff to possess collectively the knowledge and skills essential to the practice of professional internal auditing within the organization.

        3. Authorizing the director of internal auditing to meet directly and as needed with the audit committee of the board without management being present.

        4. Having both management and the board of directors review and approve a formal written charter for the internal auditing department.

    b. Which of the following statements describes a major difference in scope of work between the internal and external auditors of an organization?

        1. Internal auditors are responsible for reviewing and evaluating internal administrative control, while the external auditors are responsible for reviewing and evaluating internal accounting control.

        2. External auditors are obligated to report to management identified weaknesses in the system of internal control, while the internal auditors are not so obligated.

        3. Internal auditors do some of the work normally undertaken by the external auditors as a cost-saving measure, but external auditors do not normally perform work undertaken by the internal auditors.

        4. Internal auditors are responsible for measuring and evaluating the effectiveness of established systems of internal control, while the measurement and evaluation of the effectiveness of established systems of internal control are of secondary importance to external auditors.

    c. In developing the overall audit plan for the internal auditing function, the internal auditing manager should

        1. Avoid scheduling internal audits of those areas reviewed in detail by the external auditor.

        2. Place audit emphasis on those operations characterized by the highest levels of risk and exposure.

        3. Obtain the audit committee's approval of internal audit plans, including the detailed auditing procedures to be followed.

        4. All of the above.

 d. Organization charts are useful to the internal auditor because they
   1. Provide good internal control.
   2. Ensure the proper allocation of responsibilities.
   3. Provide a starting point for evaluating control.
   4. Depict informal lines of communication.
 e. Which of the following is generally considered to be a major reason for establishing an internal auditing function?
   1. To relieve overburdened management of the responsibility for establishing effective systems of internal control.
   2. To ensure that operating activities comply with the policies, plans, and procedures established by management.
   3. To safeguard resources entrusted to the organization.
   4. To assist members of the organization in the measurement and evaluation of the effectiveness of established systems of internal control.
 f. Which of the following statements describes the responsibilities of an internal auditing department with respect to fraud? It is responsible for
   1. Detecting irregularities that would be disclosed by the application of appropriate auditing procedures.
   2. Providing an entity with its primary defense against fraud.
   3. Detecting irregularities that affect the financial statements.
   4. Irregularities that result from undetected weaknesses in the system of internal control.
 g. According to the *Standards for the Professional Practice of Internal Auditing,*
   1. The director of internal auditing should provide written policies and procedures to guide members of the audit staff.
   2. Internal auditing organizations should have formal administrative and technical audit manuals for use in providing guidance to members of the audit staff.
   3. A small internal auditing department can be managed without any written policies and procedures.
   4. Comprehensive policies and procedures are established primarily to promote on-the-job technical training of the members of the audit staff.
 h. Which of the following elements is most important in an effective performance appraisal system for an audit staff?
   1. Completion of performance appraisals by one person or a designated group to provide reasonable assurance of consistency in the appraisals.
   2. Use of objective, measurable, and well-defined performance standards.
   3. Completion of performance appraisals on a predetermined time schedule.
   4. Comparison of the performance of each staff person against the performance of peers to promote equity in the salary administration program.
 i. Auditees are most likely to accept and act upon audit recommendations if they believe that
   1. Implementation of the recommendations will assist in achieving their personal goals.
   2. Implementation of the recommendations will result in significantly increased revenues or reduced costs for the organization.
   3. Upper-level management will require that the recommendations be implemented.
   4. A follow-up audit of action taken on the recommendations will be conducted in the near future.

j. Which of the following constitutes a sound practice of organizational control?
   1. Assigning overall responsibility for credit authorization activities to the senior marketing executive.
   2. Assigning overall responsibility for the corporate risk management activities in a diversified financial organization to the executive responsible for insurance sales.
   3. Having the person responsible for the development of company-wide administrative procedures report directly to the corporate controller.
   4. Having the director of internal auditing report to the controller.

(IIA adapted)

P24-2 Select the best answer for each of the following items relating to internal auditing techniques.
   a. Flowcharting a disbursements/payments cycle would require information on the use of the following documents and records: purchase requisition, purchase order, receiving report, voucher, and
      1. Bill of materials.
      2. Vendor's invoice.
      3. Canceled check.
      4. Economic order quantity document.
   b. In making a preliminary survey of the financial controls over an organization's research and development activity, which question would be the least appropriate one to ask?
      1. Who compares actual and budgeted costs?
      2. What procedures are employed for project authorization?
      3. Are the outputs of the research effort worth the costs being incurred?
      4. Does the R & D director regularly report on the progress of each research project?
   c. When auditing the purchasing activities of a manufacturing organization in a computer system environment, which of the following should be included in the permanent file portion of the audit working papers?
      1. Copies (or details relating thereto) of the computer program documentation.
      2. Printouts using auditor-prepared programs and test data.
      3. Prior year's working papers revised to reflect changes taking place during the current year.
      4. Information concerning administrative controls over the computer operations at each location.
   d. Internal auditors frequently use the audit technique of observation. Which of the following statements best reflects the auditors' view of observation? Observation
      1. Should be done separately from any other audit field work function.
      2. Is essentially related to the review of work flow and plant layout.
      3. Is generally considered to be less authentic evidence than copies of basic documents describing the control process.
      4. Can be supported by photography, flowcharts, drawings, and narrative.
   e. During the audit of a large sales organization, several salespeople complained to the internal auditor about errors in their commission payments. The working papers relative to this audit should include:
      1. Commission computations for the organization's sales personnel for selected periods.
      2. Copies of the organization's commission-computation worksheets.

3. The detailed procedures covering computation of sales commissions.
4. Evaluations of the efficiency and effectiveness of the complaining personnel.
f. In determining that purchase requisitions were authorized by appropriate personnel, the internal auditor should review
1. Procedures for selecting authorizing individuals to approve purchase requisitions.
2. Evidence of approval by an official having authority for the type of purchase.
3. The matching of requisitions with the corresponding purchase orders.
4. Control over the security of the requisition process.
g. Which of the following is usually the most important procedure that an internal auditor uses in validating a general ledger accounts payable balance as of a particular date?
1. Confirm recorded accounts payable balances with vendors.
2. Examine all vendors' statements on hand.
3. Prepare a trial balance of all open accounts payable balances.
4. Conduct a search for unrecorded accounts payable.
h. When you audit the expense allocations of an organization, which one of the following four steps should you perform first?
1. Evaluate the materiality of expense items under consideration.
2. Compare the expense total with those of preceding periods.
3. Consider the reasonableness of the company's basis for expense allocation of the item under consideration.
4. Compare the basis used to allocate the expense item under consideration with the basis used by other companies in the same industry.
i. You have undertaken a preliminary survey of a manufacturing operation. Which of the following is the objective of a *walk-through*?
1. Determine the layout of the plant facilities.
2. Observe the physical flow of materials among production departments.
3. Obtain an understanding of the process and control points by following the process style.
4. All of the above.
j. Which of the following statements in an audit finding in an effectiveness audit of a government personnel office would not be a necessary part of an audit finding?
1. "The activity is directed by Ordinance 485 of 19X8?"
2. "The activity being measured covers interviewing, recordkeeping, and job placement."
3. "The salary of the department head was increased on June 1, 19X0, to $30,000."
4. "An extrapolation of the conditions found disclosed a significant loss of $XX."

(IIA adapted)

P24-3 Select the best answer to the following items relating to operational auditing.
a. Operational audits generally have been conducted by internal auditors and governmental audit agencies but may be performed by certified public accountants. A primary purpose of an operational audit is to provide
1. A means of assurance that internal accounting controls are functioning as planned.
2. Aid to the independent auditor, who is conducting the examination of the financial statements.

     3. The results of internal examinations of financial and accounting matters to a company's top-level management.

     4. A measure of management performance in meeting organizational goals.

  b. Which of the following *best* describes the operational audit?

     1. It requires the constant review by internal auditors of the administrative controls as they relate to the operations of the company.

     2. It concentrates on implementing financial and accounting control in a newly organized company.

     3. It attempts and is designed to verify the fair presentation of a company's results of operations.

     4. It concentrates on seeking out aspects of operations in which waste would be reduced by the introduction of controls.

  c. In comparison to the external auditor, an internal auditor is more likely to be concerned with

     1. Internal administrative control.

     2. Cost accounting procedures.

     3. Operational auditing.

     4. Internal accounting control.

(AICPA adapted)

P24-4 Following are two lists. The first is a list of control procedures, and the second is a list of related control objectives for the lending function in a commercial bank.

Required: Place numbers 1 through 10 on your answer sheet. Next to each number, write the *one* letter that corresponds to the control objective most closely related to the control procedure referenced with the number. Some letters may be used more than once, but each number should have only *one* letter.

Control Procedures:

1. Establishing a monitoring of lending limits for all loan officers.

2. Assigning responsibilities for receiving and investigating all customers' inquiries about loan balances to individuals having no control over cash receipts and collection procedures.

3. Sending periodic statements of loan activity to all credit customers.

4. Monitoring geographic concentrations in the loan portfolio.

5. Periodically reviewing and pricing the value of loan collateral to determine its adequacy in protecting the bank's investment.

6. Requiring the approval by an independent officer of all waivers of loan fees.

7. Reconciling the totals of the loan interest receivable ledgers to the corresponding control balance at least quarterly.

8. Assigning responsibilities for maintaining and safekeeping actual loan instruments (notes, collateral receipts, etc.) to individuals who do not receive loan payments.

9. Requiring that written appraisals be performed by competent, independent individuals to determine the value of real property that will be used to secure a loan.

10. Routing a copy of a computer-generated report of all changes made to loan payment due dates to a high-level, independent official for careful review on a daily basis.

Control objectives

A. To ensure that potentially uncollectible amounts are promptly identified, evaluated, and accounted for.

B. To ensure that loan interest, fees, and other charges are recorded correctly as to account, amount, and period.

C. To ensure that each loan and its terms are reviewed and properly authorized before the transaction is consummated.

D. To ensure that physical loss or misuse of loan documents, collateral, and repossessed property is prevented or promptly detected.

E. To ensure that all lending transactions completed are recorded correctly as to account, amount, and period.

F. To ensure that loan interest, fees, and other charges are billed to customers in the correct amounts.

(IIA adapted)

P24-5 The year-end physical inventory of a large wholesaler of automotive parts has just been completed. The internal auditor reviewed the inventory-taking instructions before the start of the physical inventory, made and recorded test counts, and observed the controls over the inventory-taking process. No significant exceptions to the process were observed. Subsequent comparisons by the auditor of the quantities shown on the count sheets with those listed on the perpetual inventory cards disclosed numerous discrepancies.

Required:

a. List *five* likely causes of such discrepancies (for example, theft).

b. List *five* inappropriate management actions that might have been taken as a result of relying on incorrect perpetual inventory data.

(IIA adapted)

P24-6 James and Tidwell, a local CPA firm, responded to an invitation to bid for the audit of a local federally assisted program. They have had no previous experience with audits of federally assisted programs. They have, however, heard of GAO audit standards, and are aware that a great deal of federal programs exist that are in need of audits.

Required:

a. Name and describe the federal law that requires audits of federally assisted programs. Why is this program probably contacting auditors with invitations to bid their audit?

b. Describe the types of audits that James and Tidwell could perform on this engagement. What should they use as the criteria for deciding which type to perform?

c. Describe the basic differences between GAO auditing standards and AICPA auditing standards.

d. Why would materiality thresholds and audit risk levels be lower for audits of federally assisted programs than for entities in the private sector?

e. Describe the contents of a typical GAO financial audit report.

Index